CUSTOMS OF INDIA

CUSTOMS OF INDIA

(In Six Volumes)

Volume 2

Western: Maharashtra, Goa, Gujarat, Daman & Diu, Dadra & Nagar Haveli

Editor

Gopal Bhargava

ISHA

Customs of India

ISBN: 978-81-8205-524-7 (Set)
ISBN: 978-81-8205-526-1 (Vol. 2)

Published in 2012 in India by
Isha Books
B-69, New Gupta Colony
New DDA Market
Delhi - 110009

Lasser Type Setting : Rajender Vashist, Delhi
Printed at : Chawla Offset Printers, Delhi

Contents

List of Illustrations

Daman and Diu

1. Men and women are dancing during festival.
2. In traditional dress people are celebrating a festival.
3. Decorated boats in a festival at Daman.
4. Women are participating in a festival.

Preface

This painstakingly researched work on the customs of the western region is a vast treasure trove of information on various individual tribes and castes. This volume contains an introduction on the customs, characteristics of the castes and tribes and also the generic attributes of the states concerned. The volume also takes stock of the probable origin of the customs and transitions in the due course of time. Besides, the work contains seven chapters including conceiving and birth, puberty, betrothal, marriage ceremony, death rituals : cremation, death rituals: burial and social customs. The book also describes at length the ancient forms of customs, rites, rituals and usages, in addition to various superstitions and religio-magical practices, as recorded by numerous British and Indian ethnographers, gazetteer-writers, surveyors of land settlement reports, monograph writers, anthropologists christian missionaries, social scientists, etc.

Following independence in 1947, the entire scenario of social, economic life, customs, rites and rituals of both the castes and tribes in the western region, as well as the entire India, changed dramatically, the process of which was earlier set in motion with the arrival of Railways in India. Again the region had been impinged upon by the Pan-Indian and global influence and factors. All these changes in the rites and rituals had been incorporated in this monumental work.

The entire mass of information and knowledge had been carefully researched, written and edited with the anthropological view that makes this work all the more valuable for the purpose of scholars, social scientists, anthropologists, researchers, teachers and students in various disciplines. Every detail of the information, collected, collated and formatted, has gone through meticulous validation, checks and rechecks. In line with the constant evolution of the text, this work, too, would have to be updated and improved in the successive editions. In a country as vast and complex as India, there will always be a scope for improving the work through suggestions, deletions, and additions pointed out for rectification. We thus invite the beneficiaries of this work to participate in its evolution.

Disclaimer

This work contains the collected, collated, formatted and validated information on customs of India on a 'best and sincere effort' basis for presentation in a single comprehensive work. This work neither constitutes an advisory for research, analysis or investment planning, nor constitutes, in general, any professional advice. The reader should seek the services of qualified professionals for such advice.

The information presented here is to be regarded as a 'first information service' on this work. The reader should make his/her own deeper investigation of the information on any particular matter before making any decision or investment of any kind. The Editorial Board or the Publishers cannot be held responsible for loss, if any, incurred as a result of specific planning or decisions or investments made by the reader in pursuance of this work.

Our sincere thanks are due to the scholars, researchers, authors, journalists, Publication Division, Government of India, Ministry of Culture, Census Commissioner, Land Settlement Reports, Anthropological Survey of India, State Editor (Gazetteers), ethnographers and others. We have drawn the contents from a large number of published works. The credit for producing and furnishing authentic information and knowledge goes to them. We have merely weaved, consolidated and formulated the contents collected from them.

Editor

Introduction

The Western region of India comprises the states of Maharashtra, Goa, Gujarat and union territories of Daman and Diu and Dadra and Nagar Haveli Each state and the union territory has diverse customs, rites, rituals and usages in ceremonials, life-cycle events and the daily life of its inhabitants. To begin with, the diversity of physical features and geography of Maharashtra is reflected in its people and culture. Virtually, every major caste and community is represented in the state. The Deccan Plateau in Central Maharashtra is largely populated by tribal communities *i.e.* the Bhils, Mahadeo Kolis, Gonds and Warlis. On the northwestern coast, the Warlis continue their sparse reflective existence, worshipping the mother goddess. Warli myths reveal that death came upon the human race as a result of the humiliation to Mother Earth which propitiates this goddess of creative energy, the corn goddess and the goddess of trees and plants. Their death songs attempt to unravel the unfathomable mysteries of life and death, revealing their simple awe of nature in all its innocence. The Warlis, who are the aboriginal settlers from the foothills of the Sahyadri ranges in the Thane district, north of Mumbai, live in a small cluster of huts called *padas*.

Another major tribe, the Gonds, the inhabitants of central India, are spread between the forested regions of Madhya Pradesh, Maharashtra, Andhra Pradesh and Orissa. They have distinctive customs and speak a Dravidian language called *Gondi*. Today, many Gond youth have taken on the dominant language of their regions, and the cultural variations among tribal communities are expanding. Where their forest habitats are still intact, however, their lifestyles remain unchanged and such communities provide anthropologists with a splendid window into a past.

Although Maharashtra has predominantly Hindu culture and customs, it has always had a tradition of secularism. Jewish people have established several synagogues in Mumbai, Pune, Alibag, Pen, Thane and Revdanda. Besides numerous mosques and dargahs, churches and Zoroastrian fire temples, all find a space to function here. A sprinkling of Jain and Buddhist temples is also found in the region. During the recent decades, Dr. Bhimrao Ambedkar's conversion to Buddhism caused resurgence of Buddhism in Maharashtra.

About the people of Maharashtra and their customs, their caste structures and practice of endogamy, exogamy, Mr. R.E. Enthovenon notes, "In the course of revising existing materials for the caste accounts, a number of new caste divisions have been discovered, both in connection with the groups inside which marriage is essential, and the smaller division inside which marriage is forbidden. These are referred to in this work, respectively, as endogamous and exogamous groups. They are of special interest as the interior structure of a caste is frequently a valuable evidence of its origin. It has also been found that certain caste names are synonyms. Castes have in such cases been re-grouped. In connection with castes of converts from Hinduism to Islam, useful information has been obtained from the marriage registers of the *Kazis*, showing the cases in which intermarriage between such castes is allowed. Many Musalman castes adhere to the Hindu practice of endogamy. Those Muslaman castes which intermarry are found to be armourers, butchers, farriers, elephant-drivers, and similar occupational groups which are probably descendants of the camp followers of the Mughal armies. It is interesting to note that contact with the Muhammadan armies has left its influence in the greater freedom with which intermarriage is allowed. The social prejudice which prevents members of many Muhammadan castes from marrying outside the caste is a relic of the previously existing Hindu custom, such castes being clearly traceable to a Hindu origin before conversion.

They are found chiefly in areas where Musalman rule has stimulated conversion either by example, as in Bijapur, or by force as in north *Kanara*, once under the dominion of Hyder and Tipu. A great deal of new information has been obtained regarding the interesting Lingayat community, which is found to be based partly on religious and partly on caste distinctions.

Late Dr. J.F. Fleet, C.I.E., supplied some valuable notes which form the basis of a new account of Lingayats contributed by the Superintendent to Dr. Hasting's Dictionary of Religion. The special interest of the community lies in the fact that it exhibits the process by which a religious movement, starting with the abolition of caste distinctions, develops slowly into a community where the most recent converts adhere strictly to the non-intermarrying caste distinctions of their Hindu ancestors.

"The Survey has brought to light a great deal of new information regarding totemistic divisions in the Deccan and Southern Maratha Country. The identification of Maratha guardians or *devaks* with Kanarese *balis* is an indication of a similarity of origin between certain castes and tribes of the Presidency which has not hitherto been suspected. The subject is one which will repay a very careful study.

"Broadly speaking, the term tribe is used for a unit based on common descent as opposed to the term caste which is applied to a social unit founded on common occupation, common residence, common language or common political control. A social unit based on religion is described as a sect.

"A great deal of time and research has been devoted to attempts to arrive at an explanation of the origin of caste. I do not propose to recapitulate the various theories that have been put forward by numerous scholars to explain the origin and continuance of caste in India. It may, however, be remarked that, given the conditions which have prevailed in this country since the first Aryan invasion, a caste system involving the formation of a number of non-intermarrying groups must from the beginning have been inevitable.

"From the dawn of history, India has been subject to invasion by land and sea, and the invaders, who were themselves very probably of mixed origin, have seldom refrained from intermarriage with the heterogeneous populations already established in the country. In the institutes of Manu, we find an attempt to classify names. The process of admixture of blood has continued to the present day. Probably, its influence was especially marked during the series of post-Aryan invasions between the third century BC and the sixth century AD. By this time Aryan, Dravidian, and mixed Aryo-Dravidian castes were numerous. Intermarriage with the invading tribes such as the Ahirs, Gujars and other Scythian units must have led to a great complexity of racial types, each naturally tending to preserve itself from further admixture of blood, by forming a marriage group excluded by the purer groups from intermarriage, and itself refusing to countenance union with those who were members of groups regarded as inferior owing to greater impurity of blood.

"To the influence of race, in itself of great importance, was added the effect of varying occupations as the tribal units passed from the pastoral to the agricultural state and from that to the practice of arts and handicrafts. Thus, true castes were formed, but occupation would not ordinarily obliterate the racial distinctions already referred to. The occupational group would contain various ethnic groups remaining endogamous. In this way, if we start with the idea of descent, we can show the population in tribes divided into groups (castes) following different occupations or starting from the occupation, we may show the caste including a number of different tribal groups. The Ahirs and Gujars, immigrant tribes of great importance, are now divided into many sub-castes such as those found in the Shimpis, Sonars, Sutars, Chambhars, etc. We may, therefore, show Ahirs and Gujars with their occupational divisions as forming part of the tribe, or the castes as a whole, with Ahir and Gujar as sub-castes. In both cases, the sub-divisions are the endogamous units.

"Tribes and castes, therefore, are different ways of looking at the same social groups, the tribe being the forerunner of the caste. Unfortunately, the question of the correct classification of such groups is further complicated by other influences besides those of descent and occupation. Of these, the principals are religion and domicile.

"The effect of religious movements, such as Jainism, Lingayatism, Islam and Christianity on social grouping is specially interesting. Jains, found almost entirely in Gujarat and the Bombay city, usually form an endogamous division of the occupational caste, though dining with the Hindu element may be permissible. Lingayatism is more complex. Starting with

Performance of the Parsi's initiation Ceremony.

A Parsi women burning incense of invite
spiritual power during a festival.

Ganesh Chaturthi celebration.

Photograph of Shirdi Baba during the festival.

Celebration of festival in the memory of Lord Vithoba of Pandharpur.

Celebration of Kolis festival.

Celebration of Gokulashtmi, the birthday of Lord Krishna.

Carnival festival.

A person showing sea food in Goa food festival.

Persons demonstrating a dance in Food and Cultural festival

Beach wedding

People gathered around a temple and the pond in a festival.

Women in traditional dress at Saloon festival.

Bhils of Gujarat celebrating Holi festival.

Dandia dance in a Gujarat festival.

Siddhi dance festival being celebrated in traditional dress.

Performance of garba dance.

Ancient folk dance during festival.

Tarpa dance: Men and women are dancing during festival.

Bohad dance during festival.

Men are dancing in colourfull dresses during festival.

Men and women are dancing during festival.

In traditional dress people are celebrating a festival.

Decorated boats in a festival at Daman.

Women are participating in a festival.

a repudiation of caste distinctions, Lingayats have passed through several phases, the earlier converts coming in time to separate themselves from those who joined later and, ultimately, as in the case of Jains, Lingayats merely form an endogamous division of the Hindu group from which they were converted... Islam should not recognise caste, but the practice varies. There are Muhammadan castes that marry with other castes of the same faith. There are may that will only marry within their own caste, though, of course, not with the Hindu members. Even Christianity has been a source of caste division in places. There are three caste divisions of Christians in the Goanese territory, known as Brahman, Chardo and Sudra and certain castes such as Bhandaris, Kolis and Kunbis contain Christian sections that only marry within such sections.

"Most important in its effect on caste formation is the influence of domicile and language. A portion of a caste separated by migration from its parent body tends to develop certain differences in customs, occupation or interests. Owing to the common tendency to exaggerate the importance of such differences which is a specially Indian characteristic, marriage with the original body of the caste is frequently abandoned on account of these small differences. In the past, no doubt, the difficulty of communication accelerated this process. Marriages with caste fellows separated by a lengthy and tedious journey from a remote section of the caste would tend to be of rare occurrence, and eventually be looked on as in some way contrary to the caste practice, that is to say, as unlawful. The result can be traced in numerous cases where the sub-castes have a territorial name.

"Mr. A.M.T. Jackson has drawn attention to the fact that a change in domicile on the part of a portion of a caste was peculiarly liable to create new sub-castes owing to the powers exercised by Hindu rulers over the caste organisations. As the supreme authority, the king must decide on questions of caste practice and he might well do so in such a way as to create local practices at variance with the custom of sections of the caste under another jurisdiction. Here again the proneness of the people to attach undue importance to small points of differences would lead to intermarriage being abandoned between the sections of the caste under different political control. This is no doubt a good instance of the effect of domicile on caste fission. Mr. Jackson's theory will be found to derive much support from the close resemblance between the sub-divisions of the two leading castes in Gujarat, the Brahmans and Vanis, which have many of the same territorial names...

"In the Deccan, where in Hindu times political control was more uniform than in Gujarat, castes have retained a greater measure of cohesion. This has been preserved under the Muhammadan rule, even though the Deccan was then divided between five, and subsequently three, kingdoms. These territories, unlike the early Gujarat states, were ruled by Muhammadan kings, who did not interfere in caste disputes. That Bijapur, Ahmednagar and Golconda have not given their names to caste divisions is not therefore evidence against the validity of Mr. Jackson's political theory.

"It will be gathered from the foregoing remarks that caste is, in reality, a system of 'self-determination' based on the habit of attaching more importance to the differences between social groups than to that which they have in common. Social union is fostered and maintained by attaching importance to all that human beings, whatever their race, occupation or domicile, may have in common. Social cleavage is inevitable when an exaggerated importance is attached to differences of race, occupation or domicile between two groups of individuals. The barrier of religion may be expected to give rise to groups that will not intermarry, for it is based on fundamentals. But when to this is added an endless series of social fences erected on account of differences in origin, occupation or custom, it is inevitable that society should break into a number of self-contained elements to which there can scarcely be a limit. Too frequently, the bar on inter-marriage and inter-dining, which is the essence of caste organisation, is based on an assumed superiority of one group of individuals over another, so that, broadly speaking, the Indian caste system might be described as the most complete system of social exclusiveness that the world has ever witnessed. A common sentiment of Indian nationality might provide in time a sufficient motive for pulling down caste barriers. But in India habits and customs, readily formed, are adhered to with great tenacity. An inter-caste marriage law, now under discussion, does not promise to achieve any great measure of success. Recently, inter-marriages have been recorded between endogamous castes such as Deshasth and Chitpavan Brahmans. These, however, are exceptional, and there is no present indication that caste barriers on inter-dining and inter-marriage are likely to be rapidly removed.

"The Survey, therefore, has had to deal with a number of groups which cannot accurately be described as being racial, occupational, sectarian or geographical though one or more of these influences has produced the group in each case. It is almost impossible in such circumstances to avoid cross-divisions when drawing up a list of caste units, particularly in the case of Lingayats. 'The aim of the Survey has been to show in each case the groups that form endogamous units, combined for convenience of description under the heading of a major group which must in some cases be religious, *e.g.,* Lingayats, sometimes occupational, Vanis and in rare instances tribals, for instance, Bils, Kolis, Kathis, etc.

"It is of interest to note that when, owing to the influence of the four main causes of caste evolution already described, a group divides into sub-castes, the process occasionally has two distinct stages. To commence with, a group that formerly allowed inter-marriage freely between all its members develops a section that for racial, functional or similar reasons holds itself superior in status to the rest of the group. This is shown by the former declining to allow their daughters to marry the sons of the other caste members, but accepting brides for their own sons from the main body of the caste. In Punjab, a great many castes are thus related to each other to the present day, and completely endogamous castes are of rare occurrence. In the Bombay Presidency, the practice is less common, but it is found among Rajputs, Marathas, Lingayats and even among the lowest castes. Maratha, who were once one with Kunbis, will still marry Kunbi girls in some parts of the Presidency. Lingayat Panchamsalis are divided into Jangams and Banjigs, of which the former will marry the daughters of the latter after a process of initiation, though in no circumstances would they allow their own daughters to marry Banjigs. Two such groups, of which the lower is known technically as hypergamous, will usually tend to develop into completely separate castes in the due course of time. The marriage of girls from the lower section is abandoned as soon as the breach between the social status of the two sections is sufficiently wide. In the writer's experience, one of the lowest castes of the Presidency, the Mahars, developed an embryo new caste recently in this way, owing to a number of Mahars having learnt to drive motor vehicles. The added wealth and prestige that this occupation brought with it showed itself in a 'Driver' section, which was disinclined to continue free intermarriage with the caste as a whole. It only requires time in such circumstances for the caste to develop a completely endogamous 'Driver' division.

"In the course of the work of the Survey, it has been possible to accumulate some interesting facts bearing on the extent to which primitives, *i.e.,* pre-Aryan as well as foreign or immigrant elements, can be traced in the castes of the Presidency excluding Sind. The result of investigations in the southern portion of the Presidency, where castes are clearly organised on primitive lines, has brought to light a regular system of totemistic divisions of special interest and significance. These divisions are locally known as *balis* and are named after animals such as the elk, the hog deer, the elephant, the monkey, the tortoise, certain fish, and trees or plants such as the banyan, pipal, screw pine, plantain, etc. There is a division named after the white ant's nest. These *balis* are exogamous and display the usual totemistic features, *i.e.,* members worship the tree, plant, animal or other object giving its name to the *bali* on special occasions such as marriage or the occupation of a new house. They will not cut or injure it in any way and in no circumstances may those who have a common *bali* be allowed to intermarry. Children appear originally to have inherited the mother's totem. Later, this system has been modified into one of tracing the totem through the male parent.

"Further north in the Presidency we find that many castes show traces of having originally possessed a similar organisation. There is a remarkable resemblance traceable between the guardians or *devaks* of the Maratha castes in the Deccan and the *balis* of North Kanara. The same trees, for instance, the *pagchamna* (Mesua ferrea) and screw pine (Pandanus odoratissimus), are found as *devaks* and as *balis*. Being regularly worshipped, carefully preserved and governing inter-marriages, they appear to possess the leading characteristics of totems. It is reasonable to assume that the *devak* with its suggestive resemblance to the *bali* is strong evidence of the primitive origin of at least an important element in the castes in which it is found. From this assumption, very interesting results may follow—clearly Marathas contain a much stronger pre-Aryan element than has hitherto been supposed.

"We are on more difficult ground when we endeavour to trace the remains of foreign elements in the caste formations of the Presidency. Late Sir James Campbell attached much importance to the survival of the names of post-Aryan invading tribes such as Yavans, Parthians, Ahirs, Gujars and Yadavs or of the early ruling Indian dynasties, *e.g.,* Maurya, Kadamba, Chalukhya, among the castes of the Presidency. It has been seen that Ahir and Gujar divisions are still found in many castes. Maurya, Kadamba and Chalukhya survive in the form of surnames, *i.e.,* More, Kadam and Cholke, among Marathas, Kunbis, Mahars and Kolis. But it is unsafe to attach much significance to names in India. They probably bear little more significance than the term 'Shivajis' which was formerly applied by the English to numerous castes enlisted under the banner of the Maratha hero, that is to say, they indicate subservience to a common leader or dynasty, but do not connote common descent. The Ahir and Gujar elements stand on a somewhat different footing to the surnames, but it is impossible at the present day to arrive at the exact relation which such sub-castes bear to the original Ahir and Gujar tribes. The subject has been very ably treated by D.R. Bhandarkar in his study of the foreign elements in Hindu society, where both Nagar Brahman and Sisode Rajput have been shown to have been Gujars originally. It is certain that inter-marriage with local elements has largely obscured the extent to which Ahir and Gujar have contributed to modern caste formations, even in cases where the name survives.

"The general impression conveyed by the Survey is that the original foreign element in many of the castes has been greatly obscured by inter-marriage with the indigenous population. Even the Parsis, the most exclusive of immigrant castes, have admittedly mixed with the jungle tribes of Gujarat and the issue, until recently, has been admitted to the Parsi community. Ultimately, we may perhaps be prepared to the conclusion that the tribes and castes of the Presidency have far more in common as regards their origin than has hitherto been admitted.

"The pages of the Survey contain much evidence in support of this contention. There is scarcely a caste that is not found to possess a section known as Akaramashe, Bande, Shinde, Dasa, kale, etc., signifying that there has been irregular union either with women of a lower caste or with men of a higher one. The institutes of Manu allow seven generations of marriage within the caste to restore the full status to the issue of such a union. The evidence available tends to show that a much less drastic test was imposed in recent times. The Abyssinian Angria married a Maratha girl, and history equally records instances of Koli chieftains who have been allowed a similar privilege, the children being doubtlessly classed as Marathas in both instances. For many years, Maratha Kunbi women have served in Brahman houses in the Konkan, the issue being classed as Shinde under Marathas."

As for the description of birth, marriage, death and other important social ceremonies, Mr. Enthoven states, "The conclusions to be drawn from a comparison of these ceremonies must await the results of a detailed study. There are certain special ceremonies derived from Dravidian castes in Southern India which tend to occur in the Deccan and thus suggest some connection with non-Aryan elements. Until recently, the social status of a caste has been greatly affected by the prevalence of infant or adult marriages, and the existence or prohibition of widow re-marriage. It is of interest to note that, while lower castes have been endeavouring to raise their social status by introducing child marriages and abandoning the marriage of widows, a reform movement among the highest castes is aiming at a return to adult marriage and the re-marriage of widows. The development is one that has far-reaching effects in the near future.

"A number of reports have borne witness to the prevalence, among certain wild tribes and lower castes, of the practice of marriage with trees. The occasion selected is when a bachelor desires to marry a widow. In this case, the unmarried partner first goes through the ceremony with one of the totem trees, *e.g.,* the *shami* Prosopis spicigera or *rui* Calotropis gigantea. In some cases, this tree must belong to a different village from that of the bridegroom's which shows that it represents a woman selected similarly from another exogamous section. The tree is then cut down and destroyed. It seems probable that the tree bride is intended to form a spirit companion to be widow's first partner, who might, if not so satisfied, devote an unwelcome amount of attention to the re-married couple. This curious custom is in vogue in all parts of the Presidency. It is not to be confused with the ceremony known as *Ark-vivaha, i.e.,* marriage with a *rui* bush, as prescribed in the Sacred Books for Hindus, who lose two wives, before they marry for the third time. Most probably the primitive custom gave rise to the Hindu rite, which is restricted to special cases of marriages with third wives, but the original ceremony is clearly a spirit-scaring rite designed to protect a bachelor who marries a widow.

"In the early days of the Survey, a trained operator was employed for a short time, under the direction of late Sir Herbert Risley, in taking anthropometrical records of some of the leading caste types in Mumbai. The number selected for measurement in the case of each caste was very small, and this in itself would render it desirable to view the results with caution. As they stand in their published form, they exhibit such an unexpected jumble of castes and tribes, whether placed by cephalic measurement or nasal index, that it is impossible to deduce from them conclusions of value. Risley was at one time inclined to the view that measurements recorded among the Marathas afforded evidence of their Scythic origin. He based this conclusion on the discovery of broad-headed people in the Deccan. But measurements which bring together the Brahman and the Mahar require a great deal of collateral evidence from reliable sources before they can safely be used as the basis of a theory of racial origin. A reference to Risley tables (vide People of India—Appendix IV) will show the Mumbai castes or which measurements were taken grouped in the following order :

A. By Cephalic Index

1. Deshasth Brahman, 2. Mahar, 3. Chitpavan Brahman, 4. Kunbi, 5. Koli, 6. Maratha, 7. Shenvi Brahman, 8. Vania, 9. Nagar Brahman, 10. Prabhu.

B. By Nasal Index

1. Deshasth Brahman, 2. Nagar Brahman, 3. Shenvi Brahman, 4. Vania, 5. Prabhu, 6. Koli, 7. Chitpavan Brahman, 8. Kunbi, 9. Deshasth Brahman, 10. Maratha, 11. Mahar.

"It will be seen that in the first of these groups a low cephalic index is shared by the Mahar, one of the lowest castes of the Presidency, with the Deshasth and Chitpavan Brahmans. This is at least disconcerting. The Mahar would not be expected in such strange company. Again, in the case of the nasal index, to which Risley at one time attached so much importance as to hazard the theory that a man's social status would be found to vary in inverse ratio to the mean relative width of his nose, we find the lead rightly taken by three Brahman castes, which are followed by the Vani and Prabhu. After that, the classification is very suspicious. The Koli is found above the Chitpavan Brahman, the Maratha Kunbi above the Deshasth Brahman, and both of these are higher in the scale than the Maratha. It is impossible from the known facts to find any satisfactory explanation of these two lists of precedence. The Mahars and Kolis must be typical representatives of the early types in the Presidency as can well be found. Yet these measurements give them a place close to the Brahmans, and even above the Deshasth. The Maratha is found below the Koli and the Mahar in cephalic measurement, and placed below the Koli by nasal index. His history and social position would lead to the expectation that the position should be reversed. Unfortunately, it has not been found possible, owing to the withdrawal of financial support from the Survey, to pursue these enquiries and test the recorded data by making additional measurements for each selected caste, or by measuring other typical castes not included in the scope of Risley's observations. This might have thrown some further light on the very curious results already recorded. If any theory at all is to be based on the Risley tables, then it would seem to be that the tribes and castes of the Bombay Presidency are much more closely connected, racially, from the highest to the lowest, than history, tradition, customs and appearance have hitherto led us to suppose."

Mr. Enthoven further observes, "To illustrate the difficulties in which the classification of the people of the Presidency by tribe and caste is involved I will describe briefly a few typical groups representing important units of the population—Vanis, Marathas, Lingayats, Bhils and Kolis.

"The Vani, Banya or Banjig is a trader corresponding to the Vaishya of the fourtold classification of the Manu. As Vaishyas, they claim a twice-born status but here their common interest ceases, for they are divided into a large number of groups that will not intermarry. Of these in Gujarat, the following divisions are common to the Brahman and Vani :

1. Agarval, 2. Desaval, 3. Gujar, 4. Harsola, 5. Jharola, 6. Khadayata, 7. Kapol, 8. Mevada, 9. Modh, 10. Nagar, 11. Nandora, 12. Osval, 13. Palival, 14. Porvad, 15. Shrimali, 16. Sorathia and 17. Vayada,

"These being mainly geographical in origin, tend to bear out Mr. Jackson's theory of caste fission to which reference has already been made. These numerous groups contain Jain and Hindu divisions, known as *Sharavak* and *Meshri*, that will not intermarry. They have also divisions known as Visa (20), Dasa (10), Panch (5), Adhich (2½), representing an increasing admixture of some lower element.

"In the Deccan, the Vani caste is more homogeneous, only a few divisions being found, leading to the fact that political control has been more uniform in that area than in Gujarat.

"Further South, the Vani is known as a Banjig, and is generally a Lingayat. As such, he will not marry with Hindu or Jain Vanis.

"Marathas are the chief unit in the Deccan and Konkan, probably deriving their name from Maharashtra, *i.e.,* the Deccan, and representing a tribe with some Northern elements but largely aboriginal. There is probably no substantial difference in origin between the landholding and warrior sections, *i.e.*, Marathas Proper, the cultivators, *i.e.,* Maratha Kunbis, and the numerous local occupational castes such as Maratha Vanis, Sonars, Sutars, Partis, etc. Intermarriage is not ordinarily allowed between these groups, although, in remote parts, Marathas Proper will take girls in marriage from the Kunbi or Kulvadi caste. They will not marry their girls to boys of the Kulvadi caste. The Kunbi, again, is at times recruited from the Koli who settles down to agriculture and acquires a 'Kunbi' or cultivator status. The rise of the Maratha power in the seventeenth century induced the fighting classes (land-holders) to claim for themselves the Kshatriya rank, and to discourage widow remarriage. It is chiefly on this ground that they claim to be superior to the Kunbis. But, by descent, the Maratha appears to be one with the Maratha Kunbi and certain other occupational castes in the Deccan.

"Lingayats are a religious body dating from the eleventh century, when they separated from the Hindu fold by denying the authority of the Brahman, rejecting the scriptures, and abandoning Hindu ceremonies and pilgrimages. Largely recruited from Jain traders or Banjigs, these with their priests, known as Jangams, formed originally one body ignoring caste distinctions. Later converts, however, were in course of time relegated to an inferior social status, thus giving rise to endogamous groups resembling the ordinary Hindu caste in exclusiveness, though adopting the special religious rites of Lingayatism. Hindus and Lingayats do not intermarry, even if they have a common caste name and occupation. The original rejection of caste distinctions has thus, it will be seen, given place to caste distinction has thus, it will be seen, given place to the formation of castes containing Lingayats bearing the same relation to Hindus in such castes as the Jains in the Vani divisions of Gujarat bear to the Hindu members.

"The Bhils and Kolis are aboriginal tribes which probably do not differ at all in origin. They are undoubtedly the former inhabitants of the greater part of the Presidency, now largely confined to hilly or jungle tracts of country. The common bond between Bhils is one of descent, as is the case with Kolis. Changes in occupation and a certain admixture of foreign blood have led to the formation of a number of divisions in each case. Among the Kolis, we find divisions with the names of Ahir, Bhil, Dhangar and Maratha. Ahirs and divisions with Maratha names are found among the Bhils. Other primitive tribes besides the Kolis, such as the Berads, have Bhil divisions. It has been seen that the Koli, by taking to cultivation, may rise to the position of a Maratha Kunbi. For the most part, the Bhils and Kolis remain good examples of purely tribal stocks.

Intermarriage with inferior Rajputs has in places produced mixed castes from both sources.

"During the progress of the Survey, the Superintendent has automatically become a tribunal for settling disputes regarding caste precedence. The circulation of the draft monographs led to the formulation of claims, for instance, those of Panchals to be classed as Bishva Brahmans, of Sonars to be described as Daivadnya Brahmans, and of Vadvals to be admitted to the rank of Panchkalshis or Somvanshi Kashatriyas. Interesting documents have been produced bearing on these disputed points. Manbhavs have been proved to be entirely distinct from the degraded caste of Mangs with which they were formerly supposed to be connected. A very striking resemblance has been brought to light between Manbhavs and the ancient Caristian seet of Manicheans (273 AD). The Savashe Brahmans have established their appeal against their former classification as Sahavasi Brahmans. If in the decisions arrived at on these and similar points, the Superintendent's views fail to meet with general acceptance, it may at least be agreed in support of them that the evidence on both sides has been very carefully examined in arriving at these results," adds Mr. Enthoven.

Customs of Gujarat

Gujarat comprises diverse ethnic groups that may broadly be categorised as Indic (*i.e.,* northern-derived) or Dravidian (southern-derived). The former consists of the Nagar Brahman, Bhatia, Bhadela, Rabari and Mina castes (the Parsis, originally from Persia, represent a much later northern influx) and the latter consists of the Bhangi, Koli, Dubla, Naikda, and Macchi-Kharwa tribes. The rest of the population, including the aboriginal Bhil tribe, exhibits mixed characteristics. Members of the Scheduled Castes and of the aboriginal tribes account for nearly one-fifth of the state's population. There is one entirely tribal district of Dangs and Ahmedabad district has the highest population of Scheduled Castes.

About 70% of the population are Hindus ahead of minorities of Muslims and Jains. The most urbanised part of the state is the Ahmedabad-Vadodara (Baroda) industrial belt. Major towns that were once capitals of princely states are Rajkot, Junagadh, Bhavnagar (Bhavnagar), and Jamnagar. The folklore and folk culture of Gujarat had its origin in the mythology of Lord Krishna. Dance forms and festivals in honour of Lord Krishna exist, *Garba* and *Bhavai* being two examples.

The main constituents of the state population are Hindus, Muslims, Jains and Zorastrians or Parsis. The caste system is strictly followed by the Hindus of Gujarat. Besides the 'Brahmins' and the 'Banias' whose functions and occupations are fairly well determined, the community of '*Patidars*' owning land is the strongest force in the state. *Patidars*, also called *Patels*, are the best agriculturists of Gujarat, grouped into four categories: Levas, Kadawas, Anjana and Uda. The *Levas* are most shrewd and are concentrated in central Gujarat. The *Kadawas* are most numerous in the Mehsana district.

The fourth group of population which may have been a native of Gujarat is the community of aboriginals, locally known as '*Bhils*', inhabiting the hilly tracts of Gujarat that border the plains from *Abu* in the north to *Dangs* in the south. The Bhils may be regarded as a mixed group in Gujarat, on absorbing Rajput blood and that of the tribals. The Bhils regard themselves as the Kshatriya caste who had to take shelter in the hills of the Vindhyas and the Satpuras, along the lower Narmada, to save themselves from the wrath of a Brahmin hero, Parashuram. The Bhils of Gujarat thus do not possess any racial basis distinct from the other inhabitants of the region. The other tribals of Gujarat are concentrated in the south-eastern Gujarat particularly in Panchmahals, Surat, Baroda, and Broach districts. The main tribal groups are the Bhils, the Dublas, the Naika-Narkdas, the Gamits and the Dhankas.

Different groups which are distinct from one another in their language and social and cultural traits, customs and traditions indicate their successive immigration from the land as well as from the sea. While the Aryans came by land, the Persians, the Arbas and the Africans came by sea, but in course of time, they fused into a mass of humanity with distinct social and cultural traits. The Aryans were perhaps the first immigrants to come from the north who either conquered or drove away the aboriginal Bhils. The Aryans are now commonly recognised as Hindus along with the Bhils. A third class of people known as

Kolis are equally important who occupy an intermediate social position between the Aryans and the Bhils. The immigration in the medieval period brought Islam and Zoroastrianism to Gujarat and initiated the growth of a multi-religious society. Subsequent developments and the internal migrations in the country led to the growth of a society in Gujarat.

Though the peninsula of Kathiawar is named after the Kathis, the latter are no longer the majority community in Saurashtra. Successive waves of immigrants from other parts of India have led to predominance of different communities and cultures in Kathiawar. The powerful royal families, which conquered Saurashtra later established their rule, coercing the Kathis to accept their dominance and follow their own pastoral occupations or take to more settled occupations like farming. The nomadic people of Kathiawar without any past royal glory like that of the Kathis are the 'Rabasis', essentially a community of cattle-breeders who had migrated from Sindh, and Marwar who claim a Rajput ancestry. Tall, strong and well-built, the Rabaris stand out prominently by their physical features and dress. The generic Gujaratis are found all over the state, who trace their lineage from Gurjars after whom Gujarat is named. They are believed to have migrated to India with the Huns and passing through Punjab settled in Gujarat. Gujaratis had been highly influenced by the cultural waves from the mainland. Various religious traditions like Shaivism and Vaishnavism that sprang upon the mainland were imbibed by Gujarat which in turn developed its own saints and devotees. Thus, various successive waves of immigration were absorbed in the society that was fast evolving.

As a result of this amalgamation, the general term 'Gujaratis' can be applied to the entire population of the state. The Kutchis, the natives of the peninsula of Kutch, a district of Gujarat, have their own dialects, and while identifying themselves as 'Gujaratis' outside the state, they prefer to retain their identity as people within the state. The Kutchis are both Hindus and Muslims who have mainly migrated from Sindh. The Jadeja Rajputs, the Lohanas, and even the Muslims, many of whom are 'Maldharis', the cattle-breeders, have all come from Sindh due to their defeat by some kings and their religious persecution.

However, the Kathis, the settlers of Kaithiawar, after whom the peninsula was named, arrived in Saurashtra during the fourteenth century. Earlier, they were a nomadic tribe in Central Asia from where they were driven southwards by the Muslim invaders. 'Khachar' and 'Chotila' had been the important seats of the Kathis. Worshippers of the sun, they were essentially nomadic people.

As mentioned above, the castes and sub-castes among the Hindus of Gujarat are strictly adhered to. A few religious groups have a particular geographical affinity. The Hindus and Jains are diffused all over. The other minority groups, by and large, show regional variations in their distribution, sometimes disproportionately concentrated in certain areas. For instance, the Muslims have a much larger population in Ahmedabad, Surat, Junagadh and Kaira than anywhere else. The first three cities have been the seats of Muslim rule for some time and the Muslim population, a vital element in the royal 'entourage', shifted to these cities. The Zoroastrians had migrated from Diu, the place where they originally landed from Iran. Some of the towns in the Surat and Bulsar districts, like Billimora and Navasari, seem to be largely planned and developed by the Zoroastrians, who never took to farming and engaged themselves mostly in commercial and industrial endeavours. The place where the Parsis landed first on the Gujarat coast is Sanjan from where they spread in all directions. The Parsis then moved to Vankaner, Broach, Variav, Ankaleshwar, Cambay and Navasari. The most important of these towns is Navasari, which is also the seat of Parsi priesthood. Even today, a large number of Parsis who have migrated to other parts of the country, particularly Mumbai, still consider Surat or Navasari as their ancestral home. The community, though divided into two sub-sects, the Shahenshahi and the Kadmi, has its own customs, rituals and religious ceremonies. Being the worshippers of fire, their fire temples are called 'Agyaris'.

In Gujarat, the Muslims can be divided into two sub-groups: those who have foreign blood and others who are of the Indian origin converted to Islam by hook or by crook. The immigrant Muslims and their descendants are divided into four traditional sub-groups : Saiyads, Shaikhs, Moghuls and Pathans, and the convert Muslims are usually called as Bohras. These distinctions are intra-communal and are perhaps considered in matrimonial alliances, but the Muslims as a community are governed by Islamic codes and Mohammedan law.

The most important of these communities are the Hindus who are the most comprehensive with its *Varnas*, castes and religious sects, all of which have come to overshadow the general significance of the word Hindu which symbolises a group of humanity that has been living in India since the earliest times of history. The social life of the Hindus is characterised by many religious customs, ceremonies and rituals. Their group life thrives on the common religious and caste groupings. Though the customs and traditional practices are fast disappearing under the impact of the modern trends, the castes and sub-castes still retain their hold in the social hierarchy and marriage alliances. the Brahmins, Rajputs and Banias particularly believe in endogamous marriages and marry in their own caste or sub-caste. The Hindus as a whole are ridden with religious and social prejudices and hierarchies. Law does not always acclaim social approval and what is socially approved and often encouraged may be anachronistic.

In the state, the Hindus are divided between the followers of Lord Vishnu and those of Lord Shiva. As a result, there are old shrines dedicated to both these deities. Most of the Brahmins are the followers of Lord Shiva. The Banias, the merchant class, as a rule are devotees of Vallabhachari, while the Rajputs also show great attachment to Shiva.

The main sects among Hindus include: *Shaivaites, sub-sects: Shankar,* and *Lingayats (*not many); and *Vaishnavas, sub-sects: Ramanujacharis, Vallabhacharis, Madhavacharis, Swaminarayans and Kabirapanthis.*

Among them, the Vaishnavas are more numerous and among the Vaishnavas, the Ramanujacharis have a commanding position. However, a vast majority of Hindus do not believe in any of these sects and their religious affiliations are limited to their castes.

Life in a Gujarati village is largely controlled by the forces of tradition and the needs of the agricultural economy. The community life of a village does not represent a smooth collective living of simple village folks. The recent land reforms have brought a sense of security among the farmers and a greater awareness of their rights. The impact of industrial developments and the planned efforts of the Government to improve agricultural production and village life, in general, is spectacular. The social relations, often characterised by stratification from the higher to the lower, from the landowner to the land tiller and the existence of extremes, are undergoing a vast change. The result is that the old tyranny of the landlords or money-lenders has become largely a thing of the past. Ownership of land by land tillers has given them more strength.

However, no big change in the social attitudes of the village people is seen. Village society is ridden with factions and feuds. Caste-hierarchy still has its sway and the increasing economic freedom of the individuals has not liberated them from age-long social bondage. The commonest and perhaps the strongest bond among the villagers is a common village site. Besides a common ancestry, a common religion and a common association of interests linked up with the village people. Socially, they follow common customs and observe common festivals rites. They feel themselves part of a group in so far as certain social obligations and taboos are concerned. The common social codes are a check on the behaviour of an individual and every villager is a custodian of these codes and is free to criticise and enlist the support of others in condemning the behaviour which is not consistent with past practices. The social classes, the castes and the sub-castes are as distinct as had been during the old times.

Every caste has its own peculiar customs, rites and rituals, and marriages, though inter-village affairs, remain confined to the caste itself. Several festivals are celebrated in the course of a year, in some of which all villagers participate. A visit to periodic fairs at a village is something to which an average villager looks forward with great joy and delight. The family in Gujarati society is an institution inherited from the hoary past. The family has not broken up though it is bit weakened because of the increasing migration of earning members from villages to towns. A large part of the family responsibility is borne by housewives. A Gujarati villager is still a greater believer in god than a town's man, and finds merit in bathing in a sacred river or going on a pilgrimage.

Customs of Goa

In the Indian Union, Goa is the smallest state with only 3700 sq km. territory and a population density of 272 people per sq km according to the Census of 1991. Today it exceeds the density prevailing in the adjacent states of Maharashtra and Karnataka, and also the All-India average. There was little comfort to be drawn in the projected population density of Goa in the year 2001, which was expected to be 351 people per sq km. Goan cities, towns and villages are already teeming with people from all over India.

Of the total Goan population, Hindus account for a little more than 64.68%, Christians (Roman Catholics) nearly 29.86% and Muslims 5.25%. The remaining 1.21% includes other religions including Buddhism, Jainism, and Sikh, etc. The scheduled castes amount to 2% of the population and there are no scheduled tribes in Goa. Earlier, the Catholic population, which was about 40%, has now declined to about 30% after independence of Goa, which has relegated the Christians to an ethnic minority.

Goa has remained a Portuguese colony for 451 years from 1510 to 1961. During the period, a large number of Hindus were converted to Christianity forcibly. This was a dark phase that witnessed ruthless oppression in the name of proslytisation. On the other hand, there was also a great deal of interaction between the indigenous and alien cultures, which is reflected in art and architecture and language and various other aspects of culture. This enriched the cultural traditions and strengthened the sense of identity. The Goans distinguish themselves because of their vibrant folk culture, their cuisine and their dialect which has a mixture of Konkani and Portuguese words. The establishment of the Goa-Portugal and Goa-Brazil sea route made possible the transfer of ideas and information on a large scale, which enriched the material culture in Goa.

A significant result of the Portuguese colonial rule in Goa was the rise of an indigenous population of Christians and their westernisation. The members of the upper crust of the indigenous Christian society intermarried with the Portuguese. However, the population of the mixed people (*sankirna jati* in Konkani) is small today. It is the survival of caste system and *varna* hierarchy among the Christian converts that sprang surprise. The Catholics are grouped into Brahman Catholics (the sub-castes of the Brahmans have merged), Chardo Catholics (Kashtriyas and Vaishyas put together) and Sudra Catholics. While the converts maintain many elements of traditional customs and culture, they do not practice *gotra* exogamy and consanguinity. In Goa, there are 34 communities. Their salient features are as below.

A number of communities identify themselves as local communities or as regional communities—they perceive themselves as part of the larger communities in Maharashtra—and some at national level like Christians, Muslims, Sikh, Jain and Brahmans. A number of the communities have ethnographic accounts or *Jati Purana* and recall their references in religious legends and history. A number of them again identify themselves as immigrants to the present habitat or recall their migration in old folklore or their migration in very recent years. The Christian communities inhabit mainly the coastal belt. The Hindu communities are dominant in the regions adjacent to the borders of Maharashtra and Karnataka. One Goan Catholic community called Catholic Gauda has reconverted to Hinduism. The Hindu communities of Goa share a great many social traits with their neighbours in adjoining states.

The people of Goa generally follow the norm of clan exogamy whereas *gotra* exogamy and surname exogamy have been specifically reported by 12% of the Goan communities.

The state of Goa is separated from the mainland by the rivers the Mandovi and the Zuari which join together and empty their discharge into the ocean forming on both sides of the island two spacious anchorages. The Portuguese occupied some area in 1510 as traders and thereafter tried to propagate Christianity. Their philosophy was *Cujuio regio Lillus region, i.e.,* 'the religion of the king is the religion of the subjects. Hence, since

1542, they attempted to impose Christianity on the Goans. The first Archbishop of Goa, Dom Fr. Joao de Albuquerque, founded churches in various corners and very soon there started a number of forcible conversions. The inquisition started from 1560 onwards, creating an atmosphere of horrible torment and harassment. In 1722, the number of the Catholics in Goa was reported to be 1,81,565, while in 1931, the total number of the Catholics is reported to be 2,47,570. Currently, the number of the Catholics in Goa is about 30%. This shows that, in spite of the inquisition by the Portuguese, there was persisting resistance from the Hindus of Goa to maintain their traditional religion. Hinduism and various Hindu temples have co-existed in Goa with the Catholic churches even after 451 years of Portuguese tyranny. In Goa, temples of Santeri, Durga, Vetal, Shiva and other deities have flourished and the traditional institutions of Bhavin and Kalawant associated with their traditional temples have functioned with the patronage of the rich Hindus who have been instrumental in maintaining excellence in music and dance.

Goa has always proved to be a confluence of various creeds and ethnic groups. Currently, it has about 395 settlements (including four major towns). During the inquisition of 1560 AD, 350 temples were destroyed and about 1360 Hindus were converted. Some of the Hindus fled from Goa to Maharashtra and Karnataka. This happened with the connivance of the Crown of Portugal and the tyranny continued unabated till the 19th century. In the early 20th century, however, a section of the Gaudas, who were converted forcibly to Christianity, sought the path of reconversion and obtained purification (shuddhi). On 26th February, 1928, at the initiative of Santan S. Carneiro of the Chimbel village, about 800 Hindu Gaudas were reconverted, ensued by other reconversions at intervals. These reconversions continued till 1929. The reconverted Gaudas formed a new sub-group adopting the name Nav-Hindu Gaudas and thus became alienated from the Gaudas who retained the original religion of Hinduism. Thus, in Goa, there is a strange factor of division of the Gauda community by conversion and reconversion into three sub-groups: Gauda, Gauda Catholic and Nav-Hindu Gauda.

The Portuguese influence is obvious in the area of place names and personal names on account of 450 years of rule. An early convert Loqu, his wife and nephew, after conversion, were re-christened as Lucas, Isabel and Antonio, respectively. Hence, Inas, Franics, Diogo, Jose, Rita, Isabel, Maria, Nicholas, Pedro are some of the common names among the Goan Christians. Some place names like St. Jacinto, St. Pedro, Pilar, Goa Velha, Dona Paula, Vasco da Gama bear the testimony of Portuguese and Catholic influence.

In South Goa, the Kunbis are traditionally supposed to be the autochthones of Goa but some claim that the Kunbis together with the Gaudas and Velips are the original settlers of Goa. The name of Goa is said to have been derived from Gopa Rashtra, *i.e.,* the area of cowherds and shepherds. Goa still is the habitat of the Dhangar whose traditional and present occupation is herding of sheep and cattle.

As for the Hindu caste system, the Bamonn or the Brahmins belonged to the originally priestly class adopting other occupations like agriculture, trade and commerce (merchants), and goldsmithy, etc. The Chaddho or the Kshatriyas were the noblemen, warriors and related soldiers taking up commercial avocations also. The Vaishya or Vanis were traditionally engaged in trade and commerce and among them were the 'shetts' or goldsmiths pursuing the craft of gold and gold ornaments. The *Sudir* or the *Sudras* were the workers and agricultural labourers engaged in the servicing professions. The *Gavddi* or *Kunnbi* were the landless labourers, earlier dislodged by the above high castes.

There were the *Gauddo* or *Gaudde*, probably the Vaishya counterparts in Goa of the neighbouring Karnataka's Gowda, as there is 'Gaud' found in the Canacona taluka of Goa on Karnataka's border. The caste structure in Goa was somewhat like pre-eminence in the social hierarchy based on the nobility of blood, very much resembling the idea of family nobility in the rest of India. All other castes or sub-castes or jatis like Saraswats, Karades, Chitpavans, and Padhyes among various segments of the population of Goa, particularly the goldsmiths and some merchants probably, as seen from the surnames of members of communes purportedly all-Brahmin, were lumped into the Christian caste of Bamonn or Brahmin after their forcible conversion during the successive inquests by the Portuguese.

Various groups among the Kshatriyas or locally known as *Chaddho* were mainly the noble and warrior class. Some of them engaged in the trading known as Chatim, an occupational appellation common to Brahmins also. The caste name of Chaddho gradually fell into disuse. Later, among the people of this caste, who did not embrace Christianity, began preferring the appellation of Maratha. However, the Marathas and Vanis were incorporated into the Christian caste of *Chaddho*.

The Vaishya-Vani caste men who could not get themselves merged as Christian Bamonn or Chaddho group appear as *Gauddo* in place in Bardez Taluka of Goa among Christians and those among the Hindu remnants of this caste in the present Canacona taluka etc. *Gauddo* caste is treated among Christians as one of the three high castes. A large number of Vaishya-Vanis emigrated to the adjoining district of Sindhudurg in Maharashtra. Their descendants trace their origin to Goa and the flight of their ancestors at the time of the tyranny of conversion.

The Christian counterpart of the Hindu Vani is the Gauddo Christian caste. The goldsmiths call themselves 'Daivednya Brahmins' and are called in Goa as '*Shetti*'. They were put into the Christian caste of *Sudir* or *Sudras*, which is a lower caste. They did not get into the caste deemed superior because they were known as 'Panchal' or the artisan group of castes.

In Goa, the aboriginal stock is called the '*Gavddi*', a higher caste. The Christian convert of the Gavdi aboriginal was termed as Kunbi. The Kunbis are found in larger number in the Salcete taluka than in any other taluka of Goa. At the time of the conversions and inquests by the Portuguese missionaries, there were untouchables like the 'Mahara' and Chambars, who were converted to Christianity and were found in the Chandor village. Chambars have later merged with the *Sudras* among Christians. Bamonn and Chaddho are the two high castes among the Hindus in Goa, who continued to attach their caste to the Christian names and surnames even after conversion.

The Portuguese effected the first mass baptism or conversion to Christianity in the two prominent villages in the vicinity of the then city of Goa, Divar Island and Carambolim villages, the first of the *Bamonn* and the second of the *Chaddho*. The majority of the total village communes converted to Christianity belonged to the two high castes. The priests in the Goan community should be recruited from the Bamonn and Chaddho. At some places, the Christian name is also mentioned along with the old Hindu name while at others the Christian name is mentioned with the person's father name in the Hindu original or in case of the father being a Hindu.

The surnames like Poi, Kamat or Vamotim, Naik, Desai Kudav, Prabhu or Porbu, etc. are common to both the high castes of Bamonn and Chaddho. Christian Bahmonns and Chaddhos are the two leading rival classes among the Goans. The continued maintenance of the caste system among the Christians in Goa is due to the mass conversion of entire villages. As a result of which the religious complexion of the entire village was given a new coat of Christianity without affecting its age-old social structure which was rooted in caste foundations. The old usages and customs and age-old traditions, including superstitions of a varied order, especially the caste-system, were transferred. The Portuguese rulers and missionaries, fearing the relapses of their converts to Hinduism, destroyed all available material related to the old religion including literary works which are stated by historians to have been in Konkani, mainly religious or socio-religious in nature. Moreover, the Telis are a very small community in Goa have has merged with the broader Maratha stratum. Unlike in Maharashtra, the Telis of Goa form a single group without any sub-division. Currently, in regard to marriage and other social activities, they do not strictly adhere to their endogamy and often marry outside their community, especially those who have come under the Maratha caste. Earlier, the Telis used to extract oil from coconut, sesamum and groundnut. But now many of them have given up their traditional occupation and have adopted agriculture and petty trading. The Telis are very small in number and are spread over the north and south of Goa. They are covered by two Devaks, Rumad and Kallan. The

Devaks are strictly exogamous. In other customs and rituals, they follow the Marathas and the importance of Bhatji (priest) is seen much in this group. After the death of a Teli, the Bhatji invokes the soul of the dead and brings it within the house, to be placed in one sacred corner called *daam*. The worship of *daam* on every ceremonial occasion is important in the ritual life of the Telis.

Similarly, the Shimpis existed earlier in Goa. As this region is not a cotton-growing area, cotton thread was imported in Goa during the Portuguese regime. Besides weaving cotton textiles, the Shimpis were also known for tailoring. There is a possibility that the members of the Shimpi community came from the neighbouring Maharashtra because they use surnames like Hirve, Dhekane, Wadkar and Rellekar. Since tailoring has now become a specialised occupation learnt by anybody through training, the tailors who often call themselves *Shimpi* are not necessarily the original Shimpi found in Goa about 50 years ago. The Shimpis were mostly Hindus. But then there were the Muslim tailors also, who were called *Darzi* and most of the Muslim *Darzis* came either from Gujarat or Maharashtra and settled down in Goa. The traditional customs and ritual habits of the Shimpis (a few of them can still be seen in Goa) are similar to the Namdeo Shimpis of Maharashtra. Both the groups of Teli and Shimpi now cannot be easily traced in Goa and even if found, they exist in a very small number.

The caste structure existing in India is more or less followed by the Goan Hindus with a few modifications as warranted by the local social conditions. The Brahman groups of *jati* consists of—the *Bhat* or the priests who officiate at the various temples and are mainly the descendants of those who migrated into the state from neighbouring Maharashtra and Karnataka to man the temples including the *Chitpavan, Karhade, Dravid*, and *Padhye*, the *Saraswats*, who are further sub-divided into the *Vaishnava* and *Smarta* or in Konkani *ube* and *addve* repectively, the term indicating the smear of consecrated ash on their forehead as vertical or across in that order. While the former groups has surnames like Phadke Bhave, Pujari, the later group. Saraswats have Shenvi village. They also take up other occupations like agriculture, trade, teaching, and commerce, the

The Kashtriya varna is headed by the *Chaddhi*. The term, however, has fallen into disuse, now they have adopted the surname of *Maratha*, that was very much prevalent at the time of the Portuguese arrival in Goa in 1510 and much later till the ascendance of Marathas on the political firmament of India. Still some temples continue to have *Chaddhi purus* venerated by them along with *Brahmani purus*, as in Sanguem and Sattari conunties of Goa. The Desai landlords and others with surnames like Naik, Prabhu, Kamat, belong to this varna. There were also other claimants to this caste from the related soldiery of the historical times. These people began calling themselves Marathas. Many other castes of lower hierarchy could be put into the *Sudra* category, including the toddytappers, temple-attached personnel and even the tribal *Gauddi*.

The *Vaishya-Vani* and the sub-castes are the merchants and traders, some of whom have been doing extremely well. The community of goldsmiths and gold dealers go by the surname of *Shet* indicative of *Daivednya* Brahmin, though the latter group refute them. The main surnames of the *Vani* group are Amonkar, Munz, Verenkar, etc. while those of the *Shet* are Raikar, Anvekar, Vernekar. There is a small group in Canacona called Gaud or Gowd, of this caste.

Inferior to them are the occupational groups of the various sub-castes categorized under the Sudra *varna*. They include mostly the craftsmen and artisans like tinsmiths, carpenters, blacksmiths, as well as other professionals like fitters, toddytappers, fishermen, and washermen, etc. There are others also like barbers, wicker-workers and labourers who are outside the pale of the caste-system, as they are regarded as outcastes virtually, though this does not happen so rigidly in Goa. Still further down come the aboriginals called *Gauddi, Kunnbi*, and *Vellip*, who demand schedule tribe status, while they have been included under "Other Backward Classes." There were other marginal communities like *devadasi* (women attached to the temple) and *cheddvvanle* (those born of kept women.)

The *Varna* system of the Goan Hindus that persists to this day, got transferred to the neo-Christian sub-society in Goa, with the active assistance of the Portuguese clergy during the sixteenth and seventeenth centuries. For the Baptism record mention specifically caste of the convert, along with the Hindu as well as the new Christian name. This practice of co-joining the two names together, to indicate their origin, among the upper castes, continued till the 18th century. There must have been on the part of the Portuguese an attempt to hammer out a separate society of Goan Christians, to overcome the stigma of the loss of Superior caste that would fall on them inevitably upon conversion, as found in records and opinions o n the subject. This converted society could only be formed in the image of the social structure of Portugal. The hierarchy there contained the clergy, the nobility and the commoners. On finding that the caste structure in Goa was somewhat similar to the pre-eminence in the Portuguese social hierarchy based on the nobility of blood claimed, they adapted it. Thus, all cases and sub-castes which were then distinct by themselves among the Brahmins or some other claimants to that varna including goldsmiths and even some *Vani* merchants as seen from the caste-coloured surnames of village commune members purportedly all-Brahmin now, were merged into the new Christian caste of *Bamonn* (Brahmin).

In the same way, various group among Kshatriyas, locally known as *Chaddhi* were called so a practice which continues even today, with pride, while it has been disowned by the Hindus of that caste, who now call themselves as Marathas and some even Brahmin. These groups included, mainly the noble and warrior class (*Rajaputras* or *Khetri* as the early Portuguese chroniclers mention them), some of them possibly engaged in the trading profession, known as *Chatim* or *Shet* on that account, which was an occupational term of the goldsmiths mainly but applicable commonly to the Brahmins and Kshtriyas practicing it. A Konkani writer and scholar Shennoy Goembab, himself a Saraswat Brahmin, traced the *jati* term *Chaddhi* to *Chaturathi*, meaning noblemen meriting the honour of four chariots. There is no evidence to suggest that Kshatriyas and Vanis were merged to form a 'new caste' of *Chardo*, as it is called in Portuguese.

The Vaishya-Vanis who could failed in their bid to get merged into the Brahman community and Kshatriya superior castes among the Christians, still appear as *Gauddo* mainly mainly in Bardez county. The Christian counterpart of the Hindu Vaishya-Vani caste is called as the *Gauddo* caste, treated as one of the higher castes, as distinct from *Gauddi* of tribal stock. The other castes and sub-castes who did not get themselves merged into the above three upper castes, among

Goan Christians, and interestingly even some goldsmiths and *Bhanddari*—toddytappers among Goan Hindus—were all clumped together under the category of the Christian caste *Sudir* or Sudras.

The tribal people in Goa are termed as *Gauddi*. The Christian converts from this group continued in some cases to carry the same surname but in most cases were called *Kunnbi*, which is a term different from the one used in Maharashtra for an agricultural caste. They are found in their bulk in the Salcete county of South Goa and in their day-do-day life, are slightly different from their Hindu counterparts and are the faithful adherents of Christianity. Besides, there were a some 'untouchable' castes, like the *Mahar*—wicker-workers and those engaged in menial asks and *Chamar* of the leather workers, who had converted to Christinanity but their social status did not improve a bit. In course of time some of them have merged into the *Sudir* caste of Christians. A few still continue to be in a degraded status.

In the early period, the Portuguese records refer to the upper castes of *Bamonn* and *Chaddhi* as being the two advanced castes among the Hindus in Goa of that time; they continued to attach their caste to their Christian names and surnames even after conversion. In fact, the missionaries attempted hard to convert the Brahmins and Kshatriya first all, either individually or in groups, expecting those lower down the hierarchy to follow suit. But this was contrary to the situation in most parts of India, where the converts generally came from the lower classes.

The initial mass conversions to Christianity are graphically described in respect of the villages of the Brahman and Kshatriyas, which were mostly exclusive of each other, by the missionaries in their letters to home or in books. The earliest large conversions, took place in two prominent villages close to the then city of Goa (now called as Old Goa) named as Carambolim and Divar, comprising the Kshatriyas and Brahmans respectively. Of the total number of villages converted during the 16th and 17th centuries in the three (now four) coastal, better-developed counties of Goa, the majority belonged to these two high castes.

In fact, the Church, bowing to the realities of society at that time in Goa, even directed that the priests in the community should be recruited exclusively from "the two nobler castes." Conversions to Christianity changed no thing except just the faith. The old customs, usages, traditions and superstitions of varied order, including the caste system, were taken to the neo-Christian society.

Thus the Christian Brahmins in Goa continued to be a dominant caste, who occupy some of the highest positions in the administration, clergy and the liberal professions, and the Christian kshatriyas formed a rural aristocracy preponderant Portuguese nobility... occupying a privileged position in the contemporary social hierarchy also in the highest positions in stock of peasants, artisans, today practically free though with memories none too far of the times they 'belonged' to their landlords; this does not mean that there are no cases in which in a relatively-veiled manner there still exists dependence.

The *Kunnbis*, are Christians of aboriginal stock, mostly the landless labourers who work on the plantations of coconut trees, mango-tees and other random jubs on land and around houses of the landlords being employed for hard and risky menial task and particularly as for coconut plucking. But in the course of time, Christianity has bought about a visible relaxation in the rigidity of the Hindu caste system and a better integration of the people of differing social status into one composite community. Education has opened up new opportunities of socio-economic mobility for the lower castes in the state.

Muslims compose a very small religious group in Goa but it has been considerably reinforced over a tiny core of ethnic Goan Muslims, by accretion from the neighbouring Karnataka and Kerala. Earlier the Muslims had the caste divisions of Sayyad and Sheik at the top of the hierarchy corresponding roughly to the Brahmins and Kshatriyas respectively among the Hindus. The Memons, and Muzawars, etc. corresponded to the Vaishya-Vanis among Hindus and the artisans like weavers, tailors, fitters, and labourers with corresponding caste surnames, were approximately equivalent to the Hindu *varna* of *Sudras* or *Sudir*. The Goan Muslims followed the uniform Civil Code enjoined upon all communities irrespective of their caste divisions.

Most of the Muslims are that of the Sunni sect. There are, however, some Shias as well, particularly those owing allegiance to the Aga Khan, and some Bohras also.

Important changes are taking place in the entrenched social system, especially among the Christians, and some relaxation of caste rigidity even among the Hindus. Though mostly the Christian Brahmins and kshatriyas continue to seek marriage partners in their own castes there appears to be operating closer alliance between these upper castes, though at one time due to antagonism, one caste never conceding ground to the other. The mutual prejudices are still in vogue, though their overt expression is suppressed. They appear to have arrived at some amicability in their social relations. They have also begun inter-marrying now if the economic and educational status and social ranking are compatible. Whereas among the Hindus, the Brahmins including the Saraswats are reluctant to give up their dominant position and have little to do with sub-castes in terms of marriage, but shown some leniency. Their treatment of the other castes lower down the hierarchy is becoming lenient now. The educated young men and women of the Sudir castes among Hindus and Christians move rather freely with their peers among the high castes. There is less fear shown to the higher caste people as earlier. Because they mix together as friends now, thought the difference in castes does to a certain extent obviate an open friendship of a more intimate character among them. Because the old members of upper castes still views the lower castes as beneath themselves. The new generation of the lower castes are giving up their old avocations and taking up white-collared jobs, in the opened up society. Emigration to foreign countries of Christians especially in the Gulf which fetch a lot of money have brought more income into the hands of the lower castes who are now able to afford a better living.

Important changes in the political milieu with the bulk of votes in hand have catapulted the Sudirs to positions of dominance in village Panchayat as well as in social organizations like the Jayceias and the Loions Club. The result of all this social churning has been a gradual erosion of the rigid caste system of the old days and the consequent segregation. This had been prompted further particularly after Goa's merger with India.

However, there has been more coalescence among the various occupational group of the Sudir groups. The consequence of all these changes has been a gradual harmony in the society.

As for the religious sphere, among Hindus, there were the *Bhat* among the Brahmin-held temples as well as *Gurav* in the Kshatriya-owned one. There is no change among the priestly orders amongst them. But in the matter of entry into temples, for the lower castes people there is a certain leniency. On certain dates during the year such entry was the privilege of some lower castes and even that of the so-called 'untouchable' *mhar* (mahar). Among the Christians there is a no segregation for various castes or classes in the church or in the cemetery. In the confraternities, however, there was a distinctive uniform for the processions, which was a red shoulder-cape for the upper castes to be worn over a white gauze-like full length gown, while it was a shoulder-cape yellow for some, white and blue or some other colour for still others, according to the caste. But these distinctions are now things of past with in most cases due to being prohibited by the famous Archbishop-Patriarch of the East Indies (Goa), D. Jose da Costa Nunes, in his well-argued circular letter of 1943, thus all are allowed to wear the red cape and white gown. The consequence of this salutary step has been that the upper castes hardly now participate in processions with their uniform over their suit. But there are now members of the lower castes sporting the distinctive uniform with understandable pride.

The Brahman and Kshatriyas among Goan Christians held the monopoly of priesthood for a long time during the four centuries, with a few from the *Gauddo* caste, too. The *Sudir* were not accorded the honour. Now, with a shortage of candidates for the vocation from the higher castes, the *Sudir* have been encouraged by the Church to scale up that ladder. Even the *Kunnbi* aboriginals have been preening with their aspirations to enter the *sanctrum sanctorum* of the Church, and a few of them have achieved the priesthood in this essentially egalitarian religion. There was an interesting saying among Goan Christians of the upper castes epitomizing the careers available to their sons, as put into the mouth of the mother of famed Dr. Jose Inacio de Loyola, a physician, and founder-leader of the *Indian Party*. On being asked what her three sons were doing, she said in Konkani: *Ek Devak, ek Denvcharak ani ek Povak*, meaning (I have offered) one to God (as the priest), another to the Devil (as the lawyer), and the other for the People (as the physician-politician (wedded to the people).

Dadra and Nagar Haveli

Of the 14 communities of Dadra and Nagar Haveli six are tribals and one, Chamar, is the scheduled caste. Besides, there is one Muslim community, Makrana. The Parsis, with their legendary number of 12,000, had arrived in India and landed at Diu first from where they spread to other parts of India. They are still a land-owning, trading and god-fearing community. The Rajput community originally came from the North and took shelter in the Dharampur state. The Kahars and other communities such as Agari, Kapadia and Bharwad are also there. The Warlis are the autochthones of the region. The tribal population which was 88.5% of the total population in 1961 census got reduced to 78.82% (1981), with the influx of non-tribals. The socio-cultural system here is only an extension of the larger system prevailing in Gujarat. The local communities, except for the four tribal groups who represent an overflow of the populations from Maharashtra, have mostly migrated from South Gujarat. Therefore, as many as 12 communities have their presence at the regional level and only the Parsi community has its presence at the national level. Most of the tribal communities dwell in the hilly terrain which has only a thin forest cover left. Most of the men and women are non-vegetarian and consume mainly rice, wheat, *bajra, tur* and gram. Mostly, men folk consume alcoholic drink.

In all the regional communities, there exist social divisions particularly in the form of clan organisation and are endogamous. The tribes stand outside of the Hindu varna system. Adult marriage is being increasingly practised and marriage by negotiation is the norm. Marriage by service exists in four tribal communities. Some tribal groups have both sororal and non-sororal polygyny. Junior sororate is also widespread. Interestingly, *tali* or *mangalsutra* or *ganthi* as it is called is used as a marriage symbol making Union Territory an extension of the southern region particularly Konkan. Payment of bride price is common. Dowry in kind rather than cash has been prevalent in two communities. The rule of residence among them is entirely patrilocal. Divorce is permitted in most of the communities for reasons of adultery and witchcraft, etc. Remarriage of both widow and widower is permitted in many communities. Both extended and nuclear families exist in most of the communities. Male equigeniture is the norm and no property right of the female is found in spite of the substantial role played by the women in the economic activities like agriculture, handicraft, maintaining household by collecting fuel, and fetching potable water. The status of women is generally considered low in the Union Territory.

Clan deities exist in most of the local communities, their worship being an integral part of their social organisation, as do village deities, which are also an integral part of village communities in tribal areas. Since the Portuguese arrival, conversion to Christianity has been reported among two castes, Kokna and Warli. Many religious movements from Gujarat have penetrated into this area and there are followers of many sects such as Jala Ram, Jai Gurudev, Shanti Panth, Gayatri Pariwar and Swami Narayan. The old pattern of commensal restrictions still exists among many tribes except in tribal areas. In the Union Territory, there has been a visible impact of the development process on all communities. The impact of some of the development processes has been most widespread in the Union Territory compared to the rest of the country. However, the gender bias in the matter of access to education and employment persists in all communities in the region. All the communities of Dadra and Nagar Haveli enjoy monopoly over traditional occupation. The system makes people to unite as well as to divide into certain sub-groups. In one way, they co-operate with each other and are inter-dependent, providing assistance to the village life. They are divided in the sense that there is stratification among them as they regard themselves superior or inferior to the other in the social hierarchy. The Mauri Rajputs are considered superior to all followed by the Kapadia, Agri, Bharwad, Parsi, Dhodia, Kahar, Dubla, Varli, Kokna, Makrana, Chamar, Kathodi and Koli Dhor. The rule of residence is patrilocal, except among some of the tribals who practice *khandaria* or marriage by service and the matrilocal residence. Extended and nuclear families are common, its members can be expelled after giving them due share or a member can walk out voluntarily. Unmarried women and other family members who have their own property nevertheless have right to live in the family which has an obligation to feed them. The tribals are independent by nature and their houses are so small that the sons, after marriage, generally build their separate house. The youngest son inherits the residential land and the head of the family is competent to make all acts and enter all contracts. The people still abide by the Code of Usages and Custom of Non-Christian Act of 1854 under which the eldest person in the family is empowered to administer all properties, ceremonies, rites and rituals. When a person living in the extended family dies suddenly without leaving any heir, the extended family inherits all the property of the deceased. A widow succeeds her husband in preference to all other relatives who live separately, including the son. In Dadra and Nagar Haveli, the marriage of a boy and a girl belonging to the same *kurh/kul* (clan) usually does not take place and such marriages are considered bad according to social customs. The rules of exogamy among the non-tribals are applied upto certain degrees which vary according to the customs prevalent in different communities. The tribals, however, practice cross-cousin marriages, among them adult marriage takes place instead of child marriage. Among the regional tribals, the mates are acquired through negotiation, khandaria (marriage by-service) and mutual consent, whereas the non-tribals acquire spouses through negotiation. Both *dej* or dowry and *pend* or bride price in cash and kind are in existence among various communities, while *mehar* is in practice among the Muslim Makrana. Though polygyny is allowed, the people generally practice monogamy. *Natra* (remarriage) or *pat* (widow re-marriage) prevails among the communities other than the Rajputs.

Among the Muslims and Christians of the territory the life-cycle rituals are governed by the Christian and Islamic laws. The tribals have their own set of customs for every occasion, being observed for many years and are considered as good as the customery laws.

A woman among the tribals has to observe certain taboos during her pregnancy to ward off malevolent spirit. Tribals do not have any pre-birth ritual. Elderly female members conduct delivery with the help of *suin,* the locally trained mid-wife from the community. *Pansuthi* is the first post-birth ritual performed on the fifth day after birth when both the child and mother are given bath and the child is placed ceremonially in the *jholi* or cradle and thus both become free from pollution. Kurh (clan) deities are worshipped on the sixth day and the mother herself names the child. Among the Christian tribal converts, children are named by the pastor of the Church. *Babri* or tonsure of a male child is performed by the maternal uncle after completion of one year. A girl, after her puberty and menstruation, is called *banni*, who remains confined for three or four days and cannot enter the kitchen and sacred places. However, she is allowed to carry on working on fields or collecting forest produces or other labour works after four days. She is supposed to wash her hair and bathe to become free from pollution. Premarital sex is common among the tribals and such cases are not taken seriously. However, if a girl conceives, then the boy is forced to marry the girl.

For marriage, *Ram-Ram* or negotiations are initiated by the boy's side. *Bol-dhan* or betrothal takes place one year prior to marriage. Marriage is performed at the bride's residence. In case of the Kokna, traditionally, the marriage used to be solemnised at the bride groom's residence, but now there are no firm rules. The venue for marriage is often decided according to the economic conditions of the parties. Marriage rituals are conducted for three days and begin with the erection of *mandva* or marriage booth on the first day, followed by *harad* or rubbing of turmeric on the bodies of both the bride and bride groom and worship of *kurh* deity on the second day. The bridegroom with the *barhadi* (marriage procession) arrives in the bride's village on the third day. Both the bride and the bridegroom are taken to *mandva* where they make five rounds of the *umar* tree stick erected in the *mandva* to conduct *fera* (circumambulation) in the midst of the verses recited by the *bhagat* (magico-religious specialist). Tying of *ganthi* (chain of beads) round the neck of the bride by the bridegroom is the main ritual. Brothers of both the spouses lift the couple on their shoulders and thus the rituals are concluded. The bridegroom, with his bride, returns to his village the next day where the marriage is consummated.

Among the Dhodia and Dubla, the ceremonies of *hastmilap, barmal, kanyadan* and tying of *ganthi* are the principal rituals performed in the *chauri* (celestial fire in *mandva*), which are common to all the Hindus. The bride is taken back to her parent's house after five days. After five to ten days, the bridegroom with his parents visit the bride's village and brings her back.

Customs of Daman and Diu

The Union Territory of Daman and Diu comprises 25 communities. Out of these communities, five are fisherfolk, five peasants, three tribes, two Muslim and three are scheduled castes. Daman and Diu are historically and culturally an extension of South Gujarat and Saurashtra regions, respectively.

The ethnic composition of Daman and Diu comprises Hindus, including the castes of the Brahman, Bania, Vanja, Kharwa, Koli Patel, Koli, Sangharia, Salat, Sagar, Baria, Kamli, Mitna, Mangela, Bhandari, Kumbhar, Machhi, Bhoi Raj, Dhobi, Vankar, Hadi, Bhangi and Mahyavanshi; the tribals, including the Dhodia, Dubla and Siddi; the Muslims, including Momin and Khoja; and the Catholic Christians. Most of the Hindu caste groups consider themselves the descendants of Rajputs owing to the *atak* or (surname) *gotra* or clan names. While the Kharwa, Koli, Koli Patel, Vanja, Mangela, Bhandari, Sagar and Salat claim to be the aboriginals of the Union Territory, others perceive them as migrants from the various places of Gujarat and Saurashtra. *Tribal sub-plan for Daman-1971 to 1979*-(1987:3) states that 'tribals of Daman migrated to Daman generations before from the adjoining areas. Though they belong to original tribal groups, they have now adopted the life of the common people but still maintain the individuality of their tribe.' The Parsis firstly landed in Diu in the 7th century and then migrated to Sanjan. The *Agyari* (holy fire temple) and *dakhma* or the tower of silence are still found in Diu. They seem to have lived in Diu for a longer period. The statue of a Parsi near Port and the presence of *dakhma* or the tower of silence, place of the disposal of the dead, and a settlement in the name of a Parsi at Diu stand testimony to their claim. Now, there is not a single Parsi in Diu. A few live in Daman but being big businessmen, they have settled in big cities like Mumbai, Surat, Navsari and Baroda. The ethnic composition around the places of Gujarat is similar and represents the communities as found in Daman and Diu. The economic blockage of Daman and Diu by the Government of India during 1954-1961 caused a large-scale migration of some communities, especially the fishing communities, viz. the Kharwa, Machhi and Khoja, to Gujarat, Mumbai, and other Portuguese colonies in East Africa.

However, Daman and Diu do not represent a single instance in which the various communities share a common and compact settlement, but a nucleus consisting of 21 villages was established on the seashore in the west of Daman and east and west of Diu. The scattered settlements of the villages are in the range of three to seven kilometers on way to the towns. The nucleus settlement is inhabited by the Christian, Koli Patel, Khoja, Machhi, Momin, Brahman, Bania, Vanja, Salat and Sanghria, whereas the scattered settlements are inhabited by all other ethnic groups of Daman and Diu.

In the Union Territory, people practise four religions, including Hinduism, Islam, Christianity and Animism. Though the Khojas profess Islam, they are the followers of Imam Hajrat Ali and their present prophet is Agha Khan, the 49th descendant of Imam Hazrat Ali. The distinctive feature of the religious beliefs among the Daman fishermen, especially of the Mangela and Machhi, is that they have also expressed their faith in Nossa Senhora dos Remidios (Our Lady of Remedy), a Christian shrine which the regional fishermen consider as one of the seven sisters of Goddess Laxmi who lost her caste. They visit the shrine, in Nani Daman, once a year at the end of June to show their deep reverence for the safe fishing expeditions and good catches and make offerings to the Goddess of bread, eggs and vegetables. Mothers place their new born babies on the steps of the altar of the church for blessings. The chapel of Our Lady of Remedy, whom they consider the mother of sea, was constructed by a Portuguese named Rey de Mello Sanpalo, the Captain Governor of Daman in 1607 after they had conquered Daman, and it was subsequently converted into a church. Apart from these major religions, people are the followers of other religions including Sanatan Dharma, Swaydhya Parivar, Jalan

Ram and Kabir Panth. Though the temples of various deities have been built here from time to time but there is no pilgrim centre in the territory. However, the devotees visit Somnath, Dwaraka, Amba Mata, Shiva temple at Palsana, Mahalakshmi temple near Dahanu for their pilgrimage which are located in Gujarat and Maharashtra. Birpore, Chardad village in Varoda and Tattva Gyan Vidyapeeth at Thane in Maharashtra are the centres of religious importance for tribals like the Koli, Koli Patel, Machhi, Mangela, Sagar, Baria, and the Mahya Vanshi. The Kalinki Mata temple in the Buchodwada village of Diu has been important not only for the Hindu communities of Diu, but also for the people of the neighbouring districts of Gujarat who pay obeisance once a year during *Poonam Mela*.

In the Union Territory of Daman and Diu, the Koli is a dominant community which broke up into three sub-groups including Rajput Koli, Khedut Koli and Kadiya Koli. Rajputisation is the dominant model for many groups seeking upward social mobility. The Portuguese rule of about 450 years introduced many elements of change in the society. Besides the rise of a Christian community, the period also witnessed introduction of new practices such as dropping or banning of surname, worship of the Christian shrine *Nossa Senhora dos Remidios* (our Lady of Remedy) considered by the Machhi and Mangela as one of the seven sisters of Goddess Laxmi who had lost her caste (the Chapel dedicated to the Goddess was erected in 1607 by the Portuguese), upgradation of status of the outcaste Hadis as cooks and government servants, etc. As in other territories, the Portuguese law did not permit consanguinity among the Christians except with the permission of the Church. The Portuguese also introduced new crafts such as manufacture of bangles out of turtle shell.

After the liberation, the communities have gone back to affixing their surnames as their titles and have revived their affinity with the members of their larger communities in Gujarat, Maharashtra, and the rest of the Konkan region. Most of the communities of Daman and Diu therefore perceive their identity at regional level in terms of their linkages with larger communities. They have their ethnographic accounts. Most of them consider themselves as migrants to Daman and Diu from other regions. Social division exists in all communities except the Momin (Muslims) who claim that they have no social division. Notably, there exist the vansha division including Suryavanshi or Chandravanshi or which are endogamous among the Machhi and Sagar. Such divisions as clans and lineages, etc., exist to regulate marriages. Varna hierarchy is widely recognised and many communities claim the status of Kshatriya, though others do not accept this claim. Exogamy exists in many communities at the village level and also at the surname level. Consanguinity exists mainly among the scheduled castes, scheduled tribes and Muslims. Both junior sororate and junior levirate are widely among the people of the Union Territory. Incidence of polygyny has been reported from various communities, even though monogamy is the general rule. The rule of residence is patrilocal. Divorce is permissible among most of the communities. Like the rest of Gujarat and Maharashtra, an interesting practice is the remarriage of widows first to the trees and the full observance of rites and rituals in case of the marriage of an unmarried girl to a widower and in case of inter-community remarriage of a widow. *Neel* or the ghost marriage which seems to be an important feature is the marriage of the unmarried deceased person to a cow because the belief generally held is that unless the deceased person is 'married off' even after death, other marriages in the family will not be auspicious. Most of the communities in the Union Territory have both extended and nuclear families except the Christians. The norms of avoidance in the family and among kins are almost all pervasive among all communities including the Muslims. Many of the Hindu practices customs, rites and rituals survive among Muslim and Christian communities such as pre-delivery ritual birth, menstruation and death pollution, etc. An interesting feature of the social scenario is the rule of male ultimogeniture for paternal residence and residential land, while the rule of male equilgeniture exists for other forms of property inheritance including cultivable land in most of the communities. While the women continue to play a major role in all fields, particularly economic maintenance of family, their status is generally low. They have little role in decision making with regard to the family matters.

1

Conceiving and Birth

In the western region of India, consisting of Maharashtra, Gujarat, Goa, Dadra and Nagar Haveli and Daman and Diu, the customs relating to life cycle particularly conceiving and birth are diverse, and differing in details in different neighbouring communities and tribes. They also differ in the same tribe and caste in different geographical locations in the same state, or different states. The form of custom indicates the status of the family, clan, tribe or the caste concerned in the social hierarchy. The primitive and savage tribes have many uncouth and strange customs, whereas the urbane castes like Brahman, Rajput and Bania have refined customs, indicating their social status in the society.

The life-cycle rituals and rites are very important in the Life of any individual in the world, and so is the case with the Goans. The life of a Goan Hindu, very much like his counterpart in the rest of India, is governed by the customary rituals and rites known as *samskaras* or sacraments which are rather long-drawn, yet impressive and meaningful. These samskaras are classified into two groups: the *nitya* (customary and imperative), numbering sixteen, which must be performed compulsorily, and the *naimittika* (special performance on particular occasions) the observance of which is left to the discretion of the individual, and these are as many as 24 in number. The life-cycle rituals begin to be performed right from the time of conception of the child in the mother's womb in a rite called *garbhadana* (or earlier on the young woman attaining puberty) and go through the ritual of thread-girdling, naming and other ceremonies, and end with the *antyesthi* rite or the last rite, that is the funeral at a person's death.

Ritual of *Garbhadana*

The rite of *garbhadana* is conducted at the woman's husband's house. When the time of delivery draws near, the pregnant woman is dispatched to her natal place, or the beloved *kullar* in Konkani, and she goes through a ritual called *fulam mallttat* in Konkani—the bedecking or adorning the coiffure of the expectant mother with flowers in the fifth, seventh and ninth months of pregnancy. The first two flower-offering rites are conducted at her husband's house. In the fifth month of pregnancy her lap is filled with the offerings of green clothes. After 'filling her lap' or the rite of *vontti bhortat* in Konkoni, in the seventh month of pregnancy, she is sent to her parental house, where she is adorned with flowers in the ninth month.

Only married women with living husbands, the *sovasnni* in Konkani, from the group of relatives, can participate in these auspicious ceremonies. The birth of a child causes great rejoicing in the family. On the sixth day from the birth, there is a prescribed ritual called *sotti* in Konkani, or *shastti-pujan* in Sanskrit, which is performed by most of the Hindus. That night a local female deity called *Sottvai* is revered and food served to the few people present, with great clan. The whole of the night resounds to the beat of the *ghumatt*, a special local percussion instrument made from a mud-pot contraption, with one end open and the other covered with taut, paste-tuned lizard or snake skin. This ritual is now shorn of its original glory and éclat, but it is still observed in a very simple manner.

From the birth of a child, a period of ten days of taboo and seclusion is observed on the woman who has delivered the baby, when she is prevented from touching any thing in the household. On the eleventh day she is bathed and offered *panchgavya* consisting of cow's urine, basil-plant (*tulasi*) leave, and cowdung, etc. A *homa* or sacrifice ceremony is performed to please God and water from the *tulasi* plant is brought into the house and sprinkled on household objects for their ritual purification. The new mother, is given coconut, sweet preparations in lifuid pasty form called *goddshem*, cakes, rice, and pulses, etc. This observance is now on the wane particularly among the higher castes who seem to attach less importance to rituals. On the twelfth day of the birth of the child, there is performed a ritual *Barso* or the naming ceremony, called elsewhere in India as *Namakaran*. Married women of the extended family with living husbands meet and fill up the lap of the woman who has delivered the baby, with flowers and gifts of all sorts. The child is then placed in the cradle and bestowed a name.

No Special Custom Relating to Conceiving and Birth

In the primitive tribe of the Son Kolis, the period of pregnancy is left without any special custom or religious practice. The only restriction observed by the mother during pregnancy is that if an eclipse, lunar or solar falls during the period, she has to be completely in bed during the *vedh* of the eclipse and during the eclipse. *Vedh* is the period of nine hours before a partial lunar eclipse and the span of twelve hours before a full lunar eclipse or a solar eclipse, whether full or partial; it ends when the eclipse begins. The tribal belief is that any movement by the woman at that time results in the child's body being deformed. A more reasonable and practical restriction is that the expectant mothers are needed to avoid spicy food and meat, for an excessive intake of these victuals results in the child suffering from *garami* or excessive heat. For the same reason, cashewnut, its fruit, jackfruit, and fruit of the *tad* palm are also prohibited.

About them, Vijaya B. Punekar writes, "A Son Koli woman believes that the delivery takes place nine months and nine days after the last menstruation. The woman continues her regular routine work until labour begins. This accounts for the easy delivery for which the women of this community are known. The delivery today generally takes place in a maternity hospital. Sample study reveals that 76.46% of the total number of births in the four localities studied took place in a maternity home, while 23.54% of the deliveries took place at home. Most of the deliveries that took place at home did so nearly twenty year ago... the proportion of birth in a maternity home varies inversely with the distance of the locality from the city.

"When the delivery was at home it was usually at the woman's husband's place. A midwife (*suin*) was engaged and the mother-in-law of the woman and one or two experienced elderly women used to be present at the time of the delivery. A part of the room was reserved for the purpose by throwing a curtain across it. In corner was dug a temporary sink or *mori* for bath and other purposes. The mother and child were given a cot which after forty days was soaked in the sea for three days. As soon as the labour started, a coconut was offered to the deity. The coconut was broken on the thirteenth day. The practice continues to this day. The umbilical cord was buried in a corner of the room.

Twins are rare and so far there have been cases of only twins. Mr. Punekar writes further, "Son Kolis profess to have no preference either for a son or for a daughter. A child is a God's gift and must be accepted as given, they say. However, when asked for the second time, most of them expressed preference for a son. Of the total households studied, 65.45% preferred a son, 28% had no preference and 11% preferred a daughter. The reasons given for the particular preference are economic, religious or sentimental. Those given for the preference for a daughter are more sentimental than anything else. Preference for a son is due to either economic or religious reasons: firstly, sons are helpful to the parents in old age while daughters leave the home; secondly, the son continues the family name; and lastly, unless the son offers funeral oblations (*Pinda*) after one's death, it is believed, one's soul will not reach Heaven. The majority of the people (64.70%) who preferred a son, however, could not express any reason for the preference '...a Son Koli likes to have both sons and daughters. Daughters are an economic asset as long as they are unmarried. Sons will look after the parents in old age and will give them *moothmati* (funeral oblations) after death. They will also carry forward the family name. Hence, the question of preference arises when there are more than one daughter and no son or vice versa, adds Mr. Punekar. The custom relates to the Son Koli tribals of the western region.

Horror of Leaving no issue behind

Mr. R.E. Enthoven writes about the Muslim Customs "The Urdu proverb *Margae mardud, na fatiha na darud*: Here lies the wretch eternally damned without the *Fatiha* or the *Darud* (*Fatiha* is the opening chapter of the Kuran in praise of God: *Darud* the calling down of blessings on the Prophet.) shows the horror felt by the Musalman at the prospect of leaving no issue to perform these ceremonies on his behalf. His desire for the immortality given by children, especially by male children, is much akin to the Hindu hankering after issue to save him from the hell of oblivion by performing his *shraddha* or mind feast. After a year or two of married life, if their union is not blessed by issue, some Musalman women resort of remedies to obtain children. Saints, living or dead, are appealed to, the former to bless by giving charms or medicines to the wife who yearns to be a mother. The law doctor or exorcists also give charms, written on a piece of paper to wash in rose-water and drink.

"Some *Amils* or exorcists give their applicants cardamoms of cloves or pieces of candid sugar on which the mystic and powerful names of God have been blown. These are supposed to possess the virtue of casting out the spirit of barrenness, since as a rule barrenness is believed to be due to spirit-possession. Others direct strands of thread to be worn round the abdomen or the neck; others again simply write or trace some name or charm of words with the tip of the finger over the womb of the woman or the loins of the man. The exorcist or *Amil* has also to help after conception to secure that the issue may be male. He gives charms to be washed and drunk every month or some written charm to be washed in water for a monthly bath. Some dead saints have a reputation as child-givers. To tie knots on bits of string or ribbon with one end attached to a post or pillar supporting a canopy over a saint's grave or to a trellis or balustrade around a shrine is considered by barren women one of the surest means of obtaining issue. Blochmann (*Ain-i-Akbari*, 267, note 1, paragraph 3) notices that the tomb of Shaikh Salim-i-Chishti at Fatehpur Sikhri, in whose house the Emperor Jehangir (A.D. 1605-1627) was born, is up to the present day visited by childless Hindu and Musalman women. A tree in the compound of the saint Shah-i-Alam of Ahmedabad yields a peculiar acorn-like fruit which is sought after far and wide by issue-seekers and carried away and given to their wives, who eat the fruit, and from the moment the fruit is eaten, conceive. If the birth of a child follows the eating of the acorn, the man or woman who took the acorn should for a certain number of years come at every anniversary of the saint and nourish the tree with a supply of milk. The leaves of the tree near the grave of the Miran Saheb of Unjha are also said to favour conception. In addition to these, jasmin and rose bushed at the shrines of certain saints are supposed to possess issue-giving properties. To draw virtue from the saint's jasmin, the woman who yearns for a child bathes and purifies herself and goes to the shrine and seats herself under or near the jasmin bush with her skirt spread out. As many flowers as fall into her lap so many children will she have. In north Gujarat, if after the birth of a child no male issue follows, or being born does not live, the first-born child is believed to be the cause of the evil. The first-born is looked on as possessed by some malignant spirit who destroys the young lives of the new-born brothers and sisters. So at the mother's next confinement molasses and sesame seed are passed seven or nine times over the new-born infant from head to foot, and the elder boy or girl is given these to eat. The molasses represent the life of the young one given to the spirit who possesses the first-born. Children born deformed or with one or two teeth are supposed to exercise a baneful influence over their parents and near relatives. A child born with teeth is believed to exercise so malignant an influence that the early death of one of the parents is almost certain.

"If the treatment of the live, or the relics of the dead, saint result in pregnancy the greatest care is taken that no baneful influences interfere with a safe delivery. The lady is made to wear a number of charms and always to carry a knife or other piece of iron. She must not go out of doors, especially on new-moons and Thursdays, and on all days at sunset must avoid groves and the sea and river side. Charmed silk threads called *bhardori*, literally the spirit-laden cord, are worn round her waist and abdomen, and, especially if any portion of the period of her pregnancy falls on or about the days of *Diwali*, which is considered an evil spirit-time, she requires the greatest care. She is not allowed to go under the *mandwa* or alcove built before a house on marriage or other festive occasions. She must avoid marriage or death ceremonies, must not pass under the city gates, and must cross no river or sea. During eclipses of the sun and the moon particular care must be taken that neither she nor her husband, nor even the relatives of her husband, eat or drink or smoke or cut or clip or break anything. If any of them eat a *pan* or betel-leaf or even fold a *pan* the child is sure to be born with ears folded like a '*pan*' leaf: if the relation cuts or clips anything the child is sure to have a deformed finger or a hare-lip.

"The *bhardori* or weight that is the spirit-laden cord, in the sense of the ill-luck imprisoning cord is regarded as a preservation of the child from conception to delivery. It is a seven-braided piece of silk upon which the Mulla or exorcist spends time and trouble, repeating over it verses of the Kuran or charms and tying a knot at each repetition, making the number of knots correspond with the number of pregnancy months and giving the silk to be wound round the womb. The braids are particoloured white, red, green, black and fine variations of these leading colours. This silk cord is a guard against miscarriage and all the evils, spiritual as well as physical, that cause miscarriage. At the end or beginning of the ninth month the braid is unwound and some incense is burned under it and together with some flowers it is thrown into an unused well, or, if no well is at hand, into a river or a lake or other water. During the period of pregnancy the woman may not wear new clothes, jewels, even bangles, the symbol of married life which the married woman holds most sacred. All the usual adornments of the person otherwise considered necessary are during pregnancy laid aside and looked upon as forbidden. No eyelid is darkened with antimony, no finger or toe-tip, no palm or sole is reddened with henna, no tooth is blackened with *missi*, and certain kinds of food are forbidden. The pregnant lady is not to touch a cocoa-kernel, nor to taste any underground root except the exotic potato. The ban against ornaments lasts till the *satmasa* or seventh month celebration." adds Mr. Enthoven. The customs are practised by the Muslims in Maharashtra and Gujarat.

About the Muslim customs, rites and superstitions, Bombay Gazetteer records, "Women who desire children resort to the shrines of saints, who are supposed to be able to induce fertility. Blochmann notes that the tomb of Saint Salim-i-Chishti at Fatehpur-Sikri, in whose house the Emperor Jahangir was born, is up to the present day visited by childless Hindu and Musalman women. A tree in the compound of the saint Shaih Alam of Ahmedabad yields a peculiar acorn-like fruit, which is sought after far and wife by those desiring children; the woman is believed to conceive from the moment of eating the fruit. If the birth of a child follows the eating of the acorn, the man and woman who took it from the tree should for a certain number of years come at every anniversary of the saint and nourish the tree with a supply of milk. In addition to this, jasmin and rose-bushes at the shrines of certain saints are supposed to possess issue-giving properties. To draw virtue from the saint's jasmine the woman who yearns for a child bathes and purifies herself and goes to the shrine, and seats herself under or near the jasmine bush with her skirt spread out. As many flowers as fall into her lap, so many children will she have. In some localities if after the birth of one child no other son is born, or being born does not live, it is supposed that the first-born child is possessed by a malignant spirit who destroys the young lives of the new-born brothers and sisters. So at the mother's next confinement sugar and sesame-seed are passed seven or nine times over the newborn infant from head to foot, and the elder boy or girl is given them to eat. The sugar represents the life of the young one given to the spirit who possesses the first-born. A child born with teeth already visible is believed to exercise a very malignant influence over its parents, and to render the early death of one of them almost certain.' *Bomb. Gaz. Muh. Guj.* pp. I47, I48.

Fertility Rites of filling the Lap

Mr. Russell and Hira Lal writes, "In the seventh or ninth month of pregnancy a fertility rite is performed as among the Hindus. The woman is dressed in new clothes, and her lap is filled with fruit and vegetables by her friends. In some localities a large number of pots are obtained, and a little water is placed in each of them by a fertile married woman who has never lost a child. Prayers are repeated over the pots in the names of the male and female ancestors of the family, and especially of the women who have died in childbirth. This appears to be a propitiation of the spirits of ancestors."

Ceremony of *Fulam Mallap*

Among the Saraswat Brahmans, pre-delivery rituals, locally called *fulam mallap,* are performed in the fifth, seventh, or ninth month of pregnancy. On this ceremony, the pregnant woman is presented with a green sari and green bangles (especially in the fifth month) by her parents and close relatives. She is placed in a hammock and women folk sing some songs. Thereafter, they offer the expectant mother garlands and five fruits. For the first delivery, the pregnant woman is sent to her parental house to take special care of her health.

The Karhade Brahmans also conduct pre-delivery rituals. When the first sign of pregnancy is noticed, it is a moment of great joy for the newly married woman, her husband as well as for the entire family. The young wife goes to her parent's house for her first confinement and delivery.

Cohabitation During Pregnancy

The customs are pertinent to the Saraswat and Karhade Brahmans. An anthropologist Mr. D. Hazra wrote about the Kolam motherhood and other related customs, "The Kolam are aware of the physiological cause of paternity. The conception of a woman, as they think, is indicated by the cessation of her menstrual flow. When a woman conceives, it is her husband to whom she informs first about the onset of her pregnancy. The other senior female members of the family, if there are any, also get a hint about it when they notice that the woman in question does not have her menses (*daueddin* or *malaeddin*) continuously for few months and confirm about the matter after inquiring her.

"A man continues to cohabit with his wife upto fifth or sixth month of her pregnancy after which it gradually stops. A pregnant woman without any restriction carries out all her usual routine works including strainuous activities in field, cutting and bringing fire-wood, etc. She continues to carry out fieldwork even in her advanced stage of pregnancy. She is not subjected to any food taboo or food restriction, except those which are, as a general rule, tabooed to all women. However, she usually avoids hot things like tea, etc.

"If a pregnant woman gets separated from her husband and even if she remarries, the child gets the clan and phratry affiliation of its begetter. If an unmarried girl bears a child, the village-council makes enquiries from her in order to know about the begetter of the child and, accordingly, the clan affiliation is given to it and if it is possible, the girl is married to the man.

"There is no ceremony or function during the gestation period till the child is born. Delivery takes place in a corner of the hut, and if required it is covered with bamboo mats. At present, the people of Khekadwai call a Pardhan woman from Gokuldora to act as a midwife (*matte-murtal*) at the time of a childbirth. If necessary, an experienced elderly Kolam woman may also act as a midwife. Formerly, many of the Kolam villages, including Khekadwai, used to have a *matte-murtal* recruited from their own community on village basis. She was recruited from among elderly Kolam women of the village. She remains in the profession, serving the village only. She used to get 1 *kuro* (about 10 kg) of *jowar* annually from each family annually for her service. At present a Pardhan midwife gets from the concerned family 1.5 *kuro* of *jowar* and 75 paise for the delivery of a male child, and 1 *kuro* of *jowar* and 50 paise if the child is female."

Taboos for the Pregnant Woman

About the pregnancy customs of Mahadev Kolis, Mr. G.S. Ghurye notes, "As a rule a pregnant woman is given whatever food she desires for. This privileged treatment results from a belief, common in this region, that the woman's discontent has an undesirable effect on the child in her womb. She is, however, advised to abstain from abnormally hot or hard-to-digest stuff, particularly in summer, as such food is believed to develop ear trouble in her child. A pregnant woman might wade through a shallow river but might not cross the river in a ferry or use any other contrivance to do so. She is not to officiate as a 'karavali', that is, the bride's companion accompanying her with the auspicious pot. She is neither considered eligible for receiving the gifts of grain and cloth of the 'lap-filling' ceremony, nor considered eligible to play the host in such a ceremony. She is neither supposed to pay a condolence visit to a bereaved family, unless she has an opportunity to do so, nor supposed to see a funeral procession during the course of her first pregnancy. There are also some restrictions on the behaviour of the husband. He might not kill a fish or a serpent. He might participate in obsequies, but might not carry a corpse to the burial ground or offer water to the dead. Modern youths are found ignoring these taboos, treating them as superstitious and irrational and proclaiming that their unconventional behaviour has done them no harm.

"A lullaby frequently sung by Mahadev Koli women describes the progress of pregnancy: paleness of the first month, awareness of the existence of the child in embryo and nausea of the third month and longing for delicacies of the sixth month.

There are some indications pointing to the sex of the child-to-be. Thus, weakness and pallid expression of the woman are the signs of a male child, while her better health points to a female child. Her likes and dislikes are also similarly interpreted. Predilection for 'dodka' vegetable indicates a female issue while that for a pumpkin indicates a male one. A son is always coveted; he is described in songs as much more valuable than wealth.

"The first delivery of a woman usually takes place at the house of her parents-in-law. Many people, particularly elderly men and, more so, women, do not know either the place or the year of their birth. At Manik Ozar, of the seventy people about whom definite information was available, only thirteen were born in the house of their mother's parents.

"A woman continues to do her routine work till the pains of childbirth make that impracticable. There have been cases of a woman's delivery in a forest where they she gone to bring firewood. Theoretically, there is no restriction on sexual intercourse either before or after parturition. Two or three husbands reported to Dr. Chapekar that they had intercourse on the night previous to the birth. A woman told Dr. Chapekar that she heard her friend speaking at the village well that her husband could not leave her alone even for the first twelve days after her parturition. When a woman feels birth pains, she retires to an inner chamber in the house and a midwife is sent for. But many times the house is only a one-apartment construction. In such cases, men and children leave the house to allow women full privacy. In every predominant Mahadev Koli village, there are women of this community who are reputed for their skill in midwifery. The services of one of them are adequate in normal cases of delivery. In difficult cases, experienced midwives from other castes, including the scheduled castes, are called in," adds Mr. Gharye. The custom is prevalent among the Mahadev Kolis of the region.

For delivery, women go to parental house

About customs regarding delivery among the Muslims, R.V. Russell and Hira Lal record, "A woman goes to her parents' home after the last pregnancy rite and stays there till her confinement is over. The rites performed by the midwife at birth resemble those of the Hindus. When the child is born the *azan* or summons to prayer is uttered aloud in his right ear, and the *takbir* or Muhammadan creed in his left. The child is named on the sixth or seventh day. Sometimes the name of an ancestor is given, or the initial letter is selected from the Koran at a venture and a name beginning with that letter is chosen. Some common names are those of the hundred titles of God combined with the prefix *abd* or servant. Such are Abdul Aziz, servant of the all-honoured; Ghani, the everlasting; Karim, the gracious; Rahim, the pitiful; Rahman, the merciful; Razzak, the bread-giver; Sattar, the concealer; and so on, with the prefix Abdul, or servant of, in each case. Similarly Abdullah, or servant of God, was the name of Muhammad's father, and is a very favourite one. Other names end with Baksh or 'given by', as Haidar Baksh, given by the lion (Ali); these are similar to the Hindu names ending in Prasad. The prefix Ghulam, or slave of, is also used, as Ghulam Hussain, slave of Hussain; and names of Hebrew patriarchs mentioned in the Koran are not uncommon, as Ayub Job, Harum Aaron, Ishaq Isaac, Musa Moses, Yakub Jacob, Yusaf Joseph, and so on.

"After childbirth the mother must not pray or fast, touch the Koran or enter a mosque for forty days; on the expiry of this period she is bathes and dressed in good clothes, and her relatives bring presents for the child. Some people do not let her oil or comb her hair during these days. The custom would seem to be a relic of the period of impurity of women after childbirth. On the fortieth day the child is placed in a cradle for the first time. In some localities a rite called *Ukika* is performed after the birth of a child. It consists of a sacrifice in the name of the child of two he-goats for a boy and one for a girl. The goats must be above a year old, and without spot or blemish. The meat must be separated from the bones so that not a bone is broken, and the bones, skin, feet and head are afterwards buried in the earth. When the flesh is served the following prayer is said by the father: 'O, Almighty God, I offer in the stead of my own offspring life for life, blood for blood, head for head, bone for bone, hair for hair, and skin for skin. In the name of God do I sacrifice this he-goat.' This is apparently a relic of the substitution of a goat for Ishmael when Abraham was offering him as a sacrifice. The Muhammadans say that it was Ishmael instead of Isaac who was thus offered, and they think that Ishmael or Ismail was the ancestor of all the Arabs.

"Either on the same day as the *Ukika* sacrifice or soon afterwards the child's hair is shaved for the first time. By the rich the hair is weighed against silver and this sum is distributed to beggars. It is then tied up in a piece of cloth and either buried or thrown into a river, or sometimes set afloat on a little toy raft in the name of a saint. Occasionally tufts of hair or even the whole head may be left unshaven in the name of a saint, and after one or more years the child is taken to the saints' tomb and the hair shaved there; or if this cannot be done it is cut off at home in the name of the saint.

"When a girl is one or two years old the lobes of her ears are bored. By degrees other holes are bored along the edge of the ear and even in the centre, till by the time she has attained the age of two or three years she has thirteen holes in the right ear and twelve in the left. Little silver rings and various kinds of earrings are inserted and worn in the holes. But the practice of boring so many holes has now been abandoned by the better-class Muhammadans," add Mr. Russell and Hira Lal.

About the Muslim birth customs Mr. RE Enthoven writes, "After the last pregnancy ceremony the wife goes to her father's house and stays there till her confinement is over. Among the rich and middle classes the servant who first brings his master news of the birth of a child gets a present of Re. 1 to Rs. 2. Soon bands of musicians and the hated *hijdas* or eunuchs crowd round the house on the lookout for gifts. The eunuchs beat a drum and sing, while one of their numbers, with the help of a pad or pillow, acts the part of a woman with child, in child-birth, and nursing. At Ahmedabad not only the *Hijdas* but some of the *Bhawayyas* or Hindu strolling players claim presents on the birth of a boy with a pertinacity that is not satisfied till the whole of their demand is paid. The person claiming the gift is generally the clown or fool of the troop. He does not dance or sing, but by his obstreperous sallies of coarse abuse tries to make his stay so annoying that to get rid of him no expense is thought too great. To avoid the nuisance some people satisfy his demands at his house by sending him a present of eight annas or a rupee. Some peculiar customs are observed at the birth of a child. No sooner does the stranger appear than the midwife or *dai* announces its sex. If a boy she says, nominally to save the mother a shock of happy surprise, but at heart to deceive the evil spirits of jealousy, 'It is only a girl blind of one eye.' If a girl is born, the fact is stated since the birth of a girl can cause no jealousy. Boy or girl, the new born child is laid in a bamboo *supla* or winnowing-fan while the more pressing needs of its mother are being ministered to. A piece of new red cloth is wound rather tightly round the little one's head and the young one is ready to hear the *takbir* or call to prayer. That its Creater's name may be the first word it hears, the father, as soon as the child is bathed, repeats in its ear the call to prayer, *azan*, beginning with the words Allah-o-Akbar God is great. Occasionally at the time of birth a Brahman is called and told to draw up a horoscope. He chooses certain letters, with one of which the child's name should begin. The paper is kept by the parents of the child and referenced to on great occasions. The Brahman is paid Rs. 5 to Rs. 20. As soon as the first bath is over pieces of black-thread are wound rather tightly round the child's wrists and ankles as its first armour against the evil eye. Its eyes or rather eyelids are stained with soot made of *ghi* and lampblack, its eyebrows are pencilled with soot, dots of lampblack are made on its little cheeks, palms and sole and a lock of its hair is gummed or waxed so that any one with an evil eye feeling them or looking at them may not meet an even glossy surface. Every morning and evening frankincense and the *rai-ispand*, corruptly termed *rai-band*, that is mustard and henna seed, is passed seven or nine times over the mother and the child from head to foot, and thrown into the fireplace and burned. In his Urdu Dictionary Forbes says the seed of the henna plant is burnt at marriages to drive away evil spirits. Henna seed mixed with mustard seed is also burnt after a child is born, particularly at the door, to prevent demons from entering. Often red chilly seeds are thrown into the fire, especially to judge whether an ailment of the child is physical or spirit-caused. If the burning of the chillies creates no pungent vapour, a spirit is surely the cause of the disease. If the burning chilly has its proper pungent smell the ailment is natural. Sometimes a piece of alum is burned with the mustard-seed, the burning alum swelling into fantastic forms which to the wise show the sex of the person who owns the evil eye. During the five days before the *chatti* or sixth-day celebration no fire or salt or water is to be given to any one from the house in which a woman is confined. To accustom the child to noise a copper or brass dish is struck at his ear before the father repeats to him the *takbir* or call to prayer. To harden the child cold water is sprinkled over him before his bath.

"Early in the morning of the sixth-day the child is named. The father, grandfather or other male relative opens the Kuran at a venture, and the first letter of the first word of the third line is the initial of the child's name." The class of names recommended by the Prophet are the slave or servant of Allah or servant of the most Merciful, Abd-ullah or Abd-ur-Rehman. Among Sayads, boys' names generally end in Ali, as *Ahmad-ali, Akbar-ali, Mumtaz-ali*, or in *Husain* as *Fazl Husain*, and sometimes though rarely in *Shah*, as *Muhammad Shah* and *Taj-Shah*. Among *Shaikhs*, boys are called *Umar Usman, Muhammad, Mahmud, Husain, Ghulam-husain, Ghulam-ali, Gulamam-ahmed*. These names are common in all families. The following are used almost solely in families of good position: *Shams-ud-din, Moin-ud-din, Saadullah, Fazhullah*, and the like. The names of Shaikhs are preceded either by the word *Muhammad* or *Shaikh* as *Muhammad Asadullah* or *Shaikh Ghulam Ali*. Among Mughals, boys are called *Amir, Muhammad, Hasan, Husain* and *Ali*, the word *Mirza* always preceding and *Beg* following the name. Pathan boys have the same names as Mughal boys, only there is no *Mirza* and *Khan* is added instead of *Beg*. The commonest names for women are for all classes and grades, taken from the Kuran, such as *Fatimah, Khadijah*, or *Aishah*. Among the higher Musalman families such Arabic phrases as best of women *Khair-un-nisa*, Noblest of women *Amir-un-nisa*, or Moon of women *Badra-un-nisa* are commonly used. Among Sayads a woman's name is followed by *Begam*; among *Shaikhs* by *Bibi*; among Mughals by *Khanam*; and among Pathans by *Khan*. Besides these parents who have lost children or whose children do not live give curious names showing deformity or the most abject humility. *Nathihu*, literally nose-bored, is a name which accompanies the actual boring of the nose of the new born child on the principle of deforming the child and so making it less liable to spirit attacks. Another name is *Punju* or *Kachra*, that is, refuse. Sometimes when a child is born after the death of several children the child is thrown into a grain-winnowing fan *supla* with a lot of dirt or refuse and the fan is dragged outside the door with the child in it and made over to some other member of the family as whose property the child re-enters the house. After his ride in the winnowing-fan the child is named, Ghasita, that is, The Dragged. If he is a Pathan this becomes

Ghasitkhan, if a Sayad or Shaikh Mir or Shaikh Ghassu or Bhisu, names which occur among all ranks of Muslim and Hindu society in Gujarat. These old naming practices have their root in the belief that untimely births or the death of the new-born are due to the anger or jealousy of uneasy family ghostas, chiefly of women who have died in child-birth with the main object of life unfulfilled. To this belief there attaches the further experience that the unfriendly ghost is easily outwitted. The ghost or other spirit on the lookout for the soul of the new-born hears the child is deformed or worthless and so turns its mind to some more gainful mischief. Further the ill will of the ghost is not towards the child but to the child's father or mother. The ghost's aim is to harm the child of the father or the mother; against the aunt's child the ghost has no manner or grudge. This is similar to the Jewish custom according to which the infant Joseph was supposed to steal a sash of one of his aunt's, which being found on his person he was according to patriarchal law claimed by his aunt for a certain number of years. Sometimes a name is chosen because it had been borne by one of the child's forefathers or because the giver thinks it lucky. In the evening of the same day the husband's kindred bringing gold or silver anklets or necklaces, money or clothes, go to the wife's father's house. Sweet cakes are distributed, and, after sunset, the husband gives a dinner to the wife's relations. In the women's rooms the child and its mother are dresses in their best and the midwife makes a six cornered lamp of flour with as many wicks as corners. This is lighted, fed with clarified butter, and kept in a plate along with parched rice or millet *jowari*, and fruit. The presents brought by the husband's friends are now offered and a few small silver coins are given to the midwife. The young mother is then led to a casement and made to counts even stars. When this is over, the husband's people return to their homes. The sixth-day ceremony includes another propitiation of the female relatives that have died in child-birth. Food untouched by unclean persons is cooked and the *Fatiha* repeated for the souls of women who have thus died, and the food is distributed to the poor. The value of the presents made by the husband's friends would, in the case of a rich family, vary from Rs. 20 to Rs. 50, and from Rs. 10 to 20 in the case of a middle class family. Among the poor, silver necklaces *hansli*, or anklets *kadian*, and a pair or so of ornamented shirts worth Rs. 5 to Rs. 10 are sometimes given.

"On the seventh, fourteenth or twenty-first day after birth

comes the purely Muhammadan and by all classes carefully kept rite of sacrifice *akika*. In this rite there are two parts, the shaving of the child's head and the killing of one or two goats. If the child is a girl, one goat, and if the child is the child is a boy, two goats, are bought. Some friends are asked and a barber is called. When all is ready the father of the child, or some one specially named by him, at a given sign, as the barber passes the razor along the head of the child, draws a knife across the goat's throat saying, 'I sacrifice this animal or animals for the child named *Wali*, blood for blood skin for skin, flesh for flesh, hair for hair." When the shaving is over, the child's hair and nails are laid on a flat half-baked cake and carried away to be thrown into a river. The barber goes round among the men guests and each drops a small coin into his cup. Before they leave, the guests are entertained at dinner. In preparing the goat for cooking none of its bones may be broken. The bones must be separated from the flesh and buried. The flesh and skin are divided into three shares. One share is given in charity, a second is distributed among friends, and the rest, except that the child's father and mother may not join, is eaten by relations.

"On the fortieth day, in honour of the mother's recovery, *naos* or grass boats of the same kind as those made by the water-carrier for the seventh-month pregnancy ceremonies, are with music taken to the nearest water, a lamp is lighted, and the boat set adrift as a thank-offering to Khaja Khizr or Elias. The father of the child's mother presents her with clothes and the child with some small quilts and a cradle.

"When the child is four and a half months old and able to take food stronger than milk, comes the ceremony of mutton sucking *botan*, or, as the Persians call it, salt-tasting *namak-chashi*. Friends bring the child presents of clothes worth Re. 1 to Rs. 5. In the evening dressed in his best, the child is offered by his father's sisters some rice and milk *khir*, on a rupee, and after the rice and milk is given a piece of flesh to suck." adds Mr. Enthoven.

Ritual Called *Dohale*

Dohale was a ritual of giving desired food to women during the prenatal period, particularly during their first pregnancy. After two or three months of the first pregnancy, women were taken to their parents' house for celebrating *Dohale*. On a designated day, pregnant women were offered new green bangles, oil was poured in their ears and applied to their hair and they were bathed usually by their mother or grandmother. Prayers were offered to a family deity and Goddess *Mariai* (Mariai meaning death Mother) for protecting them. This is done due to the high mortality rate in the caste particularly during the first delivery—the reasons being the pregnant girls' young age, physiologically under-developed constitution lack of nutritious food and lack of health or medical facilities. On the day of the *Dohale* ceremony, women were given desired food, of course, within financial limits of the family. They were kept in a good humour for some days and then sent back to their husband's residence. This custom was common even among many other castes in Maharashtra. However, the custom is disappearing fast. The custom is prevalent among the Mahar caste of Maharashtra.

No Superstition about Childbirth

The critical conditions in the life of an individual centre round important events like Puberty, Marriage, Pregnancy, Birth, Climacteric, Old Age and Death. These turning points in individual life-cycle are observed with a certain amount of reverence and sometimes accompanied by care and anxiety, often relieved by festivities and celebrations of dinner, dance or singing. The individual is helped in tiding over these afflictions by the relatives or the tribe joining in general celebrations. The customs pertaining to such events have a great value in the life of a tribe.

About the Dubla Tribal customs in Gujarat, Mr. P.G. Shah notes, "The Dublas are among the liberal tribes of the country and do not possess any superstition about the birth of a child being a gift from Heaven. There is a certain amount of freedom of contact between the sexes; the boys and girls meet on the grazing fields when in charge of cattle, and during dances on marriage occasions and festivities like Holi and Norata. This leads to a kind of premarital sexual liberty among young persons of both sexes who are not unaware of the periodical menstruation among women on maturity and of the taboos observed by them. There is no special celebrations as in some other communities to announce the attainment of puberty and no peculiar ceremonies are performed on that occasion. However, menstruation involves taboos in many a primitive society and these taboos have been strengthened by constant contact with the Hindu community of farmers to which the

Dublas are usually attached as labourers. The general pollution for three nights and the bath on the fourth morning are observed in most Dubla families. The fourth day bath for the hair is supposed to be an elaborate affair, requiring a special shampoo, called *mathu cholvu*, for the hair which is to be made free from oil. This monthly wash of the hair is considered unnecessary as soon as menstruation stops in a pregnant woman. This is technically described as stoppage of the monthly hair washing. This description indicates that sufficient knowledge about menstruation and pregnancy is prevalent among the Dublas. They keep a count of the month in which pregnancy has begun. This makes it easy for them to celebrate various ceremonies connected with the first pregnancy.

"The Dublas celebrate only the first pregnancy of a young wife. This celebration known as *Kholobharvo,* is organised on the fifth or seventh month after conception. The main ceremony consists of filling the lap of the pregnant woman on the ceremonious occasion with presents, consisting of varying amounts of wheat grain, generally a seer and half by measure, seven arecanuts, one coconut, etc. The woman is seated on a *patld* or a higher pedestal according to the means available. The sister-in-law, that is, the wife of her husband's elder brother called *Jeth* (real or classificatory) takes a prominent part in this *Kholo-bharavo* ceremony and it is she who takes initiative in singing appropriate songs on the occasion. She also wears her a new *sari,* puts on a *kumkum* mark on her forehead, sprinkles rice on her head and gives her blessings. In the same way, other elderly women of her conjugal and natal families give her blessings for getting a son and happy married life.

The parents of the pregnant woman come from long distances to attend this ceremony, as it is their social duty to give presents usually in the form of garments, etc., to the husband and the mother's younger brother called (*Mama*) on this occasion. The parents generally leave the home of their son-in-law on the same day or the next one. The husband's parents and other relatives bid them goodbye with some formality and give them a rupee or two as a token of gift. The ceremony brings together the families of the young husband and wife, all of whom take interest in the arrival of the new baby.

Rite of Garbhadhan

"A brief description here of the standard Hindu ceremonies described in the Grihyasutras would be helpful in understanding the acculturation that has taken place. The birth of a male child is essential in Hindu culture and the *Garbhadhan* ceremony performed after the marriage ensures the birth of a hero. The *punsavan* is performed in the beginning of the third month of the first pregnancy when the pounded powder of a Nyagrodha shoot (which has fruits on both sides) is inserted in the woman's right nostril with ceremonies and mantras. The *Garbha-rakshana* ceremony (for the protection of the embryo) and the *Simantonnayana* ceremony (parting of the hair) are performed during the seventh month and *Kshepra-prasavana* (the quick delivery) ceremony seem to have been in later times compressed into one ceremony—the *Kholo-Bharvo*—the lap filling as mentioned above. The lying-in-chamber is to be besmeared with pounded roots of a certain plant to drive away the *Rakshasas.* A water pot is then placed near the head and a Turyanti plant near the feet of the pregnant woman; her body is then touched and stroked with some mantras which ensures a safe and speedy delivery. During the labour itself, *Soshyanti-homa* (sacrifice) is performed, when Darbha grass is strewn round the fire and prayer is offered for the birth of a son. These ceremonies offer material for a comparative study of the simple practices followed by the Dubla tribe. However, the main difference is that there is no chanting of mantras and no Brahmin is present. The tribal priest performs some sort of invocations to the tribal goddess on each occasion *e.g.* the offering made to the *pet-fodi-devi* (the goddess which opens the stomach (uterus) adds Mr. Shah. The customs, rites and rituals are related to the Dubla Tribals of Gujarat.

Birth Pollution

About the prevalent custom of birth pollution, Mr. R.E. Enthoven records, "A woman is held impure for five weeks after childbirth, but after the twelfth day she is touched, though nothing is eaten from her hands. On the fifth day, after the child is born, they worship a dough image of *Satvai* or simple five pebbles arranged in a line in the mother's room and offer them cooked rice and split pulse or *dalbhat*. Two dough lamps are kept burning the whole night and a feast is held. On the twelfth day, the mother and the child are bathed, mother's clothes are washed and the laying-in room is cowdunged. Seven pebbles are then placed outside the house in a line and worshipped by the mother in the name of the goddess *Satvai*. The child is named on the same day, the name being given by a Brahman astrologer. Female guests are called and boiled grain or wheat is distributed among them. A month later new bangles are put round the mother's wrists. The hair of the boy child is cut at any time when he is between one and three years old and relatives and friends are invited and feasted." These customs, rituals and rites are observed amongst the Mang people.

Tying of Linga Round the Infant's Neck

Mr. R.E. Enthoven states, "After a birth a Kabbaligar, Lingayat, or Maratha midwife washes the mother and the child in warm water, and lays them on a bedstead. The family priest ties a *linga* round the neck of the child and withdraws. The mother is given dry dates, dry ginger, anise-seed or *shep* (*Pimpindla anisum*), raw sugar and clarified butter, and is fed on boiled rice which is eaten with garlic. She is kept warm by having a chafing dish set under her bedstead on which garlic rind is burnt. On the fifth evening, the midwife places in the lying-in room an image of goddess *Jivati*, sprinkles turmeric and red powder on the goddess, lays cooked food before her, waves a lamp about her, and carries the lamp under cover, for if the lamp is seen by anyone but the midwife, then the mother and child will become sick. On the twelfth day the child is cradled and named. Each of the women, who come for the naming, bring with them a robe or a bodice-cloth for the mother, a jacket or a cap for the child, and two halves of cocoa kernel and a pound of Indian millet, wheat, or spiked millet." These rites and rituals are celebrated by the community of Lingayats in the region.

Birth Follows the Circumcision of the Male Child

The main ceremonies among *Bene-Israels* are birth, circumcision, marriage, a girl's coming of age, and death. Formerly, their ceremonies were quite as important and complicated as those of the local Hindus and had curious mixture of Hindu and Jewish customs, but the recent tendency is to do away with the old and unnecessary customs and have as few customs and rituals as possible. Nevertheless, on account of their residence in India for several centuries, they possess certain customs which differentiate them from the Jews of the rest of the world. These customs are fully discussed by a Christian missionary Rev. J.H. Lord and the following is a summary of his account:

(1) *The use of frankincense*: While the Jews of other countries have not used incense, since the burning of the second temple, the Bene-Israels did so until the middle of the last century. This practice might have been either a relic of pre-Talmudic Jewish customs or a late imitation of Hindu ritual.

(2) *The Nazarite vow* : Such vows are generally made by a woman without male issue. In the event of her bearing a son, the son would be kept with head uncropped till the age of six or seven. His hair would then be clipped off and weighed against gold or silver, according to the vow, and the equivalent money is distributed in charity (or in recent times handed over to the synagogue funds). The clipped hair instead of being burned (Num. VI, 14) is thrown into the sea or any other water. This latter divergence Lord attributes to the imitation of Hindu customs.

(3) *The use of 'subjah'* : This plant (apparently *Ocimum basilicum var thyrsiflora* Benty. Cooke Fl. Bom. Pres. II 442), according to Lord, is used in many ceremonials. He suggests that it was used as the nearest approach to the hyssop. On the other hand, it is of course closely allied to the Hindu *tulsi* (*O. santum L*).

(4) The *use of 'malida'* : This is a sweet cake made of rice, milk, *gul*, butter, etc. It is used, according to Lord, in many ceremonies. The point is that the word is Persian and is especially used of offerings at the tomb of Muhammadan *Pir*.

(5) *The practice of giving cooked liver of a fowl or goat to the officiating priest* : For this no origin has yet been suggested.

(6) *The 'cup of blessing'* : The name is given by Dr. Wilson. The ceremony consists of handing round in the synagogue a cup of wine previously blessed. Lord considers it a modification of the ceremony of *Habdalah* or a ceremony marking the separation of a holy day from an ordinary one.

(7) *The 'kiss of peace'* : At the close of the service in the synagogue, kiss is first given by the chief minister and then followed by the elders and people throughout the congregation. The bestower of the blessing as between any pair holds out both hands. The receiver first places one hand between the two hands of the bestower and then the other hand over the same. Each of them then withdraw their hands and kiss the tips of their own fingers. Lord mentions that the practice is in vogue among the Syrian Christians of Malabar, the Nestorians of Kurdistan, and the 'Assyrian Christians'.

"As among Jews of other countries, the male child is circumcised and named on the eighth day after birth. This is one of those customs which have been kept up by the Bene-Israels from the very beginning, and its observance led David Rahabi to consider that they were the descendants of Jews. There is no fixed rule as to when female children must be named, but usually they are named on or after eight days from birth," adds Rev. Lord.

Custom of *Kholobharni* or Lap-filling

According to the Bombay Gazetteer, "During the seventh month of a woman's first pregnancy, on a day fixed by the astrologer, the lap-filling or *kholobharni* takes place. A woman who has all her children alive lays in the pregnant woman's lap 5.25 or 10.25 lb. of clean rice, plantains, betelnuts, a coconut and red powder. The pregnant woman empties the rice from her lap into a winnowing fan, and from the winnowing fan the rice is again passed to the pregnant woman's lap. After this has been repeated seven times, the rice is put into a new earthen jar.

Seven balls made of the dung of a goat and a mouse, seven bundles of cotton thread, seven figs of the banyan tree, seven betelnuts, seven almonds, seven dry dates and seven copper coins, and a rupee and a quarter worth of silver coins are put along with the rice in the jar. A red cotton thread is wound round the jar's mouth and in the jar's mouth a coconut is placed. The pregnant woman, with the help of a family priest, worships the coconut and the jar. After the worship is over, besides small cash presents, the priest receives the seven copper coins from the jar. The jar and its other contents are put aside and are carefully preserved. The pregnant woman receives presents in the form of clothes from her father and on the wrist of her right arm a silver armlet called a *rdkhdi* or guard with a golden bead is tied by her husband's sister. The woman continues to wear the silver armlet till her delivery, after which it is returned to the husband's sister with an additional cash present if the child is a boy. The ceremony ends with a dinner for friends and relations. After this ceremony when the woman goes to her father's house for confinement, she is invited to dinner by her relatives and friends and receives a present of Re. 1 to Rs. 5 or a robe. This is known as *vdyanu.* In the course of the seventh or ninth month, the woman goes to her father's house to be confined" (*Bombay Gazetteer*, Vol. IX, Part I, p. 161). The customs are observed by the Kanbis in Maharashtra and Gujarat.

Special Feast for the Pregnant Woman

Mr. R.E. Enthoven writes, "When a woman is pregnant for the first time, her good longings are satisfied, and a special feast called *dohalejevan* or the longing dinner is held in the fifth or seventh month of her pregnancy. She is presented with a green robe and a green bodice, or a bodice only if her husband is poor, and some ten or fifteen unmarried women are asked to dine with her. Lamps are placed by the side and the feast is made as grand as the giver can afford. To guard against the danger of miscarriage from violent movements or a sudden fright, a pregnant woman is made to sit in a railing boat or a cart, shown funeral processions, made to craw the leather rope attached to the bag in a bullock-drawn well, and cross the boundaries of a village or a town." The ritual is celebrated by the Kunbi community in the western region.

Expectant Mother Goes to Natal Place

According to Mr. R.E. Enthoven, "Kanbi women go to their father's house to be confined. When a woman's time is come, a barber's wife or any other skilled woman is called and attends the child and its mother every morning—generally for ten days. Besides a set of woman's clothes, she is given about Re. 1 if the child is a boy and about 50p if the child is a girl. On the birth of a child, the family astrologer is asked to note the time by some of the Patidars and, in the case of the birth of a son, a barber or a messenger of any caste is sent to give the news to the child's father. The messenger takes with him the footmarks of the child impressed on a piece of paper with red-powder. The relations and friends of the child's father gather on hearing the news. The barber is feasted and paid from Rs. 2 to Rs. 5. The child's father distributes molasses and sugar to his relations and friends. As soon as the child is born, it is bathed in warm water, and about ten inches of the navel cord is left uncut and tied to a red cotton thread, which is wound round the child's neck. For three days, the child is fed on a liquid mixture of clarified butter, molasses and castor oil called *golthuthi* or *chatu,* and on the fourth day it is suckled. Cowdung ashes are rubbed on the navel daily for three or four days. At the end, the cord dries and is separated from the navel. On the sixth day, the *chhati* ceremony is performed. In the evening, on a footstool near the mother's bed, are laid a piece of paper, an inkstand, a reed pen, red rice, flowers, a rupee, a few copper pice, a lamp fed with clarified butter, some molasses, some cocoa-kernel, and a piece of the waistcloth of a man whose children are all alive. These things are taken away in the morning. The silver and copper coins are melted along with other similar coins and made into an anklet or wristlet for the child, and the piece of the waistcloth is made into a *jabhla* or small coat. On the morning of the tenth day, the woman bathes, but remains unbathed for another twenty-five days in the case of a son and for thirty days in the case of a daughter. On the morning of the thirty-fifth or fortieth day, she bathes, worships the sun, the well and the door-post. Four or five months after the birth, the woman is sent to her husband's house. The woman's father, besides making presents of cash, ornaments and clothes to the child and its mother, give the child a cradle, a small mattress and pillows. Except that the name is fixed by the family astrologer, no naming ceremony is performed. The child is named on the sixth or twelfth day or on a lucky day in the first, second or third month when a Brahman priest attends and worships Ganpati. Four boys in the case of a boy or four girls in the case of a girl rock the child in a piece of cloth and the father's sister names the child. The father's sister receives a robe or *sadi*, a piece of silk for a bodice, and the Brahman priest receives from Re. 1 to Rs. 2 in cash."

Delivering the Baby out of Villages

"Among the wandering Vanjaris, children are often born away from villages, and in the absence of midwives, women attend women and no ceremonies are performed. Afterwards, when the caravan, tdnda, meets a Brahman, a council is called. The time of the child's birth is explained to the Brahman, who fixes the name and the father pays him for his assistance. Among settled families, when a child is born, the relations beat drums, fire guns, and distribute sugar among their friends, the Bhats and priests. On the fifth day, the women worship Sati and are given grain, pulse and flowers. Some sections of the Vanjaris in Gujarat and the Lad Vanjaris gird their boys with the sacred thread before marriage," adds Mr. Enthoven. The custom is prevalent amongst the *Vanjaras* in the western region of Maharashtra and Gujarat.

Burying Navel Cord in the Yard at the front of the House

Mr. R.E. Enthoven writes "When a child is born, its navel cord is cut and buried in the yard at the front of the house. A stone is laid over it, and the mother and child are bathed upon the stone. On the fifth day, Indian millet is cooked into a thick gruel, a small stone is kept in the lying-in room, and five lumps of Indian millet gruel are set round the stone on a piece of cloth which has been dipped in a solution of turmeric powder and water. The five lumps of porridge and a little coarse sugar are served in five dishes, and five married unwidowed women are asked to eat the food. On the ninth day, five sorts of grain, Indian millet, *togari* (Cajanduinsicus), *besru* (Pshaseolus mungo), wheat and *madki* (Phaseolus acouotifolius) are boiled together and seasoned in a little oil, and *five* unwidowed women are called and fed with it. The women lay the child in a cradle and sing. On the twenty-ninth day, the child is taken to the temple of their goddess Adchava and is laid before the idol. The *pujari* or ministrant cuts a betel leaf in the shape of a pair of scissors, and with them goes through the form of cutting the child's hair, whether it is a boy or a girl. Then the ministrant is asked to find from the goddess what name should be given to the child. The ministrant consults the goddess, and remains for a while in silent study. He then, suddenly utters a name and that name is given to the child. Flowers, turmeric and red powder are laid before the goddess and all go home. On the next day, or on some future day, the hair of the child's head is cut."

"Amongst the Deccan Holars, on the fifth day, two figures are traced in charcoal on the door of the lying-in room, and an elderly woman worships them as the goddess Satvai. The figures of the goddess are offered wheat, bread and rice and the mother brings her child and bows before them, and the ceremony is over. On the twelfth day, the mother worships five pebbles outdoor and offers them bread and rice. A child is named when it is a month old, the name being given by a Brahman priest. Their children's hair is clipped any day between four months and four to eight years of age after birth. Five pebbles are worshipped at some distance from the house or in the bush, a goat is offered, and they return and feast," adds Mr. R.E. Enthoven.

These customs and rituals are also observed by the Holaya community.

No Rejoicing at a Girl's Birth

"For her first confinement, a young wife generally goes to her parents' house. After delivery, the position of the woman is not changed for some time. If the child is a boy, the midwife beats a metal pot; if a girl is born, the father is told without any signs of rejoicing. The father notes the time of birth so that the Brahman astrologer may be able to choose a lucky name. The midwife cuts the child's navel cord with a knife, and, holding the cord in her left hand, she passes it through the child's mouth.

She puts the cord in an earthen jar along with a little turmeric and red powder, and rice, and buries it in a hole in the mother's room. She touches the spot, with ashes where the navel cord was cut and rubs the mother and the child with turmeric and oil, bathes them in hot water, and swathes the child in cloth bandages. The mother is given butter and myrrh pills, and the child is dosed with three or four drops of castor oil and honey. The mother is purified by burning Embelia Ribes, *Ova* Zigusticum ajwaen, and *Balantshep* Anothus gravoelus in the room, and then, with her child beside her, she is laid on a cot, quite naked, under which a small fire of live coal is set. The mother is fed on fine rice, butter, pepper, and warm water. Near the door of the room, an earthen pot of cow's urine is set with a *Nim* branch floating on it. That no evil spirit may come in with them, all visitors sprinkle a few drops of cow's urine on their feet before entering the room. At noon, the mother is bathed in hot water, and elderly women begin to drop in to ask how she is. If the child is a boy, they congratulate her warmly, if it is a girl, they say, 'The first daughter is bread and butter' *(Pahili beti tup-roti)*. If the child's aunt is present at the time of delivery, she cowdungs the threshold of the room, places a packet of betelnuts and leaves near it, and says, looking towards the child, 'This child is to be my son's wife.' The mother smiles, and if she has a son says, 'When you get a daughter, she will become my daughter-in-law.' In the evening, the mother is again bathed, *Nim* juice is given to her to drink and she is fed, as in the morning, on rice, butter and pepper, and is given some hot water to drink. The child, as before, is dosed with three or four drops of castor oil and laid by the mother's side on the cot. A lump of coal is kept burning during the night, and next morning, after rubbing them with turmeric and oil, both mother and child are bathed. The mother is purified with *vishesh* (-incense), and the child is given a dose of castor oil. The mother takes some *Nim* juice, has a meal of rice, butter, and pepper, and is given some hot water to drink. At noon, women neighbours and Kinswomen begin to drop in. Each visitor touches the soles of her feet as if taking a pinch of dust therefrom, waves it round the child, and blows the dust partly onto the air and partly onto the ground. Then, cracking the finger joints of both her hands, she takes her seat, and is given turmeric and red powder. Should she be unlucky enough not to crack all her finger joints, she is thought to have no friendly feelings for the mother and child, and is not given the powder. In the evening, if the child takes to crying, frank incense is burnt in the names of Bahiroba and the goddess Satvai and they are prayed to save the child and prolong his/her life. On the third and fourth days, other than bathing the mother in hot water, no ceremony takes place. On the morning of the fifth day, the following articles are brought: a coconut, five pieces of cocoa kernel, five dry dates, five grains of pepper, dry ginger, poppy cardamoms, cloves, nutmeg, betelnut and leaves, catechu, scented and red powders, tooth powder, a coloured cord with a small parcel of red and scented powder or *Nada-pudi*, frankincense, turmeric, and a small copper or brass image of Satvai. Dishes of mutton and rice flour balls are cooked, and kinspeople and friends are asked to a feast. The women guests bring with them, on a brass plate, a few grains of rice, a coconut, and betel leaves, and set them before the goddess Satvai. Then the child's grandmother or some other elderly woman of the house sets a low wooden stool in the lying-in room, and places the image of Satvai on the stool. She sprinkles red powder on the image, burns frankincense, offers fruit and cooked food, and, wrapping the child in a cloth, lays it before the goddess, and prays her to accept the offerings, be kind to the child, and overlook any shortcomings in the worship. The mother comes forward, bows before the image and eats of all the dishes. The other women bow before the goddess, and after eating, return to their homes. When the women go, the men begin to drop in. They are seated on blankets and dinner is served outside as the woman is not allowed to see any man for twelve days. After dinner a pipe of tobacco is handed round, first to the *patil,* then to the senior guests, and then to the rest, but youths must go out if they desire to smoke. Singing, smoking and drinking go on till morning when all go home. The custom of the worship of Satvai varies according to family usage. Next mornin, the mother and child are rubbed with coconut oil and bathed in warm water, and the former goes back to her special diet of rice, butter, pepper, and hot water. On the morning of the seventh day, the cot and earthern waterpot are smeared with red powder and turmeric, *five* lighted rice flour lamps are placed in the waterpot, and cooked food is offered. Five unmarried girls are rubbed with red powder and turmeric and their laps are filled with wet gram, a piece of cocoa-kernel, betel leaves and nuts, find small balls of powdered ginger mixed with molasses. After the mother has prostrated herself five times and bowed twice before the girls, a dinner is served to one or two women neighbours. On the morning of the eighth day, the mother and child are bathed, and after eating her usual special food, the former is given betel leaves and nut to chew, and a dish of live coals is placed under her cot. Cocoa-kernel and dry date *(Kharik)* are pounded together and mixed with molasses, a little being given to the mother and the rest is distributed among the neighbours. On the tenth day, two or three women come and wash all the clothes and bedding, and in return are given breakfasts. All the house walls and floors get a fresh plaster of cowdung, and when the singers come, cow's urine is sprinkled on their bodies and clothes. Then they, together with the house people, feast on bread, relishes white *shepu* (Anethum foenic tum), and green chillies. On the eleventh day, preparations are made for the twelfth-day ceremony. Articles are laid in and the Brahman priest and guests are invited.

"On the morning of the twelfth day, the women of the house bathe the mother and again purify the walls and floor of the house with a plaster of cowdung. They take some cakes and begin to cook dishes of rice, vegetables, and pulse. A goat is killed, and its blood is gathered in a metal plate and mixed with spices and boiling water. This dish is called *rakti.* The bones and flesh are cooked into two separate pots and the liver or *kalij* in the third. A girl goes to tell the neighbours that the feast is ready, and when a few women come, the mother goes along with them to a spot outside the village and makes offerings to Satvai. On their return, a bangle-seller puts green bangles round the mother's and black bangles round the midwife's wrists. Men guests have by this time begun to drop in, and as they come, they are seated on blankets spread in the verandah. The Brahman priest arrives next with his almanac, and he too takes his seat in the verandah. The women of the house tell the Brahman the day and time at which the child was born, and he, spreading his almanac before him and counting his fingers, gives the child a name and tells his fortune. The child is dressed in a new frock and cap. Soot is rubbed on his cheeks and eyelids, and he is allowed to sit facing the east. The priest is given about two pounds of rice, and split pulse, a little molasses, and betelnut and leaves. A cradle is hung from the ceiling and worshipped, turmeric and red powder are thrown over it, cooked food is offered, a blanket is spread in it with some wet gram and betelnut and leaves in the corners and a string is tied in the middle. The mother sits near the cradle, and as they rock the cradle, they sing songs. The mother lifts the child, and turning it thrice round the cradle, they say, 'Take Harpal and give Gopal, take Govind and give Krishna, take Mahadev and give Ram, take Bharat and give Shatrughna'. The child is then laid in the cradle and the paternal aunt of the child along with the rest slap her all the time on the back, puts her mouth close to the child's ear, and says, 'Quietly quietly receive pulse and take Somji (the name given to the child) Patel to play'. Then the mother's lap is filled with a coconut, rice, glass beads, turmeric, pieces of cocoa-kernel and betelnut, and she is taken to bow to the family gods. A piece of thread is tied round the child's loins and the guests are feasted, the men and women in separate rooms. After they have done, they are given betelnut and leaves, wet pulse, and rice cakes. When the guests begin to leave, an old man and woman sit in the doorway and refuse to let the women pass till each mentions her husband's name. After some coquetting, the boldest of the women repeats some verses in which her husband's name occurs.

"On the thirteenth day, the mother begins to go about the house, washing, cooking and cleaning, as usual. Except on the full and new moon, the child is bathed every day. When two months old, as a safeguard against liver disease, the mother gives the child toothpowder mixed with cow's milk and liquor, and rubs its stomach with black nut and ashes, while a sorcerer says a charm or a mystic verse. To increase her supply of milk, the mother is given rice, butter, and split peas. When the child is three months old, to help it to holdup its head, the mother is given a cooked goat's head and round the child's neck is hung a black thread with two black nuts or *bajarbatus* and an image of the goddess Satvai. In this month, a black thread is tied round the child's waist and copper rings are put on its feet so that teething may be accomplished safely, and to ward off the evil eye, the eyelids of both the child and the mother are touched with soot. In the same month, the mother and the child with other relations go to visit the shrine of the goddess Satvai. A goat, toothpowder, turmeric, red powder, betelnut and leaves, soot, two coconuts, a robe and bodice, some grains of rice, dry cocoa-kernel, and frankincense are offered to the goddess and a goat is killed by a Mahar or Mang before her. The head and four legs are placed behind the goddess and the body is taken away presented to the goddess, cooked and eaten. The temple priest or ministrant tells the goddess the reason of the offering and, taking a pinch of ashes, rubs them on the brow of the child and its mother. After feasting on the flesh of the goat and on other dishes, the party buys back the goat's head, paying to 25p, and go home. All the religious parts of this ceremony are performed by the temple servant, who is generally a Gurav by caste. On reaching the house, the mother and child stand at the door, and a woman comes from the house and waves a piece of bread round them and pours water over the mother's feet.

"When a child is four or five months old, it is bathed outside the house, and when it is about a year old and begins to walk, its head is shaved, except a tuft on the crown, and the hair is offered to the goddess Satvai. The barber gets a present of a pair of scissors and the mother gives a feast to a party of married women. Six months later, when the child begins to eat, any flow of saliva is stopped by the mother passing a live fish three or four times round its face. When four years old, the child begins to run about the streets and lanes and plays at marbles, bat and ball, tops, and hide and seek. After about seven, the child begins to be of use to his parents, taking the cattle to graze and bringing them home in the evening. When ten or twelve years old, he is branded as a cowherd either on the right or left hand or on both hands. A few pellets of hare's dung are brought from a hill, pounded and set in four or five places about the boy's wrist and burnt. The other boys hold the child so as to keep him quiet, and when he can no longer bear the pain, the burning pellets are knocked off and the skin rubbed," adds Mr. Enthoven. The customs, rites and rituals are celebrated by the *Kunbi* community of Maharashtra, and other neighbouring regions.

Horrible Torment of Mahar Woman

Generally, the pregnant woman used to be pale and weak due to malnutrition and lack of medical aid. A few days before delivery, she was brought to her parent's residence. At the time of delivery, a village quack midwife and few selected old women used to sit around her to give her courage. Cry of the pregnant woman could be heard outside the house for hours as the village midwife used to employ crude methods of pressing womb, stretching body and limbs of the pregnant woman, as they did for cow and goat. Delivery without casualty of either child or mother was a great relief among the Mahars. After delivery, both child and mother were given hot water bath and were kept on a cot, under which burning charcoal or cowdung cakes used to be kept presumably for contraction of expanded organs of the mother and for keeping the mother and child warm to protect them from cold, cough, fever and resultant pneumonia, etc. Generally, the mother used to be extremely weak, pale and anaemic because of which she was prone to diseases of one kind or the other in the aftermath. Subsequently, child was also a victim of malnutrition. Probably, because of these reasons, post-natal and infant mortality rates were very high among the Mahars who suffered the social stigma of being an outcaste.

During recent times, some of them are availing of the facility of primary health centres and Government hospitals, dispensary, etc. Consequently, old crude methods of delivery by the quack midwife are being replaced by the modern and safe ones. Two pits were dug inside the house, one for burying the umbilical cord and placenta seeing which an evil spirit was believed to cause death of a newly born baby. Second pit known as *Nahani* (bathing place) was for storing bathed water, etc., of the child and mother as they were supposed to confine to their house for twelve days.

As a custom in the caste, a woman is not allowed to venture out of her house for twelve days, but she is not allowed to work inside house after five days of delivery due to pollution. During these twelve days, both child and mother are considered impure. The ritual of pollution is observed in the same manner as in case of menses, and purification methods employed were also similar to that of menses pollution.

The Ritual of *Pachvi* (Fifth day)

On the fifth day of delivery, the mother and child are given ritual hot water bath as usual inside the house. A lamp of *Jowar, Bajra* or wheat flour was made and filled with edible oil. Small three or five pieces of the same flour mixed with water were taken in the clockwise direction around both the mother and child and then taken to Goddess Satvai for purification. Goddess Satvai, according to them, as well as other castes in Maharashtra, wrote fate on a child's forehead. Afterwards, a red thread was tied round the neck and wrists of the child and the mother. After the fifth day, the mother invariably worked inside the house without breaking the custom of pollution.

On the twelfth day after delivery, house floor is plastered with cowdung and walls with mud and aches. Clothes and utensils in the house are washed. Cow urine is sprinkled on everything for purpose of purification and then the child and the mother are given the final ritual bath inside the house to remove pollution. *Nahani* (the bathing water pit) is worshipped, called *Nahani Puja,* by applying vermillion, turmeric powder and offering a small piece of flour mixed with water. After *Nahani Puja* is over, the pit is closed.

The customs, rites and rituals are pertinent to the *Mahar* caste in Maharashtra.

Engaging no Brahmans

Mr. RE Enthoven notes, "Before the birth of a child a midwife is called in, and after the birth, she stays for five days washing the child and the mother twice a day. Among the Dhors, if the child is a girl, the midwife stays for four days only. They employ no Brahman to draw up a horoscope or to name the child. Among Sons the name is given on the fifth day after birth by some elderly relation when caste fellows and friends are treated to liquor and a dance. Among Dhors, no limit is set to the number of days within which a child should be named, and the name is chosen not by some elderly relation, but by a medium into whose body a spirit, *dev*, has entered. They wait till some one is possessed, and then go and ask him to name their child. They do not generally, have to wait long, as spirit possession is common among Katkaris. In Gujarat, on the sixth day after a birth, the goddess Chathi is worshipped, and some rice figures of the goddess are set on the ground with a lamp near them. The father or mother names the child and the guests are fed on thick cakes and liquor."

The customs are pertinent to the Katkari community.

Worshipping the Mother's Breasts

The ceremonies and customs of the Brahma Kshatriya caste differ in some particulars from those among the higher castes of Gujarat. They are as follows:

"On the evening of the day on which a child is born, the mother's breasts are worshipped and the child suckled. Among a few families in Kathiawar, a woman while in confinement eats only fruit and roots or such food as is used on fast days. On the sixth day after birth, the goddess of fortune *Vidhata* or *Chhathi* is worshipped. The first giving of cooked food or *botan* takes place in the sixth month after birth. The rite of hair-cutting or *mundan* takes place between the age of five and seven when girls as well as boys have their hair cut. Like thread-girding and pregnancy ceremonies, hair-cutting is performed at the place sacred to the family goddess. Except in Kathiawar, at the first hair-cutting a minor ceremony called *devka* is performed. The child's mother and father go to the mother's house with music and a following of women. There the pair tie the ends of their garments together and bathe, and then wait in their wet clothes until some woman of the mother's family whose husband is alive spots with saffron the clothes of the father's maternal uncle and gives him sweets to eat. When this is done, the mother and father put on fresh clothes, return home, and worship the family goddess.

"Three, four or five days before the hair-cutting, as also at thread and pregnancy ceremonies, the family goddess is worshipped. A black male kid five or six months old is brought, kept in the house, and fed with green grass and grain till the last day of the ceremony. On that day, the family priest slits the kids' right ear and touches with blood the forehead of the child, its parents, and other members of the family. The kid is then let loose in one of Devi's temples and allowed to roam at pleasure. This custom is kept by many families. In a few families, during the eight or nine days of the ceremony, six or seven male black kids are brought every day and their foreheads are marked with red powder. The priest kills the kids, and the flesh is cooked, offered to the goddess, and eaten by the members of the family, friends and relations, including the priest himself. In almost every family, one or other of these customs is kept." The custom pertains to the Brahma Kshatriya caste in the western region.

Mr. R.E. Enthoven notes, "It is very difficult to ascertain the customs proper to the original Bhil race, as the tribes belonging to it represent various grades of civilization, from the primitive man to the fully Hinduised Kunbi or cultivator. Again, they vary from place to place. The following details may, therefore, be taken as applying to certain typical localities in which Bhils are found.

"In Gujarat, five days after a birth, the child and mother are bathed. In the Rewa Kantha, no ceremony is performed. But in the Panch Mahals, the mother makes a circle of flour, piles little heaps of flour on all sides, and sits in the middle of the circle when her female relations make her presents of money or clothes. On the tenth day, the father and mother name the child. On the twelfth day, in the Rewa Kantha, the house is cleaned and a feast is given, but this is not done in the Panch Mahals. When five years old, the child's head is shaved. The child's aunt takes the hair in her lap and wrapping it in her clothes, receives a cow, buffalo or other present from the child's father.

"In Khandesh at the birth of a child, a midwife is employed, and besides a bottle of liquor, a rupee is paid if the child is a boy, and 50p if it is a girl. For four days, no one but the midwife touches the mother. On the morning of the fifth day, a party of women are called, and both mother and child are bathed in warm water. Just outside the threshold of the hut, the mother cowdungs the ground and traces turmeric lines. In the middle of the drawing, she places a lighted lamp, setting round it five flint stones corresponding to the number of days since the child was born. Round these pebbles, she lays pieces of coca kernel, and over the whole sprinkles turmeric, millet, red powder and liquor. The guests drop a few grains of millet over the mother and child, and then re-enter the house. Next, the guests are feasted with wheat and rice bread, mutton and liquor, and the whole night is spent in singing, smoking and drinking. The lamp is allowed to burn for twenty-four hours.

"On the twelfth day, a dish of boiled millet and split pulse is made ready. Some of it is laid on a brass platter in which are also placed twelve wheaten cakes and lighted lamps, corresponding to the number of days since the child's birth. In another dish, a lamp, *arti*, is set, and along with the mother, women go in procession, singing and beating the drum, towards the nearest running water, where the mother arranges the twelve lamps. The cakes are placed in a line between the lamps, and a little of the boiled food is laid on each cake. The mother worships the water goddess, *Faldevta*, throws a little red lead, red powder and some grains mixed with turmeric into the water and on the twelve lamps, and lighting a fire before the lamps, feeds it with oil. They then go home and feast on mixed rice and pulse and oil," adds Mr. Enthoven. The custom prevails among the Bhil Tribals in Maharashtra and Gujarat.

Observing *Chhathi* ritual on Sixth Day

To attend to the delivery *suin* (tribal trained midwife) is called among the Parsis. *Chhathi* is performed on the sixth day following birth. The parents procure the *rashi* name or zodiac name after examining the stars and planets. The child is named by the parents on the sixth day of birth. They observe birth pollution for forty days. The ritual of *Mahino ugadiyo* is performed after one month and after forty days, *babri* or tonsure of male child is performed by any elderly women of the household. *Kusthee* and *shudre* or *navjyot* ceremonies are performed at the age of seven to nine years during which period the sacred thread is tied on the child's body by the *mobid* (priest). *Kusthi* is made of seventy-two threads and *shudre* is of cotton shirt with half sleeves. *Kushthi* is tied over the *shudre* round the waist of the male infant.

Following delivery, the mother of the newborn baby is not permitted to undertake any household chores and participate in any religious ceremony due to the pollution period. They observe eleven days pollution period following delivery. On the eleventh day, they clean their house and invite *Bhatji* or a Chitpavan Brahman to conduct the naming ceremony called *barsa* attended mostly by neighbours, relatives and friends. After the end of the ceremony, the host distributes sweets to invitees. They observe *jaival* ceremony for the boy at the age of one or two years. They invite Bhatji Brahman on the occasion to perform the stivals and the Mhalo to shave the male child's hair.

The rites and rituals are related to the Saraswat Brahmans of the western region.

Woman in Labour Lies on Palm-leaf Mat

A special cot made of Kathi or the coconut-bark string is prepared for the woman in labour. The cot is spread over with a palm-leaf-mat on which the woman is made to lie during the period of confinement. The expectant mother is given fresh hot semi-liquid food for a few days in the beginning of labour but later the usual food is considered sufficient. A village midwife or *dai* is considered indispensable for delivery. The job of midwife is sometimes taken over by elderly Dubla women themselves, but in the absence of such a woman, the neighbouring women of experience are called for help. In the case of difficult delivery, a more experienced midwife of Muslim-barbour caste is called. No male member is allowed to stay near the labour room at the time of delivery. If villages are near dispensaries and maternity hospitals, a qualified doctor may be available, but in tribal areas, this facility is still wanting.

When a woman is passing through an intense pain or delay in labour, a vow is made to propitiate the deity called *Pet-fodi mata* (lit, the mother-goddess capable of releasing the stomach). Sometimes the *Pet-fodi Mata* is offered the sacrifice of a fowl or a goat according to the financial status of the vow-maker when the vow alone does not give adequate relief. Sometimes a vow is made to 'offer a baby' to the *Pet-fodi Mata*. In this case, not a real baby but the miniature effigy of a child made of flour, clay or metal is offered to the deity.

The navel cord of the baby is cut with the blade of the jawar stalk, and the navel cord and afterbirth are buried in the backyard of the hut. The use of wood for this purpose is reminiscent of the ancient times when the use of metal was not familiar to the members of this tribe. A stone slab is put on the ground where the navel cord is buried and it is on this stone slab that the mother and the infant are bathed every day. The mother also keeps a sickle by her side in the bed, and she carries the same with her when she happens to go out of the hut; the use of the sickle is also practised by the neighbouring Hindu women for protecting the mother and the child from being molested by malevolent spirits.

The mother of the woman or the midwife massages with oil the body of the newborn baby for some days, with the object of giving good blood circulation and shape to the baby. Similar treatment is also given to the mother if she is in delicate health.

The sixth day after the birth is very important for the newly born, being the day when the Goddess of Fortune is supposed to come at the time of this ceremony and write the fortune of the newborn child. A lamp of clarified butter in an earthen dish is placed near the mother's cot at night and the same is offered to the goddess. The neighbouring women are invited to attend the function when a feast or a tea party is given. The Dubla custom is different from that followed by Hindus. In the case of the Hindus, a slate and pen or paper and pencil are left overnight near the baby; the object being that the goddess *Vidhata* may come over at night and write out the 'fortune' of the future of the child on his forehead with the writing material left for the purpose. The illiterate Dubla does not think of writing instruments though he believes in a goddess of luck. The mother emerges from the house only after the eleventh day. On the twelfth day, she is, after the usual bath, led to a well where she puts an earthen lamp to propitiate the water goddess. Then she returns home and applies red and yellow turmeric paste on the threshold of the door. At the end of this ceremony, one seer of rice or wheat and a rupee is gifted to the midwife concerned. The mother is now considered pollution free and is permitted to perform usual domestic work except cooking. On the thirty-seventh day of delivery, the mother resumes her normal cooking after taking a special purificatory bath. The customs, rites and rituals are practised by the *Dubla* tribals of Gujarat.

Custom of Ritual Uncleanliness

About the *Son Kolis* of Maharashtra, Vijaya B. Punekar writes, "Upon giving birth, the mother enters a period of ceremonial uncleanliness. She rests in bed at least for twelve days, and then resumes her household duties. Circumstances permitting, she does not go for her outdoor work for a month or two. In the Alibag region, it was stated by the elderly women that the woman would be confined to the house at the most for a couple of weeks after delivery, and then she would take the child and the cradle to the drying-ground when she goes for work.

"For the first five or six days, the mother is given *pej* (gruel) prepared from *bajari, halim,,* rice or wheat. The grains, whatever they be, are parched lightly before cooking and ghee and sugar may be added to the gruel. In Alibag, it is called *ghatla. Dhan* is usually given after five or six days. *Pankdnji* is the special food given to the mother for a few months after delivery. It is known as *mirkanji* in and around Alibag. It is a special preparation of *jira* (cumin seed), pepper, turmeric, coriander, *kokam,* garlic, grated coconut, ghee and salt. At first the *pankanji* is prepared with vegetables; fish is introduced after two or three weeks. Only particular varieties of fish and vegetables are used. The fish varieties that such a woman may eat are *morya, nivte, chimori* (crabs), *ovshi, sarangd, chendi* and *mushi.* From among the vegetables, she is given tomatoes, *bhendi, methi, shektdchyd shengd, dudh bhopald and shiravld Vdvari;* flatulent varieties of fish and vegetables are prohibited till the umbilicus wound of the child is healed. Oil and chillies are not given to her for six months. *Roti* is introduced in her diet anytime after twelve days, depending on her health. *Churandche Idru* is used to be a special item of the diet of a mother; they were balls made from a mixture of nutritive articles like almond, pistachio-nuts, dried dates, dried grapes, ghee and sugar, but they contained *methi* and other bitter substances too; hence today, young mothers refuse to eat them. A few substitute *dinkdche Idru (Idru* prepared from gum and sugar and the other ingredients) for them. *Onvd* is consumed in various forms.

A special kind of *supdri* is prepared from *onvd* and *shep* (sweet fennel). If she enjoys a favoured position in the family, or if she is very weak, once a month or a fortnight, she is given *kdl* (chicken soup) prepared with spices.

"From the very first day, the mother and the child are given oil massage and bath twice a day. For this, a *suin* is engaged for twelve days or a month, but later the woman's mother or mother-in-law does the needful. An attempt is made to correct the shape of the child's head and limbs by massage. When massaging *(maltan),* the *suin,* sitting on a *pira* with legs stretched out on a *parat* (circular shallow plate), lays the baby on the legs. After the massage and before giving bath, the baby is given a teaspoonful of gripe water. This is done in a ritualistic way: a drop is dropped on the right of the baby, then one on the left, then the spoon is taken to the forehead and the chest of the child, and then it is emptied in its mouth. Formerly, a little *shep*-water was given instead of gripe water. Tepid water and gram flour are used for bath.

"Today, since the delivery takes place in a maternity home, for the first ten days the mother and the baby are under the care of the physician. After coming home, the usual Koli diet and routine of a woman in confinement are followed, along with the doctor's directions, if any.

"Sometime after the birth, word is sent to the relatives, who usually reside within the locality itself. The latter may have already received the news, as it spreads very fast in the locality. Neighbours are also formally informed. From the first day, the women relatives and neighbours come to visit the newborn baby and the mother. They are served tea brought from a tea-shop. When the delivery takes place in the hospital, only the very close relations visit the woman there, the rest visit she after her returns home.

"A child's first religious ceremony is *sati*. As the term signifies, the ceremony is performed on the sixth day after birth. It starts at about nine or ten at night and continues till midnight. The whole ceremony is performed by the *suin*. When the delivery takes place in a hospital, the *sati* is performed on the eleventh or twelfth day. If for some reason it is not possible to perform it on that day, it is postponed to the next earliest available opportunity.

"On a *pata* (the grinding slab), placed near the woman's cot *(bdjald),* are arranged the following articles: a handful or more of *bhunguli* (parched rice or *jowar),* five betel leaves, five betel nuts, five almonds, five dried dates, five dates, one coconut, some *ruicha pala* (leaves of carded cotton plant), *vanaicha pala* (neem leaves) ten *dive,* ten *dandya,* ten small *gharya,* and ten *umbar.* The *dive, dandya, gharya* and *umbar* are prepared by the *suin*, from wheat flour. Along with these, Rs. 1.25 is placed on the *pata.* A lighted oil lamp (*thamnyacha diva)* is kept at the centre of these things on the *pata.* Besides the *pata* is another lamp lighted in a drinking vessel containing water. Some neem *(vanai)* and *rui* twigs are tied to the *bajala* on all sides. Frankincence is burnt. This is called *pata bharavcha.*

"The child is laid down uncovered on a *mandra* (mat) near the *pata.* The mother lies beside the child. Five fingers of *shendur* (red lead) are applied to the *pata.* The *suin* carries out of the house a brass drinking vessel containing water and a *soop* (winnowing fan) with four fingers of red lead and four of *mas* (black soot) applied to it. These are placed near the entrance, *puja* is offered to the *soop,* and the *suin* comes in. With a neem twig, she sprinkles water from a *pitli* (a small circular shallow vessel) on the child, saying in a typical tone, '*Kavlyala bhiv nako* (do not fear a crow); *vaghala bhiv nako* (do not fear a tiger); *janvarala bhiv nako* (do not fear an animal); *mansala bhiv nako* (do not fear a man); *dolila jashi tayan bhiv nako* (do not be afraid when you go for fishing)' and so on. (In Versova, the *suin* beats near the child's ears a *thali* (small circular vessel) with a twig, and takes a vesselful of water from over the child from head to feet.) The mother is asked to put a *vira* (betel leaf, a betel nut, some rice) and near the *pata* and kneel before it. The *suin* puts red lead in the parting of her (the mother's) hair, applies vermilion on her forehead, makes her wear flowers and neem leaves in her hair and fills her lap with a coconut, some rice, betel nuts, dried dates, almonds, (each of these five or three in number) and a few copper coins. The *suin* asks the mother thrice, '*Satitun uskal jhayli kay?* (Has the release from the *sati* been secured?)' The mother replies thrice, 'Yes', kneels before her and takes the child. All the members of the family place a copper coin each on the *pata* and kneel before it. The neighhours and near relations who are invited[9] bring a handful of rice and a copper coin, which they offer to the *pata*. They are served tea or liquor and they go home. Before retiring to sleep, a paper and a pencil (or ink and pen) are placed near the *pata*. The belief is that at night when everybody is asleep Goddess Sati comes and writes the life and fortune for the child. The oil lamp is kept burning throughout the night.

"The next morning, before other people are out of their beds, somebody from the family removes the things on the *pata* and the water placed at the entrance and disposes them off in the sea. Nobody is supposed to see him when he goes. The *suins* share of money and rice left there, while the *soop* is taken into the house for use.

"On the twelfth day, sweets are placed on the cot used by the woman, on the place where the umbilical cord was buried and on the temporary sink, which is now filled up. *Puja* is offered to these. The sweets on the cot are later distributed to children. The mother and the child are bathed and taken out by the *suin* to pay obeisance to the sun. After this ceremony of *baltila bena karavcha* (taking out the woman in confinement), the mother is free to move out of the house.

"The *suver* or the pollution of the house due to childbirth being over on the twelfth day, the Brahmin is invited to purify the house. The latter sprinkles milk and cow-urine (*go-mutar*) everywhere in the house. The members of the family take bath, and the women take a head-bath," adds Mr. Pumekar. The customs, rites and rituals are practised among the *Son Kolis* of Maharashtra and adjoining region.

Umbilical Cord Cut by Bamboo Strip

About the *Kolam Tribals,* D. Hazra writes, "A few elderly women of the village also remain present along with the *matte-murtal* in a delivery, case to assist the midwife and the mother. After the delivery, the umbilical cord is cut with a bamboo strip *(beyera)*. The child is washed thoroughly and a piece of thread is wound round its navel-stump *(nar)*. The placenta *(jaroam)* is buried by the midwife in a pit made near the bathing place for the mother, which is kept ready outside the house beforehand for such purpose. After the mother takes her bath (inside the house), she suckles the child.

"The midwife continues to come for the next five days consecutively to bathe the mother and the child in the bathing place twice a day, morning and afternoon, for which she charges one *paili* of *jowar* per day. Before bath, both the mother and the child are thoroughly smeared with oil. They are bathed on a wooden plank below which a pit is dug. When the navel stump of the child falls off, the midwife puts it into the pit.

"On the second or third day, a function called *kumli-tinakad* takes place in the daytime. On that day, a mixture of *til*, *gur* and dried coconut is distributed to the village women who attend the function. They are also entertained with boiled *jowar* and *dal*. If one can afford, a feast may be given to all the villagers. The function of *divel-olakad* takes place on the fifth day. On that day, after the bath of the mother and the child, the midwife fills up the pit at the bathing place with earth by applying turmeric powder and *kuku* (a red powder) to it. The name-giving ceremony of the child takes place in the morning of the fifth day. It is not an elaborate function and is attended only by women. Some names are suggested by those who assemble in the house, and one of these names is finally selected. On the same night, five earthen lamps are lighted near the bed of the child. The village women are entertained with boiled *jowar* and *dal*; this feast is called *divel-ambal*.

"The mother observes pollution for a period (*sendar-anda*) of thirty days after childbirth during which she refrains from doing any work and does not eat with others. She does not eat bread during this period. She eats *khichri-java* made of *jowar* or rice mixed with *tuor* pulse and little chilli. Usually, she avoids taking vegetables. Fish, meat or egg is tabooed during this period, and she is given betel leaf, betel nut, cloves, cardamom, etc. After thirty days, the pollution period is over, and no elaborate function takes place in this regard.

"A child is fed with mother's milk till it becomes accustomed to taking solid food, which is gradually introduced to it after the *talkerkakad* ceremony. A child is not usually given cow's or buffalo's milk. When the child is still very young, it is not given solid food regularly; it eats on its own whatever little food it gets from the members of the house during their meals.

"The function of *talkerkakad,* which is associated with the first shaving of hair, takes place when a child (male or female) is about six months old. This may also take place one or two months earlier or later. It is preferred to perform this function in the month of Siurati. A man, related to the child as *mama,* real or classificatory, is invited to perform the function. He makes a leaf-cup of *palas* leaf. Five coins and some water are put into it. He then takes the child on his lap and shaves its hair which is collected in a cup. He then bathes the child and he also takes a bath. After the bath, he ties a red cotton-thread *(kordora)* round the waist of the child and ties a similar thread round his own waist. He then dresses the child with new clothes and ornaments provided by the parents of the child.

"He then makes five cakes *(kurmul)* out of one *paili* of wheat-flour. While preparing them, each of the flour doughs in the form of flat cakes is put in between two *palas* leaves and all these cakes are then steamed by placing them at the mouth of a boiling pot by covering them from top. He goes to a nearby field carrying one *kurmul* and the leaf-cup containing the shaved hair (of the child), coins, etc. He picks up the coins and keeps the cup concealed in grass, after putting a bit of the *kurmul* into it. He eats the rest of the *kurmul* and comes back. He breaks the rest of the four *kurmul* into pieces with a sickle and puts them into a bamboo measure. He takes the child on his lap and puts a cloth, usually red in colour, on its head in the form of a pad *(summa).* He places the measure on it and makes the child bow down. As a result the *kurmul* pieces from the measure fall off in front. He collects the pieces and again puts them into the measure. The whole process is repeated five times. After this is over, some *kurmul* pieces are distributed among five children, male or female, who are asked to eat them behind the house. The rest of the *kurmul* pieces are given to those who are present there. The parents of the child, if, they can afford, entertain their relatives with food.," adds Mr. Harzara. The customs and rituals are practised by the Kolam tribals.

Cutting Umbilical Cord with Sickle

About the Mahadev Koli Customs, Mr. G.S. Ghurey writes, "The woman lies for her delivery on the floor, no cot being used. Doors are closed to avoid breeze which, if the parturient woman is exposed to, is believed to develop rheumatic pain in her. At Jawhar and the adjoining areas, the midwife serves the mother and her child for five days. She massages and bathes them once a day and washes their clothes during this period. Sesamum oil is used for massaging and washing soap for bathing. Formerly, gram flour was rubbed on the body in place of soap. For her services, she receives about a seer (two lbs.) of grain every day, and 50p in cash on the last day. She is honoured on that day when at a 'lap-filling' ceremony she is offered some rice and copra. In Akola and Igatpuri talukas, the midwife attends to the mother in the same way but for twelve days. On the first day, she receives a copra-half and about 25p in cash. On the twelfth day, she is again given a rupee. One rupee is the standard payment in the area, although some well-to-do families might give her a piece of bodice cloth as a gift. At Devargaon and the adjoining villages in the Nasik district, the payment is from 50p to a rupee, although the well-to-do families give the midwives a sheet of cloth, particularly in difficult cases. When a non-Koli midwife attends on the first day, she usually holds on only until the woman is safely delivered. All the subsequent work during the first few days is then done by some elderly women in the house, usually the mother or the mother-in-law of the woman. For her work, the non-Koli midwife receives a rupee on the fifth day.

"As the news of the impending delivery spreads in the village, women gather in the house of the parturient woman to advise and help the members of her family. When the woman has delivered and bathed, these women are each given a copra half and some grain, at a lap-filling ceremony.

"There are experienced midwives who manipulate the foetus to facilitate delivery. Women do not deal with a dead foetus, as it is taken to be a man's job and it is reported that there are male experts who cut the foetus and free the woman. The umbilical cord is cut with a sickle. Some midwives keep a special small-size sickle for this purpose, but the practice is not common.

Before use, the sickle is worshipped with an offering of turmeric and vermilion powders, some rice and an anna. The mother keeps the sickle by her side till the twelfth day when it is washed and removed. The placenta is buried in the bathpit. There are two varieties of the pit where water with which the mother and the child are bathed is directed for twelve days. One is called *vahati nahani*, the flowing drain, and the other is called *kondan nahani*, the enclosed drain. *Kondan nahani* is more common. Only in some families, it is said, that there is a custom for the use of the *vahati nahani.* No family was found to be using the *vahati nahani* as a family tradition. Some who used it explained the practice as due to modern influence. Placenta is buried either at the first sunrise or at sundown after it is cut by the midwife. The pit is closed on the twelfth day after cooked rice is put in it as an offering.

"When parturition is delayed so as to cause anxiety and the case is feared to be serious, the help of a *bhagat* is solicited. In addition to the esoteric charms of the *bhagat,* there are herbal prescriptions which are believed to be efficacious in such serious cases. The *bhagat* first squeezes a tuber of the 'kala-lavi' plant and then with his moist hands holds those of the woman. Another prescription is to put a piece of the root of 'rui' plant in a leaf of the same plant and tie the packet to the woman's hair. The effect is said to be instant that if the herb is not removed immediately after the woman delivers, it is feared to lead to the prolapsus of the uterus. The efficacy of these methods was vouched by a local physician from Manik Ozar and also by a carpenter from Mulund. (A bit of the root of 'chitrak' plant of the red variety tied in a piece of cloth and placed in the vagina is reported to be an efficacious prescription for abortion. The physician of Manik Ozar who supplied this information said that he had no personal experience about the use of this herb and its efficacy because, although his help was solicited for securing an abortion on a couple of occasions, he refused to associate in an activity so grossly sinful.)

"If death occurs in a family in which there is a pregnant woman, the dead member is expected to be reborn as the woman's child. A mark is made with turmeric or vermilion on the face, forehead or one of the feet of the dead body before it is removed from the house, and when the child is born in the family, it is examined for the mark to ascertain if it is the deceased reborn.

"Twins are said to be rare. Actually, there is none on my record. The Kolis assert that twins with a common placenta do not survive. Abnormal children are called *viparya* (a corrupt form of *viparit*, the Marathi word for abnormal). Such children are born with teeth or with long hair on the head. They are either stillborn or have to be cut and removed to save the mother's life.

"When a woman gives birth to a daughter, the threshold of her house is plastered with cowdung by her husband's sister. This is considered to be the registration of her demand for the newborn girl as a bride for her son. On the fifth day, she draws on the threshold a line with ash to prevent evil spirits from entering the house and harming the baby.

"As soon as the child is born, cold water is sprinkled over it to 'awaken' it. This sprinkling is called *opsavni.* The midwife pats the head and the nose of the child to give them proper shape and then bathing the mother and the child in warm water leaves them to rest. If the midwife is a Mahadev Koli woman, she takes a bath on the first and the fifth day. Her clothes on these two days are washed by the women of the family. The mother starts suckling the child only from the fourth day. Normally, the child needs no feeding during this period, but if it cries and seems hungry, it is given water mixed with molasses. Infants that have lost their mothers are fed on goat's or cow's milk or, when practicable, by an obliging neighbouring woman who acts as a wet nurse.

"If the mother has not enough supply of milk, 'bajri' flour cooked with 'katbol' is fed to the mother. On the other hand, if there is an overflow of it, they apply to the breasts a paste made with the flour of 'raybhog' variety of rice which soon decreases the supply. The child is fed at the breast even for four years depending on the onset of the next pregnancy.

"All visitors sprinkle some drops of cow's urine on their feet before entering the lying-in room as a precaution against evil spirits trying to enter with them.

"For the first five days, the mother eats cooked 'sava' or 'vari' grain or wheat flour boiled in ghee with molasses. She eats 'bajri' if that grain is available. Some women during their subsequent confinements restrict themselves to the grain which they had eaten at the time of their first confinement. They are afraid that their family deities will resent any change in their diet. Meat and fish are forbidden during this period. The stirabout of one of the aforesaid grains that the mother is fed on for the first five days is called pat, a corrupt form of the Sanskrit word *pathya* meaning salutary. Copra and molasses are also given to the mother twice a day, as they are taken to be nourishing food. After five days, she eats rice and curry of 'tur' pulse. She eats this food for four to six weeks. Chicken and eggs are also given for nourishment in this period.

"The goddess Sati is worshipped on the fifth day. The function is called *Satipujan*, the worship of Sati or, alternately, Panchavi, that is, the fifth day festival. The mother and the child do not bathe on this day. During the first five months, the child is not bathed on the day of the week on which it was born. On this fifth day, the parents present to their daughters-in-law dried dates, copra oil, jaggery and some other provisions. In the evening, the midwife moves the mother's bed from the place where it lays for five days to another place in the lying-in room and moves the child from the right side of the mother, where it had been so far, to her left. She then plasters with cow dung a small area near the mother's bed for the worship and then takes a bath. Thereafter, she prepares by steaming five breads of 'nagali' flour and cooks some wheat or gram. The latter are called 'ghugrya' and are distributed to guests in celebration of the childbirth, the practice being common to all Hindu communities in the Marathi-speaking areas. She then places some husked 'sava' grain in two small heaps on the plastered portion of the floor. These heaps represent deities. Turmeric and vermilion powders are sprinkled on the heaps and five balls of cooked rice and molasses are placed on well-spread grass in front of them. The mother takes a ball and molasses and offers a part to the bath-pit, keeping the rest back in its place. She then does obeisance to the deities after which she and the midwife dine. Eleven small human figures are then drawn on the wall, two at the head of the mother's bed, two at the foot of it, one on each side of the entrance, two on the side walls and three near the bath-pit. The figure is called *bahula* or *bali* and its body is drawn with lamp-black and the head with red lead. A stalk of hemp and a strut of the prickly pear are placed vertically near each of these figures. The figures are worshipped in the usual way. The offering consists of milk and curds, and a fish and a crab. One from each of these two pairs must be offered. Sometimes men have to walk a good deal before a crab can be secured. At the time of the worship, the midwife ties a piece of orris root with a coloured string and puts it round the neck of the mother who wears it till the twelfth day. Coloured strings are also tied on the child's wrists. Its maternal uncle presents the child new clothes and it is dressed in them, for the first time on this day. Relatives and friends are feasted and entertained on this occasion. The figures with the accompaniments are later removed on the twelfth day. Hereafter, the mother eats 'ajwa' with copra every day for about a month.

"The deities represented by the 'sava' heaps are removed the next morning, that is, on the sixth day, by the midwife. Special invitation has to be sent to her for this purpose. The deities are worshipped for the last time by the midwife who then removes, carries home and uses the grain that represented the deities. At the time of the worship, the midwife holds the child over the fuming incense to purify it and protect it against all evil.

"In Devargaon and the adjoining villages, the midwife places a twig each of mango, plum, the glomerous fig tree, 'rui' and 'sabar' at the two sides of the entrance on the fifth day. The cooked gram or 'ghugrya' is distributed on the seventh day at the 'satora' ceremony to which all women excluding widows are invited. Each guest brings with her a handful of some grain, usually rice or 'nagali', and puts it in a basket placed by the host for the purpose in the house. The child is then placed on the corn in the basket.

"In Ambegaon, Junnar and the neighbouring areas in the Pune district, the grinding stone in the house is worshipped on the fifth day. An offering of rice and curds is made to it. A lamp, which is a stone receptacle with oil and wick in it, is lighted at the time of the worship. In Jawhar taluka, some use a grinding stone and others a winnowing fan.

"The mother worships the well when she goes there to fetch water for the first time after her parturition. The worship known as *barav-puja*, that is, 'worship of the well' is usually done on the twelfth day. It might, however, be done any time during the first month. She first offers rice to the well and then draws ten vertical lines on the inner wall, five with turmeric and five with vermilion. She makes obeisance to the well and returns home with a well cleaned pot filled with water.

"The worship of *panch pavli* represents the worship of the family god and is performed sometime before the child begins to move or crawl. 'Panch pavli' means 'five steps'. For practical difficulties, the parents cannot take their child to the temple of the family god; therefore, they console themselves by walking 'five steps' in the direction of the temple and offering worship there. For the worship, the family moves outside the village in the direction of the temple of the family god and selecting a clean spot places on the ground five small stones which represent the family god and his associate deities. The stones are washed and turmeric and vermilion put on them. The offering consists of rice and molasses. Incense is burnt, and the child is held over the fumes for a while. The mother makes obeisance, copra is distributed and the party returns home. It may be noted that 'panch pavli' is dispensed with when the worship is offered to the family god in its temple," adds Mr. Ghurey. The customs, rites and rituals are peculiar to the Mahadev Koli Tribe of Maharashtra.

***Barse* or the Naming Ceremony**

By the time *Nahani Puja* is performed, men and women return home after work. Women lead mother and child out of house and sing auspicious songs in a chorus. Each one of them lifts the baby and wishes it a good fortune and a better life.

Since ages, names have been given to persons in accordance with their caste status in caste hierarchy; Hindu scriptures like *Vishnu Smriti* and *Manu Smriti,* etc., prescribed that the name of a Brahmin should be auspicious, a *Kshatriya* indicative of power, a *Vaishya* indicative of wealth and a *Sudra* indicative of contempt. As the Mahars were *Avarnas* or the outcastes and were branded lower even than the *Sudras,* they were not allowed to give auspicious names to their children; they were required to be indicative of filth, dirt, inauspicious, and low status. Accordingly, the names of the Mahar men were like *Kachrya* (filthy, dirty), *Kondya* (straw), *Gavary* (dung cake), *Kuppya* (dirty pit), *Chotya* (pigmy), *Ukandya* (piled dirt), *Zadu* (groom), *Chindhya* (torn dirty piece of cloth), *Sukya* (*dry*), *Chimnya* (sparrow), *Dagadya* or *Dhondya* (stone), *Kalu* (black), *Kalya* (famine, inauspicious), *Marya* (dead), *Bhikkya* (beggar), *Dhulya* (dust), *Kadu* (bitter), *Tanhya* (ignorant infant), *Chendu/ Chendya* (kicking ball), *Meghya* (cloud), *Dhebya* (shapeless leg), *Tangya* (shortage), etc. Similar names were given to women, but they were not suffixed by *Ya,* instead were suffixed by *i.* Besides names indicating filth and low status, it used to be suffixed by *Ya* conveying contempt and hatred. Suffixing *Ya* to the name of a *Mahar* man started under the Peshwa rule, who superimposed their authority on the Maratha rule. Before and during the Maratha rule, names of the Mahar men were suffixed by *Nayak* or *Nak* (leader, head). After giving name to the baby, boiled bengal gram mixed with *Jowar* was distributed as a token of their joy, which only was affordable for them in their stark poverty.

At about one year of age, a day is fixed for shaving the child's head for the first time, in front of the Goddess *Satvi* (Goddess who wrote fate, or Goddess *Mariai,* mother of death) or the family deity. People of the caste go to the shrine of the Goddess in a procession led by drum beating and pipe playing men. At the Goddess shrine made of stone, people take five rounds clockwise. At times, mother of the child takes rounds by *Dondwat* (prostrating and touching ones own palms to forehead) and again walks two to three meters and repeats *Dandwat* as a mark of respect and veneration to the Goddess, for protecting her child from disease and death, and ensuring his/her well-being.

The cairn or stone shrine of the Goddess is given water bath followed by curd or buttermilk bath for making her *Sital* (cool). Goddess's shrine is smeared with vermillion and turmeric powders, and green bangales, small piece of green cloth, little rice, a piece of coconut, a piece of turmeric, *Naivedhya* or *Nivad* (five/six centimeter diameter baked thin five breads) is kept in line on which boiled rice and *Bone* (lamps) made of *Jowar* flour are kept kindled. Sometimes, even a goat or sheep or fowl is sacrificed to propitiate the Goddess by applying blood to the shrine. It was said to be a substitute for the life of child. All devotees would prostrate before the Goddess and apply ashes or dust lying in front of it, on the forehead.

On the occasion, the maternal uncle or maternal grandmother of the newborn baby presents new clothes to the baby and its mother. After putting on new clothes, the mother takes the child in her left arm and the maternal uncle of the baby is required to cut its hair, in front of the Goddess, as the barbar who himself a low caste in *Sudra Varna* would not touch or serve the Mahars. Sometimes, maternal uncle, not being conversant in the art of shaving or hair cutting, used to cut a bunch of hair of the baby from front side and offered it to the Goddess.

Depending on the economic condition of the maternal uncle, he would present a cow to the baby for supplying milk. Relatives would also give him presents. By this time, the sacrificed goat would be cooked and ready for feasting. However, vegetarian Mahars and those following the *Warkari sect*, used to perform this ceremony on the bank of a river or stream, preferably *Sangam* (confluence point of two or three rivers), for avoiding blood sacrifice of an animal or a bird.

Soon thereafter, both ear lobes of a child are pierced by a copper wire, and in holes the copper wire rings are fixed. It was said that this would protect the child from diseases. The customs and rituals are related to the *Mahar* community.

Family Members Selecting a Name for Baby

P.G. Shah writes, "Unlike the Hindus, the Dublas do not call upon a Brahmin to prepare a horoscope or to give a name to a child. Generally, the family members jointly select the name of the baby, but the father's sister is given a priority in this respect. The name-giving ceremony takes place on the same weekday on which the baby is born. Sometimes, the child is given the name of the day itself, e.g. a child born on a Saturday is named *Shanio* and one born on Wednesday is named *Budhio.* It has been observed that the day of Thursday, i.e. *guruvar,* is not generally selected for name-giving. Nowadays adopting names from high caste people has become common. The name is also chosen from those given to the children of their relatives or neighbours. When the children of a person happen to die one after the other, this is considered as due to ill-will of some godling or spirit. To escape this, it is customary to name the child after an unattractive or repulsive person. The names of the lowest category which refer to mean professions or objects, e.g., *Bhikhalo* or *Bhikhli,* meaning beggar or *Ukadio* or *Ukadj,* meaning a heap of refuse or cowdung, are chosen.

Dr. Apte (*Dr V. M. Apte's Social and Religious Life in the Grihya Sutras*, p. 68) gives the Hindu version, of the name-giving ceremony *(Namakarana)* during which there is a prayer for a long life of 100 autumns, and a name of two to four or six syllables is given by the father. His name may be that of *Nakshatra* based on the stars under which he is born and is different from that given on the tenth-day. The double name probably indicates that the tenth-day ceremony was common among all people including the tribal people, while the second elaborate sanskritised ceremony was evolved later by the Indo-aryan settlers."

Mr. Shah further notes, "The custom of removing the hair from the head of a boy is present among the Dublas, as among the high caste Hindus. This ceremony is known as *Mundan* or *Choulikarma* in Sanskrit and is performed when the boy attains the age of three or four. As the child is supposed to be a gift of a god or goddess according to their traditional belief, they consider it to be their duty to offer the boy first to the deity. It is believed that the deities have full right over the life of children and a boy in particular. So when the children die in a family one after the other, it is thought that these unpacified deities have devoured them; with a view to admit the right of the deity over the children and to give due recognition to its authority, a vow is taken to pacify it by making some offerings. It is also believed that the child with original hair on the head is not accepted by the deity and that a growth of hair on the head is supposed to protect the life of the child from the unpacified deities. They consider the hair to be so important that on the day selected for the ceremonial tonsure they offer a hair and a coconut to the goddess and request her to accept the gift as a substitute for the child offering. We heard a Dubla saying, 'Till today the boy belonged to the Goddess but as we have now given her the offerings (in hair, coconut, a lamp, etc.) in compensation, she is pleased to give to us the son back, to live with us permanently.'

He writes, "The mother is supposed to remain contaminated for one full month after delivery. During this state of pollution, she is not allowed to fetch water, enter the kitchen, touch earthenware, brass and copperware, clothes, etc. She observes this upto a month and a quarter. It is only after this period that she is allowed to resume her normal duties. This limit is sometimes raised to 40 or 45 days which closely follows that observed by the Hindu community in the area.

"A woman is bathed with hot water boiled with a herb called *nagol,* which is supposed to remove foul smell and to invigorate the health of the mother in confinement. The bathing continues for eleven days after childbirth, and it is performed by the midwife who also cleans the utensils used by the woman.

"If it is possible for her parents or husband, the pregnant woman is given nourishing food, but generally poverty and the strain of daily domestic life keep her ill-fed and ill-nourished till the day of delivery. But after delivery, she is given more rest and looked after better to some extent, and given nutritious food to compensate for the loss of her health and vitality.

"The importance of the mother in Dubla life, as judged by the general considerations given to her, is not small. Cases of ill-treatment of the young wife by the mother-in-law are few because the joint family does not last long. On the other hand, the husband being occupied in agriculture or household work at the Dhaniama, the wife slowly gets a superior position with growing maturity, and her voice and counsel are generally appreciated. The woman has no position in tribal councils, but she is given a more lenient and favourable treatment in divorce proceedings. Further, the custom of bride price has placed an economic value on the wife, who cannot be displaced without a fresh monetary investment and thus secures an increasingly higher social status.

"The Dublas believe that conception takes place only by the will of God. They do not generally make a grievance about sterility or barrenness. Unlike the Hindus, they do not believe in the necessity of a male child to perform *Shraddha* after a deceased Dubla. On the other hand, when they want to avoid getting more children, the advice of a midwife or some other experienced woman, nowadays that of a doctor, is sought after for this purpose. They often indulge in abortion, and this is specially done when an unmarried girl becomes pregnant. On the whole, the demand for more children is not perceptible among Dublas. It is their poverty that is responsible for such an attitude towards children. The average size of a Dubla family consists of about two to three children; they manage to have a considerable gap of years between the births of two children. Some of them avoid sexual intercourse till the child is weaned, and often the weaning of the child is prolonged for two or three years in the belief that such a delay prevents the coming of another child.

"The social and cultural aspects of pregnancy are important and affect the daily life of all the members of the family. The birth of a healthy child is not considered to be an accident but the event which requires careful preparation. Even the husband of the pregnant woman has to observe several restrictions if an eclipse falls within the period of pregnancy. Some of the restrictions are as follows:

(*i*) The husband should not make a *bidi* out of leaves and smoke. If he does so, it is believed that the baby's ears get rolled up like the *bidi* itself.

(*ii*) He should not cut anything with the aid of a penknife. If he does so, it causes cuts on the body of the baby in the womb.

(*iii*) If he hurls a stick at anybody, it is supposed to create a hollow in the body of the embryo.

Similar taboos and restrictions are observed by the husband of a pregnant woman in the Anavil community. This is an additional feature in the culture of the Anavils and Dublas, who have been living together as farmers and labourers for centuries."

Brahmans Suggest Baby's Name

About the naming ceremony, Vijay B. Punekar writes, "For the naming of the child, after purifying the house, the Brahmin, reading his *panchang* (almanac) and studying the position of the stars at the time of the child's birth, tells with what letter or letters the name of the child should begin. The name is given accordingly. Sweets or sugar is distributed to everyone present. Today, besides this official name, the child may be given some pet name. In some places in Alibag, at this ceremony, the child is formally laid in the cradle by the aunt *(atu),* who is given a sari or a *choli* piece by the child's parents. In Mumbai, the practice is unknown. The Brahmin is given an *anchni,* consisting of a coconut, rice, *vira,* and Rs. 1.25. Women visitors bring a *choli* piece for the mother, and some clothes, toys and small vessels for the baby. Near relations present some gold and silver ornament to the child. The visitors are served tea and are given sweets or sugar. This continues for a month or so.

"Many of the traditional Koli names are common to both the sexes. The suffix *I* or *bâi* is added to the male name with the necessary changes to get the female name, such as Joma—Jomai and Poshâ—Poshibâi. Some of the Koli names are taken from the days of the week: Itwar—Itwâribâi *(Itwâr*=Sunday), Budhyâ—Budhubâi (*Budhwâr*=Wednesday) and so on. A new trend has been discernible in the names in the last twenty years. The new names given by the Kolis were the popular, ones among other Maharashtrian groups. Such names were chosen more for the boys than for the girls. Girls' names were still to some extent traditional. Within the last ten years or so, names from the Marathi novels and movies have become popular, and here the change is more in the names of girls than in those of boys. Names in Marathi novels are preferred to popular names. Names like Kalpanâ, Sandhyâ, Kâmini and Râgini found among the Kolis of today are not common even among the higher classes of Maharashtrians of Mumbai. Although the traditional names are not out of vogue, names like Hirâbai, Mânkubâi, Kisan and Shrâvan are still given to the children.

"The baby is vaccinated *(sike devâche* or *phâshitâri)* in the sixth month. *Bâyâi* (the goddess of smallpox) is believed to live in the baby for twenty-one days after vaccination. For the first nine days, the baby is not bathed but *pujâ* is offered to it. On the ninth day, a ceremonial bath is given to it. A *ghat* (sacred pot) is installed and worshipped every day. Seven *suvâsinis* (usually small girls) are invited. Turmeric and vermilion are applied to their forhead, and they are given *bhunguli* and *vird.* They are also served tea. This is again repeated on the twenty-first day, Y-'hen it is *kavalâsâychyâ,* that is, the flowers and other *pujâ* materials offered to the ghat. Along with the water in the ghat other things are immersed in the sea. For all the twenty-one days, a *kanâ* (a figure drawn in flour) is described on one side of the entrance. Colours are filled in it. Turmeric, vermilion and flowers are offered. Camphor, frankincence and scented sticks are burnt. Dried cowdung cakes are burnt and their ashes are applied to the vaccination marks for healing. Later, a goat is offered to *Bâyâ*.

"The 'birth' (first) hair of boys and girls is ceremonially removed. It is called *'kes kârâvche* or *jâvli devâchi*. The children are taken by the parents either to Ekveri or Jejuri according to the family tradition. The children can be taken for the tonsure only with the *Ponvâ,* which may go every alternate year or once in five years. If the *Ponvâ* is not taken in procession for a period more than that, the *Bhagat* of the *Mandli* (the priest or the spiritual head of a group of families) may take such children and their parents once a year. In the Versova and Kolaba district, the practice is to perform the ceremonial tonsure at either of these places, only if a vow to that effect is made. In some families in these places, the practice is to take only the first child for ceremonial tonsure. In some other families, the child may be taken to any holy place, not necessarily Ekveri or Jejuri.

"For removing the hair, the barber is given rice, coconut and 5¼ annas per head. A goat is sacrificed. Around Alibag, the practice is for the paternal grandparents and paternal uncle and aunt to accompany the child. The hair is given in the aunt's lap. She is presented with a sari and a *choli,"* adds Mr. Punekar. The custom and rituals are practised by the Kohis of Maharashtra.

Ceremony of *Barai*

About the naming ceremony of Mahadev Kolis, G.S. Ghurye

writes, "The naming ceremony is not a traditional item of Mahadev Koli culture. Even the practice of consulting the astrologer-cum-priest for referring to the almanac for a name for the child is not very old. So convinced are some of the people of the newness of the naming ceremony that they assert about themselves as not having gone through the ceremony for the names that they bear. Consulting the almanac is much in vogue now and the formal name-giving ceremony, similar to the one observed by the neighbouring communities, is gaining in popularity, particularly in the urban and semi-urban areas. The function is more social in nature than religious, and friends are invariably feasted. Today, educated Mahadev Kolis are found here and there who use an almanac and select the right name for those who approach them for it. Names based on some characteristic of the child or on the day of the week on which it was born are common. Parents who lose a number of children name their child *Dagadu*—stone, *Bhikya*—beggar, *Kerya*—litter, or *Gavrya*—cow dung cake. This practice is common among all sections of Hindus and is a strategy to mislead the God of Death into thinking the child to be an insignificant or dirty object, and thus to dissuade him from putting his heavy hand on it. The naming is often postponed for some months for the same reason.

"There is a function called *barai* which is performed sometime within six months of the child's birth, although properly speaking it should be performed on the twelfth day. It depends upon the family tradition whether the function is to take place at the village of the mother's parents or that of the father. The main item is the offering of a goat to the family gods and inviting the villagers to a feast. If the offering is not made, it is believed that things will not go well with the child. Dr. Chapekar was informed that no naming takes place on the occasion.

"The ceremonial cutting of the child's hair is called by the usual Marathi term javal. The practice is common amongst Hindus and is based on the belief that the hair with which a child is born is impure. Although for poverty or some other reason, the ceremony might be postponed until the time of the marriage of the child or the well-to-do might arrange it quite early, it is normally performed when the child is running its second year. Tuesday, Friday and Sunday are the favourite days of the goddess Bhavani, the god Kaloba and the god Bhairoba, respectively, and the ceremony has to be performed on the day sacred to the family god. The villagers are invited for the ceremony which is performed outside the village and in the direction of the family god, as in the case of *panch pavli*. Five stones are placed on a cleaned spot and worshipped in the same manner as at the time of *panch pavli*. After the worship, a goat or a cock is sacrificed and the villagers feasted. It depends upon the family tradition as to whether a goat, a cock or both are sacrificed. 'Malakari' families who eschew meat and abstain from animal sacrifice offer only a vegetarian feast on this occasion. When the goat is killed, villagers take charge of the cooking, and the host and his relatives arrange the ceremonial hair-cutting of the child. The maternal uncle of the child keeps the child on his lap and cuts a lock from its hair with scissors to which the father of the child has earlier made an offering of an anna or two. The money is taken by the maternal uncle. The child's father's sister collects the lock in the hem of her sari, a service for which she is honoured by her brother with a gift of a pair of bangles or a bodice cloth. She keeps the lock under a pot of cold water, so that the child might grow into a coolheaded adult. The barber who is present by special invitation cuts the child's hair in the usual way after the maternal uncle has done the ceremonial cutting. The maternal uncle then presents some clothes, or a rupee or two, to the child. He is followed by the villagers who, one by one, give the child a copra-half, some jaggery or an anna. Because of the grain and other expenses, people prefer the harvesting season for performing this ceremony. A poor man invites his wife's brother to his house and performs the ceremony in the house, but this might be done only in the case of girls; for the hair-cutting ceremony of a boy, one is required to go beyond the outskirts of the village.

"When the child begins to toddle, five breads of steamed rice flour of the size and shape of a human foot are prepared and distributed to five neighbours.

"The institution of adoption prevails, although it is not very common. The adopted boy usually changes his name so as to signify the new relationship in the place of the old one, but it seems that this is not considered obligatory. The formal ceremony of adoption is a simple one. The headmen of the neighbouring villages are invited to the ceremony and are presented with head dresses. In their presence, the adopter keeps the boy on his lap, puts vermilion on his brows and makes an announcement of the adoption. Betel leaves are distributed and a feast follows. The ceremony does not need the services of a Brahmin priest," adds Mr. Ghurye. The customs and rituals are practised by the community of *Mahadev Kolis*.

References

1. *Bombay Gazetteer*, Vol. IX, Part I.
2. Enthoven, R.E., *The Tribes and Castes of Bombay,* Low Price Publications, Delhi (reprint) 1997, first published 1922.
3. Russell, R.V. and Lal, Hira, *The Tribes and Castes of the Central Provinces of India*, Low Price Publications, Delhi (reprint) 1997, Originally Published Macmillan, London, 1916.
4. Roy, Shibani, *Koli culture*, Cosmo Publications, New Delhi, 1983.
5. Kamble, ND., *Deprived Castes and their Struggle for equality*, Ashish Publishing House, New Delhi, 1983.
6. Shah, P.G. *The Dublas of Gujarat*, Bharatiya Adimjati Sewak Sangh, Delhi, 1958.
7. Hazra, Dr. *The Kolam of Yoetmal, Anthropological Survey of India*, Ministry of Culture, Govt. of India, 1983.
8. Punekar, Vijay, B., *The Sonkolis of Bombay*, Popular Book Depot, Bombay, 1959.
9. Shah, P.G., *Tribal Life in Gujarat*, Gujarat Research Society, Bombay.

2
Puberty

Puberty customs for girls are not observed in the region: rather the first menstruation of the girl is concealed by the woman folk out of shyness. Even the practice of child marriage is not present in all castes and tribes. Initiation rites for the boys are, on the other hand, are observed in various castes, communities, religions and tribes. Among the Brahmans, this rite is called *upanayan;* initiation rites are also celebrated among the Lingayats, Jains among others. The Christians call this rite baptism.

Ritual Connected with Bhuri Bhimayak

About the initiation rite of young lads conducted by the Kolams, Mr. D. Hazra writes, "A sort of initiatory rite is performed for the boys when they attain the age of about five to six years. It is performed during the Kargul festival and some of its ritual functions are associated with the village-god, Bhuri Bhimayak. The father of the boy, who is to be initiated, selects a man belonging to any of his affinal groups, irrespective of the age and marital status of the man. He is taken to the boy's house to act as an *iltam* (son-in-law) or the groom of the boy. Two girls act as *peror-rasikul* (attendants to a bride or a groom during a marriage). They anoint this assumed couple with oil and turmeric paste and bathe them. They dress the boy with a new cloth and a blouse like a bride. The *iltam,* of course, need not wear any new clothes. *Kuku* (a kind of red powder) is put on their head and feet, *akdal* (*jowar*) or rice grains mixed with turmeric) is thrown over their head and a few other rituals, that are part of a marriage, are observed in imitation of them. Five breads are prepared out of one *paili* of wheat flour. Some *jowar-ambal* is also prepared. These five breads are put over the *ambal* and a stick of *ambari* plant is fixed vertically right through the breads and *ambal,* reaching to the bottom of the container."

"One man carries this pot on his head in a procession, along with the couple, to the spot of Bhuri-Bhimayak. The boy sits before Bhimayak and the *iltam* offers *ambal* and bread to the deity. He also sacrifices a fowl to it. The fowl is cooked there. The *iltam* distributes a little quantity of meat, *ambal,* etc, to all those who are present there. Next day the parents of the boy feeds the *iltam* with good food. Until this function is performed in respect of a boy, he cannot attend any feast or pertake the food in connection with any ritual performed in association with Bhimayak." adds Mr. Hazra.

The custom prevails amongst the Kolam tribals.

First Christian Sacrament–Baptism

All the Goan Christians are Catholics, who have seven sacraments to conduct their religious life. The first of them is Baptism or *Batism* or *Baltim* in Konkani or christening in the social sense, where a young one or a new initiate is spiritually reborn through pouring of water blessed by the churah priest, and is admitted formally into the Christian religion. This ceremony is conducted in the presence of witnesses who act as the godfather and godmother to a child. Officially a name is given to the child at the ceremony, confirmed by its registration at the Civil Registrar's office. This sacrament can also be conducted on an adult Christian in name, who had not been baptised earlier due to some circumstances beyond control, or on an adult from another faith who is converted forcibly into Christianity. The birth of a child, incidentally, is announced to the world outside with two bursts of crackers in the case of a girl and three in the event of a male baby, as is the practice among the Gaon Hindus too.

They celebrate the 'Wake' or *Sotti* on the sixth day of the birth of a child (as among the Hindus), an observance that is disappearing gradually, especialy among the upper castes and educated people, with others following suit. But its memory keeps most of the people on the alert during that night, for it is believed that the fate of the child is written or decided on that day by the Almighty. These beliefs still continue to linger in the minds of the people long after the practice of keeping the *wake* has disappeared and hence some basic precautions are taken about the child's well being throughout that night, considered as crucial to its future life.

At about the age of eight, the child is prepared with instructions in the prayers of day-to-day life to receive the first Holy Communion (or *Poilo Komunheano* in Konkani). Before that sacrament comes another one of a preparatory kind called Penance or Confession or *Kum'sar* in Konkani. It is the one in which the sins of a repentant person are pardoned by the absolution given by the priest during the confession. The first holy communion of a child is an important event in the family and for the child's life, as it is the base of his spiritual growth. The ceremony of ritual marks the communion with the fellowmen and involves receiving the holy host (wafer) representing God, in a ceremony in which the child is dressed in white like a bride/bridegroom, with a decorated and lit white candle in hand. The fourth sacrament is the Confirmation or *Krism* in Konkani performed by the bishop or archbishop of the diocese or archdiocese respectively entire Goa is an archdiocese with an Archbishop-Patriarch at the helm of affairs. Confirmation is normally administered at a mature age. However, it may so happen that some persons might have missed it during their younger years, as the bishop in the old days rarely visited villages in the interior of Goa, and hence have to receive it at the earliest opportunity afforded to them by the visit of the Archbishop/Bishop at their parish, which takes place more frequently in the present times.

The Goan Catholics are very particular about the rite of baptism of their baby. At the time of baptism, the parents should be accompanied by the god-parents, *Kumpar* (Godfather) and *Kumar* (Godmother), who on behalf of the baby, answer questions put to the baby by the church priest (*Padre*). The priest asks the child whether he desires to receive the baptism and the answer is given by the god-parents. In the absence of parents, the god-parents usually take the sole responsibility of the baby. When the baby is brought for baptism, the priest comes to the main gate of the church and invites the child into the church. The rituals are administered by the priest. The Easter candle (special type of candle which indicates the presence of Jesus Christ) is lit. The baby is anointed with the holy oil and the priest pours Holy water on his head saying, 'I baptise you in the name of the Father, the Son and the Holy Spirit.' Henceforth, the baby is addressed by the name given to him by the godfather or the godmother and conveyed by the priest at the time of baptism. The baby is dressed in a white garment, a symbol of purity and innocence. The ceremony is generally attended by the relatives, friends and well-wishers who also present gifts to the baby. A grand feast is arranged by the parents for the invitees for their blessings and good wishes to the baby.

Seven years after christening they organise a function for the Communion (which is one of the sacraments of the Catholic) performed by the church priest by laying his hands on the child by to confirm or complete the baptismal vow. After holding faith in baptism, the Catholic children at the age of 12 to 14 years join the Holy Chrism, one of the sacraments of the Catholic church and a ritual where bread and wine are blessed by the Bishop and offered to the incumbent and also to the worshippers. It has its origin in the Last Supper which Lord Christ took on earth with his disciples, when he blessed the bread and wine.

Customs and Rites practised among the Goan Catholics

Various rituals and ceremonies conducted by the Catholic Nadvol during the important events of the life-cycle like birth, marriage and death, are conducted as per their tradition. During the childbirth, a woman from the village (called *vaigin* i.e. midwife) or a doctor is called to facilitate the delivery. On the 8th day of birth, baptism (*bathizm*) is conducted but now it is conducted on any possible day before the child completes one month. In this ceremony, the god-parents (mostly family friends of the child's family) carry the infant to the priest (*Padre*) at the local church. The *Padre* takes some promises from the god-parents on behalf of the baby. The god-parents make the promises and the *Padre* blesses the child with Holy water. On the same day a name is given to the baby, which is also pronounced by the *Padre*. A feast is served to the relatives and the church members on this day. Between 12-15 years of age, the Holy Communion is organised when the *Padre* blesses the grown up and offers bread and wine. From then onwards, he or she can participate in the Lord's Supper. Among the caste people, Chrism is another ritual conducted before attaining adulthood, when the bishop blesses the youngster by anointing him with the Holy oil.

The custom has been adopted by the Catholic Nadvol or Dhobis of Goa.

Among the Catholic Candas, the life-cycle rituals are very simple. Neither any restriction exists in the prenatal period, nor is there any ritual. Twenty years ago, the delivery of a child was conducted at home with the aid of a *vaigin*. Because of easy access to hospitals, now delivery is performed there. Two decades ago, a pollution period of 9 days was obligatory but not now. Birth must be registered with the church officials within 15 days and baptism must be held within a month. Twenty years ago naming was done on the day of baptism. But as baptism without registration is now refused by the *Padre*, naming is conducted within fifteen days to facilitate the baby's registration. If a birth is not registered within fifteen days, a fine of one rupee is imposed on the parents with a relaxation period of another 15 days. In case of further delay to register, an affidavit from the court of law must be submitted to the satisfaction of the church authority. The rituals and ceremonies observed by the Catholic Capenters are similar to those common among the other Goan Catholics. In the earlier times, during childbirth, a woman from the village referred to as the traditional midwife, (*vaigin*) used to attend the mother during the delivery, but at present times women go to hospitals for their delivery under the supervision of a doctor or trained midwife. On the 8th day after birth, the child is baptised by the pastor or church priest. Now some of them are baptising their children even after one month. On the same day, the godmother and the godfather, usually family friends of the child's parents, carry the baby to the church where the church priest (*Padre*) baptises him with the Holy water and gives him a name chosen by the parents. The god-parents make a vow that the child will be brought up as a true Christian. On the third day, the family invites friends and some church members to a feast at their house. At the age of 14 to 15 years, a person is confirmed which means that he or she is a full member of the Christian Community and can thereby partake the sacrament of the Holy Communion. *Chrism* is another important ritual performed before attaining adulthood, in which the boy is produced before the Bishop who blesses him with the Holy oil.

As for the rituals and ceremonies observed by the Catholic Mahars, during the seventh month of pregnancy, the woman is sent to her parental house and small prayer by the church pastor is arranged. Childbirth may take place either in the house or in the hospital. Mostly, midwives (*vaigin*) from the same community facilitates the delivery and cut and dispose off the navel cord. On the 6th day after birth, they break a coconut and light candles before the goddess Boa Morte (Good death, believed to be an incarnation of Vargin Mary) at home and present the *vaigin* with clothes and cash; on the 8th day after birth, the baptism (*batism*) ceremony is conducted as usual. A god-father carry the child to the church-priest who blesses him with Holy water. The promises to be made by the child, to be a Christian, are uttered by the god-parents on behalf of the new-born baby. On this day, the *Vicar* (*Padre*) announces the name of the newborn baby and a feast is served to the friends and church officials. After 8 years of age, 'Holy Communion' is observed for the child, when again, the *Padre* blesses the child and offers him bread and wine. From then onwards, the child can participate in the Lord's Supper. The only change in observance of the above ritual is that now a days the ritual of *baptism* is not performed exactly on the eighth day. *Chrism* is another important ritual observed for the child before adulthood, especially after the age of 12. At the ceremony, the boy is produced before the Bishop for his blessing who blesses the child by anointing him with Holy oil while praying.

The Catholic Kharvis also observe important events of life-cycle, like birth, marriage and death. Earlier, *vaigin* used to attend the mother in labour during the delivery, but now childbirths either take place in the hospitals or a trained nurse or a doctor is called for the purpose. On the 8th day, (in some cases after that) *bathiza* or Baptism is given to the new-born baby by the *Padre* who blesses the child with the Holy water. During the ceremony, only the *Padre* announces the name of the child selected by the parents. A feast is served to the church officials, friends and relatives on the occasion. After 8 years of age, mostly around 10-12 years, Holy Communion (Confirmation of Baptism) is given to the child when the Padre or church-priest blesses him with Holy water and gives him blessed bread and wine, *i.e.* the initiation of participation in the Lord's Supper. The next important Catholic rite is the *Chrism*, observed at any time between 12 to 15 years or even after that. In this rite, the child is produced before the Bishop for his blessings, who blesses the child by anointing the forehead with the Holy oil while praying to the God. Whenever the Bishop visits a church, *Chrism* is arranged for all the children who have not undergone the ceremony and the ritual till that time is observed only once. There are no important changes in the above observance after birth except that in some cases baptism is not done on the 8th day exactly, but performed after a month. The custom pertains to the Goan Catholic Kharvis.

Custom of *Sal-girah* and *Sunnat* (circumcision)

About the birth day and circumcision rites among the Muslim in Maharashtra Mr. RV Russell and Hira Lal write, "The child's birthday is known as *sal-girah* and is celebrated by a feast. A knot is tied in a red thread and annually thereafter a fresh knot to mark his age, and prayers are offered in the child's name to the patriarch Noah, who is believed to have lived to five hundred or a thousand years, and hence to have the power of conferring longevity on the child. When a child is four years, four months and four days old the ceremony of Bismillah or taking the name of God is held, which is obligatory on all Muhammadans. Friends are invited, and the child is dressed in a flowered robe (*sahra*) and repeats the first chapters of the Koran after his or her tutor.

"A boy is usually circumcised at the age of six or seven, but among some classes of Shiahs and the Arabs the operation is performed a few days after birth. The barber operates and the child is usually given a little *bhang* or other opiate. Some Muhammadans leave circumcision till an age bordering on puberty, and then perform it with a pomp and ceremony almost equaling those of a marriage. When a girl arrives at the age of puberty she is secluded for seven days, and for this period eats only butter, bread and sugar, all fish, flesh, salt and acid food being prohibited. In the evening she is bathed, warm water is poured on her head, and among the lower classes an entertainment is given to friends."

About the rites and rituals in Maharashtra and Gujarat Mr. RE Enthoven adds. "The child's first birthday *salgirah* is the next time for merry-making. The word *salgirah* or yearly knot owes its origin among Indian Musalmans to the Mughal practice of the emperor's mother keeping a silken string in the *harem* and adding a knot for each year of the emperor's life. As a rule only female relations are asked. These come and in the women's quarters pass the day in feasting and the night, except in some strict higher class families, in playing the drum *dhol*, and singing. Sometimes men also are asked, given a dinner, and afterwards entertained by professional musician. Before they leave each of the guests gives the child Re. 1 to Rs. 5. This birthday feast is given only by the rich and by some of the middle class. Poor families do not give it.

"When a child, whether a boy or a girl, has reached the age of four years four months and four days comes *bismillah*, the taking the Name of God, a ceremony no Muhammadan neglects. On this day a rich man will feast from a hundred to two hundred guests. In the evening after the dinner is over, the child, covered by a skillfully woven flower-sheet called *sehra* is taken to the men's room where the priest *mulla*, the guests, and a band of young children are waiting. The child is seated on a rich cushion or *masnad*, sweetmeats are laid before it, and of these, two covered with gold-paper are given to it, and after the priest, the child repeats the opening chapter of the Kuran. When this is done, the priest chants some Hindustani verses in praise of the child's parents, invoking blessings on the child's head, and at every pause the young band of choristers shout a loud Amen. When the children are eating the sweetmeats a procession is formed and the child is taken to kiss the tomb or *dargah* of the family guardian saint. As soon as the procession returns, presents are made to the child, silver or gold coins rolled in paper with the name of the giver written on it. As the child passes into the women's quarters the women guests crowd round it, each striving to be the first to take on herself the child's sorrows. After this is over and the child has put off its flower-robe, the women guests amuse themselves listening to the women players or *domnis*.

"At the age of six or seven comes circumcision or *khatna*. Friends send presents of sugarcandy, clarified butter, and sweetmeats, and, though this is commoner among the middle than among the higher classes, the recovery of the child is celebrated with great rejoicing. Among north Gujarat Musalmans circumcision is neglected till an age bordering on puberty, when it is performed with a pomp and circumstance almost equaling those at a marriage, and all the preliminary rites like the *birat* or arranging the pots of clay, a remnant of the pot rites, are observed. In north Gujarat circumcision is styled a *shadi* or joy-time, a word applied in south Gujarat only to marriages.

"After circumcision come rejoicings and a dinner in honour of a boy or girl keeping their first *Ramzan* fast. This is chiefly celebrated by people belonging to the upper and middle classes. It is said that the merit of a boy's or girl's first fast passes to their parents. At its seventh or eight year, a child, if strong enough to hear the privation, is made to fast one day in the *Ramzan*, and that day is marked by a dinner to which a choice party of friends and relations is called.

"Soon after the first *Ramzan* fast, when its Kuran lessons come to an end, the child's parents give its teacher a present *hadya*. A small party is asked, and, before them, the child repeats the beautiful Chapter LV from the holy book styled *Surah Ar-Rehman*, that is, The Most Compassionate, being a description of the bounties Allah has showered on man. Except the teacher's present of clothes and money worth Re. 1 to Rs. 50, a suit of clothes for the child, and parched rice, almonds and walnuts distributed among children costing Rs. 1¼ to Rs. 5 there are no expenses." *Bom. Gaz.*, Vol. IX, Part II, pp. 147-162.

Custom of *Khatna* or *Sunnat* or Circumcision

The Muslims of Goa follow, by and large, the procedures observed in the rest of the country in regard to their sacraments, with a few local variations. The first Muslim sacrament is that of *Paidaish* that concerns the birth of a child. The *Pesh Imam* or the *Baangi* from a neighbourhood Mosque is called after the birth of a child, and two holy phrases are whispered into the ears of the new-born baby, the *aazan* into the right ear and the *ikaayat* into the left one. Then honey is applied to its tongue and it is given a suitable name. If the priest from the mosque is not available, the ceremony may be conducted at home by an elder member of the family. Later, according to convenience, the *akika* ceremony is performed on the seventh or the fourteenth day, the twenty-first or the fortieth day after the birth of a child by the clergyman, when a goat is slaughtered, one goat in the case of a girl and two in the event of a boy, as is ordained by the custom. The second sacrament is that of *khatna* intended for male children, meaning circumcision, called *'sunta korunk'* or *'sun' not'* is Konkani, which is now a days performed in hospitals. The third sacrament among them is *Bismillah,* meant to initiate the child into the system of education, for thereafter the child is taught the *Quran* and other essentials of the Islamic religious persuasion with a strong determination and dedication. According to Olivinho J.F. Gomes, "The religious picture of the State at present, with a large injection of non-native Goan population, shows the Hindus in a numerical majority (around 66%), with Christians further dropping behind (around 29%), and the Muslims around 4%, the rest making up around 1%. The rest of the faiths represented are the Sikhs, the Jains, the Buddhists, the Parsees, and others who have made their way into the State for trade or employment in government, private firms or in self-run businesses. As a large majority of ethnic Goans are mainly Hindus, Christians and Muslims, who have a local orientation in their religious observances of distinctive character. This distinctiveness is not prevalent among other religious persuasions who follow the all-India pattern."

Rituals of Upanayana

The life-cycle of a Goan Hindu, very much like his counterpart in the rest of India, revolves around customary rituals and ceremonies called as *samskaras* or sacraments that are rather long-drawn yet impressive and meaningful. These are grouped into categories: the *nitya* (customary and prescribed), numbering sixteen, need to be performed compulsorily, and the *naimittika* (special performances on occasions of importance) the observance of which is left to the discretion of the individual concerned and these are as many as twenty-four. The sacraments begin to be performed right from the time of conception of the child in the mother's womb in a ceremony called *garbhadana* (or earlier on the young woman attaining puberty) and go through the thread-girdling, christening and other ceremonies, and end with the *antyesthi* ceremony of the funeral rite, after a person's death.

Mr. Obivinho J.F. Gomes writes, "The *garbhadana* ceremony is performed at the woman's husband's home. When her confinement draws near, the pregnant woman is dispatched to her mother's haven, the beloved *kullar* in Konkani, and she goes through a ritual called the *fulam malltat* in Konkani, the bedecking or adorning the coiffure of the woman with flowers in the fifth, seventh and ninth months of pregnancy. The first two flower-offerings are held at her husband's house. In the fifth month of pregnancy her lap is filled with offerings of green clothes. After 'filling her lap' (*vontti bhortat* in Konkani), in the seventh month of pregnancy, she is sent to her mother's haven, where she is adorned with flowers in the ninth month. Only married women with living husbands, the *sovasnni* in Konkani, from the group of relatives, can participate in these important ceremonies."

"The birth of a child makes for great rejoicing in the family. On the sixth day from birth, there is prescribed a ceremony called *sotti* in Konkani, or *shastti-pujan* in Sanskrit, which is performed by most of the people. That night the female deity called *Sottvai* is honoured and food served to the few people present, with great unction. The whole of that night resounds to the beat of the *ghumatt*, a special local percussion instrument made from a mud-pot contraption, with one end open and the other covered with taut, paste-tuned lizard or snake skin. This ritual is now shorn of its original sheen and eclat but it is still observed in a very simple manner. From the birth of a child, a period of ten days of seclusion is imposed on the woman who has delivered it, when the latter is prevented from even touching any thing. On the eleventh day she is bathed and offered *panchgavya* consisting of cow's urine, basil-plant (*tulasi*) leaves, cow-dung, etc. A *homa* sacrifice of a ceremony is offered to God and water from the *tulasi* plant is brought into the house and sprinkled on household objects for their purification. The woman is offered coconut, sweet preparations in liquidpasty form called *goddshem,* cakes, rice, pulses, etc. This observance is now on the wane particularly among the higher castes who seem to attach less importance to it."

"On the twelfth day of the birth of the child, there is performed a ritual called *Barso* in Konkani, or the naming ceremony, called elsewhere in India as *Namakaran.* Married women of the extended family with living husbands meet and fill up the lap of the woman who has delivered the child, with flowers and gifts of all sorts. The child is then placed in the cradle and bestowed a name. Normally in all castes among Hindus, three names are given to the child including a surname. They are the first, proper name of the boy or girl, as the case may be, the second being the father's name and the third the surname."

"When the child cuts its first tooth or grinder there is a ceremony held to celebrate the occasion with refreshments, food, etc. after it. This is known in Konkani as *'datollem ghalta'.* Little fried cakes, biscuits etc. are strewn over the head of the child and then distributed to the children gathered on the occasion. This practice is also on the decline these days and wherever it is prevalent, the fried *vodde* (flat bread cakes) have been replaced by chocolate, toffee, peppermint, etc. *Chaul* or tonsure of the head was done at the age of two or earlier. It consisted, according to precept, of shaving off the entire head of the child of the hair on it, leaving only a tiny pigtail behind. This practice has almost disappeared among all the castes."

"*Moonz* or the *Upanayana* that is the thread ceremony is performed among the higher castes of the Saraswats and other Brahmin groups, the Kshatriyas, the Daivednyas, the Vaishya-Vanis etc. The sacred thread is known as *zaan'vem* in Konkani. This ceremony is not performed among the Sudir group of castes, as they are not eligible ritually to perform it. The *Munz* ceremony was ordained for performance and was done between the ages of eight and ten. Even today marriages do not take place unless this ceremony has been performed, which is done sometimes on the eve of marriage. As it is well-known. *Upanayana* was meant to usher in the period of education of a student in what was called the Brahmacharya ashram. That has lost much of its relevance now with a different calendar being followed in modern education. During the Portuguese times, the child started his/her schooling in the sixth year of age, inscribing on his slate a picture of Saraswati, the goddess of learning, and began his first lesson with *Sri Ganesha Namah*, an invocation to Lord Ganpati. But now a days the child, in a highly competitive spirit that is fostered by the parents and sanctioned by the educational system, starts its formal education at an earlier age and without the obeisance customarily accorded to Sri Ganesha, the deity of wisdom. The thread-girdling ceremony amounts to purificatory rite when the boy is initiated into the intricacies of a worldly life." adds Mr. Gomes.

At the age of 8 to 10 years the Saraswat-Brahmans observe *munz* or a sacred thread-wearing ceremony when *mundan* or tonsuring the head is a must. Two or three Bhatjis are required to perform these rituals and *hom* is one of the religious rituals connected to this occasion. They observe first-feeding ceremony which is called *ushtauan*. The onset of the male puberty is also ritually observed. The custom is related to the Saraswat Brahmans of Maharashtra.

The thread ceremony is performed when the boy is between the age of six and eight in mainland Gujarat and between the age of six and eleven in Kathiawar. Betrothals generally take place two or three years before marriage. At betrothals, the boy, accompanied by the women of the family, is brought on horseback to the girl's house. Here he is taken by the girl's mother, who makes him sit on her lap and fed with sugarcandy and almonds. In some families, the betrothal ceremony is performed on the booth-consecrating (mandva murt) day, that is, three days before the marriage-day. During the time between betrothal and marriage, presents are exchanged; and on holidays the boy is asked to dine at girl's house or the girl at the boy's house. The custom is related to the *Brahma Kshatriya* community of Gujarat.

Custom of Sipping Bull's Urine

About Parsi custom of initiation, R.V. Russell and Hira Lal write, *Bombay Gazetteer*, Vol. IX, Part II, p. 231. Thus, "Parsi boys and girls are received into the Zoroastrian faith between the ages of seven and nine. The child is purified by being bathed, sipping bulls' urine and chewing a pomegranate leaf, and makes the profession of belief in the faith. He or she is then invested with the sacred shirt, *sadra*, and the sacred cord or thread called *kusti*. The shirt is of thin muslin, with short sleeves and falling a little below the hip. The sacred cord is of wool, and can be made only by the wives and daughters of Parsi priests."

Binding Linga on the Child

About the customs of the *Lingayat* community in the western region of Maharashtra and the adjoining region, Mr. R.E. Enthoven records, "It is commonly asserted now a days by prominent members of the Lingayat community that the true test of the Lingayat is the right to receive the full *ashtavarna*, and that the possession of a few of these eight rites only does not entitle the possessor to be styled a member of the community. The contention seems scarcely in harmony with the popular usage of the term 'Lingayat'."

"The *ashtavarna* consists of eight rites known as : 1. Guru, 2. Linga, 3. Vibhuti, 4. Rudraksha, 5. Mantra, 6. Jangam, 7. Tirth and 8. Prasad."

"On the birth of the Lingayat the parents send for the *guru*, or spiritual adviser, of the family, who is the representative of one of the five *acharyas*, or holy men, from whom the father claims descent, The *guru* binds the *linga* on the child, besmears it with *vivhuti* (ashes)], places a garland of *rudraksha* (seeds of *Elaeocarpus ganiturs*) round its neck, and teaches it the mystic *mantra* or prayer known as *Namah Shivaya-i.e.*, 'Obeisance to the god Shiva'. The child being incapable of acquiring of knowledge of the sacred text at this early stage of its existence, the prayer is merely recited in its ear by the *guru*. The child has then to be presented to the God Shiva, in the person of a Jangam, or Lingayat priest, who is summoned for this purpose. On his arrival, the parents wash his feet, and the water in which the feet are washed is described as the *tirtha* or *charanatirtha* of Shiva. This water is then poured over the linga attached to the infant. The Jangam is fed, and a portion of the food from the dish is placed in the child's mouth. This final ceremony is known as *prasad*. Occasionally, the double characters of *guru* and jangam are combined in one person.

When the child attains the age of eight or ten, the ceremony is repeated with slight modifications."

"It will be seen that this eightfold ceremony forms a very concise test of a Lingayat's religious status, and may be not unfitly compared to rites of baptism and confirmation which are, outward and visible signs of admission to the Catholic Church. But not all Christians are confirmed, and in the same way not all members of the Lingayat community undergo the full ceremony of initiation. It would probably be safer to apply the term 'Lingayat' to all wearers of the linga, whether they are entitled to the full ashtavarna on birth or conversion, or to a few only of the eight sacraments. In so doing, the lower orders from a social standpoint, of the Lingayat community, will not be excluded, as they would otherwise be, from the fold."

"Lingayats are not permitted to touch meat, or to drink any kind of liquor. The greater number of them are either occupied in agriculture or are traders. They are generally reputed to be peaceful and law-abiding; but at times they are capable of dividing into violent factions with such rancour and hostility that the dispute culminates in riots, and occasionally in murder. Among the educated members of the community there is a strong spirit of rivalry with the Brahamans, whose intellect and capacity have secured them a preponderating share of Government appointments and often a preponderating influence in municipal affairs. This rivalry between the two sects may be said to dominate the whole social and political life of Bombay and Karnataka. Except for these defects the community may be described as steady and industrious, devoted to honest toil, whether in professional employment, or occupied in trading or the cultivation of the soil." adds Mr. Enthoven.

According to the *Bombay Gazetteer*, "The rite of *aitan* or initiation is performed on the unmarried sons of the Jangams. When *aitan* is performed one becomes fit to hold the highest religious house. A Jangam who has no sons hadayya or the head of a religious posts; he may become a *matkadayya* or the head of a religious house. A Jangam who has no sons has the rite performed at the expense of one of the sons of a lay disciple who is not below the Panchamsali group. The boy who is chosen from a lay Lingayat faimily should be of respectable parents. and his ancestors, both male and female, even to the eleventh generation should not be children of married widows. For this reason the sons of *mathpatis* or beadles and of *ganacharis* or managers seldom undergo initiation or *aitan*. A boy is initiated when he is between eight and sixteen years old. The ceremony takes place at night, so that no non-linga-wearing Hindu may see it. It should take place in one of the seven months from *Vaishakh* (April-May) to *Phalgun* (February-March) inclusive – on one out of eight days in either fortnight. viz.: the second, third, fifth, seventh, tenth, eleventh, twelfth, or thirteenth—on either a Monday, Wednesday, Thursday, or Friday, and in one of the following lunar mansions or nakshatras. viz:- *Anuradha, Hast, Magha, Mrig, Mul, Revti, Rohini, Uttara, Uttarashdda,* and *Uttarbhadrapada*. If the boy is to become a *Virakt* to celibates, his initiation is performed in the dark half of the month, and when he is intended to be a *Grihasth* or householder, the ceremony takes place in the bright half of the month. In an initiation the *bhushuddhi* or earth purifying is it the observance. Either in a religious house or a dwelling house a piece of ground, eleven and a quarter, twelve, or twelve and three-quarters feet, is six and three-quarters, seven and a half, or eight and a quarter feet, is dug seven and half to eight and a quarter feet deep. Bits of stone and tiles and other large objects which may be in the pit are removed, and it is filled with fine earth, which is afterwards beaten hard. At the same time the house is whitewashed and painted and its floor is cowdunged. On the day fixed a small bower with a canopy of silk cloth is raised on the sacred spot. At the entrance of the bower an arch is made of two plantain trees or sugarcane stalks. The floor of the bower is plastered with *gorochan* or bezoar, cowdung, clarified cow's butter, cow's milk, and cow's urine, and on it is drawn a large parallelogram with lines of quartz powder, and within it, three small parallelograms.

Of these, the first, which lies farthest from the entrance, measures three feet and a quarter by two feet and a quarter. It is covered with a folded silk or woollen cloth and is set apart for the guru or initiator. The second or middle one is six feet by two and a half feet. In the centre and at each corner is set a kalash or brass or copper vessel with a narrow mouth and a dome-shaped bottom. These five vessels represent the five mouths of Shiva and the five *gotras* or family stocks which are believed to have sprung from them. The names of the five mouths are Aghor, Ishanya, Sadyojat, Tatpurush, and Vamdev, and the names of the corresponding family stocks are Uddan, Panchvanigi, Padudi. Muthin-kanti, and Mali. In the elaborate scheme of five-fold classifications, these names do not occur. For the *gotras* he gives Vira, Nandi, Vrishabha, Bhringi, and Skands (see above). The names given in the text perhaps belong to his *pravaras* (family stocks) for all of which he curiously gives simply Virshaiva. Of the five jars the Sadyojat is set at the corner next to the *guru's* right hand and the Vamdev at the corner next to his left hand. Opposite the Sadyojat is set the Tatpurush and opposite the Vamdev, the Aghor. In the centre is placed the Ishanya. Each jar is covered with five pieces of cloth—white, black, red, green, and yellow, and before each of them are laid five halves of dry cocoa-kernels, five dry dates, five betelnuts, five turmeric roots, five betel leaves, and five copper coins. The third or last design, which is not a parallelogram but a square two-feet each way, is close to the entrance of the bower. This square is covered with a woollen cloth seat, and is occupied by the boy, whose head has been completely shaved in the morning, since when he has been naked and fasting. Near the *guru* are placed a small brass vessel called *gilalu*, a conch shell, and a cane. Behind the boy sits a man belonging to the boy's *gotra* with a coconut in his hands. This man bows to the *guru*, and says—"Excellent teacher, purify this body of flesh and blood." After him the boy also bows to the *guru*, and worships an earthen vessel filled with water, in whose mouth is a coconut covered with a piece of cloth. The boy first marks the vessel with sandal paste, burns frankincense before it, and offers it molasses, fruit, betelnut, betel leaves, and money. At the end of the jar worship, a string composed of five strands is wound five times round the jar, the *guru* and the boy in the following elaborate order, each object mentioned being encircled five times before passing on to the next :

"Ishanya, Sadyojat, Ishanya, guru Ishanya, Vamdev, Ishanya, Aghora, Ishanya, boy, Ishanya, Tatpurush."

"When the *guru* and the boy are thus seated, the *mathpati*, or *Lingayat* beadle, worships the *linga* which the boy wears and his hand and head. He first washes the boy's *linga* with seven holy waters in the order, *Gandhodak* or sandal paste water, *dhulodek* or dust water, *bhasmodak* or ash water, *suvarnodak* or gold water, *ratnodak* or jewel water, and *pushpodak* or flower water. He then washes the *linga* seven times with the mixture called *panchamrit*, or five nectars, namely, milk, curds, clarified butter, honey and sugar. In the same way he wahses the boy's hands and his head. The *guru* then gives the boy a *jholi* or beggar's four-mouthed wallet and a staff, and tells him to beg alms of those who have come to witness the ceremony. The boy is given *dhatubhiksha* or metal alms, that is, gold, silver or copper coins. After gathering the alms, the boy gives them with the bag to his *guru*, bows low before him, and asks him to return the bag, promising to obey all his commands to the letter. The *guru*, after commanding him to live on alms, to share them with the helpless, and to lead a virtuous life, returns his bag. The boy gives him gold, vessels, and clothes, and gives other Jangams, money and clothes. Besides these gifts the *guru* takes a handful of copper coins from a heap worth Rs. 3-8-0, the rest of which is distributed to ordinary or Samanya Jangama. The friends and kinspeople of the boy's parents present the boy with clothes and vessels; and he takes a light repast. Next morning the boy's father gives a caste feast to Jangams of all orders and to friends and kinspeople. *Aitan* can be performed on one or more boys at the same time and by the same initiator." (*Bombay Gazetteer*, Vol. XXIII, pp. 230-3.)

Diksha, or cleansing rite, is performed on any Panchamali Lingayat, entitled to the *ashtavarna* rites, who wishes to enter into a grade higher than his own or to readmit one who has been put out of caste. In the main points, diksha does not differ from *aitan* or initiation; the only difference is that in the purifying it is not necessary that a celibate Jangam should be the performer. His place is often taken by a family priest. As the person on whom the rite is to be performed is old enough to pray for himself, no man of his family stock is required to sit behind him. The *diksha* rite can be performed on twenty or thirty persons at the same time. When a person has undergone this rite and has entered into a higher grade, he or she does not eat with the former kinspeople. But this contingency rarely arises except when a girl marries into a higher grade. The ceremony performed at the time of tying a linga on a child's neck or arm is also called *diksha*. (Bombay Gazetteer, Vol. xxiii, p, 233.) The customs and rituals pertain to the Lingayat community.

Girding Boys with Sacred Thread

About the investiture of sacred thread and its ceremony held for boys in the Jain community, Mr. R.E. Enthoven writes, "Boys are girt with the sacred thread between eight and sixteen. A boy must not be gird until he is eight. If, for any reason, it suits the parents to hold the thread-girding before the boy is eight, they add to his age the nine months he passed in the womb. A Jain astrologer names a lucky day for the thread-girding, a booth is raised before the house and an earth altar or *bahule,* a foot and a half square is built in the booth, and plantain trees are set at its corners. Pots are brought from the potter's and piled in each corner of the altar and a yellow cotton thread is passed round their necks. Over the altar is a canopy and in front is a small entrance hung with evergreens. Invitation cards are sent to distant friends and kinsfolk. A day or two before the thread-girding, the invitation procession consisting of men and women of the boy's house, with music and friends, starts from the boy's house. They first go to the Jain temple, and the father or some other relative of the family priest lay a coconut before the god, bows before him, and asks him to the ceremony. They visit the houses of their friends and relations and ask them to attend the ceremony. The Jains have to *devak* or family guardian worship. The boy and his parent go through the preliminary ceremonies as at a Brahman thread-girding. The boy's head is shaved and he is bathed and rubbed with turmeric. The astrologer marks the lucky moment by means of his water-clock or *ghatka,* and as it draws near, music plays and guns are fired. The priest repeats the lucky verses and throws red rice over the boy. The boy is seated on his father's or, if the father is dead, on some other kinsman's knee is already seated on a low stool. A knot is tied in his hair and he is girt with a sacred thread or *janve* and a string of *kush* grass is tied round his waist. The priest kindles the sacred fire, betel is served to the guests, the money gifts are distributed among priests and beggars. The boy has to go and beg at five Jain houses. He stands at the door of each house and asks the mistress of the house to give him alms saying. "Oh lady be pleased to give alms". The alms usually consists of a waistcloth, rice, or cash. Great merit is gained by giving alms to a newly girded boy, and many women visit the boy's house for three or four days to present him with silver or clothes. After begging at five houses the boy returns home, and a feast to friends and kinsfolk ends the first day. The *sodmunj* or grass-cord loosening is performed usually after a week and sometimes between a week from the thread-girding and the marriage day. The loosening is generally performed near a *pipal* (Ficus religiosa) tree. The boy is bathed, the rite of holi day calling or *punyahavachan* is gone through as on the first day, music plays, and flowers, sandal paste, burnt frankincense, and sweetmeat are offered to the *pipal* tree. The boy bows before the tree and the priest unties the cord, from round his waist. The boy is dressed in a full suit of clothes, declares that he means to go to Benaras and spend the rest of his life in study and worship, and sets out on his journey. Before he has gone some yards, his maternal uncle meets him, promises him his daughter's hand in marriage, and asks him to return home and live among them as a householder or *grihasth*. The boy is escorted home with music and a band of friends and a small feast to friends and kinsfolk ends the ceremony." adds Mr. Enthoven. The custom pertains to the Jain community in the region.

Rituals of *Padur Jhevacha*

Till marriage, there is no ceremony either for a Son Koli boy or girl, except that among Thalkars, when a girl attains puberty, on some auspicious day, especially *Gaurya, Shimaga* or *Dasara*, she is 'given' *padur* (allowed to throw the end of the *lugut* on the shoulders) and sweets are distributed to her friends, relatives and neighbours on the occasion.

According to Mr. Vijay B. Punekar, "Among the Son Kolis the rules of sex morality have always been stringent. A few decades ago, when early marriages were in vogue, pre-marital chastity was not a serious problem: but as the age of marriage went on advancing, the parents of young men have had to make sure of the virginity of the brides. Due to the nature of their work, rigorous control of the parents over the daughters has never been possible. Pre-marital unchastity is detected, however, only if it results in pregnancy. In that case, the usual practise is to marry off the couple. Where the boy could not be compelled to consent for the marriage, the girl, it is said, had to resort to abortion. This, however, besides being illegal, is socially prohibited. Marital faithfulness is certainly expected, at least on the part of the women. Even among the men extra-marital intercourse has been very rare, as bigamy was common and polygamy was permitted, till recently. The Bombay Prevention of Hindu Bigamous Marriages Act, passed in 1946, has altered the state of affairs now. It is interesting to note that the community does not have trade in women. In fact, majority of people do not know the meaning of the corresponding Koli terms, *kamavtya baya*. Rarely a married woman may have her paramour, but such a women is looked down upon by the society."

"Continence is rigidly observed during the wife's menstrual period for seven to eight days. Some fifteen years back, the husband and wife were segregated for six months or a year immediately after marriage: today, this custom is observed at the most for a month. There is no fixed period of continence after the child-birth."

"Contraception is virtually unknown. Only a few young women know of or have submitted themselves to sterilization, 7on the physician's advice. The majority of women, however, regard it as a serious sin (*pap yete*), since children are the gift of God (*Devachi dengi*)," adds Mr. Punekar. The custom is practised among the Son Kolis of the Western region.

Keeping Menarche under Wrap

According to Mr. G.S. Ghurye, "At the appearance of the first menses, a girl tries to avoid her condition from being widely known. If the mother be near, she confides only to her. As a result of freedom from any rigorous taboo, women in menses are not easy to make out. There are at least two beliefs which take notice of this freedom. When women go in a team for fishing, failure to catch fish is attributed to one of the participants being in menses. At the annual Katha fair at Sakirwadi in Akola taluka of Ahmednagar district, failure of a devotee to complete his usual rounds of circumambulations is also taken to be due to the defiling presence of such a woman. Although full freedom is the rule, there appears to be some change taking place. Women in some families are not allowed to milk cows and buffaloes during the period, and they do not eat onions, milk-products or milk. Some informants suggested that the taboo is a recent innovation and seems to be neither widespread nor strict. The authors of the Bombay Gazetteer writing in 1884, about the Mahadev Kolis from Ahmednagar district have recorded that when a girl comes of age she sits apart for three days, is bathed on the fourth and her lap is filled with rice and coconut. This record is quite inconsistent with the prevailing practice of avoiding the condition from being known. Moreover, people have not known nor have they heard of such restrictions and rites prevailing in the community any time in the past. In Mulund, a cosmopolitan satellite town of Bombay, some women in the condition under discussion observe seclusion. The practice was explained to be due to the influence of neighbours in whose eyes freedom from such restrictions is a sign of backwardness" adds Mr. Ghurye. The custom is prevalent among the Mahadev Kolis of Maharashtra.

Adorning the Girl at Menarche

Mr. Enthoven writes, "When a girl comes of age, her feet are rubbed with turmeric powder, moistened with water and her brow with redpowder with or without oil; and she is fed on *varan* or split pulse cooked in water with turmeric powder, and salt, rice, vegetables, and unstuffed cakes or *polis*. If her father-in-law is rich, the girl is for four days, seated in a gaily dressed frame called a *makhar*. Oh the fifth day she and her husband are bathed, and while they bathe music is played. She is dressed in a green robe and green bodice, and her hands are adorned with fresh green grass bangles. Her father, if rich enough, gives her husband a waistcloth and turban and to his mother a robe and a bodice, and beds, a carpet, a set of betel, dishes, and a *samai* or metal lamp for her and her husband's use. Some unwidowed women with relations are asked to feast on cakes or *polis,* and the girl and her husband are made to feed each other from the same dish. In the evening the girl is sent to sleep in a separate room and the wife's brother or other near relation leads the boy to the room and shuts him in." The custom pertains to the Kunbi tribals of Maharashtra.

Rituals of the Vat-Bharan Puberty Ceremony

In the Mahar community of Maharashtra, a puberty ceremony at the time of attaining puberty was performed. Among them, the normal age of bride at the time of attaining puberty used to be around 12 to 13 years. However, only few Mahars performed the *Vat-Bharan* ceremony in a grand way due to stark poverty. Due to the practice of child marriage, girls would attain puberty several years after marriage. The appearance of menarche was celebrated by them probably for making the girl feel less frightened due to physiological changes and also to express their joy over her reaching fertility age which would possibly add new members in the family.

An astrologer, who normally used to be a non-Mahar, would made forecast on the basis of the time of reaching puberty, her name, day, time and star position at the time of appearance of menses. He would also suggest rituals and methods of observance of puberty. In case of inauspicious zodiac signs, some kind of worship to propitiate the heavenly stars was performed by the astrologer himself. However, it was neither popular among the Maharas nor they were obliged often by a Brahman astrologer. However, the *Vat-Bharan* ceremony was very much popular among the Hindus. On the first day of attaining menstruation, ceremonious bath like the one given during the marriage time was given to the girl. Five grain flour balls were made by keeping in each one of them pieces of coconut, arecanut, turmeric, vermillion and old cloth.

The girl was asked to pick up and break them one by one; if contents were coconut, arecanut or vermillion, then the first baby was believed to be a male child; in case of turmeric, a female, in case of vermillion, a happy marital life; and in case of cloth, she would be foreseen as barren. On the fifth day of puberty, house floor, walls and roof were smeared by cowdung paste, and all clothes and utensils were washed to remove the ritualistic pollution as a purifying measure. Turmeric powder paste and at times even scents were applied to her body and vermillion paste and rice were applied to her forhead. The custom of application of turmeric paste to body existed probably due to antiseptic values of turmeric paste. Oil was applied to her hair and poured in her ears. Ceremonious bath was given to her in public by five *Suhasinis* (five married women) amidst singing of songs and traditional music of drum beating and playing of pipes. After the ritualistic bath, again turmeric paste was applied to her body, vermillion and rice were pasted on the forehead; foot and palm were decorated by vermillion and *Mehandi, Kajal* (collyrium) was applied to her eye lids and ornaments, if any, were presented to her. Sometimes, the girls and their husbands used to sit together during the ceremony. These rituals were followed by a community feast, and at times it was restricted to close relatives due to the poor economic condition of the family.

Later on the same day, the girl was given only green-coloured bangles, green sarees and green blouse to put on. Five *Suhasinis* or the married women used to keep the rice and five pieces each of coconut, arecanut, and turmeric, etc., in the lap of her green saree, usually in front below navel. This ceremony was called as *Vatibharan* (filled lap). On this occasion, relatives gave *Aher* (presents), mostly new clothes, to each other and also to the girl and his family. However, this ceremony, related to puberty, is fast disappearing even among other castes as the age of marriage of girl has gone up. These days practically all girls are getting married after attaining puberty.

However, on the occasion of the first as well as every successive menstruation, a woman becomes impure or her very touch to any animate or inanimate thing was believed to be polluting. Then, the polluted person could be purified only by taking a purifying bath and washing all clothes on the body. If such polluted person touches other person before taking bath, he would cause further pollution. Pollution-related taboos were meticulously observed. A naked child, however, was not supposed to be polluted even if directly touched by a woman during the menstrual period. Probably, this permission was granted to enable a mother to feed her child with her breast during the menstrual period.

The non-inflammable articles were purified by putting them on fire and inflammable things were purified by washing and sprinkling cow uring on them. It was said that pollution due to menses would aggravate illness, eye patient or smallpox patient would become blind, serious patient would die, sacredness of temple and even the God in it would vanish, family would be cursed by supernatural powers and plant, flowers, fruits, etc., would perish. Therefore, woman during the menstruation period was not allowed to work in fruit and vegetable gardens due to fear of their destruction. A woman during her menses period was completely seggregated and was asked to sit in a corner of the house. Menses pollution related taboos and prohibitions are meticulously observed. Such rigid observance of menses pollution was common in most of the castes in Maharashtra be they high or low. The customs are related to the Mahar caste of Maharashtra.

Rituals Related to Sane-eddin

About the puberty-related customs and rituals among the Kolams, Mr. D. Hazra writes, "Some rites are observed when a girl first attains her puberty. The first appearance of menses is called *Sane-eddin,* which is usually attained by a girl when she becomes about 13 or 14 years of age. Marriage may take place even before it, but in that case consummation takes place only after she attains her puberty."

"When a girl has the first experience of her menstrual flow, she tells about it to her mother or some other senior female member of the family. She is at once secluded and she goes inside her house to occupy a corner, which is covered with a wicker work partition. She remains secluded till she takes her bath on the eighth day. The following day of her having first menstruation, some rites are performed during the day-time which is attended only by women. One *tendu* stick is laid across the entrance of the house covering its whole extent breadthways, and one husking pestle is put across the stick at its middle along the door-way passage by her mother or any other elderly woman. The girl walks over the pestle by putting her steps at either side of it and enters the house. The pestle is then removed, but not the stick. An old woman digs a hole at the threshold of the door at the middle. She puts one egg in upright position into the hole and applies *kvku* and turmeric. Then she closes the hole.

The girl remains indoors during the day-time, as she must not show her face to any grown-up male person. She only comes out in the early part of the morning or in the darkness of the night to attend nature's call. She is served food inside the house, the utensils, which are used by her, are kept separate. During this pollution period she may wash her body, but cannot put water on her head. For all sorts of washing, she has to go beyond the *bandhi* limit of the village. She is not subjected to any food restriction, and can eat meat available from a sacrificed animal. But she is debarred from doing any work."

"On the seventh day, a function called *kumli'-tinakad* takes place. Some old women (those who have attained menopause) go to the *nullah* with *puja* articles like *kuku, gulal,* turmeric, *till, gur,* dried coconut etc.; they also carry one cock and some cooked *jowar (ambal).* At the *nullah* they perform worship in the name of Asrai. water-spirit, and offer it all the *puja* articles. The cock is also sacrificed there. It is cooked there. Then the women eat *ambal* and the meat on the spot. After they return, the mixture of *til, gur, soera,* coconut, etc., and *ambal* are distributed to all the woman and girls who are present there."

"The girl takes her bath on the eighth day. If there is water in the *nullah,* she goes there for bath, otherwise, she is supplied with water and she has her bath beyond the *bandhi.* But she never goes to the village well for such a bath. She applies only oil to her head before the bath. She washes her clothes and cleans the spot where she remained secluded. The *tendu* stick from the door is also removed on this day."

"On the subsequent periods of her monthly courses she has not to observe any such formality, except that which is prescribed for a normal menstruating woman. When a woman has her monthly courses *(daueddin* or *malaeddin)* she is debarred from doing any domestic work. She cannot go to a well for drawing or fetching water; cooking, cleaning of utensils, plastering of floor, husking and grinding of grains, etc., are also not done by her. But she may go to jungles to bring fire-wood, may do harvesting work, but cannot do sowing. She is also debarred from attending any ceremonial function, social or religious. Her husband during this time, cannot offer anything to a deity.

During this period, either the husband or any member of the family does the cooking, and the menstruating woman is given food in a place which is kept separately for her use."

"On the fifth day (it may be extended to seventh day even) she takes her purificatory bath, either in the *nullah,* or with the water supplied to her by any woman outside the *bandhi.* She rubs her hair with mud, takes her bath, cleans her clothes and utensils. Now she is purified and attains her normal life." adds Mr. Hazra. The customs rites and rituals are practised by the *Kolam* people of Maharashtra."

Custom of Training and Education

About the childhood and rearing up of children, Mr. Vajaya B. Punekar writes, "Among the Son Kolis, infancy is a period of indulgence, particularly until the child is succeeded by a new baby. The indulgence takes the form of complying with the child's wishes and satisfying his demands. So far as training and education are concerned they are more or less left to nature."

"No serious effort is made to regulate the child's habits of feeding. For the first four to six months the child is regularly fed. Afterwards, its crying dictates the timing. The breast is given whenever it cries. The time for feeding water and gruel is more or less fixed. Fostering is not practised. A motherless baby is fed on rice gruel and cow's milk or even buffalo's milk, mixed with water. Weaning automatically follows the birth of a new baby. Otherwise it is done after the child is two years of age. Normally the mother experiences no difficulty in weaning the child, but if she does, she rubs her nipples with gall-nut paste or any other bitter substance every time the child insists on the feed."

"Children are, however, accustomed to solid food long before the weaning time. By the end of the first year, the child is given a piece of *roti,* a little *dhan* and *ambat* without chillies. But no attempt is made to regulate the child's eating habits. It has its share with every member of the family. The women of the house, on their way home from the market, bring fruits, sweets, peppermint and other eatables. Besides, the pedlars have their regular rounds in the locality, the daily allowance of a few annas given to the children for eatables is a substantial item of expenditure in every household. To complete the list, during the drying-season, eatables are bought in exchange for *kutâ* (the waste from the dried fish sold as manure). As the child grows older, its habits of eating are automatically regulated."

"The child is usually trained with regard to toilet habits. After three months, till the child is able to sit, whenever the mother feels that it is uncomfortable, she lays it on her outstretched legs, with its head towards her. When the child is able to sit, she seats it on her legs, supported by her feet. After the child is about two years of age, it is occasionally instructed to go out for the purpose. At times it may be scolded too, if the instructions are not followed. There is, however, no physical punishment. By the age of three, the training is fairly complete and the child knows what is expected of him or her."

"The sense of general cleanliness is acquired by the child later. From the day of birth, the child is given two baths daily. Of late, talcum powder is occasionally used by some mothers ; *kajal* (lamp-black collyrium) may be used for the eyes. But apart from these, no care is taken to keep the baby clean; nor is the child taught cleanliness habits. Filthy children, inadequately clothed, snotty-nosed, and with stains of mud all over the body are not a rare sight in the streets of the Koli localities. The mother and every other woman in the house are too busy to look after the child. At the most, occasionally, when the child comes to her for *dirkya* (money) the mother may clean its nose with her *pharki.* As in the case of the eating habits, the child becomes more and more conscious of personal cleanliness as he (or she) grows up. Many boys and girls of ten or twelve spend an hour or so a day looking in the mirror. Whenever a girl (especially between ages ten and twenty) is dressed up, say for a festival, it is amusing to see her admiringly looking at herself in the mirror every few minutes."

"As already stated, the mother has no time to look after the baby. She never takes him to the market when she goes to sell. The baby is left with the elder children, usually an elder daughter, to be looked after. But the latter is still too young to know her responsibility, and so, in reality, the child is left to himself. When going to the drying-ground, the mother takes her little ones with her. But the children rarely stay with the mother. They find their playmates there or play by themselves: with earth and stones."

"The child being left to himself, as a result of this careless attitude of the elders, becomes bold, and grows up independently. Rarely any effort is made to teach the child to walk or talk. Very early in life, he learns to take care of himself. By the age of three or four, the child knows his neighbourhood perfectly well. At the age of five he bargains with the hawker on his own."

"The first years' indulgence results in spoiling the children. They show little respect for the parents and other elders. Children, three and four years old, frequently answer back to the parents when the latter scold or, occasionally, strike them. This is only laughed at indulgently in the earlier years. Discipline is mostly stressed in the form of reprimand along with a few abusive words, and occasionally, threats of punishment. Physical punishment is usually avoided. It consists of striking or slapping. Children are, normally, not allowed to scream or whimper. If one person in the family tries to be stern, another will yield and satisfy the child's demand. Whenever grand-parents or uncles and aunts of the child stay in the same house, the latter, after it is weaned, sleeps with one of these."

"Children up to the age of five or six, that is, till they join school, spend the whole day in play. Up to the age of seven or eight, boys and girls play together. The most popular game for them is *bhurkuli.* It is the representation of adult occupations and ceremonies: the 'husband-boy' going out for fishing and mending nets, the 'wife-girl' cooking, going to the market and - bringing eatables, and so on. All the details of the family life are played out in a make-believe way. The little toys and dolls bought by the elders are used for these 'miniature households'. I heard a three or four year old girl rebuking her 'husband-boy', more or less of the same age, for joining a particular gossip group (which really was a notorious group, condemned by the people). The girl must have heard it at home.)"

"As the children enter school, the separation between the boys and the girls begins, though it is not complete before they are fourteen or so. Moreover, by now the girl starts assisting her mother in her household duties and hardly has any time to play. Occasionally, once in three or four months, a few girls in the neighbourhood may accidentally come together, say on the drying-grounds or on the sea-shore, and decide to play. These days, (within the last twenty years or so), girls sometimes join a group of boys for play," adds Mr. Punekar.

He further adds, "The usual pastime of the Koli boys is to play in the creek waters. Little boys of seven to ten spend hours in the creek. They build boats from the spikes of the coconut palm and sail them in water. During the *bhang* or neap-tide, when the boats are anchored on the shore, the boys row the smaller boats *(shipil)* within the creek or climb up the bigger ones and spend hours there, running from one end to the other and from one boat to another."

"The other games played by the Son Koli boys and girls are the Indian native games, which commonly have their respective seasons lasting for a couple of months in the year. The games, commonly played by boys of ten to twelve, are: *âtyâ-pâtyâ,* various forms of hide-and-seek, and *gârâ.* The girls also play these games, independently or joining with the boys. For the older boys there are *gotyâ* (marbles), *bhovrâ* (top), *patang* (kite-flying), *iti-dându* and *lagori.* Besides these there are certain games that do not need much exertion, such as *kâchauryâ, khube* (only for the girls) and *ât-chamak.*"

"In the game of Atyâ-Pâtyâ the players are divided into two teams. The method of forming the teams is very simple. It is called *vân-hanâvcha.* The players form themselves into pairs, go aside, take a name for each, come back and ask the leaders to choose between the two names. The player who has taken the chosen name joins the leader who chose him. Sometimes, instead of names, two articles may be offered for the choice. When the teams are formed, lines are drawn on the ground as shown in the diagram."

"The playing team and the fielding team are decided by lots *(oli-suki).* One of the leaders spits on one side of a little flat stone. The stone is then thrown in the air. Before the stone falls to the ground the other leader calls out '*Oli*' (wet) or '*Suki*' (dry) just as in the spin of coin they choose head or tail. If his guess is correct his team will play; otherwise it will have to field."

"The players stand on one side of the rectangle and the leader of the rival team takes stand at the centre on the front line of the bigger rectangle facing the players of the other team. He is known as *Murdâvâlâ* and has some privileges. He can move anywhere on the central vertical line (in the diagram) to catch the players. The rest of the fielders take their stand on the horizontal lines. Once he has taken his stand, a fielder cannot move from the spot. Nor can he change his position. He has, however, one chance of turning back, but once turned he cannot revert back."

"With these limitations they must touch at least one of the players, who enter the rectangle one by one as they think safe. Their aim is to reach the end of the rectangle and come back without being touched by any of the fielders and without going out of the bigger rectangle. If one of the fielders succeeds in touching one of the players, the latter lose the game. Then the game starts again, the players now taking fielding and vice versa; if all the players escape untouched the game continues as before."

"The rectangle is wide enough to keep the players out of the fielders' reach, but at the same time not so wide as to allow them easy passage."

Mr. Punekar records, "At the age of six or seven, children are sent to school. *A* year or two spent at school, more or less, decides the future career of the child."

"Within two or three years a girl leaves school and joins her mother in work. Sixty-eight out of 260 women, according to the sample survey, had primary education. This comes to 26.15%. Out of these sixty-eight, forty-two are below twenty years of age (61.76%) and only twenty-six above that age. The reason for this difference is that it is only within the last twenty years or so that the girls are mostly being sent to school."

"However, very few girls go beyond primary education. The limit of education for the Son Koli girls is generally the fourth standard. Only ten out of 260 women (3.85%) have taken secondary education. Of these ten, only one has gone beyond the seventh standard. As in the case of primary education, here too, six out of the ten women educated beyond the primary stage, are below twenty years of age."

"A large number of women, 176 out of the total of 260 (67.69%), are illiterate. The percentage of the illiterate women, in contrast to that of the women who have taken primary and secondary education, rises with the age-groups. Of the total number of illiterate women (above six years of age), 68.64% are above twenty years of age. The illiteracy is minimum in the age-group of 11-15. (6.25%)."

"Another important fact noticeable, in the education of women, is that the percentage of the literate women is higher, both in the cases of primary and secondary education, in Worli and Colaba than in Versova and Danda. Out of the sixty-eight women who have taken primary education, fourteen (20.58%) are from Versova and Danda while fifty-four (79.41%) are from Worli and Colaba. In these latter localities the literacy among girls has started earlier too. Of the twenty-six women in the age-group above twenty, twenty-two are from Worli and Colaba. Studying the secondary education group, the same results are obtained. Out of the ten women fortunate in having secondary education, seven are from Worli and Colaba. And all the four who are above twenty years of age are from Worli and Colaba only. Correspondingly, the percentage of illiterate women in Worli and Colaba is much lower than in Versova and Danda."

"Boys too usually leave school at an early age, say after one or two years' study. A fisherman, to be successful, must be introduced to the work at an early age. The Son Kolis sincerely believe that once accustomed to the easy life of the school, a boy will never succeed as a fisherman, for fishing needs hard work and a strenuous life. Again, education, according to them, is not essential for their occupation. The result is that even to this day quite a few parents consciously neglect the education of their children."

"It should not be concluded from this that the boys who leave school within two or three years are taken up in fishing. It is not till the age of fifteen or twenty that a boy is entrusted with regular fishing work, and then too more or less on the shore. Occasionally, he is taken to the fishing stakes, just to accustom him to the sea weather. Till the age of fifteen he spends his time in playing with his friends, and running errands. The parents ignore him, saying he is too young for work."

"The boy who takes up education, or rather whose parents in some way or other have realised the importance of education, continues it as long as he can. Education after the primary instruction, that is given free in Municipal Schools, depends on the financial condition of the parents, their interest in education, and also that of the boy, and on the facilities available for such education."

"From the study of the material obtained from the sample survey, one may venture to say that the boys, as a rule have been taking more education and from much earlier times (since the end of the last century) than the girls. Besides this, the facts noticed in the case of the education of girls are also observed in their case. These are: steady increase in the percentage of literates and the corresponding decrease in that of illiterates with the fall in the limits of the age-group, and a marked difference in the percentages of literates and illiterates between the localities of Danda and Versova on the one hand, and Worli and Colaba on the other. But the rise or fall in the percentages of the two zones, however, is not as sharp as in the case of the females. The numbers of illiterates, of men with primary education, and of men with secondary education, are more or less proportionate. Out of a total of 270 men, 88 are illiterate, 95 have received primary education, while 84 have reached the secondary stage."

"Out of the 88 illiterates 61, that is, nearly 70% are above the age of twenty. In the case of primary education, the number of men below twenty and above twenty are almost equal (namely, 54.74% below twenty and 45.26% above). However, the percentage of those above twenty is still lower than that of those below twenty. So far as secondary education is concerned, the facts of late show a change. Out of the 84 men educated beyond the primary stage 51 (60.71%) are above twenty. This change can be easily explained by the fact, that, in the case of men's education beyond the primary stage includes the matriculation and graduation too, while in the case of women, the sample study shows that there is only one woman educated beyond the seventh standard."

"Considering the difference in education localitywise, it can be seen, that more than 70% of the illiterates are from Versova and Danda and less than 30% are from the other two localities. In the case of primary education the position is reversed from what it was in the case of primary education of women. There are more educated persons in this group in Versova and Danda than in Worli and Colaba. More than 63% are in the former while nearly 37% are from the latter. The reason for this is the rise in the number of men going for education beyond the primary stage. With regard to secondary education, it has been noticed that nearly 62% of the men in this category are from Worli and Colaba."

"Another important distinction that can be noticed between the female education and the male education among the Son Kolis is that, today, while boys are almost compulsorily sent to school at the age of six or seven or sometimes even a little later, such compulsion is not enforced in the case of girls. Only 27 out of a total of 114 boys between the age limits of six and twenty are illiterate (23.68%). Out of these twenty-seven, only six (22.22%) are from Worli and Colaba. Among girls, out of the total number of 103 between the ages six and twenty, 55 are illiterate (53.40%)."

"Again, there is a wide gap between the two sexes in the case of secondary education. While only 10 out of 260 women studied have been fortunate enough to reach that stage (and as already stated only one beyond the seventh standard), there are 84 men out of 270 studied who have had secondary education."

"Apart from the sample survey, from personal observations in the course of the present study, it appears that interest in education is on the increase. Normally, even among the illiterates, respect for educated is clearly discernible. Quite a few parents are sorry for their uneducated children, while a number of them feel that there should be better facilities for the education of the Son Koli children."

"Though interest is being taken in the education of the boys, the degree of education is not as high as it should be. Very few boys, as already seen, reach even the matriculation stage. Due to their surroundings, by the time they reach the sixth or seventh standard, the boys feel they are 'educated'. And so do their elders. The boys think too highly of themselves; and fishing becomes a low occupation for them. But their meagre education has practically no value outside the community. So, after a few years of unemployment, they take to jobs like fitters and welders. If this is the case of the less educated, the more educated feel even more strongly that going in for fishing, after all their education, is below their dignity. Hence, as the standard of education rises in a particular locality, fishing industry dwindles in that locality."

"There is an important distinction between the 'educated' Son Koli boys and girls. As seen earlier, a Koli boy after reaching the fifth or sixth standard feels that fishing is a low occupation; on the other hand, the girls, even after matriculation, are not ashamed to sell fish in the market. The reason given by the Son Kolis for this distinction is worth noting. They say a girl has an incentive to selling fish: the mother gives her a part of the day's income whenever she sells fish. But when a boy joins his father in fishing, the income goes to the father, and the son has to ask for money from his parents or sisters. To some extent, therefore, economic dependence is the cause of fishing being despised by the educated boys," adds Mr. Punekar. This trend of education is related to the Son Kolis of Bombay.

References

1. Enthoven, R.E., *The Tribes and Castes of Bombay*, Low Price Publications, Delhi (reprint) 1997, first published 1922.
2. Russel, R.V., and Lal, Hira, *The Tribes and Castes of the Central Provinces of India*, Low Price Publications, Delhi (reprint) 1997, Originally Published MacMillan Pvt. Ltd., London 1916.
3. Singh, K.S. (Gen. ed.), *People of India : Goa*, Popular Prakashan, Bombay, 1993.

4. Bahadur, K.P., *Castes, Tribes and Culture of India*, ESS ESS Publications, Vol. VIII, Western Maharashtra and Gujarat, Delhi 1981.
5. Kamble, N.D., *Deprived Castes and their Struggle for Equality*, Ashish Publications House, New Delhi, 1983.
6. Ghurey, G.S., *The Mahadev Kolis*, Popular Book Depot, Bombay, 1957.
7. Shah, P.G., *The Dublas of Gujarat*, Bharatiya Adimjati Sevak Sangh, Delhi 1958.
8. Gomes, Olivivho J.F., *India–Land and People*; *Goa*, National Book Trust, New Delhi, 2004.
9. Hazra, D., *The Kolam of Yoetmal*, Anthropological Survey of India, Calcutta, 1983.
10. Punekar, Vijay B., *The Son Kolis of Bombay*, Popular Book Depot, Bombay, 1959.

3

Betrothal

In the matter of Hindu betrothal, and marriage, the rules exogamy and endogamy hold a big sway. Even to primitive tribals, Muslims and Christians converted from Hinduism are influenced by those notions, which though may differ in minute details from caste to caste and depending upon the geographical region, the level of being civilized, and the economic status. Mr. R.V. Russell and Hira Lal described the rules of exogamy totemism and betrothal in detail, stating, "The caste or subcaste forms the outer circle within which a man must marry. Inside it are a set of further sub-divisions which prohibit the marriage of persons related through males. These are called exogamous groups or clans, and their name among the higher castes is *gotra*. The theory is that all persons belonging to the same *gotra* are descended from the same male ancestor, and so related. The relationship in the *gotra* now only goes by the father's side; when a woman marries she is taken into the clan of her husband and her children belong to it. Marriage is not allowed within the clan and in the course of a few generations the marriage of persons related through males or agnates is prohibited within a very wide circle. But on the mother's side the *gotra* does not serve as a bar to marriage and the union of first cousins would be possible, other than the children of two brothers. According to Hindu law, inter-marriage is prohibited within four degrees between persons related through females. But generally the children of first cousins are allowed to marry, when related partly through females and several castes allow the intermarriage of the first cousins, that of a brother's daughter to a sister's son and in a less degree of a brother's son to a sister's daughter being specially favoured. One or two Madras castes allow a man to marry his niece and the small Dhoba caste of Mandla permits the union of children of the same mother but different fathers.

"Sir Herbert Risley classed the names of exogamous divisions as eponymous, territorial or local, titular and totemistic. In this work, the word clan is usually applied only to the large exogamous groups of the Râjputs and one or two other military castes. The small local or titular groups of ordinary Hindu castes are called 'section' and the totemic groups of the primitive tribes are called 'sept'. But perhaps it is simpler to use the word 'clan' throughout according to the practice of Sir J.G. Frazer. The vernacular designations of the clans or sections are *gotra,* which originally meant a stall or cow-pen; *khero,* a village; *dih,* a village site; *baink,* a title; *mul* or *mur,* literally a root, hence an origin; and *kul* or *kuri,* a family. The sections called eponymous are named after Rishis or saints mentioned in the Vedas and other scriptures and are found among the Brahmans and a few of the higher castes, such as Vasishta, Garga, Bharadwaj, Vishvamitra, Kashyap etc.A few Rajput clans are named after kings or heroes, as the Raghuvansis from king Raghu of Ajodhia and the Tilokchandi Bais from a famous king of that name. The titular class of names comprise names of offices, supposed to have been held by the founder of the clan, or titles and names referring to a personal defect or quality, and nicknames. Instances of the former are Kotwar (village watchman), Chaudhri, Meher or Mahto (caste headman), Bhagat (saint), Thakuria and Rawat (lord or prince), Vaidya (physician), and instances of titular names and nicknames are Kuldip (lamp of the family), Mohjaria (one with a burnt mouth), 'Jâchak (beggar), Garkata (cut-throat), Bhatpagar (one serving on a pittance of boiled rice), Kangâli (poor), Chikat (dirty), Petdukh (stomach-ache), Ghunnere (worm-eater) etc. A special class of names are those of offices held at the caste feasts; thus the clans of the Chitrakathi caste are the Atak or Mânkari, who furnish the headman of the caste *ponchâyat* or committee; the Bhojin who serve the food at marriages and other ceremonies; the Kâkra who arrange for the lighting; the Gotharya who keep the provisions, and the Ghorerao (*ghora,* a horse) who have the duty of looking after the horses and bullock-carts of the caste-men who assemble. Similarly, the five principal clans of the small Turi caste are named after the five sons of Singhbonga or the sun: the eldest son was called Mailuar and his descendants are the leaders or headmen of the caste; the descendants of the second son, Chardhagia, purify and readmit offenders to caste intercourse; those of the third son, Suremar, conduct the ceremonial shaving of such offenders, and those of the fourth son bring water for the ceremony and are called Tirkuar. The youngest brother, Hasdagia, is said to have committed some caste offence, and the four other brothers took the parts which are still played by their descendants in his ceremony of purification. In many cases, exogamous clans are named after other castes or subcastes. Many low castes have adopted the names of the Rajput clans, either from simple vanity as people may take an aristocratic surname, or because they were in the service of Rajputs, and have adopted the names of their masters or are partly descended from them. Other names of castes found among exogamous groups probably indicate that an ancestor belonging to that caste was taken into the one in which the group is found. The Bhaina tribe have clans named after the Dhobi, Ahir, Gond, Mali and Panka castes. The members of such clans pay respect to any man belonging to the caste after which they are named and avoid picking a quarrel with him; they also worship the family gods of the caste, add Mr. R.V. Russell and Hira Lal.

Totemism and Caste Clan

"Territorial names are very common and are taken from that of some town or village in which the ancestor of the clan or the members of the clan themselves resided. The names are frequently distorted, and it seems probable that the majority of the large number of clan names for which no meaning can be discovered were those of villages. These unknown names are probably more numerous than the total of all those classes of names to which a meaning can be assigned.

"The last class of exogamous divisions are those called totemistic, when the clan is named after a plant or animal or other natural object. These are almost universal among the non-Aryan or primitive tribes, but occur also in most Hindu castes, including some of the highest. The commonest totem names are those of the prominent animals, including several which are held sacred by the Hindus, as *bâgh* or *nâhar,* the tiger; *bachâs,* the calf; *morkuria,* the peacock; *kachhwâha* or *limuân,* the tortoise;

nâgas, the cobra; *hasti,* the elephant; *bandar,* the monkey; *bhainsa,* the buffalo; *richharia,* the bear; *kuliha,* the jackal; *kukura,* the dog; *karsayâl,* the deer; *hearn,* the black-buck, etc. The utmost variety of names is found and numerous trees as well as rice, kodon and other crops, salt, sandalwood, cucumber, pepper, and some household implements, such as the pestle and rolling-slab, serve as names of clans. Names which may be held to have a totemistic origin occur even in the highest castes. Thus, among the names of eponymous Rishis or saints, Bhâradwâj means a lark, Kaushik may be from the *kusha* grass, Agastya from the *agasti* flower, Kashyap from *kachhap,* a-tortoise; Taittiri from *titart* a partridge, etc. Similarly, the origin of other Rishis is attributed to animals, as Rishishringa to an antelope, Mandavya to a frog, and Kanâda to an owl (Wilson's *Indian Caste*, p. 439). An inferior Rajput clan, Meshbansi, signifies descendants of the sheep, while the name of the Baghel clan is derived from the tiger (bagh), that of the Kachhwaha clan perhaps from *kachhap,* a tortoise, of the Haihaivansi from the horse, of the Nâgvansi from the cobra, and of the Tomara clan from *tomar,* a club. The Karan or Writer caste of Orissa, similarly, has clans derived from the cobra, tortoise and calf, and most of the cultivating and other middle castes have clans with totemistic names. The usual characteristics of totemism, in its later and more common form at any rate, are that members of a clan regard themselves as related to, or descended from, the animal or tree from which the clan takes its name, and abstain from killing or eating it. This was perhaps not the original relation of the clan to its clan totem in the hunting stage, but it is the one commonly found in India, where the settled agricultural stage has long been reached. The Bhaina tribe have among their totems the cobra, tiger, leopard, vulture, hawk, monkey, wild dog, quail, black ant, etc. Members of a clan will not injure the animal after which it is named, and if they see the corpse of the animal or heat of its death, they throw away an earthen cooking-pot, and bathe and shave themselves as for one of the family. At a wedding, the bride's father makes an image in clay of the bird or animal of the groom's sept and places it beside the marriage-pest. The bridegroom worships the image, lighting a sacrificial fire before it and offers to it the vermilion which he afterwards smears on the forehead of the bride. Women are often tattooed with representations of their totem animal, and men swear by it as their most sacred oath. A similar respect is paid to the inanimate objects after which certain septs are named. Thus, members of the Gawad or cowdung clan will not burn cowdung cakes for fuel; and those of the Mircha clan do not use chillies. One clan is named after the sun, and when an eclipse occurs they perform the same formal rites of mourning as others do on the death of their totem animal. The Bâghani clan of Majhwârs, named after the tiger, thinks that a tiger will not attack any member of their clan, unless he has committed an offence entailing temporary excommunication from caste. Until this offence has been expiated, his relationship with the tiger as head of the clan is in abeyance, and the tiger will eat him as he would any other stranger. If a tiger meets a member of the clan who is free from sin, he will ran away. Members of the Khoba or peg clan will not make a peg nor drive one into the ground. Those of the Dumar or fig-tree clan say that their first ancestor was born under this tree. They consider the tree to be sacred and never eat its fruit, and worship it once a year. Sometimes the members of the clan do not revere the object after which it is named but some other important animal or plant. Thus, the Markam clan of Gonds, named after the mango-tree, venerates the tortoise and do not kill it. The Kathotia clan of Kols is named after *kathota,* a bowl, but they revere the tiger. Bâgheshwar Deo, the tiger-god, resides on a little platform in their verandas. They may not join in a tiger-beat nor sit up for a tiger over a kill. In the latter case, they think that the tiger would not come and would be deprived of his food, and all the members of their family would get ill. The Katharia clan take their name from *kathri,* a mattress. A member of this sept must never have a mattress in his house, nor wear clothes sewn in cross-pieces as mattresses are sewn. The name of the Mudia or Mudmudia clan is said to mean shaven head, but they apparently revere the white *kumhra* or gourd, perhaps because it has some resemblance to a shaven head. They give a white gourd to a woman on the day after she a child, and her family then do not eat this vegetable for three years. The Kumraya sept reveres the brown *kumhra* or gourd. They grow this vegetable on the thatch of their house-roof and from the time of planting it till the fruits have been plucked they do not touch it, though of course they afterwards eat the fruits. The Bhuwar sept are named after *bhu* or *bhumi*, the earth. They must always sleep on the earth and not on cots. The Nun (salt) and Dhân (rice) clans of Oraons cannot dispense with eating their totems or titular ancestors. But the Dhan Oraons content themselves with refusing to consume the scum which thickens on the surface of the boiled rice, and the Nun sept will not lick a plate in which salt and water have been mixed. At the weddings of the Vulture clan of the small Bhona caste, one member of the clan kills a small chicken by biting off the head and then eats it in imitation of a vulture. Definite instances of the sacrificial eating of the totem animal have not been found, but it is said that the tiger and snake clans of the Bhatra tribe formerly ate their totems at a sacrificial meal. The Gonds also worship the cobra as a household god, and once a year they eat the flesh of the snake and think that by doing so they will be immune from snake-bite throughout the year. On the festival of Nâg-Panchmi, the Mahârs make an image of a snake with flour and sugar and eat it. It is reported that the Singrore Dhimars who work on rivers and tanks must eat the flesh of a crocodile at their weddings, while the Sonjharas who wash the sands of rivers for gold should catch a live crocodile for the occasion of the wedding and afterwards put it back into the river. These latter customs may probably have fallen into abeyance owing to the difficulty of catching a crocodile, and in any case the animals are tribal gods rather than totems," add Mr. R.V. Russell and Hira Lal.

Exogamy and Totemism

"Exogamy and totemism are found not only in India, but are the characteristics of primitive social groups over the greater part of the world. Totemism establishes a relation of kinship between persons belonging to one clan who are not related by blood, and exogamy prescribes that the persons held to be so related shall not intermarry. Further, when terms of relationship come into existence, it is found that they are applied lot to members of one family, but to all the persons of the clan who might have stood in each particular relationship to the person addressing them. Thus, a man will address as mother not only his own mother, but also all the women of his clan who might have stood to him in the relation of mother. Similarly, he will address all the old men and women as grandfather or grandmother or aunt, and the boys and girls of his own generation as brother and sister, etc. With the development of the recognition of the consanguineous family, the use of terms of relationship tends to be restricted to persons who have actual kinship; thus, a boy will address only his father's brothers as father, and his cousins as brothers and sisters; but sufficient traces of the older system of clan kinship remain to attest its former existence. However, it also seems clear that some, at least, of the terms of relationship were first used between persons really related; thus, the word for mother must have been taught by mothers to their own babies beginning to speak, as it is a paramount necessity for a small child to have a name by which to call its mother when it is wholly dependent on her; if the period of infancy is got over without the use of this term of address there is no reason why it should be introduced in later life, when in the primitive clan the child quickly ceased to be dependent on its mother or to retain any strong affection for her. Similarly, as shown by Sir J. G. Frazer in *Totemism and Exogamy,* there is often a special name for the mother's brother when other uncles or aunts are addressed simply as father or mother. This name must therefore have been brought into existence to distinguish the mother's brother at the time when, under the system of female descent, he stood in the relation of a protector and parent to the child. Where the names for grandfather and grandmother are a form of duplication of those for father and mother as in English, they would appear to imply a definite recognition of the idea of family descent. The majority of the special names for other relatives, such as fraternal and maternal uncles and aunts, must also have been devised to designate those relatives in particular, and hence there is a probability that the terms for father and brother and sister, which on *a priori* grounds may be considered doubtful, were also first applied to real or putative fathers and brothers and sisters. But as already seen, under the classificatory system of relationship, these same terms are addressed to members of the same clan who might by age and sex have stood in such a relationship to the person addressing them, but are not actually akin to him at all. Hence, it seems a valid and necessary conclusion that at the time when the family terms of relationship came into existence, the clan sentiment of kinship was stronger than the family sentiment; that is, a boy was taught or made to feel that all the women of the clan of about the same age as his mother were as nearly akin to him as his own mother, and that he should regard them all in the same relation. Similarly he looked on all the men of the clan of an age enabling them to be his fathers in the same light as his own father, and all the children of or about his own age as his brothers and sisters. The above seems a necessary conclusion from the existence of the classificatory system of relationship, which is very widely spread among savages, and if admitted, it follows that the sentiment of kinship within the clan was already established when the family terms of relationship were devised, and therefore that the clan was prior to the family as a social unit. This conclusion is fortified by the rule of exogamy which prohibits marriage between persons of the same clan between whom no blood-relationship can be traced, and therefore shows that some kind of kinship was believed to exist between them, independent of and stronger than the link of consanguinity. Further, Mr. Hartland shows in *Primitive Paternity,* Vol. I. pp. 272, 276, that during the period of female descent when physical paternity has been recognised, but the father and mother belong to different clans, the children, being of the mother's clan, will avenge a blood-feud of their clan upon their own father, and this custom seems to show clearly that the sentiment of clan-kinship was prior to and stronger than that of family kinship.

"The same argument seems to demonstrate that the idea of kinship within the clan was prior to the idea of descent from a common ancestor, whether an animal or plant, a god, hero or nicknamed ancestor. Because it is obvious that a set of persons otherwise unconnected could not suddenly and without reason have believed themselves to be descended from a common ancestor and hence related. If a number of persons not demonstrably connected by blood believe themselves to be akin simply on account of their descent from a common ancestor, it can only be because they are an expanded family, either actually or by fiction, which really had or might have had a common ancestor, that is, the clan tracing its descent from a common ancestor, if this was the primary type of clean, must have been subsequent to the family as a social institution. But as already seen the sentiment of kinship within the clan was prior to that within the family, and therefore the genesis of the clan from an expanded family is an impossible hypothesis, and it follows that the members of the clan must first have believed themselves to be bound together by some tie equivalent to or stronger than that of consanguineous kinship, and afterwards, when the primary belief was falling into abeyance, that of descent from a common ancestor came into existence to account for the clan sentiment of kinship already existing. If then the first form of association of human beings was in small groups, which led a migratory life and subsisted mainly by hunting and the consumption of fruits and roots, as the Australian natives still do, the sentiment of kinship must first have arisen, as stated by Mr. M'Lennan, in that small body which lived and hunted together, and was simply due to the fact that they were so associated that they obtained food for each other, and on occasion protected and preserved each other's lives. These small bodies of persons were the first social units, and according to our knowledge of the savage peoples who are nearest to the original migratory and hunting condition of life, without settled habitations, domestic animals or cultivated plants, they first called themselves after some animal or plant, usually, as Sir J. G. Frazer has shown in *Totemsm and Exogamy,* after some edible animal or plant. The most probable theory of totemism on *a priori* grounds seems therefore to be that the original small bodies who lived and hunted together, or totem-clans, called themselves after the edible animal or plant from which they principally derived their sustenance, or that which gave them life. While the real tie which connected them was that of living together, they did not realise this and supposed themselves to be akin because they commonly ate this animal or plant together. This theory of totenism was first promulgated by Professor Robertson Smith and, though much disputed, appears to me to be the most probable. It has also been advocated by Dr. A.C. Haddon, F.R.S. The Gaelic names for family, *teadhloch* and *cuedichc* or *coedichc,* mean 'having a common residence' and 'those who eat together,' respectively. The detailed accounts of the totems of the Australian, Red Indian and African tribes, now brought together by Sir J.G. Frazer in *Totemism and Exogamy,* show a considerable amount of evidence that the early totems were not only as rule edible animals, but the animals eaten by the totem-clans which bore their names. But after the domestication of animals and the culture of plants had been attained to, the totems ceased to be the chief means of subsistence. Hence, the original tie of kinship was supplanted by another and wider one in the tribe, and though the totem-clans remained and continued to fulfil an important purpose, they were no longer the chief social group and in many cases, as man had also by now begun to speculate on his origin, the totems came to be regarded as ancestors, and the totem-clans, retaining their sentiment of kinship, accounted for it by supposing themselves to be descended from a common ancestor. They thus also came to base the belief in clan-kinship on the tie of consanguinity recognised in the family, which had by now come into existence. This late and secondary form of totemism is that which obtains in India, where the migratory and hunting stage has long been passed. The Indian evidence is, however, of great value because we find here in the same community, occasionally in the same caste, exogamous clans which trace their descent sometimes from animals and plants, or totems, and sometimes from gods, heroes, or titular ancestors, while many of the clans are named after villages or have names to which no meaning can be attached. As has been seen, there is good reason to suppose that all these forms of the exogamous clan are developed from the earliest form of the totem-clan, and since this later type of clan has developed from the totem-clan in India, it is a legitimate deduction that wherever elsewhere exogamous clans are found tracing their descent from a common ancestor or with unintelligible names, probably derived from places, they were probably also evolved from the totem-clan. This type of clan is shown in Professor Hearn's *Aryan Household* to have been the common unit of society over much of Europe, where no traces of the existence of totemism are established, and from the Indian analogy it is therefore legitimate to presume that the totem-clan may have been the original unit of society among several European races as well as in America, Africa, Australia and India. Similar exogamous clans exist in China, and many of them have the names of plants and animals," add Mr. Russel and Hiralal.

Reckoning of Patrilineal Clan and Exogamy

They further add, "The transfer of the reckoning of kinship and descent from the mother's to the father's side may perhaps be associated with the full recognition of the physical fact of paternity. Though they may not have been contemporaneous in all or even the majority of societies, it would seem that the former was in most cases the logical outcome of the later, regard being had also to the man's natural function as protector of the family and provider of its sustenance. But this transition from female to male kinship was a social revolution of the first importance. Under the system of female descent, there had been generally no transfer of clanship; both the woman and her partner or husband retained their own clans, and the children belonged to their mother's clan. In the totemic stage of society, the totem-clan was the vital organism, and the individual scarcely realised his own separate existence, but regarded himself as a member of his totem-clan, being a piece or fraction of a common life which extended through all the members of the clan and all the totem animals of the species. They may have thought also that each species of animals and plants had a different kind of life, and consequently also each clan whose life was derived from, and linked to, that of its totem-species. For the name, and life, and qualities, and flesh and blood were not separate conceptions, but only one conception, and since the name and qualities were part of the life, the life of one species could not be the same as that of another, and every species which had a separate name must have been thought to have a different kind of life. Nor would man have been regarded as a distinct species in the early totem-stage, and there would be no word for man; but each totem-clan would regard itself as having the same life as its totem-species. With the introduction of the system of male kinship also came the practice of transferring a woman from her own clan to that of her husband. It may be suggested that this was the origin of the social institution of marriage. Primitive society had no provision for such a procedure, which was opposed to its one fundamental idea of its own constitution, and involved a change in the life and personality of the woman transferred".

Marriage by Capture

"The view seems to have been long held that this transfer could only be effected by violence or capture, the manner in which presumably it was first practised. Marriage by capture is very widely prevalent among savage races, as shown by Mr. M'Lennan in *Primitive Marriage* and by Dr. Westermarck in *The History of Human Marriage.* Where the custom has given place to more peaceable methods of procuring a wife, survivals commonly occur. In Bastar, the regular capture of the girl is still sometimes carried out, though the business is usually arranged by the couple beforehand, and the same is the case among the Kolams of Wardha. A regular part of the marriage procedure among the Gonds and other tribes is that the bade should weep formally for some hours, or a day before the wedding, and she is sometimes taught to cry in the proper note. At the wedding, the bride hides somewhere and has to be found or carried off by the bridegroom or his brother. This ritualistic display of grief and coyness appears to be of considerable interest. It cannot be explained by the girl's reluctance to marriage as involving the loss of her virginity, inasmuch as she is still frequently not a virgin at her wedding, and to judge from the analogy of other tribes, could seldom or never have been one a few generations back. Nor is affection for her family or grief at the approaching separation from them a satisfactory motive. This would not account for the hiding at all, and not properly for the wedding, since she will after all only live a few miles away and will often return home and sometimes she does not only weep at her own house but at all the houses of the village. The suggestion may be made that the procedure really indicates the girl's reluctance to be severed from her own clan and transferred to another and that the sentiment is a survival of the resistance to marriage by capture which was at first imposed on the women by the men from loyalty to the clan totem and its common life, and had nothing to do with the conjugal relationship of marriage. But out of this feeling the sexual modesty of women, which had been non-existent in the matriarchal condition of society, was perhaps gradually developed. The Chamars of Bilâspur have sham fights on the approach of the wedding party, and in most Hindu castes the bridegroom on his arrival performs some violent action, such as striking the marriage-shed or breaking one of its festoons. After the marriage, the bride is nearly always sent home with the bridegroom's party for a few days, even though she may be a child and the consummation of the marriage impossible. This may be in memory of her having formerly been carried off, and some analogous significance may attach to our honeymoon. When the custom of capture had died down, it was succeeded by the milder form of elopement or the bride was sold or exchanged against a girl from the bridegroom's family or clan, but there is usually a relic of a formal transfer, such as the Hindu *Kanyadan* or gift of the virgin, the Roman *Traditio in manum* or her transfer from her father's to her husband's power, and the giving away of the bride.

"These customs seem to mark the transfer of the woman from her father's to her husband's clan, which was in the first instance effected forcibly and afterwards by the free gift of her father or guardian, and the change of surname would be a relic of the change of clan. Among the Hindus, a girl is never called by her proper name in her husband's house, but always by some other name or nickname. This custom seems to be a relic of the period when the name denoted the clan, though it no longer has any reference either to the girl's clan or family. Another rite portraying the transfer in India is the marking of the bride's forehead with vermilion, which is no doubt a substitute for blood. The ceremony would be a relic of participation in the clan sacrifice when the bride would in the first place drink the blood of the totem animal or tribal god with the bridegroom in sign of her admission to his clan and afterwards be marked with the blood as a substitute. A married woman always continues to wear this smear of vermilion as a sign of her state, unless she wears pink powder or a spangle as a substitute. Where this pink powder (*kunku*) or spangles are used, they must always be given by the bridegroom to the bride as part of the *Sohâg* or trousseau. At a Bhaina wedding, the bride's father makes an image in clay of the bird or animal of the groom's sept and places it beside the marriage-post. The bridegroom worships the image, lighting a sacrificial fire before it, or offers to it the vermilion which he afterward smears upon the forehead of the bride. The Khadâls at their marriages worship their totem animal or tree, and offer to it flowers, sandalwood, vermilion, uncooked rice, and the new clothes and ornament intended for the bride, which she may not wear until this ceremony has been performed. Again, the sacrament of the Meher or marriage cakes is sometimes connected with the clan totem in India. These cakes are cooked and eaten sacramentally by all the members of the family and their relatives, the bride and bridegroom commenting first. Among the Kols, the relatives to whom these cakes are distributed cannot intermarry and this indicates that the eating of them was formerly a sacrament of the exogamous clan. The association of the totem with the marriage, cakes is sometimes clearly shown. Thus, in the Dahait caste, members of the clans named after certain trees go to the tree at the time of their weddings and invite it to be present at the ceremony. They offer the marriage cakes to the tree. Those of the Nagotia or cobra clan deposit the cakes at a snake's hole. Members of the Singh (lion) and Bagh (tiger) clans draw images of these animals on the wall at the time of their weddings and offer the cakes to them. The Basors of the Kulatia or somersault clan do somersaults at the time of eating the cakes; those of the Karai Nor clan, who venerate a well, eat the cakes at a well and not at home. Basors of the Lurhia clan, who venerate a grinding-stone, worship this implement at the time of eating the marriage cakes. M. Fustel de Coulanges states that the Roman Confarreatio, or eating of a cake together by the bride and bridegroom in the presence of the family gods of the latter, constituted their holy union or marriage. By this act, the wife was transferred to the gods and religion of her husband. Here the gods referred to are clearly held to be the family gods, and in the historical period it seems doubtful whether the Roman *gens* was still exogamous. But if the patriarchal family developed within the exogamous clan tracing descent through males, and finally supplanted the clan as the most important social unit, then it would follow that the family gods were only a substitute for the clan gods, and the bride came to be transferred to her husband's family instead of to his clan. The marriage ceremony in Greece consisted of a common meal of a precisely similar character, and the English wedding-cake seems to be a survival of such a rite. At their weddings, the Bhils make cakes of the large millet juari, calling it Juari Mata or Mother Juari. These cakes are eaten at the houses of the bride and bridegroom by the members of their respective clans, and the remains are buried inside the house as sacred food. About the Kurnai tribe, Dr. Howitt states, "By and by, when the bruises and perhaps wounds received in these fights (between the young men and women) had healed, a young man and a young woman might meet, and he, looking at her, would say, for instance, 'Djiitgun! What does the Djiitgun eat?' The reply would be 'she eats kangaroo, opossum,' or some other game. This constituted a formal offer and acceptance, and would be followed by the elopement of the couple as described in the chapter on Marriage, *Native tribes of S.E. Australia,* p. 149. There is no statement that the question about eating refers to the totem, but this must apparently have been the original bearing of the question, which otherwise would be meaningless. Since this proposal of marriage followed on a fight between the boys and girls arising from the fact that one party had injured the other party's sex-totem, the fight may perhaps really have been a preliminary to the proposal and have represented symbolic substitute for or survival of marriage by capture. About the Santals, Colonel Dalton says, "the social meal that the boy and girl eat together is the most important part of the ceremony, as by the act the girl ceases to belong to her father's tribe and becomes a member of the husband's family." Since the terms tribe and family are obviously used loosely in the above statement, we may perhaps substitute clan in both cases. Many other instances of the rite of eating together at a wedding are given by Dr. Westermarck, *History of Human Marriage,* pp. 418-420. If, therefore, it be supposed that the wedding ceremony consisted originally of the formal transfer of the bride to the bridegroom's clan, and further that the original tie which united the totem-clan was the common eating of the totem animal, then the practice of the bride and bridegroom eating together as a symbol of marriage can be fully understood. When the totem animal had ceased to be the principal means of subsistence, bread, which to a people in the agricultural stage had become the staff or chief support of life, was substituted for it, as argued by Professor Robertson Smith in *The Religion of the Semites.* If the institution of marriage was thus originally based on the forcible transfer of a woman from her own to her husband's clan, certain Indian customs become easily explicable in light of this view. We can understand why a Brahman or Rajput thought it essential to marry his daughter into a clan or family of higher status than his own; because the disgrace of having his daughter taken from him by what had been originally an act of force was atoned for by the superior rank of the captor or abductor and similarly the terms father-in-law and brother-in-law would be regarded as opprobrious because they originally implied not only that the speaker had married the sister or daughter of the person addressed, but also that they had married her forcibly, thereby placing him in a position of inferiority. A Rajput formerly felt it derogatory that any man should address him either as father or brother-in-law and the analogous custom of a man refusing to take food in the house of his son-in-law's family and sometimes even refusing to drink water in their village would be explicable on precisely the same grounds. This view of marriage would also account for the wide prevalence of female infanticide. Because in the primitive condition of exogamy with male descent, girls could not be married in their own clan, as this would transgress the binding law of exogamy, and they could not be transferred from their own totem-clan and married in another except by force and rape. Hence, it was thought better to kill girl children than to suffer the ignominy of their being forcibly carried off. Both kinds of female infanticide as distinguished by Sir H. Risley, *The People of India* (Thacker & Co.) pp. 171, 173 would thus originally be due to the same belief. The Khond killed his daughter because she could not be married otherwise than by forcible abduction not necessarily because he was unable to protect her, but because he could not conceive of her being transferred from one totem-clan to another by any other means and he was bound to resist the transfer because by acquiescing in it, he would have been guilty of disloyalty to this own totem, whose common life was injured by the loss of the girl. Rajputs killed their daughter, because it was a disgrace to them to get their daughters married at all outside their clan, and she could not be married within it. Afterwards, the disgrace was removed by marrying her into a higher clan than his own and by lavish expenditure on the wedding and the practice of female infanticide was continued to avoid the ruinous outlay which this primitive view of marriage had originally entailed. The Hindu custom of the Swayamvara or armed contest for the hand of a Rajput princess, and the curious recognition by the Hindu law-books of simple rape as a legitimate form of marriage would be explained on the same ground.

"It has been seen that the exogamous clan with female descent contained no married couples, and therefore it was necessary either that outside men should live with it, or that the clans should continually meet each other or that two or more should live in the same village. With the change to male descent and the transfer of women to their husbands' clans, this unstable characteristic was removed. Henceforth, the clan was self-contained, having its married couples, both members of it, whose children would also be born in and belong to it. Since the clan was originally a body of persons who wandered about and hunted together, its character would be maintained by living together, and there is reason to suppose that the Indian exogamous clan with male descent took its special character, because its members usually lived in one or more villages. This fact would account for the large number and multiplication of clans in India as compared with other places. As already seen, one of the names of a clan is *khera,* which also means a village, and a large number of the clan names are derived from, or the same, those of villages. Among the Khonds, all the members of one clan live in the same locality about some central village. Thus, the Tupa clan are collected about the village of Tepgârh in the Patna state, the Loa clan round Sindhekala, the Borga clan round Bangomunda etc. About the Nunias of Mirzapur, Mr. Crooke remarks, '*tribes and castes of the N.W.P.* have a system of local subdivisions called *dih,* each subdivision being named after the village which is supposed to be its home'. The word *dih* itself means a site or village. Those who have the same *dih* do not intermarry. About the villages first settled by the Oraons, Father Dehon, (*Religion and customs of the Oraons, Memoirs* As. Socy. of Bengal, Vol. I, No. 9) states, the population is divided into three *khunt* or branches, the founders of the three branches being held to have been sons of the first settler.

Members of each branch belong to the same clan or *got*. Each *khunt* or branch has a share of the village lands. The Mochis or cobblers have forty exogamous sections or *gotras,* mostly named after Rajput clans, and they also have an equal number of *kheras* or groups named after villages. The limits of the two groups seem to be identical and members of each group have an ancestral village from which they are supposed to have come. Marriage is now regulated by the Rajput sept-names, but the probability is that the *Kheras* were the original divisions, and the Rajput *gotras* have been more recently adopted in support of the claims already noticed. The Parjas have totemistic exogamous clans and marriage is prohibited in theory between members of the same clan. But as the number of clans is rather small, the rule is not adhered to, and members of the same clan are permitted to marry so long as they do not come from the same village. The Minas of Rajputana are divided into twelve exogamous *pals* or clans; the original meaning of the word *pal* was a defile or valley suitable for defence, where the members of the clan would live together as in a Scotch glen.

"Thus, among the cultivating castes, apparently, each exogamous clan consisted originally of the residents of one village, though they afterwards spread to a number of villages. The servile labouring castes may also have arranged their clans by villages as the primitive forest-tribes did. How the menial castes formed exogamous clans is not altogether clear, as the numbers in one village would be only small. But it may be supposed that as they gradually increased, clans came into existence either in one large village or a number of adjacent ones, and sometimes traced their descent from a single family or from an ancestor with a nickname. As a rule, the artisan castes do not appear to have formed villages of their own in India, as they did in Russia, though this may occasionally have happened. When among the cultivating castes, the lands were divided, separate joint families would be constituted; the head only of each family would be its representative in the clan, as he would hold the share of the village land assigned to the family, which was their joint means of subsistence, and the family would live in one household. Thus, perhaps the Hindu joint family came into existence as a sub-division of the exogamous clan with male descent, on which its constitution was modelled. In Chhattisgarh, families still live together in large enclosures with separate huts for the married couples. A human ancestor gradually took the place of the totem as the giver of life to the clan. The members thought themselves bound together by the tie of his blood which flowed through all their veins, and frequently, as in Athens, Rome and Scotland, every member of the clan bore his name. In this capacity, as the source of the clan's life, the original ancestor was perhaps venerated, and on the development of the family system within the clan, the ancestors of the family were held in a similar regard, and the feeling extended to the living ancestor or father, who is treated with the greatest deference in the early patriarchal family. Even now Hindu boys, though they may be better educated and more intelligent than their fathers, will not as rule address him at meals unless he speaks to them first, on account of their traditional respect for him. The regard for the father may be strengthened by his position as the stay and support of the family, but could scarcely have arisen solely from this cause.

"Dr. Westermarck's view that the origin of exogamy lies in the feeling against the marriage of persons who lived together, receives support from the fact that a feeling of kinship still subsists between Hindus living in the same village, even though they may belong to different castes and clans. It is commonly found that all the households of a village believe themselves in a manner related. A man will address all the men of the generation above his own as uncle, though they may be of different castes, and the children of the generation below his own as niece and nephew. When a girl is married, all the old men of the village call her husband 'son-in-law'. This extends even to the impure castes who cannot be touched. Yet owing to the fact that they live together they are considered by fiction to be related. The Gowari caste do not employ Brahmans for their weddings, but the ceremony is performed by the *bhânja* or sister's son either of the girl's father or the boy's father. If he is not available, anyone whom either the girl's father or the boy's father addresses as *bhânja* or nephew in the village, even though he may be no relation and may belong to another caste, may perform the ceremony as a substitute. Among the Oraons and other tribes, prenuptial intercourse between boys and girls of the same village is regularly allowed. It is not considered right, however, that these unions should end in marriage, for which partners should be sought from other villages (Mr. S.C. Roy, *The Oraons,* p. 247). In the Maratha country the villagers have a communal feast on the occasion of the Dasahra festival, the Kunbis or cultivators eating first and the members of the menial and labouring castes afterwards.

"The Brâhmans and Rajputs, however, and one or two other military castes, as the Marathas and Lodhis, do not have the small exogamous clans (which probably, as has been seen, represented the persons who lived together in a village), but large ones. Thus, the Rajputs were divided into thirty-six royal races, and theoretically all these should have been exogamous, marrying with each other. Each great clan was afterwards, as a rule, split into a number of branches, and it is probable that these became exogamous; while in cases where a community of Rajputs have settled on the land and become ordinary cultivators, they have developed into an endogamous subcaste containing small clans of the ordinary type. It seems likely that the Rajput clan originally consisted of those who followed the chief to battle and fought together, and hence considered themselves to be related. This was, as a matter of fact, the case. Colonel Tod states that the great Rathor clan, who said that they could muster a hundred thousand swords, spoke of themselves as the song of one father. The members of the Scotch clans considered themselves related in the same manner, and they were probably of similar character to the Rajput clans. I do not know, however, that there is any definite evidence as to the exogamy of the Scotch clans, which would have disappeared with their conversion to Christianity. The original Rajput clan may perhaps have lived round the chief's castle or headquarters and been supported by the produce of his private fief or demesne. The regular Brahman *gotras* are also few in number, possibly because they were limited by the paucity of eponymous saints of the first rank. The word *gotra* means a stall or cow-pen, and would thus originally signify those who lived together in one place like a herd of cattle. But the *gotras* are now exceedingly large, the same ones being found in most or all of the Brahman subcastes, and it is believed that they do not regulate 'marriage as a rule. Sometimes, ordinary surnames have taken the place of clan names, and persons with the same surname consider themselves related and do not marry. But usually Brahmans prohibit marriage between *Sapindas* or persons related to each other within seven degrees from a common ancestor. The word *Sapinda* signifies those who partake together of the *pindas* or funeral cakes offered to the dead. The *Sapindas* are also a man's heirs in the absence of closer relations; the group of the *Sapindas* is thus an exact replica within the *gotra* of the primitive totem clan which was exogamous and constituted by the tie of living and citing together. Similarly, marriage at Rome was prohibited to seven degrees of relationship through males within the *gens* [Professor W.E. Hearn's *Aryan Household* (London, Longmans, Green & Co.) p. 160], and this exogamous group of kinsmen appear to have been the body of agnatic kinsmen within the *gens* who are referred to by Sir M. Maine as a man's ultimate heirs. At Athens, when a contest arose upon a question of inheritance, the proper legal evidence to establish kinship was the proof that the alleged ancestor and the alleged heir observed a common worship and shared in the same repast in honour of the dead. The distant heirs were thus a group within the Athenian *yevos* corresponding to the Sapindas and bound by the same tie of eating together. Professor Hearn states that there is no certain evidence that the Roman *gens* and Greek *yevos* were originally exogamous, but we find that of the Roman matrons whose names are known to us, none married a husband with her own Gentile name, and further Plutarch, in writing of the Romans, says that in former days men did not marry women of their own blood or, as in the preceding sentence he calls them, kinswomen just as in his own day they did not marry their aunts or sisters; he adds that it was long before they consented to wed with cousins (*Aryan Houshold,* p. 60, quoting Plutarch, *Quaestions Romanae* c. 6). Professor Hearn's opinion was that the Hindu *gotra,* the Roman *gens* and the Greek *gense* were originally the same institution, the exogamous clan with male descent, and all the evidence available as well as the close correspondence in other respects of early Hindu institutions with those of the Greek and Latin cities would tend to support this view", they add.

Rule of Hypergamy

About the practice of hypergamy, R.V. Russell and Hira Lal write, "The detailed rules prescribed for the status of legitimacy and inheritance show that recognised unions of this kind between men of a higher class and women of a lower one were at one time fairly frequent, though they were afterwards prohibited and they must necessarily have led to much mixture of blood in the different castes. A trace of them seems to survive in the practice of hypergamy, still widely prevalent in northern India, by which men of the higher subcastes of a caste will take daughters in marriage from lower ones but will not give their daughters in return. This custom prevails largely among the higher castes of the Punjab, as the Rajputs and Khatris, and among the Brahmans of Bengal. Only a few cases are found in the Central Provinces, among Brahmans, Sunars and other castes. Occasionally, intermarriage between two castes takes place on a hypergamous basis; thus, Rajputs are said to take daughters from the highest clans of the cultivating caste of Dangis. More commonly families of the lower sub-castes or clans in the same caste consider the marriage of their daughters into a higher group a great honour and will give large sums of money for a bridegroom. Until quite recently, a Rajput was bound to marry his daughters into a clan of equal or higher rank than his own, in order to maintain the position of his family. It is not easy to see why so much importance should be attached to the marriage of a daughter, since she passed into another clan and family, to whom her offspring would belong. On the other hand, a son might take a wife from a lower group without loss of status, though his children would be the future representatives of the family. Another point, possibly connected with hypergamy, is that a peculiar relation exists between a man and the family into which his daughter has married. Sometimes he will accept no food or even water in his son-in-law's village. The word *sala,* signifying wife's brother, when addressed to a man, is also a common and extremely offensive term of abuse. The meaning is now perhaps supposed to be that one has violated the sister of the person spoken to, but this can hardly have been the original significance as *sasur* or father-in-law is also considered in a minor degree an opprobrious term of address.

"But though among the four classical castes it was possible for the descendants of mixed unions between fathers of higher caste and mothers of lower caste to be admitted into their father's caste, this would not have been the general rule. Such connections were very frequent and the Hindu classics account through them for the multiplication of castes. Long lists are given of new castes formed by the children of mixed marriages. The details of these genealogies seem to be destitute of any probability, and perhaps, therefore, instances of them are unnecessary. Matches between a man of higher and a woman of lower caste were called *anuloma,* or 'with the hair' or 'grain', and were regarded as suitable and becoming. These between a man of lower and a woman of higher caste were, on the other hand, known as *pratiloma* or 'against the hair', and were considered as disgraceful and almost incestuous. The offspring of such unions are held to have constituted the lowest and most impure castes of scavengers, dog-eaters, etc. This doctrine is to be accounted for by the necessity of safeguarding the morality of women in a state of society where kinship is reckoned solely by male descent. The blood of the tribe and clan, and hence the right to membership and participation in the communal sacrifices, is then communicated to the child through the father; hence, if the women are unchaste, children may be born into the family who have no such rights, and the whole basis of society is destroyed. For the same reason, since the tribal blood and life is communicated through males, the birth and standing of the mother are of little importance, and children are, as has been seen, easily admitted to their father's rank," add R.V. Russell and Hira Lal.

Beef-eaters Deemed to be Impure

The Katkaris have five endogamous divisions such as : 1. Athavar, 2. Dhed or Dhor, 3. Sidhi, 4. Son or Maratha, and 5. Varap.

According to Mr. R.E. Enthoven, "The Son or Maratha Katkaris do not eat cow's flesh, and are allowed to draw water at the village well and to enter Kunbis' houses and temples. The Dhors eat cow's flesh, and, like the Mahars, are held to be impure. Athavars are looked down on as inferior by the Son Katkaris. Sidhis are doubtless African immigrants in origin. Varaps or reverts may have been either Christian or Musalman.

Dhors or Dheds are beef-eaters and therefore the lowest of the tribe, socially. Son and Dhor divisions are found also among the Kolis. Dhor is commonly supposed to mean cattle-eating, and Son either golden, red (Sanskrit *shon),* or foreign (Dravidian *son* or *sonag*). The Son Katkaris declare that at one time there was no such division as the Dhor Katkaris, but that many generations ago, under stress of famine, some of the tribe took to feeding on the carcasses of cattle, and since that time the two sections have been distinct. There is some probability in this explanation, as in many places, notably in the Kolaba district, the customs of both sections are identical. But it is equally possible that the Son division arose from abandoning the primitive habit of feeding on beef, with a view to rise in the social scale.

"It is commonly alleged that, more, Vaghmare, ect., are totemistic in origin, though reverence for the totem is no longer observable. Thus, the headman of the Katkari *vada* of Wawarls, near Karjat in the Kolaba district, Dhakumarya Vaghmare, of name, had a son who fell ill. He went to a Thakur who was supposed to have some skill as a doctor, and asked for medicine. The Thakur prescribed a draught of water and earth on which a tiger had micturated. Traces of a tiger's presence were found and the required earth carefully collected. The medicine was prepared and given to the boy, who rapidly came out in eruptions like large blisters. The father hastened to the Thakur, who was for a moment non-plussed. Then anidea occured to him and he asked Dhaku what his surname was. 'Vaghmare', was the reply. 'That explains it', said the Thakur. Since your name is Vaghmare, we should not have used the tiger in your son's case.

"Dhors have no restriction on intermarriage among different families. But amongst Sons marriage is prohibited between members bearing the same surname. First cousins are not allowed to marry, though second cousins may. Marriage with a wife's younger sister is allowed. Two brothers are allowed to marry two sisters. Girls are generally married between twelve to fifteen years of age and boys between twelve and twenty-five. Sexual licence before marriage is not recognised. Should a girl become pregnant before marriage, the fault would be condoned by marriage, but the ceremony would be performed with widow remarriage rites. Polygamy is permitted when the first wife is barren. Sometimes when a man becomes well-to-do and owns a number of cattle, he takes a second wife as an additional helper. In this case it is looked upon rather as a mark of a man of substance. Polyandry is unknown.

"The religion of the Katkaris, so far as they have any, is animism. They have no sacred books, neither have they any spiritual guides. They do not appear to say any prayers themselves, or to employ others to say prayers for them. Their chief object of worship is the tiger-god, who is supposed to look with peculiar favour upon them and very seldom harms them, and they are disinclined to shoot him. His image is generally set up in the forest or on the boundary of the village. But in parts, as in Knrjat, where forests and tigers are scarce, there are many Katkari hamlets without a tiger-god. What worship there is among the Katkaris is paid to the Kunbi village god, *gamdev,* and to such minor gods as Maolya, Mhasha, Vetal, Jarimari and Hirva. Red lead, coconuts and fowls are offered to these gods and to evil spirits, which are greatly dreaded. In Gujarat, Bhildev is worshipped. In a Dhor Katkari's house, there may sometimes be seen devil gods whom they call *Cheda.* This is the soul of a dead relation which has become a spirit, *bhut,* capable of entering the bodies of men. It is this close connection with and power over spirits that makes the Katkari so dreaded by the Kunbi. The latter credits him with the power of the evil eye, and with being able by means of his spirits to compass the death of his enemies. Among the Dhors, the only holidays are *Shimga* and *Divali,* to which the Sons add the fifteenth of *Bhadrapad* when they perform ceremonies in honour of the deceased," adds Mr. Enthover. The custom is practised by the community members of Katkari.

Not Marrying to Anybody Socially Inferior

About the custom of betrothal, R.V. Russell and Hira Lal write, "As the tribe is sprung from one ancestor, any marriage in the tribe is incestuous and forbidden. Poverty does not lower a Rajput's social position. But his position is injured if he marries a woman who is not a Rajput. He also lowers himself if he marries his daughter to some one who is socially his own inferior.

The daughter of a Chudasama Rajput is considered fit for the hand of a ruling chief, and a Chavada maiden may marry a Mevad Sisodiya. The names of daughters given in marriage to a husband of lower rank are not entered by the genealogist in the list of the women of the family. Daughters married into a family of inferior birth are not entitled to any special honour at any family gathering or feast. A peculiarity of the Jadejas is the extent to which they practised female infanticide. The probable explanation is that, on attempting to return to Hinduism, though they could get wives for their sons, no one of proper position would take their daughters in marriage. The story is that a chief of the Samma tribe had a beautiful and accomplished daughter for whom he wished to find a suitable match. He accordingly sent his family priest to travel in search of a young chief who should be her equal not only in rank and age but also in beauty and accomplishments. The Brahman travelled in vain and finally returned unsuccessful, reporting to his master that such a paragon was not to be found. The chief in despair asked the Brahman what to do and was advised to put his daughter to death. He did the same and other Jadejas followed the chief's example. In Kathiawar, the marriageable age among girls is between fifteen and twenty, while among Palanpur Thakors the marriageable age is between eight and ten. Rajputs are never careful about the age of the husband, who is sometimes two or three years older or younger than the girl. Betrothals take place either immediately before or some years before marriage. Betrothals are always verbal and never written.

On a lucky day, the relations of the girl go to the boy's house taking with them a small gold coconut and some ornaments and dresses and a horse, if the gift of a horse has been previously agreed to. When they reach the boy's village, the boy's father receives them with friends and music. Before leaving the house the boy's priest hands to some husband-owing woman of the house a gold or silver spouted vessel called *jhari* filled with water, with a coconut stopper in its mouth. When the boy's father meets the girl's party, he welcomes them. The girl's father puts some cash into the vessel and makes money presents to the priest and musicians, and distributes dry dates to the women who sing marriage songs and accompany the woman who holds the spouted vessel. The woman who holds the vessel with the spout leads the procession to a house specially furnished for the girl's party, and here the boy's father feeds the bride's party with rice cooked with sugar and clarified butter, acid and pungent articles being scrupulously avoided. A lucky day is fixed for the acceptance of the gold coconut of betrothal, when the girl's party go with music and friends to the boy's house carrying a brass platter containing the gold coconut and the presents for the boy with packets of sugar, red powder *gulal,* cloves, cardamoms and raisins, vermilion, rice and flowers. If a horse is among the presents it is led in front of the party. Women sing songs and men throw red powder. The boy's relations and friends meet at his house. The boy is richly dressed and seated on a raised seat. On reaching the boy's house the girl's priest marks the boy's brow with vermilion and presents him with the gold coconut and other articles brought from the girl's house. He then asks the mother of the boy to accept the brass salver containing the presents. A servant girl of the house comes and takes the salver and daubs the forehead of the boy with the vermilion from the dish, and sticks grains of rice on the spots of vermilion. If there be more servant girls in the house, each of them in turn daubs the boy's brow with vermilion and rice, and the boy drops the gold coconut in the lap of the last of them. The boy's father then removes the presents and fills the dish with dry dates and money. He opens the sugar packets and takes a little sugar into his hollow hands and offers it to four men of each party. Sugar is then distributed to friends and relations met at the house and the girl's party is treated to opium-water *kusumba.* On the next day, the girl's party asks the boy's party to their lodgings to sip *kusumba* and distribute sugar to the guests. The boy's father afterwards presents the girl's party with dresses and feeds them so long as they stay in his village. After this, on a lucky day fixed by the astrologer, the boy's party goes to the girl's village to make her a present of ornaments and dresses. The girl's father receives the boy in the same manner as his own party was received. The girl is seated on a low stool and presented with ornaments and a petticoat, bodice and headscarf, which she puts on. The other presents consisting of packets of sugar, rice, flowers, cloves, cardamoms and dry dates are received by a woman of the family who marks the girl's forehead with vermilion. The boy's father presents the girl with a coconut and a rupee. The girl's father is required to treat the boy'a party in the same way and for the same number of days as his party was treated at the boy's village. The boy's party asks the girl's party to a *kusumba* entertainment and distributes sugar to all who are present. The boy's relations are presented with dresses before they leave, and the ceremony is complete.

"Afterwards, when the father of the girl wants to marry his daughter, he sends for an astrologer, who, consulting the birth papers of the boy and girl, finds out a lucky day for the wedding ceremony. If the birth papers are not available, the astrologer is guided by the names of the boy and the girl. He takes a slip of Ahmedabad-made paper and writes an invitation or *lagan patrika* to the boy's father, naming the day and the time. On this paper, a silver coin, some rice and five dry dates are laid and it is marked with saffron and vermilion, and the whole is formed into a conical packet and wound round with a *nada chhadi* or yellow and red cotton thread. The girl's priest takes this invitation packet called *laganno pado* with four conical shaped packets of 1.25 pounds of sugarcandy, 1.25 pounds of sugar, 1.25 pounds of raisins 1.25 pounds of vermilion and five coconuts to the boy's house, where the boy's father welcomes him to some place in his neighbourhood and asks him to his house at some lucky time of the day. Friends and relations meet at the house, music plays, and the women sing marriage songs.

"The boy's priest then asks the girl's priest to seat himself on a low stool. An unmarried girl of the boy's family marks the forehead of the girl's priest with vermilion and on the vermilion sticks grains of rice. She then throws four pinches of vermilion and rice on the invitation packet and takes it into her hand. The boy's priest offers the girl's priest four handfulls of sugar, and, dipping his open right hand in the vermilion and water, marks the chest and back of the girl's priest with the lucky red right hand. The girl's priest then leaves the stool and the boy takes his place. The boy's priest daubs the boy's forehead with vermilion, and four unmarried girls one by one drop on him pinches of vermilion and rice. The boy's priest reads the invitation. A local astrologer is consulted, and if the moon at the time proposed for the wedding is favourable to the boy, the invitation is accepted and the day for the girl to put on the bangles and for the marriage are fixed. Sugar or molasses are distributed to the guests and they are treated to opium-water. The girl's priest is told whether the boy is to come personally to the girl's house for the marriage or is to send his *khándu* or sword. He then leaves the boy's house with the present of some article of dress or cash or both. As by sending the sword the bridegroom escapes expensive presents to bards and singers, the practice has become common. From the day the bride's priest leaves the bridegroom's village, the bride and bridegroom are dressed in rich clothes and ornaments and at both houses a party of women sing marriage songs morning and evening. At the house of both the bride and the bridegroom on the third, fifth or seventh day before the marriage, day booths are erected. On the same day at both houses takes place the ceremony of fixing the *manak stambh* or ruby pillar. The wooden post is made by a carpenter. It is about a foot long and is handed to the women of the house, who give the carpenter five measures of wheat and a coconut. A hole is dug either on the right side of the main door of the house or in a place specially chosen by the astrologer. In front of this hole, the parents of the bride or of the bridegroom, as the case may be, are made to sit on low stools facing east, their foreheads are marked with vermilion, and the ends of their garments are knotted together by the family priest. They throw in the hole a few drops of water mixed with vermilion, curds and milk, a copper, and a betelnut. Their garments are then untied. The wooden post is bound with a cotton thread and *pipal* leaf, a betelnut, a copper, a bamboo rod and a branch of the *khijda* (Prosopis spicigera) tree, and the post is planted in the hole. While the post is being planted, music plays and women neighbours and friends sing songs. On the same day, the bride's and bridegroom's mother and father, each at their village, go with music and a party of male and female relations to the potter's to worship his wheel and to bring earthen vessels. The Brahman priest walks in front with a brass platter filled with rice, a coconut, molasses and turmeric powder. The women follow him singing songs. The bride's and bridegroom's mother and father throw rice and turmeric powder over the wheel and present the potter with the coconut, rice and molasses. The women then sing *phatánás* or jest songs and return in procession with the earthen vessels required for the wedding. When they reach home, dry dates are distributed to the guests and the ceremony of *chák vadhávani* or wheel-inviting is over. On the same day, at both houses follows the installation of Ganpati and of Gotraj, the family goddess. Inside the house a portion of the northern or eastern wall is whitewashed with *khadi* or white clay and daubed with vermilion. Near the wall is set a low wooden stool covered with a piece of white or red cloth a cubit and a quarter square. On this cloth are laid five measures of rice or wheat and a coconut and a lamp fed with clarified butter. The boy or the girl sits on a bed before the low stool. A betelnut Ganpati is laid in a brass salver and washed in milk and afterwards placed on the stool. Sandal-paste, rice and flowers are offered to the god, incense is burned before him, and round him is waved a light fed with clarified butter, *kansar* or wheat-flour cooked in clarified butter and sugar is laid before him, and a lamp fed with clarified butter is again waved round him. The boy or girl is made to repeat verses in praise of the god. On the same day, the boy's and the girl's fathers, at their respective houses, invoke the family goddess. A portion of the wall is whitewashed, and on the white part a picture of the family goddess is drawn with vermilion water. Rice, flowers and turmeric paste are stuck upon the picture, incense is burned before it, a light fed with clarified butter is waved round it, and sugar is offered to it. The members of the house eat *kansar* on that day and the family priest is feasted. After the invocation of Ganpati and the family goddess, both at the boy's and at the girl's house comes the *randal* ceremony. A small ornamental booth is erected in the house, and in it is placed a stool covered with white or red cloth a cubit and a quarter long. On the cloth are laid five measures of rice or wheat, and on the rice or wheat is set a jar with its mouth covered by a green silk cloth. On the jar is laid a coconut draped in a woman's robe so as to represent a female face. Near the jar a lamp fed with clarified butter is kept burning day and night. Another ceremony, that of *gotardo bharvo* or pot-filling, takes place at both the houses. The father and mother or a brother and his wife have the ends of their garments tied together and go with a party of men and women and music to buy a new *bedu,* that is, a pair of earthen pots. With these pots, they visit a well, pond or river and bring water to bathe the bride and the bridegroom. The pair, that is, either the father and mother or the brother and his wife, first worship the river, well or pond and then the earthen pots. The earthen pots are filled and carried by the mother or the brother's wife. A day or two before the marriage the bride and bridegroom are rubbed with turmeric paste and scented oil, and *mindhals* or marriage-nuts are tied round their right wrists.

"In the case of a sword-marriage, when the *khdndu* or sword is to be sent to the girl's house, the boy sits in a litter with a sword and a coconut and passes with music and a company of friends and relations as far as the boundary of his village. There he alights, leaving the sword and a coconut in charge of a maid-servant who takes his place in the litter. The procession marches to the bride's village and is welcomed at the boundary by the girl's party, who take the guests to a house specially furnished for them and feast them. After the feast is over, at a lucky moment for the girl to put on the marriage bangles, the boy's Brahman takes to the girl's house a robe and a pair of bangles. The girl is seated on a low stool before the family goddess who has been previously installed in the house; the Brahman repeats verses and the girl bows before the goddess and puts on the robe and the bangles and again bows before the goddess. The bridegroom's party then carries the sword in procession to the bride's house, where, under an arch or *toran,* the maid in charge of the sword waits till a *varmáchi* or bridegroom's chair is brought for her to stand upon. The bride's mother comes, wearing on her head a *mod* or three-cornered tiara of gold set with pearls, and over it a *chundadi* or female robe and stands before the maid. The girl's priest holds a cloth between them. He then sends for the *dhoshru* or miniature yoke, marks it with vermilion, covers it with one end of a robe, and, after waving it over the handle of the sword, passes it to a man standing behind. He repeats the same process with the miniature *sámbela* or pestle, the *ravai* or churning stick, and the *trak* or ladle. The girl's priest waves over the handle of the sword four balls, two made of rice or wheat-flour and two made of ashes. Of the two flour balls, one is thrown to the north, the other to the east, and of the two ash balls one is thrown to the south, the other to the west. Two *kodias* or earthen lamp saucers filled with rice put brim to brim and bound together with cotton thread are waved over the sword and placed on the ground. The maidservant breaks them with her foot, and enters the booth. In the booth are placed a *varmachi* or chair and a stool opposite to it. The maid-servant with the sword sits on the chair and the girl sits on the low stool opposite to her. At the lucky moment, the right hands of the girl and the maidservant are joined together. At each corner of the booth, a brass jar is placed and in the north-east a stone daubed with redlead is set to represent the *khetrapal* or field-guardian. Near the field-guardian is laid a copper pot containing rice and pulse with a coconut laid on its mouth. The girl's father performs the ceremony of *kanyadan* or girl-giving by taking a little water in the hollow of his joined hands and pouring it on the ground. The priest repeats verses and the *kanyadan* is complete when the water is poured on the ground," they add. The customs rites and rituals are practised by the Rajput community.

Child Marriage on Wave

Pre-puberty marriages of girls existed among the Son Kolis about forty years ago. The marriages did not take place earlier than a year or two before puberty. Thus, there have never been child marriages in the sense that we find in many other Hindu castes. The wife is always younger than the husband. Due to the complete ignorance of age, no definite difference of age could be found; but generally the difference has been somewhere between five and ten years. Almost all the marriages are settled by the elders. However, with the freedom of movement given to the girls and the comparatively higher age of marriage, such high incidence of marriages settled by the elders seems a condition too good to be true. Moreover, most of the marriages take place within the locality. In fact, a large number of arranged marriages are settled by the spouses but consented to and celebrated by the elders, willingly or otherwise, because marriages settled by the spouses are not favoured by the society.

Even when the marriages are settled by the elders, the approval of the boy and the bride is always sought. Very few Sons Kolis, have married outside the community, though a few cases of keeping mistresses from other communities are found.

Customarily, marriages within the family are forbidden, while marriages within relations are not favoured. Though, a marriage with maternal uncle's daughter can take place, however, in practice, even that is rare. Due to the old tradition, preference is given to the non-relatives. However, some women felt that the reason was a precaution that any failure of the bride to accommodate herself in the new home should not spoil the relations between the two related families. Among them, marriage by exchange called mas-*palat* is practised around Alibag. Such marriages are favoured because neither party has to pay bride-price and the marriage expenses also are comparatively lower.

The first step in arranging a marriage is for the household of the young man to find a proper match form him from among the marriageable girls. The ideal bride is a strong, healthy and hard-working girls, with no physical defects. The selection being made, a Brahmin priest is consulted. From the names of the boy and the girl and their horoscope, the Brahmin finds out whether there is any astrological hitch in the union of the two. If the Brahmin approves of the match, the next step is to find from the neighbours or friends of the girl's family whether her parents intend to get her married. If the reply is positive, some influential persons, usually with a relative of the boy, are sent with marriage proposal. The intermediaries may be men or women, but very often the services of the latter are preferred in this negotiation. If they get a favourable answer, which they would rarely get on the first visit, the boy's parents make the formal proposal. Whenever, the go-between is asked to come some other time, the match is discussed over with relations, about the boy his family members, their nature and their financial status. If the boy is not approved for some reason, the refusal is always conveyed as due to non-intention of the girl to marry: no fault is to be pointed out with the boy or his family. If the match is approved, the parents of the prospective bride are approached by the boy's parents, along with a couple of relatives to discuss bride-price, ornaments and other marriage expenses.

The involved bride-price depends on the financial status of both the parties. Formerly, after the amount was fixed the father of the bride-groom had to swear before the *Panch* that he would give a particular sum in the particular form. Besides the bride price, the bridegroom's father had to gift certain ornaments to the bride. The list of the ornaments that had to be compulsorily given to the bride was given by an informant.

Nowadays, most of the traditional ornaments are out of fashion and the bride is given modern ornaments; however, it is not obligatory to do so. The bridegroom's father has to pay a marriage tax to the bride's *Jamat*, which varies in different regions. Efforts have been made from time to time to get rid of the custom of bride-price. For quite sometime they seem to have succeeded, but the evil practice started again with vengence. Today, the practice varies from one extreme, namely of not taking any bride-price (when they say, 'Sokari dharmis devachi,' meaning 'To give the daughter as a charitable or virtuous act') to the other, of demanding thousand of rupees as bride-price. Another tendency, possibly resulting from the contact with the higher classes of Maharashtrian Hindus, is to demand money from the bride's parent in dowry. The custom is related to the Son Kolis of Maharashtra.

No Marriage of Minors

The tribal people do not believe in early marriage, or in the prevention of widow-re-marriage, or in minor food and caste taboos, prevalent among the Hindu Castes. The practice of early marriage among the Hindus, which has a long historical origin enforced with greater rigour as a measure of social protection during the domination of foreign culture, does not exist among the tribal people. The Dublas have the usual age of marriage about 18 for boys and 15 for girls. Even then marriage among them is not always a simple affair of love and courtship between a young man and a girl, but the tribal society imposes the marriage through certain some social institutions.

The Vito means an endogamous marriage circle within which the selection of bride is generally allowed. Marriage connections are permissible under certain sub-sections of Dublas within certain geographical areas e.g. a number of villages within a particular area of *Navasari* taluka would form an endogamous group beyond which brides could not be given or exchanged; and so also those in Bardoli or Gandevi would form another *Vito*. This zone may overcome sub-group differences of Dublas e.g. Talavias and non-Talavia dublas may form one Vito and exchange brides between themselves, provided they come within this *Vito*. The concept of *Vito* as a geographical unit, is borrowed from the majority community of the Hindu. It saves the participants' long journeys in connection with marriage arrangements, numersons negotiations or of the wedding ceremonies, the Anu or the first formal exchange of visits of the bridegroom and bride after marriage, or the pregnancy or ceremony child-birth visits, etc. The closeness of marriage has strengthened the solidarity of the local culture and led to its enforcement with a sense of rigid reality.

This practice is probably the result of poverty but its social significance also cannot be over-emphasised. It gives a definite clue as to whether the Dublas were or at all connected with Rajputs. A Rajput never marries within a clan *e.g.* a Solanki Rajput would not accept a bride from another Solanki family but from a non-Solanki Rajput family. However, a Dubla takes the bride from a local Dubla or Talavia or Dubla-Rathod—the geographical tie being more important. The idea of a gotra or a clan responsible for the avoidance of local marriages among some Hindu castes, is not observed rigidly by the Dubla Tribals. This supports the theory that the Dublas a constitute group with foreign origin and with certain concepts which are not accepted by Rajputs or the other Hindu castemen.

When a Dubla boy reaches a marriageable age of 18 years, his parents communicate with their relatives asking them to suggest the names of suitable girls for their son. Usually, the maternal uncle or the brother-in-law (sister's husband) of the boy as well as other relatives on the mother's and father's side approach girl's parents. The relatives take all possible case to search for a girl amongst their relatives and acquintances, and make suggestions to the prospective bride's parents to think over the proposal. The girl's parents also make inquiries as to the general nature of the members of the boy's family, behaviour, boy's habits, his temper, his general pose and whether any person from the boy's family suffer from any serious disease or hereditary ailment. If any disease is found, the boy's parents straightaway refuse the proposal and go in search of another bride. In villages, a girl with high education may not be preferred due to apprehension that education may make her indifferent to the simple life in Dubla huts, where cooking, domestic work and field works are overwhelming. The well-being and stability of a Dubla family brings upon the capacity of the womenfolk to work in harmony in the dull and heavy household and field work. The accetance of the bride into the husband's family is always a slow business in all communities. The bride is often looked upon by her mother-in-law as an inferior person and she has to bear her own share of household chores and farm work. The parents on both the sides, therefore, make enquiries as to how far these adjustments would be possible before they finally agree to the marriage alliance between the two families. If the information supplied is found satisfactory, then they convey the message to the boy's parents through intermediary known as *Vastario* or *Vastalia* among the Dublas of Dharampur side. The Naikdas of Chikhali and Gandevi also follow this custom.

The bridgroom's parents formally go to see the girl at her house and the bridegroom also does the same after some days. If he does not approve of the girl, the parents do not ignore his wishes even through they might be in favour of the girl. If a girl is refused at the stage, it is not considered out of etiquette among the Dublas, and the girl's prestige is not supposed to have been affected by the refusal. But sometimes, the boy and girl meet each other and make up their mind to enter the wedlock. Sometimes they elope and live together for a few days with the connivance of the parents. This kind of marital alliance is generally accepted by the parents who consider themselves lucky that they have been saved the trouble of making preparations and also the consequent expenses at the various stages. However, when everything else is agreed to by parents on both parties, then comes the settling date of betrothal known, in their languages as *nani tadi* i.e. 'a minor drinking occasion'. The custom prevails among the Dubla tribesmen of Gujarat.

Sexual Licence Before Marriage Not Allowed

About the betrothal customs, rites and rituals, Mr. R.E. Enthoven writes, "Marriage with a maternal uncle's daughter, father's sister's daughter, and mother's sister daughter is allowed. Marriage with a wife's sister is allowed. Two brothers may marry two sisters. Girls are married from ten and boys from twelve upwards. Girls are married even after they attain the age of puberty among the rich as well as the poor. Sexual license before marriage is not allowed. If before marriage a girl commits sexual indiscretions with a man of her caste, her father is fined, and she is married to a poor man of her caste. The man involved is fined or compelled to give a dinner to his caste-men. When a girl commits sexual indiscretions with an outsider, she is excommunicated. Polygamy is permitted, but polyandry is unknown.

"The offer of marriage generally comes from the boy's father. The father of the boy pays from forty to one hundred rupees to the girl's father as the price of the bride. A Brahman fixes the auspicious day for marriage and conducts the service of marriage. When a marriage is settled, the father of the boy treats the girl's party to liquor. A period of one or two years may intervene between the betrothal and marriage. The ceremonies of Ganpati worship, *telpithi, varghoda,* marriage and *kanyadan* are performed in order. A feast to the caste-men ends the marriage ceremony. The *telpithi* ceremony consists in anointing the bride and bridegroom with turmeric paste and bathing them. The bride and bridegroom fold their hands and place them over one another. This is known as *hasta-mela,* and is supposed to be the binding portion of the ceremony. They have the *panchpalvi* or leaves of five kinds for their *devak.* These are hung in the marriage pandal.

"Widow remarriage is allowed. A widow cannot marry her maternal aunt's uncle's son, or her father's sister's son. She may marry a younger brother of her dead husband. Permission of the headman of the caste is usually essential for a widow remarriage. Widow remarriage is celebrated on Tuesday or Sunday at about ten at night. On that occasion, the widow, her new husband, and a couple who have been remarried, are present. The widow gives liquor or food to her new husband and receives the same from him. The remarried couple then join their hands and the ceremony ends. The joining of hands is the binding portion of the ceremony. But in some districts this is substituted by the striking together to the bride and bridegroom's heads, or by both striking a coconut with their heads. A bachelor is allowed to marry a widow after first being married to a *shami* tree.

"Divorce is allowed with the consent of the caste-men. The husband or wife may ask for a divorce, and permission is granted when it is proved that the husband is impotant or that the wife dislikes him for some adequate reason. A deed of divorce is passed on a stamped paper. A woman divorced for adultery with a man of her caste is allowed to remain in the caste and to marry a second time. But when she is divorced for adultery with an outsider, she is excommunicated," adds Mr. R.E. Enthoven. The custom, rites and rituals are practised among the *Machhis*.

Marriage with Maternal Uncle's Daughter Allowed

Mr. R.E. Enthoven notes, "Marriage with a mother's sisters' daughter or father's sister's daughter is not allowed. It is allowed with a maternal uncle's daughter. Marriages with a wife's sister are allowed. Two brothers may marry two sisters. Girls are married before they are twelve. There is no limit of age for the marriage of boys. Sexual licence before marriage is neither allowed nor tolerated. If a girl commits sexual indiscretions before marriage with a man of her caste, she is married to him. The man is compelled to undergo certain purifcations and to pay a fine and give a dinner to his caste-men. They are then classed as *kadu, akaramashe* or bastard, and treated as being of an inferior division. If a girl commits sexual indiscretions with an outsider, she is excommunicated, and cannot be readmitted into her caste either by paying a fine or by giving a dinner to her caste-men. Polygamy is permitted, but polyandry is unknown.

A man marries another wife when his first wife is barren or is physically defective. There is no limit to the number of wives." The custom is related to the *Lonaris* in the Western region.

No Marriage in the Same or Allied Clan

"The members of the Sadhu division are said to be converts from other castes. They have no connection in food or marriage with any of the above divisions."

"Marriages are prohibited between members of the same clan or of allied clans. Thus, Devijivals are forbidden to marry not only with other Devijivals, but also with the Bahons, Babisivals and many other clan or *kuls* because they are branches of one stock. Marriage with a father's sister's, mother's sisters, or mother's brother's daughter is prohibited. Marriage with a wife's sister is allowed, and two brothers are allowed to marry two sisters. Polygamy is allowed and practised, but polyandry is unknown. In some divisions of the tribe such as Charans, divorce is not allowed. In others it is allowed on the ground of the wife's misconduct. Sexual intercourse before marriage appears to be connived at in some places, while in others, the offending parties are compelled to marry. Among Charans, Mathuas and Labhanas, who are of Upper India origin, girls remain unmarried to twenty and thirty, but among Deccan Vanjaris the marriageable limit for girls is from ten to twelve and for boys from twelve to twenty. In the Kanarese districts, marriage is mostly an adult affair, and in some places, girls are kept unmarried permanently. Black glass beads are fastened to the left ankles of such girls, who frequently live immoral lives," adds Mr. Enthoven.

No Consanguineous or Affinal Marriage Valid

About the Parsi betrothal and marriage customs, Mr. Enthoven writes, "Differences arose, and the community was divided into two sects or divisions, the majority holding to the old calendar of the Indian Parsis. Those who stuck to the old calendar made themselves known as Shahanshahi, *i.e.,* following the procedure of the Persian Emperors or Kings of Kings. The others called themselves Kadmi (kadmini), *i.e.,* following old

(Kadim) procedure as observed in Persia. In the heat of the preliminary differences when first schism took place, each sect called the other by a nick-name. The Shahanshahis called the Kadmis 'Churigars', *i.e.,* bangle-makers, from the fact, that, among the first few who joined the new movement in Surat, there were several who prepared bangles (Churis). In an Gujarati document which lately came to my hand, wherein the first Kadmis bind themselves to the Fire-temple, many signatories place before their names the abbreviated word (chu) to signify that they were *churigars* by profession (*vide* the *Jam-i-Jamshed* of 11th June 1919 for the text of the document.

"Up to a few years, there were certain restrictions in the matter of intermarriage, based upon a supposed social or rather professional status. The Athornans (A'thravans) or the Mobeds, *i.e.,* the priestly class claimed to be endogamous. From times immemorial the ancient Iranians, the ancestors f the modern Parsis, were divided into four classes, based on their profession or occupation. According to the Avesta, the people were at first divided into the following three classes:

1. A'thravan, *i.e.,* the priests, whose class corresponded to that of Brahmans among the Hindus.

2. Rathaeshtar, *i.e.,* the warriors or soldiers, whose class corresponded to that of the Kshatriyas of the Hindus.

3. Vactirya (Vactirya fshuyant) *i.e.,* the Agriculturists, whose class seems to correspond to that of the Hindu Vaishyas.]

4. Latterly, as civilization grew, a fourth class—the Huiti. (Pahl. Hutokhsh)—was added. It included the arizans or traders. It may correspond, to some extent, to theSudras of the Hindus.

"According to Firdousi, it was King Jamshed (the Yima Khshaeta of the Avesta, the Yama of the Vedas), who first made this division. Firdousi names the division as follows: 1. Amuzian, 2. Nisariyan, 3. Nasoudi, and 4. Ahnukhushi.

"Ardeshir (Artaxerxes) Babegan, the founder of the Sassanian dynasty and principal supporter of the Iranina Renaissance, is reported to have made a similar division, with a slight variation in the order of precedence in the case of the last two division.

His division was as follows: 1. Achab-i-Din, *i.e.,* the priests, 2. Mukatel (mardan-i-Karzar, *i.e.,* Army). 3. Kuttab, *i.e.,* the writers. This class included clerks, medical men, literary men, and scientific men. 4. Muhana, *i.e.,* men of the ordinary class of work.

"This class included merchants, agriculturists, workmen, etc. Ardeshir is said to have made these professions well-nigh heredi tary. Members of one profession or class could not join or pass into another without the sanction of the Government. From all these three sources,—*viz.,* (*a*) the Avesta, (*b*) the Shahnameh and (*c*) the letter of Taosar, the minister of Ardeshir Babegan—we learn that the priestly class was placed at the top.

"In two Silhara grants of the 10th, and 11th, centuries the priestly class of the Parsis is referred to as "*trivagarg*", *i.e.,* of three classes. Dr. Buhler, translates the word as "three castes" and adds the "twice born" in brackets after the word "three"

"In the Avesta, the Athravans—the priestly class corresponding to the Brahmans—are called *Thrayavan, i.e.,* of the three orders. These three orders are said to be those of the three grades of the priests, the Dasturs, the Mobeds and the Herbads. The above grants speak of them as "the holy men". The word *Thrayavan* of the Avesta corresponds to the "trivagarg" or the Silhara copper plate grants. Whatever the precise signification of the word "*trivagarg*" may be, it seems pretty clear, that the priestly class of the Parsis was held to be superior and, as it were, "twice born" like the Brahmans.

"Now, imbued with the idea of preserving this supremacy, the priestly class at one time allowed no free intermarriage with the laymen (Bedhins) who formed the other classes. At times, and that even very rarely, they took the girls of the laymen class in marriage, but never gave the girls of their class to the laymen. This practice at one time led to several internal disputes among the community. About 1727 the Parsi priests of Surat regularly resolved among themselves that they might take in marriage the daughters of laymen, but not give theirs in return. When they sought to put this resolution into force in Bombay, it was resented by the laity, who, at a public meeting convened by the Punchayat in 1777, resolved that there should be no intermarriages between the clergy and the laity. The priests did not accept this resolution.

"In 1785, a breach of this resolution occurred, and, at a public meeting of the community convened by the Punchayat, the offending parties were excommunicated. The point in dispute being represented to Mr. R.H. Bodham, the then Governor of Bombay, he appointed a committee of three European members to inquire into the matter and report. The committee decided, that it was not fair for the priests to take in marriage the daughters of the laymen, and to refuse to give theirs in return. The decision of this Committee seems strangely inconsistent with caste practice prevailing in many parts of India, particularly in the Punjab, where many castes take daughters from other castes but will not marry their sons to members of such castes.—R.E.E. Now-a-days, though the members of the priestly class generally preter to give their daughters in marriage to the sons of the priestly class only, the former strict prohibition is obsolete, and there are a number of cases of intermarriage.

"Looking to the religious books and ancient tradition we find that intermarriages with aliens, *i.e.,* those who followed a religion other than Zoroastrian, were disliked. The Vendidad (XVIII, 62) speaks of prohibition of marriage between the righteous (*dahma*) and the unrighteous (*a-dahma*), between the Mazda-worshipper (*a-daeva-yacna*) and the Daeva-worshippers (*daeva-yacna*), between the unsinful (*a-tanuperetha*) and the sinful (*tanu-peretha*). This prohibition is generally taken to cover intermarriage with aliens or non-Zoroastrians. History presents some examples of Persian kings marrying princesses of other creeds. But, as a rule, such marriages were disliked. The Dinkard says: 'Men who are bound by the precepts of the religion ought, with the object of avoiding sin and strife, to tie the knot of marriage with such believers in the religion, as that strength might accrue to them and to the people of their race for deliverance from hell by means of prayers and devotions to god. The prosperity of the progeny of men is (secured) by marriages entered into with this object of receiving mutual assistance. Khetiodath (*i.e.,* relationship by marriage) is then said to be formed when it is formed within one's own race.

Mr. Enthoven continues further, "As to the marriage of a Persian woman marrying a non-Persian, there has been only one solitary instance recorded by Herodotus, *viz.,* that of Metiochus, the son of the Greek Miltiades, marrying a Persian woman.[(1)] When Noshirwan the Just (Chosroes I) made peace with the Arabs of the country of Yemen, Arabia Felix, which he had invaded, in the treaty of peace there was a special condition that no Arab was ever to marry a Persian woman, though Persian soldiers might marry Arab women. Thus, when for some special reason as, for example, the long stay of an army in a foreign country, intermarriages were permitted, they took the form of marriages between Persian men and non-Persian women, but Persian women were not allowed to wed non-Persian men. These prohibitions and restrictions derived from the country of their ancestors, the Parsis of India have generally observed, and as a rule, they have avoided intermarriage with non-Parsis, though there have been rare instances of civil marriage here and there. During the last decade or two, meeting in general assemblies, they have more than once affirmed their determination to follow their ancestral custom. The Parsi marriage Act has embodied that determination in legal form.

"Parsis have adult marriages at present. No sexual license before marriage is recognized or tolerated. It appears from their marriage service that adult marriage was the rule in old times. They very fact that the officiating senior priest asked, during the marriage service, questions to the marrying couple, whether they chose to enter into marriage till the end of their life with good faith, shows that the marriage was celebrated between adults.

"But latterly the community in passing through various vicissitudes of fortunes in India under different Hindu and Muhammadan rulers, had departed form the old custom of adult marriages and allowed infant marriages. These were common up to about 40 to 50 years ago. But, now, with very rare exceptions, infant marriages are unknown. The few cases of infant marriages that do occur take place in some remote towns.

"Polyandry was never known among Parsis in their long history' whether in Iran or India, their mother or adopted country. Polygamy, in the sense of marrying several wives in the ordinary course, was and is never permitted. But up to about 50 year ago, a man was permitted to take another wife in the life-time of his first wife in exceptional cases, such as continued illness, barrenness, faithlessness or bad conduct, etc., of the wife. In such cases it was necessary to ask the permission of the Panchayat or the elders of the community, who made inquiries and gave the necessary permission in case of necessity. There have been cases, wherein, the first wife, finding herself incapable of bearing children to her husband, has of her own accord desired the husband to marry a second wife, with whom she lived very peacefully. The elder wife generally managed the household. The Parsi Marriage Act of 1856, given to the community by the British Government at the well-nigh unanimous desire of the community, has now put an end to the practice altogether. But in some of the Native States, where Parsis are not strictly governed by British laws, there still occur occasionally cases of persons having a second wife with the consent of the first wife or on the dissolution of the marriage obtained with the consent of the first wife. The form of marriage is known as the Ashirvad (lit. blessing) ceremony, which is performed by two priests."

Consangineous and affinal Marriage Prohibited

About the betrothal customs and rituals, Mr Enthoven writes, "Marriage is prohibited to the ordinary near relations, but not between first cousins. A man cannot marry his foster-mother or foster-sister, unless the foster brother and sister were nursed by the same women at intervals widely separated. A man may not marry his wife's sister during his wife's life-time unless she has been divorced. A Muhammadan cannot marry a polytheist, but he may marry a Jewess or a Christian. Polygamy is permitted to the number of four wives, but is rare in practice. Divorce is at the option of the husband, but is rare among the gentler classes, both the parties to it being looked upon with opprobrium. A divorcer finds it hard to marry a second time, and a woman once divorced tires as far as she can to shun matrimony for the rest of her life on the grounds of the homely Zenanah proverb: by changing the bed, fate cannot be altered. The dislike, almost loathing, with which an Indian Musalman looks upon divorce is so great that one of the strongest of his oaths is: May she who has given me birth be thrice divorced if I do so.

"Of the three forms of divorce two are easily recalled; but in the third, which is called the severer *bayin*, when the word divorce is repeated three several times it is final until the wife has married and is again free. After divorce a woman cannot marry for three months called the *iddat* or term during which the husband is bound to maintain her."

About the customs of endogamy, exogamy among the Muslims, RV Russell and Hira Lal write, "Formerly the Saiyads and Mughals constituted the superior class of Muhammadan gentry, and never touched a plough themselves, like the Hindu Brahmans and Rajputs. These four divisions are not proper subcastes, as they are not endogamous. A man of one group can marry a woman of any other and she becomes a member of her husband's group; but the daughters of Saiyads do not usually marry others than Saiyads. Nor is there any real distinction of occupation between them, the men following any occupation indifferently. In fact, the divisions are now little more than titular, a certain distinction attaching to the titles Saiyad and Shaikh when borne by families who have a hereditary or prescriptive right to use them."

They write further, "The age of marriage of boys may therefore be taken at I8 to 25 or later, and that of girls at I0 to 20. The age of marriage both of girls and boys is probably getting later, especially among the better classes.

"Marriage is prohibited to the ordinary near relatives, but not between first cousins. A man cannot marry his foster-mother of foster-sister, unless the foster-brother and sister were nursed by the same woman at intervals widely separated. A man may not marry his wife's sister during his wife's lifetime unless she has been divorced. A Muhammadan cannot marry a polytheist, but he may marry a Jewess or a Christian. No specific religious ceremony is appointed, nor are any rites essential for the contraction of a valid marriage. If both persons are legally competent, and contract marriage with persons are legally competent, and contract marriage with each other in the presence of two male or one male and two female witnesses, it is sufficient. And the Shiah law even dispenses with witnesses. As a rule the Kazi performs the ceremony, and reads four chapters of the Koran with the profession of belief, the bridegroom repeating them after him. The parties then express their mutual consent, and the Kazi, raising his hands, says, 'The great God grant that mutual love may reign between this couple as it existed between Adam and Eve, Abraham and Sarah, Joseph and Zuleika, Moses and Zipporah, His Highness Muhammad and Ayesha, and His Highness Ali and Fatimah. 'Hughes' *Dictionary of Islam, s.v.* Marriage. A dowry or *meher* must be paid to the wife, which under the law must not be less than ten silver *dirhams* or drachmas; but is is customary to fix it at Rs. I7. the dowry of Fatimah, the Prophet's favourite daughter, or at Rs. 50, that of the Prophet's wife, Ayesha. *Bomb. Gaz. Muh. Guj*. P. I66. The wedding is, however, usually accompanied by feasts and celebration not less elaborate or costly than those of the Hindus. Several Hindu ceremonies are also included, such as the anointing of the bride and bridegroom with oil and turmeric, and setting out earthen vessels, which are meant to afford a dwelling-place for the spirits of ancestors, at least among the lower classes. Op. cit p. 66. Another essential rite is the rubbing of the hands and feet of the bridegroom with *mehndi* or red henna. The marriage is usually arranged and a ceremony of betrothal held at least a year before it actually takes place.

"A husband can divorce his wife at pleasure by merely repeating the prescribed sentences. A wife can obtain divorce from her husband for impotence, madness, leprosy or non-payment of the dowry. A woman who is divorced can claim her dowry if it has not been paid. Polygamy is permitted among Muhammadans to the number of four wives, but it is very rare... Owing to the fact that members of the immigrant trading castes leave their wives at home in Gujarat, the number of married women returned at the census was substantially less than that of married men. A feeling in favour of the legal prohibition of polygamy is growing up among educated Muhammadans, and many of them sign a contract at marriage not to take a second wife during the lifetime of the first. There is no prohibition on the remarriage of widows in Muhammadan law, but the Hindu rule on the subject has had considerable influence, and some Muhammadans of good position object to the marriage of widows in their family. The customs of the seclusion of women also, as Mr. Marten points out, operates as a bar to a widow finding a husband for herself." They add.

References

1. Russell, R.V., and Lal, Hira, *The Tribes and Castes of the Central Provinces of India*, Low Price Publications, New Delhi (reprint) 1997, originally published MacMilan and co., London, 1916.
2. Enthoven, R.E., *The Tribes and Castes of Bombay*, Low Price Publications, Delhi (reprint) 1997, first published 1922.

3. Roy, Dr. Shivani, *Koli Culture*, Cosmo Publications, New Delhi, 1983.
4. Ghurye, G.S., *The Mahadev Kolis*, Popular Book Depot, Bombay, 1967.
5. Shah, P.G., *The Dublas of Gujarat*, Bharatiya Adimjati Sevak Sangh, Delhi, 1958.
6. Punekar, Vijay B., *The Son Kolis of Bombay*, Popular Book Depot, Bombay, 1959.
7. Shah, P.G., *Tribals Life in Gujarat*, Research Society, Bombay.

4

Marriage Ceremony

In the western region of India comprising Goa, Maharashtra, Gujarat, Daman and Diu and Dadra and Nagar Haveli, the marriage of a boy and a girl belonging to the same clan and sept usually does not take place and such marriages are considered by the society valid and lawful. The rules of exogamy is practised to certain prohibited degrees which vary according to the customs followed by the various communities. Child marriage was the traditional custom which has been replaced by adult marriage due to the spread of education prohibition by the law and changes in the social norms. Negotiations for marriage are started by the girl's party in higher Hindu castes, while among the *Scheduled Castes* and *Tribes* and *Muslims* the boy's parents make the approach. Both dowry and brideprice are practised among various communities in the region both in cash and in kind. Muslims have the practise of *mehar* (mehr) while the Christians have no such practise; *natra* (remarriage) is allowed among all the communities except the Brahmans, Salat, Sangharia, Baria and Bania. Divorce is also allowed to both men and women in all communities except among the Brahman, Vania, Sangharia and Baria as they consider marriage a sacrament. Marriage is settled by parents among all the communities except the Christians where they practise self-arranged marriages.

In a number of castes, *Sagai/Vevisar* (betrothal) is ceremonised one-to-three years prior to marriage solemnised at the bride's parental residence. Marriage is celebrated for three days and rituals are performed at both the places. The important rituals connected with marriage are *gharia* (rice powdering), rubbing of *pithee* on the bodies of both the bridegroom and the bride and erection of *mandva* or marriage booth and *deva* or *graha shanthi* (worship of clan deity) on the first day. The *jan* (marriage procession) arrives at the bride's village on the third day where marriage is to be solemnised. The main rituals connected with marriage ceremony are *jaimal, hartoda* (exchange of garland), *hast-milap* (joining of hands), *agniparikrama / saptapadi, chauri-ferwa* (making five or seven rounds of the holy fire lighted in *mandva*, and handing over the bride *kanyadan*. These rituals are conducted on the third day at night. The ritual called *Ana* (return of the bride) is performed after fifteen days to three months but this period varies in different communities. Feast, in the marriage, is given by the bride's parents. Marriage is consummated at the bridegroom's residence.

In most of communities in Daman and Diu and Gujarat, *Bithi chandla* or betrothal takes place after one month to one year prior to marriage at the bride's house. White dress is worn by the bride for marriage ceremony. The bridegroom wears coat, pant and black cap and bride wears white *saree* and blouse. After the arrival of the bridegroom alongwith the marriage party at the bride's residence, both sit on the chairs in front of the gathering. *Dasturs* (priests) from both the sides officiate the marriage ceremony. Parents or both the sides apply *tilla* (dot) on the forehead with the paste of *kanku*. The ritual of *Hast milap* (joining of hands) is conducted by the priest and *awastha* (their holy verses in Pasand language) and *ashirwad* (blessings in Sanskrit) are recited by the priest while sprinkling rice over the bride and the bridegroom and the couple receive pomegranate as a token of blessings. The bride's father presents *sambha* or dowry which includes clothing, cash and other valuable things as per economic status. The couple returns to bridegroom's village after some rituals according to Hindu customs are performed.

Visting Naik of Another Village

According to the enthological account given by Mr. R.E. Enthoven in *The Tribes and Castes of Bombay*, the marriage ceremonies of the Kolaba Katkaris are as follows : "The elders of the bridegroom's village take the boy to another Katkari hamlet. They call on the *Naik* and ask him if there is any marriageable girl there. The *Naik* asks who the boy is. He is produced and the party is invited to spend the night there. In the evening, the villagers are summoned and are informed of the object of the visit. The *Naik* invites any one who has a girl to give in marriage to speak. The father of a possible bride asks who that boy is. Again he is produced, and if he finds favour and there is no objection otherwise, the parent or guardian of the girl says so and agrees to give her in marriage. The girl is brought and shown to the strangers. If she finds favour, the boy's father distributes *pansupari*, which he has brought with him for the purpose. This ceremony being over, the bride's party ask for the usual betrothal money—generally one rupee, though in the case of the bridegroom's father being comparatively well-off, a larger sum might be given. The father of the bride is also asked to give his contribution to the betrothal money, which amounts to four annas as a rule for every rupee contributed by the bridegroom's father. The bride's father then asks if the wedding is to take place at once or the following year. If it is to be deferred, then they proceed to the ceremony of tying on the marriage necklace, for which a further contribution of two rupees is levied on the bridegroom's father. The visitors remain as guests for the following day and the ceremony of fastening the necklace takes place in the evening. The necklace is put into the boy's hands who fastens it on the girl's neck in the presence of the *panch*. The day after the bridegroom's party return home.

"If the wedding is to take place without delay, after the ceremony just described is over, the boy's father fixes the wedding day in consultation with the *panch*. The Katkaris do not consult Brahmans in these question. Anyone present who has a reputation for special knowledge of days and seasons may be consulted. The months for weddings are *Margashirsha*, *Magha*, *Vaishakh* and *Shimga*. Two days before the wedding day, the boy's father sends a messenger to the girl's parents to remind them and to tell them to put on the *halad* or turmeric powder. Afterwards, he takes five mango leaves and places them in a row. On each leaf he places a little turmeric powder, red powder, red lead and lampblack. He places these leaves in some spot outside the village, thereby propitiating the *vansh* or typical five ancestors of the tribe, whch is the custom of most primitive tribes.

"Then five girls are selected to apply the turmeric powder to the bridegroom, which they proceed to do, reserving half the quantity, which is sent with half a maund of rice, some salt and spices to the bride, who takes the gift from the messengers wth her own hands. On the next day the bridegroom's party sets out for the wedding, accompanied by musicians. On leaving the village a coconut is broken, and on reaching the bride's village, the bridegroom alights at the house of the headman or *Naik*. The bride's maternal aunt comes there with a present, and he gives her a small sum of money, from two to four annas. She accompanies him to the marriage pandal in front of the bride's dwelling, whither he is carried on someone's shoulder. The bride's brother is seated on the top of the pandal and, as the bridegroom is about to enter, he sprinkles him with water. The bridegroom gives him a small present of money, generally two pice, and enters. The bride is then brought out into the pandal and the couple are made to sit together.

"Preparations are then made for bathing. The bride is told to place her hand on the bridegroom's head. She then takes off her outer garments, and the two are made to stand opposite each other. The bridegroom places his left hand on the bride's head and as they stand in this position, five girls pour water over them. When the bathing is over, a cloth is held between them, and a new robe is put in the bridegroom's hand. He throws it to the bride and says, 'take it'. She throws it back to him and says, 'it is not enough'. Again he throws it to her, saying, it is very big: there is enough and to spare'.

"The bride then goes into the house, puts on the robe and comes out to sit beside the bridegroom. Then five married women sit down in front of them. In their hands, they hold a betelnut, a pice, and some rice, with which they make a circle on the ground. On this a brass tray is placed and rubbed backwards and forwards until the rice, pice and betelnuts are mixed up, and the shape of the figure is gone. The bride and bridegroom are then told to grasp their great toes. The five men lift them up in this position and deposit them on the rice. The bridemaids place the brass tray behind the bride. The men then throw rice on the heads of the couple and what is left is thrown into the tray. Of the money, three pice are given to the bride and two pice to the bridegroom. When this is done, the marriage ceremony is complete.

"Following this, however, the bridegroom has to fasten a necklance of black beads on the bride's neck. Two balls of rice are then made, and one is given to each. The bridegroom puts this in his mouth, takes it out again immediately, and gives it to the bride to eat. She gives her ball of rice to him, which he eats. The pair then put some more turmeric powder on each other's faces and repeat each other's names, always a source of amusement owing to the reluctance of the bride to pronounce her husband's name in public.

"Next day the married couple go to the bridegroom's village, escorted by a party of musicians. The headman comes out to meet them, ties a little money, a betelnut and some rice in a corner of the husband's cloth, and again tying this to a corner of the bride's robe, accompanies them round the village, where they visit each house in turn.

"The day after, the bridegroom bathes the bride, and washes off the turmeric powder. Before entering the house again, the bridegroom's sister puts a bar across the door and they have to remain without. He asks his sister why she is keeping him there. She replies, 'You must give your daughter to my son'. The bridegroom says to the bride, 'She asks for our daughter. Shall we give her?' The bride says, 'Yes. The bridegroom tells his sister that they agree to give their daughter to her son, and then, withdrawing the bar, she lets them in.

"Afterwards they take off the bride and bridegroom's *bashings* or marriage coronets and fasten them on the bridegroom's head back and front. The headman goes out of the village and the bride and bridegroom, following him, ask, 'Whether are you going?'. He replies, 'To Banaras'. They beg him not to go and return home. They all come back. The *bashings* are taken from the bridegroom and placed in the bride's hands. He then lifts her up and carries her to the house. For five days, the couple remain, at home. On the sixth day, they prepare balls of rice flour which they cook. Of these the bride breaks one, which they share. The remainder are sent to the bride's parents, who distribute them one to each household. This terminates the marriage ceremonies.

"The remarriage of widows is permitted. A widow cannot marry her mother's sister's or mother's brother's son or a member of her late husband's section. A widow remarriage can be celebrated on any day. The widow's intended husband presents her with a robe and bodice and glass bangles and her father with Rs 2 or 3, if he can afford it. Next, he ties a *mithla* (a neck ornament) round the widow's neck and the widow puts a turban over his head, which completes the ceremony. In some places, the ceremony consists simply in holding a meeting of the tribesmen at night and in treating them to liquor, while in other places, joining the hands of the couple is sufficient to validate the marriage.

"Should a bachelor desire to marry a widow, he has first to marry a *rui* bush (*Calotropis gigantea*). This ceremony consists in the bachelor putting a marriage coronet on his head and going round the bush five times. As he walks, he passes a cotton thread round the tree. In some places, bachelors are allowed to marry widows without any ceremony," adds Mr. Enthoven. The custom, rites and rituals are pertinent to the Katkari Tribals.

Marriage Proposal Comes from Boy's Side

According to the *Bombay Gazetteer*, Vol. XVIII, "Marriages are prohibited between member of the same *kul* and *devak*. In some places however sameness of *kul* alone is considered a bar to intermarriage. A Maratha Kunbi cannot marry his mother's sister's daughter. He may marry his father's sister's or mother's brother's daughter. Marriage with a wife's sister is allowed after the death of the wife. Brothers are allowed to marry sisters. Polygamy is allowed and practised, but polyandry is unknown. Girls are generally married between the age of three to twelve years and boys between the age of sixteen to twenty-five years. Girls can be married even after they attain puberty. Widows are generally allowed to marry, but some families consider widow-marriage disreputable and do not practice it. As a rule, only widowers marry widows, and the children do not get so large a share of the property as those of first marriages. Divorce is allowed. Divorced women can marry again by the widow re-marriage form.

"As a rule, the proposals of marriage come from the boy's parents. Before accepting the offer the boy's father makes a full enquiry regarding the surname, family, and relations of the girl's father. When he is satisfied on these points, the boy's father goes with friends and kinsfolk to the girl's marks her brow with redpowder, touches her brow with a rupee, and lays the rupee in her hands. The girl is given a small robe, a bodice, and some ornaments, and her grandmother and maternal uncle's wife are presented with two robes. The girl's father asks the boy's father and his kinsfolk, and his own friends and kinspeople, to a feast of cakes or *polis* either stuffed or unstuffed. When the feast is over, a Brahman is called to fix the marriage day and is paid by both fathers. If the girl's father is poor, he takes Rs 100 to Rs 150 as her price; if he is rich, he gives Rs 50 to Rs 100 as her dowry. Before the marriage in front of both the boy's and girl's houses, a marriage porch is built, and in the girl's marriage porch is set an earthen altar or *bahule*. The *muhuria-medha* or auspicious post of the marriage booth is planted on the marriage day. Supplies of clothes, grain, oil and other articles are also laid in. Not more than five days before the marriage, the bride and bridegroom are rubbed with turmeric powder. Three or four unwidowed women grind this turmeric in a handmill, and to the handle, in a yellow cloth, are tied a betelnut and three or four sprouted turmeric roots. In country parts, except the headman and other *mankaris* or honourables, most of the men of the village take part in the turmeric grinding, sitting four or five at a handmill. They sing the women's corn-grinding songs. These handmills are not used till the marriage ceremony is over. On the morning of the marriage day, a low wooden stool is set in the doorway and round the stool *five* metal water pots for bathing are arranged and a thread is passed *five* times round them. Some betelnuts and a few grains of rose are laid in the girl's hands, and a metal pot filled with cold water is laid in the hand of the bridesmaid, or *karavli*, and the two go round the pots *five* times. Then the bridesmaid, walking behind the girl, pours a little water on the low wooden stool and the girl *five* times drops a few grains of rice on the water, and setting first her right foot and then her left foot on the stool, sits on it. Her head is rubbed with oil and she is bathed. Meanwhile, the girl bathes five little children who stand in front of her, and the musicians from time to time play their pipes. When all the children have been bathed, the girl's mother comes forward and baths her daughter sitting close to her on the low wooden stool, is bathed. When the bath is over, she is presented with a robe and bodice, and if she is not a widow, her arms are rubbed with turmeric, red powder is rubbed on her brow, and a coconut and rice are laid in her lap. The girl is dressed in a robe and green bodice and her clothes are stained with wet turmeric, her forehead is daubed with red powder and rice, her cheek and the space between the eyebrows are marked with soot, and in her lap are laid a coconut, *five* dry cocoa-kernels, *five* betelnuts, *five* turmeric roots, and some grains of wheat or rice. After this a chaplet, either of flowers or of tinsel, is tied round her brow and her head is covered with her husband's blanket. Without letting the cotton thread that encircles them touch the four women standing with water-pots in their hands, a fifth loosens one end of the thread and ties it to the *muhurtamedha* and plants the post on one side of the doorway. By this time, at the boy's house, the Brahman priest has come, and is given a coconut, pieces of cocoa karnel, thread, turmeric, a piece of yellow cloth, a winnowing fan and rice. The priest sets two lighted lamps on a low wooden stool, and between the two lamps, sets a bathing tub or *ghangal*. He picks up a winnowing fan, lays grain of rice in it, and filling a metal water-pot with cold water, sets it on the rice. He spreads a few mango leaves on the water-pot or sets a coconut on it. He ties in a yellow cloth a few grains of rice, and some betelnut and turmeric. He daubs the bundle with red powder and lays it in the winnowing fan, beside the water-pot. The priest opens his almanac at a picture of Ganpati, tells the host to worship the picture, repeats verses, and the host sprinkles over the picture sandalwood, rice and red and scented powder, lays betelnut and leaves and a copper coin before it, offers it sugar and bows to it. When the worship of Ganpati is over, the priest rolls up his almanac and lays it beside him. Then, after worshipping the winnowing fan and its contents and seeing that it is put in a safe place, the priest goes home. A near relation of the girl, taking turmeric powder and accompanied by music, goes to the boy's house, makes over the turmeric to the people of the house and returns. The boy is seated on a low wooden stool in the midst of the *five* earthen pots, bathed, and dressed in a new waist-cloth, a turban and a shoulder-cloth. His forehead, like the girl's forehead, is marked with red power, and over the powder a few grains of rice are stuck. A tinsel chaplet is tied to his brow, and, as at the girl's house, the thread that was wound round the earthen pots is tied to the *muhurtamedha*. The village barbers lay a cloth on the grinding stone or *pata*, and worship it by laying grains of rice before it. To the wooden pestle or *musal* are then tied a betel leaf, a millet stalk, and a needle, and it is set in the mortar. The women of the house seat the boy in front of the mortar on a low wooden stool, take coconut oil in a metal cup and, dipping mango leaves in the oil, allows it to drop on his head. The washerwoman, holding the pestle her left hand, stands in front of the boy singing songs. A chaplet of flowers, a coconut, and a few grains of wet pulse are sent to the village god with the prayer that he may be kind that the marriage ceremony may pass without mishap and that he may give the marriage guests a safe return to their homes. When this is over, the guests are treated to a dinner. During the two or three days, after the boy has been rubbed with turmeric, friends and kinspeople ask him to dine, and when he goes young girls sometimes go with him. If one of the friends is wealthy, he invites the boy and all the members of the boy's family to his house with musicians playing before them, feasts them on cakes and *polis*, and hangs flower garlands or *mundavals* round the boy's head. If the houses of the bride and bridegroom are in the same village or town, installation of the *devak* is held on the marriage day. If the boy and girl live in different places, then the worship is held two or three days before the marriage. In installing the *devak,* the first step is to worship the house gods. After the house gods have been worshipped, a near kinsman of the boy's father and his wife have the skirts of their garments tied together, and, under a waist-cloth held over their heads by four persons, go, preceded by musicians, to the village Maruti. The husband carries on his shoulder an axe or some other iron field tool and a rope twelve to fifteen feet long, and his wife walks close behind him carrying a platter with the family *devak* and an offering of food. Behind the pair walk four or five unwidowed women, each carrying a brass water cup, filled with water. At Maruti's temple, the Gurav or ministrant has supply of *panch palvi* or springs of *five* trees, the mango, the *rui* (Calotropis gigantea), the *saundad* or *shami* (Prosopis spicigera), the Indian fig or *vad* and the *jambhul* (Eugenia jambolana). These five trees or shrubs vary, the mango, *rui* and banyan (*vad*) being frequently used, but the *kadamba* (Anthocephalus cadumba), the *bel* (*egle* marmelos), the say Indian teak and *pipal* (Ficus religiosa) being sometimes included in place of others mentioned in the text.

"The party bow before the god and lay sandal, flowers, frankincense, and food before him, and the ministrant presents them with the five sprigs or *panch palvis*. On their return to their house, they tie the five sprigs to a pole in the marriage porch and along with the sprigs tie a cake or *poli* and the spiced gram relish called *besan*, which is eaten with bread. On this day, some ten to twenty friends and kinspeople are asked to a feast of unstuffed cakes. They sit on square blankets and after the serving of betel withdraw. When the guests are gone, the women of the house sit on the bare ground and eat. When a marriage party has to go to a distant village, they travel in bullock carts with music. On reaching the boundary of the girl's village or town, water is fetched and poured on the boundary by a Koli of the place, who is given a coconut and occasionally a turban. In some places, a lemon is cut, waved round the boy's head, and thrown away, and his eyes are touched with cold water or soot. On entering the village, if he has not ridden the whole way, the bridegroom mounts a horse and goes to the village Maruti with music, and halts there with his sisters or other young girls who are called *karavlis* or groom's maids. In the village, the girl's father provides for a lodging facility or *janvasghar* for the boy's party. In the evening, from Maruti's temple, the bridegroom's brother or other near relation, called the *vardhava* or groom-seat, mounts a horse and, with friends and music, goes to the bride's village. On reaching the bride's village, her father asks him to dine, and, if he is rich, gives him a turban. When the groom-sent has taken some food, the bride's father gives him, for the bridegroom, a tinsel, chaplet, a turban, a red chintz overcoat, a pair of waist-cloths, a pair of shoes and a shoulder-cloth. The harbinger mounts his horse and starts for Maruti's temple with the bride's father and some of the bride's kinsmen, who carry *five* bodice-banners or *dhvajas* tied to poles and held over his head, and followed by a married unwidowed woman, with a coconut and betel-leaves in a platter. As he goes, the bride's brother pelts him with onions. At Maruti's temple, the bride's father lays the platter with the dress before the bridegroom. A Brahman priest, who is in attendance, tells the bridegroom to wash his eyes with water, loosens the brocaded end of the bridegroom's turban, and winds it twice or thrice round the bridegroom's neck. He sets up a betelnut Ganpati and tells the bridegroom to wash it and lay sandal-powder and flowers before it. After this the priest touches the new clothes with turmeric powder, marks the bridegroom's brow with sandal-powder, and gives him the clothes. If the bridegroom's old turban is of little value, it is given to the barber who is to lead his horse; if the turban is of high value, the barber is given a coconut. Betel leaves are handed to all present and money is given to the Brahman. The bridegroom's left cheek is touched with lampblack. He lays before Maruti two betel leaves, a betelnut, and a copper coin and walks round him. He carries a dagger or poniard with a lemon stuck on its point. Before starting for the bride's, a coconut is broken at the village gate to keep off evil influences and given to the Mahars. The village Mahar stands before the bridegroom as if to stop him and is given a white turban or shoulder-cloth worth 25p to 50p. When he reaches the bride's house, a Mahar woman comes with an iron lamp in a platter and waves it round his head, saying, 'May all your pains and troubles vanish and the riches of Bali be poured on you.' For this she is given a cheap bodice cloth. Near the door of the bride's house the wife of her maternal uncle waves round the bridegroom's head a lighted lamp of wheaten flour with two wheat flour balls at its sides and is given a bodice and a robe. This lamp-waving is called *varovalni* or the bridegroom-waving. The boys' party are seated in the marriage porch, and the bridegroom is made to stand near the earth altar in the centre of which is placed a mango sprig stuck in a ball of mud and at each corner a cloured earthern pot called *vahi*. The bride is carried out of the house and set in front of the bridegroom facing him. The priest and some begging Brahmans come forward and divide into two parties. A cloth or *antarpat* is held between the bride and bridegroom, so that they cannot see each other's faces. They touch finger tips with the cloth between them. The two parties of Brahmans hand the guests turmeric or red-coloured rice or millet to throw on the heads of the bride and bridegroom. The two parties of priests in turn recite *mangalashtaks* or lucky verses, at the end of each verse throwing some cloured grains on the heads of the pair, and the guests, like the Brahmans at the end of each verse, throw coloured grains. When the verses are over, the Brahmans clap their hands and the guests clap their hands, and musicians raise a din of music. Shortly after the maternal uncles of the bride and bridegroom sit on stools with the bride and bridegroom on their knees and with their faces turned to each other. The priest tells the bride and bridegroom to fold their hands and touch finger tips, while he winds a yellow thread round their necks. This ceremony is called *sutavane* or thread-winding. When they are thus seated, the girl-giving or *kanyadan* is performed by the bride's maternal uncle, or, in his absence, by her father. When he gives her away, the uncle presents the girl with copper vessels according to his means. The priest, muttering some verses, cuts the yellow thread that was passed round the pair's necks and tells them to sit on the altar or *bahule*. The bride sits on the bridegroom's left. In front of the pair a burnt offering is made, called *lajahom* of clarified butter, pieces of wood and fried rice. A winnowing-fan with rice, split pulse, wafer biscuits, fried rice cakes and vermicelli is laid before the bridegroom. The priest suddenly puts his hand over one of the articles on the fan and asks the bridegroom to say what he has hid. If the bridegroom guesses right, the priest says that his patron has got an intelligent son-in-law; if he answers wrong, he calls him a dull fellow. After this a low stool, covered with wheat flour and with lines drawn on it, is set before the bride and bridegroom, and they are told to say each other's name, money is given to the Brahman, and he retires. On the same day, after the marriage is over, a party from the bride's go to the village Maruti, and, with the same rites as those described in the case of the bridegroom's party, bring and tie in the marriage porch the bride's father's *devak* or marriage guardian. After the bride's *devak* has been installed, a party of the bride's kinswomen got in procession to the bridegroom, with platters full of fried rice, cakes and rice vermicelli or *shevya*. They are received with honour and are given turmeric and red powder. They empty their platters, and in return, in one of them, the bridegroom's kinswomen put 50p to Rs 10 in cash. This food-gift to the bridegroom is called *rukhvat*. Then some of the bride's near kinsmen with music go to ask kinsmen to dine, and bring them home with music, and in the same way the women of the bride's family bring kinswomen. The relations are feasted on unstuffed cakes or *polis*, rice, split pulse, *alan* or boiled rice flour, seasoned with spices, and fried rice cakes. Early next morning, with music and friends, the bride and bridegroom seated on a horse, the bride in front, are taken to a river or garden and, after retiring, have their feet rubbed with wet turmeric powder and oiled red powder, and return with music. About then, the boy and girl are bathed on low stools in the booth. Round the bathing place are set five *tambyas* or cooper drinking pots with a white thread passed round their necks. At the time of bathing, the bridegroom is seated on a low stool and the bride on another low stool or a large platter. While bathing they fill their mouths with water and blow it over each other's faces. The boy holds a betelnut in his hand and the girl using both her hands tries to force it out; then the girl holds the nut and the boy tries to force it out with his left hand. If the boy fails the guests jeer at him calling him *bulga* or impotent. When the bathing is over, the bridegroom tries to lift the bride by his left hand and set her at his left side while the bride tries to prevent him lifting her from the ground. These struggles greatly amuse the guests and relations. The boy and girl are then dressed and their brows are rubbed with red powder and their bodies with turmeric. They are given a dish of *shevya*, that is milk, clarified butter, rice vermicelli, and raw sugar, and feed each other. After dinner they sit on the altar in the booth. In the evening the bride's father gives a caste feast, and on one of the days the boy's father treat the caste to rice, split pulse, vegetables, and unsuffed cakes or *polis*. On this day or, if this is not a lucky day, then on the next, the bride's lap is filled. The priest folds a waist-cloth four times, covers it with rice or wheat grains, and tells the bride and bridegroom to sit on it. While the priest chants verses, the bridegroom fills the bride's lap with *five* half cocoa-kernels, *five* dates, *five* sprouted turmeric roots, *five* betelnuts, a quarter of a pound of rice, a comb, a small casket, and a variously coloured cord. The bridegroom's father presents the bride with coloured cord. The bridegroom's father presents the bride with what he can afford and the guests present the fathers of the bride and bridegroom with clothes or cash of 50p or more. These presents are called *aher*. After this the twelve *balutedars* or village servants come in and according to his means, the boy's father gives their wives bodies-clothes or cash. If he is rich, he gives the headman or *patil* a turban. In the evening, the bride's and bridegroom's skirts are tied together and they walk to the bridegroom's house or lodging. After lamplight, the bridegroom's mother, with a band of kinspeople, walks towards the bride's, on cloths spread by the village washerman, and at the same time the bride's mother starts with a band of friends to visit the boy's mother. When the parties meet, they stop ten or fifteen paces from each other. A waist-cloth is held in front of each party and they begin throwing red powder on one another. They jest with one another showing in front of the cloth a ladle, a rolling-pin, a dog or a cat. While this is going on, the bridegroom and his mother pretend to be offended and leave the party. The bride's father and mother follow them and appease them with presents. Then the two parties move on to the bride's where the bridegroom's mother is seated in the booth on a three-legged stool. Round her are arranged *five* metal drinking pots or *tambyas* with a thread passed round their necks, and the boy girl are seated on her lap. *Five* women of the bride's family wash the feet of the bridegroom's mother. The bride's father gives a robe to the bridegroom's mother and the bridegroom's father gives a robe to the bride's mother. This interchange of robes is called *potjhakni* or stomacher. While the bridegroom's mother is seated on the stool, the *jhal* or hanging ceremony is performed. A bamboo basket or round metal dish with a comb, a looking-glass, a basket, a rolling-pin, *five* sweet things and *five* wheat flour lamps is set on the bridegroom's mother's head, and four or five women stand about her and sing the *jhal* song which runs, 'The bridegroom has reached the village boundary, I will worship the boundary and win the bridegroom'. Meanwhile a kinsman of the bridegroom's runs away with the basket or dish to the bridegroom's and is pursued and pelted with onions by the bride's people. The bride's father, mother and other near relatives hold the bride and seated on their crossed hands set her on her husband's lap and then on the laps of his father, mother and other near relatives. At the time of handing her over, the girl's relatives with sobs and tears say, 'Up to this time she was ours, now she is yours.' This ceremony is seldom over till the morning cock-crow, and, after it is over sometimes as late as five, they sit to a feast. When the feast is over, the bride and bridegroom are led into the god-house and bow before the images. As he bows, the bridegroom steals one of the gods and refuses to give it until the bride's father makes him a present. All then go to the bridegroom's. In the evening, the bridegroom's father gives betel leaves with nuts to the guests and bids them good-bye. If the bridegroom belongs to another village, the guests, who belong to his village, accompany him home. When they reach the village the bride and bridegroom, are taken to the temple of the village Maruti. In the evening, at about seven or eight, the bride and bridegroom are seated on a horse and led to his house with a procession, music, and, if they can afford them, fireworks. In the house a dish with coconuts, saffron, and betel leaves is waved round the image of Khandoba, a ceremony which is called the lifting of Khandoba's *tali* or plate. After the plate-waving, comes the *jhenda nachne* or flag-dance when one man sets the bride on his back and another sets the bridegroom on his back and they dance. Sometimes the bride sits on the bridegroom's back and a man dances with both on his back. After the dance, the bridegroom, holding the full box of a seed drill in his hand, sprinkles grain on the ground as if sowing, and along with the bride, who carries resin in her hand, goes to the god-room. At the door of the god room they find the boy's sister, who refuses to let them pass till they promise to give their first daughter in marriage to her son. They agree though the promise is practically never kept, and pass in, and laying a betelnut and copper coin before them, bow to the house gods. The girl is considered the goddess of wealth and her brow is marked with redpowder. Some wheat with a piece of gold in it is heaped between the bride and bridegroom and they are told to divide the heap. If the bride gets the gold in her half she is applauded, and it is taken as an omen that the rule in the house will be hers. On the next or some other lucky day, the bride and bridegroom are bathed and the turmeric is taken off. If the boy's mother can afford it, then she feeds them on boiled rice and clarified butter for another fourteen days. (*Bombay Gazetteer*, Vol. XVIII, Part I, pp. 300-307).

Custom of Simant Poojan

The actual Chitpavan Brahman marriage with a lengthy procedure consists of numerous steps. *Simant poojan* is one of them, which is mainly the reception of the bridegroom at the entrance of the town by the bride's side. Now it is performed at the residence of the bride. The bride is brought to the marriage hall by her maternal uncle. Similarly, the bridegroom is also ushered by his maternal uncle, to the same place and both the bride and the bridegroom are asked to stand face to face on their wooden seats (*patt*). A mixture of rice grains, cummin seeds (*jira*) and sugar is given to both. The maternal uncles of both the bride and the bridegroom stand behind them. The priest stands on either side of the curtain called *antarpat* and asks the pair to look at the lucky symbol *swastika* and pray to their family deity. He then starts reciting the *mangalashtak*. The persons who are attending the marriage, throw rice mixed with vermillion called *akshata* on the couple by way of blessing them. After the *mangalashtak* is over, the curtain is removed by the priest. The bride and the bride-groom then put their garlands on one another's neck. The womenfolk take active part in the marriage ceremony. After *mangalashtak*, the bride-groom puts *mangalsutra* in the neck of the bride. They perform the *kanyadan* ceremony on this occasion. The hands of the bride and bride-groom are joined by the girl's father over an auspicious pot of bell-metal and the girl's mother pours water over the hands. This is called *kanyadan*.

Another ceremony at this stage of the marriage is *lajjahom*. The last step of the function is *saptapadi*. At this time, the bride and the bride-groom walk around the sacred fire seven times making the marriage irrevocable. The marriage symbol of the Chitpavan woman is *mangalsutra* and green bangles. Residence after marriage is patrilocal, after marriage the bride goes to the bridegroom's house to live there. Sometimes, formation of neolocal residence is set up if the bride cannot harmonize with the parents of the husband. Dowry system exists, but is not rigid. Divorce among them is allowed. If the spouses are not willing to live together or if it is proved that there are justifiable reasons, such as cruelty, adultery or impotence etc. A divorcee can remarry.

The customs, rites and rituals are prevalent among the Chitpavan Brahmans in Goa.

Marriage to be performed with Permission of Church

It is the strict customs of the Catholic marriage system that the marriage should be performed with permission of the church priest. The Catholics observe the rules of monogamy and marry among themselves only. Marriage is usually negotiated within their own persuasion when the boys and girls reach the adult age varying from 28 years to 35 years for boys and 22 years to 25 years for girls. If one of the couple is not Catholic, the non-Catholic one should be baptized first, before the marriage is solemnized in church. Both cross-cousin and parallel cousin marriages are allowed but the cross-cousin marriage among the Catholics of Goa is preferable, as it is largely prevalent among the Hindus of the Konkan region. Junior sororate is allowed after the death of the wife. Levirate is also allowed, but is very rare among the higher caste Catholics. Under the Portuguese Civil Code, the rule of monogamy was imperative for all, whether Hindus, Christians or Muslims, and all the marriages were to be registered in the Civil Registration Office situated in the headquarters of every county in Goa. The Catholics of Goa observe this rule strictly even todays as a customery law.

The wedding ring is the symbol of the Christian marriage. Divorce is allowed but it should be certified by the church as well as by the Civil Court. The decision about the maintenance and other liabilities of the children after divorce should be taken either by the church or by the court. The widow, widower and divorcee can remarry. But, in case of a widow remarriage, the bride cannot put on white garments, when her subsequent marriage is solemnized. They generally wear pink, lemon or any other light coloured flowing wedding robe. Dowry is given either in cash or in kind specially among the higher caste Catholics. They follow the patrilocal rule of residence.

FINDING SUITABLE MATCH

Sunni Marriage

In past, among the Sunni sect, as the rest other Muslims, polygyny was permitted but now monogamy is the rule. Cross-cousin and parallel-cousin marriages are permitted. Child marriage is not performed in their society. The age of marriage varies from 18 to 23 for the girls and from 23 to 28 years for the boys. Generally marriage is settled by negotiation between the parents. When a girl's father finds a suitable match for his daughter, he approaches the boy's father with the marriage proposal. The boy's father is requested to approve the girl for his son. If the girl is found suitable, they fix a date of marriage with the consultation of the priest, *kazi*. Earlier, marriage used to be performed at the bride's residence but now. It is generally conducted in a common hall and the expenditure involved in the marriage ceremony is borne by both the parties. The marriage is performed according to time or *ghadi* and is held during the day only. The *kazi* is consulted for the auspicious hour. At the time of marriage, when the bridegroom comes alongwith his kins and friends to the wedding place, he is received by the bride's father and relatives.

The bride's and bridegroom's party sit separately leaving some space between them. Three seats are kept reserved, one for the bridegroom, the second for the Muslim *kazi* and the third for the *kazi's* deputy for registration of marriage. The Registrar charges a fee called *jamat* from both the parties. An agreement form is signed by the bride, bridegroom and their witnesses and the amount of the money *mehar* which is give by the bridegroom to the bride, at the time of marriage, is fixed. At the departure of the bride and bridegroom, the parents of the former come and offer their daughter to the care of the bridegroom. This system is called *jalwa*. Blackbeads studded with gold *lachcha* are the marriage symbol of the Muslim woman. Residence after marriage is patrilocal, *i.e.,* the bride after marriage goes to bridegroom's house to live there with his family. Divorce is permitted which is called *talaq*, uttered three times before it is enforced according to the Islamic customary law. However, there should be adequate reasons to take divorce. The reasons may be barrenness, cruelty, adultery, impotence and insanity, etc. A divorcee, widow or widower are free to remarry.

Custom of Monogamy

Thus the prevalent form of marriage in Goa state is monogamy, a condition in which one man is married to one woman. Among the Christians, if the proposal was found to the liking of the bridegroom's elders, *Soirik Korunk* (arrange of alliance) or rather entering the preliminary talks concerning a marriage alliance. If the girl finds acceptance in the eyes of visitor, a sweetmeat or some article of value like a wrist-watch or dress piece or gold ornaments brought by the bridegroom's party, is gifted to the bride-to be, signifying the acceptance of the proposal. For the Christians, the church has prescribed a brief course or instruction to be taken by the prospective bridegroom and bride at the church or at the pastoral institute Pius-x at old Goa. Among *Sudras*, there was the practice of the bridegroom to be, to take away the handkerchief and soap kept for him, being a sign of acceptance of the proposal. Later a ring was sent for the engagement.

Among the Goan Hindus, marriage within the same '*gotra*' are not permitted. If the '*gotra*' happens to be the same for the bridegroom and bride and it is still every one's wish that the concerned marriage should take place, then the marriage ceremony is gone through by a special ritual called *Dattak Vidhan* or adoption of the bride and her 'gotra' changed.

The betrothal ceremony is called *Mudi* (literally the ring), it is same for Hindus and Christians. The engagement ceremony among the Muslims is called *Mangani*.

For the bride, the bangle-wearing ceremony that is held once in her life time to be is called the *Chuddo*. The bangles symbolise married life for the bride, as they are broken only on her dead husband's coffin. The *Chuddo* among the upper castes consists of a set of seven glass bangles of a green colour on each wrist. Among the lower castes, the bangles are of the seven colours of rainbow. This ceremony is conducted on the eve of marriage or a day or two days before, at the house of bride's maternal uncle. Generally, these bangles are put on her hand by the bangle seller. Other relatives and those present at the ceremony are also given by him a pair or more of their choice free of cost.

The women of the family and relatives sing songs all the while which are typical and appropriate to the occasion. Offerings of money in token of blessing are put in a tray placed before the bangle seller. The money collected thus is taken by the bangle-seller over and above the payment that he gets for the work done. Many women are experts in singing in parables and pointed metaphor in the form of *Zotis* as well as throwing aside all taunts to them and other people, *i.e.,* relatives. Next, the maternal uncles sends the niece home with a *vojem* (a parcel in a big special type of bamboo woven basket) containing sweet meats, bananas, bread–twelve each in number. This gift is known as Perkund. Similar Perkunds without the festive bangle are made when other relatives invite her at their place for lunch or dinner of farewell. She receives a special bunch of flowers from her uncle and others during the ceremony.

Even if the bride's parents do not happen to be on speaking terms with the maternal uncle or relatives, she has to go and obtain at least water from their well. If they have no well or it is not possible to get water from there, then some water has to be obtained by the bride from their house. Relatives visit the two houses of the bride and of the bridegroom, with flowers and other gifts. Special 'fole' cakes made of rice-flour stuffed with shredded coconut mixed with jaggery, cupped into a wrapping of jack fruit tree leaves and pinned by a thin stick-pin are served at the maternal uncle's house in the feast or it may be '*mankeo*' something like dosas stuffed with coconut-shredding and jaggery. The *Chuddo* ceremony is same for both Hindus and Muslims converts. The 'Saddo' a variant of the saree is a special dress, usually flowery or plain red or pink, worn by the bride in the house at the wedding day after the main function is over. It is given by the maternal uncle to the bride among Hindus and Christians. The Muslims have no such practice.

On the day prior to the marriage, the bridegroom sits on a ceremonial stool or chair at home and the family barber, gives him hair cut. Songs are sung on the occasion and friends and relatives gather to witness it. The barber is paid a handsome amount in cash as well as the presents in the form of coconut and a measure of rice and sweetmeats. This ceremony is conducted prior to the bath with coconut-pulp, juice or milk held among all communities. The bath with coconut water pulp and is held thus: Among Christians, on the evening preceding the wedding day, the bride at her place and the bridegroom at his take a ceremonial bath with coconut pulp-juice or milk. It starts with applying ceremonially to the accompaniment of special verses called *Zotis*, peculiar to the occasion, sung by trained women. On the head or a part of the body of the bride or bridegroom, clad in bathing dress, at his/her own place, a tumbler full or cup full of juice extracted from coconut-shredded pulp kept in a pot is applied by relatives in a proper order of priority, followed by friends. This is done first, outside the bathing room, in the hall. In the second part of the bathing ceremony, a bath with water possibly warm is taken in the bathroom, again in a ceremonial manner, with songs being sung in a group of relatives and friends. After bathing with a tumbler of water, a few coins are dropped into the pot of water, kept for the purpose. All the money dropped into the pots is taken by the maids who helped or were called for preparing the bath water and coconut pulp juice.

The Goan Hindus, too, have a similar bath but not so elaborate. They have an additional application of turmeric (halad) and mustard oil on the body of the bride. The Muslims, do not have this practice.

Among Gaon Catholic Christians, a lavish feast called the Beggar's lunch or Bhick Reamfevon is performed a day or two before the wedding day, preferably on a Tuesday. Seven or nine poor people, both men and women, are treated to a sumptuous lunch with pork, beef, fish, rice and a special curry called *samrachi koddi*. They sat squat on the floor mat and specially prepared jack fruit tree leaves, well plaited into plates, are placed before them into which food is served or ladled out by the bride and bridegroom at each one's place of residence. The main object behind the service is to feed and satisfy the manes of ancestors on this auspicious occasion in their house through the medium of these beggars. Coconut oil is also given for their hair and a bidi or cigarette, according to the preference expressed by them. They are also given a sweet dish of gram dal and *soji* a sweet composed of wheat preparation and bananas. Instead of coconut-feni, a sweet wine could also be served to the destitutes.

The wedding ceremony in proper Goa does not take place on Thursdays and Fridays in the normal course. On the wedding day, the bridegroom's sister and another close relative go with the bride's dress and assorted materials and dress her up. The wedding ceremony of Goa is the same as all over Christian dom in the world. There will be a wedding dance function in the hall. After the dance function is over, the whole group of the marriage party or part of it that remains to the end.

The groom's side cross over a line of demarcation, imaginary but conventionally drawn called '*shim*' (literally, boundary line in Konkani), the bride's guests remaining on the hither side of the boundary. The boundary being normally the place where the roads going towards the residence of the spouses part from each other in a fork. Here a prayer is said and a wish is expressed for the prosperity and happiness of the married couple. Some liquor from a bottle brought by the bridegroom's or bride's side is taken in little cupfuls by the guests and without crossing the boundary line. At this time of pouring the liquor, the *shim* should not be crossed, until this brief ritual is over. Later one or two relatives from the bride's side come and cross the '*shim*' to formally invite the bridal couple to the bride's place which in Konkani is called '*Apovnnem*' (invitation) for the return of the couple on the next day for what is known as the *Portovnnem* (ceremonial return). This practice of pouring the liquor and observing the shim is being given up now.

Among the Hindus, at both houses, the priest is called to perform the *punnyavaham* and *nandhishradha* readings in the presence of the groom/bride and their parents. Then oil and turmeric are applied to them after which they take bath from a water barrel placed there for the purpose. Married women with husbands living or *sovashnni* go with oil and turmeric from bride to bridegroom and vice versa. The wedding ritual is held at the bride's place where the maternal uncle takes the lead in the ceremonies. At the groom's place, the groom's married sister ties the wedding turban called the bashing. Then the marriage procession sets out, with the bridegroom's sister carrying a pot with mango leaves placed on a coconut. Another sister carries a wicker basket with a lighted lamp, followed by the bridegroom in his full regalia. He is received at the bride's place ceremonially and led into the marriage chamber where the sacramental ceremony is performed by the priest.

Among the Christians, the day following the wedding, at the bridegroom's place a brief ceremony of wearing the bangles is held at the home by the bangle-vendor of the village. They are put on the wrist of the bride. The vendor is later given a coconut, a measure of rice and payment in cash for his services. At the bridegroom's place, in the morning, following the wedding day, a session of ceremonial blessing in kind is held. In that session, close relatives, from the mother-in-law of the bride onwards, give presents in the form of gold ornaments to the bride. This was done earlier to the accompaniment of songs, verses and prayers.

Later for the lunch, the bride and bridegroom with a small retinue of close relatives go to the bride's parental place. They are received at the bride's place ceremoniously and there may be a dance or simply a litany (ladin) in thanks giving and a small party and service of drinks and food.

On this occasion, at the bride's place in Goa, is also held the 'folle-fevonn' a sumptuous bride for close relatives. After this feast, the bride and bridegroom among the high caste and wealthy people used to go sitting in a machila (palanquin) led by boias (bearers) along with a red coloured rush-mat or floor-mat with a '*vojem*', a parcel of sweetmeats, bananas, etc., to accompany them to the bridegroom's place of residence.

On the day following the wedding day, *among the Sudras*, a group of masked friends from the bridegroom's side comes to the bride's place along with their retinue. They sing songs and wash the feet of the bridal couple who tip them liberally. A ceremony called '*Tollvar*' sitting was held consisting of *kurponn* (mat of bamboo placed on the pot of rice while draining water from it) and turbaned men approach the married couple with salt and chillies and chant some incantations so as to take away the evil eye from the couple. After this they go through the movements of shaving the bridegroom. There was another *Tollvar* sitting at the bride's place at the time of the return of the bride to her place in the *Portovnnem* (ceremonial return).

Among the Hindus, after the bride becomes a part of the bridegroom's household a ceremony is held to join her into the fold of his (husband's) *gotra* in a ritual called *Gotraint haddop*. The bride has to show a lit lamp before eight people, all from the bridegroom's side, and also offer them ghee, bananas and snacks. Before leaving for the bridegroom's place, five couples along with the bride and the bridegroom are seated and rice is thrown on them in a ceremony called *Sensorbhorp*.

Among the Christians, all the elders of the house gift ornaments or cash as presents to the new son-in-law. The new bride would be given things necessary to set up her new household like kitchenware, bed mattresses, pillows, etc. After the marriage ceremony is over, the bridegroom with his bride has to sit on the mattress and get himself acquainted with all the elders of his in-laws. The bride's handicrafts, trousseau, and jewel box, etc., would then be displayed for the relatives, friends and the other guests present to see and then sent to her in-laws. After the *ghar-pravesh* (entry of the bride to the bridegroom's house), there used to be a ritual of giving a fresh name to the new bride. The bridegroom had to write the proposed name for the bride by his own fingers in the rice grains from a stand proffered to him. The practice, however, is on the wane now.

In the northern Goa, there is celebrated a beautiful ceremony called the *Saddo,* involving the ceremonial cutting of the cloth, normally flowery red, to be worn by the bride in the house after the wedding. A tiny image of child Jesus is placed on the floor mat where the tailor is sitting with the clothes, at their house, and two tiny length-wise pieces of clothes are cut by him and placed there in the form of a cross. To begin with, there is the 'Nomon' celebration in which blessing of God almighty and especially of the virgin Mary, mother of Jesus are invoked in the form of *Zot* (a special song peculiar to the occasion sung by an expert song-stress.

Then each relative, from the particular order of hierarchy to begin with, followed by others to the accompaniment of references to them made in beautiful metaphor in the form of Zotis, walks up to the spot where lies the Infant Jesus and lays his or her offerings of money before the image. Then a piece of betel nut and betel leaf with calcined lime and some sweets are disturbed to the relatives and guests present. The elder men are served with wine, women and children with sweet red wine and other soft drinks. The money collected on the occasion is appropriated by the tailor, beside his wages. The tailor will later stitch the main wedding dress or gown in milky white colour and other necessary apparel for the bride and close relatives and brides' maids, etc. The bride's gown, ornaments and trousseau are displayed in a special ceremony at which relatives are invited, and then they are sent to the bridegroom's place for display there.

Match-making by Parents

About the match-making and other marriage celebration of Lingayats, *Bombay Gazetter*, (Vol. XXIII) records, "The choosing of the bride and bridegroom is managed entirely by the parents. Among Lingayats marriage is much cheaper than among Brahmanical Hindus, as no price is paid for the girl. The offer of marriage comes from the boy's parents. When a boy's father can afford to pay for his son's marriage, he goes to a family who have a daughter likely to make a suitable match. If the girl's parents agree, he returns home and tells his wife that he has secured a bridge for their son. After some days the boy's father, with friends and relations goes to the girl's village, and, through a *Mathpali* or a Lingayat Gurav, calls those of his castemen and Jangams who live in the village. When all have come and taken their seats at the girl's house, a blanket is spread, some grains of rice are strewn on the blanket, and the boy and girl are made to sit on the rice. A kinswoman of the boy's dresses the girl in a new robe bought by the boy's father and gives her five pieces of bodicecloth, out of which one must be white and the remaining four of any colour except black. The woman dresses the girl, puts on her a gold ring and other ornaments, and fills her lap with two coconuts, five lemons, five dry dates, five plantains, and a few betel leaves. The girl's father presents the boy with a complete suit of clothes, including a turban, a shouldercloth, a coat and a gold ring. The boy and girl then rise, bow to the Jangams and house gods and resume their seats. The Jangams on both sides, naming the father of the boy and girl, declare to the people that the boy and girl are engaged, and the guests are dismissed with betel leaves and nuts. This ceremony is called the *sakshivike* or engagement. On the next day it is followed by the *bashtagi* or betrothal. In the betrothal, the girl's father gives a caste feast, presents clothes to the relations of the boy's father, and leads them out of the village in procession with music. When the boy's father reaches home, he asks an astrologer to fix the days on which the wedding rite and other ceremonies relating to the wedding should take place, makes a list of the days, and sends a copy of it to the girl's father. Preparations then begin. On the first day, the laps of five married women are filled with bits of dry cocoa-kernal, dry dates, soaked gram, and betel. A grind-stone and a wooden mortar are brought out, whitewashed with lime, and marked with stripes of *hurmanj* or red colour. Before them are laid bits of coca-kernel, dry dates, soaked gram and betel leaves and nuts, and incense is burnt. The women, whose laps have been filled at a lucky moment, begin to pound the turmeric roots in the mortar and grind them on the grind-stone. On another lucky day, the marriage booth is raised, the number of posts in each row being always uneven. The ornamenting of the booth depends on the parent's means. When all preparations are finished, both parties invite their kinswomen to live with them during the ceremony. A marriage takes five days. It is held at the boy's house. On the first day, the bride and bride-groom sit together on a blanket, and, about eight at night, a Jangam begins to rub their bodies with turmeric paste. The rubbing is completed by a party of married kinswomen, whose first husbands are alive, after which the bride and bridegroom rub turmeric on each other. The women wave a light before the pair and chant. This day is called the *arshan* or turmeric day; and when the *arshan* has been put on, the boy and girl are considered *madmaklu* that is husband and wife. The second day is called the *devkarya* or god-humouring day. The boy's father gives a great dinner to Jangama and friends, the marriage garments are laid beside the house god and worshipped and the *guru's* feet are washed and the water is taken and drunk by the bride and bridegroom and all other members of the family. In a house in which Virbhadra is one of the house gods, the third day is called the *guggul* or Bdellium gum day. A new earthern vessel is brought to the boy's house, the neck is broken off, and a piece of sandalwood set in it, tipped with oil, and lighted, and camphor and *guggul* are burnt. The earthen vessel is held by a Jangam, and the boy and girl stand in front of them with the image of Virbhadra in their hands. The Jangam takes up the vessel, and the boy and girl carry the god and, with music playing in front of them and followed by a band of friends, they go to Basavanna's temple. In front of the musicians walks a *vadab* or bard, dressed in silk, with a dagger in his hand, and an image of Virbhadra tied at his waist, chanting the praises of Virbhadra. At the temple, the pair worship Basavanna, break a coconut, lay down the earthen vessel, and then return to the boy's house. Next day the actual marriage ceremony, the chief feature of which is the tying on of the bride's lucky neck-thread or *mangalsutra* is performed by a Jangam.

"Other persons of special positions who ought to attend a Lingayat wedding are the personal *guru,* the *mathadayya,* or head of the local religious house, and the *panchacharus* or "five pots" namely the *ganachari* or manager, the *mathpati* or beadle, the *meligauda* or village head, the *desai* or hereditary district revenue superintendent, and the *deshpande* or hereditary district revenue accountant. A dais or raised seat called *sheshikate* or rice-dais is made ready, a blanket is spread on the dais, and on the blanket women strew rice. On this rice-strewn blanket, the bride and bridegroom are seated. In front of them, lines of rice are arranged in the form of a square and, at each corner of the square and in the centre, a *kalash* or drinking-pot is set with betel leaves and a betelnut on it, some molasses and twenty-five copper coins, five close to each pot. Two strings are wound five times round the necks of the drinking-pots placed at four corners of the square. One end of the strings is held by the bride and bridegroom and the other end by the *guru*, who sits opposite them beyond the rice square. Between the teacher and the rice square sits the *mathadayya* with the *metigauda* on his right and the *mathpati* on his left. In the row behind, on each side of the teacher who holds the threads, sit the *deshpande* and the *ganachori*, the *dashpande* on the teacher's right and the *ganachari* on the teacher's left. The bride and bridegroom do not sit opposite each other but side by side and no curtain is held between them. Near the drinking pot in the middle of the square is set an image of Ishvar or Basavanna, and the *mangalsutra* is kept in a cup of milk and clarified butter. The ceremony begins by the *mathpati* bowing to the *mangalsutra,* and proclaiming that it is about to be tied to the bride's neck. The bridegroom lays his right hand on the bride's right hand, the *mathpati* lays the lucky thread on the boy's hand, and the *ganachari* drops water, *vibhuti*, or cowdung ashes, and *kunku* or vermilion on the lucky thread, and marks the bride's forehead with red and the boys with sandal paste. The teacher gives the order to tie on the lucky thread and the *ganachari* ties it on the girl's neck, and calls *Sumuhurta Savdhan* that is, the moment has come, beware. When the priest says, 'Beware, the lucky time has come' the guests throw rice over the boy and the girl. The *ganachari* ties the hems of the bride's and bridegroom's robes together and, in the knot ties a little rice, salt and split pulse. The teacher lets go the end of the two strings, ties a piece of turmeric root into each of them, and binds one to the boy's right wrist and the other to the girl's left wrist. The married couple fall down before the teacher, who ends the rite by dropping sugar into their mouths. The rice is given to the beadle, and first he and then the other four *panchahcharus* are presented with five quarter-anna pieces which had been lying besides the *kalashas.* On the last evening, the bride and bridegroom ride on one horse in state to a temple of Basava, break a coconut before the god, and return and take off the marriage wristlets. On their return, friends wave boiled rice and curds round the heads of the bride and bridegroom and throw the rice to the evil spirits. During the passage to end from the temple, when they reach a street crossing or when they pass a ruined house, they break a coconut to the evil spirits (*Bombay Gazetteer*, Vol. XXIII, pp. 233-35).

"According to their religion, the wearer of the *linga* cannot be made impure. As a matter of fact Bombay Lingayats mostly observe ceremonial impurity during a woman's monthly sickness, and after a birth or a death. The feeling about ceremonial uncleanliness which has its basis in the fear of spirit possession, seems to be stronger in the north than in the south. Among the Lingayats in the south, near Mysore, a woman's monthly sickness is not considered to cause impurity, while to the north of Bijapur in some families women sit by themselves on the first day of their monthly sickness and in other families a woman has to bathe on the first day, and to mark her forehead with ashes. Hence, the Marathi proverb, "The Lingayat woman puts on ashes and is pure." Families in which this rule is kept do not let their women touch the house gods during their sickness. If a Lingayat girl comes of age before she is married, the fact that she has come of age is kept secret. When a married girl comes of age, she is seated gaily dressed upon a canopied chair for four to sixteen days. During the time, her kinswomen feed her with sweetmeats and at the end she is sent to live with her husband. On the last day, the boy's father feasts Jangams and kinspeople. The boy's father gives the girl a rich robe and the girl's father gives the boy a dress. In the fifth month of her first pregnancy, her mother gives the girl a green robe and a green bodice, and her kinswomen make similar presents.

"The marriage of widows was one of the points on which Basava insisted, and was probably one of the biggest bones of contention with the Brahmans. Widow remarriage is allowed at the present day, but the authorities at Ujjini disregard it. They say that amongst Jangams it is prohibited and that amongst the other classes of Lingayats it is the growth of custom. Divorce is permissible. The ordinary law of Hindus is followed in regard to inheritance. A special feature of Lingayat life is the frequency of adoptions."

Proposal Comes from Boy's Father

About the Dubla (ST) marriage custom, Mr. R.E. Enthoven writes, "Of the above divisions, the Talavias are the highest in social rank. They take to wife the girls of the Saravias, but do not give their daughters in marriage to them. The Talavias and Mandvias eat together and intermarry. With these exceptions, the members of the above mentioned clans seldom eat together and never intermarry.

"Marriages are prohibited when relationship can be traced between the two contracting parties. Marriage with a mother's sister's daughter, father's sister's daughter and maternal uncle's daughter is not allowed. A wife's younger sister can be married during the wife's life-time or after her death, and two brothers may marry two sisters. Boys are married in the age group of ten to twenty years and girls in the age group of ten to eighteen years. An unmarried girl cannot openly cohabit with any person. When she has cohabited with a man of a higher, or of her, caste and the fact has gained publicity, the girl is fined. In some places, sexual intercourse before marriage is connived at. When the man involved is of her caste, the girl is sometimes married to him. If a girl is guilty of misconduct with a member of the Kokna, Chodhra or Gamta caste, she can remain in the caste by giving a caste dinner and a fine; but if with a member of a very low caste such as a Dheda or Bhangia, she is permanently expelled.

"The offer of marriage comes from the boy's father. In some places, the marriage day is fixed and the service conducted by a priest belonging to the degraded class of Tapodhan Brahmans, or by a member of any other caste wearing the sacred thread. In others, the service is conducted either by a casteman or by a member of another caste who knows the rites. The boy's father pays to the girl's father fifteen to twenty rupees. Sometimes the amount, which is known as *Dej,* is paid in the form of grain. The *Khandalia* form of marriage, *i.e.,* by serving the parents of the wife, also prevails. When a marriage is settled, the bride's party go to the house of the bridegroom and throw grains of rice coloored with red powder into his house and present him with as many seeds of castor oil plant as there are number of days intervening between that day and the marriage day. Out of these seeds, one is thrown away daily. The day on which the last seed, is thrown away is thus held to be the marriage day. Five days before marriage the bride and bridegroom are rubbed with *pithi* turmeric paste. The planet pleasing ceremony is performed the day before the marriage day at the bridegroom's house, and again on the marriage day at the bride's house. In the afternoon, with a company of his friends, the bridegroom with his eyes painted and a spot on each cheek marked black to keep off the evil eye starts with music and singing for the bride's house. He is led by the bride's father to the square space in the centre of the booth. The bride is brought in and the skirts of the bride's and bridegroom's garments are tied into a knot. As the sun sets, a Brahman or a casteman calls out three or four times "*Savdhan, Kaligranthi Savdhan*" "Beware of the auspicious knot" and joins the hands of the bride and bridegroom. The bride and bridegroom then walk round the *chori* four times and are fed with sweetmeats and cooked rice. Then they make a bow to their patron deity. Walking round the *chori* and making a bow to the patron deity are supposed to be the binding portions of the ceremony. At night, men and women dance together and the marriage ceremony closes with two dinners, one at the bride's and the other at the bridegroom's house. If the bride's father is a well-to-do man, then he, like the Gamits or Dhodias, selects a bridegroom and keeps him at his house. If the girl desires the match, the usual ceremony is performed. The bridegroom in such cases is termed *Ghar Jamai* or *Khandalio*.

"Widow remarriage is allowed. A widow cannot marry her maternal uncle's son, father's sister's son, or mother's sister's son. She may marry, if she chooses, the younger brother or any other relative of her deceased husband younger than him. A remarriage is arranged by the near relatives of a widow and is celebrated on a Sunday, Tuesday or Thursday. At the time of remarriage, kinspeople on both the sides are present. The ceremony is conducted by a remarried widow. The widow wears brass ornaments *Chhali* and *Kalla*. The couple are seated on low wooden stools near each other and their brows marked with red powder. A cloth sheet is held over them by four men, and rice grains coloured red are thrown over their heads by four women. This last ceremony of throwing rice grain is supposed to be the binding portion of the ceremony. Some perform this ceremony in two different ways. First, the bride stands opposite the bridegroom on a mortar, and two widows, one on each side of her, bring together the heads of the bride and bridegroom seven times, and the bridegroom pays to the bride a sum of 25p. This completes the ceremony. Secondly, Coconuts are placed on the heads of the bride and bridegroom, and their heads are brought together. A bachelor is allowed to marry a widow after first being married to a *shami* tree. In some places, the *shami* tree must be of a different village from that of the bachelor.

"Both a husband or a wife may obtain a divorce with the permission of the headman of the caste and of the relatives. Divorce is termed *Chhuta Chheda Karva* or *Fargati Apvi*. Divorce is allowed on account of incompatibility of temper or when the husband is suffering from some incurable disease or is impotent," adds Mr. R.E. Enthoven. The customs pertain to the Dubla tribe (ST) of Gujarat and the Daman and Diu region.

Bride-price being Negotiable

Mr. Enthoven records, "The offer of marriage comes from the boy's father, who has to pay to the girl's father a sum varying from Rs. 15 to 150, and some bullocks. If he is unable to pay this amount, the bridegroom has instead to serve his father-in-law for two or three years. Marriage ceremonies differ among the different sections of the Vanjaris. In some places, when the bride-price has been fixed, the bridegroom's party distribute molasses and liquor. A part of the amount is paid in cash and a part in bullocks. On a convenient day fixed by a Brahman astrologer, the boy goes in procession with his house-people and guests to the bride's house, where he is received by four or a larger number of men, and the bride's father feasts the bridegroom's party on boiled rice and curry. After the feast, the bride and bridegroom are led to a square marked out with quartz powder and stand opposite each other. A Brahman gives coloured rice to the guests, the bride and bridegroom stand inside the square, the guests throw rice over them, and the priest repeats verses. It a Brahman is not available, the ceremony is performed by an elderly Lamani. When the rice-throwing is over, the bridegroom's father serves the bride's people with a meal of mutton and bread. Then the bridegroom returns with the bride to his house. At night, he retires to some lonely part of the dwelling and lies on the ground with a coconut under his head, feigning to be asleep, while the bride sits in another part of the house near an elderly woman who rubs her feet. One of her husband's kinswomen walks to the bride and tells her that her husband wants her, and guides her to the place where he is waiting for her. The husband gives the woman the coconut and in return receives his wife. Among Lamans, the nuptials are often performed by married women, of whom the bride's mother or other nearest kinswoman is one. In the bride's house, a square is traced with quartz powder. At each corner, a large water pot or *ghagar* is placed and the bride's mother winds a thread seven times round the necks of the water pots. The bride sits on a bag filled with rice in the centre of the square. The thread is taken from the necks of the pots and cut in two, one part being tied round the bride's neck and the other round her arm. One of the women splashes water on her and bathes her, another rubs her body with turmeric paste, a third takes off her wet clothes and dresses her in fresh clothes, and a fourth sprinkles her brow with rice. They join in lifting her off the bag of rice. The bridegroom then takes her place and undergoes the same ceremonies. At the end, the bride's mother marks both their backs with a Jain cross in turmeric paste. The boy and girl sit together, a tub in set before them and filled with water, and a couple of shells are dropped into it. The bridegroom takes the shells out seven times and again drops them into the water. The bride picks out the shells seven times and at the end of the seventh time keeps them. In some families, at each corner of the marriage parallelogram, branches of the *rui* plant *(Calotropis gigantea)* are stooped, bound together. Underneath each stoop are placed five water pots and a copper coin. In the heart of the parallelogram, a cross with a circle round it is drawn. In the middle of the east and west sides of the parallelogram a rice pounder or *musal* is erected. The bride holds on her open palm a cowry shell and a rupee and the bridegroom, placing his open palm over the bride's and over the cowry shell and rupee, leads her seven times round the two *musals,* from west to east. The bride and bridegroom then sit together in the square and eat molasses out of one dish. A near cotton thread is brought and divided in two. One-half is tied round the boy's wrist and the other round the girl's and their clothes are marked on the back with turmeric paste. On the next day, there are games and amusements. On the third day, a kinswoman leads the bride to the bridegroom's chamber, thus ending the marriage.

"In Khandesh, the boy's party go to the girl's village for the marriage, riding on ponies or walking, for carts are forbidden.

On arrival they are given separate apartments facing a booth covered with mango and *nim* (Melia azadirachta) leaves. The marriage takes place at midnight. A post of *palasa* (Butea frondosa) or *umbar* (Ficus glomerata) is smeared with turmeric paste and fixed in the ground, and alighted lamp is placed on the top of the post. The marriage ceremony, which is very simple, is performed near this post. Grains of *juvari* dipped in turmeric water are thrown over the bridal pair by the party, and the *homa* or marriage sacrifice is performed. The bride and bridegroom walk five times round the sacrificial fire, thus completing the marriage. In some places, two posts of *kher* (Acacia catechu) are fixed in the ground. On each corner of a square, nine earthen pots are piled one on one another and are covered with leaves of the *rui* (Calotropis gigantea). The nine pots probably represent the nine planets, *navagraha.* Near the post sit the bride and bridegroom, who have been rubbed, with turmeric and bathed. Then the Brahman priest worships Ganpati, joins the hands of the pair, and ties the knot in the same way as at a Kunbi wedding, except that a rupee, given by the bride's father, is tied to the knot. Then, between the posts, the Brahman lights the sacred fire, and muttering sacred verses, leads the pair seven times round the fire from right to left. This ends the nuptial ceremonies. The Lad Vanjaris have a *devak* consisting of the *panchpalvi* or leaves of five kinds of trees, which they install in Kunbi fashion. Among them, the *devak* is installed on the fifth day after the birth of a child. The *devaka* of the Ravjin Vanjparis consists of the *panchpalvi,* the feathers of the *tas* or blue jay *Coracias indica* and of leaves of the *nagvel* betelvine. In Nasik, it is customary to carry the *devak,* consisting of the leaves of the mango, *jambul, umbar, shami* and *rui,* known as *panchpalvi,* to Maruti's temple, after which the *devak* is brought back and tied to the marriage booth. Without the *devak,* marriage cannot take place.

"The marriages of Gujarat Vanjaris are celebrated in the months of *Jyeshtha* and *Asaddh,* the binding portion consisting in walking five times round the sacrificial fire. The bride goes to live with her husband three years after the marriage, when her father gives her a bullock laden with clothes and untensils and corn.

"Except among Mathuras and Labhanas, the remarriage of widows is permitted. Among the Charans, if a widow marries an outsider in preference to her deceased husband's brother or relative, a fine is levied by the *panch.* The ceremony of widow marriage is extremely simple. It consists in locking up the widow and her intended husband for the night or in their eating from one plate. A bachelor is not allowed to marry a widow. In some sections of the Gujarat Vanjaris, the head of a widow is shaved ten days after the death of her husband, and she is forced to betake herself to a secluded place for one year, during which period she is only allowed one meal a day, which must be taken at night, without salt," adds Mr. Enthoven. The custom is practised among the *Lawani* community.

Ritual of Making 27 Heaps of Rice

Mr. Enthoven writes, "The offer of marriage generally comes from the boy's father. It is arranged throught the mediation of four or five men of their caste, who are termed *pudhail.* A Brahman priest fixes an auspicious date for the marriage and also conducts the service. When an offer is received, two men from both the sides go to an astrologer with the bride and bridegroom's horoscopes and get them compared. When the horoscopes are not available, the marriage is settled by the religious names of the bride and bridegroom. Twenty-seven heaps of rice corresponding to the twenty-seven stars are prepared. Over each heap a betelnut and a pice is placed. Red and turmeric powders are offered to these heaps, and a smael girl is asked to pick up a betelnut. From the number of the betelnut, the bridegroom's star is marked. Similarly, the bride's star is marked and then the astrologer decides whether the proposed match will be happy and prosperous. The principal ceremonies are *kunku-lavne* or betrothal, *logna-chithi* or fixing the date of marriage, turmeric rubbing, *devtarya* or the ceremony of enshrining the marriage guardian deity which consists of *panchpalvi, i.e.,* leaves of the mango, *jambul* (Eugenia jambolana), *shami* (Prosopis spioigera), *umbar* (Ficus glomerata), and *rui* (Calotropis gigantea), *vardhava* or taking the bridegroom to the bride's house, *simant-pujan* or the reception of the bridegroom by the bride's father, *kanyadan* or the bride-giving ceremony, *rukhurat* or offering food articles to the bridegroom party, and *sade.* Their marriage ceremonies do not differ materially from those of the Marathas except that at the time of marriage the bride and bridegroom are made to stand on bamboo baskets, or the bride on a grindstone and the bridegroom on a coil of rope. The *saptapadi,* or taking of seven steps by the bride and bridegroom, or the throwing of rice over the bride and bridegroom's heads is the binding portion of the ceremony," adds Mr. Enthoven. The custom is popular among the Lonari Community.

Rituals of Sword-Marriage

About the marriage custom among the Rajputs, Mr. R.V. Russell and Hira Lal says, "In the centre of the booth a *chori* or square is made. At each, corner of the square a pillar of nine metal or earthen vessels, piled one above the other, is kept upright by bamboo supports. In the centre of the *chori,* a heap of cowdung cakes is piled. The bride's priest kindles the pile of cakes and feeds the fire with clarified butter, barley and sesame. He then makes the bride and the maidservant go round the fire twice in such a way as to make their right feet touch the *khetrapal* or field-guardian. Then the boy's party present the girl with rich robes and bodices, ornaments and cash, and the girl's father pays the boy the sum of money or gold agreed upon, first laying it on a brass platter and showing the amount of money to the boy's party. The chief of the boy's party accepts the amount on behalf of the boy and returns the silver after laying some cash upon it. The girl bows to the family goddess and after the girl's father has presented dresses to the boy's party and cash to the assembled Bhats and Charans, the boy's party are allowed to leave in good time to reach their village before the arrival of the bride.

"Two or three days after the sword-marriage the bride is sent to the bridegroom's house seated in a carriage with the maid who brought the sword. Before starting, the bride's mother worships the wheel of the carriage and lays a coconut and copper coins under the wheel. As the carriage starts, the coconut is crushed and the pieces are laid in the bride's lap to be kept during her journey to the bridegroom's house. When the bride's party reaches the village boundary, the bridegroom marches on horseback with his friends and relations and music to receive the bride. The march turns into a race among the bridegroom's friends for the honour of being first to reach the bride, and the winner is rewarded with a coconut and a silver coin and the others with sweets. When he reaches the bride's carriage, the bridegroom asks the maidservant to give him her place. She refuses and he offers her money. When she is satisfied, she leaves the carriage and the bridegroom takes her place. When they reach the bridegroom's house, the pair leave the carriage and enter the booth, where, under a silk canopy, at each corner of a square, is placed an earthen pot fresh-fly brought from the potter, and, in the middle, two low stools for the pair. Under the arch of the booth, the bridegroom's mother waves round the pair a miniature pestle and mortar, a ladle, a plough-yoke, and a roller, and the pair are then led to their seats in the canopy. A sacred fire is kindled by the bridegroom's priest. The hands of the couple are joined and they are made to move round the fire. The pair are then taken inside to worship the *gotraj* or family goddess. Next they play the game of *eki beki* odds or evens with betelnuts, dry dates and coins. The women affirm that the mastery in wedded life falls to the victor in this game. After the game, the priest unties the *mindhals* or wedding nut-bracelets and the marriage is complete.

"On the next day presents are made to Bhats and Charans. When the bridegroom goes personally to the bride's house he takes the place of the maidservant and performs all the necessary rites at the bride's house. When this is done, the rites of hand-joining and going round the sacred fire are not repeated at his house.

"After marriage Rajput women, as a rule, remain within the *zenana* or private apartments. As, among the rich, polygamy is usual, the inmates of the *zenana* always enjoy the interest of rivalry or affection," add Russull and Hira Lal. The customs, rites and rituals are prevalent among the *Rajputs*.

Taking consent of Bride and Bridegroom

About the marriage customs and rituals of Parsis, it is recorded, "Polygamy among the Parsis has been forbidden by the Parsi Marriage and Divorce Act of 1865. The remarriage of widows is allowed but is celebrated at midnight. If a bachelor is to marry a widow, he first goes through a sham rite with the branch of a tree, as among the Hindus. Similarly before the wedding the bride and bridegroom are rubbed with turmeric, and for the ceremony a marriage-shed is erected. At a feast before the wedding one of the women beats a copper dish and asks the ancestral spirits to attend, calling them by name. Another woman comes running in, barking like a dog. The women drive her away, and with fun and laughing eat all the things they can lay their hands on. Prior to the rite the bride and bridegroom are purified in the same manner as when invested with the sacred shirt and cord. The bridegroom wears a long white robe reaching to his ankles and a white sash round his waist; he has a garland of flowers round his neck, a red mark on his forehead, and carries a bunch of flowers and a coconut in his right hand. At every street corner on his way to the bride's home a coconut is waved round his head, broken and thrown away. He sets his right foot in the house first, and as he enters rice and water are thrown under his feet and an egg and coconut are broken. At the wedding the couple throw rice on each other, and it is supposed that whoever is quickest in throwing the rice will rule the other. They are then seated side by side, and two priests stand before them with a witness on each side, holding brass plates full of rice. The two priests pronounce the marriage blessing in old Persian and Sanskrit, at each sentence throwing rice on the bride's and bridegroom's heads. At intervals in the midst of the blessing the bridegroom and bride are asked in Persian, 'Have you chosen her?' and 'Have you chosen him?' They answer in Persian, or if they are too young their mothers answer for them, 'I have chosen.' *Bombay Gazetteer*, Vol. IX. Part II, *Parsis of Gujarat*, pp. 233, 237.

Mr. Enthoven adds further about their marriage customs, "Marriage is taken to be an institution finding favour with God (Ahura Mazda), who prefers a married man to an unmarried man, and one with a family and children to one without them (Vendidad IV, 47). A place where a married man lives feels, as it were, happy (*Ibid* III, 2).

"After the several vicissitude of fortune which the community has gone through, it is not possible to say with certainty which of their marriage customs are originally Iranian or Zoroastrian and which Indian or alien. But the strictly solemn or religious part, wherein the priests participate, is Iranian, and is the essential or binding portion. The marriage is celebrated in the presence of an assembly which consists of at least five persons, two of whom are the officiating priests and two witnesses.

"The marriage ceremony consists of the following parts:

I. The Preliminary Ritual.

II. The Ashirvad (the marriage ceremony proper).

I. The Preliminary Ritual consists of following ceremonies:—

(a) The *A'da antar* or the curtain ceremony, wherein the couple are at first separated by a curtain and made to sit opposite each other.

(b) The tying by the senior officiating priest of a marriage knot, wherein the couple are enclosed in a circle by a piece of cloth, the ends of which are tied during the recital of the sacred formula of *Ahunavar*.

(c) The Hand-fastening (*Hathevaro*), wherein the priest places the right hand of one in the right hand of the other, and then fastens the hands with raw twist during the recital of the above sacred formula.

(d) The encircling of the couple with raw twist passed round them seven times during seven recitals of the above formula.

(e) The throwing of the rice, wherein, the couple, who are provided with a few grains of rice in their left hands, at a certain signal given by burning frankincense on fire presented before them in a vase, throw rice upon one another. The one who throws first indicates thereby that he or she will be the foremost in loving and respecting the other.

"This preliminary part of the ceremony, not being the solemn and religious part, is now dispensed with by many.

II. The *Ashirvad* recital is the ceremony proper, being the essential or binding part of the marriage ceremony. It consists of the following:—

(*a*) A preliminary blessing, wherein the senior priest blesses the couple, wishing them a healthy and prosperous long life of 150 years and a healthy progeny of sons and grandsons.

(*b*) The asking of consent, wherein the senior priest takes the consent of the couple and their respective witnesses to the marriage. For a brief account of the marriage ceremony, *vide* my paper on the "Marriage Customs of the Parsees," Journal of the Anthropological Society of Bombay, Vol. V, No. 4, pp. 242-82. This consent is asked thrice.

(c) A joint address by both the officiating priests, wherein they admonish the marrying couple and say prayers and benedictions. They throw rice over the couple while giving these admonitions and reciting these prayers and benedictions.

"The re-marriage of widows is permitted. The widow may marry, if she likes, her husband's younger or elder brother, but there is no compulsion. As to the limits within which she may marry, there are no particular special limits other than those for a woman marrying for the first time.

"The form of marriage and the essential binding portion are the same as in the case of the first marriage. But the affair is a quiet one. The few points of difference are the following:

(*a*) In the case of first marriages, the ceremony was, at one time, performed twice, once in the evening and again at midnight. But in the case of a re-marriage, it was performed only once, and that even rather quietly at some odd hour between the early part of the night and midnight.

(*b*) In first marriages, rice was thrown by the priests with the palm of the hand lower down, but in the second marriage, with the palm of the hand open above.

(*c*) A change of few words in the preliminary blessing, to say that the lady is not a virgin and that the marriage is a second marriage.

"It may be observed that now-a-days the first two differences are not generally observed. According to the Parsi Marriage Act divorce or dissolution of marriage was permitted in the following cases:

1. Lunacy or mental unsoundness, at time of marriage, of which one of the contracting parties did not know.

2. Impotence.

3. Continued absence for seven years of either party, without being heard of as alive.

4. Adultery of the wife.

5. Adultery or bigamy with adultery, or adultery with cruelty or adultery with willful desertion for two years or upwards, or rape or unnatural offence on the part of the husband.

"Formerly divorce was permitted by the elders for some other reasons besides the above, such as a continued quarrelsome disposition, and when the wife bore no child or was a hopeless invalid.

"It appears from old Pahlavi books that in Iran also there was a regular procedure for divorce. In the case of a wife misbehaving, she was sent back to her parents, who had, if aggrieved, the option of sueing the husband before judges who tried the case assisted by some members of the community. It appears that there was some set form of speech whereby the husband declared his intentions to divorce his wife.

"It appears from an allusion in Herodotus that barrenness of the wife was held from very ancient times to be a justifiable cause of divorce or for taking a second wife.

"The form by which the divorce was formerly effected in India was a written document known as *fargati* meaning a release (from Persian *farag* free)," add Russell and Lal.

Ceremony of *Nikkah*

About the Muslim ceremony of Nikkah, Mr. RE Enthoven writes, "Boys are generally married between sixteen and twenty-two and girls between ten and eighteen. When their sons reach manhood, parents generally consult professional matchmakers or go betweens, women free to enter the houses even of the strictest. Some girl likely to make a good match is before long chosen, and the women of the lad's family pay a visit at the girl's home. After seeing her and talking together, the guests are offered a glass of sugared water. This they drink if they think well of the girl, but if they think she will not suit, they decline. After drinking, in sign that they ask her in marriage, they drop some sugarcandy into the girl's mouth. Then they talk of ornaments and fix the day for the betrothal. On the betrothal day, both at the boy's and girl's houses, there is a meeting of kindred. In the evening at the boy's house ornaments and sweetmeats are laid out on neatly covered trays and are generally sent to the girl's house with music. With the presents go the women of the bridegroom's family and a gay procession of children of their relations and friends. On reaching the bride's house the men and children who formed the procession sit in a booth outside of the house, or, if there is no booth, in some part of the house prepared for their reception. Here *sherbat* sugared water is handed round, the person serving it, generally a relation or a near friend of the wife's family stating that in honour of the betrothal. Each person on putting down his cup drops, for the good of the man who has served it, annas 2 to Rs. 2 into the saucer. Meanwhile the women guests going into the house deck the bride with ornaments, put the troth ring on her finger, and cover her with a scarf *dupatta*. Then drinking sugared-water and coffee and getting flowers and rosewater they leave, taking with them trays filled with fresh presents, a handkerchief, a ring, a gold turban on *mandil*, and sweetmeats. Except when things are hurried and the betrothal and marriage take place at the same time, the betrothal lasts for at least a year. During this time on every holiday gifts pass between the betrothed couple.

"Some months before the marriage day the bride's female relations meet at her house and make ready the smaller articles of dress. Every night when their work is over, for about a fortnight before the marriage day, the women sing together to the accompaniment of the drum or *dhol*. Eight days before the marriage the bride keeps to one room, and both she and the bridegroom are made to wear yellow clothes. Two or three days before the marriage, both at the house of the bridegroom and of the bride, a store of earthen pots is laid in. If the women observe the *pardah* or veiling, the pots are arranged in the inner apartments, but if the women are not *pardah*, they are arranged in a temporary booth or alcove in front of the house. That the object of arranging these pots is to house and so please ancestral spirits is known and admitted. Food is laid on the pots, and the opening chapter of the Kuran or *Faliha* is repeated. After the pots have been arranged both at the bride's and the bridegroom's the women of the family, while female musician sing songs, rub the bride or bridegroom with gram flour mixed with oil and perfumes called *ubatna*. The chief ingredients in this cosmetic are the flour of washed wheat and *mung* (*Phasoleus munga*) turmeric and sesame oil. As this cosmetic has to ward off all the evil influences which hover round the bride and bridegroom, every care must be taken that no element of evil enters into the guardian *vbatna*. To stop the approach of evil the hand-mill in which the grain is ground has its handle smeared with sandal paint, and a *midhal* (*Vangueiria spinosa*) nut and some *pan* or betel-leaves and betelnuts wrapped in a piece of new red cloth are tied to it. Then seven *suhagans*, that is married women whose husband are alive, sit to grind the grain and into the flour pour clarified butter or sesame or jasmine oil. When the *ubatna* is ready henna leaves are ground in the same way. A square diagram is traced on the floor with rice and a stool is set in the square. The bride or bridebroom in suit of her or his oldest clothes dyed yellow is led forth and seated on the stool. The *vbatna*, amidst the songs of women either the relations of the family or hired female musicians, is rubbed all over the body and henna is applied to the hands and feet. In rubbing on the cosmetic each of the seven matrons takes her turn. She puts a piece of candid sugar into the bridegroom's mouth, throws a handful of rice over the bride or bridegroom's head, passes the mustard seed seven times over the bride or bridegroom's body, and takes on herself the ill-luck or *balas* of the bride or bridegroom by cracking the joints of her fingers across her temples. Finally she passes a pice or more over the bride or bridegroom, hands the coin to the musicians if hired or lays it at the foot of the stool to be given in charity and retires. When all seven matrons have performed their task, a knife, dagger or other sharp iron instrument and a lemon are handed to the bride or bridegroom which she or he is to be careful to keep till the bath on the marriage day. During these days, to keep off the evil eye, a bracelet or a garland of gold must also be worn. Seven songs called *tonas* or charms sung by *domnis* or hired female singers before the *julwah* or unveiling of the bride in the presence of the bridegroom, which form a portion of the marriage ceremony, are said to possess special anti-magic and spirit-power. If the bride be spirit possessed to the slightest extent the sound of the *tonas* makes the spirit instantly declare itself. When the bridegroom comes songs are again sung and has height is measured by an odd number of red and white braids. These braids are woven into a thick cord which is used by the bride in her trouser string. The bride and bridegroom's houses are put in order, painted or whitewashed, and outside of each house is built a booth or hall, sometimes very splendid with gilt pillars, friezes and cornices and hung with glass-lamps and pictures. The first post of the booth is driven into the ground after the point has been rubbed with sandal oil and enveloped with a piece of new red muslin in which are warpped betelnuts, betel-leaves and the lucky wedding *midhal* nut Vanguieria spinosa. A coconut is broken and the kernel distributed among the workmen who built the booth and the members of the family. As the whole house is given over to the women this hall is for the time the men's room. For some days before the marriage, musicians are hired to play in front of the house. This is a time of great merry-making. One day, outside of the house for men and inside for women, earthen vessels are filled with the red and yellow colours used in dyeing cloth. In the evening the men among themselves and the women among themselves each with a little jar full of colour, chasing and waylaying, cover one another with the dye. At such times from Rs. 5 to Rs 20 or at most Rs 30 of colour is used one amusement for the women during the days before a marriage is the twisting, knotting and tying of silver rings into silk and gold thread wristbands *kangna*. Of these one is given to the bride and the other to the bridegroom, and after marriage each has to unravel the knots and twists in the other's bracelet. On the evening of the marriage day, the bridegroom's party send to the bride's with a procession of children in carriages and on horseback with music and led horses, a band of hired women and servants carrying as many as two hundred or more earthen pots painted in gold and green filled with sweetmeats and dried fruits, and trays with dresses. This procession is called the *cart* or *sachak*, that is, the present. On arrival the children are seated in the marriage hall or shed with the men and are treated to *sherbat*, each of the little guests dropping silver coins the smallest of which is a two-anna piece into the cup or saucer in acknowledgment of the trouble of the server, who is often either a poor or juvenile relation of the bride. In her room the bride is bathed by the women of her family, clothed in new robes, and decked in some of the jewels. Then with trays refilled with clothes for the bridegroom, with henna *mendhi* and with the wife's chattels *jahez*, *Jahez* or paraphernalia includes clothes, jewels, furniture and ornaments for a lady's sitting room and bedroom and a set of cooking vessels. This continues to be the wife's property, and has to be returned to her in case of divorce. The company goes back to the bridegroom's on their return the bridegroom is dressed in his wedding clothes, and the furniture of what is to be his room is set in order. At nightfall, an occasion of much merriment, the sister of the bride comes to apply henna to the bridegroom's hand. On one side of a screen or partition sits the lady and on the other the bridegroom and some of his friends. Only the bridegroom's hand should be passed under the screen. But instead of this, many hands are thrust through, and the lady has to trust to her wit to choose the hand she should punish by pinching and the hand she should adorn with henna. Her mistakes are greeted with much laughter, and when in the end she paints the bridegroom's little finger with henna she receives a present of Rs. 5 to Rs. 10. When this play is over, the bridegroom's guests sit listening to dancing girls and buffoons *bhands* or to a company of Arab nativity hymn-signers called *Mauludias*. *Mauluds*, that is, Muhammad-mas carols, are gradually displacing dancing girls and buffoons. At the close of the *maulud* coffee, warm sweet-milk in small coffee cups, and sweets or sugar-cakes called *batashas* are distributed to singers and hearers.

"About ten, the time comes for the bridegroom to fetch the bride. The bridegroom is clothed in a *sehra* or flower-sheet fastened round his head by a string which the father ties with thankful heart that to him has been granted the wish of every Indian Musalman; May I live to tie my son's *sehra* knot. Then the father or some other male relation lifts the bridegroom on a horse and with music and followed by all his friends he starts for the brides. As he passes under her window the bride lets fall on the bridegroom some grains of rice. He is led before the door of the house, and is handed a cup of sugared-water by his brother-in-law, to whom in return he gives Rs. 5 to Rs. 10. The women of the bridegroom's family and the wives of his chief friends follow the procession in closed carriages. On their arrival at the bride's they retire to the ladies' quarters, where, till the bridegroom is called in to see the bride, they are entertained by women singers *domnis*. When the bridegroom comes, those who do not appear before him, retire. The men of the bridegroom's party when they arrive, seat themselves in the brightly lighted marriage hall, the bridegroom's party ranged on one side and the bride's on the other. In the space between are three seats; one in front of his party for the bridegroom, one in front of the bride's party for her agents and the third between the two for the registrar, the *Kazi* or his deputy. The bridegroom, if very young, is carried, or, if grown is led to his seat and the bride's agents find their way to theirs. Then the registrar, seating himself, asks the bride's agents whether she with a certain portion or *meher* Though the rich sometimes give more, the portion of *meher* is generally fixed at Rs. 17 the dower of Fatimah the Prophet's favourite daughter, or at Rs. 750, the dower of the Prophet's wife Aishah. Among the rich and the middle class the marriage portion of a girl is what is legally termed the *meheri misl* or the portion of her peers, that is, the girl's grandmother, aunts and sisters, accepts so and so as her husband. If told she will have him, he takes the declaration of two other witnesses. He then making the bridegroom repeat the creed, puts to him the same question. The proceedings are recorded, and the guests, raising their hands, offer the marriage thanksgiving. When the ceremony is over, the registrar receives a shawl and Rs. 5 his fee, and leaves the house taking his share of the marriage sugarcandy, trayfuls of which are distributed among all present. The hired musicians, who so far have been silent owing to the presence of the representative of the law of Islam, strike up a loud discordant peal. Then, till the bridegroom is called to receive his bride, the men pass their time in listening to hired dancers and singers. When the husband is called, In north Gujarat the husband walks alone, and this at five or six in the morning instead of about three or four in the afternoon.) a dancing girl, stepping backwards, singing and keeping time by beating him with flower twigs, slowly lead the bridegroom into the ladies quarters. Here she hand him over to the *domnis* or female musicians, who in the same way lead him to a seat. On his way to his seat the bridegroom is jealously guarded by his sisters or other near relatives from the onslaughts of the younger sisters or relatives of the bride who hang about unobserved, and if they get an opportunity, dart on the bridegroom and if his female relatives are not on the alert wring his ears unmercifully. Soon the bride, veiled and arrayed in her wedding garment, is carried in by one of her relations and seated before the bridegroom, and a set of ceremonies, in which the rest of the night passes, are begun. These seem to be the humorous survival of the eating together form of marriage. The bride, who should not voluntarily move a muscle, is by one of the musicians made to take in her hand a piece of sugarcandy, some pounded sweet bread, or a dry date, then her hand is stretched out to her husband's mouth, and as he tries to secure the morsel her hand is drawn away. This in different forms with much merriment goes on for a long time. At dawn the bridegroom is for the first time shown his wife's face in a mirror, and from a Kuran placed between them the chapter of Peace is read. This is the sign that the time has come for the bride to leave her father's house.

"After the marriage the husband with his wife and family pass some days in a garden-house, spending their time in amusements and singing.

"On each of the first four Fridays or *char jumagis* after marriage the bride and bridegroom are asked to dine at the bride's father's house. On the first and perhaps the second Friday some of the bridegroom's friends and relations, both men and women, are asked. In north Gujarat the young couple stay from the evening of a Thursday to the following evening. In the south they go on the Friday evening and generally leave next morning. Much is thought of these Friday dinners, and if they are not given, a man seldom visits his father-in-law's house. So too, after marriage, the relatives of the bridegroom and the bride do not visit each other till each party has once formally invited the other." (*Bombay Gazetteer*, Vol. IX, Part II, p. 162-167)

Marriage Comes Two to Three Years after Betrothal

About the custom of marrying two to three years after marriage among the Jain, Mr. Enthoven writes, "Boys are married between fifteen to twenty-five years of age and girls before they come of age. As a rule the boy's father proposes the match to the girl's father and, when they agree, an astrologer is consulted, who compares the birth papers of the boy and the girl and approves the match if he thinks the result will be lucky and if the family stocks and branches or *shakhat* of the boy and the girl are different. Then on a lucky day the boy's father visits the girl's house with a few friends, including five kinswomen, and are received by the girl's father and mother. The girl is seated on a low stool in front of the house gods and the boy's father presents her with a robe and bodice and a pair of silver chains or *sankhlis* and anklets or *valis*. Her brow is marked with vermilion and decked with a network of flowers. The women of the boy's house dress the girl in the clothes and ornaments brought by the boy's father and the boy's father puts a little sugar in her mouth. Packets of sugar and betel are handed among the guests and the asking or *magni* ends in a feast to the guests. As a rule, marriage takes place two or three years after betrothal. Every year the boy's parents have to send a present of a string of cocoa-kurnel and some fried rice on the Cobra's Fifth or *Nagpanchmi* in July-August and this they have to continue to do till the girl comes of age. When the boy is fifteen or sixteen years of age and the girl is ten or eleven, the parents consider it the right time for them to get married, and send for and consult an astrologer. He compares their horoscopes, consults his almanac, and names a lucky day for the marriage. The ceremony as a rule lasts for five days. On the first day, two married girls in the bride's house bathe early in the morning, wear a ceremonial dress, and with music and a band of friends go to a pond or a river with copper pots on their heads, sandal-paste, flowers, rice, vermilion, burnt frankincense, and sweet meats on the bank in the name of the water, goddess, fill the pota with water, and mark them with vermilion, net a coconut and betel leaves in the mouth of each, cover them with bodice-cloths, and deck them with gold necklaces. They then set the waterpots on their heads, return home, and lay them on the earthen altars. Flowers, vermilion, burnt frankincense and sweetmeat are offered to the pots and five dishes filled with earth are set before them sprinkled with water from the waterpots and mixed seed grain is sown in the earth. Friends and kinsfolk are asked to dine at the house and the sprout offering or ankurarpan is over. The bridegroom is bathed at his house and lights a sacred *fire* or *hom*, puts on a rich dress, and goes on horseback with music and friends carrying clothes, ornaments, sugar, and betel packets to the bride's house. The bride's party meet him on the way and the bridegroom is taken to the bride's house and seated outside of the house on a sent of *audumbar* or *umbar* (Ficus glomerata). The bride's parents come out with a vessel full of water, the father washes his future son-in-law's feet and the mother pours water over them. The bridegroom is then taken to a raised seat in the house, seated on it and presented with clothes, a gold ring, and a necklace. The bridegroom's parents present the ornaments and clothes they have brought for the bride, packets of betel and sugar are handed among friends and kinspeople, and the first day ends with a feast to the bridegroom's party. The bridegroom returns home with his party, is rubbed with turmeric and clarified butter, bathed by five married women seated in a square with an earthen pot at each corner and a yellow thread is passed five times round their necks. The bride is bathed in a similar square at her house. On the third day, the bride and bridegroom bathe, dress in newly washed clothes, and starting from their homes meet at the Jain temple. The priest attends them and the pair bow before the idol. The priest makes them repeat the five-solutation hymn which every Jain ought to know and warns them to keep the Jain vow or *Jain vart* of not killing or *ahinsa* and of leading a pure moral life. The pair are treated to sweetmeats, each by their own people, and the family gods and the cork marriage coronet or *bashing* are worshipped at both houses. Men and women from both houses go with music and ask their friends and kinspeople. In the afternoon, when all meet, the women take their seats in the booth and the men inside of the house, and all eat at the same time. On the fourth day, the actual marriage ceremony begins. Friends and relations are asked to both houses. The bridegroom is rubbed with fragrant oil and, with about fifteen of his relatives, again kindles the sacred fire, dresses in rich clothes, and goes to the bride's house on horseback with music and friends. On the way he is met by the bride's party and taken to a raised *umbar* (Ficus glomerata) seat. While he is seated on the *umbar* seat, a couple from the bride's house, generally the bride's parents, come and wash his feet. The bridegroom sips water thrice, puts on the new sacred thread offered him by the bride's priest, and swallows curds mixed with sugar which the couple have poured over his hands. The father-in-law leads the bridegroom by the hand to a ready-made seat in the house. Before the seat, a curtain is held and two heaps of rice, one on each side of the curtain, marked with the lucky cross or *svastik* and crowned with the sacred *kush* grass. A short *time* before the lucky moment the bride is let out by her friends and made to stand on the rice heap behind the curtain, the bridegroom standing on the rice heap on the other side. The guests stand around and the priests recite the nice-planet lucky verses or *navgrah mangalashtaks.* The astrologer marks the lucky moment by clapping his hands, the musicians redouble their noise, the priests draw inside the curtain, and the pair look at each other and become husband and wife. The bridegroom marks the bride's brow with vermilion and she throws a flower garland round his neck. They fold their hands together and the bride's father pours water over their hands. They then throw rice over each other's head and the priests and guests throw rice at the pair. The priests tie the marriage wristlets on the hands of the pair. The bridegroom then sits on a low stool facing east and the bride on another stool to his left. The priest kindles the sacred or *hom* fire and the bridegroom feeds the fire with offerings of parched rice held in a dish before him by the bride. Then the priest lays seven small heaps of rice each with a small stone at the top in one row. The bridegroom, holding the bride by the hand, touches the rice and the stone on each heap with his right toe, moves five times round the heaps, the priest shows the pair the Polar Star or *dhrav*, and the payment of a money gift to the priest completes the day's ceremonies. The hems of the pairs' garments are knotted together and they walk into home and bow before the waterpots which are arranged on the first day, and are fed with a dish of milk and clarified butter. On the next day, the bride's parents give a feast to the bridegroom's party and to their own kinspeople. In the morning, the pair are seated in the booth and young girls on both sides join them. The pair first play betelnuts for a time and the bridegroom takes some wet turmeric powder and rubs it five times on the brides face, who gathers it and rubs it on the bridegroom's face. The bridegroom is given a betel packet to chew, chews half of it and hands the rest to the bride. Thus, he chews the five betel packets, and the bride in her turn chews another five, each time handing half of the betel packets to the bridegroom to chew. Next morning the sacred fire is again kindled and the serpent is worshipped. The pair then dine at the bride's place and play with betelnuts. The pair are seated on horseback, the bride before the bridegroom, and taken to the Jain temple, where they walk round the god, bow before him and ask for his blessing. They then walk to the bridegroom's with music and friends.

"Before they reach it every part of the house is lighted and a long white sheet is spread on the ground from the booth door to the godroom. When the pair attempt to cross the threshold, the bridegroom's sister blocks the door and does not allow them to enter. The bridegroom asks her why she blocks the door. She says, "Will you give your daughter in marriage to my son?" He answers, "Ask my wife". The sister asks the wife and she says, "I will give one of my three pearls in marriage to your son". Then she leaves the door, the pair walk into the house, bow before the house gods, and a feast of uncooked provisions to those who do not eat from them and of cooked food to friends of their own caste and to kinspeople ends the ceremony," adds Mr. Enthoven. The custom, rites and rituals are pertinent to the community of Jains in the region.

A Maze of Rituals Within Rituals

The Brahmans are divided into ten exogamous *gotras* or subgroups, said to be originated from the name of mythological sages like Upamanyu, Bundal, Bhargave, Shandilya, Kaushik, Vatsa, Gurg, Gautam, Vashistha and Parashar. They bore surnames like Joshi, Trivedi, Dave, Pandia, Samarth and Bhatt. The basis of differentiation is social. The principal function of *gotra* is to trace descent in order to regulate marriage alliances and to help in the life-cycle rituals. They perceive their status in the social hierarchy as well as in *varna* position and are so placed by others, too. The Brahmans resort to sept and clan exogamy and the community endogamy. Marriage is prohibited within *sapinda,* within seven ascending generations of patrilineal side and five ascending generations of mother's side. Traditionally, they practice child marriage when girls used to be married before attaining puberty. The practice of adult marriage is a recent change under the force of law. Marriage is settled by parents through negotiation and they practise monogamy. *Bangdi* (bangles of turtle shell and of ivory) and *mangalsutra* are their traditional marriage symbols. The Brahmans have practice of *dej* or dowry in kind fixed during the negotiation. Divorce and remarriage are never allowed. The Brahmans practise the patrilocal rule of residence.

The ritual of *Sagai* or betrothal is conducted one to two months prior to *vivah* or marriage at the bridegroom's residence. Marriage is the procedure of three days performed at both the places and solemnised at the bride's residence. The three-day's marriage rituals start with the installation of *manek-stambh* (sacred pole for the Ganpati) doubed with turmeric and near it is placed a *kalash* (earthen pot) filled with water. The marriage booth *Mandava* is erected thereafter. *Pithee* (paste of barely flour turmeric mixing with ground nut oil) is rubbed on the bodies of both the bride and bridegroom for three days by the relatives at their respective houses. *Maushals* (ceremonial marriage gift) is presented to both at their houses by their maternal uncles on the second day. The family deity called *Devsantak* is performed at night. The *jan* (marriage procession) starts for the bride's village on the third day where the bridegroom, relatives and guests are given *janawas* or separate lodging on their arrival. The bridegroom, with the *jan,* arrives at bride's house where *ponkhavan* or reception is conducted near the *toran* (entrance of the marriage booth) by the bride's mother. The ritual of *Har toda* (exchange of garland) is conducted at *otah* (inner varandah) and the bridegroom is led to *chauri* (square of sacrificial fire) in the *mandava* and is made to sit there. The bride also comes to the *chauri*, escorted by her maternal uncle, and is seated on the left side of the bridegroom. Thereafter, *Kanyadan* is performed and the bridegroom is presented with a golden ring by the bride's father. The Brahman priest recites the appropriate mantras and the robes of the bride and bridegroom are knotted together. The ceremony of *Hast milap* is performed when the priest holds the right hand of the bride and places it on the right hand of bridegroom covered by a piece of cloth and recites mantras. *Saptpadi* is the principal ritual performed thereafter when both the bride and the bridegroom circumambulates seven times the *chauri* amidst the mantras recited by the priest. The family deity is worshipped by both and the bridegroom returns to *janawas*. *Chaturthi-karma* is conducted the next day in *chauri* when both the newly-married spouses feeds each other *kansar* (rice boiled in milk mixing jaggery). *Dej* (dowry) in kind is paid to the bridegroom's father and the bridegroom is presented with gifts by the bride's parents relatives. The bridegroom with his bride returns back to his village in the evening and pays homage to his family deity. The consummation of marriage takes place in the *suhag-ghar*, at the bridegroom's residence. *Ana* (return of bride) takes place after 29 days or three months. The custom is related to the *Gujarati Brahmans* of Daman and Diu.

Rite of *Mandva Murl*

About the peculiar marriage customs, rites and rituals, Mr. Enthoven writes, "Three days before the marriage, booth-consecrating *mandva murl* and Ganesh-invoking ceremonies are performed. The day before the marriage at the boy's house the *sakranman* or sweet-curd ceremony is performed. Two big clay pots, one containing 1 cwt. 3 qrs. 4 lbs. and the other 1cwt. 8 lbs. (5 and 3 *mans*) are filled with curds mixed with sugar and a little clarified butter. An old woman whose husband is alive and who is a relation of the bridegroom stirs the curds with her hand. The family-priest worships the pots, and presents are made to the woman who stirred the curds. Next the priest takes the pots, accompanied with music, to the bride's house and there gets the bride to worship them. The big pot is kept at the bride's house and the little pot is sent to her maternal uncle, and the contents of both pots are distributed among the caste-people. When this is done the priest brings what is called *dahiani* from the bride's house. This *dahiani* consists of a brass dish with two clay pots *kodia*, a letter naming the day and hour of marriage and a certain amount of cash. After these presents, the betrothal cannot be broken. On the wedding-day, shortly before the marriage hour, the bridegroom, with his face covered with flower garlands and wearing a long tunic and a silk waistcloth *pitamber,* escorted by the women of his family, goes to the bride's house on horseback in procession. Here, in presence of a company of the bride's friends, he stands at the central square of the marriage hall, and looking down into a large earthen pan full of water, from their reflection in the water, touches with the point of his sword four saucers hung over his head. He then goes back to his father's house and after two or three hours his friends, making him sitted on the horseback, escort him to the bride. Before the bridegroom's party arrive, the bride, dressed in a headcloth, bodice and loose *Musalman*-like trousers, is seated in a closed palanquin or *balai* set in front of the house. The bridegroom, on dismounting, walks seven times round the palanquin, the bride's brother at each turn gives him a cut with an oleander *karena* twig and the women of the family throw showers of cakes from the windows. He retires, and while mounting his horse and before he is in the saddle, the bride's father comes out and, giving him a present, leads him into the marriage-hall. In Kathiawar, on the morning of the marriage-day, the bride bathes in water drawn from seven wells. She then puts on *chatudi* or Punjab bracelets sent by her maternal uncle. She wears yellow trousers reaching to the knee and a red robe. The girl keeps her eyes closed throughout the whole day, not opening them until the bridegroom is ushered into the marriage booth, so that the first object she sees is her intended husband. On the first Monday, Thursday or Friday after the marriage, the bride is hidden either in her own or in a neighbour's house. The bridegroom comes in state and with the points of his sword touches the outer doors of seven houses and then begins to search for his wife. The time is one of much fun and merriment, the women of the house bantering and taunting the bridegroom, especially when he is long in finding his wife's hiding place. When she is found, the bridegroom leads the bride to the marriage hall and they sit there combing each other's hair. After a while, the women of the party in sport douse the bridegroom with dirty water. Then the couple have to bathe and sit together on a cot and gamble with dice. Fresh clothes are put on instead of the wedding garments, and the marriage ceremonies are over," adds Mr. Enthoven. The customs, rites and rituals are practised among the *Brahman Kshatriyas* of Maharashtra, Gujarat and Daman and Diu.

No Tribe-price Among *Catholic Mahars*

For setting the marriage alliances, they refer to the birth registers and find if a parallel-cousin matrimonial has been contracted. So the Catholic marriages are possible even between spouses with the same surname. For instance, a Fernandes of one village can marry a Fernandes of another distant village, if no close relation between them can be found through the marriage registers. Though they are aware of the Hindu *varna* system, they could not place themselves in that hierarchy. Among the Catholic broad divisions, they are, however, considered to be under the rubric of Sudra Catholics. The Catholic Mahar do not marry a Hindu Mahar, their marriages are allowed, however, with any other Catholics. Catholic church officials claim that any Catholic can marry any other Catholic, though the distinctions and community discriminations are evident among the Catholics in Goa. Consanguineous marriages are allowed and practised but only with legal sanction in case of maladjustment. In the current times, boys marry around 25 years of age and the girls around 20 years of age. The age for marriage has slightly increased during the recent times due to the spread of education in the younger generation. Widow and widower remarriages are allowed and performed in the same way as the first marriage. The custom of marriage through negotiation is prevalent among them though by mutual consent of the spouses and nowadays the love marriage also takes place occasionally. No compulsory payments are made at the time of marriage either from the bride's side or from the bridegroom's side, but the brides are given fifty gifts at the time of marriage by their parents. The wedding ring is the Catholic symbol of marriage.

Marriage Proposal Coming from Girl's Side

Among the *Catholic Madvol*, marriage proposals come from first the girls's parents. When both the parties feel satisfied with the proposal, they go for the civil registeration of the marriage in the Rigistear's Office in their Taluka alongwith the witnesses from both side. Then the Registration Certificate is produced compulsorily in the church where the actual marriage is to be celebrated, and the prospective merriage alliance is announced there twice on three occasions in the mass. After making each announcement, the *Padre* seeks the approval of the memebers by asking them to raise objections, if any, to the marital union. The next cermony is betrothal locally called *soirlk*. In this ceremony, the bride and the bridegroom exchange rings in the presence of the community memebers and church officaials and a feast follows. The principal marriage ceremony (*cazar*) is traditionally celebrated in the Church of the bridegroom's village and again repeated in the church of the bride's village. But currently the *cazar* is celebrated only in one church convenient to both the parties to save time and expenditure both. For marriage celebration in the church, a special mass is arranged when the *Padre* or the priest utters some scriptures and extracts promises from both bride and bridegroom. He blesses both the spouses with Holy water. The marriage feast follows immediately and people drink wine and enjoy themselves after raising the toast to the welfare and happiness of the bridal couple. Then, the new couple visits the bride's house and spend two or three days there. This visit is called *appoune,* invitation or calling. The nuptial rituals are usually arranged on the same nights of the wedding.

Different Brahman Sub-castes Fuse into Catholic Brahmans

In Goa all the Catholic belong to the Roman Catholic Church apparently without any division and discrimination. But, since they are the Hindu converts, they prefer to preserve their core-culture and maintain the traditional caste and *varna* system of the Hindus even after four hundred years of their conversion into Christianity. However, they do not believe in system of *gotras.* Sheltering behind a special decree by Pope Gregory XV, given in 1623 that Brahmans converted to Catholicism might wear their sacred threads and caste-marks, they virtually transported the entire caste structure of the Hindu Brahmans into their adopted religion.

The different Brahman sub-castes Brahman have got fused into the single caste of Catholic Brahman or Saraswat. The Kshatriya and Vani (Vaishya) converts have also merged into one single caste of Charddo Catholic and all the remaining castes have merged into the caste of Catholic Sudras being treated as an inferior class. Besides this caste distinction, a small section of Catholics is also identified as *Mesticos* who are the offspring of the Portuguese white males and the Goan Catholic female, but their number is very small in Goa.

But in the present times, the Brahman and the Charddo Catholics have merged into a single entity recognised as the upper class Catholics and both of them do not hesitate to establish social and commensal relationship or enter into connubial relations. The Catholic Sudras, including the Mahar and some fisher folks, still prefer to maintain their endogamous entity in making their marriage alliances.

In principle, the Catholic marriage should be solemnised with the permission of the Parish priest. The Catholics follow the rules of monogamy and marry with in the bounds of their community only. Marriage is usually negotiated within their own group when the boys and girls reach the adult age varying from 28 years to 35 years for boys and 22 years to 25 years for girls. If one of the spouses not happens to be Catholic, the non-Catholic should be converted and baptised first. Then the marriage is solemnised in Church. Both cross-cousin and parallel cousin marriages are allowed, but the cross-cousin marriage among the Catholics of Goa is preferable, as largely prevalent among the Konkan Hindus. Under the Portuguese Civil Code, monogamy was a must for all, whether Hindus, Christians or Muslims and all the marriages were to be registered in the Civil Registration Office located in the headquarters of every taluka in Goa. The Catholics of Goa follow this rule strictly even today, besides many other Portuguese laws.

Their wedding ring is symbol of their marriage. Divorce is allowed but it should be certified by the Church as well as by the Civil Court. The decision about the maintenance and liabilities of the children, following divorce, should be taken either by the Church or by the court. The widow, widower and divorcee can remarry. Dowry is given either in cash or in kind especially among the higher caste Catholics.

Among the Catholics, the marriage proposal generally comes from the girl's side. After negotiation is over to the satisfaction of both the sides, the betrothal is performed is done at the bride's place and wedding rings alongwith some presents are exchanged. But before the betrothal, three announcements on three consecutive Sunday masses are made by the priest in the church regarding objection, if any, from any person to solemnising the marriage. Prior to the wedding, a fortnight or a week before it, the bride puts on bangles (*chuda*) like the Hindu brides but all the twelve bangles like those of the latter are of different colours which are worn till a few days after the wedding. The marriage is solemnised in the church by the *Padre* or the Vicar (parish priest), who blesses the couple and prays to the Almighty for their better future ahead. The marriage ceremony takes place in the afternoon, when the bride dressed in the bridal white ceremonial gown offered by the bridegroom and the bridegroom in suit are brought to the altar by their parents or relatives along with specially invited guests. The Church priest delivers a sermon giving his councel to the couple and blesses both the rings of the couple which are also exchanged by them as per the priest's instruction. After the ritual is over, registration for marriage is performed by the priest with at least two witnesses from both sides before the mass. The registration of the marriage in the church is the Christian customary law, but after betrothal their marriage is registered in the Civil Registration Office.

A reception is given either in the Church, usually near the bride's residence or in a common hall by both the parties. If the reception is held in a common hall, the *Var* comprising the bride and the bridegroom, brides-maids (*dhedyo*), flower girls, Best Man (*Dhedo*) and page boys are brought to the bride's house or some relative's house before they proceed to the bridegroom's residence. Sometimes, the bride's father organises a feast on the return of the wedding party. In the wedding party, both men and women taste wine, if offered. After the wedding, a toast is raised, usually by a prominent person or a family elder to the newly-married couple followed by thanks from the bridegroom and a prolonged dance in which both the guest couples and the bridal couple dance to Western music. When the newly married couple enters the bridegroom's house, they are received and greeted by the patriarch of the family through offering a golden chain with a locket or a gold coin (*pod*) and a red scarf (*sad*) to the bride while reciting prayers in front of the altar in the residence. The next day the bridal couple is invited to the bride's residence for a party and feast and the bridegroom is offered an ornament depending upon the financial status of the bride's father. In the same evening, the bridal couple returns home. They, however, do not observe any puberty rites or the menstruation-related pollution. Moreover, abortion is a taboo among the Goan Christians.

Custom of Tying Bridal Robes

About the Bhilalas primitive customs and rituals, Mr. Enthoven writes, They celebrate their marriages at sun-down, one of the caste being set to watch. As the sun disappears, the watchman claps his hands, and the young women of both bride and bridegroom's families fasten the bridegroom's waist cloth to the bride's lugda robe. Presents are made and a feast follows.

Bhilalas are chiefly husbandmen, being the principal cultivators in the native states on the north-west boundary of Khandesh."

Custom of Giving Pallun

About the Bhisti customs and rituals, Mr. Enthoven writes "The offer of marriage comes from the girl's father. They boy's father has to pay to the girl a *pallun* (woman's property) consisting of ornaments worth Rs 25 and clothes worth Rs 15. The day for the marriage is fixed by an astrologer or by the family priest who conducts the service. The marriage ceremonies of Bhistis resemble those of the Galiaras except that they perform the *mata vavava* ceremony. If this ceremony is not performed at the time of marriage, it is required to be performed at the time of first pregnoncy. From the commencement of the marriage till it is over, the bridegroom holds in his hand a dagger, a knife or a pair of scissors, which is ultimately thrown into a river or well. The binding portion of the marriage service is the joining of the hands of the bride and bridegroom.

"The remarriage of widows is permitted with the sanction of the caste *panch*. A widow may marry her late husband's younger brother. A widow remarriage is celebrated on a Tuesday. Thursday or Sunday. A bachelor desirous of marrying a widow has first to marry a *shami* bush (Prosopis spicigera).

"A husband can divorce a wife on the ground of her misconduct. A wife can divorce a husband if he ill-treats her. A divorced woman has to pay a fine of from Rs 100 to 200 to the caste-people in order to remain in the caste. Divorce is not much in vogue. The caste follows the Hindu law of inheritance," adds Mr. Enthoven. The customs and rituals pertain to the Bhisti caste.

Performing Ceremony at Bride's House

Mr. Enthoven records, "Till about thirty years ago boys and girls were married at a very early age, but at present the marriageable age for a boy is about twenty to twenty-two and for a girl it is fourteen to sixteen, or even later.

"The offer of marriage generally comes from the boy's side. The engagement ceremony is performed at the girl's house in the evening, when the girl is presented with a ring or a small golden ornament. The marriage is celebrated on some subsequent Sunday. On the preceding night, which is called "*Halad Mendi night*" the boy and girl, at their respective houses, are rubbed with turmeric paste and moistened powder of the leaves of the *mehndi* plant (*Lawsona incermis*). On the next morning, a feast is given to relatives and friends at both houses. In the evening, either before or after sunset, the marriage is celebrated at a synagogue or any other convenient place and the married pair are then taken to the house of the bride. In the evening of the next day, the pair are taken to the bridegroom's house, and a few day's later feasts are given to the bridegroom's house, and a few days later feasts are given to the nearest kinsfolk at both houses. This ends the marriage.

"A necessary function of the marriage ceremony is the execution of the marriage contract by the bridegroom. The contract is attested by the officiating priest and by two or more other persons present, and is handed over to the bride, who gives it to her parents for safe custody.

"The Bene-Israels, though not prevented from practising polygamy, have as a rule only one wife. A second wife is married only in case the first is barren, but even this custom is rapidly dying out.

"The marriage covenant is generally rigidly observed. However, in cases of violation of the contract, the innocent party is allowed a divorce and given the liberty of remarriage; however, cases of divorce are rare. Intermarriage with alien women is discouraged. The children born of such unions necessarily pass into the Kale endogamous group, even though the Bene-Israel parent was of the Gore," adds Mr. Enthoven. The custom is related to the community of Bene-Israels.

References

1. Enthoven R.E., *The Tribes and Castes of Bombay*, Low Price Publications, Delhi (reprint) 1997, originally published 1922.
2. Russell, R.V. and Lal, Hira, *The tribes and Castes of the Central Provinces of India*, Low Price Publications, Delhi (reprint) 1997, originally published MacMillan & Co, London, 1966.
3. Singh, K.S. (Gen. Ed.), *People of India : Daman and Diu*, Popular Prakashan, Bombay 1994.

4. Singh, K.S. (Gen. Ed.). *People of India : Dadra and Nagar Haveli*, Popular Prakashan, Bombay, 1994.
5. Singh, K.S. (Gen. Ed.). *People of India : Goa*, Popular Prakashan, Bombay 1993.
6. *Bombay Gazetter*, Vol. XXIII.
7. *Bombay Gazetter*, Vol. XVIII.
8. Risley, Sir Herbert, *The People of India*, Munshiram Manohar Lal Publishers, New Delhi, 1991 (reprint), originally published 1915.
9. Gome, Olivinho J.F., *India—Land and People : Goa*, National Book Trust, New Delhi, 2004.

5

Death Rituals : Cremation

Most of the Hindu castes and communities in Maharashtra, Gujarat, Goa, Daman and Diu, Dadra and Nagar Haveli, cremate their dead except those below one year and whose death is caused by smallpox and snake-bite who are buried. Generally, the eldest son acts as the chief mourner. The funeral rites generally begin on the third day after death when the chief mourner visits the cremation ground, pours milk and water over the cold embers, collects the ashes and charred bones and immersed in sea with flowers. The ritual is called *phool-padhraw*. The consecutive funeral rites are performed on the tenth, eleventh, twelfth and thirteenth days after death. The chief mourner and the other male members of the bereaved family shave their heads and moustaches on eleventh day and take bath to rid themselves of the ritualisite pollution. *Shraddha* ceremony is performed on the eleventh and twelfth days when *got* men shave their heads and rice is offered in the names of the departed soul and ancestors. The thirteenth day *shraddha* is performed when the articles designated for the use of departed soul in the next world are gifted to the low-caste priest. The fisherman also perform certain magico-religious rites to pacify the ghost of departed soul. These rites include are *madhejawawan, darah, tutke,* and *neel* (ghost marriage). When a death occurs in sea, while on fishing expedition and the body is not found, all the funeral rites are performed in absentia, as usual when all the remaining fishermen and their relatives return from the high sea finishing their fishing expedition. An effigy of the deceased, made from banana plant, the eyes from oyster and the teeth from pomegranate seeds, is carried away on the date fixed by the *gynat samaj* Patel, to the cremation ground and then cremated. This rite is of multiple significance, firstly, it is for taking over of the interest of certain supernatural power. It provides relief to the tormented soul of the deceased, and finally, the departed soul remains friendly to the fraternity of the fishing expedition as a result of such rites.

In the western region, the Parsi way of disposal of the dead is well known. The dead body is exposed to a particular place called *dakhma* (tower of silence). They take the body to Nargal in Maharashtra for the disposal as there is no *dakhma* in the Union Territory of Daman and Diu. The body is given bath and is covered with white clothes. However, the clothes are taken off from the corpse and donated in charity before disposal. *Khandliya* carry the dead to the *dokhama.* The *Parsis* observe death pollution for three days. On the fourth day, *chautha* is performed and a feast is given to the relatives and the members of the community. The mourning period extends for eighteen days and *mukhtad* is performed by the *mobid* (priest) and another feast is given in the memory of the deceased.

Exposing Corpse to be Devoured by Vultures

About the Parsi method of the disposal of dead, Mr. R.V. Russell and Hira Lal write, "The Parsi method of exposing the dead in Dakhmas or towers of silence to be devoured by vultures has often been described. It has objectionable features, and the smaller communities in the interior of India do not as a rule erect towers of silence, and are content simply of bury the dead. It seems probable that the original custom was simply to expose the dead on waste land, the towers of silence being a substitute which became necessary when the Parsis began to live in towns. This hypothesis would explain some points in their funeral customs recorded in the *Bombay Gazetteer*. The dead body is washed, dressed in an old clean cloth and laid on the floor of the house, the space being marked off. If the floor is of earth the surface of this enclosed space is broken up. If the floor is of cement or stone one or two stone slabs are set on it and the body laid on them; it is never laid on a wooden floor, nor on stone slabs placed on such a floor. The space where the body was laid is marked off, and is not used for a month if the death occurs between the eighth and twelfth months of the year, and for ten days if the death occurs between the first and seventh months. The last are said to be the hottest months. (*Bombay Gazetteer*, Vol. IX. Part II, *Parsis of Gujarat*, pp. 239-242). It would appear that these rules are a reminiscence of the time when the body was simply exposed. It was then naturally always laid on earth or rock, and never on wood, hence the prohibition of a wooden floor. The fact that spot where the body is now laid in the house is held impure for a shorter period during the summer months may be explained on the ground that all traces of the decaying corpse, after it had been devoured by wild animals and vultures, would have been dried up by the sun more quickly at this time than during the winter months. In the latter period, as the process would take longer, the place in the home is similarly held impure for a month, as against ten days in summer, though at present neither the sun nor weather can possibly affect a site inside the house. The fact that when the floor is of earth the site for the corpse is broken up may indicate that it was formerly laid on rough waste ground, and not on a floor beaten smooth, though it might also be simply a means of avoiding contamination of the floor. But if this was the object it would be simpler to avoid letting the body come into contact with the floor at all. The corpse may still be wrapped in an old cloth because it was originally exposed in the cloth worn at death. The body is carried to the tower on an iron bier by special bearers; if the journey is a long one a bullock cart may be used, but in this case the cart must be broken up and the pieces buried near the tower. Before the funeral starts a number of priests attend at the house and recite the prayers for the dead. During the service a dog is brought in to look on the face of the dead. The mourners follow in the usual manner, and on arrival at the tower the bearers alone take the corpse inside and lay it naked on one of the slabs, which are built in circular terraces in the interior. The mourners must be purified at the tower by pouring a little cow's urine into their hands, and on returning home they wash their face and hands, and recite a prayer before entering the house. They must bathe and have their clothes washed before these are again used. When a married man dies his widow breaks her glass bangles and wears only metal bracelets, and so long as she remains a widow she takes no part in any festal celebration. Every morning for three days after a death rice is cooked and laid in the veranda for dogs to eat. No other food is cooked in the house of death, the family being supplied by their friends. During these three days prayers are said for the dead several times a day by priests, and kinsmen pay short visits of condolence. On the third day, a meeting is held in the house and prayers are said for the dead; trays of flowers and burning incense are placed before the spot where the body lay, and a list of charitable gifts made by the family in memory of the dead man is read. On the fourth day a feast is held specially for priests, and friends are also asked to join in it. A little of the food cooked on this day is sent to all relations and friends, who make a point of eating or at least of tasting it. On the tenth and thirtieth days after death, and on monthly anniversaries for the first year, and subsequently on annual anniversaries, ceremonies in honour of the dead are performed. (*Bombay Gazetteer*, Vol. IX, Part II, *Parsis of Gujarat*, pp. 241, 243.)

"Some of these customs are peculiar and interesting. It has been seen that for three days the home is impure, and no food is cooked in it except what is given to dogs; and since on the third day offerings are made on the spot where the body lay, it seems to be supposed that the dead man's spirit is still there. On the fourth day is the funeral feast, in which all relations and friends join, and after this the house becomes pure, it being presumably held that the dead man's spirit has taken its departure. For these three days food is cooked in the house and given to dogs, and immediately after the man is dead a dog is brought in to look at his face. It has been suggested that the manner of laying out the body recalls the time when it was simply exposed. But when it was exposed the body would have been devoured principally by dogs and vultures, and the customs connected with dogs seem to arise from this. The cooked food given to dogs for three days is perhaps a substitute for the flesh of the dead man which they would have eaten, and the display of the body to a dog is in substitution for its being devoured by these animals, who now that it is exposed in a tower of silence no longer have access to it. It has further been seen how during the marriage rites, after an invitation has been issued to the ancestors to attend, a woman comes in barking like a dog. The other women drive her away and laughingly eat everything they can lay their hands on, perhaps in imitation of the way dogs devour their food. This custom seems to indicate that the Parsis formerly believed that the spirits of their ancestors went into the dogs which devoured their bodies, a belief which would be quite natural to primitive people. Such a hypothesis would explain the peculiar customs mentioned, and also the great sanctity which the Parsis attach to dogs. On the same analogy they should apparently also have believed that the spirits of ancestors went into vultures; but it is not recorded that they show any special veneration for these birds, though it must be almost certain that they do not kill them. The explanation given for the custom of the exposure of the dead is that none of the holy elements, earth, fire or water, can be polluted by receiving dead bodies. But, as already stated, towers of silence cannot be a primitive institution, and the bodies in all probability were previously exposed on the ground. The custom of exposure probably dates from a period prior to the belief in the extreme sanctity of the earth. It may have been retained in order that the spirits of ancestors might find a fresh home in the animals which devoured their bodies; and some platform, from which the towers of silence subsequently developed, may have been made to avoid defilement of the earth; while in after times this necessity of not defiling the earth and other elements might be advanced as a reason justifying the custom of exposure," they add.

About the disposal of dead among the Parsis, Mr. RE Enthoven says, "The Parsis expose their dead in round structures known by them as *dokhmas* and ordinarily known as Towers of Silence. In place, where there are no such Towers; they unavoidably bury but never burn. Their practice of exposure is very old. Classical writers like Herodotus and Strabo refer to it.

"The Towers of Silence are constructed of solid masonry work on sanitary principles. The bodies are soon devoured by vultures. which are the scavengers of Nature. The sun, air and rain do the rest of the work to keep the place clean. There are in all seven Towers in Bombay five of which are public Towers and two private. A tower costs from about Rs 7,000 to Rs 1,00,000 according to its size. They carry the bodies to the Tower during the day hours only.

"In some big centres of Parsi population, there are paid professional carriers. Those who carry the dead body are required to bathe before they mix with others and to change their clothes, which are altogether rejected or used once or twice again for the purpose of carrying the dead bodies of poor Parsis, who cannot afford to furnish suits of clothes to the carrier for such a purpose. The clothes over the dead body are rejected altogether. Even those that attend the funeral are required to wash their faces and other parts of their body that are exposed. The carriers are at least two, and when more are required, they are always in pairs, *i.e.,* in even numbers, never in odd numbers. The mourners who follow the bier also walk in pairs, holding a *paiwand* (lit. connection) between them in the form of a handkerchief.

"They perform some ceremonies in honour of the dead during the first three days. They are known as the Sarosh ceremonies. Most of these are performed in their fire-temples. The other principal occasions for the performance of the ceremonies are the fourth (*chahurm*), the tenth (dehum), the thirtieth (*si-roz*), and the anniversary (*sal roz*) day after death. Those who can afford perform a few ceremonies continuously for the first ten days or for the first month or for the first year.

"In the recital of prayers for the ceremonies, the name of the particular individual, in whose honour they are performed, is mentioned first, and then, the names of the ancestors and other near relatives. Even the names of some great and good Parsis of the past, who have done good to the community, to the city or to the country are remembered. For example, the name of Zoroaster, the Prophet, kings like Jamshed, Ardeshir Babegan and Noshirvan the Just (Chosroes I), saintly persons of old like Earch, Shiavax and Agriras, national warriors like the great Rustam, Dasturs or Prelates like Ardai Virai and Adrbad Marespand, all of ancient Persia, learned Dasturs like Neryosang Dhaval and Meherji Rana and benefactors like the first Sir Jamsetjee Jeejeebhoy. Bombay, are still remembered generally during the public, and often during the private recitals in honour of the dead. The modern form of recital is: "May the soul of the pious souled... (here the name of the deceased is mentioned) be remembered here." At the end of the recital of the names of particular deceased persons, as said above, there is a general remembrance of all (hama) good men of the past, whether priests (athornan) soldiers (ratheshtraran), agriculturists (vactrayocan) and others practising various professions, trades and arts (hutohkshan).

"In the performance of these ceremonies, no particular distinction is made in the case of childless persons. The only thing that is done extra, in the case of a childless man, is that if he is of the age of 15 or above, he is given a son in adoption at the *uthamna* ceremony in the afternoon of the third day or at the dawn of the fourth night. It is announced that such and such a person is selected as the adopted son of the deceased and a *Tandarusti* (a benedictory prayer) is recited for the welfare of that adopted son. His name is also mentioned occasionally in the prayers in honour of the deceased, as one directing the ceremonies to be performed (farmayashne). A near member of the family, generally a younger brother or a nephew or such near relative, especially from the father's side, is adopted.

"There is nothing extra or special in the funeral ceremonies for a person who has met a violent death.

"The ceremonies in honour of the dead performed after the third day are generally spoken as the Baj Rojgar ceremonies, and they correspond, to some extent, to the Shraddha of the Hindus, and remind us of the ceremonies in honour of the Lares among the ancient Romans" add Mr. Enthoven. The customs are practised among the Parsis.

Dressing the Corpse in New Robe and New Shroud

About the custom of cremation by the Gujarat tribals, Mr. Enthoven writes, "Except a few of the poorest who bury, they burn the dead. Persons dying of leprosy, small-pox and such other contagious diseases are buried to prevent the spread of the disease. Children below four years are buried. While burying, they place the deceased in the grave with head northwards. When the deceased is burnt, the ashes and bones are washed away with water. On this occasion, friends and relatives meet at the house of the deceased, the women weep and beat their breasts. When the deceased is an unwidowed woman, the brow is marked with red powder, the eyes are painted with lamp black, and red lead is sprinkled over the sinciput. The body is dressed in a new robe, and covered with a new shroud. If the deceased is a male, a white shroud is used. The body is set on a bamboo bier, and is carried by four relatives, who, as they pass to the burning-ground, chant the refrain *Ram bolo bhai Ram,* Call Ram brothers, Call Ram. At the halting station every member throws grains of rice over the corpse. On reaching the burning-ground, which is generally on the bank of a stream, the pyre is made ready. Half a seer of rice is cooked in a jar in which fire is brought by the chief mourner. A ball of cooked rice is prepared and is placed on the mouth of the deceased. Four balls are offered to crows on a leaf of banyan tree. This is called *Vas Mukvi.* Copper coins are placed in the hands of the deceased, and a particle of silver is put into the mouth. The chief mourner then kindles the pyre. The party waits till the pyre is consumed, receiving on return a draught of *tadi,* palm beer. Ceremonies are performed on the second, fourth and sixth days after death, and on the twelfth day a caste dinner is given. A poor man delays the ceremonies to a later date, and when they are performed, an image of *kush* grass is made and burnt in the burning-ground, after which the ceremony is commenced. When funeral ceremonies are not observed owing to the poverty of the relations, they bathe at the *Holi* (March-April), *vali* (October-November) and *Divaso* (July-August), and before taking food make offerings of a portion of crows. This is known as *Pandadu Mukvu.*"

"Every year in the month of *Chaitra* or *Magh* the following ceremony is performed for the pacification of the *manes."*

"A devotee called *jangio* is called. He becomes possessed and utters the names of the deceased ancestors. The members of the family then go to the bank of a river and burn images of *kush grass* in the name of the deceased ancestors. After their return home, funnel-shaped earthen pots are filled with water and placed on the ground, one in the name of each ancestor. If the deceased be a male, the earthen jar in his name is covered with a white piece of cloth, if a female, with a red piece. The mouth of the earthen pots are closed with small earthen cups, and over these cups small earthen pots are again placed. Then the devotee nods, and taking in succession the name of each of the deceased ancestor, says "I a certain ancestor have come." After each time he has repeated a name, the devotee is given water and liquor to drink and a little food to eat. After this is over, all the jars are emptied and the ceremony ends. The Dublas believe that only by the performance of this ceremony the deceased ancestors become satisfied. In some places, wooden images are made in the name of the deceased ancestors ; they are dressed in clothes and smeared with vermilion. In the mornings of Sundays and Tuesdays the images are worshipped with offering of goats, fowls, toddy and liquor."

"Dublas are peasants and labourers, most of them ploughmen or *halis,* the hereditary servants of Bhatela, Brahmans and other better class cultivators. These men work in the fields, their women acting as household servants in the master's family. They are entirely dependent on their masters for food and clothing, and on the whole seem as well off as those of their tribe who are freer in names. As they mix much with the better class of cultivators, their ways are cleaner and their manners less rough and peculiar from those of most early tribesmen. Between A.D. 1863 and 1866, when labour was dear, many Dublas left the families, they formerly served, and worked as free labourers. Since then they are said to have found their old position as ploughmen or *halis* securer and not more onerous."

Mr. Enthoven further writes, "They believe in witchcraft, sorcery and magic. Every community has a Bhagat or sorcerer, who cures diseases by means of a broom made of the leaves of the *nimb* tree. He is much respected when possessed by a spirit; he nods his head and directs the performance of certain rites to free the patient from his troubles."

"The Dublas are animists by religion. They have no knowledge of Shiva and Vishnu nor of the incarnations of the latter. Besides spirits and ancestors they worship Hanuman and different forms of goddess such as Shikotri, Agashi, Himario, etc. Offerings of goats, fowls, etc., are made to their goddesses during the *Navratra* or nine nights festival in *Aso* September-October. Stones and holy trees, especially the tree *sameer,* which is believed to be the haunt of ghosts, and the *shami,* are worshipped. They also worship the cow, the bull, the *pipal*, a scythe, a grinding mill, the serpent, the tiger, etc. Their leading holidays are *Matavi Athem* in *Astio* September-October, *Holi* March-April, *Diwali* October-November, *Makar Sankranti* in January, *Divaso* in June-July and *Balev* in July-August. The *Divaso* holiday is specially observed by them. On that day they make dolls and puppets and marry them. There is a saying that the *Divaso* is the special holiday of Dublas alone. During the *Navratra* they dance and are called *Gherias.* While dancing they wear the skirts of women, but above their waist they dress like men. They tie a belt of jingling bells round their waist and hold a stick in their hands. They collect subscriptions from the public and spend the amount on a feast. They worship the images of their ancestors. The images are prepared of sandal wood and are called *Khatruns*. Offerings of coconuts, flowers, red powder and red lead are made to them. Occasionally animal sacrifices also are made for their propitiation, and liquor is poured over the images. They revere Musalman saints. When cholera and small-pox are raging, they adore the minor deities Kalikamata and Kababalia. They treat Brahmans with respect and, except in a few of the wilder villages, on marriage occasions and sometimes at the time of the naming ceremony make use of their services."

Conducting Cremation on Bodies Buried Earlier

About the weird custom of cremation, Mr. Enthoven writes, "Among Katkaris, when a person dies of cholera, he is buried until the outbreak of cholera is over, when the body is dug up and burnt. In the same way, in some parts of Kolaba, if a death takes place in wet weather, the corpse is buried for a time between two hurdles and is afterwards dug up and burnt. The men who have to carry out the exhumation are plied with drink and have their nostrils stuffed with onions to enable them to carry out the task. In other cases the dead are burnt at once. If the death happens at night, the funeral is put off till the next day. But the corpse has to be watched all night, and to cheer the watchers special music is played. On the upper surface of a common brass plate a lump of wax is stuck, and, in the wax, a thin stick about nine inches long. When the finger and thumb are passed down this stick, it vibrates with a weird drone or hum. To this accompaniment the mourners chant all night long, crouching round a fire outside the house. When the time comes to prepare the body, it is washed with warm water mixed with turmeric. The waistcord and loincloth are thrown away and new clothes put on. If they can afford it, a piece of new cloth is wound round the head and another cloth is laid under and drawn over the body. The cloth is sprinkled over with red and sweet-scented powder and a pillow of rice is laid under the head. About half way to the burning ground, the pall-bearers stop and lower the bier, while the chief mourner hides a copper coin under a stone. At the burning ground the corpse is laid on the pile. A hole is torn in the face cloth, some rice and a piece of silver or copper are laid in mouth, and the pile is lighted at both ends. While it burns the chief mourner walks round it five times with an earthen water jar in his hand. Then, knocking a hole in the jar, he sprinkled the pyre and dashes the jar to pieces on the ground. When the burning is over the Dhors leave the bones and embers as they are; but the Sons gather them into a heap, quench the embers, and lay a stone over them. On the twelfth day after the death the Sons of Karjat cook a hen with spilt pulse and some rice. The hen and pulse are divided into two equal parts, and one-half left in the house and the other half, with the whole of the rice, taken by the chief mourner to the stone under which the copper coin was left. He lays part of the rice and half of the hen and pulse on the stone, and the rest of the food he sets on the stone that covers the dead man's ashes. Over this stone he builds a little hut to shade the deceased's resting place. On his return home, he divides the share of victuals that he left in the house among some fasting children, and entertains his neighbours, friends and relations with rice and liquor.

"In Gujarat, on the third day, the mourners visit the burning ground and gather the ashes, throw a little into the village, and, on the top of the ash-heap, place some cooked rice. Then, in front of them, in the deceased's name, the chief mourner feeds young children on cooked rice.

"Katkari children are great plunderers of birds-nests and very sharp in finding them. The men seldom commit deeds of violence, but are notorious for constant petty thefts. Many of them, both men and women, have found permanent employment in Bhiwandi as rice cleaners, and numbers, both in Bhiwandi and Karjat, have two or three months' steady work a year as field labourers. Some of them still make kath or catechu, the thickened juice of the *khain* (Acacia catechu). A few partly support themselves by tillage. They never take land on a regular lease or grow rice. They till uplands, *varkas,* either waste or taken from the Government holders, or on agreement to share the produce. They burn brushwood, *rab,* on the plot of ground and use the hoe, but never the plough. When their supply of grain is finished, they gather and sell firewood and wild honey, and, with their bows and arrows, kill small deer, hares and monkeys. When these fail, they dig in old threshing floor for rats, eating the rats and taking their stores of grain, or they steal from fields and threshing floors. In the rains, they build dams across the streams, under which ingenious basket-traps are inserted. A small opening in the dam just over the mouth of the basket creates an eddy in which the fish are caught and carried into the basket. Their women work hard, both as labourers and in bringing into market the head-loads of wood their husbands have gathered in the forests." Add Mr. Enthoven. The custom is peculiar to the Katkari caste.

Mr. Enthoven states further, "The Katkaris, who are probably of Bhil origin, are believed to have come from the north, and to have been originally settled in the Gujarat Athavisi, the present district of Surat. They have a division named Athavar to this way. According to their story, they are descended from the monkeys which the god Rama took with him in his expedition against the demon-king Ravan of Ceylon. They say that when Rama became victorious, he blessed the monkeys and made them human beings. From their appearance, customs and religion it would appear that they are an aboriginal tribe little influenced by Brahmanism. Their peculiar dialect contains certains words common among the Bhils and their customs, to some extent, indicate a Bhil origin.

"Katkari women were formerly said to carry off men of other castes. The youth's friends regarded him as an outcaste and he then joined the Katkaris, living with one of their women. (Trans. Bom. Geog. Sec., Vol. I, 329). The Katharis are reported by Dr. Wilson to have similarly compelled strangers to join their community (Dr. Wilson's Aboriginal Tribes, p. 20). No relic of the custom has been traced, but in some parts of the Thana district members from higher castes such as Varlis, Kolis, Thakurs and Kubis are still admitted into the tribe on the paying a sum of Rs. 5, which is spent in treating the tribesmen to liquor."

"Formerly the Katkaris chose their settlements in the forest to suit their convenience, selecting a spot that promised good hunting or tillage, and leaving it as convenience dictated. Even to the present day, an epidemic of sickness will induce the people of a *vada* to vacate it and settle elsewhere in the neighbourhood, following a practice common among the Bhils. Their dwellings are low thatched huts, built of *karvi* and mud. The huts are square or rectangular."

"Katkaris, according to the *Bombay Gazetteer,* are much darker and slimmer than the order forest tribes. The Sons and some of the Dhors shave the face and head, and wear a very marked top-knot. But the northern cow-eating Katkaris generally have long matted hair and wild beard. The women of both divisions are tall and slim, singularly dirty and unkempt. They are strong, healthy and hardy, and pass through child-birth with little-trouble or pain. They are said, sometimes when at work in the fields during the rains, to retire behind a rice bank, and give birth to a child, and after washing it cold water, to put it under a teak-leaf rain-shape and go back to their work. The Katkari children can always be known by their gaunt pinched look."

"The chief peculiarity of the dress of Katkari women is the number of bead necklaces they wear, and the glass and metal bangles which cover almost the whole of the forearm. They wear a robe tightly wound round the waist and drawn up between the thighs. One end is thrown loosely over the shoulder, and for the rest, body and limbs are bare. Bodices are worn only on great occasions. They also wear long hanging ear-rings in both the top and bottom of the ear. The unmarried women may wear coloured necklaces, but no toe-rings. The married women wear black necklaces along with the coloured ones, and toe-rings."

Consigning the Charred Bones and Ashes to Stream

About the custom, Mr. Enthoven writes, "The dead are burnt. Children who have not out their teeth are buried. The ordinary funeral rites are observed. The bones and ashes are consigned to water. For the propitiation of deceased ancestors the *Shraddha* and *Muhalay* are performed every year.

"The caste follow the Hindu law of inheritance and belong to the Hindu religion. Most of them are followers of the Varkari sect. They worship all Brahmanic and local gods, observe all the

Hindu fasts and feasts, and make pilgrimages to all the sacred places of the Hindus, but particularly to Shiva Kanchi or the modern Conjeveram in Madras, where there is a shrine of Muktadev, the supposed founder of the caste. All the plants and animals held sacred by the Hindus are worshipped. The family deities of the Deccan Jingars are Khandoba, Bahiroba, Narsoba and the goddess Bhavani of Tuljapur and Kolapur ; of those residing in Kanara, Venkatarama and Mailarling ; and of the Karnatak Jingars, Malaya. Goats and fowls are offered to the goddess Mhalsa on the full-moon days of all months excepts *Shravan.* These offerings are received by the officiating priests. When an epidemic breaks out, a cart filled with cooked rice sprinkled over with red powder and a he-buffalo are moved in procession through all the streets of the village, and the cart is left beyond the village boundary, the buffalo being set at liberty. This ceremony is known as a *Bali kadhane* or the procession of the offering. The spiritual guide of the Deccan Jingars is the Shankaracharya of Shringeri, of the Karnatak Jingars, Shankar Bharati. It is said that the Jingars keep the sixteen Brahmanic *Sanskars* or sacraments, but enquiries show that this is not the case, the caste members being not even award of the names of most of the *Sanskars.* There appear to be only two such *Sanskars* observed by the Jingars as are not observed by the lower castes. They are the *Chaul,* that is the hairclipping ceremony, and *Upanayan* or the thread-girding. The latter ceremony is not performed after the Brahmanical ritual, but the boys is invested with the sacred thread when the other members of the caste renew theirs in the month of *Shravan.* The priests of the Deccan Jingars are the Yajurvedi Deshasth Brahmans, those of the Karnatak and Kanara Jingars are either Deshasth, Konkanath or Havik Brahmans." he adds. The custom is practised by the Jingar caste.

Cash given to Brahman to Facilitiate the Soul to Heaven

About the custom, Mr. Enthoven writes, "Kunbis generally burn their dead. When a person is on the point of death, his son or his wife lays the dying man's head on his or her right knee and lets a few drops of water fall into his mouth. Money and grain are given to the poor and a cow or from annas 8 to Rs. 5 in cash is given to the family Brahman to help the flight of the soul to heaven. When the dying man has breathed his last, the women of the house raise a loud cry and dishevel their hair. A small piece of gold is put into the dead mouth, and after an hour or two, friends and neighbours come and mourn. The dead body is bathed in water heated on a hearth set in front of the house. To carry the body a ladder like bier is made of two poles, six or seven feet long, with three or four small cross pieces. Two new earthen pots, a large one for water and a small one for fire, redpowder, betel leaves and cloth about seven and-a-half feet long are brought from the market or village cloth shop. Word is sent to the village Mahar, who carries cowdung cakes and firewood to the burning ground, which is generally on river bank. Except the face the body is covered with a new waistcloth and a cord is passed several times round the body to secure the cloth firmly. Betel leaves and *gulal* or red powder are sprinkled over it and a basil leaf is put in the mouth and some rice, a copper coin and the quarter of a cake are laid beside the body. Four kinsmen of the deceased bear the body and the son bathes and walks in front carrying the firepot on a triangular frame fastened to a sling. Before setting out he is warned not to look back. About half way to the burning ground at a place called the *visavyachi jaga* or rest place the party stops and the bearers set the bier on the ground and change places. They throw away the rice, the copper coin and the quarter of a cake which were laid on the bier beside the body and pick up a stone, which is usually called the life stone or *jiv-khada*. When they reach the burning ground, they raise a pile of four layers of cowdung cakes. They then take off the waistcloth, cut the thread tied round the wrist, and loosen the loincloth. The body is laid on the pyre and is covered with other layers of cakes. When the mouth is being covered, the son pours a little water into it. The son sets fire to the pyre, bathes, brings water in the large earthen pot, and stands at the head of the pyre. Another person comes and with a small stone makes a hole in the earthen pot. As the water spouts from the pot, the son goes five times round the pyre and at the end throws the pot on the ground at the head of the pyre, and calls aloud, beating his mouth with the back of his hand. He then goes and sits among the other men without touching them. After a short time the sound made by the bursting of the skull is heard and the chief-mourner and others at least the four bearers, bathe. The stone with which the earthen pot was pierced is kept with great care somewhere in the burning place. On their return to the house of mourning the funeral party are given *nimb* leaves to eat; or they go to a temple and then to their houses. The mourners do not cook but are fed on that day by a relation or friend with food prepared at his house."

"In the evening after the funeral, a lighted lamp is set on the spot where the deceased breathed his last. Flour is strewn round the lamp, and the lamp is covered with a basket. Next morning the basket is moved and the flour is examined. If a human foot-print appears on the floor, the deceased is believed to be re-born as human being ; and if the foot-print is that of a bird or beast, the spirit of the person is believed to have entered that beast or bird.

"Next morning the son with some friends and relatives goes to the burning ground with three small earthen pots with their mouths covered with three small wheaten cakes and three *pimpal* leaves. He places the small pots in a winnowing basket and fills them with milk, cow-urine, and honey or sugar, and lays some cowdung in the basket. On reaching the rest-place the son lays on the ground a cake with a little raw sugar. He goes on to the burning ground and from the spot where the body was burnt, he takes the ashes except one bone which he puts aside and throws them into the nearest river. If he is rich, he gathers the bone and afterwards takes them to a holy river. After removing the ashes the son sprinkles the spot with cowdung and cow-urine and place the two pots with the cakes, one where the head lay and the other where the feet lay. When the ash-gathering or *vakshavadhne* is over, the son and the other mourners bathe and return home. On the third day the bearers' shoulders are rubbed with oil and they are given dry cocoa-kerel to eat. On the tenth all the household bathe and wash their clothes in the river; and the son shaves his moustache and bathes. While a Brahman repeats verses the son washes with cow-urine, the life-stone or *jiv-khada* and the bone he kept, prepares ten balls and three little banners made of ochre-coloured cloths, each tied to a stick. The Brahman is given some money, shoes, and sometimes even a cow, presents which are supposed to help the deceased on his way to heaven. After preparing the offering balls the son sits at a distance that crows may come and eat them. If a crow touches them soon after they have been laid but, the deceased is supposed to have died with no unfulfilled wish. If crows do not touch the balls, the son and his relations promise to fulful the dead person's wish, and when the promise is given, the crows are believed to fall the offering and eat it. After this is over, the son and the other mourners bathe and return home. On the thirteenth day the priest is given money and provisions, and a feast of unstuffed cakes of *polis,* rice, and split pulse is given to friends and relations in honour of the deceased. Some food is put in the platter and the platter is kept aside that crows may eat out of it. In the evening, one of his near relations ties a small white rurban round the son's head and takes him with the other mourners and generally some of the villagers of Maruti's temple, where the son lays a copper coin and a betelnut before the god. Every month a man is asked to dine in the name of the deceased, and, after five months and a half, a feast of unstuffed cakes of *polis* is given to the near relations of deceased. In the dark half of *Bhadrapad* the spirit of the deceased is worshipped on the day of the fortnight which corresponds with the death day.

""The staple food of Maratha Kunbia is millet, rice and vegetables, and, in some places in the Konkan, *nachni.* They eat the flesh of goats, sheep, hare, deer, wild hogs, fowls, and fish, and drink."

Deaths Believed to Becaused by Witchcraft

Most of the volis currently had adopted the custom of cremating the dead, but earlier the practised both cremation and bonial. About their custom, Mr. Enthven writes, "The lead are either burnt or buried. When buried, the head is turned to the south. The bodies of persons woh die of a lingering disease are burnt, as such deaths are believed to have been caused by witchcraft. Either the same evening or the next morning they examine the ashes to see if they can find any unconsumed bits of cloth or some article of food. If they find a piece of cloth or some grain, they believe that what they have found was the cause of death and that it was worked into the dead man's intestines by a witch who had been employed to do this by some one from whom the dead man had stolen some cloth or some grain. Under Maratha rule, if the friends of the deceased found articles of this kind, the magician, unless he bribed some local officer, was sent for a time to some hill fort. The death ceremonies of Mahadev Kolis resemble those of local Kunbis. The deceased are propitiated in the latter half of *Bhadrapad* when rice mixed with milk is offered to the crow and feast is given. Those who die in battle or in the performances of an act of bravery are called *Virs* and are worshipped with the gods, a silver ball with two owners being offered to them and on the first day of *Phalgun* a fowl or goat is sacrificed to them. The *Shraddha* is performed only on the tenth to thirteenth day after death, and subsequently on the first anniversary.

"The original occupation of Mahadev Kolis is supposed to have been that of an infantry soldier. They are now husbandmen, cattle-keepers and labourers. In some places they are boatmen, carrying passengers across rivers and streams during the rainy season. Some are hereditary ministrants at Mahadev temples and take to themselves the offerings laid before the god. In Kolhapur they also gather slake and sell lime nodules, and catch and sell fish. Many are land holders, and many till the lands of others though they are not so skilful as Kunbis. Many Kolis are employed as watchmen, a considerable number are *patils* or village headmen, and a few are *deshmukhs* or hereditary district officers.

"Mahadev Kolis eat the usual kind of flesh except beef and pork and drink country liquor to excess. Their staple food is *nagli* or *sava* bread and vegetables. In some outlying parts many, after finishing their stones of grain, live for a time on wild roots, herbs and fruits and on the flesh of game animals and birds. They eat with Marathas and Kunbis, but no lower caste. Kunbis and Marathas eat with them above ghats, but below ghats may only take water from them."

"Malhar Kolis or the Kolis worshipping the god Malhar, also called panbhari or water-filling Kolis, are, according to Captain Mackintosh, one of the purest and most respectable of all Kolis tribes. They are also called Chumlis from the cloth-fenders they wear on their heads as water-pot rests, and Kunum Koli, because according to Mackintosh, they eat and associate with Kunbis. They are found in almost every village in the Deccan, in Bombay City and along the sea coast in the Thana district.

Their common surnames are Bhoir, Jadhav, Kerav, Langa, Povar, Sharanpad, Shelar, Sojval and Vekhande. In speech, dress, customes and ceremonies they do not differ from the Mahadev Kolis. As the name Panbhari or water filler shows, their usual calling is to supply villagers and strangers with water and to clean out the village rest-house and office. Near Pandharpur, many Malhar Kolis are *yeskars* or village door-keepers and in Khandesh and Ahmednagar a few are husbandmen. During the Maratha rule, to the south of Poona, Mulhar Kolis were the hereditary guardians of the hill forts of Purandhar, Sinhgad, Torna and Rajgad. According to Mr. A.M.T. Jackson, Malhar Kolis in the Thana district frequently become Maratha Kunbis, and the prcess has been recognised in many parts of the Poona district.

"Son Kolis are found along the North Konkan coast from Bassein to Ratnagiri in the south. They are numerous in Kolaba and form the most interesting of the castes found in the district. Distinguished physically from the other inhabitants by their light-brown complexion, the round curves of the face and their smiling expression, they are equally distinguished by their aristocratic constitution, their separate dialect and their occupation. History is not clear as to their arrival on the coast, but a probable inference from tradition is that a majority of the present Kolis is descended from immigrants from the hills, who arrived some four hundred years ago. If this be correct, it would certainly go far to explain the marked difference in type. But doubt is thrown upon the tradition by the difficulty of understanding the sudden conversion of hillmen into fishers," adds Mr. Enthoven.

The Rite of Martikacha

About their current custom, Mr. Vijay B. Punekar writes, "As a Hindu, the Son Koli after death is cremated. A few exceptions must be noted. An unteethed child and a victim of smallpox, cholera or any other infectious disease is, however, buried and never cremated. If a pregnant woman dies, her embryo is removed and buried and the corpse cremated."

"When a person is about to die, all the family members, relatives staying nearby and the neighbours, assemble round the person's bed. Each one puts a spoonful of Ganges water in the dying person's mouth. The water is usually preserved in a small vessel in the family shrine. After the death, all the relatives are informed and the obsequial ceremonies do not start until they arrive. Meanwhile, the dead body, decked with fine clothes and ornaments, is seated in a chair. (To prevent the stiffening of the body ghee is applied to the joints immediately after the person has breathed his last). Continuous *bhajan* (hymns) is sung at the door-step."

"On the arrival of the relatives, all the clothes except the lower garment, and ornaments are removed; the dead body is given in the lap of the son, who is seated on a small table placed on a *kana.* All the people apply turmeric paste, sprinkle a little coconut juice and pour a vesselful of water on the head of the deceased ; and so they pay their last respect to the dead. Again, new clothes and ornaments are put on the body and it is seated in a chair till all the arrangements for the funeral are over. Photographs of the dead with the relatives are taken.

"A bier *(tirdi)* is constructed of bamboos. Two of these are about six feet long, and the other two, three feet long. Coir rope is used for tying these into a rectangular ladder-like frame. Then a mat of date-palm leaves is put on the bier; a piece of cloth about two yards in length, called *kaphan,* is spread on it. The body is laid on the bier and is covered with another piece of cloth. Only the face is left uncovered. *Gulal* (red powder) and *abir* (black powder) are applied to the forehead. These and black sesame and some red and white flowers are thrown on the corpse. A garland of holy basil leaves is worn round its neck. If the deceased leaves his widow behind, she sits at his feet all this while, bewailing and praising the dead husband. At this stage, her glass bangles are broken, the *mangalsut* is removed and the vermilion mark on the forehead is wiped out. Before the bier is lifted, all the women put a little milk in the mouth of the deceased."

"The funeral procession starts. Four or more men carry the bier. From time to time they are relieved by others walking with the procession. The procession is headed by the chief mourner carrying *akta,* an earthen pot containing live coal, a few dried cow-dung pieces, and a bunch of joss-sticks. Behind him is the bier followed by other mourners, including relatives and neighbours."

"The women accompany the procession a few steps. All along the route the men in the procession repeat *Ram-nam* (name of Rama) and rose water and red powder are sprinkled on the bier from time to time. On the boundary of the locality, the corpse is touched with a stone from the street, and the stone is preserved there only, to be used later on the tenth day for the *kirya* ('rites' after death)."

"On reaching the burning ground, which usually lies a little further away from the locality, the bier is placed on the ground. A pyre *(saran)* is constructed, and the corpse is laid on it facing south, after all the clothes and ornaments are removed. The head and face of the chief mourner are shaved off. He takes a dip in the sea. All the relations put a little coconut water or milk in the mouth of the deceased. The fire is taken round the pyre and the pyre is lit. When the skull bursts, a coconut is broken and offered to the pyre along with some fruits. Every piece of cloth is removed from the body so that the corpse may burn completely. For the same purpose, a little salt is thrown from time to time as the pyre is burning. While the pyre is burning, two weapons are thrown from the two sides (east and west) across the pyre, as a protection for the dead from the evil spirits. The *bhajan* continues till the pyre has completely burnt down. The assembled people are given *bidis,* and sometimes, some cold drinks too on behalf of the bereaved family."

"When the pyre is burnt down, a few close relatives and friends return home and a bath is given to the members of the family. For twelve days the family remains in pollution. Everyone who attended the funeral takes a bath. No one in the village eats anything as long as the corpse is in the village."

"When a person, man or woman, dies unmarried a sort of marriage ceremony is performed on the corpse. The corpse is taken through two plantain trees and *chiiv* are thrown on it as it passes through. These plantains are later erected at the head and feet of the pyre when it is burning. Also, for the unmarried, the funeral procession is accompanied by a *vajata,* for it is his or her marriage procession."

"For a married woman, *at bharan* is done by suvasinis and vermilion applied to her forehead. All the married women who are present kneel before her."

"The death of an old person, long foreseen, is not an occasion of great sadness for most of the members of the household, especially if he does not leave a widow behind. It is on occasion for rejoicing, when liquor is consumed in great quantity."

"For three days the neighbours bring their own food and eat with the bereaved members who prepare their own. The next day after the death, a few relations and neighbours go to the burning ground to bring the remains of the dead body. A coconut is broken and pieces of the coconut, milk and roti are left there for the crows to eat. The remains are collected in an earthen pot, which is covered with a new cloth. The pot is hung to the roof inside the house until it is taken to some holy place, usually Nasik, for immersion."

"The third day is *bena karavcha.* The male members of the family and the chief mourner are taken out of the house and given tea and sweets. The *vol,* with which they covered themselves since the death, is removed. The chief mourner is given a cap. If the deceased was old, liquor is bought and consumed. Women neighbours apply coconut juice to the hair of the women members of the family. If the family can afford it, a Brahman is employed to read the *Garuda Purana,* and the members of the family and neighbours listen," adds Mr. Punekar.

"For twelve consecutive days, an oil lamp is kept burning day and night, in the house. No *puja* is offered to the deities and no alms are given. Everyday, meals and tea are kept on the roof for the spirit of the deceased. Sometimes the practice is continued for a year or more. For the first three days it may be taken to the cremation ground too."

The *kirya* or the ceremonies for the dead are conducted on the tenth, eleventh and twelfth day.

However, some people perform it only on the twelfth day. If an *ambosha* (new-moon day) falls in between the twelve days the ceremony is performed on that day. The *kirya* needs a Brahmin, though the actual offerings to the spirit of the dead are made by the chief mourner. Usually, the chief mourner for the parents is the eldest or the youngest son. For an unmarried boy or girl, the uncle may perform the obsequies, the father not having been permitted to light the child's pyre. From the tenth day onwards, a *pinda* (a ball of dough or boiled rice) is offered daily to the spirit of the deceased, but the important ceremony takes place on the twelfth day. The kins and neighbours are informed about the time and the place of it, because it takes place on the sea-shore. On a piece of cloth, a yard square, are placed five dollops of *tur dal,* four smaller ones in the four corners and a larger one in the centre. The central dollop also contains almonds, dried dates and betelnuts. On this heap is placed a copper drinking-vessel, with a small plate on it, holding *chav* and betel-nut. On the cloth are also put eight coconuts facing the four directions, five types of fruits, *vire* and a little sugar, and a joss-stick; and beside these a lamp is kept burning.

The chief mourner, who makes the offering of holy basil leaves to the copper vessel, sits in front of it with crossed legs. Sacred grass is tied to his third finger, to his tuft of hair and to his sacred thread (temporarily worn). When the offerings to the spirit of the dead are over, vermilion, turmeric, *chav* and flowers and offered in the plate. In front of them are offered water libations, across the thumb of the right hand. The water offered has milk and flowers in it. In front of them, on a plantain leaf, are put, with a little water and black sesamum seed sprinkled, on three or four blades of sacred grass, sixteen small *pindas* in a row. The *pindas* are prepared from the dough of wheat flour, with a little ghee and sugar, a few holy basil leaves, some black sesamum seeds and milk. Water, a thread, *abir, gopi-chandan* (also called *gandhgoli*), vermilion, turmeric, *gulul*, black sesamum seeds, *jav* (barley seeds), leaves of *agasta, maka* and holy basil, and flowers are offered to the *pindas.* A little sugar and incence are also offered.

Besides these *pindas,* the chief mourner places, on three on four blades of sacred grass, a bigger *pinda.* The smaller *pindas*, about the size of a big coconut, is for the spirit of the deceased. It is hollowed; some honey is applied to it from inside ; a holy basil leaf and an old two-anna silver coin and a handful of a mixture of crumbs of *roti (damaki* as it is called*)* and *halva* (sweats) are also placed in it. After him the widow of the deceased and the rest of the mourners assembled there offer a little of this mixture to the *pinda* as food to the dead. Then the *pinda* is closed with ghee. The chief mourner, and then the rest of the mourners offer thread, *abir, sandalwood,* vermilion, *gulal,* turmeric, black sesamum seeds, *jav, chav,* leaves of *agasta, maka* and holy basil, flowers, water, *vira* and copper coins to the *pinda.* An ornament is placed on the *pinda,* which is removed and preserved as a memento when the *pinda* is immersed in the sea. Camphor and coconut are also offered to it. Food is served on plantain leaves to the *pinda,* a crow and a cow. A number of dishes are cooked for the purpose by the bereaved family. A low-caste Brahmin is given all the necessaries of life—clothes, chappals, utensils, an umbrella and bedding; he is also given a boat prepared from sugar-cane candy. The general belief is that, whatever is given to the low-caste Brahmin here is received by the spirit of the deceased in the next world. Some even give him a cow; all other things arranged on the cloth also go to the Brahmin.

The chief mourner takes all the *pindas* to the sea for immersion ; he carries the larger *pinda* between the two halves of a coconut ; the rest of the *pindas* are taken by another mourner usually a son of the deceased. Young children are served a sweet dish and a vegetable after the chief mourner, and others come home. (On the death of an unmarried person *satavra* is performed on the seventh day. Sweets and sugar are distributed to seven children. No *pinda* ceremony is performed in that case). Again the same day or the next day, at home, four more *pindas* are offered to the waves of the deceased and his ancestors. Offerings are also made to the sacred fire (*hom*).

After two or three weeks or a month, the females of the household are taken out to the drying-ground or a tea-shop, where tea is served to them. When bringing them back home, their *pharki* (mourning covers) are removed; liquor is served to them on the occasion. Then, they become free to move out of the house. The closer the relation of the members, the longer the interval of this ceremony called as *bena karavcha.* From the very first day to the end of the after-death ceremonies, no solemnity is observed by the assembled primitive people. There is shouting and quarrelling and even an occasional joke. The family members exercise perfect self-control except at the time of ceremonial mourning, when neighbours and relatives and friends come on formal condolence visits. Otherwise, even the nearest relatives refer to the deceased very casually in conversation with the visitors.

Ashes of the Dead Thrown in Sea

Mr. Enthoven writes, "The dead are burnt, except children under eighteen months, who are buried in a lying position with head to the north. The ashes are thrown into the sea, if near, or buried in a pit near a watercourse so as to be carried away by the rain water. The unburnt bones are carried to Nakatinga (Nishkalanka) which is about sixteen miles from Bhavnagar. In honour of the dead a *shraddha* is held once a year on the ninth day of the dark half of *Bhadrapad.* If the deceased has no child a male calf is married to a female calf by a mock ceremony called *Nil parnavavi*," adds Mr. Enthoven. The custom is prevalent among the *Kharaks.*

Consigning the Ashes of the Dead to Stream

About the custom of cremation Mr. Enthoven writes, "The dead are either burnt or buried. The ashes of the burnt are consigned to water on the third day after death. The bones are thrown into a river on the full-moon day of *Kartik.* The caste is feasted on the third day after death, and on the day following the anniversary of the deceased. For the propitiation of the deceased ancestors, uncooked articles of food are given to the caste priest and castemen are feasted on the *Akshatritiya* day. The *shraddha* is not performed."

"Kachhis belong to the Hindu religion. They worship the usual Hindu gods and goddesses and observe all the Hindu holidays. The chief object of their devotion is the goddess Balaji. They make pilgrimages to Tuljapur in the Nizam's dominions, Chatarshingi in Poona, Saptashring in Nasik and Mahurgad in the Berars. Their priests are Upper India Brahmans." The custom is related to the *Kachhi* caste.

Putting Silver Coin in the Mouth of Deceased

"Kayasths burn their dead except children under two years

of age, who are buried. The funeral rites are of the standard type except that a small silver coin is placed in the mouth of the deceased before cremation. The ceremony of *shraddha* is performed annually on the anniversary of the death and on the day corresponding to the day of death in the dark half of *Bhadrapad.* A ceremony called *dhro* is performed also in the bright half of *Bhadrapad,* for the well-being of the deceased. In the case of children, ancestors and persons who have died a violent death, in addition to the usual rites, ceremonies called *Narayan Bali* and *Bawan Kriya* are performed at some holy place, such as Bet Dwarka, Sidhapur, Patan or Gaya, on or about the full moon day either of *Chaitra* or *Kartik,"* adds Mr. Enthoven. The customs are practised among the *Kayastha* caste.

Taking Three Rounds of Pyre

About the custom of cremation Mr. Enthoven notes, "The dead are burnt. After death the body is bathed, set close to a wall, and tied in a sitting position to a peg fixed in the wall. It is wrapped in a blanket, laid on a bier, and taken by four men to the burning ground, where the pile is prepared, and the body burnt. When the pile is nearly consumed, the chief mourner walks three times round it with an earthen pot on his shoulder, pierces three holes in the pot, throws the pot over his shoulder, and beats his mouth with the back of his right hand. Gifts are given to Brahmans and the Mahar, who is called the son of the soil, is given something as the price of the land which was used for the pyre. On the third day, the ashes of the deceased are gathered and thrown into water. On the fifth, the chief mourner worships three stones in the name of the deceased, and offers them boiled rice without looking to see whether or not it is touched by a crow. On the eleventh day, the friends and relations are treated to a rich feast of boiled mutton and wheat cakes. A month after the death, goats are killed and caste people are feasted. The anniversary or death-day, mind-feast or *shraddha* at the end of the year is optional.

"Khetris belong to the Hindu religion. Their family deities are Kalamma, Maruti, Venkatarama of Tirupati and Yellamma, and they also worship other Brahmanic and local gods. They keep the usual Brahmanic and local Hindu fasts and feasts, make pilgrimages to the shrines of their family gods, and visit local fairs held in honour of Hindu and Musalman saints. They keep two special holidays, the full-moon of *Ashvin* and *Bahulashtami* or the dark eighth of *Margashirsha*. They believe in soothsaying and evil spirits. They ask Deshasth Brahmans to officiate at their ceremonies, and after a birth or death ask Oshtama Brahmans to purify them with *tulsi* (sweet basil) water. Their marriage are conducted by three men, a Deshasth Brahman, the *Kattimani* or caste headman, and an Oshtama," he writes. The customs pertain to *Khetris* caste.

Mahar Making Funeral Pyre

"The dead are burnt. On reaching the burning ground the body is placed on the funeral pile which has been made ready by a Mahar or some other low-caste man. The shroud is taken off and given with $1^1/_3$ annas and two pounds of rice, to the Mahar. Logs of wood are piled over the body and the chief mourner sets fire to the pile. When the body is consumed, the chief mourner offers the deceased cooked rice, and all except the mourners go to bathe in some pond or spring. When they have bathed, they accompany the chief mourner to his house and retire to their homes. On the twelfth day after death, all the mourners shave their faces and swallow the five products of the cow. Crows are then fed and caste people feasted. A *shraddha* is held on every anniversary day," writes Mr. Enthoven.

"The Kanara Khetris are Hindus of the Vaishnava sect. They worship all Vaishnava gods, especially Venkatarama, who is their family god. . ." adds Mr. Enthoven. The custom is related to the Kanara Khetris.

Removing the Old Sacred Thread From Neck

"When a man is on the point of death, he is laid on a freshly cowdunged space on the floor strewn with *darbha* grass and *java* grains. The old sacred thread on his neck is removed, and a new one is put in its place. The water of the Jumna river is poured into his mouth. When life is gone, the body is tied to the bier, which is carried by the mourners after they have bathed. The body is burnt in the same way as among other high class Hindus. If a person meets death by drowning, an idol is made in his name, and the funeral rites are performed thereon.

"They mourn for twelve days. On the eleventh day, wheat flour balls or *pindas* are offered to the deceased, and thrown in a running steam. They feast Brahmans on the twelfth and the caste-fellows on the thirteenth day."

"A large number of Bhatias are merchants, traders, bankers and brokers; and within the last fifty years, they have become a very wealthy and important class. Numbers have moved either permanently or for a time to Bombay and many of them are settled in the west, in the ports of the Persian Gulf, the Red Sea and Zanzibar, and in the east as far as Japan. In Cutch they are traders, clerks, bankers and shopkeepers. Some of them are landowners," he writes. The custom is prevalent among the *Bhatias*.

Obsequies being Elaborate and Complex

About the Kanbi funeral rites and ceremonies, *Bombay Gazetteer,* (Vol. IX, Part I) notes, "When a Kanbi is on the point of death the family-priest, who is generally an Audich Brahman, and other Brahmans of the village are called, and a lamp fed with clarifed butter is placed near his bed. The dying person worships Vishnu, and gives, besides presents in cash and clothes, a cow or the value of a cow in cash to the priest. To each of the other Brahmans, besides presents of cash, the dying man makes gifts of wheat, husked rice, pulse, salt, and rusty nails and shovels. If well off, he sets apart sums of money to be spent after his death on works of public charity, sinking wells, making halting places on the roadside, and supplying water to thirsty travellers. Friends and relations come to visit the dying man, and as the end draws near, they utter the name of Ram near his ear. One of the female relations sweeps the floor of the entrance room and cow-dungs a portion of it which is equal to the length and breadth of a man. The cowdunged space is strewn with sesame and barley seeds, *tulsi* leaves, and *darbha* grass. The head of the dying man is shaved, he is bathed with hot water and his brow is marked with *gopichandan* or milkmaid's earth, and the body is laid on its back with the head towards the north, on the freshly cowdunged floor. Ganges water and some gold, silver and coral, a pearl, a piece of crystal, and a basil leaf are placed in the mouth. A ball of unbaked millet flour and a rupee are given to a Brahman. When life is gone, the nearest relations raise the life-cry or *pran-pok,* a call to bring back the spirit. Among the Patidars of Ahmedabad the name of the deceased is written on a tile with a piece of charcoal and it is sent to the relations of the deceased by a Bhangi to inform them of the occurrence. Caste-people go to the house of death, the men to bear the body to the burning ground, the women to mourn. The Kanbi funeral procession is large as by caste rules the attnedance of one man from each house is enforced on pain of fine. Two or three of the mourners bring from the market two bamboo poles, several short lengths of bamboo, coir string, and a piece of red silk if the deceased is a married woman, or of white cotton cloth if the deceased is either a man or a widow. The poles, pieces of bamboo and the coir string are made into a ladder-shaped bier and from each corner a coconut is hung. The corpse is laid on the bier and tied to it by the coir strings. The body is covered with the white or red cloth, and over the cloth red powder and flowers are strewn. The bier is raised on the shoulders of four of the nearest relations and is borne forth feet first, preceded by one of the nearest relations carrying an earthen or copper vessel with fire and cakes of cowdung. The relations and caste-fellows follow calling the words *Ram bolo bhai, Ram* (Call Ram, brothers, call Ram). The female mourners follow the body for some distance, weeping. Then they stop, beat their breasts, return to the house and bathe either in well-water or in a river. Midway between the house and burning-ground the male mourners halt and set down the bier. The nearest relations cease to weep and the bier is borne head foremost to the burning-ground. When the burning-ground is reached, the bearers lay the corpse almost uncovered with the head to the north on a pile of a man's length of wood and cowdung cakes. A little butter is dropped into the mouth of the dead and the chief-mourner, generally the eldest son of the deceased, puts some fire near the face, and the other mourners set the pyre ablaze. Two or three of the older men stay near the body while it is being burnt, keeping the pile in order ; others sit afar, talking and making merry if the deceased was old, and with a certain sadness and regret, if the deceased was young. When the body is almost consumed, a little clarified butter is poured on the flames. The mourners bathe and return weeping to the house of the deceased and then to their homes. Letters, telling friends and relations in distant villages, are sent either by post or by a carrier. On the second or third day, the chief-mourner and two or three of the nearest relations go to the burning-ground. The ashes and bones are gathered and are thrown into a river or a pond, and an earthen jar filled with water is set where the body was burned. The mourners bathe, and with wet clothes return home, weeping. They take with them a few of the bones and keep them in the house till some member of the family goes on a pilgrimage and throws them into the sacred Narbada or Ganges. After the mourners return from the burning-ground, an earthen pot is filled with water and milk and placed on the roof of the house. The nearest relations remain impure for ten days, during which they touch no one, do not approach the house gods, do not visit the temples, do not change their clothes, and do not shave. On the tenth day, men shave their head and moustaches; girls and married women wash their hair with clay or with soapnut, the floors are cowdunged, and all earthen drinking pots, which have been touched during the ten days, are replaced by new ones. The mind-rite or *shraddha* ceremony is performed by the chief-mourner from the tenth to the thirteenth day, on the eleventh with the help of a Kayatia Brahman, and on the other three days with the help of the family priest. During the four days of the *shraddha* ceremony the chief mourner, instead of a turban, wears a linen cloth wound round his head. On the thirteenth day, his father-in-law presents him with a new turban and the linen cloth is removed. On the thirteenth day, the family-priest is given, besides a few ornaments and a complete set of clothes, a sleeping cot, some pillows, and some brass or copper vessels. Friends and relations are feasted from the tenth to the thirteenth day, and the caste-people on the twelfth and the thirteenth. If the deceased was a wealthy man, presents in grain, clothes, and cash are given to Brahmans, to religious *beggars,* and to the poor. Female mourners go to the house of the deceased to weep and mourn, morning and evening, for a month if the deceased was of mature age, and for six months if the deceased was young. During the first year, as among other Hindus, monthly, half-yearly and yearly mind-rites or *shraddha* are performed, and a yearly *shraddha* in all subsequent years and an additional *shraddha* during the latter half of *Bhodrarvo* (September-October). Landlords or Patidars and headmen of villages call all the villagers to dinner on marriage and death feasts. This custom has ruined many families." (Bombay Gazetteer, Vol. IX, Part I, pp. 161-163).

Mr Enthoven adds "Except Anjnas, Kanbis neither eat flesh, nor drink liquor.

"Though many town Kanbis are skilled weavers of silk and cotton, dealers in cloth and grain, and some have risen to high positions in Governments service or made money in trade or as money-lenders, the bulk of the Kanbis are husbandmen. Many village are headmen or *mukhis*, that is, police headmen, and enjoy allowances in cash and land. The officiators are chosen from the *Matadars,* that is, those who have the right to sign village papers. They are very jealous of their rights, which give them a certain position and influence, and which go to show that they are the original *vatandars* of the village. Gujarat Kanbis do not enlist as soldiers. Kanbis, especially those of the Kadva and Leva divisions, are capital husbandmen. They are learned in the properties of every soil and minutely acquainted with the wants of every crop.

Anjna Kanbis are found chiefly in North Gujarat. In appearances they are more like Kolis than other Kanbis and like Rajputs, some of their names end in *sing*, such as Dansing, Harising, Rajsing, Umsing. They have twenty-three clans, who eat together and intermarry. Some of the anjnas of Cutch are Jains.

Dangi Kanbis are found in Mahi Kantha. Originally Anjnas, with whom they dine but do not intermarry, they are said to have lost their position by adopting the dress and language of Bhils. Many of them live in Mewar and have marriage and other relations with the Mahi Kantha Dangis.

"Gujar Kanbis are found in East and West Khandesh. They consist of eight sub-division, (1) Anala, (2) Dale, (3) Dore, (4) Gari, (5) Kadva, (6) Khapra, (7) Londhari or Bad and (8) Reva or Leva. There are a few families of Dales on the banks of the Tapti in Shahada and Taloda and in Raver towards Barhanpur. The Deshmukhs of Jamner are said to be Gari Gujars, but they claim equality with and call themselves Reva Gujars. Revas or Levas appear to be an offshoot of the Gujarat Levas. They consider themselves a very superior caste, eschew flesh and liquor and eat only at the hands of Brahmans. Kadvas, Analas and Dales are found only in small numbers. Kadvas appear to be a branch of the Gujarat Kanbis of the same name, and like the parent stock, celebrate their marriages once in twelve years. The Londharis are said to have acquired the name Londhari from their being exclusively employed in ginning cotton. The Khapras are a mixed or inferior class.

"Kadva Kanbis are chiefly found in Ahmedabad and in the Kadi *taluka* of the Baroda State. They are closely connected with the Levas. According to one story, the Kadvas are descendants or followers of Kush, the second son of Ram and Sita ; according to another, they are sprung from clay figures fashioned by Uma or Parvati, the wifr of Shiva. Shiva at Uma's request inspired the figures with life and founded for them the village of Unja about forty miles north of Ahmedabad, where a temple was raised in Uma's honour. This village and temple all Kadva Kanbis consider the chief seat of their tribe, and to it they resort from long distances to pay their vows. Some state that they came to Gujarat from Kabul through the Punjab, which is supported by the names of some of their *shakhas* or sections. Except in Surat they have no sub-divisions. In Surat there are three sub-divisions, one calling themselves Lalchudawalas from their women wearing red bracelets, the other Kalachudawalas from their women wearing black bracelets, and the third Ahmedabadis from Ahmedabad. These three divisions eat together, but for the last thirty-five years have ceased to intermarry. As among Leva Kanbis they have Kulia and Akulia sections in south Gujarat, the relations between which are the same as those between similar branches of the Levas. A Kadva Kanbi can divorce his wife at will, but in north Gujarat the wife cannot divorce the husband without his consent or after she has borne a child. Kadva's marriages are celebrated once in every nine, ten or eleven years. Efforts are of late being made to reduce this period to five years by some and to one year by others, and a few marriage have also been celebrated accordingly. But the community as a whole has not yet accepted the reform. There are fifty-two original *shakkas* or exogamous sections, mostly called after the names of villages in the Punjab." Adds Mr. Enthoven. The customs, rites and rituals are pertinent to the Kanbis.

Married Dead are Cremated

"The Karnatak Kabbaligars bury their dead, except persons dying of leprosy, who are burnt under the belief that, if buried they prevent the rain falling. In Kanara, the married dead are burnt, the unmarried being buried. At burial the unmarried are laid with the head to the north, the married are seated. The funeral rites of the Kanara Kabbaligars resemble those of the Banjigs. In the Karnatak also their death ceremonies mostly resemble those of the Lingayats, the marked difference being that, after the funeral party returns home, they bathe in cold water holding *durva* grass and *patri* or *bel* leaves in their hands, which they wash in a metal pot full of water placed on the cow-dunged spot where the deceased breathed his last. On the third days the mourners take *ragi* gruel or *ambli* and millet bread to the grave, lay them on the grave, and burn incense close by. They retire to some distance to allow the crows to feed on the offerings. If the crows do not eat the cakes, it is held as a bad omen, and the food is given to a cow. On the fifth day the corpse bearers are feasted. They slaughter a sheep and feed the castemen on the ninth. In some places, on the ninth or eleventh day, water, in which a Jangam's feet have been washed, is sprinkled all over the house of the deceased. Next, a jar filled with water is placed near the gods and, if the deceased was a male, it is covered with a man's waistcloth, and if a female, with a woman's robe. The jar is then worshipped with an offering of cooked food containing goat's or fowl's flesh. Some of the food is laid on the spot where the corpse was buried and the caste is feasted. During the fifth or some other odd month after death, a mask or *mukhavata,* if the deceased was a man, or a top-like vessel if the deceased was a woman, is brought from a local goldsmith and is laid among the house gods. To these a waistcloth or a robe is offered and a goat is killed before them. If the deceased was a great drinker, spirituous liquor is also offered; and if he leaves a son, the latter presents clothes to a person of same age and sex of the deceased on the *marnavami,* that is, the day before the *Dasara,* and during the *Diwali* holidays. Once in every two, three, four or five years, the castemen are feasted for the propitiation of the deceased ancestors, when the masks of the deceased, or in their absence the household gods, are worshipped with offerings of articles of dress.

"Among the Kanara Kabbaligars, on the twelfth day after death, a feast is given to the corpse-bearers and caste people, and crows are fed. At night, an exorcist is called to release the spirit of the deceased from the control of the ill-disposed spirit Rahu, and to give it over to that of the favourable disposed spirit, Guttu. On the thirtieth day after death, a man of the same age and sex of the deceased is feasted, and crows are fed, when the spirit of the deceased is supposed to have joined the spirits of the other ancestors. This is repeated every thirtieth day during the first twelve months, and after that once a year during the latter half of the month of *Bhadrapad.*" Adds Mr. Enthoven. The customs are practised by the community of Kabbaligars.

Pouring Warm Water Over the Body

"When a person dies, relations, friends and castefellows are told, the body is brought out of the house and laid on the house steps and warm water is poured over it. A piece of cloth is rolled round its loins, it is laid on a bier and sweet flowers are strewn over the body. This bier is carried on the shoulders of four men, and the chief mourner walks in front, carrying an earthen pot with burning cowdung cakes. On the way to the burning ground the body is rested and pieces of bread are left for the evil spirits to eat. At the burning ground a pile is raised, the body is laid on the pile, and the pile is kindled by the chief mourner. When the pile is completely burnt, the chief mourner walks thrice round it with an earthen jar full of water. At the end of the third turn he dashes the jar on the ground and cries aloud, beating his mouth with the back of his right hand. The mourners return home. On the third day, the chief mourner goes to the burning ground, removes the ashes, shaves his moustache, bathes and sprinkles cow's urine and dung on the ashes. On the spot, where the body was burnt, he sets three earthen jars filled with cooked rice, curd, honey and milk, and after bathing, returns home. They mourn for ten days and on the eleventh, the chief mourner goes to the river-side, prepares ten wheat flour balls, offers one to the crows and throws the rest into the water. On the eleventh or twelfth day the memorial or *shrdadha* ceremony is performed at the mourner's house, and either on the twelfth or thirteenth day the caste is feasted, chiefly on sweet cakes or *puran polis*.

"Bhavasars in the Deccan prepare dyes and print and dye cloth." writes Mr. Enthoven. The custom prevails among the *Bhavasars*.

Hanging Coconut from Bier

"The poor bury and the well-to-do burn the dead. The body is washed, perfumed and covered with a clean cloth, and is laid on a bier, from each corner of which a coconut hangs. One of the relatives carries fire before the body in a black earthen pot, and the bier is carried by four men who sing hymns as they go. On their way, near the burial ground, the bearers stop and rest the bier. On reaching the burning ground, the body is laid in a pit with its head turned to the north, a copper is thrown in and the pit is filled with earth. When the body is burnt or buried the mourners bathe and return home. At the house of mourning, when the funeral party returns, one of the relations of the deceased places an upturned basket over the spot where the head of the deceased lay. On the second day an earthen pot full of water is placed at the spot where the bearers halted near the burning ground, and is allowed to remain there for ten days. The upturned basket in the house is also allowed to remain for ten days. On the eleventh day, the basket is set right, the earth underneath the basket is scraped away, and the basket is given to a priest of their own caste. If the body is buried, for ten days after the death one of the family members lays a tooth-twig or *datvan* on the grave, and a little opium, if the deceased was an opium-eater. Some Bhangias do, and others do not, consider themselves impure for ten days after a death. All perform death ceremonies on the eleventh, twelfth and thirteenth. Balls of wheat flour are offered, the clothes of the deceased are given to the officiating priest, and caste-people are feasted on the twelfth and thirteenth.

He adds further, "Bhangis are Hindus by religion. They honour almost all Brahman divinities, and their favourite objects of worship are : in Central Gujarat—Hanuman, Meldi and Shikotri, and in South Gujarat—Ganpati, Devi and the *basil* plant. As they are not allowed to enter Hindu temples, they bow to the idol from a distance. Many Bhangias are followers of the sects of Kabir, Ramanand and Nanak. Some of them keep in their houses, an image which represents some woman of the family who has been possessed by a spirit. They honour the *Navaratri* or nine-night festival in *A' so* (October). Some teachers or *gurus* of their own caste visit the Bhangias yearly and receive 50p to 1 rupee from each house. There have been several Bhangia saints or *bhagats,* of whom the chief are Chiko, Dhiro, Harkho, Kipro, Lallo, Manor and Valo. Their leading holidays are *Sankrant* in January, *Holi* in February-March, *Akhatrij* in April-May, *Divaso* in June-July, *Sitalasatem* and *Gokulashtami* and *Balev* in July-August, *Dasara in* September-October, and *Diwali* in October-November. They go to Bachucharaji, Dakor, Dwarka, Shukaltirth and Unai, where they pay their respects to the idols from a distance or content themselves by worshipping the banner which flies from the top of the temple.

They honour Musalman saints, and some of them are Lalbegis, that is, disciples of the Musalman saint Lalbeg. In South Gujarat, their great day is the *chaddi* or dark ninth of *Shravan* in August. The day is marked in honour of a certain Zahir Pir (Zahir Pir lived in the Hissar district of Panjab during the reign of the Emperor Firuz Shah, A.D. 1350-1390), who, besides by Bhangias, is held in esteem, by many Gujarat Hindus and Parsis. On this day, the Bhangias form a procession and carry a model of the saint's tomb. In front of the tomb the more devout dance and sing, beating themselves with heavy iron chains, but by the power of the saint, receive no harm. When small-pox is raging they worship the Kakabalia deity. They respect Brahmans, who tell them lucky days, and Garudas or Dheda priests, who, except in South Gujarat, conduct their marriage ceremonies." The customs, rites and rituals are related to the *Bhangis* of the western region.

Performing Ritual of Mahalaya

"As a rule Bhandaris burn their dead, though burying is not regarded as objectionable, and is not uncommon in the case of poor people. At burial, the corpse is either seated or is laid with head to the south. The bones and ashes are thrown into the sea or a river in the vicinity. Those who have the means, carry a few of the bones to a sacred river to be thrown into the holy waters. The ordinary funeral rites are observed. For the propitiation of the deceased ancestors the *mahalaya* is performed in the latter half of *Bhadrapad* and the *shraddha* on the anniversary of the deceased.

"Bhandaris follow the Hindu law of inheritance and belong to the Hindu religion. They are followers of the Shaiva sect. They worship all Brahmanic and local gods, observe all the Hindu fasts and feasts, and make pilgrimages to all the sacred places of the Hindus. Their family gods are Mahadeva, Rawalnath, Nagnath, Ramnath, Shejjeshwar, Shivanath, Mahamaye, Kalika, Chandika, Kolamba, Mahakali, etc., whose shrines are in Goa, Vengurla, Ratnagiri, Rajapur, and other places in the Southern Konkan. Their spiritual guide is the Shankaracharya of the Shringeri monastery," writes thus Mr. Enthoven.

The Bhandaris' priests include Konkanasth, Karhada, or Karnatak Brahmans.

Rubbing the Deceased's Brow with Ashes

"The dead are either burnt or buried. The dead bodies of those who have been branded with a religious seal by the *pujaris* (worshippers) of Yelgurdappa (Hanumant Dev) of Yelgur on the Krishna in the Bagevadi taluka of the Bijapur district, must be buried. At burial, the unmarried dead are placed in a lying position with head to the south, and the married in a sitting position with the face towards the east. The body is washed and dressed, the brow of the dead man is rubbed with ashes and the head of a dead woman is decked with a flower-net. They carry their dead on a bier, except for the poor, who carry them in an old blanket. After burning or burying the body the funeral party bathes and returns to the house of mourning.

On the third day the mourners take rice *kanolas* or semi-circular cakes and water to the burning ground in a small new earthen pot and lay them near the spot where the deceased was burnt or buried. They wait till a crow touches the offering. If no crow come to eat, the chief mourner promises to take care of the children of the deceased. If, even after this, the crows refuse to eat, they give the food to a cow and go home. A dinner is given to the corpse bearers, and mourning is ended by smoking together. On the seventh, ninth or eleventh day, the ashes and the bones of the deceased are gathered up and thrown into the water, and friends and relations are feasted. At the end of a month, friends and relations are asked to a feast, at which goat's flesh is served. In Belgaum, a Mahar always goes with the dead body and is paid one anna. On the twelfth day, the chief mourner brings water from the village Brahman, sprinkles it in the house, and, if the deceased was married, a silver plate impressed with the figure of the deceased is brought from a goldsmith for annas 4 or 8. On the thirteenth day, the relations of the deceased worship the silver plate which is kept in the house and worshipped once in a year. For the propitiations of the deceased ancestors, a dinner is given to the tribesmen by every family on the new moon of either *Bhadrapad, Ashvin* or *Phalgun.* The ceremony of *shraddha* is not performed.

"Berads were formerly a warlike and dangerous class, notorious as thieves and highway robbers. In the Belgaum district, even now, some of them are clever thieves, skilful in eluding search and hiding stolen property, and are much feared by travellers. They steal cattle with such cleverness, and send the stolen animals such long distances, that the greatest energy and cautions often fail to find any trace of them. The owner has to go and ask for the Berad's help, and if he promises a reward, the animal is found and restored. If an animal is missing, it is almost sure to have fallen into the hands of the Berads. As a class they are orderly, hard working, hospitable and free from crime. Some are husbandmen, some village watchmen or *talvars* holding free grants of lands, some are *patils* and *shetsanadis,* some are labourers, some are hunters and snarers, and some are cartmen. Many hold lands under the

Rayatvari system. The *patils* and *shetsanadis* hold *watan* lands. The Berads observe all the field rites and ceremonies of local Kunbis," writes Mr. Enthoven.

Donating Grain, Valuables to Brahman

According to R.V. Russell and Hiralal, the Rajput funeral ceremony is performed thus : "A short time before death, according to his means, a Rajput gives a cow, a horse, grain, and gold to Brahmans, and a Brahman priest reads the Bhagvatgita to the dying person. On the near approach of death, the dying person is laid on his back with his feet to the south on a portion of the floor which has been freshwashed with cowdung, sprinkled with water from some holy river, and strewn with sacred *durbha* grass. On the left of the dying person is set a zinc cup with a ball of wheat flour and ashes, and a lamp fed with clarified butter is kept burning near the zinc cup. In the dying mouth are laid five jewels, that is, clarified butter, curd, basil leaves, holy water and gold. The relations sit near and repeat *Ram Ram* till life is gone. The deceased, if a male, a shouldercloth, a coat, a waistcoat and a turban. A bamboo bier is prepared and furnished with a mattress and cushions and a white sheet. The body is laid on the bier and covered with a silk or brocade cloth according to the means of the dead. A coconut is tied to each of the four corners of the bier. In the case of the chiefs and the members of chief's families a *sinhasan* or lion seat is made to carry the dead to the burning ground. To carry the bier, five persons bathe and put on the sacred thread. Four of them bear the bier, and the fifth walks in front carrying fire in an earthen pot set in a bamboo frame hanging from his hand. The widow dresses in a holiday robe and bodice and ornaments. When the bier is carried out of the house she goes to some river or pond with women neighbours and friends crying bitterly, she breaks her ivory bangles and puts off her gay clothes and ornaments, bathes in the pond or river, and, dressed in plain dark garments, returns home weeping. At a short distance from the burning ground the bearers halt and lay a ball of rice flour and a silver coin in the right hand of the dead. The bier is again lifted and taken to the burning ground, which is generally near a pond or river. A pile of wood and cowdung cakes is prepared and the body is again bathed and laid on the pile. On the body are dropped sacred basil leaves, pieces of sandalwood, *gugal* or incense, and coconuts. The hands and feet of the dead are rubbed with clarified butter. The Brahman priest repeats the sacred verses; the chief mourner moves five times round the pile with a burning brand in his hand and touches the mouth of the dead with the brand, repeating the words *Nas prani Ag* avi, that is, Flee Oh soul, fire has come. The pile in then kindled; when it is completely burnt, water is poured over it and the embers extinguished. Then they go to a neighbouring river or pond, bathe, and return home crying aloud. On that day no food is prepared in the house of the dead. The inmates are fed with cooked rice, pulse and clarifed butter prepared at the house of the chief mourner's wife or at the house of some near relations or neighbours. For nine days cooked rice with pulse called *kadvani khichadi* is eaten in the house. For the first ten days a Brahman priest pours sugar, water, milk and opium-water into leaf cups and the cups are placed on the roof of the house. On the third day letters bearing the sad news are sent to relations and friends who do not live in the same village, stating the time of death and the time when the death rites are to be performed. On the same day, the chief mourner, with relations and friends goes to the burning ground taking a new earthen vessel covered with a new earthen saucer called *Ramvatra* or Ram's saucer, and a little milk in a brass or copper vessel also covered with a metal saucer and flowers. He pours the milk over the cold embers, gathers the ashes and, except a few bones which are preserved to be sent to some holy place or river, such as Benares, Gaya or Sidhpur, removes them to some neighbouring tank or river. In the place of the ashes he lays the earthen vessel filled with water and on the vessel's mouth Ram's saucer with a wheat-flour ball in it. He then bathes and returns home. For the first ten days after a death, the inmates of the house are considered impure and keep apart even when visitors come to console them. For these comforters the chief mourner keeps dry opium and water and a smoking pipe ready. Every morning, from the first to the ninth, balls of rice flour are offered to the dead. On the tenth day the chief mourner, who is generally the eldest son, shaves his face, the eyebrows and the head except the topknot, and performs the tenth day *shraddha* or mind-feast. For the other men of the family, the rule is that only those younger than the dead shave the moustache. On the eleventh day, all the members of the mourning family bathe and put on fresh washed clothes. On the morning of the eleventh the waistclothes, bamboo baskets, metal idols, rice and other grains and flour, turmeric, sandal paste, flowers, earthen vessels, sesame and molasses required for the eleventh-day rites are taken to the village river or pond, and during the course of the day a *shraddha* or mind-rite is performed. A young bull and a heifer are wedded, balls of rice-flour are offered to the spirit of the dead, and the chief mourner returns weeping aloud. A caste feast is given to the relations of the dead. On the twelfth, as on the eleventh, the mourners go to the village river or pond and perform the twelfth day rites. When they return, the priest lays before the house twelve balls of wheat-flour each in an earthen saucer covered with a rim-down cup of brass, copper or, in the case of a chief, of silver. Each cup and saucer is tied together with a cotton-thread. On the thirteenth day, the village potter hand a cup for his trouble. Of the remaining vessels, half go to the Brahman and half to the daughter's or sister's sons of the dead. Castepeople and servants as well as ascetics and beggars are then fed with sweetmeats and *mori biranj,* that is, pounded rice and pulse cooked in clarified butter and condiments, or *lapsi* wheat flour cooked with molasses and mixed with clarified butter, pulse and *khichdi,* that is, cooked rice and pulse, or *shiro,* that is, wheat flour cooked in clarified butter and molasses. If the deceased, is a woman thirteen shallow bamboo baskets called *chhdbdis,* each containing a petticoat, a bodice and a robe, are presented in the name of the dead person to near relations. If the deceased is a man, thirteen deep baskets are filled each with a headscarf, a waistcoat, a shouldercloth and a waistcloth, and are given to near relations. At night a cot is laid out furnished with a mattress, pillows and cushions and a pair of shoes. A metal lamp, five garments—a waistcloth, a shouldercloth, a headscarf, a coat and a waistcoat—wheat, rice, *juvar,* molasses and clarified butter, dice and playing cards, betelnuts, brass salvers, jars, cups, and smoking pipes are also placed on the cot. A cow is brought in, the wife of the dead comes and holds the tail of the cow with both hands, and over her hands the priest pours water. The bedding or *sejja,* with the rest of the articles, are presented to a Brahman, who is generally called *Kayatiya,* that is, funeral Brahman. The Brahman is laid on the bedding, and the cot is lifted by four men and carried out of the house to the village boundary. The men and women of the house follow for a short distance crying bitterly, and burning cowdung cakes are thrown after the *Kayatiya.* They then return home. If the family is well-to-do, two sets of bed with presents or *sejjas* are given—one to the *Kayatiya* the other to the family-priest.

"On the thirteenth day, the thirteenth-day rites are performed and the family priest is given a milch cow, a cot with mattresses, pillows and cushions, a cup, a lampstand, waistclothes, robes, bodices and packets of sugar. Friends and relations are asked to dine at the house and Brahmans are feasted and presented with money. The chief mourner is given a turban or cash by his father-in-law or maternal uncle, and such friends and relations as are present, are entertained with *kusumba* and betel-leaves and nuts. The sister or daughter of the dead distributes sweet balls of wheat flour to relations and friends in the village. On the fifteenth day, a dinner is given to Brahmans and castepeople; and till another month is over, that is for six weeks in all, the members of the family do not join in marriage or other feasts nor do they eat the special dishes which are taken on festive occasions. At the same time as the seclusion of the mourning family ceases, that is a month and a half after the death, the third fortnightly *shraddha* is performed; and four and a half months later the sixth-monthly *shrddha* follows. On the bright fifth of *Bhadrapad* (Sept.-Oct.), grain is cooked and served to Brahmans. On the next day, the members of the house feed on sweet balls. Three days later, on the bright eighth of *Bhadrapad* (Sep.-Oct.), balls of rice or Indian millet flour mixed with molasses or sugar and clarified butter are made and given to Brahmans with cash. A bamboo lantern is made and in it are put a head scraf, a waistcloth, a shouldercloth, a coat and a jacket, with copper-pots, ornaments, a looking glass, a silk waistcord and articles used in games. All of these, including the bamboo lantern, are presented to Brahmans in the presence of the relations who add gifts of cash. On the bright tenth of *Aso* (Oct.-Nov.) Brahmans are fed. And on the *Diwali* a wheat-flour lamp in a leaf cup is launched in the nearest river. On the *Sankrant* (Jany. 12) Brahmans are fed with balls of *mag*

Phaseolus radiatus flour mixed with sugar and clarified butter and are presented with earthen vessels and cash. On the *Akhatrij* or bright third of *Vaishakh* (May-June), earthen vessels filled with water are presented with cash to Brahmans. A little less than twelve months after the death, the first year feast is held, when bamboo baskets and earthen and metal vessels and a cot with bedding, waistclothes and metal vessels are given to the Brahman priest, and Brahmans and castepeople are feasted. From this day to the actual anniversary, counting by months, a Brahman and an ascetic are fed daily, and, on the twelfth month death-day, they are presented with dresses and cash. On the twelfth month death-day Brahmans are presented with money. The widow and the sons of the dead leave off mourning and the widow goes to her father's house. On each anniversary, a *shraddha* or mind rite is performed and Brahmans are fed.

"Except for their clan and local pecularities, Rajputs do not differ from other Hindus in their religious observances and practices. Before A.D. 1818 Cutch Jadejas were half Hindu half Musalman. They visited mosques and gave their daughters in marriage to Musalmans. Since A.D. 1818 the example of several strictly Hindu Ravs, the decline of infanticide, the divisions of land and the spread of proverty have combined to make the Jedejas give up several of their un-Hindu ways. Of their former Musalman beliefs and practices nothing remains but for the reverence for certain Musalman saints and occasional marriage into Musalman families. Though many are followers of the special forms of Vashnavism preached by Vallabhacharya and by Ramanuja, and though the modern sect of Svaminarayan still gathers adherents, Rajputs from remote ages have been partial to the worship of Shiva. At the same time, they worship all Hindu gods and goddesses, and their house-shrines contain the images of Shiva, Vishnu, Ganapat, and of the tutelary goddess of the clan," add Russell and Lal.

Chief Mourner Sitting Near the Body

"Among Gujarat Bhils, except in the case of a very young child or when the cause of death has been small-pox, the dead are burnt as they say 'with the sun as a witness', that is, only during the day. When life is gone, the relations bathe the body, spread a waistcloth *dhotar* over it, and carry it on a rough bamboo bier to the burning ground. At the burning ground the chief mourners sit near the body while the rest of the party gathers wood for the pyre. The son or other next-of-kin sets the pyre alight. When the body is half burnt the mourners bathe. On the way back to the house of the deceased the party rests half-way between house of the deceased and the burning ground, place five stones near each other, and to the branch of a neighbouring tree ties a small piece of the winding sheet of the deceased. On returning to the house of the deceased the party smoke tobacco for a short time and after saluting each other go home. On the fifth day after death, ten to twenty friends and relations of the deceased come to the place where the small stones were laid and, without drinking any liquor eat boiled maize, *ghugari.* After the meal they throw away the stones and the piece of the winding sheet, and return to their homes. On the fifth day as well as on the day of the *kaita* or death dinner, the Jhalod Bhils have the special practice of shaving their moustaches. In Jhalod, where they are well to do, Bhils give a death dinner or *kaita* on the twelfth day like upper class Hindus. Among the poorer Bhils the families of five or six deceased persons subscribe and give one combined death-dinner, in some cases two or three years after the death. For this death-dinner much liquor is distilled and a dish called *ghugari* made of Indian corn, gram and wheat boiled together, is prepared. When the guests, who often number two or three thousand, come together, a Raval pours a quart of milk into a metal salver and in the milk sets a brass horse. Two of the near relations of the deceased squat down holding the dish at arm's length above their heads. Then, while the Raval plays a one-stringed guitar or *tamburo* with a hand drum accompaniment, the mourners for an hour or two keep throwing into the dish money, rice and Indian corn. At last the salver shakes and the image of the horse falls on its side in the milk. The mourners weep and wail. Liquor is handed round, and, in a leaf, each guest is given a small dole of boiled Indian corn, gram and wheat. When the meal is over, all but relations leave, the Raval taking his perquisites, the brass horse and the salver full of grain. The relations usually bring a goat or young buffalo or a few yards of country cloth as a present for the son of the deceased. If they bring cloth it is given when the villagers leave ; if they bring a goat or young buffalo it is at once beheaded and the head thrown on the roof of the house of the deceased. The body is taken to a distance, cut up, cooked and eaten, the relations bringing liquor to drink with it. If the deceased was a man of importance, year or two after his death, his relations go to a stone mason and make him cut on a stone slab the figure of a man on horseback with a spear in his hand, paying him by the gift of a cow or a she-buffalo. On the first *kalichaudas* or dark fourteenth of *Ashvin* (September-October), the stone, with procession and drum beating, is carried in a cart to the house of the deceased, where it is washed, daubed with red powder, covered with a white cloth and again placed in a cart, and taken to the village spirit yard or *devasthan.* There a goat is killed, its blood sprinkled on the stone, and its flesh cooked a and eaten with as much liquor as the party can afford," writes Mr. Enthoven.

"In Khandesh, when a Bhil is on the point of death, his relations distribute money among the poor in his name. When he dies, the body is laid on a blanket or a piece of cloth spread over a blanket. An earthen pot full of cold water is placed near the door of the house and the body is brought out, held in a sitting position outside the door, and water poured over it. The old clothes are taken off, and tying a new piece of cloth round the loins, the body is laid on the bier and covered with a new white sheet, leaving the face bare, and the head covered with a turban. Red powder, *gulal*, is sprinkled over the face, and some red powder and cooked rice are tied together in a piece of cloth and placed on the bier. The body is then tied with a string to the bier, and carried to the burning ground on the shoulders of four near male relations. In front of them go the sons of the deceased, the chief mourner carrying fire in an earthen jar, and one of the others carrying an earthen jug full of water. Half-way to the grave, the bier is lowered, and some of the cooked food is laid near a bush. The bearers change places, and without further halt, the body is carried to the burning ground. Here the bier is lowered and the mourners help in digging a grave, long enough for the body, and to prevent it being opened by wild animals, about five or six feet deep. In this the body is laid, the head to the south and the arms stretched along either side. Cooked rice and bread are placed in the mouth, and the body is sprinkled with water. Before leaving the grave, the man who is last arranging the body tears a small hole in the winding sheet. Then the whole party sits round the grave, so far off that they cannot see the body, and the chief mourner throws a handful of earth on the corpse, and all joining, cover the corpse with earth. When the body is covered, they rise and fill the grave, cutting a small trench round it. In this trench, beginning from the north, they pour water out of an earthen jug, and when the circuit of the grave is complete, drop the jug and break it to pieces. Then the bier is turned upside down and burned, and the funeral party, going to the nearest water, bathe and accompany the chief mourner to his house. In front of his house a fire is lit, and into it some woman's hair is dropped, and each of the funeral party, taking some *nim, Melia azadirachta,* leaves, throws them on the fire, and passing his open palms through the smoke, rubs them over his face. The mourners are now pure, and after taking a draught of liquor, go to their homes.

"On the third day, one of the women of the mourning household rubs the right shoulders of the pall-bearers with oil, milk and cowdung, and washes them with *nim* twigs steeped in cow's urine. Then the four men bathe and are treated to a dinner. In the house the only sign of mourning is that every morning, for five days, the women wail for about a quarter of an hour.

"On the eleventh day, the chief mourner goes to a river, and there has his head, beard and face shaved, and bathes. Next he makes a dough cow, sprinkles it with red powder, and setting it on a leaf plate, bows to it, and throws it into the water. He then bathes and goes home.

"Either on the twelfth or the forty-fifth day a potter, Kumbhar, is called and a seven-step hemp ladder, *chodhvan,* is set against the wall of the house that the soul of the dead may climb by it to heaven. The priest sits at the foot of the ladder and chants a verse from the *Purans*, the string by which the ladder is fastened to the ground is burnt, and the ladder pulled down and thrown away. The spot where the ladder was tied is then covered with flour, and a small plate with a piece of bread and cooked rice is laid on it. In the plate is set a small water pot, and alongside of the water pot a lighted lamp covered by an empty bamboo basket with a cloth drawn over it. This day a grand dinner is prepared, and before it is eaten, five mouthfuls are burnt near the basket. The burial rites for a woman are the same as those of a man. When a child dies the father carries the body in his arms and buries it, and on the seventh day a small dinner is given. In some rare cases the Bhils burn instead of burying their dead," adds Mr. Enthoven. The customs, rites and rituals are pertinent to the *Bhil* community.

References

1. Singh, K.S., (Gen. Ed.) *People of India : Daman and Diu*, Popular Prakashan, Bombay, 1994.
2. Singh, K.S., (Gen. Ed.) *People of India, Goa*, Popular Prakashan, Bombay, 1993.
3. Punekar, Vijay B., *The Son Kolis of Bombay*, Popular Book Depot, Bombay, 1959.
4. Enthoven, R.E., *The Tribes and Castes of Bombay*, Low Price Publications, Delhi (reprint) 1997, first published 1922.
5. Russell, R.V. and Lal, Hira, *The Tribes and Castes of the Central Provinces of India*, Low Price Publications, Delhi (reprint) 1977, originally published 1916.
6. Gomes, Olivinho, J.F., *India—Land and People : Goa*, National Book Trust, New Delhi, 2004.
7. *Bombay Gazetteer*, Vol. IX, Part I.

6

Death Rituals : Burial

Disposal of the dead through burial is a common practice among Muslims and Christians. Yet many primitive tribals, low-caste Hindus also bury their corpses out of poverty and due to some superstitions. Thus, the primitive tribals practising animalism and the low caste Hindu in Gujarat, Maharashtra, Daman and Diu, Dadra and Nagar Haveli practise burial. In his ethnography, *The Tribes and Castes of Bombay* Mr. R.E. Enthoven has given much details about them, besides *The Tribes and Castes of the Central Provinces of India* by R.V. Russell and Hira Lal.

Muttering Half-Hindu, Half-Muslim prayer

About the burial custom of the Matias, Mr. R.E. Enthoven writes, "The Matias bury the dead. A dying person is bathed and laid on the ground, the *kaka* standing near and reading tera. When life is gone, the body of the deceased, if a man, is dressed in cotton trousers, a shirt and a cap and, if a woman, in a silk robe, a bodice and a petticoat. It is laid in a Musalman bier and carried to the burial-ground, which is generally on the bank of a stream. The bearers do not take off any of their clothes or their shoes. On reaching the burial ground, the bearers, without removing any of the clothes, lay the body in a pit and fill the pit with earth. After the body is buried, the mourners purify themselves by each holding a piece of frankincense in his hand and muttering two half-Hindu half-Musalman prayers. The first prayer runs, 'In the name of Allah the pitiful, the merciful, of Satgor or Satgur Patrs, of Brahma and Indra, of Imam Shah, of the spotless spiritual Vishnu and of Ali Muhammad Shah'. The second prayer is in these words, 'The incense burns, evil goes and faith wins (now is the time to) mercy implore'.

"The funeral party go to the house of mourning, and there the deceased's family feast them with sweet wheat-balls. The mourners eat a mixture of split pulse and rice cooked in a neighbour's house. Like Hindus, Matia women weep and beat their breasts for ten days, and for ten days the sin-removing *lahc-utarni* ceremony is performed daily. Friends and relations from the villages round, summoned by a Bhangia, come to mourn and are feasted with wheat-flour mixed with clarified butter and sugar. Unlike Hindus, the nearest relations do not consider themselves impure for ten days. No death ceremonies are performed and no rice balls are offered to the spirits of the deceased. Caste people are feasted on the tenth and eleventh days after a death or on any day between the thirteenth and the twentieth, if the eleventh or twelfth falls on a Sunday or a Tuesday. On the first feast-day after a death, each family of Matias sends the chief mourner half a *man* (twenty-pounds) of husked rice and, besides the rice, friends and relatives give 50p. These presents, along with the clothes, bed and bedstead of the deceased, are sent to the shrine of the saints at Burhanpur, Navsari, Ahmedabad, or Vemal. Besides these presents, the chief mourner sends on his own account a money present, and if rich he sets apart a mango tree for the exclusive use of the saint. The aggregate amount of death presents which go to their saints varies from Rs. 15 to Rs. 100. The Brahman priest receives some presents on the eleventh day, not in his character of priest, but in return for the help he gives in feasting the caste-people," adds Mr. Enthoven. The burial custom is prevalent among the Matia Kanbis.

Koli Dhor Abandoning Burial

Earlier the Koli Dhor used to bury their dead, but now all the tribals, except the Christian converts, cremate their dead. Ashes and bones are collected and disposed off in water. *Daru* (liquor) is served after cremation to the funeral party members on their return from the cremation. The ritual of *Darhoo* is performed after one month by the *bhagat* to remove the death-related pollution. *Kurh* members are invited and liquor is served. *Cheda* or stone memorial is erected near the crematorium in the name of the deceased. The Koli Dhors throw boiled rice on the roof of their houses every year on Diwali for use of the departed soul.

The Ritual of *Santesaon*

In Goa, the *Catholic Mahar* observe the ritual of the Last

Sacrament (common Catholic custom), locally called *santesaon*, prior to the death of a person. In this ritual, *Padre* or the parish priest comes and prays anointing the person's forehead with Holy oil. This ritual originates from a belief that the Almighty may extend the life of the dying person. The dead are disposed off through burial, keeping the corpse in a coffin with the wedding suit or dress on. The coffin is carried to the church by the mourners attired in black for last prayers prior to the burial in the cemetery. Before taking the coffin to the church and cemetery, the widow of the deceased is adorned specially with flowers tucked in the hair and coloured glass bangles by hitting them on the coffin. Then on the grave, flowers are kept. On returning from the cemetery, the mourners depart after a prayer. Traditionally, on the third and seventh day and after a month special Masses in the local church are arranged for the soul to rest in peace. But at present, this is being performed only once on any convenient day and a feast is given to the church officials on the same day. One year after death, a mourning prayer is arranged in the church in a specially convened Mass. Though no observance of pollution exists among them, the family pays respect to the departed soul. All the adult members of the bereaved family wear black dresses regularly for one year However, in current times people do not wear the black dress for a full year, but discard it after a short time.

The custom is practised among the *Catholic Mahars*.

Ritual of Extreme Unction

In Goa, when a person is on the deathbed, the *Padre* or the parish priest is invited to the house of the ailing person to perform Extreme Unction, the last sacrament of anointing with the consecrated oil in the last hours the dying man so that he may either recover by the blessings of God or die in peace. The body is generally carried in the church bier to their cemetery in the vicinity of the village church. When the corpse is lowered in the grave, the hands of the deceased are tied together across the chest and a small crucifix is placed in them. Then the *Padre* or the parish priest spreads a handful of earth over the body and others follow the suit until it is properly buried. The mourners are dressed in black symbolizing their grief. On the third day, a special mass (mourning prayer) is arranged by the family of the bereaved in the church when all pray to the Almightly for the peace of the soul. The same is repeated on the seventh day and after one month a feast is organised. After one year, a mourning prayer is convened by the bereaved family to observe the death anniversary, administered by the *Padre* or the vicar in the church. Though the Catholics do not observe any ritual of pollution period related to death, the sons and the close relatives observe mourning for one year. They usually do not attend any festive or ceremonial occasion for a year and wear black dress during this period as a mark of respect to the soul of deceased. The Custom is Prevalent Among the Goan Catholic.

The corpses of the dead are buried. The widow of the deceased dresses in her nuptial attire. Then she breaks her bangles on the arrival of the *Padre* in the house through striking against the coffin. The priest recites a prayer in the house and leads the funeral procession to church prayer and thereafter to the burial ground. The married women may accompany the funeral procession but widows are not allowed sometime ago, even married women were not allowed. All deaths must be registered with the Registrar of Births and Deaths according to law. The pollution period after death is not observed among the Catholic Gauda now.

A little prior to death, the *Last Sacrament*, locally called *santesaom,* is performed. In this ritual, the *Padre* offers a prayer at the dying person's bedside and applies sacred oil on his forehead in a belief that the Almighty may extend his life span, even when there is no hope of survival. The body is buried in the cemetery after placing at in a coffin, but before the burial coffin is taken to the Church where the last prayers are offered. After burial, flowers are placed on the grave and the mourners return to the house of the deceased and get dismissed after saying a prayer. As per tradition, special Masses are arranged on the third and the seventh day and on completion of one month following death. But in the current times only one Mass is arranged and a funeral feast follows it. On the death anniversary, a mourning prayer organised in the church or chapel by the bereaved family. Though there is no observance of death pollution among the Catholics, the bereaved family does not participate in any celebrations for a period. They are expected to wear a black dress as a mark of mourning. But, currently some people wear the black dress for a short period only, instead of one year.

The custom is prevalent among the *Goan Catholic* carpenters.

Dying on Thursday or Friday during Ramazan most Propitious

About the death customs of Muslims, Mr. RE Enthoven writes, "That death may not attack him unawares, or in a foreign land, is the wish of every Muhammadan. To one on the point of death the chapter of the Kuran, telling of death and the glorious future of the true believer, is read, the creed and prayer for forgiveness are repeated, and a few drops of honey are dropped into the mouth. After death the eyes and mouth are closed, the body is laid on a wooden platform, carefully washed and perfumed, and covered with a scented shroud of white cloth. For a woman to die in the evening is a hopeful sign of her future forgiveness. She has lived within the veil and within the veil she goes to her Maker. It is well to die on a Thursday or a Friday or any day in the month of Ramazan and on any other holiday. Death on a Wednesday is unlucky. Four deaths take place in the family which loses one of its members on a Wednesday. If the death happens at night the body is not taken away till dawn. Otherwise, so soon as it is shrouded and the friends have taken their last look, (When the deceased is the head of a family his widow is brought in dressed in her richest robes, to take a last look at her lord. A husband is not allowed to look at his dead wife. Among the wails of the women, the wailing of women is against the order of the Prophet. In Surat and Broach it is practised only among the poor. In north Gujarat it is common among all classes except Arabs all of whom stay behind, the body is laid on the bier, lifted on the bearers' Biers or *janazahs* are used only in south Gujarat; in the north the body is laid on a cot. It is unusual to lay the body in a coffin. The bearers are never hired men, always the nearest relations and friends. An exception is made at the funeral of a married woman, when, unless he means never again to marry, the husband is not allowed to join in carrying the bier shoulders, and borne away, the company of men raising the cry *Lailaha illallah* There is no God but Allah, and trained singers chanting solemn hymns. Over the bier four bearers carry a piece of brocade called the canopy *shamianah*. Upon the bier is a shawl, green or other dark colour for men and red for women. The grave is either where the deceased has asked to be buried or in the family burial ground. At the mosque the bier is set down in the outer court, the mourners wash, and, standing in a row, repeat the funeral prayer *Allaho-Akbar* God is great. They move to the ready dug grave, laying the body in it, the head to the north and leaning on the right side so that the face turns towards Mecca. The grave may be in one of three forms. The most common is a pit where the body is placed and earth thrown in. The other is a hollow formed by planks placed aslant. The third is a hole of soft yielding mud into which the body is gently left to sink. Coffins also are used, but only by the very rich. They lay clods of consecrated earth close to the body, and the mourners fill the grave repeating the verse of the Kuran, "Of earth We made you, to earth we return you, and from earth will raise you on the resurrection day." They retire to the house of mourning and standing at the door repeat a prayer for the soul of the dead, and all but near relatives and friends who stay to dine, go to their homes. The duty of helping at funerals and of praying for the souls of the dead is solemnly enjoined on all Musalmans and is carefully observed by them. Though a *farz*, that is, a divine behest, it is also a *farz-i-kifayah* or duty which if attended to by a sufficient number of the faithful does not demand the presence of all. Among the rich the clothes of the dead are given in charity and grain is distributed. Till the third day no food is cooked in the house of mourning. At Ahmedabad the friends and relations of the deceased send ready-cooked dinners. In south Gujarat dinners called *bhathi* are cooked at the house of mourning at the expense of near relations. On the morning of the third day after a death a feast called *Ziarat* is held. A large company of relations, friends and others meet in the mosque, where each of them, reading from small books a chapter of the Kuran, finish with a prayer that the merit of the act may pass to the soul of the deceased. A sermon *waaz* is preached by a Maulvi. After the sermon a tray full of flowers and a vessel with a sweet-smelling mixture and oil in a small metal or porcelain cup is passes among the guests. Each guest as the tray passes picks a flower and drops it into the vessel and the whole is poured over the grave. Sweetmeats or *batashas* are distributed and the friends present shawls to the son or sons of the deceased; and before leaving the mosque and again on arrival before the house of the deceased, prayers are offered for his soul. After this, among the rich and some of the middle class a dinner is given on as grand a scale as a wedding dinner. A man may without disgrace avoid this third day feast. At Ahmedabad the great dinner is given on the fortieth day. On the third day a smaller number of friends and beggars only are fed. But on the fortieth day, the fourth month, the sixth month, the ninth month, and the last day of the first year he must give choice dinners.

"The only form of mourning laid down by Muhammadan law is in the case of the death of the head of a house, the strict seclusion of his widow. This lasts for four months and ten days and during that time the widow, unless she is forced to do so, never leaves the house. Besides this strictly Muhammadan observance, other customs have been adopted from the Hindus. As soon as life is gone, the mother and the widow of the dead break their bangles. The mother may get new bangles but except when they are of gold or silver the widow, unless she marries, never again wears bracelets or a nosering. In south Gujarat the women of the poorer classes, and in the north all except those of Arab families or of families entertaining strict religious opinions wail in Hindu fashion. In the north, too, when a woman first visits the widow, on seating herself she bursts into a wail. The chief mourner joins in the cry, keeping it up until she is soothed by her friend. This custom is known as the *munh dhankna* or facehiding. The shortest term of mourning is six months. For the first forty days the rooms are stripped of their furniture, cots, cushions and pillows are put out of sight, and all members of the household sleep on the bare ground and no food is cooked in the house. During the whole six months no holiday is observed, no gaieties attended, and no music heard. At the end comes the *seg uthana* or grief-lifting, when some friend asks the family to visit him. For his nearest relations a man for about a year wears a white turban. If young, a widow wears some dark coloured dress; if old, she wears white but never either yellow or red."

About their funeral customs, Mr. R.V. Russell and Hira Lal note, "The same word *janazah* is used for the corpse, the bier and the funeral. When a man is at the point of death a chapter of the Koran, telling of the happiness awaiting the true believer in the future life, is read, and some money or sherbet is dropped into his mouth. After death the body is carefully washed and wrapped in three or five cloths for a male or female respectively. Some camphor or other sweet-smelling stuff is placed on the bier. Women do not usually attend funerals, and the friends and relatives of the deceased walk behind the bier. There is a tradition among some Muhammadans that no one should precede the corpse, as the angels go before. To carry a bier is considered a very meritorious act, and four of the relations, relieving each other in turn, bear it on their shoulders. Muhammadans carry their dead quickly to the place of interment, for Muhammad is stated to have said that it is good to carry the dead quickly to the grave, so as to cause the righteous person to attain the sooner to bliss; and, on the other hand, in the case of a bad man it is well to put wickedness away from one's shoulders. Funerals should always be attended on foot, for it is said that Muhammad once rebuked people who were following a bier on horseback, saying, 'Have you no shame, since God's angles go on foot and you go upon the backs of quadrupeds?' It is a highly meritorious act to attend a funeral whether it be that of a Muslim, a Jew or a Christian. The funeral service is not recited in the cemetery, this being too polluted a place for so sacred an office, but either in a mosque or in some open space close to the dwelling of the deceased person or to the graveyard. The nearest relative is the proper person to recite the service, but it is usually said by the family priest or the village Kazi. The grave sometimes has a recess at the side, in which the body is laid to prevent the earth falling upon it, or planks may be laid over the body slantwise or supported on bricks for the same purpose. Coffins are only used by the rich. When the body has been placed in the grave each person takes up a clod of earth and pronouncing over it a verse of the Koran, 'From earth we made you, to earth we return you and out of earth we shall raise you on the resurrection day,' places it gently in the grave over the corpse. The building of stone or brick tombs and writing verses of the Koran on them is prohibited by the Traditions, but large masonry tombs are common in all Muhammadan countries and very frequently they bear inscriptions. On the third day a feast is given in the morning and after it trays of flowers with a vessel containing scented oil are handed round and the guests pick flowers and dip them into the oil. They then proceed to the grave, where the oil and flowers are placed. Maulvis are employed to read the whole of the Koran over the grave, which they accomplish by dividing it into sections and reading them at the same time. Rich people sometimes have the whole Koran read several times over in this manner. A sheet of white or red cloth is spread over the grave, green being usually reserved for Fakirs or saints. On the evening of the ninth day another feast is given, to which friends and neighbours, and religious and ordinary beggars are invited, and a portion is sent to the Fakir or mendicant in charge of the burying-ground. Some people will not eat any food from this feast in their houses but take it outside. On the morning of the tenth day they go again to the grave and repeat the offering of flowers and scented oil as before. Other feasts are given on the fortieth day, and at the expiration of four, six and nine months, and one year from the date of the death, and the rich sometimes spend large sums on them. None of these observances are prescribed by the Koran but have either been retained from pre-Islamic times or adopted in imitation of the Hindus. For forty days all furniture is removed from the rooms and the whole family sleep on the bare ground. Sometimes a cup of water and a wheaten cake are placed nightly for forty days on the spot where the deceased died, and a similar provision is sent to the mosque. When man dies his mother and widow break their glass bangles. The mother can get new ones, but the widow does not wear glass bangles or a nose-ring again unless she takes a second husband. For four months and ten days the widow is strictly secluded and does not leave the house. Prayers for ancestors are offered annually at the Shab-i-Barat or Bakr-Id festival. The property of a deceased Muhammadan is applicable in the first place to the payment of his funeral expenses; secondly, to the discharge of his debts; and thirdly, to the payment of legacies up to one-third of the residue. If the legacies exceed this amount they are proportionately reduced. The remainder of the property is distributed by a complicated system of shares to those of the deceased's relatives who rank as sharers and residuaries, legacies to any of them in excess of the amount of their shares being void. The consequence of this law is that most Muhammadans die intestate," they add. The customs are prevalent among the Muslims.

Custom of Seven Sacraments

In Goa, all the Christians are Catholics, followers of that core religious persuasion. They perform seven sacraments to regulate their religious life. The first of it is Baptism or *Batism* or '*Baltim* in Konkani or christening in the social terms, where one is spiritually reborn through the pouring of water blessed by the officiating priest, and is admitted into the Christian faith. The ceremony is conducted in presence of eyewitnesses who act as the godfather and godmother to the child. A name is bestowed officially on the child at the ceremony, which is then confirmed by its registration at the Civil Registrar's office. This sacrament can also be bestowed on an adult Christian in name, but who had not been baptized earlier due to some circumstances beyond control or on an adult undergoing conversion wishing to embrace Christianity.

The birth of a child, incidentally, is announced to the world with two bursts of crackers in case of a girl and three in the event of a boy, as is the old practice among the Hindus also in Goa.

Then the rite of 'Wake' or *Sotti* is held on the sixth day of the birth of a child, (as among the Hindus), an observance which is gradually disappearing, especially among the upper castes and educated Catholics, with others following the suit. But the memory of it keeps most of the people on the alert that night. Because it is believed that the fate of the child is written or decided on that day. These beliefs still continue to persist on in the mind of the people, long after the practice of observing wake has disappeared, hence some basic precautions are taken about the child's wellbeing throughout that night considered as crucial to its future.

When the child is about the age of eight years, he is prepared with instructions in the prayers of day-to-day life, to receive his first Holy Communion or *Poilo Komunheanv* in Konkani. Before that sacrament comes another one of a preparatory nature called Penance, or commonly known as Confession or *Kum'sar* in Konkani is observed. It is one in which the sins of a repentant person are forgiven by the absolution given by the priest in the church. The first holy communion of a child is an important ceremony in the family and for the child's life, as is the base of its spiritual growth. It marks the communion with his fellowmen and involves receiving the holy host or wafer, representing God, in a ceremony in which the child is dressed in white like a bride or bridegroom, with a decorated white candle in hand.

The fourth sacrament is called as the Confirmation or *Krism* in Konkani or rather *Thiravnni* in its modern chaster form: this is performed by the bishop of archbishop of the diocese, or archdiocese accordingly. The whole of Goa is an archdiocese with an Archbishop-Patriarch at its helm of affairs. The Confirmation is generally administered at a mature age. However, it may so happen that some persons might have missed it during their younger years, as the bishop in the old days rarely visited villages in the interior of Goa, and hence have to receive it at the earliest opportunity afforded them on the visit of the archbishop or bishop at their parish is performed more frequently in the modern times.

The fifth sacrament is called as Extreme Unction or *Sontesanu* which is normally administered in the last, before the imminent death of a person, rather when a person is felt to be on verge of death. It may have to be given again if, once imparted, the person concerned who received it does not die thereafter but continues to live. It is administered by anointing the person concerned, with consecrated olive oil, accompanied by the prayers by the officiating priest.

The sixth sacrament is that of the Holy Orders, with ordination to the priesthood by the bishop/archbishop of the diocese of candidates after due training and preparation of several years of tenets, philosophy and theology. Among Catholics, the ordained priest has to take the vow of celibacy, for the rest of life. The seventh sacrament is that of Marriage or Holy Matrimony; the ceremony of which is conducted by the priest, but administered to each other, on beings blessed by the priest, by the guests and participants in the marriage. They also hold an exchange of marriage vows between them, when the bride and bridegroom pledge fidelity and unity to their bond till death do them part. The rings, blessed by the priest, are exchanged by the bride and the bridegroom. It is taken as a contract between the baptized persons, elevated to the level of a sacrament by Jesus Christ.

However in the modern times out of the seven sacraments, such as Baptism. Confession, Confirmation, Holy Communion, (Penance), Holy Orders, Matrimony and Extreme Unction only the Baptism and matrimony are the most important in the life of the Catholics.

In the modern times the high caste catholics particularly do not observe any pre-delivery ritual, but they take special care of a pregnant woman. The expectant mother is usually brought to the hospital for delivery. They do not observe any pollution related taboo after the delivery. Though there is no taboo on the mother of the new-born baby either to cook or to attend any religious function, yet they are not absolutely free from the influence of the Hindu culture. The woman after delivery, however, is restricted for about a fortnight. Forty day after delivery, the mother goes to the church with the baby for the ritual purification.

The Catholics are very particular about the baptism of the new born baby. At the time of baptism, the parents of the baby should be accompanied by the god parents (*Kumpar* or Godfather) and (*Kumar* or Godmother), who on behalf of the baby, answer the question put to the child by the church priests or (*Padre*). The priest asks the baby whether he desires to receive the baptism and the answer is given by the god-parents. In absence of baby's parents, the godparents usually take the sole responsibility of the baby. When the baby is brought for baptism, the priest comes to the main gate of the church and invites the child to come inside. The rituals are administered by the *Padre*. The Easter candle (special type of candle that symbolises the presence of Jesus Christ, is lit. The child is anointed with the holy oil and the priest pour Holy water on his head declaring: 'I baptize you in the name of the Father, the Son and the Holy Spirit'. Henceforth, the child is addressed by the name given to him by the godfather or the godmother and conveyed by the priest at the time of baptism.

The baby is dressed in a white garment, a symbol of purity and innocence. The function is generally attended by the relatives, friends and well-wishers who also present gifts to the new-born. A grand feast is organised by the parents to the invitees for their blessings and good wishes to the baby.

Seven years after christening they hold a function for Communion one of the sacraments of the Catholic, which is performed by the church priest laying his hands on the person to confirm or complete the baptismal vow. After holding the faith in baptism, the children of the Catholics at the age of 12 to 14 years join the Holy Chrism, one of the sacraments of the Catholic church and a ritual where bread and wine are blessed by the Bishop and offered to the candidate and also to the worshippers. It has its origin in the Last Supper which Jesus Christ took on earth with his disciples, when he blessed the bread and wine.

The Catholics do not observe any puberty rites or any restriction or pollution during the menstruation period for girls. Abortion is a taboo in Goan Catholics. The marriage proposal generally comes from the girl's side. After negotiation is over to the satisfaction of both the parties, the engagement is made at the brides' place and wedding rings alongwith some presents are exchanged. But before the engagement, three announcements on three consecutive Sundays are made by the priest in the church before the Mass, regarding any objection, if any, from any side to solemnizing the marriage. Prior to the wedding, a fortnight or a week before it, the bride wears bangles or *chuda* like the Hindu brides, but all the twelve bangles like those of the Hindus are of different colours and are worn till a few days after the wedding. The marriage is solemnised in the church in the presence of the priest who blesses the couple and prays to the God for their welfare. The marriage ceremony is solemnised in the afternoon, when the bride dressed in the bridal gown (white ceremonial dress offered by the bridegroom) and the bride-groom in suit are brought to the altar by their parents or relatives alongwith specially invited guests.

The priest addresses a sermon giving his congest to the couple and blesses both the rings of the couple which are also exchanged as per the instruction of the priest. After the ritual is over, registration for marriage is made by the priest with at least two witnesses from both sides before the Mass in the church; such registration of the marriage is their customary law, but after engagement their marriage is registered in the Civil Registration Office of Goa. A reception is given either in the Church, usually near the bride's residence or in a common hall by both the parties. If the reception is held in a common hall, the *Var* comprising the bride and the bride-groom, brides-maids (*dhedyo*), flower girls. Best Man (*Dhedo*) and page boys are brought to the bride's house or some relation's house before they proceed to the groom's residence in procession. Sometimes, the bride's father holds a feast on the return of the wedding party. In the wedding party, both men and women accept wine, if offered. After the wedding, a toast is raised, usually by a prominent person or an elderly family friend to the couple followed by thanks from the bridegroom, and a prolonged dance in which both the guest couples and the bridal couple dance to the tune of Western music. When the couple enters the bridegroom's house, they are received and greeted by the patriarch of the family by offering a golden chain with a locket or a gold coin or *pod* and a red scarf or *sad* to the bride, while reciting prayers in front of the altar of the residence.

The next day the bridal couple is invited to the bride's residence for a party, and the bridegroom is offered an ornament depending upon the financial status of the bride's family. On the same day, the couple returns groom's house.

As a the last sacrament, when a person is on his deathbed, the priest is invited to the house of the ailing persons to perform Extreme Unction, the last sacrament of anointing one with consecrated oil the last hours of the dying man so that he may either recover by the blessings of God or die in peace. The corpse is generally carried by the church bier to their cemetery in the vicinity of church. When the body in the coffin is lowered in the graveyard, the hands of the deceased are tied together across the chest and a small crucifix is placed in them. Then, the priest spreads a handful of earth over the coffin and others follow until it is properly buried.

The mourners are dressed in black symbolizing their grief. Traditionally, on the third day, a special mass or mourning prayer, is arranged by the bereaved family when all pray to the Almightly for the peace of the departed soul. The same is repeated on the seventh day and after one month and feast is hosted. After one year, a mourning prayer is arranged by the bereaved family to observe the death anniversary which is administered by the priest or *Padre* or the vicar in the church. Though, the Catholics do not observe any pollution related taboo for death, the sons and the close relatives observe mourning for one year. They usually do not attend any festive or ceremonial functions for a year and wear black dress during the period as a mark of respect to the departed soul.

Muslims Sacraments

The Islamic customs among the Goan are Muslims by and large the same as observed in rest of the country, with a few exceptions. The first sacrament is that of *Paidaish*, that concerns the birth of a baby. The *Pesh Imam* or the *Baangi* from a Masjid is called after the birth of a child, and two holy phrases are whispered into the ears of the baby, the *aazan* into the right ear and the *ikaayat* into the left one. Then honey is applied to its tongue and it is given a suitable name. If the priest is not available, the ceremony may be conducted at home by the elder of the family house. Later, according to convenience, the *akika* ceremony is performed on the seventh or the fourteenth day, or the twenty-first or the fortieth day after the birth of a child, when a goat is sacrificed, one goat in the case of a girl and two in case of a boy, goat in the case of a girl and two in case of a boy, as is their custom.

Khatna is the second sacrament intended for male children, meaning circumcision, called '*sunta korunk*' or '*sun*' *not*' in Konkani, which is nowadays being performed in hospitals. The third sacrament *Bismillah* is akin to the *Upanayana* Samskar among the Hindus, in order to initiate the child into the discipline of education, for thereafter the child is taught the *Quran* and other religious texts.

The fourth sacrament is *Nikah* or Marriage. Caste endogamy is still prevalent among Goan Muslims, but it is the gradually giving way to modern trends and a more progressive view among a privileged few of them. The priest or the *Kaazi* reads out from the *Quran* the prescribed prayers before the groom his bride the fathers of both the parties and two family elders, while the bride and the womenfolk from both sides watch the proceedings. The practice of having the *dheddo* (accompanying young man) and the *dheddi* (accompanying young female) for the groom and the bride respectively, is popular among Muslim also as among the Christians and Hindus in Goa.

The fifth Muslim sacrament is the *Vafat* or death when holy phrases relating to God are read out to the dying person. After a person is dead, his legs and arms are straightened out, eyes and mouth closed, and then he is laid to rest, with his face turning towards Mecca. Before the corpse is taken out to the graveyard for burial, it is bathed somewhat like they do in other communities, with soap and aromatic essence, the ceremony beings called as *Gusul*, after which new clothes are put on it. It is then laid in the *Kaphan* (coffin) and three sets of clothes for men and five of them for women are kept separately in it. Some verses from the *Quran* are read out and then the body is taken out to the cemetery where it is kept for some time for public homage and the last prayers.

Later, three days of *Ziyarat* are observed at the house of the deceased, with frequent recitations from the holy book. On the third day after the demise, snacks, and fruits, etc. are served to all the participants in the funeral held earlier. Food is served to the people on behalf of the deceased on the ninth and the fortieth day after death as well as after three months and after six months after the death.

Apart from Shias and other low caste Muslims, the Sunnis observe puberty rites. When a girl attains puberty she is restricted for seven days and during this period she eats butter bread and sugar only. Non-vegetarian dishes and salt are strictly prohibited. In the evening, she takes a bath in warm water. Pre-delivery rites are not observed by the Sunni's. At the time of delivery they take the help of a quack midwife (*dai*). Generally birth takes place in their house. But now, the pregnant women are brought to the maternity centre or hospitals, for delivery. After delivery, they observe a 40-day pollution taboo. The mother of the new-born baby is not allowed to enter the mosque for prayer. She can neither cook, nor take part in religious functions. At the end of this pollution period, she is bathed and dressed in new clothes. After the birth of a child, either the patriarch of the family or the maternal uncle of the baby, or the *kazi* reads *azan* into the ear of new-born baby for his welfare. They hold the naming ceremony on the sixth or seventh day. Sometimes the name of an ancestor is given or an initial latter is selected from the Quran. This function is attended by the kins and friends. They bring some gifts for the new born baby. After this, the father of the baby offers some sweets and non-vegetarian dishes to the invitees. After 40 days, they observe the *aquia* ceremony. On this day, the child is placed in a cradle for the first time. To celebrate the function, they sacrifice a goat, which must be more than a year old. When the mutton is served, the father of the new-born baby prays to the Almightly, saying. 'O Almightly God, I offer this lamb instead of my own offspring, life for life, blood for blood, head for head, bone for bone, hair for hair and skin for skin". The barber or Mhalo is summoned to tonsure the baby. His hair is buried under the ground. The family offers a non-vegetarian feast to the invitees.

However, the child and his parents take only vegetarian food. This ceremony is performed when the boy is of 6 to 8 years. They perform the circumcision ceremony for the male child between one to six years. They invite the barber to carry out this minor surgical operation. The child is usually given a little *bhang* to render him unconscious. The affiens and agnates are invited to attend the ritual.

The body of Sunni Muslims is buried in the community's burial ground. Before the body is brought to the burial ground, it is covered by 18 yards of shroud. The body is buried with the head turned towards the North. The *kazi* recites the *namaz* which is called the *Janazah namaz* before the body is interred. At the time of burial, they put a piece of coir or a drop of *sharbai* into the mouth of the dead person. The women do not attend the burial ground. Only the male friends and relatives of the deceased are allowed.

The Married Deceased Buried in Sitting Position

On the peculiar burial custom, Mr. R.E. Enthoven writes, "The dead are buried in a grave like a *Lingayat* grave. When a *Kiliket* dies, the body is washed with warm water and dressed, and if it is a married woman the hair is decked with a network of flowers. If the deceased was married, the body is kept in a sitting position by a string fastened to a peg driven in the wall; if unmarried, the body is laid on its back. So long as the body remains in the house, it is covered with garlands and bouquets of flowers and with red and scented powders. It is carried to the burial ground in a worn-out blanket and is buried in a sitting position, if married and in a lying position if single. When the burial is over, the funeral party bathe and return to the house of mourning, throw blades of *durva* grass in a pot filled with water which is placed on the spot where the dead person breathed his last, smoke tobacco, and go home. The mourners do not dine at home. Their friends and relations ask them to eat a meal of bread and *chatni* or relish. On the third day, the mourners go to the burial ground and lay two offerings, one on the stone which was placed on the top of the grave and the other twenty-four feet from the grave. These offerings are of millet grit mixed with molasses and and oil and laid on two leaves. They stand far off for fear that they may frighten the crows. If the crows eat the offering, then it means that the deceased has left no wish unfulfilled. If the crows refuse to eat, the mourners pray to the dead. If even then the crows do not eat, they give the offerings to a cow. The mourners bathe, return home and ask the four persons who carried the body to a meal. On the eleventh day, the house is washed with cowdung, the clothes are washed and a feast is given. Before a month passes a goat is killed in honour of the house gods, a brass image of the deceased is made and placed among them and the caste is feasted. As is the case with several other castes, the bodies of pregnant women are burnt to prevent the Garudis digging them up and using their bones as charms." adds Mr. Enthoven.

The burial custom is related to the *Kiliket* community.

Burial of Dead in Sitting or Lying Position

Dwelling on the burial custom and rites of *Mahars*, Mr. Enthoven writes, "The dead are generally buried. A few who have the means burn. At burial the corpse is either seated or laid with the head to the north or south. The body is carried to the burning ground either on a bamboo bier or in a sling. In Khandesh, the thumbs are tied with a piece of silver wire over the breast, the body is shrouded in a new cloth, and grains of rice are tied to one of the hems of the cloth. The chief mourner walks in front with fire in a new earthen jar and music if he has the means. The mourners follow. On the way to the grave, the party halts and the rice from the hem of the deceased's robe is laid on the ground. A pit five feet deep is dug and the body is tripped of all its clothing, even the loincloth, according to the saying, 'Naked hast thou come and naked shalt thou go.' In some places, the clothing is not removed. The body is then lowered into the grave, the chief mourner scatters a handful of earth on the body, the rest also scatter earth and the grave is filled. The chief mourner fills the fire pot with water, sets it on his shoulder and goes thrice round the grave, crying aloud and striking his open mouth with the palm of his right hand.

At the end of the third turn he pours water from the jar on the grave and dashes the jar to pieces on the ground. All bathe in running water, and go to the mourner's house each carrying a *nim* branch. At the house an earthen pot of cow's urine is set on the spot where the deceased breathed his last. The mourners dip the *nim* branches into the urine, sprinkle it over their heads and bodies, and go to their homes. On the third day a few of the deceased's kinsmen go to the burial ground, the chief mourner carrying in his hands a winnowing fan with two pieces of cocoa-kernel and some molasses in each piece. At the rest-place, where the bearers halted, they lay a piece of cocoa-kernel with molasses on it under five stones. The other piece is laid on the heaped grave. They beat the grave down to the level of the rest of the ground, bathe, and go to the chief mourner's house. The four bearers are seated in a line on the bare ground in the front room of the house. Each holds a *nim* branch under his arm, the chief mourner drops a little molasses into his mouth, and they go to their homes. On the third, seventh or eleventh day a bread and vegetable caste feast is given. In the Savantvadi State, on the eleventh day after death, an earthen jar is worshipped with an offering of a cook, the people assembled put coins into the jar, sing praises of gods all the night, worship a flour image of a cow and at daybreak the chief mourner gets his face and moustanches clean shaved, and the flour image is taken and thrown into a pool.

"For the propitiation of the deceased ancestors *mahalaya* is performed in the dark half of *Bhadrapada*, when crews are fed and castemen are feasted. The ceremony shraddha is not performed. "The Mahars are hereditary village servants and are considered authorities in all boundary matters. They escort Government treasure, act as guides and messengers to public officers, watch boundaries and the village office, repair the village office and village gate or *gaonkusu* and sweep the village roads. Most of them enjoy a small Government payment, partly in cash and partly in land. The chief source of their income is the yearly grain allowance or *baluta*. They say that they used to have fifty-two dues, but now the number is greatly reduced."

Mr. Enthoven writes further about the Mahar occupation, "The duties of the Mahars to the villagers are to cut firewood, carry letters, sweep and clean the yards in front of their houses, carry cowdung cakes to the burning ground and to dig graves. For their private services, they are paid in cash or, what they like better, in cooked food. They have a monopoly of the dead village animals, of the shrouds used in carrying the village dead and of the copper coins which in the name of the dead are thrown to one side at the resting place or *visaviachi jaga*. Mahars are largely employed by Europeans as domestic servants and, as grooms, or syces, they perform service in all parts of India. Recently, they have taken readily to attending motor-cars and earn high wages in that capacity. As unskilled labourers they are employed in very large numbers. Of recent years complaints have arisen in villages near large centres of industry that the Mahars have been so depleted in numbers by emigration to the cities as to leave an inadequate staff for village requirements. Some are husbandmen. Many are contractors and money-lenders and manage their business without the help of any high-caste clerk. Mahars make excellent railway gang labourers, and have gained almost a monopoly of the unskilled railway labour market in some districts." The custom rites and ritual pertain to the much exploited, tormented and depressed caste of Mahars in Maharashtra and Gujarat.

In the recent times, the body of the deceased is kept in sitting posture against a wall by folding its knees and men and women in mourning sit near it. The relatives were informed about the death. Hot water bath was given to corpse, new clothes put on it and the body kept in sitting posture as before. A coin was affixed on its forehead, which was removed before the burial, to be given to the daughter or sister of the dead as a last present from him. Later the corpse was put on a bier made of bamboos and straw heading north-south, a new earthern pot tied with a rope containing fire was carried ahead by the eldest son and, in the absence of a son, by any close relative but never by a woman. In some places, a drum was beaten ahead of cortege heading for the graveyard.

The chief mourner who carried the fire pot was required to shave his head, beard and moustaches. Then the chief mourner, followed by four carriers of the corpse and other mourners, take clockwise five rounds of burial pit. The corpse was to be restednorth-south parallel to the pit before lowering it in two-metre deep burial pit and then little water was poured in the corpse's mouth by chief mourner.

Then all the mourners take bath and wash their clothes at any running stream before going to their homes. Children were not allowed to see corpse, follow corpse, and cross the road by which corpse was carried. Direct or indirect touch of the corpse was strictly avoided by a pregnant woman, newly delivered woman, patients, etc.

Next day the family members and close relatives go to the burial ground to level the graveyard and erect a stone as an identification mark. Now the custom of carrying fire pot is abandoned by the Mahars who have converted Buddhists, beside the custom of shaving head, beard or moustaches. Most of the ritual and customs associated with funeral are not followed by them. However, the bereaved family members do not cook food on that day; therefore, neighbouring Mahars supply food to them. Family members of deceased do not wear ornaments, new clothes, hair oil, join any feast, festival, fair, ceremony, etc. Women would not use vermillion or beautifying aids for twelve days of mourning.

On the thirteenth day, the chief mourner takes cooked food to the graveyard. He holds food in his right hand and stands on grave till a crow eats it. The food was believed to have been eaten by the deceased's soul in the form of a crow. If the crow does not turn up, it was believed that the departed soul had unfulfilled desire needed to be fulfilled by the chief mourner. The oath of fulfilling the desire was treated as sacred and was fulfilled in a stipulated time. Otherwise, the departed spirit was believed to wander, not allowing happy and peaceful family life. Illness, death or any unpleasant happenings in a family were attributed to the wandering spirit of deceased or the unfulfilled vow.

On the same day in the evening, oil was applied with betel-leaf to the shoulders of the persons who carried corpse on their shoulders. Filtered ashes were neatly levelled and kept in a place where the corpse was kept before taking it to the graveyard. Baked lumps of *jawar* or *wheat* flour were kept burning on it covered with a bamboo or cane basket. The bereaved family hosts a *Divas* (Community dinner); however, it was not given in case of the death of a minor child. On the fourteenth day morning, ashes on which the lamp was kept burning was carefully observed and then somebody would discover or imagine pug marks animal and would declare that the departed soul was reborn in the particular species. This belief exists among all Hindu castes because of the belief in re-birth. Invariably, the Mahars would find footprints only of an animal or bird and not of human beings, as they were made to believe that they would never attain rebirth as the human beings.

Many people believe that the deceased at times does not take rebirth and moves around his old house and family either for taking care of his family members or his children or for taking revenge of his enemy or for taking away the beloved ones. At times due to too much love and attachment one would die as a result of a shock of hearing news of death. Such death was regarded as a meeting of two beloved souls in the next world. Spirit of a pregnant or newly delivered woman was believed to be the most dangerous who would haunt anyone during night or noon.

Propitiating the hovering spirits with favourite cooked food or other victuals was believed to cure illness of the family members. Newly born baby was given the name of recently died person. According to a superstition, if the spirit of the dead took possession of a person, a coin was stuck to the backside of a plate kept in vertical position by taking names of dead persons in the vicinity one by one. The coin adheres to the surface of the plate and ashes were applied to the forehead of a sick person in the name of the departed by making a vow to propitiate it through offering food or animal sacrifice. This rite was known as *Navas*. This practice, however, was discontinued by the Mahars after their embracing Buddhism.

They also worship the dead ancestors known as *Pitru* (Parents) on Amavasya (the first day of *lunar* month of Bhadrapad) that falls in the month of October. Similar ritual was also performed on *Akshya Tratiya*, the third day of the *Vaishak* month of the Hindu calendar that falls in May. *Pitru* was to be performed only by the eldest son. After taking purifying bath, he used to place inside his house two new earthen pots filled with water by applying vermillion and turmeric powder from outside, perfumed fire was lit in front of it and the food was offered in the name of the ancestors. Thereafter, sweetmeats mixed with *ghee* were thrown on the roof of the house in the name of ancestors by the eldest son, which was eaten by crows, believed to be the spirits of the ancestors. This ritual was performed every year only by the eldest son.

In the name of a dead father, a man known as *Pitarkari* was invited to meal. The one who performed rite or *Pitru* has to wash the feet of *Pitarkari* after applying vermillion mark on his forehead and wishing him by touching his feet. After the sumptuous meal *Pitarkari* was served betel-leaves.

Burying the Dead in Lying Position

About the customs and rites related to the burial, Mr. Enthoven writes, "The dead are generally buried in a lying position with head to the north. Those who can afford the expenses burn their dead. Persons who have made pilgrimages to Tirupati and other sacred places must be buried in a sitting position. The standard funeral rites in use among the lower castes are observed. Even in the case of burial, fire is carried with the corpse to the burning ground and is enkindled on the grave after the corpse has been buried. The bones and ashes are collected on any odd day between the third and eleventh day after death, and thrown into a stream or the sea. On this occasion, an offering of cooked rice, cakes, fish curry and a coconut is made to the deceased near the grave, and the chief mourner gets his head and moustaches shaved. The mourning ends on the eleventh day when all the male members of the family who are fatherless have their heads and moustaches shaved. The house is purified by sprinkling soda and ashes brought from a washerman, and all members of the deceased's family sip *panchagavia* (five products of the cow) brought by the family priest. On the twelfth day, a casteman having no father is invited to dinner and is presented with articles of dress, five pice, a metal plate and a metal drinking pot.

"For the propitiation of the deceased ancestors, cows are fed on the new-moon day of every month, and every year on the new-moon day of *Bhadrapad* crows are fed and castemen are feasted. Persons meeting a violent death are considered to become violent spirits, and in order to prevent disturbance from them, they are consulted through mediums and their desires are fulfilled," adds Mr. Enthoven. The custom is related to the *Harakantra* community.

Burial with Head to the East

"The dead are buried without coffins in graves about six feet deep with head to the east. A burial cannot take place after sunset on Fridays and before sunset on Saturdays. Similarly, interment is not allowed from 5 p.m. on the day before the day of Atonement till after sunset on that day. Mourning is generally observed for three days in the case of a child and for seven days in the case of an adult during which time flesh is eschewed. The mourners visit the grave on the third day after death in the case of a child and on the seventh day in the case of an adult, and offer prayers for the soul of the deceased. On the same day, prayers are also offered at the house of the deceased and a feast is given to those present. Such ceremonies are also held at the end of a fortnight, a month, three months, six months, and eleven months after death. During the period of mourning, the relatives of the mourners used to carry cooked food to the house of the mourners and share it with them, but this custom has now almost vanished.

"Bene-Israels are chiefly husbandmen, oil pressers, carpenters, but some are schoolmasters, hospital assistants, shopkeepers and cart-drivers. Formerly, a large proportion of the regiments of Bombay Foot were of this caste, and an especially large proportion of the native officers. But conditions no longer exist in which it is worth their while to take up this profession. A large number are turners and fitters in Mumbai and many have availed themselves of English education and taken up clerical appointments. A good many women become nurses and midwives," writes Mr. Enthroven. The custom is practised by the Bene-Israel community.

Nuns Carry Body to Grave

"All Manbhavs bury their dead. Manbhav nuns attend the

funerals both of monks and of nuns. At a monk's funeral, they walk far behind. At a nun's funeral, men dig the grave, and then withdraw. The body is carried to the grave by nuns, the monks walking at a distance behind. When they reach the grave, the nuns take the body out of the palanquin, strip it of its clothes except a waistcloth, lay it in the grave, cover it with earth and walk away. When the nuns retire, the monks who followed at a distance come and fill the grave. When a Mahant dies, his body is washed, placed on a raised seat and worshipped by the monks. It is then tied to a palanquin in a sitting position. The palanquin is carried by the disciples on their shoulders to a place chosen for the occasion. As they walk, they ceaselessly repeat the names of Krishna and Dattatraya from the moment of the death till the body is buried. Manbhivs do not use the ordinary burial grounds. They choose a clean spot, and a grave is dug lengthwise, north and south, and spread with salt. The body is taken out of the palanquin, stripped of its clothes, a loincloth of buff silk is tied round the loins, and it is laid in the grave with its head to the north and its feet to the south. It is laid on its left side so as to face the east. A sash or *shela* or other valuable cloth is spread over the body and salt is spread on the sash followed by earth. After the earth has been spread on the salt, each of the mourners lays a coconut and a betel packet over it, the grave is filled and the ground is levelled so as to leave no trace of the burial. No tomb is ever raised over a Manbhav. For ten days after the death the members of the religious house are fed. In Punjab, the dead are immersed in water," writes Mr. Enthoven. The custom is pertinent to the community of *Manbhavs*.

Burying Unmarried Man in Lying Position

About the burial custom of Madigs, Mr. Enthoven writes, "The dead are generally buried, the married in a sitting position and the unmarried in a lying position. The dead body is washed, dressed in its every day dress, and set leaning against a wall in a sitting position. It is carried to the burial ground in an old blanket. The mouth of the grave is closed with three stones to which, on the second day, are offered rice, molasses and clarified butter on a castor-oil leaf. When a crow has pecked this offering, the chief mourner bathes and returns home. On the fourth day, a sheep is killed, its flesh is offered to the spirit of the deceased and a feast is given to the caste people. In some places, the castemen are feasted on *polies* or sugar rolly-polies on the fifth day. For the propitiation of the deceased, a feast is given every year in the latter half of *Bhadrapad*," adds Mr. Enthoven. The custom is peculiar to Madigs.

Sprinkling Betel Leaves and Red Powder on Body

"Mangs generally bury their dead. The corpse is bathed and dressed in a waistcloth, turban and coat and laid on a bier. Red powder and betel leaves are sprinkled over it and a copper coin and some grains are tied to the hem of its garment. The chief mourner walks in front with an earthen firepot and his own turban under his arm, and music and the mourners follow. The musicians belong to the Mang caste. On the way to the burying ground, the bearers halt, but the firepot is not allowed to touch the ground lest it should become impure, and the copper coin in the shroud hem is thrown away. On reaching the burying ground, a hole is dug and the body is lowered into the hole and laid on its back. The chief mourner dips the end of his turban in water, squeezes a little water into the dead mouth, and strikes his own mouth with his open hand that the gods may hear and open the gates of heaven, *Svargi ghat vajte*, that is, the bell of heaven rings. The grave is filled and the mourners bathe in a river or stream close by and return to the deceased's house each carrying some grass and *nimb* branches. At the house of mourning, cow's urine is sprinkled on the spot where the deceased breathed his last and the grass and *nimb* leaves are thrown over the urine. The mourners return to their homes. On the third day, the chief mourner with the four bearers and a kinsman or two goes to the burial ground taking three *juari* cakes, cooked rice and curds, or only milk if the deceased is a child. They leave one of the cakes at the rest place and the other two on the grave. They bathe and return to the deceased's house, and are sprinkled with cow's urine. The four corpse bearers sit in a line and their shoulders are touched with *nimb* leaves dipped in sweet oil. They are then fed on *juari*, molasses, oil and *sanja*, sweet preparation of wheat flour, red sugar and *ghi*. The chief mourner is held impure for twelve days. On the thirteenth day, he goes to the burying ground with his friends, has his whole face and head shaven, and bathes. He sets thirteen leaf saucers or *drons* side by side, fills them with water, and returns home with his friends. On the same day, friends and kinsfolk are asked to dine at the house of mourning. They present the chief mourner with a turban and the mourning comes to an end," writes Mr. Enthoven. The custom is related to the community of outcaste Mangs.

"Gujarat Mangs or Mangelas are found in Bansda and other states to the south-east of Surat. They stand lowest in the social scale. No Hindu will touch them and even the Vitohas, themselves impure, will not eat at their houses. Their occupation is making baskets and winnowing fans. They worship Hanuman and Mari Mata. They neither make use of a Brahman's services, nor pay him any respect. Among them is a class of men called Bhats who claim to be of Brahman descent and act as their priests. More than other wild tribes, their ceremonies resemble those of high-class Hindus," notes Mr. Enthoven.

Getting a Leper Buried by a *Mahar*

"Except lepers, persons who have died of cholera and small-pox, women dying in child-birth and children under two or three months, who, as a rule, are buried, the Pavras either burn or bury their dead. So great is their aversion to a leper that, when living, he is kept in a distant cottage and, when dead, he is buried by a Mahar untouched by a Pavra. In ordinary funerals, a party of them carry the corpse. A rupee, or, if the family is poor, a pice is placed in the deceased's mouth, a little rice, turmeric and red powder *gulal* are rubbed on the forehead, and his sword and bows and arrows are placed on the bier by his side. To the sound of drums and music, the body is carried to the burying ground. The widow wears good clothes on the day of her husband's death, cooks rice in an earthen pot, and after the corpse is carried away, breaks the pot outside the house door, and follows the burial party dressed in new clothes. On her return, she puts on her old clothes, and unless she wishes to marry, never again wears gay clothes or ornaments. All the furniture of the deceased, dishes, cots and pots, except drinking pots, are buried or burnt with him. If the dead did not own these articles, they are bought and laid by his side. His silver ornaments also are sometimes burnt. But shoes, cows and money are given to his sister's son *bhacha*. On the return of the funeral party, some drink, and all bathe. On the eighth day after death, friends and relatives meet at the house of the deceased and drink a jar of liquor. Though the death is not considered to have made the family impure, they perform ceremonies on the twelfth day after death. The ground is smeared with cowdung, leaf plates are spread, straws are laid to represent the dead man's forefathers, liquor is sprinkled on the ground, and a dinner of rice or mixed rice and pulse is given to the caste-fellows. On that day, they drink, but do not dance. It is not obligatory to perform these ceremonies on the twelfth day; if that day does not suit, they can be performed on any day within the month. Till these ceremonies are over, the nearest relatives do not wear turbans. Like other Bhils, Pavras leave a house in which two or three deaths have taken place," writes Mr. Enthoven. The customs are prevalent among the Bhil Pavras.

Burying with Head Bound to North

Mr. Enthoven writes, "They bury their dead. The body is laid on its back in the grave with the head turned northwards. It is washed with hot water and is laid on a bamboo bier covered with a new shroud. Red powder and flowers are sprinkled over it. If the deceased is a woman whose husband is still alive, the body is washed by a married woman and wrapped in a new waist-cloth, bangles being put on the arms. Red powder, turmeric powder, and flowers are offered to the dead. The chief mourner walks ahead of the bier holding in his hand a burning cowdung cake. A halt is made midway to the burial ground, and grains of rice and a pice are thrown over the place where the bier is put down. The bearers change sides without looking back. When the interment is complete, the chief mourner applies his hand to his mouth and calls aloud. All then retire to their houses. The grave is levelled on the third day. The chief mourner goes to the burial ground taking with him in a winnowing-fan milk, cow's urines, cooked rice and three cakes. One cake and a little of the cooked rice are thrown on the place where the bier was put down on the way to the grave. The grave is then levelled, cow's urine and milk are sprinkled over it, and a cake and some rice are placed at each end of the grave. This is known as *mati-savadne*. On the eleventh day, all go to the burial ground and prepare a small triangular platform of earth, a cone of which must point to the south. Three small porcelain pots of earth filled with water are placed at each cone, and in their mouths are placed three cakes and three balls of rice. Red flags are also pitched close by. A crow is required to touch the ball pointing to the west." The custom is practised among the *Kolhatis*.

All Lingayat Dead are Buried

Dwelling on the Lingayat death ceremony, the *Bombay Gazetteer* (Vol. XXIII, pp. 225-9) elaborates, "Lingayats always bury their dead. They make no exception even in the case of a leper, or of a woman dying in child-birth. According to the Lingayat theory, death is a cause of gladness. Death changes the course of life for the joy of *kailas,* the heaven of Shiva. When a Lingayat dies and a few rites are performed, he is believed by the people to go straight to heaven. It is well with the dead, and the Lingayats are less nervous about the dead walking and coming to worry the living than most Brahman Hindus. Still, the loss to the living remains. A Lingayat death scene is a curious mixture. The Jangams feast with merry music, the widow and children mourn and bewail the dead. When fatal symptoms set in, a *mathadayya* or head of a monastery is called. When he comes, the dying person gives him ashes and a packet of betel leaves and nuts and says, 'I go to become one with your lotus-like feet'. When the dying man has breathed his last wish, the Jangam whispers a text or *mantra* into his right ear, and those who stand round say, 'His soul is cleansed'. When all is over the body is bathed and set on the verandah (*katta* or *soja*), and the brow is rubbed with cowdung ashes. In front of the body, a Jangam sits reading texts out of the Lingayat scriptures to help the soul in its flight to heaven. A feast is made ready in the inner room and the Jangams go in and eat. Before sitting, each Jangam sets his right foot on the dead head. When the feast is over, the Jangams are given money and clothes. The body is dressed in fine clothes and ornaments and flowers are tucked in the head dress. The body is set in a *viman* or gaily canopied chair and sprinkled with powder and betel leaves. The beadle takes a cloth, tears it in two, keeps one and lays the other half on the dead face, and seats himself in front of the chair and rings a bell. Exactly on the day of the death, but sometimes not until two or three days have passed, the chair is carried to the grave. The chair is carried by any four castemen, and the procession is headed by a band of music. The poor, though contrary to the rule, sometimes carry the dead on a bier. While the Jangam's feast goes on in the house of death, the length of the dead man's foot is taken and the grave is dug. The grave is of two kinds, a married person's grave and a celibate's grave. The grave is nine of the dead man's feet long and five of the dead man's feet broad. It is entered in three steps, the first step is one foot wide and one foot deep, the second step is two feet wide and two feet deep and the third step is three feet wide and three feet deep. At the bottom of the grave is raised an altar one foot high and three feet broad. In the side of the grave, facing either east or north, a five-cornered niche is cut, each of the three sides measuring three feet and each of the two sides measuring one and a half feet. On either side of the large niche is a small niche one foot across for keeping lamps. Such a grave is called *gomukh samadhi* or the cow-mouth grave and is used for married men. A celibate's grave is called *shikhar samadhi* or the peak grave. The celibate's grave has three steps equal in breadth and depth to those of a married man's grave, but of unequal length. The first is one foot long, the second two feet, and the third three feet. When the funeral party come, the grave the body is stripped off its rich clothes and ornaments, which are either given to a Jangam or kept by the mourners. It is carried into the grave by two kinsmen and seated cross-legged on the central altar. The body is generally bare except for a loincloth and a face cloth. Sometimes it is shrouded in a sack. In either case, the *linga* is taken out of its silver cover. The cover is given to a Jangam and the *linga* is tied either round the neck or round the upper right arm of the body. The large niche is partly filled with ashes and faded *bel* leaves and flowers that have been offered to Shiva, the body is set in the niche, and the niche is filled with cowdung ashes and fresh *bel* leaves. The grave is then filled with earth. On the grave, the beadle lays a stone, and on the stone the Jangam stands and the chief mourner washes his feet, lays *bel* leaves on them and gives him and the beadle each five copper coins. Sometimes the beadle washes the Samanya Jangam's feet, lays *bel* leaves on them, and gives him five copper coins. Alms are distributed to all Jangams and poor people who are present. Those who have been at the funeral go home and bathe. After they have bathed, the mourners wash their teacher's feet and purify themselves by drinking the water with which his feet are washed. Strictly speaking, Lingayat funeral rites end with the purifying of the mourners. In practice, the rich, for five days after the funeral, daily send for a Jangam, wash his feet and drink the water, and do not eat wheat bread or sugar. On the eleventh day, friends are feasted. Nothing is taken to the grave and there is no yearly mind feast (*Bombay Gazetteer*, Vol. XXIII, pp. 236-238)".

About the Lingayat's custom of burying, R.V. Russel and Hira Lal state, "The corpse is separated from the *lingam*, as this is considered to be the incarnation of Shiva and must not be destroyed in the fire. If it is lost, the owner must be invested with a fresh one by the Jangam in the presence of the caste. It is worshipped three times a day, being washed in the morning with the ashes of cowdung cakes, and in the afternoon with the leaves of the *bel* tree and food is offered to it. When a man is initiated as a Lingayat in after-life, the Jangam invests him with the *lingam*, pours holy water on his head and mutters in his ear the sacred text, '*Aham so akam*' or 'I and you are now one and the same."

Custom of *Garipeng Kosakad*

Dwelling on the burial custom of *Kolam* tribals of Maharashtra, Mr. Hazra notes, "The Kolams dispose off their dead bodies by burial (*garipeng kosakad*) whatever may be the cause of a death. The burial-place (*mas-nkuti*) remains in the outskirts of a village, usually in a jungle. They have their own burial ground separate from that of others, where the people of their own community are buried. When a death occurs in a village, the villagers gather in the house of the deceased. The message is sent to the close relatives of the dead person who are residing in other neighbouring villages, and the people wait for their arrival. In the meantime, necessary arrangements are made for the funeral. All the activities in a village are kept suspended as soon as the news about any death in the village is known to the people; the household activities like grinding of grains, cooking of food, fetching of water, cleaning of house, etc., are kept pending until the funeral party return from the burial-ground and the village is ceremonially purified. The Kolams regard a village to be polluted (*dulung*) if a death occurs within its *bandhi*. But if anyone dies outside the *bandhi*, and if the dead body in question is not brought inside it, the villagers go on with their usual activities, as in that case the village is considered to remain unaffected by any pollution.

"After the death of a person, the body is placed in a prostrate position on a new cloth by spreading it on the floor of the house. It is completely wrapped with the cloth afterwards and is tied at the neck, middle part, knees and ankles from outside. The corpse is brought out of the house and is placed in front of the door in such a way that it lies at its back with its head pointing towards the west. The feet are, after uncovering a little portion of the cloth, washed with water by a woman of the family. In case of a married man, it is done by the widow who also applies a little kuku, *gulal* and *haldi* to it. But if a woman dies during childbirth, her feet are not washed. The body is kept lying there for sometime. The villagers (elderly), both men and women, come to the corpse one by one to pay their last homage to it. They salute it and put some money at its feet inside the cover. One man belonging to the family of the deceased, during this time, collects some thatching grass from the caves of the house of the deceased by standing with his back towards the house and facing towards the dead. He puts the grass inside the cover of the dead.

"The corpse is carried in a procession to the burial-place, either on a bier *(satta)* or as it is, being covered with a new cloth, by six men—two at the middle and two at each of the extremities. While carrying, the head of the dead points opposite to the direction of the movement. A man goes in front of the party, carrying one axe and one crow-bar. This man belongs to the affinal group of the dead person, and is usually of the same generation. The bearers of the corpse follow him from behind. The rest of the people follow them in a row. The party consists of only elderly persons, the majority being men. The persons going for a burial do not wear any foot-wear. They are to keep their head covered, in case of a man, either with a cap or a turban and, in case of a woman with her *sari*. A woman carries a pot containing water and a plate containing food articles like *jowar,* paddy, *tuor* pulse, *till, gur* and salt.

"After crossing the *bandhi* of the village, the corpse is placed on the ground for a short while, when the carriers interchange their position; the two men who were holding the head portion, now come to hold the feet portion, while the two men at the feet portion go behind to take the position of the former.

"On reaching the burial-ground, the dead body is placed on the ground with its head pointing to the east, instead of west. The grave *(masuti)* is dug beside the spot where the corpse is laid. Digging is started first by a man belonging to the dead person's family or lineage, failing that by a member belonging to the same clan. Then others join hands. A grave measures about waist-deep in depth and two feet in width; the length depends on that of the dead body.

"When the pit is ready, a man, who led the funeral procession, takes out the thatching grass from inside the cover of the dead and also collects a kind of wild grass *(tikhandi-gaddi)* obtained from the neighbouring ground and puts the both into pit. He then collects the money which was put by different individuals inside the shroud at the time of treatment of the dead body. A few of the coins are also put into the grave by him. The rest of the money is kept hiding at a spot beyond the *bandhi* of the village. (It is utilised to purchase drink *(nira)* at a market-place during any occasion and is consumed by male persons.) The men and women come to the grave and put tobacco leaves into it. The corpse is then lifted from the ground by some men and slowly lowered down into the grave; the man who led the funeral procession holds the feet. The body is laid sidewise with its face pointing towards the north and head towards the east. The water and food articles which were brought from the village are dropped into the grave (over the body). All the knots of the cloth that covers the corpse are untied and all the clothes of the dead person are torn off and if there is any attachment of cord to any part of the body, like waistcord, etc., then it is broken. The new cloth, that is used for covering, is also torn a little, and is placed loosely over the body, covering its whole part. In case of a woman died of childbirth, five iron nails are thrust at several parts of her body—one on the forehead and one each in the palms and feet— after placing of the corpse in the grave. The pit is then filled with earth by men and women; it is started first by a family or clan member of the deceased. Some thorny branches of ber tree are placed over the grave and a few boulders are put on it by the men.

"If the deceased person is a man and leaves behind a widow, some lineage member of the deceased, belonging to the same generation preferably the younger brother, breaks the bangles of the widow with the blunt end of an axe and tears off her *gelsori*. If a woman dies, leaving behind her husband, it is his duty to break the *gelsori* of his dead wife before the body is buried. When a man dies after suffering from an illness and, if, in the mean while, there is any vow made to a deity by some member in his family for his recovery which remains unfulfilled, a rite is performed after the burial to indicate symbolically the fulfillment of such an outstanding vow. In such case, a male member of the family or lineage of the deceased takes a small branch of a *char* tree and stands beside the grave. He tears and drops the required number of leaves one by one on the grave, the number of which corresponds to the number of vows made which remain unfulfilled. But in no case a vow, if made to Amma, can be fulfilled symbolically in this way, and requires to be actually observed according to the terms of the vow. Before leaving the funeral place, all the mourners gather round the grave and offer tobacco, food articles, etc., on it. The axe-head is separated from its wooden handle and the latter is left there. The crow-bar is put into the socket of the axe by the man, who carried it while coming to the burial-ground; he throws it from the northern side of the grave to the opposite side. It is collected by another man who throws back the same to the first man on the northern side which is then collected and carried by him on his shoulders. The party of the mourners makes a complete movement round the grave in anticlockwise direction before it finally starts for the village.

"The people first come to a water-source, usually to a *nullah* outside the *bandhi* where they wash their hands, feet and mouth. Those who carried the corpse may take their bath there. The axe and the crow-bar are thoroughly washed. One man goes to hide the money collected from under the cover of the dead person in some bushy place. After returning he washes his hands and feet. One man holds two leaf-cups made of *char* leaves in his two hands facing the west. One of the leaf-cups contains water and the other contains urine of a cow (failing that, cowdung mixed in water). The carriers of the bier stand before him in a row, facing towards the east. Another man takes a *tikhandi* grass and holds it with his two hands in form of 'V'. He dips the two ends of the grass into the cup containing the urine and applies the same to a carrier from head to feet; again he treats the man in a similar way by dipping the grass into the cup containing water. In this way, each of the carriers is treated one by one. They now turn to face the opposite direction, *i.e.,* west, and the whole process is again repeated in the similar way for each person. All the persons, who have attended the funeral, now stand facing the east, and a man sprinkles a mixture of water and cow-urine on them with bunch of *arre* leaves *(bhosa* in Marathi). If a woman dies of childbirth, gold is dipped in water and is sprinkled on all the members of the funeral party; an egg is broken and its contents are also sprinkled on them. This is performed in addition to the usual rites performed at this time. Then all the members of the funeral party gather at a spot outside the village *bandhi.* One female member from each of the Kolam houses of the settlement by then reaches there (if no woman is available from a house, one man comes instead) and stands within the *bandhi* with a pot of water, all standing in a row. As soon as the funeral party reaches near the *bandhi,* they come one by one and pour water on the ground, a little outside the *bandhi.* Those who attended the funeral now enter the village across the ground where water is poured and come to the house of the deceased. A pot of water and a cup of oil (which they use for cooking) are kept ready in the courtyard. After reaching there, each of them washes the hands and feet with the water and applies the oil to them. Two men then go jointly to move inside the village to sprinkle water and urine of a cow (contained in two separate pots) to each of the houses situated within the *bandhi* (including the vacant ones). The sprinkling *arre-alkakad* is done with *arre* leaves. They also sprinkle the same to all the sacred spots and cow-sheds of the village which lie within the *bandhi.* All domestic activities start after this rite. The water which was stored beforehand is thrown away and, if there is any cooked food, then it is given to the dogs. The sprinkling of water, etc., is done by the affinal kins of the deceased.

"Tea is prepared in the house (courtyard) of the deceased. A man takes a cup of tea and stands facing the east. Villagers, including men, women and children, come to the house of the deceased and each of them touches the tea with the finger and sprinkles a little of it on the ground, and then drinks a cup of tea there. Then one man holds a plate containing *jawar*-flour and a cup containing water. The villagers, including men and women, at least one from each house, take little *jowar*-forum from the plate and water from the cup, and throw the same on the ground in memory of the dead. This rite is called *uperam eratad.* After this they can have their usual meals at their houses.

"The family members of the deceased person observe pollution for a period of three days; during this period, they refrain from doing any fieldwork and avoid eating fish and meat. They also do not have their hair cut. These restrictions are usually observed only by the members of the concerned family living under the same roof. The family members of a brother are not affected directly by the pollution caused by the death of another brother living separately. But if the two brothers have joint cultivation, one brother abstains from fieldwork for three days when the other dies. The whole village also remains ritually unclean during this pollution period during which no social or religious function can take place. The pollution period comes to an end with the performance of *ella-olakad* ceremony on the third day of a death. In case of urgent necessity, *ella-olakad* may be performed on the very same day of a funeral, so that the village is free to have a marriage or a festival performed according to the schedule fixed beforehand. Sometimes a death-pollution is observed for five days and accordingly the *ella-olakad* ceremony falls on the fifth day.

"In the morning of the *ella-olakad* day, a party consisting of some men and a few women go to the grave. Some cooked food and water are carried by a female member of the dead person's family. They stand in a line beside the grave facing towards the north. All sorts of offering, which are made here, are made on the eastern end of the grave towards which the head of the deceased directs. After offering is over, all bow down and make one complete movement around the grave in anticlockwise direction. While returning, they wash their hands and feet at a water-source. They come to the deceased person's house and again wash their hands and feet, and smear them with oil. The axe and the crow-bar, which is brought to use on the funeral day, is washed by the man who carried it on that day, and is returned to the owner. Two persons again sprinkle water and urine of cow on each house, as done on the funeral day.

"On this day, the concerned house is cleaned with mud and cow-dung. One fowl is sacrificed inside the house, on the spot where the person breathed his or her last. In case of a male, a cock is sacrificed, while a hen is sacrificed in case of a woman. The sacrifice is done by an affinal kin belonging to the same generation of the deceased, if the deceased person happens to be a man or an unmarried girl, but in case of a married woman, the sacrifice is performed by a consanguineal kin of her husband belonging to the same generation. The fowl is sacrificed by thrashing it against a stone inside the house.

"Tea is prepared and one man holds a cup containing tea and stands facing the east, as it was done on the funeral day. The villagers, before they have their tea in this house, sprinkle a little tea on the ground by dipping the finger into the cup held by the man. Food consisting of *ambal* and meat (of the sacrificed fowl) is served on two *palas* leaf-plates spread on the courtyard of the house. This feast is given to the old and elderly persons of the village. The men and the women, in their respective groups, sit separately around these two plates and eat together. Each of them offers little food on the ground in memory of the deceased before they start eating. After food, they wash their hands and smear little oil to it. The bones, left-over, plates, feathers of the fowl, the ashes of the hearth (where the food was cooked), etc., are collected in a basket and thrown away outside the *bandhi.*

"The services of a medicineman *(supari),* belonging to their own community, are often taken to ascertain the cause of a death on the *ella-olakad* day. After this death rite, the concerned family members and the village become ritually clean.

"The second important post-funeral ceremony which is associated with a deceased person (male or female) is *tukpusakad.* It is performed in relation to the annual oblation in commemorating the deceased; this ceremony is always observed in the month of *Pusi* (December-January). *Tukpusakad* of a dead person cannot be performed before the completion of one full year from the time of his or her death. It may be kept delayed for more than a year; sometimes it may be kept pending (on account of financial difficulty) even for several years. It is performed by a man for a dead member of his family. In time of performing this ceremony for a particular dead relative, if there occur a few more deaths in the family, and if one full year is completed in each case, then *tukpu-sakad for* all these relatives is performed jointly on the same day. Sometimes it is also found that a few unrelated families, belonging to the same or different clans, or inhabiting the same or different villages, jointly perform this function for their respective dead relatives at one place. The main reason for such joint participation is economic consideration. All the participants share jointly the burden of expenditure incurred on such occasion.

"It is obligatory on the part of a celebrant to feed all his villagers on this occasion. The ceremony is performed outside the village *bandhi.* The villagers give full cooperation and help him in various ways. New earthen pots are purchased for cooking in connection with the communal feast. Rice and jowar are cooked; vegetables and meat are prepared as side-dishes. Bread *(pange)* is made out of *jowar* or wheat-flour.

"In the morning of the *tukpusakad* day, the participants visits the burial-place accompanied by a few men. Here he cleans a small area of ground. He sacrifices a chicken here in memory of the dead person, for whom *tukpusakad* is to be performed on this day. The number of chickens depends on the number of dead ancestors for whom the rite is to be performed. After the sacrifice, the head of the chicken is buried. Some food articles like gram, *gur,* etc., are also offered to the dead. A little earth from this place is collected in a strip of new cloth. They return to the village and assemble near a water-source outside the village *bandhi* where some rites are performed, and cooking and feasting take place. While coming back, they take with them the sacrificed chicken and the earth tied in the cloth strip.

"The celebrant gets his head hair, moustache, beard and eyebrows shaved by one of his fellowmen. The shaved hair is put into a *palas* leaf-cup into which is also put the earth, collected from the burial-place. He puts the cup on his head along with a piece of stone and carries the same to the water-source (which is in usual cases, a *nullah*); some men accompany him. He faces the east and takes a few dips in the *nullah* holding the leaf-cup with his two hands. Finally, he buries the cup in the bed of the *nullah* by keeping his head submerged under water. He puts the stone on the spot where he buries the cup. After final bath, he comes out of water and changes his dress.

"The village priest, in the meanwhile, makes an arrangement for a sacrifice of a cock in memory of the dead. He cleans a small area of ground and offers *gulal, haldi,* fried grams, *gur,* etc., on this spot in memory of the dead. A sugar-cane is also offered and the fowl is sacrificed. Its blood is poured on this spot. He performs all these rites facing towards the north. With this, the ritual part of *tukpusakad* is over.

"The chicken that was sacrificed in the burial-ground is roasted and eaten by some old men. The other fowl is cut into pieces and is cooked by men; it is served to all the villagers during the time of feast. Men also prepare *pange* made of *jowar* and wheat-flour. *Tuor dal (togarpaf)* and rice *(biam ambal)* are cooked by women. Brinjals, *methi* leaves and green leaves of onion, which are essentially required for consumption on this occasion, are cooked and mixed with *tuor dal* by women. Food is served to all the villagers at about midday. After meals, they wash their hands and smear it with oil. The food which is cooked on this occasion is not taken inside the *bandhi.* The earthen pots which are used for cooking are also left behind outside it.

"*Dev-karon* or *karon* is another post-funeral ceremony which is performed by a man for his any dead ancestor. It is usually performed by a son for his dead father. As it entails a heavy expenditure, it is difficult for a man of common status to bear the expenditure necessary for the function. It is performed by a man for his deceased father, usually in case he (father) happened to be a man of influence and commanded the respect of people during his lifetime. Sometimes, it is also felt necessary to perform the ceremony, if a number of mishaps take place one after another in a family within a short span of time, because, people think that all these calamities may be due to the displeasure of the ancestral spirits (or the concerned family), caused to them by certain activities of some of the family members. Though this function is performed for a particular dead ancestor, the *elladiam* of the concerned family as a whole, which includes all the ancestral spirits, is appeased on this occasion, invoking for the blessings.

"This ceremony is performed in the month of Siurati (January-February). All the rituals and functions, associated with it, take place before the house of a celebrant. The function starts in the evening and continues upto the middle of the following day. In the evening of the first day, one forked post of a *meri* tree *(Ficus glomerata)* is erected by an affinal kin, usually a *soiriak* of the celebrant, in front of his house. One rope of *palas-bark* is also made by any such kin which is attached to the post. The ground below the post is cleaned with mud and cowdung. *Kuku,* vermilion, etc., are applied to the post and a design is made on the ground below it with *jowar*-flour, *kuku,* haldi, etc. One *paili* of *jowar* grain is kept below it on which a lemon is put; a plate containing some cooked *jowar (ambal)* and *jowar*-bread *(ippate)* is also kept here. One burning lamp is kept here which burns for the whole night. One pit (about 2 feet in depth and 1 foot in diameter) is dug in the courtyard or near it by any man. This is called *rarhi,* meaning the storehouse of the concerned dead ancestor.

"On the occasion of this ceremony the services of a *supari* (medicine-man) are sought. The people believe that he, in his trance, can commune with the spiritual world. He can say if any displeasure is caused to the ancestral spirits and, if there is any, then he can prescribe the means by which they can be propitiated in the right way during this function. He is also consulted by the concerned family members in his trance to know about the well-being of the family in general. Under the state of possession, he also acts as a medium in certain rites associated with this functions.

"Sacrifices are made on this occasion to the *meri* post and *elladiam* and at some important sacred spots of the village. These are done by an affinal kin of the celebrant. One fowl is sacrificed in front of his house, meant for his *elladiam,* and another at the *mudol-kon* (northeast corner) of the *bandhi.* A pig is sacrificed to Devi. Finally, a goat is sacrificed in the name of the dead ancestor, for whom this ceremony is being performed. The goat is ceremonially offered to the dead ancestor by washing its feet and anointing *kuku, haldi,* etc., on its head. It is tied to the *meri* post with the *palas* fibre-rape. One *soiriak* of the celebrant stands near it, facing the east. He holds an axe. He strikes the head of the goat with the blunt end of the axe with a great force. It becomes senseless and falls on the ground. It dies after inflicting it with some more strokes. Then the skinning of the goat is done; the hoofs, skin and such other remains, including the water used for cleaning, are put into the *rarhi* pit. The body of the goat is kept suspended from the *meri* post for the whole night. The fowls and the pig, which are sacrificed, are dressed and the meat of the two is cooked separately. This meat is tabooed to women and children. It is eaten by some elderly men with *ambal* and *ippate,* prepared in the house of the celebrant. The cooked food which is kept on a plate near the *meri* post is also consumed at this time. The people who assemble at the spot, particularly those who take the food here, spend the whole night by gossiping, though there is no restriction for them to go back and sleep in their houses.

"In the morning of the following day, villagers gather near *rarhi*; the elderly persons, both men and women, belonging to the family and lineage of the concerned dead ancestor, put *haldi, kuku,* etc., into the *rarhi* pit. The *supari,* under the state of trance, remains near *rarhi.* He gives an egg to a man, related as a *soiriak* to the dead person, who, in his turn, puts it into the pit in upright position. He also puts a burning *chutta,* which is lighted by an agnate of the dead, in memory of the dead person. The *soiriak* first puts earth into the pit at the time of filling it and others follow him. A *soiriak* of the celebrant takes out the *meri* post and keeps it on a new cloth along with the *palas* fibre rope.

"In the mean time, a trench, measuring about 5 feet in length and 1 foot in depth and width, is dug in the east-west direction near the house of the celebrant to serve as a hearth. Here the meat of the sacrificed goat and *ambal* are cooked in some big pots for the communal feast arranged for the villagers in connection with this ceremony. Cooking is done by men. The villagers, including men, women and children, attend the feast during the noon. After the meals they wash their hands; the water which is used for washing is collected in a big pot. All the bones and left-over are also collected in this pot. The members of the lower social groups, who live outside the *bandhi,* are also fed on this occasion. But after meals they must clean the spot themselves where they eat, and they must not wash their hands over the pot which is used for collecting such water and left-over of the Kolam villagers. After the feast is over, the water, left-over, etc., which are collected in the big pot, are put into the narrow pit which is used as the hearth. Vermilion, *haldi, kuku,* etc., are applied to it before it is filled up. The elderly men of the village stand around the filled-up pit, shake hands with one another, bow down to the ground and jointly pronounce '*Ram*' '*Ram*'. One woman of the concerned family sprinkles cowdung water on this spot. She also sprinkles cowdung water at *rarhi.* Some big boulders are put on the *rarhi* spot which are thoroughly besmeared with vermilion.

"The *meri* post is then taken up by a *soiriak* of the celebrant. The *jowar* grains which are kept near the *meri* post are tied in the new cloth and are given to the *supari* along with some money. A man takes a pot of water; he and the *soiriak* carry the post to the grave of the concerned dead man, the latter following the former. A little water is put on the grave and the *soiriak* simply puts the post over it. The *soiriak* washes his hands and feet and both return to the village.

"*Sek-korakad* is the concluding post-funeral ceremony which is performed for a deceased person to get his or her soul united finally with those of the other dead ancestors in respect of a particular lineage group. It cannot be performed for a person, unless his or her *tukpusakad* is observed. So, in some cases if the members of a family want to perform *sek-korakad* for its any dead member, whose *tukpusakad* has yet to be observed, it is done in a short form during the time of performing *sek-korakad*. *Sek-korakad* is performed jointly by the members of a particular lineage group to enshrine formally the souls of those in the house of a senior member who happen to die in a particular time-period. These souls are, as a part, supplemented to the *elladiam* or house-deity of the concerned lineage group. The house where *elladiam* is enshrined is called *do-ella,* meaning 'great house', *i.e.,* house of the senior and as such, the ceremony is held here.

"The *elladiam* or house-deity of a particular lineage group is essentially constituted by the concerned ancestral spirits, each of which is symbolically represented by small wooden chips *(bomma)* obtained from *char* trees *(Buchanania angustifolia).* A few of such emblems are sometimes made of silver or gold, called *bauli-bomma*. In some cases, an *elladiam* may include, besides the ancestral spirits, one or two deities prescribed for the clan to which the concerned lineage group is affiliated. These emblems gradually lose their original form as they gradually increase in size due to the thick deposition of layers of vermilion-paste applied to them every year on several occasions. The older is a *bomma,* the bigger is its size. All these emblems are kept in a closed basket called *diala-topla,* including the symbol of a clan-deity, if there is any. The lineage members who are settled in different villages, living detached from the main village, construct in their houses a small square altar *(thapna)* in name of their *elladiam,* so that in time of necessity they can invoke and make necessary offerings to it at this altar. If there are a few families, belonging to the same lineage, settled in a village, they may have a common *thapna* for their *elladiam* in the house of a senior member, where in time of its worship they assemble and observe the function jointly. But it is obligatory on their part to assemble in the main village (where *do-ella* which enshrines the *diala-topla* is located) during the time of an important ceremony associated with their *elladiam,* particularly in the *sek-korakad* ceremony, in order to participate in it jointly with their fellow lineage members. On such occasion, prior information is sent from the main village to all the concerned lineage members, settled in different villages, regarding the date and programme of the function.

"The *sek-korakad* ceremony is to be performed conventionally by the members of a descending generation for those of the next generation ascending one periodically at one time, usually when all the persons of this level are dead. But in practice it is not possible to follow this rule rigidly. Usually, the stretch of time between two such successive ceremonies is very long, varying from 10 years to 20 years, or even more. Obviously, all the members of a particular lineage group, irrespective of their generation level, who die subsequently after a certain *sek-korakad* ceremony, are included for the next ceremony to follow on the subsequent occasion.

"*Sek-korakad* is a big affair and involves a heavy expenditure, which is shared jointly by all the participants. Though it is an affair of a particular group, all the people of the concerned village also attend it with equal enthusiasm. It is performed in the month of Siurati (January-February) and commences on an auspicious day, usually on Sunday, and continues for three consecutive days.

"In the morning of first day of the ceremony, a booth is erected *pandri irakad* near the *do-ella* where *elladiam is* enshrined. The roof of the booth is covered with the leaves of a blackberry tree. An affinal kin of the participant group goes to cut a post from a *salai* tree *(Boswellia serrata),* but he does not go in a party, nor any worship is performed to the tree, as is done in time of a marriage. After he returns, a housewife of any family of the participant group washes the lower end of the post and puts *haldi* and *kuku* to it. She also washes the feet of the man and puts *kuku,* etc., on his forehead. He fixes this post at the centre of the booth. A small rectangular mud platform *(boley)* is made at the base of this central post to serve as the altar of the *elladiam.* Beside the door of the *do-ella,* two small brass pots are put side by side on a coiled rope placed below the leaves. These are called *ghottam.*

"In the noon, the villagers go to a stream in a party to observe the next ritual, called *kaie-sumakad* or fishing. The participants take with them a new cloth and a new earthen pot (with a lid) for catching fish, a cock for sacrificing, some *puja* articles including vermilion, *haldi, kuku, gulal, gur,* fried gram, etc., and some cooked food, like *ambal, ippate,* etc. The worship of *asrasil* or water-spirit is performed by offering *haldi*, *kuku,* etc., to the stream, and by sacrificing the cock to it. This worship is done by the village priest or any man. Then the fishing starts in the stream. Two men of the participant group hold the cloth a little above water. One woman, either a wife or a widow of any of the concerned lineage member, or an unmarried girl of that lineage group, stands near them, holding the earthen pot. Other participants also stand in water. One man from each of the participant families comes by turn to call the respective dead members of his family, for whom the *sek-korakad* rite is going to be performed. He throws *ambal* in water in their names one at a time, calling him or her to come. When a fish (usually very small) jumps out of water, it is caught in the cloth (held by two men); it is thought that the concerned dead person has responded to their prayer by coming in form of a fish. In this way, the man calls out for all the concerned dead members of his family one by one, and in each case a fish is caught in the cloth. If there is any delay in catching a fish in some case, the people earnestly pray to the concerned dead member to come early, and the man goes on throwing *ambal* in water, and some people throw *haldi, kuku,* etc., in it on all sides, so long no fish is caught in respect of that particular member. When this man gets all the required number of fishes caught for all his dead relatives, men from other families come by turn to get fish for their respective dead family members in the same manner. In all the cases, as soon as a fish is caught, all shout that the concerned dead person, for whom they pray, has come; the fish is caught then and there from the cloth by any person and is put into the earthen pot (held by the woman), and is covered with the lid. The pot contains little water in it.

"The meat of the sacrificed cock is roasted and it is distributed to all the persons along with *ambal.* The liver and the head of the cock are eaten by the elderly men. While returning to the village, the pot containing the fishes is kept carefully inside a bin *(dhola)* outside the village-*bandhi.* A feast is given to all the villagers in the night; dancing and playing of drums *(tappate)* continue for the whole night.

"In the morning of following day, all the villagers go to a *char* tree to observe the most important function of the day called *sek-korakad.* Two men collect the pot containing the fish caught in the previous day and come there with it. The people, while going, take with them one cock and the usual *puja* articles. The ground below the *char* tree is cleaned with cowdung and the fish-pot is kept here. Two men of the participant group hold one cloth near the tree-trunk. One man belonging to the affinal group of the participants cuts a piece of wood *(sire-sekka)* from the trunk of the *char* tree with an axe by two strokes. It is readily collected in the cloth held near the tree. The man, who cuts the piece, makes some small chips (about 1.5 inch long and circular in cross-section) out of it. These are called *bomma*; the making of *bomma* is done on a new cloth spread on the ground. The number of *bomma,* made by him, depends on the total number of dead persons included for the function. If any participant gets a *bauli (bomma)* made of silver or gold for any of his dead relatives, no wooden *bomma* is required to be made by him or her. All the *bomma,* wooden, silver or gold, are tied together in a strip of new cloth and the bundle is kept hiding inside the turban-cloth of a man of the affinal group.

"After cutting of the *sire-sekka,* the village priest performs the worshipping of the tree by putting marks of *haldi, kuku,* vermilion, etc., to it and by sacrificing the cock. The roasted meat is distributed to all the persons. The pot containing the fish is left below the tree as it is.

"All then return to the booth. One medicine-man *(supari)* remains present in the booth when the party reaches there. In a short time, the *supari* gets possessed when the drums are being played rhythmically in high pitch. If he possesses really any supernatural qualities, which are essential for a *supari,* he can at once identify the man, who is carrying the *bomma,* without fail. He comes forward and puts his hand on the head of the man, indicating that the *bomma* is hidden there. He then hands over the bundle of *bomma* to the *supari.* A wife of any of the lineage members washes the feet of the man, who carries the *bomma.*

"In front of the *salai munde* or central post, *i.e.,* towards its eastern side, is kept 1.25 *paili* of *jowar* grain along with an amount of Rs 1.25 and 1 betelnut, all being obtained from the *do-ella.* One pot full of water is placed on the grain. One cotton thread *(nara)* dyed in turmeric water is kept suspended from the top of the booth the tree end of which remains inside the pot containing water. A few betel-leaves are attached in a row to the suspended thread. The *diala-topla, i.e.,* the basket which contains the *bomma,* is placed in between the central post and the water-pot. The *supari* puts the new *bomma* into this basket; thus, the union between the old and the new *bomma* is brought about. The new *bomma* are then thoroughly besmeared with vermilion paste. A goat is vowed (vao) on the occasion of unification of the old and the new *bomma* in order to effect their unification concordantly. After sacrificing the goat, its roasted lever is offered to the *bomma.* The head and the forelegs of the goat are cooked separately and are eaten by elderly men. All the villagers are fed with meat and *jowar-ambal* during the day. Drums are played during the whole night. Sometimes *do-veta* is performed as it is done during a marriage.

"The main function on the third or concluding day is *potor-pusakad. Haldi, kuku,* etc., are applied to the *bomma* in the morning. A new earthen pot is made into two halves. Any man of the participant group puts some cotton seeds into the lower-half of the pot and pours some oil to it. Some marks of *haldi, kuku)* etc., are also put on its outer surface. It is then put on the upper-half of the pot. The whole thing *(potor)* is held by the *tupari.* Any male participant puts fire to it and as a result, the contents of the pot start blazing. This rite is called *potor-pusakad.* The *supari* dances by holding the pot of fire. From time to time he gives the fire-pot to any person, who has to dance with it for a while. When the fire becomes slow, anybody puts oil into the pot. The dance continues for sometime. Finally, it is kept on the altar of the *bomma.* One goat is sacrificed in name of the important deities, including those of the clan of the participant group. Sometimes the services of the people of the Gondri caste (Mang Gondri or Maratha Gondri) are taken to play musical instruments. After the sacrifice of the goat, the roasted liver is offered to the *bomma.* The forelegs and the head are cooked separately and are consumed as usual by men, usually by elderly ones. The villagers are entertained with meat and *ambal* during the day. They are also entertained with *paf* and *ippate.* In the morning *gur,* fried grams, betel-leaf, etc., are also distributed to them, as is done during a marriage. The members of the participant group exchange presents of new clothes among themselves before the noon-meals.

"In the afternoon, a male participant brings the *diala-topla* from the booth and places the same on the altar *(thapna)* of *elladiam* inside the *do-ella.* All the things, like *potor, nara, munde,* etc., are left deposited to the sacred spot or any of the clan-deities of the participant groups," adds Mr. Hazra.

Rites Related to Abortion

The tribals usually attribute miscarriage to some supernatural power. They consider it is due to the any deity's wrath. Deity may get angry if it is not propitiated or if it is not offered with the thing which was vowed to it, or in some other ways. If necessary, the family members may seek councel of a *supari* to know the cause of this misfortune and the means of its reparation. A woman, after miscarriage, remains in the state of ritual pollution till she takes her purificatory bath on the day the house-deity or *elladiam* is propitiated. On the day of miscarriage, the husband of the woman sacrifices a cock to the goddess and offers either eggs or chickens to the four corners of the village *bandhi.* Vermilion or *kuku* is applied to some other malevolent deities. The sacrificed cock, chickens, etc., are consumed by some village elders with *ambal*, supplied by the family concerned.

After two to four days, the husband worships his house-deity or *elladiam.* A cock is sacrificed and vermilion and coconut are offered to it. Before such worship is performed, the entire house is pasted with cowdung and mud. The woman's clothes are washed and all the members of the household take their bath in water mixed with little cow urine. Such propitiatory rites are essential for the general welfare of the village as well as for the family concerned. If these are not done, the village may face misfortunes very often.

References

1. Singh, K.S. (Gen. Ed), *People of India: Goa*, Popular Prakashan, Bombay, 1993.
2. Singh, K.S. (Gen. ed), *People of India: Daman and Diu*, Popular Prakash, 1994.
3. Enthoven, R.E., *The Tribes and Castes of Bombay*, Low Price Publications, Delhi (reprint) first published 1922.
4. Russell, R.V. and Lal, Hira, *The Tribes and Castes of the Central Provinces of India*, Low Price Publications, Delhi (reprint) 1997, originally published 1916.
5. Gurye, G.S., *The Mahadev Kolis*, Popular Book Depot, Bombay, 1957.
6. Gome, Olivinho J.F, *India—Land and People: Goa*, National Book Trust, New Delhi, 2004.
7. Hazra. D., *The Kolam of Yoetmal*, Anthropological Survey of India, Ministry of Culture, Govt of India, Calcutta, 1983.
8. *Bombay Gazetteer*, Vol. XXIII.

7

Social Customs

In the western region, there are many and widely varied social customs, originated mostly from the primitive ideas and weird notions about life, nature, god, godlings, and countless other phenomena. These social customs give a sly peep into working of human mind and, how it operated in the absence of civilisation, logic, restraining of mind, natural tendencies and how it worked in the absence of scientific development. However, in the recent times, most of such weird practices, social customs and rituals have been abandoned. The primitive tribals and the savages hiding in the dense forests come into the contact with the outside world, and as a result learned a new way of life and abandoned their primitive practices and bizarre behaviour. Now after a few generations of contact, they disown such practices, and out of shame even refuse to admit that their forefathers had in the past had anything to do with these customs and practices.

Hindu Sacraments

Normally in all castes among Hindus, three names are given to the child including a surname. They are the first, proper name of the boy or girl, as the case may be, the second being the father's name and the third is surname. When the child grows its first tooth or grinder a ceremony is held to celebrate the occasion with refreshments, and food, etc. This is called as '*datollem ghalta*'. Little fried cakes, and biscuits etc. are strewn over the head of the child and then distributed to the children gathered on the occasion. This practice is also on decline these days and wherever it is prevalent, the fried *vodde*—flat bread cakes—have been replaced by chocolate, toffee, and peppermint etc.

Chaul or tonsure of baby's head was done at the age of two or earlier. It consisted, according to precept, of saving off the entire head of the baby, leaving only a tiny hairtuft behind. This practice has almost disappeared among all the castes Hindus. *Moonz* or the *Upanayana* or thread ceremony is performed among the higher castes of Saraswats and other Brahmin groups, Kshatriyas, Daivednyas, and Vaishya-Vanis etc. The sacred thread is called as *zaan'vem* in Konkani. This ceremony is not performed among the Sudir castes groups as they are not eligible ritually to perform it. The *Munz* ceremony was ordained for performance and was done between the ages of eight and ten in respect of a male child. Even today marriages do not take place in Goa before this ceremony has been performed, which is done sometimes on the eve of marriage. As it is well-known, *Upanayana* ceremony was meant to usher in the period of education of a student in what was called the *Brahmacharya ashram*. That has lost much of its relevance now with a different method being followed in modern education. During the Portuguese times, the child started its schooling in the sixth year of age, drawing on his slate a picture of Saraswati, the goddess of learning, and began his first lesson with the chanting of *Sri Ganesha Namah*, an invocation to Lord Ganapati who removes all obstacles. But nowadays the child, in a highly competitive spirit that is fostered by the parents and sanctioned by the educational system, starts its formal education at an earlier age and without paying obeisance customarily to Sri Ganesha, the deity of wisdom. The thread-girdling ceremony amounts to a purificatory rite when the boy is initiated into the intricacies of a worldly life.

The next Sanskara in the life-cycle of Goan Hindu is the '*Lagn*' or '*Vhaarddik*' in the religious and profane senses respectively in Konkani, or the '*Vivaha*' in the Sanskritised language, or Marriage, in which one goes through the prescribed procedures and rituals ordained, according to the *Sastras* or scriptures for a marriage, particularly as formulated in the *manusmriti*. The priest or the *bhatji* is called at both the houses, those of the bride and of the groom, to perform the *punyavachan* and the *nandishradha* readings in the presence of the groom and the bride, as the case may be, and their parents. Then oil and turmeric are applied on their body after which they take a ceremonial bath from a barrel of water placed there for the purpose. The wedding ceremony is held normally at the bride's residence, where her maternal uncle takes the lead in the arrangement and performance of the rituals and rites with the bride fully-bedecked in her special attire of the nuptial occasion.

At the groom's patrilocal residence, his married sister ties the wedding turban called *baashing*. It may be noted that sisters are normally married off first before the brothers can get married; these custom, however, is being relaxed now-a-day.

The marriage procession or *vor* or *barat* in Hindi then sets out, with the groom's sister carrying a pot with mango leaves in it, on which is placed a coconut. Another sister carries a lighted lamp in a wicker basket and goes ahead. They are followed by the bride groom in his full wedding attire, who reaches the bride's place either in a palanquin or *palkhi* in Konkani or on horseback, and nowadays in a car hired and fitted for the purpose. He is received ceremonially at the bride's place and ushered into the marriage chamber or hall, where the religious ceremony is performed by the priest. All the marriage ceremonies like '*lajahoma*', and '*saptapadi*', etc., ordained according to the Vedic rites, are performed among the upper castes and according to Puranic rites for other castes. They also include the garlanding of each other by the bride and groom or '*mall ghaltat*' as called in Konkani, declaring the couple as husband and wife, and the husband's gift to her of the *mangalsutra* a necklace, to be worn as the married status.

Thereafter the bride becomes a part of the groom's household a ceremony is held to welcome her formally into the fold of her husband's family's *gotra* or endogamic group, in a ritual called '*gotrant haddchem*' meaning 'incorporation into the gotra' in Konkani. It is perhaps a reminder of the olden days when the women of the local tribes existing in Goa at the time of the arrival of the Indo-Aryan castes, were selectively taken in marriage after going through this ritual of a purificatory or adoptive ceremony. The bride has to show a lit lamp to eight agnate persons, all from the groom's side. She also offers them ;*ghee*' (clarified butter), bananas and snacks. Before leaving for the groom's place of residence five couples along with the bride and the groom are seated in a prominent position and rice thrown on them in a ceremony called *sensor bhortat* in Konkani.

But the marriage ceremony as everything else in the modern times days, is changing fast since the time Goa came into the

Indian mainstream, with all the long rituals being pruned down to their essentials and preparations of various lavish feasts, etc., which used to take so many days, are no longer being practised. The people concerned, instead, make use of the ready-made village or city hall and employ service from catering professionals.

The last *samskara* among the Goan Hindus however, is the funeral rite or *antyesthi* performed on the death of an individual. This is carried out in the form of cremation for all Hindu castes in Goa, the funeral pyre being lit by the eldest son, with the accompanying prayers, on the cremation ground.

Following the death of a person, mourning is observed for a period of twelve days. On the tenth day after the death, a *homa* is performed at home and *panchgavya* offered for the purpose of purification. On the twelfth day is performed ritual the *Baravo* (literally the twelfth day in Konkani), on which day there is held the performance of the *shraddhavidhan* of the passing away of the deceased with offerings being given to the public and food to the priests. Food is also served to those who participated in the funeral. Friends and relatives who could not attend the funeral service come later on a visit to offer condolences in what, in Konkani, is known as '*pacharunk*'. Earlier, there used to a practise of having the *shraddha* ceremony as *bharni-shraddha*, monthly *shraddha* and yearly *shraddha*. But nowadays only the annual *shraddha* ceremony is performed on the death of a person in the family.

Wild Fetish and Nature Worshipping

The British rulers appointed a number of ethnographers and anthropologists to gather information about these savage people and their weird customs. About the Bhil customs, Mr. Enthoven writes, "It is not easy to describe the religion of the Bhils as they are in all stages of civilisation from the wild fetish and nature worshippers having no idea of a divine being to the peaceful peasant who observes most of the details of popular Hinduism.

"Except the Nirdhis and Tadvis, who are now half Hindus half Musalmans, the original religion of the Bhils was perhaps a form of nature worship, and even now they worship the Vagh-deva or tiger god, Sivariya-deva or boundary god, Nimaji-deva or the god of the *Apta* plant or trees, Dungarya deva or the mountain god, Barabij or Barbij, the moon, etc. Other minor deities worshipped by them are Kali, Hatipava, Vaghacha Kunver, Hal-Kamata, Khodiyarmata, Devikanai, Behyee, Baji, Ghora Raja, Hallam, Gaukondamata, Hanivanamata, Bhadribaimata, Ghona, Ginva Deva, Shalu Pandar, Pachchhaya, Mata Panda, Kaksat, etc. They believe greatly in demonical influence, witchcraft and omens. Captain Prescott says that they are superstitious beyond all belief. Mr. Willoughby mentions the same characteristics and how they desert villages on the outbreak of an epidemic. 'Their religion' he says, 'is one of fear'. Sir J. Maeom is of the opinion that the original worship was that of deceased ancestors. Of the gods of their adopted religion, they chiefly worship Mahadev, whose fiercer aspects would appeal to original nature worshippers.

"Bhils have no temples. Over some of their most sacred images, they raise open sheds, but, in general, for a place of worship they choose some tree consecrated by a few large stones set on a mud terrace built round its roots. They respect Musalman shrines and make offerings to Musalman saints. Although they worship the deities mentioned above, their chief objects of worship are spirits and ghosts. In the forests near an old tree or well, but often apparently at some chance spot, they offer to ghosts and spirits earthen horses, jars and beehive-shaped vessels. In honour of the spirits in most of these god-yards or *devasthans,* they also raise beams of timber, sometimes as much as twelve feet long, poised on two uprights in the form of a rough seat. Here they offer a goat and a cock, numbers of Bhils come together to eat the sacrifice and to drink.

"The animal held in most veneration by the Bhils is the horse, and in Kbandesh also the dog. If a prayer has been granted, they often make small clay horses and range them round an idol or in the spirit-yard. In many of their legends, the principal event depends on the assistance or advice of an enchanted horse. Except for the Modasa and Khandesh Bhils who kill neither the cow nor the blue bull *Portax pictus*, Bhils have no special feeling for the cow. Most of them eat its flesh and freely take its life. Except in some parts of Khandesh, they do not worship snakes, and kill them when they have the chance. Except a few who reverence the *pipal* or *apta,* they have no holy trees or plants.

"With Bhils the chief festivals are those in honour of the dead. The only regular Hindu festivals they specially observe are the *Shimga* or *Holi*, the *Dasara* and *Divali.* Besides these three regular festivals, the Gujarat Bhils perform three sacrifices or *jatars*, one on the *Dasara* day, bright tenth of *Ashvin* (September-October), and the other two, both of them field festivals, in *Ashad* (June-July) when the groom grass shoots and in *Ashvin* (September-October) when the early or rainy season harvest is reaped. On the *Dasara* day, the sacrifice is offered either to the goddess Kalika or Chamund or to the god Kachumbhar, in *Ashad* to the god Sarsel or Salun, and in *Ashvin* when the crop ripens, to the goddess Chamund. On all these occasions, the sacrifice or *jatar* is performed with the same rites. On the day before the *jatar*, the Badva to recite incantations. The Pujari, or in the absence of the Pujari the Badva, with a loud voice, calls the gods to be present. Throughout the night the Badva continues singing. He first invokes the aid of Sarda the goddess of learning and then sings the praises of Ganpati and other divinities, including the goddess Chamund and the god Kachumbhar. He recited the tale of Jasma, the old woman who rejected the love of king Siddhraj Jaising (A.D. 1100). Early next morning the Badva becomes inspired by the god Kachumbhar. To ascertain if he is really inspired or, as the Bhils say, if 'the breath has entered him' they send the Badva to bathe, and in his absence they place in a line on the ground seven billas or apples of the *bel* Egle marmelos tree. On his return, the Badva is asked to point out which apple was first laid down. If he chooses the right one, he is believed to be really inspired. Some of those present then ask the Badva questions regarding their future, regarding the cause and cure of some sickness, the next rainfall, or the cattle plague. The people then accompany the Badva outside of the village to the spirit yard, or *devasthan* of the god or goddess in whose honour the festival or *jatar* is held. In this spirit-yard, the Badva sings, becomes inspired, and is again asked a number of questions. After the breath or spirit of the god has passed, the Badva offers the sacrifice of a buffalo or a goat, generally a buffalo on the *Dasara* day. The Badva throws a little water on the head of the sacrifice and if the animal shakes its head, the offering is believed to be accepted. The headman then cuts the neck of the animal with a sword. The head is separated from the trunk and placed near the image of the god or goddess. As a libation to the deity, the headman pours on the ground a little home-made liquor. The liver of the sacrifice is dropped into the fire, which is kept burning at the time. The head of the animal is taken by the village headman and the rest of the meat and liquor is distributed on the spot. Sometimes, besides the three regular *jatars* to obtain rain or for some other purpose, the Panch Mahals Bhils hold special *jatars* in the honour of Ghodadev the horse-god whose temple stands on a hill in the Shahada village of Dohad.

"The Khandesh Bhils go to the caves of the hills, in which the Dungarya Deva is supposed to reside, in the months of *Kartik* and Margashirsha. For a fortnight before they approach the shrine, they practise a sort of penance as a preparation for approaching the god. This penance consists in bathing morning and evening each day and living on gram and maize. They keep on puffing, blowing, shivering and chattering as if they were possessed, and at intervals blow aloud and beat their mouth, shouting the name of Dungarya Deva. On the *Paurnima* or full-moon day, they ascend the hill. It is supposed that a fissure or passage is made in the hill by their prayers, and a goat or a hen is first driven through the passage and if the animal returns with a red mark on its forehead, the god is supposed to be pleased. The chief *Bhagat* or devotee then enters the cave followed by others who have also taken the vow. Then they worship the god and stand with outstretched hand and offer prayers. Then it is said that some cowdung drops into the hands of some and grains of maize into those of others. Some get nothing at all. Those who get cowdung are considered to be blest with cattle and those who get grains of maize feel assured of a plentiful harvest. After this ceremony, they offer sheep, and having fulfilled their vow, return home puffing, blowing and shouting the name of Dungarya Deva."

". . . When an epidemic breaks out, heads of the villages go to the Badya with offerings and ask him to tell them the cause of their misfortune. He is always ready, after a due amount of mummery, to point out an old woman as the head and fount of the offence. Small mercy is shown to the luckless creature after she is named. She is seized by a crowd of fanatics, swung by the heels and otherwise ill-treated, and unless timely notice is given to the authorities, her life is in great danger," adds Mr. Enthoven.

Changing Dress Style

Mr. R.V. Russell and Hira Lal write, "Parsi men usually wear a turban of dark cloth spotted with white, folded to stand up straight from the forehead, and looking somewhat as if it was made of pasteboard. This is very unbecoming, and younger men often abandon it and simply wear the now common felt cap. They usually have long coats, white or dark, and white cotton trousers. Well-to-do Parsi women dress very prettily in silks of various colours. The men formerly shaved the head, either entirely, or leaving a scalp-lock and two ear-locks. But now many of them simply cut their hair short like the English. They wear whiskers and moustaches, but with the exception of the priests, not usually beards. Neither men nor women ever put off the sacred shirt of the thread. They eat the flesh only of goats and sheep among animals, and also consume fish, fowls and other birds; but they do not eat a cock after it has begun to crow, holding the bird sacred, because they think that its crowing drives away evil spirits. If Ahura Mazda represented the sun and the light of day, the cock, the herald of the dawn, might be regarded as his sacred bird. Sometimes when a cock or parrot dies the body is wrapped in a sacred shirt or thread and carefully buried. Palm-juice toddy is a favourite drink at almost all meals in Gujarat, and mahua spirit is also taken. Parsis must never smoke, as this would be derogatory to the sacred element fire."

They further write, "Though they have a common Aryan ancestry and their religion is so closely connected with Hinduism, the Parsis feel themselves a race alien to the Hindus and probably have no great sympathy with them. Their wealth and position have been mainly obtained under British rule, and the bulk of them are believed to be its warm adherents. The Parsis now make no proselytes, and no regular provision exists for admitting outsiders to their religion, though it is believed that, in one or two cases, wives taken from outside the community have been admitted. They object strongly to the adoption of any other religion, such as Christianity, by member of their body. The Parsis are notable for the fact that their women are very well educated and appear quite freely in society. This is a comparatively recent reform and may be ascribed to the English example, though the credit they deserve for having broken through prejudice and tradition is in no way diminished on that account."

Mr. R.E. Enthoven writes, "The Parsis follow the religion of Zoroaster, who was born in the region of Azarbaizan in Persia, and who first promulgated his religion in Balkh or Bactria. Opinions vary as to the time when he flourished, Classical authors refer to him and give as his date, years varying from 7,000 B.C. to 252 B.C. Parsi books well-nigh unanimously give his age as about three centuries before Alexander the Great, *i.e.,* about 700 B.C.

Ancient Muhammadan authors closely support the Pahlavi authors. Present European scholars, though not unanimous generally, accept the date given by the Pahlavi works. But strange to say, the Parsis themselves are disposed to lay aside the testimony of their own books and to accept that of Classical authors.

"Their religion is monotheistic. *i.e.,* a belief in one omnipotent, omniscient, omnipresent God Ahura Mazda, whose existence is manifested by the grand and sublime objects of Nature. The harmony, order, law, system, observed in Nature leads the mind from Nature to Nature's God. He is the Creator as well as the preserver of this great universe. He is the ruler of the Physical world as well as the Spiritual world. He is the most Spiritual among the Spiritual ones. His distinguished attributes are Good Mind, Righteousness, Desirable Control, Piety, Perfection and Immortality. He is the Beneficient Spirit from whom emanates all good, all piety. In His moral rule, virtue has its own reward and vice its own punishment. He not only rewards the good but punishes the wicked. All that is created is His work.

"The Philosophy of Zoroastrianism supposed 'two primeval causes,—the Spenta Mainyu or the Increasing Spirit and Angra Mainyu or the Decreasing Spirit,—which, though different, were untied, and produced the world of material things, as well as that of the spirit.' The world is the work of these two hostile principles—the Good and the Evil Spirit—both serving under Ahura Mazda. 'The history of the world is the history of their conflict... Man is active in the conflict.' In the end, the Evil spirit will be destroyed, and all happiness will prevail in the world. It is incumbent upon man to do actions that would support the cause of the Good principle and destroy that of the Evil Principle.

"The moral Philosophy of Zoroaster was moving in the triad of thought, word and action. These three form the ground work upon which the whole edifice of Zoroastrian morality rests. Think of nothing but what is good, speak of nothing but what is true, do nothing but what is proper, and you are saved.

Worship of Fire

Mr. Russell and Hira Lal write, "The religious ritual of the Parsis consists of the worship of fire, temples are single storey and contain three rooms. On reaching the outer hall the worshipper washes his face, hands and feet, and recites a prayer. Then, carrying a piece of sandalwood and some money for the officiating priest, he passes to the inner hall, in which a carpet is spread. He takes off his shoes and rings one of four brass bells hanging at the corners of the room. The priest also rings one of these bells at each watch when he performs worship. He then proceeds to the threshold of the central fire-room, kneels there, and again standing begins to recite prayers. None may enter the fire-room except the priests. Here the fire is kept always blazing in a silver or copper urn on a solid stone pedestal, and is fed day and night with sandal and other commoner woods. A priest is always present, dressed in long white robes, his hands covered with white cloths and his face veiled. The worshipper lays down his offering of sandalwood at the entrance, and the priest takes it up with a pair of tongs, and gives him some ashes from the urn in a silver or brass ladle. These the worshipper rubs on his forehead and eyebrows. On concluding his prayers, which are in the Avesta language, he walks backward to where he left his shoes and goes home. A Parsi man never allows his hearth fire to go out, and if he changes his residence he carries it with him to the next place of abode.

"Like the Hindus, the Iranian ancestors of the Parsis revered the sacred liquor made from the Soma or Homa plant. It was considered a panacea for all diseases, and many stories about the miraculous effects obtained from drinking the juice are contained in a hymn of the Zend-Avesta composed in its honour. According to Dr. Mitchell the offering of Homa is still made at Parsi temples, though apparently some substitute must have been obtained for the original plant, which does not grow in the plains of India. At any rate the offering and sacrificial drinking of the liquor were probably continued so long as the Parsis remained in Persia. As this is a comparatively cool country, the bad effects of alcohol did not perhaps become apparent to the Parsis as they did to the Hindus in the plains of India, and hence the sanctity attaching to the liquor underwent no similar decline. From this it perhaps results that the Parsis have no feeling at all against alcohol, and drink it for pleasure, like Europeans. Both the toddy of the date-palm and mahua spirit are freely consumed at their feasts, while the rich members of the community drink European wines and spirits. As any dealing in alcohol is practically prohibited to high-caste Hindus and also to Muhammadans, and low-caste Hindus have hitherto scarcely ever been literate, the Parsis on account of this peculiarity have found a profitable opening in the wholesale liquor trade, and until recently have had very little effective competition to face. This is perhaps a reason for their special addiction to it, and also for their engaging in the sale of European stores and wines.

"The Parsi priests form a hereditary caste, and are all supposed to be descended from one Shapur Sheheriar, who with his sons and grandsons, one of whom translated the Zend-Avesta into Sanskrit, are believed to have been among the first Parsi settlers of the priestly caste at Sanjan in north Thana. The training of a priest consists of learning substantial portions of the Zend-Avesta by heart, and in going through elaborate ceremonies of purification, in which the drinking of *nerang* and *nerangdin*, or cow's and bull's urine, being bathed, chewing pomegranate leaves and rubbing the same urine and sand on his body are leading features. Priests always dress in white and wear full beard. They must never shave the head or face, and never allow the head to be bare nor wear coloured clothes. If a priest's turban happens to fall off, or if he travels by rail or sea, his state of purity ends, and he must go through the whole ceremony of purification again and pass nine days in retreat at a temple. The principal business of a priest, as already seen, is the tending of the sacred fire in the temples, and he also conducts marriage and other ceremonies."

Religious Sectarianism

About the Islamis scism between the Sunnis and Shiahs, Mr. Enthoven writes, "Both the leading forms of the Musalman faith, the Sunni and Shiah, are found in the Bombay Presidency, the former being more common than the latter. Except some of the Sayads, and Mughals of Gujarat, the trading Bohoras, the Tais and some of the Momnas who are Shiahs, all are Sunnis.

"The original question in dispute between Sunnis and Shiahs, whether as the Sunnis hold, Abubakur, Umar and Uthman were the lawful successors of the Prophet, or were, as the Shiahs contened, usurpers, defrauding Ali of his right to the Khilafat, has given rise to several differences in belief and practice. The chief of the differences are that the Shiahs leave out of the Kuran certain passages which they say were written by Uthman; they add a chapter in praise of Ali which they say Uthman kept back; and to other parts they give a different meaning from that accepted by the Sunnis. The Shiahs do not believe in saints, and follow the precepts of the twelve instead of the four Imams. (The twelve Shiah Imams are: (1) Murtuza Ali (date of birth not known) died at Kufa, A.D. 660; (2) Imam Hasan, born A.D. 625; (3) Imam Husain, A.D. 626; (4) Zain-ul-Abidin, A.D. 653; (5) Muhammad Bakir, A.D. 675; (6) Jafar Sadik, A.D. 698; (7) Musi Kazim, A.D. 745; (8) Musi Raza, A.D. 770; (9) Taki Abu Jaafar, A.D. 810; (10) Abdul Hasan Askari, A.D. 829; (11) Abu Muhammad Askari, A.D. 845; (12) Al-mehdi, A.D. 971. The four Sunni Imams are: Shafai, A.D. 767-819, Abu Hanifah, A.D. 700-733, Malik (A.D. 708-713, died A.D. 735), and Hamba (born A.D. 780, date of death not known). They claim for their head doctors in Persia, the *mujtahids* or religious superiors, the power of altering the spiritual and temporal law; the Sunnis say that the time for change ceased with the four Imams Shafai, Abu Hanifah, Malik and Hambal. The four Sunni Imams have given rise to the four schools, the Hanafi, Shafai, Maliki, and Hambali. Except the Arabs who belong to the Shafai school, Gujarat Sunni Musalmans are Hanafis. In practice some sects of Shiahs differ from Sunnis, chiefly by counting the month from the fading of the old moon and not as the Sunnis do, from the shining of the new moon. They pray thrice instead of five times a day, and in praying hold their hand open by their sides instead of folding them below the breast. When praying with a *jammat* of the Sunnis the Shiah deports himself according to the orthodox part of the company in obedience to the Shiah doctrine of *takiyyah* literally fear or caution. Where the Shiahs are in a minority they practice this doctrine and while acting upon they even vilify their own sect if their personal safety requires. Except these and a few other particulars, the belief and customs of the rival sects are the same.

"Belief in the unity of God; in his angels; in his books, the Jewish Christian and Muhammadan scriptures; in his prophets; in his government of the world; in good evil as coming from Him; and in the day of resurrection, are the chief articles of a Musalman's faith. A Muslim should pray The Sunni prays five times: before sunrise *fajr*, at noon *zuhr*, between four and sunset *asar*, at sunset *maghrib*, and from 8 to 12 p.m. *isha*. Some very religious Sunnis say a sixth prayer *tahajjud* at midnight, and a seventh called *ishrak* two hours after the morning prayers. The Shiah prays three times: before sunrise *fajr*, at noon, when he repeats both the *zuhr* and the *asar* prayers, and at sunset, when he says the *maghrib* and *isha* prayers. Some of them say also the midnight *tahajjud* prayers. five or three times a day, give a part of his goods to the poor, The poor tax *zakat*, literally purification, is 2½ per cent. On all incomes over a hundred rupees a year, and from the poor seven and a quarter pounds of wheat a head to be paid in the *Ramazan* month fast in the month of *Ramazan*, and make a pilgrimage to Mecca and if a Shiah, to Karbala and Shah Najaf if he has no debt and is rich enough. Muslim worship consists of a number of bows and prostrations accompanied with prayers and verses from the Kuran. The body of the person praying as well as the place of prayer must be free from anything causing legal uncleanness.

The prayer must always be preceded by ablution *wuzu*, unless nothing that constitutes legal defilement has taken place since the former ablutions. Praying in company at a mosque is considered more meritorious than saying prayers at home. Each of the five daily prayers has its separate form, and on Fridays and on the days of the *Ramazan* and *Bakr* festivals, the reading of prayers is accompanied by a sermon. The funeral prayer is simply repeating several times the words *Allah-o-Akbar*, God is great.

"Though as a body not very zealous, Musalmans are on the whole careful to observe the chief rules of their faith. Few of them go to the daily public prayers. But the Friday service is well attended; and crowds join with fervour in the long night prayers *tarawih* of the *Ramazan*. Though among Sunnis it is chiefly a time of noisy merriment, to Shiahs, both men and women, the *Muhrram* is a season of the keenest grief and real self-denial. Almost all observe the month of fasting and attend services on the *Ramazan* and *Bakr Id* feasts. All who can afford it give alms freely, and few, except those of Hindu origin, lend money at interest or drink spirits. They reverence the name of the Prophet and the Kuran and accept the doctrines of their faith. The irregular classes of Shiahs and most of the Sunnis become *murids* or disciples, the former to their *mullas* and the latter to some religious person called their *prizadah* or *murshid*. Among the women, a few, chiefly unmarried daughters of Sayads and some Shaikhs, and may of the trading Bohoras, both Sunnis and Shiahs, are well taught in the Kuran and other religious books. Many are pious, and, though not allowed to appear at places of public worship, are careful to repeat their daily prayers and to keep fasts and other religious observances," add Mr. Enthoven.

Division on basis of castes among the Muslims

About the Muslims social customs Mr. R.V. Russell and Hira Lal write, "The principal castes are the Bohra and Khoja merchants, who are of the Shiah sect, and the Cutchis or Memans from Gujarat, who are also traders; these classes are foreigners in the Province, and many of them do not bring their wives, though they have now begun to settle here. The resident castes of Muhammadans are the Bhanas or cotton-cleaners; Julahas, weavers; Kacheras, glass bangle-makers; Kunjras, greengrocers; Kasais, butchers; and the Rangrez caste of dyers who dye with safflower... a section of the Bhils are at least nominally Muhammadans, and the Fakirs or Muhammadan beggars are also considered a separate caste. But no caste of good standing such as the Rajput and Jat includes and considerable number of Muhammadans in the Central Provinces, though in northern India large numbers of them belong to this religion, while retaining substantially their caste usages. The Muhammadan castes in the Central Provinces probably consist to a large extent of the descendants of Hindu converts. Their religious observances present a curious mixture of Hindu and Muhammadan rites, as shown in the separate articles on these castes. Proper Muhammadans look down on them and decline to take food or intermarry with them.

The Muhammadans proper are usually divided into four classes, Shaikh, Saiyad, Mughal and Pathan... The term Saiyad properly means a descendant of Ali, the son-in-law, and the lady Fatimah, the daughter of the Prophet. They use the title Saiyad or Mir before, and sometimes Shah after, their name, while women employ that of Begum. Many Saiyads act as Pirs or spiritual guides to other Muhammadan families. The external mark of a Saiyad is the right to wear a green turban, but this is of course no longer legally secured to them. The title Shaikh properly belongs only to three branches of the Quraish tribe or that of Muhammad: the Siddikis, who claim descent from Abu Bakr Siddik, Siddik means veracious or truthful, and he was given the name on account of his straightforward character — *Bombay Gazetteer*, the father-in-law of the Prophet and the second Caliph; the Farukis claiming it from Umar ul Faruk, the third Caliph, and also the father-in-law of the Prophet; and the Abbasis, descended from Abbas, one of the Prophet's nine uncles. The Farukis are divided into two families, the Chistis and Faridis. Both these titles, however, and especially Shaikh, are now arrogated by large numbers of persons who cannot have any pretence to the above descent. Sir D. Ibbetson quotes a proverb, 'Last year I was a butcher; this year I am a Shaikh; next year if prices rise I shall become a Saiyad. And Sir H.M. Elliot relates that much amusement was caused in 1860 at Gujarat by the Sherishtadar or principal officer of the judicial department describing himself in an official return as Saiyad Hashimi Quraishi, that is of the family and lineage of the

Prophet. His father, who was living in obscurity in his native town, was discovered to be a Lohar or blacksmith. The term Shaikh means properly an elder, and is freely taken by persons of respectable position. Shaikhs commonly use either Shaikh or Muhammad as their first names. The Pathans were originally the descendants of Afghan immigrants. The name is probably the Indian form of the word Pushtun (plural Pushtanah), now given to themselves by speakers of the Pushtu language. Mr. A. M. T. Jackson in *Bomb. Gaz. Muh. Guj.* p. 10. The men add Khan to their names and the women Khatun or Khatu. It is not at all likely either that the bulk of the Muhammadans who returned themselves as Pathans in the Central Provinces are really of Afghan descent. The Mughals proper are of two classes, Irani or Persian, who belong to the Shiah sect, and Turani, Turkish or Tartar, who are Sunnis. Mughals use the title Mirza (short for Amirzada, son of a prince) before their names, and add Beg after them. It is said that the Prophet addressed a Mughal by the title of Beg after winning a victory, and since then it has always been used. Mughal women have the designation Khanum after their names. They add.

Religion with No Priest, No Idol

Mr. Enthoven writes further, "Their religion is simple. They have neither priests, temples, nor idols. They worship a supreme creator, *bhagvan*, and strive to please him with sacrifices and offerings. In the forest near each village is a sacred three round which, before harvest, the villagers meet and prostrate themselves before the rising sun, offer corn, and sacrifice goats and fowls. The deity to whom these offerings are made is called Bava Kumba. Offerings are also made to his wife, Rani Kajhal, a sacred tree not far from her husband not far from her husband's, a sacred tree to which offerings are made. They worship the tiger god *vaghdev* but only to propitiate it and prevent it attacking their cattle, or when it has carried off any of their people. Though they acknowledge no household or village deities and reverence no rivers or fire, they are very superstitious, believing in witchcraft and sorcery. Before the British rule, many an old woman had her nose slit under the suspicion of being a witch, *dakin*, the idea being that the loss of the nose destroys all power to work evil. A belief in omens is common. Odd numbers are lucky, but to see a blackbird called *pichi* is most ill-omened. At the beginning of any undertaking they cast omens with a bow and arrows. They salute friends by taking the two hands of the person saluted, and saying *bhaj-bhaj*, that is, worship.

"Pavras have three chief holidays, *Indraja, Divali* and *Shimga* or *Holi*. *Indraja*, apparently in honour of Indra, is held only when the year is good or when a vow has to be discharged. It is celebrated on any Sunday, Wednesday or other lucky day between *Dasara* and *Divali*. Its chief ceremony consists in planting a *kadamb* Nauclea parvifolia branch in front of a landlord's, *jamindar's*, house so as to remain one cubit underground and a man's height above. The branch is rubbed with vermilion and worship begins at midnight. A goat and hen are killed and offered, and dancing is kept up till day-break. Next morning at about ten they pull up the branch and throw it into some neighbouring river or pond. On returning they drink and dance, and eat the goat and hen offered overnight.

"*Devali*, sometimes called *Nagdivali*, is a yearly festival celebrated in the month of *Posh* (January) on different dates in different villages, so as to last on the whole for nearly a month. Four or five stones are brought from a neighbouring river and placed outside the village but within the limits of the village lands. They are then painted red, and next day at noon worship begins. Liquor is sprinkled on the ground and freely drunk, and goats and hens are killed. Dancing begins at nightfall. Two men, holding two lighted bamboo sticks, go from house to house followed by the villagers. Every housewife comes out with a lighted lamp in her hand, waves it before them, marks their foreheads with lamp oil, and gives them drink. After dancing for a few minutes, the procession passes to another house and there go through the same routine. Next day they feed their bullocks with Indian millet, rice, *banti* and *paral*, and give them drink.

"The *Shimga* or *Holi* takes place, as elsewhere, on the fifteenth of the bright half of *Phalgun* (March). Immense crowds meet at Dhedogaon, the central village and police headquarters of the Akrani territory. A pit is dug, and a wooden rod thrust into it an lighted about ten or eleven at night. Everyone present brings a piece of bread, some rice and a cock.

Portions of these are thrown into the fire, and the rest is handed round among friends. Then, with the help of an occasional draught, they dance till dawn."

The customs, and rituals are related to the Bhil community and its sub-caste Pavras.

Magico-religious Practices, Witchcraft, Sorcery

"The Mangs profess Hinduism. Most of them are Shaivas, their chief god being Mahadeva. Their favorite goddess is Mariai or the cholera goddess. Their family deities are Bahiroba, Khandoba, Mhasoba, Ambabai, Bahiri, Janai, Taki, Vithobs and Yamai. They are not allowed to enter the village shrine, but stand at a distance and bow to the god. Goats and fowls are offered to the goddesses on Tuesdays or Fridays and to the gods on Sundays, Musalman saints are venerated. Embossed images of deceased ancestors are installed and worshipped with offerings of cooked food. They make pilgrimages to alandi, Kondanpur, Dehu, Pandharpur, and Singnapur. They observe the leading Hindu holidays, such as *Shivratr, Holi, Ramnavami, Ashadhiekadashi, Gokukishtami, Dasara* and *Divali*. When cholera rages in a village, an offering of a goat is made to the goddess Mariai by the villagers through the village Mangs. They have a strong faith in soothsaying, witchcraft and sorcery. Their priests are the village Brahmans. In some places, Gosavis, Bhats or Sadhus of their own caste officiate at all their ceremonies. In the Southern Maratha Country, Jangams are also sometimes employed. Unlike Mahars who use the word *johar* that is 'Oh Warrior' in saluting, the Mangs say *pharman* probably the Persian *Farman* or command to their caste fellows; to others they say Maharaj, at the same time passing the right palm to their forehead." adds Mr. Enthoven.

The custom is prevalent among the Mang caste.

Beggars acting as Priests

Mr. Enthoven notes, "The religious teachers and priests of Mahars are members of their won caste, who are called *gurus, sadhus, vachaks, pandits, gosavis*, ro *mendhe joshis*. In Khandesh, there is a class of beggars known as Mahar *thakurs*, who also act as their priests. The *gurus* are those who have been initiated by other *gosdvis*, and who have devoted themselves to a religious life, chiefly to the worship of Vithoba. The Mahar *thakurs* are probably Bhats who have been degraded by mixing among Mahars. Their form of greeting is different from the Mahar saying *ram ram* to each other and *brahma* to strangers. Besides officiating as their priest the *thakur* acts as the Mahar's banker. He eats from a Mahar but no Mahar will eat from him. Besides *gurus* and *thakurs*, Brahmans are sometimes employed to conduct marriages in the Southern Maratha Country. The *Jangams* also officiate at times.

"In the time of namdev and Tukaram, the Mahars were admitted to the Varkari cult of the *Bhaki Marg*. Their great saint Chokhamela has a shrine at Pandharpur close to Namdev's preaching place.

"The saddhus read and explain their sacred books, the *Bhaktivijaya, Dasbodh, Jnyaneshvari, Harivijaya, Ramvijaya, Sonthla*, and the poems of Jnyanoba, Tukoba and others. Some of them are very fluent preachers and expounders of the *purans*. Every Mahar, both a male and female, has a *guru*. If one has no *guru* he is not allowed to dine in the same line with the *gurus*. A child is first brought to be taught by its *guru* when it is about a year old, the rite is called *kanshrami* or ear-whispering and more commonly *kavphnkne* or ear-blowing. About seven or eight at night, the parents take the child in their arms and go to the teacher's house, carrying frankincense, camphor, red and scented powders, flowers, betelnut and leaves, a coconut, dry dates and sugar. In the teacher's house a room is cowdunged and a square is traced with white quartz powder. At each corner of the square a lighted lamp is set, and in the middle on a wooden plank or on a low wooden stool is a metal pot or *ghat* filled with cold water. Another board or stool is set facing the square and the teacher sits on it cross-legged. He sets flowers, sandal paste and rice on the water pot and takes the child in his lap, resting its head on his right knee. He shrouds himself and the child in a blanket or a waistcloth, mutters the sacred verse into child's right ear, pulls off the blanket and hands the child to its parents. The priest is presented with money gifts and, if they are well-to-do, the parents give him a waistcloth, one or two metal water vessels and a plate. A feast is given to the teacher and a few near relations, or, if the parents cannot afford a feast, sugar is handed round. After the dinner the parents retire with the child.

The Mahars believe in sorcery, witchcraft and soothsaying and attribute all diseases to the working of evil spirits. They have many spirit scarers or exorcists among them, some of whom are *gosavis*, and the rest *potras* or devotees of Lakshmi, who cover their brows with red powder and carry a whip with which they lash their bodies while they beg, singing and dancing.

The custom is practiced by the Mahar caste.

Professing Animism

"The religion of the Katkaris, so far as they have any, is animism. They have no sacred books, neither have they any spiritual guides. They do not appear to say any prayers themselves, or to employ others to say prayers for them. Their chief object of worship is the tiger-god, who is supposed to look with peculiar favour upon them and very seldom harms them, and they are disinclined to shoot him. His image is generally set up in the forest or on the boundary of the village. But in parts, as in Karjat, where forests and tigers are scarce, there are many Kathari hamlets without a tiger-god. What worship there is among the Katkaris is paid to the Kunbi village god, *gamdev*, and to such minor gods as Molya, Mhasha, Vetal, Jariuari and Hirva. Red lead, coconuts and fowls are offered to these gods and to evil spirits, which are greatly dreaded. In Gujarat, Bhildev is worshipped. In a Dhor Katkari's house there may sometimes be seen devil gods whom they call *Cheda*. This is the soul of a dead relation which has become a spirit, *bhut*, capable of entering the bodies of men. It is this close connection with, and power over, spirits that makes the Katkari so dreaded by the Kunbi. The latter credits him with the power of the evil eye, and with being able by means of his spirits to compass the death of his enemies. Among the Dhors the only holidays are *Shimga* and *Divali*, to which the Sons add the fifteenth of

Bhadrapad when they perform ceremonies in honour of the deceased." adds Mr. Enthoven.

The custom is prevalent among the Katkaris.

A Motley Faith Called Satpanthi

According to the Bombay Gazetteer (Vol. IX, Part I), "They follow the Atharva or fourth *Ved* and call themselves *Satpanthis*, followers of truth. They worship the tombs of the Musalman saints whose mausoleums are at Pirana, Ahmedabad, Navsari, and Burhanpur. Their sacred book is the collection of religious precepts called *Shiksha Patri* made by Imam Shah, the saint of Pirana. Some of them learn the book by heart and gain the name of *kaku* or devotee. The *kakas* are laymen, and like the rest of the Matias maintain themselves by tilling the soil. One special family of *kakas* officiated at some of their ceremonies and are the agents through whose hands all presents pass to the saintly descendants of Imam Shah at Ahmedabad, Navsari and Burhanpur. The Matias include three religious division, *Panchias* or followers of Surabhai's mausoleum, the third of the five Pirana shrines, so called from the five devotees who at first managed the institution, *Satias*, form the eight devotees who managed the institution, who are the followers of Bakar Ali's mausoleum, the fifth Pirana shrine. Except in being called after different saints, these divisions do not differ in belief or in practice. Sin-removing or *lahe-utarni* is their chief ceremony. A woman after child-birth or monthly sickness, a cow or a buffalo after calving, a person who has accidentally defiled himself by the sight of a woman in child-bed, and all those who have broken caste rules by using forbidden articles of food, are made to pass through the sin-removing ceremony. At the house where the purifying ceremony is to be performed various dishes of sweetmeats are prepared. The village *kaka* is called and comes accompanied by an assistant called *khal kaka*. The *kaka* brings with him four copper coins, an earthenware cup, and frankincense. He also brings with him in a small portable tin or brass box, peashaped balls made of white chalk or rice-flour mixed with milk or sandal dust brought from the tomb of one of the saints. On entering the house the *kaka* goes into the kitchen, lights a lamp fed with clarified butter, and mutters a text. While his chief is saying a prayer the *khal kaka* call for a brass plate and in the plate piles from five to eight heaps of cooked rice according as the host is a Panchia, a Satia, or Athia Matia. After the *kalmo* or prayer is over the *kaka* sits bowing on a waistcloth spread on the ground. He then burns frankincense and murmurs a second prayer. After the second prayer he spills a circle of wheat grains in a brass plate, and, inside the circle, sets four coins and on the coins a cup. Into the cup he pours a mixture called *nur* or light made of sugared-water, milk and white chalk or rice from the saints' tomb. When this is ready the *khal taka* brings the brass plate with the heaps of rice, and over each heap the *kaka* sprinkles. The text for each sprinkling is different, but each ends in *La-ilaha-illalah, Muhammad ar-Rasulallah or Imam Shah-Ali Muhammad Shah*. The brass plate with the heaps of cooked rice s then put aside and the person to be purified is called in. the man or woman to be purified stand near the *kaka* and bows to him, and after being sprinkled with the mixture from the earthenware cup, sits down. He or she then presents a silver or copper coin to the *kaka*, who washed it with water, and gives the water along with the mixture from the cup to the man or the woman to drink. The heaps of rice in the brass plate are mixed by the *khal kaka* with the rest of the cooked articles and distributed among the guests. The puriying fee is 8 annas for a woman after childbirth and for a buffalo after she has calved, 4 annas for a cow after she has calved, and ¼ anna for those who have broken caste rules. These fees are sent by the *kaka* to the saint's tomb at Ahmedabad, Navsari, or Burhanpur. Besides these presents every Matia cultivator sends once a year to the saitns through the *kaka* three and a half *mans* (140 pounds) of husked rice and one rupee for each of his ploughs.

"Matias hold the second day of every Hindu lunar month sacred, and when the second falls on a Friday they fast for the whole day and do not eat until they have seen the moon. They keep the Ramzan fast, some of them eating no solid food during the whole month. Their other Musalman holidays are the *Uras* or Saint's Day and the two preceding Sandal Days. On these days they do no work, and spend their time in feasting or in visiting the shrines of their saints in Navasari. Besides these Musalman holidays they observe as days of feasting *Holi* February-March, *Akhatrij* April-May, *Divaso* June-July, *Balev* July-August, and *Divali* October-November. Their chief places of pilgrim-age are Navsari, Pirana, Burhanpur, and Vemal, seven miles from Miagam in Broach, which they visit on great days or whenever they have leisure. The *kaka* accompanies the pilgrims to these places. At Pirana; Navsari and Vemal the pilgrims visit only the saints' tombs. But at Burhanpur the pilgrims worship the great toe of their living saint. The spiritual guide sets his foot on a heap of not less than a hundred rupees contributed by one or two pilgrims. After it has been set on the heap of rupees the leader's foot is washed, rubbed with a fragrant substance, and the right great toe is kissed by each pilgrim in turn. The *kaka* who accompanies the pilgrims receives from the spiritual head presents in clothes and ornaments both for himself and his wife.

The ritual and superstitions are related to the Kanbi community.

> "Instead of the Brahmanic thread, some of the Kanbis wear a rosary of bead made of the stem of the basil plant or some other material. Some of the Patidars in Kaira and Broach have of late taken to wearing the sacred thread and claiming to twice-born. Among those who wear the rosary, some time when they are between seven and eleven years old, both boys and girls are taken to the religious head or *guru*, who binds the rosary round the neck of the novice. Besides a day's food the *guru* received about Rs. 2 as the initiate in fee. The offer of marriage comes form either side. If the boy's father accepts the offer the girl's father's family-priest goes to the boys' house, where, in the presence of the assembled guests, the boy worships a Ganpati painted in red on a low wooden stool. The boy's brow is marked with red powder, and he is given a turban, a coconut and a rupee. Cash presents are made to the priest and the barber, and a dinner is given to the family. Betrothals may be broken at any time before marriage. If the betrothal is broken by the boys' father, the girl's father gets back the

amount he has paid, but if the girl's father breaks off the engagement none of the betrothal money is returned. As a rule, the amount to be paid to the bridegroom is settled at the time of betrothal. The amount varies according as the parties are of family *kulia* or of no-family *akulia*. A bridegroom of high family gets a dowry of from Rs. 1,000 to Rs. 2,000 while a no-family bridegroom has to pay from Rs. 500 to Rs. 1,000 to the bride. Landlords or *Patidars* marry their daughters before they are eleven, and the ordinary peasant Kanbis between eleven and sixteen." Bombay Gazetteer, Vol. IX, Part I, pp. 157-158.

"As a class, Kanbis are very religious. Unlike Vanias and other high classes, the Kanbis belong to many sects, Bijmargis, Dadupanthis, Kabirpanthis, Madhavgarnis, Pranamis, Ramanandis, Shaivs, Svami-narayans, and Vallabbacharyas. A few are Jains. They worship all Hindu gods and goddesses, and respect Musalman saints. Though very few keep images in their houses, they often visit the temple of their sects. They are careful to respect Brahmans and their spiritual leaders and to give grain in charity to the poor of the village and to travelers. To their religious heads or *gurus* they show much reverence, paying them about Re. 1 on occasions of a marriage or of a death, and besides food about Rs. 2.5 on the *kanthi* or rosary ceremony. To their *guru* they also pay a small fee whenever he goes to their town or village. They have much faith in sorcery, witchcraft, and the influence of the evil eye. In sickness or in difficulty they consult a sorcerer, generally a Koli or Vaghri, a Brahman, or a religious beggar, Hindu or Musalman. They believe in omens and sings. On the lucky *Akhatrij* or third day of *Vaishakh sud* (April) they begin to take manure to their helds. On the fourth of the first fortnight of *Bhadarvo* (September) they worship Ganpati in order that his carrier the rat may not destroy their crops. Before sinking a well and before each season's first ploughing the ground is worshipped by making *kanku* or vermilion marks and sprinkling rice over the marks. Before watering the ground for the first time, the water in the well is worshipped to increase its nourishing power. Rice and *kanku* are thrown into the water, a lamp fed with clarified butter is laid near the well's mouth, and a cocoa-kernel is offered to the water-god. To guard against too great rainfall the village headman and other husbandmen go with music to the village reservoir and offer powers, *kanku* and a coconut. Of four-footed animals, they hold the cow sacred, and of birds the *nilkanth* or jay and the *chas* or kingfisher on *Dasara* Day (September-October). For three days from the 13th to the 15th of *Bhadarva sud* (September-October), Kanbi women fast and worship a cow and feed her with barley, and on the fourth day they drink cow's milk mixed with a few grains of barley found in the dung. They observe the ordinary Hindu fasts and feasts and occasionally make pilgrimages locally to Ambaji, Bahucharaji, Daker, Dwarka, and Unai; and among more distant holy places to Allahabad, Banuires, Badrikedar, Gokul, Jagannath, Mathura, and Shrinathji, Rameshwar, Nasik and Pandharpur. *Bombay Gazetteer,* Volume IX, Part I, pp. 156-157.

Linga—a Symbol of Creation

Dwelling on the Lingayat custom *Bombay Gazetteer* states, "The three main objects of reverence are the *linga*, the Jangam and the *guru*. The *linga* is stone home of the deity, the Jangam is the human abode of the deity, and the *guru* is the teacher who preaches the sacred spell into the disciple's ear. The *linga* worn by Lingayats is generally made of light-gray late stone, and consists of two discs, each about three-fourths of an inch in diameter, the lower one about one eighth of an inch thick the upper slightly thicker, and is separated from the lower by a deep grove about an eighth of an inch broad. From its centre, which is slightly rounded, rises a pea-like knob about a quarter of an inch long and broad, giving the stone *linga* a total height of nearly three-quarters of an inch. This knob is called the *ban* or arrow. The upper disc is called *jalhari* that is the water carrier, because this part of a full sized *linga* is proved to carry off the water which if poured over the central knob. It is also called *pith*, that is, the seat and *panak* the little seat. Over the *linga*, to keep it from harm, is plastered a black mixture of clay, cowdung ashes, and marking-nut juice. This coating, which is called *kanthis,* or the covering, entirely hides the shape of the enclosed *linga*. It forms a smooth black slightly truncated cone, not unlike a dark betelnut, about three-quarters of an inch high and narrowing from three-quarters of an inch at the base to half an inch across the top. The stone of which the *linga* is made comes from Parvatgiri in North Arkot. It is brought by a class of people called Kambi Jangams, because besides the *linga* stone they bring slung from a shoulder bamboo (*kambi*) the holy water of the Patal Ganga a pool on Parvatgiri, whose water Lingayats hold as sacred as Brahmanical Hindus hold the water of the Ganges. A *linga* should be tied to the arm of a pregnant woman in the eighth month of pregnancy and to the arm of a child as soon as it is born. This rule is not strictly kept. The *linga* is sometimes tied on the fifth day but generally not till a day between a fortnight or three weeks after birth. A child's *linga* has generally no case or *kanthi*; the *kanthi* is sometimes not added for months, sometimes not for years. The *linga* is sometimes tied to the cradle in which the child sleeps, instead of to the child. It is rarely allowed to remain on the child till the child is five or six years old. Till then it is generally kept in the house shrine along with the house gods. The *linga* is worn either on the wrist, the arm, the neck, or the head. Some wear the *linga* slung from the left shoulder like a sacred thread and some carry it in the waistband of the lower garments. The last two ways are contrary to the rule that the *linga* should never be worn below the navel. It is worn either tied round by a ribbon or in a silver box fastened by a silver chain. Each family has generally a few spare *linga* in stock. The *linga* is never shown to any one who does not wear a *linga* himself. It should be taken out three times a day, washed, rubbed with ashes and a string of *rudraksh* bead bound round it. A man or a woman keeps the same *linga* all through life and in the grave it is taken out of its case and tied round the neck or arm of the corpse. If the *linga* is accidentally lost, the loner has to fast, give a caste dinner, go through the ceremony of *shuddhi* or cleansing, and received new *linga* from his *guru*. For the cleansing he bathes and washes a Virakt Jangam's feet, rubs cowdung ashes on his head, and bows before him. He sprinkles on his body the water in which the Jangam's feet were washed and sips a little of it along with the five cow-gifts. The Jangam places a new *linga* on his left palm, washes it with water, rubs cowdung ashes on it, lays a *bel* leaf on it, mutters some texts or *mantras* over it, and ties it round the neck of the worshipper.

When a Jangam loses his *linga*, the case becomes serious, and many a Jangam is said to have lost his caste on account of losing his *linga*. The *guru* or religious teacher, the third watchword of the Lingayat faith, is either a Virakt or celibate or a *Samanya* (ordinary) Jangam. Their head teacher is the head of the monastery at Chitaldurg in North-West Mysore. Like other Hindu teachers, the head teacher during his life-time generally chooses a successor, who acts under his orders so long as he lives. The head teacher may belong to any of the higher classes of Lingayats. He lives in celibacy in his monastery at Chitaldurg with great pomp, and receives divine honours from his followers. He goes on tour once every three or four years, receiving contributions, and in return giving his followers the water in which his feet are washed, which they rub on their eyes and drink. The ordinary *maths* or religious houses are under married or unmarried Jangams. When the head of a religious house is a celibate, or Virakt Jangam, he is succeeded by his pupil. These pupils remain unmarried and are the sons either of married clergy or of laymen, who, under a vow or for some other cause have, as children, been devoted to a religious house. Boys devoted to a religious house under a vow are called *maris* or youths. The *gurus* or teachers are of five kinds. The *guru* who ties on the *linga* is called the *Dikshaguru* (from *diksha* ceremonial purification). The *guru* who teaches religion is called the Shikshaguru (from *Shiksha* instruction), and the religious guide is called the Mokshguru (from *Moksha* absorbtion into the deity). The *guru* of the Mokshguru is called the Gurvinguru or the teacher of teachers and the highest priest is called the Paramguru or the chief teacher. According to tradition, Basava taught that there was only one God, namely Shiva. In practice, like their Brahmanic neighbours, Lingayats worship many gods. First among their gods comes Basaya, Basvanna or Basvandev, the founder of their faith, whom they identify with Nandi or Mahadev's bull. They also worship Virbhadra and Ganpati, whom they consider the sons, and Ganga and Parvati, whom they consider the wives, of Shiva, and keep their images in their houses. Besides these members—of Shiva's family they worship Yellamma. The origin of Yellamma is obscure. She is now identified with Renuka, the mother of Parsuram. However, there is also a village godling,

Yellavva or Yel-Makkaltai (mother of seven children, probably crop pests), represnted by painted stones in fields (C.W.M. Hudson in Journ, Bomb. Anthro. Soc. vii. p. 110). of Hampi in Bellari, and Saundatti in the Belgaum district, Malaya, Mallikarjun, and Tulja Bhavani of Tuljapur in the Nizam's country. (Lingayats also worship the village goddess Durgavva and Dyamavva. The former is simple Parvati. The latter is said to have been a Brahman girl who was reduced by and married a Holava (one of the untouchable castes) and subsequently destroyed him on finding out the deception (Bombay Gaz., 1884 Vol. XXII, p. 807). As a guardian against evil, that is against evil spirits, the great rival of the *linga* is the sun. Worship of the heavenly bodies was specially forbidden in the original faith. Shilvants and other strict Lingayats veil their drinking water so that the sun may not see it ; they say the sun is Brahma, But common Lingayats worship the sun on new moon day, and the moon on full moon day. Again, according to the books, Basava removed fasts and feasts, penance and pilgrimage, rosari and holy water, and reverence for cows. This change probably never passed beyond the sphere of books. At present Bombay Lingayats all fast on *Shivratra* or Shiva's Night on the dark thirteenth of *Magh* (January-February), and on *Nagpanchmi* or the bright fifth of *Shravan* (July-August) and follow their fasts by a feast. They keep partial fasts, that is, they take only one evening meal, on Mondays in *Shravan* (July-August). They make pilgrimages to Gokarn and to Ulvi in Kanara where Basava died, to Sangameshvar, to Yellamma Hill in Belgaum, to Parvatgiri in North Arkot, to Hampi in Bellary, and to Tuljapur in the Nizam's country. Contrary to the rule forbidding the worship of the *Sthaviralingas* a few devout Lingayats even visit the twelve Jyotirlingas at the famous shrines of Shiva in different parts of India. Mnay Jangams wear rosaries and tell their beads; the water in which a Jangam's feet have been washed is drunk as holy water or *tirth,* and Lingayats show the cow as much reverence as Brahmanic Hindus show her. As regards mediators, Basava's efforts to drive Brahmans out of their place as mediators between men and god have been successful. No Lingayats of the first two orders, except that they consult them as astrologers, ever employ or show respect to Brahmans. But in practice the Jangam is as much a mediator to the Lingayat as the Brahman is a mediator to the Brahmanic Hindu.

"Lingavats have two peculiar religions processions, the *Nandi kodu* or Nandi's horn and the Vyasantol or *Vyas* hand. The story about Nandi's horn is that in a fight with a demon Nandi once lost a horn. His followers found his horn and carried it in procession. The horn is now long bamboo pole wound round with strips of coloured cloth and the top is surmounted by a conical globe. About four and a half feet from each side of the pole, a plank is fastened, and on each plank is set a brass bull. This is paraded chiefly in the month of *Shravan* (July-August). Vyasantol or the hand of Vyas, the reputed author of the *Purans,* is a hand made of raga which, in theory, means that the *linga* wearer is safe from evil spirits. Lingayats are as much afraid of ghosts as other Hindus, and one of their five holy ashes is specially valued as a ghost scarer. When a person is possessed, his brow is marked with ashes from a censer placed before the house image of Virbhadra, or he is sometimes given charmed water to drink. They have also faith in soothsaying and astrology, and occasionally consult Brahman astrologers to find the lucky time to hold marriage and other ceremonies.

"Except in religious houses and when a priest is present, the different Lingayat sub-divisions are socially as exclusive as the different Brahmanical castes. Their feeling to the Mahars, Mangs, and other castes deemed impure is in no way kinder or more generous than the Brahman feeling. The theory that nothing can defile the wearer of the *linga* has toned down in practice. Coming of age and monthly sickness, a birth and a death are all believed to cause impurity, though, as among Jains, the impurity is much less thought of and is much more easily and quickly cleansed than among Brahmanic Hindus. That the dead Lingayat goes to Shiva's heaven seems to be a practical belief which has greatly reduced the rites to the dead, and probably the fear of spirits. Still in practice the *linga* has not been found to protect its wearers against all evil. Lingayats consult astrologers, fear and get possessed by evil spirits and employ knowing men to cast out spirits, lay ghosts, and counteract charms and spells. Little if at all less freely than their neighbours among Brahmanic Hindus. On the whole, Lingayats are less lettered than Brahmanic Hindus by ceremonial details and observances. They have fewer gods and have less fear of the dead, they perform no mind rites—*Shraddha* and they allow the widows of laymen to marry. When you have said this, and said that they do not read Brahmanic holy books, that they hate Brahmans, that when men meet instead of calling Ram they say Sharthi that is Help Prav and when you have added that they wear a *linga* and not a sacred-thread, that the men shave the topknot and do not shave the widow's head or the mourner's lip, you have nearly exhausted the difference between the two parties.

"It has been seen that the Lingayats are believers in the god Shiva, the third person of the Hindu trinity, signifying the creative and destructive forces in the universe. Thence they derive the phallus or *linga,* emblematic of reproduction, and the sacred bull, Nandi or Basava, found in all their temples, and in all probability the emblem of strength. The principal Lingayat ceremony known as the *ashtarana* or eightfold sacrament has been already referred to in some detail. The essentially Lingayat beliefs and ceremonies, such as the wearing of the *linga*, the worship of the *jangam,* and the administration of *ashtavarna* rites are, however, usual in India, constantly mingled with many commonplace Hindu beliefs and customs. It is a common practice in India for Hindu to worship at the shrine of Musalman *pirs* or saints, and in the same way Lingayats will combine the worship of the special objects prescribed by Basava, with the worship of purely Hindu deities, such as Hanuman, Ganpati, Yellamma, Maruti and many others. The investigations hitherto conducted do not clearly show how far Linhayat and Hindu rituals are liable to be combined, but it can be securely predicted that the lower orders of the community, who still keep in touch with the unconverted section of the caste to which, professionally speaking, they belong, will be found to adhere in many instances to the beliefs and customs of their unconverted fellow castement, despite the teaching and influence of the Jangams." The customs are related to Lingayat community.

Propitiating Evil Spirits

Dwelling on their jumble of faith, superstition and sorcery, Mr. Enthoven writes, "Maratha Kunbis follow the Hindu law of inheritance and belong to the Hindu religion. They cannot tell whether they are Smarts or Bhagvats. Many of them are Varkaris who are also called Malkaris as they wear necklaces of basil beads. They worship all Brahmanic gods and goddesses, but their chief objects of worship are Bhairay, Bhavani, Biroba, Jakhai, Janai, Jokhai, Khandola, Maruti, Metisai, Mhasoba, Mukai, Navlai, Phringai, Satvai, Tukai, Vaghoba and Vetal, whom they greatly fear and whose images or *taks* they keep in their house. Bhairav is the usual village guardian. He has two forms, Kal Bhairav and Bal Bhairav. Kal Bhairav is shown as a standing man with two hands, an hour-glass-shaped drum or *damaru* in his right hand, and a trident in his left. He is encircled by a serpent. Bal Bhairav lives in an unhewn stone covered with red lead or *shendur* mixed with oil. If kept pleased by a coating of oil and red lead and if he given offerings of clarified butter, Bhairav is kindly. He cures snake-bites and tells whether an undertaking will do well or will fail. In the chest of the rough figure of Bhairav are two small holes. The person who wishes to consult the oracle places a betelnut in each of the holes and explains to Bhairav that if the right betelnut falls first it will mean that the undertaking will prosper, and that if the left betelnut falls first it will mean that the undertaking will fail. He asks the god, according as the event is to be, to let the lucky or unlucky nut fall first. He tells the god that, if he will drop the lucky nut and if his undertaking prospers, he will give the god a cock or a goat. Twice a year, before they begin to sow and before they begin to reap, the villagers come in procession and worship Bhairav. Bhavani, that is, Parvati the wife of Shiva, is known by many names such as Phringai, Tukai, etc. She shares with Bhairav the honour of being the village guardian; she is generally shown as a rude image, either with two hands, a sword being in the right hand, or with eight hands holding a conch, a wheel and other articles the same as Vishnu holds. Like Bhairav she is asked the cause of sickness or ill-luck and to advise regarding the future, and like him, if she removes trouble or advises well, she is given a goat or cock. Biroba is worshipped mainly by Dhangars or shepherd. He lives in an unhewn stone outside of the village. Like Mhasoba, he is an unkindly spirit to whom people pray when they are anxious to plague or ruin their enemies. Jakhai, Janai, Jokhai, Kalkai, Metisai, Muskai and

Nevlai are all local mothers. According to the people's account, they are unkindly forms of Bhavani. With the help of two attendants, Naikji and Birji, they do much mischief. They blast crops of grain, plague men with sickness, and carry off travellers. People who owe their neighbours a grudge pray to Janai, Mukai, or one of the mothers to send them sickness, to kill their cattle, or to ruin their fields. Khandoba, literally swordfather, guards the country as Bhairav guards the village. Khandoba is the Ishvar Dev or guardian diety of the Deccan. As a guardian, he is shown sometimes at his chief shrine at Jejuri as a *linga,* the great protector, and more often as a horseman with a sword in his right hand, and his Mhalsabai sitting beside him. As a horseman, he is Malhari, the form he took when he came to destroy the demons Mani and Malla. As an animal, he is the dog who runs beside his horse, and in the Deccan is generally called Khandi. As a plant, he is turmeric powder under the name Bhandar. His house image is always of metal, never of wood or of stone. He drives away the evil which causes sickness. No class honours Khandoba so highly as the Ramoshis. If a Ramoshi makes a promise while laying his hand on turmeric powder or *bhadai,* that is, on Khandoba, nothing will bring him to break his promise. Maruti, also called Hanuman, is the monkey god. No village in the Deccan is without a Maruti, a rudely embossed monkey figure, sometimes within the village and sometimes outside, but generally near the gate. He is a kind god, the great saviour of those into whom evil spirits have entered. He is fond of coconuts, but does not care for blood offerings. Mhasoba or Mhaskoba is perhaps the commonest and most widely feared of the local evil spirits. He lives in an unhewn stone coated with red lead. These stones are all old dwellings of Mhasoba—some get forgotten. Then sickness falls on the village, and the people go to the village guardian and ask him a series of questions, which he answers by dropping a betelnut or by some other sign. In the end, they find out from the guardian that there is an old neglected dwelling of Mhasoba. The villagers find the stone, cover it with oil and red lead, and kill a goat or a fowl in front of it. Besides, to prevent his working mischief, Mhasoba is worshipped by men who have a grudge to clear off or a wrong to avenge. They go to Mhasoba, name their enemy, and promise, if he ruins their enemy with sickness, that they will give him a goat or a fowl. So much is he feared that when a man knows that some one whom he has ill used has arranged to set Mhasoba on him, he makes such amends that the god is not forced to exert his powers. Satvai, or Mother Sixth, is the goddess of pregnant and lying-in women. She is worshipped by barren women, and by lying-in women on the fifth or sixth day after the child is born. Her image is an armless bust.Vaghoba, or Father Tiger, lives in an unhewn stone. If he is cared for, he guards the village herds from the attacks of tigers. *Vetal* is the leader of demons and evil spirits. He seems to be the earliest form of Shiva, the leader of spirits, and Ganesh, the lord of spirit troops. *Vetal* lives in an unhewn stone, three or four feet high, surrounded at a distance of a few yards by a circle of smaller stones in which his leading attendants live. Unlike most shrines, the stones in which Vetal and his attendants live are covered both with white and red wash. *Vetal* and his guard are generally at some distance outside of the village. Vetal's great day is the *Mahashivaratri* or great night of Shiva on the full-moon of *Magh* in February. On that night the villagers, each with a bundle of lighted straw in his hand, walk round the circle of stones howling and bawling. When a Kunbi or one of his family is possessed by an evil spirit, he goes to Vetal and promises, if he orders his spirit to give up troubling him, that he will give him a goat or a fowl. Vetal is the patron of wrestlers and athletes. On one of the holidays, the villagers go and wrestle at Vetal's circle. Vetal's sign is a cane called *vet* or *bet,* from which he seems to get his name. From his apparent similarity with the early forms of Shiva, and from the resemblance of his circle of guards to a rude Buddhist rail, and to the circles of unhewn stones found in Western Europe and in other parts of the world, the worship of Vetal is specially interesting.

". . . . Maratha Kunbis believe in incantations, witchcraft, ghosts and evil spirits, oracles and the evil eye. Partly because they are much more sober and partly because fever is much less common, the Deccan Kunbis are much less afraid of spirits than the Konkan Kunbis. Still, the belief in spirits, witchcraft and the evil eye has a great effect on the lives of the Deccan Kunbis. If a Kunbi is seized with uncommon sickness or suffers from any calamity, he first finds out whether his misfortunes are due to natural causes or due to the displeasure of the gods or due to witchcraft or due to the evil eye or due to an evil spirit. To find out the cause, the sufferer and his friends make several experiments. A flower is stuck on the breast of an idol and its fall on one side or the other determines the cause of the misfortune, or a sacrificial vessel is hung by a string and, as is agreed beforehand, the direction to which it points when it comes to rest settles the cause of the evil. If these trials are not satisfactory, a *Janta* or knowing man is asked. If the evil has come from the gods, the knowing man says how the gods are to be pleased; if the cause is witchcraft, either the knowing man breaks the spell by counter-charms or the witch is caught and either forced to remove the spell or made to drink water from the hands of a cobbler, which destroys her power; if the cause is the evil, either the knowing man breaks the spell or the mother of the sick child throws salt and red pepper into the fire saying, *Drisht-Misht ali gelichi, Bhutkhet papi chandalchi,* that is, 'The evil eye of passers-by, of evil spirits and fifthy wights'. The evil eye is much feared. The owner of the eye is not though to blame, but he is shunned and cattle are not driven past his door. To draw the evil eye from the crops, a white-washed pot is stuck on a pole; the walls of houses are decked with figures and gaudy stripes; beautiful women and children wear necklaces and cattle wear necklaces and anklets. A Kunbi never congratulates a friend on his prosperity, his fine oxen or his beautiful wife. If he does, ill-luck will hear and carry away the excess of good fortune. Every place teems with ghosts and evil spirits, who are included under the general name *bhut,* literally a being. The male ghosts are called Keins or Jhotings and the female ghosts Hadals. Among the worst female ghosts are the seven water-nymphs called Aija or Jaldevtas, who carry off handsome youths. There are distinct names for the ghosts of Brahmans, Musalmans and outcastes. A ghost wanders and ill-uses the living either because he was murdered or ill-treated or because he hankers after a house, a wife or a treasure. Ghosts live in large trees, lonely places, empty houses and old wells. They are generally seen or heard at noon and at midnight. They take many shapes, that of a deer, a tall figure, a strange ox or a goat. If a person sleeps under a haunted tree, or cuts a brunch of a haunted tree or defiles the ghost's ruin or old wall or jostles a ghost on a road, the person sickens or is unlucky. The ghosts of the murdered or of ill-used are chiefly dangerous to those ill-treated them. The ghost enters into the culprit, maddens him, destroys his sleep, kills his family and turns his joy to sorrow. Many people make a living by appeasing or casting out angry spirits. One plan is for the excorciser to take the possessed person in front of an idol, seize him by the top-knot, scourge him, and abuse him till the spirit says what offering or penance will satisfy him.

"Maratha Kunbis have great faith in omens. They consider it unlucky if a crow flies to the right and *tas* or the blue jay Coracias Indica flies to the left. On going out they think it lucky to meet an unwidowed woman with a full waterpot on her head, a milkmaid with milk pots or anybody with a dish of cooked food. If a cat or a widow happen to pass before them while going out, they consider it unlucky and go back. They hold it very unlucky if a lighted lamp falls on the ground and goes out or if a house lizard drops in front of them. The priests of Maratha Kunbis are the local or Deshasth Brahmans. Their religious teachers are Gosavis, whose advice or *updesh* they take," adds Mr. Enthoven. The custom, rites and rituals and related to Kunbis in Maharashtra.

Worship of Cattle

About the custom of worshipping the cattle by the savages, R.V. Russell and Hira Lal write, "The Banjaras worshipped their pack cattle. When sickness occurs, they lead the sick man to the feet of the bullock called Hatadiya. On this animal no burden is ever laid, but he is decorated with streamers of red-dyed silk, and tinkling bells with many brass chains and rings on neck and feet, and silken tassels hanging in all directions; he moves steadily at the head of the convoy, and at the place where he lies down when he gets tired they pitch their camp for the day; at his feet they make their vows when difficulties overtake them, and in illness, whether of themselves or their cattle, they trust to his worship for a cure."

"The Banjaras," Sir A. Lyall writes, "are terribly vexed by witchcraft, to which their wandering and precarious existence especially exposes them in the shape of fever, rheumatism and dysentery. Solemn enquiries are still held in the wild jungles where these people camp out like gypsies, and many an unlucky hag has been strangled by sentence of their secret tribunals." (Asiatic Studies, Vol. I p. 118. ed-1899). The business of magic and witchcraft was in the hands of two classes of Bhagats or magicians, one good and the other bad, who may correspond to the European practitioners of black and white magic. The good Bhagat is called *Nimbu-katna* or lemon-cutter, a lemon spreading on a knife being a powerful averter of evil spirits. He is a total abstainer from sacred to the diety whom he venerates, usually Mahadeo; he is highly respected and never panders to vice. But the Janta, the 'Wise or Cunning Man', is of the different type, and the following is an account of the devilry often enacted when a deputation visited him to inquire into the cause of a prolonged illness, a cattle murrain, a sudden death or other misfortune. A woman might often be called a Dakun or witch in spite, and once this word had been used, the husband or nearest male relative would be regularly bullied into consulting the Janta, or if some woman had been ill for a week, an avaricioius husband or brother would begin to whisper foul play. Witchcraft would be mentioned, and the wise man called in. He would give the sufferer a quid of betel, muttering an incantation, but this rarely effected a cure, as it was against the interest of all parties that it should do so. The sufferer's relatives would then go to their Naik, tell him that the sick person was bewitched, and ask him to send a deputation to the Janta or witch-doctor. This would be at once despatched, consisting of one male adult from each house in the hamlet, with one of the sufferer's relatives. On the road, the party would bury a bone or other article to test the wisdom of the witch-doctor. But he was not to be caught out, and on their arrival he would bid the deputation rest, and come to him for consultation on the following day. Meanwhile during the night the Janta would be thoroughly coached by some accomplice in the party. Next morning, after meeting the deputation, he would tell every man all particulars of his name and family, name the invalid, and tell the party to bring materials for consulting the spirits, such as oil, vermilion, sugar, dates, coconut, *chironji,* and sesamum. In the evening, holding a lamp, the Janta would be possessed by Mariai, the goddess of cholera; he would mention all particulars of the sick man's illness, and indignantly inquire why they had buried the bone on the road, naming it and describing the place. If this did not satisfy the deputation, a goat would be brought, and he would name its sex with any distinguishing marks on the body. The sick person's representative would then produce his *nazar* or fee, formerly Rs. 25, but lately the double of this or more. The Janta would now begin a sort of chant, introducing the names of the families of the *kuri* other than that containing her who was to be proclaimed a witch, and heap on them all kinds of abuse. Finally, he would assume an ironic tone, extol the virtues of a certain family, become facetious, and praise its representative then present. This man would then question the Janta on all points regarding his own family, his connections, worldly goods, and what gods he worshipped, ask who was the witch, who taught her sorcery, and how and why she practised it in this particular instance. But the witch-doctor, having taken care to be well coached, would answer everything correctly and fix the guilt on to the witch. A goat would be sacrificed and eaten with liquor, and the deputation would return. The punishment for being proclaimed a Dakun or witch was formerly death to the woman and a fine to be paid by her relatives to the bewitched person's family. The woman's husband or her sons would be directed to kill her, and if they refused, other men were deputed to murder her, and bury the body at once with all the clothing and ornaments then on her person, while a further fine would be extracted from the family for not doing away with her themselves. But murder for witchcraft has been almost entirely stopped, and nowadays the husband, after being fined a few head of cattle, which are given to the sick man, is turned out of the village with his wife. It is quite possible, however, that an obnoxious old hag would even now not escape death, especially if the money fine were not forthcoming, and an instance is known in recent times of a mother being murdered by her three sons. The whole village combined to screen these amiable young men, and eventually they made the Janta the scapegoat, and he got seven years, while the murderers could not be touched. Colonel Mackenzie writes, "Curious to relate, the Jantas, known locally as Bhagats, in order to become possessed of their alleged powers of divination and prophecy, require to travel to Kazhe, beyond Surat, to learn and be instructed by low-caste Koli impostors. This is interesting as an instance of the powers of witchcraft being attributed by the Hindus or higher race to the indigenous primitive tribes, a rule which Dr. Tylor and Dr. Jevons consider to hold good generally in the history of magic."

Custom of Human Sacrifice

Several instances are also known of the Banjaras having practised human sacrifice. Mr. Thurston states, "In former times the Lambadis, before setting out on a journey, used to procure a little child and bury it in the ground up to the shoulders, and then drive their loaded bullocks over the unfortunate victim. In proportion to the bullocks thoroughly trampling the child to death, so their belief in a successful journey increased." [*Ethnographic Notes in Southern India*, p. 507, quoting from the Rev. J. Cain, *Ind. Ant. viii.* (1879)]. The Abbe Dubois describes another form of sacrifice: (*Hindu Manners, Customs and Ceremonies,* p. 70).

The Lambadis are accused of the still more atrocious crime of offering human sacrifices. When they wish to perform this horrible act, it is said, they secretly carry off the first person they meet. Having conducted the victim to some lonely spot, they dig a hole in which they bury him up to the neck. While he is still alive they make a sort of lamp of dough made of flour, which they place on his head; this they fill with oil and light four wicks in it. Having done this, the men and women join hands and, forming a circle, dance round their victim, singing and making a great noise until he expires. Mr. Cumberlege records the following statement of a child kidnapped by a Banjara caravan in 1871. After explaining how he was kidnapped and the tip of his tongue cut off to give him a defect in speech, the Kunbi lad, taken from Sahungarhi, in the Bhandara district, went on to say that, "The *tanda* (caravan) encamped for the night in the jungle. In the morning, a woman named Gangi said that the devil was in her and that a sacrifice must be made. On this four men and three women took a boy to a place they had made for *puja* (worship). They fed him with milk, rice and sugar, and then made him to stand up. Then, Gangi drew a sword and approached the child. The child tried to run away but caught and brought back to this place, Gangi, holding the sword with both hands and standing on the child's right side, cut off his head with one blow. Gangi collected the blood and sprinkled it on the idol; this idol is made of stone and is about 9 inches high, and has something sparkling in its forehead. The camp marched that day, and for four or five days consecutively, without another sacrifice; but on the fifth day a young woman came to the camp to sell curds, and having bought some, the Banjaras asked her to come in the evening and eat with them. She did come, and after eating with the women slept in the camp. Early, next morning she was sacrificed in the same way as the boy had been, but it took three blows to cut off her head; it was done by Gangi, and the blood was sprinkled on the stone idol. About a month ago Sitaram, a Gond lad, who had also been kidnapped and was in the camp, told me to run away as it had been decided to offer me up in sacrifice at the next Jiuti festival, so I ran away. The child having been brought to the police, a searching and protracted enquiry was held, which, however, determined nothing, though it did not disprove his story."

R.V. Russell and Hira Lal further write, "The Banjara caste is not closed closed to outsiders, but the general rule is to admit only women who have been married to Banjara men. Women of the lowest and impure castes are excluded, and for some unknown reason the Patwas (The Patwas are weavers of silk thread and the Nunias are masons and navvies)." Nunias arc bracketed with these. In Nimar it is stated that formerly Gonds, Korkus and even Balahis might become Banjaras, but this does not happen now, because the caste has lost its occupation of carrying goods, and there is therefore no inducement to enter it. In former times, they were much addicted to kidnapping children—these were whipped up or enticed away whenever an opportunity presented itself during their expeditions. The children were first put into the *gonis* or grain bags of the bullocks and so carried for a few days, being made over at each halt to the care of a woman, who would pop the child back into its bag if any stranger passed by the encampment. The tongues of boys were sometimes slit or branded with hot gold. This ceremony of initiation into the caste is still used in Nimar. Girls, if they were as old as seven, were sometimes disfigured for fear of recognition, and for this purpose the juice of the marking-nut (*Semecarpus Anacardium*) tree would be smeared on one side of the face, which burned into the skin and entirely altered the appearance. Such children were known as Jangar. Girls would be used as concubines and servants of the married wife, and boys would also be employed as servants. Jangar boys would be married to Jangar girls, both remaining in their condition of servitude. But sometimes the more enterprising of them would abscond and settle down in a village. The rule was that for seven generations the children of Jangars or slaves continued in that condition, after which they were recognised as proper Banjaras. The Jangar could not draw in smoke through the stem of the huqqa when it was passed round in the assembly, but must take off the stem and inhale from the bowl. The Jangar also could not eat off the bell-metal plates of his master, because these were liable to pollution, but must use brass plates. At one time, the Banjaras conducted a regular traffic in female slaves between Gujarat and Central India, selling in each country the girls whom they had kidnapped in the other (Malcolm, *Memoir of Central India,* ii, p. 296).

Propitiating *Bera Pennu* with Human Sacrifice

Dwelling on the Khond custom of human sacrifice, R.V. Russell and Hira Lal further add, "The Khond pantheon consists of eighty-four gods, of whom Dharni Deota, the earth god, is the chief. In former times the earth goddess was apparently female and was known as Tari Pennu or Bera Pennu. To her were offered the terrible human sacrifices presently to be described. There is nothing surprising in the change of sex of the divine being, for which parallels are forthcoming. Thus, in Chhattisgarh, the deity of the earth, who also received human sacrifices, is either Thakur Deo, a god, or Thakurani Mai, a goddess. Deota is an Aryan term, and the proper Khond name for a god is Pennu. The earth god is usually accompanied by Bhatbarsi Deota, the god of hunting. Dharni Deota is represented by a rectangular peg of wood driven into the ground, while Bhatbarsi has a place at his feet in the shape of a piece of conglomerate stone covered with circular granules. Once in four or five years a buffalo is offered to the earth god, in lieu of the human sacrifice which was formerly in vogue. The animal is predestined for sacrifice from its birth, and is allowed to wander loose and graze on the crops at its will. The stone representing Bhatbarsi is examined periodically, and when the granules on it appear to have increased, it is decided that the time has come for the sacrifice. In Kalahandi, a lamb is sacrificed every year, and strips of its flesh distributed to all the villagers, who bury it in their fields as a divine agent of fertilisation, in the same way as the flesh of the human victim was formerly buried. The Khond worships his bow and arrows before he goes out hunting, and believes that every hill and valley has its separate deity, who must be propitiated with the promise of a sacrifice before his territory is entered, or he will hide the animals within it from the hunter, and enable them to escape when wounded. These deities are closely related to each other, and it is important when arranging for an expedition to know the connection between them all, this information can be obtained from any one on whom the divine afflatus from time to time descends."

The following account of the well-known system of human sacrifice, formerly practised by the Khonds, is contained in Sir James Frazer's *Golden Bough,* having been compiled by him from the accounts of Major Macpherson and Major-General John Campbell, two of the officers deputed to suppress it: "The best known case of human sacrifices systematically offered to ensure good crops is supplied by the Khonds or Kandhs, another Dravidian race in Bengal. Our knowledge of them is derived from the accounts written by British officers who, forty or fifty years ago, were engaged in putting them down. The sacrifices were offered to the Earth-Goddess, Tari Pennu or Bera Pennu, and were believed to ensure good crops and immunity from all disease and accidents. In particular, they were considered necessary in the cultivation of turmeric, the Khonds arguing that the turmeric could not have a deep red colour without the shedding of blood.The victim or Meriah was acceptable to the goddess only if he had been purchased, or had been born a victim—that is the son of a victim father—or had been devoted as a child by his father or guardian. Khonds in distress often sold their children for victims, 'considering the beatification of their souls certain, and their death, for the benefit of mankind, the most honourable possible.' A man of the Panua (Pan) tribe was once seen to load a Khond with curses, and finally to spit in his face, because the Khond had sold for a victim his own child, whom the Panua had wished to marry. A party of Khonds, who saw this, immediately pressed forward to comfort the seller of his child, saying, 'Your child has died that all the world may live, and the Earth-Goddess herself will wipe that spittle from your face.' The victims were often kept for years before they were sacrificed. Being regarded as consecrated beings, they were treated with extreme affection, mingled with diference, and were welcomed wherever they went. A Meriah youth, on attaining maturity, was generally given a wife, who was herself usually a Meriah or victim, and with her he received a portion of land and farm-stock.Their offspring were also victims. Human sacrifices were offered to the Earth-Goddess by tribes, branches of tribes, or villages, both at periodical festivals and on extraordinary occasions. The periodical sacrifices were generally so arranged by tribes and divisions of tribes that each head of a family was enabled, at least once a year, to procure a shred of flesh for his fields, generally about the time when his chief crop was laid down. The mode of performing these tribal sacrifices was as follows. Ten or twelve days before the sacrifice, the victim was devoted by cutting off his hair, which, until then, had been kept unshorn. Crowds of men and women assembled to witness the sacrifice; none might be excluded, since the sacrifice was declared to be for all mankind. It was preceded by several days of wild revelry and gross debauchery. On the day before the sacrifice, the victim, dressed in a new garment, was led forth from the village in solemn procession, with music and dancing, to the Meriah grove, a clump of high forest trees standing a little away from the village and untouched by the axe. Here they tied him to a post, which was sometimes placed between two plants of the *sankissar* shrub. He was then anointed with oil, ghee and turmeric, and adorned with flowers; and 'a species of reverence, which it is not easy to distinguish from adoration,' was paid to him throughout the day. A great struggle now arose to obtain the smallest relic from his person; a particle of the turmeric paste with which he was smeared, or a drop of his spittle, was esteemed of sovereign virtue, especially by the women. The crowd danced round the post to music, and addressing the Earth said, 'O God, we offer this sacrifice to you; give us good crops, seasons, and health.'

"On the last morning the orgies, which had been scarcely interrupted during the night, were resumed and continued till noon, when they ceased, and the assembly proceeded to consummate the sacrifice. The victim was again anointed with oil, and each person touched the anointed part, and wiped the oil on his own head. In some places they took the victim in procession round the village, from door to door, where some plucked hair from his head, and others begged for a drop of his spittle, with which they anointed their heads. As the victim might not be bound nor make any show of resistance, the bones of his arms and, if necessary, his legs were broken; but often this precaution was rendered unnecessary by stupefying him with opium. The mode of putting him to death varied in different places. One of the commonest modes seems to have been strangulation, or squeezing to death. The branch of a green tree was cleft several feet down the middle; the victim's neck (in other places, his chest) was inserted in the cleft, which the priest, aided by his assistants, strove with all his force to close. Then he wounded the victim slightly with his axe, whereupon the crowd rushed at the wretch and cut the flesh from the bones, leaving the head and bowels untouched. Sometimes he was cut up alive. In Chinna Kimedy, he was dragged along the fields, surrounded by the crowd, who, avoiding his head and intestines, hacked the flesh from his body with their knives till he died. Another very common mode of sacrifice in the same district was to fasten the victim to the proboscis of a wooden elephant, which revolved on a stout post, and, as it whirled round, the crowd cut the flesh from the victim while life remained. In some villages Major Campbell found as many as fourteen of these wooden elephants, which had been used at sacrifices. (Sir H. Risley notes that the elephant represented the earth-goddess herself, who was here conceived in elephant form. In the hill tracts of Gumsur she was represented in peacock form, and the post to which the victim was bound bore the effigy of a peacock. Macpherson also records that when the Khonds attacked the victim they shouted, 'No sin rests on us; we have bought you with a price'). In one district the victim was put to death slowly by fire. A low stage was formed, sloping on either side like a roof; upon it they laid the victim, his limbs wound round with cords to confine his struggles. Fires were then lighted and hot brands applied, to make him roll up and down the slopes of the stage as long as possible; for the more tears he shed the more abundant would be the supply of rain. Next day the body was cut to pieces.

"The flesh cut from the victim was instantly taken home by the persons who had been deputed by each village to bring it. To secure its rapid arrival it was sometimes forwarded by relays of men, and conveyed with postal fleetness fifty or sixty miles. In each village all who stayed at home fasted rigidly until the flesh arrived. The bearer deposited it in the place of public assembly, where it was received by the priest and the heads of families. The priest divided it into two portions, one of which he offered to the Earth-Goddess by burying it in a hole in the ground with his back turned, and without looking. Then each man added a little earth to bury it, and the priest poured water on the spot from a hill gourd. The other portion of flesh he divided into as many shares as there were heads of houses present. Each head of a house rolled his shred of flesh in leaves and buried it in his favourite field, placing it in the earth behind his back without looking. In some places, each man carried his portion of flesh to the stream which watered his fields, and there hung it on a pole. For three days thereafter no house was swept; and, in one district, strict silence was observed, no fire might be given out, no wood cut, and no strangers received. The remains of the human victim (namely, the head, bowels and bones) were watched by strong parties the night after the sacrifice, and next morning they were burned along with a whole sheep, on a funeral pile. The ashes were, scattered over the fields, laid as paste over the houses and granaries, or mixed with the new corn to preserve it from insects. Sometimes, however, the head and bones were buried, not burnt. After the suppression of the human sacrifices, inferior victims were substituted in some places; for instance, in the capital of Chinna Kimedy a goat took the place of a human victim.

"In these Khond sacrifices, the Meriahs are represented by our authorities as victims offered to propitiate the Earth-Goddess. But from the treatment of the victims both before and after death it appears that the custom cannot be explained as merely a propitiatory sacrifice. A part of the flesh certainly was offered to the Earth-Goddess, but the rest of the flesh was buried by each householder in his fields, and the ashes of the other parts of the body were scattered over the fields, laid as paste on the granaries, or mixed with the new corn. These latter customs imply that to the body of the Meriah there was ascribed a direct or intrinsic power of making the crops to grow, quite independent of the indirect efficacy which it might have as an offering to secure the good-will of the deity. In other words, the flesh and ashes of the victim were believed to be endowed with a magical or physical power of fertilising the land. The same intrinsic power was ascribed to the blood and tears of the Meriah, his blood causing the redness of the turmeric, and his tears producing rain; for it can hardly be doubted that, originally at least, the tears were supposed to bring down the rain, not merely to prognosticate it. Similarly the custom of pouring water on the buried flesh of the Meriah was no doubt a rain-charm. Again, magical power as an attribute of the Meriah appears in the sovereign virtue believed to reside in anything that came from his person, as his hair or spittle. The ascription of such power to the Meriah indicates that he was much more than a mere man sacrificed to propitiate a deity. Once more, the extreme reverence paid him points to the same conclusion. Major Campbell speaks of the Meriah as 'being regarded as something more than mortal,' and Major Macpherson says, 'A species of reverence, which it is not easy to distinguish from adoration, is paid to him.' In short, the Meriah appears to have been regarded as divine. As such, he may originally have represented the Earth-Goddess, or perhaps a deity of vegetation, though in later times he came to be regarded rather as a victim offered to a deity than as himself an incarnate god. The later view of the Meriah as a victim rather than a divinity may perhaps have received undue emphasis from the European writers who have described the Khond religion. Habituated to the later idea of sacrifice as an offering made to a god for the purpose of conciliating his favour, European observers are apt to interpret all religious slaughter in this sense, and to suppose that wherever such slaughter takes place, there must necessarily be a deity to whom the carnage is believed by the slayers to be acceptable. Thus their preconceived ideas unconsciously colour and warp their descriptions of savage rites. (*Golden Bough,* 2nd ed. Vol. ii. p. 241)."

In his *Ethnographic Notes in Southern India,* Mr Thurston states (1906, pp. 517-519), "The last recorded Meriah sacrifice in the Ganjam Maliahs occurred in 1852, and there are still Khonds alive who were present at it. Twenty-five descendants of persons who were reserved for sacrifice, but were rescued by Government officers, returned themselves as Meriah at the Census of 1901. The Khonds have now substituted a buffalo for a human being. The animal is hewn to pieces while alive, and the villagers rush home to their villages to bury the flesh in the soil, and so secure prosperous crops. The sacrifice is not unaccompanied by risk to the performers, as the buffalo, before dying, frequently kills one or more of its tormentors. It was stated by the officiers of the Maliah Agency that there was reason to believe that the Raja of Jaipur (Madras), when he was installed at his father's decease in 1860-61, sacrificed a girl thirteen years of age at the shrine of the Goddess Durga in the town of Jaipur. The last attempted human sacrifice (which was nearly successful) in the Vizagapatam District, among the Kutia Khonds, was, I believe, in 1880. But the memory of the abandoned practice is kept green by one of the Khond songs, for a translation of which we are indebted to Mr. J. E. Friend-Pereira (*Journal, A. S. of Bengal,* 1898):

> At the time of the great Kiabon (Campbell) Sahib's coming, the country was in darkness; it was enveloped in mist.
>
> Having sent paiks to collect the people of the land, they, having surrounded them, caught the Meriah sacrificers.
>
> Having caught the Meriah sacrificers, they brought them; and again they went and sized the evil councillors.
>
> Having seen the chains and shackles, the people were afraid ; murder and bloodshed were quelled.
>
> Then the land became beautiful; and a certain Mokodella (Macpherson) Sahib came.
>
> He destroyed the lairs of the tigers and bears in the hills and rocks, and taught wisdom to the people.

After the lapse of a month he built bungalows and schools; and he adviced them to learn reading and law.

They learnt wisdom and reading ; they acquired silver and gold. Then all the people became wealthy.

Wearing Charms and Amulets

About the Bhil custom of wearing charm, Talisman and belief in sorcery, Mr. R.V. Russell and Hiralal write, "They wear charms and amulets to keep off evil spirits; the charms are generally pieces of blue string with seven knots in them, which their witch-finder or Badwa ties, reciting an incantation on each; the knots were sometimes covered with metal to keep them undefiled and the charms were tied on at the Holi, Dasahra or some other festival.) *Asiatic Studies,* Ist series, p. 352. In Bombay the Bhils still believe in witches as the agents of any misfortunes that may befall them. If a man was sick and thought some woman had bewitched him, the suspected woman was thrown into a stream or swung from a tree. If the branch broke and the woman fell and suffered serious injury, or if she could not swim across the stream and sank, she was considered to be innocent and efforts were made to save her. But if she escaped without injury she was held to be a witch, and it frequently happened that the woman would admit herself to be one either from fear of the infliction of a harder ordeal, or to keep up the belief in her powers as a witch, which often secured her a free supper of milk and chickens. She would then admit that she had really bewitched the sick man and undertake to cure him on some sacrifice being made. If he recovered, the animal named by the witch was sacrificed and its blood given her to drink while still warm; either from fear or in order to keep up the character she would drink it, and would be permitted to stay on in the village. If, on the other hand, the sick person died, the witch would often be driven into the forest to die of hunger or to be devoured by wild animals. *Bombay* Bombay *Gazetteer, Hindus of Gujarat,* p. 302. These practices have now disappeared in the Central Provinces, though occasionally murders of suspected witches may still occur. The Bhils are firm believers in omens the nature of which is much the same as among the Hindus. When a Bhil is persistently unlucky in hunting, he sometimes says *'Nat laga'*, meaning that some bad spirit is causing his ill-success. Then he will make an image of a man in the sand or dust of the road, or sometimes two images of a man and woman, and throwing straw or grass over the images set it alight, and pound it down on them with a stick with abusive yells. This he calls killing his bad luck. *Bombay Gazetteer, Vol. xii.* p. 87. Major Hendley notes that the men danced before the different festivals and before battles. The men danced in a ring holding sticks and striking them against each other, much like the Baiga dance. Before battle they had a war-dance in which the performers were armed and imitated a combat. To be carried on the shoulders of one of the combatants was a great honour, perhaps because it symbolised being on horseback. The dance was probably in the nature of a magical rite, designed to obtain success in battle by going through an imitation of it beforehand. The priests are the chief physicians among the Bhils, though most old men were supposed to know something about medicine *(An Account of the Bhils,* pp. 362, 363).

"The Hindu Bhils say that they do not admit outsiders into the caste, but the Muhammadans will admit a man of any but the impure castes. The neophyte must be shaved and circumcised, and the Kazi gives him some holy water to drink and teaches him the profession of belief in Islam. If a man is not circumcised, the Tadvi or Muhammadan Bhils will not bury his body. Both classes of Bhils employ Brahmans at their ceremonies. The tribe eat almost all kinds of flesh and drink liquor, but the Hindus now abjure beef and the Muhammadans pork. Some Bhils now refuse to take the skins off dead cattle, but others will do so. The Bhils will take food from any caste except the impure ones, and none except these castes will now take food from them. Temporary or permanent exclusion from caste is imposed for the same offences as among the Hindus," add Mr. Russell and Hira Lal.

Non-Linga Man Must not See Lingayat Food

Mr. Enthoven notes, "Lingayats are strict vegetarians, the staple food being Indian or spiked millet, pulse, vegetables, onions, garlic, condiments, milk curds, and clarified butter, rice replacing the millets in the Mallad. As regards eating, a member of any one of the main divisions will eat in the house of any member of his own or of any higher division. None of the division below the Jangam eat in the house of any member of an inferior division. But in a field, in a rest house, or in any place except the host's house, so long as the host has used a new set of earthern cooking vessels, they will eat food cooked by the host even though he is of an inferior division. In a *math* or religious house any Lingayat without question will eat bread which a Jangam has gathered in his begging. If the Jangam has brought it, it is all right if cooked by any *linga* wearer. Though the rule is that a member of a lower division is allowed to eat with members of higher divisions in a religious house when a Jangam is present, this privilege is not granted to all classes who profess Lingayatism, but only to the higher of them. In the same way there is no objection to any *Linga*-wearing man coming into a Lingayat's house and seeing the food; but if a Musalman, or a Maratha or anyone without a *linga* sees the food it must be thrown away. This rule applies only to food in one's own house; it does not apply to food in the field or in the rest-house." The custom is peculiar to the community of Lingayats in the western region.

Abhoring Pig-eaters

"Bene-Israels eat the flesh of animals, fowl and fish, as admissible under the Levitical Law. It was this observation and the dietary laws enjoined in Leviticus that convinced David Rahabi that they were the descendants of Jews.

"The following very interesting story of their identification is current among them One day David Rahabi to test conclusively whether the ancestors of the Bene-Israels were the descendants of Jews, bought different sorts of fish in the market and gave them to his hostess. The house-wife, who was a very simple woman, was greatly astonished to find that the learned Rabbi had brought some kinds which they were forbidden to eat, but considered that there was some mistake on his part. She selected only such as had fins and scales and threw away the rest. The Rabbi on seeing this was convinced that those among whom he lived were the descendants of Jews. This test, it will be seen, was necessary to differentiate them from the Muhammadans who like them circumcised their male children.

"Among four-footed animal they eat only such as chew the cud and have divided hoofs. They so abhor swine's flesh that "pig-eater" (*suvar khau*) is their grossest term of abuse. Of birds the rule is that only those may be eaten which do not hold their prey in their feet, and of fish, only those with fins and scales. They drink liquor, both country and European.

"No man can be admitted as a member of the Bene-Israel community without being circumcised. Before a man (or woman), who has been put out of caste, is again received, the back is stripped bare, he is seated on a plate filled with cold water and the priest gives him thirty-nine gentle lashes with a twisted handkerchief or *korda,*" adds Mr. Enthoven. The customs are pertinent to the Bene-Israel community.

Eating Rats, Snakes and Lizards

About the eating habits of the Khonds, Mr. R.V. Russell and Hiralal write, "The Khonds will admit into the community a male orphan child of any superior caste, including the Binjhwars and Gonds. A virgin of any age of one of these castes will also be admitted. A Gond man who takes a Khond girl to wife can become a Khond by giving a feast. As might be expected the tribe are closely connected with the Gaurs or Uriya shepherds, whose business leads them to frequent the forests. Either a man or woman of the Gaurs can be taken into the community on marrying a Khond, and if a Khond girl marries a Gaur her children, though not herself, can become members of that caste. The Khonds will eat all kinds of animals, including rats, snakes and lizards, but with the exception of the Kutia Khonds they have now given up beef. In Kalahandi social delinquencies are punished by a fine of so many field-mice, which the Khond considers a great delicacy. Catching of twenty to forty field-mice to liquidate the fine imposes on the culprit a large amount of trouble and labour, and when his task is completed his friends and neighbours fry the mice and have a feast with plenty of liquor, but he himself is not allowed to participate. Khond women are profusely tattooed with figures of trees, flowers, fishes, crocodiles, lizards and scorpions on the calf of the leg and the arms, hands and chest, but seldom on the face. This is done for purposes of ornament. Husband and wife do not mention each other's names, and a woman may not speak the names of any of her husband's younger brothers, as, if left a widow, she might subsequently have to marry one of them. A paternal or maternal aunt may not name her nephew, nor a man his younger brother's wife."

Women Eating to Become Witch

"The every-day food of a well-to-do Gujarat Bhil is rice cooked with salt and mixed with butter-milk, and of an ordinary Bhil, Indian corn and butter-milk boiled with chillies, and sometimes split peas or beans and grain mixed with vegetables. Except the ass, horse, camel, rat, snake and monkey, the Gujarat Bhil objects to no form of flesh, eating animals he has found dead as well as those he has killed. As there is a belief among them that if women eat or even cook a cock or hen they will become witches, they will not let a fowl be cooked in the house or even in one of the household vessels. The men eat and cook them at their spirit yard or *devasthan*. They are extremely fond of toddy and liquor.

"The every-day food of the civilized sections of the Khandesh Bhils is millet bread, curry, curds, vegetables, fish, and when they can afford it, goat's flesh or mutton. The wilder sections of the tribe eat carrion, animals that have died a natural death, cows, buffaloes, rats, jackals and monkeys. They feed on wild roots and fruits and on all sorts of vermin and garbage. Like their Gujarati brethren, all Khandesh Bhils indulge in drink to excess.

"In Gujarat, from his indiscriminate fondness for flesh and his want of reverence for life, the Bhil holds a very low place among Hindus, and though his touch does not defile, his is one of the few classes from whom a high caste Gujarat Hindu will not take water. Gujarat Bhils have no objection to eat food cooked by Musalmans.

"In Khandesh, the more civilized sections of the Bhils will not eat pakki or kachchi or smoke with Mahars, Mangs, Chambhars, Mochis, Dhors or Bhangis. The latter will eat the leavings of Bhils. Marathas and Kunbis will smoke with them, but some will not use their *chchapi* (the piece of cloth through which smoke is inhaled from the chillum)."

Dirty Eaters

Dangchis or Dang Bhils, living below the Sahyadris, are the most uncivilized of all the wild tribes, stunted in body by their drunken dissolute life and dulled in mind by hardships and bitter poverty. They are very dirty feeders, eating monkeys, rats and all small vermin, not to mention cattle killed by tigers or by themselves. Even on grand occasions their dress is only a loincloth, *langoti*, and a wisp of rag round the head. They always carry materials for producing fire, flint and steel and some silk cotton in a small gourd hung round the waist by a strong thin cord. They have a very high idea of their dignity, as Rajas' kith and kin. The Konkanas and Varlis are not above helping about camp and carrying loads. But the Bhil Rajas never condescend to such work fit only for their subjects, and when they are not resting or idling, wander about with bows and arrows in search of small game such as peacocks and hares. Thoroughly unwilling to work, they do very little cultivation, and live on the share they take of the harvests of their so-called ryots, the Konkanas and Varlis. They hold the tiger sacred and worship Vaghdev.

Eater of Carrion

Khotils are chiefly found along the south face of the Satipudas and at Dhauli, Vaijapur and in many of the Chopda and Chirpur villages in Khandesh. The Tadvis and people of Savda call all Bhils Khotils. But they are a distinct class, regarded by the pure Bhil as degraded, because they indulge in carrion and do not hesitate to touch the dead body of the cow. Their common surnames are Ghania, Ghartia and Takria. Their ceremonies are very simple. The child is named by its parents or tribesmen...

"Many of the Khotils worship the tiger-god and refuse to join in a tiger hunt. They do not employ Brahman priests. They bury their dead without form or ceremony, piling a few stones to mark the grave. They are great huntsmen and very fond of liquor. They make their living by catching fish and gathering leaves, lac, honey, wild berries and other forest produce, which they barter for cash or credit," adds Mr. Enthoven.

Guzzling Liquor before Setting Out for Dacoity

The Banjaras consume all kinds of meat, including fowls and pork, and drink liquor. But the Mathuria Banjaras abstain from both flesh and liquor. Major Gunthorpe states that the Banjaras are accustomed to drink before setting out for a dacoity or robbery and, as they smoke after drinking, the remains of leaf-pipes lying about the scene of action may indicate their handiwork. They rank below the cultivating castes, and Brahmans will not take water to drink from them. When engaged in the carrying trade, they usually lived in *kuris* or hamlets attaches to such regular villages as had considerable tracts of waste land belonging to them. When the *tanda* or caravan started on its long carrying trips, the young men and some of the women went with it with the working bullocks, while the old men and the remainder of the women and children remained to tend the breeding cattle in the hamlet. In Nimar they generally rented a little land in the village to give them a footing, and paid also a carrying fee on the number of cattle present. Their spare time was constantly occupied in the manufacture of hempen twine and sacking, which was much superior to that obtainable in towns. Even in Captain Forsyth's[3] time, who wasted *Author of the Nimar Settlement Report,* (1866) the construction of railways and roads had seriously interfered with the Banjaras' calling, and they had perforce taken to agriculture. Many of them have settled in the new ryotwari villages in Nimar as Government tenants. They still grow *tilli* sesamum in preference to other crops, because this oilseed can be raised without much labour or skill, and during their former nomadic life they were accustomed to sow it on any poor strip of land which they might rent for a season. Some of them also are accustomed to leave a part of their holding untilled in memory of their former and more prosperous life. In many villages they have not yet built proper houses, but continue to live in mud huts thatched with a cement or tiled roof; this being no doubt a superstition arising from their camp life. Their houses must also be built so that the main beams do not cross, that is, the main beam of a house must never be in such a position that if projected it would cut another main beam; but the beams may be parallel. The same rule probably governed the arrangement of tents in their camps. They prefer to live at some distance from water, probably that is of a tank or river; and this seems to be a survival of a usage mentioned by the Abbe Dubois (*Hindu Manners, Customs and Ceremonies,* p. 21) : "Among other curious customs of this odious caste is one that obliges them to drink no water which is not drawn from springs or wells. The water from rivers and tanks being thus forbidden, they are obliged in case of necessity to dig a little hole by the side of a tank or river and take the water filtering through, which, by this means, is supposed to become spring water." It is possible that this rule may have had its origin in a sanitary precaution. Colonel Sleeman notes (*Report on the Badhak or Bagri Dacoits,* p. 310) that the Banjaras on their carrying trips preferred by-paths through jungles to the high roads along cultivated plains, as grass, wood and water were more the high roads, they commonly encamped as far as they could not avoid the high roads, they commonly encamped as far as they could from villages and towns, and upon the banks of rivers and streams, with the same object of obtaining a sufficient supply of grass, wood and water. Now it is well known that the decaying vegetation in these hill streams renders the water noxious and highly productive of malaria and it seems possible that the perception of this fact led the Banjaras to dig shallow wells by the sides of the streams for their drinking-water, so that the supply thus obtained might be in some degree filtered by percolation through the intervening soil and freed from its vegetable germs. The custom may have grown into a taboo, its underlying reason being unknown to the bulk of them, and is still practised, though no longer necessary when they do not travel. If this explanation is correct, it would be an interesting conclusion that the Banjaras anticipated so far as they were able the sanitary precaution by which our soldiers are supplied with portable filters when on the march," adds Colonel Sleeman.

The custom is practised by the Banjaras in the western region.

References

1. Captain Forsyth, *Nimar Settlement Report*, 1866.
2. Dubois, Abbe, J., *Hindu Manners, Customs and Ceremonies*, Oxford University Press London, Trans. Beauchamp, K. Henry, London 1906 (Third edition).
3. Risley, Sir Herbert, *Tribes and Caste of Bengal: Ethnographic Glossary*, Firma KLM Pvt. Ltd, Calcutta 1998 (reprint), originally printed Bengal Secretariat Press, Calcutta 1891.
4. Russell, R.V. and Lal, Hira, *The Tribes and Castes of the central Provinces of India*, Low Price Publications, Delhi (reprint) 1997, first published 1916.
5. Enthoven, R.E., *The Tribes and Castes of Bombay*, Low Price Publications, Delhi (reprint) 1997, originally published 1922.
6. Sleeman, Colonel, *Report on the Badhak or Bagri Dacoits*, Govt. Press.
7. Hendley, Major, *An Account of the Bhils.*
8. Asiatic Studies, Ist series.
9. Bombay Gazetteer, Vol. IX, Part I.
10. Thurston, E., *Ethnographic Notes in Southern India*, The Government Press, Madras, 1906.
11. Sherring, M.A., *The Hindu Tribes and Castes*, Vols. I and II, Thakar and Spink, Calcutta, 1872 and 1879.

Bibliography

...*Aspects of the Goan Cultural Heritage*-in Proceedings of the First International Goan convention (1988)-Academic Deliberations-pub. by G.O.A., Toronto, 1990.

...*A History of Christianity in India (from early times to St. Francis Xavier*-52 to 1542)-P.C. Manaktalas and Sons, Bombay, 1964.

—1891. Vol. XI: *The Central Provinces and Feudatories*, Part I—Report, Calcutta 1893.

—1891. Vol. XXII: *His Highness the Nizam's Dominion*, Part I—Report. Bombay 1894.

—1901. Vol. VIII: *Berar, Part I—Report*. Allahabad 1902.

—1931. Vol. XII: *Central Provinces and Berar, Part I—Report*. Nagpur 1933.

—1941. Vol. XXI: *H.E.H. the Nizam's Dominion* (Hyderabad State). Hyderabad 1945.

—1948. *The Raj Gonds of Adilabad: the aboriginal tribes of Hyderabad*, Vol. III. London.

—1951. *District Census Hand-book*, Yeotmal (Maharashtra). Bombay 1965.

—1952. *Among the Gonds of Adilabad* (second edition). Bombay.

—1952. *The Cult of Ayak among the Kolams of Hyderabad*. Wiener Bietrage zur Kulturgeschichtee und Linguistik, Vol. 9.

—1961. Vol II: *Andhra Pradesh*—the village survey monograph, Laindiguda. Delhi 1965.

Andrew D.: *British Attitude Towards India: 1784-1858*, Oxford University Press, London, 1961.

Bahadur, K.P., *Castes, Tribes and Culture of India*, Ess Ess Publication, Vol. VIII, Western Maharashtra and Gujarat, Delhi, 1981.

Bahadur, K.P., *Castes, Tribes and Cultures of India,* Vol. III, Ess Ess Publication, New Delhi, 1981.

Bains, Strathestane, *Ethnography, Castes and Tribes,* Reprint, Concept Publication, Delhi, 1976.

Ballal, K.D., *Dapada: A Village in Dadra and Nagar Haveli,* Census of India, Registrar General of India, Delhi, series I, Part VI-C; 1974.

Ballal, K.D., *Socio-economic Profile of Dadra and Nagar Haveli,* Census of India, New Delhi, series-1, Monograph NV 2: 1974.

Ballhatchet, K. : *Social Policy and Social Change in Western India,* Oxford, London, 1957.

Banerjee, A.C.: *Peshwa Madhavrao*, Veenit Pub., Calcutta, 1968.

Bhatia, R.C., *On Perpetuating the Original Sin Religious conversions of Adivasis* in Ex-Portuguese pockets, AARSI Publication, Moti Daman, Daman: 1986.

Bhattacharjee, J.N., *Hindu Caste and Sects,* Edition India, Part X, A&B Series-2, Calcutta, 1968.

Bhattacharya, S. 1961. Naiki of Chanda. *Indo-Iranian Journal,* Vol. V:2.

Bhattacharyya: *British Residents at Poona*, Veenit Pub., Calcutta, 1984.

Bhawe, V.L.: *Maharashtra Saraswat*, Popular Prakashan, Bombay, 1982.

Bhobe, Gopalakrishna–*Kalatma Gomantak*–Goa Kala Akademi, Panjim–Goa, 1972.

Braganza, Alfred–*The Discovery of Goa*–Brooks Publications, Bombay, 1964.

Briggi, W.G., *The Chamars*, Reprint, B.R. Publications, Delhi: 1920.

Brown, C. and Russel, R.V. 1908. *Central Provinces District Gazetteers, Yeotmal District*, Vol. A. Calcutta.

Burakdar, M.P. 1947. *The Clan Organisation of the Gonds*. Man in India, Vol. XXVII: 2.

C.A.P., *The Gazetteers of Orissa and the Feudatory States,* Part I, Vol. XXII, 1910.

Cabrale Sa, Mario (ed.) *Winds of Change*, Commemorative volume of Silver Jubilee of Liberation of Goa, Daman and Diu, Department of Information, Govt. of Goa, Daman and Diu, Panaji, 1987.

Campbel, James M., *Hindu Castes and Tribes of Gujarat*, Vintage Books, Gurgaon, Haryana, Vol I and II: 1988.

Census of India 1891. Vol. VI: *Berar of Hyderabad Assigned Districts*. Calcutta 1892.

Census of India 1971, *General economic, social and cultural tables*, Series-27, Part III, A and B and part IV-A, Delhi, 1974.

Census of India, 1991, *Final Population Totals,* paper 3 of 1991, India, Series-I, Controller of Publications, Delhi, 1993.

Census of India, *District Census Hand Book,* Series 29, Goa, Daman and Diu, Vol. XIII, part A&B, Panaji, 1981.

Census of India, *Final Population Totals,* paper 3 of 1991, India Series I, Controller of Publication, Delhi, 1993.

Census of India, *Goa, Daman and Diu,* Registrar General of India, Panaji, 1971.

Census of India, *Provisional Population Totals*, Paper I of 1991. Series 6. Goa, 1991.

Census of India, *Socio-economic Survey of Ponda*, Monograph No. 2, Vol. II, Part IV, 1961, Census of India, Delhi, 1961.

Census of India, *Socio-economic Survey of Village of Goa*: Part IV, Census of India, Delhi, 1961.

Chanda, Sudhendu, *Nature of Changes in the Goan Society: A Preliminary Observation* in *Acculturation and Social Change*, A.K. Danda (ed.) Anthropological Survey of India, Calcutta, 1989.

Chavda, Vijay Singh: Modern Gujarat, New Order Book Company, Ahmedabad, 1982.

Chib, S.S., *The Beautiful India, Union Territories of India,* Light and Life Publications, Delhi, 1977.

Cottineau-de-Klequeen, D.H., *History of Goa,* Bombay, 1910.

Crooke, W., *Tribes and Castes of North Western Province and Oudh,* Vol. I, II and IV, 1896, Calcutta, The Government Press; Reprint, *The Tribes and Castes of the North Western India,* Vol. I, II and III, 1975, Cosmo Publications, Delhi.

Crooke, William, *The Tribes and Castes of North Western India*, Vol. I, Cosmo Publications, Reprint 1974, Delhi.

Dalton, E.T. 1872. *Descriptive Ethnology of Bengal.* Calcutta (reprinted in 1960).

Das, A.K., Roychoudhary and M.K. Raha, *Handbook of SC and ST of West Bengal,* Director of Tribal Welfare Department, Calcutta, 1966.

Davidar, David, *Paradise Lost* in The Sunday Weekly, 16-22 April, Calcutta, 1989.

De Souza, Teotonio, R. Enthoven, R.E. *Medieval Goa* (A Socio-economic History), Concept Publishing Company, New Delhi, 1979.

Department of Planning and Statistics, *Indicators of Socio-Economic Development,* Daman, 1987.

Desai, Neera: *Social change in Gujarat*, Vora and Co., Bombay, 1978.

Dessai, S.S., *States of Union; Goa, Daman and Diu, Dadra and Nagar Haveli,* Delhi, 1976.

Dey, S.K.: *Community Development: A Bird's Eye-view*, Asia Publishing House, Bombay, 1962.

Dhume, Ananta R.S.–*Gomantakacya Vasahatici Rupresa*–(Sketch of settlements in Goa)–in Gomatakaci Pratima (Image of Goa)–Vol.I–Shree Saraswati Mandir, Panjim–Goa, 1976.

Doshi, J.K.: *Social Structure and Cultural Change in a Bhil Village*, Kishor Pub., Delhi, 1991.

Dube, S.C.: *India's Changing Villages*, Routledge and Kegan Paul, London, 1958.

Dumont Louis: *Home Hierarchicus: the Caste System and its Implications*, Vikas Publishing House, Delhi, 1970.

Eckehard Kulke: *The Parsees in India: A Minority as Agent of Social Change*, Welforum Verlage, Munche, 1974.

Elliot, H.M. 1869, *The Races of North-West Provinces of India*, Vol. I. London.

Ensminger, Douglas: *Community Development: Aims and Methods Marathi version, Gargoti*, Mauni Vidyapeeth, Kolhapur, 1959.

Enthoven, R.E., *The Tribes and Castes of Bombay,* Vol. I to IV, 1920-1922, The Government Central Press; Reprint, Vol. I to IV, 1975, Cosmo Publications, Delhi.

Enthoven, R.E., *Tribes and Castes of Bombay,* Vol. I: 1920, Vol. III, 1922, Bombay, The Government Central Press, Reprint, I and III, 1975, Cosmo Publications, Delhi.

Enthoven, R.E., *The Tribes and Castes of Bombay,* Vol. 1, 1920, II and III, 1922, Bombay, The Government Central Press. Reprint I and III, 1975, Cosmo Publications, Delhi.

Fthoven, R.E.: *The Tribes and Castes of Bombay*, Popular Prakshan, Bombay, 1920.

Faquir Chand, *Socio Economic Development of Dadra and Nagar Haveli Since Its Liberation* (1987-88). Administration of Dadra and Nagar Haveli, Statistical Wing, Silvasa: 1987.

Farquhar J.N.: *Modern Religious Movements in India*, Munshiram Manoharlal, New Delhi, 1967.

Fonseca, Jose Nicolauda, *An Historical and Archaeological Sketch of the city of Goa*. Thacker and Company Limited. Bombay 1978, Reprint 1986, Asian Educational Services, New Delhi.

Fiirer-Haimendorf, C.V. 1941. *Tribal Population of Hyderabad: Yesterday and To-day*. Hyderabad (reprinted from the Census of India 1941, Vol. XXI).

Fiirer-Haimendorf, C.V. 1945. *Tribal Hyderabad*. Hyderabad, the Revenue Department, Government of H.E.H., the Nizam.

Gandhi, S.K. *Census of India, Series* 29, Goa, Daman and Diu, Part XIII A and B, 1981.

Gandhi, S.K. *Goa, Daman and Diu-A Portrait of Population*, Census of India, 1971.

Gandhi, S.K., *Census of India 1971,* Series-28 part (X-A) and (X-B) page III, Directorate of Census Operation, Goa, Daman, Diu, Dadra and Nagar Haveli, 1972.

Gazetteer of Baroda State *General Information,* Times Press, Bombay, Vol. I, 1923.

Gazetteer of India, Goa, Daman and Diu, Part II and III, pp. 18, Panaji, 1979.

Gazetteer of India, Gujarat State, *Junagadh District* Registrar General, Delhi, 1975.

Gazetteer of the Bombay Presidency, *Gujarat Population, Muslims and Parsees,* Govt. Central Press, Bombay, Vol. IX, part II, 1899.

Gomes, Olivinho J.F.–*Village Goa–study of Goan social structure and change*, S.Chand and Co., New Delhi–1987–2nd ed. 1996.

Grant Duff: *A History of the Marathas*, Oxford, 1921.

Grigson, W.V. 1944. *The Aboriginal Problems in the Central Provinces and Berar*. Nagpur.

Guha, J.P.: *James Grant Duff: History of the Marathas*, APH, New Delhi, 1971.

Gune, V.T. *Gazetteer of the Union Territory: Goa, Daman and Diu*, Part I Goa Gazetteer Deptt: Govt. of Goa, Daman and Diu, Panaji, 1979.

Gune, V.T.-(ed.) *Gazetteer of the Union Territory-Goa, Daman and Diu-District GOA Part-I, Panjim, Goa*, 1979.

Gune, V.T., *Gazetteer of Union Territory of Goa, Daman and Diu,* Part II and III. Daman and Diu, Panaji, Goa, 1979.

Gustav, Oppert. *On the Original Inhabitants of Bharatvarsha or India*, 1893. Madras, Reprint, 1972. Oriental Publishers, Delhi.

Hislop, S. 1866. *Papers relating to the Aboriginal Tribes of the Central Provinces* (*ed.* R. Temple). Nagpur.

Hussain, S.K.M. 1949. *Social services and tribal welfare in Hyderabad*, Hyderabad.

Hutton, J.H., *Castes of India,* Oxford University Press, Oxford, (reprint) 1969.

Imperial Gazetteer *of India Codapoor to Edwardesabad*, Today and Tomorrow's Publishers, New Delhi, Vol. IX: 1908.

Imperial Gazetteer of India, *Condapoor to Edwardesabad,* Clarendon Press, Vol. XI, Oxford, 1908.

Kakodkar, Archana "Shuddhi: Reconversion to Hinduism", published in *Goa: Cultural trends*, P.P. Shirodkar (ed.) Directorate of Archives, Archaeology, and Museum, Panaji, 1986.

Kales, D.N., *Agri: A Socio-Economic Survey*, Asia Publishing House, Bombay: 1952.

Karaka, D.F., *History of the Parsi*, Discovery Publishers, Delhi, Vol. I and II: 1986.

Karve, I.: *Hindu Society An Interpretation*, Luxmi Pub., Poona, 1961.

Kaye, Sir John William: *Selections from the Papers of Lord Metcalf*, London, 1855.

Khera, S.S.: *District Administration in India*, Asia Publishing House, Bombay, 1964.

Kincaid, C.A. and Parasnis, D.B.: *A History of the Maratha People*, Delhi, 1968.

Kulkarni, M.G.: *Problems of Tribal Development: A Case Study of Harsul Block*, Gokhale Institute of Politics and Economics, Poona, 1967.

Lyall, A. (*ed.*) 1870. *Gazetteer for the Hyderabad Assigned Districts* (*Berar*).

Malbari, Behramji M.: *Infant Marriage and Enforced Widowhood*, Popular Prakashan, Bombay, 1887.

Malgaonkar, Manohar *Inside Goa*, Directorate of Information and Publicity, Govt. of Goa, Daman and Diu, Panaji, 1982.

Malhotra, K.C. "Population Structure among the Dhangar Caste Cluster of Maharashtra, India" *The People of South Asia*, (ed.)., Lukaes, J.R., New York, Plenum press, 1984.

Malik, S.C.: *Dissent Protest and Reform in Indian Civilisation,* Indian Institute of Advanced Study, Shimla, 1977.

Malley O', L.S.S.: *Modern India and the West.* Oxford University Press, London, 1968.

Menezes, Antonie De, "Daman and Diu, Union Territory", *Herald Magazine,* Panaji, Goa, 1987.

Misra, B.B.: *The Indian Middle Classes: Their Growth in Modern Times*, Oxford University Press, London, 1961.

Moraes, George M., *Pre-Portuguese Culture of Goa*-in Proceedings of the First International Goan Convention (1988)-Academic Deliberations-pub. by G.O.A., Toronto, Canada-1990.

Mukherji, B.: *Community Development in India,* Orient Longmans, Calcutta, 1961.

Murdeshwar, B.G.: *Slavery Under the Peshwas* Bombay, 1987. Oke, Pramila: *Maha Vidarbha*, Akola Matrubhumi Prakashan, Bombay, 1948.

Nanekar, K.R. 1968. Land reforms in Vidarbha: an inquiry into the implementation of land reforms in the Vidarbha Region. Calcutta.

Natarajan, S.: A Century of Social Reform Movement, Asia Publishing House, Bombay: 1954.

Parmar, Y.A., *The Mahyawanshi: The Success Story of a Scheduled Caste,* Mittal Publications, Delhi, 1987.

Pereira, Gerald, *An Outline of the Pre-Portuguese History of Goa*-Vasco da Gama, Goa, 1973.

Priolkar, A.K. *The Goa Inquisition*, University of Bombay, 1961.

Priolkar, A.K.—The Goa Inquisition—Pub. By Author—Bombay, 1961.

Rajendran, S., *A Portrait of Population,* Census of India, 1981, Directorate of Census Population, Daman and Diu, Controller of Publication, Delhi, 1988.

Rajendran, S., *Census of India, 1981*, part III, Series-27, Dadra and Nagar Haveli, Directorate of Census Operation, Panaji, p. 150, 1988.

Rao, R.P., *Portuguese rule in Goa* (1510-1961), Asia Publishing House, Delhi, 1963.

Rose, H.A., *Glossary of the Tribes and Castes of the Punjab and North West Frontier Provinces,* Vol. II, 1919, Lahore, Punjab Government; Reprint, Vol. II, 1980, Amar Prakashan, Delhi.

Roy Shibni and S.H.M. Rizvi., *Dhodia Identity*, B.R. Publication, Delhi: 1985.

Roy, Shibani, *Koli Culture,* Cosmo Publications, New Delhi, 1983.

Russel, R.V. and Hiralal 1916. *The Tribes and Castes of the Central Provinces of India*, Vol. III. London.

Russel, R.V. and Rai Bahadur Hira Lal, *Castes and Tribes of Central Provinces of India*, Vol. II, 1916, London: Macmillan and Company; Reprint II, 1975, Cosmo Publications, Delhi.

Russel, R.V. and Hiralal, *The Tribes and Castes of Central Provinces of India,* Vol. II, 1916, Macmillan and Co. London. Reprint 1975, Cosmo Publications, Delhi.

Russell, R.V., and Rai Bahadur Hiralal, *The Tribes and Castes of Central Provinces.* Vol. I, III and IV, 1916, London, Macmillan and Company; Reprint, Vol., I, III and IV, 1975, Cosmo Publications, Delhi.

Sahay, K.N., *Christianity and Culture Change,* Inter-India Publication, New Delhi, 1986.

Saldanha, C.F., *A Short History of Goa*-Imprensa Nacional-Nova Goa-1957.

Saldanha, M.J. Gabriel-*Historia de Goa*-2 vols. Nova Goa-1925 and 1926.

Sane, K.J., *The Varli*, Padma Publications Limited, Bombay: 1945.

Satoskar, B.D., *Gomantak-Prakriti and Sanskruti*-(Goa-nature and Culture)-Vol. I, *Samaj Rachana ani Samaj Jivan* (Social Structure and Social Life)-Shubada Saraswat, Pune, 1979.

Shah, P.G., *The Dubla of Gujarat,* Bharatiya Adim Jati Sevak Samaj, Delhi, 1958.

Shah, P.G., *The Tribal Life in Gujarat,* Gujarat Research Society, Bombay, 1964.

Sherring, M.A., *Hindu Tribes and Castes*, Vol. II, 1979, Calcutta, Thapar Spinks and Co: Reprint, Cosmo Publications, Delhi, Vol. II: 1974.

Sherring, M.A., *The Hindu Tribes and Castes,* Vol. I and II, 1872 and 1879, Calcutta, Thakar Spinks and Co.; Reprint, Vol. I and II, 1974, Cosmo Publications, Delhi.

Shrinivas, M.N.: *Social Change in Modern India*, Allied Publishers, Bombay, 1966.

Singer, Milton: *When a Great Tradition Modernizes*, Vikas Publishing House, Delhi, 1972.

Singh, Yogendra: *Modernization of Indian Tradition*, Thomson Press, Faridabad, 1977.

Sinha, N.K., "Funeral Rites among the Fishfolk of Diu", *Indian Anthropologist,* Vol. X, No. 9, Delhi, 1977.

The Goa League *Report of the New Administration of the conditions in Nagar Haveli and Dadra before and after the Liberation from Portuguese Colonialism*, Independent Publishing Company, London: 1975.

The Tribes and Castes of Bombay, Vol. I, 1920, II and III, 1922, Bombay, The Government Central Press. Reprint I and III, 1975. Cosmo Publications, Delhi.

Thornton, D.M., *Parsi, Jain and Sikh: Some Minor Religious Sections in India*, Mittal Publications, Delhi: 1987.

Thurston, E., *Castes and Tribes of Southern India,* Vol. V, 1909, Madras, The Government Press; Reprint, Vol. V, 1975, Cosmo Publications, Delhi.

Thurston, E., *Castes and Tribes of Southern India*, Vol. I: 1909, Government Press, Reprint, Vol. I, 1975, Cosmo Publications, Delhi.

Toothi, N.A.: *The Vaishnavas of Gujarat*, Asia Pub., Bombay, 1935.

Trivedi, R.K., *Siddi: A Negroid Tribe of Gujarat,* Census of India 1961, Ethnographic Series, Gujarat, Vol. V, Part V-B. No. 1, Delhi.

Wilberforce, Bell H.: *The History of Gujarat*, MacMillan, London, 1916.

Wilson, John, *Indian Castes*, Vol. II. 1877. Times of India Office, Bombay. Reprint, 1985, K.K. Book Distributors, Delhi.

Wilson, John: *History of the Suppression of Infanticide in Western India*, Rawat Pub., Jaipur, 1998.

Index

H

T

CUSTOMS OF INDIA

CUSTOMS OF INDIA

(In Six Volumes)

Volume 4

Northern: Chandigarh, Delhi, Haryana, Himachal Pradesh, Jammu & Kashmir, Punjab and Rajasthan

Editor

Gopal Bhargava

ISHA

Customs of India

ISBN: 978-81-8205-524-7 (Set)
ISBN: 978-81-8205-528-5 (Vol. 4)

Published in 2012 in India by
Isha Books
B-69, New Gupta Colony
New DDA Market
Delhi - 110009

Laser Type Setting : Quick Media, Delhi
Printed at : G. Print Process, Delhi

Contents

List of Illustrations

Preface

This scientifically researched work on customs of Madhya Pradesh, Uttar Pradesh, Chhattisgarh and Uttarakhand is a vast treasure-trove of information on individual tribes and castes and their customs, rites, rituals and ceremonies etc. Each volume contains an introduction on the customs, characteristics of people of all the states concerned, also taking stock of the probable origin of customs. Besides, the work contains seven chapters including: *Conceiving and birth, Puberty, Betrothal, Marriage ceremony, Death rituals: Cremation, Death rituals: Burial, and social customs.* The book describes at length the ancient forms of customs, rites, rituals and usages as recorded by numerous British and Indian ethnographers, gazetteer writers, surveryors of the settlement reports the monograph writers and anthropologist etc. Following Independence in 1947, the entire scenario of social, economic life, customs, rites, rituals and culture belonging to both castes and tribes in the central states of India have been in a constant transition. The region has been impinged upon by pan-Indian and global influences and factors. All the recent changes in the rites and rituals have also been incorporated in this work.

The entire mass of information and knowledge has been painstakingly researched, written and edited with the anthropological point of view that makes this works all the more valuable for purpose of scholars, researchers teachers and students in different discipline.

Every detail of the information collected, collated and formatted has gone through meticulous validation checks and rechecks. In live with the constant evolution of the text, this work, too, will have to be updated and improved in the successive editions. In a country as vast and complex as India, there will always be a scope for improving this work through suggestions, deletions and additions pointed out for rectification. We invite the beneficiaries of this work to participate thus in its evolution.

In this work are incorporated, the collected, collated, formatted and validated informations on customs of India on a 'best and sincere effort' basis for presentation in single comprehensive work. This work, however, is not deemed to be advisory for research, analysis or investment planning, or in general professional advice. The reader, thus, should seek services of qualified professional for such advice. The mass of information provided in volume is to be taken as a 'first information service'. The reader should make his own investigation on any given point of information about the rite, ritual or custom prior to making any investment related decision. The author, editor or the publisher do not take the responsibility for any loss, if any, incurred as a result of investment planning or any other specific·project made by the reader on basis of the information provided in this work.

In the end, we acknowledge our indebtedness and express gratitude to the researchers, administrator-cum-academicians, scholars, Publication Division (Government of India), various state information departments, Union Ministry of Culture, census commissioners, authors of the settlement reports, various ethnographers, Anthropological Survey of India, state editors of Gazetteers and others. We studied a large number of published works, and drew from them. The credit for producing and furnishing first hand survey reports and other data goes, infact, to them. We merely reshaped and reformulated contents of the surveys and reports produced by them.

Editor

Introduction

This volume contains the customs of north Indian States and Union Territories including Chandigarh, Delhi, Haryana, Himachal Pradesh, Jammu & Kashmir, Punjab and Rajasthan. The northern region has been the most progressive, forward-looking and pro-development in the spheres of economy, education, culture, industry, agriculture etc. Delhi being the seat of political power had been on the forefront of the cultural changes also followed closely by Punjab, Haryana and Himachal Pradesh. The total population of Delhi on March 1, 2001 stood at 13,782,976 as per the provisional results of the Census of India 2001. In terms of population, it holds the top position among all the Union Territories and ranked 18th among all States and Union Territories in the country. The density of population in Delhi (9,294) is also the highest among all states and Union Territories. Its population sharply rose by 46.31% during the decade 1991-2001. Men-women ratio in Delhi has further widened when compared to 1991 Census. The sex ratio (i.e., the number of females per thousand males) of population was recorded as 821, which has declined from 827 in the previous census. Total literacy of Delhi rose to 81.82% from 75.29% in 1991.

Even though the Hindus are in the majority numbering, almost 85%, India does not impose any official religion on its people. Through the ages, though Delhi has accepted, adapted and moulded itself to everything from Islam, rather from the Aryan culture to Christianity. She adapted herself with the changing faces of history. The country got destroyed many times, but it has retained the culture, heritage, religion and the tradition of its time for the generations to come.

While visiting architecturally magnificent spiritual places, it require a set of age old etiquettes to be followed. Taking off shoes and other leather articles and even covering the head and body in the sanctum sanctora might be mandatory at many places. One should avoid hugging and holding hands at these places people take a break from the hurried life during the ancient fairs and festivals like *phoolwalo-ki-sair* which are still organised in traditional way.

The capital of India, Delhi reflects the cultural diversity and religious unity of India. It is difficult to define the culture and religion of Delhi. As there is a continuous inflow of people in the capital city from all parts of India, the cultural diversity is very prominent. Being an ancient city, Delhi has the shadows of its past. It is said that though Delhi is losing its charm, but still the glory of the past looms large over its life-style. Delhi might be changing in culture and customs with time, it has always done so, but it has never shelved the past. Ranging from discos for youngsters to swing their body throughout the night, there are *Quwallies* at the Nizamuddin Shrine which float in the air and the silence of the night is broken by the *Prabhat ferries* and the singing of *Gurbani* (the verses from the *Granth Sahaib*), the bells in the temples still tell about God being everywhere, the Sunday masses in Churches continue to attract the otherwise busy residents of India. Delhi shares its borders with Haryana, Rajasthan, Uttar Pradesh and Punjab, which influence the life-styles and language of the local people. Migrations from various parts of India have led to pockets of many diverse cultural streams coming together in various parts of Delhi. For example, R.K. Puram has a concentration of South Indians, while C.R. Park has a concentration of Bengalies. Jama Masjid of the Walled City is an excellent example of Indo-Persian architecture, whereas the Birla Temple and the Chattarpur Temple complex are considered as a blend of the North and South Indian architectural styles. Gurudwaras Raquab Ganj, Sheesh Ganj and Bangla Sahib stand tall for Sikhism, whereas St. Thomas and St. Columbus toll their bells for Christians. The Bahai Lotus temple has introduced the Bahai way of worship in Delhi. Not to forget the ancient religions of Jainism and Buddhism whose genesis is in India. The Buddhist monastery near the Interstate bus terminus is the hub of Buddhist culture in the capital city.

Custom of Jammu & Kashmir

The state of Jammu & Kashmir comprises almost all the major religions of India including Hinduism, Buddhism, Jainism, Christianity, Islam and Sikhism. A study of communities the state shows the predominance of Islam followed by Hinduism, Buddhism, Christianity, Jainism and Sikhism.

The Hindus has their bastion in Jammu region whereas Buddhism is confined to Ladakh, Jainism also has been confined to Jammu except a few families which have migrated to Kashmir in connection whith their business. Christianity exists in Jammu and Kadakh regions. Sikhsism is confined to Jammu though a sizeable number of Kashmiri Sikhs and around Baramula district of Kashmir. There Sikhs are not different from their brethren living in Punch district of Jammu region. Islam as a common faith is present in all three regions though with a varying numerical strength. Th Muslims in Jammu region are mostly the converted Rajputs, the nocadic Gujjars and those Kashmiris who have migrated to Jammu region and populace the region adjacent to Doda district. The size of Muslim population saw a considerable change after the formation of Pakistan and the subsequent forced and illegal dismemberment of the region. That was certainly the beginning of undermining the secular character of the state of Jammu & Kashmir which had earned a name for mutual coexistence, tolerance and of various faiths stressed by the Rishi and Sufi traditions. Once this binding force got weakened, which had bound the state into a single politico-cultural entity during the past five centuries, the three regions started drifting wide apart in different directions. The only way to stem this chasm is to strengthen the glorious tradition of securarism in ths state. Political opportunism has caused a havoc with the secular fabric of the state. The Common masses belonging is different religions of the state are still willing to live as brothers but they are not allowed to have their own natural way of living by the forces alien to the traditional politicocultural fabric of the Jammu and Kashmir

The Hincu sects present in Jammu region are Arya Samaj, Shaivites and Vaishnoists, Shwetamber and Pitamber and Pitamber among the Jains, Wahhabi and Hanafi among the Muslim. Most of the Christians People belong toe the Protestant Church though Roman Catholics also exist in certain regious. Coming to the Kashmir scenario the Hindu population of the Valley is a solid entity which follows a blend of both Shaivism and Vaishnavism and do not show any sect demarcations or acrimony but the followers of Islam are divided into three visible sects, like the Sunni, the Wahhabi and the Shia (Ethna-e-Ashri). The Buddhists in Kadakh are the Followers of Gelukpa and Drukpa sects which are of Mahayani order.

Meanwhile, it is to be noted that the Afghans came to the Valley of Kashmir 200 to 250 years ago. A siqeable number of them came to India before and during the Mughal rule, and entered Kahmir Territary during the time of Ahmad shah Durrani, around AD 1753. They belong to various clans and had settled in different parts of the Valley. The prominent Afghan cland of the present day Kashmir are Yousufzai, Khankhal, Afridi, Swati, Malik, Durrani and Qais. They are popularly called as Khans by the local peo;e in Kahmir, but they prefer to be known as Pakhtoons. Over a period of time various batches of immigrant Afghans settled in the upper reaches of the Valley of Kashmir with a view to occupy the virgin lands with abundance of natural spring water. Now the afghan settlements have grown in size and have become full-fledged state subjects since 1947. The Afghans, especially in rural areas, still maintain their indigenous identity. The Afghans initially came to Kashmir during the time of Ahmad shah Durrani, and thereafter in batches due to the inter-tribal feuds in their homeland creating insecure conditions. Later on it was Maharaja Gulab Singh, the ruler of Kashmir, who offered them employment opportunities, especially, for guarding the frontiers and, granted them agricultured land and *jagirs* and allowed them to settle in colonies of their choice.The Afghans are stated to have entered Kashmir via Baramula, where they camped for quite some time. Some batches moved to the the west Baramula and settled in Uri. Other Afghans moved moved upwards in the north-west to south-east of Kashmir in search of suitable green pastures and arable land. This is how they came to Pattan, Ganderabal (Gutlibagh), Mattan, and other places in the valley.

However, the Kashmiri Afghans claim Aryan ancestry though there is no consensus among historians of their ethnic origin. Some consider them to be of Israeli origin while others consider them of TurkoIranian stock. Though ethnographic and historical accounts about the Afghans in general exist in abundance, the historical account about their migration to Kashmir is Sacauty. The Afghans of the Valley perceive their concentration mostly in the settlements at the local level though they are aware of the afghan population is other parts of India as well. The Afghans in Kashmir live in cold hilly terrains and plateaus with abundance of forests and lwo humidity in the Sno cled, inhospitable terrain, the state Government extended aid to the rural huseless or landless and to assist them to raise husts and tenements on the same Integrated housing scheme have been taken up for industrial emplowyees, housing boards and cooperatives of industrial workers of economically weaker sections of the society run on contingency basis. The housing scheme has evoked a good response and more employees are being beenifitted by it. Under the low income group housing sscheme advances for construction of houses are made to government employees as well as to private citizens. For the middle-income group the scheme was started in 1959-60. Under this scheme too, loans are provided for construction of houses. Maximum demand for loand is made by this category. Education also has always been accorded a high priority in the state. The On the development front state is making swift strides The people appear better fed and dressed than what they appeared twenty-five years ago. High rise structures have sprung up in the city of Srinagar and Jammu. Laddakh also has caught up with the trends of development sweeping the state. Kargil, a sleeping township, has emerged as a bustling tourist spot with the opening of more and more areas to the Indian and foreign topurists, The oil boom in the Middle East has absorbed many Muslim Kashmiri artisans and medical experts generating a good income for the state in the form of foreign exchange on the one hand and giving a boost to Kashmiri fruits and handicrafts on the other.

Customs of Punjab

The state of Punjab was reorganized on November 1, 1966. The twelve districts are Gurdaspur, Amritsar, Ferozepur, Ludhiana, Jalandhar, Kapurthala, Hoshiarpur, Rupnagar, Patiala, Sangrur, Bhatinda, and Faridkot with a total area of 50,372sq.km. The state economy is mainly egriculture based followed by the modern industry and small cottage industry. The Scheduled Castes constitute 26.87percent of the total population of the state. There is no Scheduled Tribe in the state of Punja. The literacy rate is 41.28 per cent. The women (33.70 per cent) are less educated than men (35.21per cent).

In the history of Punjab, the most important event which took place in the medieval Times was the emergence of Guru Nanak Dev, a contemporary of Babar.The faith Sikhism, he preached, was a synthesis of Hinduism and Islam, but more than that Guru Nanak Dev was a reforemer par excellance. He protested against many practices of the predominant Hindu society and the arrogant and aggressive behaviour of the ruling Muslims. Guru Nanak Dev would think of himself as neither Hindu nor Muslim, but as an enlightend member of humanity proclaiming without fear the oneness of all mankind. This humanistic approach to the solution of all the prevalent social ills led Guru Nanak to forge and develop altogether a new system of human values and faith that stressed the oneness of man; that men of all beliefs and religions are brothers born of the same source and created by the Supreme Creator. Guru Nanak visualized and proponded a Utopia. He merged the concept of a welfare state with religion, raised his voice against caste discrimination and disagreed with the Muslims, who thought that the non-believers were inferior infidels. The caste hierarchy in Hindu society of which the Brahmans. And the superior (conformist) and inferior (nonconformist) dichotomy as imposed by the Muslim rulers were repugnant to him. Thus, Guru Nanak Dev is the most important landmark in the history of the recent religions in the history of world religions.

The Guru Nanak Dev chief propounder of Bhakti movement in Punjab was the founder of Sikhism. He preached the theory of *samsarg*- of birth, death and rebirth in a cyclic manner. God is the cause of all creations and sets this world and the life within in motion. Human beings being oblivious of death indulge in sensual pleasure, but the virtuous ones abstain from indulging in worldly pleasures; they seek and find Truth. To him God was a spiritual concept-if God is the ultimate Truth, to speak untruth is to be ungodly. Guru Nanak Dev established the institution of Sikh 'Guru'. Without a guru, he stressed, no one can attain moksha (salvation). The Guru guides his followers to the path of Truth. He disciplines the disciples as a rogue elephant is disciplined from running amok; he applies the jyan anjan (salve of knowledge) to a follower's eyes enabling him to see the Truth (God); He is the divine ferryman, who takes them across the bhav sagar (ocean of life) Guru Nanakinsisted on the separation of God and Guru; Guru is to be consulted, respected and cherished, but not to be worshipped. He is a teacher, but no incarnation of God. Asceticism, penance or torturing one's body as a step towards enlightenment was anathema to him. 'Be in the world but not wordly', he said. Human birth, he explained, is a priceless gift, an opportunity that God offers to humans to escape the cycle of birth, death and birth. The aim of life is yoga, the union with God.

In the Sikh Guru's lineage, Guru Nanak Dev was followed by Guru Angad, Guru Amar Das, Guru Ram Das, Guru Arjan Dev, Guru Tegh Bahadur and Guru Gobind Singh. Each of the succeeding Gurus added his own reflections, ideologies and thoughts in *Shree Guru Granth Sahib*, the Holy Sikh scripture, compiled by the fifth Guru, Shri Guru Arjan Dev. The Holy scripture contains hymns composed by Hindu and Muslim saints as well as the contributions by various Gurus. The tenth Guru, Guru Gobind Singh laid the foundation of the Khalsa (the pure) on 1April 1699at Anandpur Sahib and gave Sikhs their identity, and a family name, Singh (lion). Anandpur Sahib is also known as the Keshgarh Sahib because it was here that the Sikhs were told by Guru Gobind Singh to keep their *kesh* (hair), alongwith the other four identification markers. Later, Guru Gobind Singh discontinued the custom of a nointing, the newt Guru after him.

Another illustrious personage of Punjab, Maharaja Ranjit Singh (A.D.1780 to 1839) extended his kingdom from Satluj to Khyber Pass and from Kashmir to Sind. The kingdom of Maharaja Ranjit Singh was annexed by the British. In the colonial period the landlords of Punjab benefited from the canal system introduced by the British. The Sikhs, a martial race were also recruited in the British army. However, the Sikhs had to suffer a lot during the partition of the Punjab in 1947. Their high spirits and hard work have enabled the Sikhs of the Pujab to one again establish themselves and became prosperous.

Punjab is said to have derived its name from the five rivers that flow through the state: The Indus, the Sutlej, the Beas, the Ravi and the Ghaggar which water this state and make it a part of the northern fertile plain. Prior to Persian period, this region was called by different names at different times. Probably, at the height of its glory it was known as *Sapta Sindhu*, land of the seven rivers, namely Sindhu (Indus), Vitasta (Jehlum), Asuhi (Chenab), Purshin (Ravi), Vipasa (Beas), Satadru (Sutlej) and Saruri (Saraswati). The last one is dried up now and its traces are found in the present seasonal streams that flow near Pehowa in Haryana. During the Greek occupation, the territory had shrunk into the area covering the five rivers. It was a region that constituted the parts of the Indus Valley Civilization. The Aryans settled in this region in about 1500 B.C. It was in about 900 B.C., when the battle of Kurukshetra took place. In 326 B. C.,Alexander the Great of Macedonia invaded Punjab. After this was the rule of Chandragupta Maurya that lasted till about Ist century A.D. By 318 A.D. the Gupta dynasty exercised their influence. In 1947, when India was partitioned, the larger half of Punjab went to Pakistan. In 1966, the Indian smaller half was further divided into three states: Punjab, Haryana and Himachal Pradesh. The rich and fertile land of the Punjab is the meeting ground of different people and races. Its population descends from various stocks, and consists of heterogeneous racial elements.

In ancient times it was mostly inhabited by a race whom the Aryans later called as *Dasyus*. They were pushed towards the south by the Indo-Aryans. But a small section of *Dasyus* remained in Punjab. Later on, the Persians, the Greeks, the Parthians, the Scythians, the Kushans, the Huns, the Turks, the Mongols and the Afghans made successive inroads into Punjab and some of them settled there permanently and adjusted themselves to the new social system, adopting the customs and tradition of the conquered land. They soon merged into the indigenous population and in the process, some of their own cultural traits became part of the culture of the Punjab.

The present inhabitants of the Punjab are the descendants of the various mixed racial stocks which entered into it during the different stages of its history. The Archeologists have traced the signs of human habitation to the ancient times. The upper basin of Indus and the Baluchistan Plateau hosted one of the earliest human civilizations known as the Indus valley civilization. The earliest signs of life and human activity date as far back as 7000 B.C. The Indus Valley Civilization grew from small village and settlements to highly refined urban life. At its height, around 3000 B.C., it boasted the splendid cities of Harappa and Mohenjodaro in the lower Indus Valley. The story of the decline, whose reasons are still not completely explained of civilization is also told through the remains of these cities. Among other reasons, like the change in the weather patterns, urbanization without any rural agricultural production base, one factor is reported to be the series of raids or small scale migrations by the Aryans from the North-West (1500-1000 B.C.). The next thousand year history of Punjab (or *Arya-Varta*, the land of Aryan as Aryan called it) is dominated by the Aryans and their interactions with the natives of the Indus basin.

The total population of Punjab on March , 2001 stood 24,289,296 persons as per the provisional results of the Census of India 2001. The State has registered a lower decennial growth rate of 19.76% when compared to national average of 21.34%. The sex ratio (i.e., the number of females per thousand males) of population has come down from 882 in 1991 to 874 in the present census. Total literacy rose to 69.95% during 1991 Census. The people of Punjab have very light brown skin. They have wavy black hair, sometimes their hair is a chestnut brown. Their eyes are a dark or light brown, very occasionally a person will have blue eyes. They tend to range between 5 ft 5 in. to 5ft. 7 in. They tend to

Celebration of Gurpurb.

Cultural festival being celebrated by different communities.

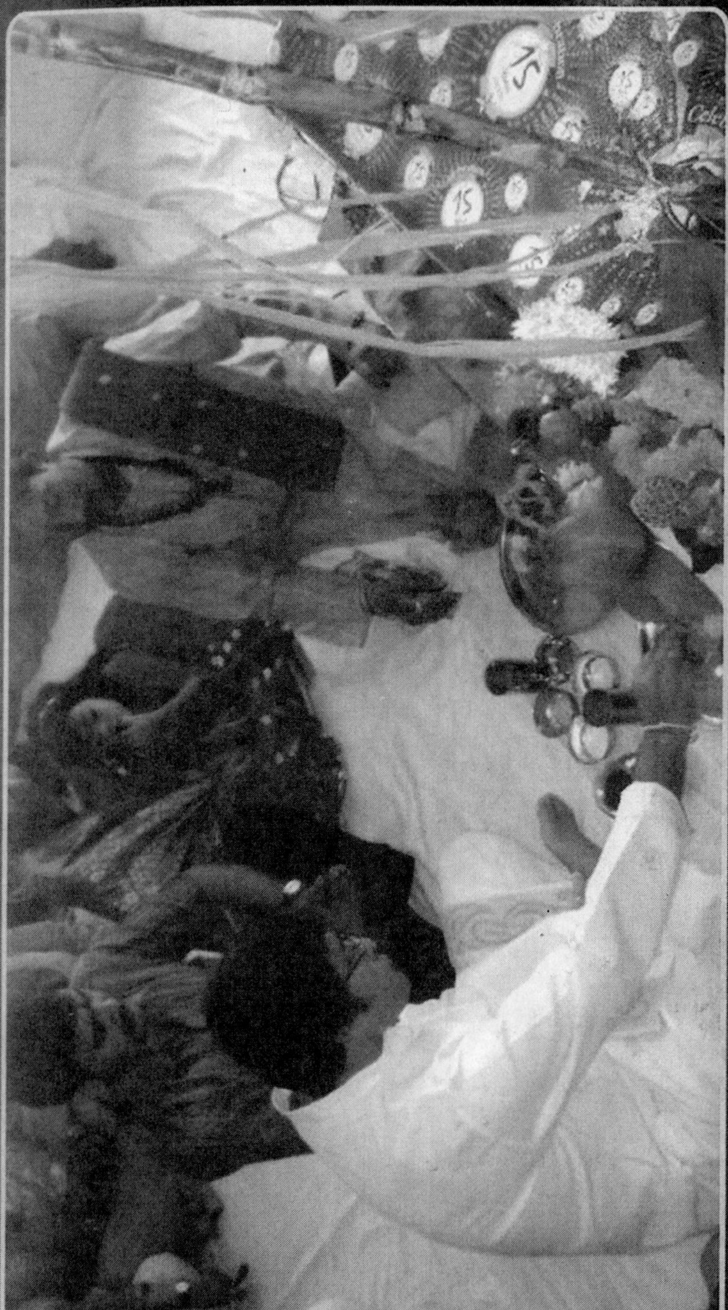

Diwali Pujan.

Lohri Festival.

Women dancing at sawan mela (July-August) in Traditional dress.

Annual Art and Craft mela at Suraj Kund.

Haryanvi people singing folk song in traditional dress in a festival.

People beating drums and Playing Other musical instruments.

Men and Women dancing in Phag mahotsav.

Dancers waiting for their turn in a festival.

Shivaratri procession at Mandi.

Celebration of Dussehra festival at Kulu.

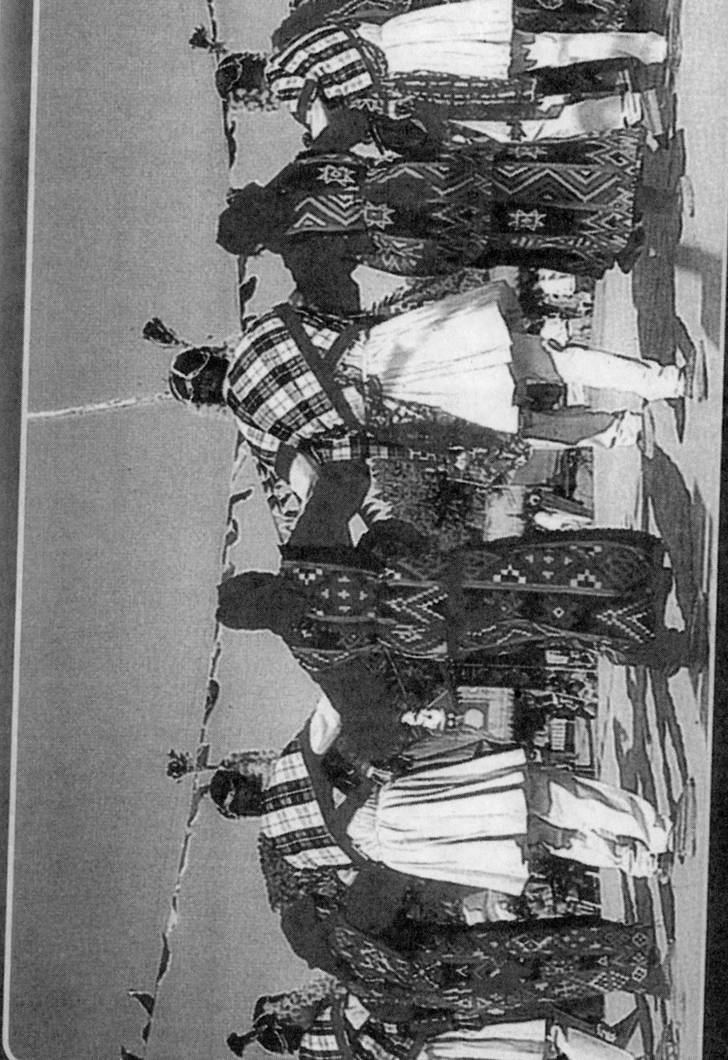

Men and women Dancing in a Circle in tradition dress.

Women dancing at Nainadevi, Bilaspur.

Kinnauri women in festive gear.

Celebration of winter festival with multi-artificial flowers.

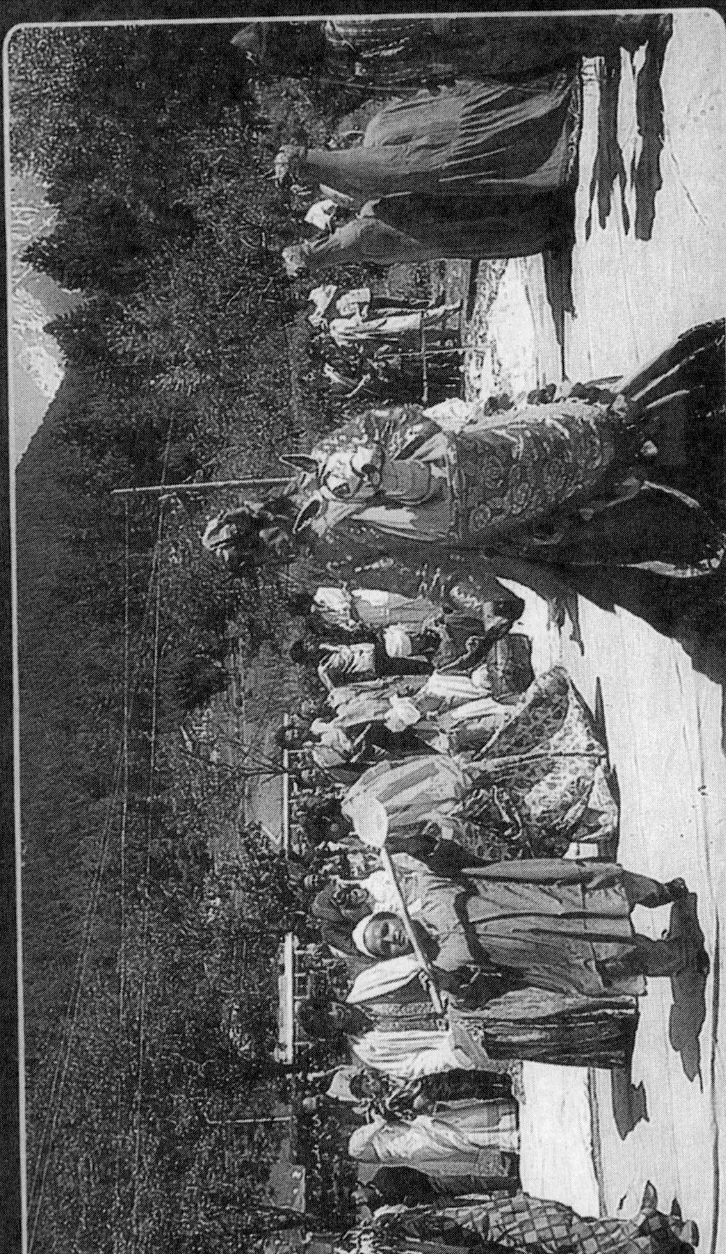

Persons dancing in traditional dress using artificial pony.

Mask dancers in Hemis festival.

Amarnath Yatra in progress.

Buddhist monks blow on these long musical instruments in a festival.

Punj Pyaras with folded hands during Gurpurb.

Celebration of Baisakhi at Anandpur Sahib.

Woman dancing in baisakhi festival in traditional dress.

Devotees at the Dargah of Panch Pir Baba fair.

The Nihangs at the Hola Mohla celebration.

Celebration of Gangaur in its traditional way.

Woman performing dancing.

At Gair festival people are dancing in traditional dress.

Camel fair at Bikaner.

Huge gathering at Chaksu fair.

A crowd of people taking dip in the Pushkar Lake.

Mahot on very well-decorated elephant during the Elephant festival.

have H⁻ long faces with medium or thick lips. Their noses are long and thin, either straight or hooked. There are over 3000 castes and subcastes. Each caste marries only within its caste and the members of different castes may not eat with other castes. Castes are most often determined by occupation and area. Since castes were endogamous, members tend to have similar physical characteristics. There are five basic types of caste. These are listed from the most privileged to the least privileged.

Brahmans-A religious and intellectual caste; *Kshatriyas*- The warrior caste; *Vaisyas* caste of businessmen and landowners; *Sudras*- made up of those that serve others such as artisans, workmen and peasants and *Untouchables*- other names include Chandala which means 'poor' or 'uncultured person' and *antyaja* which means 'the lowest by birth'. If a higher casteman is touched by an Untouchable, the one touched must go through a ritual bathing. If the Untouchable passes over a meal, the meal must be abandoned.

In the modern day Punjab, marriage is arranged by parents. To select proper mates, the parents will consult matchmakers and astrologers. Marriages are solemn affairs. The marriage ceremony is performed by chanting of verses from religious books with the couple sitting around a fire surrounded by a large number of relatives and members of the couple's caste. The marriage processions includes musicians, dancers, jugglers, lamp-bearers and fireworks. During the pre-independence days father was the head of the family. With him lived his sons, his grandsons, their wives and children and his unmarried daughters. Women were very subordinate to husbands and sons. At the death of their husbands, wives a rural expected to throw themselves on his funeral pyre. Each caste had its own system of jurisdiction with a council which would condemn and fine violators. One punishment for serious crimes was leading the criminal in a procession round the village streets, mounted on a donkey with his face painted in a grotesque manner. As the majority of its population was rural, village was the unit that determined the social and economic set up of the Punjab. Every village is linked in one way of another with the adjoining villages. Agriculture being the main occupation of the people, their economic dependence upon each other mainly pertains to their agricultural activities. All of them carpenters, blacksmiths, oilmen, sweepers and others invest their interests in agriculture. Carpenters and blacksmiths make and repair agricultural implements for the farmers. Labourers lend a hand at harvesting and in return get wages. Similarly, barbers, water-carriers, cobblers, potters and all others earn their living by serving the farmer in one way or another.

Many villages have grown up in the middle of large fields. A village in the Punjab generally springs up on the land of an ancestor, his offspring forming the nucleus. Many villages of *Majha* are divided into *pattis*, and each member of a *patti* is said to have descended from a common ancestor. In some villages, each patti has its separate Panchayat to sort out its quarrels and bring about reconciliation. But in case of inter *patti* disputes, the Panchayat of the main village decides the issues. Working classes like labourers and backward classes, like sweepers live in mud houses on the outskirts of the village, or in some remote corners. The artisans and craftsmen like, carpenters, blacksmiths, cobblers etc, have their own separate settlements.

Although the villages of Punjab are inhabited by different castes and creeds, the people of one village do not marry into the same village and in this respect each caste and village is an exogamous unit; matrimonial relations are transacted in nearly villages only. If a distant village has to be chosen, it must be of the same geographical strip. In the urban side there is no such consideration.

The partition of Punjab in 1947 left a very deep mark upon the social and economic life of its villages. The older patterns gave way to the new, and the long preserved purity of village life was disturbed. Millions of uprooted Sikhs and Hindus came and settled down here and started their life afresh. At present almost every fifth Punjabi is a rehabilitated refugee. The exogamous character of the villages, the inter-community relationships, the old traditions of social behaviour and the economic inter-dependence have all changed. The upheaval caused by the partition also changed the pattern of trade and agriculture of Punjab.

Those who migrated from Rawalpindi and Jhelum districts were mostly traders, shopkeepers and businessmen by profession. Wherever they settled down in East Punjab, they set up new trade links and re-oriented the shopping and trade centres. Even in the most remote villages, new shops sprang up giving a great impetus to the trade and industry of Punjab. The Sikhs and the Hindus who migrated from Lyallpur, Montgomery and Sheikhupura were the experienced agriculturists. They were the people who had cultivated the barren jungles and made them so rich that the entire region came to be called the granarey of Punjab.

They introduced novel ideas and made them practicable in the new settlements.

In Punjab, co-operative farming and gardening has been tried over one-fourth of the total cultivated area in the state. Similarly, the work of consolidating fragmented holdings has gathered momentum. Conditions of tenancy have improved, and the adoption of new techniques in farming have given a fillip to production. Partition brought about changes in occupational patterns also. Caste hierarchy, for instance, received a big blow. The so-called low caste people who until now had been continuing in their ancestral professions suddenly decided to discard them and take to the new ones. This brought about a new awakening among them, and they began to make a conscious effort to raise their status.

The five-year plans, particularly the community development projects and the national extension schemes, have brought about far-reaching changes in the social, cultural and economic life of the village farmer by introducing many novel ideas in his daily life. The villages of Punjab have been virtually metamorphosed. Many new roads have been constructed to link them with urban areas. Opening of new schools in pursuance of literacy campaigns have helped the demolition of blind faith and superstition. Introduction of electricity has opened up new vistas in agriculture and industry, all adding up to greater prosperity. The status of women is also undergoing a vast change. The *purdah* system is dying out and a new social awakening is spreading all over.

Kinship plays a significant role in Customs and tradition of Punjab. There is a divease range whose pattern vary considerably from group to group, but the general mode of behaviour and attitude is more or less the same. Each relation has certain duties and responsibilities towards others in his group in the day-to-day life, birth and marriage ceremonies, funerals and other social occasions. Different sets of terms are used for addressing the patrilineal and matrilineal kinfolks. The father's brother is addressed as *chacha*, while the mother's brother is *mama*. Even the terms used for addressing the elder or younger agnates are different. The father's elder brother is addressed as *taya* and the younger one as *chacha.* Generally, most of the kinsmen of a person reside in the same village, or in the adjoining villages. Because of the joint family system, the real brothers, even married ones, often live in the same household.

There are some other agnates, who generally reside in the same locality, or *patti*, participate in all social functions and exchange gifts.

Some of the cognates reside in the adjoining villages and very often they participate in social or festive occasions like the initiation and marriage ceremonies, as also other occasions like funerals etc. Kinship plays a very vital role in the social and cultural life of the people, because most of the kins have to perform certain specified and obligatory functions on social occasions. Thus, for instance, the *choora* (red ivory bangles) which bride wears at her wedding has necessarily to come as a gift from her maternal uncle. The maternal uncle has to put the bangles on her forearm, while going through certain rituals.

Similarly, the maternal grandparents must send their *khat* (bridal gift) to the girl on the occasion of marriage. This gift generally comprises a set of clothes, some jewellery and other household objects for the bride. At an initiation ceremony, like the first haircutting or wedding, each relative gives something in cash or kind according to his social standing or nearness of relation. The exchange of gifts is a prominent custom and keeps the kins, in a way, well- knit in the social fabric. Presence of all relatives at social functions is considered very essential and special efforts are made to patch up differences with all those with whom relations have been strained for some reason or the other. The joint family system having been in vogue for ages, the entire responsibility for the maintenance of the household and of social relations falls upon the father. No one in the family can question his authority. Even in such personal matters as contracting a marriage, the father as the head of the family, has the ultimate say.

After his death, the patriarchal powers pass on to the eldest son who becomes the head of the family and its chief representative on all social occasions. At home, the head of the family inspires awe among the members. Younger members of the family dare not talk flippantly or joke in his presence and, it is not considered befitting for them to smoke or drink when he is around. All conversation in his presence is conducted in subdued voices. Daughters-in-law observe *purdah* when the father-in-law is present; and it is generally understood that when he comes into the house, he would either cough aloud, or indicate in some other way that he is around, so that they may cover their faces and tone down their voices. As a general rule, there is no direct conversation between the father-in-law and the daughter-in-law, but if a situation or an occasion necessitates it, it is brief to the extent of being monosyllabic, and the daughter-in-law is barely audible. *Purdah* is observed before the husband's elder brother also. The same customary respect as is shown to the father-in-law is also shown to him. But the younger brother of the husband or *devar*, enjoys a privileged position. He is free to talk, laugh and joke with the *bhabi* or brother's wife.

Among some clans, there is a custom that when the bride is brought home, the husband's younger brother is the first person who lifts her veil and peeps at her face. In certain clans, the oldest *bhabi* is given a status equal to that of the mother, and she is treated with great respect. In Malwa, where the *devar* generally marries the widow of the elder brother, the relationship is very free. Generally speaking, relations between the mother-in-law and the daughter-in-law are not very cordial in many families. A lot of friction is caused over the domestic chores; and sometimes even small mistakes on the part of the daughter-in-law are made much of by the mother-in-law. The offended mother-in-law in her outburst does not spare even the parental family of the daughter-in-law.

However, although the position of the wife varies in different societies, the mother occupies a very respectable position everywhere in Punjab. Relations among brothers are often very friendly and cordial. They are always out to help one another. The elder brother generally commands the same respect as is given to the father. But a great change comes in this behaviour when the brothers get married and their wives start wrangling on petty matters. Over the distribution of ancestral property, sometimes the filial love and respect change into life-long enmity. The relationship between a brother and a sister is the warmest and cleanest of all relations. Right from her childhood, a sister idealises her brother. When she plays the folk games *kikli* and *thaal* with her friends, she sings praises of her brother.

After marriage when she is in her husband's house, she always looks forward to the arrival of her brother, because whenever she goes to her parents on a customary visit, it is the brother who fetches her. She looks up to him as her sole protector, and expects help from him when she is in difficulties. The agnates who live in a separate house though in the same village are generally the brothers or first cousins of the head of the family. Relations with them are generally kept pleasant and they in their turn join in all sorts of festive as well as sad occasions. Regular dealings of exchange of cash and gifts are maintained with them on all festive occasions. Relatives from the maternal side generally reside in the adjacent villages.

Children are, as a matter of course, more attached to their maternal relatives. Among many clans, eating or even drinking water in the house of married daughter is taboo. It is believed that one who eats in the house of one's married daughter goes to hell. Among some, even elder brothers are not supposed to accept the hospitality of theirs. However, there is no restriction on children accepting such gifts or hospitality. But now with the change of times people's views have changed, and the rule has been relaxed.

Sometimes, close friends and associates enter into a putative relationship. They often exchange their turbans, and are known as *pagwat* brothers. They go to a temple or a gurudwara, exchange turbans and eat from the same plate. It is quite an occasion and many near relatives are invited. This sort of ritualistic relationship is frequent. Sometimes, even a girl ties *rakhi* on the wrist of a boy outside her own kin and makes him her *dharam bhra* or the brother in faith. The approach to these ritual relationships is very serious and all obligations are as earnestly observed as in the case of real kin ties. Among the villagers of the Punjab, there is an unusual sense of kinship. So, relative terms of address are used by the fellow-villagers unrelated by either real or ritual ties. In all social communication, modes of address are very respectable. An elderly woman is always addressed as *chachi* or *masi* (aunt) and as elderly man as *chacha* or *mama* (uncle). Similarly boys and girls of the same age-group generally address one another as brother or sister. A daughter is the most privileged person, as she is given a daughter's status in every household of the village.

The expectant mother is put in a separate room where no one else, except the midwife and some elderly women of the family are allowed to go. When the midwife comes, some lentil and salt are taken over the head of the mother-to-be and made over to the midwife. A small pitcher of water, some grains and a small lighted lamp made of flour are kept in the room. An iron knife and an iron bangle are kept under the pillow as a protection against malignant spirits. When the child is born, the women present at the time, call out that a baby girl is born even if it is a boy. This is done on purpose because it is feared that with the happiness resulting from the birth of a son, the new mother's placenta may not be released fully thus spreading poison in her body. If the infant is a son, *shirin* leaves are hung outside the house, as an indication of the lucky incident.

Often the happy event is announced by the beat of a metal tray outside the main door by some female relative. Among some clans, the new mother after the birth of a son has to sleep on the floor even at the time of confinement. Some people make the mother count the beams of the roof after delivery in the belief that she will bear as many sons. Shortly after its birth, the baby's navel string is cut. If it is a boy, the Hindus in Malwa cut a piece of the holy thread worn by an old person in the family and tie it round the severed part. In case it is a girl, they take a piece of home-spun thread to tie it with. When the umbilical cord dries up, it is thrown over a *peepal* tree along with the thread with which it was tied. The placenta and the severed cord are both buried in a corner of the house, for if someone unwittingly steps over it, some calamity is expected to befall either the mother or the child.

A child's life is supposed to be greatly influenced by the placenta. This belief is based on continuous magic. If the child falls ill during the early days of the mother's confinement, a flour lamp is lit at the place where the placenta is buried. Light is the symbol of life in Punjabi folklore, otherwise also light is kept on day and night in the room of the mother and the baby for five, seven, eleven or thirteen days after the birth. The lamp is generally kept on an unused pitcher containing some food grains, *gur* and money which are later given over to the midwife. The baby is made to taste its first liquid food (*gurhuti*) which is generally administered by some elderly member of the family. After that the "breast washing" rite is performed.

One of the father's unmarried sisters or some other related girl soaks a few petals of grass in milk-and-water and washes the mother's breasts with it. In return for this performance, the girl is given some money as a gift. After this rite, the baby is put to the mother's breast. Making a baby wear its first set of clothes is also done ceremoniously, though the ritual varies from clan to clan. If a child is born after many daughters or long after marriage, the members of the family go about from house to house virtually begging. Out of the money thus collected, they buy clothes for the new-born. The Vij sub-caste of Khatris has a different custom. For their new-born, no clothes from the family or even those gifted by relatives or friends of the same sub-caste are used. Generally, all that the baby wears has to come from the parents of the mother, or from friends belonging to different sub-castes. Some years ago, at the birth of a baby, village-folk tied a string to a beam in the roof and every year thereafter added a knot to that string. That helped them to determine his age. This method is still in practice in some of the remote villages. Five or seven days after the childbirth, the mother is allowed to bathe. A few grains or rice or a few leaves of *methi* are added to the bathing water.

The house, where a child is born, is considered impure for the first ten days or more. This impurity is called *sootak*. On the eleventh day of childbirth, the Khatris make the mother bathe and also wash her hair, after which the whole house is washed and smeared with cow dung mixture. Sugar candy or pieces of jaggery are distributed among all relatives and friends. This ceremony is called *Dhaman*. Women from the families of friends and relatives come to offer congratulations, and give money in the form of *Shagan* (gift) to the child. Khatris and Aroras from the area, now in west Punjab, perform the name giving ceremony of the child on the day of *dhaman*, but some castes or tribes do it later.

The Sikhs read the Holy Book, recite a hymn from Gurugranth Saheb and build up the child's name on the first letter of that hymn. The Hindus call the family priest who performs the *havan* and then gives the child its name. When the mother steps out of the house after eleven days, a rite is performed. In Gurdaspur, before stepping out of the house, the mother throws some cotton seeds and barley to the moon and the stars. In Malwa, this going out, first time after confinement is considered very important. This is called *Bahar Vadhavan*. This is performed on the thirteenth day. On this day, the mother bathes and washes her hair first in the urine of a cow, and then in curds. After that she dresses up and receives relatives and neighbours who come to wish the baby luck. If the child is a son, all the functionaries and servants come to congratulate and bring toys for him. The toys are representative of their respective trades; for instance, the water-carrier brings a *sehra* (garland) made of the *mauli* thread and *shirin* leaves; the carpenter may bring a toy-cart; the sweeper a bow and arrow; and the potter a little earthen pot, etc. In return, they are all given something in cash or kind according to their social status.

The *Nain* or wife of the village barber makes out of dung, an image of *Vedmata* (goddess of luck) , wraps it up in silk, makes a heap of grain in the courtyard and buries the image in that heap. The midwife brings a waistband with bells and ties it round the baby's waist. After this, the mother is made to wear the shoes of the barber and to go out. She sits with the child in her lap, facing the buried figure of the goddess *Vedmata* and bows to it. In the evening she carries a bowl of water outside, brings back a little grass and keeps it under her pillow.

When the child cuts his first tooth, fresh coconut is distributed. If a child cuts his upper teeth first, it is considered an ill-omen for the maternal uncle. The maternal uncle, on seeing the child, performs a rite and touchs his teeth with a silver cup and then offers it to the child as a gift.

Marriage is celebrated in Punjab with a great gusto. Until a few decades ago, a marriage celebration meant a long chain of ceremonies and rituals, but now it has become a comparatively simple affair. Nevertheless, marriage still means rituals and festivity. Mainly a girl has no say in the choice of her husband. Formerly it was the *Parohat* (priest) or *Nai* (barber) of the family who negotiated with the boy's family on behalf of the girl's family or vice versa. If what he fixed up met with the approval of the girl's parents, the matters were finalised. This procedure is still followed by some orthodox families, but the more advanced ones almost always take the girl's consent before making a commitment.

Of the various considerations that influence the choice of a bride or bridegroom, caste and clan are the most important. Normally, out of the caste marriages are not allowed. The Khatris marry their daughters into Khater families only, but it is very interesting that they do not mind taking a bride from another caste, like the Aroras. There is a system of social graduation in accordance with which certain Khatri tribes refuse to intermarry, except in a certain specified few of their fellow groups, such as Dhaighara, Charzati or Bahri, etc.

Thus, for instance, a *Dhaighara* (literally, two and a half houses) Khatri marries only in one of three castes-*Kapure*, *Khannas*, and *Mehras* or *Malhotras*. The Jats are also very particular about their *gotra* (clans) who do not marry into the *gotras* of the parents and grandparents on both sides. The villages of the Punjab are exogamous units and marry their children in villages which are near about. Each village is said to have a traditional set of villages to which its girls regularly go in marriage and another set from which it regularly receives wives.

After completing all the initial negotiations, the girl's father takes the initiative towards ceremonial commitments, through the family barber. He sends a coconut, *chhuhare* (dry dates), sugar and some money to the boy's family in the form of the first auspicious gifts. When these things are received by the boy's father, he calls all the relatives and the

Tilak or *Shagan* ceremony is performed. Among Hindus, this ceremony is performed by the *parohat* (family priest) who draws a *chauk* on the ground, seats the boy facing it, recites some mantras, applies a *tilak* on his forehead and then makes him eat one of the dates sent by the girl's father. Sikhs have this ceremony performed by a *Bhaiji* (preacher) from the Gurudwara, who first reads five stanzas from the *Japji Sahib* (a hymn of Guru Nanak) makes the boy taste a date and then applies *tilak* on his forehead out of a mixture of saffron powder and rice. A little saffron dissolved in water is then sprinkled on the clothes.

After this ceremony, the boy's father sends to the affianced bride some gifts through the same barber which include sugar, coconut, rice, dry dates, money, ornaments, clothes and henna. The girl's people receive the gifts and then on an auspicious day, they call the village *Nain* (family barber's wife) and make her perform the engagement ceremony. The girl is made to wear the things sent by her prospective in-laws and is seated facing east. The *Nain* then makes her eat the sugar and dry dates received from the boy's parents and that completes the ceremony. Among the *Khatris*, the first rite performed after the completion of negotiations is called *Thaka*. This also known as the 'milk drinking' ceremony. On a fixed day, the bridegroom-to-be and his relatives go to the girl's house, where the girl's mother brings milk for the boy to drink, and thereafter gives him some money, sweets etc, as a gift. The boy's parents also give to the girl clothes, jewellery and other gifts.

Sometime after the *Thaka* the regular engagement takes place. Generally, this is done shortly before the wedding. On the fixed day the girl's people, accompanied by some relatives, take the betrothal, gifts-sweets etc, to the boy's house. Sometimes, the boy's parents accompanied by the near relatives go to the girl's house to receive these gifts. This is a very expensive ceremony for the girl's family. Besides, money and large *thals* full of sweets and fruit, the boy is given a golden ring and a bangle.

Towards the end of the ceremony, perfumed or coloured water is sprinkled over every one. The *tika* ceremony is performed at this time. Sometimes after the betrothal a date for the marriage is fixed. Hindus are very particular about the auspiciousness of the day. They call the family priest who consults his books and the almanac and then fixes a day which is called *Saha*. Sikhs do not bother about these things. They see the convenience of both the families concerned and generally fix the solemnization of the marriage on a holiday, which is convenient to all. The months of *Kartik* and *Poh* and the *Shradh* days are considered inauspicious *Maghar* is the most favoured month for marriages. When the *Saha* is fixed, the girl's father informs the boy's father of the same through a formal letter. Earlier, this letter used to be written in saffron water is sprinkled over it and a functionary is deputed to take it to the boy's father and to read it out in the presence of all relatives. A few days before the marriage, *bhaji* (literally 'share'- share of sweets) is distributed among relatives and friends and invitations to attend the wedding is given.

A few days before the marriage, women from the neighbourhood and female relatives start coming every evening to participate in singing bridal songs. They sing, dance, mimic and act. Every night, the house resounds to the gay exuberance of feminine revelry and the fun goes on till midnight, sometimes even till the small hours of the following day. This continues till the day of marriage. A very peculiar custom generally followed as part of preparations for the marriage is that of *Maiyan*. It is a sort of confinement of the bride and the bridegroom for a few days before the marriage. The boys and the girls are not allowed to go out of the house or change clothes. They are, however, allowed to have their close friends around. During these days, *Kangna* is tied on the right wrist of the boy and the left wrist of the girl.

A couple of days before the wedding, *vatna*, a scented powder consisting of barley flour, turmeric, *kachur* and mustard oil, is applied to the boy and the girl. In the case of the girl, she is made to sit on a square stool while four girls hold a cloth over her forming a sort of a cover or canopy. The women of the house sing songs specially meant for this occasion and apply *vatna* on her body. In some caste, this ceremony is performed only one day before the marriage, but in Malwa, it starts a few days before the marriage, and continues to be repeated every day till the eve of marriage.

The wedding-eve is called *Mehndi Raat* or the night of Henna. Once again the women assemble and to the accompaniment of bridal songs apply henna to the hands of the bride or the bridegroom. The henna left over is then used by the other women present on the occasion. On the morning of the day fixed for the departure of the *barat* (marriage procession), the ceremony of *gharoli* is performed. The bridegroom's *bhabi* (brother's wife), dressed in her best and accompanied by some other female relatives, goes singing to a nearby pool or well and fills a *gharoli* (small earthen pitcher) with water. This water is ceremoniously brought mixed with more water and after *vatna* has been nicely applied, the person to be married is bathed in it. This is called *Khare Charna* (sitting on the basket). Under the stool on which the boy is seated one small lamp is lighted. It is made of flour and is filled with *ghee*. Women keep singing songs meant for this occasion. Four girls hold a cloth overhead forming a sort of canopy.

After the bath, the boy gets up from the stool and breaks with his feet five earthen lids which have already been kept there for the purpose. After that he goes and puts on his new clothes. The same ceremony is performed at the girl's house, the only difference being that the girl's maternal uncle helps her get up from the stool, and after she has changed clothes, takes her into one corner of the house, where she keeps sitting till it is time for the marriage ceremony. This is called sitting on *Chhandalian*. It is here that she wears *choora* (red ivory bangles). She also receives at this time a gift brought by the family barber from her in–laws, which is known as *Kuar Dhoti* (dhoti for the virgin). The packet actually includes clothes for the bride, a coconut and various other things.

All this time the girl is supposed to be observing a fast. After this gift has been received, she is made to wear the clothes and break her fast. As for the boy, when he gets ready after wearing his new clothes, his sisters tie *Sehra* (flower garland) on his head to the accompaniment of appropriate songs. The boy gets on to the back of decked mare and is ready to proceed to the bride's place. The bridegroom's *bhabi* at this time puts collyrium in his eyes, and his sisters hold the reins of the mare. In return, the bridegroom gives them money. Before proceeding to the bride's house, the ceremony of cutting the *Jandi* tree is performed. To ward off evil, the bridegroom cuts off with his sword, which hangs on his side, a branch from the *Jandi* tree. After that he is taken to a temple to pay his homage there, and then the whole party proceeds to the bride's house. Before entering the bride's house, the *Barat* stops at the gate and the *Milni* (meeting) ceremony is performed. The chief male relatives of both the parties hug their counterparts one by one. The first person to do this is the father. After the introductory embrace, the girl's relatives give to their counterparts money according to their means. While this goes on, the female relatives of the girl sing or just recite *Sithanis*, which are verses replete with humour and satire. They seek to make great fun of the boy's family, but everybody takes it lightly. That over, the party goes in for dinner. The boy is escorted to the place where the girl is seated. Before he steps across the threshold, some oil is poured on the hinges of the door, and the family barber lights a lamp in a sieve and welcomes him with that. The bridegroom then steps in and is made to recite some *chhands* (verses) which he has already learnt. Next starts the ceremony proper. Among the Hindus, this ceremony is generally performed late at night and goes on till dawn. In the courtyard of the house or out in the open, a *chauk* of flour is drawn by the priest, and the girl and the boy are made to sit before it facing east.

The family priest then chants hymns and verses from the scriptures and goes through the whole gamut of rituals, culminating in the father giving away his daughter to the boy, and the boy and the girl taking wedding vows as they go round the sacred fire. At the conclusion of the ceremony, both families exhibit to each other and the relatives, the clothes and jewellery which they have presented to the bride. The gifts brought by the boy's family are called *Vari* and those given by the girl's parents are called *Daaj* (Dowry). *Daaj* also includes clothes for the bridegroom, his parents, and his other near relatives. The next ceremony after the marriage is the bride's departure, the *Doli* (palanquin). To the accompaniment of the songs of separation, the *Doli* is sent away. At the time of parting, the parents of the girl and her brothers and sisters present a touching sight, moved at separation from one so dear. In some villages even today, a maid servant, generally the Nain (barber's wife), is sent with the bride. She is there to help the girl in case she is faced with any difficulties in her new family.

Moreover, when the Nain returns home, she supplies the parents of the girl first-hand information regarding the family into which the girl has gone to spend the rest of her life. But this system is fast fading out. When the wedding party along with the bride reaches home, the *Pani Varna* ceremony is performed. Diluted milk, called *Kachchi lassi*, is put in a small vessel and the bridegroom's mother and sisters turn by turn take it over the head of the bride, three times each. Each time they pretend to make an attempt to drink it, but the bridegroom puts his hand across and stops them. Thereafter, some oil is poured over the threshold and the couple enters the house. The bride is escorted to a separate room where she is seated. All relatives and women from the neighbourhood give her gifts, mostly in the form of money.

After this, another ceremony called *Mundri Chhalla* (playing with a ring) is performed. The *Nain* throws a small ring in a broad vessel of diluted milk. As soon as she throws the ring, the bride and the bridegroom both try to fish it out, even snatching it from each other's hand. Friend's and relatives stand all round, watching and cracking jokes. This is done seven times. The next day the ceremony of *Got Kunala* is performed. The following day, the bride accompanied by her husband, goes to her parents on her first short visit after her wedding. This is called *Phere Pana*. After this visit when the girl has to leave for her husband's home again, it is customary for her parents to give her clothes and other gifts. This ceremony, known as *Muklawa*, is performed immediately after the marriage.

Among the less known types of marriages in the Punjab, mention may be made of the *Punn* (virtuous) marriage which is considered the best of all types. The girl's parents do not accept any money or gifts in any form, the merit of the boy and the family are the only consideration. Then there is the *Dohathi* (two-handed) marriage. It is a sort of marriage by exchange between two families. A daughter is married off into one family and one of that family's daughters is similarly received back in marriage. Such marriages are very common at the lower social level. The third type is called *Taka* marriage, in which the boy's father pays something in cash to the girl's father and for all practical purposes, purchases her. This type of marriage is not unknown among the artisan castes.

Sikhs and Hindus of Punjab look upon the marriage as a sacred and indissoluble bond and do not, therefore, recognize divorce. According to the Sikh scriptures, husband and wife are one spirit of two bodies. Both Hindus and Sikhs consider marriage as a spiritual tie which does not break even after death. Therefore, divorce is seldom thought of, not even when men turn their wives out of their houses on the basis of adultery. A woman generally does not seek separation from her husband even when he is idle, vicious, cruel and characterless. Only at the low social levels does one come across some cases of divorce. The Bagri Jats of Ferozepur, for instance, perform the following ceremony for dissolution of marriage. Some of the brotherhood assemble and the woman is made to stand in their presence, her husband tears his white loin-cloth (*dhoti*) into two and places half of it on the head, saying that he has given her up, this ceremony is called *Dhola Urna*.

Widow remarriage does not exist as a custom in Punjab. Among some clans, an issueless widow is allowed to remarry. Widow remarriage is mostly performed with a near relative of the deceased husband. Widow remarriage is comparatively common among the Jats of the Punjab. This marriage is called *Kareva* or *Chadar Andazi*. In the presence of near relatives, the prospective husband puts a *Chadar* (white sheet) over the head of the prospective wife, and puts bangles on her wrists. The corners of the sheet are dyed yellow. Hindus sometimes call the family priest on this occasion, and he chants some sacred verses. The Sikhs go to the Gurudwara and perform the ceremony there, before the Holy Book. Among the erstwhile lower and backward tribes of the Punjab such as Sansi, Pakhiwals and Bazigards, widow remarriage is not only permitted and customary, but also obligatory.

When a person in Punjab is about to die, he is often shifted from the cot and put onto the floor, his feet turned towards the north. Before doing so, some people smear the floor with cow dung paste and spread darab grass over it. (There is a common belief that a person who dies on his cot becomes a ghost). Thereafter, the ceremony of *Deeva Batti* is performed. A lamp made from flour dough is lighted and put near the head or on the right palm and then something is given in charity on his behalf. A cow given away at this time is considered the best form of charity among the Hindus, for it is believed that on his way to the other world, the dead man has to cross a wide river. It is believed that he can do it easily if he holds on to the tail of the '*Vaitarani*', that is, the cow given in charity. The cow and other articles or money given in charity are made over to the Brahmins or the family priest. Those who cannot afford to give a cow, give away some food grains and money. Among the Hindus when a person is on the death-bed, someone recites verses from the *Geeta*; the Sikhs offer strength to the departing soul by reading *Sukhmani,* the psalm of peace.

When the death takes place, the women of the house sit around the corpse and lament loudly. Men spread a cover in the courtyard and sit silently, while friends, neighbours and relatives come in to condole. Among some Hindus, the sons and some other male relatives of the deceased have their heads shaved off. The widow of the deceased takes off all her jewellery and if she happens to be young and is still wearing the wedding bangles, these are broken. Certain rites and rituals are performed before the body of the deceased is taken for cremation. The body is rubbed with curds, washed and wrapped in a shroud. If the deceased happens to be woman and if her husband is alive, some jewellery is put on her body and vermilion applied in the parting of her hair. Her nose-ring is also not removed. A woman who dies thus, is considered lucky and is believed to go to heaven.

When a man dies after living a full span of life, his *Baban* (viman or bier) is made in the shape of a boat decorated with balloons and buntings and strips of golden lace. His funeral procession is often accompanied by musical bands; conches are blown and gongs are struck. Some coins, dry fruits and other edibles are thrown over the bier. These are collected and kept by the poor and considered very prized possessions. It is believed that a person who keeps such articles as souvenirs or eats them also lives to be as old. A close relation of the deceased grinds in a grindstone seven grains, viz., wheat, gram, barley, maize, moth, lintels and rice. Some grind only rice, sesame and barley. A Brahmin makes a *pind* out of this flour to be offered in the name of the dead. Before the bier is lifted to be taken out of the house, the widow, children and daughters-in-law of the deceased touch his feet.

Thereafter, four close relatives lift it on their shoulders and walk towards the cremation ground. The body is always taken out of the house feet first. The Sikhs sing hymns on the way. Relatives of the deceased and mourners help the carriers of the bier and share the burden with them. This is called *moda dena* (offering the shoulder). This gesture has a great religious significance. If the deceased has a grandson, he follows the bier with a *Chauri* (whisk), fanning the corpse. On the way to the cremation ground a halt called *adhmarg* (half way) is made. Here a pitcher full of water is broken by the eldest son near the corpse's head. The widow and other female relatives of the deceased bow down to the corpse and touch his feet again.

The pyre is made at the cremation ground. The corpse is placed on it and *ghee* is poured in the mouth, eyes and nose. The left-over dough-balls are given in offering, after which the eldest son sets fire to it, starting at the head and then going round clock-wise. Some Hindus perform *havan* before igniting the pyre. Sikhs recite hymns from the Holy Book, read *Sohila,* and offer prayers for the peace of the departed soul. When the body is almost burnt, the ritual *Kapal Kirya* (breaking the skull) is performed. The chief mourner, generally the eldest son, breaks the skull with a bamboo, the idea behind the ritual being that the skull burns up completely. On their way back, mourners bathe at a pond or well, wash all their clothes and perform another ritual in which each one sits on the ground, bends forward, takes a blade of grass in his hands and after the priest has chanted a verse, breaks it into two and throws it back behind his head, thus severing all worldly relations with the dead man. Sikhs generally go to Gurudwara before going home and offer prayers for the benefit of the departed soul, and distribute the traditional pudding, *Karah Parshad*. After this, the funeral party disperses. In earlier times, the mourners invariably stayed on near the pyre till sunset. Small children are generally buried and not cremated, but the Sikhs cremate their children also. Till decades ago, if a person died of small-pox or of an epidemic, his body was immersed in water and not cremated. It was believed that epidemics were caused by the anger of some gods or goddesses, and a person who caught any of those diseases was actually possessed of those gods and goddesses. Burning such a body would mean torturing the god or goddess along with it, which would further offend the already angered deity.

On the fourth day after the death, but not on a Wednesday, the rite of *Phul Chunana* (picking the charred bones) is performed. In the evening the *Chautha* ceremony is performed, a condolence meeting at which all the relatives and friends assemble. If the *Chautha* falls on a Wednesday, it is observed a day earlier. While picking the bones, diluted milk is put in one vessel and all bones which are picked up are washed in it and then put either into a bag or an earthen vessel. The ashes are also collected and immersed in a stream, if there is one nearby. But the bones are also taken to Hardwar and immersed in the Ganga. Some Sikhs take these bones to Kiratpur and immerse them in the river Beas. *Kirya*, the chief ceremony after death, is performed on different days by different clans. Some perform it on the 10th or 11th day, some on the 13th, and some on the 16th day after death. In rare cases, it is even performed on the 21st day. The Jats of the Punjab perform it on the 10th day and call it *Dasahi*. Brahmans perform it on the 11th day. Other Hindus perform it on the 13th day and call it *Tehravan*. On this day, all relatives and friends assemble in the afternoon in condolence. Some Hindus perform *Havan* on this day. Sikhs have a non-stop reading of the Adi Granth, Kirtan and prayers. The chief mourner, mainly the eldest son is ceremonially installed as the head of the household in place of his father and as a token he wears the turban usually given for this occasion by his father-in-law. If the wife of the deceased is alive, the *Nain* comes and ties her hair after which all relatives according to the nearness of their relationship give her some money. This is called *Sarvanna*. This is a sort of financial aid to the widow. When a woman dies, her parents bring the turban which her husband wears on this day. If, however, he intends to remarry, he does not wear this turban. All friends and relatives are served food on this day. If a man dies of old age, his death is celebrated and *halwa* and *puri* are served to all mourners assembled. Utensils, clothes, beddings and fruits are given in charity in the name of the deceased. After one year the death anniversary is performed, this is known as *Varina*. Hindus feed Brahmins on this day. Sikhs have a non-stop reading of the Adigranth, Kirtan and arrange to serve food to the *Panj Piyaras*.

Customs

The marriage ceremony is one of the oldest customs of mankind and the Indian culture is not an exception, and it is considered one of the most important events of one's life. In Delhi, the *Kanyadana* (literally meaning, donating a virgin) or giving away one's daughter in marriage, was considered the greatest sacrifice a man could perform. It was also a duty performed by the bridegroom to perpetuate his lineage. By making marriage a sacrament, the Hindus elevated the physical union to the spiritual dimensions. Many in India consider marriage an integral part of human condition, binding not only in this life, but in the after-life as well. From the hymns and verses about marriage in the *Vedas*, we learn that adult individuals were considered ready for marriage after puberty. In subsequent times, however, brides were married even in childhood, perhaps due to a series of foreign invasions in North India. In an attempt to protect their women from the invaders, early marriages became the norm. According to the scriptures of Manu, divorce and remarriage were not permitted. Most references to marriage in the ancient Sanskritic texts suggest that the Aryans were monogamous. However, some references to polygamy and polyandry have been found in the Hindu epic of *Mahabharata*.

In the medieval times, the marriage was compulsory for all the girls except for those opted for asceticism. Brahmin girls were married between ages eight and ten from sixth or century onwards up to the modern times. Polygamy was permitted to all who could afford, and it was especially popular among Kshatriyas for political reasons. According to the *Mansasollasa*, the king should marry a Kshatriya girl of noble birth for a chief queen though he is permitted to have Vaishya or Shudra wives for pleasure.

However, in the modern times both divorce and remarriage have been completely legal, whereas polygamy and polyandry are both criminal offences for Hindus punishable by law. The Islamic personal law of Shariat allows upto four wives for a man, and it is legal for a Muslim to have multiple wives in India. From its initial simplicity, the wedding ceremony became complicated (involving such issues as the dowry) over time to reinforce the extended family.

Today, a marriage is perhaps the most important social occasion for any family, reflecting the regional colour that overlays the basic Vedic rites. A *muhurat* or auspicious moment is chosen for the date after the horoscopes of the bride and groom are inter-changed. Wedding preparations begin well beforehand. The wedding is usually conducted at the bride's home, or in temples, and nowadays, in parks, hotels, or in special marriage halls. Entire families congregate, with evenings spent in singing, dancing, and eating. The customs during the wedding ceremony in India are varied and reflect the vast diversity of cultures of the land. The cultures have influenced each other with mutual borrowing of practices. A day before the wedding, the bride and her friends and female relatives gather for the ceremony of *Mehendi*, in which their palms and feet are decorated with henna. The bride is teased with music and dance by the other women about her future husband and in-laws.

People of Haryana

The people of Haryana belong to the Indo-Aryan stock and in parts to the Indo-Dravidian stock. Haryana's population is divided into a number of castes. The main classes of people in Haryana are the Brahmins, the Rajputs, the Jats, the Ahirs and the allied agricultural communities. From the ancient past to the present, religion provides the main basis of the structure of the Haryana society. In the medieval times, there came the Islam, followed by Sikhism and Christianity. The Hindu Jats occupy a prominent place in Haryana, being the single largest group in the region. It was the Jats who formed the ethnic nucleus of the people now called the Punjabis. The Jats are divided into twelve chief clans (gotras) and about 137 minor gotras. The main gotras are *Maliks* (also called Gatwallas), *Dahiya*, *Ahlawat*, *Rathi*, *Dalal*, *Sahrawat*, *Kadian*, *Jakhar*, *Golia* and *Deswal*. The Muslim Jats, called *Mullas* are a separate group. The Jats form a predominant proportion in the districts of Hissar and Karnal and are also found in good strength in Ambala.

The caste of Rajputs occupy a respectable position in Haryana. The various Rajput clans trace their ancestry to the ancient warriors

(Kshatriya) who figure so prominently in legend and ancient lore. The Brahmins constitute an important section of the people in Haryana. Most of the Brahmins in Haryana are Gaur Brahmins. The other common gotras among Brahmins are *Saraswat*, *Bharadwaja*, *Vashishta*, *Gaudama*, *Bacchhasas*, *Parsira*, *Sandlasa*, *Gujarati* or *Bias* and the *Dakaut*. The Sarawat Brahmins, less numerous than the Gaur are not so strict in their caste habits. The Gujarati or Bias who came from Gujarat are regarded in some respects as the highest class of Brahmins. Brahmins constitute the most orthodox community. Not only do they keep aloof from others, but also practise taboos among themselves. But now the situation is changing and the Brahmins even take up other profession than the priesthood. *Tyagis* or *Tagas* are of Brahmin origin who gave up priestly profession and took to agriculture. Tyagis wear the sacred thread, but the other Brahmins will not inter-marry or eat with them.

The Ahirs are mainly concentrated in Mahendergarh, the neighbouring district of Gurgaon and the Jhajjar tehsil of Rohtak. In habits and customs, they are similar to the Jats and they also have a number of *gotras* like the Jats. Rors, a small tribe, is mostly concentrated in Karnal. The *Vazhyas* are divided into three main classes, the Aggarwalas, the Oswals and Maheshwaris. The Meos are an important community mainly concentrated in Mewat, comprising the hill tract of Gurgaon, Alwar and Bharatpur. They take their name from the place of their residence the Mewat. They claim to have a Rajput origin, descendants of an ancestor who was converted to Islam in the time of Kutub-ud-din. Meos are a happy blend of Islam and Hinduism. They observe the feasts of both but fasts of none. On the occasion of marriage, birth and other ceremonies Hindu customs and practices are observed.

The Harijans constitute roughly about one fifth of the population of the state. The several categories of Harijans (schedule castes) are the *Chamars, Chhuras, Dhanaks* and *Julahas*. As a single community the *Chamars* are the most predominant. The *Gujars* were originally a pastoral and nomadic concentrated in large numbers in the Khadar and canal villages of the Karnal district. They are of the same physical type as the Jats, Rajputs and Ahirs. In another category are the village artisans, craftsmen and certain other menials. These include the village blacksmith, the carpenter, the oilman (*teli*), the barber (*nai*), the washer-man (*dhobi*), the village potter (*kumhar*) and some others.

The caste and community inhabiting a village also impart to it a certain type of character. A Jat village will be a little different from the one in which Rajputs dominate. A Brahman village can be distinguished from a Gujjar village. All Jat villages are not similar. The sub-caste or gotra will impart certain distinguishing features. All the villages have certain features which stamp them with general character, irrespective of their location and caste or gotra of the dominating sections.

The life of the villagers remains rooted in their age old customs and traditions. The villagers have retained their essential framework of rites and rituals, fairs and festivals, taboos and superstitions. The people remain deeply attached to the caste or sub-caste to which they belong. Their social relations, marriages, eating, drinking and other dealings are still confined to the caste.

The people of Haryana are still conservative and they continue to follow old practices as a matter of routine and custom. The *Mundan* ceremony is still prevalent among people who have settled in Haryana. The people being religious minded adhere to scriptural injunctions. The *birth ceremony* is accompanied by feasting, the scale of celebration depending on the economic position of the house-holder. In the case of a son it is elaborate with much show of rejoicing. The girls are really seldom welcome. Birth of a child is followed by its *Nam-Karan-Sanskar* i.e. ceremony of giving a name to the child, male or female. The woman who has been in confinement for several days due to ritual pollution is declared fit to come out after ten or twelve days after the ceremony called *Hom* sacred fire is performed where mother and child are given a bath and given new clothes.

The ceremony of wearing the sacred thread by the boys is important among the Brahmins and is performed at about the age of fifteen. Child marriage was common in Haryana. Now among the upper and educated classes, marriages are held at a comparatively late age. Even in rural areas child marriages are rare. *Sati* was practised particularly among certain communities. Widow-remarriage is less restricted even among the higher classes.

Among the Hindus, the dead are cremated as a rule. *Janpara-Jogis* bury their dead like Muslims and Christians. Post-cremation rites include a twelve day mourning in the case of females and a thirteen day mourning in the case of males. The last ceremony is called *Tehravee*, feasts after death are now less common. Hindus as a rule believe in transmigration and rebirth. The idea was that if one feeds people in the memory of the dead, they would also benefit from it. They believe that the elderly dead of the family have been born elsewhere. All the Hindus believe that for the salvation of the soul of the dead certain ceremonies are essential. One of these is to carry the bone of the dead to Hardwar, and throw them in the Ganges which purifies everything.

The influence of the Brahmins is still predominant and without them most of the ceremonies would be incomplete. The women still observe *purdah*, at least among certain communities. In former days, *purdah* was observed quite rigidly. It is now considerably relaxed mainly due to economic causes. It is still observed in certain forms. Village girls cover their heads while daughters-in-law cover their face in the presence of elderly persons in the house or outside. The position is different in urban areas. With the spread of education, social barriers against the employment of women in offices are disappearing rapidly. Women are increasingly replacing men in many fields or participating with them in parallel fields of social work, arts and crafts. Working women still occupy a subordinate position in social life, but they do not observe *purdah*.

In ancient times, people of Haryana believed in omens and charms. They were very prone to superstitions. Some of these superstitions still influence the behaviour of many. For instance, they believe that the crow and the black duck must pass on one's right, the snake on the left. If a *mantis* is to the right, one will recoup his loss. A *mantis* is called the horse or crow of Ram, it is always auspicious specially during Dussera. If a man wishes to build a house and the first stroke of the spade turns up charcoal, he will change the site. Iron is a sovereign safeguard against the evil eye. Owls portend desolate homes, black things in general are bad omens. Charms are in common use. The leaves of the *Siras* and the mango tree are powerful especially those of the *Siras*. They are hung up in garlands with a mystic inscription on an earthen platter in the middle and the whole is called *Totka*.

The *jand* is another very sacred tree. In illness, it is a good thing to have an inscription made on an earthen vessel by a fakir and to wash it off and drink the water. Superstitions are innumerable. Odd numbers are lucky, but three and thirteen are unlucky. If a man with two wives wants to marry a third, he will first marry a tree, so that the new wife may be the fourth. Hindus consider the south a quarter to be avoided, for the spirits of the dead are supposed to live there. To sneeze is auspicious, it indicates that you will not die for some time more. A *bania* (shopkeeper) will not make the first transaction of the day on credit. It must be paid in cash and it is called *bohni*. It is inauspicious to confront a Brahman, who has no *tilak* mark on his forehead. On Mondays and Saturdays people do not go to the east. The evil spirit '*Dasa Sul*' resides in that direction on these days. On Sundays and Thursdays people do not go to the west. A woman carrying a child or a pitcher is a happy omen. Two pitchers are happier still. A she-buffalo which tries to loosen a peg by striking it with her head is considered inauspicious. The one that makes its tighter and faster by striking down upon it, is regarded as auspicious. A bullock which shakes its head is also considered inauspicious

A cow that calves in *Bhadon* and a she-buffalo that calves in *Magh* are considered inauspicious. If a mare foals in *Sawan* in the day time, it is inauspicious and offering of alms is the remedy. If a crop has grown exceedingly well, a black pot or tattered shoe is suspended on a pole in the field. This is to avert the evil eye. Three men together will not start on a journey. If they have to do so, two will go first, the third joining them later. They will start after eating some *gur* (jaggery), *laddu* (sweet gram flour balls) or *dahi* (curd). A house with a broad front and narrow back is considered inauspicious. The reverse is auspicious. Hell and heaven on earth are described tersely: small cereals such as *china-dhan* to eat, goat or sheep as wealth, a shrew for a wife, dirty clothes – these are four signs of hell. The reverse of this is : a cart to load, a she-buffalo for property, a woman of good family and a mare to ride, these are the signs of heaven.

Customs of Himachal Pradesh

The total population of Himachal Pradesh stood at 6,077,248 on March 2001 as per the provisional results of the Census of India 2001. The population of Himachal Pradesh includes estimated population of entire Kinnaur district. The majority of population is rural (91.3%). Most of the villages are small dwellings with population less than 500 (81.5%). Only five villages have population more than 5000. The state has a large area under tribal belt which covers two districts of Lahaul and Spiti and Kinnaur and Bharmaur and Pangi Development Blocks of Chamba district. The sex ratio is 976 females per 1000 males as per 1991 census. District Hamirpur has sex ratio of 1105. This is the second highest in the country after Kerala NFHS–2 has estimated the sex ratio for the state at 1013 in 1998-99. In contrast to the country, the sex ratio has been steadily increasing in the state.

The population consists of various hill tribes, all speaking their own dialects. These tribes include the Gadis, Gujaris, Kinnauris, Lahulis, and Pangwalis. More than 95 percent of the people are Hindus, although the caste system of social groupings is less rigid than elsewhere in India. Sikhs, Muslim, Buddhist and Christian minorities total about five percent of the population. Himachal Pradesh is the least urbanized state in India. Its urban population accounts for less than 10 percent of the total.

The ancient inhabitants of this region were tribals called Dasas, who entered the hills from the Gangetic plains, between the third and second millennium B.C. They were joined by the Aryans around 2000 BC and a number of tribal republics, called the *Janapadas*, began to emerge in geographically separate regions of this state. The close of the 10th century saw the entry of Muslim rulers, in North India, through the north western passes. The people of Himachal Pradesh are simple and unsophisticated, lively and good natured, with a penchant for fairs and festivals.

These people are a close knit community. These tribes also help each other in performing the rituals and customs at the time of a death or a birth. Each village follow the caste pattern. The villages of the higher caste Brahmins, the Rajputs, the Mahajans (money-lenders) are beautifully kept and well looked after. The villages attach a great importance to brotherhood. When arranging wedding-matches, the caste and *gotra* is given importance. People prefer to marry into families with similar backgrounds both religious and economic and into neighbouring villages so that kinship may grow. Each caste is keen to retain its traditions and customs. The joint family system is encouraged and the familiar relationships are cherished and filial devotion is given high priority. The sister is highly respected and other relationships are also given due importance.

Tribal and non-tribal communities live together all over the state. The villages follow their own hierarchies of caste and community patterns, which follows the demands of a life style. The village is perceived as a large family. People have established close familiar relationship with each other and address the elder as *Chacha-Tau* (uncle), *Bhabhi* (sister-in-law), *Mausi* (aunt) or *Nani* (grandmother) according to their ages. The relationship between the wife and the husband's younger brother (*Bhabi-Devar*) carries a special romanticized aura. Each bride addresses men younger than her husband, as *Devar*. An elder is addressed as *Jija*, a woman about the same age as one's mother as *Mausi* and a man younger than one's father as *Chacha*. All old women in the mother's village are addressed as *Nanis* and the ones in own village a *Dadi*. People close in age address each other as *Bhau* (male) or *Bhain* (female). These relationships are looked upon as precious among individuals and in the community. In the tribal areas also this is a common practice.

A woman may choose a man as her brother and then they are known as *Mitra* and *Mitrani*. At the time of a marriage, the untying of the thread *Kankan* and at the time of the *Karva Chauth* fast, the exchange of *karwa* (clay pots with a snout) are also occasions for making a brother or a sister. The families always treat these relationships with respect. The maternal uncle or Mama plays an important role at the time of wedding or other family festivities. He presents his sister and her family with gifts of sweets and clothes when the sister has a baby and also when the sacred thread ceremony, or *Yagyopavit* is performed for her sons. At the time of sister's wedding, it is the brother who supports her and puts her in palanquin. Most brothers perform their traditional duties towards their sister with affection and respect. The sister as *Nanad* or sister-in-law plays an important role in her father's family. The older brother is known as *Jeth* and his wife as *Jethani*.

These two come next in importance to the parents. The parents enjoy the highest place in the family hierarchy and if the son and his wife live in their own houses separately, while the parents are alive, it is frowned upon. The older uncles are also highly respected and at the time of a wedding, they are honoured with gifts of pink turbans. Aunts, uncles, cousins are all considered equal to one's own parents and brothers and sisters are loved and respected. The Rajputs and the Brahmins lay particular stress on the purity of race, caste, *gotra* and family. Among the higher castes, the daughter's father's house (*Maika*) enjoys a great importance. At the time of festivals and major family occasions like a wedding or a birth, various gifts including foodstuffs, jewellery and clothes are sent to the girl's husband's house (*sasural*). It is also taboo for the girl's family members to eat or drink anything in her *sasural*. They must pay an equivalent sum of money as compensation.

Among the lower castes such taboos are not enforced strictly. The higher castes follow a custom of *Purdah*. Women veil their faces in front of all elders. When a girl comes out of her quarters after delivering a child, she must touch the feet of all the elders in her husband's family and leave some money at their feet. This customs is known as *Pair Bandai* (worshipping the feet). Marriages are settled at an early age. There are instances of matches being settled between families before the babies are born, based on assumptions that one will be a boy and other a girl. The relationship between a brother-in-law and a sister-in-law is an informal and a close one. It is customary for the young brother-in-law to be seated in the bride's lap and to be the first to see her face. Among the tribals, it is permissible for the younger brother to marry the older brother's widow, but the higher castes do not permit this. Among them the older brother's wife is equal to one's mother. All the brothers and their wives must live with the parents when they are alive. The older brother is considered equal to the father. The polyandrous customs of Kinnaur region also point at the close bond between the brothers. The occasion of a girl child's birth is not celebrated with great joy. Girls are respected as *De* (short for Devi or goddess). At the time of the Navratra, special Puja is offered to the young girls and at the time of festivals, she is given special gifts of clothing and sweets.

Marriage is an important ceremony, when the parents and also the closer elders relatives begin to look around for suitable matches as soon as the child is old enough. Sometimes, a middleman is used as a match-maker known as *Roovary, Dhamu* or *Mazomi*. He finds out the details about the social and financial standing of the family and final decision is taken on the basis of horoscopes. Matches in the same *gotra* are not considered very good. When the match is settled the ritual gift called *Tika* is sent. The groom and his family are invited to tea. On this occasion, ritual songs are sung and sweets are distributed. In the tribal areas, both the parties exchange *Chhang* (rice wine) and close relatives are invited to participate in the ceremony. In some areas during various festivals, gifts of jewellery and clothes are sent to the betrothed. In Kinnaur, this system is known as *Chharmi Nata*, elsewhere it is known as sending the *Tihar*. The date for the wedding is fixed in consultation with the priest, in some places the permission of the deities is also sought.

Customarily, all the wedding preparations are to be kept a secret from the bride. In Kinnaur as the wedding party approaches the house, the bride and her friends begin to wail and weep. Marriage customs differ from place to place in the state. The bride and the bridegroom are carried in palanquins except in the Lahaul area. The girl touches her father's feet at the time of her departure. People in Kinnaur follow a matriarchal system where all the brothers share a wife and if there are more than six brothers then another woman may be brought in. All the brothers are looked upon as common fathers to the children. The eldest one is known as *Teg Bawal* and the youngest as *Gota Bawal*. A maid (barber's wife or *Pachekan*) accompanies the bride temporarily from her father's house to help her settle down in the midst of her new family. In Lahaul when the groom departs with the bride, the girl friends of the bride block his path till the bridegroom promises them that he will take good care of their dear friend. The day the bride enters the new household, a special *Havan* is performed under the guidance of the family priest. The bride and the bridegroom cook *kheer* (rice pudding) and it is served to all the assembled relatives who bless them. At the time of *Feroni* (the ritual return of the bride after her first visit from her father's house, also known as *Dwiragaman*) the bride and groom are welcomed with great joy and fed sweets and butter. At the time of the wedding, the *Suhagi* jewellery (marriage symbols) is presented by the maternal uncle and the rest is given by the parents of the bride and the groom. The bridegroom's family displays their gifts or Barasuhi to the bride, to all assembled, so that they may judge their financial status. Among the poorer sections, the gifts and the cash to be given to the bride by her family at the time of the wedding are fixed in advance. In the plains, the bride's brother presents the bridegroom with a *dhoti* and a ring and ushers him to the place where the marriage ceremony is to take place. In the areas of Kinnaur, the bride's father presents the bridegroom with a white turban and ties a sword or a dagger to his waist band to indicate the start of the ceremonies. All this time wine cups are also presented to both the match-maker and the bridegroom. When the marriage party returns with the bride, it is greeted by the fellow villagers holding torches. Goats are sacrificed and special rituals are performed to ward off evil spirits and ghosts.

There are many rituals relating to the coming of a new bride into the family. The bride first performs the puja to the deities of her new family under the guidance of the older women and is then made to distribute sweets (*Gune*) in front of the *Dehre* which is a traditional wall-painting done as a religious ritual after marriage. The bride distributes *Gune* with both hands. The bridegroom is the first to get these and gives his bride, money or jewellery in return. Ritual songs are sung at this time by women sitting around the bride. *Munh Dikhai* is a custom which reveals the face of the bride. The mother-in-law comes first who presents the bride the jewellery and sees her face and then follows the uncle's wives, sister-in-law, etc. Each one of them presents the bride with money or pieces of jewellery. *Pair Bandai* (worshipping the feet) is another custom which helps introduce the bride to husband's family. In this, the bride first offers the close relatives a gift of money and then covering her hands with the edge of her sari, touches their feet. She is then blessed by the elders to be well-loved by her husband and produce sons. *Darosh Dab Dhab*, *Dam-Chalshish*, *Dual* or *Har*, *Batta-Satta*, *Jhajhara*, *Gadar*, *Mool Biah*, *Jhindphook* and *Yuth Vivah* are some other interesting forms of marriage prevalent in the area.

Darosh Dab Dhab is a tribal system prevalent in Kinnaur. In this, the girl is forcibly dragged away from a fair ground or a festival meeting. She pretends to scream, scratch, bite and show annoyance, but the boy holding her does not relent his hold. At night, the village tries to bring the girl round and if she agrees then the next day a match-maker goes to her family with a gift of five rupees and a bottle of wine (*ijit*) and tries to get their permission. Similar gifts are presented to the village deities. In *Dam-Chalshish*, the lovers elope together and the boy's father sends the Mazomi to the girl's house and tries to placate them and their relatives with gifts. If the family agrees, then a ritual marriage follows. In *Jhindphook* custom, the lovers go to a lonely spot and set some shrubs on fire and then go round the fire seven times. This makes them husband and wife. In the *Chalshish* system as the girl departs from her home, sad tunes are played and the son-in-law presents the mother of the daughter with a sum of five hundred rupees as *Masore* or the price of her milk. *Hari* or *Har* means that a woman who is dissatisfied with her husband, goes and begins to live with another man. Her new husband has to settle it with the previous one by offering him a price acceptable to him. Such marriages are known as *Jhanjhara* or *Jhanhrada*. The new husband also invites all his relatives and at night offers a special *puja* known as *Nuala* to lord Shiva. When the priest or the Chela gives him the lord's blessings, he in turn puts his *Balu* (a piece of Jewellery) on the woman and this makes her his lawful wife. The Gaddis follow this custom more than the others. The Gaddis and some labourer families follows the *Batta-Satta* System of marriage in which the bride's brother has to marry the bridegroom's sister or vice versa. If one of the girls refuses to go to her husband, the other one also will stay back. In case of complications, the village assembly of *Pachi* (Panchayat) is called. They listen to arguments from both sides and give their verdict in writing, copies of which are preserved by both sides.

The higher castes do not allow the widows to remarry, but the lower castes allow remarriage. In some cases after the death of the older brother, the younger one marries the widow. Sometimes the widow leaves her husband's house and moves in with someone else. This is known as *Ghar Karna* (taking another house). Among the lower castes a woman may make four to five such changes of spouse in her lifetime. In such cases, the new husband has to undertake the responsibilities for all the children born of previous marriages. The *Dehris* (monuments) outside most villages are reminders of the prevalence of the system of *Sati* in which the widow burnt herself on the funeral pyre of her husband. Among the higher castes, the husband's presence is the only security for most women. They observe a lot of fasts and perform many rituals to prolong their husband's life. Among them, even if widowed young, a woman must suffer her widowhood till her dying day but may not take another husband.

Some tribal communities have a divorce law known as *Dehri*, *Hari* or *Har* which is held above all the courts of law. In this, the couple seeking divorce takes a twig of *Shur* wood and snap it in front of witnesses and throw it behind them. In Lahaul, a woollen thread is similarly snapped symbolising the termination of marital ties. In some villages, the couple must break a *sal* leaf into two in the presence of fellow-villagers. In case of a divorce, the woman forfeits all rights to the husband's property. The *Har* and the *Dehri* systems decree that the party applying for divorce must pay compensation to the aggrieved party. Among the Gaddis, this payment of compensation is known as giving *Fargati*. This is paid to the *Numberdar* (head) of the village who takes down the whole case in writing and settles the accounts peacefully. Due to the spread of literacy, such divorces have now decreased. People also choose mates more carefully now, which has reduced the risk of breakups. Most divorces have personal, rather than financial causes. In some areas, the divorce procedures are conducted by the Panchayat (village assembly) whose verdict is acceptable to both the parties.

The Gaddis perform the marriage ceremony twice. First comes the *Jooth Pana* when the bridegroom's party goes to the girl's house (who is usually a minor of 8-10 years) and breaks a lump of jaggery in the girl's name, and the girl's family smears them with red colour. On their way back, the bridegroom's party distributes lumps of jaggery to all the passers by thus announcing the confirming of the betrothal. Then the real marriage ceremony follows in which the woman from the girl's family help her through the rituals. There is no system of dowry. After five or ten years, comes the second half known as *Sadnoj*. By now the girl is mature. On a fixed day the bridegroom in ritual finery, goes to his wife's house with a few relatives and after staying there for a couple of days, departs with his bride for his own village. At this time, gifts are presented and dances and celebrations begin in the bridegroom's house to welcome the party. In Pangi, at the time of the marriage, the bridegroom's younger brother presents the bride's mother with a silver rupee. This gives him the right of a second husband over the bride, but the bride is not to be shared by more than two brothers. The people in Pangi are monogamous and a widow may remarry, but such marriages are not held in high esteem.

The birth of a male baby is a great occasion in the villages. People light lamps and the women from the neighbourhood come and sing songs of joy and congratulations. The mother is treated with great reverence. The baby is delivered by old and experienced midwives who are paid both in cash and in kind. In the Kinnaur area, the palanquins of the gods are brought within their houses after a male child is delivered and a feast of rich food and liquor is given to the villagers. This custom is known as *Shukud*. At this time a goat may also be sacrificed. Among the Brahmins, the *Namkaran* (the naming of the infant), *Chudakaran* (first snipping off of his locks) and *Annaprashan* (the first tasting of cereals by the baby) are all performed with a great joy. In some areas in Solan, the infant is taken to a waterfall and lodged near it for the first three days. Getting a horoscope written for the baby is also a must. Marriages cannot be settled before the horoscopes of the couple have been matched properly. At the time of child birth, the mother is housed in a separate room. In the tribal areas, she is lodged in a cattle-manor (*Khudd*). After delivery, the infant is bathed and wrapped in a clean cloth.

The first twenty days are called *Sootak* or pollution and during this period, the family observes abstention from all religious rituals. If touched by mistake, the idol is said to become polluted, and an animal sacrifice becomes necessary to placate the god. Some other important ceremonies connected with child-birth are the first sighting of the baby by the father and the first feeding of the tonic *ghutti* to the infant. It is believed that the child imbibes the temperament of the person who gives him his first dose of *ghutti*. Therefore, the *ghutti* is administered by some exceptionally good-natured member of the family. After the twenty day, *Sootak* the pollution period is over, the 'cleansing up' ceremony takes place. This occasion is celebrated with a great fun. They call the ceremony *Goontar,* and on this occasion special *Sunds* (sweet cookies) are made and distributed among the close relatives.

In the tribal areas, when a family is blessed with a son, goats are sacrificed to the deities, and the other fathers of boys in the village joyfully clobber the new father with chunks of meat. Money is also offered to the temples. The birth of a daughter is considered the beginning of heavy responsibilities and so few celebrate it as a joyous occasion. In some areas, the girls from the village chase the girl's father round and round, and he pretends to run away. After the baby's birth and the casting of the horoscopes, people make special efforts to propitiate the evil stars in the child's horoscope. For this, special *Pujas* are offered and alms are distributed. People hang a little silver or copper *Jantar* (amulets) around the child's neck to ward off the bad effect of evil stars. Children born in the *Gandmool* hour are considered unlucky and are often gifted away ritually as soon as they are born.

When the child is seven months old, he is given the first taste of cereal in the form of *kheer* (rice pudding). This ceremony is known as *Kheerpoo*. The child is fed *kheer* with a silver article shaped like the blade of grass. Female children are also fed *kheer* and special songs are sung. At this time, a basket full of various things of daily use are also placed before the child. It is believed that the child shall pick up an article which foretells his future occupation.

The custom associated with death are quite strange and interesting. As death approaches, the sick man's body is lowered on the ground, smeared with fresh cow dung. His head must point to the north and as soon as death occurs, conch shells are blown. This is a signal for the relatives to burst out crying. It is inauspicious to die on a bed and alms must be given by the sick person prior to his or her death. After the death has occurred, a linseed oil lamp with a cotton wick is lit and placed in a corner of the room and covered with a woven grass basket. The lamp symbolizes the spirit of the dead man. The mourners come and sit in this room and the ritual mourning is done here.

The corpse is laid on plantain leaves in the courtyard, bathed and then placed in a wooden coffin or upon a bier, and covered with a colourful shroud and taken to the cremation ground. On the way, the funeral procession stops at a few places where some stones and leaves are placed in the name of the dead man. Before consigning the body to the flames a *Pind Dan* (ritual feeding of balls made of cooked rice, sesame seeds and curds to the birds and elements in the name of the dead one) is performed. It is considered propitious to add fuel wood to the pyre. After the cremation, people bathe and come back to the deceased's house. So long as the dead body lies within the house, no food can be cooked therein. After this for a month the close relatives observe *Sootak* or pollution.

During the pollution period, the use of things like meat, fish, garlic, onions, asafoetida is taboo. At the end of this period either the daughter's or the son's father-in-law (*Kudam*) brings food items cooked with asafoetida and feeds it to the bereaved family, after this the taboo is lifted. In some families, the death of an aged member is celebrated with the slaying of goats and feasting. On the third day, the bones and ashes are immersed in a holy place like Haridwar, Rivalsar or Manasarovar.

For ten days the house memberes observe a mourning period. Mondays, Wednesdays, Thursdays and Fridays are taboo for condolence visits. The daughters come at the end of the month long *Sootak*. The close relatives have their heads shaven and the widow removes her marriage jewellery. On the tenth day, clothes are washed (*Kapad Dhulai*) and the holy *Garud Purana* is recited by *Charjee* (a special class that recites scriptures in houses where death has occurred). In the tribal families, the *Lama* reads out the scriptures. For a year each month, the day of the death is observed with special rituals. A plaster statue of the dead one is placed near a stream and the articles of his use are immersed in the water. If someone dies an untimely death, a special ritual called *Sapindi* is performed. Each year an annual *Shradda* is performed to commemorate the dead one. Each four years a *Chatur Varshik* is done.

People, usually Brahmins, numbering in three, five, seven, nine or eleven are invited, feasted and presented with pots, *pans* and clothes. The whole village is then feasted.

The tribal people follow a slightly different set of customs. In Kinnaur, when someone dies, all the villagers gather at his house at night. This custom is known as *Drum Rating*. The dead body is then bathed in a large vessel called *Lam Kunyal* and then wrapped up in a white shroud. Two people then carry the body to the cremation ground on a plank.

The legs of the body are turned behind at the knees with the help of wooden pegs. It is believed that if the legs are straight, an evil spirit might enter the body. He also recites some *mantras* and during this, it is considered auspicious if a drop of blood become visible on the forehead of the dead one. When the funeral procession leaves the house, a piece of bread stuffed with *Dal* is thrown on the roof top for the crows. It is believed that the crow can communicate with the dead person. For seven weeks, the *Lama* comes to the dead man's house to recite the sacred text (*chhos*). At the end of the seven week period, the *Lama* and *Jomo* read the text together and are then fed by the family of the dead man. On the day of the death, the *Lama* tells them about life after death and about rebirth. Sometimes, alms are given to counteract evil influences. Some tribes light a lamp in the name of the dead one for seven days. On the third day after death, the *chholya* ceremony is performed and on the thirteenth day *damkochang* is performed.

On the 15th day, the Lama performs a *havan*. The next day, those who go to collect the ashes leave a stone or a little flag upon the hill top in the name of the dead one. A year after the death, the Lama performs the *fulyach* (or the *dalhyang*) ceremony, at which he gets food and clothes in the name of the dead.

These customs are followed with some local variations in the Lahaul valley. If an old man dies, no one may touch the dead body till the Lama arrives at the house. The Lama whispers an invocation to the dead man's soul in his ear and asks it to leave the body and this is called *fuhan*. After this, the dead man is seated on a wooden or metal chair in a corner and a lamp is lit with butter in front of it. The body stays in the house for two or more days according to the economic status of the dead man's family. Then it is wrapped in a shroud and placed on a bier and carried to the cremation ground. The Lama recites prayers, the relatives cry, and conch shells are blown. Two men, one with a conch shell and another with a flag follow the funeral procession. Sometimes, an umbrella is held over the bier. On the way, the procession stops a couple of times to allow the man with the flag and the man with the conch shell to circle the body for which they are paid a sum of money. At the cremation ground, the shroud is torn into five pieces, four of which are hung upon the four corners of the funeral pyre and the fifth is placed on the forehead of the dead one. The Lama recites *mantras* and gets barley, rice and butter thrown into the pyre which is set to light. On the next day the ashes are collected by the family, and it is immersed in the Chandrabhaga river.

In the tribal areas, some customs are quite unusual. In the Spiti valley, when someone dies, the *jhavan* (witch doctor) is called to find out whether the body should be burnt, buried or cut up into pieces and thrown upon hill tops for the wild animals to consume. All communities there follow the orders of the *jhavan*. The *Sanglas* and the *Sipis* have their own customs. The *thoda* custom which probably originated in the Puranic past, can be seen in the village fairs in the tribal areas. This is a competition in archery in the memory of the Pandavas. In this, the interested parties form two teams, one called *Pashi* and other *Sathi*. The players then shoot arrows at spots marked near the feet. If the arrow hits the target the player jumps up and names one of the five Pandava brothers.

The *buhana* custom is a beautiful example of community feelings within the farming communities. In some area, this is also known as *hela* or *jwari*. The planting of seedlings, weeding, hoeing and harvesting are all community activities here, and are performed co-operatively. The custom is beneficial to the smaller and poorer farmers whose necessary chores are thus completed on time without expense. While the tasks are being performed by the entire community for one of their brethren, a drummer stands at a raised spot and beats his drum rhythmically to which all keep time as they go about their work. At the end of the day's work, all the workers are fed on *bhatedus* (thick round bread made of whole wheat flour) and other delicacies. The women also work with the men and sing to the beat of drum.

This is a custom prevalent in the Kinnaur region and is designed to ward off the evil spirits and ghosts. Even the poorest families celebrate it once in every three or four years. In this, one hundred and eight clay lamps are lit, which symbolically dispel the darkness for the coming period. Then the Lama comes and performs a special *puja* in the house to the gods known as *Vikyu*. This custom was largely prevalent in Mahasu and Kulu regions and seems to have its earliest roots in human sacrifice performed every twelve years. The last *Bhoonda* (at Vaibhai in the Sutlej valley) is said to have been performed in the following manner: A man belonging to the Beda community was chosen for the ceremony. A few days prior to it, for three months, he was housed in the village temple with great respect. During this period, he wove a rope with grass-measuring some four to five hundred *Hath* (a *Hath* is the length between the elbow and the tip of the middle finger of a mature human arm).

On the fixed day, a procession of the gods was brought out ceremoniously. The Beda led this procession holding aloft an umbrella made of blue cloth, and supported on each side by his two wives. He wore only one article of clothing and a red thread around his neck. As the procession reached the spot where the *Bhoonda* was to be performed, one end of the grass rope was tied to the pillar on the top of the hill and the other to another pillar, at the bottom of the same hill. The procession then took the Beda into the temple and sacrificed a goat. In the temple, the Beda was offered to the gods and then the procession returned to the spot where the *Bhoonda* was to be performed. Here, on the top of the hill a woollen seat was laid on the rope with bags of sand suspended on both sides to keep it balanced. The *Beda* was seated on that and at a signal from the priest he was pushed down hill. The seat flew down with the Beda. His survival depended purely on chance. If the Beda survives, he is paid a sum of some 80/- to 90/- rupees from the temple fund. The observers also give him money. The last *Bhoonda* took place in 1902 at a village near Nirat. The custom is nearly obsolete now. This is tribal exorcism designed to stop the spread of epidemics in a village, and is prevalent in the villages along the Indo-Tibetan border.

When anyone in these areas contracts a contagious disease and is critically ill, a locally available boulder of white stone is put at his door-step at a spot where anyone may see it, and know that someone within the house is lying ill with a contagious disease. Due to the taboos this custom enforces, in order to isolate the patient, even the doctors are not allowed into the patient's rooms. The entrance to each village in the area is guarded to check the entry of someone suffering from the disease. Between the villages of Raja and Kibbar, each person that enters the area has to be checked by the Lama against contagious diseases.

Animal sacrifices are performed in order to reap a good harvest, or to save a good crop from destruction by the evil forces. When the crop is ready for harvesting, a black goat is led around the fields and sacrificed. The meat of the goat is then distributed in the village as a holy '*prasad* of the gods'. Sometimes to propitiate *Yakshas*, saints, goddesses or family gods, people perform a *Jatra*. In this, a whole family along with all its numerous relatives leaves in a procession to the temple of the deity all dressed up, singing devotional songs. They carry along with them foodstuff of all kinds and the sacrificial goat. The drummer and the flag are also a part of the procession. As the womenfolk sing *Jatra* songs along the way, an old woman makes little signs on the road, shaped like footprints. These are known as '*Leekhnu*'.

As the procession reaches the deity's temple, first the *puja* is performed and then all the family members sprinkle water on the sacrificial goat and at the same time urging the tribal deity to accept the gift of the animal. When the animal gives his body a shake, it is taken as a sign from the deity signifying his acceptance. If the goat does not shiver, it is taken to be a sign of the deity's wrath, and people begin praying. When the ritual is over, the goat is sacrificed. The meat is then cooked and served to all those present.

The party spends the night in the temple premises singing songs and asking questions about sickness and crops of the devotees on whom the spirit of the deity is said to descend. In the morning after offering *puja*, the group comes back to the village. Earlier it was customary to perform a human sacrifice at the time of the building of a canal, a water tank or a bridge. But this is obsolete now, and animal sacrifice has replaced the human sacrifice. Some people who object to bloodshed offer sweets and other articles to the deity. In Malana (Kulu) and Dodra Kwar (Mahasu) the twin deities Jamlu and Mahasu are unquestionably considered as the rulers of the area. Nothing is done here without consulting them and obtaining their permission. At the time of harvesting, feasts are offered to the deities especially to *Baba*. Trees are also considered holy. On fast days the womenfolk worship the Peepal, the Banyan, the Mango and the Pomegranate trees, and offer clothes and all kinds of delicacies to them. The Banyan tree is worshipped on the day of the *Vata Savitri* fast. The pomegranate tree is worshipped at the time of weddings. Friendships are also formed beneath this tree by formally appointing the trees as the witness. When the new grains have been harvested, young virgins *kanya* are fed and relatives feasted and certain traditional delicacies like *kheer* and *halwa* are cooked.

Women fast on the first (*Sankranti*), the eleventh (*Ekadashi*) and the fifteenth day of the full moon (*Poornima*). Among the higher castes, fasting by women is taken to guarantee the prolonged prosperity and physical well-being among the family members. Giving up a fast after a fixed period, is known as '*Mokh*'. On the day of a fast, the women clean the house and paint ritual '*Lekhnu*' on the floor and then collect all the required articles for the particular fast and offer *puja* to the deity. Unmarried girls are also supposed to fast on the full moon day. On the

'*Sankranti*' day, the Brahmin priests visit their clients who give them alms according to their means. As the guest arrives he is offered a bed, food, a hookah and a tea. He is looked upon as an incarnation of the gods. If he comes on the day of festival he must not leave without having a meal. Visiting relatives and married daughters must not be sent back without gifts of sweets and clothes. The guests also never arrive empty-handed. If they can manage nothing else, they bring some fruits for the hosts. The women embrace each other when departing and touch the feet of the elders. Married daughters and children are also given gifts of money. The married daughters often weep at leaving their fathers house after a visit. In some areas the customs for welcoming a guest are very strange. In Chachyot area, when the guest reaches a house, the family does not open the door to him. Neither they come out or offer him a seat. The guest lets himself in and finds a seat. In a little while, the host family files in and welcomes him.

His feet are washed with warm water, and he is given delicacies to eat. The guest as also the married daughter's husband are called *Prahuna*. Before a wedding or a sacred thread ceremony for a boy, the boy and the bride-to-be are invited specially and presented with gifts. This custom is known as *Lodhak*. The relatives cook many delicacies at this time and send it for the bride and the bridegroom. Special foods are offered to them and songs are sung. The gifts bestowed by the relatives on this occasion are to be remembered and returned when a similar occasion arises in the other relative house. This custom promotes mutual good-will and co-operation.

Untouchability has fossilized in the area into a rigid and ugly custom. The untouchables may not talk direct to someone from a high caste or dare to use their wells or enter their houses with shoes on. They must leave the road if a man from a high caste is passing by and in wedding feasts they cannot sit with everyone else. They are served food on leaves which they must accept after repeated bowings, and they must remove the carcasses of dead animals from the village for which they are paid in kind at the time of the harvesting season.

People in Himachal are simple and peace loving. Stealing, killing or taking away someone else's share is considered sinful. Long litigations are sometimes caused due to land or women related problems. Among the lower castes, abducting someone's wife or the wife's elopement causes minor scuffles but none of them are very serious. People here forgive easily. The women are more prone to suicide as the social pressures are more intense on them. The quarrels within a clan, caste or community are usually decided by *Doom* or *Khumli* (the community panchayat). The local priest and *Kardar* (head) are members of this. The *Kardar* signifies the date and the priest calls the assembly. An emergency meeting is known as *Thek*, *Dadhi* or *Dal* in which each absentee has to pay a fine of a rupee.

In some areas of Kulu, Kinnaur and Mahasu, the gods are called upon to decide matters. In Malana, the god Jamlu and the god Mahasu in Dodra Kwar decide the cases through their oracles. Their judgment are final and irrevocable. People who defy the caste laws are ostracized. This custom is known as *Chekka* or *Banaj*. A family which has been ostracized is not visited by the fellow villagers. Such people or families can be accepted back into the community only if the whole community assembles in the village and agrees to call the defaulter. He is then made to drink the holy *Panch Gava* (a holy mixture of five products of the cow comprising of her milk, butter, ghee, urine and dung) and then he may sit with the members of his community at a feast. After this, he offers a gift to the god.

Killing a cow is considered the biggest crime and sin. A man who commits it, is debarred from the village, till he goes to holy places like Mattan or Haridwar and has a *Havan* performed at his house. People trust each other and often leave their property and animals in each other's care without any formal written documents. To dig into someone else's savings is considered highly sinful.

Charging an interest on a loan, selling milk or charging a rent for lodging someone in one's house are all looked down upon. These customs are undergoing changes now. State money-lender usually takes advantage of the illiteracy of the villagers by charging them exorbitant interest rates. Some of such loans can never be paid in full. The opening of banks in villages by the government has greatly improved the situation.

The woman in Himachal are bound strictly by traditions. They must not utter the first name of an older relative, but imply it symbolically or by pointing at an article with a similar name. On feast days and festivals all of them barring widows dress up in all their finery with colourful skirts and scarves and waistcoats and rows of jewellery all over their bodies. The laws of heredity differ from area to area. Generally, the hereditary rights pass direct from the father to the son or sons. In case of having more than one wife, children of all the wives may claim an equal share. If some one has no son, his property is shared equally by the daughters. If the daughter dies issueless, the property then passes on to the father's relatives.

In Spiti the customs are a little different. The family system is called *Jethansi*. As the eldest son gets married, he shall become the head of the house, and the father shall retire to a smaller house. The eldest son then comes to be known as *Rambagchepa* and the retired father as *Ravangechugpa*. The father gets a small plot of land to live by and the younger sons join a monastery. In case the eldest son produces no male heirs, the younger brother may become the head and shoulder the family responsibilities. The land in the area is thus prevented from getting sub-divided. In case none of the sons produces a son, the daughter of the house is then married to a man who agrees to come and live in his father-in-law's house, and carry on the family traditions. Such a son-in-law is known as *Makpa*. If the girl dies, or does not have children, the husband may then marry a cousin of hers who then stand to inherit the property. In Kinnaur and Mahasu, many families follow the system of polyandry. In such families when the husband dies, the wife as also property, passes to the next brother and after him the right of property then reverts back to the sons. Illegitimate children or children born of a widow or an unmarried girl have no property rights. They are known as *Poltu* or *Chukandu*. Earlier, they were used by families as domestic servants and in exchange for their services a small plot of land was given to them. Now they have legal protection against such exploitation, and if they can establish their paternity, they can inherit a share of the paternal property. Some areas follow the customs of *Jethand*, *Paghand* and *Chundband*. In *Jethand* the eldest son inherits a larger share of the property plus a larger share of his family debts. In *Chundaband* system, all the sons of the various wives have equal share in the paternal property. In *Paghand* system, the property shall first be distributed among the daughter and then among the sons. This custom is prevalent among the Gaddis. Among the Rajputs there existed a system known as *Daya Bhag* (the rightful position). In this, the eldest son stands to inherit a special portion in addition to his other share by virtue of being the eldest son.

1

Conceiving and Birth

Custom of Rajasthan

The people of Rajasthan identify themselves more easily in the modern Times within a system of three tier ranking rather than the chaturvarna system of theancient Times. This is very clear from the way they place themselves and are placed by others as high, middle and low in the economic states. As in other states, so in Rajasthan, the largest number of communities are placed by others at the middle level followed by those who are placed at lower level and those who are placed at a high level. The communities placed at high level control rich economic resources such as land and water, and enjoy a higher status. The middle category consists of the landowning peasant and artisan castes, who are considered clean, and have acquired considerable economic and social clout. They represent strength of the burgeoning middle class. The low class consists of the residual communities who generally saffer from low social status and poor economic condition incluincluding small marginal farmers. Landless labourers and so on placed lowest in the social hierarchy, by themselves and by others. This condition prevails in spite of the fact that land transfer has been promoted in recent years under the land distribution policy of the central and state governments. And some members of the Scheduled Castes have acquired land. The high, middle and low category exist not only among the Hindu castes but but also among the Muslims, Jains, Sikhs also including and Scheduled Castes and Scheduled Tribes.

The ethnography of Rajputs in Rajasthan generally deals with the dominant lineages and clans and glosses over the stratification that exists in the community. There exist two to three recognizable strata among the Rajputs in the north-western states. The threefold stratification of Rajputs in terms is of (a) the dominant lineages, (b)a lower stratum which consists of the communities who work as labourers and practice widow remarriage and junior levirate such as Natarayat, and (c)a middle level, owning land and related to the upper groups, which has become dynamic during the recent Times.

Here many low communities tend to recognize the meselves as Rajputs or claiming the status of RajputsThus, the state of Rajasthan has projected the model of Rajputsation. Clan names of Rajputs carried by the Banjaras and wondering and homeless castes exist from Himachal Pradesh and Punjab to Andhra and Maharashtra. There are also a number of communities called borderline communities which have segments following different religions like Islam and Jainism. In fact, there are Hindu and Jain segments among the Agarwal, Oswal and Shrimali; The Cheeta and Singhiwale have both Hindu and Muslim segments. The relationships among these segments vary. There are both commensal and connubial relationships among the Hindu and Jain segments. In case of Hindu and Muslim segments, there is marriage among communities such as Singhiwale, Bhangi and Cheeta. With the rise of religious bigotry and fundamentalism on al sides, such segments are now drifting apart as they try to define themselves more aggressively in terms of the supposedly pristine element of their society and religion. In the process of bigotry they are distancing away themselves from each other. However, in Rajasthan, the shared cultural space among all search segments is still large.

In the state people's folklore is rich in accounts of interaction between the indigenous tribals and the Rajputs. Bhil-Rajpt struggle and cooperation is part of Mewar folklore. Bundi was founded on the territory belonging to the Bhil tribals Their Chief tain was Kotiya who was killed in the battlefield and the foundation of the city of Bundi was laid on his body. However, there are also stories of conciliation and collaboration among the segments. Sheikh Burhan blessed the Rajputs chiefs request for a male issue: Shekhawati was named after the fakir. Jain occupied important administrative positions and were supported in their religious architechture activities by the Ranas of Mewar.

The state is generally known for its long traditions of communal harmony which have been reflected in and reinforced by folklore and stories of friendship that existed across the religious divisions. The battles glorified in the historical records were more of a secular nature in which communities cutting across the religious lines participated on both sides. A reason for this could be the presence of a relatively large number of the minorities belonging to both Islam and Jainism. Rajasthani ethos, its tradition of chivalry, and so on.

The process of the migration of the trading and business commuities including the marwaris from northwestern India to the rest of the country, whether from Haryana (Agroha)or from various parts of Rajasthan are too well known to be repeated. As for the housing pattern in the state in the rural side, the walls are made of mud and are about 4 to 5 feet high. The roof is conical and consists of wooden supports thatched with a combination of the akra bushes and wild grass, the whole structure being secured by the means of a coarse string. The circular form of hut is favoured here in the rural side, because of the strong winds that blow throughout the year. Apart from a low door, there is no opening in the structure. Usually a family builds three jhumpas and cncloses them with a hedge of thorns to keep animals away. This type of hut costs little to build. From time to time the roof of thatch is patched or renewed, and the walls and the floor re-plastered with clay mixed with cowdung. A dharni consists of a few such family huts. The agricultural implements consist of plough, harrow, levelers, clod crushers, seed drillers and hoes. Clod crusher is a heavy log dragged over the fields by bullocks to level the grounds and gather the needs together. The leveler is made of wood, the seed drill being of bamboo. Besides, there are several other implements like kurhad (axe), kuladi (pick axe), phawada (spade), khurpi (weeding hoe), dortli (sickle), korata (bill hostk), paner (crowbar) and dantali (rake with wooden teeth). Sickle is the basic harvesting tool. Iron plough, and other modern appliances are also being utilised by some.

The people in the state are differentiated by caste, status and the dialect of the cultural zones they inhabit. The differentiation is also reflected in their dresses and ornaments albeit there a certain basic similarity. Traditionally the rural males still wear dhoti, angrakhi (shirt) and pagdi or safa (headgear). There are of course regional differences in the attire. The dhoti is worn in a different way in Marwar (Jodhpur area) or Shekhawati (Jaipur area)or Hadoti (Bundi area). Earlier the people in cities used to wear another traditional dress of chudidar payjama (puckered trousers), and sherwani (a typical long-tight coat) and safa (heat gear). In the modern times, these traditional dresses are not worn so much. The people are taking to modern western style dresses like trousers, and shirts, etc, However, the pagri and safa are still worn at times in Rajasthan. There are a few differences between a pagdi and a safa despite both being Rajasthani headgear. Mewar has the tradition of pagdi while Marwar has the tradition of safa. The pattern of wearing pagdivaries with the caste as well as in the regions in which people live. These headgears are worn on occasions of festivals, marriages and other special ceremonies. Though the elder wear these at one time or the other, but these are becoming less popular. The women wear lenga, lugdi, chunri, dupatta, petticoat, angrakkhi. In the rural areas they still wear kanchli, but in urban areas the use of ghagra and kanchli has nearly finished .the woman prefer bright coloured ,printed and artistic clothes .During fairs and festivals pink, saffron and yellow coloured, beautifully embroidered, dresses are considered auspicious.

In the present-day context in urban areas the women wear sari, blouse and petticoat. The young girls wear puckered payjama, T-shirt, pant, skirts among other. In rural areas the young girls wear kurta and payjama with chunri or dupatta. Ghagra and choli are also in use. Rajasthan is also famous for its ornaments and jewelry. From ancient times the people have been fond of jewellery. The Bhils, wear silver ornaments The rich people prefer to wear gold and jems-studded ornaments. In the state capital and other cities the well to do people wear gold and silver jewellery. During medieval not only dresses but also curtains, horse dress, elephant dress, seat cushions, chariot clothes etc. were decorated with silver or gold ornaments. One can imagine the fondness for ornamets from the jewellery on swords, shields, knives, pistols, fifless, cannon, doors, thrones, etc., which were studded with ivory, gold, silver and many costly jems.

In Rajasthan women wear *bichhia* (toe ring), *angudia* (finger ring), *kada* (wrist bangle)and *chudi* (rings), necklace or chain, *pajeb* (ring chain in ankles), *lavung* (nose stud), *jhumka* (ear ring). These ornaments are worm by all classes of women. There are many other ornaments that women wear, viz., shisful, borla, tika, fini, sankhli, nath, bali, patti, surlia, matarmala, jhalar, janjir, bajuband (bracelet), thadda, takaya, abtta, chuda, bangdi, challa, anguthi, munddi, tagdi, karghani, kangati, and payal etc. Silver toerings are considered auspicious.

The Muslim women wear mainly silver ornaments. The Bhil and Garasia tribes adorn ivory banles. Gujjar, Mina Kumhar women wear heavy silver rings in the legs. In the cities now a days the use of ornaments is less. The use of jewellery is not restricted to somen only. Men also wear ornaments like *murkhi* (ear ring) *kada* (bangle) chain and ring.

With the Aravalli mountain ranges, stretching from southwest to northeast, Thar Desert in the west, and plains in the eastern part of the state, the agro-climatic conditions vary greatly. As a result, agricultuaral production varies and so do the food havits of the people of Rajastan. In western Rajasthan bajra is the staple food. Due to the absence of irrigation facilities, the people depend mainly on the animal husbandry who consume milk and proucts in huge amount. They eat handmade bread of bajra along with other various locally available vegetables, therefore their staple food is rice. In Harauti region the production of jowar predominates, hence the people of this region take more jowar than other cereals. In eastern plains both rabi and kharif crops are raised so the people of this region take wheat, jowar, rice, bajra, tilhan, maize, gram etc. There is little difference in the food habits in rural and urban areas. In cities and urban areas wheat and gram are consumed more while in rural areas maize, jowar, bajra are given preference. The rural folk prepare rabid and butter milk with ground maize or jowar or bajra. In the cities its use is very rare, rather tea or coffee, is preferred. A special dish dal-bati (churma)is very popular in Rajasthan, particularly during festivals. Milk and curd are consumed throughout Rajasthan. Earlier meat was consumed only by Rajput and Muslims, but now many other communities have started devowring it veraciously.

Earlier the consumption of opium and alcohol was confined to the people attached to the principalities, viz., Rajput and tribals like Bhil, Garasia, Mina, etc., but now almost all communities consume it in varying degrees. In Kota, Jhalawar and some parts of Chittorgarh opium is cultivated, therefore the consumption and consezuently rate of addictin are greater in this region. They also consume the opium seeds in the form of vegetables. In southern Rajasthan the tribal communities of Bhil, Mina and Gamit prepare country liquor from mahuda (Bassia Letifolia) flowers for self-consumption. Now, however, communites have also started consuming it. In southwest and northe-west part of the state country liquor is consumed more while in the eastern part of the state commercially brewed liquor is preferred.

In his linguistic survey of India, Sir Grierson has categorized the languages of Rajasthan in the following manner:in its east, Rajasthan is bounded(going from regions of north to south) by the *Braj Bhasha* and *Bundeli* dialects. On its south (from east to west). It has *Bundeli*, Marathi, Bhili, Khandesi and Gujarati. Bhil is also spoken in two mountain tracts (the Vindhya hills and the Aravalli hills) in the heart of Rajasthan. On its north (from west to east) it has *Labanda*, *Punjabi* and the *Bagri* dialect. Pf these, *Marathi*, *Sindhi* and *Labanda* belong to the outer circle of Indo-Arayan Languages. The different dialects spoken in different parts of Rajasthan are grouped together to designate them as the Rajasthani language. Rajasthani language is divided into four groups: *Marwari*, *Dhundhari*, *Harauti* and *Malvi*, the biggest of these being *Marwar.*

Stamdard Marwari is spoken mainly in and around Jodhpur district and has some influences on the dialectin Barmer, Jalor, Pali and parts of Nagaur district all of which comprised the erstwhile Jodhpur state. The dialect, in more or less mixed form, is also spoken in the east in Ajmer, and, Bhilara district. In the south it is spoken, Sirohi district, in the sest in Jaisalmer districts, and in the north in Bikaner, Churu, Sikar and Jhunjhunu districts, It is also spoken with some Punjabi influence in Ganganagar district. Norther forms of Marwari are spoken in Bikaner, Churu, Ganganagar, Sikar and Jhunjhunu districts. In Bikaner it is called Bianeri. While in the northeastern part of Churu, the whole of Sikar and Jhunjhunu districts it is known as Shekhavati.

In the south east, i.e., *Mewar* (Udaipur, and chittorgarh districts) and its neighbourgood, there is the well-known eastern form of Marwari known as *Mewati.* In the districts of Banswarea and Dungarpur slightly different form of Mewari is spolen called as *Bagri* and has an influence of northern Gujarati dialect. In the southern Pali and Jalor districts, and the whole of Sihori district there is a souther sub-dialcet. In the western parts of Barmer and Jaisalmer, the influence of *Sindhi* can be felt.

The second biggest groups of Rajasthan lanuage is formed by eastern Rajasthani or Jaipuri, better known as Dhundhari. It covers the districts of Jaipur, Alwar Bharatpur, Dholpur, Sawaimadhopur, Tonk an parts of Ajmer district. The north-east Dhundhari has the (i) Mewati dialect of the same lanuage (spoken of Alwar districts), (ii)Further east, from north to south, Brij, Bhasha is spoken in Bharatpur, and Dholpur districts and (iii) the Dang sub-dialect of Brij Bhasha is spoken in Sawaimadhopur district.

The dialct of Bundi and Kota is Harauti, also spoken in Jhalawar and in the neighbouring parts of Tonk district.Malvi is spolen in the Indor, Rajgarth, Mandsor and Ujjain area of Madhya Pradesh. It extends to parts of the Jhalawar and Kota districts.Malvi is a distinctly Rajasthani dialect having relations with Marwari and Dhundhari.

Sir Griesrson states that the Bhils have a separate dialect. The Bhili sploken forn extends from the south of Mewar in the Aravalli range to further south in the districts of Dungarpur and Banswara, and finally extends to Gujarat and Madhya Pradesh, Thus, except for a portion of its eastern frontiers, Rajasthan is entirely covered by Rajasthani dialects.

Rajasthan being the citadel of feudalism has had a number of commuities whose oritin could be traced to fendalism for example, there was the custom of sending maid servants with the bride to her new home. Slowly their progeny emerged as a distinct class and started claiming the Rajput descent indentified by different names in different preincipalities, and now trying to form a coomon identity.The groups like Hajuri, Wajer, Daroga, Gona Rajput are uniting under the banner of Raona Rajput. One group got differentiated due to the adoption of the practice of widow remarriage. Th natrayet are given a lwo staus in the broad Rajput category, because their widows remarry. The *Chhut-Bhaiya* are descended from the younger brothers of the rulers. They are allotted small *jagirs* for an independent category.

There is a whole range of commuities in Rajasthan at different sages of economy, i.e., from hunting to settled agriculture. In the arid and semi-arid areas of Rajasthan a few small games still survive.The Van Baoria, Tirgar, Kanjar, Vagri, etc., were traditionally hunters and gatherers. Now only the Van Baoria adhere to hunting while others treat it as a subsidiary occupation. Rajputisation provided the dominant model for emulation in the past as seen from the adoption of Rajput clan names by a number of communities.

The tradition-bound society in the northern states of Jammu & Kashmir, Punjab, Himachal Pradesh, Chandigarh, Rajasthan and Delhi is changing fast, with the entire social life, culture, economic life and prospectives being in a state of constant flux hovering between age old traditions and degrees of westernisation. The traditional society which before the independance of India was almost a closed system suddenly became open to the outside influences, trends and forces released by the community development, various social movements, urbanisation, globalisation, education, new technology and the last but not least, the economic liberalisation. However, here we deal with the entire cultural cycle starting from the old times to the current age.

Praying to Goddess Tara

Among the *Kanaur Kanets* (HP/ST) during pregnancy, the following chant is sung : 'O Goddess Tara, I bow down to thee, be pleased to bestow on this woman thy choicest blessings.' And a charm written on a piece of paper or birch-tree bark is tied round the woman's neck.

Custom of *Thakni*

The observance of the third month of pregnancy is called *thakni.* Dried dates and pieces of coconut are given to the pregnant wife and of these she eats a little, the rest being distributed among her kinsmen. In Hoshiarpur, a similar rite is observed; loaves of wheat flour fried in *ghee* are distributed among the brotherhood, and both husband and wife put on new clothes and worship the family god daily. The custom is popularly practised in parts of Punjab adjoining Pakistan. But in Gurdaspur, the rite known as *thanni* (*thankni*) is said to be observed on the first day of the sixth month. The woman on the day washes her head with curd and puts on new clothes: saltish eatables, such as *papars*, *pakauras* and sewian, or vermicelli, being distributed among the brotherhood. The *thankni* is followed by the great *rit*, held early in the eighth month, which is a religious ceremony. The woman's parents send her presents, and she washes her head etc., as in the *thankni*. But a *pandit* is called in who performs certain religious rites. The women of the family also sing certain ritual hymns, and the occasion is one of great rejoicing. *Pun-savan*, meaning "causing the birth of a male child- the first of the essential ceremonies of Hindu initiation- held on the mother's first perceiving signs of a living conception," is now obsolete in the Simla hills. So, too, is the ritual *sisani*, which used to be performed in the sixth month.

In Fazilka an observance, though nearly extinct now, was observed sometime ago by Hindu Aroras during the third month of a first pregnancy. It is called the *ankh salai*, because after it the wife ceases to apply antimony to her eyes. Her parents send her rice which is distributed among her kin. In *Hissar, Haryana,* the *Kanif* rite is in popular practice. But elsewhere in the state such observances are somewhat elaborate. Thus, in Jind during a first pregnancy or *jetha hamal*, the people practise the *mitha bohia,* a social ceremony in which at the end of the third month a basket full of sweets is sent to the pregnant woman by her mother, with a suit and a half of clothes, and some money. At the fifth month, a second similar ceremony, the *sadh,* is observed, when the mother sends her daughter two and a half suits of clothes, one and a quarter maunds of sweetmeats and also some cash.

Observance of Chhoti Ritan

The rite of *chhoti ritan* is observed at or about the time when half the period of gestation has elapsed and, indeed, the rite is called the *adh-gabh* in Amritsar, Gujranwala, and in Bahawalpur. In Hoshiarpur, it is not known by that name, but it is observed on the second evening of the lunar month in the fifth month of pregnancy, and a second rite corresponding to it is observed on the second day of the ninth lunar month. In Jhelum, it is observed on an auspicious day in the fourth or fifth month of pregnancy. The woman bathes, and is dressed in new clothes, her hair is plaited and her hands stained with henna. Her kinswomen sing auspicious songs throughout the night. All this is supposed to prevent miscarriage. Her parents also send her some sweets which are put in her lap. In Sialkot, the *adh-gabh* is also said to be observed, but not by the *Jats*, and is described as simply consisting in the distribution of salty preparations *papars*, *pakauras* etc. among the brotherhood. In Sialkot, the mid-pregnancy rite is called the *paon bhari* or the heavy feet. In Rajanpur tahsil a rite is called *chilwan* from *chihi*, 'loin', is commonly observed among Hindus as well as Muhammadans.

After six months in every conception, the pregnant woman is required to bathe under the direction of datri or midwife who ties magical beads round her loins, thereby implying the safe completion of the conception and easy labour.

But Banias, who come from the south-east do not observe the *adh-gabh.* One account says it is observed in different ways, 'by all sects of Brahmans and Hindus, another, that it is called *rit* and is observed, in different ways by Brahmans, Mahajans, Khatris, Sunars and Jhiwars, but not by Jats, while a third claims that the *adh-gabh* is performed in different ways, but on the same principle by all Hindus, whereas the *Kanji* is confined to Brahman, Khatris and Aroras. In Hoshiarpur, the wife's parents send her a piece of red *salu* and some rice. She bathes and puts on the salu. Rice is also distributed among the brotherhood.

Rites in Advanced Stage of Pregnancy

During the seventh month is observed a rite of a religious character called the *bibian ka bhojan bharna*. This consists in the woman's offering four and a quarter *sers* of rice to the *bibis* or spirits, in ten *thalis* or plates of which one is given to a Dumni, another to a landholder's wife, a third to the husband, a fourth being allotted to the woman herself, and the rest to other relatives. The pregnancy rites, however, strictly speaking, religious are the *garbh sanskar,* and foreshadow the *janm, mundan* and *janeo sanskars* or rites at birth (first) tonsure and initiation.

Among the Hindus, the *garbh sanskar* or the pregnancy rites includes two distinct rites, the *chhoti* or lesser and the *bari ritan* or greater rites, which are conducted in the fifth and seventh months respectively of the pregnancy throughout the Central Punjab. In the former, the woman bathes, her hair is plaited and she is dressed in clothes presented by her parents. Her neighbours and kinswomen also assemble to sing songs and fill her lap ritually with grain and cakes made of grain flour fried in *ghee*. Her mother-in-law also congratulates her and similar eatables are distributed among the husband's brotherhood. At the commencement of the seventh month, the husband's parents celebrate the *bari ritan*; but first of all the wife's parents send her a new *tewar,* a coconut, dried dates and money, together with a present of clothes to her husband's parents, who on their part present her with new clothes.

On a lucky day chosen by the *Brahman,* the husband and wife dressed in new clothes, sit side by side and worship images of the gods drawn by the Brahman on the floor. The husband's mother then places a coconut and dried dates in the wife's lap, and congratulations are exchanged. Huge sweetened loaves of flour fried in *ghee* are then distributed among the relatives and friends. In Ferozepur, these rites are replaced by the *jar bharneki* and *bhog bharneki* observances. Of these the former simply consists in making *kachchi pinni* or rolls, of which two are marked with saffron and given to the wife who either eats them or distributes them among young girls and the other male relatives. The second rite is, however, far more elaborate.

The woman's parents send her a double *tewar*, with a shawl and turban for the husband and other things. Then on the day of the new moon, the wife visits each member of the family in her house, and gives him some rice as a summon to the rite. Before the kinswomen assemble, a corner of the eastern wall of the house is plastered and seven hand marks made on it with rice-flour mixed in water. A wooden plank is also set up before the wall and a lamp lighted. The kinswomen bring with them some of the grain and rice given them the previous day, and scatter the rice near the lamp, piling the grain, in a heap close to it. The plates are then put in one place; twenty-two *sers kham* of rice are then boiled with five of sugar and two and one half of *ghee,* the mixture being divided in precisely equal portions on the plates among the kinswomen, who object if one gets more than another. The idea, doubtless, is to convey equal fertility to all. The clothes gifted by the woman's parents are next put on her, and her skirt tied to that of an unmarried kinsman. The pair then walk round the plates seven times, and are asked to bow to the lamp. It is believed that the boy will thus soon be himself married. Their skirts are then untied.

A utensil is now placed in the woman's hands and each kinswoman gives her a little rice from their plates which she eats. Her husband's mother is then congratulated. The grain brought by the kinswoman is shared equally by the *Maihra* (waterman) and her Brahman priest.

Custom of Bari Kanji

Similar to the *bari ritan,* is the custom of *Kanji*, which is usually performed during the seventh month, though sometimes postponed to the ninth. It is very generally observed except in the extreme south-eastern region, but it varies in details and often bears no distinctive name. In Hissar, it is observed during the seventh or ninth month and among the *Bagris* the wife's parents send clothes for herself and her husband. In Hoshiarpur, the ceremony of Kanji is called *rit*, and is observed in the first of the lunar month (seventh or eighth). The presents wife's parents send her include ten to twenty loaves fried in *ghee, papars* and *pakoras*, clothes for herself and her husband, one-two ornaments and some in cash. Food is also distributed to the brotherhood and menials, Brahmans being also fed in the name of ancestors. In some places, the wife's parents feed Brahmans, giving them wheat-flour and *Kari.* Or again the wife's parents send her clothes and money, after which she bathes and then the woman and her husband both pray that the child may be a boy. In Amritsar, the *Kanji* is observed in the seventh or ninth month, by all castes but not in all parts of the district. In Ajnala, it is called *ritan.* In the adjoining regions the *Kanji* or *rit* is very similar. It is observed in the eighth month and is sometimes held in the house of the wife's parents. In Gurdaspur, a wife when pregnant for the first time is sent to her parents house in the seventh month and presented with a measure of jaggery, as an intimation to them of her condition. Her parents give her clothes for herself, her husband and his mother, and other presents, with which she returns to her husband's house for delivery.

On the rising of the new moon in the seventh month, a Brahman is called in and the husband and wife become seated side by side with their near kinsmen. An earthenware called *kumbh* is then filled with water and a lamp filled with *ghee* put over it and lighted. The Brahman makes an idol of Ganesh out of flour and worships their ancestors. The garments of the pair are then tied together as part of a rite called *gand chitrawa,* and their pedigrees to the third degree recited, their ancestors names being also written on a piece of paper which is hung up on the wall. Rice is next distributed among the brotherhood. A small gold ornament presented by her parents is also hung round the wife's neck and this is eventually given to the baby when born.

The Hindus who migrated from Muzaffargarh (Pakistan) to India usually observe the *malhwan* and *kanji* during the 6th and 8th months when a woman is pregnant for the first time. This is an occasion for feasting and rejoicing. The parents of the pregnant woman send her clothes and other presents at the *kanji;* she bathes, washes her hair and puts on her new clothes and ornaments. This ceremony is intended *inter alia* to make the fact of the first pregnancy of a bride public, or at least well known among the relatives. In *Jind* during the seventh month among Hindus *Chhimbas*, the pregnant woman performs the rite of *bhog bharna* offering rice *Bibis* or spirits, while rice with *gur* is distributed among the brotherhood. Among Muhammadan *Saqqas* during the seventh month the woman's parents send her a suit of clothes which she puts on and a feast is given to the brotherhood.

Elsewhere in Punjab, the rite is not very dissimilar. The expectant-mother's parents send her presents and on the appearance of the new moon,i.e. on the second of the lunar month, she is bathed and dressed. Ancestors are worshipped. This rite called *rit* in Panjabi, and *simanat* in Sanskrit, is known as *sawani* in Jammu, in which region the Dogras, a Scheduled caste in HP, Punjab and Haryana, celebrate it by feasting kinsmen. In Jhelum, the rite is observed in the seventh or ninth month. The wife's parents send her sweets and fruits and these are put in her lap. After this, she must not leave her house. Both at the *kanji* and *adh-gabh* in this district, the wife bathes and then receives a gift of clothes from her husband's younger brothers or other young kinsman, in whose face she gazes before she puts them on. The *kanji* or *rit* is observed on an auspicious day in the seventh month at the house of the wife's parents, and all males are excluded from it, and not even informed of it, though boiled rice is distributed to the brotherhood on this occasion. In Hazro this *rite* is observed at 4 p.m. on the day of the new moon in the seventh month, and the priest's wife conducts it. Some jaggery is cut up with a knife and a portion given to her, while the rest is distributed among the near kins.

The Rite of *Dewa- dhami*

Another ceremony with which the husband's parents are closely associated is called as the *dewa-dhami*. Among the Hindus who migrated from Montgomery, this rite is observed in the seventh or eighth month. The family priestess lights a lamp filled with clarified butter or *ghee* in a corner of the house, making a hearth and seven cakes of earth, and covering the latter with vermilion. Before these things the husband and wife prostrate themselves and big loaves of flour fried in *ghee* are then distributed among the brotherhood. Until these articles have all been removed, the women of the family do not spin cotton thread or undertake any other work. The things are then collected and given to the parents who in return present the wife with a *trewar*, a rupee and a half *ser* of jaggery. This rite is observed three days before the *anji* ceremony. But among the Hindus who migrated from Gujranwala it is said to be held at the same time as the *rit,* and it must be held in the lower storey of their house, by night the lamp being lighted in the southern corner.

Among the people hailing from *Hazro,* the *dewa-dhami* is also observed on the same *rit*, by the kinswomen and the priest's wife, all males being excluded. The priestess begins by kindling a lamp and making the pregnant woman worship the deity of Ganesha. Sweetened rice or bread is then distributed. Next morning rice is boiled or *halwa* made and the wife is bathed amd dressed in the clothes sent by her parents. Another woman is then seated by her to represent her husband, and on her knees are put all the clothes received for him. Seven vessels and covers of cowdung are then made and cardamoms, rice, barley, *mung* (pulse), *piwa* and two rupee coins are placed in each. These vessels are then put between the two women, and the wife removes the covers, which the other woman replaces. This is done thrice. Then both dip their fingers thrice. Both then chew cardamoms, which they spit over each other, and finally the rice or *halwa* is given to the priestess, who also gets some money. Next day she is called in again and lights the lamp which she extinguishes with milk and water. This ends the *rit*.

In Bahawalpur, on the other hand, the *dewa-dhami* is conducted by the husband's father who lights a lamp in a corner of the house making an effigy of Ganesha and worshipping the names of his ancestors with his face turned to the north or toward the Ganges. While worshipping he must unloose the string of his *chola* or shirt, or the gods will not accept his devotions.

In Mandi in Himachal Pradesh, the rits of the fifth and seventh months are not observed at all, but in the beginning of the eighth month, the *athwa* is celebrated through putting an idol of Ganpati on a red *chauki* and this the pregnant woman worships for a month during which period she must not bathe, change her clothes or cross a river. In the parent state of Suket, the *athwan* in observed in the eighth or ninth month. The woman's parents send her clothes for herself and the child. The clothes are perfumed. A rupee is also sent. They also send one or two garments for the husband's mother.

In the beginning of the ninth month follows the *baranwin,* at which the wife's kinswomen assemble to bathe her, make her put on new clothes and look at a handsome boy to ensure her own child being a son. This boy is dismissed with a present of money. Then, the wife is made to stand up and a kerchief is tied round her waist, and cakes, money, gold and silver, flowers, cocoanut, pomegranate, and a mixture of rice, sesame and sugar sent by her parents are put in her lap. Of the money, part goes to the priest and the rest to the midwife. On this occasion, her nearest relative also gives the wife money and ornaments for her own use. Then the wife worships Ganpati, and a vessel or *kalas* of earth, brass or copper, is put in an octagonal *jantar* or diagram and in it is placed a cocoanut with an image of Lord Vishnu. The woman is then directed to worship the *kalas* and after that a *hawan* is performed, a he-goat being sacrificed to appease the fire deity. Brahmans and near relatives are then fed, and the kinwomen sing songs and make merry all night. This rite is observed in every pregnancy.

Rituals during the Eighth and Ninth Months

In Hissar, the *kanji* is observed in the seventh or ninth month, and in some places the *adhi-garbh* is actually said to be deferred till the ninth month. In Fazilka, the rite of *kanji* is observed only in the ninth month. In parts of Hoshiarpur, there is, however, a distinct rite in the ninth month, on the second day, thus corresponding to the rite in the seventh. A corner of the house is plastered with cowdung and the wife is seated there with her face to the east and made to worship Ganesha. A cocoanut and a rupee are also put in her lap by way of *shagun* or good augury and boiled rice is set before. Sweets, clothes and dry fruits etc, sent by her parents are distributed among the brotherhood. In the northern part of the same district, it is said that the *rit* is held in the ninth month and consists simply in the distribution of *kari,* that is the gram flour cooked in whey, to the brotherhood in order to proclaim the pregnancy. It is also said that the *rit* in this part varies in different castes and that it is repeated several times. It is specifically described as being observed thrice in the fifth month (when *Kanji* and *pakoras* are distributed), in the seventh (when boiled rice and pulse are sent round) and in the ninth (when moist gram and jaggery are distributed among the brotherhood).

The Rite of Athwansa

At the beginning of the eighth month of pregnancy, the *Shaikhawat* Rajputs observe a rite called the *athwansa*. The wife's parents send her clothes, ornaments, fruits, money, and on their receipt all her kinswomen assemble. Brahmans then worship the gods and the pregnant woman bathes after which she puts on the new clothes. With this, the following custom among the same people appears to be connected. After birth, a child of either sex is bathed in the blood of a he-goat and a necklet of its flesh is put round the child's neck. Then, it is dressed in a blue *kurta* and cap, with a belt of blue silk round its waist. These clothes are worn for six or seven months, but the necklet is retained for two years and the belt worn till it reaches the age of five.

The rite of *Mawali*

The Hindus who revere the god *Mawali* perform the following rite in the seventh months: a mixture of rice, *mung* and barley is made and an earthen vessel sent for from the potter's house. This is marked seven times with three things henna, black and red colouring. Then boiled rice and the dish described above are placed in her lap seven times, some cooked *mung* being also put in the middle of the vessel. Lastly, a red thread is put in it and taken out by the midwife who deposits it under a plum or *ber* tree. All the members of the family then eat the food.

Taboos for the Pregnant Women

In Chamba (Himachal Pradesh), the pregnant woman should not go near a dead body even of a near relative, or cross a stream, especially in the evening lest the water spirit exert an evil influence on her, nor should she visit a woman newly delivered. In all these cases, the danger feared is of abortion due to the influences of evil spirits. If a snake appears and is trying to escape, the people believe that the shadow of a pregnant woman falling on it will cause it to crawl slowly. During pregnancy, the parents are both peculiarly susceptible to the effects of an eclipse, and it is safest for the wife to keep her bed and not even see the eclipse, in Haryana, but the father is not under any such necessity. However, either parent must avoid applying antimony to the eyelids, or a *tilak* to the forehead during an eclipse, lest the child be so marked. Both parents should also avoid locking or unlocking a lock, lest its fingers be bent and powerless. If they cut wood with an axe, the child will have a hare-lip; or if they break anything, such as a piece of wood, its fingers will be marked. In short, anything such as stamping or printing done during an eclipse is liable to leave its impression on the child's body. During an eclipse of the sun or moon, a pregnant woman should lie with her body straight, lest the child be born crooked. Every morning, she should be careful to look first at her husband's face, so that the child may resemble him. If anyone else is frequently seen it will take after him. If her husband is absent, she should look at the faces of her other children or at her own face in a looking glass, or at her sister's face, but not at her brother's.

Charms to Pre-empt Abortion

If abortion has ever occurred, or is feared for the woman, *sayanas* or wizards prevent it by giving her (i) a piece of wood from a scaffold on which a man has been hanged, or (ii) a piece which has been thrown over the *biwan* or hearse of an old person, or (iii) a tiger's flesh or claw. The idea in each of these charms is to increase the vitality or prolong the life of the child.

Observances at Birth

The auspiciousness or inauspiciousness of a birth depends upon several factors, such as the season or time of its occurrence, its sequence relative to preceding birth in the family, position of the zodiac signs and the child's position at birth. A birth in the eighth month of pregnancy is attributed to a cat having entered the mother's room in a former confinement. A child born in this month will, it is believed, die on the eighth day, in the eighth month, or eighth or eighteenth year, after birth. Hence, the number *eight* is never mentioned in speaking of a child's age, *un-ginat* or 'uncounted' being used instead, like *an-ginat* din=eighth day, *an-ginat barha*=eighth year.

The Athwaha Ritual

In the Dera tahsil of Kangra in Himachal, a child born in the eighth month is called an *athwaha* and is regarded as unlucky to both its parents foreboding the father's death. As a remedy, a spinning-wheel is passed thrice round the mother's head and then given to the midwife. In Kangra, a child which dies at birth or immediately after the birth is inauspicious, and its nose is bored, for a gold ring to be inserted, in order to avert its evil influence. Monday is an unlucky day for birth, and as a remedy the child's nose or ear is bored. Among orthodox Hindus in Bahawalpur, Ferozepur and Mandi, the following remedies of zodiac signs or *griha* are used to counteract the evil influences of the various planets:

Saturn: Seven kinds of grain or anything black such as iron or a black buffalo should be given away in charity.

Mars: Articles such as copper, *gur*, cloth dyed red, oil etc.

The sun : reddish things, such as *ghee*, gold, wheat, a red-coloured cow etc.

The Moon : white articles, such as silver, rice, a white cow, white cloth etc.

Mercury and Venus : green articles such as *mung* (a kind of pulse), green cloth or fruit, such as oranges etc.

Jupiter : yellow things such as yellow cloth, gram-pulse, yellow sweetmeats (*nukhti* and *laddu*), gold etc.

To avert the evil influence of *Rahu* (or ascending node) : coconuts, *ghee,* sugar (*khand*) and *mash* (a kind of pulse) ; and that is Kret or typhon (the descending node) : *samosa* (a kind of sweetmeat) and bluish cloth are given in charity. This is called as *girah-puja* (or worship of the planets). A birth which occurs during the *panchak* period will, it is believed, be followed by the birth of three children of the same sex.

Birth in Ill-omens

The *gandes* are five days which fall in the dark half of the lunar month, and a child born on any of these dates bodes ill to its parents. Accordingly, the father must not see the child until, in the recurrence of the *nakshatra* or planet in which it was born, he has worshipped the gods, or until five dolls have been made, put in a copper vessel and anxiously propitiated. Fruit is placed before them, as they are belived to eat; and Brahmans recite *mantras*. Lastly, an earthen jar is pierced with twenty eight holes and filled with water and various drugs. It is then hung up on a tree at some distance from the ground and the water allowed to trickle on to the parent's heads. After this the Brahmans are rewarded with eatables and money. The eclipse affects parents during pregnancy. So too a child, of either sex, born during an eclipse brings ill-luck, to avert which the following observances are made in Kangra (HP): First, the image in gold of the deity connected with the asterism in which the eclipse occurred, and one of the sun (if it was eclipsed), or of the moon (in the case of its eclipse), together with an image of Rahu, are worshipped. A *hawan* is also performed, *ak* wood being used if the sun was eclipsed,or, if the moon, *palas*. Like other unlucky children, a child born under an eclipse is weighed every month, on the *sankrant* day, against seven kinds of grain, all of which are given away. A child born during the month of *Bhadon* is lucky, while one born in *Katak* is inauspicious, and the mother of such a child should be turned out of the house, though she may be given to a Brahman and then redeemed from him. Children born under certain asterism are peculiarly liable not only to misfortune themselves, but to cause evil to others, and various rites are performed to avert the consequences of their birth.

A child born in *Katak* must either undergo symbolical birth from a cow (*gopareab*), or also both it and the parents must bathe on the first *sankrant* after the end of *Katak* in water drawn from seven wells and mixed with turmeric, sandal, ginger and other herbs. These are termed *sarbokhadi*, and are placed in an unbaked earthen jar with 1000 orifices and a lip, the appropriate *mantras* being duly recited. Water from seven wells or rivers is then similarly purified by *mantras*. The parents, with the child in its mother's lap, are then placed under a sieve, through which the water is poured. *Hawan* is then performed, and lastly a tray of *ghee* is given away by the parents in charity to Brahmans.

A baby born when the moon is in the sixth or eighth zodiacal sign is ill-omened, and to avert its influence a rite is observed: On the 27th day after the birth a basket made of bamboo is filled with sixteen *sers* (thirty two lbs.) of rice, some camphor, a pearl, a piece of white cloth and some silver and given away in charity, together with a team of white calves yoked and vessel of milk and *ghee*. Worship in which white sandalwood and white flowers figure, is also performed. This, however, is an orthodox rite, and the popular idea in Kangra (HP), is that a child born in the *ghati-chandarman*, in auspicious moon is not ill-omened. The unlucky *tithi* or lunar days for birth are the *amawas*, or last day of the dark half; and the *chaturdashi* which is the fourteenth, the last day but one.

Children born on the former day are unpropitious to the father, those born on the latter to the mother. To avert their evil influence, an idol of Shiva is made of silver, and in an earthen jar are placed leaves from various trees, *mango, palas*, *pipal* etc. A coconut is then placed on the jar, which is covered with a red cloth; and on this is put the idol of Shiva, after it has been purified by *mantras*. *Hawan* or fire sacrifice is performed with sesame, pulse (*mash*) and white mustard. The idol of the deity is given to a Brahman. In Nurpur Tahsil of Kangra (HP), the evil influence of a birth in any unlucky *nakshatras* is averted by bathing the parents and child with water from a jar, containing 1000 holes, into which leaves from 108 male trees (mango, *pipal*, banian, are male ; while *nakh*, 'pear', and beri, 'plum' are feminine). Children born in the remaining seven of the thirteen *nakshatras* specified are not very unlucky, and the planets are merely worshipped by more rigid observers of Hindus precepts. To avert the evil influence five, earthen jars, filled with water and leaves (*pipal* etc.) are covered with a red cloth, and the golden image of a serpent placed on them and worshipped. The person to whom the birth forebodes evil gives alms, and a *hawan* is performed with *ghee* in Kangra. The five jars should contain gold images of Brahma, Vishnu, Mahesh, Indra and Varuna. Special attention may be directed here to the position of the mother's brother in astrology. The part played by him in weddings may conceivably have an astrological basis. He is curiously affected by his sister's child cutting its upper teeth first.

To avert the evil a piece of ground is plastered with cow-dung and a platform for a *hawan* made on it. On this platform *mantras* are written in immersed with flour. Five jars, full of water are the leaves of five trees (*pipal*, mango, *palkhar*, *palas*, and a fifth), with *panchamrit* and *panchgarbh*. In a sixth jar, unbaked, with 1000 orifices are placed 107 different drugs. The parents and child are then drenched through a sieve, and then they join in the *hawan*, which must be celebrated by sixteen Brahmans. Finally, parents and child bathe in the water from the five jars. [Kangra]

The rites are the same as in the case of a Jesbta birth, except that the idol made is a gold one of a rakhshasa in Kangra.

Among Hindus in Ambala, astrologers are consulted about the auspiciousness of the birth. If the child was born at an inauspicious time, called *gandmul*, 27days after the birth, the child and its mother are bathed in water containing drugs in solution. The water is poured on them from a pitcher with a hundred holes bored in it. In some parts, if the child is a male the father gets certain incantations recited over food, which is given to the poor so that his ancestors' souls may benefit thereby.

Inauspicious Mul Asterism

In the *Mul* asterism the first *charan* is unpropitious to the father, the second to the mother, and the third to wealth. The fourth *charan* in the *Shalkhan Jeshtha* and *Reoti* asterisms, and the first in the *Mul, Ashwini* and *Magha* are called *gands* and a birth in these is unlucky : if it occurs by day, to the father; if by night to the mother; and if in the morning or evening to the child itself. But all these refinements are hardly known to the popular astrology, and the general practice is to regard births in *Jeshtha, Mula, Ashlekhan* and *Maghan* asterisms only as unlucky. In the Simla hills, the evil influence of a birth in the Krishnpak *chaudas* is averted by propitiating the nine planets. A birth at the end of a month and in the Jamgandhjag, Kalijag etc, is unlucky to the parents etc. ; and they should not see the child's face until the alms have been given to Brahmans. Triplets portend the speedy death of parents, and to avert the evil, *hawan* is performed, alms are given to the purohit and the *shonti maukat* is chanted . The rites resemble those in the *Jeshtha* or *Mul* cases, but a cow is also given as alms in the child's name in Kangra.

In the Dera tahsil of Kangra, the rites observed on such births, or in those which occur under an inauspicious (*ghatak*) moon, are simple. Images of Brahman, Indar, Suraj (Sun) and the Moon (Chandraman) are placed in four jars with the leaves of seven trees; the jars are then filled with water and covered with a red and white cloth. Mother and child are then sprinkled with the water.

Rites Related to the First-born Son

Generally speaking, the birth of the first-born child, provided it is not a girl, is the occasion for special rejoicings and in Kangra a pilgrimage is made to the family deity *kul-deota*, and a he-goat, called the *kudnu randa*, is let loose in his honour, another being also sacrificed at his shrine, and a feast given. In Saraj, a few people of the village visit the parent's house and fire off guns. The father feasts them, and gives each guest a small turban and a rupee ; the village *deota* and musician also receive each a rupee. This money is called *wadhai ka rupiya,* and it is all deposited with an honorary treasurer, and when enough has been collected a great feast is held.

In Hamirpur the Panjab rite, which consists in giving alms to the poor, is observed on the eleventh day after the birth. Brahmans and the kinsmen are also feasted, menials also receive gifts. A good deal of money is thus spent. The first-born son has always held a peculiarly sacred position, especially if born to the parents who have long been without offspring in answer to a vow, in which case sacrifice of the child was common in India. The Mairs used to sacrifice a first-born son to Seetala Mata, or the small-pox goddess, while Muhammadans throughout Northern India believe that first-born children can stop excessive rain by certain rites. On the other hand a first born son will in Telingana attract lightning. A first-born child (*Jesth*) must not be married in the month of *Jesth*.

The Third Born-Trikhal

Many remarkable ideas cluster round the third conception or round a child of one sex born after three children of the other sex. Thus, in the South-West Punjab the former superstition prevails and its results are thus :

Trikhal is the third conception after two births (without regard to the sexes of the former children). It is a *Jatki* word, meaning 'third' and implies contempt. This conception is considered unlucky among Hindus. Every effort is made by them to effect abortion, and in many cases it undoubtedly takes place. It is also suspected that the third child is killed at birth if the attempts to cause abortion have failed, but fear of the law prevents any attempt to kill it if it survives its birth. The *Trikhal*, however, appears to be a local variant as the other superstition is far more prevalent and its effects and the measures taken to avert them are thus: A child of one sex born after three children of the other sex is called in Punjabi, *trikhal*, as, for example, a boy born after three girls. Such a child is considered unlucky, and its birth portends, the death of a parent; or loss of wealth by the parents; or the burning of the house in which it was born; or some other calamity, such as lightning or snake-bite. If this child grows up without its parents suffering any injury, and is taller than the parents, they are benefited instead of injured by the birth, their lives are prolonged, or if poor they become rich and are protected against all misfortunes. Many Hindus also believe that the children born after a *trikhal* cannot live long.

A number of magical remedies are adopted at the birth of such a child to avert its evil effects which include:

(i) The father pours a quantity of *ghee* down the gutter of the roof of the room in which the child was born.

(ii) A brass tray is broken in the centre and the child passed through the hole.

(iii) A horse-shoe is painted with *sindur* (red oxide of mercury) and scented with *gugal* (a drug) and attached to the bed of the mother. The shoe is re-painted with *sindur* and scented every Tuesday.

(iv) If the third day after the birth be a Sunday, a ceremony known as *trikhal shanti* (or propitiation of the *trikhal*) is performed. Green leaves from seven trees are collected and put in an earthen pitcher with 101 holes in its bottom. Another pitcher is filled with water taken from seven wells. The mother, with her child, sits under the drain of the roof of the house on which the child was born. A *pandit* recites to her a *katha* from the *trikhal shanti shastra,* while a kinswoman of the mother holds a sieve over her head. The pitcher containing the green leaves is placed on the sieve, and the father pours the water of the seven wells down the drain of the roof, so that the water passing through the pitcher and the sieve may trickle slowly over the mother's head.

This belief relates mainly to the first *trikhal* born in the family: it applies to boys more than to girls (and indeed it is said in Kasur that a girl after three boys is not unlucky at all) and evil is to be feared by both parents but principally to the parent of corresponding sex. Moreover, a boy born after three girls is also apt to be himself unlucky. The ceremonies used to avert the ill-effects are often those employed when a child is born under an evil *nakshatra* but for a *trikhal*: five earthen pitchers filled with water containing gold images of Brahma, Vishnu, Mahesh, Indra and Rudra are worshipped, whereas in the case of a birth under the asterisms of *Jesta, Mula, Asmetkan* and *Magan,* the leaves of seven trees are used, and in the case of a child born in Katak four images of Brahma, Indra, Rudra and Suraj are placed in four pitchers covered with red and white cloth and a little of the water sprinkled over the mother and child.

Lastly, for a child born during an eclipse, three gold images, one of the *Nakshatra* of birth, another of Rahu and a third of the sun or moon (as the eclipse may have been) are worshipped.

Another name for the *trikhal* is *tretar* (derived from Sanskrit) and in Hoshiarpur the performance of a fire sacrifice with the aid of a Brahman after the *sutak* period is usual. *Pala* wood is burnt and sugar etc, thrown on to it. In Karnal and Rohtak, a son born after three girls is usually called *tetar* (or named telu Ram) and in Rohtak various ways of averting the evil he may bring are described. In one, the parents sit on a plough and bathe from an earthern vessel containing 108 or 101 holes with water from the Ganges and 27 wells, 108 medicines and milk. The water is passed through a sieve, but in some places a sieve is held to be unlucky. In another ceremony, the parents bathe in water (passed through a sieve) drawn from 27 wells and in which stones from 27 places and leaves from 27 trees have been placed. This must be done 27 days after the birth. A number of 14 or 27 Brahmins are also feasted. After these ceremonies, a pair of snakes are made of a precious metal and given with seven kinds of grain to a Dakaut Brahman. In another rite, a horse-shoe, painted with vermilion figures, is burnt on the third or tenth day after the birth. It is lucky if this day falls on a Sunday.

This superstition appears then to take various forms and the rites practised are very diverse, those used to aviod other unlucky births being often resorted to, though it appears that strictly speaking special rites should be performed. It is said to be confined in Sirmur to the immigrants from Hoshiarpur. It is possibly connected with the astrological doctrine but the powers of the first- born are not thereby explained. The belief and rites are said to be described in the *shastras.* In 1885, a Sanskrit book called *Trikhal-shanti* was published at Lahore giving an account of the belief. The saying goes that it should be abandoned as it will cause the death of its parents and maternal uncle within seven months and also destroy itself.

Rites Related to 8th Child

The eighth child is very unlucky if a son as he is sure to cause the father's death. But in Karnal the 8th child is regarded as especially dangerous to the mother. The remedy is to pass a *charkha* or spinning wheel thrice round the mother and give it to the midwife. The *charkha* or spinning wheel must be in perfect order.

Two and a Half Heads

Dhai sira or two and a half heads: In Jhelum *trikhal* is drilled with two and a half holes - a local expression meaning two holes in one ear and one in the other, or 1 in each ear and one in the nose. In Muzaffargarh, a *dhai-sira, Mula* or *sat-sira* is a child whose head has not been properly shaped.There is no objection to twins. But in Kangra, if a boy and a girl be born together it is sometimes regarded as unlucky. In Karnal, different classes have different ideas about twins. Among both Hindus and Muhammadans some consider them a good omen, while other Hindus think they forebode ill-luck. Women do not consider their birth evil and they have a proverb that the woman who gives birth to twins goes straight to paradise on her death. In Ambala, twins being weaker than single children frequently die, and so they are considered ominous. It is believed that if at intercourse air gets in, it splits the seed in two and thus gives rise to twins. It is also said that if a pregnant woman eats a fruit which has grown in a pair, she will give birth to twins.

Unlucky Teethings

In Hoshiarpur, a child which cuts its first teeth from its upper jaw is considered unlucky to its maternal uncle. To remove the evil effects, its mother goes beyond the limits of her village on the path leading to her parents' house. From the opposite direction comes the maternal uncle of the child, bringing with him a white brass tray, one and a quarter *sers* of rice, seven piece, a yard of cloth and four iron nails, all except the tray and seven nails knotted in the cloth. The maternal uncle drives the four nails in the ground in a square, touches the child's teeth with the tray, and then puts the tray and the cloth with the other articles wrapped in it within the square between the nails and returns home. The uncle and his sister must not talk.The sister sits with her child clinging to her shoulder, her veil drawn and her back towards her brother, and he returns in silence after the ritual which is called *danton ka thakna* or 'the charm of the teeth'.

In Karnal, when a child of either sex cuts the front teeth of its upper jaw first, it is a bad omen to the maternal uncle. His sister, the mother of the child, sends him a word of the event. On receiving the message, the maternal uncle takes a bronze cup of medium size, a quarter of a *sers* of *kasar* (wheat flour baked in *ghee* and mixed with sugar) and half a coconut in piece of red cloth (*kharwa*) and proceeds to his sister's house without informing her or any other person in the house of his arrival, which is kept strictly secret. He goes quickly on to the roof of the house in which his sister lives and puts the cup etc, on it, or if there is no staircase, he throws them upon it. After this rite, he retraces his steps silently without speaking to, or even seeing the face of his sister and returns home. When it is known that the ceremony has been conducted, the things are taken from the roof and used without scruple.

It is conducted differently in different villages situated in the neighbourhood of Patiala. A time is fixed and a place appointed for the ceremony. The child's mother goes to the place which is always fixed beyond the limits of the village on the road to her brother's house. He starts from his own village and halts a mile from the place till he gets news of his sister's arrival. He brings with him an old coin with an iron nail, but nothing else. When he is informed that everything is ready, he proceeds to the place. His sister takes her child up in her arms, so that its face is towards the way her brother is coming. The brother comes silently and opens the mouth of the child, touches its teeth with the paisa and iron nail, without showing himself or seeing his sister's face and after burying these things on the spot, returns to his village.

Prospective Mother Goes to her Natal Home

It is a very general, but by no means universal custom for the wife to return to her own parents' house for her first confinement. A child born in the house of his nana, or the maternal grandfather, often receives the name of Nanak. Care is taken not to let the fact that the pains of labour have begun be noised abroad, lest publicity increase their severity. And if the pains are severe, a tray (*thali*), on which a charm is written, is shown to the patient in order to remove them. It appears to be the universal custom for delivery to be effected on the ground. But after it is over, the mother is usually seated on a mat or cassock. It appears to be almost the universal custom to tell her that she has given birth to a girl, in the curious belief that if she were to learn that she had became the mother of a son, the after-birth would not come away. As a rule, the umbilical cord is cut with a sharp knife, but in Ludhiana, it is tied with the *janeo* of an elderly man belonging to the family. This is also the usage in Hoshiarpur and Sialkot, but in these districts, if the child be a girl, the cord is tied with the thread of a spinning wheel. Any other method is supposed to injure the child. Among the people hailing from Gujranwala, the umbilical cord is not cut till two or three hours after birth.

Disposal of Placenta

In Ferozepore, the secundines are buried in a corner of the house. In Mandi, (Himachal) the after-birth is buried at the spot where the child was born, after the eldest matron of the family has made the new mother worship it.

Death after Delivery

If a woman dies within thirteen days of her delivery, it is believed that she will return in the guise of a malignant spirit to torment her husband and family. To avert this, a *shanti* rite is performed at her funeral, a piece of red cloth and the grass image of her child being placed on the bier. Some people also drive nails through her head and eyes, while others also fasten nails on either side of the door of their house. In Hoshiarpur, a woman whose child has died within forty days is called a *parchhawan*, and she must not see a woman in confinement during the first forty days after birth.

Rites Related to Birth

The observances after birth are manifold, and their character complex, so that it is as difficult to distinguish between the religious and social observances, as it is to say what usage are based on superstition and magic and what on the first glimmerings of medical skill. Nevertheless, there are traces of more rational ideas regarding cleanliness, and even a kind of primitive anticipation of antiseptic treatment. One important point to note is that the performances are far less elaborate in case of a girl child, and this idea, that the birth of a girl is a misfortune, reacts injuriously on the mother, less care being bestowed upon her, and every observance being hurried over and many stinted, if the child is not male.

Thus, the mother of a son is carefully tended for forty days, but if the child is a girl for only twenty-one.

The period of ritualistic impurity is most commonly called *sutak,* but it is known as *chhut*, especially in the north-west of the Punjab. Its duration is, in theory, ten days among Brahmins, twelve among Khatris, fifteen among Vaisyas and thirty among Sudras, thus varying inversely with the purity of the caste. But in practice, it is eleven days among Brahmans and thirteen among Khatris; or only eleven or thirteen for all castes.

In Rohtak and Loharu, it would appear to be only ten, expiring with the *dasuthan*. Among the Hindu arrivals from Gujranwala, it is said to be thirteen days for Brahmans and sixteen for others.

In *Patiala*, it is generally believed that death in child-bed is ominous for the other women of the family who may yet bear children, and more or less so for the husband also, should he take a second wife, because the dead woman's evil spirit will vex her; the prophylactic measures, generally undertaken with slight modification in different localities are :- Just after the death four iron nails are driven into the ground round the corpse, and when it is taken from the house-door to the burning-ground-rape seed is scattered all the way behind it, and a voodooman follows it reciting incantations. Midway the bearers set the body on the ground and four more nails are driven into it. On reaching the burning ground, it is cremated without any ceremony, but on the third or fourth day when the ashes have cooled the unburnt bones are picked up and the ashes collected into a conical heap on which the lower part of a hand flour-mill is placed while two iron nails are driven towards the head and two towards the feet of the body as it lay when placed on the pile, and the wizard reading some incantation completes the ceremony. After all this the husband still has to go to Pehowa where he undergoes purification under the guidance of the Brahmans of that place. In Sangrur, the *Gayatri Mantra* is recited by a Brahman when a woman dies in child-birth among the *Nais*, to prevent her becoming an evil spirit. The sweepers drive an iron nail in the ground for the same purpose, and the *Jhinwars* send for a Qazi to recite some words called *kilna*. No unusual treatment is practised among other low castes in this tahsil.

Among the Jats of Hoshiarpur, who may in this connection be regarded as typical of the Hindus of the Punjab proper, the midwife washes the new born baby in a vessel into which silver has been thrown, before she gives it to the mother. But the child is not suckled for one and a half days. The *pap* must be washed by the husband's sister before the child can be fed. For this she receives a reward in cash. As on all auspicious occasions, oil is thrown on the ground and under the mother's bed, beneath which green *dub* grass is also placed, as it is a sign of prosperity; and as such some is also presented to the child's father by his friends. To prevent any harm to the mother or the child, a number of precautions are taken: Fire must be kept in the room, as must also; grain close to the bed, as an emblem of good luck: water must also be kept there, as it is a purifier; and a weapon should be placed close by the mother. Under the bed should also be kept the handle of a plough. There should be a lock on the bed, or else it should have a chain round it, this is termed *bel maria*. On no account should a cat be allowed in the room, or should the mother hear its call, or even mention the word 'cat'. It is most unlucky for her to dream of the animal, and if one is seen in the room, ashes should be thrown over it. The house should not be swept with a broom lest the luck be swept out of it. No small drain into the room should be left open, lest ill-luck enter by an aperture which must be unclean and, a lamp must be kept burning all night, and allowed to burn itself out in the morning. A son is called *ghar ka diwa*, so if the lamp were blown out, he too would be destroyed.

Neither mother, nor child must come out of the room for thirteen days of impurity. On the thirteenth day, the mother gives away her old clothes to the midwife, who sometimes shares them with the *nain*. The latter brings some cow's urine in a *thikra* or jar, with green grass, a *supara*, and a *naherna*, or nail-parer. She sprinkles the cow's urine over the mother with the grass, burns some incense, and pares her nails for the first time, since her confinement in the labour room. Then the mother must put on the *nain*'s (the nain's husband's, not the nain's) slippers, and walk out of the room carrying the child. The nain sprinkles oil on the ground outside the door, and there the *jhiwari*, or some other menial, stands with a pot of water and some green grass. Both she and the *nain* are paid a reward in cash for their services. In the outer room Vidhata Mata is worshipped, no men, not even a Brahman, being present. The women make a figure of *gobar* or cowdung covering it with a red cloth and offering to it the food cooked for the feast. Drums are then beaten, Brahmans and relatives fed, and the members of the household congratulated. The idol is kept for one and a quarter months and then deposited near the village well.

The period of confinement lasts forty days, and the mother must not stain the palms of her hands with henna, or wear clothes dyed with *kasumbha*, until the ancestors have been worshipped and kinsmen feasted. On this occasion the *dhianis*, or girls born in the tribe, must also be fed, and revered.

On the third day, the rite called *bahir* is in vogue in Rohtak, and, as the name denotes, the mother on this day comes 'outside' from the room in which she was confined, at an auspicious hour fixed by a Brahman. The women of the clan assemble at her house, each bringing 125 gms of grain. The *nain* makes a *chauk* or geometrical design on the ground, in which are depicted the planets. The eldest woman of the family then puts five *sers* of grain, some jaggery and oil on the *chauk*, and all the others follow suit. Then the mother comes out of her house and touches the grain, which is divided, with the jaggery and oil, between the *nain*, the Brahmani and the midwife. A *chhatak* of jaggery is then given to each female of the brotherhood present, and songs are sung. Low caste men also get their dues, and, when the mother comes out of the house, the *nai* waits at the door with a *naherna* with which he touches the boy, for which he gets a rupee. He also puts blades of *dabh* grass in the turbans of the child's forbears, in order that they may multiply like the grass. For this he receives a second rupee.

In Hoshiarpur, in Punjab, the mother in some places is bathed on the third day, if she has given birth to a girl, a ceremony postponed to the fifth day if her child is a boy. In Sirmur, too, she bathes on the third or fifth day; and in Mandi a rite called the *Tirphal ka gontar* is observed on the former day. Elsewhere the mother bathes on the third, fifth or seventh day, and *churi* (baked bread, sugar, and *ghee*) is then distributed among the female relatives. In the evening of the same day, she puts the child in a winnowing basket and takes it outside the village gate accompanied by the midwife.

In Mandi(HP), as part of the rite, the courtyard of the house is swept, and circles drawn on it with mud. These circles are called *makol*. The threshold of the house is painted red. The person who sweeps the yard gets *pura tar* (rice, sugar, cash etc.). Then the mother is bathed in hot water and made to worship Ganpati, whose idol is put on a yellow *chauk*, and offerings made to it. A Brahman now makes *panchgabh*, mixing it up in a jar with a blade of *dabh* grass. He gives three spoonfuls of this mixture to the mother and thus removes her impurity. He next receives his fee in money, and then places a ball of cowdung, containing gold, silver, a pearl, and a bead of coral, near the idol. This ball is called *biyahi*, and is worshipped like the feeds. After all this, the mother's breasts are washed and she suckles the child. Then balls of boiled rice are placed daily in the *chauk* for three days, until the impurity has been removed - and are then given to the midwife. The mother's brother then goes to the forest with a Brahman and a musician, and cuts four branches from a *thohar* (*Euphoria Royleana*), and these he is made to worship by the Brahman, who receives a fee for this from the mother's brother. Of those four branches, the Brahman places two, one on each side of the door of the house in which the birth took place, and sticks two in cowdung near Ganpati's *chauk*. They are then covered with a red cloth. The mother's brother's forehead is then marked with the *tilak*, and the nearest kinsmen are fed. Songs are also sung. The eldest matron of the family also gives the mother rice mixed with salt, a dish called *pichhlagra*.

As a rule, the mother bathes on the third day, or on one bearing an odd number after it, but in the Dasuya tahsil of Hoshiarpur she is bathed on the fourth, seventh, thirteenth, twenty-first, thirtieth, and forty-eighth days.

Excluding the bathing, the rites of the fifth day are confined to Jhelum, in which district the *panjwan* or fifth-day observance simply consists in a bath. In Hoshiarpur, a foster-brother is made for the child out of cowdung, and grain, sweets and bread placed beneath it. A red cloth is then thrown over it. All these things are the midwife's perquisite. The rite is performed both for a girl and a boy. The mother also bathes on this occasion, and her head is washed with milk and cow's urine. Elsewhere in the district the mother is bathed on the fifth or seventh day, and the *nain* plaits her hair. Then, she is brought out into the courtyard, wearing the *nain's dopatta* or shawl. The yard is previously plastered with cowdung, and in it the mother is seated on a stool, and given cow's urine and Ganges water to drink. She then re-enters the room in the house, which has in the meanwhile been re-plastered with cow-dung.

Inside she sits by a wall, close to which is placed some grain on which a lamp is lit. Each of the kinswomen then brings some grain and money and puts them by the lamp. Then rice, loaves and *mash* are distributed among the brotherhood, the grain and money brought being divided by the midwife and the *nain*.

Chhati Ceremony

The ceremony called the *chhati* was doubtless originally, as the name implies, observed on the sixth day, but it is now extinct (in Sirmur), or else held on the sixth or any subsequent date. Only in Mandi must the rite called *chhati gontar* actually be held on the sixth day. This rite resembles the *tirphalla*. The house is swept, as before, and Ganpati again worshipped. Then images of a cow, a calf, and a herdsman are made of brass. These are known as *dada wachha,* and are placed near the goddess idol. *Panchgabh* is given to the mother. The females of the brotherhood assemble and sing songs. They are regaled on moist grain, and red thread is then sent to the mother's parents, a custom called *dart dena*, or 'giving the thread.' In return they send money and sweetmeats. In Mandi is also performed the third or last *gontar*. On the evening preceding the day fixed for this rite, the house is swept. All the near kinswomen are invited, and they spend the night in singing, while the priest makes the mother worship Ganpati. Alms are also given to avert evil planetary influences.

On the following day the priest performs a *hawan (hom)*, in much the usual way. The mother and all the members of her family are then purified, and finally a *biyahi* of cowdung is made, and the mother instructed to clean her teeth with twigs of a fragrant plant. These twigs are struck in the *biyahi* and preserved as long as the child lives, being worshipped at its birthdays. The *biyahi*, with the twigs struck in it, must, at this *gontar*, be set afloat on a river or stream. Elsewhere the *chhati* is called as the *dhaman*, and is held only in cases when the child was a male. When the mother goes to her parents' house for her confinement, the *chhati* is observed on her return to her husband's house, and in Ferozepur it is in this case postponed till the twenty-first day. In Ludhiana, the rite is simple. The mother is bathed *(chatti ka ashnan)*, and boiled rice and sweets are distributed among the members of family and other relatives. The mother fasts all day until sunset, when she is given starch to eat and then she is brought out of the room by the midwife with a lamp burning in the winnowing basket. After the sixth day, the mother is not so carefully looked after.

In Amritsar, the *chhati* is said not to be observed by Brahmans or Khatris, but only by Aroras. Among the Hindus hailing from Montgomery, the *chhati* is termed *sathi,* and the Brahman suggests the boy's name, no such observance being required for a girl. In Rohtak and Loharu, it is said to be the occasion on which the goddess of fortune will visit the house and partake of grain and water therein, so water is set forth, and pen, paper and ink placed ready for her to record a happy future for the child. The kinswomen and the priest's wife sing songs all night, the idea being that the goddess will record a better fate for the child, if they are awake and a lamp is kept burning.

After this, the mother is allowed to eat grain, and the child is dressed in a *Kurta* and cap, and ornaments are put on it. If it is a boy, mango leaves are hung on the door of the house, and *thapas* or hand-prints made on either side of it in the corners, with henna.

Special care is taken that the sounds of mourning may not reach the mother's ears if a death occurs in any neighbouring house. The term *dhaman* is applied to the custom whereby the mother keeps her bedding on the ground. On the first Sunday or Thursday after the birth, mother and child are bathed and dressed in new clothes. They are then placed on a *charpai.* Sweet porridge is also distributed among the relatives on this day. If during the *dhaman* period thunder is heard, a pewter vessel is beaten, lest the sound of the thunder reach the mother's ears. The *satwan*, or seventh-day observance is only known by that name. It consists merely of a bath in Hoshiarpur in lieu of or in addition to those previously taken. The tenth day is not generally marked by any special rites, in spite of the fact that it gives its name to the *dasuthan,* literally bathing on the tenth day after childbirth.

In Sirmur, it is also called *sondhia*, and is observed at any time before the child is five years old. In Sialkot, the *dhaman* rite is observed on the eleventh day by Brahmans, and by other castes on the thirteenth, i.e. after the *sutak* or pollution is over. Four copper coins are placed under the mother's feet, and an idol made of cowdung. After bathing and putting on new clothes the mother worships a lamp, placed before the idol on a pile of grain (which is the midwife's perquisite). Each woman relative then gives her a cocoanut and five dates. She is then taken to the kitchen, where a Brahman administers the *panchgan*, recieving a reward in cash, and a meal. Lastly, the idol is taken away outside the village and placed under a plum tree. On the same day, the child is invested with the *taragga*, a thread on which are strung a cowry, an iron ring, another of green glass, a tiger's claw, and a piece of the child's umbilical cord, cut off after its birth. The Kinswomen are also feasted on this occasion. In the Dogar, this thread is made of silk.

The thirteenth day is important, because the *sutak* or pollution period very commonly ends on that day, and it is therefore signalled by rites of purification. Very generally the mother is bathed, all the earthen vessels in the house are broken or replaced, and those of metal cleaned. Clothes also are washed and the house plastered. Brahmans are sometimes fed, and occasionally the child is named on this day or dressed for the first time. The twenty-first day is merely marked in Hoshiarpur by bathing the mother and purifying all the vessels used by her since the birth by fire. The thirtieth day is only the occasion for a bath in Hoshiarpur. On the fortieth day the mother bathes for the last time, and then ceases to be even ceremonially impure, and can take part again in the duties of the family kitchen. Strangers also can now take food from the house.

Among the Buddhists of Kanaur, on the birth of a son the goddess Dolma is worshipped, and the chant called *Bhum chung*, which runs : *Om tayatha gate gate pare gate swahaa* (May God bless the child) is sung. The old women of the family perform the midwife's functions; and for a fortnight the mother lives apart, being debarred from touching anything due to pollution. At the end of that period, she and all she possesses are sprinkled with cow's urine mixed with Ganges water, as among the Hindus. The child's horoscope is cast by a *lama,* who also names the child when it is 15 days old, or on any other auspicious day. It is generally brought out of the house for the first time at the full moon and, if possible, at an auspicious moment, when one or two months old. Charms for its long life are also made by the *lamas.* A boy's head is shaved when one year old, the lamas performing a *hom*, *puja,* or *path* sacrifice. As the Kanauris only rank as Shudras, they are not entitled to wear the sacred thread, so they wear instead a *kanthi* or necklace from the age of eight.

During pregnancy, the *kuldeota* is worshipped among the *Bashahrs* of Himachal, if necessary, and between the seventh and eighth months the *Ashtam Rahu* is also worshipped, but these observances are confined to the twice-born Hindu castes and to the better class of the *Khash Kanets*. Brahmans predict the child's sex by counting a handful of almonds, odd numbers indicating a boy, even a girl. The birth of a girl passes unnoticed, but that of a boy is the occasion for festivities and almsgiving. As a rule, the midwife is a woman of low caste, but sometimes Karan women are also employed. During the last five months of pregnancy, the midwife massages the woman at the end of each month to keep the foetus in position. The *gontrala* is observed by Brahmans, Rajputs and Vaisyas after 11, 13 and 15 days, respectively. Some of the *Khash* also observe it. On the expiry of this period, the family is deemed clean again, and other families of the tribe can eat with them.

The mother is also purified after the *gontrala.* The impurity only lasts three days among the menial tribes. The ceremony of feeding the child for the first time is called *lugru*, and is observed at an auspicious moment, with worship of Ganpati and the nine planets and various festivities. The child is named at the *annodak*, and as usual given two names. This is done when it is five or six months old as a rule. *Natwa* is observed among the three higher castes, and since recent times by some of the Khash.

Women whose children die prematurely have recourse to various magical practices and charms, but the favourite remedy is the worship of the *Ashtam Rahu,* especially in cases of *ashtamrah* or falling sickness, to which children are liable. The first tonsure (locally called *kanbal*) is done at the *kuldeota's* temple alone. It is observed by the twice-born castes on a day fixed by a *purohit* or *padha:* and by other castes with the *deota's* permission.

Among the *Baurias*, the child's name is chosen by a Brahman. On the fifth day after birth, the mother takes a *lota* full of water on her head to the nearest well, a Brahmani and Nain, with other women, accompanying her and singing songs. She takes with her *bhanjor* or moistened grain of gram or *bajra* and after worshipping the well throws some of the *bhanjor*, with a little water out of her *lota* and a *makka* brought by the Brahmani or Nain into the well. The rest of the *bhanjor* is distributed among children. The mother is deemed purified on the tenth day. Rathaur children are taken to the *sehrh* at *Nimrana* to have their heads shaved, but the Panwars, Chauhans and Badgujars all take theirs to Masani Devi at Gurgaon. On the birth of a male child in Kullu, there is a feast amongst the Kanets and a present is made to the headman *(negi)* of the Kothi. The child is christened some time within the year following, and is then produced in public, and there is another feast. It is a common custom in Outer Saraj to give two brothers the names that rhyme. The Khash observe the same rites at birth as the twice-born castes, while the Raos, like the low castes, simply offer a bunch of green grass to the child's father and he places it on his head, but gives no alms. Infant baptism is also practised by the Bisnois in Haryana and 30 days after birth the child, whether boy or girl, is baptised by the priest (*sadh*) in much the same way as an adult; only the set form of prayer is different called as *garbhgdyatri*, and the priest pours a few drops of water into the child's mouth, and gives the child's relatives each three handcups full of the consecrated water to drink at the same time, the barber clips off the child's hair. This baptismal ceremony also has the effect of purifying the house which has been made impure by the birth pollution or *sutak*. The custom is prevalent among the Bisnois.

In accouchement the *churha* woman sits, with one woman on each side of her, and one behind her. The *dai*, or midwife, sits in front. No seat is used. When the child is born the midwife places her head on the stomach of the mother to press out the blood, and with her feet and hands presses the whole body. The *dai* and women relations attend during and after confinement. As an expression of joy at the birth of a child a string of *shirin*, or acacia leaves, are hung across the door. Green symbolises joy and blessing, *mubarikbadi*. The leaves of the *akk*, a plant with poisonous milky juice, are thrown on the house to keep away evil spirits. If the child is a male born after two girls, they put the boy in a cloth, which they tie at both ends as a sort of cradle, and then they lift the child through the roof, while the nurse says :- *Trikhal ki dhar a-gai,* i.e., 'the third time thrives.' *Gur or* jaggery is given to the friends, and ten days after that a dinner, to which the relatives are invited. At the end of 21 days, the mother gets over her separation, and resumes cooking. Among them adoption of children is common, but with no special ceremonies.

Rite of *Chura Karam*

In Mandi, a religious performance called the *chura karam* or *jarolan* is held in the third or fifth year of the child's life in *Magh, Phagun, Baisakh*, *Jeth* or *Har*, which months are auspicious for it. Two children must undergo the rite together. All their relatives assemble the previous day. On the day fixed, a *chauk* is painted red, and over it is placed a platter, made of cow-dung, and containing four hollows, one of which is filled with cold water, another with hot, a third with milk, and a fourth with curds. In each a little Ganges water is also poured, and a bundle of *dubh* grass is placed on the platter. A little oil is then dropped on the children's heads, and their bodies are rubbed with *batna*. They are next bathed, and the eldest matron of the family swirls sweets round their heads to avert evil spirits from them. Then they are made to revere Ganpati and the priest parts their hair into three, tying each with red thread. A young girl is then told to apply all the contents of the platter, with the *dubh* grass, to their hair. The rite is called *Jora senchna,* Brahmans are then fed. Next day at dawn, the priest makes the two children worship the nine planets, and then he receives his reward in money.

Oil is then poured on their heads and the barber cuts their hair, which must fall into the mother's skirt. The barber is paid his due. The mothers offer the hair at the temple of their family goddesses. Then the children are bathed and dressed in new clothes, their brothers' wives, or their sisters, painting their eyes with antimony. A goldsmith then bores their ears and puts gold ear-rings in them, receiving a he-goat and some cash as his fee. Coins are finally distributed among the poor, and a feast given to the Brahmans and near kinsmen.

Rite of Worshipping Well

In Rohtak, a month or so after the birth of a boy, a rite called *doghar puja* is observed. If the mother is very weak, the other women of the house place a jar of water by her, and they themselves visit the nearest well, singing songs as they go. The well is worshipped, rice and *dubh* grass being offered to it. On their return, coins are given to the menials. Or if the mother cannot perform this rite herself, it is observed at home. In Ferozepur, the mother goes on the twenty-first day to a well, and there distributes boiled barley amongst children.

Suckling the child for the first time is the occasion for a curious rite. At sunset, the midwife washes the mother's breasts with water, using some blades of *dubh* grass as a brush. They are again washed by the child's sister or some other female. The midwife gets cash, the sister a rupee, for this. Next day the midwife brings some green *sarin* leaves and ties them with a *mauli* thread to the house door - a fee of cash being paid her for this also. In Ferozepur, the child is not suckled till the evening after its birth, and then the mother's breasts are washed by a young girl, who gets a few rupees if the child is a boy, but only one rupee if it is a girl. Jaggery is applied to the child's lips before it is given the breast. If the milk does not flow freely, the child is given sheep's milk.

Ceremony of *Chola*

The ceremony of clothing a child for the first time is usually called *chola*, and is held on various dates. A Brahman fixes a day; in Amritsar also this is the usual custom, but often Aroras and Khatris hold it on the thirteenth day. In Ferozpur, the *Chola* ceremony is celebrated. A part of the house is plastered and a figure of a cow made by the midwife-both with cowdung. This image is covered with red cloth and designated the *Bidh- mata*, or 'goddess of fortune'. Next the barber brings cow's urine in a cup, in which he also puts some blades of *dubh* grass. Then, the mother puts on the barber's shoes, and holding his skirt in her hand, she reveres the *Bidh-mata*, her children sitting on her lap. Two coins, the barber's perquisite, are also placed beneath her feet. The barber now applies the cow's urine to the child's lips, with the *dubh* grass, and then gives it to mother, who is thus purified, as is the child.

If the latter is a boy, the parents place a rupee in the cap, but if it is a girl, *annas* two or four surface. *Pinjiri* and lumps of parched wheat are distributed to the relatives, and the females belonging to it place grain before the image of Bidh-mata. This grain is divided between the barber and the midwife. The mother is given strengthning food after this. The ceremony appears to be usually observed on the thirteenth day, but this is not always the case. The accounts of the *chola* rite are very confused, because *chola* literally means a cloak, and the child is dressed in that garment on other occassions e.g. on the fifth, seventh or ninth day; when the mother is bathed, the child is dressed in a yellow *chola*, and a boy born after several successive female children is dressed in one made of cloth, which must be given by a friend in Ferozepur.

But in the community migrating from Rawalpindi, the cloth is got from a friend or the mother's relative under any circumstances. Among the people hailing from Montgomery, the *chola* also takes place on the thirteenth day, but if the boy was born on one of the six unlucky asterisms, the observance is postponed till the twenty-seventh day. Speaking generally, the customs connected with the rite are social rather than religious, but in Hoshiarpur, the family god's temple or some Muhammadin saint's shrine is usually visited. In Rohtak, the mother's parents send her clothes and ornaments for herself, the child and her husband. This present is called *chhuchak*, and it is sent in response to the *badhai*. The *Lohri* following a birth is observed with special pomp, coins and cowries being given away to the poor. So, too, the next Diwali is celebrated by a grander illumination than usual, sweets being also distributed among the brotherhood.

Rite of Tonsure

The first tonsure of a child is an important rite, but it is known by various names and celebrated in various ways by different castes and in different localities. In the south-west, it is known as the *mundan* or *bhaddan*. If the mother has made a vow prior to the birth of her child to observe the rite at a certain shrine or temple, it is duly carried out there; otherwise, it may be done at home. An auspicious hour should be fixed by a Brahman, or the rite should be performed on the marriage of a near kinsman, or on the *Baisakhi* or *Dusehra*. In Hoshiarpur, boy's ears are bored on this occasion, and some people smear his forehead with goat's blood. In Ludhiana, the rite is, like the birth observances, described as the *mundan sanskar*, and it is unlucky to shave a child's head until it has been performed. The menials receive fees, and the relatives are regaled with sweets at the first tonsure, after which *bodi* or tuft of hair is allowed to grow, but it is more usual to let the *bodi* grow after the marriage of a near kinsman. As a rule, the rite is performed between the ages of one and a quarter and four years, or, in Ferozepur as soon as the child has cut its teeth. Sometimes, the rite is repeated once or twice. Among the Hindus hailing from Gujranwala, the observance is called *rit* and is held in the third or fifth years. In short, the observance is essentially a domestic usage, varying in its details according to the ancestral custom of the caste, section or even family.

Sometimes women vow that a child's hair shall never be cut and a girl's hair is never cut. Among Sikhs, the rite is not very common, and if practised, is observed when the child is only two or three months old. In a well-to-do family, the rite is the occasion for a feast to Brahmans, otherwise Brahmans appear to have no part in it.

Investiture of the Sacred Thread

Generally, the *janeo* or 'sacred thread of caste' is invariably worn by the three higher or 'twice-born' castes and not by the fourth or *Sudra* caste, and as if the 'sacred thread' were the same or only slightly different for all the three higher castes. But an examination of the facts as they stand not only show the extraordinary variety of form which the *janeo* takes, but also prove that it is inaccurate and misleading to call the janeo 'the thread of caste.' At the present day, it is not always worn by the higher castes, but the so-called *Sudra* castes sometime wears it. As a general rule, we may say that the form of the *janeo* varies in every caste or group or sect. It will, thus, be the most convenient to deal with the form of *janeo* as worn by each caste. Earlier, it was customary among Hindus for children to wear the *tagadhri* before they reached the ages at which the *janeo* could be worn, and in some parts of Punjab the custom still survives. The *tagadhri* is worn round the waist, and is made of *munj* or if the parents are wealthy, of silver.

Voodoo against Miscarriage

If a Hindu woman's children all die, she procures in the third month of her pregnancy a piece of iron, taken out of a sunken boat, and from it has a *kari* or bangle made. This she wears on her right leg, and it is believed to prevent her future children's premature death. The custom is in vogue in Punjab. Among some northern tribes a woman who has previously miscarried wears a charm, such as a thread or amulet on her navel; other wear a cowry on that part to avert the child's being born dead. The charms are blown upon by a witch-doctor before being put on, the fee paid depending on one's means.

Muslim Rite of *Satwahin*

In Ambala, the observance in the seventh month, or *satwahin,* is said to be confined to the towns. It simply consists in the parents sending sugar and rice etc. to their daughter on her first pregnancy; a woman related to the family also drops fruits into her lap. In Sirmur, the woman's parents try to arrange for her to be sent to their house, but if this cannot be done they send her present of rice, sweets and fruit etc, with clothes for herself and the expected child. This is called *kioka*. In Kangra (Himachal Pradesh) on the commencement of the seventh month, the woman's parents bring her presents consisting of red clothes, dry fruit, henna, scented oil and missi, with other perfumes and an ornament, preferably one for the arm. These gifts are brought in a procession, musicians and singers accompanying it.

On arriving at the husband's house, they make their daughter sit on a stool, while the *nain* dresses her in the red suit and dyes her hands with the henna. She is also garlanded with flowers, and her lap filled with dry fruits, such as cocoanuts or dates. These are all eaten, apparently by her husband's parents, she herself not being permitted to partake of them. Then the husband's parents make *karhi* of flour, *gur* and *ghi*, and this is eaten by people of the *gotar*, but by no others. Persons not belonging to the *gotar* are feasted separately. Prior to this observance, a pregnant woman may not wear new clothes or ornaments. After it, she must not go to her father's house until forty days have elapsed from her confinement. In Kapurthala in Punjab, the parents first send their daughter clothes etc. in the sixth or seventh month, and then she is taken to their house, the sweets sent by them being divided among her husband's kin. Similarly in Ludhiana, it is thought that the first confinement ought to take place in the woman's own house.

In *Malar Kotla*, the Muhammadans, especially the dominant Pathan families, observe two distinct customs on a first pregnancy. As a rule the first, the *satwahan*, takes place at the husband's house. The woman's mother is formally notified of the fact that her daughter is in the seventh month of her pregnancy, and she comes to the house, bringing a suite of clothes, sweets and dried fruit. Towards the end of the seventh month, the woman bathes and puts on new clothes brought by her mother, perfuming herself with scents. Fruit is then put in her lap, and she then sits on a floor which has been plastered, while a *mirasan* sings the appointed eulogies, called *sohla*, of Shaikh Sadr Jahan, to a drum accompaniment.Throughout this performance the woman sits with her head bent down, and her hair unloosed, but combed and oiled. Occasionally, she falls into an ecstasy under the influence of the Shaikh, who often makes her his mouth-piece. Sweets are then sent round to relatives and neighbours, and the *mirasan* dismissed with her fee. In the evening, the *darweshes* are fed at the mother's expense, and next day she takes her daughter home with the husband's parents'consent.

In Abohar and Fazilka, the *rit* is observed in the beginning of the seventh month. The kinswomen assemble and eat out of one tray, the matrons of the family giving the woman fresh fruits as an auspicious omen. The mothers of the couple are also congratulated. Then the kinswomen are feasted, and a Dumni sings songs. After this, the woman is dressed in colourful garments and puts on ornaments or flowers. At night her hands are stained with henna and the girls of the family sing. This performance is only held by the lower classes of Muhammadans, such as the *Kakezais* (distillers), *Qasaba* (butchers), *Arains* (market gardeners), *Dhobis* (washermen) and *mashkis* or watermen. Among all classes, the woman's mother brings her to her own house at the commencement of the ninth month, and on the day of her arrival sends for the almonds, dates and saffron etc, required on or after her delivery.

Patashas are distributed among the family, and also among the women of the quarter, a rite called *sauda* by the women.

It is a very general rule among all Muhammadan castes in the north Jammu & Kashmir that the woman should avoid eating fruit, wearing fine clothes, or any kind of adornment until the *rit* is performed on the commencement of the seventh month. This *rit* consists merely in feasting the brotherhood, but it is also not uncommon for the woman's parents to send her a present of a *trewar* and to boil rice which is eaten at a feast in the name of their ancestors. The *trewar* is then given to the husband's sister or the daughter of his nearest kinsman. After the *rit,* the woman may use scent. Wheat, too, is parched, mixed with jaggery, and made into balls, which are distributed among the relatives.

Among Haryana Muslims, pregnant woman avoids the use of antimony, or *dandasa*. She also avoids the shade of the *dharek* and the shadow of a woman suffering from *athra* or one whose children die in infancy. An *athrawali* is a woman whose children are born prematurely and generally die. A bead, which changes its colour, is believed to counteract the effects of *athra*. This bead is rare and is sold by gypsies at fancy prices. It is also tied to the leg of a new-born child as a *talisman* against *athra* : and *athri ka manka* means one of a changeable, volatile disposition.

In *Fatehganj, rit* is observed in the seventh month, *halwa* being distributed among the relatives. This is done either in her parents house, or in her husband's, but in the former case the consent of the husband's parents is neccessary.

Observing the Rite of *Satwansa*

Muhammadans in *Hansi* observe the *satwansa* in the seventh month of pregnancy. Seven or nine jars of water are brought from as many different wells, and the woman bathes in the water thus brought. Some Muhammadans take the woman to the nearest mosque with the jars on her head, and make her draw water from the well attached to the mosque. Her nearest kinswomen accompany her and the observance is often held at night. Others simply give the woman a hot bath. The *Hammals* of Hansi have a curious custom, which looks like a relic of the *couvade.* The woman's parents send her a present of Rs 5, a suit of clothes, some scent and a comb. After bathing, she puts on her husband's trousers, and a chaplet of flowers. Dum women also sing songs on this occasion. Boiled rice is distributed among the brotherhood.

Friday, at the time of the *Asar* prayers, is an auspicious day for this ceremony, in connection with which alms are given in the names of ancestors and the Prophet. Some castes send the woman a suit of green clothes, red bangles, a *naherna*, some *mehndi*, and a silver vessel. The clothes and bangles are worn by the woman, but the *henna* is used not only by her, but by her friends as well, if they are desirous of offspring, while the *naherna* and silver vessel are kept for the *chhati*. After this one and a quarter *paos* of sugar are sent to each relative and friend. Some families boil rice with sugar, and with it feast the woman and seven others who are also married, some being also given to *faqirs*. After this, the woman is given vegetables and sweets.

In Sirsa of Haryana, the rite is called *satwansi* and simply consists in the parents sending their daughter a gift of clothes, *henna* and dried fruit in the seventh month of her pregnancy. In Rohtak, the *satwansi* is held at the beginning of the seventh month. The woman is dressed in red, and sugar also put in her lap. The Dum woman, who sings on the occasion, gets her reward in cash. In Rohtak, among the more orthodox Muhammadans there are no regular rites during pregnancy, but the barber is sent to announce it to the mother's parents, and he takes them a rupee as *til chawali*. In the seventh month one or two men, and several of the women, bring parched unhusked rice, *patashas* and fruit, with some red cloth to the woman, with cloth for her husband's parents and near kinsmen. The woman puts on the red cloth, and the rice etc, is thrown into her lap. The menials also get certain dues. This ceremony, however, is not universal.

The Determination of Embryo's Sex

If the milk in the woman's breasts before birth be thin, the birth of a boy is anticipated, otherwise a girl is expected. Or sometimes some of the milk is put in a shell and fire applied to it; if it dries up completely, a girl is expected, otherwise a boy. The custom prevails in Hissar.

In Delhi, where Muhammadans of good birth are numerous, many elaborate customs connected with pregnancy rites survive. The craving for tart, savoury food has given rise to the polite phrase : *in ka khatte-mithe ko ji chahta hai,* lit. 'her heart yearns for bitter-sweet things' meaning thereby 'she is pregnant.' Other phrases are *paon bhari* hona (to be heavy-footed), *do-jiya* hona (to have a second life), *din charhna* (to dawn), *umed hona* (to have hopes) etc. : and women friends say *mubarak salamat* ! i.e. 'may you be blessed and the child be safe !' to the expectant mother.

The Rites of Satwansa in Delhi

When the seventh month begins the woman's parents bring her *sadhar,* as per a Hindu custom. This *sadhar* consists of kinds of vegetables, dried fruits, and cakes etc., and at 4 p.m. the woman's lap is filled with these things, then she bathes and is dressed in coloured garments, with a red sheet over her head, and flower ornaments are put on her to make her, as it were, again a bride. Her husband's sisters then fill her lap with the seven kinds of fruit etc, and receive present of money in return. They get the vegetables, dried fruit, the head sheet, and the rupee of the *neg* or customary presents all the rest being divided amongst the other members of the family. A cocoanut is then broken in half; and if the kernel be white the woman will have *ujla phul* or white fruit, i.e. a boy. This cocoanut is called *jhandula,* or '*hairy*' just as a new-born child is so called.

Rite of Naumasa in Delhi

At the beginning of the ninth month, the woman's parents send her various presents, including a red veil, seven kinds of fruit, *neg* for the husband's sisters, and rupees to buy the *panjiri*, which must be made at the woman's house. Her lap is filled as in the *satwansa*, by the husband's near kinswomen. The midwife at this stage rubs the woman with oil, and receives a fee, to which all the women contribute. The fruit is the perquisite of the husband's sisters, together with the *neg* and the red veil, as before. The midwife gets the nail-parer, one of the presents given by the woman's parents and the silver oil-cup used for the oil. The woman now goes to her parents' house - an observance called *paon-pherna,* or turning the feet, with some *panjiri,* and returns some six or seven days later, bringing with her fresh fruit and sweets.

After the *naumasa* is finished, the midwife goes to buy the *kioka* or various drugs required for the confinement. Some Muhammadans have the Hindu superstitions regarding the effects of an eclipse on the foetus, if either parent undergo violent exertion.

Muslim Rites Related to Birth

When the birth-pains start, *Bibi Mariam ka panja*, a leaf whose shape resembles that of a hand is put in a jar of water. As the delivery approaches, the leaf opens out, and as it does so the birth takes place. This observance also, it is believed, facilitates the delivery. This leaf is said to be imported from Arabia. But one account speaks of it as a kind of grass or piece of wood shaped naturally like a hand, obtained from Arabia. Sayyids and *faqirs* also believe in charms, which are tied round the woman's waist or sometimes a Muhammad-Shahi rupee, on which is inscribed the *kalima*, is put into water, which is then given her to drink. In Kangra, the *bang* or call to prayer, is pronounced in the room set apart for the confinement by one of the men of the family, the call being a prayer used in any time of trouble.

Birth Ceremonies

As among Hindus, delivery is usually effected on the ground, the mother being made to lie on a quilt with her head to the north and her feet to the south. She thus faces Mecca, and if she dies in child-birth she expires in the posture in which Muhammadans are buried. If the child is a girl, the parents give some grain in an old black *handi* (an old used pot) to the midwife. But if the baby is male they give her a rupee, and the relatives also give her money, called the *wel*, according to their means. Whether it be the hot or cold season, the mother remains in confinement for one week. If in good health she is bathed on the sixth day, provided that it is a Friday or Monday, the latter being the day on which the Prophet was born. During the actual confinement only those women who are closely related to the mother are allowed to be present, but her mother is sure to be one of them.

Some stand in the courtyard in the open, without stretched arms, and, looking upwards, pray : *Ilahi ! is ki mushkil asan ho* ! (God ! grant that her troubles may be lightened !') ; others vow *dauna* (sweets put in cups made of folded leaves) to *Mushkilkusha*. Meanwhile, the midwife tells the mother : *Jheli do, jheli*,or i.e. 'bear down.'

A child born feet foremost is called a *pa'el,* and women believe that a few gentle kicks from one so born will relieve pains in the back. As soon as the child is born the mother is told that she has given birth to a one-eyed girl in order that the heat engendered by this ill news may force out the after-birth quickly, and the joy of having given birth to a male child may not retard it. Immediately after the child has been born its umbilical cord is tied up with *kalawa*, a bit of thread dyed red and yellow, and severed with a knife, the thread being thrown round the child's neck until the rest of the cord falls off. The part actually cut off is buried in a pot inside the house, a charcoal fire being kept burning on top of it for six days, until it is all burnt up. Into this pot the near kinswomen put some money as a present to the midwife. Some betel leaf and silver are also placed in it, and when buried turmeric and charcoal are thrown in to keep off evil spirits. The cord of a *pahlaunthi* or the first-born child, is invariably so buried, but if a woman's children do not live she has it buried outside the house. The midwife now gets her *nal katai*, or fee for cutting the umbilical cord, in money ; but among the wealthy the mother's parents and her husband add gold or silver bracelets, according to their economic status.

In Amritsar and Gujarat, the parents' or mothers' formal permission to the severance of the cord must be obtained by the midwife. The eldest and most respected woman of the family takes up the new-born as soon as it is born in order to communicate her own virtues to it. She also buries the secundines on the spot where the birth has taken place, and cuts the umbilical cord, which is preserved with great care. The Ghebas do not use a knife to cuts the cord, but a *narra* or *nalla* or 'spindle,' obtained by the midwife from a weaver's house. With this the midwife cuts the cord, after pressing it with her feet, and then buries it in the ground. The people of *Khattar* caste have the uncut part of the cord, after it has dried up and fallen off, encased in silver and hung round the child's neck as a charm against stomachache. Throughout the south-east Punjab the umbilical cord is carefully buried, often with the after-birth, in an earthen vessel (*thikri*) in a corner of the house. In Hissar, neither parent should touch the cord. In Kangra, the midwife cuts the cord on the coin which she gets as her fee. Besides, she receives presents from the kinswomen, etc and these are called *nar katai*. Among the Kashmiris only the secundines are buried, the piece of the cord cut off being kept to cure the child if it gets sore eyes. In Amritsar, the uncut piece is preserved with the *jhand*.

After delivery a child is bathed, its head being pressed to give it a round shape and tied up in a *qasaba* or handkerchief folded in a triangle. The nose also is pressed to prevent its hardening on exposure into a bad shape. The *mulla* is next sent for without delay. He repeats the *subah ki azan* in the child's right ear, and the *takbir* in its left. *Batashas* chewed, or something sweet, are also applied to its palate. People are believed to be deeply attached to the spot where their navel-string is buried, so that to say to a man : *Yahan tera nal to nahin gara, jo tu jane ka nam hi nahin leta !* 'Is your cord buried here that you do not even talk of going?' is equivalent to saying that nothing will induce him to budge. The *mulla* receives a gift. His fee varies, depending mainly on the child's sex. If it is a boy he gets a rupee or more, with some flour and sugar, if a girl, only an *anna*, in Hissar. Sometimes, he whispers the call to prayer through a *nara* or tube; and if the child is a girl he sometimes whispers the *takbir* in both its ears, not the *bang*. If a *mulla* is not available, any man of reputed piety may perform the rite, receiving some sweet stuff only, not a fee. In Karnal, a man of good repute is called in to perform on the third day, and he receives no fee, but sweets are distributed. Or the eldest male of the family may perform it in lieu of *mulla*. In Kangra, this duty devolves on the child's uncle, or any pious member of the family. In Maler Kotla the rite is administered with considerable solemnity. A woman stands with her back toward Mecca, holding the child so that it may face the Qibla. As the *mulla* repeats the *azan,* she turns its right ear toward him and then its left as he recites the *taqbir*. Until the *azan* is thus repeated, the belief is that the child is convulsed with fear. In Jind, some juice of the date is poured into the child's mouth, if it is a boy, in token of welcome. After bathing, the child is made to lick honey, and then the *ghutti* is administered. After the *ghutti* has been given i.e., on the third day, the child's paternal aunt washes the mother's breasts with milk or with water squeezed out of kneaded flour, and then her hair, in which some green blades of grass are woven. The following song is sung by her or on her behalf :-

Biran, bhaiya, main teri ma ki jai,
Holar sunkar, badhawa lekar ai,
Biran, bhaiya, main teri ma ki jai,
Chhati dhulai katori lungi, to lat dhulai rupaiya,
Pann dhulan ko cheri lungi; to khasm charhan ko ghora.

[*Meaning* :- Brother ! I am thy mother's own daughter, and hearing that a son has been born into the family, I have come to felicitate thee. For having washed the breasts, I expect a silver cup as a present, and money for washing her tresses. I will accept from thee a hand-maiden to wash my feet, and for my husband a horse to ride on.]

From this observance the paternal aunt receives a *neg* varied according to her brother's position, but not less than Re. 1 as 4. From the time the child is born, a knife, sword, or piece of iron is kept under the mother's pillow to ward off evil spirits. On the next or a subsequent day, the paternal aunts make and distribute the *achhwani* amongst the kinsfolk and receive a present in return; but amongst the poor the mother alone is given *achhwani*. For six days the mother is never left alone, partly lest she overlay her child, partly to keep off evil spirits. Amongst the well-to-do Muslims, a lamp is kept burning continuously for forty days (but only for six among the poor), and a stove is kept alight, in hot weather or cold. Wild rue is also burnt for six days, to keep off the evil-eye and purify the air. Lest the mother sleep on, and her blood so stagnate and gets cold, women take it in turns to sing *jachagirian* or lullabies like:

Mere babal ko likhio sandes, jhandula aj hua:
Babal hamare raja ke chakar ;
biran bale bhes: Jhandula aj hua.

"Or tell my father that his daughter has borne a son: my father is a servant of the Raja, i.e. he is well-to-do ; and that my brother is yet a child : the young one was born this day."

They also sing a lullaby that means: "The fine, beautiful, nut-brown, slender child, to show his beauty in the world, has given me the pains of childbirth : go and tell its father that he should proclaim its advent by a *naubat* (music on the upper storey or roof) ; have *nafiri* played, so that I may be rewarded for my pain by its soothing melody : and tell the mother's father of the child to arrange to brings the *khichri* with all due magnificence, for the *chhatti* (sixth day) is given by him: go and tell the mother's brother of the child also to make ready the *hansli* (necklet) and *kara* (wristlets), i.e. give orders to the goldsmith to prepare them: go also and tell the mother's sister to have ready the *kurte* (shirts) and caps, for these are supplied by her: warn the father also that on this joyous occasion he must give us a dance by the *bhand* and *bhagatie*."

This song, though it is in reality the paean of joy sung by Deokiji on the birth of her son Krishna in Mathura is still sung among the Muhammadans. The clothes worn by the mother at her confinement are given on the day of birth to the midwife, and are replaced by new ones on her *chhatti* or *chilla*. It was formerly the custom that the lobe of that side of the ear by which the child was born was pierced, the object being that the child might live-women having a belief that the piercing of a vein in the ear is a preventative of mortal disease (presumably convulsions); further with the same object, the end of the nose was also pierced on the same day and a nose-ring inserted: but this custom is now disappearing among the lower castes.

From the day of birth, the *nakti* ('nose-cut,' or noseless one, i.e. the cat) is not allowed in the mother's room, in the belief that she is possessed of genii, or more probably in order to protect the buried umbilical cord from any possibility of injury, and she is kept out till the *chhatti* or *chilla*. Notably a *hijra* (eunuch) goes daily to each *mahallah* (street) and cries *Hua beta? Kaun sa ghar jaga ?* Or,'Has a son been born?' 'Which house has awakened?' Some child, or the sweepress of that quarter informs him of the family in which a son or a daughter was born; going to that house he gets and informs all the *bhands, bhandelas* etc. (players, actors, buffoons etc.); from that time the *bhandele sanane, hijre, shah taiyam-taiya, chune-waliyan,* and *bhand, bhagatye* of the town, all those whose business it is to sing, dance, play, or amuse, begin to come, and after singing or acting for an hour or two demand their presents and go away, only to come back again on the *chhatti*.

The Rite of *Thikri*

All the females in the house at the time of the birth drop some coins, into a *thikri*, the lower part of an earthen jar, the first to do so being the patient's mother or mother-in -law. If any near kinswoman is negotiating a betrothal, she drops a rupee into the jar, and this renders the agreement irrevocable. This is called the *thikri ki sagai*. The money dropped into the jar is the midwife's perquisite.

Ritual of the Aqiqa or Tonsure

The *aqiqa is* an orthodox Muhammadan rite, consisting in shaving the child's head for the first time, on thirty-fifth day after birth, and sacrificing two goats or sheep for a boy and one for a girl. This simple rite has, however, been confused with, or influenced by the observances proper to the *jhand*; in places, it has never been adopted, or if adopted has become obsolete. In Bhiwani, it is only observed by well-to-do people, never by the peasantry. So uomine, but on the *chhatti* the child's head is shaved. Occasionally, a vow in made that the child's head shall not be shaved unless and until it can be done at a specified place. Or part of the hair is left uncut, to be subsequently shaved off in fulfilment of the vow. In some places, the *aqiqa is* displacing the old *dhaman* rite. As a rule, the *aqiqa* is celebrated within seven days of the birth. The child's head is shaved, and the weight of the hair in gold or silver given away as alms. It is very commonly held on the *chhatti,* or on the seventh, fourteenth, twenty-first, or twenty-eighth day, in Hissar; on the seventh or tenth in Bhiwani; on the seventh, fourteenth, or fortieth in Sirmur; at any time within six months in Kangra, very commonly on the fifth, or in *Nurpur*, on the eighth; in Maler Kotla on the sixth. It is also very common in the central Punjab to perform it on the sixth, thirteenth etc. day, if the birth occurred on a Monday, it would be held on the following Sunday, and so on.

The hair itself is carefully buried in the earth. For a boy two he-goats are sacrificed and for a girl one. The bones must not be broken, but carefully buried in the ground. The flesh is distributed among the brotherhood uncooked; or else they are feasted on it. But the child's parents, and its grand parents' must not eat of the flesh. Such are the main outlines of the rite. In Kangra, the goats must be young and free from blemish, and of a uniform colour for a girl; the latter is the only essential condition. Or, as carefully preserved; while the head and feet are given to the barber, and the skull to the waterman or the *mullah* in Hansi. In Kangra, the bones are buried within the house. In Amritsar, a portion of the flesh is given to the midwife, and the rest distributed among the brotherhood; both bones and blood are buried. In Shahpur, the flesh is given to the poor, and the bones are buried in the graveyard, after being placed in an earthen jar.

In Dera Ghazi Khan, both bones and blood are carefully preserved (buried) at separate places.

Rite of Beri Barhana

A blue cotton thread, called *beri*, is tied to the left foot of a child in the name of Muin-ud-Din Chishti of Ajmer, and when it is three or four years old it is taken to the shrine of that saint, and the parents there make an offering of five and a quarter *sers* of *maleda*, two pice and a trouser-string.

Bindu Bandhna

If a man's children die in infancy, he puts a bit of *bindu* or silver wire in the left ear of his next child.

Rite of Petha Charhana

Women desirous of offspring often vow to offer *peta* to the shrine of Dana Sher at Hissar. If their wish is granted, a little of the *petha* is given to the custodian of the shrine, and the rest is distributed among the brotherhood.

The *Chhatti* or Sixth Day

The religious observance of the *aqiqa* is closly associated with the *chhatti,* the *chuchak*, and the naming of the child. As among the Hindus, the *chhatti*, in spite of its name, is not necessarily held on the sixth day of the birth.Thus, in Delhi, the mother and child are bathed on the Monday or Wednesday, nearest the sixth day, the former being an auspicious day because the Prophet was born on that day, the latter because as the saying goes.: *Budh is liya ki sab kam sudh hon*, meaning 'Wednesday, in the order that all things may be right,' and thus all subsequent children may be sons. The mother sits on a stool, while her husband's sisters pour milk, or water squeezed out of flour, over her head; green grass or a thin slice of betel-leaf are put into the water or milk. In return, the sister-in-law receives her customary presents or *neg*.

Then the mother bathes, and taking the child in her arms, puts on her nose-ring and sits on the bed. The guests, mostly women, though among the higher classes near male relatives are also invited, come in. Outside the men are entertained by eunuchs, *bhands*, *Shah-iiayam-taiya*, and dancing-girls; while inside the house Domnis and *chunewalian* give displays of dancing. The mother, with her head wrapped in gold lace, sits enthroned like a queen, the child's head being also enfolded in a kerchief. *Mubarak badian* or congratulatory songs are sung, such as

Jami jam shadian,mubarak badian;
Bawen farsand salamat, salamat-badian.

Meaning: "May you be ever blessed with such happiness; nay, may you, with your son, ever enjoy peace."

In Hissar, the *chhatti* is observed on the sixth day, the mother and child being bathed, the brotherhood feasted and the mother dressed in new clothes. Her father also sends the *chhochak*, or gift of clothes, and the *aqiqa* is observed on this day. If a man does not observe the *chhatti* it is said :- *Chatti na chhilla hogaya*. Like the Hindus, Muhammadans imagine that on the sixth night the child is peculiarly subject to influences.

In Abohar, the mother and child are bathed on the first Thursday or Sunday: this is called *chhatti ka ghusal*, and food called *sudak ka khand* is sent to all the women of the family.

Gift of the *Chhuchhak*

The *chhuchhak* is very commonly observed on the *chhatti,* but it may be postponed to the fortieth day, and, indeed, there appears to be no absolutely fixed day for its observance. In the central Punjab, the first confinement ordinarily takes place at the house of the mother's parents, and in this case the mother, if the child is a boy, brings back with her some gold and silver ornaments for herself and the boy on her return to her husband's house. These gifts are called *chhuchhak*. In the south-east, the first confinement is arranged for at her husband's house, but the mother visits her father's house some four or six months later and then brings back the *chhuchhak*.

Chhuchhak is the ceremony observed after childbirth, when the mother visits her father, generally forty days after childbirth, and returns with presents made on this occasion. Generally speaking, the *chhuchhak* appears to be used for any present sent to the mother or child on the occasion of *chhatti, aqiqa* etc, by her parents or other relatives, or even by relatives of the child's father. In Rohtak, indeed, the term appears to be limited to the presents made by the father's sister of the child. In Hissar mention is made of a gift called *jamawana,* made by the mother's parents to her. It consists of gum, *ghee* and sugar, with clothes and ornaments for the child, and would appear to be distinct from the *chhuchhak*.

The Rite of *Weham*

Closely analogous to the *chhuchhak* is the *weham* observance, which is widely spread throughout the submontane and south western districts of Punjab. The *weham* is, among well-to-do people, a link in a chain of elaborate observances. On the *chhilla*, or fortieth day, the women of the family assemble and make presents to the mother and child, who are then taken to a shrine. *Churi* is then distributed among the women, and the kinswomen of the mother's mother are also given food from her house. Her mother then sends her clothes and ornaments, for herself and the child. These gifts are called *weham*. This rite is only observed on the birth of a first-born child. Poor people of Punjab also observe it, but on a smaller scale. After this observance, the midwife is dismissed. On the day after the mother goes to her parents' house and returns with her child and the *weham* presents, the women of the *mohalla* come to view them, and the child's grandmother distributes sweetmeats and *panjiri* to the close relatives. In return the women each give the child a rupee, or less. In Amritsar the term *weham* is applied to the presents made by the mother to each of the kinswomen assembled on the fortieth day. In Kapurthala, the observance is simple. On the third day, the father sends a man with *khichri* to his wife's father, and he, on the eighth day, sends in return *panjiri*, clothes and ornaments for the mother.

In Bahawalpur the parents give her when she bathes, on the eighth, twenty-first, or fortieth day, *pinnis*, and a *trewar* for herself and her child : together with other clothes for it, according to its sex. If wealthy they also give a silver bracelet, or *hasli*, a silver necklet or a gold *mohar* for the child.

Bath given to the Mother

In theory, the new mother is bathed on the tenth, twentieth, thirtieth and fortieth days, as in Rohtak, Hissar, Karnal, Ambala and Sirmur; but to this rule there are numerous exceptions. The bath on the fortieth day is called *chhilla* or fortieth, and that on the tenth *daswan*, on the twentieth *biswan*, and on the thirtieth *tiswan*. But in the Karnal District these three earlier baths are called *chhota chhilla* ; and in Delhi, the *daswan chhilla* (tenth), *biswan chhilla* (twentieth), chota chhilla (thirtieth), and *bara chilla* (fortieth), a curious instance of the confused use of precise terms.

Showing the Planets to the Mother

On the night of the *chhatti,* mother and child are both dressed, their heads being enfolded in three-cornered embroidered bands (*qasaba*), and the mother is seated on a low stool placed in the courtyard of the house. Two women, holding naked swords in their hands, bring her out; the midwife carrying a *chaumak* to light the way. Standing on the stool with the child in her arms and the Quran on her head, the mother looks towards the sky and counts seven stars, while her companions bring the points of the swords together over her head, forming a crescent so that *jinns* and *paris* may not pass over her, and from this day the danger that they may overshadow her ceases. Meanwhile, the father goes to the mother's bed, and standing there repeats the *bismillah* in full. He then shoots an arrow into the ceiling, at the *mirg*. Hence this observance is called the *mirg marna*, and the wife's mother gives her son-in-law a *neg* on the occasion. Once, on the birth of a prince in the family of Bahadur Shah, King of Delhi, the poet Shah Nazir of Delhi, described this custom thus :

Wuhin phir shah ne yih rasm ki wa'n,
Chhaparkhat par qadam rakh, ho ke shadan,
Ada kar harf i 'Bismillah' sara,
Kaman-o-tir lekar mirg mara;
Namundar is tar'h tha saqf men tir,
Falak par kahkashan ki jaise tahrir.

"Forthwith (while his consort was viewing the stars) the king observed the rite, standing on his wife's bed with a bow and arrow in his hand, and after repeating all the *bismillah*, the arrow shot by him into the roof looked like the Milky Way in the firmament."

After seeing the stars, the mother returns and seats herself on her bed; a table-cloth is spread in front, the stool being used for a table, and on this is placed food, including seven kinds of vegetables and various other dishes. The *zacha rani* or 'queen mother', together with seven other women, whose husbands are living, takes a little from each dish, and the only words heard are *mubarak*! *salamat*! Songs are also sung, which mean:

"When the mother came out to see the stars, the revolving heavens were pleased, and showered stars upon her head (showed stars over her, like the money thrown at weddings etc, upon the chief character in the ceremony). As the child that was born will be a blessing to all, tell his father to perform the *mirg marna,* whereby his courage may be proved. When the sounds of rejoicing at the *chhatti* reached the skies, the Moon and Jupiter cried: 'What joy hath God bestowed on both (the parents), that the drums have thundered forth their happiness."

Some rupees are now thrown into the *chaumak* as a present to the midwife. In the imperial family another custom, called *Bigir-bachcha*, also prevailed, and the other Mughals of Delhi also observed it with slight variations. A big, sweet loaf was made of five and quarter *sers* of flour, baked in the ground, and the middle portion taken out, leaving only the rim; on top of this naked swords were placed, and on the right and left arrows stuck into it; seven *suhagans,* three in front of the loaf and four to the left of it, stood in line; one woman passed the child through the hole, saying, *Bigir-bachcha,* 'take the child', the next one would say, *Allah nigahban, bachcha,* 'God is the protector of the child.' In this way, each of the seven *suhagans* passed the child seven times through the loaf, and between her legs. This was the only Mughal custom foreign to India, all the others being similar to those prevailing in it. This observance is very widespread, but there are several interesting local variations.

Thus, in Ludhiana the *Jats, Gujars, Arains, Dogars* etc, observe this rite on the third day, and the mother goes to the door of the house accompanied by a boy who has a *phala* (ploughshare) over his shoulder and a *parain* or ox-goad in his hand. In Maler Kotla, the rite is called *chhatti ke tare dekhana*, 'to show the stars of the sixth.'

The mother emerges out attended by the midwife and a woman carrying a lamp. A man of the family carries the *Quran,* out of which he reads certain passages to the child. In her mouth, the mother has some uncooked rice, and in her hand an iron weapon or implement, while in her lap is some uncooked *khichri*. Thrice she spits rice out of her month to the right and thrice to the left. The reader of the *Quran* gets a silver coin and some jaggery, and the midwife takes the *khichri.* On this day, the sixth, the mother is bidden to eat her fill, otherwise the child will have an insatiable appetite all its life.

In Kangra, the mother sees the stars on the seventh day, unless it falls on a Friday. She bathes and observes the chief points described above in this ceremony, but the sword is held over her head by her husband, and a woman reads out the *Quran.* In Gujarat, the Chibh Rajputs have a ritual of their own. On the third, fifth or seventh day the mother leaves her room. A square is made with whitewash or riceflour in a wall, and red lines drawn across it diagonally. At their intersection a picture of the new moon is made, and a sieve placed over it, at which one of the child's near kinsmen shoots seven arrows.

Shirdan Karne ki Rasm

Just after the *tare dikhana,* the families of the old Mughal dynasty performed another rite called the *sardan karne ki rasm,* which is also observed by the people of Delhi, but not necessarily on that date, but at any time before the child teeth will do. Women believe that if a child, which has not teethed, be lifted will show. Women believe that if a child, which has not teethed, be lifted above the head, it will pass white motions, for which this observance is a preventative, or, if the disease has begun, a cure. The rite is performed thus: The ropes used to tighten a native bed are loosened, and two women, who must be mother and daughter, are called in: one of them gets on the bed, with the child in her arms, while the other sits on the ground towards the foot of the bed. The former then passes the child through the opening in the loosened ropes down to the latter, and she passes it back again to the former. This is done seven times. The two women receive the same gifts as are given in the *bigir bachcha* ceremony. In Delhi city this observances is called *shirdan*, and is only practised if the child actually gets ill. The women add the question *shirdan gaya*? They reply *gaya* each time they pass the child through the ropes.

Offerings made by menials to the child play an important part in the observances in Gujarat. A male child is presented with a *tota* by the tailor: with a chaplet of *dharek* and *siris* leaves by the flower-woman this is hung on the outer door as a safeguard against the influence of women who have miscarried; the washerman daubs the wall near the outer door with stuff from his washtub as a charm against the evil eye : a toy made of several pieces of cloth of all colours, strung on a thread like the tail of a kite. This is hung on to the roof of the house, but without any express meaning. This is also done in Gujarat. The *machhi* makes a net and casts it over the child, as an augury that he may remain dutiful and obedient to parental control; the sweeper or *musalli* brings a small bow and arrow, placing them near the boy's head, so that he may be manly; the shoemaker presents a deerskin; and the *kamangar* or painter brings a paper horse. Each of these dependants receives his customary dues in return. In the village of Gujarat, the family Brahman of a Muhammadan family makes an imitation of *pipal* tree, before the fortieth day, and receives from rupee one to five, according to the family's position. Among the Gujars, the Brahman actually comes in on this day and makes a *chauka* in which a lamp of flour is lit. Huge loaves of bread, each weighing a *topa*, are given to the menials and the Brahman himself gets a *topa* of flour. In well-to-do families, a special kind of *halwa* is made and eaten by the members of the *got*, but no one else may partake of it. Even married daughter cannot eat this *halwa* because in marriage they cease to be members of their paternal *got*. On the other hand, a share is sent to a son's wife if she is absent.

Dhaman Rite

The *dhaman* rite is observed among Muhammadans in Sialkot and Gujarat. In the latter district, the mother bathes on the fifth or seventh day and puts on new clothes. Bread with *halwa* is distributed among the brotherhood. This is called *dhaman karna*. In Sialkot, the observance merely consists in the kinswomen assemblings a few days after the birth, and in distributing *halwa* and *chapatis* among the close relatives.

Rite of *Pichhawan*

The belief in the evil effects of the shadow *pichhawan* of a woman whose child has died young survives among the Muhammadans of Gujarat. Every precaution is taken to prevent her getting access to mother or child, and green *sarin* leaves are hung over the outer door to avert the *pichhawan*. Certain tanks are believed to have the power of curing children who are affected by *pichhawan* and so waste away, if bathed therein.

Rite of *Kunisht*

A curious custom, not very clearly described, is observed in Sialkot by certain tribes. During the first year, if the child be a male, the wives of the family prostrate themselves before a heap of sugar, which is spread out on a blanket and divided into as many shares as there are proprietors in the village, invoking the elders' goodwill. The daughters, of the tribe are strictly forbidden to use this sugar, when it has been distributed among the brotherhood, presumably because they will once married cease to be members of the tribe or of the village community.

Custom of Fosterage

In well-to-do families a wet nurse or *anna* is chosen from some decent family, with a nurse (*mani*) to dress the children; a *dada* to bring them up, and a girl *(chhochho*) to wash soiled clothes, and to play with the children, under the mother's supervision. In the morning, the *chhochho* plays with the children, humming a number of songs. If, while asleep, the child smiles, they say that *Bihai* is making it laugh. *Bihai*, or *Beh Mata*, is a Hindu goddess who, it is believed, makes the child smile at times, and at others weep, by whispering in its ear that its mother is dead or alive.

Rat-jaga or Vigil

The name *rat-jaga*, or vigil is applied to any merry-making which is kept up all night by the women. A vigil is kept on the occasion of a *chhatti dudh-chutai, sal-girah, bismillah*, or wedding. The frying-pan is kept on the fire all night, and fritters are made, *Allah miyan ka rahm* being also baked. This is done to ensure divine favour. At the same time, the *bibi ki nias*, or offering to Fatima, daughter of Muhammad is also made. Seven kinds of fruits and vegetables, in plain or sweetened rice, are served in new earthen vessels. On this offering are also placed some *missi*, *phulel* (scented oil), *surma* (antimony), henna, *kalawa* (coloured thread), sandal-wood and five rupee as *chiraghi* or lamp fee. Formerly, it was also customary to put some slaked lime in a small plate, into which the *pak-damanan* or chaste wives, who partook of the food offered in the *nias*, dipped their fingers, and licked off the lime which adhered to them, in the belief that blood would thereby be caused to flow from the mouth of those who were unfaithful.

Custom of Making Vows

A vow, in Punjabi *manaut,* is not infrequently made by a barren woman that she will offer a cloth, light a lamp, and have her child's first tonsure performed at a specified shrine if the offspring be vouchsafed to her. The period for such an observance is always specified in the vow, but it is usually limited to a time before the child attains the age of twelve years.

Another type of vow is to place a silver necklet round the child's neck every year,or to make him wear a *hama'il*, and add one rupee or more to it every year, until he attains the age of seven, ten or twelve, when the accumulated silver is sold and the proceeds given to the poor. If the necklet is sold at the age of ten the observance is called *dasaundh*. The necklet should be put on the child's neck on the last Wednesday in *Safar*, the second month of the Muhammadan year. In Amritsar, this is called Badhawa Pir Sahib.

In Sialkot, the term *badhawa* is applied to the custom of putting on the *hama'il* and adding a rupee year by year. After the twelfth year, it belongs to his wife, but the vow may stipulate that a certain share of the value shall go to a certain shrine, and the number of years may vary. In Ludhiana, the sale-proceeds are often supplemented by further gifts, and go to feed the poor. The object is to invoke God's favour on the child.

Tonsuring Half Head

In fulfilment of vows in Ludhiana, some people shave only half the child's head at a time, every week. The right half is first shaved, from back to front; then the left. This is done for some years, and then a *nias* is offered, and the whole head shaved.

Imamon-ka-paik

During the first ten days of the *Muharram*, some people get their children made messengers of the Imams (*imamon-ka-paik*), thus: ten yards of muslin are cut into four equal parts, lengthways, and two are dyed green and two black. One of each colour is then taken and made into a sheet, giving two sheets, of which one is wrapped round the head and the other round the waist. Some ten or fifteen small bells are then strung on a cotton thread which is also tied round the waist. The boy goes barefoot, but his *pagri* is adorned with feathers. On the tenth day of Hasan's martyrdom, rice and milk are cooked and distributed among Muhammadan households.

Custom of Observing *Jhand*

In contrast to the religious rite of *aqiqa* is that called the *jhand*, which is done either in accordance with an express vow, or which may be regarded as the fulfilment of a tacit vow. In Hissar, the rite is said to be extinct, but other accounts appear to contradict this. Vows appear to be made at the shrine of *Dana Sher* of Bhauna to cut the *jhand* there at a specified age but this seems to be regarded as part of the *aqiqa.* The *jhand* is commonly observed within the *chhilla*, or forty days from the birth, but it may be deferred till a much later age. In Kapurthala, the *aqiqa* is called *jhand utarna,* but in Maler Kotla, if the *aqiqa* is not performed, the *jhand, i.e.*, a lock of hair is left on the head and cut off generally at shrine of Shaikh Sadr Jahan, a vow being made that it will be done if the child live a certain time, generally twelve years. The *jhand* rite is not confined to male child, but is observed in the case of girls also, the only difference being that the barber's fee is diminished by half in the latter case.

In Kangra, the hair is mixed with flour, baked into a loaf, and thrown over running water ; but as a rule the hair is weighed and its weight in silver given to the barber. In Punjab, however, great importance is attached to the *jhand* or first tonsure. It is generally removed on the fortieth day after the *chilla* observance is over, but some people do this on the *aqiqa* day. In either case the hair is scrupulously preserved, and sometimes placed in a silver amulet or always carried about with one. The hair is deemed sacred, and kept by one on commencing any new work. Women believe that no evil influence can prevail over one who has it near her. But some people tie the hair to the child's bed.The barber is paid from Rs. 1 to 5, and another menials get their dues from the mother's mother. *Jhand*, too, is very often performed on the seventh, fourteenth, twenty-first or fortieth day, and silver equal to the weight of the hair is given away in charity, the hair being then buried in the ground.

But if a vow has been made, the rite is carried out in fulfilment of that vow, and the *jhand,* or a lock of the hair, is removed at the specified shrine. There, too, a he-goat is sacrificed, and some people even sacrifice a he-goat every year until the child attains the age of twelve or twenty-one. Besides which bracelets are put on the child until he is twelve.

Among the Chibh Rajputs of Gujarat, the first tonsure must be performed within seven years at the shrine of the martyr Shadi, ancestor of the tribe, and until it is done the mother must abstain from meat. If the hair is cut, a lock must be left. This lock is called *Babu Shahid*. At the shrine a goat is sacrificed, the mother eats the liver, and rest is given away as alms. In Shahpur, the *jhand* is observed on the seventh, eighth or ninthday, a *churi* of bread, *ghee* and *gur* being distributed among relatives or friends. But a lock of hair called *lit* is kept and removed some years later at a Pir's shrine; but the observance is not common.

Marundon ki Rasm

When the child is about five or six months old its grandmother sends some *marunde,* and these are distributed in the family. The *marunde* are balls made of wheat or parched rice mixed with sweets, or else of *moti chur ke laddu mung ki dal* mixed with sugar's syrup, together with poppy seed or boiled wheat. The balls are made by closing the fist and are sent because at this age the child begins to open and close its fists.

Rites of Kafirs

When delivery is imminent the woman goes to the Nirmali house and remains there for 20 days if the child is a girl, or 21 if it is a boy. After a ceremonial ablution to rid of pollution, she then returns home, but is allowed a further rest of 12 days there. The instant a child is born, it is given to the mother to suckle and an old woman names all its ancestors or ancestresses, as the case may be, and stops the moment it begins to feed. The name on her lips at that moment is the child's name for life. Suckling continues for two or three years. The male children may not wear trousers till they have been taken to Dizane's shrine at the Giche festival, dressed in that garb of manhood, and sacrifice has been made there. This is followed by a feast. The sons of poor men are often associated in this observance with boys who are better off. Boys who take part in the *sanauken of a kaneash* are exempt from further observances.

REFERENCES

1. Rose, H.A., *A Glossary of the Tribes and castes of the Punjab and North-West Frontier province*, Vols. I & II, Low Price Publications, Delhi 1999 (reprint), first published 1919, Government of Punjab, Lahore.
2. Ibbetson, Denzil, *Census Report for Punjab* 1883.
3. MacLagan, Edward, *Census Report for Punjab* 1892.
4. Singh, K.S. (Gen.ed.) *People of India : Haryana* : Anthropological Survey of India; Manohar, Calcutta, 1994.
5. Singh, K.S. (Gen.ed.) *People of India: Punjab,* Manohar/ Anthropological Survey of India, Calcutta, 2003.
6. Singh, K.S. (Gen.ed.) *People of India: Himachal Pradesh*, Manohar/ Anthroplogical Survey of India, Calcutta, 1996.
7. Singh, K.S. (Gen.ed.) *People of India: J &K*, Manohar, Anthropological Survey of India, Calcutta, 2003.
8. Agarwal, B.C., *Tribe, Caste and Peasantry,* Enthnographic and Folk Culture Society Lucknow, 1974.
9. Crooke, William, *The Tribes and Castes of the North Western India,* Cosmo Publication, Delhi 1974 (Originally Published, Govt-Press Calcutta 1896

2
Puberty

The custom relating to adolescence and puberty in north India have the most remarkable peculiarities of the Brahmin caste, the one of all other upper castes which clings most tenaciously to age old customs. These customs, however, do not belong exclusively to the Brahmin caste; some of them are common to the other castes of the twice-born people as well. The life of a Brahmin has to be considered under four important aspects. The first is that of the young Brahmin who has been invested with the sacred cord composed of triple threads and who is from that time onwards called *Brahmachari*.

The second is that of the Brahmin who has married, and who is thenceforward, but especially after he has become a father, called *Grahastha*. The third is that of the Brahmin who, renouncing the world, retires into the jungles along with his wife, and who is then called as *Vana-prastha* (or dweller in the jungle). The fourth, and last, is the stage of *Sannyasi*, or that of the Brahmin who decides to live entirely in solitude, apart even from his wife, a mode of life considered even more edifying than *Vana-prastha* for the seekers of redemption from the cycle of birth and death.

Upanayana Ceremony

All Brahmins wear a thin cord hung from the left shoulder and falling on to the right hip across the chest called as *yagopatam*. It is composed of three strands of cotton thread, each strand formed by nine threads. The cotton with which it is made must be gathered from the plant by the hand of a pure Brahmin, and corded and spun by persons of the same caste, so as to avoid the possibility of its being defiled by passing through unclean hands of any low caste man. After a Brahmin is married, his cord must have six or nine and not three strands. After marriage, a

Brahmin must wear six, and may wear nine. The triple cord is thus explained by one authority: 'It symbolizes the body, speech and mind. It symbolizes the control of each; and therefore when the knots are tied in it, it means that the man who wears the thread has gained control over body, speech and mind. Brahmins, and all the other castes which have the right to wear this cord, treasure it and are certainly very proud of it.

Making Pledge to Muslim Saint

In Jammu &Kashmir, married women tie a piece of thread to the tomb of a pir pledging thereby that if they conceive and bear a child they would make suitable offering at the shrine. If the woman is blessed with a child she comes again at the shrine and presents a cow or goat, the sale proceeds of which are either credited to the funds of the shrine or appropriated by the clrgyma on duty. Some people slaughter a goat and feast the priest who organizes special thanksgiving prayers. This belief is also shared by the Muslims Hindus and Sikhs and there is hardly a day in summer when women belonging to there sommunities are not seen attending the shrines.

Women are not allowed to carry heavy loads During the period of pregnancy due to the apprehension of miscarriage.Further, visitors or even members of the family returning home late in the night after a long journey are not permitted to meet the pregnant women immediately on their arrival. It is believed that such persons carry with them the malevolent influence of evil spirits meeting on the way.During moonlit nights, pregnant women are required to confine themselves indoors because moonlight might harm the eyesight of the child to be born. Women who are pregnant for the first time do not live with their husbands and spend the remaining period at their parental house.

Generally the delivery takes place at the hands of a *dai* or *warin* (midwife)who does not usually have any formal training but is only a practical hand. She is paid remuneration in cash and kind.

Immediately after birth the newborn baby is given a bath in lukewarm water, and then initiated by whispering of azaan in its ears irrespective of its sex, done by a senior male member of the family. A message is also sent to the in-laws of the woman announcing the new birth.

In case of the first birth, breads with sugar balls are distributed among the relatives, friends and neighbours. The largest share goes to the house of the child's father. In return, the woman's mother-in-law makes a personal call and offers her felicitations. She also presents theree pairs of new clothes for the baby, a larger-sized plate full of breads and sugar balls and some money in a ceremony called piaw. The mother-in-law and the guests accompanying her are served a sumptuous dinner. On the seventh day of the delivery, the mother takes her first bath with lukewarm water mixed with juices of some indigenous herbs. Some well-to-do families organize prayers on the occasion and the serving claryymen is served with a dinner and paid in cash. The child is given a name on the day in consultation with the priest or in his absence on the advice of some learned man. The rite of *sonder* is observed in some households on the seventh day when the child is given a bath and is clad in new clothes. Relatives are invited to dinner and women sing auspicious songs in chorus. On completing forty dayss the mother of the newborn child is given another bath. From this day no restrictions are placed on the conjugal ties of the parents of the nnewborn baby. First hair cutting of the baby is called zerakasi celebrated with much unfare after a child attains the age o\f six months. The ceremony of zerakasi is performed by the family *navid* (barber). Relatives and neighbours are invited and served with a dinner cooked by the *waza* or professional cook. While the haircutting is in progress, the family and neighbourhood women sing songs in chorus praising the child, the barber and even his razor and othe implements. After hair cutting the child is given a bath and clothed in a new dress. The barber is paid the remuneration in cash and kind. The hair is buried underground along with some walnuts in the belief that the tree which will eventually grow would bear superiour varity of fruits. The child is then handed over to the women present on the occasion who shower small sugar balls, almonds and dates on the child. The guests present make gifts of money to the child which is duly recorded by one of the literate relatives persent at that time. A copper bowl belonging to the barber is circulated in the gathering the guests and relatives who put some cash in it which is given to the barber along with the bowl.The birth related customs rites and rituala are pestinent to the muslim people of Kashmir region.

No Ceremony Observed at Child-birth

While, in the Jammu region, a Hindu woman in child birth is attended by a dai(midwife)or elderly family member or an experienced woman of her own caste. Now people prefer hospitals, if available in the vicinity.

Now ceremony rites and ritual is performed at the time of child birth. Nevertheless, the birth of a male child calls for celebration. Name is given to the new born by a Brahman priest invited for this purpose and also to prepare a horoscope for the child. At times parents themselves give a name to the newborn.

The rite of sune is observed around the seventh month of pregnancy whering the father sends fruits, nuts and clothes to his daughter. *Athwan* is the eighth auspicious day falling in the eighth month of pregnancy. Small laddoos (balls) made of sugar and rice flour and *sungi* (dry grapes) grams are also distributed and eaten on the occasion. The postnatal rituals include mundane-sanskar and *janeu*. In mundane-sanskar the *hari* of the child is shaved within a year of birth by a family barber economically well-off families celebrate the occasion with great fanfare. A feast is arranged for the relations. The ceremony is performed at Mansar lake.Wearing of sacred thread ceremony is now performed one day before *lagan* (marriage).

The Birth Custom and Other Observance are Pestinent to the Hindu Communities in the Jammu Region

The birth related rites, rituals and customs AMONG THE Muslim of Ladakh are more or less similar to those performed among the Kashmiri Muslims with the variation in terminology of ceremonies. The Muslims of Kargil which consist mostly of Shite Balti and Broqpa present a slightly different picture of the rituals. Recitation of *azaan* into the ears of the child by an *akhun* or *sheikh*, *nosh yoni*, seventh-day ritual when the mother takes her first bath

And a feast is given to the guests, *nomdhonru (name-giving), ghusl-e-nifaas*, which is to mark the bath taken by the mother on the fortieth day, *aqeeqa* (tonsure)and

circumcision are some of the rituals performed before marriage. The birth customs, usages and rites are performed by the Muslim people in the Ladakh region in the state of J&K.

Performing Sang Custom in Ladakh

On birth of a child a Buddhist lama is called to perform sang (purificatory ceremony). This ceremony is repeated after forty days which marks the end the ritual of pollution caused by birth. Naming ceremony is performed by a kushak (reincarnate) lama. Marriage is performed amidst prayers to protect the couple from the malevolent effects of evil spirits.Here it is note worthy that Buddhists in Ladakh in J&K. Lahul, spite and other regions of Himachal Pradesh belong to Tibetan school like Drunkpa, Sakyape and Gelugpa, schools; belonging to the Mahayana sect of Buddhism.

Whereas the Buddhists in Punjab, Haryana, Rajasthan, Delhi belong to Himayana school. The neo Buddhists in Punjab are mainly attached to the mahabodhi society of India fonded by a Sri Lankan monk Anagarike Dhammapala, in Bodh Gaya (Bihar). The Nav-Buddhist are those Scheduled Castes who have embraced Buddhis as a result of harassment by the upper caste people Dr. B.R.Ambedkar on 14 October 1956at Nagpur had himself embraced Budhism and also converted large number of his followers, who came to be known as NeoBuddhist. The Nav Buddhist of Punjab speak Punjabi and Hindi languages an use Gurmukhi or Devanagari scripts with the members of their own community and other. Wheat is their staple food and they are occasional non-vegetarians. They exchewalcoholic drinks, and have no social divisions but they marry within their religious group, which includes converts from other commuities and thus inter commuity marriages do actually take place. They have rebelled against the Brahmanical the varna system they consider themselves to be of high status but the members of caste Hindus consiter them othervise for their traditional occupation of tanning hides eating meeal and carrion, and performing low jobs.

Post-birth pollution lasts up to seven days till then the new mother is not allowed to do any work. *Bingreee* or name giving ceremony is observed on an auspicious day decited by the Buddhist *lama.* The name is given by the lama after consulting the punthi (sacred text)and almanac. Balda or tonsure ceremony is conducted on the child attaining eight years, and on the date decided by the Lama On this day, the hair is cut by the maternal uncle or the parent, and afeast is given. The Bodh, Bhot or Chazang, as theyare called are called are primarily distributed in the Spiti valley of Lahaul and Spiti district. They are a scheduled tribe and have been enumerated along with the other Buddhist groups like Jad, Lama and Khampain Uttarakhand and Eastern Himalayas. According to an account those people of Tibet an origin who came and settled here prior to 1962 chinease aggression are called as Bodh or Bhot, whereas whose who came after 1962are known as Tibetans.

Bodhs live in an inhospitable snow covered terrain with little vegetation as the area falls in the azid zone. Spiti is referred to as the cold desert of Himachal Pradesh with a very scanty rainfall. Stone boulders and loose rocks keep falling all over and on small patches of terraced fields, which are usually near the river beds. Bhoti is the dialects spoken used by the Bodhs among themselves and their script is also Bhoti, but with outsiders they speak in broken Hindustani and the literate among them can also converse in English. Some of them can write in Devanagri and English scripts. The male Bodhs wear *kera* or Cholu with woolen trousers and *pattu* (band) on their waist. The females put on *cholu* and *jeptan* (a shawl around the shoulders). Generally a Bodh house has a *harsho* (flag) in the courtyard to ward off evil eyes that are cast on the house by invisible. Malewolent spirits. The staff is also a typical identity of a Bodh household.

The Bodh are non-vegetarian, taking all kinds of edible meat including the yak and cow meat. They are very fond of locally brewed drink called *chhang* and arak, distilled illegally in almost every house hold. Their staple food consists of *thukpa* and *momo* made from *maida* (fine wheat flour without bran) and mutton. Occasionally, they also consume pulses, *rongi*, green vegetables and tubers. Fruits consumed are chulli, bahemi, grape etc. Fresh milk is available in a small quantity and is usually kept for the infants. The adults take fresh milk occasionally. Mostly mik power is used in the preparation of sweetened tea. Salted tea is also taken frequently..Special food and delicacies are cooked on festive occasions, but on solemn occasions non-vegetarian food and drenks are avoided by the pions Bodhs.

The customs are prevalent among the Bhot or Bhotia Buddhists in Himachal Pradesh.

Taking Pregnant Woman to Parental House

Among status of women the Mirasi is secondary to that of men have no right to inherit property. They collect firewood, bring drinking water and participate in religious activities. They also contribute to the family income through singing and playing drum in the house of jajmans during the marriage ceremony. In the sphre iof politics and mechanism social the participation of women is prohibited. In case of first delivery the pregnant woman is taken to her parent's house in the seventh month of pregnancy after observing god bharna. The dai (mid-wife) helps in child-birt. On the second day after childbirth the moulavi is called for whispering ajan in the ear of the new-born as well as for naming. After forty days the nursing mother takes ritual bath to end the birth pollution. The circumcision of the male child is done before three years of age. The birth cusoms are observed among the Mirasi Muslims in Rajasthan.

Performing Chhatti Ceremony

The delivery in the karai caste takes place at their house with the help of dai or midwife. They observe birth pollution for six days. On the sixth day after birth dhey celebrate chhatti ceremony. Both mother and child are given purificatory bath. Kheer (sweet dish) is prepared and distributed among the children. Naming ceremony is also peroformed with the help of maulavi after twenty-one days. The rite of Bismillah is Conducted by the a clergy man at the age of five at the mosque. A feast is given on each ceremony. Sunnat or circumcision is a must for male child which is performed during the age of five and nine.

The Customs Pertain to the Kasai Muslims in Rajasthan

In Delhi, the major life-cycle rituals in the Kasai community are those relating to birth, childhood, marriage and death. Post-delivery pollution for the mother is normally observed for eleven days during which she is not allowed to cook food or participate in *namaz*. The child is usually named by the parents two or three days after birth. As soon as a child is born, azan is recited in his or her ear. On male children circumcision is performed and no fixed time is observed, but done some time before the age of six *Aquiqa* for both male and female children is observed some time after the child is seven days old and before it completes seven years. *Ahe*-goat for a male child and a she-goat for a female child is sacrificed on this occasionin the Kasai Muslim community.

Among the sayyads in Delhi, *thepre*-delivery ritual of *godh bharai* is performed in the seventh month of pregnancy, when the woman is given good food, clothes and sweets. Chhatti is celebrated on the sixth day after birth and the mother and child are given bath and a feast is arraged for relatives. In the case of a male child, khatana is performed within seven days of birth or according to convenience. A Muslim nai performs the circumusionand a feast is organized on this occasion. Aqiqa is celebrated after the seventh, ninth or eleventh day after the birth of a child, according to convenience of the parents. Two goats are sacrificed for a boy and one for a girl in the community. The chil's head is shaved off and a name is given to the child. A feast is organized for friends and relatives on this occasion. The birth rites and rituals are pertinent to the Sayyad Muslmis in the northern region.

The Sayyad are the descendants of Ali, the son-in-law of Prophere Muhammad, and the community includes only those descended from him by Fatima, Muhammad's daughter.The Sayyad is divided into a number of subgroups such as Abidi, the worshippers of God' *Hasani* the descendants of *Hasan* and Husaini from Husain' the sons of Ali Bukhari, the residents of Bukhara; Zaidi, descended from Zaid Shahid, a grandson of Husain; and Rizvi from Ali-ibn-Musa or Raza. Beseides, the Sayyad subdivisions are also in common with both the Sunni and the Shia. Generally among the Shia are the Sayyad while among the Sunni are the 'Shaikha-Abbasi,' taking the name from Abbas, the parernal uncle of the Prophet. 'Ulvi', descened from Zaid Shahid, a grandson of Husain' and the Jafri draw the name from jafar, one of the Imams. The nick names Chishti, the followers of the saint Salim Chishti of Fatehpur Sikri; Jalali from al-Jalal; Qadiriya the name of a special sect which denies absolute predestination and believes in the power (qadr)of man's free will. The Sayyads use the title Mir after their names and they are spreas all over India. They speak Hindustani or English and Communicate in the Devanagari or Roman scripts.

Shaikh perform life-cycle rituals according to Sunni Muslim rites. Godh Bharai is celebrated in the seventh month of pregnancy, when the woman is given good food, clothes and sweets. Chatti is celebrated on the six day after birth when the mother and child are given bath and a feast is arranged for relatives; *Aqiqa* is celebrated after the seventh, ninth or eleventh day of birth. It may also be celebrated on some other day, according to convenience. Tw goats are sacrificed when a male child is born and one for a female child. The child's head is shaved off and a name is given to the child. A feast is arranged for friends and relatives on this occasion. For a male child, khatna is performed within seven days of birth, or according to convenience. A Muslim nai performs the rite and a feast is arranged on this occasion.

The customs, rites and rituals are observed by the Shaikh Muslims community.

Amongh the Aboasi Muslims, birth pollution is observed for one-and-a-quarter months. During the pollution period, the mother is not allowed to cook food and real the Quran Sharif. Delivery is generally performed at home by a midwife but nowadays a few of them have started going to the hospital for purpose. Immediately after the birth child, a mulla or maulvi is called who recites azan in the chil's ears. On the sixth day after birth chhatti is celbebrated and a feast is given to the near king, relatives and freiends. The aquiqa ceremony is generally observed on the sixth day. Circumcision in the case of a male child is performed within fortydays of birth and a feast is given to friend and relatives on the ceremonial occasion.The custom and rites are performed by the Shaikh Abbasi Muslims in Delhi.

Among the Faqirs, women observed in purdah, but now the younger generation is not observing this strictly. Women are burdened with household work, like collection of fuel, bringing potable water, cooking, cleaning etc. Some Faqir women go out to work as agricultural labourers or daily wage labourers. Women are consulted in social, religious and economic spheres, some women control family expenditures too.

On the sixth day after the birth of a child, among the Faqir Muslims in Delhi *chatti* is perfored. Prayers are offered to the moon and stars and special food is prepared for the family and guests. Presents are given to the child and the women sing auspicious songs on this occasion. A name is given to the child from the Quran by a *maulvi.*Some open the Holy Quran at random; the child is named after the first letter on the page opened. *Kathna* or circumcision is performed on males by a Muslim *nai*. The customs are prectised among the Faqir Muslims in Delhi.

Observing Pollution Period of Forty Days

Giving a somewhat detailed account of the main life-cycle rituals of the Dafalis relating to tth birth, marriage and death ceremonies willianm Crooke (1896) writes, that After delivery, *napak* (pollution period of forty days)is observed. During this period, the mother is not allowed to cook or participate in any religious affairs and she is not supposed to bathe on Thursdays and Fridays. On the third day after the birth of a male child, a *maulana* is called to read a sacred verse in the ear of the child; but this is not compulsory. Sometimes parents do this themselves if they are able to. *Aqiqa* and *chunnat* are performed at the same time, usually within five years of birth. *Aqiqa* is performed for a male child only. A goat is sacrificed at this time and ths community is supposed to be given a feast. The custom irrelated to Dafali muslims in Delhi.

Observing Pollution Period of Forty Days

Among the Arain Muslims, Post-delivery pollution for the family lasts for forty days but is not always maintained in the community. After fifteen days the mother is allowed to offer *namaz* (prayer). Within a few hours of birth, *aqan* (summons to prayer) is recited in the ear of the new-born, normally by a *maulana* or a male member of the family. A name is given to the child within a few days after birth. *Sunnat* (circumcision) is performed for male children. It is performed any time between the age of six days and six year. A barber is called to perform the circumcision. Relatives and near kins are invited and fed on this occasion. Aqiqa or tonsure ceremony is performed for both male and female children. For a male a he-goat and for a female two she-goats are sacrificed on the occasion and relatives are fed. There is no fixed date for *aqiqa* but performed generally some time between the age of seven days and six year. Boys and girls are entitled to read *namaz* after the age of twelve. For women, *namaz* is not allowed during the menstruation period. The customs, rites and rituals are observed by the *Arain* Muslims in Delhi.

Custom of Forty Day's Birth Pollution

In the community, for the enceinte mother the 40 days period of *chilla* or pollution is observed. She can start working within the house though three days after delivery. As soon as the child is born a *maulvi* is called who recites an azan in the childs ears; the child is named soon thereafter. Though no ritual ceremony is observed for naming, but it is so important that even the child who is born dead is first named and then buried as per their cusom. *Aqiqa* is observed on the sixth day of the birth, but in cases where it cannot be performed on the said day for economic reasons, it is deferred as per the perents convenience, but has to be done on the same days and month in which the child is born in any year. In the event of the birth of a son two goats are sacrificed and in case of the birth of a daughter only one goat is sacrificed called *kurbani*. On the day of *aqiqa*, the head of the male child is also tonsured *Khatna* or *sunnat* or circumcision is performed for boys before the age of six years by the jarrah or quack barber surgeon or as per the Islamic scriptures immediately after birth, but it is invariably deferred. The cusoms, and rituals are prevalent among the Bhisti Muslims in Delhi.

Maintaining Birth Pollution for Forty Days

Amongst the Bharai Muslmis, the life-cycle rituals are observed as per the Islamic customs. Pre-natal and post-natal restrictions are maintained. Birth pollution is observed for 40 days. Naming, cereal-taking, *mundane* (tonsure) and *aqiqa* ceremonies are ignored. The *sunnat* or *khatna* (male circumcision is th main childhood ritual performed by a Nai or julaha or an Abdal who is offered in remmuration a brass or steel plate, a hen and some cash which may range from Rs. 25 to Rs. 200. The community is given a *nyaz* (feast). *Nikah* is the marriage ritual when a *maulvi* takes *kaul karar* (consent)of the boy and the girl three times and the marriage is then contracted. The parents of the bride feast the bridegroom's party and the latter also reciprocate the same to the *laddhar* (persons accompanying the bride) at their place. *Muklawa* occurs on the day following the marriage. The cusoms are prevalent among the Bharai Muslims in Delhi.

Birth Rites and Rituals Common to Other Muslims

In the community of Atishbaz Muslims, The lfie–cycle rituals of birth, puberty, marriage death are common with those of other Muslim. The birth of the male child brings more joy and happiness to the family than the girl. As soon as the child is born, an Imam is called, who whispers aqan (the verses from the holy Quran) into the child's. Ears. Post-birth pollution in the community is observed for 40 days. Purificatory bath is given to the mother and the child on sixth, eleventh, twentieth and finally on the fortieth day. The woman and the infant are then taken outside the house, in a rite called as tara dikhana, symbolizing the fact that she is ritually pure to start her normal life. Khatna or circumcision is the most important ritual for boys and can be performed antime from early infancy to the fifth year. Aqiqa ceremony is also observed and it is customary to sacrifice a goat on this occasion. Two goats are sacrificed for a male child. On the occasion the head of the child is also shaved off.

The cusoms and observances are conducted by the community of Atishbaz Muslis.

Birth Custom Common with Other Muslims

The life-cycle rituals are observed as per the Islamic tenets. Pre-delivery rituals are not observed but pre-and post-delivery pollution is observed for 40days but first purification ceremony is observed on the seventh day by taking *sarbat* (juiuce)when the naming ceremony is also performed by some but this not a regular feature. *Sunnat* or *khatna* (circumcision) in boys is the only and the major ritual in childhood, usually performed between three to eight years of age. It is performed by a member of the community and a *Maulvi* (priest) recites *kalma* (excerpts) from the Quran. The cusoms are related to the Abdals Muslims in Delhi.

Cusoms of Baptism for the New-born

The Moravians in Ladakh who belonged to Buddhism until the last one hundred years ago, have switched the Christian life-cycle rituals after their conversion to ChristianityAmongst them childbirth takes place either in a maternity hospital or at home. *Baptisma* (baptism) is carried out in the church when the child attains the age of seven monghs. The child's name is either given by the church priest or by the parents themselves. No ceremonies are performed for naming of the child.

A mix of Christion and Hindu Customs

Among the Bengali cristions, Birth of a child takes place at home or in the camp and the delivery is performed by and old, experienced woman of the community. The birth of a child, whether son or daughter, is celebrated by the family and the kith and kin by drinking liquor. The *sutak* period yaries depending upon the health of the mothers and ranges between three and thirteen days, when they take cow's urine called gunt for purification-probably a borrowed custom from the local caste Hindus. Only mundane of boys is the major childhood ritual performed in an odd year from the birth. The haircut of the boys is done by maternal uncle, on the occasion some sweets are distributed among close relatives and friends. The birth customs are practiced by the community of Bengali Christians in Himachal Pradesh.

The Bangali is a scheduled caste known for its peculiar traditions of snake-charming, wandering, hunting and gathering and eating the meat of a fox, bush-lizards and tortoise etc. ibbetson (1883) and Rose (1919) offered three interpretations of the name Bangali: (1) A native of Bengal, (2) a tribe akinto the Sansis foud in Kangra driven off by the passing of the Crimingal Tribe Act, and (3) the Kanjar and Sapada or snake-charmers of the plains. In Punjabi, *bangali* means a person, who lives by begging, exhibiting snakes and hunting etc. In Bilaspur, the Bangalis claim their origin from Bengal but their peculiar dialect is not akin to the Bengali language. They also claim their origin from the Meena tribe of Rajasthan and associate themselves as helpers of Rana Pratap during his turbulent days. According to an account their ancestors did not migrate from Bengal but in order to earn their livelihood resorted to magic tricks and charms and declared that they possessed the magic for male of Bengal hence called the Bengalis. They appear to have entered Bilaspur about a century ago. The total population of the community in 1971 in Himachal Pradesh was 617. The Bengalis live generally in warm and temperate climate of low humidity in the hills and games like fox, wild boar, hare, bush-lizards, fish etc. are found in plenty. In Kangra valley they have penetrated from Punjab or its borders during the post-independence period.

Christians Observing post-natal Pollution and Restrictions

Among the christens in Delhi, post delhivery pollution is observed and the post-natal restrictions on the mother exist. However, the option of observing them is gaining ground with modern advancement and outlook in the community. Naming ceremony is conducted in the form of baptism by water or dedicating the child, both performed by the priest and socially feasted thereafter. Although emanating from Judaism, the tradition of circumcision had been done away with from the earliest times by the immediate apostles and disciples of Jesus Christ to free the Christian from any physical and mental bondage and brandishment. Among those converted from the highcastes of Hinduism the rite of, *annaprasan* or the first feeding of cereals is ceremonially performed. Each Christian has also to undergo the confirmation ceremony at adolescence, wherein he is formally made a member of the Church and becomes entitled to its sacraments. Confirmation is a must prior to the ceremony of marriage.

The customs rites and rituals perstain to the Christians in Delhi. Although Christianity came to India in 52 A.D., it remained confined mainly to the south India, states like kerala. In the North, the Moghul Court of Akbar, entertained the first Christian missionaries, the Jesuits. In Delhi, the faith as late as 1628 when Emperor Shah jehan received Jesuit missioraires at his court, in continauation of the opern-door secular policies of his grand-father, Akbar, who had received and entertained Jesuit missionaries at his court at Agra, allowed them to build the first church there, prosetytisation of the local people and even allowe himself a Christian wife. Since 1628 onwards, there existed a small congregation of Christians in Delhi, and it continued, with reverses at times, till the advent of the British whereupon came the main thrust of Christianity to Delhi due to the privilege of it being the official religion of the rulers. In the initial phases, places of worship were provided to cater to the spiritual needs of the British Christian community, proselytism being forbidden.

Only in the later stages, when freedom to practice an preach religion was declared, were Christian missionaries permitted proselytism, and thereafter the Church and its followers grew and multiplied in numbers in Delhi. An impetus in the growth became apparent when the British moved their impereial capital from Calcutta to Delhi. The oldest known surving Church in Delhi is St. Jeames' Church at Kashmiri Gate which is more than 150 years old and has a history behind it.

The three broad denominations within the Christian Church i.e., the Roman Catholics, the Orthodox Christians and the Protestants are represented in Delhi, the former and the later categories in dominant numbers. The Christians in Delhi hail from various Indian states and traditions, as well as from outside the country, and every group speak and transcribe in its own mother tongue, as well as in English and Hindi. The cross is the common symbol of all the Christians, adopted as a symbol of identification from Christ's crucifixion on the cross. Otherwise, there are no other identification markers for the Christians.

Cusom of Baptism at the Church

Among the Christians in Haryana, The women's status is quite infereior though they have an important reole to play in both economic and domestic spheres. Those who are economically dependent, are a little worse off in comparison to those who earn. The economically independent women though are not discriminated against. Initiation ceremony takes place at one to twelve years of age being called baptism in the church.After a child is twlve years old the sacrament of confirmation is performed. In this ceremony the child consciously expresses his desire to accept Chrisianity. Thereafter, there is a sacrament of reconciliation. Whenever a person commits a sin he is supposed to go to the church priest to make a confession.

In fact, the Christians in Haryana are numerically small and are popularly known as Issai. Most of them who settled in Haryana are not the original inhabitants of the state. They have migrated from Indian states. The local Christians, mainly the Hindu and sikh converts, belong to the lower segment of caste groups. Because of their migrant character, it is difficult to ascertain their exact numerical strength in Haryana. In this region, they are mainly settled in urban areas and towns, mostly employed in public and private sectors. Womenfolk of this community are primarily engaged in the nursing and teaching professions. Since they neigther own land nor engage themselves in agricultural activities, their interaction with the local people of Haryana is relatively limited and occasional.

Therefore, their food habits, language, festivals, religious faith etc. reflct the impact of the place of their original place. The cChristians of Kerala speak Malayalam; of Karnataka, Kannada, and those from Punjabi. Despite this they hae responded favourably to the assimilative pressures of the place where they have stayed fro over two or threedecades. The influence of assimilative pressures is very much evident in their day-to-day interaction and social intercourse with the local population living in Haryana. There is a small Christian population who consists mainly converts from the Scheduled Castes and other backward classes. Such people try to acquire the cultural habits of Christianity besides attending church service.

The Christians in Punjab observes only a few rituals. Some post-delivery rituals are observed for an unspecified number of days. Naming ceremony is held but there are no strict rules about it. Baptism may accompany the ceremony of naming. Baptism is performed in various ways. The Christians in Punjab, also called as Isai, have a number of denominations such as Salvation A?rmy. Catholics, adhrents of the Church of North India, Baptism, Fernicustor, and Methodist, etc., A large number of members of this community use Massey, with their names There are differences about the origins of Christianity in Punjab. According to one view, there was no Christianity in north India prior to the naineteenth century. Other maintain that Saint Thomas, the founder of Christianity in India, came to this area in the first century A.D. After the had completed his work in this area, he returned to south India. The Western traditions maintains that st. Thomas reached India, following the then well-known trade routes sometimes in the middle of the first century of the Christian era. He preached the Gospel in Parthia and India and converted many local people including members of royal families. He suffered martyrdom in India and was buried here. Saint Thomas preached in the Punjab; but he could not establish a permanent church here. History of Christianity can be dated from 1834, when John C. Lowrie established at Ludhiana the first mission station at the Ludhiana Mission of the PreshyterianChurch of U.S.A. The next mission was the Church Missionary Society. Which was set up at Amritsar in 1851 Roman Catholics started their work in Punjab in 1888. Various groups of American Methodists, the Salvation Army, New Zealand Presbyterians, Seventh Day Adventists and Penticostals followed the suit in the later period.

Rituals and Customs Common to all Christians

The life-cycle rituals commencing from birth to death are basically common to all the Christian sections and subgroups yet the manner in which they are observed varies from church to church. When a child is born, post-birth restriction and pollution is observed by the mother for 40 days. When the mother and the child are brought to the church for blessing. Baptism of the new born is the most important ceremony which symbolises the acceptance of the child into the faith of Christianity. The age at which this ceremony is to be performed varies. Some believe in adult baptism for they argue that the child should rightly be baptised when he is able to decide the faith he would like to adopt for him self, or not.The birth customs are pertinent to the Christians in himachal pradesh.

Birth Rituals and Site Conform to Christianity

In the Chinese population Himachal Pradesh is concentrated exclusively in city of Shimla. They came to this place in search of better for business prospects for this was not only the old summer capital of India but a flourishing hill resort. Some Chinese families have been inhabiting here since the pre-Independence times but others have recently migrated from Calcutta. All the families are originally from South China and, therefore, they speak Hakk a dialect that is spoken in South China. However, with outsiders, they have learnt to communicate Hindi and English. Similarly, the script used by them while writing to each other is Chinese, but while communicating with the locals, Hindi and English are used.

The majority of the Chinese life-cycle rituals are performed according to Christian Catholic cusoms but in addition to the above, some of their birth, marriage and death customs are according to their traditional Chinese customs. Pre-birth and post-birth restrictions and pollution on the mother is exist in community. Mother and the child are given a bath on the twelfth day. An egg coloured in red is given to the near and dear ones who reciprocate by giving gifts to the child. Mother and the child remain confined to the house for 40 days during the pollution period. Baptism is a must for every child and should be duly performed by the parish priest in the church. The age at which it is to be performed is not fixed. A month after the birth, they celebrate it by giving gifts. Ward off the evil eye, they burn feathers of a hen, cover them with sheet an allow the child to inhale the smoke. By doing so they believe that evil spirits are not able to cast an evil influence on the child. The birth of a male child is celebrate with a greater enthusiasm thean the girls. The birth customs, and rituals are popular among the Chinese settlers in Himachal Pradesh.

Customs and Rituals as per Ehristians Norms

Among the Anglo-Indians, Family occasions such as baptism of a new born, confirmation, wedding and death form the ritual backbone of the community. The Christian rite of baptism according to the Roman Catholic procedure is performed when the child is a few weeks old wherein he is cleansed of the (original) sin he is born with. The ceremony also signifies the acceptance of child into the Christian faith during which parents and godparents (usually from related families) take upon themselves the responsibility of bringing up and nustring the child according to the Christian tenents, usually followed by a celebratory feast to the relatives and community members. The rite of baptism differs slightly among the Protestants who do not believe in child baptis. In this case, the child fffis merely taken to church is blessed and named by the priest –according to a ritual called Churching. The actual baptism comes at a later stage when an adolescent is immersed in water in front of a congregation of the faithfuls called as the adult baptism, followed by an elaborate feast to the relatives and friends. The birth customs pertain to the Anglo-Indians in Delhi.

Among the members of the Bene Israel community, there are certain pre-delivery rituals. After birth, a male child is circumdised on the eighth day, performed by a rabbi, generally in the synagogue. In the absence of a rabbi, the rite of circumcision can be performed by a mohel or a doctor to the accompaniment to the chanting of verses from the Torah (Jewish scripture). The infant is named on the occasion and the event is feasted. In the case of a boy, at the age of thirteen, the *Bar Mitzvah* ceremony is observed to mark the boy's coming of age. Thereupon, he assumes responsibility for himself an for his religious and social duties. This entitles him to be among the ten men who are required to form the quorum at the synagogue. His shoulders are draped with the sacred prayer scarf to the accompaniment of the chanting of relevant verses from Toran. This scarf is called the *Tsisith Tallith*. It is made of silk or cotton with blue threads woven into it and 613 knots are tied in it to the recitation of the holy commandments from the *Torah*. A similar ceremony for girls is called *Bath Mitzvah*, conducted when the girl completes her twelfth year and it denotes her coming of age. She is not draped with a shawl, as her responsibilities are deemed lighter. On the conclusion of this ceremony, the girl is required to recite her prayers three times a day, either at home or at the synagogue. In either case, they are required to offer prayers of thanks giving before each meal. The birth customs, and rituals pertain to the community of Bave Israels (Jewls).

Thus, the high caste children from the age of five to nine are invested with this cord. March, April, May and June are considered the most favourable months for the investiture of the sacred thread. As the ceremony entails a considerable expenditure, the poorer Brahmins go from house to house begging and collecting funds with which to defray the necessary expenses of investiture; and members of all other Hindu castes believe that in making such contributions they are performing a pious act. This ceremony is called the *Upanayana Sanskara* which means introduction to knowledge, for by it a Brahmin acquires the right to study under a Brahman guru. Many of the rites performed on this occasion are also performed at the marriage ceremony, but we will confine here to those which are peculiar to the cord ceremony. To begin with, the father of the boy, must provide himself with many pieces of cotton cloth and plenty of small gold and silver coins to be given as presents to the guests. He must also have a large supply of rice, flour, fresh and dried vegetables, fruit, oil of sesamum, clarified butter, and milk in vermilion, plenty of betel-leaf and areca-nut.

Further, there must be an abundance of earthen vessels of all kinds, shapes and sizes, seeing that on each of the four days the feast lasts, new ones will be required; those which have been once used on this occasion, as on that of a marriage, being always broken into little shards.

When everything is ready, the father goes to consult the *purohit* or family priest, to ascertain what day will be most propitious. The *purohit* having fixed a day, a *pandal* or pavilion is erected. The preliminary ceremonies and purifications are gone through, and the invitations issued in the customary manner. Meanwhile, the women decorate the walls of the mud house, both inside and out with alternate broad bands of red and white paint. When the guests have arrived and are all assembled under the *pandal,* the *purohit* makes his appearance, bringing with him a cord and an antelope's skin. The antelope's skin is used as a mat on which the priest sits. The skins of both the antelope and the tiger are considered extremely pure; consequently one may sit on them without fear of defilement. Having performed the *sam-kalpa,* he offers *puja,* or adoration, to Vighneshwara Ganesh who is represented by a small conical heap of fresh cow-dung, placed in the centre of the pavilion. He also makes to him offerings of *durva* grass (*panicum doctylon*), sandalwood, *akshatas* or coloured rice, incense, and a lighted lamp.

Following the sacrifice to Vighneshwara, the master of the house presents betel-nut to the Brahmans, and then they all proceed to make their ablutions on the river front. On their return, the *neophyte* is made to sit on a raised platform of earth in the centre of the pavilion. The married the boy as for the ceremony of the *chaula,* though on this and finally they delicately pencil his eyelids with antimony. This is a kind of ointment. It is still a common practice amongst the people of India to embellish the faces of their children with it. Courtesans and beauties, too, often use it. It certainly enhances the brilliance of the eyes, and is a pleasing addition to a handsome face.

His toilette finished, the father and mother of the boy seat themselves by his side on the dais, and the women perform the ceremony of the *aratti.* Puja is offered to the household deities, and for *neiveddya,* or votive offering, portions of all the dishes prepared for the feast are set aside. The guests then seat themselves on the ground in rows, the women of the household bring in the rice and various dishes which have been prepared for the feast. Each guest receives his portion of food stuff on a banana leaf, or on other leaves sewn together, which are never used more than once. When the meal is over, betel and areca-nut are distributed, and the guests then retire.

The next day is called the *muhurta,* or the great day of the opening; it is that on which the actual investitutre takes place. The guests are invited to reassemble as on the preceding day. The would-be recipient of the sacred thread is seated on the dais, between his father and mother, all three having their faces turned towards the east. The boy's loins are girt with a 'pure' cotton cloth, that is to say, either a new one, or at least one that has been newly washed. It is not only on this occasion that a 'pure' cloth is obligatory. Each time a Brahmin bathes he washes his clothing, to purify. The married women with the living husband perform his toilette, singing all the while. The *purohit* then approaches, holding in his hands an earthen chafing-dish full of hot embers. He performs the *sam-kalpa,* and then formally consecrates the pan of hot coals which by virtue of his *mantram* becomes a representative of a god *Agni Deota.* To this he offers the sacrifice called *homam,* offering clarified butter on the fire some pieces of sacred fig-tree, some cooked rice, and some melted butter.

After this, nine specially selected Brahmins offer the same sacrifice of the *homam* in honour of the nine planets. Then, each having chosen a married woman, they all go off together still singing, to place the sacred fire to some place apart, where it must be carefully attended to and kept burning until the last day of the festival. It would be considered a very bad omen if, from inattention or any other cause, this fire were to be extinguished before the appointed time. The inauguration of the *ishta devata* immediately follows.

Invoking the Deity

The married women with living husbands provide themselves with a large copper vessel which must be new and whitewashed outside. They take it preceded by instruments of music, to be filled from a well or river. On returning to the house, they place some mango leaves over the mouth of the vessel and on the top of the leaves a coconut, coloured yellow with powdered saffron or turmeric. The vessel is then wrapped in a woman's cloth which has been dyed the same colour and is placed on the ground, on the top of a small heap of rice. Round its neck are then hung two leaves, leaves rolled up and coloured red and also a necklace of small black seeds, and a few other female ornaments. The *purohit* then invokes the family deity and invites him to settle on the vessel, which becomes from that moment a female divinity, to whom the women promptly made an offering of flowers, incense, *akshatas,* a lighted lamp, some betel-leaf and areca nut. The mother of the young man then places the vessel, i.e. the new goddess, on her head, and accompanied by the other women, all singing in chorus, and preceded by a band of musicians, makes a solemn progress round the village in form of procession, under a kind of canopy. On returning to the house, she replaces the vessel, and, with the assistance of some of the other women, drapes round the two central pillars of the *pandal* with two perfectly new cloths of the kind worn by women.

The same procession then starts again to fetch a mound from ant-heaps raised by white ants. With this, they fill five small pots. These again are sown with nine kinds of seed, which are well sprinkled with milk and water, to make them sprout quickly. The women then perform the customary act of *puja* before them, and after prostrating themselves place them close to the tutelary deity. Then comes the invocation of gods, planets and ancestors.

During the invocation of the gods, a piece of saffron-coloured thread is attached to the right wrist of the child. A barber then cuts the nails of his fingers and toes and shaves his head, to the sound of instrumental music and the songs sung by the family women. The young Brahmin boy next proceeds to bathe, in order to purify himself after having been defiled by the barbers's touch. After his ablutions, the women again dress him in pure new cloths. He is then purified by the *purohit's* incantations from all the sins committed through youthful ignorance since the day of his birth. The *purohit* also makes him a girdle of plaited *durbha,* a sacred grass, and winds it three times round his body, reciting Sanskrit *mantrams* all the time. At this juncture some small coins are distributed to all the Brahmins conducting the ceremony.

A *palasa* stick, three *cubits* long, is then produced, and also ten pieces of cloth called *Kaupeen* to cover their private parts. These are dyed yellow in saffron water, and are hung in a row on the *palasa* stick, which the candidate puts over his shoulders.

The *purohit* then recites the 'neck *mantram'* and invests the youth with the triple cord which constitutes him a twice born Brahmin. During this solemn performance, the women sing songs, the musicians play, bells are rung, and in addition all present sing songs.

After his investiture, the newly initiated *Brahmchari* takes part in what is known as the 'young men's feast' which is prepared for him and for other young Brahmins who have recently been invested with the sacred cord. At the termination of the repast, the young man again seats himself on the raised platform of earth, facing the east. His father seats himself by his side, but with his face turned towards the west. A cloth is then thrown over them, concealing them from the eyes of the assembly. Again the women begin to sing songs and the musicians to play.

Meanwhile, the father is whipering in the son's ear the secrets and *mantrams* which in his new position as a duly initiated Brahmin it is fitting for him to know. It is said that the following remarkable words form part of the discourse. 'Remember, O my son, that there is only one God, who is the Creator, Lord, and Source of all things; whom every Brahmin should worship in secret. But know also that this is a great mystery that must never be revealed to the vulgar and ignorant people. Should you ever reveal it, surely a great misfortune will befall upon you.'

The instructions, however, being given in Sanskrit are not likely to be understood by the child in whose ears they are uttered. The Brahmins present then place *akshatas,* consecrated by *mantrams,* on the forehead of their new colleague, and the women perform the cermony of *aratti.* Betel leaves are afterwards served out to the guests, who after bathing, return for the feast which should on this day be on a particularly splendid and liberal scale. The same evening, just when the lamps are being lighted, parents and friends again assemble under the *pandal,* and the newly initiated child seats himself on the earthen dais once more. The married women then go and fetch the pan containing the sacred fire which is solemnly placed beside him, amidst much singing. The *purohita* performs the *samkalpa* and recites *mantrams* over this fire, while singers and musicians start afresh with renewed vigour.

The young Brahmin, standing over the coals, offers for the first time in his life the sacrifice called *homam* which by his investiture with the sacred thread he has now acquired the right to do. After this sacrifice and another, which the youth performs specially to the God of Fire, the women make a procession and carry back the pan of burning coals to its place, returning to perform *aratti* to the young Brahmin.

The day terminates with a further distribution of betel to the Brahmins, after which they all separate. On the third day, there is the same assembly again, and for the most part a repetition of the ceremonies of the preceding day, particularly that ot the *homam;* while the day's proceedings are terminated as before by a feast. The ceremonial of the fourth and last day has a few additional ceremonial rites. After a repetition of the usual preliminaries, the women of the party form a procession and, singing all the time, go and fetch the sacred fire which they set down close to the newly initiated boy who, standing up, places a few stalks of *durbha* grass round the pan of hot embers. He then performs *homam* by offering on the brazier some twigs of the sacred fig-tree, some cooked rice, some butter and some coarse sugar. Thence they go to the tutelary deity, and having offered *puja* to him, they invite him to depart as he came.

At the same time, a little of the sacramental water from the deified vessel is poured into the hand of each person present, who forth with sip it, the remainder being thrown away. The deity is also despoiled of his yellow cloth and of the saffron thread with which she was decorated. After a few prayers have been addressed to these different deities, the divine essence is supposed to escape from them. The saffron-coloured thread which was fastened round the wrist of the new member is now taken off, and put to soak in some milk. One large new earthen vessel and five smaller ones, all with lids, are then brought, smeared on the outside with lime.

Five smaller vessels are filled with water to begin with, and are then all emptied into the larger one. The lid of the larger vessel is put on, and it is then placed against the central pillar of the pavilion to which is suspended a wreath of flowers falling exactly over the mouth of the vessel. An offering is made to it of sandalwood, coloured rice and flowers, and for *neiveddya* or votive offering, cakes and cooked rice. All those present are then sprinkled with the ceremonial water contained in the vessel. Then they go on to the five little vessels mentioned above, which are filled with earth. *Puja* is offered to them, and they are then placed in a row, receiving severally the name of one of the following five divinties: Brahma, Vishnu, Varuna, Rudra, and Devendra.

They are then carried separately, and placed at the foot of five of the pillars supporting the *pandal.* They are invoked in the names which have just been given to them, *puja* is offered to them, and the divinities are finally requested to return whence they came. *Puja* is offered to the five little posts, and the celestial beings they have been copresenting are also requested to retire. Then comes the turn of all the gods in general, the planets, and the ancestors whose presence was invoked at the beginning of the feast. Litanies are recited in their honour, and they too are politely requested to depart. Then the praises of the *mantapam* deity, that is to say, of the *pandal* itself, are sung; and he also is dismissed.

Then the women, singing all the time, perform the *aratti* to the new member; and every one being seated for the feast, the newly initiatd Brahmin takes his place amongst the elders of the caste. After the feast is over, he is presented to each of the principal guests in succession, and does *sashtanga,* or prostration to them; they, on their part, congratulate and bless him on his promotion, and wish him every good fortune. In the end, the master of the house distributes money amongst his guests, also pieces of cloth, the value of which is in proportion to the wealth of the giver. A cow is occasionally added to the other gifts.

The Brahmins everywhere, be it north or south of India, are unsurpassed in the art of flattery; and on these occasions they laud to the very skies those who have been prodigal in their gifts. Their liberality is exalted in all directions, and the most exaggerated eulogies are lavished on them. The recipients of all this ridiculous flattery are generally idiotic to be gratified by it, and consider that it amply repays them for the enormous outlay which their childish vanity has caused them to incur. Before seperating, all the guests, both men and women, accompany the new Brahmin initiate, who is seated in an open palanquin richly ornamented on a solemn procession through the streets. On their return, the women, in songs, tell him of all the prayers that they have offered for his future happiness, and they wind up the feast by the ceremony of *aratti.*

As for the new Brahmin initiate, he must be careful to perform the *homam,* evening and morning, for the next thirty days. Such are the formalities which accompany the most important and solemn event in a Brahmin's life. It is not by birth alone that a Brahmin is superior to other men. It is this regenerating ceremony which gives him a new existence and makes him worthy to be elevated in his capacity as a *dwija* or twice-born (*bis genitus*) to the sublime status of his ancestors. As this long ceremonial is strictly obligatory for the upper castes particularly Brahmins. Were a single detail omitted, the whole community would raise a chorus of protest.

Many other Hindu castes share with the Brahmins the honour of wearing the sacred cord. They are the Jains, the Kshatriyas or Rajahs, the Vaisyas and even the Panchalas. Rajahs receive the sacred thread from the hands of a Brahmin *purohita*; but the only ceremony necessary on this occasion is the sacrifice called *homam*. The new initiate then gives a great feast to the Brahmins to celebrate the event, also distributes gifts amongst them. Before they depart, he is admitted to their presence, and performs the *sashtanga*, perhaps in token of gratitude for the honour they have done to him, or else merely to abase himself before these 'gods of the earth.'

According to Hindu scriptures, the Brahmins used formerly to exercise such supreme power over the kings and rulers of the country that they were looked upon by the latter as beings of a different order, and superior to other mortals; princes accounting it an honour to receive some mark of distinction from them. However, the Brahmins, on their part either to enhance their own dignity, or perhaps from gratitude for the donations and favours they received from the Rajahs, granted them the especial privilege of wearing, like themselves, the triple cord. As for the Vaisyas, they do not receive the sacred thread till the day of their marriage, when the officiating Brahmin presents it to them. The *Panchalas* in south India are also decorated under similar circumstances, but it is conferred on them by *guru,* a preceptor or priest of their own caste.

After a Brahmin has been invested with the sacred thread, he is expected to keep the anniversary every year at the time of the full moon in the month of *Sravan*, or August. This anniversary is always celebrated by a feast, for which there are many prescribed rules and ceremonies. The Brahmin has to change his sacred thread on the occasion, the small rag in front of his private parts, and the cloth with which his loins are girt, all of which is done with much solemnity. The performance of this periodical duty obtains for him the remission of all the sins committed during the year, and it is, therefore, called the Feast of the Annual Atonement. The other twice borns like the Kshatriya and the Vaisyas also keep this annual feast similar to the Brahmins.

Conduct of the *Brahmachari* Solemn

The life phase of a *Brahmachari* spans from the ceremony of the *upanayana* until marriage. This period of his life is looked upon as a time of study, of grooming of trial, of subordination, and of initiation into the rules and regulations of their caste. To learn to read and write; to commit the Vedas and *mantrams* to memory; to study in those branches of knowledge for which he shows any aptitude, that is, if his parents are sufficiently wealthy to be able to give him masters; above all things, to learn arithmetic in its elementary forms, and to study various idioms of the language: these are the occupations that fill up his days. The Brahmins have their own school, to which children of other castes, particularly the *Sudras*, are never admitted. The nature of their studies, the discipline and mode of teaching, the very principle of education are all totally different.

The *Brahmanchari* must never chew betel;he must, never put flowers in his turban or in his hair, or ornament his forehead and he must never look in a looking-glass. Every day, morning and evening, he must perform *sandhya* and the *homam,* or sacrifice of fire. He must take the greatest pains to conform to the rules and customs of his caste according to the holy scriptures; he must show the most absolute and prompt obedience and subordination to his parents and his teachers; he must be modest, deferential and respectful to his superiors, and affable to his equals. His family and his masters take particular care to instruct him in living according to the religious tenets, the qualities which are fully developed in all Brahmins, and form the principal traits in their character. There are, besides, hundreds of minute and complex details most essential in a Brahmin's education, comprising rules of good manners and decorous conduct, the art of speaking and conversing in well-chosen language, the appropriate demeanour to assume on different occasions, how to hold oneself and how to use one's eyes, the different degrees of *hauteur* or humility which should be shown under various circumstances and at different times and places according to the people who are present. Nevertheless, in spite of the stress which is laid upon these pretty precepts governing the conduct of young Brahmins, there are few who conform to them in all essentials. Even of the rules of conduct many are merely matters of form.

If, from want of means or other causes, a young Brahmin is still unmarried at the age of eighteen or twenty, he ceases to be a *Brahmachari*, but at the same time he does not become a *Grahastha*. From the time that he receives the cord, he obtains the right to the six privileges which are inherent in this status. These privileges include to read the Vedas, to have them read to him, to perform the sacrifice of the *yagnam,* to be performed, to give, and also to receive, presents and alms. As to the despised and exploited Sudras, they possess only one of the privileges namely, that which allows them to give alms or presents to those Brahmins who will condescend to accept them from their polluted hands. To the Brahmins alone belongs the right of reading the Vedas, and they are so jealous of this monopoly, or rather it is so much in their interest to prevent other castes obtaining any insight into their contents, that the Brahmins have inculcated an absurd theory, which is implicitly believed, that should anybody of any other caste be so highly imprudent as even to read the title page, his head would immediately split in two due to the divine disgrace.

The very few Brahmins who are able to read these sacred scriptures in the original sanskrit text only do so in secret and in a whisper. Expulsion from the caste, without the smallest hope of re-entering it, would be the lightest punishment for a Brahmin who exposed these books to the eyes of the Sudras, women and the other unworthies. These four marvellous books are held to be the work of Lord Brahma Himself. Brahma, it is said, revealed and explained their meaning to four famous *munis*, or the penitents, to whom the scriptures were entrusted, and to whom was confided the task of explaining them to the Brahmins. Sumantu, the first of these celebrated personages, was given the *Yajur-Veda*; Pailada, the *Rig-Veda*; Jaimini, the *Sama-Veda*; and Angirasa, the *Atharva-Veda*.

Mahidhara, in the *Vajasaneyi Samhita,* says in regard to the division of the Vedas: Veda Vyasa, having regard to men of dull understanding, in kindness to them, divided the Veda into four parts which had been originally handed down by tradition from Brahma, and taught the four Vedas, called *Rig*, *Yajush*, *Saman*, and *Atharvan*, in order, to Paila, Vaisampayana, Jaimini, and Sumantu; and they again to their disciples. In this way, by tradition, the Veda of a thousand Sakhas was produced. It is from these Vedas that the Brahmins have obtained the greater number of those *mantrams* which bring them in so much money, and cause them to be held in such high esteem. This, in fact, in writ renders the Vedas so precious to the Brahmins. Such Brahmins as devta themselves to the higher branches of knowlege learn the Vedas by heart; and though to greater number do not understand the real meaning of what they have learnt, still they are looked upon in some sort as doctors of theology, and are given the name of Vipras or Vedapathis.

It is true, nevertheless, that those who devote themselves to the study of these scriptures cannot hope to extract any instruction from them, for they are written in ancient Sanskrit which has become almost wholly obsolete and hence unintelligible in the modern times, and such numberless mistakes have been introduced by copyists, either through carelessness or ignorance, that the most learned persons find themselves quite unable to interpret the original Sanskrit text.

The original text of the Vedas must not, as is often done, be confounded with the more modern introductions and commentaries written by the penitent sage Vyasa. These were interpolated with the view of rendering the text more intelligible. They are known under the general name of Upanishads, and are three in number- the Upa-Veda, the Karma- Veda, and the Sakha- Veda.

Other than these commentaries the most learned of modern Brahmins are capable of explaining nothing more. Their meaning is unintelligible except to those who have a considerable learning in Sanskrit, the language in which they are written. Many learn to read and recite them mechanically, without understanding a word of them. In the *agraharas,* or Brahmin villages, and other places where Brahmins assemble in large numbers, you may perhaps come across some who are Sanskrit scholars, but even they would be unable to produce a good interpretation of the Vedas. Some Brahmins give gratuitous instruction in those parts of the Vedas which, thanks to the commentaries, have been made intelligible, while other Brahmins, too poor to forgo the remuneration, hold classes in which the same instruction is given to paying pupils.

Many wealthy Brahmins make a point of encouraging the study of the Vedas by offering prizes and other rewards, this being in the eyes of their fellows a work of the greatest merit. The Brahmins have done the *Rajahs* the honour of allowing them also to encourage the study of the Vedas by founding schools, for that purpose and paying the professors. But be that as it may, there is not much eagerness displayed amongst the Brahmins for this tedious kind of study. Poverty prevents some of them from taking it up, while indifference and idleness prevent others.

In the *Yagnam*, a name which comprises the third and fourth Brahminical privileges, the sacrifice called *homam* is apparently included, for the *homam* of the *Rajahs* is totally different. Every Brahmin must perform the *homam* at least once a day. It is a sacrifice offered to fire under various circumstances. The sacrifice made to fire, or by means of fire, is a form of idolatry by no means peculiar to the Hindus. It is well known among the great Persians, Chaldeans, and other ancient races who carried the practice with respect. The *homam* is made by lighting a brazier, which is then consecrated by *mantrams*. Into this are offered small pieces of wood, gathered from one of the seven sacred trees, and afterwards melted clarified butter, sesamum and cooked rice; these offerings being accompanied by suitable *mantrams*.

The *homam* is almost invariably followed by another sacrifice, which is specially offered to fire, but only ordinary *puja* is performed. The fifth privilege of a *Brahmchari*, namely, the giving of alms and presents, is much less to their taste. It must, however, be admitted that wealthy Brahmins display a lavish hospitality, besides being charitable in other ways. But this is only to the members of their own caste; the rest of the human race is, if not detested, at least absolutely of no account so far as the Brahmins are concerned. Amongst the gifts which Brahmins are willing to receive, there are some which are more specially acceptable. They are called the *pancha-danas* or the five gifts; and they are gold, land, clothes, grain and cows.

The last-mentioned gift causes them particular pleasure, seeing that milk in various forms is their principal food. Brahmins also possess large landed properties originally given to them by generous princes and on which they pay no taxes. These descend from father to son, and always retain their immunity from taxation. As a rule, Brahmins do not cultivate their lands themselves, but lease them out to the Sudras, taking half the crops as rent. The Brahmins generally live on their lands, which are called *agraharas*. Numbers of these estates were to be found in the various states of India.

Then again, in their character as high priests, the Brahmins gather in the greater part of the revenue of the lands belonging to the different temples, and furthermore receive all the offerings brought by devotees to the various idols. A Brahmin sees nothing humiliating in asking for or receiving alms. According to his ideas, it is his birth right, of which he may make free use. He displays none of the importunity or impertinence of which people are subjected by the Mahomedan *fakirs,* or by the Sudra beggars who belong to the sects of Siva or Vishnu cults.

The begging Brahmin including a young *Brahmachari* boldly enters a house and states what he wants. Should he receive anything, he takes it without saying a word of thanks, goes away without any acknowledgement and without showing the smallest sign of gratitude. Should he meet with a refusal, however, he retires without any complaint or grumbling. Manu says: 'Let every man, according to his ability, give wealth to Brahmins, detached from the world and learned in scripture:

such a giver shall attain heaven after this life' (xi 6). Very early in the statutes, a universal law is proclaimed, the spirit of which pervades the whole code. This law calmly lays down that 'whatever exists in the universe is all, in effect, though not in form, the wealth of the Brahmins: since the Brahmin is entitled to it all by his own food; wears but his own apparel; and bestows but his own alms; through the benevolence of the Brahmin, indeed, other mortals enjoy life' (i. 100-101). This is a pretty broad principle to enunciate, so it is easy to see how there is nothing derogatory in a Brahmin receiving alms, since he takes but what is his own, besides leaving a blessing to the giver.

However, woe betides anyone who ventures to make the Brahmins promises which he subsequently fails to perform. That would be a fearful sin, which could not fail to draw down the divine wrath upon the defaulting person. A Hindus author provides the following example as a proof. *'Hata! Hata!'* cried a monkey one day, seeing a fox devouring a rotten carcass. 'In a former state of existence you must have committed some atrocious crimes to be condemned in your present life to eat such disgusting food'.

'Alas!' replied the fox with a groan, 'it is only what I deserve. Once upon a time I was a man, and I then promised a Brahmin a present, and failed to keep my word; that is why I was born again in my present condition which you find so revolting.'

Brahmins declare that he who fails to keep faith with them, or who injures them in any way, will be condemned after death to be born again as a devil. Such a person could live neither on the earth, nor yet in the air, but would be reduced to dwelling in a thick forest, for ever hidden amongst the foliage of a leafy tree. Day and night he would groan and bewail his unhappy fate. His only food would be the filthy juice of the palm tree, mixed with the saliva of dogs; and he would have to use a human skull as a cup. Brahmins, as a rule, are exempt from all taxes on houses and other personal property.

In many districts, they paid no customs duty under the Hindu rajahs. They are, again, not liable to be impressed into compulsory service, or called upon for those requisitions which fall so heavily on the other citizens, who are obliged to labour at public works, such as the making and mending of the high-roads, the repairing of temples, tanks, canals, etc., and who also have to carry provisions for the troops when on the march, or for magistrates and other British public servants, more often than not without any payment for their labour, or even sufficient food, and with no compensation for the losses which these requisitions cause them. Such general servants of the public as carpenters, blacksmiths, barbers and washermen are often obliged, at least in many districts, to work gratuitously for the Brahmins. This, however, is not due to any actual pressure, but to the fact that these public servants enjoy grants of land and they work gratuitously for the whole village. In the tiny states ruled by Hindus princes, Brahmins are rarely condemned to any serious corporal punishment, however heinous their crimes may be, they are never liable to the penalty of death. The murder of a Brahmin, no matter for what reason, would be considered absolutely unpardonable, for it is the greatest of all known crimes and would not fail to bring some terrible calamity to the whole state in which it had been committed.

However, in those states which are under European or Muslim ruler, where the sacred character of the Brahmin is held in much less reverence, they are liable like any other native to punishments proportioned to their crime. Sometimes, the Muslims beat them to death, unless they pay considerable sums to buy themselves off, a process which suits their persecutors who are much better pleased to have their money than their blood.

But sometimes either from avarice, or because they are afraid that if they once let their oppressors fleece them in this manner, they will never be rid of such persecutions, until they are despoiled of all that they possess, they prefer to suffer all kinds of torture, even death itself, rather than part with their money. When Brahmins find themselves in this sorry plight there are no lies, no false statements, oaths and protestations that they will not employ in the hope of extricating themselves.

External Defilement of a *Brahmachari*

All that pertains to external and internal defilement, physical and spiritual, is the very beginning and foundation of a Brahmin's education, both religious and civil. They have invented numberless minute precautions to prevent the possibility of coming in contact with anything which, would defile their persons, their clothes, their furniture and temples etc. It is principally this ineradicable prejudice which has raised such an insurmountable barrier between them and the rest of mankind. Obliged by their religious tenets to hold themselves aloof from everyone else who does not share their beliefs, they can never, under any circumstances, be on such friendly or confidential terms with any stranger as would arise from feelings of mutual esteem and respect.

It is undoubtedly from the Brahmins that the other Hindu castes have picked up this absurd prejudice, for it is in the strongest force amongst the Brahmins. The predominating idea in their general conduct, and in their every action in life, is what they call cleanliness; and it is the enormous amount of care that they take to keep themselves 'clean' to prevent any kind of defilement and to purify themselves from any uncleanliness that they may have contracted, which gives them their ascendency over other castes. It is one of the special duties of the *Brahmachari* to be well versed, at an early age, in the customs and practices regulating this important branch of Hindu religious tenets. In all countries and the rest of mankind the sight of a human corpse produces a feel of horror. Everyone has a strong aversion, amounting almost to repugnance, to touching a corpse. But Brahmins consider that the mere fact of assisting at a funeral is sufficient to defile them. When the funeral is over, they immediately hasten to plunge themselves into water, and no one would dare to return home without having thus purified himself.

Even the news of the death of a relative, though it may have happened a hundred miles away, produces the same effect, and every member of the family who receives the polluting news must purify himself. Friends and simple acquaintances, however, are not contaminated thereby. The moment a Hindu has breathed his last, the necessary preparations for his funeral begin forthwith, for as long as the corpse remains in the house, neither the inmates, nor even their neighbours, can eat or drink or attend to their usual occupations and chores. In a temple, where a large congregation had assembled, entirely suspended their worship until the body of a man who had died not far off had been removed. Neither incense, nor any other perfume would purify a house where a death had taken place. A Brahmin *purohita* must come to remove the impurity with which all the inmates are contaminated.

To this end, he offers sacrifices, recites *mantrams* suitable to the occasion, and at frequent intervals makes copious libations of holy water. But, see, according to the law of Moses, when an Israelite died in a house or in a tent, all the people living therein, and all the furniture it contained, were unclean for seven days (Number xix. 14, 15). And an undefiled person, free from all impurity, dipped a bunch of hyssop into this water, and besprinkled the furniture, the room and the people who were defiled. On the seventh day, these latter bathed themselves in water, and washed their clothes, after which they were considered perfectly cleansed.

Making of *Upanayana*

According to Mr. H.A. Rose, pure cotton is purchased in August, and on the 13th day after the new moon it is spun into thread by a Brahmin girl, or by a married woman whose husband is alive in Gujarat but never by a widow. The cotton should be picked from a field free from filth. A *janeo* may consist of one or two *agras*. The making of a one *agra* is thus described :- There are three lines on the fingers. The Brahmins should wind the single thread over the upper line 96 times, the Khatris over the central line 86 times, and the Vaisyas over the lowest 76 times. The thread is then made into three folds and twisted on a *kath*, a special tool used in preparing the *janeo*. It is then folded in three folds a second time so that there are now nine threads in the cord. To make an *agra,* it is again folded thrice, making 27 threads in each *agra*. The number of *ganthis* or knots in an *agra* depends on the number of *parearas* or famous ancestors in each *gotra*. One *agra* is allowed to a Brahmin in the *Brahmchari* or discipleship stage, the second being added when he reaches to the second, the *Grihasthashram* or house-holder stage. The second from left to right, (and so on). The second *agra* is made in the same way. When two *agra* are worn, they are knotted together by three or five knots. The most usual or orthodox rules appear to be that the material, length and age of initiation for each caste or varna.

Janeo may be put on in the *gaun kal*, i.e. up to the last year special field, after which the man is *anadhiman* or disqualified. There are, however, modifications in the rule. Thus, if a Brahmin wishes to become learned in the Vedas, he should assume the *janeo* in his fifth year, if a Kshatriya desired strength, in his 6th year, and if a Vaisya desired success in cultivation, in his 8th year : (*Manu Smriti, Chap*. it, 36 and 37.) The Khatri's *janeo* should, according to one account, be of silk thread, and the Vaisya's of *pashmina*. In Benares (U.P.), a *janeo* of silk lace is made into which certain *antras* are interwoven. Sometimes in Sirmur, it is made of fibre from the bark of the *gudala* tree. The rules as to material are not now observed in all strictness. As we shall see the *janeo* of wool is now characteristic of certain religious castes. But the rules as to length are still very generally observed.

The Ordinary janeo is of three kinds: *Brahmgandh*:

(i) with 5 knots for the higher grades of Brahmins.

(ii) with 3 knots for the lower grades of Brahmins, and

(iii) *Vishnugandh*, with 1 knot, for all other castes.

The ceremony of initiation should take place at an auspicious time. When the ceremony is performed the boy's head is shaved, only the *shakha*, *bodi* or *chota* (the lock of hair on the top of the head) being left. He then bathes. He is then seated on the skin of an animal (deer, sheep or goat according to his caste), and is given a stick or staff of a particular tree. Or according to another account he must don a deer-skin (*mrig charam*), take a *rabus dand*, or staff of *dhak* wood, in his hand, and put on *padakas* or *khuraos* (wooden shoes). The rites in ancient times included various burnt offerings made in pits (*hawan kund*), over which a wooden frame (*bedi*) was placed. The nine planets were also worshipped.

Then, the *guru* seats the boy on his left side, and after making him promise to obey the orders he will receive, covers both their heads with a long cloth (*safa*), and amidst the beating of drums and sounding of conches (to prevent others hearing what he says to the boy), whispers in his right ear a *mantra* which is never revealed to anyone but himself.

This Mantra is called Gayatri and runs: as *Tat Savitur varenyum bhargo devasya Dhimahi dhi yo yo nah prachodayat,* "Let worship the supreme light of the Sun, the God of things, who can as well guide our understanding, like an eye suspended in the vault of Heaven."

Then, the boy goes to his mother and first begs alms of her, subsequently begging of all the women of the assembled brotherhood. Alms, consisting of rice, money, both small silver and copper coins and silver rings, etc. are thrown by them into his *jholi* or pilgrim's bag. These are offered to the *guru*, who then puts the *janeo* on the boy.

The *janeo* or the sacred thread is ordinarily worn over the left shoulder, across the back and chest, and under the right shoulder. But in worshipping the gods there are three distinct ways in which the *janeo* should be worn :

(1) Nitya-Shabih: In worshipping the gods the *janeo* is still worn on the left shoulder, but is held across the palm under the thumb of the left hand. The right hand is kept over it forward.

(2) **Ap-Shabih:** In naming the *pitris,* the *janeo* is worn on the right shoulder, and the libation of water made with the fingers of the right hand, the palm being kept above them so as to pour the water to the left.This is the worship of *pitris* or the ancestral *manes.*

(3) In worship of the *rishis,* the *janeo* is placed round the neek and allowed to fall like a necklace. The libation is made with both hands so as to pour it inwards to the chest.

The *janeo* of the Jogis

All twelve *panths* or orders of the *jogis* wear the *janeo*, which is made by certain special members of the sect, and not by ordinary *jogis* or by Brahmins. Sixteen strands, each nine cubits long, are taken. These strands are divided into 8 parts, each of two strands, and each part is then wrapped round a stick and twisted to the right. All eight parts are then twisted into one rope, which is again divided into six strands. These are finally knotted together by a *Brahm* knot, and to them is attached a *pawittri* (a ring of gold or rhinoceros horn), and to this again a *nad*, also of the latter material. This, *janeo* should be of black wool, and is worn like a necklace.

The Kalli-sutar

Besides the *janeo*, Acharj Brahmins, *Vaishnav* and *Bairagi sadhus* wear *kalli-sutar*, or thread round the loins, made of wool or *munj*.

Custom of Circumcision

Around so primitive rites as circumcision, cluster, as might be anticipated, countless local and tribunal usages, accretions on the orthodox observance. This is simple. Though not even alluded to in the *Quran*, the rite is held to be *sunnat*, i.e. founded on the customs of the Prophet, but no religious observances appear to be prescribed in connection with it. The conduct of circumcision should be gone through between the ages of seven and twelve, but it is permissible on or after the seventh day after birth. It is very commonly done in the *chhatti.* As a rule, the operation is effected at home, but in places the male child is taken to the mosque, and it is done in front of the door. The keynote to the observances connected with the operation lie in the fact that it is regarded as a wedding indeed, in the south-west of Bahawalpur it is actually termed as *shadi*. In accordance with this idea, the boy is treated like a bridegroom, dressed in yellow clothes, and mounted on a horse. Before the operation, the brotherhood is sometimes notified, sugar or dates being sent out to its members.

On the day itself the brotherhood is feasted and entertained with dances. The women sing songs, and sometimes *domnis* are employed to keep the singing up all night. It is not unusual to half-intoxicate the boy with *ma'jum,* so that he may not feel the pain.

As a rule the barber operates, but in Kangra the *Abdal* is sometimes employed, and in the west of the Punjab the *Pirhain*. In Bahawalpur, the boy is told by the guests to slap the *Pirhain*, who gets as many rupees as he recieves slaps. Naturally, as the father has to pay, he urges the boy not to slap the operator. In Kangra, the boy is seated on a basket, in which is placed a cock, the barber's perquisite. In Punjab, he is seated on a stool, to which his hand is tied by a piece of *mauli* thread, and unless a companion in suffering has been found for him, the top of an earthen vessel is simultaneously cut off.

In Maler Kotla, the boy is ceremoniously bathed on a wooden stool, and then his maternal uncle ties a *kangna* of thread, called *khamani*, on which are strung a betel nut, an iron ring and a piece of liquorice. After the operation, the barber bids the uncle take the boy away, and he does so carrying him in his arms. In Bahawalpur, the boy's mother stands by with a *Quran* on her head during the operation, her women friends standing round her while she dips the hem of her petticoat in a vessel full of water.

The foreskin, when removed, is generally buried, but sometimes it is thrown on the roof, or even attached to it with a piece of straw, in Hissar. In Bahawalpur, it is called *khol*, and is carefully preserved, being sometimes buried in the floor, which, being near the water pitchers, always remains wet. In Delhi, it is tied together with a peacock's feather to the boy's left foot, so that no one's shadow may affect him; but this custom is falling into disuse.

Custom of Kafir Games

In Kafir peoples life games play an important part. With one exception boys and girls play separately, the former playing rough games. One is played by four boys on each side, each player holding a big toe with the opposite hand and hopping on the other foot. The object is to enable the 'back' to get through to the other side's goal. The game is played by girls and boys together is an imitation of the national dance. Men play a kind of touch, in which the object is to tread on a man's instep to make him prisoner, archery *aluts*, which is a kind of quoit, played with flat stones and various athletic exercises. The stone-bow is used by both men and boys and exactly resembles the Indian *gulel*.A fairly popular game is a kind of curling with walnuts on the house-tops. No game, however, plays so important a part as dancing.

Kafirs dance when they are happy and when in mourning. They dance to amuse the injured, the sick and the dying, but possibly this is really done as a form of supplication to the gods, who are propitiated by songs, dancings and feasting, which includes sacrifices, and never in any other way. The chief occasions for dancing are the dances of the *jast* to the gods, those to the illustrious dead, those performed by the women to the gods while the men are raiding, those of homicides to Gish, at a Kafir's death and on the erection of effigies. These dances are performed inside the *gromma* or dancing-place which is thus described by Sir G. Robertson:-

"The dancing-place is always the most important spot in a Kafir village. There is usually only one, but *Kamdish* and *Bragamatal* have two each. A dancing-place should consist of a house to be used in winter and in bad weather, a boarded platform, and a level piece of ground, on which particular dances are performed, furnished with a rude stone altar. A description of the upper Kamdesh dancing place will also apply, with some modifications, to all similar places in the Bashgul valley.

The whole place is called the *gromma*, a name evidently derived from the word *grom* or *brom,* the *Bashgul* term for a village.

A Kafir who had been to India with me always called the gromma the 'Church', when spoke Urdu.To the north of the Kamdesh, dancing-place is the *gromma* or dancing - house. It is 12 feet high, 35 feet long and 30 feet broad. Its sides are barred, not closed, by heavy square beams, between the intervals of which spectators can thrust their heads and shoulders restfully.

During a spectacle these apertures are generally crowded with the heads of girls and women. Down the center of the *gromma* run two rows of massive pillars which support the heavy roof. They are about six feet apart. The central four are quite plain, except at the top, where they are ornamented with carved horses' heads. The remainig four are completely covered with the ordinary basket-work carving. In the middle of the roof there is a four feet square smoke hole. Bordering the *gromma* to the south is the largest level space in the village. It is about thirty yards square. On it there is a rude altar, formed of two upright stones, with a horizontal one on top. On this altar there is almost always to be seen the remains of a recent fire. To the east this space is continuous with a platform, which is carried out from the steep slope and maintained in that position by wooden pillars and beams. It looks, and is, a shaky structure. A railing runs round its three dangerous sides. Seats are provided on it in the shape of long planks of comfortable breadth, a few inches off the floor. These platforms are always to be seen if the village is built on the side of a hill. Most of the shrines at Kamdesh are provided with a platform which only differs from that at the *gromma* in point of size. In villages built on the flat, such as those in the upper part of the Bashgul valley, the platforms are lifted off the ground on trestles. They are indeed an essential part of every dancing-place, bacause certain ceremonies cannot be performed except upon them.

The *gromma* of a Presun (Viron) village differs considerably from those of the Bashgul valley. In the first place, they are nearly all of them half underground, that at *Digrom*, for example, is like a huge bear-pit and is reached by long passages sloping down from the village level. They are very large, as they are used for guest-houses, and are capable of holding a large number of people. In one corner they generally have a small shrine, containing a quaintly carved idol of some god. The four central pillars are hewn into marvellously grotesque figures, the huge shield-shaped faces of which are more than two feet in length. There is never any doubt, however, about the sex of an effigy of this kind. The knees of the figure are made to approach one another, while the feet are far apart, as if, indeed, the god or goddess was swarming up the pole backwards.

Rite of *Khatnabal* or Circumcision

The rite of circumcision of the male child is obligatory in all Muslis communities according to the Islamic tentent. It is performed when the child is more than two years old. The circumcision is carried out by the village barber or by a qualified surgeon in cities. In villages, a large fowl is dept in a wicker basket and the child is made to sit on its inverted base. His arms and legs are held firmly by one or two persons so that he does not make any movement when the barber applies the razor to cut of the prepace from his penis. After the circumcision the fowl is given to the barber as a gift alongwith some money sugar and cereals. During the course of operation the female relatives keep singing auspicious songs in chorus. The cusoms and rituals related to circumcision are preetired among the Kashmiri Muslims. *(For further details on the rite of circumcision, please see chapter Puberty in vlume on the Eastern region).*

Rites Related to Female Puberty

The first menstruation after the marriage has been consummated is the occassion of a strict *tabu* in Mandi (Himachal Pradesh). The wife must touch no one, and should not even see any one, to secure which she is shut up in a dark room. She must not use milk, oil or meat, while she is still impure. According to Mr. H.A. Rose, the following rite is performed: " On a day chosen as auspicious by a Brahmin, all the wife's female relatives assemble, and kinswomen wash her head with *gondhana*. Then after she has bathed, five cakes of flour, walnuts and pomegranates are put in her lap, with a pretty child, in order that she too may bear such a child. Looking into its face she gives it some money and cakes, and then the family priest makes her worship Ganpati. In return he the Brahmin receives a fee in money, with the things offered to the goddess. The women spend the ensuing night in singing."

Elsewhere in north, when a Brahmin girl attains puberty and is in a state of periodical uncleanness, she is isolated in some place apart, and may have no communication with anyone during the three consecutive days that her defilement is supposed to last. The first day she must look upon herself as untouchable outcaste person. The second day she must consider herself as unclean, as if she has killed a Brahmin. The third day she is supposed to be in an intermediate state between the two preceding ones. The fourth day, she purifies herself by ablutions, observing all the rites and rituals required to these pollutions. Until then she must neither bathe, nor wash any part of her body, nor shed tears. She must be very careful not to kill any insect, or any other living creature. She must not ride on a horse, an elephant, or a bullock, nor travel in palanquin, or a carriage. She must not anoint her head with oil or play dice and any other games, or use sandalwood, musk, or perfumes of any kind. She must not lie on bed or sleep during the day. She must not brush her teeth or rinse out her mouth. The mere wish to cohabit with her husband would be a serious sin.

She must not think of the gods or of the sun, or of the sacrifices and worship due to them. She is forbidden to salute persons of high rank. If several women in this unclean state should find themselves together in one place, they must not speak to or touch each other. Any other married woman in this condition must not go near her children, or touch them, or play with them. After living thus in retirement for three consecutive days, on the fourth she must take off the garments that she has been wearing, and these must be immediately given to the washerman. She must then put on a clean cloth and another over it, and go to the river to purify herself through bathing. On her way there, she must walk with her head bent, and must take the greatest care to glance at nobody, for her looks would defile any person on whom they rested.

When she has reached the river, she must first enter the water and fill the copper vessel, which she has brought with her from the house. Then, returning to the bank, she must thoroughly cleanse her teeth, rinse out her mouth twelve times, and wash her hands and feet. She must then enter the water and plunge twelve times into it, immersing the whole of her body. She must take the greatest care, while doing this not to look at any living soul, and to this end each time her head rises above the water, she must turn her eyes towards the sun. On coming out of the water, she must take a little fresh cow-dung, some *tulsi*, and some earth. These she must mix together in a little water, until they make a thin paste, and with this she must thoroughly rub her hands and feet and then her whole body. After this, she must re-enter the water, and completely immerse herself twenty-four times. When she again leaves the water, she must rub herself over with saffron, and again dip three times in the water. Then mixing saffron in a little water, she must drink some and pour the rest on her head, after which she must put on a pure cloth freshly washed and the little bodice. She may then paint the little round red mark on her forehead called *kumkum* and return home. On entering the house, she must take special care that her eyes do not rest on her children, for they would thereby be exposed to the greatest danger. She must immediately send for a Brahmin *purohit* so that he may complete her purification. On his arrival, this venerable person first plaits together thirty-two stalks of *durbha* grass, to make the ring which he dips in consecrated water that he has brought with him. The woman then takes another bath, drinks a little of the consecrated water, places the grass ring on the ring finger of the right hand, and drinks some *pancha-gavia* or cow's five products. After these ceremonies her purification is complete.

REFERENCES

1. Dubois, Abbe, J.A, *Hindu Manners, Customs and Ceremonies*, (Translation from French by Henry K. Beauchamp), Oxford, The Claredon Press, London, 1897.
2. Rose, H.A, *A Glossary of the Tribes and Castes of the Punjab and North-West Frontier Province*, Low Price Publications, Delhi, 1999 (Reprint) first published in 1919.
3. Ibbetson, Denzil, Census Report for the Punjab 1883.
4. Maclagan, Edward, Census Report for the Punjab 1892.
5. Singh K.S. (Gen.ed), *People of India:Jammu & Kashmir*, Manohar/ Anthropological Survey of India, Calcutta, 2003.
6. Sherring, M.A., *Hindu Tribes and Castes*, Thacker & Spink, Calcutta, 1879.
7. Mamgain, M.D., *Himachal District Gezetteers*, Lahul & Spiti, Creater Punjab Press, Chandigarh, 1975.

3
Betrothal

Customs relating to betrothal have changed gradually after Independence of the nation as a result of spread of education and opening up of new economic opportunities in various sections of society in the northern states. The capital city of Delhi had been attracting a vast crowd from various states of India, and this new society, a mix of all castes and sections has been enjoying a new status through shedding their primitive customs. With modern educations men and women perceive no meaning in old customs which their ancestors attached so much importance to.

Mariage Negotiation

During the British period, the *Gaddi* wedding customs merited special notice. In betrothal, the boy's parents or guardians send their *purohit* to negotiate for a girl about whom they have information, and he brings back her parents reply. If it is favourable, the boy's parents send two or more respectable men to the girl's home to complete the bargain. Then if it is *clinched*, two of the boy's family go with the *purohit* to perform the ceremony. If the betrothal is *dharma puna,* it consists in the bride's father giving the *purohit* a bunch of *drub* grass with four copper coins or more, if they please, to be handed over to the boy's father in token that the alliance is accepted. The *purohit* hands over the *drub*, and the coins are returned to the *purohit* with a rupee added by the boy's father.

The night is spent at the bride's house, and after a meal her father gives the boy's father eight copper coins and these he places in a vessel as a perquisite to the servant who cleans it. In a betrothal by exchange (*tola*), the first observances are the same, but when all go to finally complete the alliance a grindstone and *sil* with 3 or 5 *roris* of *gur, supari, bihan* and *roli* or vermilion for marking an auspicious dot on the forehead, are placed before the party and then the *purohit* places *supari, bihan* and *roli* in the skirt of his sheet and puts them on the *sil.* Before tapping them on the *sil* with the grindstone, he receives four annas from the boy's father and mentions the names of the boy and girl whose alliance is to be formed, and then taps them. After this, the *supari,* etc., are placed in a vessel, with the balls of *jaggery* broken up, and distributed to those present after the girl's father has taken a bit. The elder members of the girl's family do not take any as it would be contrary to custom.

The boy's father puts Re. 1 to 4 in this vessel and this is made over to the bride's parents who get jewellery to that amount made for her. After this, the bride appears before the boy's father and he gives her a rupee. The rest of the ceremony is exactly as described above, but in this case the coins put in the vessel come out of the boy's father's pocket. The ceremony in the other house is performed in exactly the same way, though not on the same day for the sake of convenience. A propitious date is not fixed, but a lucky day is desirable, and Tuesday, Friday and Saturday are considered unlucky.

Sir James Lyall wrote, "Three kinds of marriage ceremonies are in use in Kullu in Himachal, viz.

(1) *Bedibiah*, the ordinary Hindu form;

(2) *ruti manai*, four or five men go from the bridegroom to the bride's house, dress her up, put a cap on her head, and then bring her home to the bridegroom;

(3) *Ganesh puja*, the form used by Brahmins, Khatris and *Suniasas*, etc., in marrying a *Kanet* girl. The bridegroom sends his priest and others to the bride's house where worship of Ganesh is performed, and the bride then brought home.

Suniaras send a knife to represent them. The children of a Brahmin and Rajput by a *Kanet* wife are called Brahmins and Rajputs ; the term *Rathi* is often added as a qualification by anyone pretending himself with unmixed blood. In the absence of other children, they are their father's full heirs, but in the presence of other children by a *lari* wife, they would ordinarily only get an allotment by way of maintenance, put by some at one-fifth, but the limit seems rather vague in practice.

Inheritance

The rule of inheritance in Kullu among all tribes at the present day is *pagvand*, or, as it is here called, *mundevand*, that is, all legitimate sons born of each wife or mother. Among the Kanets and the lower castes, the real custom hitherto has been that every son by a woman kept and treated as a wife was legitimate. It was not necessary that any ceremony should have been performed. If no one else claimed the woman, and she lived with the man as a wife, the son born from such cohabitation was legitimate. In the same way among the same classes a *pichlag*, or posthumous son (called *ronda* in Kullu), born to a widow in the house of second husband, is considered the son of the second husband ; and a widow cannot be deprived of her life tenure of her husband's estate of want of chastity so long as she does not go away to live in another man's house. It appears to be a general idea in Kullu that a father could, by formal deed of gift executed in his lifetime, give his estate to a daughter, in default of sons, without consent of next of kin. It is, doubtful also whether a distant kinsman (say, more than three or four generations apart) could claim against a daughter without gift, and, it seems, generally allowed that a *ghar jawai* or son-in-law taken into the house becomes after a time entitled to succeed as a kind of adopted son without proof of gift according to Sir James Lyall.

"Polyandry now prevails only in Saraj, and there the custom seems to be tending to fall into disuse. It is in reality a mere custom of community of wives among brothers who have a community of other goods. In one house you may find three brothers with one wife, in the next three brothers with four wives, all alike in common; in the next house there may be an only son with three wives to himself. It is a matter of means and of land; a large farm requires several women to look after it. Where there is only one wife to several brothers, it will generally be found that some of the brothers are absent for part of the year working as labourers. In former years, It is seen perplexing claims arise from this custom. The sons or grandsons of a family which has lived in polyandry agree to divide the ancestral estate, and quarrel as to the shares, some saying that each son should get an equal share, others that the sons of each another (where the fathers had several wives in common) should get an equal share, other's that the sons of each putative father should get an equal share. Of late years, such disputes have seldom arisen, as it has become a pretty generally recognised principle that, as far as our courts are concerned, the woman in these cases is the wife only of the eldest son or head of the family, and all sons she may bear must be presumed to be his. This principle agrees in results with, what is to believe to have been in former times, the general rule of inheritance, as between the children of brothers all living in community of wives (but it must be confessed that no one custom seems to have been rigidly followed in all cases); on the other hand, as between the children of brothers all of whom did not live in community of wives. The old custom of the country was, as follows: If of three brothers, one separated off his share of the estate and set up for himself, and the other two lived on in common and a son was born in their house; then such son was considered to be the child of two fathers and heir to the estate of both: the separated brother or his children could claim no share of such estate on the death of either of the united brothers. This appears to have been the custom in past times but it is opposed to the principle, above mentioned as at present in force, of only recognising the mother to be the wife of one of the brothers.

Gujar Betrothal Customs

The Gujars are often said to have 84 clans or sections and in Ludhiana their Mirasis address them as '*Chaurasi got da diwa,*' i.e., 'Light of the 84 clans'; but other accounts assign them 101, 170 or even 388 sections. Of these numerous clans, none have any definite superiority over the rest, though a few have a vague local standing above their neighbours. Such are the Khobar, Rawal, Wape and Dhalak in Karnal - because they abstain from flesh and liquor, whereas Chhokar, Kalsan, Datyar, Dhosi and Rathi sections do not. Of regular classes, there is hardly a trace, excepting the Mianas who form in Gujarat a semi-sacred class. They are descendants of men who have acquired a name for learning or sanctity and so their descendants cannot give wives to Gujars of less exalted rank. Indeed, the leading Khatana family of Dinga used to consider it derogatory to give daughters to any Gujar at all and sought bridegrooms in more exalted families, or failing them let their girls remain unwed. In Gujarat, the Gujars also possess a curious social organisation, being possessed of 84 *darrs* or lodges. Originally the number was only 54, distributed over the 7 *tappas* into which the tract was divided in Akbar's time, but 20 have been added from various families, and 5 assigned to the Gujars of Kala in Jhelum. To became a *darr-wala* or member requires money, influence and popularity.

At his son's wedding, A candidate must first, obtain the consent of the existing *darr-walas*, which is not easily done, as there must be no 'black-balls,' and he must be on good terms with the leading men. Having been thus elected he must pay so much per *darr* to the *mirasis*. During the British period, the rate was Rs. 11 per *darr,* so he has to pay 84 multiplied by that was Rs. 924, or nearly 60 guineas as entrance fee. His descendants remain *darr-walas*, but his agnates do not acquire the privilege. At a son's wedding in the family, a *darr-wala* has to pay a fee of not less than 4 annas to each *darr* for its *mirasi*. The *darr-walas* do not as a rule give daughters in marriage to those who do not possess equal social standing. The real origin of this system does not appear to be known, but it has some resemblances to the Rajput *chhat* and *makan*, and perhaps more to the lodges of the *Bara Sadat*. The social observances of the Gujars are ordinarily those of the other Hindus or Muhammadans, as the case may be among whom they live, but one or two special customs are to be noted. In Delhi, a child is betrothed in infancy by the barber and Brahmin jointly, but he is not married till the age of 10 or 12. Prior to the wedding one or the other on the bride's part go to the boy's house with the *lagan* to discuss the arrangements for the wedding. Half the dues are paid to both these functionaries at betrothal and the other half at the *lagan*, whereas Jats pay the whole at betrothal.

Ghirthas Customs

The *Ghirthas* are said to be of Rajput origin by mixed marriages or illegitimate intercourse. They are essentially agricultural, and the proverb says :- "As the rice bends in the ear, the Ghirth lifts his head." Their social position is low. "You can no more make a saint of a Ghirth than expect chastity of a buffalo," and they practise widow marriage, for "You can't make a Ghirthni a widow, any more than you can turn a hill buffalo into a barren cow." In Hoshiarpur, *Ghirthas* are called *Bathi*. In Uttar Pradesh, Madhya Pradesh and Bihar they are called *Kurmi*. *Chang* is the Punjabi name, and *Ghirth* the Pahari word. The *Ghirthas* have a few large sub-divisions. The eight largest are the *Kandal, Bhardwaj, Pathari, Chhabru, Reru, Badial, Chhora and Bhattu*. *Bhardwaj* (a Brahminical gotra), is also found as an al (sect) among the Brahmans of Chamba. Chhabru is found only in Hoshiarpur, and Chhora and Bhattu only in Kangra. The others occur in both Districts. But the Ghirthas say that they have a large number of *als* or sects - 360 in all. A great part of these are named after villages. Others are named after trades, occupations, etc. A very few are possibly totemistic in origin. Other exogamous sections (*gots*) are *Balaru, Banjara, Barol, Chakotra, Bhut, Dialu, Hangaria,*

Jalarich, Kathe, Narotra, Panjla, Panyau, Panyaria, Sakre, Sial, Thimbu, Thirku, etc., all of unknown derivation. In the Rajput hypergamous system, the Ghirth does not rank very high, for not till the seventh generation can his daughter become a queen (*Satwin pirhi Ghirthni ki dhi Rani hojali*), whereas the Rathi's daughter can attain the position in four generations and even the Kanet's reaches it in five. But the Rajahs could promote a Ghirth to be a Rathi, as Sir James Lyall records, in his Kangra seltlement Reports.

The following accounts of the Ghirth social observances are given as typical of the usages among all the Hindu castes of the Kangra Hills and not as peculiarly characteristic of the Ghirths. They resemble generally those in vogue among the Gaddis of Kangra, but the local variations appear to be endless.

In betrothal the father, mother to uncle, if alive, will tell the youth to arrange to marry such and such a girl. If these are not alive, he chooses himself; otherwise he retains passive throughout the arrangements. The father then finds a go-between who goes to the girl's parents and makes the proposal to them. If they accept, a day is arranged for the ceremony of betrothal. On this day, the *rubaris* conducts the boy's father or other guardian, the boy does not go as a rule to the girl's house. Provided the father has an infirmity renderus the son's assistances necessary, otherwise the son will not accompany him. He will generally accompany any other guardian. If the boy goes too, he is allowed to play at the girl's parents' house, if the Brahmins decide the occasion favourable otherwise he must stay in some other house. The boy's Brahmin may be one of the party. They make it a point to arrive during the particular watch hour of the particular day which the Brahmin has found to be propitious. He leads the way in followed by the father and relatives. The others stay in the enclosure outside. The things are put down and a rupee in silver and a half anna bit in copper are placed by the boy's father. This is placed of on the freshly plastered chankah. At the same time, the girl's parents put down a tray consisting of a little jaggery of their own. The boy's father puts a half *anna* in this and tastes the *gur*. He puts a pice in the *lota* of water (*garwi*) before the shrine, touches his forehead and bends down to Ganesh, the girl's Brahmin worshipping all the time in the usual way. The girl's mother puts the jewellry on the girl, and the ceremony is over. The girl's parents take all the things brought, including the rupee and pice, into shrine in the tray, out of which the girl's mother takes them, and not the girl's father as it is the mother's right.

There is a feast next morning and pice are distributed to the poor, and a few *annas* to the Brahmin, the *dai* of the girl's family and the local watchman. A few pice are also given to the girl's sisters, if any, and her other female relations. The boy's family Brahmin settles the day. About 20 days before the day is fixed, the father takes him to the house of the girl's parents, where there is a consultation between him and their Brahmin as to whether the day fixed is also auspicious for the father, paternal uncle and brother of the boy and girl respectively.

The girl's father puts some rice and *gur* and a few blades of *drub* grass and two pice, and the boy's father also one anna in copper, into a tray. These are divided by the two Brahmins who throw out the grass. In the tray the girl's mother also puts the red paste, for making the *tika* on the forehead which is used for all religious occasions, needing vermilion. The girl's Brahmin puts the *tika* on the boy's father's forehead and then on the foreheads of a few of the bystanders. Both families then make their preparations and summon their friends and relations to the wedding. On the day the boy's party, which always includes the Brahmin and the family barber, goes to the girl's house, the boy being carried in a *palki* and musicians accompanying. The boy is dressed in red with a fringe of silk tassels (*sehra*) bound round his turban and hanging in front of his face. He has been washed and dressed by the barber before starting. The *sehra* and a pair of shoes and a coat are given to him by the boy's maternal uncle.

When the party reaches the girl's house, they all wait outside until the girl's Brahmin announces that the auspicious moment (the conjunction of two stars, '*Lagan*') has arrived. The boy and his Brahmin with the barber and a friend who has the custody of the money for current expenditure go inside. The *chaukah* with the *diwa dera* is ready. The friend puts a rupee and half *anna* in the shrine while the Brahmins mutter a few words. The girl's mother takes the rupee and half *anna*. A blanket is spread inside the outer room. The boy and girl sit facing each other on it with the boy's barber supporting him and the girl's barber's wife supporting her, and the respective Brahmins facing each other on the two other sides. Both recite *mantras*. The barber's wife puts the boy's cloak over the pair and the barber lifts the *sehra* from his face and the barber's wife her cloak from the girl's, so that they can see each other.

The boy takes the ring off the little finger of his right hand and puts it on the little finger of the girl's right hand. The cloak over the pair is removed and the girl's face hidden again. Some *gur* mixed with *ghee* is put by the girl's mother in a tray and the boy takes some, after which the barber's wife gives some to the girl. The friend with money bag puts two pice into the tray. These are taken by the barber's wife. The boy comes out to his relations and the girl goes into the inner room among the women. After all have refreshed themselves, four sticks with small cross-sticks at the top are fixed in the ground in the enclosure to form a small square in which 5 or 6 can sit. The barber's wife makes a figure (chaukah) with flour on the ground and a small heap of grain at each of the two points marked with a cross, and these heaps are covered with baskets.

The boy sits on one basket, and the girl on the other supported by their Brahmins, the barber and his wife, respectively, the Brahmins being further off than the barber and his wife. A fire is lit at the point marked with a double cross. The Brahmins put rice soaked in water and *ghee* on the fire. The girl's mother brings a tray containing a little rice and a *lota* filled with water and puts them down by her Brahmin in worship. He throws soaked rice over them and gives them to the boy's Brahmin who puts them in front of the boy. The girl's mother or father then brings another tray with a little rice in it and an empty basket and puts them down by the girl's Brahmin, and the girl's parents put into the tray whatever jewellery they intend to give to their daughter, and the Brahmin hands the tray to the boy's Brahmin, who puts the jewellery down in front of the boy and returns the tray to the girl's Brahmin. Friends and relations are then called to bring their presents, and they put money in the tray, which is then offered to the girl by her Brahmin. The girl takes out as much as she can with two hands, and this is handed over to the boy's Brahmin. The remainder in the tray belongs to the girl's parents. Similarly, presents of cloth are put in the basket and these belong to the girl's parents. Next morning the barber and barber's wife again show the couple's faces to each other under the cloak as before; but this time, they are sitting on the two baskets, and the girl has all the jewellery on. The boy puts another ring on the girl's finger. They separate again as before and the ceremonies are over. In the evening, the girl will be taken off in a *palki*, the boy preceding her in his *palki*.

After this ceremony is over, he takes with him curd or Dahi in a clay vessel (*dehali*), grain, *gur* and clothes for the girl, and two rupees two pice in cash (and jewels, if rich enough); and if a price for the girl has been agreed upon, they take that too. When they get to the house they find a *ghara* of water and an oil-lamp and a vessel containing a little *gur* and *ghee* in the girl's parent's house, and her parents waiting for them, but not the girl herself. They put down the grain, *gur* and *dahi*, rupees and pice, and clothes and jewels by the water in a wicker basket put ready for them, and no one speaks a word. Square mats made of sugarcane stalks are placed for the deputation. When they have set down the grain, etc., the boy's party bows with joined hands to the lamp and water-vessel, and dipping their fingers into the *gur* and *ghee* put them in their mouths. Then the boy's party greets the girl's party, and then all sit down for the first time. Then the go-between takes the rupees and pice and clothes to the girl who is with the women in another room, gives the money to her, and gets down the clothes. Then the *rubaru* comes back, and receiving the girl's price from the boy's father, gives it to the girl's father. Then the boy's father gives pice to the girl's party's *kamins*, including, the barber, the *purohita* (family Brahmin) and the watchman. The boy's party stays till night, when the girl's party entertains it with a meal. Then the girl's mother calls in other women of the village, and they sing and the boy's father gives them pice. Next day, the boy's party having breakfasted return home. From this time until the wedding, which in the case of a virgin is called *biah*, the boy's father sends once a year rice or maize, butter, *gur* and clothes for the girl. The person who brings these gifts is entertained at night by the girl's parents and goes away the next day. The date of the wedding is arranged by the girl's father. It may take place when the girl is seven years old. There is no limit of age.

Betrothal among the Churahis

Churahi is the generic name for the people of the *Churah wizarat*, in Chamba in Himachal, who include Brahmins, Rajputs, Thakurs, Rathis, and the low castes like Halis, Kolis, Sippis, Barwalas, Lohars, Chamars, Dumnas, Riharas, Chanals and Meghs, etc. The low castes are all endogamous. Tradition makes the Thakurs descendants of the old Ranas, or petty chieftains, who held Chamba, prior to the foundation of the State by the Rajahs, and the Halis, its oldest inhabitants. It also makes the Brahmins immigrants from Brahmins and the Rajputs from the plains; but the Rathis preceded these two castes, having been expelled from the Dugar country by Gugga Chauhan - a curious legend.

The adult, and young women are allowed every license before marriage. Matrimonial alliances three degrees on either side, counting from the grandparents, are avoided, but otherwise there are few restrictions, Brahmins intermarrying with Rathis, by both forms of marriage, and also with Rajputs and Thakurs. Polyandry is not recognized, but polygamy is, and the first or head wife or *bari lari* is given some money when a second wife is admitted into the house. This fee is called *jethwagh*.

The *Churahi* observances at betrothal are simple. The initiative is taken by the boy's side, and the binding rite consists in the boy's agents placing eight coins, in the plates used for entertaining the bride's *rubarus* or representatives, and giving some cash for ornaments to the girl. Marriage is of three kinds. In the superior form, called *janai*, the rites observed are as follows: Some six months before the wedding, the boy's father or brother goes to the girl's house with one or two friends and gives her father some money and a goat as his *lag*. Some money is also given to the bride to buy ornaments, and this is called *bundha dena*. If the parents agree, an auspicious day is fixed for the wedding, and a day before it, two messengers (*dhamu*) from the bride's house come to fetch the boy, who worships the family *deva* or *devi*. Next day, accompanied by a few friends and one of the *dhamu,* he goes to the bride's house. One of the boy's menial *Halis* accompanies him, carrying the *badhai,* a present of two *manis* of grain, to her father. This Hali is called *putriar.*

On his arrival at the entrance, the boy worships the *kumbh* (a vessel full of water); throwing two copper coins into it and then seating himself on a blanket placed near the wall. The bride's sister now has a mimic fight stretched with him and does not let him sit down till he has paid her two *annas*. This perquisite is called *bhisk*. She then fetches the bride and seats her by the boy whose future brother-in-law brings a vessel of boiled rice which he and the boy's brother scatter over the floor. This rite is called *bhat chingana*. The pair are then seated, as are the guests, and a feast with songs and dancing follows. The bride's dowry called *suaj* is then given to the bride by her parents.

In the afternoon, the boy's party returns to his house with two or three of the girl's friends, and the bride herself and other men and women of the bride's party. Before leaving the threshold of the bride's house, the ceremony of *arti* is performed, a lighted lamp being waved four times round the head of the pair by a priest, who recites verses from the *Suklamber* and *Deo Lila*. At the boy's house this performance is repeated, and the *kumbh* worshipped by the bride and bridegroom at the door.

Then the boy's mother lifts up the bride's veil and presents her with a rupee or half a rupee according to her economic position. This is called *ghundu khara karna.* After this, a feast is eaten and another feast given on the following day, and songs and dances performed. The binding portion of the ceremony is when *arti* is waved round the couple's heads at the boy's house. At his wedding the boy wears a high peaked cap like a Geddi's, but not a *sehra.* Within a month after the marriage, the married pair pay a visit to the wife's parents and make them a small present. This observance is called *har-phera*. Among them, widow remarriage is recognised. Formerly the widow was obliged to marry one of the deceased husband's brothers,but now this is not the practice. She can choose her own husband within her own caste or sub-caste. This union is solemnized by an inferior form of marriage called *sargudhi*. There are no *dhamu*, and the bridegroom simply goes to the woman's house with his *putriar* and brother. The *bandha* is given as at a regular wedding, but *arti* is not performed, and there is less feasting and the cost is much less. The binding ceremony in this form is when an ornament is put on her, usually a nose-ring. Among the *Churahis* quiet form of *sargudhi* marriage is called *garib chara*. The *lag*, etc., are all rendered as in the other form, but on an auspicious day, the bridegroom accompanied by his sister simply goes to the bride's house, and at the entrance worships the *kumbh.* He then seats himself on the blanket in the usual way, and the girl's father proceeds to the boy's house where the *kumbh* is again touched. This second worship of the *kumbh* makes the marriage binding.

The third and lowest form of marriage is the *bandha luana* in which a widow, who is to marry her husband's brother, is married to him on the *kiria* day, i.e., 7th to the 11th or 13th day following the first husband's death. She puts aside her late husband's ornaments and puts on his brother's, in token that she accepts him. A he-goat is sacrificed at home to the *manes* of the deceased husband and a small feast usually given. The widow's parents need not attend, but they are entitld to a *lag,* called *bakra*, as being the price of a goat.

If the widow wishes to marry a stranger, he must pay the *bakra* of one rupee, and Re. 1-8 or Rs. 3 as *chadyali* to her parents. An auspicious day after the *kiria karm* period is ascertained from a *jotshi*, or priest and the ornaments changed as described above. However, when a man who elopes with a girl can, after a certain interval, open negotiations with her father, and if he assents, pay him some money and a goat as compensation. This observance is termed *lag rit* that operates as a valid marriage.

Custom of Gharjawantri

The custom of *gharjawantri* or service in lieu of a bride-price payment for a wife, is common among all caste in the states of Himachal Pradesh, especially in the Churah and Sadr *wizarats*. The term of service is usually three or seven years, and the marriage may take place at any time if the girl's father is agreeable. A husband may divorce his wife, if he cannot get on with her. The divorce is complete if the husband receives back his ornaments and says; "I have divorced you, *Rajah ki durohi*," i.e., on the Rajah's oath. The husband also breaks a stick in her presence. Divorced wives can remarry if they like. In inheritance and succession all sons, even bastards, if recognized by the father, succeed on equal terms, but the eldest son gets the best field as his *jethwagh*; the second a special implement, sickle, sword or axe as his *hathiar*, while the third gets the family house as his *mulwaher*. The son (*rand put*) or daughter (*rand dhia*) of a widow born in her husband's house has all the rights of the deceased husband's own children. It is, however, essential that the widow should continue to live in her husband's house and the child be begotten therein.

Betrothal Among Chuhras

For purpose of a betrothal among the *Chuhras* the *lagi*, the marriage functionary and go-between, go to the house of the boy's parents, taking with him sugar and dates for the family members. He states the purpose of his visit, and there is placed before him five or ten or more rupees, of which he takes one and goes. If the people are very poor, they intimate to the *lagi* how much he should take out of the heap. Returning to the house of the girl's parents he makes his report, describing the boy, his prospects, circumstances, and so on. A *lagi* now goes from the boy's residence, carrying clothes and jewels for the girl. He himself is presented with a *pagri* or turban and songs are sung by the family woman. The binding portion of the ceremonies is where the turban is given to the *lagi* before witnesses.

Later on, in two, three, four, or five years, the girl's parents send the *lagi* to say that it is time for the marriage. If the parents of the boy find it convenient, they declare that they are ready, and instruct the *lagi* to ask the other house to send a *nishan*, *bahcha*, *bahara*, which is a present of three garments, one to the *mirasi*, one to the *nai*, and the third to the *chuhra* who lights the fire. There is *gur* also in the basket containing the clothes, and this is distributed to the singing girls and others. The *lagi* receives a rupee or two, and goes back with the news that the *bahocha* has been accepted. Then a *triwar*, a present of seven garments, is prepared, and sent from the girl's residence, a white *phulkari* or embroidered shawl, a *chob* or *chop* (a red cotton shawl with a silk embroidered edge), a *choli* or bodice, a *kurta* (jacket), a *dariai* (narrow silk cloth), a *lungi* or *saya* (a check cloth or petticoat), two *pagris* or turbans and one *chadar*, or sheet or shawl. The jacket has a gold button, *bira*, and three silver ones called *allian*, and *gota*, or gold and silver lace, with the figure of a man embroidered on the right breast or shoulder. This present is sent to the boy's residence, where the garments are spread out on a bed to give the inmates and friends an opportunity of seeing them.

The *lagi* takes with him also *gur*, *patasse* (sweets), and a rupee as *ropna*, which he gives to the bridegroom. This *ropna* may be seven dried dates, and other things. The boy's hands are dyed with *mehndi* (henna) to signify joy. Again, rupees are placed before the *lagi*, of which he takes as many as he has been instructed to take. He then says that such and such a day has been fixed for the wedding and goes back to tell the bride's parents that the day is fixed. On this occasion, songs are sung by the boy's sister and mother. Eight or nine days before the wedding, they have what they call *rasaipana*, that is, they take *ghungnian* (wheat roasted in the husk) to the quantity of five or six *paropi*, which they put in the boy's lap. This he distributes with *gur* to his friends, of the same age as he is, seated on a basket. Wheat is distributed to the other friends, perhaps as much as four or five maunds, with *gur*. The boy is anointed with oil as many times as there are days before the marriage, and a song is sung by his friends.

The *nai* or barber anoints the bridegroom to make him sweet. The ointment is made of the flour of wheat and barley, *kachur*, *khardal* (white mustard), *chaihal charila* (a scent), and oil. This preparation is called *batna*. When the boy is taken off the basket, they bind a *gana* (ornament) or *kangna* (bracelet) on his wrist, which consists of an iron ring, a *cowrie*, and a *manka* (string) of *kanch* (glass) beads. They put a knife into his hand at the same time. All this is to keep off the evil spirits. The same operation is performed on the girl by her friends; only she puts on a *kangni* (wrist ornament) or *churi* (bracelet of iron), instead of taking a knife in her hand. Betrothal takes place at any time from five years of age and upward, the consent of the parents only being necessary. If the betrothal is cancelled, the *panch* arranges the amount to be repaid, and recovers it.

Rule of Endogamy

The *Chuhras* do not marry within their own section, but they take wives from all the other divisions. Marriage with a wife's sister is permitted after the death of the wife. Marriage with the wife's mother, or wife's aunt is not allowed. Two wives are allowed; the former of whom is considered the head, and has peculiar rights and privileges. Both wives live together in the same house. Marriage takes place before puberty even when the girl is about 7 or 8, and even 5 years of age. Marriages are arranged by the *nai* (barber), the *chhimba* (washerman), and the *mirasi* (village bard and geneologist). The consent of the parents is necessary in all cases, except when the woman is a widow, or independent of her parents. Girls are never asked whom they will marry, or if they are willing to marry. They would not give an expression of their wishes, as they say, *sharm ke mare*, for shame. There is no freedom of choice in the case of minor spouses marrying.

The bride-price is paid by the bridegroom's family, the amount of it being settled by the two contracting parties. The bride becomes the bridegroom's property after marriage. An engagement to marry may be broken off in the case of a defect or blemish in either the man or the woman, and divorce may be obtained after marriage by a regular 'writing of document for divorce'. Divorced women may marry again. Children of different mothers inherit on equal terms, and all assume the father's section. Widows remarry, but they have no price. The widow of an elder brother may marry a younger brother, and the widow of a younger brother may marry an elder brother. A widow marrying out of her husband's family takes away her children along with her.

Four *got* rule of Betrothal

Like the Khatris, the Punjabi Brahmins profess to follow the usual 'four-*got*' rule in marriage, but, precisely like the Dhaighar Khatris, the *Zat-wale* Brahmins avoid only their own section and the mother's relations. The *Bans-puj* are an exception. The *Asht-bans* obtain wives from them, but if a father has taken a *Bans-puj* wife, the son may not, he must marry an *Asht-bans* or lose status. That is to say, the *Asht-bans* may only stoop to inter-marriage with the *Bans-puj* in alternate generations. Similarly, the 'four-*got'* rule is relaxed in other cases. Thus, the *Kanchan-Kamal* section of Hoshiarpur are also called *Suraj Doaj,* (Sun-worshippers). Their ancestor came from Delhi as a *qanungo* at Haryana; hence, they are called qanungos. These Brahmins can marry in the *nanka got*, avoiding only the father's *got*. They do not take any *dan* (charity) and may either take service or engage in trade or cultivation. If anyone of them takes to receiving charity, he is considered an outcast and they do not intermarry with him.

Among the *Bunjahi Brahmins,* the age of betrothal is from 4-8 years and that of marriage from 8-12 years. It is, however, impossible to lay down any universal rules, as generally speaking, the ages of betrothal marriage depend upon the economic status of each family within the group, as is the case among the Khatris.

Aversion to Hypergamy

It will be seen how the lower subgroups of the Khatris have endeavoured to shake off the yoke of the higher in matrimonial matters. A similar revolt against the position of the Dhaighar occurred amongst the Sarsut Brahmins. About 116 years ago, says the account received from Amritsar, the Lahoria Dhaighar used to take daughters from the *Panj-zat*; but owing to the ill- treatment meted out to the girls by the Dhaighar, they resolved to discontinue the custom, and the three other groups of the *Zat-wale* followed suit, while the remaining *Bunjahis* continued to give wives to the *Zat-wale*, but no longer received them in return. The result was that the *Bunjahis* could not obtain wives and many families died out, so it was resolved by the *Bunjahis* that they should for the future break off all connection with *Zat-wale*, unless any of the latter should agree to give them daughters in return. This was prior to *Sambat* 1932 when a second meeting of the caste elders at Amritsar renewed the contract. Notably in both castes the proceedings of these conferences were conducted in a formal manner, written agreements being drawn up, and the families which agreed to the demands put forward being entered in a register from time to time.

Like the Khatris, the Brahmins have territorial sub-caste groups, but these groups do not usually correspond with the territorial groups of the former. For example, the Brahmins of the Murree Hills are divided into two sub-castes - *Paharia* and *Dhakochi* who do not intermarry or eat together. The Dugri Brahmins correspond to the Dugri Khatris of the Sialkot, sub-montane, but they are said, on the one hand, to give daughters to the *Sarsut*, and, on the other hand, to intermarry with the *Batehru* group of Brahmins in Kangra. Allusions have been already made to the *Pachhada* and to the *Lahoria*, terms which seem to be applied exclusively to the five highest sections who serve the Dhaighar Khatris.

Rites of Betrothal Among the Baurias

Betrothal is not specially initiated by either side, but as soon as the negotiations have reached a certain stage the girl's father, his Brahmin or *nai* goes with the *tika* and even the poorest man confirms the agreement by presenting a rupee to the boy. Well-to-do people give him a camel or gold ear-rings. *Bauria* men are, in their youth, sometimes branded. Most of their women are tattooed in one or more places on the face, viz, near the outer corners of the eyes, at the inner corner of the left eye, on the left cheek and on the chin; hence *Bauria* women are easily recognizable. *Baurias* do not marry within their own *got* or *sept*, and it is said that the bridegroom must not be younger than the bride, and that a blind or one-eye'd man must espouse a blind or one-eye'd woman! In some tribes, fair women are only married to fair men, and the blackskinned, which form the majority, mate with one another. The girl's father intimates the date fixed for her wedding by sending a *saha chitthi* written in Sanskrit, and on the day fixed for the wedding, party goes to the girl's house. The bridegroom wears the *sehra* and his forehead is smeared with *haldi* or turmeric. The ceremonies are all in essence the same as those observed by the Rajputs, except that no *khera* is named, for the simple reason that the *Baurias* have no fixed abodes.

Weddings are, however, not solemnised by sending the *patka* or *katar* in lieu of the bridegroom. *Bauria* brides wear a necklace made of horse hair on which are threaded gold and silver beads. This is called *sohag sutra* and it is worn till the husband's death, when it is burnt with his corpse. On a man's death, his elder and then his younger brother have the first claim to his widow's hand. Failing such near kinsmen, a stranger may espouse her on payment of *pichha*, a sum of bride price assessed by the *panches* and paid by the new husband to the nearest agnate of the deceased's father.

Among the castemen, co-habitation with a woman of another caste is punished through not allowing the offender to smoke with brotherhood, and the woman is regarded as a *suret* and her children as *suretwal* even though she be a pure Rajput by caste. Infidelity on a wife's part is purged away by pressing a red hot iron into her tongue.

Shastric Injunction on Betrothal and Marriage

The relatives who can give a binding promise of betrothal are:the father, paternal grandfather, brother, a *sakulya*, lastly the mother. But if any one of these disregard the *prikrati* or *kulachar* (family custom), he loses his or her privilege and it devolves on the next in order. For example, if the father is inclined to sell his daughter, the right to betroth devolves on the grandfather, and so on. Betrothal being governed by various considerations, it is no hardship on a boy or girl to betroth them in infancy. The guardian of the girl should not only see the boy's body, but have regard to his conduct, family, economic means, education and repute. He should choose one whose age is double that of the girl, but not treble her age or more. The boy should be sound in body and in mind, and his family should have no hereditary disease. He should not live too far away, be constantly engaged in warm or an ascetic, and, apart from these general considerations, he should have the following particular qualifications: "Broad or deep should be his chest, face and forehead, his navel, voice and *satya* (inherent power). Short his throat, back, male organ and legs. Fine (*sukhsham*) his hair, nail, teeth, flesh and the joints of his fingers. Long the distances between his eyebrows and his breasts, his arms, his nostrils and his chin. Red should be his palate and tongue, the soles of his feet and the palms of his hands, and both the corner of each eye."

Numerous other points of astrology have also to be considered. Thus, a boy with no lines, or too many, in his hand will be poor and short- lived. Lastly, horoscopes have to be consulted, and it is important that neither party should have been born in the *mangal ras*, or house of Mars, because, if so, his or her mate is doomed to an early death.

On the other hand, the girl should be *aspinda*, i.e., not related to the boy within the following degrees. The *got* of the maternal grandfather is also sometimes avoided.

The bride should be a virgin, beautiful, young and free from disease. She should also have a brother, for otherwise, according to the marriage contract, her first-born son would have to be given to her father, in order that he might become his maternal grandfather's heir. Various other qualifications are prescribed; health, good repute, a swan like gait, fine teeth and hair, delicate limbs and soft red-soled feet without prominent joints. Her fingers and toes should be separated, and the palm of her hand shaped like a lotus for luck. Her shape should be fish like, and on the soles of her feet there should be the marks of a goad and barley corns. Her knees should be round, her legs are free from hair, her forehead broad and prominent, the navel deep, with three deep wrinkles in the abdomen, the nipples round and hard, the throat like a lion's, the lips as red as a *trinha* fruit, the voice soft like a cuckoo's, the nostrils evenly matched, and the eye like a lotus. Lastly, her little toes should not touch the ground, lest she become a widow; the second toe should not project beyond the big toe, lest her character be lost, and her legs should not to be long and thin, for that, too, is an omen of widowhood. Hair on the legs presages misfortune, and a prominent abdomen lasting sickness and sterility. Her eyes should not be reddish brown or like those of a cat, for the latter denotes easy virtue. Hair on the nipples will bring misfortune on her husband. Dry hair and everted lips show a quarrelsome temper, and so on.

Scriptures classify women into four groups Padmani, Chitarni, Sankhani and Hastni. The complexion should be fair, the face and brow broad, the chin round, the nose thin and aquiline, the eyes black and (one regrets to say) lustful. The hair, eyebrows and eyelashes should all be long and black, the teeth white and the lips red: the charms of rosy cheeks are enhanced by a black or a green mole; the neck should be long, the fingers tapering and the waist slim.

When all these points have been investigated and the betrothal decided on, an auspicious day is fixed for its celebration which should not take place in the month of *Poh*, *Katik* or *Chet*, when Venus and Jupiter are on the wane, during the *shradhas,* annual or general, *dwitik* (intercalated month), or the *anatra,* when Venus and Jupiter are in the same *ras*, and so on. Sundays, Tuesdays and Saturdays are also to be avoided. Betrothal was generally performed during the favourable *Nakshatras* or asterisms.

On the day fixed for the ceremony, the boy's party goes to the girl's house and both parties are seated, while Brahmins recite the *manghla-charan* or benedictory prayers, and Shri Ganeshji is worshipped in a brass dish called as *thal*; rice is *sprinkled* on Ganeshji and the boy's party, and sometimes red-coloured water is also sprinkled over them. The girl's guardian then announces that the girl, daughter of so-and-so, is betrothed to the son of so-and-so. This is called the *wakkdan*, or 'the dan or gift by word of mouth,' and is the essence of the betrothal contract. It is now irrevocable, and there is a very strong feeling against breaking it among the Hindus.

When once the promise has passed the lips of the girl's father, it can only be withdrawn for grave causes. A Sanskrit adage says : *Sakrit pradiyate kanya*, or 'a girl is given but once.' Formerly, in respectable families, a betrothed girl whose fiance had died could not be married, and if such a marriage occurred, it brought social discredit on the family.

Then a *janeo*, or sacred thread, fruit, flowers and some clothes are given to the boy by the girl's brother or Brahmins. The girl's Brahmin applies the *tilak* to the boy and his kinsmen. The boy's parents and kinsmen make gifts to Brahmins and distribute money among them, an observance called *nawan*. The boy is next taken to his father's house when a morsel of bread, butter, sugar and *khichri* is given to him. This rite is called *Grahin dena* (or gift of a morsel of bread).

The females also distribute *khichri* to the brotherhood, who, in return, give them presents. Till far into the night, songs are sung by the women. Betrothal thus effected creates a kind of relationship, so that if one of the parties to it dies, the other is counted impure for three days. In some families, *gur* and a rupee, five pieces of turmeric, some *supari* (betel- nut), rice and fruit are thrown into the laps of the boy's party at the betrothal. Taking money for a girl is strictly forbidden by the Hindu *Shastras*, and one who takes it goes to hell. A proverb says: *Kanjar te Qasai, chut nal chut watai* - meaning that low-caste men are divided into (a) Kanjars who prostitute their girls; (b) butchers, who kill them; and (c) those who exchange their persons.

Rite of Betrothal

Amongst the Hindus, betrothal is a sacrament, and is, as a rule, an indispensable preliminary to the marriage of a girl, though a woman once married cannot again be betrothed according to the ceremonies of a first betrothal. Betrothals are of three kinds: (1) *dharm* or *pun*, in which the girl is given by her parents as a quasi-religious offering to her future husband. (2) *watta satta* (exchange), in which two or more families exchange brides. (3) *Takke or takkian di pachar*, in parts of the south-west Punjab, in which a bride-price is more or less openly paid and demanded. Such a betrothal or the price paid for it, is said to be called *dambah* in Ludhiana. *Pun* betrothal is confined to the higher caste, and instances rarely occur among them of the intiative being taken by the boy's people.

The *dharm* or ritual form of betrothal is a religious rite. In it the initiative is almost invariably taken by the girl's parents. Thus, in Gurgaon, her father sends his family barber and priest to search for a suitable boy. When they have found one they return, and, if horoscopes are kept, compare those of the pair to see if they are in accord. If the girl's father approves of the match, he sends the two delegates again to the boy's house with the signs of betrothal called *tika* or *sikka.* If the boy's father approves of the match, he calls his kindred together and in their presence, the delegates place the tokens in the boy's lap, and some sweets into his mouth, simultaneously proclaiming the girl's name. The girl's barber or priest also makes a mark (*tika*) on the boy's forehead with his thumb. During the ceremony, the boy is seated on a wooden plank (*chauki* or *patri*) slightly raised off the ground, on which, after it has been swept and smeared with cow-dung, a square (*chaukah*) has been traced with flour. The signs of betrothal vary, but in the South-East Punjab, there is almost always a rupee, often a cocoanut and sometimes clothes. Elsewhere in Punjab, the cocoanut is replaced by dates, usually five in number, but often two or seven; thus in Gurdaspur, the girl's father sends seven nuts (*chhowara*), one or more rupees and some clothes as *a shagun* or conventional gift to the boy. These are made over to him by the *lagi* (a priest, a barber, or a bard) at his parents' house in the presence of his kinsmen, and in return he sends the girl a *shagun* of ornaments and clothes.

The rite of betrothal is quite distinctively religious. Although the boy's father and kinsmen take the initiative and go empty-handed to the girl's house. They say, they have come to arrange for the *pachar* (betrothal) of so-and-so *Chaudhri's* (notable's) son. The reply is that the girl's father will consider the proposal (*wichar karna*), and it appears to be etiquette for him to promise a reply in a week or a fortnight's time, when the boy's people again approach him. They are met by her father or guardian with his kinsmen and presented with *gur*, fruits or clothes, and the Brahmin, if present, performs the worship of Ganesh and recites the *gotrachar*. The *gur* and fruits are taken to the boy's house and distributed. This rite is held on an auspicious day and must be solemnized at the girl's father's shop or pleasure-house, but not at the house where his women-kin live, and after it the boy's father is called *putreta* and the girl's *dheta*, the relationship called *sain* or *senr,* henceforth existing between them. This relationship prevents their visiting each other or even eating together, while the future son-in-law or *jawatra* may not even speak to his father-in-law or *sohra*.

Thus, betrothal in Punjab is a solemn rite and the tie it creates is irrevocable, so much so that it can only be annulled owing to impotence or incurable disease, and even when the boy or girl is thought to be dying, the tie between the pair is solemnly cancelled by the following rite: Where the rite is called *pani pilawan* (i.e., giving water to drink), the boy is called to the girl's death-bed and made to stand by her pillow and drink some water. The girl also drinks, and then the boy says, 'Thou art my sister.' This, of course, dissolves the betrothal, but it is understood that if the patient recover, the tie will hold good. In the event of the boy's not arriving till she is dead, the girl's body is not burnt until he has looked upon her face, or if the body has to be burnt before his arrival, some cotton is smeared with blood from her forehead and thrown into his house. Every effort is, however, made to prevent the cotton being thus thrown into the house and a watch is kept over it, the belief being that, if the cotton is thrown in, it will bring ruin upon the dwelling. After four days, the blood-stained cotton cannot be thrown in and the house is safe.

Elsewhere in Punjab, a very similar ceremony called *mathe lagawan* is performed to cancel the betrothal. Thus, if the girl be at the point of death, the boy goes to her and standing by her death-bed gives her some sweets, saying *"han kaki mithai ghin"* meaning' dear sister, take this sweetmeat,' and she must reply "*lia bhirawa*", meaning 'brother, give it to me'.

This ritual cancels the betrothal, but if the sick child recovers and the parents of the couple agree to the renewal of the contract, the betrothal ceremonies are again performed by the parties concerned. The *mathe lagawan* must be done at the house of the sick child, but his or her parents do their utmost to prevent it as it brings bad-luck upon their family. If they knowingly permit it, no other *Kirar* will enter an alliance with them. Consequently, guards are posted at the door of the sick child's house to keep out the intruder who makes every effort to get in. Both sides resort to violence, so much so that sticks are sometimes used and serious affrays ensure. Disguise is even sometimes resorted to in order to obtain access to the sick child; for the betrothed to strike his or her forehead against the wall of the sick child's house. This knocking the wall, which is termed *Sawan*, must be performed within four days from the sick child's death, after which it is of no avail. If a child fails to perform the ritual of *mathe lagawan* or *sawan* he or she cannot secure a second betrothal, being regarded as ill-starred, but if the ceremony be duly performed he or she is considered purified, and can readily contract a second betrothal.

Betrothal by exchange is further divisible into three or more varieties, viz: (i) *amho samhana* or simple exchange; (ii) *treabanj* or three fold barter; (iii) *chobhanj* or fourfold, and so on. In all these, the parties concerned meet at one place by appointment and enter into the contract of giving the girls, one to the other, after which each girl's guardian gives *gur* or fruits to the guardian of the boy to whom his girl is betrothed. Then the Brahmin, if present, performs worship of Ganesh and recites the *gotrachar*. The *gur* or fruits are taken home and distributed. Exchange betrothal is called *amo same*, a term which is applied to direct, as opposed to *tarain vatni* or indirect exchange. In Ludhiana, betrothal by exchange is called *hatarh*. The exchange marriage *(batte ka biyah)* sometimes takes the form called *badhe ka biyah* in which a girl of, say, eighteen years of age is exchanged for one of five. In such a case, a kind of disparity fine (*badha*) has to be paid to the party giving the adult girl.

Among the *Gaddis* of Chamba in Himachal, marriage by exchange is called *bola*, and the first of the rites observed is called as *dharma-puna* betrothal. But when all the boy's people go to complete the alliance, a grindstone, pestle and sil (mortar) with three or five lumps of *gur*, *supari*, *bihan*, and *rolian* are placed before them, and the *purohita* taking the *supari* etc., in the fold of his garment puts them in the mortar, receiving a fee of money from the boy's father before grinding them. He then mentions the names of the betrothed pair, and pounds up the spices. Then the *supari* etc., is put in a dish with the *gur* broken into small pieces, and distributed among the guests, the boy's father first taking a piece. The elder members of the bride's family do not take any, as that would be contrary to etiquette. Then, the boy's father puts silver coins of one rupee four *annas* in the dish, and from this silver the girl's parents have an ornament made for her. She also presents herself before the boy's father and he gives her a rupee. The rest of the ceremony resembles that observed in a *dharma-puna* betrothal, but the coins put in the vessel come out of the boy's father's pocket. The whole rite is repeated in the other family's house, but not neccessarily on the same day. Tuesday, Friday and Saturday is an unlucky day for these auspicious performances.

In betrothal by purchase, the essential difference is that the initiative is taken by the boy's people who go to the girl's house and there make the bargain of the bride-price to be paid. Then the girl's parents send their *lagis* (or more usually one man, the *nai*) to the boy's house where the ordinary rites are gone through. In the north-eastern (Himalayan) corner of the Punjab, the initiative is usually taken by the boy's people. After certain preliminary negotiations, they go to the girl's house with their priest called as *purohita* to perform the rites. In a *Dharma-puna* betrothal, the girl's father gives the *purohita* some *dubh* grass, with at least four copper coins, which are to be handed over to the boy's father in token that he accepts the alliance. All remain for the night at the bride's house, and after a meal, her father gives eight copper coins to the boy's father. These he puts in his dish as a perquisite for the man who cleans it. The above are in vogue among the Gaddis of Chamba, but in the Churah sub-division of that state, the custom is for the boy's father or brother to place eight copper coins or a rupee in the dish from which he has eaten. This is called *juth,* and the act *juth dalana.* On the following day the betrothal contract is made.

In Kulu, among the higher castes, the *purohit* fixes a day for the rite and is then sent with one or two men. With a present of clothes, ornaments and money to the bride's house. There he makes the girl worship Ganesh, and she is then dressed in the clothes and *gur* or jaggery is distributed among the villagers or neighbours. In return, her parents send a sacred thread and a betel-nut for the bridegroom, in whose village also *gur* is distributed on the *purohita*'s return. Among the *Kanets*, the local god fixes the auspicious day for the rite, and on that day, the boy's father or brother with two companions, the clothes and ornaments goes to the bride's house. She puts them on and *gur* is then distributed without any worship of Ganesh.

The lower classes have the same rites, but among them the boy also goes to his father-in-law's house at the betrothal. When the initiative is not taken by the girl's father, it is fairly safe to assume that the parties are of low status or caste, and that the contract was not *pun*. Thus, among the *Chuhras*, the boy's father goes to the girl's house with a female kinsman, and is then feasted, giving her father two rupees. Next, the visitors are given an ordinary meal, and the girl's father gets another rupee. After this a blanket.

In Punjab and the people originating from Multan and Muzaffargarh, now in Pakistan, there is a similar custom called *subha,* which consists in the exchanging presents of sweets at festivals. Clothes and toys are also presented. These presents, too, are sometimes returned by the girl's parents. This custom is spreading, it is said, into Sirmur.

Very similar to the *subha* observance, yet distinct is an the observance called *gur* in Multan, it consists in sending *gur* (jaggery), fruit and vegetables with two rupees to the boy's father, (some time after the betrothal has been completed).

Muzaffargarh also appears to have some distinctive local customs in the *sag* or *wat walawan,* which consists in the girl's father sending the boy's a request for *sag* (vegetables). The request is complied with and fruit of any kind in season sent. After this, the fathers may have dealings with each other, a thing wholly forbidden to them before the observance. After it too comes the *watr sakh,* in which the girl's father sends the boy's fresh fruit or green stuff, in both cases the fruit etc., is distributed among relatives and neighbours. The betrothed spouses' fathers do not even salute each other when they meet, after the betrothal has once been effected, until the *Ram sat* observance has been duly performed. For this a lucky day is chosen, and then the girl's father with some of his kinsmen takes some sweets and money in cash to the boy's home, where he finds the latter's kinsmen also assembled. He presents the boy's father with the sweets etc., and salutes him, saying '*Ram-Ram*'. After this, the two fathers may salute each other if they meet. In other parts of Punjab, some time after the betrothal a ritual called *piridas* is in vogue. The boy's kinsmen with some of his kinswomen visit the girl's home where they receive sweet stuff or some cash each, and the women of the boy's party are seated on a *piri.*

Betrothal among Hindus in large towns is arranged by the womenfolk, the mother, grandmother or some other relative of the boy visiting the girl's mother till she gives her consent or refusal. Betrothal is formally announced by the girl's parents sending a lump of *gur* or jaggery with a rupee to the boy's. In well-to-do families, this ceremony is called *shagun,* 13 to 25 rupees with 100 *kuads* (sugarcandy) are sent.

In the case of a *maju* (a widower) of good social status and well-to-do, the amount often rises to Rs. 500 or even Rs.1000. After the betrothal comes the *pair pand* (to put in one's feet) ceremony. At this the girl's people send as many as 51 trays of *laddu, luchi* and other sweets to the boy's parents, followed on the same day by a formal visit paid by the women of the boy's family (neighbours and friends are also invited, but no males) to the girl's. These women are served with light refreshments and among well-to-do families, the boy's kinswomen get a cup of milk with a rupee each. The boy's mother takes the girl in her lap and *sarwarna* of Re.1-4-0 is done. When the boy's party have left, the girl's in turn goes to his house. Where the girl's mother takes the boy in her lap and gives him a *mohar* or a half *mohar*. One rupee each is given to all the other relatives of the boy, but his father and grandfather get a whole or half a *mohar* according to the status of the family. The girl's party are not served with refreshments. The boy's parents then celebrate the *bhaji*.

In Karnal, betrothal is called *nata;* the ceremony is called *sagai.* It generally takes place in infancy. When the father of a girl wishes to betrothe her he makes inquiry for a marriageable boy of good family, the village barber acting the part of go-between. If matters are satisfactory, he sends the barber to the boy's village, who puts either a ring or one rupee into the boy's hand. This is called *ropna* and if the boy's father returns Re.1-4, called *bidaigi,* to the barber to take to the girl's father, he hereby accepts the offer and clinches the engagement. This engagement is not a necessary preliminary of betrothal; and is most customary among castes, such as the Rajputs, who marry at a comparatively late age, and who do not wish to go to the expense of a formal betrothal so long beforehand, for fear that one of the children should die and the money be wasted.

Among the Gujars, on the other hand, the above ceremony constitutes betrothal; but the *taka* is affixed at the time by the Brahmin. It is possible for the proposal to come from the boy's side, in which case he sends his sister's necklace; and if the girl keeps it, his proposal is accepted. But this is only done when the families are already acquainted. When it is decided to procced to the betrothal (*sagai)*, the barber and Brahmin are sent with the *pach-narial;* or one rupee which has been all night in the milk which is set for butter, a loin-cloth *(pich)* and a cocoanut or *narial.* The boy is seated in a chair before the relatives, the Brahmin puts the *tika* or mark on the boy's forehead and the other things into his lap, and *gur* jaggery is divided by the boy's father, who takes hold of the hand of each near relation in turn and puts some *gur* into it. The boy's father then gives Re.1-4 to the Brahmin and double the amount to the barber. This is called *nai* or *lag,* and must be brought back to the girl's father; and when so brough back completes the betrothal. Ordinarily no relation of the girl *may* take any part in the embassy *(lags)* of betrothal ; but Brahmins send the girl's brother-in-law or relation by marriage. Exchange of betrothals between two families *(santa nata)* is considered very disgraceful; and if done at all, is done by a tripartite betrothal, *a* betrothing with *B,B* with *C,* and *C* with *A.*

Among the *Jats,* if the boy dies, his father has a right to claim the girl for his other son, or, in default of another any male relation in that degree. If the girl dies, her family has no claim. Jats marry at about 5 or 7 years; Rors and Gujars at 12 to 14 ; Rajputs at 15,16 or even older. The prohibited degrees are thus described : Every *gens* (*got*) is exogamous that is, that while every man *must* marry into his own tribe, no man can marry into his own *gens.*

But this is by no means the only limitation imposed upon inter-marriage. In the first place, no man can marry into a family, of whatever gens it may be, that is settled in his own village or in any village immediately adjoining his own. The strength of this custom is shown by the virtue that the speaker could not marry into a 'family of his own *gens,* even if it lived 100 miles off'. The prohibition is based upon *simjor ki biradiri,* or the relationship founded upon a common boundary, and is clearly a survival from the time of marriage by capture. This limitation is further extended by the Rajputs, so that no man can marry into any family living in the *thapa* into any family of which his father, grandfather, or great-grandfather were married. Thus, if a Mundhar Rajput married a Chauhan Rajput of *thapa* Jundla, his own grandson, and great-grandson would not be able to marry any Chauhan of any village in the Jundla *thapa.* But beyond this, and the prohibition against marrying within the *gens,* the Rajputs have no further limitations on inter-marriage. Among the other castes, the *thapa* is not excluded; but no man can marry into any family of the *gens* to which his mother or his father's mother belongs, wherever these gens may be found.

The Gujars, however, who are generally lax in their rules, often only exclude such persons of these *gens* as live in the individual village from which the relation in question came. In some parts of Ambala, the people are beginning to add the grandmother's *gens,* or even to substitute it for the father's mother's *gens*; and this may perhaps be a last stage of the change from relationship through women to relationship through men.

Better Social and Family Status of Women

Christian women have, per individual choice, a role to play in the family economic activity, social functions and to a great extent in religious spheres, as weel as in political activity. Christian priesthood, which was till recently a male bastion universally, is no longer so with certain Christian denominations in Delhi. Women enjoy equal status within the Christian community, having, a role to play in the mechanism of social control, with decision making powers, engaging in economic activity also. Thus they may be contributing to the family income, irrespective of which they enjow a high esteem, perpectuated by religion, controlling the amily budget and expenditure. The cusoms pertain to the Christians in Delhi.

No Custom of Dowry or Bride-price

Among the north Indian Christians, *thali* and *ring* both are prevalent. The Christions do not practice dowry, but gift-giving on this occasion is common and it is given both in cash and kind. The rules of residence are guided by the Indian Christian Act. Which is quite rigid. It is only in exteme cases when there is absolute incompatibility, adultery and mental sickness that divorce is permitted. The Church of North India members regard divorce as the last resort and Catholics do not permit it at all. Rules regarding remarriage are quite liberal. In this regard men and women both have equal rights. Now the Catholics are not very rigid about divorce as they are also getting used to the idea of divorce. The Christians also have a patriarchal type of family.

The interpersonal relations with the family members are based on mutual affection and love and there are no avoidance and joking relationships. Rules of inheritance recognize male as coparcener and females are normally deprived. The Indian Christian Act also does not pay adequate attention to this fact.

The custom pertain to the Christians originating from Southern States in Haryana.

Social and Economic States Regulate Marital Alliances

The social differentiation helps to indicate status and regulates marriage alliances among the Punjab Christians. There is a tendency to het matrimonial allances with better-educated persons with non-agricultural occupations. There has been no change in the surnames, class names or titles of the converts to the Christianity. Some Christians in Punjab suffix Massey to their names. A few consider themselves of medium status. Though the community does not recognize *varna* system, it is conscious of its low status because they are the converts from the Hindu and sikh low castes. In spite oof this consciousness the caste is not pronounced in the community because most origingal converts are from lower castes in Punjab. It is generally recognized that the conversions have provided better status to them. And this is one reason why there has been no reconversions back to Hinuism under the post-independence reservation policy which provided benefits to the Scheduled Castes. Marriages are contracted at the community level and also generally at the Christian denomination level, yet inter-denomination marriages are also acceptable. They practice exogamy at village level. These marriages are contracted by negotiations or even by mutual consent, of the boy and girls which is generally asked for. Wedding ring ceremony is performed at the time marriage.Rules of residence after marriage continues to be patrilocal, the family being patriaseha. Divorce with judicial approval for various reasons is permissible by both parties. Compensation and custody of the children is decided by the court. Marriage of widows and divorced women is permissible, and is celebrated with full ceremony. The community lives in nuclear families in urban areas and in vertically extended families in rural areas. Avoidance and joking relationship have been influenced by local culture of the pre-conversion times. Jocking between *Sali* and *jeeja* and *dewar* and *bhabi* continue. Although women are legally entitled to inherit parental property, prevalent practice is of male equigeniture; succession rules also favour the eldest son. There has been a rise in the number of nuclear families among the converts. Women have generally lwo status as compared with men. However, they enjoy better status than in the Hindu and Sikh communities. In rural areas, they have role in animal husbandary and agricultural operations, they have accepted the profession of nursing and are also school teachrs. The Roman Catholic church also allows women to become nuns.

The betrothal customs are prevalent among the Christians in Punjab.

Custom of Community Endogamy

In Himachal Pradesh the Christian community is divided into a number of denominations on the bases of the church denomination to which they belong. The reformist churches in England were thus organiqed into various branches like Anglicans, Baptist, Evagelist and Seventh-day Adventist. Similarly, the church mission in Americal grouped itself into Presbyterian, Methodist, Episcopal and other territorial denominations. The growing fission and disintegration in the Christian community was a painful experience for all who cared for the spread of Christianity. As a consequence the process of unification of the different churche denominations referred to as ecumenism was started, bringing the different churches of South India and North India into a common fold. In 1947 many churches of South India were brought under a common umbrella with the inception of CSI (Church of South India) and similarly at least six different churches formed the Churches of North India (CNI) in 1970. The Christians are an endogamous community. The rule of Endogamy is both preferred and practiced at the subgroup level based on the membership of an individual in a particular church. Thus the two main arch-rituals-the Catholic and the Protestant-remain endogamous to this day. Endogamy persists at yet another level which refers to an individual's caste and community affiliations prior to accepting Christianity. For instance, a Christianity. For instance, a Christian convert from low caste is never accepted in marital alliance by a Christian convert from a high Hindu or Sikh caste.

Thre are also many educated and professionally trained women among the Christians. However, despite their high education and earning potentials they still do not enjoy full economic freedom in the family. Though legally women are to receive an equal share from the inherited property yet in practice this is not true. More often than not, they surrender their share. A widow has the right of maintenance. In religious sphere, women actively take part in the Christian festivals and attend church service along with men. They may also take to the life of nun or sister in the Roman Catholic Church who are dedicated to the service of God and Humanity. There are yet other women who may spend all their life in missionary activities serving charitable institutions and spreading the message of God while attending to their wordly responsibilities. Women are also politically conscious and their awareness of the political issues is fairly enlarged. But they generally avoid any active role in the politics at the district, state or national level.

The Betrothal customs, rites and rituals pertain to the Christians of various denomination in Himcachal Pradesh.

Chinese Christian Practising Territorial Endogamy

The Chinese Christians are divided into territorial groupings and observe endogamy at this level. There is, however, no hicrarchy as such since marriages also can take place with other territorial groups settled in India. But for the similarity of speech, dress and food habits, marriages are preferably confined to their own groups. They are further divided into a number of patrilineages which are essentially exogamous. The Chinese have an elaborate system of numberting the lineages in chronological order an interpersonal behavior is regulated in terms of the proximity and distance of a lineage with that of the other. Generation and age are very important criteria of stratification within their society. Marital alliance is settled through negotiation by the family elders is fixed usually Rs.999, and is given to the bride's parents who in turn give it back to the daughter along with other gifts. It is considered bad in the community if the amount is used by the bride's parents. There are not marriage symbols. The newly wedded bride goes to live with her husband's family after her marriage. Parallel and cross-cousing do not marry. However, distant cousing may marry but such marriages are not preferred or frequent. Divorce and remarriage in the lifetime of the first wife is exceptional and since most of them have embraced Christianity and profess Catholic faith, divorce is ruled out. Widows and widowers on the other hand can remarry.

Among the Chinese joint family is a common form. It is patripotestal with patrilineal inheritance and succession pattern, and patrilocal system of residence. Property is divided equally among all the sons. Daughters inherit only in the absence of a son. The family Elders are given great respect. For instance, food is first served to the elders and then to the children, and the elders have to be consulted on all important matters and their decisions are respected. There is no avoidance as such but the young are expected to be courteous in their behaviour towards the elders. Similarly in terms of generation, precedence is one of the major criteria of determining their behaviour towards each other. Women do not enjoy a status equal to men despite the fact that they contribute towards economy in addition to the household jobs they undertake.

Women do not enjow a status equal to men despite the fact that they contribute towards economy in addition to the household jobs they undertake. Women have an active role in social ceremonies, rituals and festivals, but lack initiative in political and religious spheres. In economic matters, the women folk find themselves generally dependent on their menfolk.

Custom of Adult Marriage

In Jammu region, marriages usually take place after attaining adulthood among the Hindus. Cross-cousin marriages are not practiced. It is a general rule that the age of the bride should not be more than that of the bridegroom. Marriage by exchange is a common practice among the local people. In backward areas of the region, hypergamy is also prevalent. Negotiations for a marriage are initiated on behalf of the girl's parents by a close common friend or a relative who is supposed to be impartial and capable of bringing the two parties together for negotiated agreement. At times this job is done by Brahman priests for a fee. The intermediary fixes a date for marriage according to the convenience of both sides entering into the marital alliance. Some of the important ceremonies connected with marriage are as follows.

In Ladakh region, the Broqpa Muslims marry later than the Baltis cross cousin and inter *gatti* marriages are allowed but marriages are avoided with children among the Broqpa. *Muta* or *nikah-e-ingatai* (temporary marriage contract terminable at the will of the husband)is predominantly prevalent. Now there seems to be a growing tendency towards *nikah-e-daimi* (permanent marriage contract). *Muta* may be *bakhstan* (through negotiation) or *khuftan* (secret). *Mahr* is payable to the wife on demand but such cases are unheard of since the incidence of divorce is absent among the Balti and Broqpa Muslims in the region. The termination of *Muta* marriages is theoretically automaticafter the expiry of the stipulated and mutually agreed period but in fact the duration of muta unions vary between forty to hundred years making termination of marriage almost an impossibility during the lifetime of both the spouses. Widow remarriages are common in the community. Rich families without male issues prefer to marry off their daughter with such person who agree to live with their maqpa (in-laws). Negotiation are initiated by a hapla (mediator) who neither demands nor is paid any remuneration for his service as the act of match making is considered as sawab (an act of merit). The parents bridegrooms's seek a date for marriage from the parents of the bride by sending a token amount of money through the halpa who also negotiates the amount of *mahr* with the Sheikh. The betrothal custom's are observed in Ladakh region among the Muslims.

As per the Christian sacraments when a child attains the age of thirteen years he or she is initiated to the church and is imparted theological teachings. A child at this age is expected to participate regularly in the Holy communion held once in a month and also attend the Last Supper. Marriages take place at the church during the day time and the parish church pastor confirms the marital union by making the couple exchange wedding rings. The ceremony is followed by an elaborate feast in which the community members participate at the bridegroom's house.

Customs, Rites, Ritual Varying in Different Regions

About the agarwal betrothal and marriage customs, rites and rituals, or Baddi Ram Gupta comments, Social customs and practices among the Aggarwals are essentially and basically the same every where, though they vary slightly from state to state. For instance, the rites and rituals connected with the celbetration of marriages among Marwari Aggarwals of Rajasthan are not precisely the same as prevailing elsewhere. Anyway, a marriage, whether of a boy or of a girl, is by far the most important event in an Aggarwal family. For them, it is an occasion for unbounded an limitless extravagance.

A popular saying is, *Bania Ki Kamai, Byah aur Makan ney Khai*-the earnings of a Bania are eaten up by a house or a marriage. The two ambitions of an Aggarwal in life are to own a palafial house and acquire the capacity or the ability to make marriages in the family splendid occasions. Though most cautious and calculating in his day-to-day spending, he would generaously loosen the strings of his purse while building a house or celebrating a marriage.

Marriages are solemnized in strict accordance with the scriptures and meticulous care is taken to observe the smallest rites and rituals prescribed by the pandits, The chief *Pani Grahan Sanskar* (the hand-golding ceremony-acceptance of the bride by the bridegroom as a partner in life) is performed in the usual way by going seven times round the sacred fire.

The use of a decorated horse, or a decorated flood-lit car, with "chavar" and "chhatra" for the ride of the bridegroom, is and innovation of Aggarwal marriage processions, which has been adopter by many other well-to-do communities in India.

A marriage is, no doubt, a rare occasion for mirth and merry-making and comes like an oasis in the midst of the boredom of daily chores. But the Aggarwals get completely lost in the function and many ruin themselves. For, each marriage means the offereing of whole life's earnings at the altar of the abominable, obnoxious practice of dowry, an evil the community is particularly plagued with.

The present system of dowry and "tika" is one of those grievous evils which are fast eating into the moral fibre of the community and sapping its social and economic structure. ' Kanya-Dan' is by far the most precious offering one house-holder can make to another. Yet most people are not content with it and openly and shamelessly, 'sell' their sons and brothers. They try to extract the maximum of casth and valuables from the bride's party. After having squandered their hard-earned resources over marriages, the bride's people live in a state of constant worry and destituation. The community is faced with virtual extinction due to this social evil.

Having said this, it must be stated in all fairness that the practice of dowry is as old as the institution of marriage it self. And it has been prevalent through out the world among all communities and societies. It has been a part of the Indian tradition and culture throughout the ages. The Aggarwals, however, are given to extreme extravagance in the observance of this practice. They have always been vying with each other in the matter of providing handsome dowries to their daughters and sisters. All this, however, was mostly voluntary in the past. The form in which the dowry system exists today is totally coercive. All kinds of fantastic arguments are advanced and theories addueced to justify on's lust for money and to estract the maximum of cash and valuables from the other party in the form of 'tika' of these, the plea of social status and prestige comes most handy and works most effectively. The size and shape of 'tika' has become the yardstick to measure anybody's position in society.

According to the scriptures, the groom's father, who accepts Kanya-dan, has to prove himself worthy of it, which he can do by giving generous donations. That is why members of the Vaish community in the past gave liberally in charities at the time of the marriage of males in the family. Now times have changed, and so have minds. Unfortunately, things have taken an ugly turn. Now people pay lip homage to the scriptures. The meanest type of horse-drading goes on in settling matches. People demand cash, jewellery and other valuable in a most unabashed fashion and even go to the extent of settling beforehand the minutest details regarding feeding of the marriage party. The irony of it all is that every single male needs a wife, and yet he dictates terms for getting one.

"Several remedies have been suggested to tackle this vexed problem. Inter-caste marriages is one; love marriages another; a stricter enforcement of Dowry Prohibition Act a tird, and building up of a strong public opinion against the evil, the fourth.

With the increasing modernization of the Hindu society in general, and that of advanced communities like the Aggarwals in particular, one does come acacross cases every now and then, when boys and girls select their partners inlife them leves according to their personal likes and preferences and without allowing the barriers of caste, creed or community to stand in their way. Such cases are, however, only marginal and many eyebrows are raised at the time of the marriage. They have failed to make any significant don't into the citabdel of the deeply embedded social prejudices against such bold steps, and do not have more than a peripheral effect upon the overall situation. Society will have to travel a long distance before intercaste and love marriages become a normal feature of Indian life. Such a radical transformation of the country's social ethos does not appear to be possible in the foreseeable future. At any rate, they cannot be depended upon to deliver a hammer blow to the obnoxious practice of dowry and stamp it out, root and branch, from the community." Mr.Gupta adds.

Customs of Muslim Betrothal

Among the Muslims, 'betrothal' is known as *mangewa, nangni,mangan* (and other forms of that word,which literally means 'asking', or 'begging'). It is also called *sagai,* especially in the south-east, and *kunmai.* Another term is *ropna*; which literally means the present or token consisting of seven dried dates and various other things sent by a (Hindu) girl's father to his prospective son-in-law at or before the betrothal. It corresponds to the *shagun* among the higher castes, like in Hoshiarpur. The Arabic word *nisbat* is also used chiefly in the towns. Another common term is *natta* or *nata,* which has a somewhat derogatory meaning, so that *nata dena* means to give girl in marriage, an admission of inferiority in status. The bridegroom is styled *mangedan* or *mangetan,* a term also applied to a betrothed girl, while *bendla* is used in the south-east. In the north-east, he is called *dulo,* or *dulha,* or *naushal, nausha, nansa,* or *nandho* being variant forms of the latter word. The bride is correspondingly *bendhani, dulhan,* or *kwar* in the South-west, and after she is married *nodh* or *bahia,* the latter term means literally son's wife. Elsewhere in Punjab, betrothal is called *koyidam.* The bridegroom is called *changlul* and the bride *chunghali.* During the days of marriage the *changlul* and *chunghali* are respectively called *khawand* and *nawi.* The boy's father is particularly, and the boy's kinsmen are generally called *putreta.* Similarly, the girl's father or party is *dhea.*

In Arabia, it is said, marriage is usually adult, and it is not regarded as indecent that the bridegroom should see his future wife, but the seclusion of women in India renders this impossble, at least amongst the better classes. In consequence, a *mashshala* or intermediary is often employed to spy on the girl and report on her looks etc. to the boy's people. These go-betweens assume: various disguises, such as clothsellers, in order to obtain access to the girl's house, while, on the other hand, a girl is very after substituted for the one seen and reported on by the go-between. Unpleasantness frequently results from such a deception. In the Muhammadans, law attaches great importance to mutual consent in marriage, but in India the practice is very often opposed to allowing even grown-up girls to express any opinion on a proposed betrothal.

In fact, among the Muhammadans of Delhi there is a custom of pre-natal betrothal which is called *thikri ki mang,* because, if a girl be born according to anticipation, the boy's mother drops a rupee into the girl baby's bath or mixes sugarcandy in the *ghutti* given to her, as an earnest of the betrothal contract thus ratified. In Rohtak, a boy's mother or any near kinswoman may drop a rupee into the vessel used by a midwife, and by so doing apparently bespeaks the new-born girl for her son. The betrothal is there and then announced and congratulations are exchanged. Contrary to the usual practice amongst Hindus, the proposal among Muslims comes almost invariably from the boy's side. The term *batana bat-jana,* to propose, is used when negotiations are opened by the boy's parents. When both sides are satisfied as to the suitability of the match a day is fixed ' for sweetening the mouth' (*muh mitha karne ka din*), and on that day a number of women, with a few men of the boy's family, go to the girl's house to perform the betrothal rites. In the Sangrur tahsil of *Jind*, the request by the boy's father is called *dhuk* and visits the girl's father in the evening. The *dua-i-khair* is then observed, the senior member of the boy's party commencing the prayer.

The negotiations are, however, not infrequently opened by the girl's people among the rural classes who are converts from Hinduism. Thus, among the Meos of Gurgaon, the girl's party first visits the boy's father, and reaches his house on the evening of an auspicious day in the lunar month. If they find the boy to their liking, they accept the feast after giving a rupee each to the boy, his father, brother, father's sister, and his *mirasi* and barber. The party is also feasted on the second and third days, after which it sets out for its home, giving the boy's parents some rupees as a farewell gift. Of this sum, a rupee is left in the vessel in which it was presented ; the barber and *mirasi* take one rupee, and the balance is given to the poor. The girl's father in turn gives a rupee to the boy's father. This is called *milap.* Among other Muslims, the observances vary. A ring or two is often sent to the boy, with other presents, and the rings are put on by the boy amongst assembled kinsmen. A ring is often presented in sugar, and the kinsmen feasted.

Among the Muslims, when such a negotiation is initiated by the girl's father, certain special observances may occur. Thus, in Sialkot, a *mirasi,* barber or even a Brahmin, is sent to the *putreta* or boys' father, and when he reaches his house, a little oil is dropped on the threshold before he enters it. This rite is called *tel dalna.* The *putreta's lagis* also assemble, and the *dhea's lagi* is given some sugar in a plate, from which he takes a little in his mouth. This observance is called *munh juthlawna* or *juthalnna* or tasting. Then the *lagi* is given *khichri.* He eats some of it and drops a rupee and some copper coins in the plate. These are distributed among the *putreta's lagis.*

Next day the boy's kinsmen feast the *lagi* on rice and sugar or mutton and bread. At the *zuhr* prayer carpets are spread in the boy's house and the whole brotherhood assemble. The boy is seated in front of the *lagi,* named, the boy's father invites his kinsfolk to his house and displays the gifts mentioned. Congratulations are then exchanged and *Patasas* distributed among those present. A customery sum of money are given to each of the bride's *lagis,* and they are then sent back. Various intermediaries are employed in the preliminary negotiation. Thus, a *Sayyid, maulavi, faqir* or any respectable elder, is sent to the girl's father by the boy's to make a request *(dhukna)* for her hand. If it is meant to accept it, an ambiguous answer is given, until the proposal has been repeated four or fives times.

Meanwhile the boy's kinswomen begin visiting the girl's family with presents, and finally the offer is accepted, provided the parties be related or the boy's father promises compensation or a girl in exchange. Among the leading families, almost all *Sayyids* and dominant *Baloch*, the first step to take when a boy reaches a marrying age is to send a *dhunk* or embassy of picked members of the family to the girl's father. His refusal will be definite, not to say abrupt, but his acceptance ostensibly reluctant and well considered. The families now begin to associate, but the girl veils herself from the males of her intended husband's family. But in other places, generally no intermediary is employed save the barber, and he is not called when the parties belong to the same brotherhood, for then the womenfolk arrange matters.

Even after these preliminary negotiations, the final betrothal does not always take place at once. Thus, a few days after the negotiations have closed, the boy's people go to the girl's house and formally present her father with a few gold or silver ornaments for her use, and after the *dua-a-khair* has been repeated, distribute sweetstuff. This observance is called *nishans,* or 'token'. The boy's father is said to place a ring on her finger and a *bhochhan* or sheet on her head, and this is called *nishani.* The betrothal follows a month or two later. But among the *Utmanzais*, the *nishani* only precedes the betrothal by a couple of days, and is observed in rather a curious way : the boy's party takes present to the girl's village. After nightfall they are invited to her house, and the *mirasi* brings a plate, into which the boy's father puts the ornaments. Of these the girl's father takes two or three by way of *nishani,* and then the betrothal is announced, the *dua-i-khair* recited, and congratulations exchanged. The *mirasi's* fee for this service varies from Rs. 4 to 8, twice that of the barber, so the part he plays must be the betrothal itself, for when a match has been arranged then pays a visit *(jirg),* which must be made on a Monday or a Friday, and by night, to her house. The *jirga* or visitors are then fed, and a barber presents sugar in a plate to one of its members. He drops Rs.30, 50, or whatever the girl's father demands into it and the barber carries it into the house. The girl's father accepts part of the money and returns the rest. The *dua-i-khair* is then recited, and a rupee given to the mosque.

A barber then gives the boy's kinsmen a cup (*katora*), into which they drop a rupee. In another cup *mahndi (henna)* is brought, and this is applied to each man by way of *nishani.* Another rupee is dropped into this cup, men take a sweetmeat called *pakwan* to the girl's house, where they spend the night. The return visit is called *mili.* At the next Id the boy's parents sent the girl clothes and uncooked food, with an ornament if well-to-do, and similar presents are sent on every Id and *Shab Barat* until the wedding. When the last *jirga* has obtained a definite reply of the girl, a body of the boy's kinsmen go to the girl's house, and take one to seven ornaments with them as *nishani.* When they arrive, they are seated on a carpet, and the barber brings a *patinos* into which each puts some money. The ornaments, too, are put in, and then the *patinos* is sent inside to the girl's women relatives. The amount of money agreed upon and the *nishani* are kept, and the *patinos* with the balance sent out again to the boy's kinsmen. The betrothal is completed by the father paying certain fees to the barber, the *imam* of the mosque, and the *mutrib.*

On the third day after this, the girl's parents send the boy a ring and a suit of clothes-a gift called *jora*-and at each fair and festival his parents send her presents till the wedding. In the *Utmannama Tappa*, the *nishani* performance appears in all essentials under the name of *thal*-the plate in which the ornaments for the girl are placed. The *thal* ceremony concludes with the return, it is said, of all the ornaments and cash offered. However this may be, at its close each person presents drinks some *sharbat* and puts some *mehndi* on his hands, a ritual called *ghunt,* which is held to make the girl's kinswomen go to the boy's house for two or three days, and when they depart, his parents give his future mother-in-law and sister-in-law a rupee each by way of *parona.* This performance is called *channa arta.* Again, two or three days later the bridegroom, with two or three friends and females, goes by night to his father-in-laws house taking with him sweetmeats and cash from Rs. 2 to 10. The party is feasted and then the bridegroom puts the money into the plate and sends it with the sweetmeats to his mother-in-law as *salamana.* Shortly afterwards, the bride's parents come, flinging jets at him, and sprinkle scented water over him. This is called *ubachwal.* At each fair and festival after these ceremonies, the bridegroom sends gold or silver ornaments for the bride.

In parts of Haryana, a very similar custom exists. To ratify the understanding already arrived at, the boy's father goes one day to the girl's and presents her with sweetstuff and a custom cash in the presence of her brotherhood. Her father accepts from Re. 1 to Rs. 5, rarely taking the whole, and coloured water is sprinkled over the whole of the boy's party. The *dua-i-khair* is recited at night, and they return next day. This is called *nishani rakhna.* The boy does not accompany the party on this occasion. On the first Id after it, the boy's father sends presents for the girl, and if he is well-to-do he sends clothes to her mother and sister as well, when the gift would be called *dhai tewar dena,* 'to gift 3 (literally two and a half) sets of clothes'. The father may also exchange gifts of clothes, but if the bride's parents only receive garments for her, they need only give sweetmeats in return. If this gift is brought by a barber, the girl's father gives him a rupee, a turban, and a *kurta,* an observance called *kapre dena.* At the next Id clothes and sweetmeats are only sent to the girl. The *nishani* is merely a present of Rs. 5 in cash and as many *paos* or sugar made, it seems, at betrothal. So, too, in Haripur tahsil, it is an ornament given to the girl at the *mangeva.* Finally, in Hoshiarpur, at least among the Pathans, we find the *nishani* following the solemn betrothal, at which a *maulavi* invokes the *niyat khair* twice and the girl's father gives dried dates and sugar to the boy's party by way of *shagun.* The contract having thus become irrevocable, some dates of the lunar month is fixed for the *nishani,* which merely consists in the interchange of presents, and the payment by the girl's father of sufficient money to buy the boy a ring.

In Mandi, the following times are considered inauspicious for a betrothal, and in fixing the date for it a Qazi is consulted :

(i) The first ten days of the month of Muharram;

(ii) The month between the'Id-ul-Fiter and the'Id-ul-Suha;

(iii) The month of Jamadi-us-Sani;

(iv) The last day of every month; and

(v) The 3rd, 8th, 13th and18th of every month.

Auspicious days for a betrothal are:-

(i) The 7th,11th, 14th, 25th, and 27th of every month and

(ii) All days except the 3rd, 8th, 13th, and 18th.

But this custom is confined to Mandi only, because,in the adjacent district of Hoshiarpur any date may be fixed for the betrothal, and at most a *maulavi* is called for the *niyat khair.* In *Dasuya tahsil,* any date of the lunar month is fixed. This is called *parna,* and on it a party of four at least visits the bride's house with presents, which differs according to the means of the parties. Among Pathans, called *Wilayati* and Muslims of Kangra generally, betrothal is styled *bale,* or 'assent.' Among the *Saddozai* and *Qizzilbash* Pathans of Hoshiarpur, for instance, the *bale* simply consists in a visit by the boy's friends to the girl's father and a formal acceptance of the proposed match. The boy himself does not take part in any of ceremonies before his wedding, though these are rather elaborate, and include the *shirini khori* (sweet-eating) and *rakht-burani* or cloth-cutting. At some date after the *bale* the boy's father, accompanied by some of his family, takes some sweetmeat, pieces of silk and rich cloth, unsewn and uncut, for the bride, but ornaments are not sent till the eve of the wedding. The sweetmeat, which is always a miture of *patasha, naugal* and *ilaichidana,* is arranged in trays carried by menials, who form a procession. Before them goes a hand. The women relatives of the boy's family follow in closed carriages. Sometimes fireworks are also used. When this procession arrives at the girl's house, the boy's mother or some elderly relative puts a ring on the bride's right-hand finger and say, '*bismillah*'. Congratulations to both the parties follow, and sweetmeat is distributed among the women inside the house as well as among the men outside. Finally, the date of the wedding is decided upon and publicly announced.

In Kangra, the *bale* is a little more formal, and it is also followed by similar rituals. The boy's father, with some respectable elders, goes to the girl's house on the 11th, 17th, 27th or 29th of the month. The girl's father also assembles some men at his house before their arrival, and soon after it he distributes sweetmeats, such as *patashas,* giving a plateful of sugar with his own hands to the boy's father, and congratulations are exchanged. The giving of the sweetmeats shows that the girl's father has agreed to give his daughter to the boy. This ceremony is called *sharfi khori,* and females take no part in it. On this day, and sometimes on the next day, the boy's father sends sweetmeats and fresh fruit to the girl. This sweetmeat is called *majma raza.* The fruit is distributed by the girl's parents among their relatives. Thereafter (till the date of betrothal) on each *Id -ul-Fitr,* the boy's parents send some *mehndi* and food to the girl, and a he-goat or ram is also sent to her on each *Id-ul-Zuha*. The animal is painted with *mehndi* (henna) and a silver *hansli* is put round its neck. It is sacrificed by the girl's parents. On each last Wednesday of the month of Safar, 20 silver rings and a gold ring, with a suit of clothes and some *mehndi*, are sent by the boy's parents to the girl's. The silver rings are meant for her friends and the gold one for the girl herself.

On the *Shab Barat,* fireworks are also sent for the girl. These practices are kept up till the *nikah,* and there is no limit to the period intervening between the betrothal and the wedding. The date of the *nikah* is fixed in consultation. First of all the date of the *rakhat bari,* or cutting of the clothes, is settled. The boy's parents take even suits of silk clothes to the girl's house. These clothes are carried by servants on their heads. A pair of laced shoes is also taken. The first cloth for the bride is cut by the oldest and most respected matron of the family. The girl's parents present the boy's parents and relatives with food for the night at the *rakhat bari,* and the men of his party depart after taking it. This ceremony is performed ten or eleven days before the wedding. The auspicious dates for a betrothal are variously given.

In some places, no regard is paid to the date of the month, but the boy's party should reach the girl's house on a Thursday night. In Loharu the usages in betrothal are typical of those in vogue in the south-east Panjab. In that state, betrothal (*sagai*) is never solemnised on the 3rd, 13th, 23rd, 8th, 18th, or 28th of a lunar month. The bridegroom (*bendha*) only accompanies his father and kinsmen to the house of the bride (*bendhani*), if specially desired to do so by the bride's father. The boy's father then presents Rs. 35 in cash and a cocoanut in a vessel, together with 5.25 *sers* of sugar, one *ser* of henna and a silk cloth, which are put in the bride's lap, an observance called *god bharana* (*literally, 'to fill the lap'). Then the girl's father gives the boy some cloth, a rupee, and a cocoanut, with clothes for himself and his mother. Next follows the *shukarana* or thank offering, a feast of rice, coarse sugar, and *ghee,* given to the boy's party, during which the girl's kinswomen fling insults (*sithinian*) at them.

In well-to-do Muslim families, a woman who makes bangles accompanies the party to the bride's house and puts glass or ivory bangles on her. In other cases, the bride is taken next day to a shop and the bangles are bought and put on there. After this the nose of the bride is bored, and as a compensation for the pain she is given 1.25 *chhalaks* or 1.25 *paos* of sugar-candy. Finally, the visitors are feasted with *choia* (rice or bread with *ghee* and sugar) by the bride's father, but nothing that has been cut with a knife, such as meat, is given to them. This ceremony is termed *nath sura*.

Rituals Subsequent to Betrothal

On the first day on which the new moon is seen in the lunar month following the betrothal, the bridegroom visits his father-in-law in order to congratulate him on the new moon, and takes his meals in his house. This is termed *chandranan khawan*. The bridegroom drops from Re. 1 to Rs. 10 according to his means in the plate in which food is given to him and his father-in-law in return gives *him* a ring. This usage is now expressly non-existent or obsolete in almost every other part of the Punjab. After the *chandranan* on both the Ids, on the Ashura (the 10th of Muharram), the *Shab Barat*, and the last Wednesday in Safar, the boy's father sends uncooked food (rice, *ghee* and *sugar*) to the bride. Here again nothing that has been cut may be sent, and this rule is observed even on the *Baqr-Id* day (the festival on which sheep or goat are sacrificed).

In parts of Haryana on the Id day after the *mangni,* the boy's party goes to the girls's house with ornaments and clothes, which are put on the girl on that auspicious day. Even poor people take a suit of clothes and ornaments worth Rs. 20 to 50, while the rich send silk clothes and ornaments costing as much as Rs. 500 to 2,000. Congratulations are exchanged between the parties, and sweets distributed on this occasion. This, custom is, however, not in vogue among cultivators. It is confined to the higher castes living in towns. This usage is subject, of course, to endless variations, not only in different localities, but also in different castes. Thus, in Ferozepur, after the *mangnan*, food, clothes, and ornaments are sent to the bride on the Id. Among Bodlas the boy's mother goes with these articles herself. The ornaments are a *hansli*, bangles, a *gokhru* (all of silver), and clothes - a gown and a *kurta*. Sayyids send 5 *sers* of rice, a rupee, for the price of *ghee*, sugar, shoes, trousers, a laced *kurta*, and *dopatta*, bangles, and *karyan*. Rajputs send all the above except the rice, and in return the bride's father sends a *lungi*, *kurta*, turban, shoes, and a finger-ring for the boy on the last Wednesday. Among Athins the boy's father sends two *sers* of rice and one of sugar. Half of this is sent by the bride's father in return.

Rite of Kawar ka Sawana

In Hoshiarpur, the presents thus sent are called *Idi* and *Shab Barati*. In Mandi, on any festival day, such as the *Id* or *Niaz*, and at any marriage in the girl's family after his betrothal, the boy is invited and feasted with rich food. This is called *kawar ka sawana*. On the other hand, among respectable families, the girl is presented with clothes and victuals etc., till her *nikah*.

A similar custom exists in Loharu. In that city *bidri* is a present of sweets etc. (including clothes, if they can be afforded sent to the girl by the boy's father on every festival between the betrothal and the wedding). If no ornaments or clothes were given to the girl, on the day of the *mangni,* they are sent with the first *bidri*. In return the girl's parents also send a *bidri* to the boy. If the Tij festival of the Hindus in *Lama* happens to fall between the betrothal and the wedding, Muslims send *sundhari* to the bride.This consists of *Khajars* (sweets shaped like dates), made of wheat flour and coarse sugar fried in oil, together with a suit of clothes for the girl.

But in Sialkot the *milni* is not carried out by the women folk at all. In that district some time after the betrothal and before the wedding, the fathers of the boy and the girl meet toghether, and this is called *milni*. The boy's father on this occasion sends the girl some ornaments and clothes, which are put on her. In return her father may give the boy's father valuable clothes and ornaments as well as a she-buffalo or a mare, but this is not generally done.

But in the Haripur tahsil of this district, it is said that on the third day, or some time afterwards, the females of the boy's family pay a visit by way of *pair gela* to the girl's mother, taking with them ornaments. On their return the girl's parents give them clothes.

REFERENCES

1. Rose, H.A., *Glossary of The Tribes and Castes of the Punjab and North-West Frontier Province*, Low Price Publications, Delhi, 1999 (reprint) first published in 1919.
2. Ibbetson, Denzil, *Census Report for the Punjab,* 1883.
3. MaeLagan, Edward, *Census Report for the Punjab* 1892.
4. Sherring, M.A., *Hindu Tribes and Castes,* Thacker & Spink, Calcutta, 1879, reprint CosmoPublicaions New Delhi,1974.

5. Singh, K.S. (ed.)*People of India, Punjab Anthropological Survey of India*, Calcutta, 2003.
6. Gupta Badlu Ram, The Aggarwls: A socio. economic study, S.Chand & Co. New Delhi 1975
7. Singh. K.S. (gen.ed.) People of India: Himachal Pradesh, Manohar Publication, New Delhi
8. Majumdar D.N. *Races and Cutures of India,* Asia Publishing House, Bombay 1944

4
Marriage Ceremony

The Hindu marriage is of two kinds-regular and irregular. The regular marriage is a sacrament, and in the religious law indissoluble, so that a formal divorce is not recognised. The irregular marriage is a civil alliance, rather than the religious union, which is often dissoluble in practice. Thus, there are degrees of marriage, with something like corresponding degrees of legitimacy.

Of the eight ancient forms of Hindu marriage traces still survive. Thus, in Gurdaspur it is said that the Brahma form of marriage is still practised by Brahmins and Khatris, while among Jats marriage generally takes place according to the *asura* form, in which a pecuniary bargain is struck. In Bahawalpur also the *Brahm biah* in which the bride's father apart from receiving a price for her gives her as much as he can afford among the higher classes, while among the lower the *asur biah* is practised.

In the latter the girl's father receives a consideration, no doubt, but neither in Gurdaspur nor in Bahawalpur does there appear to be any real difference in the ritual of these two kinds of marriage. Both are called biah in *Bahawalpur*, and such differences as exist are matters of caste, i.e., social and not ritual. In the hills, the names of one or two of the old forms are said to be still in use. Thus, in Kulu Himachal, marriage is said to be of three kinds : (i) *bedi biah*, the ordinary Hindu forms ; (ii) *ruti manai*, 4 or 5 men go from the bridegroom to the bride's house, dress her up, put a cap on her head, and then bring her home to the bridegroom; (iii) *Ganesh puja*, the form used by Brahmins, Khatris, Sunars or goldsmiths etc., in marrying a Kanet girl. But another account distinguishes the three forms as *Brahm*, *gandharb* and *gharbiah*, and a third classifies the usage in vogue thus:

Brahm and *Asur* forms of marriage are practised by the twice-born castes and Kanets; and Gandharb, by the low castes.

Side by side with these are current four forms of customary marriage, viz. (a) *Ghar-biah*, performed at the house of either party. (b) *ruti manai*, in which the bridegroom accompanied by 4 or 5 kinsmen goes to the bride's house and brings her home. (c) *madkhuia*, concubinage. (d) *randol*, widow-remarriage.

These four form are more or less practised in all primitive tribes. In (a) and (b) Ganesh worship is necessary ; whereas in (c) and (d) a goat or sheep is sacrificed and kinsmen are feasted. The inconsistencies in these accounts show how fluid the customs in Kulu have become, and before describing any of the forms it will be convenient to glance at the classifications in vogue elsewhere in the hills.

In Chamba, the Gaddis recognise only three forms, *biah,* i.e. regular marriage, *jindphuka*, and *jhanjarira* or widow-remarriage. But in the *Churah wazarat* of that state regular marriage would seem to be either (1) *janai* or (ii) *sir guddi* ; corresponding to the *jiudphuka,* is the *man-marzi* or marriage made by a couple of their own free will ; while widow-remarriage is called *bandha lana*. It appears to be also called *jar phuka* and is solemnised by burning a *karjora* or *kahmali* bush, i.e. by setting light to the bush and tying the end of the bride's sheet to the bridegroom's woollen girdle and going round the fire eight times. This form is only permissible in the case of an educated girl marrying her paramour, or when the bride's parents will not consent to the marriage though they gave their consent to the contract of betrothal. It is celebrated by the mutual concurrence of the bride and bridegroom, and no priest or relations are required to attend its celebration.

At a *janai* wedding 5 or 7 men accompany the bridegroom to his father-in-law's house and there give the members of the bride's party Rs. 3 and a he-goat : in a *sir guddi* double that amount is paid, but not always accepted, and the bridegroom is only accompanied by a man. In both forms a rupee is given to the bride for her *bandha*, an ornament.

Jandi appears to mean presents in *Kulu,* it means presents made to members of the *birdi* or wedding party.

Sir guddi means 'plaiting the hair' and is an incident in formal marriage. The term *Jhanjrara* is used for the remarriage of a widow in Kangra and Kulu as well as in Chamba. But in Sirmur, regular marriage is called as *jhajra*, in contradistinction to *rit* or marriage with a woman purchased from her former husband-the *madkhula* of Kulu; but the *jhajra* is not the orthodox Brahmanical marriage, which is all but unknown in the trans-Giri part of Sirmur. *Jhajra* is in fact solemnised without the *phera* or circumambulation round the fireplace and is thus performed : After the betrothal the bridegroom's father or in his absence any near relative with two or three other persons goes to the bride's house, taking with him a *nath*, some dresses, and as many ornaments as he wishes to present to her. The *pandit* recites certain *mantras* at an auspicious moment and the women sing the wedding songs. Then the *pandit* puts the *nath* into the bride's nose; and after that *gur* or sugar is distributed among those present. When this is over, the bride puts on a red dress and follows the visitors to her hushand's house, one or two relatives accompanying her. At an auspicious hour fixed by the *pandit* she enters her husband's house in which a pitcher of water has been placed, with quaint figures or rural deities painted on the walls and an (earthen) lamp put near them. The bride and bridegroom are made to sit in front of these and incense is burned. *Gur* or jaggery is then given to the bridegroom and he puts it in bride's palm and she eats it. In the same manner the bride gives *gur* to the bridegroom and he, too, eats it. This completes the marriage and the custom is called *gharastni*.

Two or three days after this, the bride's father goes to the bridegroom's house, accompanied by his friends and relatives to the number of 300 to 400, and the party are entertained there, first with sweet food and then with meat. No entertainment, however, is given if the bride's father has taken compensation for bringing her up. The whole ceremony is called *jhajra*. Apparently then *jhajra* means 'putting the *nath* or nose-ring in the bride's nose,' but to the west, i.e. in Kulu and Kangra, the term has come to be applied to widow-remarriage.

Marriage Rituals in Himachal

In Kulu the *purohit* is sent for and given sweets and money. He then fixes an auspicious date for the wedding and prepares a *lakhnotari* or programme. This he takes to the bride's house and expounds to her family. The day of marriage once fixed cannot be changed even if a death occurs in either family. In Chamba among the *Gaddis* after the *purohit* has fixed a day, two men are sent to the girl's house with some *ghee* and if her people approve of it messengers from both sides go to the *purohita* and get him to prepare the *lakhnotari*.

When both the parties are ready for the wedding, an astrologer is asked to examine their horoscopes for matching of planets and fix a propitious time for the ceremony. The wedding is generally celebrated at night but in special cases it is solemmised during the day (*hathlewan*). In the twice-born castes of Brahmin, Kshatria and Vaisya, the boy must be in-vested with the sacred thread before the wedding can take place. This is the first of the wedding ceremonies. *Pera* is made of *mash* or pulse, finely ground, called *pithi*. The bride groom takes his seat on a wooden plate and the help of the principal deities is invoked, especially that of the goddess of wealth, who is represented by a current coin. This coin is used in every rite and is carefully preserved. After the marriage is over, these deities are represented by images of goddess made of flour. *Pithi* is distributed among all the relatives and friends with a sweetmeat made out of it.

The bride's father sends of to boy's party clothes, jewels, cash, and cattle according to his means and status. Among the Hill Rajputs, these presents are made by the bridegroom's father.

A letter fixing the date for the wedding and setting the number of followers in the bridal party is despatched by the bride's father. Later a barber is sent by the boy's father to measure the girl for her wedding garments. Among the Khatris and Brahmins of Gurdaspur, along with the '*saha chitthi*' are sent some cash, from Rs 1 to Rs 250 in amount, ornaments and clothes for the *Kurmani* (boy's mother), also a *katora* (cup) resembling a *taalbaz,* some *misri* (refined sugar), a cocoanut and a rupee for the boy. These articles are known as the *tikk*. The boy's parents give the bearer of the *chitthi* a bag containing bits of cocoanut, almonds, dried dates and weighing at most 20 *sers.* They also give the bearer a bid (gift) for the girl. Nowaday in Gurdaspur, the girl's parents with the *saha chitthi* send the boy's parents a *mauli* as a *mecha* or measure for the preparation of the girl's garments.

Sweetmeats and cash are distributed among the Brahmins of the place. The distribution is three-fold, (1) per head; (2) per family; (3) per branch of that family.

Custom of *Del*

A distribution of money among Brahmins and barbers, each of whom receives so many *dels* or shares according to the number of relatives he may be connected with, in some instances one man getting as many as 60 *dels*. Barbers get half as much as Brahmins. In the trans-Satlaj districts the ceremony is called *thama*, and the number of *dels* is fixed to 252 altogether. The minimum rate per *del* is a quarter of an anna and the maximum one rupee among persons of ordinary means; and the bridegroom's father is put to wasteful expenditure on that ceremony which arises solely from a desire for ostentation. This custom prevailed generally among the Kalals, but now it is wane.

Rite of *Hath bhra, chonk ulanga*

This ceremony is observed by the women only. The bridegroom's mother or in her absence a nearest kinswoman, after bathing, dons new clothes and passes over the place where her son has performed the rites mentioned above. She then effaces the flour images used in them and stamps her handprint over the house door. It is regarded as a disastrous omen if any one apart the mother or nearest kinswoman passes over the place in question.

The bridegroom after performing the usual religious rites is made to sit on a wooden stool. The near relatives rub perfumed oil and a fragrant substance called *batna* over his face, and he is supplied with a weapon to guard himself from sudden attack ; he is girt with an auspicious thread called the *kangna*, and from this time he is never left alone till the wedding is over. On this day too, four small earthen vessels are hung up by a string in the middle of the courtyard of the house, and in these some medicines and herbs are placed to purify the air and to protect the house from evil spirits or enchantments. In Gurdaspur, the women relatives assemble and 5 or 7 of them whose husbands are alive, oil the bridegroom or bride, as the case may be. This ceremony is also called tel *charhana*, 'to apply oil.' *Watna* or *batna* is also rubbed on their bodies. On the same day, *pakauras* (lumps of flour) sweetened and fried and rice are distributed among the kindred, and the *kangna* or *gana*, a coloured thread is tied round the bridegroom's right wrist. These ceremonies are performed by both the families concerned of bride and bridegroom.

Rite of Chakhi Chung, Kothi Ata

The special millstone which is to be used to prepare the marriage feast is tasted by some women of the family, who join in grinding a little corn in it in order to ensure that it is not impregnated with any poisonous substance. They in like manner examine the place where the flour and corn to be used in the wedding are kept. These are precautionary measure for the safety of the guests invited on the occasion. There are also some other minor ceremonies observed by the women. In Gurdaspur, 5.25 *sers* of wheat are ground on an auspicious day. The flour being put in an earthen vessel (*kathi*) which is also decked with a thread (*mauli*), and some of it is mixed with the flour meant for use of the wedding party. The hand-mill, in which the wheat was ground, is also decked with a *mauli*.

The *Shan* ceremony is performed on the morning of the wedding day. The bridegroom takes *nalu*, and the help of certain deities is invoked so that no misfortune may befall during the continuance of the marriage. He dones a gorgeous red dress with a crown (*mukat*) and a garland of gold or lace on his head. All his kinsmen and friends pronounce blessing on him and money, called *bhur*, is distributed among the Brahmins present. A boy relative of the bridegroom is made his *sarbala*, and if the bridegroom die the bride is wedded to the *sarbala*, as her marriage must never be postponed, under any circumstances whatsoever, when she has once gone through the ceremony of jal *charhana*.

Ghori Charhna, Jandi Katna

In the evening the bridegroom proceeds to the bride's house with his *sarbala* riding on a horse, the whole wedding procession following him. On his way he cuts a branch of a *jand* tree with a sword. *Aphar* is made on this occasion. In Gurdaspur, after the boy has mounted the mare, the women sing songs and some cash (as *sirawara*) is waved round his head and then distributed among the *lagis,* etc.

While the *barat* or marriage party is waiting outside the town the rite of *Jutha Tikka* is performed. A line (*tikka*) is drawn in saffron on the bridegroom's forehead, the residue being sent for the use of the bride. The object is that she may always remain obedient to her husband. Then some respectable persons of the town proceed in token of respect towards the *barat* to conduct them to the place appointed for their residence. *Atshar* is now made.

On the first evening some uncooked food and sweetmeats are sent by the father of the bride for the bridal party's dinner. A small quantity of sweetmeat is sent back to the bride after the bridegroom has eaten of it. This is called the custom of *Bateri*.

At twilight the wedding party goes to the bride's house, some of whose inmates approach and receive it with due respect. First *sarnasar* is interchanged between the parties, and then an elderly kinsman of the girl presents *nazar* to the boy's father or other kinsman; sometimes a horse, cow or she-buffalo is given. This occasion is celebrated with fireworks and dancing, and the front of the house is illuminated. This done, the bridegroom enters his future father-in-law's house, and the rest of the party return to their abode.

The real rite according to the *shastras* is that the girl herself should come forward and present a *nazar* to her lord as a mark of obedience. But this custom of *Milni* is not now observed, as the marriage is celebrated in her childhood.

An examination of the bridegroom to see whether he is an expert marksman or not, a *channi* with a lamp burning in it is hung in the middle of the doorway, and the boy takes it cut with a sword. The custom is called *channi jorna*.

Before the bridegroom enters the house, the bride is brought outside the door where she meets him, kneels and makes him an obeisance as a token of homage. Under the existing custom, she is wrapped up in a blanket and taken under the bridegroom's horse. The custom is called *ghori*.

Some married women go and bring water from a neighbouring well, singing wedding songs. With some of this water they make the bride bathe, and the rest is put into small earthenware with which they make the bridegroom undergo certain ceremonies, intended to test his physical dexterity and capacity. The boy is further made to utter some rough verses called *chands*, for each of which he is given presents in cash by the kinswomen of the bride. This rite is called as *Jhilrian*.

According to the Hindu religious doctrines, either the girl's brother or a learned Brahmin should be present to examine the boy at the betrothal, and he should then address these words to him in presence of the assembly; "My father or *yajwan* (as the case may be) will bestow his daughter on you in marriage subject to the following conditions: (i) that you bathe before the nuptial rites in order to prove that you are free from all dangerous diseases; (ii) that there is no defect in any of your organs; (iii) that your manners are gentle and your life blameless; and (iv) that you are not impotent."

This custom, however, has disappeared now. The bridegroom sends the following articles for the bride as a first gift: A looking glass, a comb, perfumed oil, saffron, jewels, a shawl.

This is to signify that in future she will have to adorn herself only with what he may from time to time provide. Some sandal wood, medicines and spices are also sent with them, to express the hope that she may enjoy worldly pleasures with him in perfect health and happiness.

In the courtyard of the house is erected a quadrangular structure of trees framed in a square and beautifully decorated with split and festooned leaves. This is called *bedi* or altar and this rite is performed under it.

A priest, conversant with the Vedas, ignites the sacred fire and pours into it a libation of clarified butter with due *mantras*. Then the father of the bride welcomes the bridegroom in the prescribed form by offering water to wash his feet and by the well-known oblation called the *arghya*. He then gives his daughter's hand to the boy thrice, reciting a holy *mantra*. This time both the boy and girl are installed on two separate stools, and for the first time see each other's faces. The boy afterwards worships according to the ordinance the fire compound, and taking his wife's hand by general invocation prays to the principal deities that they both may pass their lives in comfort, faithful to each other, and that union may be blessed with healthy children. Both then walk round the nuptial fire, the bride holding the hem of her bridegroom's garments, to call to witness that effulgent light which pervades every quarter of the globe, that neither in thought, deed or word will either swerve from the path of duty.

The bridegroom then sprinkles holy water on bride, and invokes that element that she may ever remain chaste and gentle and that her eyes, heart and mind may be his and his hers always. A number of Vedic *mantras* are recited on this occasion, invoking the aid of the Natural Power, personified in different gods, as well as beseeching the one Universal Spirit pervading all to bless the marriage pair. From these *mantras* it appears that marriage among the Hindus is not a civil contract, but a spiritual union of two souls for their worldly happiness, the propagation of the race, the performance of the sacred sacrifices, the attainment of true knowledge of the secrets of nature, and the final absorption of the soul in the Absolute soul, the source of all existence, conscientiousness and bliss, marriage for the mere satisfaction of lust being held abominable. It was for that reason that the Hindu Shastras prohibited remarriage of widows, for ties once consecrated by Vedic ceremonies were considered indissoluble for ever:

> At the time when the nuptial rites are being performed, the mother of the bridegroom in her own house, in company with other female relatives, puts her feet in water mixed with milk. She then asks the old women to give her son and daughter-in-law their blessings that as the milk is mingled with the water so they may ever live in loving kindness one with another.

Ceremony of Mitha Bhat

On the second day in the bride's house in the afternoon the marriage party is entertained with a feast worthy alike of the guests and the host. Various kinds of sweetmeats are laid out in an oval form over a white *chaddar*. Before they commence eating, a senior male relative from the girl's side presents a *nazar* and sweetmeats to the father or a near kinsman of the boy. Each of them eats separately out of *pattals* made of leaves. At night supper is supplied. In Gurdaspur this usage is also called *khurli*. The rest of the sweets is given to the bridegroom's barber. Similarly on the second day the *barat* is entertained with sweets called *biha bhat*, the residue being given to the bride's barber. The sweets served on the third day are called *danda*.

On the third day in the evening costly costumes, beautiful gold and silver ornaments, prepared for the bride, are sent to her, as well as some *hennah,* almonds and cocoanuts. The pomp displayed on this occasion is proportionate to the wealth of the bridegroom's family. The parents of girl keep some of these articles for immediate use and the rest are sent back.

Dowry Custom

Khat (dowry)- Under the existing custom parents gift their daughter and son-in-law with all household articles such as clothes, kitchen utensils, cash, jewels, bedstead, *razais*, carpets, cattle, in short with every necessary articles. These are kept outside for some time for the public view. The boy and girl are then made to sit on a bed, when with an eloquent and clear voice the fathers of both the parties pronounce blessing on the girl in these words:- 'Be thou unto thy husband as Sita unto Rama, Rukmani unto Krishn, Damodri unto Rawan, Sachi unto Indra'.

At the *Khat* in Gurdaspur, the bridal pair are seated on the couch given to the bridegroom in *dower*, and Ganesh and the nine *garahas* are worshipped. Then the bride's father presents (as *sankalp*) the bridegoom with all the ornaments, clothes, untensils, sweets, etc., which he means to give his daughter in dower having regard to his means. Then the heads of the pair are made to touch each other (a usage called *sir jori)* and a rupee is waved round their heads and given to the barber. The *barat* or wedding party then departs.

Bride Entery into New Home

When the marriage party returns home, on their arrival in the town the procession moves slowly through the bazar with great splendour. The bridegroom mounted on a horse proceeds first and the bride is borne after him in a *doli*. Among the Hill Rajputs the girl is carried first. *Apshar* is made at this time.

When the couple approach the house, some women of the family receive them with due honour. The mother waves a cup of water seven times round her son and daughter-in-law, which she then drinks.This means that she, with pleasure and for her son's love, takes on herself every misfortune that may in future time befall either of them.

In Gurdaspur, this observance is also called *wapasi* or returning and the rite of waving the cup round the boy's and girl's heads is known as *pani warsa.*

The elder relatives of the boy in succession put a handful of sesamum into the hands of the girl, which she returns to them at once. This ceremony signifies that they wish the bride to bear children as numerous as the sesamum seeds which fall to the ground. Then the women sing:

Jitne dharti til giresi,
Utne baukti put janesi.

(May the bride bear as many sons as sesamum seeds have fallen to the ground). The rite is called as *til khalna.*

A purse containing money is made over to the bride. She is at liberty to take any amount out of it to spend at her pleasure. The signification of this rite is that the husband entrusts to the care of his wife all his worldly goods. She then promises that she will spend nothing without his knowledge.

A little boy is made to sit in the lap of the bride as a sign that she may also be a mother of sons. She then presents *nazars* to the elder relatives of her husband, and in return gets presents and clothes from them.

To convert the new bride into her husband's *got* all the women of the family, including the girl, eat together rice and sweetmeat out of the same dish.The mud vessels that are hung in the middle of the house are now taken out.

The sacred thread with which the waists of the husband and wife are encircled are now taken off and put into a large dish, when each of them tries to take possession of it and to achieve victory over the other. This is the last rite of marriage called as *kangna khelna.*

Muklawa- After a stay of few days the bride returns to her father's house. The husband with some servants after a period varying from one to three years from the date of marriage goes to take her back. His father-in-law on this occasion supplies him with some clothes and jewels.

Custom of Karnal

In his settlement reports of the South-East Punjab (now Haryana) Sir Denzil I Betson recorded in1893, as follow:

The boy's Brahmin fixes an auspicious day, and decides how many ceremonial oilings (*ban*) the boy is to undergo. It must be 5,7,9, or 11; and the girl will undergo two fewer than the boy. The boy's father then sends a *lagan* or *tewa*, generally 9,11, or 15 days before the wedding, which is a letter communicating the number of *ban* and the number of guests to be expected, and is accompanied by a loin-cloth or a complete suit of female clothes (*twal*) and a pair of shoes. In all these communications the Brahman who takes the letters always gets Re. 1-4.

"The boy and girl then undergo their *bans* in their respective homes. The women collect and bathe them while singing, and rub them from head to foot with oil and turmeric and peameal.The *bans* are given one each night, and are so arranged that the boy's will end the night before the procession starts, and the girl's the night before the wedding. After each *ban* the mother performs the ceremonies of *arata* and *sewal* described below to the boy. The girl has only *sewal* performed, as *arata* can under no circumstances be performed over a female. The day of the first *ban* is called *haladhat*, or 'red hand.' Seven women with living husbands husk 5.4 *sers* of rice and make sweets with it. The Brahman comes and sticks up two small round saucers, bottom outward, against the wall with flour, and in front of them a flour lamp is kept alight in honour of ancestors. On either side he makes five marks of a bloody hand on the wall. This is done in each house. In the girl's village the street turnings all the way from the village gate to the bride's house, and the house itself, are also marked with red or red and white marks. After the first *ban* the boy has the *rakri* or black woollen thread, with a small iron ring (*chhalla*) and some yellow cloth and betel-nut, tied round his left ankle. The girl has her small gold nosering put on, for up to that time she can only wear a silver one and, she must not wear a large one till she goes to live with her husband. She also takes off her silver wristlets (*chura*) which no married woman may wear; and substitutes for them at least five of glass on each arm. Those glass wristes and her nosering form her *sohag*, and a woman who has a husband living (*sohagan*) must always wear them. When her husband dies, she breaks the wristlets off her arm, and throws the pieces and nosering on to the corpse, and they are wrapped up with it in the shroud. After that she may wear silver wristlets again. And occasionally, if a widow has plenty of grown-up sons, she will continue to wear the *sohag*.

The day before the procession is to start or arrive, as the case may be, the *manda* or *mandab* is erected. At the boy's house they take five seed-stems of the long *sarkara* grass and tie them over the lintel. They dig a hole in front and to the right of the threshold, put money in it, and stand a plough beam straight up in it. To this they hang two small cakes fried in *ghee*, with three little saucers under and two above this, and two pie, all tied on a thread. Finally, some five *beran culms*, and a dogar, or two vessels of water one on top of the other, and brought by the mother, attended by singing women, and after worship of the potter wheel (*chak*) are put by the door as a good omen. At the girl's house the same is done; but instead of burying the plough beam, they erect a sort of tent with one central pole, and four cross sticks, or a stool with its four legs upwards, at the top, and on each is hung a brass water pot upside down surrounding a full one in the middle; or a curtained enclosure is formed, open to the sky, with at each corner a *lichi* or 'nest' of five earthen vessels, one on top of the other, with a tripod of bamboos over each.

On the same day the mother's brother of the boy or girl brings the *bhat*. This is provided by the mother's father and consists of a present of clothes; and necessarily includes the wedding suit for the bride or bridegroom, and in the case of the boy, the loin-cloth and head-dress he is to wear at the marriage; for all that either party then wears must always be provided by his or her mother's brother. The boy's maternal uncle also brings a girl's suit of clothes and a wedding ring, and the girl wears both suits of clothes at the wedding. When the *bhat* is given, the boy's or girl's mother performs the ceremony of *drata* or *minna*. She takes a 5-wicked lamp made of flour, places it on a tray, and while her brother stands on a stool, waves it up and down his body from head to foot. She also performs *sewal*, which consists in picking up her petticoat and touching his body all over with it. They then take the brother in-doors and feed him on *laddus* or sweetmeat balls. The people then at the boy's village collect in the village common room and the *neota* (337 *infra*) is collected the *bhati* (giver of the *bhat*) putting in his money first, which is a free gift and not entered in the account.

On the day when the marriage procession (*janet, barat*) is to start, the boy receives his last *ban* and is dressed in his wedding suits, the *kangna* or seven-knotted sacred thread is tied on his wrist, and his head-dress is tied on, consisting of a crown (called *mor*) of mica and tinsel, a *pechi* or band of silver tinsel over the turban, and a *sehra* or fringed *vizor* of gold tinsel.

He then performs the ceremony of *ghurchari*. The barber leads him, while singing women follow, and the mother with a vessel of water; and his sister puts her wrap over her right hand, and on it places rice which she flings at his crown as the boy goes along. He then gives her Re. 1, worships the gods of the homestead, and gives Re. 1 to the *Bairagi*. He is then put into a palanquin, and the procession to which every house nearly related must contribute a representative, and which consists of males only, starts as much as possible on horseback, with music of sorts. At each village they pass through, they are met by the barber, the Dum, and the Brahmins, whom they pay money to, and who put *dubh* grass on the father's head and pray that he may flourish like it. The procession must reach the girl's village after the midday meal (ibid).

A place, rigorously outside the village, has been appointed for them called *bag* or *goira*. The girl's relations come to meet them, bring in a loin-cloth and 11 *takas* and a little rice and sweetmeats in a tray. The two parties sit down, the Brahmins read sacred texts, the girl's Brahmin affixes the *tika* on the boy's forehead, and gives a loin-cloth and 11 *takas*, taking a loin-cloth and 21 *takas* in exchange. The two fathers then embrace, and the girl's father takes Re. 1 from his turban and gives it to the boy's father, who gives him in exchange the cloth which is to form the *patka* at the wedding. The girl's father then asks the boy's father for either 11 or 14 pice, the *goira ka kharch* or expenses of the *goria*; and these he distributes to the menial bystanders, and makes the boy's father pay something to the barber and Brahmin. The procession then proceeds to the girl's house, the boy being put on a horse, and pice being thrown over his head as a scramble (*bakher*) for the menials. They do not go into the house; but at the door stand women singing and holding flour lamps. The boy is stood on a stool, and the girl's elder married sister, or if she has no married sister, her brother's married daughter, performs to him the ceremonies of *arata* and *sewal* already described, and the boy's father gives her Rs. 1-4. She also performs the ceremony of *warpher* by waving a pot of water over the boy's head and then drinking a little of it, and waving a rupee round his head. The girl's and boy's relations then fight for the stool on which the boy stood, and the boy's relations win, and carry it off in triumph to the *jandalwasa* or *dandalwasa*, which is the place fixed for the residence of the guests. This should, in theory, be outside the village; but for the convenience sake it is generally in the *chopal*. Presently, the guests are bidden to the girl's house, where they eat; but the boy stays in the *jandalwasa*, as he must not enter the girl's house till the wedding itself. So, too, the girl's relations do not eat; for they cannot eat that day till the wedding ceremony is over. This ends the first day called *dhakao*.

That night, at some time after sunset, the wedding ceremony (*phera*) takes place. Shortly before it the girl's barber goes to the *jandalwasa*, where the boy's father gives him a complete suit of clothes for the girls, some jewels, sacred coloured strings to tie her hair up (*nala*), some henna for her hands, and a ring called the yoke-ring (*jua ki anguthi*). The girl wears nothing at all of her own unless it be a pair of scantly drawers (*dhola*); and she is dressed up in the above things, and also in the clothes brought in the *bhat* by her maternal uncle, one on top of the other. The ring she wears on the first finger; and on her head she wears the *cholasop*, or an unsewn and unhemmed reddish yellow cloth provided by her maternal grandfather, used only at weddings, but worn after the ceremony till it wears out. Meanwhile her relations sit down with their Brahmin under the *manda*.

There a place on the ground (*chauri, bedi* has been fresh plastered, and the Brahmin makes a square enclosure (*mandal* or *purat*) of flour, and on it puts sand and sacred fire (*hawan*) of *dhak* wood, and *ghee*, and sugar, and sesame. Meanwhile, the other party has been sent for; and the boy, dressed in the clothes brought by his maternal uncle, comes attended by his father and nearest relations only. They sit down to the north, the girl's people to the south, and two stools are placed facing the east, on which the boy and girl, who are fetched, after all have sat down by her mother's brother, are seated each next to his or her people, so that she is on his right hand. When the ceremony commences the girl's people hold up a cloth for a minute so as to hide the boy and girl from the boy's people, 'just as a matter of form.' The Brahmin puts five little earthen pots (*kulia*) in the sacred enclosure, and makes the boy and girl dip their third fingers into turmeric and touch pice, which he then puts into the pots, the boy offering twice as many as the girl. Sacred texts are then recited. The girl then turns her hand-palm upwards, her father puts one rupee and a little water into it, and takes the hand and the rupee and solemnly places them in the boy's hand, saying *main apni larki dun, kanya dun*: 'I give you my daughter; I give her virgin.' This is called *kanya dan*. Then the sacred fire is stirred up, the Brahmin ties the hem (*palla*) of the girl's wrap to a piece of cloth called the *patka*, and the boy takes the latter over his shoulder and leads her round the fire counter clockwise four times, and then she goes in front and leads him round three times. Meanwhile, the family priests recite the tribe and *gena* of each, and the names of their ancestors for four generations. This is the *phera*, and constitutes the real marriage. After this the Brahmins formally ask each whether he or she accepts the other, and is ready to perform duties which are set forth in time, in honoured and very impressive and beautiful language. The boy and girl then sit down, each where the other sat before; and this completes the ceremony. The bride and bridegroom are then taken into the girl's house, where the girl's mother unties the boy's head-dress and gives him a little *ghi* and *gur* mixed up. There two small earthen saucers have been fixed with flour against the wall, bottom outwards, and a lamp lighted in front of them. This they worship; the boy returns to the *jandalwasa* after redeeming his shoes, which the women have stolen, by paying Rs. 1-4; while the girl stays with her people (Ibid).

On the second day (*badhar*), the boy's people must not eat food of the girl's people; and they get it from their relations and friends in the village. Various ceremonies involving payment to Brahmins and barbers are performed.

At night the girl's father and friends go to the *jandalwasa*; the two fathers, who are now each other's *simdis*, embrace; the girl's father gives his *simdi* one rupee and invites the whole *barat*, including the boy, to eat at the girl's house. But when, after eating, they have returned to the *jandalwasa*, the girl's friends follow then and make them give a nominal payment for it, called *roti ka kharch*, which is given to the menials.

On the third day, called *bida*, the *neota* is collected in the girl's house just as it was in the boy's house before the *barat* started. The boy's people then eat at the girl's house, and return to the *jandalwasa*, hence they presently summoned to take leave (*bida hona*). The boy's father then presents a *bari*, which is a gift of sugar, almonds, sacred threads, fruits and clothes to the girl's people. The ceremony of *patta* is then performed. The girl's relations form a *panchayat* or council, and demand a certain sum from the boy's father from which the village menials then and there receive their fixed dues. The money is called *patta*. The girl's *panch* having ascertained that all have been paid, formally asks the boy's father whether any one in the village has taken or demanded out of him save this money; and he replies in the negative. During this ceremony the girl's father sits quite apart, as he must have nothing whatever to do with taking money from the boy's people, and in fact often insists upon paying the *patta* himself. While the *patta* is being distributed, the girl's mother makes the boy perform the ceremony of *band khulai*, which consists in untying one knot of the *manda*. She then puts the *tika* on his forehead and gives one rupee and two *laddus* (a sweetmeat made into a ball), and the other women also feed him. This a called *johari*. Then the girl's father presents the *dan* or dower, which includes money, clothes and vessels, but no female jewels; and the *barat* returns to the *jandalwasa*. The boy's father then visits all the women (*gotan*) of his own gens who live in the village, and gives each one rupee. The horses and bullocks are then got out, and should assemble at the outer gate of the village, though they sometimes go to the door of the house for convenience. Her maternal uncle takes the girl, and, followed by women singing, places her in the ox cart in which she is to travel. She is accompanied by a female barber called the *larumbi*, and the boy is kept apart. When they are just starting the two fathers embrace, and the girl's father gives the other one rupee and his blessing; but the girl's mother comes up, and having dipped her hand in henna, claps the boy's father on the back so as to leave a bloody mark of a hand (*thapa*) on his clothes. A few pice are scrambled over the heads of the happy pair; and the procession starts for home, the girl screeming and crying as a most essential form.

When the *barat* reaches the boy's village, the friends are collected at the boy's door, which has five red marks of a hand on the wall on either side. The boy and girl are stood on the stool which the *barat* have brought from the other village and the boy's mother measures them both with a *sela* or string made of the hair of a bullock's tail, which is then thrown away. She also performs the ceremony of *sewal* and waves a vessel of water over their heads and drinks a little of it. The boy's sister stands in the doorway, and will not admit them till the boy pays her one rupee. That night the boy and girl sleep on the floor, and above where they sleep are two mud saucers stuck, bottom outwards, against the wall, and a lighted lamp before them.

On the next auspicious day the girl puts on the wrap with the *patka* still knotted to it; the boy takes it over his shoulder and leads her off, attended by women only and music, to worship the god of the homestead, the sacred *tulsi* tree, the small pox goddess, and all the village deities and the wheel of the potter, who gives them a nest of vessels for good luck. They go outside the village and perform *kesora*, which consists in the boy and girl taking each a stick and fighting together by striking seven blows or more. Then comes the ceremony of *kangna khelna*. The girl unites the *kangna* or 7-knotted sacred thread which the Brahman tied round the boy's wrist before he started, and he undoes hers. The *kangnas* are then tied to the girl's yoke-ring ; and it is flung by the boy's brother's wife into a vessel of milk and water and dubh grass in it. The two then dip for it several times with their hands, the finder being rewarded with cheers. Till this ceremony is performed, the boy and girl must sleep on the ground and not on bedsteads. Then the boy's elder brother's wife (his *bhabi*) sits down, opens her legs, and takes the boy between her thighs. The girl sits similarly between the boy's thighs, and takes a little boy into her lap. The girl or his mother gives him two *laddus* ; and she says, 'a son for my sister-in-law, and two *laddus* ; for me.' Some few days after a barber comes from the girl's village, and takes her back to her home.

So far the bride and bridegroom are infants, and of course the marriage has not been consummated ; in fact, a child conceived at this stage would be illegitimate. The consummation takes place after the return of the girl to her husband's house, called *challa* or *muklawa*. This takes place when the girl attains puberty; but must be in either the 3rd, 5th, 7th, 9th, or 11th year after the wedding. The girl's people fix the day ; and the boy with some male friends, but without his father, goes to fetch her. The girl then for the first time wears a large nosering, an armlet (*tadia*), and a bodice or *angi*. The girl's father gives her some clothes and jewels, and they go off home. As they start, the girl must scream and cry bitterly, and bewail some near male relation, who has lately died, saying, 'oh ! my father is dead,' or 'oh ! my brother is dead.' After reaching home they live together as man and wife.

The girl stays with her husband a few weeks only ; and must then return to her father's home and stay there some six months or a year. She is then brought back for good by her husband, her father presenting her with her trousseau (*pitar*) of clothes and jewels. This she retains ; but all clothes given by her father to the boy's father previous to this, at marriage or *challa*, must be divided among the female relations of the boy's father and not retained by him.

This is the course of affairs when the parties marry in infancy. But among Rajputs who always marry late, and generally when the marriage has from any cause been delayed till puberty, there is no *muklawa*, but on the third day before the *barat* starts the ceremony of *patra pherna* or changing the stools is performed. The girl changes all her clothes, putting on clothes provided by her father, and also a large nosering, armlets, and bodices. The boy and girl are then seated on stools and exchange places, each sitting where the other was, and the *patka* is tied up. The girl's father presents both the dower and the trousseau at the same time ; and the pair, on reaching home, live as man and wife.

Among Musalmans there is no *phera* ; the *nikah* or Musalman marriage ceremony being substituted for it, which the *qazi* reads in presence of witnesses. Envoys (*wakils*) go into the girl's house to take her consent and come out and announce it ; the boy consents himself three times, and the ceremony is complete. But among converts to Islam, at any rate, the other customs and ceremonies are almost exactly the same. Of late years the Musalmans have begun to leave off the *sewal* and *arata* and they often use no *pechi*, though they retain the *sehra*.

Local and tribal variations are numerous, but quite unimportant. There are innumerable *minutia* which is not detailed, and which vary greatly, though quite constant for each tribe or locality. The Rajputs never use a *mor*, nor have the customs of *thapa* ; and the tent is often omitted from the *manda* in the Khadir.

The wife has to hide her face before all the elder brothers and other elder relations of her husband ; not so before the younger ones, elder and younger being, of course, a matter of genealogical degree, and not of age. Nor may she ever mention the name of any of the elder ones, or even of her husband.

When once the ceremonial goings and comings are over among Rajputs, for instance, where there is no *muklawa*, directly the wedding is over, she may never return to her father's house except with his special leave; and if he sends for her, he has to give her a fresh dower.

The village into which his daughter is married is utterly tabooed for the father, and her elder brother, and all near elder relations. They may not go to it, even drink water from a well in that village ; for it is shameful to take anything from one's daughter or her belongings. On the other hand, the father is continually giving things to his daughter and her husband as long as he lives. Even the more distant elder relations will not eat or drink from the house into which the girl is married, though they do not taboo the whole village. The boy's father can go to the girl's village by leave of her father, but not without.

There is a curious custom called *neota* by which all the branches of a family contribute towards the expenses of a marriage in any of its component households. If A and B are relations, and A first marries his daughter, B will contribute, say, Rs. 10. If B then marries his daughter, A must contribute more than this, or say Rs. 12. At further marriages, so long as the *neota* consists between them, the contribution will always be Rs. 10, so that B will always owe A Rs 2; but if either wishes to put an end to the *neota*, he will contribute, if A, only Rs. 8, if B Rs 12. This clears the account, and, *ipso facto*, closes the *neota*. The *neota* is always headed by the *bhali* or mother's brother ; but his contribution is a free gift, and does not enter into the account, which is confined to the relations of the male line. These contribute even when the relationship is very distant indeed.

This is the real *neota* ; and is only called into play on the occasion of the marriage of a daughter or son of the house. But in a somewhat similar manner, when the *bhat* is to be provided by the mother's father, he sends a little *gur* to each *neotara*, or person between whom and himself *neota* exists ; and they make small contributions, generally Rs.1 each. So, too, when the boy's father gives *gur* to his relations at his son's betrothal, they each return him Re.1.

The Rajputs call the custom *bel* instead of *neota*, and take it, in the case of the *bhat*, only from descendants of a common great-grand-father.

As said, a man may marry as often as he pleases. If he marries again on the death of his wife, he is called *dheju.* The ceremonies are exactly the same for a man's different marriages. But under no circumstances can a woman perform the *phera* twice in her life. Thus, among the Rajputs, Brahmins and *Tagas*, who do not allow *karewa* or *karao*, a widow cannot under any circumstances remarry. But among other castes a remarriage is allowed under the above name. It is, in its essence, the Jewish levirate; that is to say, on the death of a man his younger brother has first claim to the widow, then his elder brother, and after them other relations in the same degree ; though *karewa* cannot be performed while the girl is a minor, and her consent is necessary. But it has been extended so that a man may marry a widow whom he could not have married as a virgin, the only restriction being that she is not of his own gens. Thus, a Gujar may marry a Jat or Ror widow of any gens but his own. Thus, neither marriage, nor adoption, nor any other ceremony, can change the gens of a man or woman ; that being, under all circumstances, the gens of the original father. Even women of menial castes can be so in marriage. At the same time any marriage out of one's own caste, even if with a higher one, is thought disgraceful.

The marriage must not take place within a year of the husband's death. It is effected by the man throwing a red wrap over the woman's head and putting wristlets (*chura*) on her arm in presence of male and female members of the brotherhood. There is no *neota* in *karewa*, because there are no expenses.

An Account of a Marriage Ceremony in Punjab

A few days before the wedding on an auspicious day the *dhang* and *milni* ceremony is observed. On this occasion too the girl's people send 51 trays of *laddu* with a big *chati* full of *dahi* (curd) to the boy's house. No females accompany these trays, only males doing so. They are met in an open space by the men of the boy's party, assembled there for the purpose. The *milni* (to meet) is now performed, the girl's party standing on one side and the boy's on the other. To begin with the girl's people present money to the boy's through their *purohita* commencing with Rs. 3 and rising by odd numbers, 5,7 to Rs.17. Then the girl's people present jewellery and this is followed by the *salami*, which involves the gift of a rupee by the girl's relatives to each of the boy's. At the *milni,* the kinsmen formally meet one another, and the boy meets his father-in-law to be. On the wedding night, the girl's people send a mare to the boy's house to fetch him. After the necessary *puja* in his house, he dons a *mukat* and then he and his *sarbala* (a boy under 10 years of age and closely related to the bridegroom) don clothes specially prescribed and march out of the house after the *tambol* has been taken. The boy carries a sword in his hand. The boy then mounts the mare with the *sarbala* behind him. The mare is fed on *dal*. The boy's sister then holds the reins of the mare and refuses to release these until she gets some money as *wag pharai* (- to catch the reins). She sings the following song:-

Ki kuchh dena vira wag pharai
Ki kuchh vira dal charadi.

'Brother dear ! how much would you give me for catching the reins ? Dear brother, how much would you give me for feeding your mare on dal ?'

The bridegroom and his *sarbala* then ride off to the girl's home accompanied by a couple of friends and a servant. On dismounting at it, he is beaten with thin sticks (*tili marna*) by little girls who sing :-

Sas puchhdi, jawai mera kehra.
Jide hath gana sir sehra.

" The mother-in-law asks : 'who is my son-in-law ?'

One with a *gana* round his wrist and a garland of flowers on his head."

After this the girl's relatives try to put a *lahngha* (an old skirt) round the boy's neck, but he resists in every possible way, being helped in this by the friends who had accompanied him. If the girl's relatives succeed, it is anticipated that the boy will always remain obedient to the girl, otherwise it will be the other way round. This over, the boy goes into the house marching under a sieve with a lamp in it which he knocks over with his sword. He is then accommodated in a room till the time for the *lawan* comes. In this room he is surrounded by girls and other females of the bride's family, who jest with him getting him to bow down before an old shoe of the girl wrapped in red cloth which is represented to him as a goddess, but the boy does not always submit to this as he has been warned by his mother and sister near against such traps. When the time for the *lawan* draws near, he goes to the *bedi*, and is seated on a *khara* turned upside down with the girl similarly seated alongside him. Here too, a number of small girls behind him try to heat him with tiny wooden boxes called *dabbias marad* and annoy him with various tricks. He tries to snatch from them as many of the *dabble* as he can. The wedding rite having been gone through the *kha pujna* is performed. In this, the bride and bridegroom are seated on a bed with everything that forms a part of the dowry on it. The boy is asked by the bride's kinswomen to recite some *chhands* and for these he is paid a rupee each.

The *chhands* are :

Ohhand parage di jai chhand prega kesar.
Sas meri Parbati, sauhra mera Parmeshar.

After this the girl is taken to the *doli*, but before doing so the following song which moves every body to tears is sung :

Lai challe babala lai challe wai,
Mainun doli pa kahar babala lai cholle wai.
Rakh lai babala rakh lai wai.
Mainun rakh hun dihare char
Hun ki babal tera dawa.
Was pardi kera dawa.
" Father dear ! they are taking me away !
Father dear ! the kahare are taking me away in a doli!
Father dear ! Keep me with you, do keep me with you.
Keep me a little longer ! Father dear ! you can claim me no more!
"belong to some one else, your claim now is false."

When the bride has been seated in the *doli* often with a little girl beside her, she goes on crying. The *doli* is carried a few paces by her nearest relatives and then by the *kahars* a Hindu caste, and *Doli*-bearer, the bridegroom going in front of it.'

A few days before the marriage singing parties are invited to their houses by the parents of the pair. They consist of females only and sing at night when they are served with light refreshments. The songs sung at the girl's house are called *sohag* and those at the boy's *ghoria*.

SOHAG

Desap da raja bap chhadia mahlap rani map,

Patti likhda vir chhadid, chhadid sab parwar.

" I am leaving now my father, king of many a kingdom, and my mother, queen of many a palace !

I am leaving my dear brother who writes on *pattis*. I am leaving the whole family."

GHORIA

Sir tera naurangia chira, kalgi di ajab bahar.

Pair tera makhmal di juti turnde pabban de bhar.

Custom of Sending Ghee

After having the date for the wedding fixed by a *purohita* two *gaddi* men are sent to the girl's parents with a ser of *ghee* to notify them of the date, and if they approve of it, messengers from both sides go to the *purohita* and get him to write the *lakhnoteri*. For this he is paid money in cash, rice and some red tape (*dori*). At the wedding itself the *sumhurat,* rite is first performed by worshipping *Ganpati*, *kumbh* (a small pitcher filled with water, placed over a handful of rice and *peach* leaves, or a few blades of *Drub* grass put into the pitcher. The *kumbh* is worshipped like a deity and the nine planets and then the *supari* (a mixture of turmeric, flour and oil) purified by *mantras* is rubbed on the boy. Three black woollen threads are also tied round his right wrist to protect him from the evil eye any other malevolent spirit. He is then taken out into the courtyard by his mother,with part of her red sheet thrown over his head, to bathe. At the bath, the black thread is torn off and he is led back by his mother. Next, he must upset an earthen lid, containing burning charcoal and mustard placed at the entrance to the worshipping place, and this must be thrown away so as to remove any evil influence which he may have contracted in the courtyard. The *purohita* then ties nine red cotton threads round the boy's right wrist and gives him *ghee* and *gur* to taste. These wristlets are called *kangana*. This is preceded by the *tel-sand* ceremony. Again Ganpati, Brahma, Vishnu, kumbh, dia, a small earthen lamp with a burning wick, is placed over a handful of rice, and worshipped like any deity and the nine planets are worshipped, and then a he-goat is sacrificed to the planets by the boy, its blood being sprinkled on the *sandori* (*bagar* grass rope) and *munj mala* (a ring of *bagar*). The *sandori* is then spread round the room along the cornice and the bridegroom made to don a white *dhoti* or sheet round his loins, to put flour *mundras* (*jogi's* ear-rings) in his ears, sling a *satchal* over his shoulder, tie a black rope and take a timber stick in his right hand with a Brahminical thread tied round his right thumb.

This dress is assumed so that he may appear a regular *jogi* (ascetic). After this, the presiding priest asks him ; 'why hast thou become a *jogi?*' His answer is 'to receive the Brahminical cord.' Then he is further interrogated by the priest as to what kind of cord he requires, i.e., one of copper, brass, silver, gold, or cotton, and he asks for the cotton sacred thread. The priest then sends him to bathe at Badri Narain, Trilok Nath and Mani-Mahesha, and these supposed baths are taken in turn by dipping his hands and feet in and pouring some water on his face from a vessel put ready for the purpose in the doorway. After these ablutions, the pretended jogi begs, first of his relations and then at the house, and they give him a piece of bread and promise him cattle, and goats, etc., according to their means. In conclusion, the priest asks him whether he wishes to devote himself to *jatera* (worldly business) or *matera* (an ascetic life) and he invariably answers 'to *jatera*,' and then the priest makes him take off his jogi's clothes, receiving a reward for this. The cattle, etc., which the relations promised to the boy go to him and not to the priest. This over, the boy is made to sit on a wicker basket, or a sheep-skin bag for carrying grain (called *khalru*), and a dagger is placed on the *munj mala* above his head. Then the people pour oil over his head, with a few blades of grass (*drub*), taken from a vessel containing oil and held by his mother's brother or in his absence by her sister. After this, the bridegroom fits an arrow to the *fanani* (bow) and shoots it at the head of the dead goat which is placed over the nine planets, thereby pretending to slay them. The rite of tasting *gur* and *ghee* by the boy ends this ceremony. The bridegroom is then dressed. He wears a white *pagri* (turban) and *kuwa*, a red *luancha*, and a white *patka* with *gulbadan suthan* and a *jaul* thrown over the shoulders. The present (*suhag-patari*) is then arranged. The nuptial ensemble consists of a *kharbas*, *luancheri*, *ghagru*, *nau-dori*, *ungi*, *chundi*, *kangi*, *manihar*, 3 *roris* of *gur*, dates, grapes, almonds, rice and 7 *luchis*, and these are carried by the *purohita* to the bride's house, with the procession.

The bridegroom is then veiled with a purified veil (*sehra*) by his mother, brother's wife puts antimony on his eyes, and his sister fans him. After this, the bridegroom gets up and the arti is then waved thrice from right to left over his head by the *purohit*, and his mother throws three round cakes (luchis) on three sides of him. The *arti* must be sanctified by *mantras* before being used at the door. After this, the boy's father gives him the tambol (present) of Re. 1, and 4 copper coins, the latter being the *purohita's* fee. The boy then gets into a *doli* in the courtyard and his mother gives him her breast to suck. The *palki* is then carried by four bearers to the entrance, beneath the woollen parrots called *toran*, which the boy, his mother and the *purohita* worship, and then the bearers present the boy with a *kumbh* filled with water and he puts a copper coin in it. The bridal procession, consisting of the male members of the house and friends, dressed in their best clothes and preceded by tom-toms, goes to the bride's house.

On arrival, the boy with his followers is put up in a house other than the girl's or camps out in the open air. The boy's father or uncle, with one or two more, then takes a basket full of round cakes to the bride's parents : this is called *bat partana.* They return from the bride's house, after eating something and putting some coins in the plate, and rejoin the procession. This observance is called *juth pai*. Two respectable men are also deputed to the bride's *purohita*, to settle the amount he will take for performing the rites at the *lagan,* and then rejoin the camp.The boy's *purohita* then proceeds to the bride's house to deliver the *barsuhi* (bride's dress) to her. The *barsuhi* consists of a white sheet (*dupatta*), *luancheri, ghagaru, naudori, ungi, kangi* (comb), *chundi,* 3 balls of *gur*, cocoa, dates, grapes, almonds, one ser of rice and 9 *luchis,* 3 wheat cakes, 7 *puris* of *chandan chura, roliyan, kesar, sandhur, nahani, muth* and *supari.* The priest then comes back to conduct the bridegroom and his party to the bride's house with tom-toms plying. The boy is received at the entrance by his mother-in-law who performs the *arti* ceremony over him, waving it seven times over his head with her right hand, holding her left over his turban. Four turns are taken from the boy's right to his left and three in the reverse direction. Three cakes, placed in the plate with the *arti,* are also thrown out towards the courtyard.

The priest gives four *chaklis* (copper coins) to the boy who then places them in the *arti* after clasping his hands before it. The mother-in-law then retires, while the father-in-law comes to the spot and placing a *patka* (white cloth) round his own neck, washes and worships his son-in-law's feet. The boy's priest gives a *duna* (leaf-plate) with some rice, a walnut, *drub* and flowers into his hands. Both the palms are held upwards, with both thumbs joined, and held up in his hands by the father-in-law who brings the bridegroom into the *verandah* while the *mantras* are being recited. After this, the bride is brought to the place and made to stand a foot from him, face to face with the bridegroom. The priest then takes hold of the boy's neck with his right hand and of the girl's with his left and makes their shoulders thrice touch each other, first pressing the boy's right to the girl's left. This is called *chan par chan*. After this, two torches are held on either side of them. Seven small pieces of *malti* (jasmine) twigs are then put in the girl's hands, she drops them into the boy's hands and he breaks them one by one, placing them under his right foot. This breaking of the twigs is called *chiri*. It is preceded by giving *bihun* into the hands of the couple and they blow it at each other. This ritual goes by the name of *faruri*.

The couple are next made to sit down and the boy's father-in-law offers *sankalap*, that he gives his daughter away, and then washes the couple's feet as they sit before him. Certain minor rites, called *chichari,* are now performed by the bridegroom and his father-in-law. In *chichari*: Two or three blades of *drub* are tied together with red cotton thread and placed in a cup of green leaves. Then a *chakli* (copper coin), *til*, rice, *roliyan* (turmeric), *son*, flowers, water and a walnut are also placed in it. This cup is put in the bridegroom's hands and his father-in-law's hands are laid over them. The priest then recites some *mantras*, after which the *drub* is taken up by the father-in-law and with it he sprinkles water from the cup thrice over the heads of the pair. This is called the *pahla bishtar* or first *char*. This is repeated, but the second time some blades of grass, *kasar* (saffron) *savan shadhe* and flowers are thrown into the water. While the priest recites *mantras,* the father-in-law sprinkles water on the couple's feet. This second rite is called *pada*.The third or *argh* ceremony is similar, but this time the mixture is made of *dhain*, *til*, *drub* and rice, and after reciting *mantras* it is sprinkled over the boy's head. The fourth *char* is called *dua bishtar* and is an exact repetition of the first *char.*

The fifth *char* (*achmani*) is solemnised by putting water, *til*, and rice in a cup which is placed on the ground as was done in the other chars, but at the end of the ceremony the priest thrice throws a few drops of water from the cup on to the father-in-law's hands, and the boy and they drink it from his hands.

The sixth and last *char* is called *madha parak*. The cup is filled with milk, til and rice and put in the boy's left hand ; he daubs the four fingers and thumb of his right hand with it and then lifts his hand towards his mouth and putting it again into the cup, sprinkles its contents on the ground. This cup is then taken by one of the bridegroom's *jan* (one who has come with the procession) and given to the *tom-tom* plyer. This *jan* returns to the bridegroom and after being purified by *mantras* is allowed to mix again with the other men.

Then *Ganpati, Brahma*, *Vishnu, Kumbh*, *dia* and the nine planets are worshipped. After this, one end of the girl's sheet is held out by her brother and on this red *tikka* is sprinkled thrice by the boy. Similarly, the boy's waist-band is held out and anointed by the girl. The girl then holds up her hands; and into them 4 copper coins, a walnut, drub, flowers, til and rice are thrown by the priest and then the boy is made to lay his hands over her hands. The priest then takes part of the bride's sheet and wraps both pairs of hands in it by running a tape (*dori*) round it. The girl's father then performs the *kania-dan* (giving the girl away) with the proper *mantras*. At its conclusion, the girl's *maula* (mother's brother) touches her wrapper with a copper coin and it is then unknotted, the things in the girl's hands being taken by the boy and given to the *purohita*. The *gur* and *ghi* is then tasted and this concludes the ceremony called *lagan*.

The girl now retires, but the boy remains for another rite called the *manihar.* In this ritual, nine walnuts (the nine planets) are put on rice and worshipped and their blessing invoked. There must be a separate handful of rice for each of the walnuts. A bored copper coin, a betelnut and a cotton *dori* (three cords about 1½ *sparts* long)- all these together are called *manihar*- but the ceremony is performed by *taking* the boy out to the doorway where he takes out his dagger from the waist and touches the coin with its point, pretending to bore it. The string is then passed through the bored coin and put in a *mani* (grain measure) and then the *manihar* is sanctified and tied round the boy's head dress by his mother-in-law at the gateway after the *arti.*

After performing the arti over the bridegroom, the tape with the betelnut is then put on the boy's left toe and he is required to pierce the nut with his dagger. This done, the priest takes the tape up and throws it over the boy's head, passes it down to his heels and under his soles, and then ties it round the *pagri*. The boy is then drawn by the *manihar* by his mother-in-law and led inside the house to the *Kamdeo*. The girl is also brought there by her brother and dressed in the *barsuhi* clothes and placed by the boy's side before Kamdeo's picture. Finally, the remaining seven *doris* of the *barsuhi* are handed over to the boy by the girl's *mami* (mother's sister) ; he places them on the bride's head and then her hair is combed and arranged with these *doris* by her *mami* and the following song is sung by the female relatives :

Kun gori baithi sir kholi, hor
Kun baitha pith gheri,
Gaura baithi sir kholi, hor
Isar baitha pith gheri.

"Who is that beautiful girl sitting with her hair dishevelled ?
Who is sitting with his back turned ?
Oh, Gaura is sitting with her hair uncombed,
Isar (Shiva) is sitting with his back turned."

Thereafter the boy's *jaul* (shoulder-band) and the bride's *kharvas* (sheet) are knotted together and the bride is carried by her maternal uncle *(maula)* to the canopy where the wedding is to be celebrated. Under this canopy (*baid*), they are placed, on bamboo baskets covered with woollen cloths, facing east. The bridegroom sits to the right of the bride and in front of the sacred fire *(homa or havan)*. The bride's father then washes the couple's feet; after which *Ganpati, Navagirah, Brahma, Vishnu, Kumbh, Sat Rishi, Chaur Vedi, Chaur-disa* (the four quarters) and *Chaur-updes* (the four elements) are worshipped in due order, to ward off mishaps. This is followed by placing fried barley in a *chhaj* (sieve) which is brought to the *baid*. First, the bridegroom takes a handful of this grain and puts it on three different spots, while the bride's brother keeps wiping it away with his right hand as fast as it is put down. This is repeated, but the second time the bride's brother puts the grain down and the bridegroom wipes it away. This is called *khila* or parched grain *khedni* and is done to break the tie of relationship, if any exists, between the contracting parties. After this *khila khedni,* the boy's father puts 4 annas into the *chhaj* and the bride's brother takes off the red piece which he has worn on his head during the ceremony and puts it in the *chhaj* too. It is then removed and the 4 annas are claimed by the boy's brother-in-law. Then the wife of bride's brother comes and grinds turmeric (haldar) on the *sil* and sprinkles it wet on the feet of the pair, three times on each. She receives 16 copper coins, for performing this rite. Then the couple are made to stand up and walk round the sacred fire four times from right to left.

The bridegroom keeps his right hand on the bride's back all the while. After each turn they are made to halt near the baskets and their feet are worshipped, by throwing *til*, *drub*, milk, and red colour, etc., by the bride's father, and at the end the bride's brother worships the couple's feet in the same way. These four rounds are called *charlai*, and constitute the binding rite in the wedding. At the *charlai* two women sing the following song :-

Pahlia lajaria phirde kuanre,
Dujia lajaria phirde Isar Gauraja,
Trijia lajaria anjan dhrir lai,
Chauthia lajaria anjan tori nahsa.

"In the first round of the *lai* go bachelors,
In the second round of the *lai* go Ishwar and Gauraja.
In the third round they let the *anjan* drag on the ground
In the fourth round the *dulha* (bridegroom) broke it and ran away."

The bridegroom and bride now change seats and sit facing each other. The bride then holds up her hands and in them a green leaf cup *(duna)* containing some walnuts, rice, flowers, four coins, etc., is placed by the priest. The bridegroom covers the bride's hands with his hands and then the priest unknots the *manihar* from the boy's *pagri* and puts it on their hands. The bride's father then takes *til, drub,* rice, flowers and copper coins, and the *sankalap* is performed to the recitation of *mantras*. After this, he places 4 copper coins and a rupee in the vessel containing water, turmeric, milk and curd and sprinkles the mixture on the baid (canopy). This is called *saj pana* or giving of dowry. The bride's mother's brother then comes and touches the boy's and girl's hands with a *ser* of rice and a copper coin, and then they are released, the *manihar* being given to the girl to be put round her neck. The rice and coin go to the priest. After this all the girl's other relatives and friends give her presents, either in cash or in kind, according to their social position. These presents are then divided thus :- To the bride's and bridegroom's *purohitas* 2 rupees each ; to the bride's *palki-carriers* four rupees ; to the bridegroom's the same ; and to the carpenter (*badhi*) who erects the temple and the canopy *(baid)* 4 rupees. After this, the bride's *purohita* counts the things received in dowry receiving for this 8 copper coins, with four more as *dehl* (door-way) for acting as the family priest. Of the residue a fourth goes to the bride and a tenth of the remainder is appropriated by her priest. The balance with the canopy is then given by the bride's father as *sankalap* to the boy's father and forms part of the paraphernalia.

After this, the *gotra-char mantras* are recited and fried rice is thrown towards the couple by both the priests. Each gets 4 rupees for reading the *gotra-char*. This is followed by making the fathers of the couple sit under the canopy, and a blade of *drub* is put by the bride's priest into the girl's father's hands. He holds it between the tips of his middle fingers at one end, the other end being similarly held by the boy's father. The bride's father then says: "*tusmat kania*, asmat gotra," meaning "our girl passes to your *got*." The ends of the blade are then reversed and the boy's father says: "*tusmat kania, asmat gotra*," meaning "your girl has come into our *got*." At the conclusion, the bridegroom comes to the end of the canopy where he receives *rular* (salutation with a present) from his mother-in-law and the other elderly women of the bride's house. The mother-in-law gives a rupee in cash and four copper coins, the others only copper coins, and without receiving this gift from the women, it is not etiquette for him to appear before them. The boy touches the bride's mother's feet in token of her giving him this privilege. The ceremonies at the bride's are now over and the bride is taken in the *palki*, with all the paraphernalia, followed by the bridegroom, his followers and friends, to his house.

Female relatives sing song on the bride's arrival at the bridegroom's house, thus:

Soi (pichaik) aunde-jo adar de-jande-jo bhali mar;
Hallare jande-jo mochar-mar bhale bhale adar.

"Receive the *soi* (those who come with the bride) with courtesy and on their departure give them a good thrashing.

Give to this *hallar* (bastard) a shoe-beating, this is good treatment for him."

On arrival at the door-way the song is sung, thus:

Ham ku pujna kun gori ai,
Ham ku pujna Gaura ai,
Ham ku pujde putr phal mangde.

"Who is that beautiful girl who has come to worship a pomegranate tree?

It is Gaura who has come to worship,

While she is worshipping, she is praying for a son."

Then the *arti* is presented by the boy's mother and she also gives the bride a *rupee*. Next the couple are conducted to the kamdeo (picture on the wall, and Ganpati, etc., are worshipped, after which they are both made to go four times round the earthen lamp (*diwa*) and *kumbh* (pot containing water), tape and a bunch of pomegranate. This circumambulation is called the *athlai* (eight rounds). After this, the bridal veil is taken off by the purohita and the imitation birds on the veil are given to the priest, the brothers of the couple and their newly acquired *mitras* (brothers made by sacred observance).

Having done the *athlai*, the bride and bridegroom's wrist threads are loosened by two men who thus become brothers. These threads were put on by them at the commencement of the preliminary marriage observances. At the conclusion, the bridegroom receives presents (*tambol*) from the men and women, and similary *munhsani* from the women is received by the bride for unveiling her. Song are sung by the female relatives on thise occasions. The following song is sung at the bridegroom's house :-

Kuniaye chauka paya, kuni dhotores hath pair,
Janne chauka paya, soi dhotore hath pair, darohi Ram Ram,
Bhat paritha, mas paritha, upar parithe tare more,
Bhate mass khos na jane soi, bahin kardi hare hare.

"Who has smeared the floor with cowdung ; who has washed the hands and feet ?

The *jan* (followers of the bridegroom) have done it, the soi (followers of the bride) have washed their hands and feet : we appeal to Ram (for the truth of our statement),

Boiled rice has been given, meat has been given, over them have been given small pebbles,

The *soi* know not how to eat rice and meat, the sister expresses surprise (by saying) *hare hare*."

Four feasts are given in the boy's house to the relatives and guests : first, on the day of the oil ceremony; second, on the morning on which the procession starts to the bride's house; third, on the day the procession returns home, and fourth, on the morning on which the bridegroom receives presents. The first two feasts are given at the bride's house on the oil day to the guests of the girl and the last two on the marriage day to the bridegroom and his followers and to the bride's guests.

Other forms of Marriages

Another form of marriage called *bujkya* is common in which the ceremony is gone through only at the bride's house, thus saving expense. The Gaddis also practise the form of marriage called *jhind phuk,* solemnised by burning brushwood and circumambulating the fire eight times hand in hand, or with the bride's sheet tied to the boy's girdle. It is admissible in cases where a girl's parents have consented to her betrothal put refuse to carry out the marriage, and is sometimes done forcibly by the bridegroom ; or in cases in which a girl elopes with her lover. No priest or relative need attend to this form of marriage.

Among the Gaddis widow remarriage is permitted, except among the Brahmins. The rite is called *gudani* or *jhanjarara* and also *choli-dori*. As per the marriage rites, the pair are made to sit down by the *diwa* and *kumbh,* with some *dhup* burning. They worship both these objects, then the bridegroom places a *dori* (tape) on the widow's head and another woman combs her head and binds her hair with the tape. After this, the bridegroom places a nose-ring (*balu*) in the woman's hand and she puts it on. This is the binding portion of the ceremony because nosering is the symbol of marriage. A feast is given to guests and relations, and songs are sung. If no priest presides at the ceremony, the *kumbh* and *dia* etc., worship is dispensed with, but the tape and ring ceremony is gone through and the guests, relatives and friends are feasted. A widow earlier used to be compelled to marry her husband's elder or younger brother, but the custom is no longer enforced by the State or society.

Among them, divorce is permitted by mutual consent, but there is no special form. A divorcee may remarry a partner of choice.

Sons, whether by a wife married for the first time, or by a widow or divorcee remarried, succeed, but illegitimate sons do not, unless they are adopted in default of legitimate sons or heirs. The eldest son gets an extra share, called *jaithund*, but he has per contra to pay a proportionately larger share of any debts. Among the sons the property is otherwise divided *mundavand*, i.e., equally, except in Kangra, where the *chundavand* rule prevails among that small part of the tribes, which originally came from the southern side of the upper Ravi in Chamba. No money is given to the mother of the girl, except when she is a widow and has been turned out by her late husband's heir, and has alone borne the cost of the girl's upbringing.

The Gaddis also have the custom whereby a widow's child (*chaukandhu*) born at any time after her husband's death succeeds to his property, provided that the widow has continued to live in his house and has worn a red dori (tape) in the name of his *chula* (oven) or *darat* (axe). Cases have even occurred in which the widow has retained her late husband's property without complying with these conditions, though the Gaddis consider her rights disputable.

The Custom of Dawari Marriage

When the parents are agreed that their son and daughter, respectively, are suited and shall be married, a day is fixed and the bridegroom's kinsmen go to the bride's guardian's house taking with them sheep, rice and Rs. 30 and *Kabuli* with which to feast the bride's relatives and friends. The Islamic marriage contract is then ratified, the two young people are formally betrothed, and the price to be paid by the bridegroom for the bride is fixed. The bride's guardians may ask any price they like, as there is no fixed scale of prices in Dawar, and unless the guardians are amenable and remit a portion of the money demanded, the sum demanded by them for the girl must be paid. The price thus paid is taken by the girl's guardian, who is of course her father, if alive-if not her brother, and if she has no brother, then by the relative who is by custom her *wari*. The guardian, however, sometimes gives a portion of the price to the girl to fit herself out with ornaments and clothes, etc. Some years ago, a determined effort was made by the *maliks* and *mullahs* of Lower Dawar to have the price of girls in Dawar fixed at Rs 200 for a virgin and Rs. 100 for a widow. This they did because they thought that many Dawaris were prevented from marrying owing to the high prices demanded by guardians, which sometimes ran up to Rs. 1,000 and more, and showed a tendency to increase rather than decrease the bride-price. The majority of the *maliks* were in favour of the proposal, and as a test case the *mallahs* attempted to enforce the new custom on the occasion of the marriage of the sister of the chief *malik* of *Tappi*. Public opinion, however, was too strong for the reformers, still a serious riot was only prevented by the intervention of the British authorities.

The usual reference to the Political Officer on the subject was, of course, met with the reply that, although he was glad to listen to the proposal, yet he could not and would not interfere in what was a purely subjective question for the Dawaris themselves to settle. The subject was then allowed to drop and now, as before, everyone can put what fancy prices they like on their girls. The husband has no claim on the girl until this ceremony (known locally as *lasniwai* or clasping of hands) has been performed. The next ceremony is that of *nikah* which is the consummation of the marriage.

In *Dawar,* boys and girls are betrothed at the ages of 6 and 8 respectively and the marriage is consummated at their majority. Should the husband die after the *lasniwai* and before the *nikah*, the girl becomes the property of his heirs, and one of them can either marry her or they can give her in marriage elsewhere, provided that she is given to a member of the same tribe and village with her parents, consent. If the parents' do not consent, then they can buy the girl back again by returning all the money received for her, and are then free to marry her to whom ever they please. Similarly, a widow is married by one of the deceased's heirs, or they may arrange a marriage for her elsewhere. She must, however, be supported by them until she marries again, otherwise she is free to marry as she chooses, and they are not entiled to exact the bride price sum paid earlier to her parents. As a rule, the bride and bridegroom are much of an age, but occasionally here as elsewhere some aged *David* takes his *Abishag* to his bosom. These are not as a rule happy marriages. The expenses of a wedding in *Kashmir* are fairly heavy. There are no restrictions on intermarriage between Dawaris and Wazirs. They intermarry freely, and the majority of the bigger Dawar *maliks* have aWazir wife, and the Wazir *maliks* living in *Dawar* have generally at least one *Dawari* wife. As a rule *Dawaris* do not give their daughters to those living far away, which is probably due *mostly* to the fact that those living far off do not come and ask for them, but content themselves with something nearer home.

There is no law or custom regarding marriage. The ordinary Muhammadan laws hold good in Dawar with regard to inheritance.

Customs of Muslim Marriage

No rigid classification by localities or caste is possible, but speaking very generally, the marriage observances of the Muhammadans in the south-east Punjab differ a good deal from those of the centre and north-east districts. In the latter, the Muhammadans are few in numbers. The Muhammadans of the western Punjab, including the North-West Frontier Province, have a good many characteristic rites, rituals and customs not found in the centre or east. Roughly speaking, then the arrangement in this account follows their territorial differences.

In the south-east Punjab, the wedding rites vary among different castes and tribes to a bewildering degree. Those in vogue in the Loharn State may be regarded as typical together with those found among the *Meos* in Haryana and Rajasthan who are Muhammadans with a strong survival of Hindu beliefs and ideas.

Bans - Butana : Preliminary to Marriage

Ten or fifteen days before the date of the wedding, the bride's father sends the *gandh* (lit. a knot). In this observance, a piece of silk is knotted as many times as there are days remaining till the wedding day. A *kangna* or bracelet of silk (containing a ring of iron, another of lac and some *rai*) is also made for the bridegroom. The *gandh*, the *kangna* with a lump of sugar and a rupee, are carried to him by a barber and his sister or his father's sister hangs the *gandh* on a peg.

The ritual of *Bans butana* then follows. This rite consists in rubbing the bodies of the pair with *batna* three or four days before the wedding. Among the Meos of Gurgaon *ban* is said to be 'taken out of' the pair from their respective houses. He (or she) is led out of the house, holding a plate on which is a lighted lamp, to a certain distance and is then brought back. This is done seven times.

Kinswomen accompany him (or her), continue to sing songs. The bridegroom is also bathed by the women of his family and oiled. This observance is called *tel charhana*. A knot in the *gandh* is untied every day, and when only one remains tied, the boy's father sends for his kinsfolk, who are feasted and in return present their *neota* or *tambol*.

Shortly before the wedding party sets out from the boy's house, he is seated on a stool and bathed by the barber. At the same time seven women whose husbands are alive pound up barley in a mortar - a ritual called *jau chhare*. After the bridegroom has been bathed, his mother's brother lifts him down from the stool, a custom called *pata utarna* or *pirha utrarna*. After this, four women lead the boy away under a piece of cloth held over him like a canopy, and seat him on a cot. He is then dressed in new clothes and the *kangna* tied on his wrist.

Another performance which takes place a day or two before the wedding is the *nikasi*. In this the boy, dressed in his new clothes, with the *kangna* on his wrist and a chaplet of flowers tied round his head, is mounted on a mare (never on a horse) and taken to a mosque, where prayers are said by him and a congregation. On his return, he goes round the whole town and is then taken to some house other than his own home until the wedding party sets out at night. On the day of the *nikah* when the wedding party reaches the girl's house the *tuntia* observance is first held. In this, the women assembled jest with one another and hold a mock marriage, one dressed in man's attire and holding a sword in her hand being wedded to another by a third who acts as the *Qazi*. Another of the women also puts her face into the mouth of a jar and calls all the others ill names.

Custom of Sending Hari Dali

While the wedding party is still a mile or so from the bride's home, the boy's father sends a bunch of green leaves (called *hari dali*) by his barber to the father of the girl. The latter receives it seated on a wooden stool and (after giving the barber a rupee as his fee) stains his hands with red and places them on the barber's breast or loins. The latter then returns. Meanwhile the wedding party is nearing the bride's home and is met by girl's people, being conducted to a suitable place for its stay. Songs are now sung by the girl's women relatives and the potter's wheel worshipped by them. At sunset the bridegroom performs the *toran*. Five wooden sparrows are hung up at the bride's house-door and the bridegroom moves them with a stick.

After the *toran,* the bridegroom goes to the bride's house, but a barber stops the way and measures him with a thread, receiving for this his reward. Then the bridegroom enters the house of the bride who has taken her stand inside the door. Giving her a rupee, he places his hand over hers - an observance called *hath-lewa* or 'hand - taking.' The *nikah* is now solemnised according to Muhammadan Law of Shariat and the amount of the dower fixed.

Post-Marriage Ceremonies

Another usage prior to the nikah consists in the sending of *bari* by the boy's father to the bride. The *bari* consists of clothes, shoes, dried dates, almonds, maize and, if he can afford them, ornaments.

After the *bari,* the wedding party takes the boy to the girl's house where her mother places a tray of sugar before him. Into the tray he puts a rupee, called *sasuana* or the mother-in-law's due.

In Rohtak, the *bari* is also called *sachu,* and consists of presents sent to the girl by the boy's maternal relatives.

After the *bari* has been received, the women of the bride's family go to see the place where the boy's party is staying - known as *dera jhankna* or *bhir*. There they are given dried fruits.

On the morning after the *nikah,* the bridegroom and his *shahbata* with their companions are feasted on *khir*, called *kanwar kalewa*. After this, sugar on a plate is set before the bridegroom and he puts some money into the plate - an observance called *salu arta*.

Juakhelna

Next, the pair are seated facing each other with an earthen plate full of water between them, and a silver ring, a nut and two or four coins are put on the bride's head which she inclines, thus throwing the coins etc., into the water. Both then scramble for them in the plate - and the one who first gets the ring wins. This is done thrice. The rite is called *jua khelna*, ' to gamble.'

On the day on which the wedding party is to return home, the bridegroom goes to the bride's house and there the pair sit facing each other. Here again, the *shahbala* accompanies the bridegroom. The pair then comes out of the house with their clothes knotted together. The bride's father now gives her clothes etc., a couch and if he can afford it, a horse, camel or cow. The wedding party departs, with the bride in a cart or on a camel if possible.

Sat Suhagan Ka Kunda

On nearing the bridegroom's home, the clothes of the pair are again knotted together. At the entrance, the bridegroom's sister bars their way till she receives her dues, and further in stand vessels through which the bridegroom must make a way with his sword, the bride accompanying him. Both then seat themselves in the house and the *shahbala* says :-

Bhabi, bhabi mujh ghar pahla beta ser gur.
Throwing a cocoanut into the air he says also :-
Dahne goda dhakni aur bain goda sut.
Mujhe milen laddu aur bhabi ko milen put.

The pair then separates.

Rice is then boiled by women relatives whose husbands are alive and eaten by them and the bride-a rite called *sat* (seven) *suhagan ka kunda*.

Two or four days later, the bride's brother or other kinsman goes to bring her back to her own home, and he takes with him some sweets. This usage is called *len hari*.

In Kashmir, youngsters of marriageable age do not enjoy the freedom of selcting the spouses of their own choice, which is the exclusive preserve of the parents or guardians as it is believed that the children, however grown-up they may be, would not, because of lack of experience, be able to make correct choice. The unmarried persons do not even participate in the negotiation about offers received from various parties as it is regarded an act of mis demeanor. Early marriges which were once very common have been discontinued partly because of the Infant Marriage Prevention Act, 1928, and partly because of the infant Marriage Prevention Act, 1928, and partly due to the people have come to realize the bad consequences of such marriages which generally result in divorce besides damaging the health of the married persons.

In making matches services of a *manzymyor*, and intermediary, are invariably engaged for initiating the preliminary negotiations. The *manzymyor* is paid a fee for his services. In villages, a common friend starts marriage negotiatioins on the intitiative of one of the sides. The intermediary is not paid any fee for his services in villages but he remains present in all ceremonies of the marriage. Aconvenient date is fixed for a formal announcement of the marriage ceremony. On this day the bridegroom's father accompanied by close relatives visits the house of the bride where he is served tea and snacks. He then deposits some money in a cup which is collected by the host or a senior member of the family signifying the acceptance of the relationship. At times the guests are served dinner also, in a ceremony called as *gandum*. This is followed by doon-leij ceremony. On the occasion the bride's father, accompanied by his close relatives visits the house of the bridegroom where he is entertained in the same manner as on the occasion of engagement. He also places an equivalent amount in the cup in which he had tea and supplements it with a full pot of dry fruits.

As he returns the host returns the amount he he has received from the guests by adding some more money but he retains the dry fruits. The period intervening between doon-leij and the actual marriage varies according convenience of the parties concerned. If during the interval any of the four religious festivals,, Id-ul-Fitr, Id-ul-Zuha, Shab-e-Meraj or annual *urs* of a local saint takes place, the bridegroom's father sends some gift for the bride such as silver bangles and sugar candy, etc. In return, the bride's father also reciprocates the gift adding some money. Immediately after a fixed date is announced for the marriage, necessary preparations for the ceremony start. New garments are ordered for both the bride and the bridegroom's, silversmiths supply necessary ornaments for the bride. Various dishes, are made ready. Members of the two families visit the houses of their respective relatives and extend an invitation for the marriage. In return they are entertained by their relatives with lunch or dinner. This ceremony is known as *dapanbata*. As the date of marriage draws closer several ceremonies are performed in a quick succession. Beginning with *malasbeboun* wherein the bride is not permitted to take bath or attend any domestic chore and is kept on solid diet. She is not allowed to drink soup, juices or milk. This lasts for three lasts for three days after which the second function. Massmechravoun (loosening of hair plaits), is conducted. On the occasion, close relatives and women from the neighbourhood assemble and one of them combs the hair of the bride, others keep on singing in chorus. On the penultimate day of marriage, a ceremony called as *malamenz*, is performed in which female neighbours are invited and served dinner. The hands and feet of the bride are dyed in benna or mebnadi late the night while the women keep on mebndi late in the night while the women keep on singing auspicious songs. They are served tea and refreshments after mid-night.

The first day of marriage called, *menziraat*, starts with the arrival of invited guests from early morning. They stay in the house until the marriage ceremony is over. The neighbours are invited in the night and are served with dinner. Cooking is made by a professional *waza* (cook). The second day of marriage, called *yenevou*l, starts with the bridegroom's father sending off a number of copper plates containing sweets, dry fruits, clothes and ornaments for the bride. The bridegroom is made to sit on a specially laid seat in the centre of the room. The barber gives him a haircut before he takes bath. After bathing, the bridegroom is made to wear a new dress, a turban and a new pair of shoes. He then walks into a seraglio where another set of rituals is performed. Then he sits amidst relatives and guests who offer him money which is duly recorded by a family member.

Then the bridegroom is taken in a procession being accompanied by his close relatives and friends to the house of the bride. As the procession starts a group of singing women follow the procession for some distance. The procession is welcomed first by a group of women singing in praise of the bridegroom. Senior member of the bridegroom's house receive him and escort him to a seat reserved for him. Sugar balls are showered on the entire marriage party by the women of the bride's side. The guests are entertained with *qahwa* and specially made cakes.

This is followed by nikah ceremony which is presided by a Muslim clergyman. The date of wedding is in no way coterminous with the nikah. In some cases wedding takes place well after the performance of *nikah*. Usually, hoever, nikha and wedding ceremonies are performed in quick succession. When the bridegroom is personally present at the nikah ceremony he is not represented by any attorney. He answers all the questions put forward by the elergyman. The bride, however, does not make a personal appearance who is represented by her close relatives who function as attorney and witnesses. No marriage is permissible under the Islamic law unless the amount of *mahr* is fixed in advance. One third on the *mahr* is paid on the spot. The husband, during his life-time does not pay the remaining amount. Usually, however, it is paid only in case of dissolution of marriage at the instance of the bridegroom. The clergyman prepares the *nikah-nama* (marriage document)in duplicate giving full details about the bride, bridegroom, witnesses and attorneys and also the amount of *mahr* consented upon by the two parties. Both copies of the document are signed by the two parties in presence of witnesses. After nikha, dinner is served in copper *traem* (plates) from which four persons are served simultaneously. The *waza* makes several rounds appearing each time with a new dish which he serves to the guests on copper plates. The guests then leave if their houses are nearby but close relatives of the bridegroom follows the palanquin in which the bride is made to sit. The bride's female relative escorts her for some distance singing farewell songs. After bidding farewell to the bride, to her in-law house. There she is carried by her uncle to the seat reserved for her. The female members of the bridegroom's side shower sugar balls on the bride and keep on singing songs until she is seated. The bride remains sitting in a kneeling posture until her mother-in-law raises her head. The women present on the occasion make offering of cash to the bride which is duly recorded on a piece of paper. The bride stays with her husband for seven days. During the period she is invited by her relatives who present her *khabar* (gifts in kind). On the seventh day the bride's mother sends a message inviting five to seven persons for dinner. They attend the bride's house with the presentation of cooked meat and breads. The bride returns to her parental house after dinner.

On the following day, called withal, relatives and friends are again invited by the bridegroom's father for a dinner. A few close relatives of the bride also attned this feast. The bridegroom, in return, is invited by his in laws where he stays for three days. This ceremony is called *phirsal*. Before returning on the third day he is presented with some gift known as *bakhshish*. The customs and rites pertaining to the marriage ceremony are practiced among the Muslims in Kashmir region.

Custom of Drinking Liquor

About two decades ago, marriage was a simple ceremony performed in the dera (camp) or at home and followed by a small feast and by amusement play peformed by professional *swangis* (folk artist) from the Chamar or Julaha community. The bridegroom's father was suppsosed to offer one or two bottles of liquor failing which the bride's father would abuse and give him a thrashing with a stick. No services of purohit and nai were employed (in Bilaspur), but now they take the services of a priest of the Chamar community, who performs the Hindu Vedic rituals and the bridegroom and the brdie circumambulate the sacred fire. In Kangra, the Gandhila Bangalis employ a priest of their community who also conducts certain Vedic rituals and the bride circumambulate the fire. The Christian group performs marriage in a church. Marriage is consummated on the same day. The marriage customs pastain to Bengali Christians.

Conducting Marriage Ceremony in Church

The Christian marriage ceremony is conducted in Churches, the religious ceremony being followed immediately after by a civil one, within the Church precincts, in the presence of the priest who is also a civil magistrate or registrar. Certain rituals or rites are also observed at home, as per respective local traditions. Both sides respectively feast their relatives and guests the occasion on respective days. The marriage ceremony is head at the groom's residence. Economically, the Christain community in Delhi is well consolideated. The community is in a way moderately affluent, with its members to be found in all walks of life.

The customs are observed by the christens in Delhi.

Marriage Customs and Ritual being Simple

In Haryana, the Christian marriage rules are not cumbersome and lengthy. Their marriage normally takes place in the church where the church priest acts as the registrar of marriage. The Christian marriage takes place according to the Indian Christian Marriage Act of 1872. The clegyman in charge (of the church) issues the licence and certificate of marriage. In some churches the Bishop authoriqes the priest to issue a marriage certificate. The language of conducting a marriage is prescribed by the norms laid down by the law. After having received the application for marriage, the 'banns' are pronounced by the Bishop in mass in western style on three consecutive Sundays, and thereafter, he officiates over the marriage. The marriage age in case of a girl is normally 21 and for men it is 24 years.

Modes of acquiring the mate are not rigid. Therefore, along with the arranged marriage, love marriage is also popular among the local Christians. That means marrying outside the community is not desirable, but just in case it takes place, it does not arouse wide reaction from them. They refer marrying within one's own community, i.e., the

Christians of South India origin would like to keep their marriage alliance confined to the south itself. However, this practice of endogamy is not rigidely followed. Marriage symbol for this community involves wearing of a wedding ring. The south Indian women tend to wear mangal sutra also as a mark of marriage symbol. Some Catholics use versmilion as well.

The self-persception of the community in Haryana is guided by the humanitarian outlook where a fraternal attitude towards other members of their religious group is reflected. They believe that their life is meant to serve others. They are governed by egalitarian norms which do not allow discrimination within the group. Another significant feature about them is that they all strive to maintain harmony between themselves by maintaining solidarity and unity. The custom, rites and rituals are practiced by the Christians in Haryana.

Rule of Denomination and Caste Endogamy

The Christian community in Punjab has various denominations united by common reverence for the Bible which is the holy book for all. There are variations in the practices of various denominations. In Gurdaspur district, the Salvation Army has the most following in urban areas. The Church owns some agricultural land in Gurdaspur and Amritsar districts. Owning to encroachment the land holdings of the church have declined of late. A few ordained saints, such as Saint Xavier and Saint Thomas are held in great esteem among the Roman Catholics and various medical and educational institutions are named after them. Festivals such as Diwali, Lohri, etc., are celebrated Cristms is celebrated with gaiety. Other communities also participate and greet this community on this day. A midnitht mass is held in churches at all known Chuhra-Chamar conversion movement of the early decades of the 20the century was the most vigorous part of this movement. Prechange practices have been modified and even forgotten altogether. These days a few members of the community have reported as Scheduled Castes to enjoy the benefits of reservation policy. The community sings the folk songs sung by other communities.

Their Marriage rituals are performed at the church and both the sides arrge a feast at their respective places following the wedding. In case of inter-denomination marriage, the rites are performed at the bride's church. There is a practice to register the marriage at the church. There is a practice to register the marriage at the church.

Land is the main source of income for the community even though land is owned by other communities. This community itself is engaged mainly in agricultural labour. Only 5 per cent of thise people in Batala tahsil of Gurdaspur district own small patches of agricultural labour.

Others work as labour and skilled worker in hospitals and cantonments. There are only a few included in the Punjab Civil Service Personnel. Some Women work in hospitals as nurses and medical technicians, and a few are teachers in private schools. Child labour exist particularly in the agricultural operations. The agricultural labour from the community their operation as labour to the twons in mechanical outfits or work in grain markets. In Gurdaspur area about 50 per cent of the *panches* belong to this community. There are more than ten *sarpanches* in Ferozpure district belonging to the christian community. A nominated body of the community at the state level also exists. It is known as the Punjab Christain Sabha with head office at Batala. The sabha fights for the rights of the community. To maintain record and preserve peace and discipline, pastorate committees exist in Punjab.

Custom of Pronouncing ' Banns' in Church

In Himachal Pradesh, the Christian marriage is performed in the church. Before the wedding, betrothal or engagement takes place which ceremonially involves the exchange of wedding rings which is their marriage symbol. Every marriage is to be announced three times and three weeks prior to the wedding day in the mass so that if there are any objections to it, they should first be resolved before marriage. If there are still objections, such a marriage cannot be performed in the church. Under these circumstances marriage through court is the only alternative. After marriage ceremony is over the guests are entertained to a wedding feast. The customs rtes and observances relating to the marriage ceremony pertain to Christians in Himachal Pradesh.

The *baqpa* Or bridegroom is given a bath by this *chasis pa* (close friends) who receive the clothes discarded by the bridegroom before putting on wedding clothes. The *baqpa* enters the sitting room where the *agha*, sheikh and *akhun* area already sitting. The *agha* or sheikh recites some Koranic verses over a cup filled with water that is sprinkled on the dress of the bridegroom. Thereafter *qasida* in praise of *Chabarda* Masoomeen (the Fourteen Incantations)are recited. The bridegroom is taken in a procession to the bride's house. As a custom, Bridegroom's parents do not participate in marriage procession. On reaching the house of the bride the members of the marriage party seek permission from the village elders to enter the bride's house and fetch the bride's house and fetch the bride which is granted readily. The guests are served with qahwa and dry apricots. A feast called as *dawat-e-walima* follows immediately Thereafter. The *nikah* ceremony is performed in the night at the bride's place and the *segha* (statement)of nikha is ready by a mujtabid or sheikha or akhun in order to their availablility. Attorneys and witnesses from both sides remain present and reatify the marriage contract. After nikha the bride is taken to the bridegroom's house. The guests are served with sweet tea and ishnan mizan (feast)is given in the night. The guests form the bride and the bridegroom go to the bride's house where a ceremonial *shum* feast is given to them. Then, the bridegrooms parents go to the brdi's house where a ceremonial *shum* feast is also given to them. The bridegroom's parents are invited to khangso feast by the bride's parents and the bride's kin make offerings of sheep, goats and clothes to the kin. The bridegroom along with parents return to their village leaving behind the bride who stays with there parents for a couple for months and then returns to her husband's house to live there permanently.

Custom of *Muklawa*

Muklawa takes place as a rule one or two years after the marriage. The husband fetches his wife from her home, receiving a present of ornaments from her father, if he can afford to give them. The rite of *muklawa* or *chata* in Gurgaon, e.g., among the Meos who have several usages. Sometimes the bridegroom accompanies the bride to her home, stays there 3 or 4 days and then returns with her. Sometimes *muklawa* takes place after one, sometimes after three years, in which cases it is much more formal and costly to the girl's father - and less so to the bridegroom.

In the central districts fixing of wedding day is not a very prominent rite, but in some parts it survives. Thus, in Gujarat in order to fix a date for the wedding, the girl's parents send a barber and *mirasi* with Rs. 5 to Rs. 21 or a gold *mohar* for the boy, as well as Rs 2 to Rs 11 for the *lagis* which sum is also called 'village expenses' to the bridegroom house. The boy's father then invites all his kinsmen and friends. The boy is seated in the midst of the assembly and the barber gives him sugarcandy to eat. He also puts in his skirt the cash or the gold *mohar*. Then congratulations are exchanged. This ceremony is called *bhocha*. The date of the marriage is fixed at it and the barber and *mirasi* are given from Re. 1 to Rs 5 by the boy's party. His parents also dismiss the *lagis* with a *chunni* and Re 1 to Rs 11 together with a *bidh* (bundle) containing dried fruits such as almonds, cocoanuts, dried raisins and *patashas*.

In Gujranwala, to tie the knot or *gand pana* as it is termed, is the ceremony of fixing a day for the marriage. If any ceremonies connected with the betrothal have not been already performed, they are now observed. The wedding day is fixed by correspondence between the parties or at a personal meeting.

So too in Mandi, some respectable men of the boy's family go to the girl's house with a *Qazi* and he fixes there the dates of the *nikah* and *dham*, and that for applying *mehndi*. These dates are always close to one another. Congratulations are exchanged and sugar sent to relations to notify them of the date of wedding, the *lagi* deputed giving each of them sugar while they in return give him from one pice to two *annas* by way of *widaigi*.

The mehndi ceremony is performed before the *nikah*. Women of the boy's party paint his hands with *mehndi* at night. Then some *mehndi*, a silver ring and Rs 1, 5, 9 in cash are sent to the girl through the *lagi*, women also going with him. *Mehndi* is also applied to the girl. The females of both parties keep awake singing songs all night. On the next day at 4 P.M., *batnad* is rubbed over the bridegroom's body and he is bathed. Then he is seated in a special room and some of his relatives and friends sit with him. He is dressed in such clothes as are worn by a bridegroom and a *sehra* is placed round his horse and fireworks are let off. He is then taken to a slow pace with the whole of the wedding party to the bride's house, and all are seated here in a specially decorated room. The men of the girl's party and the *Qazi* also come there. The girl's guardian allows the *Qazi* to perform the *nikah*. He first fixes the amount of the bride's dower which depends on the will of her guardian. If the amount is not fixed according to the demand of the bride's guardian he is entitled to marry her to another. Thereafter two witnesses and a *vakil* are appointed by each party. They go with the *Qazi* to the bride and perform the ceremonies of offer and acceptance; she and the bridegroom are told to repeat the sacred *kalma* five times. The *khutba* ceremony is performed in the presence of all the kin. The dowry, viz, wearing apparel, bedding, a couch, household utensils and ornaments are given on this occasion. Dried fruits and sugarcandy are distributed among the people. The *Qazi* gets Rs. 1-4 for the ceremony, while his assistant gets four rupees for the *dua-i-khair*. All these expenses are borne by the bridegroom. Besides, copper coins are distributed among the poor. The bride's guardian feeds the wedding party.

Sehra Bandhna and *Ghori Charhna.*

One day before the wedding, the bridegroom is garlanded with flowers. This ceremony is called *sehra bandhna*. On this day also *tombol* (presents in money) is offered by the brotherhood and the bridegroom, and the bridegroom's father gives to his *kamins* (menials) their *lag* or dues according to his means. Before the *sehra bandhna,* the bridegroom ascends a *khara* and breaks 5 or 7 *chhunnis.*

In Hoshiarpur on the wedding day, the bridegroom bathes and a garland of flowers called *sohan sehra* is hung round his forehead. A coloured cloth is also tied round his head as a turban and saffron sprinkled over his clothes. But Muhammadans who are strict followers of the sehra do not observe these usages. Nothing of the *mami chhak* or articles sent by the maternal relatives of the bridegroom in Sialkot and forming part of the dowry. The *mami chhak* generally consists of a couch, *pirha*, 21 large cakes of flour fried in ghee, 5 suits of clothes, 5 utensils and some ornaments. The articles given by the parents of the bride generally are an *arsi*, chhalan or rings, *phul, chaunk* and *mahan* (ornaments worn on the head), *jhumke*, quilt, pillow, 21 suits of clothes, 101 *laddus* and sometime a horse, cow, she buffalo and a camel. The bridegroom sits on a couch on this occasion.

In Sialkot, the wedding party on its arrivals at the bride's house is put up in a hut outside the village. The bride's father sends it *hukkas, sharbat* etc., by a *lagi* who is given *annas* 8 or 1 as his *lag*. After this, the party is called for and the barber on behalf of the bride's father brings with him a basket full of sugar and the fathers of the bride and the bridegroom meet together. The father of the bride gives the other on this occasion some money or a horse. The wedding party is then seated close to the bride's house. The bridegroom's father drops some cash in the basket of sugar. This is followed by a feast to the wedding party. A stove is suspended in the way and is removed by a female barber on receipt of Re 0-1-3 as her due. The sweeper also stands in the way of the wedding party and does not allow it to pass without getting his *lag*. The bride's sisters also exact their *lag* which may amount from Re.1-4. Then the wedding party is served with food. This is followed by the performance of the *bera ghori* ceremony. It may be noted that after the wedding party has taken its food until the next ceremony, many *sithula* (jests) are flung at it. Many obscene songs are sung on this occasion.

In Kangra, the *nikah* is performed after midnight and after it congratulations are exchanged and sweetmeats distributed. The bridegroom is then called inside the house by the women. The bride takes her seat on a *masnad* with females, around her. The bridegroom takes his seat at her right and a piece of cloth is thrown over both of them. The *Quran* and a looking glass are placed inside this sheet with a cup of sweet water and a spoon. The bridegroom gives a spoonful of the water to the bride and her relations also give her a spoonful to be given to the bridegroom. After this, they look at each other's face in the looking glass. This ceremony is called *aina masuf*. The bride is then taken to the house of her father-in-law in a palanquin. On the third day, the females of the bride's family go to her husband's house to bring her back. The dowry is then exhibited to the kinsfolk. The bride sits on a *masnad* for three days. The bridegroom then comes, takes his wife's arm and leads her to a separate compartment in the presence of the other females. This is called *chauthi*.

When the wedding procession is about to start, the bridegroom is made to ride on a mare. This is called *ghori charhna*, and his sister asks for *bag pherai*, or a fee for holding the reins. He gives her either a she-buffalo or money according to his means and wishes. Then his mother performs the *sir warna* or sacrificing over the head, the amount of money offered being a rupee or two which sum is also given to the *kamins*. After this, the boy goes to do obeisance at the shrine of an ancestor of the Meo tribe and then the procession leaves at such a time that it may reach its destination at nightfall. Some people take with it a band, fireworks and dancing girls, but others do not. When the procession reaches the bride's village, some men come to receive it on behalf of the brides's father. It is then seated at a place where carpets have been spread. *Huqqas* or smoking pipes are first smoked and an hour or two later tea is served if it is winter and in the hot season *sharbat* by the bride's party, who then go away. Then the bride's father accompanied by some of his relatives enters the house in which the bridegroom's party has been lodged before food is served. As soon as he arrives, the ceremony of *milni* is observed. If he is well-to-do, he offers a mare as a *milni* present to his *kuram* (the bridegroom's father) and they embrace each other. On this occasion too, the *lagis* are given money as their fixed dues. After this, the bride's father takes the bridegroom and his party with him to his house and provides a feast for them.

Chhanni Turwana

Some women of the bride's party now come and take a *chhanni* or sieve which is hanging over the doorway and in which a lamp is burning. After this, he and his party sleep, but early in the morning at about 4 A.M., he is awakened by the women of the bride's house and taken to a female apartment where the bride's sister makes him play *beru ghori* and exacts some money from him.

Nikah

The actual wedding ceremony, the *nikah*, is performed at 8 or 9 A.M or at some later hour. On this occasion, some people distribute *chhokaras,* while others distribute uncooked rice mixed with sugar. When the *nikah* is over, the bride is made to ascend a *khara* and her maternal uncle causes her to descend from it and in return he gives her a she-buffalo or a sum of money which must exceed Rs 11.

Then the bride's father places on cots whatever dowry he has prepared for his daughter, whereupon the parties meet together and give *lag* to their *kamins*. This done, the dowry is packed up, the bride seated in a *palanquin* and the bridegroom's party departs with it and the dowry. When the bride arrives at her father-in-law's village, some women of his household accompanied by singing *mirasans* receive her and bring her to their house.

Sprinking of Oil on Threshold

When she reaches the house door, she alights from the doli and oil is sprinkled on the threshold. After this, the bridegroom's mother sacrifices water over his head and attempts to drink it but is dissuaded by her son. The bride is then seated on a carpet or mat or some suitable place in the house.

Munh Dikhlai or Face-Showing Ceremony

The bridegroom's mother then gives a sum of money as *munh dikhlai* or showing the face to the bride who removes the veil (*ghunghat*) from her face and is entertained with milk.The next morning, the bridegroom and bride untie the *gana*. The bride returns to her father's on the third day after the arrival at her father-in-law's house.

In Shakargarh, although the *mayan* is not performed the day before the wedding party starts for the bride's house, drums are beaten and next day the boy is seated on a *khara* and *batna* rubbed on him but the practise of breaking *chapnis* ceased 16 or 17 years ago. His party should reach the bride's house in the first part of the night. Some people take drummers with them. On their arrival, the *milni* ceremony is performed. In the *milni* the men of both the parties stand opposite one another at some distance, and representatives of each embrace. The bride's representative gives a rupee to the boy's. His barber also brings some sugar and rice in a vessel. An *ulma* recites the *niyat khire* and gets Re. 1-4 and 4 copper coins from the bride's father as his fee. The barber also gets four *annas* on this occasion.

In Sialkot the *milni* is thus described :- The girl's father takes his stand on an open site outside the village of the boy's father who comes to meet him there with all his party. Fireworks may be let off at this meeting which is called *milni*. At it too, the *mirasis* of the parties recite their genealogies. The parties pass a rupee over one another's head and give it to the *mirasis*. This is called sir *warna kuram*. On the arrival of a wedding party in Hoshiarpur the customs of *milni* and *peshkara* are observed and the party is served with *sharbat*. It is also supplied with food for one or two days.

REFERENCES

1. Rose, H.A., *A Glossary of the Tribes and Castes of the Punjab and North-West Province*, Low Price Publication, Delhi, 1999. (reprint). first published in 1919.
2. Ibbetson, Denzil, *Census Report for the Punjab 1883.*
3. Maclagan, Edward, *Census Report for the Punjab 1892.*
4. Ibbetson, Denzil, *Settlement Reports for the South-East Punjab, 1893.*
5. Bamgai, Prithvi Nath Kaul, *A History of Kashmir: Political, Social and Cultural*, Metropolitan Book Co, New Delhi 1962.

6. Singh K.S. (Gen. Ed.) *People of India : Jammu & Kashmir,* Manohar Anthropological Survey of India, Calcutta, 2003.
7. Swinson, Arthur, *North-West Frontier*, UBS Publishers, New Delhi, 1967.
8. Singh K.S. (Gen.Ed.) *People of India: Haryana,* Manohar Publication,New Delhi 1994.
9. Singh K.S. (Gen.Ed.) *People of India: Rajasthan,* Manohar Publication, New Delhi
10. Singh K.S. (Gen.Ed.) *People of India: Punjab,* Manohar Publication, New Delhi 2003.
11. Singh K.S. (Gen.Ed.) *People of India: Delhi,* Manohar Publication, New Delhi
12. Majumdar, D.N., *Races and Cultures,* Asia Publication house, Bombay 1944.

5
Death Rituals : Cremation

Death rituals in the Punjab are said to be based on two distinct schemes of rituals, one Vedic, the other based on the *Garur Purana.* In the Vedic ceremony the body of the deceased is washed and clothed in new clothes and then is taken to the place of cremation on a bier. There in the *shamshan bhumi* (place of cremation) a *vedi* (rectangular pit for sacrificial fire) some two feet deep, is dug, and the funeral pyre, of *dhak, pipal* or, in the cage of the rich, of sandal wood, is set up in it. On the pyre the body is laid and more wood placed over it. When the flames rise high, four Brahmins recite *mantras* from the Veda, and at the end of each *mantra,* at the syllable *swaha,* each casts into the fire an oblation of *ghee*, mixed wilth camphor, saffron, and other aromatics. The weight of *ghee,* if thrown into the fire in the oblations, numbering 484 in all, must equal that of the corpse or at least two *sers*. When all the oblations have been made and the corpse is completely consumed by fire, all the deceased's friends and relations bathe in a tank or river, and return home.

After expressing their condolence, some return home, others help the survivors to clean and purify their house and perform a great *havan;* which being over, all the members of the household and their friends offer prayers to the Almighty on behalf of the deceased's soul and themselves. The *havan* may be prolonged to a few days in order to purify the air of the house. On the third or fourth day, the ceremony of *asthi sanchaya* is performed, and in this the bones of the deceased are picked out of the ashes and immersed into a river. After this, nothing is done for the deceased. But if the members of his family are wealthy, they give money in alms to the poor or to some charitable movement or start a school, orphanage, *sada varta etc.,* at their own expense, to commemorate the memory of the departed.

Cremation According to Garur Purana

The other cremation as per *Garur Purana* rituals performed by all the Hindus in general, follow the *Garur Purana Yagana Valik Smriti* and other *smritis*, which are believed to be based upon old Hindu scriptures such as the *Grihya Sastras* and *Brikman Granthas.* In this, ritual, the body is washed, clothed and taken to the cremation ground as in the Vedic rite, with only this difference that a *panch ratna* (small pieces of gold, silver, brass, coral and pearls) is thrust into its mouth while it is being washed, and four *pindas* (balls of flour or boiled rice) are offered at four different places, while the dead is being carried from the house to the crematorium. A son or near kinsman of the deceased is singled out to go through all the death ceremonies, and in common parlance he is called *Karmi-dharmi* or the chief mourner. He has to go barefoot and sleep on the ground for 11 days. When the body has reached the burning place, the pyre is built generally of *dhak* wood, without the *vedi*, and the corpse is burnt without going through the *havan* described above. The *kapal kirya* or breaking of the skull is performed by the *Karmi-dharmi.*

After it, all the mourners return, wash their clothes and bodies at a tank or well and offer up *tilanjali* (an offering of water mixed with sesamum seeds) on behalf of the deceased's soul. But the *Karmi-dharmi* has still to go through a host of other ceremonies. He places a *ghara* or pitcher for a male, and a *chali* for a female, on a *pipal* tree, supported by its trunk and two branches, with a hole in the bottom which is loosely stopped by a few blades of *kusha* grass, so that the water may drip daily for 10 days. Besides this, he has to go through two other daily ceremonies; the *pinda* or offering balls of boiled rice in the morning, and that of lighting an earthen lamp and placing it on a tripod of three small *Kanas* or reeds in the evening. On the fourth day, the ceremonies of *asthi sanchaya* and the *chaturthik shradhas* are performed. Food with *dakshna* is given to a *Maha-Brahman* and the deceased's bones are picked out of the ashes and sent to Hardwar to be immersed into the sacred Ganges.

The *dasahi* or shaving of all the members of the family and washing clothes is gone through on the 10th day.

Kriya Karma

The *Kriya Karma* and *pindi chhed* ceremonies are performed on the 11th day. In the former, *pindas* are offered on behalf of the soul, and food and *shaiya* which consists of a cot, a pair of shoes, an umbrella, some pots and ornaments are given to the Maha-Brahman for the sake of the dead. In the *pindi chhed,* the *pinda* or ball representing the deceased's soul is cut into three parts and each is mixed with three other balls representing his father, grandfather and greatgrandfather if they are dead. It should not be performed if he died without male issue or unmarried, but some people do not observe this restriction.

The *barah* is performed on the 12th day. In this ceremony *12 gharas* or *chatis* (as deceased was a male or a female) filled with water, and each covered with a small piece of cloth, a *matha,* a large cake of wheat flour fried in *ghi* or a *ganffor* (a large cake of sugar) and some pice are given to Brahmans. The *brahma-bhoja* is performed on the 13th day in the case of a Brahman or Kshatriya and on the 17th in the case of a lower caste. Food with *dakshana* (two pice at least as a fee or present) is given to 13 or 17 Brahmans. With this ends the ceremony. If the family of the deceased is well-to-do, it gives a Brahman food every day in the morning only for one year; or else distributes *netakes laddus* 360 in number with some pice as departed has to walk a long distance for one year to reach the court of Dharma Raj.

Death Rituals

When a Hindu is in *extremis,* he should be made to give away some grain, money and a cow in charity, and a *pandit* is sent for to recite verses from the *Bishan Sahansar-nam* and *Bhagwat Gita.* The orthodox alms are (i) the *gaudan* or gift of a cow, whose horns are ornamented with gold or silver rings, while her neck is garlanded and her body covered with a piece of new cloth-red in the case of a female. Copper coins are placed at her feet and she is led up to the dying person who gives her to a *Vedwa* Brahman who prays that she may lead the dying man by the tail to the next world. The donor also pours a few drops of water into the *Vedwa's* hands. This ceremony is called *gaudan,* 'gift of a cow' or baifarni, 'vistifum'. Subsequently (ii) the *raskha's* gift, of sugar, alkali, soap and other necessaries of life, is given to the *Vedwa*. Lastly a *dipa*, earthen lamp, containing a silver or gold coin is placed in the palm of dying person and after the recital of *mantras* is given to the *Vedwa's* but this rite is not observed in all parts of the Punjab.

In *Kangra*, it is believed that he who dies with the cow's tail in his hand, through the help of the cow (*Baitan*) crosses the deep *Baitarni* river of *Bhanjla nadi* which is supposed to exist between this world and heaven, and which it is difficult to cross without the aid of a cow. The cow is afterwards given to Brahmans. After this, a lamp called *diva* dharyara is lighted and placed by the head of the deceased, with a wick, which must last for 10 days. No new wick may be put in it during that time and if it burns out, it is considerd a bad omen. If the sufferer should recover after all this has been done, he is asked what he desires and his wish, whatever ills may be, is fulfilled, if that be possible. If, however, he shows no signs of improvement, a space of ground near his *charpai* (cot) or some other place, is smeared with cow-dung and some *dub* grass scattered over it. On this grass a sheet is spread, and the dying person laid on it, with his feet to the east, and his head resting on the lap of his or her eldest son or next-of-kin. Some Ganges water is very commonly dropped into his mouth, together with one or two *tulsi* leaves, and, especially if he is a man of advanced age, a little gold. When death ensues, the corpse is covered with a cloth and its face turned towards the Ganges. It is extremely inauspicious to die on a bed and in Rohtak, it is believed that the soul will in that event be re-born as an evil spirit.

In cases when a child over 27 months of age, a grown up person or an old one is dying, the ground is first plastered with cow-dung. Then *kusha* grass is spread and on that again a cloth is laid. On to that the dying person is taken down from the cot so that his feet point towards the south,i.e. to Lanka or Ceylon. This is called in Urdu *manzil resani.* A Hindu must not be allowed to die on a bed or even on a mat, as it is supposed that the soul in separating itself from the body in which it is incorporated, enters into another body which leads it to the abode of bliss destined for it. But if the dying man were to expire on a bed, he would be obliged to carry it with him wherever he went, which it may be easily supposed would be very inconvenient. In Jind, the dying man is laid on the ground and grain, money, a cow etc., are given away in alms according to his means with his own hands. This is called the *chhaya dan* or *akhiri dan* (last gift) and is supposed to avert the agonies of death so that the dying person either recovers or dies without further suffering. *In* Kulu, according to a highly idealised account which can only apply to the highest castes, when a man is on his death-bed seven species of grain or *satnaja,* some iron, wool, salt and money are put, before him, and he is made to give these articles as his last alms or *ant-dan:* a cow *baitarni* is also donated. The scriptures already mentioned are read. If the sick man recovers the alms go to a Brahman, otherwise they are taken by the family *acharaj,* whose office is hereditary. Where it has no *acharaj,* the *dan* or a gift of lamp is made and a *panch-ratan* (a collection of five metals) is put in the mouth, a *sankh* (conch) is blown to make the death known to the neighbours, and the near relatives are also informed.

The next of kin or nearest agnate of the deceased is, it may be said, his chief mourner. In Ambala, he is commonly called the *karmi dharmi* or in Sialkot *bhungiwala.*

The *bhungiwala* or chief mourner (a person who is most nearly related to the deceased or who by common usage has the right to perform this function) changes his clothes, gets his head and face shaved clean and then bathes in order to purify himself from the defilement of the barber's touch. All the younger male relatives of the deceased also get their heads and faces shaved in honour of his death. The *bhungiwala* then puts on *dhoti, parna* and turban of pure white cloth and sacred thread, and performs *havan* (a sacrifice to fire) and *sankalpa* giving a few alms to the *acharaj* who appears at the lamentable scene of mourning.

The body is bathed having its head towards the north and feet to the south. Then it is shrouded in white cloth if a male and in red if a female. A *mansuri* coin is tied to the shroud.

The corpse is then washed and wrapped in a piece of ceremonial cloth and placed on a kind of state bed called *viman*. Several other costly coverings of silk and muslin are placed over it in order to show the high social status of the bereaved family. In the case of the death of an elder, the *viman* or litter which is constructed of a plank of wood and several strips of bamboo, is decorated with artificial flowers and birds. Before starting all the women of the household, in particular the daughter-in-law and grand daughter-in-law, walk round and do obeisance giving alms to the family barber.

After the death, the chief mourner shaves his head, beard and moustache, leaving only the *bodi* or scalp lock, bathes, puts on a clean loin-cloth and turban, and for a period of 14 days eschews leather shoes, but not those of cloth or jute. In theory, the chief mourner is a *Brahmachari* until all the rites due to the dead have been completed. It results from his status that he must avoid several ceremonially impure acts, such as sexual intercourse, eating more than once a day, and taking medicine. He should also avoid sleeping too long and, more especially, sleeping anywhere but on the ground. Lastly, he ought to abandon secular business for a time and meditate on God day and night.

If the deceased has left behind a widow, she loosens her hair. Moreover, she is for a time, ceremonially impure and must not sleep on a bed or touch any household utensils. For 13 days, and until she has bathed in the Ganges or Jamuna, she may only eat once a day.

In Ambala, two copper coins wrapped in red cloth are thrown over her husband's head to indicate that her married life is now over. Among the Hindus migrated from Montgomery, two garments of red cloth (given by her own parents) and two of white (given by her parents-in-law) are put on by the widow on the 11th and 13th days respectively. In Jind, directly after death has ensued, the deceased's son sits down on the ground near him and places his knee under his head, a usage called *god dena.* In some place a lighted lamp is also held by the son. He then 'sits in *kiria' (kiria baithna)*, changes all his clothes and puts on fresh ones which in the case of well-to-do people are of wool.

Before cremation, all the sons and grandsons of the deceased get themselves shaved-*bhuddar karwana* in Jind, Bhakkar and elsewhere, but the usage is not universal. Thus, in Gurgaon, only the eldest or youngest son may shave or one of his kinsmen may do so, but in some villages all the sons shave. In this district the hair shaved off is placed underneath the cloth spread on the *arthi* and taken to the burning ground. So, too, for example in Bannu, before the cremation all the deceased's children and grand-children get their heads, moustaches and foreheads shaven and very often the man who performs the *kriya* gets all the hair of his body shaved. In Isa khel if a father or a mother dies, all the sons, grandsons and great-grandsons get their moustaches, beard and head shaved, but the eyebrows are not shaved at all. Only the eldest son is allowed to perform the *kriya*. If an older brother or uncle dies without issue, only he, who performs his *kriya,* gets shaved.

If, in Gurgaon, the deceased's wife is alive, she breaks her bangles in token that she has lost her *suhag* on her husband's death. This is called *suhag utarna*. These bangles are also placed on the *arthi,* like the hair. In Karnal, she also unties her knot of hair, breaks and throws the pieces of her bangles and her nose-ring on to the corpse, with which they are wrapped up in the shroud. The other females of the household also discard their ornaments. Soon after the death, the body is washed, a man's corpse being washed by men and a women's by women. The water for washing the dead should be drawn in a particular way: the chief mourner ought to take pitcher and rope, go to a well and bathe. Then, without drying his body or changing his waist-cloth, he should draw a second pitcher full of water, using only one hand and one foot, and carry it home to wash the corpse. If the deceased was a man of high caste, the *tilak* is applied to his forehead, a *janeu* placed round his neck and a turban tied round his head. The body is invariably clothed: a man being dressed in white, and a married women, whose husband is alive, in red called *chundri*. A widow is also shrouded in red cloth, but no ornaments are used, whereas a wife whose husband is still living is decked in all her finery, a new set of bangles being put on her wrist, her teeth blackened with *missi,* her eyes darkened with antimony, her nails stained with henna, and a *bindi* fastened on her forehead. The old are dressed with special care. If the death occurs too late, for the body to be burnt before sunset it is kept in the house for the night, during which some 5 or 10 of the deceased's kinsmen watch the corpse.

In Kulu, if the death occurs early in the day, as the cremation can be effected that same day, a bier is made at once and after the corpse has been bathed and the *mrituasthan* (death-bed) and *dwarpal* (door) *pinds* have been offered, it is placed on it, and a shroud put on the body. Four of the nearest male relatives carry the bier to the burning place and midway the bier is put down, a *bisram* (rest) *pind* being given and the mat, on which the man died, burnt. All the way grain, fruits and pice are thrown over the corpse, which is then taken to the burning-place where the fourth *pind* is offered. A funeral pyre is then made, and when the corpse is put on it, the 5th or *chita pind* is given. On the corpse are piled big logs of wood to press it down and the pile is then set on fire, first by the *karm-karta* or man who gives the *pinds* and then by others. All the near relatives and neighbours, especially the brothers, sons and other agnates etc. of the deceased should go with the *arthi.* When the body is nearly burnt, the skull cracks and the *purohita* sprinkles water over the pyre: this is called *kapal* (brain) *maksh* or *kapal kirya.* The shroud is given to the *acharaj* and the other white cloth is given to the musicians or *Dagis.*

When burnt to ashes, some on the very day of the burning and others on the third day wash away the ashes and take out the *asthis* (bones or the teeth and fingers) which they keep carefully and send down to Hardwar by one of the family or some reliable person. Some rape-seed and iron nails are spread on the burning place. As a general rule, death is swiftly followed by cremation among the Sikhs and Hindus, but there are many notable exceptions. Thus, the members of several religious sects and orders are buried, as also are very young children, and in certain cases exposure, especially by floating a body down a stream, is resorted to. But whether destined to be burnt or buried, the treatment of the corpse is much the same.

The bier (*pinjri* or *arthi*) is made of the pieces of the bed on which the deceased lay prior to his death, or of bamboo or *farash* wood. Upon it is laid the hair shaved off by the next of kin, together with the wife's bangles if the deceased leaves a widow. Over the hair is spread a sheet on which the body is laid. For persons of great age or sanctity a *bawan* replaces the *arthi.*

Offering of *pinda*

After the body has been tied on to the bier, the first *pind* is placed on the deceased's breast, before the bier is lifted up. The bier is then lifted on to the shoulders of four near kinsmen of the deceased, the body being carried feet foremost.

The five *pinds* are all made of barley flour, *ghee* and in Jind they are prepared at the time by the *Nain* or barber's wife, and carried in a dish, *thal* by the Maha Brahman who also carries a *garwa* or basin full of water.

But with head foremost in Karnal: in which District, it is said, the bier is merely halted at a tank and *pinds* again placed on it. Then all the water and the body taken up again feet foremost.

As soon as it is taken out of the door of the house, a second *pind* is offered, the third being offered when it has passed the gate of the village or town, and the fourth at the *gharaban* or *adhmarag* or 'half way' between the gate and the crimation ground. Before this fourth *pind* is offered, water is sprinkled on the ground and the bier is set down, the first *pind* being replaced by this, the fourth. This rite is called *basa dena,* or the 'rest giving,' and the corpse turned round, so that the head of the corpses now in front, though the same four kinsmen continue to carry it. The fifth *pind* is offered at the burning-ground. These offerings are supposed to pacify the *duty* of *Yama* (the messengers of the god of death). The bier is set down at the burning-ground, and the chief mourner plasters a piece of ground with cow-dung and writes the name of Ram seven times to invoke god's help for the dead. On the same ground, the funeral pile raised and the body being placed, on it a *panchratans* (five metals) of gold, pearl, copper, silver and coral put in its mouth. In the case of a woman, this is done at the house.

Cremation and Kapal Kriya

The best wood for the funeral pyre is sandalwood, which is, however, rarely used owing to its prohibitive cost, *pipali, dak* or *jand* being used instead, but a piece of white sandalwood is if possible placed on the pyre. Sometimes the wood is carried by the mourners themselves. A pyre should be so constructed as to lie due north and south, in rectangular pit some two feet deep, resembling the *vedi* or pit for the sacrificial fire. When the pyre has been completed the fifth and last *pind* is offered and any valuable shawl or other cloth removed from the corpse, and given to a sweeper or a Maha- Brahman.

The corpse is then unfastened, the cords which bind it being broken with one hand and one foot, and laid on the pyre. The body is laid supine upon the pyre its hands being placed behind, therefore underneath it to prevent its being cruel in the future life. The shroud is torn near the mouth, and the *panjratni* inserted in it, while chips of sandal wood with some *tulsi* leaves are placed on the deceased's breast.

A man then takes the burning grass in his hands and walks once right round the pyre, keeping it on his right hand, and then turns back, until he reaches the feet. Here he halts and throws the burning grass on to the pyre. As soon as it is ablaze, all present withdraw out of reach of the smoke until the body is almost consumed, when the chief mourner draws near again and pulling a bamboo out of the bier with it smashes the deceased's skull. The man throws the bamboo over the corpse beyond its feet. The smashing of the skull is said to be due to the idea that the life of man is constituted of ten elements, nine of which cease their functions at death, while the action of the tenth *(dhanjiye)* continues for three days after death causing the body to swell if it remains unhurt. The seat of this, the tenth, element is in the skull, which is accordingly smashed in order to set it free. Finally, he pours over the skull a cup of *ghee,* mixed with sandal wood and camphor. This rite of smashing the skull is called *kapal kriya* or the rite of the skull. After this, all the members of the funeral party take a piece of fuel and cast it on to the pyre, and as soon as the body has been completely consumed, one of them takes the bamboo which was used to smash the skull, and with it draws a line on the ground from the head of the corpse to its feet, keeping the pyre on his left in so doing.

Custom of *siapa*

After this line has been drawn, all the deceased's kin stand at his feet with clasped hands and the next of kin raises a loud cry of sorrow, *dah marna.* After the *dah,* all the men go to a river or well where they bathe, and wash all their clothes, save those made of wool. The deceased's kinsmen and others now take a handful of water and facing southwards, cast it on the ground, saying his name and *got.* With this water sesame is mixed, whence it is called *tilanjali*, or a little water mixed with seasame is distributed in the name of the deceased. In former day a *siapa* or mourning assembly lasted 10 days, but now-a-days it is held only for one day, when the women beat their breasts. But on the death of a full-grown man, it lasts for several days and the wife of a *Bhat* leads the mourning, and for this she lets a fee which may vary from person to person.

In Sialkot, cremation is called *sanskara* and when the corpse is laid on the pyre its face is bared in order that the women of the family may have a last look at it. After pouring *ghee* and *panchrani* into the mouth the face is covered with the shroud. A piece of wood is then thrown over it from west to east and several logs of wood and splinters of sandalwood are placed on it. Before adding fire to the pile, the *bhungiwala* performs a *havan,* under the directions of the *acharaj* recites *mantras.* His example is followed by near relatives of the deceased.

The women now leave the scene and collect on the banks of a river or tank to bathe, but the rest of the mourners wait until the skull cracks. This is called the *kapal kriya* ceremony. After it, they proceed to make their ablutions, but only at a few yards from the burning pile and they sit down again to perform the straw breaking ceremony. In this, the *acharaj* recites aloud a *mantra* ending in the familiar words *yatra ae tatra gachhate* or 'whence he came, thither he goes'. At the end of this *mantra* every one takes a straw, break, it in two and throws it backwards over his head. But the *bhungiwala* throws his straw without breaking it, thus showing that some connection still subsists between himself and the deceased. After purifying themselves of the pollution of having carried a corpse, they all return to the door of the deceased's house, though no person may enter it as it is still defiled. Finally, everybody taking leave of the relatives of the deceased returns to his own house, where it is usual to sprinkle water upon the clothes in order to completely purify oneself of the ritualistic pollution. It is not until all these funeral rites and formalities have been accomplished that the people of the house are allowed to take any food, have neither eaten nor drunk anything since the moment that the deceased expired. All these practices are most rigorously observed. After the above ceremonies, the deceased's relatives spread a carpet or mat on the ground publicly and sit on it the whole day. Friends and acquaintances of the bereaved family come from far and near to sit on the mat in order to express their grief at the death as well as to condole with the relatives. This is called *phuri pana* or carpet spreading.

The same course is followed by the women of the family, but they spread a carpet in their own house and perform *siapa,* in which a hired woman of low caste *(siapa ki nain)* sings dirges and the women joining in the chorus, beat their thighs, naked breasts and heads in measured time. At night, several caste-fellows of the deceased sleep on the ground in the house in his honour. Every day for four days early in the morning, all the males of the family utter loud cries which are followed by the weeping of the women. If the death takes place late in the evening or at night then all the funeral ceremonies are postponed till the next morning and the corpse is kept indoors. But a stick just as long as the length of the deceased's body is placed beside the dead, in fear, perhaps that the corpse may not get longer.

On returning from the burning ground, the members of the party bathe at a tank and wash all their cotton clothes to purify themselves, while the *Nai* gives them *nim* leaves, which they put in their mouths. On arriving at deceased's house they sit in front of it in two rows through which the *Nai* passes pouring out water, which is also supposed to effect purification. Then they return to their homes. As a rule, no food is cooked in the deceased's house on the day of death. Those who have married, son and daughters receive food from them. But elsewhere, as in Jind, any relatives may supply the family with food, *khichri* (rice and pulse), flour and *ghee* in case the deceased was an adult, and suger and rice also in case he was an old man. This provision is called *karwa batta* or 'better food' and the remains of it are not kept but distributed among the poor. In Gurgaon, if the deceased was a Brahmin, uncooked *khichri* (a mixture of *dhal* and rice), pulse and flour are brought by his *jajmans* and if he was a Mahajan, they are purchased from the *bazar*. If the deceased was a man of any other tribe, this food is sent by some of his relations. When it is cooked a *gangaras* (some leaves of bread given to a young cow) is given. After this, the man who has performed the funeral rites, takes his food and is followed by other members of the family.

In Gurgaon, the man who has to perform funeral rites as the chief mourner cannot wear woolen clothes but only a *dhoti* (waist cloth), is he not allowed to wear leather shoes. He spreads a cloth before his house door and sits there for the whole day. Those who come to pay a visit of condolence stay with him for a short time and then leave after expressing sympathy with him and the other heirs of the deceased. A little before sunset, this man goes for *ghut bharna* a second time. He fills a pitcher after taking a bath and then returns to his house, it is not necessary that *pandit* should accompany him in the evening. In the evening an earthen lamp is lighted on the spot where the deceased breathed his last. The wick of this lamp is made so long that it may be sufficient to last for ten days of mourning.

The funeral party then returns to the village, accompanied by the Nai who has plucked a branch of a *nim* tree. From this every one takes a leave before he enters the village, and this he chews, and then spits out as a token that all contamination has been removed; or to accept another explanation, to invoke a curse on those who wilfully failed to attend the funeral. The actual funeral ceremonies are closed by a *chaudhri* or other elderly man saying after the members of the party have sat for a time close to the deceased's house, *Bhaiyo dhoti sukhao,* 'Brother, dry your clothes.'

After the men of the house have returned from the funeral, the women headed by the deceased's wife or mother (in the case of a man, or, in the case of a woman, by her daughter-in-law) or by his nearest female relative, go. She also takes with her the grass which was spread under the deceased's death-bed and the earthen vessel used in washing the corpse, and caste these away outside the village. This is called *pula uthana,* they go to bathe weeping and singing mournful dirges as they go. After bathing they return in soaked clothes to the deceased's house and leaving his heir they go to their own homes. There they take a *shudh ashnan,* bath of purification, and then resume their ordinary duties.

The *Nai* now obtains from a *Kumhar* (a Hindu caste, manufacturer of clay-build pots) all the articles required for the *ghat,* together with those required for burning the lamp at the spot where the deceased died. These articles include some *dub* grass, *jeorian,* sesame, milk, Ganges water, an earthen jar, and *tulsi* leaves. The chief mourner accompanied by a *Nai* takes these to a well by which he hangs a pitcher full of milk and sweet water or simply water, in *chhinka* or net on the trunk and two branches of a tree, which the spirits are supposed to haunt. A small hole is made in the bottom of the pitcher and stuffed with *dub* grass so that the water may trickle slowly to the ground. Hence it is called *dharra* (from *dhar* a stream) in Jind.

In Gurgaon, certain trees are set apart for this rite, which is known as *ghat marna* and for which certain *mantras* are prescribed. A little before sunset, this pitcher must be refilled, after the chief mourner has bathed, but the *pandit* need not accompany him. The pitcher has to be filled thus twice daily for 10 days. In the evening too a lamp has to be lighted at the place where the breast of the corpse was or near the spot where the death occurred. This lamp must be furnished with wick enough to last 10 days, and it must be kept burning day and night for that period, to light up the path of the departed spirit through *Yama-Loka.* A small fire must also be kept burnnig there. In Kangra this lamp, called the *diwa dhariara,* is said to be placed by the head of the corpse; and the wick must not be renewed: it is inauspious if it fails to last all the 10 days. Both this lamp and the *choaru* are taken, at the expiration of the 10 days to the river side, or to a spring, or placed under a *bar* or *pipal* tree.

At the same time a lamp is lighted and placed on the ground outside the dead man's house. Close to it but on the public road side must also be placed a *tikoni* or tripod of reeds, tied together in the middle, on top of which is placed a cup full of water and milk but with a hole in it. All this is done while a *pandit* recites *mantras.* This is repeated on the two following days, a new lamp and *tikoni* being required each day. In Ambala, this ritual is repeated daily for 10 days.

The *karam-karta* (one who gives the *pinds*), the next day after bathing, cooks some rice to make three *pinds* on which pieces of betel nut and black wool are placed. A jar containing water, milk and *ghee* is placed on some sand in the compound on a teapoy; and a very minute hole made in the bottom of the jar to let the water out slowly, and *kusha* (sacred grass) is put in the jar. On each of the nine subsequent days only one *pind* is given and more water is poured in to the jar to keep it full. A lamp is kept burning for nine days and the *Garur Puran* is read by the priest to the audience, who offer money to the lamp, which goes to the priest.

On the tenth day the lamp is taken away by a *Nai* who gets some cash, and the other things are thrown into a river or stream, everybody has his head shaved and washes his clothes; on the 11th day the *pindi karm* is performed: a bed, umbrella, shoes, a cow, cooking utensils, a suit of clothes and jewelry being given to the *acharaj.*

Custom of *Sradha*

In Himachal Pradesh, Kanets and other low castes give one *pind* every third day, putting the *pind* in a hollow piece of wood and taking it to the river, where the *karm-karta* holds it by one end and a carpenter by the other, the latter cutting the wood at the middle and thus the *pind* is dropped into the water. Water is brought from the river in a pot, with which to knead some flour which is given to cows. Then a goat is killed and relatives and neighbours are fed. This custom is called *sradha.* After the funeral a *pandit* is sent for, in Gurgaon, to ascertain the *soharni* and *teremi* days. The *soharni,* also called *astat sanchi* (or in ordinary speech *phul chugna,* is performed on the third day after the death, provided it does not fall on a Bhadra, *panchar,* a Saturday or a Tuesday, in which case it is observed on an appropriate day.

The deceased's kinsmen go in a procession to the pyre and there cook rice and pulse, each in separate vessels. A *pind* is then placed by the deceased's skull, and eight *balis* set round it in as many different directions. The bones of the deceased, which are universally called as *phul,* are now picked up with an elaborate ceremonial. First of all the chief mourner picks up three, using only his thumb and little finger. These he places in a platter of leaves and then all those present collect the remaining bones. Secondly, the ashes are collected with a wooden *hoe*.

Then the bones are washed in a *karel* (the lower half of a pitcher) with milk and Ganges water. Lastly, eight stakes are driven into the ground on either side of the pyre. The bag in which the remains are placed should be of red cloth for a woman and of white for a man. But in Jind, only the bones of the hands, toes and the teeth are gathered into a *thali,* a purse of silk or deer-skin, and then taken to the Ganges or *Pihwa tirath.* In the Kurukshetra and Devadharti on the Jumna this ritual is not observed.

The rest of the ashes are collected into a heap, about which pegs are driven into the ground, and round these a cotton thread is tied. The bones are carried by a kinsman, a Brahman or a *Kahar*.

But people originating from Montgomery do not pick up bones until the 4th day and they are then sent to the Ganges, while the ashes are cast into any running river. On the other hand in Rohtak, the Jats if well-to-do are said to despatch both bones and ashes to the Ganges while those of people dying of leprosy are cast into the Jamuna, while round Tohana in Hissar, the ashes are merely piled up in the crematorium. Hindus dwelling in the Kurukshetra do not send the bones to the Ganges, but bury them in an earthen vessel after they have been washed with milk and Ganges water. This is a purely local custom.

In Kulu Himachal, among the higher classes the *asthi* or bones should be taken to the Ganges within a year of the death. The man who takes them eats only once a day, because the *patak* is considered to have been renewed at this time. These bones are taken from the place of cremation and in an earthen pot put in a hollow of a tree or wall. When despatched they are wrapped up in silk cloth and hung round the bearer's neck. If he is not one of the family, he is paid a remuneration in addition to the fee for the *dan-pun* at Hardwar and his expenses on the journey. On reaching Hardwar the bones are immersed into the river and alms are given. Some sacred water is taken home, where it is called Gangajal and worshipped. Brahmins are fed on the return and some cloth, cash and grain are given to the *purohita*.

Offering of the *Pinds*

In addition to the five *pinds* offered during the actual funeral, other *pinds* which are believed to constitute the body of the dead man, are subsequently offered. After the bones have been sent to the Ganges, all the kinsmen and relatives return to the spot where the *ghat* is hanging. Then a patch of ground is plastered over and as many *pinds* offered as days have elapsed since the death. And from this day onwards a Brahmin is fed at this same spot, or given 10 days' supply of uncooked food. After the *phul chugna* is over in Jind, the eldest son or he who performs the *kria karm* has a *katha* (reading) of the Gurur Purana recited by a Brahmin at the deceased's house for 10 days among Vaisyas and for 13 among Brahmins, Kayasths and Jats; and some money is spent on this *katha* by the members of the family and kin.

Rites of *Patak* or Death Related Impurity

Corresponding to the *sutak* or ceremonial impurity which ensues on birth is the *patak* or *bhit,* sometimes erroneously called *sutak,* which ensues on a death. In theory, the period of this impurity is 10 days among Brahmins, 12 among Khatris,15 among Vaisyas and a month for Sudras, but it is now in practice 13 days among all classes, or less according to the degree of relationship, for example, the death of a kinsman in the 4th degree involves *patak* for 10 days, and that of one in the 10th degree for 1 day only. *Patak* extends in theory always to kinsmen of the 7th degree.

These rules are, however, subject to many variations. For instance in Sialkot, the *bhit* lasts only from the day of death to the 11th day and no outsider ventures to eat or drink in the deceased's house during this period. But among the people originating from Bahawalpur, the family in which a death has taken place is held to be impure for 13 days, when the other Hindus do not eat or drink with any of its members. The impurity extends to all the agnates for five generations. After the 13 days the members of the family remove this impurity by bathing, washing their clothes or putting on new ones, and by re-plastering their houses. A person affected by the *bhit* or impurity is called *bhittal.* In Bhakkar tahsil, the rules are the same, but the period is only one day on the death of a child of 6 months, 3 days on that of one of 5 years, 6 days if he was 10 years old and 13 days in the case of all persons whose age exceeded 10 years. It is removed by breaking old earthenware, as well as by washing cloth. On the last day an *acharaj* is fed and after taking his meal he recites *mantras* whereby the house is purified. In Bannu, the rule is that the pollution lasts for as many days as there were years in the dead child's age. If one more than seven years dies, the pollution lasts for 13 days, and affects the descendants of the four higher generations.

The rite of *kria karm* is performed, at least in theory, on the close of the period of pollution. Thus, it is performed by the eldest or youngest son on the 13th day, as the family is deemed to be in state of impurity for 13 days. This impurity affects the kin to the 3rd or 4th generation. So, too, in Kapurthala, the *kria karm* is performed among Brahmins on the 11th day after death, among Khatris on the 13th, while Vaishyas observe it on the 17th and Sudras on the 31st day after death. In Shahpur, however, the family is considered impure for only 12 days. This impurity affects all relations up to the 7th degree. On the 13th day, it is removed by donning new clothes and plastering the house. A person affected with impurity is called *marutak.* In Rohtak, the sect or the Sat-Nami sadhus does not mourn or perform any *kria karm* after death.

In some parts of the country, there is tendency to simplify the full rites. Thus, in *Kohat* after the body has been washed and five valuables like gold pieces and pearls put in its mouth, it is carried on a bier by 4 men who are relieved from time to time on the way. There appears to be no *adhmarg* and *pind karana* (as it is termed) is only performed thrice, once at the place of death, once at the outer door of the house and lastly at the burning ground. After this, the man who has offered the *pinds* carries a pitcher full of water round the body, breaks it and spills the water. The corpse is carried out with its feet towards the burning ground, but on reaching it is turned round so that its feet are towards its houses. On the way raisins, dates and pice are thrown over the coffin, and if the deceased was a very old man flowers, too, are cast upon it. At the burning ground, the body is washed a second time and *ghee* is put in its mouth. After the *kapal kria,* the man who is to perform the *kria karm* circumambulates the fire six times, being joined by all the other members of the deceased's clan in the 7th round. Then all those attending the funeral withdraw. A short distance from the pyre on their way back, all collect and each picks a few blades of grass while the *acharaj pandit* recites some *mantras,* and on their completion, all men except the one who is to do the *kria karm* cut the blades into pieces and when they come to some water bathe and wash their clothes.

Then all the clansmen take water in their hands and putting seasame in it while the *acharaj* recites *mantras,* throw it on the ground. The deceased's family then gives the *acharaj* sweetmeats and 1.5 yards of cloth are given to the man who is to perform the *kria karm* for his turban or *bhurgi*. After prayers, all may now depart accompanying of the deceased's family to their house which the *kiria karm* man or the chief mourner enters, and he or some other relation present comes out and bids them adieu. When they reach their own house, they stand at the door while some one from inside sprinkles water over them before they enter.

In the house of the deceased a lamp placed in a small pit dug at the place of the death is kept burning for 10 days during which the *pandit* recites the Garur Puran by night or day. In the morning a *pind* and in the evening *tarkashta* is offered during these 10 days outside the door of the house. The chief mourner or the *kiria* man bathes twice daily, but eats only once, though he is given good food. Very early on the morning of the 10th day, the lamp is taken to a spring or river where the *pind karm* was done on the first day and put into the water with its face to the south. While so doing a naked weapon is placed on the *kria* man's head and the same day all the deceased's clansmen bathe and the boys get shaved. The *katha* or reading ends on this day and the *pandit* is given some cloth and cash.

Rite of *khorsha*

The relations give turbans to the *kria* man, who is thus recognised as the deceased's representative. Some cash is also given to him and his kinsmen console and encourage him to do his work. Brahmins perform the *kria* on the 11th day, Khatris on the 13th and Aroras on the 15th. At this rite, the *acharaj* makes figures of the *deotas* or deities on the ground with dry flour and then reads *mantras.* After he has finished, a bed with bedding, ornaments, grain, a cow, some cash etc., are given away in charity in the deceased's name. Another rite called *khorsha* very like the *kria* is held on the 16th day when Brahmins are fed. Until the *khorsha* is performed, the deceased's clansmen are considered impure being under *sutki* and other people will not eat or drink from their hands. On the 4th day after death, the bones are picked up to be immersed into the Ganges. But the ashes are collected and cast into the nearest river. On the 10th day *khichri* (rice mixed with pulse) is cooked by a man not belonging to the family and distributed among the kinsfolk. For 10 days the females assemble together and mourn. Children dying under 5 are said to be affected by *athrah,* a kind of disease.

Death Custom in Gurgaon

In Gurgaon, from the time the bier is taken up until it reaches the burning ground, all the mourners keep saying in a loud voice *Ram nam sat hai-sat bole gat hai.* The name of Ram (God) is true and will last till eternity. He who meditates on His name will get salvation. The *kaj* or *din* ceremony is not performed on any particular day in Gurgaon, but care is taken to perform it as soon as possible.

In villages, the people cook rice with *ghee* and sugar, while Banias and Brahmins in the town fry *laddus* and *kachauris.* All kinsfolk whether living near or at a distance are invited and the people of the village, as well as Brahmins, Jogis and beggars are fed with sweetmeats. Some only entertain people of 36 castes on this occasion, while others invite men of every caste. The relatives who are precluded by kinship from eating from the bereaved house are given *pattal* or separate share, and travellers visiting the village are treated in the same way. Others in addition to inviting kinsfolk in this way give Re. 1 and a *laddu* weighing a *ser* to each man of the tribe which does not disdain to receive alms. Some people have been known to spend about a *lakh* of rupees on a deceased's *kaj*. Relatives invited on the occasion are on their departure given cash as well as sweetmeats.

Those who are bound by relationship to pay something give money when the deceased's heir binds his turban. Among the Bishnois, the dead are buried at a place called *ogara* where cattle are tethered. It is believed that the deceased will not turn into an evil spirit by reason of cows urine always falling on it. In the absence of such a place they bury the dead in a burial ground or crematory.

No ceremony is performed in the case of a child. But in that of a young or old person they perform the *tiju* or *kaj* ceremony on the 3rd day after death. The *kaj* of a youthful person is on an ordinary scale, i.e. only 20 or 22 kinsmen and 5 or 6 Brahmins are served with food. Recitations from the sacred scriptures are continued for three days. The *kaj* of an old person is celebrated with great *eclat,* large sums of money being spent on it. An ordinary Bishnoi only feasts all his villagers but rich folk spend thousands of rupees. A cow and the clothes of the deceased are given to a Brahmin in charity. The food prepared on the *kaj* day is at first placed on the deceased's tomb in the leaf of an *ak* plant together with a cup of water. It is believed that it is more auspicious if this food is eaten by crows than by any other bird. The period of impurity of *patak* is limited to three days. The actual members of the family are alone considered to be impure. An observance peculiar to the Bishnoi sect is that the marriage of a daughter or great-granddaughter of the deceased is celebrated on the *kaj* day.

This performance of *Barni Bathana* depends on the pecuniary means of the deceased's heir. On the *saharni, pandits* are sent for and made to recite the *Gayatri mantra* about 125,000 times for the deceased's benefit at a place fixed by the owner of the house. All the *pandits* rise early and after bathing recite the *mantra* till 2 P.M., when they take food. If one of them has to take water while reciting the sacred verse, he may do so but cannot resume his place without washing. Smoking is also forbidden during this time. On the 11th day, all the *pandits* assemble at the *ghat* to perform a *havan.* After this they are dismissed with some *dakhshina* or remuneration. The rite of *Banjur chhorad* is performed on the *ekadshi* or 11th day after death if the heirs are men of wealth and position. It consists in marrying a cow with a bull. The dues on this wedding are as usual given to the menials concerned, and after it the cow and bull are spotted with *mehndi* and let loose, to run wild, but the cow is generally given to a Maha-Brahman, while the bull is branded so that it may not be put to work. Agriculturists will not harass a bull so branded. It is fed by the deceased's heir until full grown. Further, it is never tethered with a rope or confined in any house. This rite is also called *barkhatsar chhorna* or *akals chhona.* It is not necessary that it should be conducted on the death of an old man, but it may be performed on the death of a young one, and generally speaking, it is done in the former case also.

The rite of *Gankhas jarna* is only performed when the *banjur chhorna* has been duly observed. It consists in planting a long bamboo (about the height of a man) in the ground outside the village with a human head dyed red on its top.

Cremtion Common to all other Hindus

In Jaamu region the Hindus burn their dead. The pyre is lit by the son or nearest male relative of the deceased however the bodies of renowned saints are buried. In the past the buring of Rajput women alive on the pyre of their husbands gave rise to a number of *sati* temples. All such pplaces are called debries. Muslims bury their dead in accordance with the provisions of shara. Mourning among the Hindus lasts for thirteen days. Ashes are collected from the cremation ground on the third day for their immersion in the sacred water of the Ganga or Basantar river. The earest male relative of the deceased who performs funeral rituals pours water under a peepal tree for all the thireen days of mourning early in the morning. The deceased's widow also sprinkles water near the door for all the thirteen days. On the tenth day of mourning the relatives of the deceased assemble near a tank to take bath and wash their clothes. The *purohit* is given a bed and a pair of clothes on this day in a belief that there would be received by the spirit of the deceased in the next world. He is also given dry rations equivalent to thirteen days for his consumption (rah kharchi). Six months after the death adh-barkhi is performed. The priest is offered chaji on this occasion too. Barkhi is a shradh ceremony performed after one year of death. Chaubarkhi is held after four year of death. The customs are related to the Hindus in Jammu region.

Custom of Funerary Phoa Ritual

Among the Buddhists in Ladakh, on death a lama is invited to perfrom phoa cermony. The body is cremated after three days if the death has occurred during winters. The ashes are collected and are kept in a chorten. The *zitsik* reast is given to the mourners in the nrighbourhood. Periodic death rituals are conducted after a month and a year of death in which a lama of the local *gompa* is invited for incantation of *mantras*. Other Buddhist communities of Ladakh like Beda, Champa, Dokhpa, Gara and Mon also observe similar cremonies with slight variations.

Building of Memorials Called Chhatris

Rich men and those of good position often raise a fine building to the memory of a deceased ancestor at the place where his body was burnt. In the middle of it they erect a structure of the shape of an umbrella called *chhatri*. Beneath this in the second storey they have the deceased's foot-print carved. These are always marked on hard ground whatever be the height of the building. Some *chhatris* in Gurgaon have cost Rs. 10,000 or Rs 12,000 each during the 19th century. They are handsome buildings containing decorated staircases, etc. They serve as shelters for travellers. Some people raise these *chhatris* to a considerable height so that they may be seen from the roofs of their houses.

The general beliefs current in Gurgaon include:

(i) One who joins in funeral procession to the burial or burning ground abstains from eating sweetmeats or drinking milk for that day.

(ii) Those who raise a funeral pyre for the first time do not drink milk or eat sweetmeats for three days.

(iii) If any one dies in the *panchak,* his death will be followed by another and so a ritual of *panchak shanti* is performed.

(iv) The man who takes the remains of a deceased to the Ganges does not re-enter his house without going to the deceased's burning place, and sprinkling Ganges water on it.

(v) If the death of a young person occurs on some festival, it is never celebrated until a male child has been born in the familly on the same festival.

(vi) A man is considered to be very lucky if he has a great-grandson at his death, and it is believed that he will go straight to paradise. But it is considered unfortunate if he leaves a great-great-grandson at his death as he will then go to hell. A body is watched till the *soharni* so that no one may take wood or coal from its pyre, as it is believed that if this be done the spirit will fall under the control of some evil person.

Fruit of some kind is given to a husband and wife in halves on the death of a child so that they may soon be blessed with another child.

The shroud of a child dying of *masan* (a wasting disease) is brought back to the house and carefully kept after being washed. On the birth of a second child it is laid on that shroud, the main object being that it may not die of that disorder. A death is considered auspicious if it occurs during the *amawas* and *kanagat* days, and it is believed that a man dying during those days will get an exalted place in heaven.

The Year of Mourning

Hindu mourning in theory lasts a year, during which period many rites have to be observed. The principal ones are:

(i) The *pinda* offering: On the day after the funeral, the *bhunghiwala* rises early and bathes, puts on a *pavitram* (a straw ring), performs a *havan,* offers one *pinda* (a ball of boiled rice) and goes out to water a sacred *pipal* tree. All these practices are repeated every morning and evening up to the 10th day under the directions of the *acharaj*. The number of *pindas* which are regularly placed side by side in water at a fixed locality are increased until it reaches 10 on the 10th day.

(ii) *The chautha*: On the 4th day, after performing these rites in the morning as usual, the *bhunghiwala* with his friends and relatives goes to the cremation ground for the bone gathering (*phul chunna).* The bones are generally picked up on the 4th day, but if it falls on an ill-omened day, the rite is performed on the 3rd. He performs a *havan* there, and taking an earthen pot full of water and milk, sprinkles it over the ashes with a small

> wooden spade, looking for any bone that may have escaped the flames, and puts them into an earthen pot reciting a *mantra*. Taking up a portion of the ashes he immerses them into any river nearby. The remainder he collects into a heap covering it with a piece of cloth supported on 4 sticks, like a canopy. Then he offers a sacrifice to it. These mementoes of the deceased he brings home and they are buried in a corner of the house to be thrown one day into the sacred water of the Ganges.

In Shahpur, on the 4th day after the death, all the bones and ashes of the deceased are immersed into the Ganges in the case of a rich person. But in that of a poor one, only one bone from each limb is thrown into that river. The ashes, however, are always thrown in a stream. An effigy of the deceased is made and sweetmeats and copper coins are distributed.

In some other areas, the remains are also collected on the 4th day. The bones washed with milk and Ganges water are put in a bag made of deer skin and immersed into the Ganges with some gold or silver, while the ashes are thrown into any running channel.

This day is called by various names. In the eastern districts it is called the *dasahi,* and in Jind two rites are observed on it : (i) All the kinsfolk and relatives (both men and women) of the deceased go to a tank and bathe there, but only the members of his family have their heads shaved as well : (ii) His eldest son distributes 10 *chhahnas* (pieces of cloth) with 10 pice and 10 *laddus* of rice each wrapped in a *chhahna,* and cooked gram among the *Nai*, *Jhiwar*, Brahmin and relatives of his family. This observance is called *dasahi ke laddu uantna.* The kinsfolk do not take these things home, but give them to the poor, merely tasting the gram and throwing the rest away. This is said *patak nikalna,* 'to avert the impurity,' or evil influences of the death.

The 10th day following death is theoretically one of ceremonial importance. In Gurgaon, it is known as the *dasgular,* and upon it the first *seja* is offered. During the time preceding days the *ghat* has been kept filled and a single *pind* offered daily, but on the 10th day all the deceased's kinsmen go to the place where the pitcher hangs and there the next of kin, with some other (near) relatives, is shaved; and after bathing they give to a Maha-Brahman all the necessaries of life. This ceremony takes fully six hours, and is concluded by giving away 360 *pindas,* and lighting 360 lamps. In addition,16 special or *khorsi pindas* are given and *tilanjali* is also distributed 360 times. After this, the *ghat* is untied, and the spot where the deceased died is plastered with cow-dung, mixed with cow's urine and Ganges water, and is thus purified.

Tenth Day of Mourning in Kullu

In *Kulu* on the 10th day after death, a goat is sacrificed and relatives are feasted. This is called *sondha.* The ceremonies of *jowasha* etc., are not observed. The higher classes perform the *shudhi* or purificatory rites on some auspicious day, and the lower on the 3rd, 5th or 7th day after the death. In this rite, Brahmins, neighbours and relatives are feasted and sometimes a sheep is sacrificed. The Kanets of Lag drink *lugri* or *sur* (hill beers) on this occasion, while the Dagis kill a sheep or goat on the 3rd day.

The lower castes, like Dagis, etc., are considered purified after a death in the family while the 3 days, *Kanets*, after 3,5,7,11, or 13 days, Brahmans 11days, Rajputs 13 days, Kshatriyas 15 days, Mahajans, Bohras, suds and goldsmiths 16 day.

The ceremony of the Tenth day in Sialkot is called the *dasahra.* And after the ceremonies usual on it, the friends and caste-fellows of the chief mourner meet on the banks of a tank or river for the final ablutions. He and his near relatives are shaved and tonsured on this day, shaving not having been allowed during the preceding 10 days. Having finally purified themselves, the deceased's relatives hold a funeral feast to which all kinsfolk from far and near are invited. They stay two days in his house and then the women wash their clothes and hair with curds and soap. The earthen pot of water and the lamp which was kept burning day and night are also cast into river. But according to another account, the purification is not attained or completed until the day of the *kiria karm,* the date of which varies.

In parts of Punjab, a few members of the community put a burning lamp before sunrise on a bundle of *khas* or *khashak* and set it afloat on a river or pond. All the members of the family shave the head, moustaches and beard, and bathe after they return home. They also pour 360 pitchers of water at the root of a *pipal* tree with the aid of the *acharaj* who recites *mantras* all the time. The women also wash their heads and all the clothes worn in performing the above ceremonies. In the afternoon all relatives and the members of the community gather together, and the Brahmin finishes reading the *Garur Puran* the same day, receiving some cloth and a little money as his fee. But of late in the towns, the Brahmins have not completed the *Garur Puran* till the 14th day, instead of the 10th, because the pollution is absolutely removed on the 14th and also because alms giving to Brahmins is most proper when no impurity remains. On the day when the *kirya* ceremony is finished, the *acharaj* is offered a bedstead, a quilt, a coverlet, a few ornaments and a sum of money and is then dismissed.

Late Sir Denzil Ibbetson had reported in the settlement Report of Karnal in 1893, "When a Hindu is on the point of death, he is taken off the bed and put with his feet to the east on the ground, on a fresh plastered spot strewn with the sacred *dubh* grass and sesame. Ganges water and milk, and tiny pearl (they can be bought for a few pice), and gold,are put into his mouth. The friends are called in and the son or nearest heir shaves completely in public, draws water with his right hand alone, bathes and puts on a clean loin-cloth, turban, and handkerchief, and no other clothes. Meanwhile the widow has broken her *sohag,* and throws it on the corpse, which the men or women of the family, according to its sex, bathe with the water the son has drawn, put on it a loin-cloth, and sew it up in a shroud (*guji* or *ghugi*). They then place it on the bier (*arti* or *pinjri*) and bear it out head foremost. At the door, a Brahmin meets it with *pindas* (balls of dough) and water which the son places on the bier by the head of the corpse. On the road, they stop by a tank or some water, and *pindas* are again put on the bier. Then all the *pindas* are flung into the water, and the bier is taken up the reverse way with the feet foremost. When they reach the burning place *(chhalla)*, the corpse is placed on the pyre (*chita*), and the son taking sacred fire, lit by the Brahmin, lights the wood (*aag dena)* and fans it. This is the *kiria karm* so often mentioned. When the bone of the skull is exposed, the son takes one of the sticks of which the bier was made, drives it through the skull (*kapal kiria*) and throws it over the corpse beyond the feet. When the corpse is completely burnt, all bathe and return together to the house, and then go off to their homes. The burning should be on the day of death, if possible; but it should always be before sunset.

If the burning was performed on the bank of the Jumuna, water is thrown on the ashes; if in the Kurukshetra, the bones are thrown into one of the sacred tanks, and all is over. Otherwise, on the third day the knucle-bones and other small fragments of bones (*phul*) are collected. If they can be taken to the Ganges at once, well and good; if not they are buried in the jungle. But they must not be brought into the village in any case; and when once ready to be taken to the Ganges, they must not be put down anywhere, but must always be hung up till finally thrown by a Brahmin in to the stream. Their bearer, who must be either a relation, or a Brahmin, or Jhawar, must sleep on the ground, and not on a bed, on his way to the Ganges. After the death a *ghara* of water with a hole in the bottom, stuffed with *dubh* grass so that water will drip from it, is hung in a *pipal* tree ; and the water is filled, and a lamp lighted daily for 11 days.

The house is impure (*patak*) till the 13th day after death. On the 10th day the Maha Brahmin or *Acharaj* comes. The household performs *dasahi*; that is, they go to the tank, wash their clothes, shave, offer 10 *pindas,* and give the *Acharaj* grain enough for 10 meals. On the 11th or day of *sapinda,* a bull calf is let loose, with a *trident* (*tirsul*) branded on his shoulder or quarter, to become a pest. The *Acharaj* is seated on the dead man's bedstead, and they make obeisance to him and lift him up, bedstead and all. He then takes the bedstead and all the wearing apparel of the dead man, and goes off on his donkey. But he is held to be so utterly impure that in many villages they will not allow him to come inside, but take the things out to him. On the 12th day the Gujrati Brahmin is fed, being given *sidha* or the uncooked materials for dinner only, as he will not eat food cooked even by Gaur Brahmins. On the 13th day the gaur Brahmins are fed, and then the whole brotherhood; the walls are plastered, the earthen vessels changed, all clothes washed and the house becomes pure. If the man died on his bed, instead of on the ground, the house is impure for 45 days; and after the 11th day special ceremonies called *jap* have to be performed to purify it. Again, if he has died on certain inauspicious days of the month, called *panchak,* 5 or 7 Brahmins have to perform *barni* in order to ease his spirit.

The same ceremonies are observed on the death of a woman. Children under 8 years of age are buried without ceremony.

There are no particular ceremonies observed at the death of a Musalman, who is, of course, buried with his feet to the south. Gosains and Jogis are buried sitting up in salt; and used to be so buried alive before our rule. Their graves are called samada. Bairagis are burnt, and in the case of an abbot a samad erected over some of the bones. Chamars are burnt while sweepers are buried upside down (*mundha*).

The disembodied spirit while on its travels is called *paret ;* and remains in this state for one year, making 12 monthly stages. For the first

12 days after death, a lamp is kept lit,and a bowl of water with a hole in the bottom for it to drip from kept full in a *pipal* tree for the use of the spirit. At the end of each month, the son gives his family priest the 'monthly *ghara*' which consists of a *sidha* or uncooked food for two meals, a *ghara* of water, a towel, an umbrella, and a pair of the wooden shoes (*kharaun*) used where the impure leather is objectionable. At the first anniversary of the death (*barsant*), he gives the Brahmin a bedstead and bedding, a complete suit of clothes, some vessels, and such other parts of a complete outfit as he can afford. This is called *sarja.* He also gives him a cow with a calf at foot and some rupees in water.

Likewise in other parts of Haryana, on the third day some of the relations of the deceased go to the crematory for the purpose of what is known as *phul chugna* (collection of fragments of charred bones of the deceased) which without being brought over to the town are despatched to be immersed into the Ganges through a relative, a Brahmin or a Kahar. The house is impure for 13 days. On the 10th day the household performs *dasahi, i.e.* they go to the tank, wash their clothes, shave and offer *pindas.* On the 13th day, a number of Brahmans are fed; the walls and the floor are besmeared with cow-dung; the earthen vessels are changed; the clothes are washed and thus the house is purified. If the deceased left sons, the eldest performs the *kirya karm.* This ceremony is performed on the 11th day among Brahmins, on the 13th among Khatris and among Vaishyas on the 16th.

Among Brahmins the ceremony is observed by the eldest son, among Khatris by the eldest or youngest son and among Vaishyas by the agent of the deceased. A family in which a death occurs is considered to be impure, until the *kirya karm* has been performed. The *bhungiwala* or the chief mourner rises early to make his ablutions. The *acharaj* draws a *chauk* (square) showing therein the symbols of various gods and goddesses on the ground and constructs a *pandal* over it in his courtyard. Rice is boiled and several kinds of flowers, vegetables and scents provided. Indeed, many other things are prepared which are indispensable for the sacrifices and offerings which he is to make. The *kirya karm* lasts for several hours and the ceremonies connected with it are a maze of superstition rituals. It is supposed that from this moment the departed soul is divested of his hideous form and joins the league of his forefathers to live among them in the abodes of bliss. This ceremony is observed by Kshatriya and other castes excepting Brahmins on the

13th day. On this day, too, many Brahmins are summoned to a feast to be eaten by proxy for the deceased. Popularly the day is called *Bura din* or the evil day and on it a widow's parents send her clothes, ornaments and cash according to their means in order that she may pass her widowhood in comfort.

The Rites of Randepa or Widowhood

The same afternoon at the conclusion of the *kirya karm,* the *randepa* ceremony is observed. The deceased's widow, after performing ablutions, decorates her body, puts on her richest garments and bedecks herself with all her jewels. Married women surround her, clasp her in their arms, and weep with her beating their beads and breasts in measured times crying and sobbing as loud as they can. Now, too, it is customary for the deceased's relatives to give his widow valuable clothes and ornaments in token of their sympathy with the widow. But she then divests herself of all her jewels and rich garments which are never to be donned again in her afterlife, thus showing her fidelity and devotion to her departed husband. On this day at the death of an elder, splendid feasts are given to his daughters, and grand-daughters, husbands and their relatives. *Ghee* and turmeric, the use of which is strictly prohibited during the preceding 10 days of mourning, are now used in the preparation of various dishes for the entertainment of the guests. The *bhungiwala* or the chief mourner puts on new clothes and turban bestowed on him, if married, by his father-in-law.

Rites of the eleventh Day

The rites on this day are either the *kirya karm* or survivals of the full *kirya* rite. Thus, in *Jind* on the 21th day after death, a Brahmin performs the *pind-dan.* The *pindas* consist of rice, flour, *ghee* and sugar, and *mantras* are recited by the Brahmin. A bedstead, clothes, utensils and grain are given in the deceased's name according to his means in alms to an *acharaj,* who is supposed to satisfy the desires of the *bhuta* or ghost body by means of his *mantras,* and other performances.. This observance is called the *kirya of gyarah* or ceremony of 11th day. The eldest son who has performed the *kirya karm* now changes his clothes and puts on a coloured turban. In Bhiwani, the *gharwin* is solemnised on the 11th or 12th night after death. Sweet-scented things are burnt in fire to the recitation of verses from the Vedas, and all tribes except the Saraogia, give the *acharaj* clothes, cash and utensils on this day.

Rites of the Twelfth Day

In Ambala and Karnal, the 12th day after death is observed.Twelve *gharas* (or *chatis* in the case of a female) are filled with water, covered with a small piece of cloth, and with a *matha* (a large cake of wheat flour fried in *ghee*) or *ganara* (a large cake of sugar) and some pice, donated to Brahmins.

Four *pindas,* one for the deceased, and one each for his father, grandfather and great-grandfather are prepared on the 12th day at the place where the death occurred. The deceased's own *pind* is cut into three parts, with a piece of silver of a blade of *dub* grass, and each part kneaded to the other three *pindas,* to typify the dead man's re-union with his forefathers. At this rite a Gujrati Brahmin is feasted. A gift of at least two utensils, a cup and a jar (*tilia*) is also made to him.

Hence, this rite is known as the *pind chedan karam.* In Karnal, it is said to be observed on the 11th day and as a rule only to be observed if the deceased left male issue. In Jind this rite is called the *apindi karm.* It is observed on the 12th day by a Brahman, and four *pindas,* money and food are given to a *Bias* Brahmin. In Gurgaon, a *hawan* is performed at the spot where the death had occurred, and at night a fire of *dhak* wood is lighted and on it is thrown a mixture of *ghee,* barley, sesame, dried fruit and sugar by means of a stick. The deceased's house is now deemed purified.

The Rites of the thirteenth day

Brahmins and Khatris celebrate the *Brahmabhoja* on 13th day, other castes on the 17th. Food, with a fee of at least 2 pice, is given to 13 or 17 Brahmins. On the 13th day at least 13 Brahmins (one of whom must be a female, if the deceased was a female) are fed. The second *seja dan,* which is precisely like the first, is also offered this day, but it is the perquisite of the *purohita*, the other 12 Brahmins each receiving a vessel of water coverd with a bit of cloth, a cup full of sweetmeat, a nut, *kambal gatta,* and a pice. This ceremony is sometimes held on the 12th day or, in Delhi, postponed to the 17th day after the death. But in Bhiwani on the 13th day only one Brahmin is fed, the house plastered with cow-dung and cow's urine mixed with Ganges water sprinkled in it. It is then considered purified.

The Rite of Dastar Bandi

The ceremony of installing the heir, of which the *dastar bandi* or tying on of the *pagri* is symbolic, is held in the afternoon of the 13th day after death. In Delhi, if the deceased had a shop, his heir is made to open it. The 13th is in a sense an auspicious day because the performance of rites is designed to secure future happiness. Thus, in Gujarat, a widow is made to don *fine* clothes and ornaments on the 13th or *kirya* day after her husband's death and clothes and money are given to her for support in the hope that she will pass the rest of her life in resignation. Nevertheless, the donors weep over her on this date. In order to secure future fertility to the bereaved family, some vegetables and water in a new pot are brought into the house on this date.

In Jind, on the 13th or 17th day after death, the whole house is plastered and a *hawan* performed, so that the house is purified. In case of a wealthy man 12 bronze *garwas* (small pots) with covers filled with the water as are placed up and in the case of a poor one as many earthen ones are filled and put up. Either 13 or 17 Brahmins are feasted and the *purohita* given a bed, utensils, clothes and money according to the donor's means. In the case of an old man, the family if wealthy of the deceased perform a *jag,* called the *bara karna* or 'making known' rite. A man of average wealth gives food to all the Brahmins of his town, and a rupee to each with a feast to his brotherhood. This custom, still prevalent in the villages of Jind tahsil, is also called *kaj karna* or *hangama karna.* The *Neota* ceremony is also practised at this time. After this, some wealthy men feast a Brahmin daily in the deceased's name, while others give him two loaves and an earthen pot filled with water every month.

The rites of Satarin

On the 17th day some food, clothes and utensils are often given to a Brahmin, in parts of Punjab and the Hindus who had migrated from Montgomery. The *tarwan* or 17th day in *Sialkot* is the occasion for just as many elaborate ceremonies as are performed in the *kirya karm,* but the gifts offered now go to the family *purohit.* In this district, it is also called *satarhwin* and on it the period of impurity ends although the *kirya karm* is performed some days earlier according to the customs of deceased's caste.

Post-death Monthly Rites

The dead are commemorated by Hindus every month during the first year and thereafter annually. This monthly commemoration consists in feeding a Brahmin (or a Brahmani if the deceased was a female) on the day of Hindu calendar *tithi* in each lunar month, consists in giving some flour and *dal* to a Gujarati Brahmin, hence called *Mahku* or 'he who receives the monthly offerings.' Elsewhere the monthly gift consists of a pitcher of water and some food, or of necessaries of all kinds. The subsequent commemorations are really a continuation of the rites on the lunar date of the death. Thus, in Kulu, the death of a man is commemorated by performing the yearly *shradhs* during the *kaniagats.* In these *shradhs* priests and Brahmins are fed according to the position of performer. Some also observe the *sambatsari shradhs,* which are not confined to the *kaniagats,* but on the contrary are performed on the lunar date of the death.

Annual Ceremonies

The annual rites are the *barsodhi* or first anniversary, the *khiabi* or recurring anniversary, and the *chaubarsi* or fourth anniversry of the death. The *barsi* and *chaubarsi* consist in the offering of a *seja-dan,* and in feeding Brahmins and the poor. After the *chaubarsi,* the annual ceremony may be said to be merged in the general commemoration of the dead ensured by the observance of the *Gangajal,* but the *khiabi* is said to be observed every year until the heir goes to Gaya and celebrates the rite there. The *khiabi,* as the term implied, merely consists in feeding a Brahmin or his wife. Generally speaking, all the ceremonies hitherto described are modified or liable to modification to meet various contingencies. For instance, in the event of a death occurring just before the date fixed for a wedding, all the funeral and other rites which are usually spread over 13 days can be completed in 3 days or even 3 *pahrs* or 3 hours each. But still more important are the modifications due to the age of the deceased, the circumstances under which death had occurred, such as its cause or the time at which it happened.

The Death-rites of Minors and Children

Very common are the customs in vogue if a child of less than six months dies, it is buried under a tree, and a cup of water is put beside the grave at its head. But in Shahpur, if a child of six months dies, the body is thrown into a river or running channel and in some cases it is buried, but no cup of water is placed near the grave. A child over six months, but under five years of age is buried or thrown into a river. But these rules are subject to endless variations. Thus, in the towns of Jind children dying when under 27 months of age are merely taken down on to the ground and then buried. There is no *mansil rasani.* Children in villages dying under the age of 6 years have similar funeral rites.

Generally, children are buried and not burnt, if they die before attaining a certain age, which is very variously stated as being 6 months or a year. Two and a quarter years or even 8 years in Hissar. Before the 1st tonsure at 22 months in Kangra.

In Hissar, the custom depends on the parents' position or caste. As a rule a child under 2.1\4 years is buried with a cup of milk at its pillow. But around Tohana, children are buried in burial-grounds up to the age of 8, except in the case of *pandit* families when they are cremated after the age of 5. As a rule, only well-to do people send the remains to the Ganges, but compulsorily the remains of a married person should be cast into river. Before the 1st tonsure at 22 months in Kangra; three in Gujarat, 5years among Hindu Rajputs, Jats and Mahajans in Rohtak; 2¼ years in towns among the higher castes, but 6 years among all castes in Jind; up to 10 years, if unmarried, in Gurgaon; after cutting the teeth in Kapurthala. It is impossible to say why the ages reported are so different and what the causes of the differences are. *In* Kangra stress is laid on the *mundan sanskar* or tonsure. If a child dies before that rite, it is buried under a tree or behind the house; but if it dies after the tonsure it is burnt. It is generally preformed before the child is 22 months old, and only in the case of male, but a girl child is also bured up to the age of 22 months. All persons more than 22 months old are said to be cremated in Kangra (Himachal). So, too, in Punjab children exceeding the age of 5 in general and those whose hair-shaving rite has been performed in particular are cremated. Thus, in Rohtak among Mahajans, whose children are generally buried if under five, those under two are carried to the burial-ground in the arms but, those over two are borne on a bier. A child over five is cremated.

But another account from this same district says that among Hindu Jats, children under the age of five are generally buried. If a Hindu boy between five and ten years dies, townsmen as well as rich people in villlage set the body afloat in the Yamuna, while ordinary villagers bury in the burial-ground. Persons *above* the age of 10 are cremated. Among Jat townsmen the procedure is not easily reconciliable with the one given in the text.

Hindus are especially careful that a child does not die on a cot as it is believed that one who dies on a bed transmigrates into an evil spirit.

A dying person is therefore laid on the ground a little before the death. In Sialkot although chilldren over two are cremated, no *kirya karm* is performed for those under 10 and both the bones and ashes of such children are set afloat or buried. Children who die after these periods are usually burnt in Hissar, though sometimes the body is set afloat on a canal or river- in Rohtak this is done only if the deah was due to small-pox, and in Gurgaon victims to that disorder are not burnt even up to the age of 12, but are set afloat on theYamuna or the Ganges, because Sitla would be displeased if they were cremated and the disease would spread. In Amritsar, all children dying under five are said to be be cast into a river or tank or if that is not possible buried, if less than one year old they are buried under a *jand* tree. Further, it is said, those exceeding five years of age are cremated.' In such cases the funeral pile is made of the reeds or sticks on which the body is carried to the crematory.

Among the Hindus originating from Isa Khel, children under one are buried near the banks of a stream or watercourse, but those who die between one and 5 are set afloat on a stream, with a bag of sand tied to the neck so that they may be eaten by fishes. And in *Gujarat,* this is also done, but a second jar, filled with sweetstuff, is also tied round the child's neck. Among townspeople, and in village, the well-to-do prefer to set the body of a child afloat on a stream, but villagers as a rule bury their children up to the age of about 10 in Rohtak: but in Montgomery children over two but under 5 (or even under 10 among the poor) are set afloat on a stream, those under two being buried in pits in a grove of trees.

Though cremation of children is not unusual, it is not the rule to vouchsafe them all the rites if they die before the age of 10, or even 14. But in Sialkot, the rule is that up to 2 or 3 children are buried, from 3-5 they are not taken to the Ganges unless their age exceeds five. In Kapurthala, the body of a child which has cut its teeth but not reached puberty is cremated, but instead of the *kirya karm* only the *dasgatri* is performed. This merely consists in both men and women bathing at a well or river.

In Gujarat, it is said to consist in giving an *acharya* a suit of clothes, which would fit the dead child, on the 4th day when its bones and ashes are cast into a stream. Though observed on that day it is called the *dasgatar.*

After marriage or attaining puberty, the rule is that the body of a child, at whatever its age it may have died, should be cremated. Children are buried in a place specially set apart for that purpose, called the *chhur gada* in Gujrat, and *masan* in Jampur. In Gurdaspur, an infant under one year of age is buried under the bed of a stream, if there be one within reach and a child under two is buried in a lonely spot far from the village and all paths, among bushes and preferably near running water.

In Bahawalpur, thse body of a child under six months is buried under a tree.The rites at the burial of a child are very simple and have already been noticed incidentally. A cup of water is often put beside the grave at its head, and in Hissar a cup of sweet water is put by the head of a male child which was not being suckled at the time of its death. Sometimes a cup of milk and some sweetmeats are also placed. It is a common custom for the relations to bring back on their return from the burial the leaves of a tree or vegetables and cast them into the mother's lap, in order that she may continue to be fertile. A similar idea underlies the custom in Gujarat, where on the 13th day some vegetables and water are brought into the house in a new earthen jar, to ensure the continuance of the family's fertility. If a Hindu child dies in Shahpur, the mother gets one of its ornaments re-made into one for her own feet, but the custom of dragging the shroud is extinct. Instead of putting greens into the mother's skirt something such as sweetmeat is put into it.

In Kapurthala, one of the ornaments belonging to a dead child is re-made into a foot-ornameant which the mother puts on in order that she may bear another child. When a child is buried and its body disinterred by jackals, there is a widespread belief that the parents will soon have another child, if the marks show that it was dragged towards their home: otherwise, their next child will be long in coming. To prevent this fire is kept burning at the grave for three days in Karnal. But in Gujarat, just the opposite occurs, for the mother places breads on the grave in the hope that it will attract dogs to it and that they will disinter the corpse.

Another widespread superstition is that when a child dies its mother should take hold of its shroud and pull it towards her, in order that she may have another child; sometimes too a small piece of the shroud is torn off and sewn on to her head-cloth. After burying a child, the relations bring leaves of vegetable (*sag*) and put them in the lap of the mother in hope that she may get another. These beliefs are found in Kangra and with a little variations elsewhere. Thus, in Tohana, the father or some other relative of the dead child brings green *dubh* grass and casts it into the mother's lap.

If a child aged between four and six dies leaving a younger brother the parents take a black thread or a red thread equal to its height in length, and tie it round the younger boy's leg where it remains until he has passed the age at which the elder child died. It is then thrown, with some sugar, into a river. This thread is called *lakh.* In Bahawalpur, if a child aged four to six years who has a younger brother dies, the parents take a red thread, touch the body with it and then fasten it round the leg of the younger boy, and it is not removed until he has passed the age at which his elder brother died. This thread is called *lakh.* In Amritsar, a child dying in such case is not buried until one of its ornaments has been put on the younger brother and a thread touched by the dead body tied on his right foot. When the younger brother has passed the age on which the child died, these are both removed.

Taboo on the Mother

Care is taken that the shadow of the dead child's mother does not fall on any other woman, until the milk disappears from her breasts, lest the other woman's child pine away and die. When the milk has disappeared from the mother's breasts, she is taken to a place outside the town, and there made to bathe and put on new clothes. On her return some green vegetable is put in her skirt.

If baby whose parents are greatly attached to him dies and another child is subsequently born to them, they are careful not to make any show of affection for it. Thus, if on the occasion of the deceased child's birth they distributed *gur* or sweetmeats, they now distribute onions instead. So, too, in Punjab those whose children die one after the other distribute *gur* instead of *batashas* or sugarcandy on the birth of another child. This custom is widely spread and the idea on which it is based gives rise to many similar customs. Thus, in Hissar the second child is dressed in clothes begged from another house. In and about Tohana, blue woollen threads with cowries on them are tied to both his feet and not removed until he has passed the age at which the elder child died. In Karnal, the father bores the nose of the son born afterwards and often gives it a girlish or worthless name, with a view to scare away death from it; it being considered that Death-god (*Yama*) strangles in his nose more male infants than female. In Kangra, nothing is distributed at the birth of such a son and no ceremony is observed on his birth or it is observed with some alterations; the kinsmen are not feasted at the observance of the *chola* ceremony. In Shahpur, a child born after 3 or 4 children have died, is given iron bangles made of the nails of a boat to put on its feet.

In *Gujarat,* if a man's children do not live, he adopts the birth ceremonies of another caste avoiding those of his own. A similar idea underlies the following custom: If a man's children do not live, he gives opprobrious names to those born afterwards. Such names are Khota Ram (*khota* an ass), Tindan (worm), Lota (an earthen vessel), Ledan (camel-dung) Chuhra (a sweeper), Chuha (rat), Giddar Mal (jackal),Lala-Lela (kid) and daddu Mal (frog) for boys: and Hirni (a doe), Rali (one mixed with others), Chuhri (a sweepress), Chuhi (she-rat), Chiri (sparrow) and Billo (cat) for girls.

Taboos on Subsequent Wives

If a man, in Bhakkar, loses his first wife and marries again, he places a *pahajri* or silver effigy of his first wife round the neck of the second, distributing, in memory of the former, sweetmeats among young girls. And for the first three nights he and his wife sleep with a naked sword between them. If he loses his second wife also, he is married the third time to a plant, or a sheep, so that the marriage to his third wife may be his fourth, not his third. His third wife wears the *pahajris* of the first two, and the other rites are also observed. In Punjab, if a betrothed child is dying, members of the opposite party take some sweetmeats to him a little before his death. Of this a small quantity is kept and the rest sent back. By this the connection between them is considered to be severed for good.

Taboo on a Betrothed Girl

If a girl lose her fiance, she is made to stand in the way of the funeral cortege and pass under the bier in order to avert all evil in the future from her own life. Thus, epecially the fiance's death is kept a secret from the girl's relatives, and rejoicings are actually held by his kinsmen, who go about their business as usual by day, and at night secretly carry out the corpse, wrapped in a blanket to the burning ground. The fiance's parents attribute his death to the girl, and her relatives perform rites to avert evil to her. In Amritsar, if either of two affianced parties die the survivor comes to the deceased's house and tries to knock his or her head against the wall. This clashing of head is considered by the deceased's heirs an unlucky omen. If the other party cannot find an opportunity to effect it, he tries to get a chance to touch a piece of cloth with one worn by the deceased.

One such attempt to get access to the house or possession of such a piece of cloth even led to blows. Thus, in 1903, a betrothed boy died of cholera. So closely was the secret of his illness kept that the most essential sanitary precaution were ignored and he was carried out stealthily to be burnt, lest his fiancee should succeed in striking her head on the *thara* or raised platform of his house, which was kept shut up. Failing in this, the girl's father got his daughter's forehead marked with small stars and placed her, clad in a red cloth, in a hackney carriage. Accompanied by three or four persons, he stopped it before the boy's house and made the girl alight from the carriage in order to strike her head on the *thara,* but she was prevented from doing so by the police posted there at the instance of the boy's father. He next tried to bribe the police but without success; then in desperation he tried to throw his daughter headlong across the *thara* from the roof of the house, but he was prevented from doing this either by the police, and a free fight resulted between his party and the police. Unsuccessful in all these attempts, he then went to the *shamshan,* but its gates had already been locked by the boy's father. The girl's partizans next tried to scale the walls, but those inside threw bricks at them, the besiegers retaliated and a hotly contested fight ensued, but at last the boy's body was burnt and his ashes together with 6 inches of the earth were put in a cart and taken by another route to the river into which they were thrown.

If the husband of a young girl dies, his ashes are wrapped in a cloth which is put round the widow's neck in the belief that she will pass the remainder of her life in patience and resignation. Thus, if a young girl becomes a widow, two pieces of red cloth and two of white are put on her on the 11th and 13th days. The red cloth is given to her by her own parents and the white by her husband's.

Death Rituals of an Adult

In Jind, when an old man is dying, the womenfolk of the family prostrate themselves before him and make an offering of money which is the barber's perquisite. If an old man dies leaving grandsons and great-grandsons, his relatives throw silver coins (or if poor, copper coins) over his bier, only Muhammadans and Acharyas will take these flowers and coins, but elsewhere people pick them up and place them round their children's necks, in hopes that they will thus live as long as the deceased old man.

But in some places, such as Hissar, they are taken by the poor. This is the case too in *Bhakkar* where the same usage prevails in the case of a 'perfect devotee' of an unspecified sect or order who is further honoured by being cast into a river. In Amritsar, much joy is displayed on the death of an old person with living grandsons and great-grandsons and his kinsmen send pitchers full of water for a bath to his eldest son. These are broken and the wood purchased for cremating the body is pilfered. Flowers of gold and silver, almonds and dried dates passed over the funeral pyre are considered auspicious and the women strive their utmost to pick them up. The pyre is built of wood, wrapped in a silk cloth, which is carried to the cremation ground.

Death from Disease or Accident

The children who die of small-pox are often floated in water. And the children dying of that disorder, measles or whooping cough are in general thrown into a river, the idea being that the goddess of small-pox must not be burnt. When thrown into a river the body is put in a big earthen vessel full of earth and sand to sink it. All who die of leprosy are cast into the Yamuna. If a man be drowned and his body cannot be found, his relatives go to Thanesar, and then make his effigy which is duly cremated on the banks of the Saraswati. In Kulu, in such a case a *Narain-bal* is performed at a sacred place, such as Kurukshetra in the manner prescribed in the Hindu Shastras. A lighted lamp is placed or the breast of the corpse, if it has been found; otherwise an image of flour of *kusha* is made and the lamp is put on its breast. It is then cremated in the usual manner.

The lower castes and the poor people take water in a pot and pour some rape-seed into it. A bee is also put in, and the *chela* buries the pot on the spot where the death occurred. A fowl is sacrificed there and then all the other performances are observed. The people say that if the *Narain-bal* be not performed the dead man goes to hell.

When a Hindu man dies in the *panchak,* idols of *kusha* grass are made, one for each of the remaining days of the *panchak* and burnt with the deceased; some perform the ceremony of *panchak shanti* on the *spindi* day. A death during a solar or lunar eclipse is considered inauspicious and in such cases *arahan shanti* is performed on the *spindi* day, but the other matters of *ras* and *nakchhattar* are not observed. In Kulu, when a man dies without issue or at enmity with his family; an image is made to represent him and worshipped by his survivors and their descendants as an *aniar deota* (sonless deity). This image is worshipped before beginning to consume a new crop and at every festival it is kept at the village spring or at home. Non-performance of this ritual is believed to cause illness, accident or some other evil. The worship is continued indefinitely, as it is believed to do good to the survivors' descendants for ever in future.

Other Beliefs and Superstitions

The Kulu, people believe in the predictions made by the *chelas* or oracles of a *deota* when at a burning place they see someone who was really elsewhere. To avert the danger, they sacrifice a sheep, a goat or a fowl and recite certain *mantras*. Some cooked rice and meat are also put in a broken earthen ware and thrown away far from home. A priest or *jotshi* is sometimes consulted who advises charity.

They believe that it is unlucky to carry a corpse through a gate or door, lest death subsequently finds its way through it. Thus, if a death occur in one of the palaces of the royalties, the body is carried out through a hole in the wall. So too in Maler Kotla it is, or used to be, forbidden to bring a body into the town unless permission be obtained to break through the town wall, in which case the body must be brought in and taken out again by that gap.

Inauspicious Time of Death Panchak Observance

The period of *Panchak* is uncanny in several ways, and it is especially inauspicious for a death or, to recall the original idea, for a cremation, to occur in it. Anyone so dying can only obtain salvation if a *shanti* or expiatory ceremony be performed on his behalf. This consists in employing five Brahmins to recite verses, and on the 27th day after the death, on which the moon is again in the asterism in which the deceased died, the *shanti* rite is performed, various things such as clothes, flowers and furniture being given away. The chief superstitions appertaining to the *panchak* related, however, to the surviving kin, for the Hindus believe that a death in this period will involve the deaths of as many others of the family as there are days remaining in the *panchak*. To avert this supposed disaster, the corpse should not be burnt until the *panchak* is over, or if this cannot be avoided as many dolls are made of cloth of the *darabh* or *dubh* grass (or among the well-to-do of copper or even gold) as there are days remaining. The dolls may also be made of cloth or cowdung, and in some places a branch of a mango tree is carried with the corpse and is burnt with it, as in Sirmur. In some other places wooden dolls are made. These are placed on the bier along with the dead body, and burnt with it. For example, if a person dies on the 2nd day of the *panchak* 3 dolls, and if on the 3rd, 2 dolls are made, and burnt with the corpse.

However, one account says that five dolls are always burnt, irrespective of the number of days remaining. These are named *Pret-bah*, *mukh-ap*, *bhumip* and *barta*, and, after being worshipped with flowers etc., are placed on the pyre, at the head, eyelids, left armpit, abdomen and feet of the corpse: *Kalsis*.

After the recitations are over, a *hawan* is performed. The Brahmins are given fee and fed, and then they take water from each jar and sprinkle it over the members of the deceased's family. This removes the evil effects of the death in the *panchak*. The head of the family also performs a *chbaya-dan*. In the Pachhad tahsil, some people fill a new earthen pot with water from five different tanks or rivers and hang it from the door of the house by a rope made of five kinds of twine. The water of the Giri, or of large tanks which never run dry, is preferred. In the Cis-Giri country a *panchak shanti* is performed by a Brahmin who recites *mantras*. The corpse is not burnt on the ordinary burning ground but in some other place and, if practicable, in the lands of another village; and Brahmins are feasted one day before the ordinary time. People do not venture to wear new clothes or jewels, buy or sell cattle, lay the foundation of a house or undertake any new work in the hand during the *panchak* days.

Notably some of the Muhammadan peasantry, in Bahawalpur, believe in the *panjak,* but according to them anyone dying in the first or last five days of a lunar month is said to have died in the *panjakan*; and the belief is that 5 or 7 members of the family must then die. To countervail the superstition, while carrying the coffin they sprinkle mustard seed on the road to the graveyard. Blue *pothas* (small beads used by girls for decorating dolls) are put into the mouth of the corpse. A piece of *ak* plant is buried with the body. After the corpse has been buried, an iron peg is driven into the ground outside the grave, towards the deceased's head.

However, if a person dies during the *panjak* and his relatives knowingly omit these ceremonies at his funeral, other deaths must ensue in the family, so they exhume the body, and ignorant people believe that it will by then have grown long teeth and eaten its shroud. Some sever the head from the corpse: others think it sufficient to drive a nail into the skull. The occurrence of a death in the *panchak* also modifies the rites observed after the usual cremation. Thus, on the 7th or 8th day after such a death orthodox Hindus sometimes make an image of 360 pieces of wood or of *dubh* grass and burn it, with full rites ; and on the 27th a special *panjak shanti* is performed. *In Gujarat* on the 13th or 27th day after death, the Hindus fill five jars with grain of various kinds and make 5 dolls of metal -gold, silver or copper, according to their means.

These images are then worshipped and fed with butter, curds, etc., and Brahmins recite *mantras*, receiving cash for their services. In Sirmur, on the corresponding day of the *panjak* in the following month, a door frame, made of *thimbu* wood, is erected beside the house-door through which the corpse was taken out ; and in this seven different kinds of grain are stuck with cowdung. A special *mantra* is recited on these before they are stuck to the door. A he goat's ear is also cut off and the blood sprinkled upon the frame. If these ceremonies are not performed as duly, as many people of the family or the village will die as there are remaining days of the *panjak*.

However, it is not easy to say what are the precise ideas originally underlying the *panchak* observances, but it would appear as if the leading idea was that anything which occurs during this period is liable to recur. For this reason it is unwise to provide anything likely to catch fire-lest it get burnt and a funeral pyre ensue-during the *panchak*. Accordingly fuel should not be bought, cloth purchased or even sewn, beds be bought or houses thatched ; nor should a pilgrimage be undertaken towards the south, or indeed at all nor should one sleep with one's head towards the south. It is, indeed, unlucky to commence any new work, but as a set-off to the prevailing gloom of the period it is peculiarly auspicious for Hindu women to wear ornaments during the *panchak* days, the idea being that they will get as many more ornaments as there remain days before the period expires.

If in Punjab a corpse has to be burnt on a Wednesday, an iron nail or peg is fixed at the spot where the death occurred, near the head, before the body is removed. Otherwise another death will occur in the house within a year. Generally speaking, this superstition is only common among Hindus, Muhammadans disregarding it. In the Simla Hills, it is believed that if a corpse be burnt on a Sunday or a Tuesday, another will soon be burnt on the same ground.

Death under *Swati Nakshatra*

If a person dies in the *Swati nakshatra,* the following ceremony is performed, lest many deaths occur among the brotherhood and the villagers. After the body has been burnt, five wooden pegs are driven into the ground, at the spot where it was burnt, in a peculiar shape, and round these an untwisted cotton thread is tied. As the mourners go back, a hole is made in the road, at a short distance from the pyre, and in this a he-goat's head is buried with a loaf made of seven kinds of grain, and a *patha* (a bamboo tube, through which seed is poured in the ploughed land, in which are fixed severn iron nails besmeared with goat's blood and over which a special *mantra* is recited. In the trans-Giri country, if a person dies during the Swati or Mul *nakshatras,* or on the 1st or 7th day of either half of the lunar month, 4 pegs of *thimbu* wood are fixed to the door of the house in which the death occurred, and a white woollen thread is tied round them, while *mantras* are recited.

Seven kinds of grain are also stuck with cowdung on the upper part of the door. Six more deaths will take place among the relations or villagers if this ceremony is not performed for a death occurring in the Swati or on the *saptami* (7th) day of either half of the month, and an indefinite number will ensue on a death in the *Mula* or on the *Purima* (first day of either half). In the Simla Hills in the country beyond *Phagu*, a death in *Makar* (Capricorn) portends the deaths of seven kinsmen, and to avert its consequences seven dolls are made and 7 arrows cut in precisely the same way as in the *panchak* rite. This superstition is called *satak* (from *sat 7*).

In the same part of the hills, it is also believed that if A dies in the nakshatra of B, both will die within the year, or fall victim to a dire disease. To avert this a rite is held in honour of Mahamurti ji, when the *nakshatra* recurs. B is covered with a white cloth and the Brahmin, after performing a *chhaya-dan,* worships with offerings of seven kinds of grain. In some places, a he-goat is sacrified over B' s head; but elsewhere by night a large loaf of wheat flour is baked, and round it lamps are lighted, a flour image of Jogni Devi being placed on its centre. About midnight, a Brahmin puts this loaf etc. before B and mutters *mantras,* offering seven kinds of grain over his head and putting them also on the loaf. Then he sacrifices it over his head and takes it with five *balis* (ordinarily he-goats) to the burning-ground, a few men following him. As he goes he signals for the sacrifices to be offered at various spots along the road, and those who follow him observe perfect silence, under pain of death, and do not look back, as that would vitiate the ceremony. The party, moreover, must not return to their homes that night but spend it in the forest or another village. At the burning-ground, the Brahmin deposits the loaf there and a he-goat is sacrificed, its flesh being consumed by the party on the spot, anything left being the Brahmin's perquisite.

In the Simla Hills, if the drum beaten at a Kanet funeral emits a loud sharp note, it is believed to portend another death in the village, and the rites in vogue are ineffective to prevent it. The Kanets and lower castes, especially after collecting the bones to take to Hardwar, drive two wooden pegs into the ground and place a mill-stone on the site of the pyre, enclosing it with thorns in order to weigh down Jam, the god of burning-grounds, for several days. Otherwise he would devour people. In the Simla Hills, the musicians and the makers of the *baman* or hearse go to the burning-ground and kindle fire in a large stove for warmth, but if anyone's shadow falls on the stove, he will, it is believed, die within the year: or if part of his shadow falls on it, he will suffer sickness. Sitting round the stove these men profess to see a spirit flying through the air, as if impelled by some force into the stove. This spirit they identify as that of some one still living and to avert the omen he worships *nakshatras* and offers sacrifices.

It is usual, especially among Kanets, to drive two pegs, one at the head, the other at the feet, of the corpse, in order to prevent a demon from entering it. If a demon does so, the body will grow to a great height and, standing erect, devour all the survivors of its family. With the same object a lamp is also lit close by the corpse, and a weapon placed near it. If, when the pyre is lighted, the corpse holds a piece of the wood in its arms, it is taken as an omen that another of the family will soon die. This superstition is held by the Kanets and lower castes of the Simla Hills, who in some parts think that if the ghostly effigy of the dead be seen wandering round the house, or if his voice be heard calling anyone by name, he who is called or sees the ghost, will die soon afterwards. It is believed that the spirit can find no home. In such cases *narain-bal* or *Gaya-pind* is also performed.

If within four years of a death in the Simla Hills, anyone of the deceased's family be attacked by *dadra*, it is supposed that the dead man's funeral rites were not duly performed. So a Brahmin is consulted to ascertain all details by astrology: and a *chela* or oracle is sent into an ecstasy *(khelna),* until he reveals who it is that has become *pitar.* An image of the *pitar* must then be made, lest the sufferer become a leper, and a rupee placed before the *chela* by the members of the family, who gives the *pitar* a certain period - six months or a year - in which to cure the patient, if he desires to be worshipped as a true *deota* or deity, otherwise they will have recourse to a doctor. For this period, the patient is left without any treatment. If he recovers a temple is built to the *pitar,* otherwise he gets nothing. Such diseases are attributed to those dead whose *gati* or funeral rites were not performed, or who died a violent death, or who when in extremism felt a longing not to quit their family or yearned for wealth and so on or who sacrificed their lives to their devotion to their families.

REFERENCES

1. Rose, H.A., *A Glossary of the Tribes and Castes of the Punjab and North-West Frontier Province*, Low Price Publications, Delhi, 1999. (reprint), First published, 1919.
2. Ibbetson, Denzil, Census Report for the Punjab 1883.
3. Ibbetson, Denzil, Settlement Report for Karnal 1893.
4. Mae Lagan, Edward,Census Report for thePunjab 1892.
5. Baines, J.A., General Report Census of India 1891, Eyre and Spattiswoode, London.
6. Bhattacharya, N., *Hindu castes and Sects*, Editions India, Calcutta, 1968.
7. Ibbetson, DGJ, *Coutlines of Punjab Ethnography,* Census of the Punjab 1821.Calcutta, Superintendent, Government Press, 1883.
8. Mamgain, M.D., *Himachal Pradesh District Gazetteers :Bilaspur, State District Gazetteers*, Simla, 1975.
9. Mamgain M.D., *Himachal District Gazetteers : Lahul & Spiti* ; Greater Punjab Press, Chandigarh, 1975.

6
Death Rituals : Burial

Disposal of dead through burial and cremation

The Crristian group among the Bengali's bury their dead but others cremate them and the ashes are immersed in a nearby river. One of their ancestors (in Bilaspur) is said to have been buried and his little finger and choti or the hairtift were burned. The Gandhila section of the Benagali's also bury the dead and pour water on the burial place for three consecutive days. In bilaspur, they observe impurity period for 10 days and perform ancestor worship with the help of an Acharaj. They also give a ceremonial feast on solia to the community members. In Kangra they observe 40 day's pollution period and no festivities are med during this period, excepting a feast on the last day. The custom is practiced among the Bengali's Christians.

The orthodox Christian observe seven sacraments during their life time. There is sacrament called as the extrometion performed by the preist on behalf of the sick person. In grave sickness, the priest prays for God's heasling by anointing the person with oil and the whole community prays for well being of the sick person. After a person dies his body is buried in the church cemetery but there are instances of cremation as well. For example, it was reported that a chrisian priest of Gurgaon, who died in May 1989, had his body cremated at Delhi and subsequently the ashes were immersed in the holy rivers. There is also a reference to Rajkumari Amrit Kaur, who was a Christian, but who was cremated. The Custom is prevalent among Christians in Haryana.

Custom of burial as well as cremation

The Christian dead are buried and a tomb is constructed to commemorate the deceased. A mourning service called as mass is held in the church for the peace of the departed soul. The mourners wear black badge a symbol of mourning. There is no ritual of pollution as such but the priest is often called to sprinkle the holy water for the purification of the house. Though burial is the most commonly observed form of disposing of the dead but even cremation can be performed if the person has so desired. After the initial ceremony of the last prayer in the church the body can be taken to the burial ground or for cremation.

The Christians as a community in Rajasthan are not associated with any one occupation; rather they are found in different pursuits in life as servants, businessmen, teachers and in white-collar professions.

Rite of burial as well as cremation

The dead among the Christians in Himachal Pradesh, are mostly buried but cremation may also take place depending on the wish of the person. A mourning service called as is held in the church for the departed ones. Whenever a death occurs, the family members wear a black badge around their arms to mark their mourning. Food is cooked by the relatives of the bereaved family in other houses. They call for the elder man of the community who reads the horoscope and decides about the time of the burial. The custom are related to the Christians in Himachal Pradesh.

Custom of burying the deceased

The bene Israel bury their dead. No pollution as such is observed. However, the mourning period for the nearest of kin lasts for a yar, for near ones six months; and for distant kith and kin only one month. During the mourning period, social or festive celebrations are avoided, held within the household. A memorial service for the peace of the depasted soul is held either on completion of a week or of a month. Ancestors are not worshipped, though prayers are offered for the repose of their souls. Thre has been no change in the Bene Israel ritual observances, though they are becoming more expensive.

Funeral rites common to all other muslims

When a Muslim is about to die, he is asked to utter *'allah'* as it is likely to bring *sawaab* or good merit to the departing soul. The body is surrounded by *lagriwadan* (crying of female relatives). The male relatives carry the corpse and place it on a wooden platform. The bath is given by a professional low casteman called *snanagor*. The body is wrapped in a *kafan* or shroud. The corpse then kept in a *taboot* (wooden coffin) which is carried to the burial ground on the shoulders of *kins*, friends and neighbours. The *taboot* is first kept outside a nearby mosque for funeral prayers. A clerggman leads *namaz-e-janaza* and all those who accompany the funeral procession also participate in the prayer. The grave is dug by a *malla* or *gorkun* in the community. After the corpse is placed in the *labad* (grave) it is filled with earth and each person in the funeral procession feels duty-bound to throw a handful of earth in the grave as the last gesture to the departed soul uttering 'Inna lLillah-e-wa-inna Alaibe Rajaoon'. After the labad is filled upto the level of the ground is is further raised up above the level ground into a small mound. There a memorial stone is placed for identification of the grave of the dead. Candels and incense are continuously burnt until the next Friday on which relatives, friends and acquaintances from near and far come to offer their condolences to the bereaved family.

During the period lying between burial and the ensuing Frideay the near kith and kin pay a daily homage to the departed through visiting the grave and reciting the fateha in order to add credit to the departed soul. On Friday morning, female relatives and guests indulge in *labriwadan till late in the day.* Thereafter, the mourners are served tea and breads. In the afternoon male relatives, friends and neighbours assemble at the grave and recite fateba. Treafter they reassemble at the house of the deceased and pay their condolences to the bereaved family. On the fourth day after death, the priests, relatives and neighbours recite Koran Sharif in honour of the decased. The funeral ceremony is repeated on the fortieth day; the two ceremonies are called *chabarum* and chebllum respectively.

The funeral customs and observances are related to the Muslims In Kashmir region.

Elaborate funary rites and rituals

Among the Muslims in ladakh, death is considered a natural phenomenon. On news of a person's demise the people recite: Inna *Lillah-e-wa-inna Alaibe Rajaoon* meaning one who cometh from Allah returneth to Him and organize themselves for making funeral preparations for *ghusl-e-janaza* (funerary bath) adiministered to the corpse to be conducted by a poor kinor a low caste professional. A sheikh or akhun, holding Mufatebul Jinan or Tohfatul Awaam, the books that contain the procedures and steps of various rituals, supervises the funerary bath. Thereafter the body, is wrapped in a black shroud and brought inside the matamsara. The akhun covers the corpse in yet another shroud to knee, sando, a piece of loin cloth that covers the body from the the abdomen to the feet, and a scarf around the head and finally a white piece of cloth covering the body from the head to the feet.

Now the coffin is brought outside and the sheikh leads the *namaz-e-janaza* (the namaz offered in honour of the departed soul). *Marsia khani* (recitation of dirges that narrate various kinds of travails faced in the battlefield of Karbala by Imam Husain and his associates and kin) is conducted. The Muslims assembled give vent to their pent up feelings by crying in unison. The face of the corpse is uncovered to pay the final homage to the departed soul. The father of the deceased, if alive, leads the mourners in paying their respects to the dead. Thereafter the body is lowered into the grave and all those assembled in the funeral procession feel duty bound to throw a handful of earth into the grave repeating '*Inna Lillah-e-wa-inna Alaihe Rajaoon*' over and over again. As the day draws to close the mourners return to their houses. Those who have come in physical contact with the corpse take purificatory bath known as *ghusl-e-maiyat* and the mourners assemble again for *namaz* prayers dedicated to the departed soul. The deceased's kin slaughter a goat, Then the mutton is distributed among the villagers. On the third day an assembly is held at the house of the deceased to recite the Holy Koran to bring peace to the departed soul. The guests extend a helping hand to the bereaved family by bringing some flour of parched barley and a little quantity of butter which, in return, is distributed by the head of the bereaved family among the widows, orphans and other needy persons in the village. In the evening all mourners assemble in the house of the bereaved family and are served a meal. On the fortieth day after death, a similar funeral ceremony is repeated with a larger number of kins of the deceased. Similar ceremonies are also observed by the Broppa (Shia) also the custom's and rituals are related to the Muslims in Ladakh region.

A number of Hindu castes and groups profess their form of funeral as burial in north India, while Muslims and Christians perform burial universally. Among the Hindu castes conducting burial indeed are

Kothodi, *Gaddis*, *Batwals*, *Jogis* and *Churhas* etc. due to different reasons.

Batwals either bury or burn their dead

The *Batwals* either burn or bury their dead. In either case on the way to the ground they halt and place two balls of leavened barley bread at the shoulders, and two at the feet, of the corpse. Thirteen days after the death they take to a Brahmin a rupee and 4 *sers* of wheat flour, and these he carries to a tank, where he recites *mantras* and prayers. As amongst Hindus *bhajjan* is performed after a death. Two yards of cotton cloth, knotted at the four corners are hung over the left shoulder, in token of mourning, by the kins and relatives.

The remains of a body are taken either to the Ganges or to *Parmandal*. The Batwals are not allowed to sell *ghi,* and after a cow has calved they do not eat *ghi,* until some has been offered to a Brahmin.

DISPOSAL OF DEAD THROUGH BURIAL AND CREMATION

Jogi's burial in sitting position

A dying Jogi is made to sit cross-legged. After death, the corpse is washed by the deceased's fellow-Jogis, a *langoti* tied round its waist and ashes smeared over the corpse. A coffin is then made, if means permit, but a poor Jogi is simply wrapped in a blanket and carried by two on two poles, and the body is floated into a river. A wealthy Jogi is, however, placed on a wooden *chauki* shaped like a palanquin, and upon this flowers are cast. The procession to the grave is called *sawari* that is headed by horses and bands playing music. The grave is made deep, with a spacious niche like that in the Muslim graves, and the body placed in it cross-legged and facing the north. The Jogi's *bairagan* is placed before him, with a gourd full of water on his right, a loin-cloth, a *kanak* or staff of Mahadeo, a loaf of wheaten flour, and two earthen plates, one full of water, the other of rice and milk. An earthen pot-sherd is also placed on his head.

But now a day Jogis are said to bury their dead facing the east, Saniasis east or north east. In the Simla hills, the Jogis were originally mendicants, but have now become householders. They *burn* the dead, and for every corpse get 4 annas in money, together with a plate of brass or *kansi* and a woollen or cotton cloth. They also get some grain at each harvest. They are considered defiled as they take offerings made at death, and the Kanets and higher castes will not drink with them. Then a mound is raised over the grave. All the *Jogis* wash their hands with water supplied by the deceased's disciples. They then bathe and the disciples give them sweets. On the third day they are also fed with *churma* alone being given if the disciples are poor. Later on the *shradh* is, if possible, performed. Jogis are invited and keep a vigil all night. About a *pahr* before dawn, they are fed with fish, or *pakauras* (vegetables coated with *baisan* or paste of powdered gram and *ghungnian,* or *pulao,* or rice, *wine, flesh* and fruit, etc. Seven thrones or *gaddis* are now erected to : (i) the Pir, (ii) Jognis, (iii) Sakhya or witness, (iv) Bir, (v) the Bhaudari of Guru Gorakh Nath, (vi) Guru Gorakh Nath, and (vii) to Neka. *Mantras* are then repeated, and clothes: *gold, silver* and *copper :* a cow and *earth* given away in charity. The wake is now attended only by *Jogis*, but formerly men of all classes, even Muslims used to take part in it. Lastly, after all these ceremonies, a council or *pindhara,* of *Jogis* is held, and one of the deceased's disciples who is elected *Guru* or *Bir Mahant*, three kinds of food, *puri, kachauri* and *pilao* being distributed. The deceased's clothes and the coffin are given to the *kotwals,* or *bankias,* or else to *Jangam faqirs.* As the *Jogi* is not burnt, his bones cannot be sent to the Ganges, so his nails are removed and taken to Hardwar.

The *samadhi* of a *Jogi* may be of earth or brick, and *belpatter* (leaves) are strewn over it. On it a lamp is also kept burning for 10 days, flowers and water being placed near it and a conch being blown. Rice balls are given in the name of the deceased for 10 days as among other Hindus. On the 10th day clothes are washed and on the 13th *kirya karam* ceremony is performed. All the ceremonies are the same as among Hindus. The following story is told to account for the fact that Jogis bury their dead : In Gorakh's time, there arose a dispute between the Hindus and the Muslims, the latter saying they were masters of the earth and of all the living and the dead. Gorakh sat on the ground, placing all his food, etc., by his side, and bade the earth yield to him, if he too had a share in it. It opened and Gorakh sank into it, and so *Jogis* usually bury their dead.

Custom of calling Muslim priest

The *Chuhras* generally bury their dead. When a person is dying they call in the Muhammadan priest to read the *sahani,* but if it is in a

Hindu village where there is no *mulla,* nothing of this nature is done, except that in some cases they lift the sick man on to the ground.

In Maler Kotla, the Chuhras bury the dead, like Muhammadans, but on their way to the grave, the carriers of the bier change places as among Hindus. And on their return they pick up straws and break them, saying, 'God bless the dead and protect those left behind', while the *faqir,* who usually accompanies the parties, recites verses of Guru Nanak, like a Sikh. Three days later the deceased's nearest relative feeds the men who carried the bier, and on the 17th day he distributes food to the poor and to unmarried girls. This they call *sathar* or a couch. The dead are carried to the grave on a bed, bound in a shroud made of cloth, which is tied at the head and the feet like a sack, and in the middle. The body, after being washed with soap and water, is dressed in a jacket, a cap, and a sheet, or in two sheets, and is sprinkled with rose water. In the grave, the shoulder is placed towards the pole star, and the feet to the east.

If it is that of a young person, they put a black blanket over the bier, if of an old person a red one. This is called *khes.* The priest sits on the west side and looks towards the east. He recites a prayer, and they repeat it after him. This is *janaza.* One rupee, called *askat* or donation is given to the priest on the *Quran*. A cloth called *jae namaz* is also given. The blanket becomes the property of the *mirasi.* The face of the dead is not placed downwards. If a very old person dies, his friends make a mock mourning : but their grief is really very great for a young person.

The women stand in a circle; the *mirasan* (wife of the family bard) stands in the centre. She sings marsia or dirge in mournful tunes, the other women following her in wailing tone. They beat their legs, breasts and forehead with their hands in time to the dirge. Nothing could be sadder. The woman that leads repeats the *alahni,* and the other women beat the breast, thus making *siapa.*

Putting food and water in grave

The *Kamad* bury their corpse in a sitting crossed-legged. Some sweets in a *thali* (plate) which they call *annapatra* and an earthen pitcher full of water are kept inside the grave. Death pollution, called *sutare* or *sot* is conducted for twelve days. Pollution period ends with *boarma* or *baroa* (rites observe on twelfth day). *Boarma* is followed by the succession ceremony. The nails of the deceased are consigned to river water at Hardwar. Their remnant of post-death ceremonies are similar to the local Hindus.

The Kathodi also bury their dead. After the death the corpse is carried to the burial ground by the sons. The chief mourner puts soil over corpse. The Kathodi observe six days pollution period, *gam,* after the death of a person. During the pollution period the sons lead a simple life. They refrain from taking fish and eat. After six days, the relatives and friends assemble in the deceased house for drinking alcohol.

Burying the corpse lying flat

If buried, the body is laid flat in the grave with the back on the ground and the palms of both hands folded on the chest. The head is kept to the *utar* (north). Children and females of the Gaddi community are burried in the same way. When burnt the ashes are collected, together with the seven bones of the finger, knee and ankle joints, on the day the corpse is burnt. They are brought to the house in a piece of *masru* and kept for ten days in the clothes in which the deceased breathed his last and in the room in which he expired. After the *daspindi,* they are washed in honey, milk, clarified butter, cowdung and *belpatri* seed and then dried and deposited in a small wooden box, wrapped in the piece of *masru* buried in a recess made in the wall of the house, with a coating of barley and mustard over it. They should be taken to Hardwar to be immersed into the holy Ganges as soon as the family has collected sufficient funds for the journey, and at most within four years.

The religion of the Gaddis contains some interesting features. The *Gaddis* are by preference *Shaivas*, but their worship is *Catholic* to a degree. Thus on Sundays and Thursdays *Nags* and *Sidha* are worshipped, on Sundays alone *Kailung*, *Devis* on *Tuesdays* and on Thursdays *Birs*. To the Nags, *ahri* or bee-stings, male kids or lambs, and *ora* (the first-fruits of all crops), incense and small cakes are offered; and to the *Sidhas* a sack, a stick of rose-wood, a crutch, sandals and *rot* or thick bread. To the *Devis* are offered vermilion, *bindli* (brow-mark), *salu* (a red chadar), *dora* (waist-rope), *sur* (a coarse spirit), and a goat. To the *Birs* a he-goat, a *chola* or thick woollen coat, a waist band, a white conical cap (*chukannij topi*) and fine bread. *Kailu Bir*, the *numen* of abortion, is only worshipped by women. *Kailung* is a *Nag*, and the father of all the *Nags*. He is worshipped, as is *Shiva*, under the form of the *darat* or sickle, which is always carried by a *Gaddi* when shepherding his flocks.

The *Gaddis* also burn their dead. Lepers and those who die of *luhar,* a kind of typhus, are first burried, but their corpses are exhumed after three months and burnt. The corpse is placed on the funeral pyre with the head of the deceased to the north, and all the jewellery and the body burnt. A copper coin is placed by the pyre as the tax of the land on which the body is burnt. Fire is first applied to the pyre under the head by the nearest relative and the other *gotris* (blood relations). The *purohita* joins the relations in this, observances, but no rites and rituals are observed. The light is applied after going round the pyre once from left to right. On the 10th day after the demise, the *daspindi* ceremony is performed by the nearest blood relations, with the aid of the *purohita.* Other relatives wash their clothes and bathe on this day and remove the *kambal* which is spread to receive the mourners.

On the 12th day at night, a he-goat is sacrificed in the deceased's name. This goat is given to the *purohita.* The clothes, utensils and cash, etc., are given to him. On the 14th day the deceased's relations on the wife's side come to the house in the morning and give a feast to the relatives and the member of the clan. A goat is sacrificed for this feast and the mourning ceases from this day. At the end of the third month, oblations are again offered to the *manes* of the deceased and the occasion is signalised by a feast to the brotherhood. All the offerings made in this ceremony go to the *purohita* who presides over rituals. Similar ceremonies are gone through at the end of the sixth month and the first and the fourth years.

Washing the corpse carefully

The Muslim *Kasai* bury the dead in their burial ground. After the death of a person the dead body is carefully washed, covered with a *kafan*, and then take to the burial ground. *Maulavi* performs *dafna-ka-sadh* (last prayer). The grave is dug by the *fakirs.* The eldest son acts as chief mourner. The *Kasai* observe mourning for a period of forty days. At the end of mourning period, *challisma* ceremony is observed. The *Kasai* have been slaughtering cows and goats and selling the meat to the people in the local markets. Besides, they also trade in raw hides and carcass. Another section of the *Kasai* is engaged in purchasing goats and sheep from villages and sell these to big slaughter houses. The *Kasai* are the Sunni Muslims. They obey *Hazarat Mohammed* as their *wasi* or Prophet (*paigambar*). The *Kasai* make to *durgah* (shrine of pir) situated in their villages and also at Ajmer. The *Kasai* engage *maulavi* (sacred specialists) for officiating their death rituals.

Custom of dying in sitting posture like Buddha

The Buddhist *lamas* of the various sects in Spiti, Himachal Pradesh, have next to nothing to do with the burial or burning of the dead, since those functions are in the hands of a certain class of people called *jaba* (pronounced *joa*). This class is, however, existent in Upper *Kanaur*, *Lahul* and *Ladakh*. As *spiti* is a woodless country, burning is seldom resorted to, except in the case of a prominent *lama* who has departed this life and as such must be burnt. The dead are also buried, sometimes in fields or near them in grounds which belong to the family, and sometimes under rocks: while strangers, poor people and more especially children, even those of the well-to-do, are floated into the streams. A fourth custom, common in Spiti, but unknown in *Phu* and its neighbourhood, is the rending of the corpse in pieces, which afford a welcome meal to fish and to the Lammergeiers which are called *jajin* or *jazas*.

However, a *lama* especially a Great Lama, must alway, be careful when on his death-bed to leave this temporal world in the posture of a sitting Buddha. If he quits it without assuming that seated attitude, his learning counts for nothing and his fame is lost for ever. Three such attitudes ar distinguished, (i) the usual one in which the dying man cannot see his feet, (ii) that in which the soles of the feet appear to be turned upwards, and (iii) the peculiarly artificial *dzogspe skyiltrung*.

The more artistic the posture of a Great Lama at his demise and the longer his corpse preserves it, the higher rises his reputation and the respect in which he is held by all the Buddhist faithfuls in the area. As soon as his body begins to lean to one side it can be carried out and burnt at the spot where the *chhorten* or grave-stone has already been set up. All corpses are said to be tightly bound before burial in the tracts under Buddhist influence.

The rigid tying up of the body is due to a fear of the *rolangs* or resurrection of the body in which a spirit or *kobhold* enters into the corpse. The *vetalas* or corpses temporarily animated by *kobholds* according to the popular belief, share the tendency of dead bodies to become stiff and so cannot stoop. Owing to this belief at Lhasa, low doors are preferred for houses in the neighbourhood of burial places.

Moreover, manifestations of *rolangs* occur generally all the more that the universal degeneracy of mankind has so increased in comparison with former times, that the demons find ample opportunities to enter into the living bodies and men's virtues are rarely great enough to enale them to withstand their entry. The *lamas,* in Lahul, are generally of the *Kanets* caste, though there are, of course, cases where even *Thakurs* have become *lamas.* The *Kanets* cuts his *choti* as does a *Gosain*, and becomes the disciple of some *lama,* and this may be even after marriage. The *lamas* of Lahul, who all belong to the *Drugpa* Order, may marry. Their sons belong to their father's original caste. *Lamas* sometimes cease to belong to the priesthood, allow their *chotis* to grow, and are again received as *Kanets*.

Women also become nuns and live in the monasteries, where the morality is far from pure. In *Spiti*, the monks of Pin are of the *Drukhpa*, and not of the *gelukpa* or celibate class to which those of the other four monasteries, *Ki*, *Dankhar* or *Lawopi*, *Tabo* and *Tang-gyut* belong. They marry in imitation of their patron saint *Guru Rimpoche*, though in their books marriage is not approved of, this saint founded several orders, of which that, to which the monks of Pin belong, is the most ancient, and is called *Ngyangma.* The wives and families of the monks live not in the monasteries, but in small houses in villages. Every son of a *lama* or monk becomes a *buzhan,* which is the name given to low order of strolling monks or friars. Sometimes, the younger son of a landholder becomes a *buzhan,* in preference to going into the monastery. These *buzhans* are a very curious set of people, they get a living by wandering in small parties though all the neighbouring regions stopping at every villages, and acting plays, chanting legends, and dancing like whirling dervishes, many also trade in a small way by bartering grain for salt with the Tibetans, and then exchanging the salt with the *Kanaur* people for iron, buck-wheat or honey, they also often undertake to carry loads for travellers across the passes, as substitutes for the landholders.

Eating of Jaggery at burial

At the time of burial of a *Sansi* deceased, *gur* is distributed amongst the men present. Seven days after the burial, a feast is given to their relatives and friends by the relatives of the deceased. The continual recurrence of the number seven is curious. When consigning the body to the grave, the tribal ancestors are invoked and propitiated. In this the malignancy of motive attributed to the deity is again apparent. To ask a just deity to be merciful to a man who has lived a virtuous life, according to the ideas of the society, of which he was a member, is superfluous and unnecessary. To ask a just deity to forgive a man who has transgressed against the laws of society and left the effects and evil influence of his actions behind him is inconsistent, absurd, and contrary to every law of justice and equity. Since to attribute such a perverted system of justice to the deity would be to credit him with a procedure which no man of sane mind and sound judgment could endorse. It is apparent that the ultimate origin of such an idea is based upon superstition rather than upon reason. The elementary train of thought which gave rise to the custom of worshipping and praying to the deity at the time of birth, marriage and death, is present amongst the *Sansis* untouched by subsequent developments and additions of the human intellect. The sole object of the propitiatory rites of the *Sansis* is to induce their tribal godlings and evil spirits to refrain from exercising their malignant influence on the fortunes of person or persons for whom intercession is made. By gradual stages and correlatively with the forward moves of the human intellect, it appears that this fundamental conception of supernatural beings, as spirits of evil influence, has been enlarged upon, and embroidered, until malignancy has become magnanimity and propitiatory rites have become moral duties.

The mode of disposing of their dead through burial has been borrowed from the Muslims and is an innovation of recent times. Previous to their settlement in various villages, where the majority of inhabitants are Muslims, their dead were disposed of in a manner similar to that of the Hindus. It is probable that they will adopt the Muslim religion altogether in the course of time, or that the Muhammadan's gods and saints will be added to their own demonology. The so-called conversion of a Sansi to the Christian or Muslim faith is merely a verbal phrase. The only result of such a conversion is that the Christian and Muslim deities are degraded into occupying positions in the Sansi demonology, similar to those held by *Sahas Mal*, *Mahla*, and *Bhidu*. The intelligence, which left to itself, can evolve a deity of no higher type than *Sahna Mal;* which can watch the inception of new lives, and the extinction of old, without feeling and curiosity regarding the mysteries of life and death, is utterly incapable of comprehending the higher ideals and aspirations of the Christian and Muslim religions.

Muslim death Rituals

Occasionally, for instance in *Gujrat*, old people, who see their end drawing nigh, build their own tombs, while still alive. And if they feel misgivings that their death rites will not be properly performed, they feast their kinsfolk and the poor in anticipation of death. In Gurgaon, a good many men get their graves constructed of masonry and filled with grain before death. The grain remains there till their death and is given away in alms at their burial.

Amulets and charms etc. are used to escape death. The *Imam zaman ka rupiya* is also protective, and as many as seven goats are sacrificed. Sometimes, a disease is taken for the influence of an evil spirit. By others it is ascribed to the displeasure of *Miran Sahib*, *Madar Sahib* and *Khwaja Sahib*.The remedy is the sacrifice of a he-goat in the saint's name. Sometimes unmarried girls are feasted to secure recovery from sickness.

However, as soon as the shadow of the Angel of Death falls on a dying person, the first duty of his (or her) kinsfolk is to straighten the limbs, close the eyes and mouth of the deceased, place his hands one over the other on the breast and set his cot north and south so that his soul may depart with its face towards *Macca*. This is called *rakh sir karad,* in Ambala. Members of his family mourn and preparations are begun by his kinsfolk for digging the grave. On the death of her husband, a wife breaks her bangles and takes off all her jewellery in sign of widowhood.

Strict followers of the Muhammadan law recite the *Sura-i-yasin* or other verses relating to pardon for sins near one who is at the point of death. They also ask him to recite them himself. It is believed that this recital will draw his attention to one direction only and that if he dies he will not suffer any difficulty at the time of death. *In Ludhiana*, when the case is seen to be hopeless, verses from the *Quran* are rected, and just prior to death the medicines are stopped and pure honey with water is given to the dying person in a spoon. The *kalima* is whispered to him and he is also bidden to recite it himself. He is now made to look toward the north. In Gujrat something sweet, honey as a rule, or if that is not procurable, *sharbat* is poured into the dying person's mouth. In Kapurthala, it is explained that the *kalima* literally means that God alone is worthy to accept devotion and that Muhammad is His Prophet, and that it is intended that the dying man may carry with him the idea of the unity of God. It is only when he is unable to speak that the *sura-i-yasin* is recited to him.

When he breathes his last, the people burst into cries of mourning and females begin to beat their breasts, but in cultured circles the shock is borne with resignation and the bereaved repeat : *Inna-lillaha-wa inna ilahie rajiun,* 'we have come from God and to Him we will return'. But in Gujrat, when the end is seen to be near, the *mullah* is sent for to recite the *Sura-i-yasin* or other passages from the *Quran* and this is called *Husaini parhna,* although the Muslims in this district are Sunnis. If a *mullah* is not available, relative or friend can officiate. Great importance is also attached to the repetition of the *kalima*. All those standing round the death-bed repeat it and the dying person is required to do so, too, until the end approaches. A person dying with its words on his or her lips is considered to have had a happy end. In the ordinary affairs of life, a Muslim will take an oath :- 'Be it my lot not to be able to repeat the *kalima* on my death-bed, should I fail to do such and such a thing.'

In some places, a form of death-bed confession is found. It is called *hadia Quran.* If the dying person is in his senses, he takes the *Quran* in his hands and confesses all his sins, saying that he has brought god's own words (in the *Quran*) as a claim to forgiveness. At the same time alms of different kinds, equal in value to the *Quran* or the book itself, is given to a poor orphan, or a *mullah* who places it in the mosque where the village boys read. If, however, the dying man is not in his senses, his rightful heir performs this rite. When the bier has been carried out of the house, the people stand in one or two rows or as many as the space permits or as there may be present, with a *mullah* in front of them to pray for the deceased. This is called *nimaz janazah.* After this, another *hadya* is given and then those not closely connected with the bereaved family return, while those of the brotherhood generally accompany the cortege to the burial ground where again, when the grave is ready and it is time to bury the body, a similar *hadya* is made by the heir.

When the grave is filled with soil and the body is buried, the *mullah* standing at the tomb calls out the *bang,* the belief being that when the deceased who, by the departure of the soul, lives in a sleeping posture hears the call, he being a Muslim pronounces the *La ilaha Illallaha -o-Muhommad-ur-rasul-Allahe;* and the two angels *Munkir* and *Nakir*, who recorded all his sins during life, go away thinking him a Muslim who according to Islam is free from all pains when he repeats the above verse.

Kauri wate di roti

If the dying man was one of a well-to-do family and died a day or two before Friday eve, his heirs engage some *hafiz* or *mullah* to sit day and night at his tomb and repeat verses until that night, it being thought that on that auspicious night he will not be called to account for his sins and that afterwards, too, God will also show him mercy. The relatives on the night after the death raise money by subscription and manage somehow to provide food for those who accompanied the coffin to the burial-ground. This is called *kauri wate di roti* or *kauri roti,* which must not be confounded with *mundr-chhor* or *munhchhor* which is the food supplied to the bereaved family by its nearest relation.

In Kangra, Himachal the face of the dying person is turned towards Mecca. If possible, the corpse is buried on the day of death but when this cannot be done, the *Quran* is recited and a knife placed upon the body to keep off evil spirits. In Gurgaon, two classes of Muslims must be distinguished. The first includes the immigrant *Shaikh*, *Sayid*, *Mughal*, *Pathan* and Baloch and the second the indigenous *Meo*, *Khanzada* and *Rajputs converted to Islam by the former*. But a large number of these *converts* have now become assimilated to the former class, and owing to this many Hindu customs have been adopted even by the immigrant classes, though in a somewhat altered form, and they are, of course, still performed by Muslims who embraced Islam recently. Other Muslims of inferior rank found as tenants in villages are the *Qasai Kunjraq*, *Bhatiara*, *Manhiar*, *Saqqa*, *Nai*, *Mirasi*, *Dhunna*, *Teli* and *Rangrez*, who are dependants of the two groups mentioned above and being affected by their influence observe the same rites and ceremonies as they do. When a corpse is taken to the graveyard, the bier is set down at least once on the way. This is called *muqam dena.* At this spot, the head is always kept to the north. After the burial some grain and copper coins are given there in alms to Muslim beggars. The place where a person breathed his last and was washed is called *lahad* and a lamp is kept burning there for 40 or at least 10 days. A man always remains sitting on the *lahad.*

The body of the deceased is washed with various rites, rituals and by various agents. For example, in Gurgaon, some of those present at the death who are acquainted with the doctrines of Islam, wash the body with the heirs' permission. If it be washed in a river or tank, it will not require *lahad*, but if washed inside the house a rectangular pit of the height of a man and 4 or 5 feet deep called *lahad* must be made for it. A flat board prepared from a public fund raised for this purpose is then put up over the *lahad*. Then the body is laid on the board, with its face to the east and feet to the west. The clothes are removed and the private parts covered with a piece of cloth. The garments of the deceased as well as the clothe of the bed on which he died are given to beggars. After this, the washing is begun. First bath is given with sandal water, the second with camphor water and the third with pure water. But Sunnis bathe the corpse with hot water. The body of a male is washed by males and that of a female by females. One of them supplies the water, another pours it on the body and the third rubs it on. The private parts are not touched. Meanwhile, the people assembled in the deceased's house recite prayers for the benefit over the deceased person from the day of his demise till the third day, and sometimes the recitations are prolonged for a full year or more. These customs are in practice among those who are to some extent educated or well-to-do. New converts observe them in a much simpler way.

In *Gujrat*, the corpse is washed on a wooden board (*patra*), kept expressly for this purpose by the *mullah*, with water drawn fresh from a well and mixed with green leaves from a *ber* tree. Only if the weather is cold, is the water moderately warmed. If the deceased was a woman, 3 or 4 of her silver ear-ring are given to the woman who washes her body. In other parts of the state, however, the *mullahs* proper perform other functions. In Jullundur *'a special class of mullahs* called *murda-sho'* washes the body of the deceased Muslim. But elsewhere such a duty does not appear to be performed by any special class. Thus, in Shahpur, each mosque is in charge of an Imam or Ulma who teaches the boys to repeat the *Quran* and officiates at weddings and funerals. But, it is also said, the mullah recites the burial service (*janaza*) accompanied by the mourners. He gets as his fee a copy of the Quran and a rupee or two, and he is also feasted with the guests. *In Ludhiana*, immediately after the death relatives are notified through barber and the *ghussal* (washer of the body) is sent for. Meanwhile, the Qazi prepares the shroud. The body is washed in hot water being kept covered down to the knees. Rose water and camphor are also sprinkled over it. After this, it is laid on a couch which is then carried to the graveyard. For the bath, hot water with *ber* leaves boiled in it, soap and sweet scented things such as rose water, camphor, sandal etc. are required.

The bath being prepared, the corpse is laid on a wooden board with its feet facing west and veiled from sight with sheets, only the washerman (or woman as the case may be) and the nearest of kin remaining inside. The deceased's clothes are removed, the waist-cloth being used to cover the body from the navel to the knees. The washerman then rubs it with soap and water, towels being used to dry it and sandalwood burnt to give it frangrance. Then the shroud, cut in two, is spread over the bed and the body is laid on one half and covered with the other down to the knees. Verses from the *Quran* are written on the shroud with burnt charcoal or clay. Camphor dissolved in rose-water is painted on every joint, the higher classes using scents instead. The lower sheet is then wrapped round the corpse, and knotted in three places, on the head, on the waist and over the feet. A copy of the *Quran* is placed at the head of the body, and the nearest of kin, friends and others are shown the face of the deceased for the last time, accompanied with weeping. A red cloth is thrown over the corpse, if the deceased is an aged person. Sometimes, the toes of the hands and feet are tied together with a piece of cloth. This is called *sanakh*. Similarly, a piece of cloth is tied round the head across the chain to shut the mouth. This is called *taht-ul-hanak*.

Rites regarding shroud

After washing the body, it is dried with white napkins and is laid on the cot on which it is to be carried to the graveyard and on which white colour shroud has been already spread. Before it is shrouded, camphor is rubbed on the body as ordained by the *shara* on all the points which touch the ground when the head is bowed in prayer. Then the shroud is wrapped round the body. In *Gurgaon*, Shia Muslims use the shroud on which verses from the *Quran* are stamped with earth from Mecca or if it be not obtainable they use white cloth as shroud and print the verses on it. As regards this the Shias believe that followers of Hazrat Ali are exempted from the sorrows of the tomb and the fires of Hell and so they print verses on the shroud to let the angels know that the deceased was a Shia and to prevent their troubling him. It is considered essential by some Muslim tribes to shroud the body of a female in red cloth. The Chhimba (tailor or washerman) comes to the house without being called to supply cloth for the shroud and Napkin etc. Country cloth is preferred for this as more durable. About 30 yards are required as the grave clothes consist of two sheets, a shroud, a prayer-cloth, four towels and a waistband.

Among the agricultural tribe such as the Rajput, Awan, Jat, Gujar, Dogar and Arain of Ludhiana women spin cotton with rolded feet in the month of Ramzan and make cloth which is kept in boxes for use as shrouds exclusively. It is always 40 yards in length. In the modern times the cloth is purchased from the markets. When the body is dressed in the shroud (*kafan*) a piece of cloth called *kafin,* wetted with *ab-i-zam sam* or water from the well at Macca and inscribed with the words *bismillah-ul-rahman-ul-rahim* and the *kalima,* together with some *khak-i-shafa* or earth from Mecca, is placed on the breast. If these articles are not obtainable, the *kafin* is wetted with ordinary water and a clean clod of earth used.

In Gujarat the *mullah* merely writes the *kalima* on the shroud in *geri.*

Death of a female in child birth

In Gurgaon if a woman dies in child-birth some superstitious female tie an *atti* (skein) of cotton thread on her legs as she is believed to have died in impurity and it is feared she may become an evil spirit and injure the family. As a further precaution a man throws mustard seed behind her bier from the place of her death all the way to the grave-yard and on reaching it he drives in four nails one at each corner, and the 5th-in the middle of the grave. By doing this, it is believed, the departed soul will not return.

The deceased woman's husband may not touch the body of his dead wife or even help to carry her coffin though comparative strangers may do so. If the deceased was old and his heirs are in easy circumstances and disposes to pomp, singers are engaged to lead the procession singing the *maulud* verses, a narration of Muhammad's birth, loudly in chorus. Every Muslim seeing a procession on its way to the grave-yard is religiously bound to join it. On arrival there ablutions are performed by the funeral party, preparatroy to prayer. The coffin being placed in front, those who are to join in prayer arrange themselves into three or five rows, the *mullah* leading the service. This over, permission is given to all present to depart, but as a rule very few leave at this stage. All present sit on the ground and the ceremony of *askat* is performed, but only in the case of adults, minors being regarded as innocent and not answerable for their doings. The *askat* is thus performed.

Ceremony of askat

Some cooked meal and cash, varying in amount according to the means of the parties, with a copy of the *Quran,* are placed before the *mullah* in a basket. Another man sits in front of him so that is lies between them. The *mullah* then says solemnly : "The deceased failed to obey certain commandments and to refrain from certain acts on Saturdays during his or her life. This meal, cash and *Quran* are given in alms to atone for those sins": and so saying he passes the basket with its contents to the other man who gives it back again. The *mullah* again hands it over to him with the same words, but refers to the deceased's sins on the Sundays in his life. This is repeated for each day of the week. The *mullah* is then paid some money with the copy of the *Quran,* and the body is interred. The sheet spread over the coffin is now given to the Nai (barber). After the interment the cash and meal in the basket are distributed in alms. Informal prayers are again said for the benefits of the deceased and the funeral proccession returns to the house of the deceased. In Sialkot, the *askat* is performed *before* the burial. Several *mullahs* sit in a circle, the leader being given a copy of the *Quran;* a rupee and some copper coins, grain, salt, sweetmeat other victuals etc. are also placed before him. Then one of the *mullahs* makes overs the sins of the deceased to another, he to a third and so on till the circle is completed. By this it is believed that the deceased's soul is freed from the penalty of sin.

Lastly, the head *mullah* distributes the cash etc. among the poor and the other *mullans.* If the deceased was old, clothes are distributed among the poor. The *Quran* and a rupee are taken by the *mullah* himself. The *ahl-i-hadis* regard *askat* as an innovation and do not observe it. In Shahpur, poor people only borrow a copy of the *Quran* which changes hands for seven days simply as a matter of form. If is borrowed from a *mullah* who is given some money.

The deceased's relatives and kins sit near the cot with the *Qazi* who takes the *Quran* in his hands, and offers it on the part of the deceased, as a sacrifice for his sins. The book then changes hands, the *Qazi* is paid a rupee or more according to the position of the parties, and the *Quran* is thus redeemed.

In the meantime, the followers and mourners have washed their hands and feets with his face towards the corpse, which is placed with its head to the north. Behind him the followers stand in old lines and pray after which the corpse is taken to the grave into which it is lowered to two men who descend and place it in the *lahd* or the burial niche. In sandy tracts, the knots tying the corpse are undone to admit of this being done. If the *lahd* is in one of the sides, the opening is closed with clods or earthen vessels, if in the centre, with fuel wood. All the by-standers take a little earth in their hands, repeat some verses over it, and drop it at the head of the corpse. The cot is turned on its side as soon as the body has been taken off and in the case of an aged person the red cloth is given to the barber or *mirasi.* While the grave is carried out a cup of water is eptied to ensure the family's future safety. The cot br he dead, standing in a circle round the body, and then lower it into the grave. The *toshe ki roti* and grain are then given to the poor. In some places, after the burial a call to prayer (*azan*) is made and a prayer offered for the soul of the departed. All then return and after expressing their sorrow and sympathy with the relations of the deceased go home. In some places the women of the family cause *fatihas* to be recited in the name of the brown worms of the tomb in the belief that they will dictate to the dead person the correct answers to the questions put by Munkir and Nakir.

So, too, in Punjab while the body is being washed *tosha,* (food for charitable purposes) consisting of *halwa,* boiled rice with sugar, and loaves is made ready in the house. The cot is lifted up, the towels and the waist-cloth going to the washerman (or woman as the case may be). Four men lift up the four legs of the cot, but as many men as can do so relieve them on the way, reciting verses from the *Quran* all the while, considering this as an act of piety. The cot and *tosha* are set down outside the cemetery. So, too, in Kangra, the carrying of the coffin is considered good for the soul of the carrier and for this reason the *corpse* is carried by the attendants turn by turn.

But in some places when a body is carried to the graveyard all except the near relatives are given twenty rupees each so that the deceased's soul may not be indebted to them for their toil. Poor people, however, only give the bearers sweetened rice on a Thursday. The food given in this way is called *khatteu.* The corpse before being taken to the burial-ground is shrouded in a cloth which is taken by the carpenter or ironsmith, who prepare the coffin.

Rituals in the graveyard

After washing and shrouding the corpse, it is taken to the graveyard, the cot on which it is laid being carried by all the collaterals in turn, but not by the nearest kinsmen such as the father, son and brother etc. On the way to the graveyard, they recite sacred verses, the *kalima* and prayers for the deceased. At a short distance from the graveyard, the bier is set down north and south at a spot swept clean and all those present recite the funeral prayers. But they do not bow the head at this rite and only invoke blessings for the departed soul. Then, the bier is carried on to the graveyard. The grave is always dug from north to south, and has two chambers the lower, called *lahad,* in which the body is placed being as long as a man's height. The face of the corpse is kept towards the *Qibla* that of a man being laid by men while that earth from the upper walls may not fall on it. The upper part of the grave is then filled in with sods and earth by all the mourners except the deceased's heir. When filled in water is sprinkled over it and the *chadar* in which the body was wrapped is spread over it. The members of the funeral party now recite the *fatiha* or verses from the *Quran* for the benefit of the departed soul and on their return condole with the heirs. They then depart to their houses. Food and *halwa* which are called *tosha* as well as grain and cash are carried in come quantities to the graveyard and distributed among beggers and other poors after the burial.

In Gurgaon while the corpse is being carried to the graveyard some water is thrown behind the bier on the way as it is believed that it will bring resignation to the deceased's heirs. The women of houses on the route taken by the bier also cast the water out of their vessels, chew *nim* leaves and spit on the ground. The water is thrown out so that the departed soul may not stay in any vessel containing water and the *nim* leaves are chewed as a token that the shock is unbearable. When the corpse is lowered into the grave the *mullah* is asked to write the *kalima sharif* with a stick on a mud brick which is put in the grave near the deceased's head. When the corpse is in the grave the *mullah* calls on each of those present to recite the *surat ikhlas* over seven clods of earth and puts them together near the head of the deceased. Then all join in filling the tomb with earth.

In Kohat, the female neighbours assemble at the house and standing round the corpse continue to wail, beat their breasts and slap their faces. A matron leads the mourning and the rest wail in chorus after her.

Meanwhile the deceased's friends and relations assemble for the funeral procession (*janaza*) which is preceded by *mullahs* carrying from 3 to 21 *Qurans* according to his rank. Women take no part in the assembly. At a short distance from the grave, the corpse is set down, while the prayers for the dead are recited, the mourners ranging themselves behind the leading *mullah* (as *imam*) in lines of old numbers varying from three to seven. After the prayers money is distributed to the *mullahs* present, with grain and salt and a few copies of the *Quran.* Cash and grain are also given to the poor there present. At a child's funeral the grain and salt are replaced by sweetmeat. The body is then taken to the grave which is dug north and south and after it has been let down and laid with the face to the west, stones are placed over it and the earth filled in. In the case of a man two tomb stones are erected, one at the head, the other at the feet. For a women a third stone is set up in the centre.

Kinds of graves

There are two kinds of graves-one on the *lahad* system containing a side sepulchre for the body, and the other a pit (*chinwan*) dug deep in the ground with an enclosing wall of stone or brick about 4 feet high. After the body has been returned to the dust, the *mullah* recites the law of inheritance (*miras ka masla*) and then all present offer prayers, invoking blessings on the deceased.

Some of the mourners then accompany his heirs home and they give them cooked rice etc. (some is also given to the poor) and then dismiss them. Next day kinsfolk assemble in a mosque and offer prayers for the deceased. On the third day 30 *siparas* of the *Quran* are handed in separate parts to *mullahs* and others who can read so that the whole recitation may be finished in a short time. After its conclusion sweetmeats are distributed by the deceased's heirs and then one of the *mullahs* observes the *kul khwani* (*a recitation of certain Suras of the Quran* called *kull)* and is given some cash as his fee. Then follows the *dastarbandi* or formal recognition of the heir.

Every evening for 40 days the heirs supply food to the *mullah* and every night a lamp is lit at the place where the body was washed. For some weeks too food is distributed every Thursdsay to the poor in his name and on the last Thursday clothing, sweetmeats etc. are given to the *mullah* and general feast to the kinsfolk. For 2 or 3 years on the aniversary of the death the heirs distribute food and alms to the poor.

The cost of a funeral of an average agriculturist including food and alms may vary according to his financial position.

Placing of *Ahdnama*

Most of the Shias and some Sunnis place a written paper called *ahdnama* in the deceased's mouth in the grave. This 'agreement' contains a declaration by him of the principles and doctrines of Islam, and it is placed on him with the idea that he may not be terrified at the questions put to him by Munkir and Nakir when they appear before him with dreadfull looks, but may answer them them with the aid of the agreement. In Gurgaon two loaves with *ghi* and sugar spread over them are tied in a handkerchief and are sent to the graveyard through a *faqir,* with a pitcher full of cold water and a goblet, placed one over the other.

After the burial the *faqir* recites the *fatiha* over the bread and takes it to his house. These breads are called *tosha* (provisions for the journey). As in life, a man requires provisions for a journey so a dead person requires *tosha* on his last journey from his house to the grave. Only two loaves are given because, it is said, Noah satisfied the hunger of Anak, who was of a great stature and whose hunger was never appeased, with only two loaves. Moreove,r it is often related in the miracles of saints and *pirs* who passed their lives in the solitude of forests that they received two loaves and a goblet of water from God. So it is believed that a man's daily food as fixed by the Almighty is two loaves and a goblet of water. Dara Shikoh also, when imprisoned by Alamgir, wrote to him that he only required two loaves and a cup of water. It is essential that no flesh should be used in the *tosha* and so sugar and *ghi* are used instead, because the food of people in Heaven generally consists of sweet things as is evident from the fact that there canals of milk and honey are believed to flow. The water of Kausar, a stream in heaven, is sweeter than honey and whiter than milk or ice.

In the time of Moses, *manna* and *salwa* (a savoury food) were received by the Israelties in the wilderness. As to this tradition the people, contrary to what is written in the religious book believe that these things were received from the sky in large plates and were softer and whiter than carded cotton and sweeter than anything on earth.

In Gurdaspur, a dying person is laid with his face towards the Qibla and verses of the *Quran,* especially the *Sura-i-yasin,* are recited. A copy of the *Quran* and a little money are caused to be given by his hand in charity to a *mullah.* Kinsmen and relatives repeat the *kalima* aloud so that on hearing it the deceased, also may do the same. In villages, grain flour, rice *ghi* etc. are distributed to the poor in alms. When life is extinct, the face is wrapped in a cloth and shroud and a bath are prepared. The shroud consists of three clothes in the case of a male and five in the case of a female. There must be one red cloth in the later case. If the deceased was a young female a *gahwara* (cradle) is also made of white cloth. Moreover a *dhodna,* consisting of a *dopatta* or sheet of white muslin (*malmal*) or striped (*doruja*) and a red *dopatta,* is put on the body and after burial one is givern to the barber and the other to the washerman This *dhodna* is given simply as a social usage.

After the bath one ear-ring is given to the woman who washed the corpse and the other to the washerman. If the deceased be an old woman, a coloured shawl or *doshala* is put on her and given to the barber after the burial. When the coffin is carried out to the graveyard some grains, *halwa* (a kind of pudding made of flour, *ghi* and sugar) and bread are taken with it and when the recital of the funeral prayers is over a rupee is given to the person who gave the bath and a rupee or a copy of the *Quran* to the *imam* of the mosque. If the deceased was an old man or woman, people generally distribute pice in charity to such beggars and blind men as may be present at the grave. The *tosha* consisting of bread, and *halwa* etc. mentioned above are also given in alms. Some people also appoint *hafis* or readers of the *Quran* to recite verses from it at the grave till the following Thursday. In the case of an old man's death *kamins* of his family are also given a rupee each. This custom is not in force among the followers of Muhammad. When after the funeral, they come back to the house any near kinsman or neighbour gives a meal to the bereaved family. One meal is always considered essential, but if there are more houses of relatives and kinsmen three meals at the outside are given.

Immediately on the return from the funeral, some rice and four loaves are sent to the person who bathed the body or to the mosque in the name of the deceased. But this custom is not observed by the *ahl-i-hadis.* the deceased's heirs do no business for three consecutive days, but stay in the *deorhi* (entrance hall) or *baithak* (sitting place) for the *faliha-khwani,* and the kinsfolk come for that purpose. On the third day the ceremony of *qul-khwani* is performed, verses of the *Quran* being recited for the benefit of the deceased's soul. Condolences are offered to the bereaved family with a request to recommence business.

On the following Thursday, the ceremony of *khatam* is conducted and the deceased's clothes are given to the person who washed his corpse. Kinsmen are invited on this occasion also. In the same way, *khatam* is conducted on every Thursday or on the 10th, 21st or 30th day after death. On the 40th day (*chihlam*) a feast is given to *ulma* (learned men) and *fakirs,* and clothes, copies of the *Quran* and cash are also distributed. Kinsmen are also invited if the deceased was an aged person. This custom is called *roti karna.* These customs are not observed by the *ahl-i-hadis.* One loaf or a man's meal (according to their means) is given daily for 40 days to the man who bathed the body or is sent to a mosque.

On the morning after the *chihlam, i.e.* early in the morning before the morning prayer, they bid farewell to the soul of the deceased. The females cook rice and send it to the *mullah* in the mosque and thus bid farewell to the soul. On this the women believe that the soul leaves the house. For a year food is given to *faqirs* at festivals and again after a year food is distributed among the poor. The rites in parts of Punjab are peculiarly interesting because of the part played in them by the *mullah* who is styled the *dindar.* After the *isqat* the deceased's body is washed by him and his old clothes are kept to be given away in alms on the third day. After this it is shrouded, and also wrapped by the near relatives in sheets called *uchhar.* They may be of ordinary long cloth or of a valuable silk and, before the body is placed in the grave, they are removed and distributed among the potters, ironsmiths and carpenters who dug the grave, and on hearing of the death went to the graveyard of their own accord for that purpose. After burial, the surface of the grave is raised a little and the coffin is buried along with the corpse.

Custom of *Kauri Roti*

The bereaved family is supplied with *kauri roti* by a brother of relative of the deceased. Fire is not kindled in their house for three following days. Relatives and friends at once join in the mourning and are served with *kauri roti.* Though the mourning mat is burnt, all the mourners sleep on the ground or on cots turned upside down. This state of affairs lasts for three days, during which the *aindar* (or washer of the dead) gets some of *kauri roti.* Contrary to the custom elsewhere, the *dindar* leads the funeral prayers. On the third day *gul khwani* is performed. The *dindar* has a basket of grain put before him with a vessel of water containing leaves of a plum tree, recites verses from *Quran* and blows them on to the water, which is then spilt at the place where the body was washed. It is believed that the deceased's soul is benefited by this. The grain and other victuals is taken by the *dindar.*

The old clothes of the deceased are now cast down at the place where the corpse was washed and are removed on the third day when the water is split. After the *gul* the mourners bathe, wash their own and the deceased's clothes which are given to the *dindar.* Rich people given him a new suit and if the deceased's widow survives some ornaments also. The eldest member of the family is next made to don a *dastar* which is given him by the relatives, to signify that he has become the deceased's success or and representative. They also give him one or two rupees. As the *fatah-khani* ceremony held immediately after the burial, the relatives also contribute a rupee each. A little before the death the whole of the *Quran* is recited and the reciters given a *Quran* or cash. On the second day after death, the relatives visit the grave and recite the whole *Quran* there.

On the first Thursday after death, sweetened rice or *halwa* is prepared, but before the relatives are served with it, it is given to the *dindar.* This practice is continued for seven day, except by the poor who can only afford it for the first Thursday, the *dindar* is also fed daily for 40 days, and it is essential that his food should be sent him before sunset. It is called *arwah* and is intended for the deceased's benefit. The *dindar,* is also fed and given an ornment of the first Id after death. The couch on which the deceased lay before death is broken to pieces and its strings are buried with the body. In the month of Shahban, *halwa* or some other sweetmeat is prepared and is sent to the *mullah* and *dindar*. This is called *ruh-rilana*. Every year in Muharram, the relatives visit the grave and pour a little water over it. For the benefit of the soul of any ancestor who died an accidental or unnatural death, and for a childless ancestor, *Qassabs* feed the poor in their names every Thursday, or at least twice a year.

The Ceremony of *Qul Khwani*

On the third day, the *qul-khwani* cermony is performed. The old clothes of the deceased are made and given away in charity for the benefit of his soul. On this day, too, the lawful heir is made to put on a *dastar* by his *pir* or a Sayyid. Sometimes on the seven day, food is given to the poor, but this is not common. On the 10th, 20th and 40th days after death relatives and friends may collect and eat together and also distribute food to the poor, but this also is not usual. From the third day to the 40th, two loaves (*i.e.* food sufficient for one man) generally flavoured with sugar and *ghi* are sent to a *fakir* daily before nightfall. These loaves are called *ubha ki rotian. Ubha* means inauspicious. On each Thursday in the first 40 days *niaz* is given for the deceased's benefit as on the 3rd day.

The Rite of *chaliswan*

The *chaliswan* ceremony in connection with a female's death is generally performed on the 28th and in the case so a male on the 30th day or in special cases on the 39th. On this day the deceased's family feast their kinsfolk according to their means, and they in return give them a turban and some money. The expenses of this ceremony generally depend on the family's means. On this occasion, too, *niaz* is given and the *fatiha* recited as on the *soyam,* but no cup of water is sent to the *fakir* with the bread. It is not necessary that the bread should be cooked by the same person who did so on the first day. On the 40th day a new suit of clothes is given away in the deceased's name, but the custom of giving away ornaments does not exist. On the same day, his soul is dismissed. In the evening a vessel full of water is placed near the *lahad* (where the dead body was washed). In it are put two copper coins and a few plates of rice, bread and *halwa* are set by it.

The near female relatives light a lamp and keep awake for the whole night. In the morning a *faqir* comes, takes the vessel of water with the plate and backs to the door with his face towards the females. On reaching the door he turns around and goes to his own house. As he quits, the deceased's house the females weep as bitterly as if his bier were being carried out. The people believe that the soul after leaving the body remains in two places, Allain and Sajjain, and maintains its connection with the grave and *lahad* for 40 days. It is also believed that the soul is allowed a walk at the time of *maghrab* prayers, and that it continues to remain anxious to receive the *niaz etc.* given for its benefit. Hence the *chaliswan* or 40th day rite is believed to be set free every Thursday and for this reason on each Thursday the *fatiha* is recited for its benefit. It is also believed to receive food given to faqirs and so several kinds of food are given them at the *fatiha.* The *timahi, chhamahi* and *barsi* ceremonies are performed after three and six months and a year respectively. One day before the 'Id, Bakar Id,' Muharram and Shab Barat as also on the 14th of Rafab, *halwa* and bread are given as *niaz.* This is usually done for one year only, but some people observe these ceremonies always. Nothing is given by way of *niaz* before the third day because the soul is not set free from Allain and Sajjain before that day.

The reason assigned for the 10 days' interval between the *daswan, biswan* and *chaliswan,* which last is generally performed on the 30th day, is that mourning lasts 10 days just as the first 10 days of *Muharram* are performed as days of mourning or the death of Hussain.

A variety of death rites

The widow of the deceased does not wear glass bangles or coloured clothes. If a woman dies married, her hands are stained with *mahndi* (henna)_and antimony is applied to her eyes after her body has been washed. On a man death his widow's parents give their daughter bangles, called the bangles of widowhood. If her parents he well off they also give her ornaments and cash by way of *khichri*. On the death of a female also her parents give some cash by way of *khichri*. When saint dies his *urs* is celebrated annually on the day of his death. All his followers and believers gather together on that day and cook food, they also offer *niaz,* recite the *fatiha* and light an earthen lamp on his grave every Thursday. Fruit and sweets are also offered at his grave. In *Qadaria* and *Naqshbandia* families the members sit near a grave, sing hymns in praise of the Almighty and recite eulogies of the saint. They also repeat verses from the *Quran*, but use no musical instruments, a prohibition not observed in Chishti circles. Singers and prostitutes dance at their tombs on the *urs*. On the 7th or 10th day after death a *khatam* is given, food is cooked and offered to the *qazi, faqirs*, the tomb-digger, and bier-bearers of the deceased. It consists of milk, *halwa*, vegetables, meat, pulse, fruit, rice and dry bread. Some people do this on four Thursdays after the death with in 40 days, give the deceased's clothes to the *qazi*, with some cash and a *Quran*. From the *tija* to the 40th day the deceased's heirs feed a needy person once a day for the good of his soul. The *daswan* and *biswan* ceremonies are performed in different by different sects of

Muhammadans. *Nan* (bread) and *halwa* or other food is distributed by them to their kinsfolk as well as to the poor. The followers of the Imamia sect also hold another assembly in honour of their martyrs in addition to those already named. After it has dispersed they recite the *fatiha* prayers first in honour of the martyrs on the field of Karbala and then for the benefit of the deceased's soul. Other Muslims including the Shi'a Qizilbash and Kashmiri communities eat nothing from the deceased's house for 40 days after a death, but they send nothing to it. The Paracha, Wastir and Qazi do not eat or drink from the house for three days. With these exceptions there are no restrictions on eating or drinking from the deceased's family at a death. All others eat and drink from the bereaved family's house during the 40 days. The menial tribes living in the city give Re.1 on the day of the *qulk-hwani* by way of *kaura watta*. This custom is not in vogue among the high castes.

On their return from the cemetry in Raya, all those taking part in the funeral turn their faces towards it when some way from it and recite the *fatiha*. The cot is carried by a menial, but not on his head in the usual way until he reaches the village. All men assemble at the *takia* and repeat the *fatiha*. Then all but the heirs depart and they must stay there three days at least. The practice of sitting for prayer between the grave and the deceased's house is termed *goda-diwana,* 'knee-resting.'

Custom of *shuma*

In Bannu tahsil on the evening of the *funeral*, the deceased's heirs feast people who come to pay them a visit of condolence. This feast is called *shuma.* All those assembled recite the *kalima* about 100,000 times for the benefit of the deceased's soul. Food is sent to the *mullah* every evening for 40 days in succession. But no other ceremony is performed. Even the *qul-khwani* is not performed on the third day. The deceased's heirs merely sit in *chauk* from the first day to the third to receive the visits of condolence from people who pray for the deceased and then depart.

Quraishis, Sayyids and Ulma sit in a mosque. But in Marwat after the burial the deceased's brother or some other near kinsman supplies the bereaved family with food for the night and this is called *kauri roti.* The mourning (*liddi*) lasts for three days, and on the third the family bathes and washes its clothes. The deceased's clothes are given away in charity. The *qul-khwani* ceremony is performed and the whole of the

Quran recited for the benefit of the soul. His clothes are washed and given to the *imam* of a mosque with some cash. The custom of giving ornaments is extinct.

The deceased's heir is invested with a *dastar* on the third day, but his kinsmen contribute no cash. Rice, *halwa* and *roti* are given in charity for 5 or 6 Thursdays, but during this time no *khatam* prayers are recited. Alms are also given for the benefit of the departed soul on the 20th day, and for 40 days a loaf with *ghi* and sugar is sent to the *imam* who washed the corpse. It is always sent in the evening and is called the *imashan di gogi.* There is no custom that it should be cooked by the man who did so on the first day. The custom of giving a goblet of sweet water does not exist. On the 40th day alms are also given according to one's means. A year or two after death the heir gives a feast called *shuma* to his kinsmen.

The Rite of *Tija*

During the day the kinsmen in *Raya* sit with the men, but after the evening meal it is essential for each sex to sit with the mourners of that sex for 3 or 4 days, obviously in order to soothe their grief. On the 3rd day or *tija* friends and relatives collect at the deceased's house or at the mosque and recite the *kalima* once over each grain in a heap of gram, so that the total recitations number 125,000. This gram is then distributed. This rite is called the *kul panchayat* in Ambala in Naryana. After this, a new tuban is put on the head of the heir and he is thus recognised the legal and religious heir of the deceased.

The ceremony known as *tija* or *soyam* or of picking up the bones is performed on the third day after a burial by strict Muhammadans. When all the heirs and relatives of the deceased rise early and assemble at his house. Those who are literate recite the *Quran,* those who are not the *kalima* over each grain of the parched gram which stands there in a heap. Sunnis close this ceremony of *tija* by reciting the five verses called *Panjat* from the *Quran*, while Shias close it by reciting the *fatiha* prayers in the names of deceased ancestors and prophets slain at Karbala. Those who embraced Islam recently such as the Rajputs, Khanzadas, Gujars, and Meos etc. excepting a few persons who are well versed in their religious principles, do not observe this rite.

Daswan ceremony

In Gurgaon, the *daswan* ceremony is conducted on the evening of the birth and the *biswan* on the evening of the 10th day. On these days, also the *fatiha* is recited and food is distributed as on the third day. These ceremonies are performed one day before the actual day because among Muslims a day includes the day and subsequent night and begins at sunrise.

On Gurgaon *soyam,* the *qul khwani* on the morning of the 3rd day, or *phul* ceremony is performed. The Muslim custom is that all assemble and some parched gram weighing 12.5 *sers* is placed before each. Each then recites the first half of the *kalima* (*La illa illilah* only) on the first 10 grains, and the whole of it on the 11th, deeping all the grain by their side. The whole *kalima* is not recited on each grain so as to maintain the distinction between the Prophet and the Almighty. After this all the grain is made into a heap and sweetened *ilachi dana* of the same weight is mixed with it. Then incense *laban* and *aggar* are burnt and verses from the *Quran* are recited for the benefit of the departed soul. Then the grain is distributed among all present.

The incense is burnt to purify the air. Camphorated water is also sprinkled on the bier and coffin. The *fatiha* is also recited on reaching the grave, and flowers are thrown on it, for which reason the *soyam* ceremony is called *phul.* On the same evening *niaz* or *fatiha* is offered for the benefit of the deceased. Seven kinds of food, *halwa, khir*, flesh, bread, rice etc. are cooked and distributed among the poor after recitation of the *fatiha.*

Rite of *Karwi khichri*

At meal times remote relations of the deceased send cooked *khichri* for his family and any guests who have come for the occasion, the relatives supplying the bereaved family by turns.

Custom of Kashmiris

After the interment, early the next morning the head of the family, repairs to the graveyard and sits by the grave, others following him as they come. Prayers are said for the benefit of the deceased till sunrise when all return to his house. This is done for three days. But this custom is not general, being confined to certain tribes such as Kashmiris. The day after the death, food-offering to the Qazi commences, and he is given one meal every day for 40 days, the earthen vessels and the cloths used being also presented to him. About two *sers* of gram, maize or some other grain is taken and the *qul* verse is read over it grain by grain 125,000 times. It is then boiled and distributed among children. In some places this custom is observed differently. Early in the morning Qazis are invited to meet in a mosque and read the *Quran.* At about midday the communtiy collects, the Qazis receive offerings from the heirs, and the whole community then bestow, the spiritual benefit of the *Quran* reading on the departed spirit.

The Rite of *Kul Khwani*

The *kul-khwani* for children is observed both in towns and the villages. The Chandias of Leiah town observe it at the tombs of the aged, but other perform it on the third day after death, at the deceased's house or a mosque. All the *mullahs* recite in turn, one *siparah* each, for the benefit of the deceased's soul. *Hadia,* money varying in amount is given by the kinsfolk either at death after the *janaza* or at the burial distributed among the poor who are present. In villages grain is distributed instead. Besides this *hadia* wealthy people also distribute alms in cash and in grain.

When the *kul-khwani* is celebrated on the third day the clothes worn by the deceased's heirs and some new ones are given, to the person who washed the body and to relatives and friends. On the day of the *Kul-khwani* the near relatives let the deceased's heir put on a turban or *dastar* and also give him a cloth for a turban and cash from annas to Re. 1 as *bhaji.* The kinsfolk pay Re.1 or flour according to their means. In villages, those who give *bhaji* are feasted; but this custom does not exist in towns. Wealthy people both in villages and towns appoint *mullahs* to recite verses from the *Quran* at the tomb for 3 or 4 days and even till the evening of the first Thursday after death. Whatever part of the *Quran* they recite, they bestow it for the benefit of the deceased's soul. Members of the bereaved family give a meal, at their own cost, to the *mullahs* who get besides a fee in cash per day. Wealthy people distribute sweet rice, meat or meals to the kinsfolk and friends every Thursday for seven weeks. They give in charity sweet rice, and pudding made of half-ground grain.

There is no custom of appointing *mullahs,* at the tombs of infants, because they are innocent. Food consisting of bread with *ghi* and sugar on it and some milk or *sharbat* is sent every day before sunset to the *mullah* for 20 or sometimes 40 days. This is called the soul's spiritual food. It need not necessarily be prepared by the same woman. Various usages and customs prevail regarding the reading of the *Quran* at the grave after death.

Thus in ambala, some well-to-do people engage *moulavis* versed in the *Quran* to recite from it at the grave for a period. In some cases, the *mullahs* are asked to recite the *Quran* on the grave till the following Thursday. This ceremony is in vogue among followers of the Hadis sect, but elsewhere it is said that the followers of the Hadis sect do not perform any ceremony. If the heirs are well-to do they build a hut near the grave and engage four *mullahs* to sit in it, and recite the *Quran* through from end to end day and night. These four *mullahs* may take it in turns to recites the *Quran,* but the recital must be continuous and not stopped even for a moment till the following Thursday evening when they are dismissed with a fee ranging from Rs. 20 to Rs.10. The deceased's heirs have to feed the *mullahs* during these days.

From the moment of burial in Raya, *Quran* readers are employed to recite the Holy Book at the tomb which they do unitermittently day and night to the close of the following Thursday. The belief is that so long as reading continues the deceased escapes the torments of the tomb. But this is not done for the one who dies on a Thursday, as the belief is that by virtue of that day, he will escape the torments. The reciters of course receive offerings.

The custom of visiting the graves of dead relatives and throwing fresh earth over them at festivals, particularly in Muharram, is fast dying out, men of the new light as the phrase goes, being very indifferent to it.

REFERENCES

1. Rose, H.A., *A Glossary of the Tribes and Castes of the Punjab and North West Frontier Provinces,* Low Price Publications, New Delhi, 1991. (reprint), first published, 1919.
2. Ibbetson, Denzil, *Census Report for the Punjab* 1883.
3. MacLagon, Edward, *Census Report for the Punjab* 1892.

4. Singh, K.S., *People of India* : Haryana, Anthropological Survey of India, Calcutta, 1994.

5. Sherring, M.A., *Hindu Tribes and Castes*, Thacker & Spink, Calcutta, 1879 (reprint) Cosmo Publications, Delhi, 1974.

6. Siddiqui, MKA; *Castes among the Muslin of Calcutta in Caste and Social Stratification among Muslins in India,* ed. Imtiaz Ahmed, Manohar Publications, Delhi 1978.

7. Singh, Mian G, *Himachal Pradesh-History, Culture and Economy,* Minerva Book House, Simla, 1988.

8. Risley, H.H., *The People of India,* Thacker & Spink Co, Calcutta, 1908.

9. Singh K.S.,(Gen. ed.), *People of India: Haryana*, Manohar/ Anthropological Survey of India, Calcutta, 1994.

10. Singh K.S., (Gen.ed), *People of India : Himachal Pradesh*, Manohar, Anthropological Survey of India, Calcutta, 1996.

7
Social Customs

Social customs in the northern region of India are numerous. They also vary widely among Hindus, Muslims, Sikhs and Christians etc. They have changed with time; however, under the impact of modernity many of them are becoming extinct. An important custom in the northern region was that of fictitious kinship and also calling non-kin with kin terms. The ideas underlying the formation of these fictitious kinships and the effects of those ties, when formed, are only of importance from a practical point of view, as illustrating such practices as adoption, rules of succession, and the like, but they are also of considerable interest while illustrating the possibilities of castes, or every tribes, having been formed by processes of accretion. Among the most primitive races on the North West Frontier of India the ties of fosterage are very strong, more stringent even than those of blood kinship for example,among the so-called Dards see Biddulph's (*Tribes and Castes of the Hindo Koosh*), pp. 82-3 ; and throughout India, at least among the non-Muhammadans, the social custom of adoption plays a very important role in the law of inheritance. Here are a few ideas and customs collected in an attempt to ascertain how far fictitious kinship has come. Here are a few formed in Punjab, Harayana and Himachal.

Ties of *Ganga bhais*

A fraternal relationship entailing the consequences of natural kinship and thus operating as a bar to marrriage between the parties, who become *Ganga-bhais* each to the other, is established by making a pilgrimage to the Ganges together and there drinking the water of the sacred river from each other's hands. It was said the exchange of *pagri* at Hardwar merely cements along an intimate relationship by creating bond of artificial kinship. This relationship is also eastablished between two women (or even between a man and a woman), irrespective of caste, and the parties should drink thrice, or seven times, while lasting friendship and sisterhood are vowed. The women thus become Dharma-bahins, if Hindus. In Gurgaon, women who exchange *dopattas* (shawls) at a sacred place, or on a pilgrimage, become Ganga-bahin, Jamna bahin (if that river is the place of pilgrimage), or generally, tirath-bahin. Such women each treat the other's husband as a *jija*, i.e. as a sister's husband, and it is said that the custom of making these alliances is more prevalent among the women than among men, and more binding also. With the extension of facilities for making pilgrimages, this custom is becoming rarer, but when a pilgrimage involved journeying and living together, the tie was often contracted, and it is still not *rare* in cases where some service of aid was rendered. A Sanskrit adage states that no wrong should be done to a person with whom one has walked seven paces, an idea to which the seven steps at a wedding owe their significance.

Ties of Pahul

Among Sikhs, the tying of the *pahul* together creates a similar tie, and those bound by it are called *gurbhais*. Here again caste is disregarded and the relationship created operates as an absolute bar to marriage.

Custom of Adoption

Adoption, as a religious rite, is not very common in the Punjab, even among Hindus. It is solemnized with few rites, and is usually called *god lena,* or 'taking in the lap.' An adopted son is termed *putrela* by Hindus. But besides the custom of formal adoption, a kind of informal adoption of a man or woman as father or mother is not unusual. The adoptive parent is thenceforth treated as a natural parent, but apparently no legal rights ensue.

Exchanging *ganans*

An analogous tie can be created between two youths by exchanging *ganans* or wedding wristlets, and eating rice and milk together. The youth who is to be married puts on a *ganan,* and his would-be friend unties it, while a Brahmin repeats a Numerous other means are adopted to create or cement enduring friendships, hardly amounting to fictitious relationship. Thus, the *mundun* ceremony affords an opportunity to swear lasting friendships *mantra.* It is a string of coloured cords or of goat's hair. The man or youth who unfastens the *ganan* of a bridegroom at his wedding is also bound to him by special ties of friendship, *batashas* being distributed among those present or a child of the same age being made to catch the boy's hair as it falls, and thus form a tie of kinship with him. Simultaneous circumcision forms a similar bond. Among the Sansi tribes, friendship is sworn by one man's pleading a sword between himself and his friend. The latter removes it, and the tie is complete.

Custom of Pagwat

But far commoner than the solemn religious bond created by the foregoing fictions is the looser social bond created by the exchange of *pagris,* or *pigwat* as it is called in Gujarat. As a rule, this is only practiced among Hindus and owls its existence due to a bar to intermarriage, and that among Muslims this is not the case. The *pagri* or turban is typical of man's honour, so that the exchange means that the honour of the one party becomes that of the other. Such 'brothers' are ordinarily termed *pag-bhai* or *dharam-bhai,* the latter term being ordinarily used to denote a brother artificially created as opposed to a natural brother.

But in Ambala for instance, it is said that no such tie is created, because *pagwat* sometimes takes place between persons of different religions (and between them no such tie *could* be created). In Jhang, it creates no such tie.

Sisterhoods or Brotherhoods Forming

Women in the same way exchange *chadars* or *orhanas,* and among Muslims become *dharm-bahin* or *imah-bahin* to each other. But these customs are more prevalent among Hindus than among the Muslims.

A custom prevalent among children in Ambala was friendship was made or broken off by placing the finger on the chin and moving it backwards and forwards, saying *meri teri yari hodi,* ' there is friendship' twixt thee and me,' or *meri teri yari kut,* ' Our friendship is broken.' *In Punjab,* children hold their thumbs in their mouths and lock their little fingers togther, one saying, 'Is thy friendship like a sieve, or a river ?' If the other reply, ' like a river' the firendship is cemented.

Occasionally instead of a sieve and a river, a brass vessel and a grinding-stone are the simile. But the friendship may be broken off by taking a little dust in the palm and blowing it away, or, in Jhang, by breaking a straw. These mode of creating fictitious relationship, or the likes which underlie them, appear to be the basis of certain practices which exist in various parts of the Punjab. These practices on the one hand find analogies in the custom of seeking asylum, while on the other they emerge in certain forms of oaths.

The custom of *pagwat* finds a curious application and popularity among cattle-lifters and other criminals. Finding himself suspected, the chief offers to restore the stolen property, on condition that the owner exchanges *pagris* with him as a pledge that he will not lodge a complaint. An apparent extension of this practice is the custom of *talli pana, talla pana, tiari pana* or *tigra satna,* as it is variously called. This custom may be thus described. The supplicant casts a piece of clothing over the head of his enemy's daughter or sister, whether he be the person whom he has actually wronged, or a witness against him or his would-be captor. If he cannot get access to the girl himself, he employs a *Mirasan* or a *Machhiani* to go to her father's house and throw the cloth over her head in his name. It suffices to give the girl a small ornament instead of casting a cloth over her. By this practice means a complainant or a hostile witness may be compelled to assist a thief or any wrong-doer instead of pressing the charge againt him; or a loan may be extorted from a mony-lender. In *Gujarat,* the supplicant party assemble all the respectable men of the locality, and they go in a body to the house of one whose favour is sought. This is called *mela* (surely mela) *pand*. Both Hindus and Muhammadans have this custom, but only the latter take a *Quran* with them.

Among Muslims the relatives of man in trouble with the police approach the complainant with a *Quran* which they place in his hands and thus constrain him to abandon the prosecution. In former times, it is said, if man who had a feud died, and his kinsman could not, or would not, continue the feud they took his corpse to his enemy and thus compelled him to friendship. This is called *pallo pana,* or *niyat khair.* Refusal involves divine displeasure. In parts of Punjab it is customary for one side to send Sayyids, Brahmins or daughters as envoys to the rival faction in order to induce it to give up its claims. If this request is refused and the rival party meets with misfortune, it is attributed to its rejection of the terms proposed by the Sayyids, or the other envoys. In the same district it is customary for a thief to send a widow (called *kali siri*) to beg for mercy from the complainant. Such an envoy refuses to sit until her request is granted. The custom of casting one's garment over an enemy's daughter is found as far west as Kohat, but in that district another method is also in vogue. The thief, or one of his relatives, goes to the complainant's house, places his hands on his *chulha* (hearth or oven) and says: *ta anghare ma waniwales da,* 'I have grasped your oven': thus claiming his hospitality.

There compurgation is also not unknown. Thus in *Gujarat,* if A is suspected of stealing B's cattle, but denies his guilt, the parties nominate an arbitrator and agree to abide by his word. This is called *sunh laina,* or taking an oath, but it is termed *rah dena in Punjab*.

The Pathan custom of *nanwati,* or *nahaura* is also a very similar idea. If a man seeks mercy, or the protection of a powerful patron, he or his relative goes to his house with a *posse* of leading men of the village and there kills a goat or a sheep by way of peace-offering. Sayyid Ahmad Dehlari furnished some curious information on the customs among Muslim women in Delhi : the princesses of the old Mughal dynasty, when resident in the palaces, used to effect a tie of sisterhood, called *zanakhi. Zanakh* is the breast-bone of a fowl or pigeon, and two women used to break it. They then became *zanakhi,* each to the other, and the tie thus created was a very strong one. The custom is said to have been brought with them from Turkestan. Similar ties were formed by women of the palace who were known as *diljan,* 'heart's life', *jan-i-man, 'dilmila, dushman* (lit,enemy'), *dugana, chhagana, etc.* but these ties were less binding. *Dilmila* may be taken to mean ' confidant.' *Dugana* is applied to two women of equal age whose friendship is strengthened by eating Phillipine almonds, 'as if they were sisters, born of one mother.' *Chhagana* would appear to be derived from *chhe,* six, and to mean one who is six times dearer than a sister. *Dushman* is used, curiously enough, to imply that the enemy of either is also the enemy of the other.

These palace terms have been some what disregarded, or have at least lost much of their original force. *Chhagana,* occurs in the verse: *Mui ne gais ashiq ko tinke chunwae. Qurban ki thi chhagana woh kahmui Laita in the chagdna* they are also said to occur in three books, the *Chata-bhanchi, Sagharsuheli,* and *Baz-i-akhir,* written by a gentleman who had been brought up in the Delhi Palace, and decribing the colloquial language used therein.

Among the women of Delhi generally, the terms applied to such adoptive sisters are *suheli* (companion), *bahneli,* and *sakhi,* or *sakheli,* but the latter term is seldom used except in poetry. Another term for adopted sister is *munh-boli*, or 'adopted by word of mouth.' Other terms remind one of the *pagri-badal* or *topi-badal* brotherhoods formed among men and include the *challa-badal-bahin,* or sister by exchange of rings, and *Dopatta-badal-bahin,* or sister by exchange of scarves. The latter tie is formed ceremoniously, each 'sister' sending the other an embroidered scarf (*dopatta*) in a tray and putting on the one received from her, after which a number of invited guests are feasted. Religious sisterhood is formed by following the same faith and becoming *chini-bahin;* by affecting the same spiritual teacher *(pir)* and becoming *pir-bahin* ; or by drinking the water from the Jumuna or Ganges from each other's hands while bathing in one of those rivers, and thus becoming Jamuna or Ganga-*bahin*. The latter is the stronger tie. Foster sisters are styled *dudh-sharik-bahin.* In northern India, from Agra as far south as Bihar, the term *saiyan* is much in use among woman and in poetry. In Marwar and Upper India, the corresponding term is *saini*, which is a synonym of *saheli*.

Kafir Feasts of Honour

The kafirs have an established social hierarchy of *mirs* and priests, *Jast* and *urJast*, members of important septs, small septs, poor free men, *patsas* or shepherds, and slaves. In this strait Tribal society, the status of *Jast* or ur *Jast* can be earned through Throwing the feasts of honour. No individual can achieve importance until he becomes a *jast* or *ur Jast*. Amongst the Kam to become a *jast* it takes three years, and involves giving 21 feasts, 10 to the corpus of *jast* and 11 to the clan. Complicated ceremonies also have to be gone through. Little boys may become *jast*, though they will still be treated as boys. A *jast* wears a woman's coronetted earrings in the upper part of the ear and any gorgeous robes he can procure for religious ceremonies and dances.

The Kafir feasts are most expensive and among the Kam, many men utterly ruin themselves in becoming *jast* and praise themselves for having been so. To go through the ceremonies a man must have a female coadjutor, but she is usually not his wife because the cost of giving a double set of feasts would be too great.

Two men therefore usually arrange for one to go through the rites with the other's wife as his companion and *vice versa.* The initiatory rites are sacrifices of bulls and he-goats to *Gish*, and the animals are jealously scrutinised to see that they are up to standard. The meat is divided among the people who carry it home. These special sacrifices at the shrine recur at intervals, but the great slaughterings take place at the feast-giver's own house, though on these occasions, too, one or two goats are offered at the shrine of *Gish*. Here, too, the flesh is not eaten but taken home, only *China* cakes, cheese, salt and wine being consumed on the spot. At the feast-giver's house, however, flesh is eaten on certain day, but on others it is skewered together in great heaps or portions for the guests to carry home, bread and *ghee,* etc., being partaken of at this house. The feasts given to the *jasts* alone are called *mezhom* and as the guests are few in number, some he-goats and a bull suffice for a day's entertainment.

The feast-givers are known as *kaneash* and those who have already completed their virtuous work are called *sunajina*. Apart from giving the costly feasts, the *kaneash* undergoes a complex ritual, which becomes more and more complex as the time approaches when they may flaunt the ear-rings. At the *sanaukan* performance, the *kaneash* is 'the simulacrum of a man in that he closely resembles one of the decked out effigie', and Sir George Robertson thus describes the initiation of a priest.

" He had on a thick stumpy turban, having in front a fringe of cowrie shells strung together with red glass beads, and furnished with a tail. A plume-like bunch of junipercedar was struck in the front of this striking bead-dress, between the folds of the cloth. His ears were covered with a most complicated collection of ear-rings of all shapes and sizes. About his neck was a massive white metal necklace, brass bracelets rudely stamped with short lines and marks adorned his wrists' while he had on his feet the ordinary dancing-boots with long tops, ending in a *markhor* hair fringe. He wore a long blue cotton tunic, reaching nearly to his kness, and the curiously worked black and white nether garments made for these occasions at Shal in th Kenar Valley. Perhaps the most striking part of the costume was Ba dakhshani silk robe of the usual gaudy pattern, which was thrown negligently across the shoulders. In his hand was the dancing axe of his fathers. He was burating with pride and delight at his own appearance. After a short interval, Utah (the *kaneash*) being unable to officiate as priest, a *jast* stepped forward and acted as deputy. He bound a white cloth round his brows, took off his boots, washed his hands, and began the nights proceedings by the sacrifice of two immense billygoats, the largest I have ever seen, the size of young heirfers. The sacrifice was conducted in the usual way with the customary details. The special feature of the ceremony was the dabbling of some of the blood on the forehead of Utah and on the forehead and legs of his son Marak, who, seated opposite his father, was still weak and ill, for he was only just recovering from small-pox. For the boy, this proceeding meant that he might thenceforth wear trousers. Besides the ordinary dough, bread, and *ghee* placed by the fire ready for the sacrifice there were some enormous *chapaties,* about 15 inches in diameter, like those given to elephants in India. At this point these were lifted up with a prig of blazing juniper-cedar thrust in the centre, and they were then solemnly circled round Utah's head three times and made to touch his shoulders, while the deputy priest who handled them cried '*such*' '*such!*' The same thing was then done to the boy. After an interval for refreshnent there was dancing ; but just before they commenced, a visitor from another village, Bragamantal, burst forth into panegyrice upon Utab and on his dead father, and spoke of the immense amount of property which had been expended on the feast. This fulsome flattery was rewarded according to custom by the present of a *lungi* or turban cloth, which was taken from the waist of the little boy. Utah's son, who was still suffering from the effects of small-pox. The fire was then taken away and four or five visitors were provided with turbans and dancing boots, as well as scarves to wear over their shoulders or round the waist."

This double rite of initiation was followed by dancing, the first three dances being in honour of Gish, and the next to Imra, Dezane and other deities. The dancers included visitors as well as the initiate's sister and her daughter, the two latter being dressed in full dancing outfit. The rite of *sanaukun* was completed next day ceremoniously changing the initiate's turban for a road-brimmed crownless hat, into the front of which a sprig of juniper was thrust. This changing of the head-dress is called *shara' ute.* The *kaneash* initiated early in February were considered pure in their uniform which they wore till the spring, and the greatest care was exercised to prevent their semi-sacred garments being defiled by dogs. A curious duty of a *kaneash* is to grow a miniature field of wheat in the living-room of his house. With this no woman must have anything to do, and it is remarkable as the only agricultural work done by the men.

Just in front and to the east of the tiny field stands a flat stone and an iron tripod, on which lie pine sticks ready for lighting. The whole forms a miniature altar and before it is placed a stool with a flat piece of wood as a footstool. Every evening the *kaneash* goes through the ritual thus:-

He seats himself on the stool and takes off his boots, while some friends or relatives light the fire, bring forward a wicker basket piled up with cedar branches, a wooden vessel containing water, a small wicker measure with a handful of wheat grain in it and a large carved wooden receptacle full of *ghee*. The *kaneash,* having washed his hands, assumes the crownless hat he must never be without except in his own house, and begins by burning and waving about a cedar branch while he cries, *Such ! such!*- 'be pure!'

He thrusts this into the water vessel before him, and then burns a second branch completely, after waving it as before, and sprinkles it with the now holy water.

A *kaneash* then proceeds to sprinkle the cedar branches, the fire, the *ghee* vessel. Next he piles cedar branches on the fire, with a few wheat grains and a handful of *ghee*, he begins his incantation while the flames are dancing merrily and the smoke rolling upwards in clouds.

He pays tribute to all the gods in regular order, every now and then pausing to sprinkle and cast his offering on the fire, as at the beginning. The temperature of the room gradually grows terrific, for the ordinary house fire is blazing on the hearth all the time. The scene altogether is a strange one ; the walls of the room are frequently adorned with grotesque figures painted in black on the clay-coloured ground. The sprig of cedar worn in front of the hat shows that the wearer is an ordinary notable who has become a *jast.* If he has gone through the ceremony before, he wears two sprigs of cedar. This is very rare indeed. The *ur or urir jast* is the chief of the *ur* nor *urir,* 13 magistrates who are all elected annually, the other 12 being merely his assistants.

As a body it is their duty to regulate the amount of water which each cultivator is to get from the irrigation channels and to keep them in good order. Another duty is to see that no one picks or eats walnuts or grapes before the appointed time, a rule relaxed in favour of guests. Disobedience is punished by fines which are the *urirs'* perquisite and the only remuneration they receive. The *urir jast* also acts as master of the ceremonies at all festivals and dances and has to light the fire at the *gromma* every Wednesday (Agar) night. He is also the official entertainer of guests. The *urir* are elected in the spring at the Durban festival, after a bull has been sacrificed to *Gish* and some simple rites. The *ur jast* receives all the flour not used in sacrifices, and basketfuls of flour are also presented to him by the women on the last day of each month. In return he has to feast all comers for several days on election, but on the whole his office is a lucrative one. It is interesting to note that slaves can be elected members of the *urir* provided they are not blacksmiths and are *jast bari, i.e.,* skilled mechanics. Bari is a slave and *jast bari* would appear to mean 'a *jast* among the *bari'*. Fines are imposed for making fun of the *urir* within days after their appointment.

Other Social customs

A form of adoption which is clearly akin to the milk-tie of *chitral* is practised by them. A goat is killed, its kidneys removed and cooked at a fire. A *Kafir* then places the adoptive father and son side by side and the Adoption of a brother is effected in precisely the same way, but the latter part of the rite is omitted. Murder, justifiable homicide and killing by inadvertence are all classed as one crime for which the penalty is an extremely heavy blood-ransom to the slain man's family, or exile combined with spoilation of the slayer's property. The murderer at once takes to flight and becomes a *chile* or *chail* or outcast, for his sept will not aid him. His house is destroyed and confiscated by the victim's clan, and his moveble property seized and distributed, even if it is held only with his relatives. Their separate property is, however, exempt, nor is his family deprived of his land. The *chile* is not compelled to leave his tribe, but he must quit his village and always avoid meeting any of the family or sept of the slain, though it suffices if he merely pretends to hide so that his face may not be looked upon. His sons, 'if not grown up, and his daughters' husbands and their descendants, also become *chiles,* and even Muslim traders who have married daughters of *chiles* must behave like any other *chile* when they visit the slayer's village. Several 'cities of refuge' are inhabited almost entirely by *chiles,* descendants of the slayers of fellow-tribesmen. The chief of these is *Mergrom.* The shedding of blood may be atoned for by a heavy payment in cash or in kind, but the amount is uncertain as it is rarely paid. It is said to be 400 rupees and if paid reflects so much honour on the slayer's family that its males are for ever afterwards permitted to carry about a particular kind of axe.

Jogi Initiation

It is said, any Hindu can become Jogi or ascetic, but in practice only those of the twice-born castes are admitted into the order. In theory caste is abandoned upon entering it, and as marriage is there forbidden, no question as to the caste can arise in connection therewith. But as marriage is tolerated, the original caste is preserved in practice for matrimonial purposes, though all Jogis are said to be the caste-less. Further, there is a tendency to avoid marriage in the same *panth,* as all the members of a *panth* are supposed to be spiritually akin. Within the order there is said to be equality and no restrictions are placed upon eating, drinking or smoking together, but even a Hindu of high caste who joins the *panth* of Jalandhar Nath is excluded by other panths. Moreover, the theoretical equality does not extend to the women, as Jogi does not allow his women-folk to eat with him. Women of every *panth* may, however, eat together.

A prospective disciple is dissuaded initiallly by the preceptor from becoming a *Jogi*, the hardships of the life being impressed upon him. If he persists, he is made to fast for two or three consecutive days. After this, a knife is driven into the earth and the novice is made to swear not to engage in trade; not to take employment; not to keep dangerous weapons; not to become angry when abused; and not to marry.

The novice is also required to protect his ears, because a Jogi whose ears were cut used to be buried alive, but is now only excommunicated. After this probation, his ears are bored by a *guru*, or an adept, who is entitled to in cash a sum as an offering which may or may not be accepted. Up to a certain point the Jogi initiatory rites resemble those of the *Saniasis*. The *choti* of the novice is removed by the *guru:* the *janeo* is also removed : and he is given saffron-coloured clothes to wear. Of these the *kafni* is worn compulsorily. The *guru-mantar* is then whispered into his ear, certain set phrases (not *mantras*) being recited. According to this account *aughar* simply means 'novice.' Nath is a title acquired by the fully initiate. An account of the Jogis of *Rat Nath* says that the candidate is given a razor and scissors seven times by his *guru* who deters him from entering the Jogi order, but if he perseveres, the *guru* cuts off a tuft of his hair and he is then shaved by a barber. Then he is made to bathe and besmeared with ashes, a *kafni* or shroud, a *langoti* and a cap being given to him. The ashes and *kafni* clearly signify his death to the world. After six months probation, his ears are pierced and earthen rings inserted in them.

According to Macauliffe, Jogis smear ashes on their naked bodies as clothing or a protection against the elements, but the ashes appear to symbolize their death to the temporal world, like the *kafni.*

One may thus safely distinguish three stages in a Jogi's initiation. At first, he is a *chela* (pupil or disciple) then an *aughar* or novice, and finally a *darshani, vulg*, *kanphatta*, or 'split-eared'. An *Aughar* is not entitled to all the privileges of the sect, *e.g.,* at a feast he only receives half the portion of *Kanphatta.* A Jogi who is fully initiated certainly loses all rights of inheritance in his natural family, but it is doubtful whether an Aughar would do so.

It is indeed said that an *aughar* can become a Saniasi, an Udasi, a Bairagi, a Suthrashshi, etc., etc., as well as a Jogi or a Jangam. On the other hand, some accounts represent the *Aughars* as a distinct order, followers of Kanipa Nath and Jalandhar Nath, while the *Kanphattas* are followers of Gorakh and Machhandra (in other words, the more perfect *Jogis*) : or again they are connected with two schools of the Pattanjali philosophy : while a third account split up the Jogis into Shiv worshippers and Serpent worshippers.

Jogis themselves do not use the word *Kanphatta*. It is a popular term. So, too, in common parlance Jogis are distinguished by various names according to their dress or the penances they observe, and so on. Such are the *bastardhari* who are decently clad and live in temples (among the Saniasis this term means 'secular'): the *dudhadhari,* who live on milk, or *jatadhari* who wear long matted hair, the *munis* who observe perpetual silence, and the *khar tapesari,* who stand in contemplation. The *atit,* 'destitute or liberated from worldly restraints does not appear to be a sect of the Jogis, as Macaulife says (Sikh Religion, I, p. 162), but a popular term for any mendicant; see Platts P. 18. It is believed that Jogis live for centuries as a result of their austerities.

The origin of the word *Aughar* is obscure. The grade or order, however, does not appear to be connected with the *Aghori* or *Ghor-panthis* who are cannibal *faqirs* of a singularly repulsive type. The *Aughars* of Kirana in Jhang are of good repute and retain large *jagirs* granted to them by the Sikh kings. They are distinguished by an other coloured turban over which is twisted a black net-work of thread covered with gold. The *mahant* is styled *pir* and once elected may never again descend the hill. To these three degrees may perhaps be added a fourth, that of *mahatma* a dignity hardly alluded to in the accounts rendered of the sect.

A Jogi who attains to great spiritual eminence is exempt from wearing *mundras,* the *janeo,* and so on. After initiation a Jogi may apparently select the function which he is to fulfil. Thus, he may become a militant member of the sect, vowed to celibacy and styled *Nanga*, *Naga*, *Sanyogi* (Samayogi), *Gharbari* or *Grihisti*. Lastly, the initiate Jogi may also join one of the varous *panths* or orders. These *panths* are in theory limited to twelve in number, but in reality they number many more than twelve.

In fact, the grouping of the Jogis is exceedingly complex and appears to vary in different parts of these provinces. Thus, in Kangra, the Hindu Jogis are accounted for. Once when Gorakh gave two goats to Machhendra's sons, bade them to slaughter the animals at a place where none would see them. One boy killed his goat, but the other came back with his alive, and said that he had found no such spot, since if no man were present the birds would witness the slaughter, or, if there were no birds, the sun or moon. Gorakh seated the latter boy by his side and he was called *Andarla*, while the other was expelled and dubbed *Bahirla*. Both groups observe the usual Hindu social customs except at death, the only distinction being that the *Bahirla* only give Brahmins food and do not feast them, and at funerals they blow a *nad* instead of the conch, which is used by the *Andarlas*.

The *Darshanis* appear as a group which is distinguished from the *Nangas*, who use flesh and spirituous liquor, which the former avoid. The latter also are said to wear no clothes as their name denotes. But the *Darshanis* are said to be further divided into two classes, of which one is clothed, while the other, which smears the body with ashes and affects the *dhuni,* is not. However, this may be, the *darshanis* must have their ears pierced and are thus identical with the *Kanphara* or *Kanphatta Jogis*. The latter are celibate and live by begging, in contra-distinction to the *Sanyogis* who can marry and passes property. *In* Jind, the Jogis are said to be classed as (1) *Bari-dargah*, 'of the greater cout,' who avoid flesh and spirits, and as (2) *Chhoti-dargah*, who do not. Both groups are disciples of Mast Nath, the famous *mahant* of Bohar.

Jalandhar Nath was the son of *rajah*, whose wife remained pregnant for 13 years without giving birth to the child, and she was thought to be afflicted with *dropsy* Jalandhars. At last the *rajah* vowed that if a son were vouchsafed him, he would dedicate him to Gorakhnath. Jalandhar Nath was born in response to this vow, and founded the *panth* named after him.

Jogi Miracles

The *Jogis* claim, *inter alia,* power to transmute any metal into gold or silver. In the time of Altamsh, says one legend, a Jogi named Dina Nath begged from a boy sitting in a shop with a heap of copper coin to give him a few coins. The boy said the money was not his, but his fathers, he gave the Jogi food. The Jogi prayed to Lord Vishnu for power to reward the boy. Then he melted down the copper and turned the mass into gold by means of charms and a powder. Altamsh heard of the occurence and witnessed the Jogi's miracle-making powers but the latter declined to accept any of the gold he had made, so it was sent to the mint and coined, with his nameas well as that of Altamish upon it. Jogis alleged that these 'Dinanathi' gold mohars are still to be found.

Similarly, the Jogi claims miraculous power over hailstorms, and in Sialkot, the *rathbana* is a *Jogi* who can check a hailstorm or divert it into waste land. The connection between *Jogis* and snake-worship is naturally a close one. In some places Jogis are said to eat snakes- a kind of ritualistic cannibalism-and the snake is often styled *jogi,* just as the parrot is designated *pandit.*

The Jogis generally were a *janeo* of black wool, which is made by certain member of the ascetic order, not by any member, nor by a Brahmin. It is 9 cubits long, made of 3 strands each, woven of 8 threads on a bobbin, and plaited into a bobbin-thread. Round the waist Jogis wear a similar thread of two separate bobbin-threads of 8 strands each, twisted together, with a loop at one end and a button at the other.

The *Kanphatta* should be branded at Kalesar near Dwarka with two concentric circles within a third incomplete one, both ends of which are finished off by a circular bend in the arm. The *rudraksha* with two facets is sacred to Shiva, and can only be worn by the *Jogi* who has his wife with him : One with 5 facets is devoted to Hanuman ; and one with 11 is highly prized, being sacred to Gauri Shankar and worn by celibate Jogis.

The cults of the Jogis contain strong elements of nature-worship which finds expression in the names assumed by them after initiation. Such are Nim-nath, Kanak-nath (wheat), Nag-nath (snake), Tota-nath (parrot). The Jogis hold everything made of earth in great respect. That is why saying goes:- *Mitti ka asan, mitti ka basan, mitti ka sarhana, mitti ka bana.* 'The earthen asan (carpet), the earthen pitcher, the earthen pillow and the earthen woof.'

But how the *kundal* was turned into a *mundra* is explained in a story. When Bhartari was made a Jogi, he was put to a severe test. Jallandaripa was his *guru,* but he was also a *sadiq* or pupil whence he was known as Bhartari Kaplani and reckoned one of the 84 *sidhs.*

One day he said to Jallandaripa: " Thou hast put me to a severe test, but henceforth the *faqirs* of this *panth* will be mostly men of the world for they will mingle with such men." Gorakh said that he would be the more pleased with them, and Bhartari asked for some mark to be given them to distinguish them from worldly people. Accordingly a hole three inches wide was made in the Jogi's ears, and clay *mundras* were inserted into the holes. Subsequently the *mundras* were made of wood, then of crystal gilt, then of ivory. By wearing the *mundras,* a Jogi becomes immortal, as Bhogu-rikh had told Shakti. When this practice was permitted, two *sidhs* Kharkai and Bhuskai began to bore each Jogi's ears, with Jogis settled at a place on the road to Hinglaj in Balochistan, a place which every Jogi of this *panth* must visit if he wished to be considered a perfect *sadhu* and attain *yoga.*

Since then it has become a common practice to bore a Jogi's ears, but once when the two *sidhs* tried to bore the ears of a Jogi who had visited that place they found that they healed as fast as they bored holes in them, so they gave up the attempt, and Gorakh exclaimed that the pilgrim was '*Aughar.*' Thenceforth *Aughars* do not have their ears bored and form a body distinct from the other Jogi's.

Chuhra Taboos

The *Gil* will not eat *bataun,* the egg-plant *(bhata bart)* : the *Lute* do not eat hare or rabbit: the *Kanare* abstain from cloves : the *Sahotre* refuse to look on a tiger; at marriages however, they made the image of a tiger which the women worship : the *Bhatti* will not sit on a bench or boards or bricks : likewise no *Chuhras* will eat *seh,* or hedgehog.

The *Sarwan Chuhras* do not dye cloth with *kasumba,* saffron, and will also wear no gold ornaments, thinking this *tabu* to be imposed on their caste by their *sati.* A few different sections revere different animals, *i.e.,* the *Sahota* respect the lion, the *Athwal* or *uthwal* the camel, and one section the porcupine, while bricks are said to be revered by the *Gil*, men bowing and women veiling their faces before them. Thus the *Sindhu muhin* or *got* respects indigo: the *Kandiara* respects the horned rat; while the *Khokhar go* is said to avoid eating the heart, which all other *Chuhras* will eat. The flesh of the hare is also avoided by *Chuhras* generally- a *tabu* explained by a legend :- Once a Chuhra by chance killed a calf, and hid it under a basket, but its owner tracked it to the *Chuhra's* house. The Chuhra declared that the basket contained a hare, and when it was opened it was found that the calf had turned into a hare-from that time all the Chuhras have given up eating hare. Some, however, do not abide by this rule.

In Kangra, it is said that once a hare sought Balmik's protection, and thus the *tabu* arose. The avoidance of hare's flesh is also ascribed to the influence of the Makhdum Jahanian of Sher Shah, those who are not his followers disregarding the prohibition. In pockets of Punjab, the current legend is that once Bala Shah, the ancestor of the Chuhra, and Mullah Nur, the Mirasi, were in God's *dargah,* or court. The latter asked Bala Shah not to sweep, where upon a quarrel arose and Bala Shah struck the bard with his broom, knocking out his right eye. Mullah Nur appealed to God and produced a hare's flesh. In Gurgaon, however, the prohibition is said to be continued to the Sus Gohar *got,* or according to another account, to the Balgher *got.* In Maler Kotla, it is confined to the Sahota *got.* About *Leiah*, women are said to eat flesh of hare, but not the men.

Various beliefs have been stated to explain the origins of the Chuhra caste as a whole and of its different groups. Most of these carry its history back to Balmik as its progenitor, or at least, its patron saint. One legend avers that Balmik used to sweep Bhagwan's courtyard, and that the god gave him a robe, which he did not put on but buried in a pit. When asked by Bhagwan why he did not wear it, Balmik went in search of it and found in it a boy whom he took to Bhagwan. The god directed him to rear the boy, who was later named Lal Beg. Balmik is said to mean, 'born of the *balmi,'* or serpent's hole. Balmik was a Bhil, a race of mountaineers, who used to rob and kill travellers passing through the forest.

One day seven Rishis journeyed by, and when Balmik attacked them they asked him why he did so, as they had nothing valuable on their person worth stealing. He replied that he had vowed to kill all whom he found in the forest. The Rishis said that he was friendless, and they urged him to give up his evil ways, and to repeat '*mara, mara,*' continously. But rapidly recited '*mara, mara'* sounds like '*Ram' Ram,*' and as he thus repeated God's name, his sins were forgiven. By the end of 12 years his body become covered with dust and overgrown with grass. Once more the seven Rishis passed by and heard a faint voice repeating 'Ram, Ram' under a covering of clay. This they removed, and, having re-clothed his boned with flesh, called him Balmik, as one who had come out of a serpent's hole.

The chuhra representative assembly, or governing body, is the *Painch, Panch, Panchayat,* the members of which are chosen by the people, and the head of which, *i.e.,* the *Pir Panch* or *Sar Panch,* is selected by the other members. The office of the *pir panch* is held permanently, and is even in some cases hereditary. If the *pir* is unable to preside at the meetings his place may be taken by a *sarbarah,* or substitute, for the time being. The *painch* settles disputes of all sorts, having to interfere specially in matters of marriage and divorce ; it also looks after the poor. It punishes the caste offenders by excommunication, *hukha pani band,* and also by imposing fines. The punishment of excommunication, of being *biradari se juda,* is a heavy one, pointing to the fact that the people, valuing so highly the opinion of their fellow-men, are amenable to the rules and customs of their society by reason of sanctions affecting their standing in the society. All over Punjab the dearest thing to a Panjabi is his *izzat, i.e.,* the estimation in which he is held by his fellow beings. In Haryana the Chuhras have *chabutras* or places of assembly at several towns such as Hansi, Hissar, Barwala, Sirsa and Bhiwani. Each *chabutra* is under a *chaudhari,* who in Gurgaon is styled *mihtar.* The *chaudhris* preside over *panchayats* at which all kinds of disputes are decided, and also act at weddings as *mukhias* or spokesmen. In Nabha, the *chaudhris* are indeed said to exercise supreme authority in case of caste disputes.

Jhunha is an iron whip which a Chuhra *faqir* beats himself with for the sake of another, so that the evil-spirit in him may be troubled and flee. They also burn oil in a *tava* (iron dish). The *faqir* puts his hand in the hot oil and pours it on his person. The evil-spirit feels it, but the *faqir* does not. The *faqir* also beats his body with a millstone. After the sick man recovers, the *faqir* takes a fowl, on it, and finally binds it round the sick man's neck, assuring him that the evil-spirit will not come again. However, if the man goes where there is impurity or *sutak,* the virtue in the string disappears.

The dreams are from evil-spirits, and the Chuhras fear them. To dream that a person who is dead is cutting flesh, is an intimation that there will be a death in the house. Muslim Sayyids give the *ta'wis* (a charm) to keep away dreams. The evil eye is universally believed in. Some men are very injurious in this way. If a man with the evil eye looks at any one taking food, sickness follows. To cure this, the sick person asks a bit from the evil-eyed man when he is at a meal. The morsel given acts as a cure. When a cow is sick, and gives no milk, they give her a bit of the evil-eyed (*bad nazr*) man's food.

Sorcerers and witches act on their victim by making a clay, flour or straw figure of him and torturing the figure by inserting a needle into it. The torture reaches the person who is represented. Nails and hairs are inserted to cause pain that the original person may be tormented. They are carefully thrown away when cut off, lest any enemy should get possession of them. Women are especially careful in this particular account. The Chuhras also believe that the sickness is caused by evil spirits.

Ceremonial Taboo

The Chuhras never touch a Gagra, or a Sansi gypsy. Women and children do not go near graves. The daughter-in-law never mentions the father-in-law's name. Chuhras do not eat monkey, or snakes, or jackals, or rats.

That they also hold that crops are cut on a Sunday, Monday, or Friday, and sown on a Monday, Tuesday, and Wednesday. If the Chuhras born a *sup* (winnowing sieve or fan) in a village, the farmer is injured. It is a curse-the curse of the poor.

All the members of the household eat together, but the women folk eat after the men. If men eat after women they are *injured*, because women are weak of intellect.

'Ya juth ya jhuth, donori nuqsan pahuchande :' 'Food touched by other and falsehood are both injurious.' They use *sharab,* (strong drink), opium (*afim, post, bhang*) and *charas.* Drunkards are despised.

In salutation, the Chuhras say *pairie pan* to greet, the answer being *tera bhala kare Khuda.* Also *matha tekna, salam.*

They eat *pakki* among themselves, and *kachi* with Gagre and Sansis. They smoke only among themselves. No caste above them eats with them.

Gaddi Social Customs

Among the Gaddis ploughings, sowing and reaping should be begun on the lucky das-Sunday, Tuesday and Thursday. If wheat does not grow on a terraced field, the plough is not put on it again that year until a goat has been sacrificed there, and neglect of this custom will result in a death in the family. When new ground is to be broken up, the *purohita* must be asked to name the day, and a he-goat sacrificed first, only then the plough is put to it. But instead on this sacrifice, some Gaddis takes four young girls to the spot and there wash their feet,, mark their foreheads with vermilion and give them *gur* or jaggery to eat before they begin to plough. And the first fruits of such land are always offered to the *deota* before being eaten by themselves. The godlings associated with *chinia* wheat, pulse maize, wheat, pulse and barley are Devi, Chaund, Kailung, Kathura Nag and Sandholu Nag respectively.

The principal fairs are seven in number, *viz.,* the Basua on first Baisakh, the Patroru on first Bhadon, the Sair on 1st Assauj, the Lahori (or Lohri) on 1st Magh, and the Dholru on 1st the Holi (in Phagan or Chet) vary. The first four festivals are celebrated by games and dances, but there are differences. At the Partroru a cake of a vegetable called *siul* is eaten : only young girls dance. At the Sair *babrus* are cooked : and at the Lohri *khichri* or a mix of rice and *dal.* At the Holi *khaddas* (parched maize) are eaten, the fire is worshipped at night and a performance called *barn* held, songs being also sung. At the Dholru again *pindiris* are eaten, but amusements are rarely allowed. There is no annual feast of dead. Shiva and the Devis are propitiated with sacrifices on Shibratri.

The Gaddi salutations are :- Among Brahmans, *namaskar* to Brahmans from other, *pairi pauna* to which they reply *asir bachan.* Rajputs give *jai jai* to one another and receive it from those beneath them; responding with *ram ram.* Khatris, Thakurs and Rathis offer *luarki* to one another and receive it from the low-castes, giving in reply *ram ram.*

Striking costume of the Gaddis

The Gaddis are an interesting people, and offer a striking contrast in several respects to the other inhabitants of Chamba in Himachal Pradesh. The costume of the Gaddis, both men and women, is characteristic and striking. The old head-dress of the men is of a peculiar shape, with a flap round the margin, and a peak-like projection in the centre, said to represent the Kailas of Mani Mahes. The flap is tied up for ordinary wear, but let down over the ears and neck in time of mourning, as well as in severely chilly weather. The front is often adorned with dried flowers or beads. But this head-dress is falling into disuse, save on special occasions its place being taken by the *pagri.* On the body a *pattu* coat called *chola,* reaching below the knee, is worn. It has a deep collar, which hangs loose in two lappets in front, and in the sewing the wearer stows away various articles, such as a beedle and thread, pieces of paper and twine. The *chola* is tightened round the waist by a black rope worn as a waist-band. This is made of sheep's wool and is called *dora.* above the waist-band the coat is loose, and in this receptacle the Gaddi carries many of his belongings. On the march a Gaddi shepherd may have four or five lambs stowed away in his bosom, along with his daily food and other articles. The legs are generally bare, but many wear *pattu* payjamas, loose to the knees for the sake of freedom in walking, but fitting tight round the calf and ankle where it rests in numerous folds.

Shoes are in common use. From the girdle hang a knife, a flint box and steel and a small leather bag, in which the wearer carries money and other small articles. The hill people are all fond of flowers, and in *topi* or *pagri* may often be seen a tuft of the wild flowers in season, red berries, or other ornament. The principal ornament is the *tabit,* a square silver plate of varying size covered with carving and hung from the neck.

Gaddi women wear a dress like that of the men, made of *pattu* and called *cholu.* It is worn straight, like a gown, from the neck to the ankles, and round the waist is the woolen cord or *dora.* A cotton gown of a special pattern is now common and is called *ghundu,* worn in the same way as the *cholu.* The head is covered with a *chadar,* and the legs and feet are bare. The Gaddi women wear special ornaments, of which the main is the *galsari,* and sometimes a *tabit,* similar like the men. They also wear heavy brass anklets, called *ghunkare* which are peculiar to the Gaddi women. Brass anklets called *riharu,* are worn by Gaddi children to ward off the evil eye, and to prevent them from crying. They are made by the menial caste, named *rihara,* which is itself supposed to have the power of injuring children by sorcery.The Gaddis state that they assumed the garb of Shiva and Parvati when they settled in Brahmaur which they call *Shiv-bhumi* or Shiva's land, but it is not their dress alone that makes them conspicuous. Their whole bearing is characteristic, conveying an impression of independence which is full borne out by closer contact with them. They are robust of frame, and accustomed to exposure in all weathers, owing to the migratory life which so many of them lead. In their manners they are frank and open, deferential to their social superiors and yet manly and dignified. They delight in festive gatherings, and are fond of singing and dancing, the latter in a style peculiar to themselves. Their women are pleasing and comely, and have the reputation of being also modest and chaste. The Gaddis are a semi-agricultural tribe, and own large flocks of sheep and goats, which are their chief source of wealth. With them they go far afield, the summers being spent in the higher mountains of Pangi and Lahul; and the winters in the low hills bordering on the plains. This duty the male members of the family take in turn, the others remaining at home to tend the cattle and look after the farm work. Many of them own land on both sides of the Dhaula Dhar, and reap the winter crop in Brahmaur. On the whole, they are better shepherds than farmers, and perhaps for this reason they are the most prosperous agricultural class in the state. The annual transhumance to Kangra takes place in October and November, and the return journey in April and May. With an appearance of candour and simplicity, the Gaddis have the reputation of being good at making a bargain ; hence the saying in the hills-

Gaddi mitr Dhola, denda tap to mangda chola. or 'The Gaddi is a simple friend, He offers his cap, and asks a coat in exchange.'

Bishnoi Social customs

Bishnoi or Pahlad Bangi, a sect founded by Jhambaji towards the end of the 15th century. Jhambaji instructed his followers, stating, "Examine your fuel wood in case any living creature be burnt with it. Show pity to all living creatures. Keep duty present to your mind as the teacher bade. Do not speak evil of others. Do not tell lies. Never quarrel. Avoid opium, tobacco, bhang and blue clothing. Flee from spirits and flesh. See that your goats are kept alive (not sold to Muslims who will kill them for food). Do not plough with bullocks. Keep a fast on the day before the new moon. Do not cut green trees. Sacrifice with fire. Say prayers. Meditate. Perform worship and attain Heaven. And the last of the 29 duties prescribed by the teacher- 'Baptize your children, if you would be called a true Bishnoi'."

However, some of these precepts are not strictly obeyed ; for instance, although ordinarily they allow no blue in their clothing, yet a Bishnoi, if he is a servant of the British government, is made to wear a blue uniform ; and Bishnois did use bullocks for purpose of ploughing and given to use bad language. But they abstain from tobacco, drugs and spirits, and are noted for their regard for animal life, which is such that not only will they not themselves kill any living but they do their utmost to prevent others from doing so. Consequently, their villages are generally swarming with antelope and other animals, and they forbid their Muslim neighbours to kill them and try to dissuade European sportsmen from interfering with them. They wanted to make a condition of their settlement, that no one should be allowed to shoot on their land, but at the same time they asked that they might be assessed at lower rates than their neighbours on the ground that the antelope being thus left undisturbed inflict more damage to their crop ; but on being told this would lose the merit (*pun*) of their good actions in protecting the animals, and they must be treated just as the surrounding villages were in tax matters. They consider it a good deed to scatter grain to pigeons and other birds, and often have a large number of half-tamed birds about their village.

The day before the new moon they observe as a *Sabbath* and fast-day, doing no work in the fields or in the house. They bathe and pray three times a day,- in the morning, afternoon, and in the evening- chanting "Bishno, Bishno" instead of the ordinary Hindu 'Ram,Ram.' Their clothing is the same as of other *Bagris*, except that their women do not allow the waist to be seen, and are fond of wearing black woollen clothing. They are more particular about ceremonial purity than the ordinary Hindus are, and it is a common saying that if a Bishnoi's food is on the first of a string of twenty camels, and a man of another caste touches the last camel of the string, the Bishnoi would consider his food defiled and throw it away.

Ceremony of initiation

"A number of representative Bishnois assemble, and before them a *sadhu* or Bishnoi priest, after lighting a sacrificial fire (*hom*) instructs the novice in the duties of the faith. He then takes some water in a new earthen vessel, over which he prays in a set form (*Bishno gayati*), stirring it the while with his string of beads (*mala*), and after asking the consent of the assembled Bishnois, he pours the water three times into the hands of the novice, who sips it off. The novice's scalp lock or *choti* is then cut off and his head shaved, for the Bishnois shave the whole head and do not leave a scalp-lock like the Hindus ; but they allow the beard to grow, only shaving the chin on the father's death.

Among them infant baptism is also practised, and 30 days after birth the child, whether boy or girl, is baptised by the priest or *sadhu* in much the same way as an adult ; only the set form of prayer is different (*garbh gayatri*), and the priest pours a few drops of water into the child's mouth, and gives the child's each relatives the consecrated water to drink three times in the cupped palms ; at the same time the barber clips off the child's hair. This baptismal ceremony also has the effect of purifying the house which has been made impure by the new birth or *sutak*.

But according to the Hissar Settlement Report, the ceremony of admission to the sect is as follows :- The priests and the people assemble together, repeat the *pahul-mantar* over a cup of water, and give it to the candidate to drink ; who thereafter goes round the assembly and bows to all. His head is then shaved after the manner of the founder of the sect. According to his means he has to pay a certain sum of money (Rs. 5 to 500 is the limit), for the purpose of buying gram which is then sent to the Samrathal sandhill in order to feed pigeons.

The Bishnois intermarry among themselves only, and by a ceremony of their own in which it seems the circumambulation of the sacred fire, which is the binding ceremony among the Brahmanical Hindus generally, is omitted. They do not revere Brahmins, but have priests, *sadhus* of their own, chosen from among the laity. They do not cremate their dead, but bury them below the cattle-stall or in a place frequented by cattle, such as a cattle-*pen* and let the cow urine flow the dead men's grave. They celebrate the Holi in a different way from other Hindus. After sunset on that day, they fast till the next forenoon, when, after hearing the read account of how Prahlad was tortured by his infidel father Hiranyakashyapu for believing in the god Vishnu, until he was delivered by the god himself in his incarnation of the Lion-man, and mourning over Prahlad's sufferings, they light a sacrificial fire and partake of consecrated water, and after distributing *gur* or jaggery in commemoration of Prahlad's delivery from the fire into which he was thrown, they break their fast.

Bishnois go on pilgrimage where Jhambaji is buried, south of Bikaner, where there is a tomb (*mat*) over his remains and a temple (*mandir*) with regular attendants (*pujari*). A festival takes place here every six months, in *Asau* and *Phagan*, when the pilgrims go to the sandhill on which Jhambaji lived, and there light sacrificial fires (*hom*) of *jandi* wood in vessels of stone, and offer a burnt offering of barley, *til, ghee* and sugar, at the same time muttering their set prayers. They also make presents to the temple attendants and distribute *moth* and other grain to the peacocks and pigeons, which live there in vast numbers. Should any one have committed an offence, such as having killed an animal, or sold a cow or goat to a Muslim or allowed an animal to be killed when he could have prevented it, he is fined by the assembled Bishnois for the good of the temple and the animals kept there.

Another place of pilgrimage is a tomb called *Chhambola* in the Jodhpur, where a festival is held once a year in the Hindu month of *Chet*. There, the pilgrims bathe in the tank and help to deepen it, and sing and play musical instruments and scatter grain to peacocks and pigeons. The Bishnois look with special attention to the sacred *hom* or sacrifice; it is only the rich who can perform this daily ; the poor meet together to carry out the rite on the *Amavas* day only. The *gaenas* or *sadhus,* who act as their priests fed by them like Brahmins, are a hereditary class and do not intermarry with other Bishnois, or take offering from any other Hindu but Bishnois. The Bishnois themselves are a real caste. It is said that a member of any of the higher Hindu castes may become a Bishnoi, but as a matter of fact they are almost entirely Jats or Khatis (carpenters) or, less frequently, Rajputs and Banias, and the Bania Bishnoi are apparently not found in the Punjab, their seat being Muradabad, 'Uttar Pradesh'. The man who becomes a Bishnoi is still bound by his caste restrictions ; he no longer calls himself a *Jat*, but he can marry only Jat Bishnois, or he is no longer a Khati, and yet can't marry anyone whois not a Khati, and further than this, the Bishnoi retains the *got* of his original tribe and may not marry within it.

Picturesque Dress of Kanets

Kanets, both male and female, wear a dress which is picturesque, and not at all oriental. A red and black woollen cap, not unlike a Scotch bonnet at first sight, a gray or brown loose woollen tunic girt in, with a rope or sash at the waist, a striped or chequered blanket worn like a Scotch plaid round the chest and over the shoulders, constitute the dress of the men. If well enough off, they add loose woollen trousers tight round the ankle. Many women wear a cap like that of the men, under which their hair hangs down in long plaits lengthened out with plaits of worsted, but most of them do without a cap, and wear their hair puffed out and twisted into a high sloping chignon, not unlike the fashion once prevailing among English women. Instead of a tunic they wear a plaid or blanket fastened around them with bodkins, and so skillfully put on that, while the neck and arms are bare, all the rest of the body is modestly covered to below the knee of the leg is bare or covered with a woollen gaiter, broad metal anklets are not uncommon, and set off the leg very prettily, the arms are generally overloaded with bracelets.

Both sexes are generally shod with sandals made of plaited straw or hemp, but may go bare foot, and a few wear leather shoes. Both sexes, especially on festival days, are fond of wearing bunches of flowers. The blood is in fact generally very mixed, for both Brahman and Rajputs hung round their necks. Some are hardly darker than Spaniards in complexion, with a ruddy colour showing in their cheeks; others are as dark as the ordinary Punjabi.

With the exception of a few families, descendants of the Rajahs priests or *purohitas,* the Kullu Brahmins differ very little in appearance, dress or custom from the Kanets. The same may be said of nearly all of the few Rajputs stuck in their caps or in their hair, and strings of flowers commonly marry Kanet girls : such wives are known as *srit* in distinction from the *lari,* or wife of the same caste taken by the regular *biah* ceremony. The social usages of the Kanets are not peculiar to the caste, but are those which are followed by the other castes in the regions concerned, the upper classes of the Kanets observing the same usages as the Brahmins or Rajputs, while the lower are content to follow much the same customs as the artisan castes below them.

Gulab Dasi Social customs

Mr. Edward Maclagan wrote about the Epicurean *gulab dasis*, who had many social customs, and usages opposed to the mainstream religions of Sikhism and brahminical Hinduism at the same time. Maclagan wrote in the census report for the Punjab-1892. "The gulabdasis have thrown over asceticism and have proceeded to the other extreme. They originally held that all that was visible in the universe was God, and that there was no other. It is said that Gulâb Dâs declared himself to be *Brahm* and many of his disciples believe themselves to be god ; and, properly speaking, their faith is that man is of the same substance as the deity, and will be absorbed in him but for the most part they are looked on by their neighbours as denying the existence of god altogether. They do not believe in a personal future life, and dispense with the veneration of saints and with pilgrimages and religious ceremonies of all kinds. Pleasure alone is their aim ; and renouncing all higher objects they seek only for the gratification of the senses, for costly dress and tobacco, wine and women, the lust of the eyes, and the pride of life. They are scrupulously neat in their attire and engage in all worldly pursuits, some of them being men of considerable wealth. They are said to have an especial abhorrence for lying, and there is certainly little or no hypocrisy in their tenets. In appearance they vary ; some always wear white clothes; others preserve the Udâsî dress; others are clothed like the Nirmalas; and others are distingushed by being always shaved. They are of course greatly distrusted and, to some extent, despised by their co-religionists, and their numbers are said to be on the decrease. The gulabdasis are returned mainly form Lahore and Jullundur. They admit any caste to the sect, but the different castes admitted do not eat with each other or intermarry."

Gulab Das abolished the *kes* or Sikh fashion of wearing the hair, allowed his followers to smoke and only acknowledged such passages of the Granth as accorded with his own views. Gulabdasis do not frequent the ordinary fairs, but have a large gathering of their own, that lasts six days during the Holi.

Gulabdasi is a Sikh sect, or rather order, founded by one Gulab Das, an Udasi of Chattha or Chattianwala near Kasur. Its ideology may be described as Epicurean though the accounts given of them vary as to the precise tenets of the sect. One version is that they disbelieve in the existence of God, and only revere living priests of their own persuasion. Gulab Das, though originally an Udasi, is said to have fallen under the influence of one Hira Das, a *sadh* of Kasur, and about 70 years ago he discarded a *faqir's* nudity for the ordinary raiment, proclaiming that he had had a vision which convinced him that there is no religious superior, that pilgrimages were waste of time and temples not possessed of any sanctity. Mr. Maclagan says that the real founder of the sect was an

Udasi named Pritam Das who received some light at a Kumbh bathing festival on the Ganges and so started a new sect. His principal disciple was Gulab Das, a Sikh Jat, who had been a *ghorchara* or trooper in Maharaja Sher Singh's army and joined the new sect on the collapse of the Sikh monarchy. He compiled the scripture called *Updes Bilâs,* and it is his tomb at Chattiân wâla which is revered by his disciples.

Lahuli rites connected with agriculture

The Lahulis perform certain ceremonies of a religious nature in connection with the cultivation of their fields. A Buddhist *lama,* who understands the astrological books, names the auspicious day on which ploughing should be done, (this day falls always between the 8th and 22nd of May). After the fields have been ploughed and sown, a procession goes round all the fields, headed by one or two *lamas* and two drums, some of the company carrying at the same time several large religious books on their backs, this done, the whole company of the procession sits down in the fields near the villages and feasts on cakes and *chang* supplied jointly by all the land-holders. All this is done to secure the sprouting up of the seeds sown, after that the water-course irrigating the fields is repaired, on which occasion a sheep is sacrificed to the *lhâ* which is supposed to have special care of the water-course. Again, as soon as the seeds have sprouted, another ceremony is performed; this consists in sticking small braches of the pencil-cedar here and there in the field, and burning incense, while some members of the family sit down, eat, and drink a little, and murmur some prayers. This is to ensure that each grain which has sprung up, may prosper and produce many ears.

When the fields are nearly ripe, a goat or sheep is killed in honour of the *lha,* in several villages horse-races are held at the same time. Till the festival of the ripening grain has been celebrated, nobody is allowed to cut grass or any green plant or grass with a sickle made of iron, as in such case the field-god would become angry and send frost to destroy or injure the harvest. If, therefore, a Lahuli wants grass before the harvest sacrifice, he must cut it with the sickle made of the horn of an ox or sheep, or tear it off with the hand. Infractions of this rule were formerly severely punished, with a fine which goes into the pocket of the *jagirdar* or the village headman. The iron sickle is used as soon as the harvest has been declared to be commenced by the performance of the sacrifice.

They seem to receive the ministrations of *Bhot* priests only, while the other local castes have various divinities, *e.g., mahadeo* in Patan : *Hirmadevi* at Sissu (said to be the *Kullu Jamlu*), *Gantal Devi* called *Chahja-mon* equivalent to *Kali Devi*, and also T'su' dag-mo=*Jan -malika* or the lady of life, Devi Yamso at Kyelang. Buddha Gaya, Shakya Tub-ba, Padma Sambha, said to have come from Ujjain, and Guru Rinpoche.

Form of Mian Salutations

The form of salutation among the Mian is *jaidiya* of which the original in Sanskrit was *Jayatu Deota,* meaning "May the king be victorious." It is thus very much the same as "long live the king." It was formerly offered only to a ruling chief or a scion of his family and could not be assumed by a Râjput of lower degree without proper sanction. Occasionally a chief, being the head of the Mian clan, might confer the privilege of using the *jaidiya* on others than the members of the royal clan but unauthorised assumption of the title was punished with fine and imprisonment. By a ruling chief or the head of a royal clan it is received and not returned unless when offered by an equal in rank or an heir-apparent. Among Mians of the first rank below the chief it was freely interchanged, the inferior in rank offering the salutaion first, and when accorded to them by others of inferior social rank, whether Rajputs or, those of lower castes, the salutation *Ram Ram* is given in return.

Other Mian customs

A distinction is made by some Mians between those who do and those who do not follow the plough, the salutation being accorded only to the latter and denied to the former even when of noble descent. This distinction is not now so marked as in former times, for the force of circumstances has compelled many *Mians* to resort to agriculture for a living.

Mr. Barnes in the Kângra Settlement Report relates incident which show the great importance formerly attached to the *jaidiya*. Raja Dhian Singh, the Sikh minister, himself a Jamwal Mian, desired to extort the *jaidiya* from Raja Bir Singh, the fallen chief of Nurpur. He held in his possession the grant of a jagir valued at Rs. 25,000, duly signed and sealed by Ranjit Singh and delayed presenting the deed until the Nurpur chief should hail him with this coveted salutation. But Bir Singh was Raja by a long line of ancestors, and Dhian Singh was a Raja only by favour of Ranjit Singh. The hereditary chief refused to compromise his honour and preferred beggary to affluence rather than to accord the *jaidiya* to one who by the rules of the brotherhood was his inferior. Considerable modifications in the popular use of the jaidiya have taken place in recent years and many now receive the honour who formerly would not have been entitled to it.

The Mians themselves, however, adhere to ancient custom in the use of their honorific salutation. Mr Barnes has the following remarks about the exclusive habits of the Mîâns in Kangra, 50 years ago. 'A Mian, to preserve his name and honour unsullied, must scrupulously observe four fundamental maxims: Firstly, he must never drive the plough; secondly, he must never give his daughter in marriage to an inferior, nor marry himself much below his rank; thirdly he must never accept money in exchange for the betrothal of his daughter, and lastly, his female househoIed must observe strict seclusion.The prejudice against the plough is perhaps the most inveterate of all: that step can never be recalled. The offender at once loses the privileged salutation, he is reduced to the second grade of Râjput: no Mîân will marry his daughter, he must go a step lower in the social scale to get a wife for himself. In every occupation of life he is made to feel his degraded position. In meetings of the tribe and at marriages the Rajputs undefiled by the plough will refuse to sit at meals with the *halbah* or plough driver as he is contemptously styled, and many to avoid the indignity of exclusion never appear at public assemblies. The prejudice against driving the plough is common to Brahmins as well as Rajput and three chief reasons are assigned by the people for it. Some say it is sacrilegious to lacerate the earth with an iron plough-share. Others consider that the offence is in subjecting oxen to labour and driving them with the goad; probably the real reason is that such labour is regarded as menial, and fit only for people of lower castes. In many if not most cases, the objection applies only to driving the plough, all other forms of farm service being freely engaged in. The actual ploughing is done by men of low caste residing in or near the village.

"The giving of one's daughter to an inferior in caste is scarcely a more unpardonable offence than agriculture. Even Ranjît Singh in the height of his prosperity and power felt the force of this prejudice. The Raja of Kangra deserted his hereditary kingdom rather than ally his sisters to Dhian Singh, himself a Mian of the Jammu stock, but not the equal of the Katoch prince. The Rajputs of Kotgarh, in the Nurpur *pargana*, voluntarily set fire to their houses and immolated their female relatives to avoid the disgrace of Ranjit Singh's alliance, and when Mian Padma, a renegade Pathania, married his daughter to the Sikh monarch, his brethren, undeterred by the menaces of Ranjit Singh, deprived him and his immediate connections of the *jaidiya* and to this day refuse to associate with his descendants. The seclusion of their women is also maintained with severe strictness. The dwellings of Rajputs can always be recognised by one familiar with the country. The houses are placed in isolated positions. Either on the crest of a hill which commands the approaches on all sides, or on the verge of a forest sedulously preserved to form an impenetrable screen. Where natural defences do not exist, an artificial growth is promoted to afford the necessary privacy. In front of their dwellings removed fifty paces from the house, stands the *mandi* or vestibule beyond whose precincts no one unconnected with the household can venture to intrude. A privileged stranger who has business with the master of the house may by favour occupy the vestibule, but even this concession is jealously guarded, and only those of decent caste and respectable character are allowed to come even as far as the *mandi*. A remarkable instance of the extremes to which the seclusion is carried occurred under my own experiences.

"A Katoch's house in Mandi territory accidently caught fire in broad day. There was no friendly wood to favour the escape of the women and rather than brave the public gaze they kept their apartments and were sacrificed to a horrible death. Those who wish to visit their parents must travel in covered palanquins and those too poor to afford a conveyance travel by night, taking unfrequented roads through thickets and ravines."

This remark apply mainly to Kangra where the Rajputs are much more tenacious of ancient custom than in other parts of the hills. The restrictions of former times are, however, much relaxed.

Mr. Barnes also draws a pathetic picture of the condition of many of the Mian families fifty years ago soon after the establishment of British rule in the hills. Too proud to follow the plough they often had great difficulty in eking out a living and had to resort to many shifts to support themselves and their families. That picture is no longer true to life, times have changed for the better, and even when unwilling to follow the plough, the Mians have many other avenues of work open to them, and a large number enter the army and other departments of Government private service. Not a few have given up their prejudice against following the plough, and become keen agriculturists, while the profits derived from land are much greater than they were fifty years ago, so that the poorest of them now live in comparative comfort.

Custom of committing crime

Mina, a caste which is, in the Punjab at least, almost invariably criminal. In *Alwar* and *Jaipur* however, in which their home lies, this does not appear to be the case. Indeed Jaipur was said to be 'really made up of petty Mina States, In Gurgaon, the Mina cultivates land, but this does not prevent his being a professional thief. The following extract of the caste is taken from Major Powlett's *Gazetter of Alwar:-*

"Minas were formerly the rulers of much of the country now held by the Jaipur Chief. They still hold a good social position, for Rajputs will eat and drink from their hands, and they are the most trusted guards in the Jaipur State. The Minas are of two classes, the 'Zamindari,' or agricultural, and the 'Chaukidari,' or watchmen. The former are excellent cultivators and are good, well-behaved people. They form a large portion of the population in Karauli, and are numerous in Jaipur.

"The 'Chaukidari' Minas, though of the same tribe as the other class, are distinct from it. They consider themselves soldiers by profession, and so somewhat superior to their agricultural brethren, from whom they take, but do not give, girls in marriage. Many of the 'Chaukidari' Minas take to agriculture, and, I believe therby lose caste to some extent. These Chaukidari Minas are the famous marauders. They travel in bands, headed by a chosen leader, as far south as Haidarabad in the Deccan, where they commit daring robberies, and they are the principal class committing *Thaggi* and Dacoity, Suppression Department has to act against. In their own villages they are often charitable; and as successful plunder has made some rich, they benefit greatly the poor of their neighbourhood, and are consequently popular. But those who have not the enterprise for distant expeditions, but steal and rob near their own homes, are numerous and felt to be a great pest. Some villages pay them highly as Chaukidars to refrain form plundering and to protect the village from others. So notorious are they as robbers that the late Chief of Alwar, Banni Singh, was afraid lest they should corrupt their agricultural brethren, and desirous of keeping them apart forbade their marrying, or even smoking or associating with members of the well-conducted class.

"In April 1863, Major Impey, then Political Agent of Alwar, issued orders placing the Chaukidari Minas under surveillance ; and under Major Cadell's direction lists of them have been made out, perodical roll-call the village and absence without leave certificate punished.

"I am not sure that, although, speaking generally, Minas are divided into Chaukidari and Zamindari, there is any hard and fast line between the two classes. There is, I believe, an intermediate class, for Maharaja Banni Singh's attempts to keep the two apart were not very successful.

There are said to be 32 clans of Minas. Out of 59 apprehended for dacoity by the dacoity Suppression department, I found that the Jab clan furnished 17, the Kagot 9, the Sira 8, and the Jarwal and Bagri 5 each. The Susawat was, I believe, formerly the most powerful clan, and that which held Ajmer."

The Minas of the Punjab appear in the Muhammadan histories as Minis or Mans. Like the Bhais all the territories of the Minis were attached to Abohar in the reign of Ada-ud-Din. Under Muhammad Shah (1389-1392) we read of Rai Kamal-ud-Din Main and Rai Daud Kamal Main, doubtless one and the same person, as serving with the Bhatti chief. The Minas are the boldest of the criminal classes in the Punjab. Their head-quarters, so far as that state is concerned, are the village of Shahjahanpur; which is attached to Gurgaon but surrounded on all sides by Rajputana territory. There they till lately defied British police, and even resisted them with armed force. Their criminal enterprises are on a large scale, and they are always prepared to use violence if nesessary. In Marwar they are armed with small bows, which do considerable execution. They travel great distances in gangs of 12 to 20 men, practising robbery and dacoity even as far as the Deccan. The gangs usualy start off immediately after the Diwali feast, and often remain absent the whole year. They have agents in all the large cities of Rajputana and the Deccan who give them information, and they are in league with the carrying castes of Marwar. After a successful foray they offer one-tenth of the proceeds at the shrine of Kali Devi.

The criminal Minas are said to inhabit a tract of country about 65 miles long and 40 miles broad, stretching from Shahpurah 40 miles north of Jaipur to Gurgora in Gurgaon on the Rohtak border, the most noted villages being Koti Putli, Bhairor, and Shahjahanpur, each of which contains some 500 robbers. Their claim to Rajput descent is probably well founded, though they are said to spring from an illegitimate son of a Rajput; and in woman's slang one woman is said to "give Mina" (*mina dena*) to another when she accuses her of illicit intercourse. They have dialect of their own ; or rather, perhaps a set of slang words and phrases which are common to the criminal classes. *Minas* are mostly confined to Gurgaon and the neighbouring portions of *Patiala* and *Nabha*. They are almost all Hindus and belong to the Chaukidari section and the Kagot clan. In Nabha the Minas are found in the Bawal *nizamat*. They claim descent from Sangwar Tawari, a Brahmin and grandson of Mir Raja Ad. As elsewhere they are habitual thieves but if a Mina is made *chaukidar* of a village, no other Mina will rob it. Hence rise two occupational groups-one of village watchmen, the other of cultivators and the former will only take daughters from the latter, though they may smoke together. Both have septs named after the place of origin, and in Bawal the *got* found is called Papri from Paproda in Jaipur. They perform the first tonsure at Raj sur in that State. At a betrothal contract, a barber, a Brahmin and a Rana (Hindu Mirasi) are sent to the house of the boy's father. The Rana marks a *tilak* on his forehead, getting Rs. 16 as his fee, and other ceremonies performed the Brahmin. Like all professional thieves, the Minas are devotees of *devi*. On all occasions and even when starting on a raid, they offer her sweetmeats.

Sansi Exorcism

Among the Sansis almost the only indications of the existence of religious beliefs are contained in the ceremonies performed at birth, marriage and death. Although these are of a very primitive and elementary type, yet the first dawnings of a belief in the supernatural and the immortalising power of death are apparent. The common belief amongst Indians is that the Sansis have neither gods nor religion. This is, however incorrect. Religion in the abstract, as it affects the conduct of man towards his fellows, is certainly almost non-existent. Superstition, however, has gone a step further and has resulted in the deification of the tribal ancestors *Sahns Mal, Mahla* and *Bhidu*. They have been magnified by the lapse of time into spirits of power and prominence whom it is right to propitiate at time of birth, marriage, and death. The powers invested in these deified ancestors appear to be rather of an evil working than a benignant type.

"In honour of Sansi Mal the Sansis distribute *karha* or halwa(a kind of sweet porridge) and offer *do gharas,* two small earthen pots, filled with water, and put cowries in them on the Holi and Diwali and other festivals to pacify him."

They also believe in Lal Beg, *guru* of the Chuhras, in Jind and offer loaves of bread and *gur* to him, distributing them among children, etc., at his *marhi* (monument). For example, they are not considered to have any power or inclination to reward the good or punish the wicked for deeds done on earth. Their sole importance lies in their ability to exert an evil influence on the fortunes of their descendants, provided that the due ceremonies for propitiation are not performed at important events, such as births, marriages and deaths. These ceremonies have their counterpart in all other religious performances where the blessing of the deity is invoked on similar occasions. The fundamental idea of the deity amongst all the races appears to be that of a malignant spirit who is naturally predisposed to exert his evil influence on the affairs of human beings unless he is duly appeased and propitaited. Otherwise the motive is not apparent which would cause him to refrain from blessing the marriage-union between parties who may have been of exemplary conduct and behaviour. If it may be taken for granted that the blessings and good-will of the godling follow as a matter of course upon a man conducting himself as a just father and faithful husband, the necessity of asking for these blessings is superflous. When a man is conscious of having performed the duties which are expected of him by the society of which he is a member, the logical sequence is that the deity will reward him accordingly, unprejudiced by the fact of his having performed or not performed certain propitiatory ceremonies.

The underlying reason for the ceremonies appears to be an innate belief that the deity is a malignant spirit who desires propitiation rather than good conduct. It is interesting to see how entirely distinct and disconnected his theologial system and his conduct appears to the Sansi intelligence. His gods are merely the spirits of his tribal ancestors invested with powers for working evil, and as such do not concern themselves with the question of his having led a good or a bad life according to his own lights. The sum total of their demands is that certain propitiatory rights should be performed on important occasions. The influence of a man's conduct during life on his destiny after death, and the exaltaion of demons and evil spirits into celestial beings who judge a man according to his works are subsequent developments of the human intellect. The question of what happens to a man after his death is still an unsettled one amongst the Sansis, and the germs of inquiry have not yet led him to formulate any definite theories on the subject.

The spirits of women who die during childbirth are supposed to linger on in this world and torment living beings. Persons who die while in an unclean state, or in an unnatural manner are said to become evil spirits after death, in the same manner that in ghost stories the spirit of the murdered man rather than that of the murderer is generally supposed to haunt the scene of the crime. The character and conduct of a man during his lifetime are not considered to be factors which determine the perpetuation of his existence after death, his immortality as an evil spirit is determined only by the outward manner and circumstances of his death. Spirits possessing a kindly and benign influence are non-existent. The inhabitants of the immaterial world are entirely spirits of a malignant type who, by the unclean or unnatural manner of their death, are condemned to haunt their former abodes and enter into the bodies of living beings. The outward signs of such demoniacal possession are insanity and vacancy of mind.

In order to terrify and exorcise the evil spirit into leaving the body of his victim, the services of a sorcerer or wizard are requisitioned. The latter have the common characteristics and stock-in-trade with which the priestcraft in all ages have performed their offices. By means of mystic symbols and ceremonies, and by the length, vigour, and potency of their incantations the evil spirit is subdued and cast out. Insincerity is by no means a necessary adjunct to these operations. The representative of the priestly caste from whom enquiries were made stated in all good faith that he had in person subjugated and turned out numbers of evil spirits. The descendants of Bhalad, one of the sons of Mahla, are the sorcerers and wizards of the Sansis, and the progenitors of what would be the priestcraft in a more advanced stage of society.

All men belonging to this caste wear a long lock of hair on one side of their head. This lock of hair is never cut from the time of birth, and grows to about a foot in length, becoming a matted and tangled mass.The

Sansis were unable to state what particular significance is attached to this distinguishing mark. Beyond exorcising and casting out evil spirits, these men have no other duties to perform in any way connected with the supernatural. They are generally welcome, and invited to the marriages of other *Sansis* but take no particular part in the ceremonies. One rupee is generally given to them when they attend a marriage, as their mere presence is considered to be of service in warding off the attacks of evil spirits. These spirits are considered to be quite immaterial and intangible. Surprisingly no Sansi can testify to having ever seen any of these spirits in material shape and form. As a rule, vagaries of the imagination or defects in vision are sufficient to conjure up innumerable ghostly beings. The method employed by the sorcerers for the purpose of casting out evil spirits is as follows:- A diagram in the form of a square is drawn on the ground. The lines of the square are traced with flour and a red pigment called *sindua*. The angles and sides of the square are joined by lines intersecting at the middle point. A second and a smaller square then formed by joining the points at which the sides of the larger square are bisected. Lamps are then placed in four triangles formed at the corners of the larger square, and the sorcerer sits on one side of the diagram, the possessed by the evil spirit on the other. A long incantation is then recited with great repidity and repeated as long as the evil spirit remains obdurate, and refuses to quit the body of its victim. The Sansis have framed certain laws and penalties among themselves to deal with offences which appear to them to be deserving of punishment. Periodical gatherings are held at which tribal disputes, marriage complications, etc., are settled by men chosen from the tribe for their intelligence and impartiality. These men are called *numberdars* and the parties in all matters under dispute agree to abide by their decision. Such a thing as Sansi taking his case into a regular court of law is entirely unknown, and reports to the police are equally unheard of. The punishments inflicted upon offending parties generally take the shape of fines varying from five to twenty and thirty rupees according to the seriousness of the offence. It is a significant fact that burglaries and thefts are not included under the heading of offences. To murder, to assault, to abduct one's neighbour's wife is an offence according to Sansi ideas, but to steal and pilfer is merely a legitimate and natural means of obtaining the necessaries of life. Thefts amongst themselves are rare, partly due to the feeling that it is very seldom that they ever possess anything worth stealing. Beyond a few simple cooking utensils nothing of value is retained. Any excess on the requiremants of the moment is allowed to remain over for future use, in pursuance of the same instinct which induces a dog to bury a bone, and unearth it on the following day ; but definite economy and foresight are never practised.

It is only very recently that the Sansis have settled down in fixed homes and abodes. Their own statements show that up to the last thirty or thirty-five years ago, they used to wander indefinitely about the district living in *pakhis* or temporary shelters of straw matting or thatch. During this life, their sole means of existence must necessarily have been either alms or theft and the thirty or thirty-five years which have elapsed since their settlement in various villages have been insufficient for them to fully recognise the fact that society does not permit its members to obey the promptings of nature, by which a man is naturally inclined to utilize anything and everything for his own sustenance, regardless of ownership. The Sansi is still in the suckling stage of human progress, where he expects to receive the means of sustaining life direct from the parent nature. To ask a Sansi to work and labour for his daily necessaries is as much an anomaly as to ask an infant at the breast to earn the nourishment it receives by personal effort. The stage in the life of the individual corresponds with the stage in the evolution of mankind. During his wandering life of a few decades the Sansi was perfectly at liberty to entrap the ownerless creatures of the jungle and to gather any fruits, plants leaves growing in a wild state. His brief acquaintanceship with a domiciliary civilisation has not been sufficient to impress him with the fact that the same liberty cannot be extended to his neighbour's cattle and crops.

The *Handbook of the Criminal Tribes of the Punjab* says that Sansi males are generally dark in complexion with bright sparkling eyes, while the females are more often fair. Their faces are cast in the aboriginal mould and are very 'foxy' in expression. The hair of the face or head is grown or removed according to the custom of the country in which they most usually reside. They are often to be found with shock heads of hair and often, again, shaved with the exception of the Hindu tuft which is sometimes the only evidence of their Hinduism. The fairness of complexion of blood is due to the kidnapping of children of higher castes, the introduction of outside elements, and the illicit connections formed by Sansis women with persons of decent status. The fleetness and agility of the males has always been noticed as has the Amazon like nature of their women-folk. But the Sansi though wiry, active and no mean-athlete is not big-boned or exceptionally powerful. Sansis, it is said, can always be detected by their smell which is described as a combination of musk-rat and rancid grease.

Changes in customs

As has been indicated in the beginning of this chapter, many old customs, conventions and usages have been changing in the recent times rapidly, and many have even become extinct. Cultural integration is currently a new national fad. To decry and lament the lack of cultural integration among the divergent social segments had become a favourite pastime. Many government agencies, social organisations, voluntary groups and even individual scholars, researchers and students had been making concerted efforts toward the cultural and linguistic welfare and integration of the underprivileged and tribal groups also into the national mainstream. For example, the Gujjar are a pastoral community with no fixed abode. But recently large number of them settled down and have taken to sedentary farming. In some areas of J&K, Himachal and Uttarakhand they continue to pursue agricultural activity alongwith animal husbandry. Traditionally, they were the cattle breeders and milkmen. During the Turkish, Afghan and Persian invasions, they earned notoriety for preying upon the dead and the wounded left in the battlefield.

A majority of the Gujjars are still pastorals eking out their livelihood through sale of milk and mild products. They have herds of milch cows and buffaloes with which they keep practising transhumance from low to and vice versa high altitudes during summer and winter seasons in search of green pastures. The pastoral land at these altitudes are allotted to them by the Forest department which are owned by the government. If overgrazing is found on the pasture land they are then heavily penalized. Due to the constant harassment by the corrupt and greedy forest officials on various pretexts, many of them have left their age-old occupation and have taken to agriculture, for which land has been alloted to them. Since such land is meagre and the produce is insufficient for a year, they have resorted to other means of livelihood, working as sharecroppers, businessmen and in government and private offices.

The Gujjars have direct links as well as through middleman to market their produce. In Himachal Pradesh, the *Gujjars* are members of the *Parvatiya Adim Jati Sevak Sangh,* founded in 1956 to extend welfare activities among the tribals of the area.The welfare programmes undertaken by the Sangh are in the field of education, cottage industry and in all socio-cultural fields. The main objective of the Sangh includes development of leadership among the tribals to encourage crafts, to eradicate untouchability and to get rid of inferiority complex among the tribals. The Sangh has been taking special care to educate the children of Gujjars by starting a number of mobile primary schools, bring the general problems of the Gujjars to the notice of the state government. The statutory *panchayats* exist and are valid for those who are now leading a sedentary life, but not for the normals. The nomadic mode of existence, coupled with their own past indifference to their franchise has deprived them of their exercise of the right to vote as an ordinary citizen of the State. In a majority of cases their very names are missing from the voters list.

The traditional economy of the Hindu Gujjars also goes around cow and buffalo herding and selling milk and milk products. The Hindu Gujjars lead a settled existence and practise agriculture. The majority of them are large landowners, who may employ agricultural labour and pay them a share from their produce. Milk and milk products like *ghee,* and curd are directly sold in the market. It is customary for each family to keep a cow, but the milk is only for self-consumption and not for sale, because they trace their origin from mythological *Yaduvansha* to which Lord Krishna belonged, whose fondness for cow herding is all too well known. Besides many of them have taken to jobs in government and semi-government sector. Some of them are education officers, forest guards, members in police, military services and even politics. Still they have their traditional rights on the forest, from where they can take wood for fuel. For building houses wood is procured by a permit from the forest department at nominal rates.

The traditional occupation of the heirs is pastoralism and sedentary agriculture. At present, however, only a few of them in Delhi continue their traditional occupation, as most of their agricultrual lands have been acquired by the Delhi development authority against cash compensation. Many of them are now involved in business including transport, paper board, and plastic moulds, etc. Some of them are serving in government and private organizations as skilled and unskilled workers.

The community of Adi-Dharmis is listed separately as the scheduled caste. They are not different from the Chamar caste. About seventy years ago, the so-called adi-Dharmis became status conscious and in order to raise their social status in the local society, they set up a committee by the name of Adi-dharmi Mandal with a few eminent Chamars in Jalandhar in lead. Its main aim was to attain gaining the social status for communities. The committee members went from village to village in Punjab and asked their caste members to adopt a new name, Ad i- dharmi, instead of Chamar. They picked up the term Adi-dharmi from the sermons of guru Ravidas where the Chamars are reported to have been the most religious-minded people, right from the beginning of the world. Thus, due to the influence of the Adi-dharmi Mandal many Chamars started calling themselves Adi-Dharmis.

In Delhi, most of the Adi-Dharmis are immigrants from Punjab who came in search of better employment. The majority of them have settled in urban Delhi. They generally converse in Hindi and Punjabi, and use the Devanagari and Gurmukhi scripts. A few of them can speak and write English. The *Adi-dharmi* are basically non-vegetarian. They also take vegetarian food including all types of pulses, seasonal vegetables and fruits, etc.

From the old time Adi-Dharmis have been skinning, skin tanning, shoe making, and weaving. However, some worked as agricultural labourers also. In Delhi, most of them have found new occupations and are now working in government and private sectors. A few of them are running small scale industries and shops as well. A majority of Adi Dharmis follow Hinduism, while a few follow Sikhism. Although they worship all Hindu gods and goddesses, they have great reverence for Saint Ravi Das and Saint Kabir. Ancestor worship is also common among them. But most of their primitive beliefs and customs have changed vastly.

Now they have free access to public hydrants, crematoria, Schools, Colleges, temples, shopping centres, other public places. Earlier, intercommunity marriages were not permitted but recently some cases have been reported. Fictitious kinship ties such as *dharam bhai* (putative brother), *dharam bahin* (putative sister), *dharam sakhi* (putative friendship) etc., are maintained with members of other communities. The community has amongst them a few teachers, singers, doctors, engineers, scholars, and businessmen. Their attitude toward change of culture and education of boys and girls is favourable. Though they are not against modern medicare, yet they do not make full use of it and resort to Shamanism.

The Banjara also is a nomadic community known as Labana in Punjab, and Lambadi and Sugali in the south. Sometimes due to their nomadic habits, they were also called as khanabadosh, but at present Banjara is the most common name for them. In Delhi, they are also addressed as 'Gour Banjara' and 'Sirkiband' because quite a number of them are engaged in keeping cows and in roof-making. Originally the word 'Banjara' is derived from the Sanskrit word *banij* meaning trader. According to HA Rose(1919) and Denzil Ibbetson (1916), the word *banjara* can be split into two : B*an*-jungle and *Jara,* goer or wanderer, together meaning 'those who wander in the forest'. Until recently they claimed their Rajput ancestry, and the place of their origin somewhere in Rajasthan. Russell and Hiralal suggested that they might have originated from the Charan and Bhat Caste of Rajputana, thus suggesting an Indian origin for them. Hutton (1946) associated them with the Bhils. But the Banjaras of Delhi emphatically assert that they are the Kshatriya Rajputs.

The traditional dress of their women is an embroidered *lehnga, orni* and decorative headgear. Men wear *kurta, dhoti* and *pagri.* However, in the recent times very few Banjara men and women are seen in their traditional dress. They wear whatever is in the latest fashion and is worn by neighbouring communities. Now look at the *agri* community. The Agri is a salt-making caste, known as Noongar in Punjab, Kharwal in Rajasthan, and Agri or Sisodia Rajput in Delhi, Gurgaon, Rohtak and Ghaziabad. The word *agri* means either a plantation of palm trees or a salt pan. The word is more commonly used to refer to those who depend upon salt pans for their livelihood. During Akbar's reign most of their ancestors were taken as war prisoners and converted to Islam by the rulers of numerous small states. But many of them didn't obey Akbar and fled took to agriculture and salt making. Many of them settled beside the Luni river in Rajasthan and took up salt making. Thus they came to be known as *Agri.* After 1952, they started calling themselves *Sisodia Rajput* and this amendment was confirmed by the authorities. Thus, many castes scaled up the social, educational, cultural, economic and linguistic ladder during the recent decades. With the attainment of independence, and the implementation of the programmes of reconstruction, specially social and educational, the rural communities underwent a vast social transformation. The recent years of planning has shown accumulative trends in village, cultural and institutional variation. The scheduled tribes too, are becoming consciouse of the changing trends. The appointment of a commissioner for scheduled tribes apparently is aimed at bridging the gulf of social distance by raising the living standards of these tribes and minimising cultural differentiation. Government work has offered ample opportunities to the scheduled tribes to come forward and integrate with the advanced social groups in various ways.

The recent changes in the *Bhil* culture can be explained with reference to the factors of education, economy, and urbanisation, which has been going on for quite a long time. The changes created in the rural environment by the government sponsored activities of village development programmes during the recent decades have further accelerated the tempo of transformation. There are innumerable facets of culture-dynamics which have brought in their wake the use of money, the market, and modern amenities of life. Better transport because of the railroad and motor led to the introduction of a new technology in the form of new tools and implements, like pumping sets, wheels, chemical fertilizers etc. and this has, to some extent, revolutionised the traditional outlook of the people. The Bhil community in the plains came in to closer contact with cultures, resulting in consequent opportunities for acculturation. Their traditional economy has also changed as many of them have started raising commercial crops and working in new industries. The spread of urbanisation has affected the social and economic set up of the people.

Acting as Snake-charmers

The Bangali-Christians are still a hunting and wandering community who earn their livelihood by snake-charming, selling wild herbs and treating certain common ailments like toothache *kundanda*, earache and otorrhoea (ear blowing supposed to be caused by an insect called *bhudarwalu*). They also earn money by catching snakes from inside the houses of the rural people and are also trusted for treating snakebite. The Bengalis sell *gidarsingi* (a horn recovered from the head of a fox) and snake *mani*, which, according to them bring joy, prosperity and victory to the possessors. People often suspect that a Bangali deliberately leaves a snake near the houses of the villagers, and then he starts playing on his flute like musical instrument *been* and tells the presence of the snake expecting money for catching the same. They also hunt water birds, tortoise, snails, fish, and crabs etc. for purpose of eating.

Christians in Delhi are non-vegetarians without any prejudice as to what to eat and what not to eat. Wheat, rice, barly *jowar, bajra, nagli, maize, ragi* etc. are staple foods, as per the tradition of the respective groups. All kinds of pulses and beans are consumed, and a wide variety of cooking mediums viz. groundnut, mustard, sesamum, rapeseed, linseed, safflower, coconut and sunflower oils, in refined or other form, and animal and vegetable fats as well as clarified butter or *ghee* are used, also as per the respective communities traditions without inhibition, they also eat pork and beef.

Special liking for non-vegetarian meal

Fond of non-vegetarian food, the Chinese people's staple diet consists of rice, noodles, pulses and beans. Beans are liked by the majority; they also, take mutton, pork, chicken and beef but are very fond of eating chicken which they like to cook on all important social festivals and rituals. Men like smoking and also drink occasionally. Among the non-alcoholic beverages, green tea is widely consumed, though they have learnt to drink red tea as well. However, the younger people, is not only taking to red tea but have adapted themselves to Indian variety of food. The majority of the Chinese settled in Himachal Pradesh are in the shoemaking business. Their entire family works in collaboration with one other in which women may look after the sales and men may actually make shoes. They do no, however, skin or tan leather. A few have also opened stalls serving Chinese food which has become quite popular amongst the local Indian urban youth. They do have no agricultural land in the state. A very few have been able to buy houses. They maintain direct link with the market. Goods are bought and sold strictly with cash. Since they manufacture shoes and also sell them, they sometimes run into financial difficulties for procuring raw material. In such financial crisis they depend solely on the resources of their community members. The Chinese abide by the law of the land, and their personal conflicts are amicably solved by the elders of the community. Each lineage has its own council. Though conflicts are rare, yet in case of any dispute the elders of both the sides are invited who invariably bring about mutual agreement among the disputing parties. Sometimes, though rarely, they have to call on *khew-teang*, their headman based in Calcutta. The expenditure involved on his traveling, stay and food is borne by the party concerned. His decision is blinding on the people in both the sides. Fines are levied in cash and are rarely opposed by those punished. Efforts are always for peaceful reconciliation. Criminal offences are taken care of by the state machinery for maintaining law and order.

The Chinese families dwelling in Himachal Pradesh have embraced the Catholic faith. They celebrate Christmas, Good Friday and All Saints' Day and regularly attend Church services. Besides, they also celebrate their traditional Chinese festivals. The Chinese New Year falling in months of January-February in celebrated with much gaiety and enthusiasm. On this day it is customary to visit each others' have where the elders give *hung pao* (gifts) to the young ones. When this gift consists of cash it is also customary to always keep two currency notes of the same denomination. The Chinese new year celebrations last for three days. Another festival called *Oom-ya-che* falls in the month of May. On this day it is customary to offer mangoes to the parents. They reciprocate it by giving gifts to their children and young ones. In the month of August on the full-moon day it is customary to eat cake after performing worship.

Proslytising local Sikhs and Hindus into their faith

Maharaja Ranjit Singh allowed no Christian preachers in his territory. Hower, he invited Dr. Lowrie of Ludhiana to Lahore and asked him to set up a school for English education. To test the closed door policy of Ranjit Singh on religion, a preacher Golaknath was sent to Phillaur. He was arrested and sent back with a warning not to return. After sometime Reg. John S. Woodside was invited to set up an American Presbyterian Mission at Kapurthala, which was temporarily closed in 1865. Later, Prince Harnam Singh of Kapurthala converted as a Christian and made a claim to the throne. However, he held high offices in the Church and the state in British India. His daughter Raj Kumari Amrit Kaur, also held high offices in India and the World Health Organization. Christian followers of Sant Hakim Singh of Raipur (near Ludhiana) were poisoned: one died and the other became the famous Sadhu Sunder Singh.

The main aim of missionary activity is Punjab was evangelism carried out by preaching gospel. Meanwhile, many schools, colleges, clinics, hospitals, asylums and orphanages were established by the missionaries. They conducted relief work in times of famine, epidemics and earthquakes. As a result the Christian community in the Punjab increased from 3,823 in 1881 to 49,301 in 1947, accompanied by the popularity of Western education in Ludhiana and Jalandhar, where many Mission schools were set up including the Baring High School (now Baring Union Christian College) in Batala, Alexandra High School, Amritsar, United Christian Schools, Suranasi near Jalandhar, Christian Medical College at Ludhiana and N.D. Victor Model School at Moga. These schools provided leadership not only for the Church but also for Brahmo Samaj, Arya Samaj, Singh Sabhas, Chief Khalsa Diwan. Anjuman-i-Himayat-i-Islam, and Muhammadan Educational Conference.

Thus a large number of low-caste people like Meghs, Chamars, and Chuhras got converted to Christianity, which led to an increase in the size of the Christian community and also changed its character. This trend of conversion to Christianity was opposed by All-India Suddhi Sabha. The rise of Adi-Dharam movement also reasserted the traditional animist religion of the Punjab outcastes and checked the trend towards conversion. The Christians of the Punjab had an 'ambiguous' position vis-à-vis the Indian nationalist movement. They preferred security under the 'autocratic regime' of the British to the uncertainties of democracy. Still, Raja Harnam Singh, S.K. Rudra, C.F. Andrews, Raj Kumari Amrit Kaur, and S.K. Dutta were the committed nationalists. Even the nationalist movement leading to transfer of power from foreign to Indian pastors and lawmen was very significant. It led to the formation of 'a Native Church for the Natives of India in 1877 and Ludhiana Mission, to transfer power from foreign mission organizations to the Indian Church bodies'. The struggle was successful by 1957. The Christians faced a crisis in the wake of partition of the Punjab. They had to show their identity as Christians by marking their houses and clothes with the cross or by recitation of the Lords Prayer, Ten Commandments and Apostles Creed. Many Christian agencies provided relief on both sides of the border.

In its long-term effects the partition split the educated Christian elite into two. There was scarcity of personnel to man church, ecclesiastical, educational and medical institutions. Moreover, the community faced an entirely new situation, when it was computed as a minority in a democratic government, with no autocratic government to support it. Effective translations of the Bible were made by American Presbyterians into the languages spoken in Punjab and North-West Frontier Province. William Carey had translated the New Testament into Punjabi. Dr. John Newton had improved this translation. Levi Janvier and John Newton were the co-authors of Punjabi grammar. An Urdu weekly, *Nur Afshan* (The Light), published from Ludhiana was a contribution to religious journalism, by American Baptists (Pathak 1967: 40-50). Many American Protestant missions were founded in the Punjab. The community in the state these days perceives its distribution at national and international levels. It has not migrated to its present place but has growing in number at the present places of settlement in the state. Originally, it came in existence by conversions from other communities.

The number of Roman Catholics had doubled between 1901 and 1911. They are fairly spread out, but are found mainly in Gurdaspur, Amritsar and Ferozepur districts. The Punjabi Christians have many denominations and is differentiated at economic and occupational levels. A predominant group is employed as agricultural labourers, others work as rickshaw-pullers, *baledar* and a few are employed in railways and defence establishments, in hospitals as nurses and medical technicians and now even as constables in the police and Border Security Force besides various other jobs. The Christians are also territorially differentiated and has different levels of education.

Migrating to the land of Jats

The history of the Christian community living in Haryana has no a detailed account of its origins and the migration to the land of Jats, but the district Gazetteers of a number of districts specially Rohtak, Jarnal, Bhiwani, Ambala and Gurgaon provide a working knowledge of the earliest missionary activities that were set up in Haryana. For example, the District Gazetteer of Karnal (1966) states: "The appearance of Christianity in the district dates back to the time of Emperor Akbar when he allowed the Roman Catholic missionaries to preach their religion in his Empire. Anyhow it was only during the British period that some tangible efforts were made to build churches at Karnal and Kaithal. A church, called St. James Church, was erected at Karnal in 1860, but with the removal of the cantonment to Ambala in 1843, a church at Karnal which was completed in 1905, serves the Protestant Christian community of the district..... In 1960 the Catholic mission was reorganized; two churches, one each at Hatiri and Panipat, were built and the mission also started a convent school at Karnal."

On the one hand there is evidence of the missionary activities initiated at the time of Emperor Akber, the District Gazetteers of other districts confirm that a systematic beginning towards founding churches and missionary activities started during the British rule itself. And by the turn of the 20th century, a good number of churches were established at various places of Haryana. *The District Gazetteer of Rohtak* (1970) states: "Christianity was introduced in the district about a century ago under the patronage of the British masters. By the beginning of the 20th century, there were churches at Sonepat Kharkhoda, Bahadurgarh, Rohat and Rohtak." *The District Gazetteer of Bhiwani* (1982) mentions: "Christians, though I a small number in the district, started missionary work in Bhiwani, in 1887. The church was organized in 1903... A church was built in Naya Bazar, Bhiwani in 1935." Similarly the *District Gazetteer of Gurgaon* (1983) has noted: "The church of Epiphany (adjacent to the District Courts), Gurgaon which was built in 1863, is among the oldest ones."

The Christian people living in Haryana are mostly educated, since the majority of them have migrated from the south Indian states and Punjab, they use the languages like Malayalam, Tamil, Kannada and Punjabi. But with the local people of Haryana, the language that they use is either Hindi or English. In some places prayers in church were performed in Hindi as well. They wear a cross tied to a chain but now people also wear it out of sheer fashion and not because of any religious requirement. The cross is usually worn around the neck which is tied to a chain.

There are a few local Scheduled Caste groups who have converted Christianity to avoid their persecution at the hand of high caste Hindus.

In Haryana exist two main divisions: Protestants and Catholics. The Protestants are affiliated to the Church of North India (CNI). Even within the CNI, there are divisions. The Anglican, Methodists, Presbyterians, Calvinists, Lutherans and Protestants are the main divisions and together these have formed a union of churches which is called the Church of North India. The Protestants constitute the major group in Haryana. The

Catholics constitute the other major division within Christianity who have churches located in different districts of Haryana. The hierarchy exists between the priest and the lay people. The bishop, who is the head of the diocese, is on the top, then comes the priest and at the bottom are placed the lay people. Among the Catholics, only males are allowed to be priests who are not allowed to marry; but among the Protestants, a bishop may lead a married life. Depending upon the composition of parishes, the churches in Haryana come under two dioceses: Simla-Chandigarh diocese and Delhi diocese. Under Simla-Chandigarh diocese there are eight churches located in different districts of Haryana, and under Delhi diocese there are seven churches.

In order to signify their distinct identity as Christians, they do not retain their caste names. The first name that they retain is the original name which is suffixed by titles such as Thomas, George, Paul, Henry, Mathew, etc. These titles are associated either with saints' name or the name of the British kings. These days there is no strict regulation on retaining these Christian titles. Nowadays, there is tendency among the Indian Christians to retain their original Hindu names with surnames.

Among the Christians the mechanism of social control is quite formal. In Indian altogether the churches fall under 24 dioceses. In Haryana the churches come under two dioceses and the church itself is controlled by the priest and the bishop. One bishop may look after the services of thirty to forty churches. The churches have their own constitution and accordingly, they take decisions on various issues. Besides the church, there are a number of committees of senates and councils which take decisions on vital issues like marriage, law, education, hospital and property. The disputes are settled either by the priest or the bishop. Now there is a move among the Christians to do away with minor denominational differences by merging both the church of South India (created around 1950s) and Church of North India (created around 1970) into the Church of India. The Protestants have no holy places in India places but the Catholics have some. The nearest sacred place for the Catholics of Haryana is in Meerut in a place called Sardhana.

Priests have different methods of offering prayers and they are the Eucharist (every Sunday prayer), services, i.e., singing and praying aloud, Holy Hour – a form of pray service performed silently. Their major festivals are Easter, which falls in summer between April and May, to commemorate Christ's resurrection and Christmas (25th December) signifies the birth of Christ. Good Friday is a day of fast as it commemorates the death of Christ. Besides, Catholics have a parish feast on a fixed date. They have also launched a movement which tried to restore democratic norms by bringing all the churches under one umbrella. Christians in Haryana take part in the festivals of the local people such as Holi, Dussehra, Diwali, Rakhi, etc.

Mixed Parentage

Children born of such wedlock were brought up according to the British social custom which accounted for the close affiliation felt with the whites. This socio-cultural and political identification with the ruling White who unfortunately for their part never treated them as equal and the natives who eyed them suspiciously, has given rise to what is often described as a typical hybrid mentality. Thus it is not unusual that the Anglo Indians speak of England they have never seen as their Home.

According to the Article 366(2) of the Indian Constitution the term Anglo Indian has been explained as "as person whose father or any of whose other male progenitors in the male line is or was of European descent but who is domiciled within the territory of India and is or was born within such territory of parents habitually resident therein and not established there for temporary reasons only." If however, asked, an Anglo - Indian will define himself as a person of British parentage or as a person whose father was of pure British origin domiciled at some stage in India. As such the generic term European or Eurasians (a term used earlier), it is felt, is misleading.

Interestingly, the Anglo Indians were offered, at the time of independence, the protection of 'Queen's Protectorate' which meant that if they registered with the British Commission on or before 26 January 1948 they could settle in England as their rightful homeland. This came to an end in 1968. Meanwhile, in 1949, at the time of framing of the Constitution of India, the sheer number of this community led the Government to recognize it as a distinct group. Due to the socio-political peculiarity of the community (most of the members being employed in administrative and civil services, such as railway, postal services, army etc.) for some time i.e., upto 1957) it enjoyed certain privileges guaranteed under the Constitution. However, during the first ten years after

Independence, many of them left for England or other British dominions such as Australia, New Zealand and Canada. Today's Anglo Indians are descendants of this community though their number is fast dwindling. Yet, till this day they can be identified in the different parts of the country. Their mother tongue, quite obviously, is English, having been brought up and schooled in an English – like environ.

Going out for educational ; academic, administrative or managerial posts has been almost a hereditary trait. Very few of them can be said to engage in business or be self-employed, same is true for the industrial and skilled labour sector. Their women like men, are also engaged in different professions in public and private sectors apart from managing home affairs. The Anglo Indian woman enjoys an equal status and decision making powers within the community. They contribute as well as control, family expenditure. The community has scholars, academicians, teachers, doctors, engineers and defence officers apart from political representation in both the Upper and Lower House of Parliament and the state Assemblies. The community has an All Indian Anglo Indian Association, an organisation which has played a pivotal role in bringing together and uniting the community members. The Anglo-Indian Education Society runs schools all over the country with the help of special educational grant and other assistance from the government that also helps secure scholarships for deserving Anglo-Indian students.

The Christianity forms an essential part of the socio-cultural make up of the community. Thus, festivals and occasions celebrated in the community are closely linked to their religious tenets. Major festivals celebrated include Easter, Christmas and New Year's Day. Both men and omen equally participate in such festivities.

The businessmen par excellence

The Bene Israel group of the Jews numbered in Delhi. The 1961 Census 20,000; but the majority of them migrated to Israel, their promised land, in subsequent years. The Jewish community is divided into twelve groups after the twelve sons of Jacob, who was the grandson of Abraham, from whom the Jews derive their heritage The community is one of the twelve tribes named after Benjamin, the youngest son of Jacob called as Bene Israel. Earlier, the circumstances led the ancestors of the Jews to settle in India. The history of their settlement in India goes back some 2,000 years. At that time there was regular trade between Palestine and India. During one of the voyages, a shipwreck occurred near Alibagh on the Maharashtra coast.

According to the records, only seven men and seven women survived the wreck. Being in a quandary in an alien land and unable to undertake the return journey home, they sought refuge in the coastal area and were hospitably treated by the local people. Gradually, they developed a sentimental attachment to their adopted land and its people, and gave up the idea of returning home. They gradually adopted the local customs and acquired the local traits, but did not forget the faith of their forefathers. The new settlers gradually mastered the local language while maintaining, at the same time, the language spoken and written by their ancestors, namely, Hebrew. Their names also underwent transformation and phonetically sounded like Marathi, a language they had been exposed to in the earlier stages. Gradually, they spread all over the country, specially northward, and learnt Hindi. With the coming of the British, they were also got exposed to English.

Hence today, they read and write in four languages: Marathi and Hindi using the Devanagari script, Hebrew using its own script and English using the Roman script. With north being the seat of power, and since they were in business, they gradually moved towards Delhi. And ever since Delhi became the capital of the Imperial British Government of India, they settled in and around it. Their present settlement in the north is invariably in the urban areas, particularly in Delhi. On religious occasions and festivals, their ceremonial identification markers are the male shawl, the male headgear, the female headdress, the flag, and the emblem, which is a six-pointed star, the Star of David. The sacred prayer shawl of the male is draped around him at a ceremony, when they pay a visit to their Synagogue.

REFERENCES

1. Rose, H.A., *A Glossary of the tribes and castes of the Punjab and North-West Frontier Province*, Low Price publications, Delhi, 1999 (reprint), First Published, 1919.
2. Ibbetson, Denzil, *Census Report for the Punjab 1883*.

3. Machagan, Edward, *Census Report for the Punjab 1892*.
4. Singh D.S., *The People of India Haryana*, An thropological survery of India. Calcutta,1994.
5. Singh K.S., *The People of India*: Delhi , Anthropologic Survey of India, Calcutta.
6. Doshi, Shambhu Lal, *Bhils: Between Societal self-awareness and cultural synthesis*, Sterling Publisher, Delhi, 1971.
7. Sherring MA, *Hindu tribes and Castes*, Thaker & Spink, Calcutta, 1908.
8. Resley H.H., *The People of India*, Thaker &Spink, Calcutta, 1908.
9. Ibbetson D., *Outlines of Punjab Geography, in Census of the Punjab 1881*, Superintendent, Government Press, Calcutta, 1883.

Bibliography

Agarwal, B.C. (ed.). *Tribe, Caste and Peasantry.* Ethnographic and Folk Culture Society, Lucknow: 1974.

Ahmad, Imtiaz (ed.). *Caste and Social Stratification among Muslims of India.* Manohar Publications, Delhi 1978.

Anonymous, *Encyclopaedia Britannica.* Encyclopaedia Britannica Inc, Chicago1969.

Bahadur, K.P. Castes, *Tribes and Culture of India.* New Ess Ess Publications, Delhi1978, Vol. VI.

Baines, J.A. General Report (*Census of India, 1891*). Eyre and Spattiswoode. London

Bajpai, S.C. *Kinnaur in the Himalayas.* New Delhi: Concept Publishing Company, 1987.

Bhattacharya, J.N. *Hindu Castes and Sects.* Editions India, Calcutta:1968.

Bingley, A.H. *History, Caste and Culture of Jats and Gujjars.* Calcutta: Superintendent Government Printing, 1904; Ess Ess Publications.reprint 1978, New Delhi

Campbell, George. "Ethnology of India'. In *A Glossary of Tribes and Castes of Punjab and North West Frontier Province.* Comp. H.A. Rose, Government Printing Press, Lahore:

Diack, A.H., The Kulu Dialect of Hindi' in Census of India (1891). Ed. E.D.

Gispert Sauch, G.S.J. 'Christianity', *in Religions of India*, ed. Karan Singh. Clarion Books, Delhi: 1983.

Granquist, H. *Marriage Condition in a Palestinian Village.* Helsinki Societas Scnebtuaryn Fenrica, commentationes Humanurum Litterarum III. B., 1931.

Grierson, G.A. (ed). 'Tibeto Burman Family', in *Linguistic Survey of India.* Superintendent of Government Printing, Vol. III, Part I, Calcutta: 1909.

Haimendorf, C. von Furer (ed.). *Caste and Kinship in Nepal, India and Ceylon.* Asia Publishing House, New York:1966.

Hutchison, J. and J.P.H. Vogel. *History of Punjab Hill States*. Lahore: Superintendent of Government Printing, 1933, (reprinted 1982), Department of Language and Culture, Himachal Pradesh. Shimla:

Ibbetson, D. *Punjab Castes*. Punjab: Government Press, 1916, reprint 1974, Delhi B.R. Publishing Corpn.

Ibbetson, D.C.J. *'Outlines of Punjab Ethnography'*, in *Cenus of the Punjab* 1881. Calcutta: Superintendent of Government Printing, 1883.

Mamgain, M.D. *Himachal Pradesh District Gazetteers*. Bilaspur, State District Gazetteers, Shimla: Himachal Pradesh, 1975.

Mamgain, M.D. *Himachal Pradesh District Gazetteers, Lahaul & Spiti*. Chandigarh: Greater Punjab Press, 1975.

Mathur, K.S. and B.C. Agarwal (eds.). *Tribe, Caste and Peasantry*. Lucknow: Ethnography & Folk Culture Society, 1974.

McLagan, E.D. (ed). *'The Punjab and its feudatories'*, in *Census of India* 1891. Calcutta: Superintendent of Government Printing, 1892, Vol. 19 Part I.

Mushir-ul-Haq, 'Islam', in *Religions of India*. ed. Karan Singh, Clarion Books, Delhi 1983.

Negi, T.S. *Himachal Pradesh District Gazetteer, Chamba*. Standard Printing Press, Batala: 1963.

Negi, T.S. *Himachal Pradesh District Gazetteer, Kinnur,* Oriental Printing Press, Aligarh: 1969.

Negi, T.S. *Scheduled Tribes of Himachal Pradesh* – A Profile. Meerut: Raj Printers, 1976.

Newell, W.H. *Report on Scheduled Castes and Scheduled Tribes, Bharmaur Tehsil of Chamba District, Himachal Pradesh*. Manager of Publications, Delhi:1967, Vol. XX, Pt. V-B.

Parmar, Y.S. *Polyandry in the Himalayas*. Vikas Publishing House Pvt. Ltd., Delhi:1975.

Prince Peter, H.R.H. A *Study of Polyandry*. Netherlands: Mouton and Company, 1964.

Raghviah, V. *Nomads*. Adim Jati Sweak Sangh, Secunderabad: 1968.

Raha, M.K. *'The Khandan System of the Kinnaura of the Western Himalayas'*, In *The Himalayan Heritage*, Delhi: Gyan Publishing House, 1987.

Rahul, Ram. *The Himalayan Borderland*. Vikas Publishing House Pvt. Ltd., Delhi :1970.

Risley, H.H. *The People of India*. Calcutta: Thacker & Spink, 1908.

Rose, H.A. (Comp.). *A Glossary of the Castes and Tribes of Punjab and North-West Frontier Province*. Lahore: Government Press, 1914.

Rosser, C. 'An Aspect of political organization of Malana', in *Tribe, Caste and Peasantry.* Eds. K.S. Mathur and B.C. Aggarwal. Ethnographic and Folk Culture Society, Lucknow:1974.

Saraswati, B.N. *Brahmanic Ritual Traditions in the Crucible of Time.* Indian Institute of Advance Studies, Simla 1977.

Sashi, S.S. *The Gaddi Tribe* of H.P.: *A Sociological Study*, Sterling Publishers Pvt. Ltd., New Delhi: 1977.

Sher, S.S. The *Sansis of Punjab*. Munshilal Manoharlal, Delhi: 1965.

Sherring, M.A. *Hindu Tribes and Castes*. Thacker Spink, 1879; reprint, Delhi: Cosmo Publications, Calcutta: 1974.

Siddiqui, M.K.A. 'Caste among the Muslims of Calcutta', in Caste *and Social Stratification among Muslims in India,* ed. Imtiaz Ahmad. Manohar Publications, Delhi: 1978.

Singh, Mian G. *Himachal Pradesh – History, Culture and Economy.* Minerva Book House, Simla:1988.

Sinha, S.B. 'Twelve Sons of Lord Chitragupta' in *Souvenir of 61st*, All India Kayastha Conference. Calcutta, (n.d.).

Swinson, Arthur. *North-West Frontier*. U B S Publishers, Delhi: 1967.

Thornton, D.M. *Parsi, Jains and Sikhs-Some Minor Religious Sects in India*. Mittal Publications, Delhi: 1987.

Tobdan. *History and Religions of Lahul*: From the Earliest to circa A.D. 1950. Books Today, New Delhi: 1984.

Vidyasankar, Satyakehi. *Agarwal Jati ka Prachin Itihas (Hindi)*. Akhil Bhartiya Marwari Jati Kosh, Bombay: 1938.

Abdul Fazl, *Ain-i-Akbari*, Calcutta: Bibliotheca Indica, 1872-73, English translation, Vol. I by Blochmann, Calcutta, 1927; Vols II & III by H.S. Jarret, Calcutta, 1868-94.

________, *Akbarnama* (3 vols), English translation by Henry Beveridge, Calcutta, 1897-1939.

Ahluwalia, Major H.P.S., *Hermit Kingdom: Ladakh*, Himalayan Books, New Delhi: 1987.

Angeli, Mam, 'Hanjis of Dal Lake, Origin and Demographic Characteristics', *Geography of J. & K.*, Kashmir University, Srinagar.

Atkinson, Edwin T., *The Himalayan Districts of the North Western Provinces of India*, 5 vols (rpt 1981, New Delhi: Cosmo Publications under the title *The Himalayan Gazetteers*).

Baloria, Thakur Kahan Singh, *Tarikh-e-Rajputana-Mulk-e-Punjab*, Govt. Press, Jammu:1931.

________, *Tarikh-i-Rajgan-i-Jammu-wa-Kashmir*, Part I, Lahore: Prakash Steam Press; Lahore: Diwan Printing Press, 1986.

Bamzai, Anand Kaul, *The Kashmir Pandit,* Thackers Spink & Co., Calcutta: 1924.

Bamzai, Prithvi Nath Kaul, *A History of Kashmir. Political, Social and Cultural,* Metropolitan Book Company Pvt. Ltd., New Delhi: 1962.

Bates, Charles Euison, *A Gazetteer of Kashmir and the Adjacent Districts of Koshtwar, Badrawar, Jammu, Naoshera, Punch and the Valley of the Kishen Ganga*, New Delhi: Light & Life Publishers, (rpt) 1980.

Bellow, H.W., *An Inquiry of Ethnography of Afghanistan*, London, 1891.

________, *Kashmir and Kashghar*, London, 1875.

Bodfour, Edward, *The Encyclopaedia of India*, Eastern and Southern Asia, Vol. I, 1967.

Campbell, George, *The Afghan Frontier*, London, 1879.

Campbell, Jeffrey Young, 'Ladakh', *in India*, edited by Israel and Bikram Grewal, Singapore: APA, 1983.

Census of India, 1991, Punjab (Report), New Delhi: Govt. of India Publication.

________, *Punjab Castes*, New Delhi: B.R. Publishing Corporation, rpt 1974.

________, 1901, Vol. XXIII, Part I, Kashmir (Report), Lahore.

________, 1921, Vol. XXII, Part I, Kashmir (Report), Lahore.

________, 1931, *Report on Jammu and Kashmir State*, Calcutta.

________, 1931, *Jammu and Kashmir State*, Vol. XXIV, Part I, rpt, Jammu: Ranbir Govt. Press, 1933.

________, 1961, Vol. VI, Part VI, No. 1, *Jammu and Kashmir*, New Delhi: Publication Div., Govt. of India, 1971.

________, 1971, *Report on Jammu and Kashmir State*, New Delhi: Publication Div., Govt. of India, 1971.

________, 1981, *Primary Census Abstract, Jammu and Kashmir*, New Delhi Publication Div., Govt. of India, 1981.

Charak, SDS, (ed.), *Introduction to the History and Culture of the Dogras*, Ajaya Prakashan, Pathankot: 1977

Cunningham, Col. W.B., *Dogras*, Calcutta, 1932.

Cunningham, Alexander, *Ladakh: Physical Statistical and Historical*, with notices of the surrounding countries, Sagar Publications, rpt. New Delhi: 1970.

Dass, Bhagwan, *Bajigars of Punjab. A Case Study in Patiala District* (mimeo), 1978.

Deb, P.C. *Bajigars of Punjab: A Socio-Economic Study*, Mittal Publications, New Delhi: 1987.

Dutt, Yogesh Chandra, *The Kings of Kashmir – 2nd Series; A translation the Sanskrit work Rajatarangini of Kalhana Pandita, Jonaraj-shrivara, and of Prajyabhatta and Shuka*, Gyan Publishing House, New Delhi:1986 (original translation Published in 1879 and 1887).

Earl of Dunmore, 1893, *The Pamris* (2 Vol), London, 1893, Oriental Publisher, rpt, New Delhi: 1971.

Ferishta, *Tarikh-i-Ferishta (History of the Rise of the Muhammadan Power in India till 1612)* 12, translated by J. Briggs, Calcutta, 1808-10.

Francke, A.H., A History of Ladakh, Sumit Publication, New Delhi: 1981.

Garbe R., *'Yogis', in Encyclopedia of Religion and Ethics*, Vol. 12, Edinburgh: T. and T. Clark, 1980.

Govt. of India, *Gazetteer of Kashmir and Ladakh*, Calcutta: The Superintendent Govt. Printing Press; New Vivek Publishing House, rpt Delhi:1980.

Griffin, Sir Jepel and C.F. Massey, *Chief and Families of Nat in the Punjab*, Lahore, 1909.

Gupta, N.S. and N.C. Prabhakar, *Socio-Economic Development of Jammu and Kashmir,* Jay Kay Book House, *Jammu*: 1988.

Hassan, Mohibul, *Kashmir under Sultans*, Iran Society, Calcutta:1959.

Hassan, Tazkir-i-Awalia, *Kashmir*, Noor Mohammad and Sons, translation by Molvi Abdul Kadir Spori, Srinagar: 1960.

Heber, A.R. and M.H. Heber, *Himalayan Tibet and Ladakh*, ESS Publications, New Delhi: 1978.

Hedin Swen, *Trans Himalaya*, London: Mac Millan & Co., 1913.

Herodotus, *History*, Oxford, 1913-14.

Hindu Marriage Act 1955.

Iqbal, S.M. and K.L. Nirash (eds), The Culture of Kashmir, Marwah Publications, New Delhi: 1978.

John Bray, 'A History of Moravian Church in India', *The Himalayan Mission*, 1985.

Joldan, F., *Harvest Festival if Buddhist & Dards of Ladakh*, Kapoor Bros., Srinagar: 1985.

Jonaraja, Pandit, *Rajatarangini*, Calcutta and Bombay editions, 1835 and 1875; English trans, by J.C. Dutt under the title of *The Kings of Kashmir*, Vol. III, Calcutta, 1935; Delhi: Gyan Publishing House, rpt 1986.

Kaul, Arun, 'Kesar: The Cultural Geography of Kashmir', in Geeti Sen and Ashis Banerjee (eds), *The Human Landscape*, Orient Longman and India International Centre, New Delhi: 2001.

Khajuria, Hardev Singh, *The Punjabi Lok Sahit*, New Age Centre, Amritsar: 1987.

Khan, Mohammad, *History of Kashmir* 1847-1947, Amir, Srinagar:1958.

Khan, M. Ishaq. *Kashmir's Tansition to Islam*: The Role of Muslim Rishis, Manohar, New Delhi: 1997.

Khemendra, Pandit, *Lakaprakasa*, English translation of some extracts by Dr. A. Weber, Indische Studien XVIII, 1898.

Kilam, Jia Lal, *A History of Kashmiri Pandits, Srinagar*. Gandhi Memorial College, rpt 1955.

Knight, E.F., *Where Three Empires Meet*, London, 1895.

Kumari, Ved (Dr.) *Nilamata Purana*, translation, Vol. 1, Srinagar: Jammu and Kashmir, Academy of Culture, 1968.

Lawrence, W.R., *The Valley of Kashmir*, Srinagar: Kesar Publishers, rpt 1967, Oxford University Press, London: 1895.

________, *Provincial Gazetteer of Kashmir and Jammu*, Rima Publishing House, rpt New Delhi: 1985.

________, *The India We Served, London*: Cassell & Co Ltd., 1928.

Lidhoo, M.L., *Kashmir Tribals*, Minakshi Publishers, Srinagar: 1987.

Madan, T.N., *Family and Kinship*. A Study of Pandits of Rural Kashmir, Asia Publishing House, Bombay: 1965.

Mann, R.S., *The Ladakhi: A Study in Ethnography and Change*, Anthropological Survey of India, Calcutta:1986.

Mckim Marriot, 'Little Community in an Indigenous Civilisation', *Village India*, edited by Mckim Marriot, Chicago university Press, Chicago: 1955.

Miskin, Haji Mohi-ud-Din, *Tarikh-i-Kabir-i-Kashmir*, Amritsar, AH 1322.

Moorcroft, William and G. Trebeck, *Travels in the Himalayan Province of Hindustan and the Punjab, Ladakh and Kashmir*, 2 vols. (1819-35), illustrated and edited by H.H. Wilson, John Murray, London:1841.

Narain, A.K., *The Indo-Greeks*, Oxford University Press, rpt Delhi:1980.

Pandita, K.N., *A Chronicle of Mediaeval Kashmir*, Calcutta, 1984.

________, *Ladakh: Life and Culture*, Srinagar: Centre of Central Asian Studies, University of Kashmir, 1986.

Parmer, R.K., *A History of Sikh Rule in Kashmir* (1819-46), Srinagar, 1977.

Pathik, Jyoteeshwar, *Cultural Heritage of the Dogras*, Light & Life Publishers, New Delhi: 1980.

Przyluski, J., 1890, *Ancient People of the Punjab*: The Audumbaras and the Salavas, Sagar Publications, rpt New Delhi:1971.

Prui, Balraj, 'Major Identities of Jammu and Kashmir State', India *International Centre Quarterly*, Vol. 1, No. 28, 2001, pp 69-79.

Regional Autonomy Committee Report, Jammu, 13 April 1999.

Rizvi, Janet, Ladakh: *Crossroads of High Asia*, New Oxford University Press, Delhi:1983.

Rose, H.A. (compiled), *A Glossary of the Tribes and Castes of the Punjab and N.W. Frontier* Province, Based on the *Census Report for the Punjab 1883*, by Sir Denzil Ibbetson and the *Census Report for the Punjab 1892*, by Sir Edward Maclagan, Amar Prakashan, rpt New Delhi: 1980.

Russell, R.V. and Hiralal, *The Tribes and Castes of the Central Province of India*, Vol. IV, Cosmo Publications, (Reprint) New Delhi:1975.

Sarkar, R., V. Sarkar and M.K. Raha, 'The Gujjars and Their Society', in P.K. Misra and K.C. Malhotra (eds), *Nomads in India*, Anthropological Survey of India, Calcutta: 1982.

Sharma, D.C., *Kashmir Under Sikhs*, Seema Publication, New Delhi:1983.

Srivara, Pandit, Rajataangini (Sanskrit), English translation by Y.C. Dutt as The Kings of Kashmir, Vol III, Calcutta, 1935.

Stein, M.A., *Kalhan's Rajtarangini* (Eng. Tr.), 2 vols, London: West Minister, 1900; rpt, Motilal, New Delhi:1962.

Sufi, G.M.D., *Kashmir, Being a History o Kashmir from the Earliest Times to our own*, 2 vols, Lahore: University of Lahore, 1948-9; rpt, Light & Life Publishers, New Delhi, 1974.

________, *Kashmir*, Light & Life Publishers, New Delhi: Vols I and II, 1974.

Simi, Tokan, D. Oki Kassato and Hassnain Fida M., *Ladakh: The Moonland*, Light & Life Publishers, New Delhi: 1975.

Vogel, J. Ph. And J. Hutchison, *History of Punjab Hill States*, Govt. Press, Calcutta: 1934.

Wahid, Siddiq, 'Ladakh: Political Convergence and Human Geography', in Geeti Sen and Ashis Banerjee (eds), *The Human Landscape*, Orient Longman and India International Centre, New Delhi: 2001.

Affairs pf the East India Company being the Fifth Report from the Select Committee of the House of Commons, edited with notes and Introduction by Walter Kelly Firminger, 3 vols., Neeraj Publishing, Delhi: 28July 1812, rpt 1984.

Archer, John Clark, *The Sikhs in Relation to Hindus, Muslims, Christians and Ahmadiyyas*. A Study in Comparative Religion, Princeton: PWP, 1946.

Baines, Athelstane, 1976, *Ethnography*, Concept Pub. House, Delhi: 1912.

Bakshi, R., R. Singh and I.P. Singh, 'Secular trend in age at menarche in Punjabis', in *Proceedings of the Xth International Congress of Anthropological and Ethnological Sciences*, Delhi, 1978.

Balfour, Edward, *Encyclopaedia Asiatica: comprising Indian Subcontinent, Eastern and Southern Asia*, Vol. V, Cosmo Publications, Delhi: 1976.

Banga, Indu (ed.), *Five Punjabi Centuries: Polity, Economy, Society and Culture, c. 1500-1990*, Essays for J.S. Grewal, Manohar, Delhi:2000.

Banerjee, Himadri, 'The Kamins of the Punjab (1889-1901)', in *Punjab Past and Present*, Vol XI, Pt. I, 1977.

Barnes, G.C. and J.B. Lyall, Report of the Land Revenue Settlement of the Kangra District, Punjab Civil and Military Gazetteer Press, Lahore:1850.

Bingley, A.H., History, *Caste and Culture of the Jats and Gujjars*, ESS Publications, Delhi:1978 (1st pub. 1904: Calentt: Superintendent Govt. Printers).

Biswas, N., 'Age at menarche among Punjabi girls of Delhi', *Anthropologist*, Vol. 14, 1976.

Blunt, E.A.H., *The Caste System of Northern India*, London: Oxford University Press, 1931 and S. Chand & Co, Delhi: 1969 (rpt).

Budha, Prakash, *Glimpses of Ancient Punjab*, Punjab University, Patiala:1966.

________, 1891, Vol. XX, Part II.

________, 1901, Punjab and NWFP, Vol. 17A, Parts I and II, Castes, Races and Nationality.

________, 1911, Punjab, Vol. XIX, Part II, Tables. Civil and Military Gazetteer Press, Lahore.

________, 1911, Punjab, Vol. XIV, Part I, Report, Civil and Military Gazetteer Press,Lahore.

________, 1911, Punjab Census Report 1901, Vol. XIV, Part II, Tables, Civil and Military Gazetteer Press, Lahore.

________, 1921, Punjab, Vol. 15, Part IV.

________, 1921, Punjab and Delhi, Vol. XV, Part I, Report, Superintendent Census Operations, Punjab, Lahore.

________, 1931, Vol. I, Punjab: Report by Khan Ahmad Hassan Khan, Superintendent of Census Operations, Punjab and Delhi.

________, 1931, Punjab, Vol. XVIII, Part I, Report.

________, 1931, Punjab Vol. XVII, Part II, Lahore.

________, 1941, Vol I, Part I, Tables.

________, 1961, Vol. I, India, Part V B (II), A. Mitra, ICS, Registrar General & Census Commissioner.

________, 1961, Punjab, Vol. XIII, Part II C (I) and Part I A (I).

Channa, V.C., *Caste: Identity and Continuity*, B.R. Publishing Corporation, Delhi:1979.

Conran, W.L., H.D. *Craik, Chiefs and Families of the note in the Punjab*, Vo. II, Lahore: Govt. Printing Press (revd. Edn. By Lepa. H. Griffen), 1940.

Crooke, W., 'Kayasth, Kayastha', in Encyclopaedia of Religion and Ethics, Vol. III, James Hastings (ed.), New York, Edinburgh: T.T. Clark, 1896 (rpt. 1971). [________, *The Tribes and Castes of the North-Western India*, Vol. I to IV, Cosmo Publications, Delhi:1896 (rpt. 1974).

Darling, M.L., *The Old Light and the New in Punjab*, Oxford University Press, London:1930.

Datta, R.C., *A History of Civilisation in Ancient India*, Vishal Publishers, Delhi: 1972.

Douie, James Sir, *The Punjab North-West Frontier Province and Kashmir*, Seema Publications, Delhi:1974.

District Gazetteer, 'Punjab', Vol. XIX A, Jalandhar Division, 1904.

________, 'Gurdaspur', Govt. Printing Press, Lahore:1936.

Eliade, Mircea, *The Encyclopedia of Religion*, Vol. 6, Macmillan Publishing Company, New York: 1987.

Encyclopedia of Religion, The, Vol. XIII, Macmillan Publishing Company, New York:1987.

Gait, E.A., 'Caste', in James Hastings (ed), *Encyclopedia of Religion and Ethics*, Vol. III, Edinburgh: T.T. Clark, New York 1971.

Grewal, J.S., *The Sikhs of the Punjab*, (in the New Cambridge History of India Series), Cambridge: Cambridge University Press: Hyderabad: Orient Longman, 1991: Foundation Books, Delhi:1994.

Grierson, G.A., *Linguistic Survey of India,* Vol. IX, Part III, Motilal Banarasidass, Delhi:1907 (rpt. 1968).

Guha, B.S., *Census of India*, Vol. I, Part III, Ethnographical, Govt. of India Press, Simla: 1935.

Gupta, Hari Ram, *History of the Sikhs*, 'The Sikh Gurus 1469-1708', Vol. I, Munshiram Manoharlal, Delhi: 1984.

Gupta, B.R., 'Aggarwals', in The Illustrated Weekly of India, 11 March 1973.

Habib, Irfan; *An Atlas of Mughal Empire*, Oxford University Press, Delhi:1982.

Hershman Paul, Punjabi Kinship and Marriage, Hindustan Publishing Corporation, Delhi:1981.

Hutton, J.H., Caste *in India: Its Nature, Functions and Origins*, Oxford University Press, London:1981.

Ibbetson, Sir Denzil, C.J., *Punjab Ethnography*, [a reprint of those portions of the report on the Punjab Census of 1981 which dealt with the Religions, the Languages, and the Races, Castes and Tribes of the People], Lahore, 1883.

________, *Punjab Castes*, (Being a reprint of the chapter on 'The Races, Castes and Tribes of the People', in the Report on the Census of Punjab published in 1883 by the late Sir Denzil Ibbetson), Lahore, 1916.

________, *Punjab Castes*, Patiala: Punjabi University, 1916 (rpt. 1970); Cosmo Publications, Delhi:1916 (rpt. 1981).

The Imperial Gazetteer of India, Vols. I-XXV, Today and Tomorrow Printers and Publishers, Delhi.

Jamait, Rai Diwan, The domicited Hindus, B.R. Publishing Corporation, Delhi: 1974.

Judge, Paramjit, 'Religion, Caste, and Communalism in Punjab' (mimeo) at the seminar on 'Punjab Ethnography' held at Amritsar in December 2001 to mark the Golden Jubilee of Indian Sociological Association.

Kamboj, Bishan Singh, *Kamboj Prakash*, R.M.S. Azad Prakashan, Patiala:1980.

Kamble, J.R. *Rise and Awakening of Depressed Classes in India*, National Publishing House, Delhi: 1979.

Kane, P.V., 'A Note on the Kayasthas', *in New Indian Antiquary,* Vol. I, 1938-9, pp. 740-3.

Karve, Irawati, 'Jat', in *Encyclopedia Britannica*, Vol. XII, Chicago, 1964.

Khalsa, Gurudharm Singh, 'The End of Syncretism: Anti-Syncretism in Sikh Tradition', in Pashaura Singh and N. Gerald Barrier (eds.), *Sikh Identity: Continuity and Change*, Manohar, Delhi:2001.

Khare, R.S., " A Case of Anomalous Values in Indian Civilization', *The Journal of Asian Studies*, Vol. XXV, No. II, 1966.

Kler, Swinde, 'A study of some hereditary traits among Jats and Khatris of Punjab', unpublished thesis, Punjabi University, Patiala:1972.

Kohli, Surinder Singh, Bulhe Shah: Marker of Indian Literature, Sahitya Akademi, Delhi:1987.

Lakshmanna, C., *Caste Dynamics in Village India*, Navchetan Publications Limited, Bombay: 1973.

Lal, Bhai Harbans, 'Sahajdhari Sikh: Their Origin and Current Status within the Panth', in Pashaura Singh and N. Gerald Barrier (eds), *Sikh Identity: Continuity and Change,* Manohar, Delhi: 2001.

Leef, Murray J., *Information and behaviour in a Sikh village: Social organization reconsidered*, Oxford University Press, Delhi:1972.

Lewis, Oskar, *Village life in Northern India*, University of Illinois Press,Urbana: 1958.

Lochlin, C.H., 'The History of Christianity in Punjab', in *Punjab Past and Present*, Vol. VII, Part I, 1973.

Madan, T.N., 'Structural Implications of Marriage in North India: Wife-Givers and Wife-Takers Among the Pandits of Kashmir', *Contributions to IndianSociology* (NS), Vol. 9, No. 2, 1975, pp. 217-43.

Majumdar, R.C., *History and Culture of the Indian People*, Bhartiya Vidya Bhawan, Bombay: 1966.

Malhotra, Anshu, *Gender, Caste and Religious Identities: Restructuring Class in Colonial Punjab,* Oxford University Press, Delhi:2002.

Martindale, D. and Gerth H. Max Weber, *The Religion of India:* The Sociology of Hinduism and Buddhism, Noble Offset Printers, New York: 1966.

McLeod, W.H., 'The Turban: Symbol of Sikh Identity', in Pashaura Singh and N. Gerald Barrier (eds.), *Sikh Identity, Continuity and Change*, Manohar, Delhi: 2001.

________, The Evolution of the Sikh Community, Oxford University Press, Delhi: 1996.

________, Guru Nanak and the Sikh Religion, Delhi: Oxford University Press, 1996.

McMullen, G.O., J.C.B. Webster and M. Cable, *The Amritsar Diocese*, Preliminary Survey, Batala: CISS.

Munshi, K.M., *Glory that was Gurjara Desha* (A.D. 550 – 1300), Bombay: Bhartiya Vidya Bhawan, 1954.

Naval, Chandanmal, *Rigar Jati ka Itihas* (Hindi), Shyam Printing Press, Jodhpur:1986.

Oberoi, Harjot, The *Construction of Religious Boundaries: Culture, Identity and Diversity in the Sikh Tradition*, Delhi: Oxford University Press, 1994; University of Chicago Press, Chicago:1994.

Pandit Mohanlal, Shami Potra, *Asli-Twarikh-i-Arorbans*, cf. Rai Diwan Jamait, 1974 (rpt).

Pathak, Sushil Madhawe, *The Social, Economic and Political problems of the Christian community in Punjab*, Christian Institute for the Study of Religion and Society Publication Trust, Bangalore: 1961.

Pathak, Sushil Madhawe, *American Missionaries and Hinduism: A study of their contacts from 1813 to 1918*, Munshiram Manoharlal, Delhi:1967.

Pettligrew, Joyce, *Robber Nobleman: A study of the political system of Jats*, Ambika Publications, Delhi:1978.

Pocock, David, F., *Kanbi and Patidar: A study of the Patidar community of Gujarat,* Oxford University Press, Delhi: 1972.

Population Research Centre, 'Source Distribution of Population by Religion and Scheduled Caste', *Census of India*, Series No. XVII, Part II, Punjab University, Chandigarh: 1971.

Ram, Pt. Sant, *Sood Bansawali* (in Hindi, n.d.).

Rapson, E.J. *Cambridge History of India*, Vol. 1, S. Chand & Co., Delhi: 1968.

Risley, H.H., *The People of India*, 2nd edn., by W. Crooke, Calcutta: Thacker & Spink, 1915; Oriental Book, 2nd edn., Delhi:1969.

Rose, H.A. *Glossary of the Tribes and Castes of the Punjab and North-West Frontier Province*, Civil and Military Gazette Press, Lahore:1919.

________, *Rites and Ceremonies of Hindus and Muslims*, Amar Prakashan, Delhi:1983 (rpt).

Russell, R.V. and Hiralal, *The Tribes and Castes of the Central Province of India,* Macmillan Co., London:1916.

Sharma, Satya P., 'Marriage, Family and Kinship among the Jats and the Thakurs of North India: Some Comparisons', in *Indian Sociology*; Series No. VIII, 1973.

Shashi, S.S., *The Shepherds of India: A socio-cultural study of sheep and cattle rearing communities*, Sundeep Prakashan, Delhi:1978.

Sher, Sher Singh, *The Sikligars of Punjab*, Sterling Publishers, Delhi:1966.

________, *Sansis of Punjab*, Munshiram Manoharlal, Delhi:1965.

Singh, Gurusharan, 'Labana Sikhs and Guru-Ghar', *Labana Sewak*, July-September 1985.

Singh, Khushwant, *A History of the Sikhs,* Vol. I, 1469-1839, Oxford University Press, Delhi:1986.

Sing, Joginder, 'The Sikh Community: Demography and Occupational Change 1881-1931', in Indu Banga (ed.), *Five Punjabi Centuries: Polity, Economy, Society and Culture*, c. 1500-1900, Manohar, Delhi:2000.

Sircar, D.C., *Iranians and Greeks in Ancient Punjab*, Department of Punjab Historical Studies, Punjabi University, Patiala:1973.

Smith, V.A., *The Early History of India*, Clarendon Press, Oxford:1924.

Sood, Madan Mohan and Ram Rattan Sood, *Origin of Soods:* A critical Analysis, Lakshmi Printer, Delhi:1979.

Tandon, P., *Punjabi Century*, Orient Paperbacks, Delhi:1961.

Thakur, V., *Some Aspects of Ancient Indian History and Culture*, Abhinav Publications, Delhi:1974.

Thapar, Romila, *A History of India*, Penguin Books, Middlesex:1977.

Thind, Harbans Singh, *Kamboj Itihas* (in Punjabi), Jalandhar, 1973.

Tod, James, *Annals and Antiquities of Rajasthan: The Central and Western Rajpoot States of India*, 2 vols., London: Routledge and Kegan Paul, 1957.

________, *Annals of Rajasthan: The Annals of Mewar*, S. Chand & Co., Delhi: 1960.

Vaidya, C.V., *History of Medieval Hindu India*, Gyan Publishing House, Delhi, 1985 (rpt).

Verma, K.K., *Changing Role of Castes Association*, National Publishing House, Delhi:1979.

Wakefield, H.E.A., *Kangra District Gazetteer*, 1893.

Webster, J.C.B., *The Christian Community and Change in Nineteenth Century North India*, Macmillan, Delhi:1976.

Ali, Hashim Ameer. (1967), *The Meos of Mewat*, Oxford and IBH Publishing Co.

Baines, Athelstane. (176), *Ethnography*, Concept Publishing Company, Delhi.

Bhargava, B.S. (1949), *The Criminal Tribes: A Socio-economic Study of the Principal Criminal Tribes in Northern India.*

Bingley, A.H. (1984), *History of Sikhs*, Sumit Publications, New Delhi.

Blunt, E.A.H. (1969), *The Caste System of Northern India*, S. Chand and Company, New Delhi.

Castes, Haryana Series 6, Part 9(1), Controller of Publications, Delhi: 1988.

Chakravarti, A. ;Jainism', *Cultural Heritage of India*, Calcutta, Vol. 1, p. 185.

Crooke, W. (1896), *The Tribes and Castes of the North-Western India*. (Calcutta: Government Printing Press, rpt. 1975, Delhi: Cosmo Publications.

Cunninghan, J. (1918), *A History of the Sikhs from the Origin of the Nation to the Battle of Satluj*. Bombay: Oxford University Press.

Datta V.N. and H.A. Phadke. (1985), *History of Kurukshetra*. Vishal Publications Kurukshetra.

Elliot, Sir Henry, *The North-West Provinces of India*, Beams (eds) London Press.

Fyzee, A.A. (1974), *Outlines of Mohammadan Law*, Oxford University Press, Bombay.

Gahlot, J.S. (1966), *Rajputana Ka Itihas* (Jaipur and Alwar State). Hindi Sahitya Mandir, Jodhpur.

Giriwar, Giri (1982), 'Bhaksha Vrata Tatha Badalati Manyataen'. *Goswami smaj Darpan*, 3(9): 5-20.

Grierson, G.A. (ed) (1916), *Linguistic Survey of India*, Reprint edition; (1967) Motilal Banarasidas, Delhi.

Haryana District Gazetteers, (1982), *Bhiwani*, Haryana Gazetteers Organization, Chandigarh.

Haryana District Gazetteers, (1983), *Gurgaon*, Haryana Gazetteers Organization, Chandigarh.

Haryana District Gazetteers, (1976), *Karnal*, Haryana Gazetteers Organization, Chandigarh.

Haryana District Gazetteers, (1970), *Rohtak*, Haryana Gazetteers Organization, Chandigarh.

Hunter, W.W. (1908), *Imperial Gazetteer of India*. Vol. XVII. Oxford University Press.

Jain, Manjusha. (186), 'Changing Social Values Among Jains in Haryana; A study of Intergenerational gap.' Unpublished Ph.D. Dissertation, Haryana Agricultural University, Hissar.

Goswami Magan Giri (1986). 'Goswami Utpati Banam Pratikriya' *Goswami Kalyan*, 2(8): Dec-Jan. 13-15.

Maheshwari, H.L. (1970) Jambhoj; *Vishnoi Sampardaya Sahitya*. B.R. Publications, Calcutta.

Munilal, *Haryana*, Vikas Publishing House Ltd.: Delhi 1974.

Giri, Om Prakash (1984-85), 'Goswami Smaj Aaj Kahan', *Goswami Kalyan*, No. 4, Dec. Jan.

Powlett. (1916), Major *Powlett's Gazetteer of Alwar* (Cf. Ibbetson, 1916).

Prem, K. (1970), *Gazetteer of India (Haryana) Rohtak:* Controller of Printing & Stationery, Govt. of Haryana, Chandigarh.

Rajasthan District Gazetteer. (1971), *Bharatpur,* Government of Rajasthan.

Rajputana Gazetteer. (1879), 'Rajputana' (3 vols.) Calcutta : Office of the Superintendent of Govt. Printing.

Rose, H.A. (1919), *Glossary of the Tribes and Castes of the Punjab and N.W. F. Province.* (Lahore: Civil & Military Gazette Press, rpt. 1980, Delhi: Amar Prakashan).

Russell, R.V. and Hiralal. (1916), The *Tribes and Castes of the Central Provinces of India* London: Macmilland and Company, rpt. 1975, Cosmo Publications, Delhi.

Saini, Shiv Lal. (1970), *Shoor Saini Jati ka Itihas*, Delhi and Haryana Saini Sabha, Delhi.

Sangave, V.A. (1980), *Jaina Community*: A Social Survey, Popular Prakashan, Bombay.

Sethi, S.S. (1985), *A Glossary of the Tribes and Castes*. Rima Publishing House, New Delhi.

Shams, Shamsuddin. (1981), 'Customs of Meos of Mewat', in *Haryana Review.*

Shams, Shamsuddin. (1981), Marriage Customs Among Meos of India, *Journal of Indian Law Institute*, 2.

Sher, Sher Singh (1963), *The Sikligars of Punjab* (Gypsy Tribe) Sterling Publishers Pvt. Ltd., Delhi.

Sherring, M.A. (1879), *Hindu Tribes and Castes. (together with an account of the Mahomedan Tribes of the North-West Frontier and of the Aboriginal Tribes of Central Provinces).* (London: rpt. 1974, Delhi: Cosmo Publications).

Singh, K.S. and Mann, R.S. (1993), Ethnography of Haryana: A preliminary study. *Journal of the Anthropological Survey of India*. 42: 18-29.

Singh, Raj. (1989), *Haryana – Its Land and People*. Souvenir XIX All India Sociological Conference, Hissar.

The Catholic Directory of India. (1984), Catholic Bishop Conference of India Centre, New Delhi, 1984.

Webb, A.W.T. (1953), The Bhils of Rajputana: in *The Census of India. 1951.* Vol X, Part I, Appendices, Rajasthan & Ajmer. Government Press, Jodhpur.

Agarwal, G. *Churu Mandal ka Shodhpurna Itihas,* (in Hindi), Lok Sanskrit Shodh Sansthan, Nagarshri :1974.

Ahuja, D.R. *Folklore of Rajasthan*, National Book Trust, Delhi, 1980.

Ambedkar, B.R., *The Untouchables – Who were They and why They Became Untouchables*, Amrik Book Co., Delhi 1948.

Asopa, J. *Cultural Heritage of Jaipur*, United Book Traders, Jodhpur 1982.

Bahadur, K.P., *Caste, Tribes and Culture of India*, E.E. Publication, Delhi 1978.

Banerjee, A.C. *The Rajput States and the East India Company*, A Mukherjee & Co., Calcutta 1951.

Basham, A.L., *The Wonder That was India*. Grove Press, reprint New York:1974, Fontana Books, London, 1954.

Bedi, M.S., *Drinking Behaviour and Development in Tribal Areas*. Himanshu Publishers, Udaipur 1980.

Beteille, Andre, *Caste : Old and New*. Asia Publishing House, Bombay, 1969.

Bhanavat, M. 1983 *Abhijat Adivasi.* (in Hindi), Shilpi Prakashan, Jaipur 1983.

Bhandari, S. 1934 *Maheswari Jati ka Itihas*. (in Hindi), Bhanpur, Indore.

Bhandari, S.R. 1934 *Oswal Jati ka Itihas*, (in Hindi), Bhanpur, Indore.

Bhatt, R.S., *Mewar ke Maharana aur Shahnshah Akbar* (in Hindi), Sphatik Sansthan, Jaipur, 1976.

Bhatt, S.S. *Scheduled Caste in Rajasthan: A Spatial Analysis,* Unpublished, M.Phil Dissertation in Jawaharlal Nehru University, Delhi, 1974.

Bhattacharya, A.N. & R.N. Vyas, *Habitat, Economy and Society, A Study of Dangis,* Concept Publishing Company, New Delhi 1979.

Bose, A.B. & S.P. Malhotra, 1964 Some Characteristics of Occupational Castes in Central and Lower Luni in Western Rajasthan, *Eastern Anthropologist*, Sept-Dec. 17(3) 137-56.

Briggs, G.W. 1920. *The Chamars*, Oxford University Press, London.

Brooks, J.C. *History of Maywar*, Calcutta: 1959.

Brunel, Francis (not dated) *Rajasthan*; Roli Books International, Delhi.

Carstairs G.M. *Death of a Witch: A village in North India* 1950-1981, Hutchinson, London, 1983.

Carstairs, G.M. *Bhil villages of Western Udaipur; The Economy and Political Weekly*: 4(9), 1952.

Carstairs, G.M. *The Bhills of Kotra Bhomat: The Eastern Anthropologist*, 8 (3-4) pp. 169-81, 1954.

Census of India, Rajasthan District Census Hand Book: Kota, 1972, General Administration Deptt. Govt. of Rajasthan, Jaipur 1971.

Census of India, Rajasthan District Census Hand Book: Jodhpur, 1972, General Administration Deptt. Govt. of Rajasthan, Jaipur 1971.

Census of India, 1981 Rajasthan, District Census Hand Book: Alwar, 1982, General Administration Deptt. Govt. of Rajasthan.

Census of India, 1981 Rajasthan, District Census Hand Book: Bharatpur, 1982, General Administration Deptt. Govt. of Rajasthan.

Census of India, 1961 Rajasthan, District Census Hand Book: Bhilwara, 1966,

Census of India, Jaipur: Govt. of Rajasthan. 1961 Rajasthan. Vol. XIV, Pt. III. Household Economic Tables, 1965, Jaipur: Supdt. of Census Operations Rajasthan.

Census of India, 1961 Rajasthan Pt. II-B (II) General Economic Tables, Jaipur: Supdt. Census Operations Rajasthan:1965.

Census of India, 1981 Rajasthan District Census Hand Book Churu. Part X A-B. Jaipur: General Administration Deptt. Govt. of Rajasthan.

Census of India, 1931, Vol. VII Part-I Bombay Presidency, General Report 1933; Delhi Manager of Publlications.

Census of India, 1981 Rajasthan Census Atlas, Part XII Series 18, Supdt. Census of Operations, Rajasthan.

Census of India, 1981 Primary Census Abstract: Scheduled Caste 'Series I' Part II B (II), Controller of Publications, Delhi.

Chakravarti, M.R. 1963 *Ethnic Bearing of the Dermatoglyphic Study in India*, Acta. Genet Med, Gemelo (4) 374-404.

Chatursen, A. *Goli* Hind Pocket Books, Delhi: 1985.

Chaudhari, N.R. *Population Growth and Distribution of the Bhils in India, Tribe*, Vol. VIII, No. 3 & 4 p. 29, 1971.

Chaudhari, N.R. and R. Kumar 1979: *Demographic profiles of Bhill*, Eastern Anthropologist XXXII : 3 pp. 273-280.

Chauhan, B.R. *A Rajasthan Village.* Vir Publishing House, New Delhi: 1967.

Chauhan, B.R. *Towns in the Tribal Setting*, National Publishing House. Delhi :1970.

Chauhan, B.R. and B.H. Swaroop B.H. Nyaya Panchayats and Leadership Opportunities in Tribal Areas of Rajasthan, *The Eastern Anthropologist*, Vol. 28, No. 4. 1975.

Chine, E.A. Memorandum on the Prevailing Castes, *Census of North Western Province.* Vol. I: General Report and Appendices. Allahabad, 1865, 1967.

Crooke, W. *The Tribes and Castes of North Western India* (4 Vols.) Calcutta 1896: Government Printing Press; reprint Cosmo Publications, Delhi 1974.

Dandiya, C.K., *Women in Rajasthan*, Rajasthan University Publications, Jaipur 1975.

Das, K.R.S., The Mina Tribes of Jaipur in Mewar, *Journal of the Asiatic Society of Bengal*, 55 (1), 1924.

Dave, P.C. *The Garasias*, Bhartiya Adim Jati Sevak Sangh, Kingsway, Delhi 1960.

Dholi, R.S. *Dholi ka Itihas* (in Hindi). Rao Kelan Smriti Pratisthan, Bikaner, 1990.

Doshi, J.K. *Social Structure and Cultural Change in a Bhil Village*, New Heights Publications, Delhi,1967.

Doshi, S.L., *Tribal Ethnicity*, Class and Integration, Rawat Publications, p. 150, Jaipur 1990.

Dumont, Louis, *Homo Hierarchicus – The Caste system and its Implications*, Vikas Publishing House, Delhi 1970.

Engineer, A.A., *The Bohras*, Vikas Publishing House, New Delhi 1980.

Enthoven, R.E., *The Tribes and Castes of Bombay*, 3 Vols. Bombay: Government Central Press 1920-22. (reprint), Cosmo Publications, Delhi 1975.

Erskine, K.D. *Rajputana Gazetteers*, Vol. II-A, Scotish Mission Industries, Ajmer 1908.

Gahlot, J.S. *Rajasthan ka Samajik Jeewan,* (in Hindi), Hindi Sahitya Mandir, Jodhpur 1974.

Gahlot, J.S. *Rajasthan – A Socio-Economic Study*, Rajasthan Sahitya Mandir, Jodhpur 1981.

Hutton, J.H. *Census of India with Complete Survey of Tribal Life and System,* reprint 1986, Gian Publishing House, Delhi, 1931.

Kanungo, J.R. *Know Your Rajasthan*, Jain Brothers, Delhi 1965.

Katiyar, T.S. *Social Life in Publishing Rajasthan*, Kitab Mahal, Allahabad, 1964.

Kaul, H.K. *Census of India*, Punjab, Vol. XII, Part I, Lahore 1912.

Lal, R.B. *Sons of the Aravallis : The Garasias*, Ahmedabad: Tribal Research and Training Institute, Ahmedabad, 1979.

Metcalfe, C.T. *The Rajput Tribes*, Vols. Reprint 1975, Cosmo Publication, Delhi, 1982.

Naik, T.B. *The Bhils: A Study*, Adimjati Sevak Sangh, Delhi, 1956.

Pal, H.B. *Historic Rajasthan*, Sagar Publications, Delhi 1974.

Rajasthan District Gazetteer, Tonk, Director of Distt. Gazetteers of Rajasthan, Jodhpur, 1970.

Rajputana Gazetteers, Rajputna (3 vols), Office of the Superintendent of Government Printing, Calcutta, 1879.

Rizvi, S.H.M. 1987 *Mina: The Ruling Tribe of Rajasthan*, B.R. Publishing Co., Delhi, 1987.

Russell, R.V. & Hiralal, *The Tribes and Castes of Central Provinces of India*: Macmillan and Co; London, 1916 reprint Cosmo Publications, Delhi 1975.

Sharma, Dasrath, *Rajasthan through the Ages*, Bikaner, 196.

Sharma, G.N. 1960 *Social Life in Medieval Rajasthan*, Uni. Press, Delhi, 1960.

Sherring, M.A. 1881 *The Tribes and Castes of Rajasthan,* 1975 reprint. Cosmo Publications, Delhi, 1881.

Sheering, M.A. *Hindu Tribes and Castes*. As Represented in Banaras, 1872. reprint 1974, Cosmo Publications, Delhi, 1974.

Shyamal Das, The Mina Tribes of Jaipur in Mewar, *Journal of the Asiatic Society of Bengal*, Vol. 55, Part I, pp. 109-13, 1924.

Tod, Col. James, Damor: *A Border Tribe of Rajasthan,* (Mimeo) 1967. *Tribe* 4(1) pp 8-50, Udaipur 1967.

Tod, Col. James, *Enthnographic Study of Meena*, Udaipur (Mimeo) 1967.

Tod, Col. James *Kathodis – A Planned Change*, Udaipur (Mimeo) 1969.

Tod, Col. James *Annals and Antiquities of Rajasthan*, 3 Vols. (edited with an introduction and noted by W. Crooke) reprint, Motilal Banarsidass, Delhi 1971.

Vyas, N.N. & Choudhury, N.D., *The Frontier Bhils and Meghwals, Tribe,* Vol. VII, No. 2, 1970.

Vyas, N.N. Banjara: *The Mercantile Nomads of Rajasthan, Tribe* 3(2) T.R.T.I., Udaipur.

Index

CUSTOMS OF INDIA

CUSTOMS OF INDIA

(In Six Volumes)

Volume 5

Eastern : Bihar, Jharkhand, Orissa, West Bengal

Editor

Gopal Bhargava

ISHA

Customs of India

ISBN: 978-81-8205-524-8 (Set)
ISBN: 978-81-8205-529-3 (Vol. 5)

Published in 2013 in India by
Isha Books
B-69, New Gupta Colony
New DDA Market
Delhi - 110009

Lasser Type Setting : Rajender Vashist, Delhi
Printed at : G. Print Process, Delhi

Contents

List of Illustrations

Preface

This painstakingly researched work on the customs of West Bengal, Orissa, Bihar and Jharkhand is an invaluable treasure trove of information on the tribes and castes of the eastern region. This volume contains an introduction on the customs, characteristics of people of all the states concerned, also taking stock of the probable origin of customs. Besides, the work contains seven chapters including : conceiving and birth, Puberty, Betrothal, Marriage ceremony, Death rituals : Cremation, Death Rituals : Burial and Social Customs. The book describes at length the ancient forms of customs, rites, rituals and usages as recorded by numerous British and Indian ethnographers, gazetteer writers, surveyors of the settlement reports. The Monograph writers and anthropologists etc. Following Independence in 1947, the entire scenario of social, economic life, customs, rites, rituals and culture belonging both castes and tribes in the eastern states of India had been in a constant transition. The region had been impinged upon by pan-Indian and global influences and factors. All these changes in the rites and rituals had been duly incorporated in this work.

The entire mass of information and knowledge has been painstakingly researched, written and edited with the anthropological point of view that makes this works all the more valuable for purpose of scholars, scientists, teachers and students in different discipline.

Every details of the information, collected, collated and formatted has gone through meticulous validation checks and rechecks. In line with the constant evolution of the text, this work, too will have to be updated and improved in successive editions. A country as vast and complex as India, there will always be a scope for improving this work through suggestions, deletions and additions pointed out for rectification. We invite the beneficiaries of this work to participate this in process of its evolution.

Disclaimer

This work contains the collected, collated, formatted and validated information on customs of India on a 'best and sincere effort' basis for presentation in a single comprehensive work. This work does not constitute an advisory for research, analysis or investment planning, nor, in general, any professional advice. The reader should seek the services of qualified professionals for such advice.

The information presented here is to be regarded as a 'first information service' on this work. The reader should make his/her own deeper investigation of the information on any particular matter before making any decision or investment of any kind. The Editorial Board or the Publishers cannot be held responsible for loss, if any, incurred as a result of specific planning or decisions or investments made by the reader in pursuance of this work.

Our sincere thanks are due to the scholars, researchers, authors, journalists, Publication Division, Government of India, Ministry of Culture, Census Commissioner, Land Settlement Reports, Ethnographers, Anthropological Survey of India, State Editor (Gazetteers), and others. We have studied the contents of a large number of published works, and drawn from them. The credit for producing and furnishing authentic information and knowledge goes to them. We have merely weaved, consolidated and formulated the contents of the mass of information collected from them.

Editor

Introduction

This volume covers customs, rites, rituals and usages of the eastern region of India, including West Bengal, Orissa, Bihar and Jharkhand, which are varied in different tribes, castes and communities being at different stages of civilisation, social and customary laws, economy, finance and education. The majority of population in West Bengal is grouped under the generic denomination of Hindu and a sizeable Muslim minority. The other minority communities include Christians, Buddhist, Sikhs and Jains. The term Hindu covers a number of religious sect ranging from monotheists to polytheists in various degrees and stages of civilization. The largest religious sect in the state is Vaishnavism, mainly of the Chaitanya cult.

Of the minor Bhakti cult sects the most interesting is the Sahajiya sect, which does not recognize difference of caste and community and the traditional social life. The next in order are the *Shaktas* and *Saivas*. Ritual Brahmanism derived from the Vedic Aryan cult is practised by a fraction of the Brahmin caste. Popular Hinduism in Bengal is an amalgam of pre- and post-Aryan sects. These influences are evident not only among the Hindu Community but also among the Muslims and Christians in a considerable degree. The Bhakti cult of which Vaishnavism is a refinement, has been an ancient feature of the religious philosophy of Bengal and is perhaps the strongest element in the spiritual beliefs of the people irrespective of community.

In West Bengal, Hinduism is traditionally divided in the caste system. Earlier, the undivided Bengal was the home of numerous castes and sub-castes which did not conform to the Varna system but which were arranged according to the hereditary occupations. The Bengal Brahmans are divided into five endogamous sub-castes: Rarhi, Barendra, Vaidic, Saptasti and Madhyasreni and into numerous sub-groups with in each sub-caste according to hereditary precedence and so-called purity of blood. The Kayasthas are divided into four endogamous sub-castes: Uttar-Rarhi, Dakshin-Rarhi, Barendra and Bangaja, with numerous sub-divisions. The *Vaidyas* are a numerically small community with a preponderant representation in the higher professions and services. Notably members of all the three 'high' castes are mainly *Shaktas* by religious persuasion while the majority of the lower castes are Vaishnanavas of the Chaitanya cult and other cults. The essential ritual observances of the *Vaidyas*, *Kayasthas* and the wealthier sub-castes of the 'lower' order closely follow those of the Brahmins with additional observances inherited from the aboriginal ancestors.

The great majority of Hindus, constituting more than three-fourths of the community are lumped together as *Sudras*. The classical denomination of Sudras covers all who follow manual occupations. The demotion of the great trading community, a hereditary group akin to the Vaisyas to the position of *Sudras* was made by the royal arbitrary command. They have their traditional hierarchy and their endogamous and commensal groups, the clean *Sudras* enjoy the services of Brahmins for their rites and worship and those in 'unclean' occupations like scavenging, hide-curing etc. are considered as the real Harijans.

In the Muslim community also a division is observed between families of 'pure' stock and the indigenous stock which forms the vast majority in the Community. Similarly among the Christians, a firm line divides those who claim varying mix of European blood and the native converts mostly from the peasant stock. Caste consciousness has weakened and has ceased to be an important factor in public life, in the state. A powerful influence against caste distinctions was in operation since the early nineteenth century, when Ram Mohan Roy preached basic social and religious reforms. He propounded Vedantic monotheism, abolition of caste and communal division, and pleaded for a society guided by rationalism. Closely after him Ramakrishna Paramahamsa also preached the gospel of a universal theism by confirming the equal validity of all methods of religious enquiry. The moral and social implications of Ramkrishna's teachings were brought out forcefully by his brilliant disciple Swami Vivekananda who drove home the realization that the days of the upper caste were gone by for ever and that the India of the future would arise out of those very classes who were depressed.

Vivekananda aroused the elite enjoying caste privileges to a realization of the immortality, of depriving a large section of the people of their human right to equality. Moreover Rabindranath Tagore propounded a universal faith which recognized no social barriers between man and man. The process was given further impetus by Mahatma Gandhi's drive against caste and other divisive social customs.

As for the people of West Bengal follow all the major religions prevalent in India. According to the 1981 Census, the maximum number of the people of the state profess Hinduism. The Muslim stand next with a total population of 11,743,259 who are more numerous in West Bengal than the national average. Apart from the Hindus and Muslims, there are people who profess Christianity, Buddhism, Sikhism and Jainism etc. The rest follow various other religions. The tribals profess their own animist religions, which are various forms of nature worship.

In fact, Bengal had been a centre of the Vedic religion in the hoary past. The Buddhists and Jains at one time had converted almost the whole of Bengal to their creed. Brahmanic influences remained for centuries at a very low ebb. Several Buddhist scholars and reformers were born in Bengal, among whom Atisa Dipankar and Shilabhadra are known throughout the entire Buddhist world. Out of 24 Jain *tirthankaras* (divine men) 23 attained *moksha* (salvation) in the then undivided Bengal. *Tirthankars* such as Sriranganath and Vasupujya were born in Bengal. The greatest of the Jain *tirthankars* Mahavir spent eight years of his life term preaching his faith in Radh Desh (Western Bengal). The Dharam cult flourished towards the end of the tenth century. Revival of Hinduism in Bengal was, however, mainly responsible for the almost disappearance of these two religious faiths from Bengal. Buddhist and Jain influences can at present be traced mainly in Darjeeling Himalayas and the sporadic areas of the Radh region respectively.

Out of the five schools of Vedanta, the Gaudiya Vaishnava school founded by Chaitanya Mahaprabhu is the most prevalent. The ideology of Shri Chaitanya Mahaprabhu, nourished by his school of devotees and codified by the great Baladeva Vidyabhusan gave rise to this sect. Their doctrine may be called *achintya bhedabhedavada* (doctrine of inconceivable difference and non-difference). Vaishnavism or the *bhakti* movement flourished in Bengal due to the towering influence of Shri Chaitanya (AD 1485-1533). Devotion to Radha and Krishna had taken root in the soil of Bengal. Sri Chaitanya elevated the divine passion of the couple to a high spiritual plane and stressed the emotional at the cost of the ceremonial side of religion. The Bengal Vaishnavas were worshippers of Radha and Krishna. The cult originated with Madhavendra Puri Goswami while Shri Chaitanya and their followers developed it into a full grown system with a philosophy of its own. The sect has a very strong influence among the low caste population of West Bengal. While, the *Matua Dharam* founded by Hari Chand Thakur and Guru Chand Thakur had a deep penetrating influence among the Namasudra caste.

Shiva and Shakti cult are also very popular in West Bengal. The Radh region has a large number of pilgrim centres where it is said that parts of the body of Sati fell. Shiva temples and the worship of *shivalinga* are commonly found throughout the length and breadth of West Bengal. Bengal was also the seat of *tantra*. Numerous Buddhist and Hindu *tantrik* traditions were very strong at one point of time. Even today in some areas of West Bengal the *tantra* tradition remains active.

As for Islam, *Sufism* began to spread its wings from the eleventh century onwards and by the twelveth or thirteenth century it was in full swing in Bengal. It flourished at four centres, namely, Varendra, Radh, Banga and Chittagong last two now in Bangladesh. The Varendra centre comprises Medinipur, Rajmahal, Purnea and surrounding places. At this centre the holy names of Jalauddin Badayuni, and Allauddin Bhukhari Sayed etc. are well known. The Radh centre comprises Bardhaman, Birbhum, Bankura and Hooghly. At the Radh centre the well known *Sufis* were Makdum Shah, Muhammad Gajnavi, Anwar Kuli, Habi, Shah Sultan Ansari and so on. The *Sufis* were the wandering mendicants who roamed from place to place, preaching and singing the holy names of god and his exhilarating message. Through the combined effort of the *bhakti* and *sufi* traditions a composite of Hindu and Muslim cultures was developed in Bengal during the 15th and 16th centuries AD as found in the heart-captivating, soul-stirring, life-inspiring songs and verses of the Baul tradition of Bengal. The name of Lalan Fakir will shine forever as an enchanting symbol of the *bhakti* and *sufi* traditions.

In fact the Baul cult of Bengal is a transformed form of the Natha cult. Natha means a master-lord. The Bauls have adopted the Yogic practice of the Nathas and have inherited their mystic poetry and riddles. But they outwardly admit God and call him Krishna or Chaitanya as the Vaishnavites do. A strong presence of the Baul cult can be seen in the Radh region. A distinct class of the natha Yogi Nicknamed as Bengal Jugi has survived in North Bengal and other parts of West Bengal. The influence of visionaries and mystics like Ramanand, Kabir, Nanak, Dadu are also marked in Bengal.

Islam claimed a large number of converts particularly among the lower Hindu castes. A large number of these people did not accept neo-Brahmanism and converted to Islam. But when Islam arrived in the Indian sub-continent carrying a liberating message of social equality as preached by the *Sufis*, some oppressed castes, in order to escape the yoke of Brahmanic oppression were converted to Islam en masse. However, no evidence can be found in support of this theory. In fact, the idea that Islam fosters social equality seems to be a recent notion, dating only from the period of the Enlightenment and more particularly from the legacy of the French Revolution among the 19th century. In fact, not only people in the lower orders but a large number of upper caste people were also converted forcibly to Islam. Some Buddhists of Bengal also accepted Islam. A large section of the Muslims in the population of Bengal are removed from Pathan and Mughal power. These neo-Muslims of Bengal gave Indian Islam an indigenous temper. At present barring the Himalayan and sub-Himalayan region of West Bengal, large populations of Muslims are found everywhere in the state.

Finally, Christianity came to in Bengal from Europe mainly through the missionaries. The Augustinian missionaries with the Portuguese factory at Hooghly, using it as the base of their operation in the early years of 16th century, established a number of Christian churches in lower Bengal. William Carey, who arrived in Serampore, set up the Baptist Mission during the last decade of the 18th century, which opened a new vista in the history of Christianity in India. Though before him John Kiermander of Sweden (AD 1758-1786) had built the Old Mission Church of Calcutta with the help of Lord Clive, William Carey was the first missionary sent by a missionary society of the West. He emerged as the father of modern missionary enterprises in West Bengal. His work in the fields of translation of the Bible, primary education, journalism, teaching of the gospel gives him a unique place in the spread of Christianity in Bengal. Bishop Middleton, the first Bishop of Calcutta (AD 1815-1822) founded the Bishop's College with a view to train Indian Christian preachers and teachers, and it served the cause of general education and the spread of Christianity in Bengal. Now a notable presence of Christianity is seen in Kolkata and other parts of West Bengal including the tribal areas and north Bengal.

Apart from their indigenous tribal faith, among the tribal people of West Bengal, the impact of the *bhakti* tradition and Christianity is marked. In the Darjeeling Himalayas, the Buddhist tradition is strongly established among the tribal communities like Lepchas, and Gorkhas. Sanskritization processes has also penetrated, leading to their cultural integration with the Hindu fold.

In Bengal the Brahmo Samaj Movement also flourished. Raja Ram Mohun Roy in the last quarter of the 18th century founded Brahmo Dharma based on an age-old principle of unity underlying the Vedantic monism. After Ram Mohun, Pandit Ishwarchandra Vidyasagar, Devendranath Tagore and others kept the tradition alive. In 1868, Keshav Chandra Sen founded the *mandir* (temple) of the *Bharatvarsiya Brahmo Samaj* (Brahmo Society of India) and in 1878 at a meeting at the Town Hall the Sadharan Brahmo Samaj was formed. The spiritual renaissance of Bengal that followed the social and intellectual renaissance was largely due to the influence of Ramakrishna-Vivekananda movement. This school preaches the doctrine of *sarba-dharma samanvaya* (synchronization of all religions) and practical Vedanta. Swami Vivekananda spread the message of self-realization through meditation informed with knowledge. As a religious reformer he devoted most of his time and labour to bring solace and relief to the suffering people. The Ramakrishna Mission founded by him remains the first and foremost voluntary service organization in the country.

In the traditional caste hierarchy, the Brahmins stand the highest who claim descent from pure Aryan stock. In fact they have had the monopoly of the priestly occupation and almost the sole guardianship of Sanskritic learning particularly the sacred scriptures, until the reform movement launched during the 19th century when other castes admitted themselves to the study of the scriptures in the original Sanskrit and in Bengali translations. The next in order of the precedence are the *Vaidyas* supposed to have evolved from inter-caste unions of Brahmins and the immediately lower castes who hereditarily practiced the science and art of Hindu medicine. Backed by their learning in Sanskrit they recently laid claim to the status of Brahmins. The third in order are the *Kayasthas* the most numerous among the higher castes who claim to be of the Kshatriya descent. The fact that the Kayastha caste is fairly ancient can be proved by reference in the later Puranas and Samhitas and by their geographical distribution from Bengal to Punjab. Their traditional occupation was white collar jobs like clerks, book keepers, scribers for the ruling authority and the like. The Bengal Brahmins and Kayasthas are not admitted to marriage relationship with their counterpart in other regions. In certain late *Puranas* which seem to have originated in Bengal the Kayasthas are classed as Sat-Sudras or good Sudras.

The rural West Bengal and in the most of the municipal areas nowadays the primary education is free and compulsory. Free supply of text books have been undertaken. Girls education up to standard VIII has been made free in rural and urban areas, including Calcutta. The common Bengali dress is the *dhoti* and a stitched upper garment - a shirt, a Punjabi Kurta or a half-sleeved vest. The urban population has started favouring pyjama and trousers for convenience and economy. The western style of dress is also being adopted by the more affluent as a status symbol replacing the achakan-pyjama and the Shamla Pugree, there is a general absence of any kind of headdresses, Muslims cover their head during prayer and religious ceremonies.

The women folk invariably wear the waist to ankle length sari in a graceful style. The upper part is covered by different styles of blouses. The Bengali is predominantly a rice eater. All but the very devout Hindus eat fish as a staple food item. He has a sweet tooth and everyone who can afford them enjoys sweetmeats made with milk casein (chhan) of which a large variety have been evolved. Another staple food item is dal (pulses) which supplements their protein requirements. A large assortment of vegetables and seasonal fruits completes the dietary. Bengalis prefer to other beverages,

The cattle fair at Sonepur.

Chhat Puja is being celebrated with great pomp and show.

A gathering of Buddhists at Bodh Gaya.

At Chhat Puja, a women in engaged in rituals.

Tribals with bows and arrows in their hands.

Tribal women

Traditional costume

Chhat Puja

Baliyatra Festival: Stems of bananas are floated in the river to celebrate their rich maritime past.

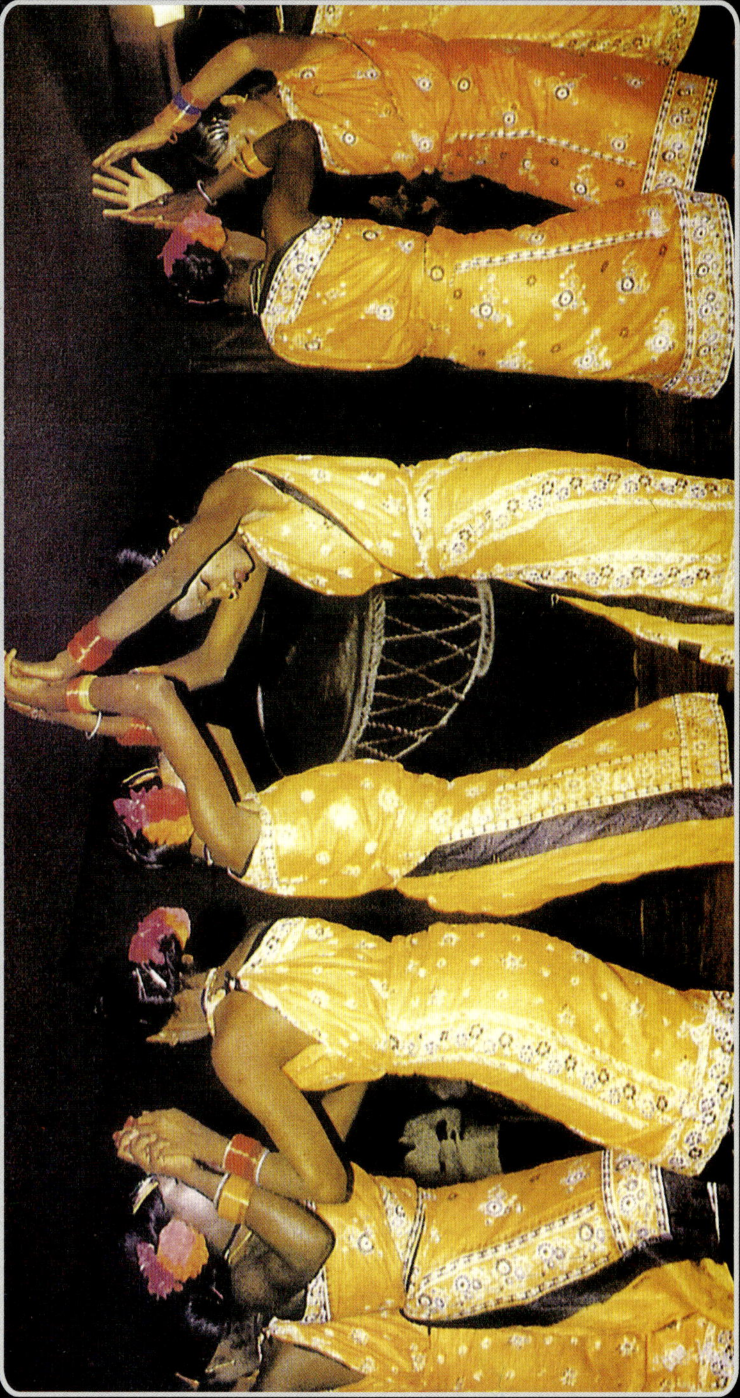

Tribal women dancing in a festival.

Huge crowd at the celebration of Jagannath Rath Yatra.

Sun-worship by ladies at Konark.

A huge crowd carrying Durga Kali during Durga Puja festival.

Women dancing in yellow garments in a festival.

A huge gathering in Gangasagar festival

Celebration of the Spring festival at Santiniketan.

the habit of taking sweetened tea has a spread to there remotest villages. Chewing of pan laced with lime, Kattha and arecanut is universal; so is smoking of tobacco, either plain in the form of bidi or mixed with treacle and spices for the hookah. Cigarette smoking has been spreading to rural areas but is still something of a symbol. Drinking of palm juice toddy and home made alcoholic brews is mainly confined to industrial labour and the tribal population.

The community of Banik, one of the traditional business communities have their largest concentration in this region. The communities of Kalwar Karan, Raju, Khandait, Kela, Kakmara (semi-nomadic migrated from Andhra Pradesh) and a small community of Portuguese are concentrated in this region. The only metropolis of eastern India, Calcutta has attracted people like the Punjabi, Bihari, Gujarati, Maharastrians, South Indians, Marwari, and also Anglo Indians, Armenian and Chinese. Some of the indigenous communities of West Bengal include the Kayastha; Karan, Prabhu, Brahman, Bagdi, Rajbanshi Mahishya, and Namasudra, while the immigrant people include the Bihari, Chinese Gujarati, and Jew or Bene Israel. The minorities in the state are Anglo-Indian, Bihari, Jew or Bene Israel and Sikhs. The Lodha is a denotified community while Anglo-Indian is a typical example of a miscegenated group. The service castes and communities which extend their specialized service include Baidya, Brahman, Nai, Bhat, and Jogi to mention a few. The non-pastoral nomadic communities include Kakmara and Nat. The Birhor, Chik Barak, Chirimar, Kharia, and Birjia are some of the communities whose traditional occupation centred on hunting, gathering, trapping and catching of birds and animals. The Gurung and the Limbu are the traditional terrace-cultivators in Darjiling and Kalimpong while the Mech have nowadays abandoned their traditional shifting cultivation. The peasant communities of West Bengal include the Ugra Kshatriya Bhuimali, Chasa Dhoba, Khen, Angarosk, Paliya, Sadgop, Mahishya, Kisan, Chasot and so on, the communities engaged in fishing are Bagdi, Jalia Kaibarta, Jhalo Malo, Kondara Kandra, Keora or Kewra, Kewat Keyot or Keot, and Namasudra. The Ahir and Goala are the communities who still practice pastoralism. The communities engaged in business and trade include Bohra, Gujarati, Subarna Banik, Jew or Bene Israel, Sikh and Parsi. While the people like the Bauri, Ghasi, Kalal, Keora, Kharia are by and large unskilled labourers. The people like the Chero, Hela, Lalbegi, Patni are engaged in unorganized services.

The state has an indigenous group of artisans called *nabasankh*, which comprises Gandha Banik, Napit, Tambuli, a section of Kumhar and such other castes which are considered clean from whom the Brahman can accept water. These *nabasankh* castes are socially superior to the artisan castes such as the Kamar or blacksmith, Chhutor or carpenter, Tanti (weaver) etc. In the

Western part of the state in Purulia and the neighbouring districts these *nabasankhs* are called as 'Lob Sena' giving a mythological touch to the ritual status. However, in the rural areas the related positions in the local caste hierarchy and the exact ritual status of the *nabasankh* groups is different. The major artisan communities in the state include the Dom or basket-maker, Kamar (black-smith and metal worker), Kansari (bell metal worker), Kumbhar (potter), Mahali (basket-maker), Malakar (manufacturer of exquisite ornament and decoration of *sola*), Malhar (*dokra* art and tattooing), Mali (garland maker), Muchi or Chamar (footwear maker and leather worker), Sutradhar (carpenter), Swarnakar or goldsmith etc. The Kunni, Pan, Tanti are engaged in textile weaving.

A unique feature of Old Bengal is the territorial endogamy. In West Bengal many of the Hindu communities have territorial segments like Radhi, Panchakoti, Banga, Barendra, and so on. Many segments have been sub-divided. For example, Kulin has been further subdivided into Kulin, Banga Kulin and so on, while Radhi have been sub-divided into Uttar and Dakshin Radhi. The origin of this practice lay in the inaccessibility of the territories divided by rivers and hills. Now with the improvement of road communication this practice is being abandoned.

A unique feature of the eastern part of West Bengal including Bangladesh and Assam is the proliferation of endogamous units within the large occupation group with sub-occupational variations. For example, the artisans are broadly divided into two endogamous units of those who manufacture and those who sell. This may probably be due to the land now being available for reclamation and cultivation, and peasant castes and artisan groups dependent on them taking advantage of the opportunity to expand, evolve and involve.

In West Bengal, the name and surname is an indication of identity and status. In ancient times, according to *Manusanghita* and *Brihadharmpuran*, the Brahmans used the surname Sharma or Dev Sharma; Kshatriyas used Burman or Roy Burman; Vaishays used Bhuti, while Sudras used the surname of Das. Before the advent of Sri Chaitanya the Brahmanical surnames became the symbol of social hierarchy. In *Bangalir Samajik Itihaser Bhumika* (1974) Prof. S. Chattopadhyay states that before the 5th century we have come across surnames like Mitra, Dutta, Dhara etc., which show the influence of Buddhist era. Various forms of Upadhyay like Mukhopadhyay and Bandyopadhyay etc. come in much later period and the name is by and large originated from the name of the places. The family surnames was changed enormously when the British Government passed Affidavit Act., 1875. Many peoples use titles as surnames. Majhi, Mandal, Sarkar, Singhas, Chakraborty,

Roy, Samanta, Majumdar, Choudhury, Pandit, and Shastri etc., are some of the titles used as surname. The surnames which are commonly in vogue in West Bengal includes Bose, Dey, Ghosh, Das, Dutta, Bandopadhyay, Mitra, Maity, Dhar, Bagchi and Lahiri. The most interesting feature is the presence of composite surnames like Sengupta, Dasgupta, Duttagupta, Roy Choudhury, Sinha Ray, Mitra Majumdar, Dutta Majumdar, Ghosh Moulik, Das Sharma and so on.

In the state, a number of groups either sanskritise their name or link up their name with traditional occupations or to raise their status in social hierarchy by adopting surnames with or without formulation of any myth like Ugra Kshatriya, Malla Kshatriya, Byagra Kshatriya and Poundra Kshatriya are the synonym of Aguri, Mal, Bagdi and Pod respectively. Similarly Bhat Brahman is the synonym of the Bhat, Baisya Behara is the synonym of Daoi. Some surname synonyms reveal the traditional occupation of the communities. Some of the surname synonyms are the sanskritised form of the community name, like Barujibi, Kansari and Sankhakara. Some synonyms reveal about their larger affiliation like. Chai Mandal, Kol, Kudmi Mahato, Malla Bagdi, Bagar Nabdak, Chamar are the synonyms of the Chain, Ho, Kudmi, Mete, Nagar and Muchi respectively.

Orissa Customs

The state of Orissa offers a kaleidoscope of sensitive visuals and of natural landscapes for her ancient cultural heritage washed by the waters of the Bay of Bengal on one side, and separated from the rest of country by various mountain ranges, is the state of Orissa on the east coast of India. Orissa is today one of the least developed states in India. Away from the main cities, one sees, nothing more pretentious than a mud hut with a thatched roof.

The tribes of Orissa are at various stages of civilization and socio-economic development. At one extreme are the group which lead a relatively secluded and primitive life keeping their core culture intact, while the other communities are indistinguishable from the general agricultural communities. Any society—tribal or otherwise, is comprised of organized groups of people who have learnt to live and work together for attaining common goals. Each society has its own rules of business and trade which helps people to define their relationship with one another and live and work together. Therefore a society is a going concern and functions on basis of the rules for living together.

In Orissa, the tribal people exhibit their cultural identity and distinctiveness in their social organization, language, food, dress, rituals and festivals and also in their ornament, art and craft. They have retained their own way of managing internal village affairs mainly through the institutions village council and the youth dormitory. The dormitory is the core of tribal culture and it reinforces the age-old traditions. In Orissa, this institution exists in many tribal communities in some form or other. The Juangs call it *Majang* and *Darbar*, the Kondhs call it *Dindaghar*, the Bhuyans call it *Dhangarabasa* and among the Bondos it goes by the name *Ingersin.* Of all the tribes, the dormitory system is well organized among the Juang. Conspicuous in the village, the Mandaghar is the largest hut. It has wall on three sides and is open in front. The wooden parts and side walls are carried with decorative figures depicting animals. The boys hang their *changu*, a flat tambourine like drum used at the time of dancing. In front of the *Mandaghar* is the small open space where dance takes place almost every night after the day's back-breaking work. The dormitory is, so to say, a school of dancing and expression of the communal art of the primitive people. The village elders assemble at the dormitory every day for every important event in their corporate life in order to discuss matters concerning the village welfare, settle the distribution of swidden and fix date and time for celebration of the village festivals, etc.

In these respects the dormitory may be considered as the centre of social, economic and religious life of the tribal village. The amazing conglomeration of traditions, customs, rituals beliefs, sorrows and philosophies that together constitute and vitalize the rituals and festivals of the tribal people, has descended from antiquity and has been preserved unimpaired to the present day. Every aspect of their life covering round- the year activities is intimately connected with religious beliefs and ritualistic practices. It is these aspects of their culture that give meaning and depth to their lives, and solidarity to the social structure of the tribal groups.

The tribal people believe that their life fortunes and destinies are controlled by supernatural beings whose abode is around them in hills, forests, rivers and houses. It is very difficult to standardize various Gods and spirits as their composition continually changes when old ones are forgotten with the introduction of new ones. Their godlings and spooks differ from one another in composition, function, character and nature; some are benevolent; some are neutral and some are out rightly malevolent. The malevolent spirits and Gods are cared more than their benevolent counterparts as they can bring misery.

Manipulation of environment being the main concern of the tribals, all the customs and ritual acts are directed towards stimulating natural forces. Illness or misfortune is attributed to the displeasure and malicious act of the

Gods ghosts or ancestors. The sacrifice of different kinds of livestock accompanied by all the rites and ceremonials of fetishism is considered the appropriate appeasement. Moreover, their extremely superstitious nature prohibits undertaking of any enterprise unless the Gods are first propitiated and the omens, after being carefully considered, are adjudged to be propitious.

There are religious functionaries among the tribes who cater to their spiritual needs. For example, the hierarchy of magician priests among the Saoras may be divided into three categories. The Buyya is a priest who presides over the agricultural festivals and offers sacrifices that especially characterize these occasions. The Kudan is a shaman who combines the functions of priest, prophet and medicine-man. The sacerdotal head among the Juang is called *Nagam* or *Buita*, *Pujari* or *Sisa* among the Bondos and *Jani* among the Khondhs. The post of these officials are mostly ascribed but not achieved.

As an institution marriage is recognised by all the tribes and castes of Orissa. Marriage is not an occasion for happiness, but when the bride takes leave of her parents, elders and friends, sorrowful verses are recited dolefully by the bride and sometimes by other family men and women of whom she takes leave. These verses, recited while weeping are known as '*Kandana*'. Many folk tales and folk songs take as their theme the day-to-day family scene in a typical joint household. The newly-wed young bride must not only cater to the varying tastes and humour, the changing moods of various in-laws, but also observe the in laws' family customs, rituals, fasts and other observances peculiar to them and their village.

Some of the forms of marriage popular among the tribes are marriage by capture or institutionalised force (often a mock-capture arranged with agreement between the spouses), marriage by intrusion when a partner intrudes into the family of the unwilling partner or unrelenting parents-in-law, or marriage by elopement when two lovers escape into the forest or to some distant place because their marriage was opposed by their family and relatives, marriage by agreeing to serve in the bride's parents house either on a trial basis or under a custom of bondage. In most of the tribalcommunities the very fact of living together of a man and woman through any of the traditionally recognised manners constitutes a marriage for all social customary and economic purposes.

Before marriage, in some tribal communities such as the Juang, the Bhuniyan, the Ho, the Khond, the Oraon, the Bondo and the Gadaba, youth dormitories offered opportunities for a lot of pre-marital sex-play and experimentation in youthful companionship. Pre-marital sex relationship is also known to be common among the Santhals, the Saora and certain other tribal communities. Even then this pre-marital sex is disciplined and institutionalised through observance of certain social taboos on sexual liaison between girls and boys belonging to the same clan. But faithfulness in marriage at least on part of the woman is insisted upon and rigidly enforced. All over tribal India, divorce is granted on persistent cases of adultery and the wronged husband, often also the wronged wife, has the right to claim compensation or restoration of the bride-price money and goods given to the other party at the time of marriage.

In the former princely states, as also during the zamindaries till their abolition after independence in 1947, concubinage was a recognized custom. The concubine or '*poili*' or '*rakhni*' was given a social status much lower than that of the married wife, but placed higher above the prostitutes. The children of the concubine were customarily given some share in the ancestral property of the father, and the concubine enjoyed the right of maintenance and alimony from her man and her sons and step-sons. The custom was so widespread that it was often institutionalized. In tribal societies or among the Hindu peasants in Orissa, to remain unmarried is a curse, not only for the man and woman, but also for the parents and the other relatives. Similarly widowhood is considered a punishment for some serious sin committed either in this life or in the previous life. Because, among the higher castes Hindus widows were not given in marriage and had to undergo a number of fasts and penances and a veritable self-denial, closing their eyes to all the pleasures of life.

The widows were not treated well either in their father's house or in their in-laws' as they were considered inauspicious persons and hence a burden. The widows among the so called lower castes and the tribals did not though have to face such an ordeal, provided they were of a marriageable age and not considered as the witches. Widow remarriage was usually practised apart for the inheritance of the elder brother's widow by one of the younger brothers.

In the state society, a barren woman is regarded so inauspicious that it is believed that no other woman should take a bath where she takes her bath. They blame the woman and not the man in almost all cases of barenness. A large number of fasts, penances and other observances aimed at the propitiation of several primitive gods and goddesses including Shiva and Parvati and many local deities, devotion to the spiritually powerful Sanyasis, bathing at and visiting some famous pilgrimage centresall these are done to remove the evil of barrenness. In tribal society barrenness is also a matter of concern for the relatives that may lead to a divorce or marriage with a second or even a third woman. The preference for having sons is widespread in tribal and non-tribal societies. The ceremonies connected with childbirth are more elaborate and lively in case of the male child, than that of the female one. The Hindu higher castes become anxious to have at least one male child, so that he would be ritually qualified to offer the proper oblations to the manes of ancestral spirits. They believe that, unless such oblations are offered by a male descendant, who perpetuates the patrilineal descent, the ancestors will be tormented in the hell.

In Orissa, the Hindus cremate their dead, except the young children, the adults who die of epidemics or of snake bite, and sanyasi who has forsaken the world who are all given a burial and in some cases thrown into the river. In tribal society, the custom varies from community to community. Those who are Hinduised like Gond, the Bhuiyan and others cremate their dead, whereas other tribals bury them. But if a tiger kills a victim he or she is not cremated, even if cremation is the usual custom.

In case of death of a pregnant woman, the foetus is taken out of the womb to be given a separate burial. As the pregnant woman is universally believed to become a dangerous ghost which tries to snatch away babies out of frustration, her grave in order to pin her down at the place where she is buried. Whether Hindus, Christian, Muslim or the primitive tribal, all have the common belief of the immortality of the soul. Among the Hindus the soul is reborn in human or in some other form according to the religious merits earned by the dead in the previous lives. The disembodies soul may go to heaven or hell in accordance with one's *Karmaphala* or the balance of the fruits of action through a series of former lives. Every yearthe ancestral spirits are offered *Shraddha* oblations at least once.

The Muslim and Christian souls of the dead await the final judgment from God at the end of the world. But among the tribal people, the soul usually goes to the underground world but always keep watch on the living descendants, protecting or punishing them through bringing illness or misfortune if they morally or spiritually go astray. Funeral ceremonies in almost all communities are so intricate and expensive that many tribal families get themselves literally bound to richer brethren or to neighbours for generations because of the debts they incur to meet the expenses. On completion of the funeral ceremony, the close relatives, and among the tribal group, the entire, village, indulge in merriment.

Almost all the castes in Orissa have the caste panchyat at various levels, at the village in whole or in a small group of villages, in a region and in a few cases for the caste group as a whole. This panchayat of sub-castes elders had the right to supervise the social interactions especially in taking of food and drink from the members of other castes and avoiding sexual contact with members of the so called lower castes. Besides the panchayat used to pass judgment on cases transgression of marriage regulations, divorce, and adultery or in cases of partition in a family and choice of occupation and client etc. Further, the panchayat was competent to excommunicate members of the sub-castes when they contravened its regulations and injunctions and it could also prescribe ritual expiations in case of some specific sins committed (incest, killing a cow, killing of a Brahman, one's wounds getting gangrenous and infested with maggots—all of which were considered great transgressions). Though the Hindu Raja was the highest court of appeal in social and caste matters, and he had to rely up on his family Brahman Purohit or the other learned Brahmans, the caste panchayats were left much to themselves and led a semi-autonomous and self-regulatory authority.

Every tribal community in Orissa had at least a village council looking after the village affairs, rituals social, economic and political. Among the Oraons, the Mundas, the Santhals and the Hos etc., there was an inter-village tribal organisation with a series of functionaries holding hereditary positions as periodically selected. Among the tribes of Orissa murders are rarely committed for the gain of property. But murder for revenge is rather frequent, as also murder for jealousy in sex.

Bihar Customs

In Bihar there has been a good deal of mixture among various castes and tribes. Though Brahmans and Kshatriyas belong to the same racial stock. The lower castes like the Koiri, Kurmi, Kahar and Ahir represent various racial strains. Caste rivalries and prejudices are numerous in Bihar. The narrow-mindedness of the people is one of the main causes of unsatisfactory state of Bihar politics. But now though modern life, better education and above all the efforts of its enlightened youth, are gradually doing away with such narrow prejudices. In the state, Brahman, Bhumihar, Rajput, Banias and Kayastha are the dominant castes. Kayasthas and Banias are the two important caste groups in the urban areas.

The Kayasthas are prominent in all modern professional occupations and are generally given the status of elite castes. The Banias predominate in industry, trade and commerce. Bhumihars are regarded as a caste different from the Brahmans who consider the former inferior in the social hierarchy. Members of all these caste groups have occupied prominent positions in the educational and political sphere in the state. The other land owning castes are Ahirs (Yadavas), Kurmis and Koiris in the plains of Bihar. The Ahirs or Yadavas are the agriculturists and pastoral caste. Cattle-raising is their hereditary occupation, most of them are settled cultivators. Some still roam about selling milk and ghee. Koiris are agriculturists, distinguished from Kurmis and other purely cultivating castes by their skill in growing vegetables and other special cash crops. In the neighbourhood of large towns they work as market-gardeners. Many Koiris are rich land owners. Some of them are still prosperous cultivators, holding occupancy rights.

The most notable among the schedule castes are Bhumij, Chamar (Mochi), Dhobi, Dom, Dusadh, Musahar, Nat and Pasi. Their means of livelihood still being hard manual and menial. About 92 percent of the total population of these castes are confined to the rural side while those in the towns and cities are slum-dwellers who also work on pavements. Although education is free for them, a vast majority of them still continue to wallow in illiteracy and thus in poverty.

The Musahars are field-labours whose wages are paid in cash or in kind according to the traditional custom in the villages. Most of them live outside the village. Only a few have attained the dignity of cultivating on their own land. Another caste, Dusadhs are probably of aboriginal descent. A large number of the Pusadhs serve as watchmen, they are also employed as village messengers, grooms, elephant drivers and wood-cutters, punkha coolies and porters. The Dhanuks are servant class found in every place in Bihar where there are high caste Hindus. The poor among them perform the menial household duties along with their family. Some Dhanuks are also cultivators while their females act as maid-servants.

Rabid prejudice prevalent earlier against the lower castes in Bihar gradually disappearing. The rich classes are regarded as ordinary plebeians. But in the rural side the influence of Zamindar (landlords) families is still considerable. It depends more on their position as landlords than as persons of title. In small towns they weild a certain influence on account of their high caste descent. In the larger towns the members of the upper classes are of small account unless possessing wealth. The middle classes in Bihar are mostly caste-ridden. They include mostly professionals and doesn't have rabid caste prejudices. They are the ones who almost monopolize the bar, the bench in judiciary the medical profession, trade and industry, the civil service and educational appointments. Many important posts in the Bihar secretariat are held by people of humble birth. The middle classes merge imperceptibly into the lower middle class and then into the plebeians.

In Bihar some socially inferior Brahmins are connected with the actual ritual of temple worship and include miscellaneous groups such as the *pujari* who performs the *pujas* in shrines and temples, the *Ojhas* or the occultists propensities who exorcise demons and evil spirits, the *Jyotishis* or astrologers who cast horoscopes and determine auspicious occasions, the *Pandas* who act as guides at pilgrim centres and *Mahapatras* who conduct ceremonies connected with the funeral rites of the upper castes in Bihar. The village priests pujaris among the masses are usually uneducated. There is a large proportion of hereditary priests. Many of the Brahmin *pujaris* are men from good families. The average Brahman priest knows little beyond reading the Karmakanda and he is often shaky at that. From the point of view of ethics and morality, certain priests as a rule lead pure and austere life. There are also a few Brahmin *pandits* who devote themselves to teaching Hindu scriptures to the Brahman boys.

Making gifts of land and cows to Brahmins was in the past considered very meritorious by the *Puranas*. Brahmins are generally strict about personal cleanliness and begin their private devotions well before sunrise, repeat the prayers at noon and again just before sunset calling it as sandhyas.

The Maithila Brahmins are divided into five hypergamous groups *Shrotriyas, Yogyas, Panjibadhs, Nagars and Jaiwars*. The religion of the average Brahmin is a curious mixture of Hinduism and Animism, in which belief in both evil spirits and godlings is the principal elements. Most of the Brahmins have their idols to which they make simple offerings in the open air. A few of the Maithil Brahmins are Shaivites who believe in the unity and immanence of god and have a deep sense of personal sins. Among the Brahmins there are hundreds of Agradanis or Kantahas who perform and supervise ceremonies when Hindus are cremated and receive offerings made on the eleventh day after a person's death. Bihar is also the ancient place of settlement of the Sakaldwipi Brahmins and they continue to be one of the most numerous classes of the priestly order. Some of these *Sakaldwipis* act as a *purohits* for people and explain to them the decree of fate with the help of an almanac. Many of them are of the Shakta sect and are guided by the *tantras*. Among the Brahmins of Kanoj greater part live by acting as *purohits*. Many of them are in service and some live by trade, and a great majority of them possess land which they cultivate by the help of servants, but they do not work with their own hand. They belong mostly to the sect of Rama, a few worship Krishna or the Shaktis. The worshippers of Rama have no objection to repeat the ceremonies used in the adoration of Shiva or of any other deity. Some of Saraswat Brahmins were former they landlords. Now some of them are merchants while others are priests. The Kanyakubjas act as teachers, priests, cultivators, soldiers, messengers, clerks and accountants, traders or cooks etc.

In Bihar the Muslims are commonly settled in Purnia, Darbhanga, Muzaffarpur and Champaran districts. In the Purnia district, Hindus and Muslims live together and has imbibed each others religious beliefs. Many of the Hindu and Muslim festivals are celebrated jointly with equal zeal. The Muharram 'Tazias' are usually borne on the shoulder by the Hindus and the Durga puja 'Akharas' are filled up by the Muslim enthusiasts.

Caste system was foreign to Islam, still it appears to have made foreys into the Muslim social system as a result of the contact with the Hindus. The Muslims are divided into two main classes, the *Ashroff* and *Ajlaf*. The Syeds, who belong to the first category claim descent from the prophet Mohammed himself, others in this category are Mughals, Iranis, Afghans, Pathans etc. The Momins, Kunjras and the Muslim castes-Julaha, Dhunia, Dhobe, Kulal, Chik, Lalbegi and others belong to the second group called as Ajlaf. The Mulick of Shahabad are all *Ashroff* and live by reciting poetry describing the love of Radha and Govindha; they worship certain saints and make offering at tombs and dargahs. In pre-Mughal Bihar, all the *Ulema, Mullas and Sufis were Sunni Muslims,* there were no sectarian division between Shias and Sunnis. However, the Christians and their missions found throughout the state not only engage themselves in evangelistic work but also run schools and colleges, manage several well-equipped hospitals and have many orphanages at Patna and else where. At Patna alone, the Roman Catholic Mission has five boarding schools, two for boys and three for girls, and a woman's college. The first Jesuit Missionary to have come to Patna was Fathe Simon Figuieredo.

The profession whose members stand highest for respectability and skill is medicine, Bihari medical men are among the best in India. The typical businessman in Bihar is generally a Bania, a Marwari or a Punjabi. In some examples, a person educated in a commercial college starts his career as his father's assistant in the shop. He earns a far larger income than the majority of professional men. Bihari businessmen are very practical and utilitarian. Another important profession in Bihar is the Bar. The purely professional lawyers and advocates are as a rule highly corrupt, breaking every rule of book, and detrimental to the interests of their clients. In Bihar, there is a little distinction between the upper middle class and the lower class. This in its turn lapses imperceptibly into the lowest strata society the peasant and the artisan.

Older modes in dress and ornaments are still in practice in rural Bihar and among Bihari women. The educated higher classes prefer native ornaments to the western type. Hindus and Muslims wear *dhotis* or pyjamas, kurtas or shirts, their women wear saris and heavy ornaments especially on joyous occasions. Educated people working in towns and cities wear western style trousers, shirts and bush-shirts. On special ceremonial occasions, they wear especially made Kurtas, Chudidar Pyjamas and Sherwanis etc. Most of the Hindus, rich and poor, perform their ablutions everyday. The Muslims, Sikhs and Christians use 'attar' and other perfumes. Perfumed oils are also widely used. The menfolk usually wear bala or bali in Shahabads, Kanausi in Patna and Gaya, the Gowalas wore Kundals. These ornaments are now fast disappearing except *malas* or bead necklaces.

In every part of Bihar women use aromatic oils. They wear profuse jewellery on special occasions and take particular care to wash their hair and arrange it in different hairdoes. Tattooing is a prevalent practice. Married women put in the parting of the hair vermilion. Tikli, a silver spot and bindi, a round one are placed on the forehead between the eyebrows. Many women pencil their eye with kajal or antimony preparations called *surma*. Poor women wear of silver necklaces *Chandrahar, tilri, panchlari, satlari, sikri* are different types of necklaces which women in Bihar wear. They have various ornaments for arms, wrists and fingers. Rings are in worn even among men. Bangles have always been popular among all classes of women. The position of women varies very greatly from one part of the state to the other. The written laws may be uniform throughout the country. In the unwritten laws the position of women is very unequal and wretched. Whatever a daughter receives from her parents, when she marries becomes the property of her husband, at her death it goes to her children.

The unmarried woman may not venture out alone, even if well over forty. A middle aged spinster has an unhappy life. A few women of exceptional ability though have succeeded in overcoming these disadvantages and acquiring considerable influence. Modern day girls are slowly beginning to obtain greater freedom. In the so-called lower classes, the position of the women is different. In the rural areas and among the so-called lower castes tribes husband leave their wives at their will and let them re-marry. There are many families in every village and city where the custom of *purdah* is still observed.

The region of Bihar finds mention in the Vedas, Puranas, and epics etc., and was the main scene of activities of the Buddha and the 24 Jain Tirthankaras. The hermitages of ancient monastic orders cluster in the plains and hill sides. The teachings of *Buddha* and *Mahavira,* deeply engraved in the enduring ruins and relics have with stood the ravages of time. Religion is very prominent in the daily life of the people. Besides the prominent ones like Hindusim, Buddhism and Jainism, other religions like Islam, Christianity, Sikhism etc. are also found in Bihar. The Hindus constitute the largest religious community in Bihar. Hindu piety involves rituals and ceremonies, celebrating festivals, making pilgrimages, building temples, reading and reciting the *Ramacharitmanas,* the *Ramayana* and chanting the *Gayatri Mantra.* There are a huge number of temples in Bihar. The Hindusim of the people of Bihar is chiefly characterized by *polytheism* which has given rise to many cults such as Shakta, Shaivism, Vaishnavism etc. Each cult and sect has its own special gods or goddesses, but all combine to revere other deities of the Hindu pantheon and join in their worship on occasion of different Hindu festivals.

The working Hindu religion of the peasant's everyday life consists of the propitiation of his '*Ishta Devata*' (favourite deity), ghosts (*bhuts*) and spirits (*prets*), in order that they may not afflict their worshippers or may grant them material blessings. The primitive propitiation of evil spirits and godlings and the worship of the Hindu gods go on side by side and quite often the same men make offering to both.

Besides the major Hindu deities Brahma, Vishnu, Shiva and Durga, one of the most important local deity is the elephant headed deity, Ganesha. Ritualistic greeting of the rising sun and the Ceremonial morning and the evening ablutions are widely observed by all devout Brahmins. Hindus believe in karma, image worship, rebirth and fatalism. Worship in the temples is conducted by Brahmin priests. He recites *mantras* and makes offerings for the worshipper, priests weild a considerable hold over the devout people especially in the rural areas. Their advice is sought when a difficulty arises usually by the women. There are countless grotesque and degrading superstitions in which so many of the peasants and labourers still seek councel from the priest.

The priests hope to retain their hold on masses through such means and even the more educated and liberal minded among them do little actively to combat such superstitious beliefs. In Bihar Hinduism is a religion of caste customs and usages. Its sanctions are ultimately social, its laws immemorial group customs and its tribunal the committee of the fraternity, it presents itself to the ordinary man not as a statement of the eternal principles of morality, but as a formidable code of etiquette ruling the details of his routine personal life. He finds himself greatly concerned that he should not marry a woman not belonging to his caste or sub-caste or dine with a man not of his own community, he should not help the wrong man or entertain vain caste prejudices against the right one. Bihar is known for factionalism, while others think of themselves as Bengalis or Punjabis, Parsis or Muslims their compatriots think of themselves only as Bhumihars, Rajputs, Kayasthas or Maithil Brahmins. Hinduism offers them the hope of salvation from the hard life they lead.

The people of Bihar follow a rich cultural customs, rites and rituals. In the north, the predominant themes are from the myths and legends of Hinduism. The Hindu deities, Lord Rama and His consort Sita and Lord Shiva and His consort, Parvati, form the main theme of folk paintings. Lord Krishna and His consort, Radha, are not as common a theme as they are in the neighbouring states of Uttar Pradesh and West Bengal. Also included, either under the guise of the Hindu deities as couples, or more overtly by paintings of man and woman as husband and wife, is the theme of procreation. These paintings frequently adorn the nuptial chamber, the Kohbar, of a newly married couple on their wedding night. One of the art forms of Bihar, the Madhubani School of Painting, has lately received much acclaim and popularity. Mention must be made of the Patna School of Painting or the Patna Qalaam which however does not exist any more. This offshoot of the well-known Mughal Miniature School of Painting flourished in Bihar during early 18th to mid-20th century. The practitioners of this art form were descendants of Hindu artists of Mughal painting who facing persecution from the Mughal Emperor, Aurangzeb found refuge, via Murshidabad, in Patna during late 18th century. They settled in the eastern part of Modern-day Patna, in Patna City, in areas of Lodikatra, the Chowk, Diwan Muhalla, and Machharhatti. They found patronage from zamindars (landlords) and the British officials. They shared characteristics of the Mughal painters, but unlike them (whose subjects include only royalty and court scenes), the Patna painters also started painting bazaar scenes and the plebeians.

It is this school of painting that constituted the nucleus for the formation of the Patna Art School under the leadership of Shri Radha Mohan. From a modest beginning in single room on the Govind Mitra Road in Patna, it has blossomed into the Government School of Arts and Crafts, currently housed in a large building near the Patna Museum. Radha Mohan was a disciple of Mahadev Lal (1860-1942), the last Master of the Patna qalaam. Some examples can be found at the Gallery located in the School mentioned before.

The modern districts of Gaya, Nawada, Aurangabad, Nalanda and Patna may be described as the holy of ***Buddhism***. These regions contain a fairly large number of places associated with the life and teachings of *Buddha*, the great founder of Buddhism. It was at Gaya that *Gautama* spent long years of penance and meditation before he finally attained *Nirvana*. It was to Gaya that he turned at an early stage in his search of truth. The tree under which he attained enlightenment thus became most sacred to the Buddhists and worship has consequently centred it from the earliest period of Buddhism. Since the times of Emperor Ashoka, Bihar became the last refuge of Buddhism in northern India up to the time of the Muslim conquests. The

Biharis still revere the Buddha today just as deeply as they honour Krishna, Rama, Shankara, Ramanuja, Kabir (poet) and Nanak (Sikh guru). They honour him as an incarnation.

In Bihar, Jains are the followers of the Tirthankaras. Vardhamana Mahavira, their last Trithankara was born about the middle of the sixth century B.C. at Kundagrama near Vaishali, about 27 miles north of Patna. Vardhamana Mahavira renounced the mendane world and became an ascetic. He led a life of extreme self-mortification under a shala tree on the banks of the river, *Rijupalika*, where he achieved the state called *nirvana* or *Kaivalya*. He was acclaimed as a *Kevalin* (supreme omniscient), *jina* (conqueror), *arhat* (blessed one) and *Tirthankara* (ford-finder). In a long wandering life of 42 years in north and south Bihar, he gathered a considerable following of monks known as *Nirgrathas*, or men who discarded all social bonds who after Mahavira's death became known as Jains. The Jains believe that God as such does not exist. A liberated soul, that of a prophet or *Jinas* is god. Absolute truth comes only to these periodic Redeemers. The universe-plants, animals and human is a plurality of *Jivas*, all subject to the cosmic process of Karma and rebirth. One can free onseself through austerity and penance. Mahavira breathed his last at a place called Pavapuri near Patna. A large number of Jain monks, too, breathed their last on the famous *Parasnath*, a mountain take its name from the 23rd Jain Trithankara.

Patna was also the birthplace of Gobind Singh, the tenth and last guru of the Sikh brotherhood and the place where the Guru was born is marked by a temple containing his cradle and shoes. It was Guru Gobind Singh who gave the present militaristic form and character to the originally pacifist Sikh following of Guru Nanak.

Tribal Society

Bihar and Jharkhand are the least developed states in India far removed from the modern-day civilization. In them some regions, and groups of people show extreme tribalism and primitiveness. About the tribals, Sachchidananda writes, "Older anthropologists thought that in primitive societies classes did not exist or might exist only in an embryonic form. The Evolutionists imagined a classless structure in the dawn of human history. While this may be true of some societies which are in the collectional stage, it is no longer true for the tribal Bihar where class and caste cut through society as deeply as in any other village in the non-tribal area. In most cases the class structure is intermingled with caste. Tribal people have themselves evolved social and political distinctions between groups in village consequent upon the development of certain politico-economic factors. They have also been living in contact with non-tribals who have a well defined caste and class structure. As the non-tribals are more advanced than the tribals in material culture and also in social status, the latter think it elevating to emulate their example. The continuous impact has been both regular and casual. Many Hindu castes have been living together with tribals in tribal villages for centuries and have been integrated into the social system of the village. Without them perhaps the economic structure of the village may fall to pieces. Indeed, it is these 'foreign' elements which complete the self-sufficiency of the tribal village. These two social groups have acted and reacted on each other and though they maintain their distinct identity, they are united for the one common purpose viz. to promote the prosperity and welfare of the village and its denizens. As for casual contact petty traders and low grade government servants who are representatives of a caste conscious society appear on the village scene every now and then. The total effect of such impact has been in some cases to transform the tribal group into a separate caste group like many of such groups in the village. When this metamorphosis is complete the village may no longer be called a tribal village.

"In some tribal villages in Bihar, tribes have tended to assume characteristics of caste. Ketkar defines caste as 'a social group having two characteristics : (1) Membership is confined to those who are born of members and includes all persons so born; (2) Members are forbidden by an inexorable social law to marry outside the group. (*History of Caste in India*, p. 15). Dutt adds that there are eating and drinking restrictions with members of other castes. (*Origin and Growth of Caste in India*, p. 3). Besides these within each such social group there are numerous exogamous units which may vary in social status. All these features are found in tribal Bihar. All the tribes are closed social groups and membership is confined to those who are born in that group. Natural members can be denied membership only as a punishment for some serious transgression of the tribal group and only in very special cases marriage with outsiders is tolerated. This transgression is allowed with one or two tribes which originally belonged to the same group. In other cases this results in excommunication and in Santal Parganas an extreme form of social punishment called Sitlaha is resorted to right such social wrong. Not only is intermarriage between two tribal groups forbidden but social distance is also expressed in eating and drinking restrictions between members of different tribes. If a person is guilty of the breach of this rule, he is liable to be excommunicated though this guilt is not so severe as the one mentioned before. In such cases on payment of the usual fine to the tribal social authorities the culprit may be readmitted into the tribal fold.

"Among the Munda and the Oraon the tribal community in the village is divided into two groups. One group consists of Khutkattidars or the descendants of the original settlers of the village who generally belong to one clan and the other comprises of later settlers. In most cases the majority of the second group consists of cognatic relations of the Khutkattidars. They are known as *Parja* and used to pay rent for their land to the Khutkattidars. They are not considered socially inferior to the Khutkattidars and are admitted to all social, religious and economic activities of the village. In the sasan of a Munda village only the bones of the Bhuinhars or Khutkattidar may be buried. But if a non-Bhuinhari family has lived in a village for several generations and is treated for matrimonial purposes as belonging to one of the clans of the village, the bones of its members may be interred in the sasan of one of the Bhuinhar clans. These villagers who are neither Bhuinhars nor residents of long standing are buried in a separate burial ground called masara. But even those alien families which have been accorded the privilege of being interred in the sasan may not have Samandiri (memorial slabs) erected to their memory. Thus even death does not blur the social distinction between descendants of village founders and later arrivals. The clan of the original settlers is the dominant clan in the village and most of the officers like Munda and the Pahan are recruited from it. In this dominant clan are two lineages, the Mahto or Munda Khut and the Pahan Khut. These two lineages are more or less equally important and enjoy greater prestige than rest of the village community.

"In the early days of British rule the Pahan was the supreme head of the village and acted as the elder or patriarch of the village family. He not only regulated the relations between the villagers and the supernatural but presided over the village Panchayat and collected tribute on behalf of the Raja. It is true that in his secular duties he was assisted by the Munda. After a lapse of time when the impact of foreign rule made deep impression on village life there was a reversal in the position of the Pahan and Munda. The Munda now became supreme in village affairs and the Pahan was relegated into background with only sacerdotal functions. In the gradual process of this reversal the nearest relatives of the Munda supported him against the Pahan who in his turn was backed by those Khut-kattidars who were his kin. Thus factions arose which brought the so-called Munda and Pahan lineage into exaggerated importance. The strife between two lineages spread to all villages. In the village of Anigara I even found the sasans of the two lineages situated separately though as members of one clan they should have been buried in the same sasan or bone burial ground.

"The entire Munda tribe consists of an elder and younger branch, the Mahali Mundako and the Kompat Mundako respectively. The former are found mainly in Tamar Pargana of the Ranchi District and are also known as Patar. Ordinary Munda or those belonging to the younger branch form the bulk of the Munda population. Both these branches are endogamous. The former are considered socially inferior to the latter. The reason given for this lower status is contained in a story which tells how the progenitor of this group ate a piece of umbilical cord of a member of the other group. But the real reason is to be found in the fact that this group has come less under the influence of Hinduism." (Koppors: *India and Dual Organization*: *Acta Tropica*, Vol. I, 1944, p. 80).

"In Tamar area the social stratification among the Munda has reached a developed form. Six distinct classes or castes may be distinguished. These may be grouped into two viz. (a) The Zamindars or landords and (b) the tenants. In group A we have at the top, landlords called Thakur who hold above fifteen villages each. Next come Manki who are lesser landlords holding upto ten or eleven villages each. Some of these landlords got themselves enumerated as Kshatriyas in the last census with a view to raise themselves in the eyes of their Hindu neighbours. But for all practical purposes they are Munda. Both these classes are endogamous and only in rare cases does an intermarriage takes place between the two. In the third class may be placed Munda or the village headman who owns only one village either in Khutkatti right or as a lesee of the landlord. He settles land with some members of his family and those landholders are known as Babu who form the fourth class of the social hierarchy. In group B are the Mundari who are Munda tenants. Intermarriage between Mundari and the above mentioned four classes is well nigh impossible due to great disparity in economic and social status. At the bottom of the Munda society in Tamar are the Patar who belong to the *Mahali-Mundako* branch of the tribe. Though they hold small bits of land there is no social intercourse between them and the upper five groups. Not only is intermarriage unthinkable but even water cannot be taken from the hands of a Patar.

"Thus we see that although the Munda community in Tamar belongs to a single tribe deep seated social distinctions have come to be formed. If somebody from one of the higher classes takes a fancy for a girl of the lower class he may keep her as a mistress without marrying her. A separate apartment in the house may be given to her and the man would not accept cooked food from her hands. Even in the same social class people would be chary of accepting food from the hands of a stranger. Relationship of some sort direct and indirect must be traced before food may be accepted. This social stratification resembling the caste system is evidently the result of continuous impact of the Hindu Caste system in Tamar.

"'One of the most important results of culture contact among the Ho (of Kolhan) has been the fission of the tribe into classes which share the same economic environment, co-operate with one another in all their economic undertakings, offer prayers and sacrifices to the same Bongas, participate in customary feasts and festivities, recognize relationship between themselves as members of the clan and the tribe and yet maintain their identity.' (D.N. Majumdar: Affairs Of A Tribe, p. 232). Any person who breaks social taboos is branded as Kajomesin (one from whom a Ho does not take food). No social relationship with an ordinary Ho and a Kajomesin is possible unless society readmits him after the necessary purificatory ritual. Even if he dies his corpse cannot be touched by members of his clan or village nor interred in the Sasan. Even when readmitted he does not attain full social status within the village. He finds it difficult to arrange the marriage of his children and has often to pay a higher bride-price than people of his status. The stigma endures and this has resulted in the formation of a class within class as the Kajomesins find it convenient to marry amongst themselves.

"Among the Ho two clans Kedenkel and Bage are considered to have the lowest social status. People of this clan even if taken in matrimony by other clans are not allowed to eat together. Like the Munda, the Ho do not accept food from persons with whom no relationship can be traced either directly or indirectly.

"Among the Dhelki Kharia we have a striking example of social stratification. Of their eight original clans the *Mail* and the *Topno* are regarded as lower in rank than the others. Members of other Kharia clans do not take food cooked by persons of these clans although they eat cooked food at the hands of Bhuiyas, Kherwar and Kawar tribes and Rantia and Mahakur castes. There is no bar however to intermarriage between the above mentioned two clans and the other class. The Mura clan on the other hand is regarded as highest in social rank. This is followed in status by the Samad clan. Men belonging only to these clans can act as heads of tribal council or panchayat. In tribal gatherings or feasts; such as at birth, death and marriage celebrations, men of the Muru clan are given the rank of *Pandiha* or giver of water and men of the Samad clan act as *Bhandari* or steward. A man of the Muru clan must eat the first morsel at a social feast of the Dhelki Kharias after which others may start. Social heads of the tribe and the tribal councils must be selected from either of the three clans of Dung dung, Kulu, Samad or Kerketta, who take rank one after the other and have social precedence over all the remaining clans. (S. C. Roy & R. C. Roy: *The Kharias*, Vol. I, pp. 128 and 193).

"Besides the cleavages in tribal society mentioned above amost all villages contain a number of outside castes which are employed in trades in which the tribals think it derogatory to engage. Oraon do not engage in weaving, basketry, wicker work and pottery. So in Oraon villages we may find one or two families of Ahirs or Hindu cowherds, Ghasi, Gorait, Julaha and Mahali etc. In Munda villages we find Lohar, Kumhar, Turi, Ghasi, Baraik, Tanti etc. All these little communities regard the tribals of their own village as occupying a higher social status than themselves. They have been integrated into the functional framework of the village because they do certain specialized tasks for the dominant community. Though considered apart from the tribals they co-operate in the working of the village economy and only in social matters do they form a separate entity. These castes now use the same types of household utensils, agricultural implements, tools and weapons, live in the same style of huts and wear the same kind of ornaments as the dominant community. At times they are so thick and thin with the tribals, most of them speaking the tribal languages, that it is difficult to identify them.

"In Tamar area each Munda family has its own set of Brahman, barbers and Gosain. Mundas in that area have almost adopted all Hindu religious ceremonials and hence the importance of these castes in that area. In some areas under the Khunti police station we find a caste called Manjhi who are landlords. Now almost Hinduized, they still have some relics of their tribal heritage.

"The Ahirs are important as they tend cattle of the villagers on a fixed customary annual payment varying with the number of cattle given to them for grazing.

"The Ghasi cut grass, tend horses and act as musicians at village festivals. The men are feared as petty thieves and their woman are reputed to have easy morals. Col. Dalton speaks of them as 'an extra-ordinary tribe, foul parasites of Central Indian Hill tribes.' Some times their woman act as midwives or nurses. (Russell and Hiralal : *Tribes and Castes of Central Provinces of India,* Vol. III, p. 27).

"The Goraits are a Hinduized aboriginal caste who carry messages, act as drummers, make combs and card cotton. Their women do the work of tatooers. In some villages the Gorait family hold what is called Geraiti Khet (service lands).

"In Oraon areas we find the Muslim caste of Julaha or weavers while in Tamar this work is done by the Tanti caste. Turi and Mahali are engaged in the making of baskets and other wicker work. Barhi (carpenter), Lohar (blacksmith) and Kumhar (potter) are also found in some villages.

"Apart from the tribal group and the Hindu or Muslim caste groups we have the converted tribal group. These Christian converts even if they do not form a substantial part of the village population lead a separate existence. They are usually closely knit group except in villages where they are converts of more than one denomination *e.g.* Roman Catholic, G.E.L. Mission and the S.P.G. Mission etc. as in village Birhu, three miles from Khunti. The level of aspiration of this group is much higher than that of other groups. Almost all of them are literate if not better educated, keep their houses clean, wear shirts and shorts and send their children to mission schools. Their centre of activity is the nearby church. The preacher but only looks after their spiritual welfare, but advises them on mundane problems of daily life. They have implicit faith in the leadership of the priest and at times where there is a conflict of loyalty between their village and their faith it is the latter that triumphs. In some villages they take part in the social life of the village but they have nothing to do with the ritual activities of the village. Other communities in the village maintain considerable social distance from the Christians. While the Christians have no objection to take food from the hands of non-Christian tribals, the latter can not do so. There is of course no question of any marriage between tribal Christian and non-Christian tribals.

"The effect of foreign contact on the incipient class and caste system in tribal Bihar may be seen in two stages. It may be that before contact began to produce effective results the social stratification based on the command over economic resources as in Tamar may not have come into being. The craze for imitation of the social system of the Hindus which characterised the first phase of the psychological reaction to the politico- economic changes must have led to the fossilization of the class system. Growth of education and of missionary activity brought about the second psychological phase. The rising tide political consciousness is bridging the gaps between the social classes. Members of all clans are thinking that they are all equal, one and same. Even people belonging to different tribes are forging new bonds of unity to strengthen their demand for more autonomy than hitherto enjoyed by them. But the two kinds of reaction cannot be put into chronological periods as both are present but at different places and even at different levels at the same place.

"At a time when resurgent Hinduism is forcing caste system to shed its rigidity and lose its stings tribal society has been striving to imbibe it from the low Hindu castes. It is a happy augury for the whole Indian social system that the second psychological reaction is strengthening our efforts for a classless and casteless society. What the picture will be after some time will depend on how swiftly we move to the goal of socialist society."

Jharkhand Customs

The recent agitations over the domicile policy of the newly-born state of Jharkhand is nothing, but an expression of the century old discontentment of the tribal groups of central India settled in Chhota Nagpur plateau over the influx of the non-tribal emigrants into their territory. Geographically, the present Jharkhand state is a part of Chhotanagpur plateau a traditional habitat of racially and linguistically different tribal groups including the Munda, Ho, Santhal, Kharia and Oraon. While the first four belong to Austro-Asian group the last one is known to be of Dravidian origin. All these primitive tribes speak different dialects.

Though, for anthropologists the region is a cultural synthesis converging three racial streams including Aryan, Austro-Asian and Dravidian, historically, these tribals pursued their calendar of activities in their respective societal norms and preferred to lead their life in isolation. Prior to the effective penetration and establishment of British colonial rule the principal conflict in Jharkhand region was between the tribals and the non-tribal emigrants, who settled here permanently under the influence of the then Hindu and Mughal feudal Lords. These non-tribal-settlers in the region, called '*Sadans*' emerged the dominating class and maintained their hegemony over the tribals with the help of the contemporary feudal lords. The tribals on the other hand persistently refused to reconcile with the feudal character of the *Sadans*, who though lived in the area maintained their separate identity.

To keep their isolation and separate identity from the non-tribal population, the respective ethnic groups launched various movements like Maler revolt (1772), Tika Manjhi revolt (1784), Kol insurrection (1832), Ganga Narayan revolt (1832), Santhal Hul (1855) and Birsa Revolt (1895), which were all against the outsiders. By nature these primitive people are aggressive militant, which they have even proved today. Extreme tribalism prevented them from coming under a unified leadership. Remaining in isolation and feeling aversion to non-tribals were common meeting points for these different tribal groups, they failed to develop a qualified and united leadership in the absence of an educated class, required for the success of any movement. Thus, the sporadic and localized revolts in absence of any unified leadership and ideology failed to turn into a social or economic revolution at massive scale. The British colonial power in order to create a class for manning its ruling apparatus utilized Christian missionaries to convert them to Christianity educated them and provide them the leadership. But this effort could achieve only a marginal success.

The tribals call themselves *Adivasi*, the first dwellers of this land, the people from the beginning. Where they came from, nobody knows for sure. Some came from the East through Assam; others from the North-West by way of the Khyber Pass through Baluchistan. The latter were the Dravidian speaking tribes, one branch of which found final refuge in the wild region that was Jharkhand. These were the Oraons. The former include the Munda, who claim they were the very first settlers in Chotanagpur region.

Today the Munda, the Oraon, the Kharia, Ho and Aanthal, the five largest groups of tribes on the Plateau, are included among the 29 Scheduled Tribes listed by the Government of India. They have found 'a lodging place in the turbulent mass of Indian civilization'. These three tribes – Munda, Oraon, Kharia – speak their own primitive dialects, have their own racial features, follow customs rites and rituals peculiar to them, withal living together on the Chotanagpur Plateau. They have many things in common: a lingua franca known as Nagpuria or Sadri; Sacred Groves of Sal; ritual Hunts, Sacrifices, Festivals, Witchcraft and sorcery. All three tribes are made up of exogamous septs, forbidding marriages between the members of the same septs. Among the tribals marriages are endogamous, restricting marriages within the tribe.

The centre of their culture and the source of their customs is the village, depending on which members of what tribe are in the majority. Each village has its own Sacred Grove, the sarna, consisting of five place to huts and fields to form a new village. In the village is the Akhara or Dancing Square meant solely for the young men and women of the village. In the village fields is the original water-hole, the Danri, whose water is necessary for marriage rites and for divination.

If the clans do not meet at the Jatras or fairs as they used to do in past, the confederacy of certain villages gather together on the high fields of Murma and Lohardaga every year to sing and dance the live long day and the long night through.

Animists, belief in the existence of spirits, worthy of respect as Singbonga or Dharmes "the Old One" who is the origin of every thing; the tutelary spirits, who guard their villages; the spirits of their ancestors, also known as the household spirits, the Tribes also believe in 'wandering spirits' who are not worthy of respect and reverence. Such spirits are the ghosts of people who have suffered violent deaths. And being evil in nature they are ever bent on harming men and cattle, bringing blights to crops sowing jealousy and rancour in the community. Another belief that the Tribes share with many other people in India is 'The Evil Eye' attributed to persons, men and women, whose looks and words can bring sickness, wither crops on what is good and beautiful, prosperous, promising.

As in every village there is a Cult Priest or Pahan who offers sacrifice in the name of the community to which he is accredited; there is also a sorcerer or witch-finder who claims power over the 'wandering spirits' who can neutralize the power of the Evil Eye and the poisonous praise. Implicit faith binds the entire Tribes to their sorcerers. Every village has its share of Baids or herbalists, versed in the curative properties of root, bark, leaf and fruit. Many of these Baids are sincere; some are quacks hoping to achieve results by magical means such as 'blowing', 'sucking' and 'sweeping' etc.

In Jharkhand, marriages are still arranged by intending in-laws. Brides are no more bought for head of cattre or money, however small a sum. The Tribes in Chotanagpur have not need of a presiding priest at their marriages. They marry following a specific ritual, under a Sal arbour known as Marwa erected for the purpose, in the courtyard of the bride's house, and often also in the courtyard of the bridegroom.

The Tribes bury their dead. After death rites deal with the re-entry of the spirit, or shade of the deceased, into the house in which the deceased lived. Such spirits become household deities commanding the respect and reverence of the family members. Only the shades of those who have died natural deaths are eligible for re-entry into their homes after death. Those who have died violent deaths are consigned to trees, ant-hills, and thorny bushes. The Mundas have recourse to a second burial, exhuming part of the skull, submitting that piece to a nominal cremation, then interring the charred bone under the clan burial stone known as Sasan Diri. There are other stones Bid Diriko which take the form of *menhirs* commemorating the memory of great men.

The state of Jharkhand was carved out of southern Bihar, home to several tribes. They have been living here for thousands of years and not much has changed in their life and culture till recently. The largest among them are the Santhals. Ethnically they are Proto-Austroloids and speak their own dialect. Their main occupation is agriculture but many of them work as daily-wage labourers in factories and coal mines today. Their social structure is clearly defined and seasonal festivals are joyously celebrated with dance, music and much revelry. The second largest tribe are the Mundas. Also an agricultural tribe, they are traditionally endogamous. Some clans among the Mundas have lately begun practicing exogamy. The other important tribes in Jharkhand are Ho, Kharia and Oraon. Most of the tribes inhabit the minerally rich Chotanagpur plateau. Most of the tribes are nature worshippers and animists before converting to more institutionalised religions like Christianity and Hinduism. Around 17 per cent of the tribal population of Jharkhand practice Christianity. The tribals rationalise the forces of nature by endowing objects of nature with imaginary supernatural qualities and worship them as manifestation of the Supreme God.

Jharkhand is home to such major tribes like Asur, Birhor, Chik Bariak, Ho, Hill Khariya, Kharia, Kharwar, Korwa, Mahli, Mal Paharia, Munda, Oraon, Phariya, Santhal, Saavar, Sauria Paharia, etc. The tribals of the state inhabit the resource rich Chotanagpur sifting plateau, practice hunting-gathering, and agriculture and settled-culture societies. Having spent centuries in the lap of nature, they have acquired a unique knowledge about their herbs and other natural resources. They can, therefore be, better described as a natural environmentalists. Tribals down the ages, have been fiercely protective of their habitat and customs. Consequently they have maintained their traditions and customs in its pristine form, till today. Several of the so-called advanced communities of India may not be able to compete with the egalitarian social structure of many primitive tribes. The status enjoyed by the tribal women is, indeed, enviable, in certain case. In fact, these societies have placed men and women on equal footing be it working in agricultural fields or other vocations.

Anthropologists define a tribe as a group of primitive persons having a common definite descant territory, dialect, name, religion and culture. Members of a tribes have a blood relationship and consequent strong kinship bonds. They have their peculiar social organisation and marriages are mostly between members of the same tribe. The Oraons are ethnically Dravidian and speak Khurukh dialect of Dravidian linguistic family. Oraons also speak Sadani, Hindi and other local dialects. The Oraons are the settled agriculturists. The economic values of forests to the Oraons is great because they still depend on minor forest produces for their subsistence. Occupation such as hunting, fishing, cattle rearing and crafts are subsidiary to agriculture for other peasants. Some of them also work as agricultural labourers and unskilled labourers.

The Oraons are divided into numerous exogamous clans which derive their names from birds, fish, animals, vegetables, plants or minerals. The main clans of Oraons are Toppo, Minz, Khalkho, Bakhlas, Khess, Munjni, Lakra, Tirkey, Panna, Beck etc. As regards marriage, monogamy is common among Oraons but polygamy is not exceptional. Bride price is in practice among Oraons for the marriage.

Widow remarriage is widely practised. Divorce is permissible on various grounds. The family of Oraons is patrilineal, patrilocal and patriarchal.

The *Dhumkuria* or Youth Dormitory has been among the Oraons as an important educational and economic institution. The Oraons believe in supernatural power, so all the offerings and sacrifices made are meant to protect them from the evil influences of these supernatural beings. Dharmes is their supreme god. They also worship their deceased ancestors. The Oraons mainly celebrate festivals like Karma, Khaddi, Sohrai, Maghe, Fagu etc. The *Karma* festival is celebrated in the month of September especially on Bhado Ekadashi. A branch of Karam tree is brought by unmarried girl with the help of unmarried boys of the village, who are under fasting.

In the beginning they keep it in *Akhara* which is worshipped by the Pahan (Priest) Khaddi is celebrated in the month of March-April. This festival is celebrated at Sarna place, where fowls are sacrificed by pahan (priest). The flowers of Sal tree are placed on every thing of the house.

In the state, Munda tribe is mainly settled in the districts of Ranchi. Gumla, Lohardaga, West and East Singhbhum, Hazaribagh, Palamau and Dhanbad of Jharkhand state. The Mundas are an endogamous tribe. Within the tribe, there are a large number of exogamous clans like, Bhengra, Bodra. Parti, Hansa, Kandru, Aind, Jirhul, Mundari, Nimak Munda tribe belongs Proto-Austroloid race and speaks Mundari of Austro-Asiatic language family. The Mundas also speak Hindi, Sadari and other local dialects. Amba, Balun, Gondli etc. Clan exogamy is the rule among them; the Bride price is generally paid prior to the marriage. The practice of widow marriage and divorce is common. The family of Munda tribe is patrilineal, patrilocal and patriarchal. The youth dormitory system called *Gitiora* was found among them, but nowadays this is out of practice. The Munda believe in numerous Gods and Deities. Their supreme benevolent God is called *Singbonga*. Next in importance are the presiding Deities of the village namely *Hatu Bogkao* such as Desauli, Jaher Buri, Chandi Bonga etc. These deities are of particular significance during agriculture and hunting operations. The Pahan, the village priest at Sarna, the sacred grove of the village, worships them. Then come the ancestral spirits, the *Ora Bangako*. Their blessings are invoked on every social and religious ceremony like the Hatu Bongako, which calamities are sure to overpower them. Besides, propitiate a large number of malevolent spirits and ghosts on different occasions of crisis and calamity. The Munda tribe celebrates several festivals like Mage, Phagu, Karam, Sarhul, and Sohrai etc.

In Jharkhand the Kharia tribe belongs to Proto-Austroloid race and speaks Kharia dialects of Austro-Asiatic language family. They also speak Hindi, Sadani and other local dialects. The main sources of Kharia livelihood is agriculture, hunting-gathering in forests and labour on daily wages.

Fishing, Hunting and Animal Husbandry are practiced as subsidiary occupations. The Kharias are divided into three sub-sections. The Dudh, Dhelki and Hill Kharia. The Hill Kharias are a most primitive among them. They depend upon forest resources such as honey edible roots, fruits tubers and herbs. The other sub-sections of the Kharias have been taken to plough cultivation and are better off than the Hill Kharias. The Hill Kharia is most primitive tribal group. A Hill Kharia house consists of only one room used as bed room, store room, kitchen and guest room.

Family is the centre of social organization in the Kharia society. Most of the families of this tribe are nuclear. Generally, the children set up their independent family following marriage. The Kharias have patrilineal, patrilocal and patriarchal family. Among them, clan system is strongly prevalent. The totem objects and animals are not injured or eaten.

The clans names among the Kharias are Gulgu, Bhuiya, Jaru, Badya, Tesa and Hembrom etc. The names of clans among Delkhi Kharia tribe are Muru, Soren, Samad, Barliha, Charha, Hansda, Topno and Mail etc. are the names of clans among Dudh. The marriage within the exogamous clan does not have sanction of the society.

The Kharia Kinship organizations is of the classificatory type. The Kharias are monogamous but polygamy is tolerated. The bride price is an essential part of the marriage in Kharia tribe. To avoid the brideprice, Kharias practice marriage by exchange in which sisters are exchanged by two men as wives.

The Kharias worships numerous Gods, deities and spirits. Their religious head is called *Pahan* by the Dudh and Dhelki Kharias and Dihuri by the Hill Kharias. This is a hereditary post. The Kharias worship the Giring or Bero at all religious ceremonies. They also perform ancestor worship called as Burha Burhi or Marsi Masan.

In the family, the deceased ancestors are invoked at all religious ceremonies. They dwell near the oven. The mountain spirits are known by the names of the hill in which they dwell in. They are invoked before hunting and for rain. The Kharias follow all the local religious ceremonies and festivals along with the traditional local ones. Their main festivals are Karma, Sohrai, Sarhul, Nawakhani etc. as Munda and Oraon tribes celebrate.

Ethnically Santhals are Proto-Austroloids who speak Santhali of the Austro-Asiatic language family. Apart from there traditional dialect, they also speak Hindi and other local dialects. The main occupation of Santhal is hunting and agriculture. They also collect minor forest products and involve in fishing and animal husbandary. Besides, they also work as labourers in coal, iron and other mines, factories and other fields. The social life of Santhals is highly organised. Santhals are divided into exogamous totemistic septs or clans including Baska, Pannria, Chore etc. The kinship terminologies used by Santhals is classificatory in nature. There are several kinds of marriage prevalent among the Santhals, like Kirring Bahu, Ghandi Jawae, Kiring Jawae, Itut, Nirbolk, Tunki Dipli Bapla, Sanga etc. The family of Santhal is patrilineal, patriarchal and patrilocal.

The Santhal religion centres on the worship and ceremonies of numerous Gods and Deities. Their principal god is Singh Bonga, who is the sun god. Marang Buru is the highest god after him. The important village Deities of Santhals is Jaher-era. Besides these Santhals also believe in other Deities like osai-era, Pargana Bonga, Manjhi Haram Bonga, Orak Bonga and Abge Bonga. The important seasonal festivals and ceremonies of the Santhals are Sohrai, which is celebrated in the month of Pous (November-December) when pigs, goats, fowls and eggs are offered by the Naike (Priest) in the Jaherthan. Baha or Ba festival is celebrated during the month of Falgun (February-March) with the coming of the flower on sal tree. This is the spring festival when the Santhals dance and sing to the accompaniment of Flutes and Pipes, Drums and cymbals. Bandhana puja usually takes place during Chait or Baisakh (April-May), when all the Gods and Deities are worshiped and offered their due and appropriate sacrifices and puja. Dancing, singing and drinking go on for a week or more during this festival with friends and close kinsmen. Ancestor worship crucial of their pantheon and every house and household has its own ancestor gods whom sacrifices and offerings are made during all important occasions, social and religious, in Santal life. In their religion there has been lots of changes. Some Hindu Gods and Deities have gone in the Santhal Pantheon including Shiva, Durga and such other Gods and Goddesses.

The Santhals as mentioned above are divided into a number of totemistic septs and sub-septs mostly named after some animals, plants, fruits or other material objects. It is a matter of investigation how far the septs and sub-septs have totemic relations with such objects. Totemism, in its true form is not present amongst the Santals. Nowadays, they do not believe in the actual descent of a clan from its totem, and the few legends of the Santals about the origin of some of their clans do not point to any belief in the descent of men from their so-called totems. All that they indicate is that the totem animal and plant had some accidental connection with the birth of their clan's ancestor. For example, the sept Pauria is called after the pigeon and Chonrey after the lizard; and the legend is that on the occasion of a famous tribal hunting party, the members of these two septs failed to kill anything but pigeons and lizards, so they were called by the names of these creatures. As with other totemic primitive tribes, a Santal also abstains from eating, killing, hunting or destroying the animal, plant or other objects that is his clan totem. Eating, killing, hunting, and destroying one's clan totem is decreed by the Santal as equivalent to killing a human member of his own clan. The idea of brotherly sentiments between the members of the same clan is present among them. The marriage between persons of the same clan is considered incestuous which may be taken as a confirmatory test of the above idea.

The Santals descent always reckoned in the patriline and a man has the same totem as his father; the totem of the mother's paternal line is not respected. As a female has no clan of her own, she is not a recognized member of her father's or of husband's clan and therefore need not to observe the taboos relating to their totems. But actually the Santal women do not kill any totem animal or any totem plant, just as their husbands do not kill or destroy any totem animal, plant and other object. Individual or sex totem is unknown to the Santals. Their totem is hereditary and not acquired. The members of a clan do not wear any distinguishing emblem or peculiar dress nor have they representations of their totem cut or tattooed on their persons or carved or painted on their houses or any personal belongings.

About the general customs prevalent amongst the Hindus, Sir Herbert Risley writes, "The doctrine of spiritual benefit would require her to devote her life to the annual performance of her husband's *sraddh. Tagore Law Lectures*, 1879, pp. 187, 188. Technical obstacles to her remarriage also arise from the Brahmanical theory of marriage itself. That ceremony being regarded as a sacrament ordained for the purification of women, and its essential portion being the gift of the woman by her father to her husband, the effect of the gift is to transfer her from her own *gotra* or exogamous group into that of her husband's. The bearing of this transfer on the question of her remarriage is thus stated by an orthodox Hindoo at pp. 276-77 of the *Papers relating to Infant Marriage and Enforced Widowhood* published by the Government of India : 'Her father being thus out of the question, it may be said that she may give herself in marriage. But this she cannot do, because she never had anything like disposal of herself. When young she was given away, so the ownership over her (if I may be permitted to use the phrase), vested then in the father, was transferred by a solemn religious act to the husband, and he being no more, there is no one to give her away; and since Hindu marriage must take the form of a religious gift, her marriage becomes impossible.'

"A powerful influence must also have been exerted by a cause which, so far as I am aware, has not hitherto been noticed in this connection. This is the custom which Mr. Ibbetson has called '*hypergamy,* or the law of superior marriage'—the rule which compels a man to wed his daughter with a member of a group which shall be equal or superior in rank to his own, while he himself may take his wife, of at any rate his second wife, from a group of inferior standing. *Panjab Census Report,* p. 856. Mr. Ibbetson adds in a note:— 'I am indebted to Mr. Coldstream for these two words [hypergamy and isogamy].' Hypergamy, indeed, would appear rather to mean 'too much marriage' than 'marriage in a higher rank,' but the highest classical authority in India prefers it to anoterogamy, the only alternative which suggested itself. The Kulinism of Bengal is perhaps the best known illustration of this law; but instances of its working are found all over India, and it clearly may have tuition wherever great pride of blood co-existed with a mode of life demanding the continual maintenance of a high standard of ceremonial purity. In a society so organised it must needs be that offences come, and that they affect the matrimonial status of the family by whom they come. The tribe or caste would then be broken up, like the Jews in modern Germany, into divisions of varying social position and purity of lineage, and intermarriage between these would in India be regulated by the law stated above, which appears to owe its form to the passages in the early texts which admit of the marriage of a man of a higher caste to a woman of a lower caste, but condemn the converse practice in the strongest terms. The first consequence of this restriction would be a surplus of marriageable women in the superior groups; for the men of a given superior group might, and presumably in some instances would, marry women of an inferior group, while men of this group would be barred for the women of the superior group. Competition for husbands would follow; the bride-price of early usage would disappear, and would be replaced by the *bridegroom-price* now paid among most of the higher castes in India; and in extreme cases female infanticide would be resorted to. Widows certainly would be the first to be excluded from the marriage market, for in their case the interests of the individual families would be identical with those of the group. The family would already have paid a bridegroom-price to get their daughter or sister married, and would naturally be indisposed to pay a second and probably higher, price to get her married again. The group, in its turn, would be equally adverse to an arrangement which tended to increase the number of marriageable women. Members of the higher castes, indeed, have frequently told me that these reasons of themselves were sufficient to make them regard with disfavour the modern movement in favour of widow marriage. For, they said, we find it hard enough already to gut our daughters married into families of our own rank, and things will be worse still if widow enter the competition with all the advantages they derive from having got over the first shyness, and acquired some experience of the ways of men. The sentiments of Mr. Weller sounded strange in the mouth of a Kulin Brahman, but the argument was used in entire good faith, and was backed up by much lamentation over the speaker's ill-luck in being the father of four daughters, all unmarried.

"The considerations stated above are entitled to whatever support they may derive from the fact that the castes which permit widows to remarry know nothing of the custom of hypergamy, and as a rule pay for brides, not for bridegrooms. Among these groups the normal proportion of the sexes, whatever that may be, at the age of marriage has not been affected by any artificial divisions, and there is every reason to believe that widows who are in other respects eligible have no particular difficulty in finding husbands. Polygamy prevails on a limited scale, and a large proportion of the men have two wives, the second wife being often a young widow chosen by the man himself for her personal attractions, after the first wife, whom his parents selected for him, has lost her looks and become little more than a household drudge. Another point is that the lower castes seem to have a greater capacity than the higher for throwing of sub-castes. Deviations from caste usage, trivial changes of occupation, settlement outside the traditional habitat of the caste, and a variety of similar causes which in the higher castes would, as a rule, merely affect the standing of certain families in the scale of hypergamy, tend in the lower castes to form endogamous groups, the members of which intermarry only among themselves. The difference is important, as the latter process does not disturb the balance of the sexes, and the former does.

"Let me now state as concisely as possible the actual practice which rules in respect of widow marriage in the four great Provinces—Bohar, Bengal Proper, Orissa, and Chotanagpore—which make up the Lieutenant Governorship of Bengal. In Behar a fairly liberal tendency seems to prevail. All castes except Brahmans, Rajputs, Babhans, Kayasths, and certain castes belonging to the Baniya class, which are not properly native to Behar, permit widows to marry again by the form known as *sagai.* The etymology of the word *sagai* is obscure. It has been supposed to be a corruption of *sa-gotra* or *sva-gotra;* the idea being that as a woman passes by marriage into her husband's *gotra* or exogamous group, if she marries again *within that gotra* (as she usually does), she constitutes an exception to the ordinary rule of exogamy. The Bengal term (*sanga* or *senga)* does not, however, bear out this view, and it seems probable that the word simply denotes cohabitation *(sanga),* and has reference to the fact that a widow marriage is established by the parties living together, and is accompanied by a very meagre ceremony, or none at all. The *phera* or pacing round the sacred fire is never practised on such occasions: the husband merely smears some vermilion on the woman's forehead and takes her to live with him.

"Widow marriages in Behar are usually brought about by the relatives of the widow. In some causes she may herself take the initiative, 'but,' as one of my Behar correspondents writes to me, 'public opinion is against love marriages.' The *sardar* or head of the caste council (*panchayat*) has also to be consulted, but this is mostly a matter of form, as he rarely withholds his consent. Although by marriage every woman is supposed to pass into her husband's *gotra*, no regard is paid to that *gotra* in arranging for the remarriage of a widow. Whether her husband's death is supposed to dissolve the *gotra* tie or not is a point I am unable to clear up. Certain it is that the persons whom she may not marry as a widow are the persons who would have been barred for her as a maiden. She may marry her late husband's younger brother, or younger cousin, and in some castes she is under a sort of obligation to do so. Marriage, however, with her late husband's elder brother or elder cousin, or with any of his direct or collateral ascendants, is strictly prohibited. To this extent her table of prohibited degrees is enlarged.

"The ceremony varies in certain respects according as the bridegroom is himself a widower or a bachelor. If he is a widower, he goes at nightfall to the bride's house in his ordinary dress with a few of his friends. There they are feasted during the night. Towards daybreak the "bridegroom, dressed in a new suit of clothes presented by the bride's relations, meets the bride, who wears a new cloth (*sari*) given her by the bridegroom, in one of the inner rooms of the house. There in the presence of her female relations he smears powdered vermilion *(sindur)* on her forehead and the parting of her hair. This completes the ceremony. Some castes add to it the form of throwing a sheet *(chadar)* over both parties, and under this sheet the smearing of vermilion is gone through. Brahmans take no part in the ritual, nor are any calculation entered into to find out an auspicious day. Early next morning the married couple go home to the husband's house without the final ceremony (*rukhsati*) which is used in bringing home a virgin bride. Even in the case of a virgin widow no *rukhsati* is performed; but as a child-widow is never married again until she has attained puberty, there is no necessity for a ceremony designed to celebrate that event.

"When a bachelor marries a widow, the ritual is more elaborate. Astrologers are called in to fix a lucky day; a bridal canopy (*marwa*) is erected in the bridegroom's house, and his ancestors are solemnly propitiated by Brahmans. In none of these ceremonies, however, does the bride take part, nor does she approach the *marwa*. She is brought to the house by night, and towards daybreak is conducted to an inner room, where the bridegroom puts vermilion on her forehead in the presence of the females of the family.

"Such marriages are not considered disreputable. The *sagai* bride has all the rights and position of a wife married by the full-blown Brahmanical ceremony. Her children by her second husband inherit equally with any children whom he may have had by a former virgin bride; they offer sacrifices to their father and his ancestors; they are received as members of his *gotra*, and they marry among the women of the caste. In these respects their position differs materially from that of the widow's children by her late husband, who properly belong to his family and are usually taken care of by his relations. Should they decline the charge, the children follow the widow; but they are not deemed members of the family into which she has married, and they are not allowed to join in the domestic worship or to share in the inheritance.

"So far, it may be said, the question of widow marriage in Behar seems to rest upon a reasonable footing. Symptoms of a tendency in the opposite direction are, however, not wanting. The Kurmis are a case in point. Some months ago I had a large body of them before me, and was asking 'what sort of Kurmis' they were. One group answered promptly, 'We are Ayodhya Kurmis: we do not allow widows to marry again.' Another group, of Jeswar Kurmis, admitted with considerable reluctance that their widows did remarry. In fact, the tone in which both sets spoke on the subject made it clear that the Ayodhya had adopted this restriction in comparatively recent times, and were very proud of the distinction. The Jeswars, on the other hand, were rather ashamed of themselves, and were particularly anxious to explain that did not allow the widow to marry any one she chose, but expected her to marry her deceased husband's younger brother. If she married an outsider, she forfeited all claim not only to her husband's property, but also to the custody of her children. It is possible that remarriage restricted by these conditions may represent an advance from the promiscuous remarriage practiced by the lower castes towards the total prohibition in vogue among the higher castes. It should be mentioned that the Kurmis of Behar are a perfectly distinct race from the aboriginal Kurmis of Chotanagpore and parts of Orissa... Both Jesar and Ayodhya Kurmis approach closely to the Aryan type of feature, and some of them are very fine-looking men.

"Other Behar castes in a state of transition as regards widow marriage are the Sonars, Sunris, Koiris, and Telis. Among the Sonar, the Bhojpuria and Kanaujia allow widows to remarry, while the Kamarkalla, Mairh and Ayodhiabasi do not. All five sub-castes are endogamous, and are subdivided into smaller exogamous sections, called *muls*. In Durbhunga, the Biyahut Sunris prohibit widow marriage; the Sagahut and Darchua allow it. In Gya, the Koiris belong for the most part to three sub-castes—the Barkidangi, Chutki-dangi, and Jaruhar, of whom the last-mentioned practice widow remarriage; the former do not. So also the Telis of Saran have five sub-castes, four permitting widow remarriage, and one, the Behuta (corruption of Biyahuta, 'the married ones') forbidding it.

"In Chotanagpore the castes which are, or pretend to be, of Behar origin follow the Behar rules in the matter of widow marriage. The aboriginal tribes—Santals, Bhumij, Mundas, Oraons, and Hos—permit widows to marry again without imposing any restrictions on their selection of a second husband, except that the prohibited degrees must be avoided. They also sanction considerable liberty of divorce at the instance of either husband or wife, and permit divorces wives to marry again. A step higher in the social scale, the transition to orthodox habits is well marked by the Koiris of Manbhum. These people, while retaining exogamous groups which stamp them as of aboriginal descent, forbid, at least in theory, the remarriage of widows, though they allow them to live in a sort of licensed concubinage not preceded by any kind of ceremony. Even this concession is unknown to the Lohars and Dhobis, who though occupying a very low social position in relation to the higher castes, have completely thrown off a practice which they regard as a badge of social degradation. They absolutely prohibit the remarriage of widows and divorced wives.

"The tendency to imitate the usages of the higher castes, which has been remarked in Behar and Chota Nagpore, operates much more strongly in Bengal Proper and Orissa. In Orissa, for instance, the Goalas take a higher position than in Behar, and rigorously prohibit widow remarriage. Throughout Bengal the Kaibrattas, though ranking below the Nabasakh or group of thirteen (formerly nine) castes from whose hands an orthodox Brahman can take water, marry their daughters as infants, and forbid their widows to remarry. In Dacca the gunny-weaving and mat-making Kapalis, and the Chandals, spoken of in Mau as 'the vilest of mankind,' have given up widow remarriage, and the practice appears to be confined to the Gareri, Rishi, Koch-Mandai, and other aboriginal and semi-aboriginal castes. Similar evidence of the gradual spread of practices prevalent among the higher castes comes to us from Northern Bengal. The Rajbansis of Rungpre, people of distinctly non-Aryan type, who have abandoned their tribal name of Koch in quite recent times, now pose as high-easte Hindus, and affect great indignation if asked whether their widows can remarry. The Paliyas of Dinagepore, also demonstrably Koch, fall into two sections—Rajbansi Paliyas and Byabahari, or 'common' Paliyas. The latter practice widow marriage, but are beginning to be ashamed of it, and in this and other matters show signs of a leaning towards orthodox usage. The former are as strict as the extreme ignorance of the 'fallen' Brahmans who act as their family priests admits; and as education spreads among them, they will go on continually raising their standard of ceremonial purity.

"The present attitude of the Hindu community towards the recent proposals to recognize and extend the practice of widow marriage may, I think, be briefly stated somewhat to the following effect:—The most advanced class of educated men sympathise in a general way with the movement, but their sympathy is clouded by the apprehension that any considerable addition to the number of marriageable women would add to the existing difficulty and expense of getting their daughters married. Below these we find a very numerous class of men who are educated enough to appreciate the prohibition of widow marriage supposed to be contained in certain texts, and who have no desire to go behind that or any similar injunction in support of which tolerably ancient authority can be quoted. Then come the great mass of the uneducated working classes, with rather vague notions as to the Shastras, but strong in their reverence for Brahmans and keen to appreciate points of social precedence. To them widow marriage is a badge of social degradation, a link which connects those who practice it with Doms, Boonas, Bagdis and 'low people' of various kinds. Lastly, at the bottom of society, as understood by the average Hindu, we find a large group of castes and tribes of which the lower section is represented by pure aborigines practicing adult marriage and widow remarriage, while the upper section consists of castes of doubtful origin, most of whom, retaining widow marriage, have taken to infant marriage, while some have got so far as to throw off sub-castes distinguished by their abstention from widow marriage.

"It is not suggested that the groups indicated above can be marked off with absolute accuracy. But without insisting upon this, it is clear that the tendency of the lower strata of Hindu society is continually towards closer and closer conformity with the usages of the higher castes. These alone present a definite pattern which admits, up to a certain point, of ready imitation, and the whole Brahmanical system works in this direction. Of late years, moreover, the strength of the Hindusing movement has been greatly augmented by the improvement of communications. People travel more, pilgrimages can be more easily made, and the influence of the orthodox section of society is thus much more widely diffused. The case of the Rajbansis–the fourth largest caste in Bengal—is an excellent illustration of the scale on which this force does its work.

"The practice of infant marriage has spread much further and taken root more deeply among the lower castes than its social complement, the prohibition of widow marriage. Both customs, the positive as well as the negative, have been borrowed from the higher castes, and are now regarded as paths leading towards social distinction. But the one is much easier to follow than the other. A man must get his daughter married at latest when she is fourteen or fifteen years old. To marry her five or six years earlier causes him no particular inconvenience, and confers on him whatever consideration may attach to religious orthodoxy and social property. On the other hand, to stop the remarriage of widows, in castes where the balance of the sexes has not been disturbed by hypergamy, must at starting cause some practical inconvenience. Among the lower castes women are much more of a power than they are among the higher' they assert themselves freely on a variety of public cecasions, and in many cases they have secured for themselves the right to initiate proceedings for divorce. One can hardly doubt that their influence would be exercised in favour of widow marriage, and that it would tend on the whole towards keeping that institution alive. Some allowance must also be made for the fact that the lower castes do not keep their women in seclusion. A good-looking widow shut up in the family zenana can be more easily sacrificed to notions of social property than a woman who goes out and meets possible suitors every day of her life. To whatever cause the difference may be due, it is certain that of two customs, both adopted under pressure of the same motives, the one—infant marriage—is almost universal, while the other—the prohibition of widow marriage—has only the comparatively limited currency already explained. Infant marriage in fact is now so widely diffused as to have almost entirely displaced adult marriage within the limits of the caste system proper. The aboriginal races of Chota Nagpore and the Orissa hills, the semi-Mongolian tribes of the Himalayan region and the Indo-Chinese people of the Chittagong Hill Tracts still maintain a system of courtship and marriage between full-grown youths and maidens which has been minutely described by several sympathetic observers. Directly we leave these tolerably compact tribes, and pass on to the less definite groups which form a debateable land between the tribe and the caste, we find either infant marriage in undisputed possession, or a mixed system which tolerates adult marriage as a resource open to those who cannot afford to do anything better for their children, but at the same time enjoins the more respectable custom of infant marriage for all parents whose circumstances admit of it.

"In the case of the lower castes there is little room for doubt but that the custom of infant marriage has been consciously borrowed from the higher castes in obedience to that tendency to imitation which we may almost describe as an ultimate law of the caste system. But how did the higher castes come by a custom which is without a parallel (at any rate on so large a scale) elsewhere in the world, and which cannot be referred to any of those primitive instincts which have usually determined the relations of the sexes? Neither sexual passion nor the desire for companionship and service can be called into account for a man marrying a girl at an age when she is physically incapable of fulfilling any of the duties of a wife. Primitive man knows nothing of infant marriage, nor is it easy to conceive how such an institution could have arisen in the struggle for existence out of which society has been evolved. The modern savage woos in a summary and not over delicate fashion a sturdy young woman who can cook his food, carry his baggage, collect edible grubs, and make herself generally useful. To his untutored mind the Hindu child-bride would seem about as suitable a helpmate as an American professional beauty. If, then, infant marriage is in no way a normal product of social evolution, and in fact is met with only in India, to what casess shall we look for its origin? The standard Brahmanical explanation is palpably inadequate. It represents marriage as a sort of sacrament, of which every maiden must partake in order that she may cleanse her own being from the taint of original sin, that she may accomplish the salvation of her father and his ancestors, and that she may bring forth a son to carry on the domestic worship (*sacra privata*) of her husband's family. So far as marriage itself goes, all this is intelligible enough as a highly specialised development of certain well-known ancient ideas. But it does not touch the question of age. Granted that the begetting of a son is essential for the continuance of the *sacra privata*, as Greek and Roman examples teach us, why should the householder, on whom this solemn duty devolves, go out of his way to defer its fulfilment by marrying a girl who has not yet attained the age of child-bearing? The Brahmans reply that the earlier in a girl's life she accomplishes her mystical functions, the better. But this clearly belongs to the large class of *ex post facto* explanations of which sacerdotal and legal literature is in all ages and countries so full. The priests and lawyers who compile the text-books find certain customs in force, and feel bound to invent reasons for their existence. Being unfettered by the historical sense, and disposed to give free play to their inner consciousness, it is hardly surprising that their reasons should be as often false as true. An ingenious explanation of a more scientific character has been given by Mr. John Nesfield in an article on the Tharus and Bogshas of Upper India. Mr. Nesfield says *Calcutta Review*, January 1885 :

"In the oldest type of society a woman was exposed to a double evil—the stain of communism within her own clan so long as she remained there, and the risk of forcible abduction into an alien clan, where she become the wife-slave of the man who captured her. And herein, I think, lies the secret of the seemingly irrational and certainly unnatural customs of Hindus, by which a girl is betrothed at six or eight and married at ten or eleven. The betrothal ceremony is considered by all classes of the Hindu community to be of immense importance. The force of public opinion has made it as binding as marriage itself. If the boy dies before the marriage is performed, the child who has been betrothed remains a widow for life. A father is publicly disgraced in the eyes of his countrymen if he neglects to get his daughter finally married before she has completed the age of twelve. There are few points in which the social customs of the Hindus have been more severely condemned. But though it may be granted that the time has long passed when any good could be gained from their retention, it may yet be contended that they have been of some use in their day, and that customs so opposed to the plain dictates of nature could not have been accepted by a rational people without some rational purpose. It must be remembered that the natives of Hindustan, at the time when they first appear in history as antagonists to the invading Aryans, were in the savage stage, and that they have owed their subsequent reclamation, imperfect as it is, to the subtle and ever-widening influence of Hinduism—a composite and very elastic creed, made up of the fusion of Aryan with native or aboriginal elements. I conceive, then, that the customs, to which so much exception has been taken, were the restraints imposed by this creed upon the rough matrimonial usages of the races amongst whom its lot was cast, some of which usages were formerly countenanced even by Hinduism itself as a concession to the prevailing savagery. Marriage by stealth, marriage by capture, and marriage by the ancient Hindu lawgivers as permissible to certain castes; and even. Brahmans, the holy priests, and teachers of Hinduism were allowed to indulge, in the kind last named. It is no wonder, then, that a religion which was forced to concede so much to existing custom should have sought to provide safeguards for the protection of the weaker sex through some counter-teaching of its own. By ruling, as it did, that a girl must be betrothed and married at a tender age to a youth of some outside clan, and by making this rule binding for life on pain of the severest penalties, it protected her both from the stain of communism within her own clan, and from the risk of forcible abduction into another. This explains, too, how it has come to pass that amongst Hindus, and Hindus only, the larger price is paid for the youth, and the smaller one for the maid—an exact inversion of the rule which prevails everywhere else. The Hindi word for betrothal is *mangni*, that is, 'begging' for a boy, for until the boy had been secured, the girl was not safe.'

"I have quoted Mr. Nesfield's views at length in order to guard against the danger of misstating an argument which I think inapplicable to the particular society with which we are concerned. The motives to which his theory appeals are no doubt highly intelligible, and in certain states of society would possibly be sufficient to account for the institution of infant marriage. It seems to me, however, that the society depicted in the Rig and Atharva Vedas must have got far beyond, if indeed they ever passed through, the stage of communal marriage and forcible abduction of wives. Courtship of a very modern type was fully recognized, and the consent of the girl's father or brother was sought only after the young people had themselves come to an understanding. As an additional and conclusive indication that the kind of marriage contemplated by the Vedas was the *individual* marriage of comparatively advanced civilization, I may refer to a remarkable custom, traces of which have survived in modern Italy—the lustration of the bride's night-dress after the wedding night. Zimmer, *Altindisches Leben*, p. 314; Gubernati's *Usi Nuziali*, p. 234. This custom is clearly incompatible with communal marriage, and could only have arisen in a society which set a high value on female chastity and had left primitive communism ages behind.

"For these reasons I prefer to seek the origin of infant marriage in the custom of hypergamy described above. But the fact that the social status of a family is determined not so much by the class from which it takes its wives as by the class from which it gets its husbands, would put the men of the lowest class and the women of the highest at a great comparative disadvantage, and would thus tend to produce infant marriage; for the number of possible husbands being limited, the natural tendency is to endeavour to secure them as soon as possible. That this motive operates strongly at the present day is plainly stated by one of the writers in the official publication *Papers relating to Infant Marriage and Enforced Widowhood in India,* p. 178, who says:

"Under these circumstances, when, in the case of a daughter, parents see that, unless they marry her at once, the one or two bridegrooms that there are open for their selection would be availed of by others, and that they would be disabled from marrying her before the eleventh year, and that they would thereby incur a religious sin and social degradation as regards the caste, they would seize that opportunity to marry their daughter, quite disregardful of the evil effects of infant marriages.

"Again, when the custom of infant marriage had once been started, under pressure of social necessity, by the families of the highest group, who had the largest surplus of marriageable daughters, a sort of fashion would have been set and would be blindly followed through all the grades.

"Two forces are thus at work in the same direction, both tending to disturb the balance of the sexes and to produce abnormal matrimonial relations between the members of different social groups. Enforced competition for husbands on the part of the higher groups, and the desire to imitate their superiors which animates the lower groups, combine to run up the price of husbands in the upper classes; while the demand for wives by the men of the lowest class, which ought by rights to produce equilibrium, is artificially restricted in its operation by the rule that they can under no circumstances marry a woman of the classes above their own. These men, therefore, are left very much out in the cold, and often do not get wives until late in life. An unmarried son does not disgrace the family, but there is no greater reproach than to have a daughter unmarried at the age of puberty. Husbands are bought for the girls, and the family gets its money's worth in social estimation. Bargains, however, must be taken when they are to be had; and no father dares run the risk of waiting till his daughter is physically mature. He is bound to be on the safe side, and therefore he marries her, child as she may be, whenever a good match offers.

"Many hard things have been said of infant marriage, and the modern tendency is to assume that a population which countenances such a practice must be in a fair way towards great moral degradation, if not to ultimate extinction. Much of this criticism seems to me to be greatly exaggerated, and to be founded on considerable ignorance of the present conditions and future possibilities of Oriental life. In truth, excluding the poetical view, that marriages are made in heaven, two working theories of the institution are at present in existence—one which leaves marriages to make themselves by the process of unrestricted courtship, and another which required them to be made by the parents or guardians of the persons who are to be married. The first, which we may perhaps call the method of natural selection, is accepted and more or less acted up to by all Western nations, except those who follow the French custom of *marriages de convenance*. The second, a system of avowedly artificial selection, is in force, with few exceptions, throughout the East. For all Hindus, except the handful of declasses who have adopted more less completely European ideas on the subject of marriage, and seem now to be on the high road to form a new caste, the bare idea that a girl can have any voice in the selection of her husband is excluded by the operation of three inexorable sanctions—by the ordinances of the Hindu religion, by the internal structure of the caste system, and by the general tone and conditions of social life in India. Religion prescribes that, like the Roman bride of early days, a Hindu girl shall be given (*tradita in manum*) by her father into the power of her husband; caste complications demand that the ceremonial portion of the transfer shall be effected while she is still a child; while the character of society, the moral tone of the men, the seclusion of the women, the immemorial taboos and conventions of family etiquette, render it impossible that she should be wooed and won like her European sister. To persons of a romantic turn of mind the admission that infant marriage in some shape must be accepted as an ultimate fact of the Hindu social system will sound like a final abandonment of all hope of reform. But there is more to be said for the custom than appears at first sight.

A moment's dispassionate consideration will show that if any sort of controlling authority is to make people's marriage for them, the earlier it commences and completes its operations, the better. Where the choice of a husband must in any case be undertaken by the parents, it is clearly tempting Providence for them to defer it until their daughter has grown up, and may have formed an embarrassing attachment on her own account. As for love, that may come—and, from all one hears of Hindu unions, usually does come—as readily after marriage as before, provided that opportunities for falling in love with the wrong man are judiciously withheld. This may seem a cynical way of handling the matter, but it is the only way that accords with the lines of oriental life as at present ordered, and it were folly to dream of making all things new." Adds Sir Risley in his monumental work *The Tribes and Castes of Bengal: Ethnographic Glossary* (1891).

1
Conceiving and Birth

A renowoned scholar Sachchidananda writes about the birth customs in Bihar, "The birth of a child is an occasion of great joy for the parents. The house is rendered ritually impure for a certain period which differs from tribe to tribe. At the close of the period the *chathi* or purification ceremony is performed with feasting and merry-making. The child is usually named after an ancestor, dead or living who becomes his *mita* or after the name of the day of the week on which the child was born. The formal incorporation of the child into the tribe takes place at his ear-boring ceremony. Whatever early training and discipling tribal children have is given at home by parents. Most tribal children have no formal education in schools. Little boys are allotted work in the family as soon as they are fit for it. They tend goats and look after cattle. Girls collect leaves and twigs from the forest, besides looking after younger children and helping mothers in the kitchen."

The customs relating to conceiving and pregnancy differ in different castes and tribes in the eastern region, including West Bengal, Orissa, Bihar and Jharkhand.

Seeking God's Benevolence

According to Amal Kumar Das and Manis Kumar Raha, the Rabhas believe that pregnancy takes place due to the sexual union between man and woman, still God's mercy is sought for in this regard as they think it plays an important role in successful conceiving and conduct of delivery. They strongly feel that without God's mercy no woman can become pregnant or no husband can impregnate a woman even if he has much vigour. The Rabhas of West Bengal often say that due to lack of God's mercy it is seen that even the wife of a strong and healthy man cannot become pregnant for a long time whereas a very weak man gets child within a year after marriage. The pregnancy of a woman is ascertained from physical changes in the body of the woman. When a woman feels herself pregnant from the stoppage of menstruation after copulation with her husband, she reveals about the same to her husband, mother-in-law, or husband's elder married sister.

Amal Kumar Das and Manis Kumar Raha write, "When the husband comes to know that his wife has become pregnant, he generally starts observing some prohibitions such as he refrains himself from killing certain living creatures, but he can catch living fish or bird. Moreover he tries to forbid himself also from doing any sinful deed. Beside these he controls himself from co-habiting with his wife when she attains her maturity in pregnancy (i.e after 7th month of pregnancy). All these prohibitions as observed by the husband, are for the welfare of the expectant mother and the baby in the womb.

"The wife (the pregnant woman) also on her part, observe a number of prohibitions for the same reason. She generally refrains herself from going to any burial or cremation ground or the house where any pollution (death or birth) has taken place or crossing a leveller or ladder or a rope with which is tied a cattle or a goat nor she can go alone to any jungle or lonely pond or some unearthly place, riverside, etc., nor can she take active part in any socio-religious ceremony, nor allowed to bring water with a pitcher taking in her waist. She is also not allowed to stay outside the house after dust in beheavelled hair nor can she take food from a stranger nor can she give anything to any outsider. In the same way husking anything with mortar and pestle and doing such other heavy jobs are considered to be injurious to herself and to the baby in her womb too.

"Many of these restrictions are observed by the husband and wife both from the third month of pregnancy and onward and usually much stress on these prohibitions are given after attaining the maturity of pregnancy.

"Generally the Rabhas do not observe any particular ceremony in connection with the first or successive pregnancies. To them pregnancy is a normal and usual matter of life. They know that after marriage husband and wife will have the sex-relation, the wife will be pregnant (of course if God bestows mercy on them) and ultimately a child will be born. But it is true that at the time of first pregnancy, both the husband and the wife become much more cautious regarding the spirit intrusion and harm caused by the evil-spirit, evil-eye, etc., and also by malevolent deities, and thus observe the prohibitions and restrictions more rigidly than in cases of subsequent pregnancies.

"Along with the restrictions on movement and work, a Rabha pregnant woman also observes some restrictions regarding sex-life and food. They believe that sex-relation with a pregnant woman is injurious to both expectant mother and also the child in the womb, and as such a general rule is followed that the husband should not have any sex-relation with his pregnant wife after 5th month of her pregnancy. It is believed that if a husband co-habits with his wife being pregnant over 5 months, the cohabitation causes injury to the child in her womb. Inspite of this belief it is often seen that the husband and wife cohabit even when the wife is bearing 6th or 7th months of pregnancy. Some times the husband compels his pregnant wife even at her maturity to satisfy his sex-desire, or the sex-crazy wife even at her maturity hounds her husband to cohabit with her.

"Regarding restriction on food the Rabha pregnant woman generally does not take in any form egg *(Touchi)* and flower of banana *(Latai Laylang)* as they consider these two items to be injurious. Except the above two articles, Rabha women take all other articles during their pregnancy.

"In the Rabha society it is often seen that the *Roja* (medicine man) gives *Jab* (a kind of sanctified thread) which the pregnant woman ties in her waist as a prophilectic charm in order to protect herself and the child in her womb from various evil powers. Add the writers, the customs and pregnancy related prohibitions are related to the Rabha community of West Bengal.

Dread of Infertility

Santal married couple dreads the prospect of infertility. They would secure adult respect only when they beget a child. In additions, children are also considered very important because of their potential working ability. So important is a child, especially a son to them, that a husband can lawfully divorce his woman if she is found to be barren, and a woman can also divorce her husband if he is found to be impotent or sterile. In some cases, the husband is persuaded to take a second wife. This, however, is done only with the consent of the first wife. Normally if a couple cannot beget any children, they consult a *raranic* who prescribes various herbal medicines. Archer, W.G. (1974:273-4) and Bodding, P.O., 'Santal Medicine', *Memoirs of the Asiatic Society of Bengal,* Calcutta, 10(2), 1927, pp. 133-426. If these prove to be of no effect, a recourse is had to supernatural aids. The woman approaches an *ojha* who divines whether *bonga* or ghosts are obstructing the way'. If this is so the *bonga* is said to be transferred into a fowl. If, however, all these means of securing the birth of a child fail the couple, as a last resort, approaches the *bonga* or *bangas* that are said to be latent in certain Hindu shrines, Culshaw, W.J. (1949:120).

Mr. J. Troisi writes, "The Santals believe that at no time of life is a human being more exposed to supernatural evil influences than while still in the mother's womb and at birth. Because of this, as Malinow ski in his study of the Trobriand Islanders points out, the very beginnings of human life are surrounded by an inextricably mixed-up medley of beliefs and practices (1954 : 37). Added to this, there are many precautions which have to be observed so as to protect the mother and the child in her womb.

The various precautions which a pregnant Santal mother must observe may be broadly divided into two categories (i) those meant to protect the mother and child from the unsatisfied souls of the dead, and (ii) those enjoined because of their effect on the physical appearance or the character of the child. Among the precautions in the first category, we find that a pregnant woman must not take any life, nor must she look upon or touch a human corpse. Contact with a corpse is believed to transmit danger. She must not weep when a death occurs. She must never go near rivers and streams where *curins* are supposed to dwell. She must not walk over the straw rope *(bor)* used for binding *bandis* (bundles for storing grain). She must not lie down in the courtyard or any other open space lest *bongas,* and a particular type of bird called *Puni-care,* might fly across her body. She must not put a flower of the *kanthar* tree (jackfruit) in her hair, lest the child should shrivel in the womb as a *Kanthar* flower does when it dries.

Among the precautions in the second category, we find that during a thunderstorm a pregnant woman must keep indoors and put her fingers in her ears so that the child will not hear the noise and be born a coward. She is not to make bread, lest her child's ears be wrinkled, nor must she plant or break turmeric roots, lest the fingers of her child be forked, or the child gets an extra finger. She must not make leaf cups lest child be born with a split lip, nor look upon an elephant, lest her child's tongue be very long and his ears be large and floppy. Certain restrictions are also imposed on the child's father. Thus, for example, he must strictly observe the rule against taking any life and must avoid all contact with dead bodies. He is to refrain from eating the flesh from the head of an animal offered in sacrifice or slain in the hunt," adds Mr. Troisi, the custom is related to the Santals.

But, according to Mr. P.C. Biswas, "when the Santal woman in Jharkhand and Bihar becomes pregnant, she and her husband observe certain taboos. The husband during his wife's pregnancy never kills any animal or any other creature, or participates in any burial or cremation ceremony and does not come in contact with any corpse. During the evening, the pregnant woman very rarely emerge out of the house, she never crosses any stream or river or she does not weep when any death occurs of her relations. On the occasion of the moon-eclipse she does not come out of the hut. She should not sit on the verandah with her hair or her cloth hanging down on the courtyard side. All these prohibitions signify that the Santals have a strong belief that malevolent spirits or witches can create mischief to their pregnant women.

Seeking grace of spirits

The community of Hill Kharia believe traditionally that successful birth of a baby depends on the grace of the spirits called as *Painsa-burhi* and *Painsa-burha.* Sometimes, the malevolent spirit called *Panchua bhut* causes the death of an infant either in the womb or soon after the birth. At least five kinds of *Panchua bhut* are distinguished in the community: (i) *Damra Panchua,* who causes death when the child grows to two or three years old. (ii) *Kachi Khaoa Panchua,* who kills the full grown embryo in the womb. (iii) *Bahurupa Panchua* who causes much labour pain and difficulty in delivery and the body is born with unnatural colour, (iv) *Tarpa Panchua* who causes the child to fret too much, and (v) *Barma Panchua* who attacks the all on a sudden. For appeasing these spirits prayer is observed at the crossing of two roads *(dopotha)* with sundried rice, vermilion, red cloth, red fowl, a small plank of *vela* wood *(Semocarpus anacardium),* a small winnowing fan, one earthen pot and a new piece of cloth. Whenever a woman stops menstruating *(dangua),* it is taken as symptom of conception. She is then placed under seven kinds of prohibitions: (i) Should not eat from the end of her *sari* or *khari chenga (anchar pati khas nak),* (ii) Should not eat rat, (iii) should not eat *dhamna* snake, (iv) Should not go to a hut where death has occurred, (v) Should not cross any stream river or drain by leaping over it, (vi) Should not eat fishes caught by trap, net, or rod and line and (vii) Should not wear new clothes and buy new pots from the village potter's hut. The custom is related to the Hill Kharias of the custom region.

Considering Barrenness as Misfortune

Mr. Himanshu Mohan Roy notes, in his book *Savara the Snake-charmers*, "The data on birth and pregnancy were collected by the author after an intensive study among the women of ten Savaras villages in the district of Midnapur. The data were also collected from the 'Dhais' or midwives and the medicinemen who attended the delivery cases.

"It was their opinion that the Savaras regard barrenness as a matter of misfortune. They generally believe that barrenness is caused by the machination of evil spirits. Sometimes it is supposed that barrenness is caused by witches of their own community. Some women among them are believed to be such witches and when detected in their nefarious act, or on mere suspicion, they receive a cruel treatment from the community. If no witch is found in the locality to be made the scapegoat, they think that barrenness has been caused by the curse of God. When a woman does not beget a child by the curse of God or for any other reason after a few years of her marriage, they perform some rites and rituals for induction of fecundity. They are of opinion that pregnancy or the blessing of children is due to two causes: one is the natural cause of cohabitation; and the other good fortune of previous life's deeds. When the natural cause becomes ineffective, the women perform certain rites and rituals or make Manasik or vow to a local deity for fulfillment of their desire to beget a child."

He states further, "They also believe in the efficacy of indigenous plants and medicines in curing barrenness. They believe that if the barren-women takes certain medicinal plants she may become pregnant. Such medicinal plants are, however, prescribed by a medicineman or a midwife.

"Stoppage of menstruation and all other symptoms of pregnancy are noticed. The desire for choicest meals increases at this stage, as the baby inside the womb also needs nourishment. Women generally dislike and avoid sexual intercourse with their husbands during the advanced stage of pregnancy. They also dislike certain types of food, such as, rice, fish, meat, etc. at the initial stage of pregnancy. It varies from individual to individual. The vomiting tendency is also reckoned as a symptom of pregnancy. . . "

Mr. Ray records, "The expectant mother among the Savaras generally does the household chores, e.g. cooking, cleaning, fetching water from the pond, etc. till the advanced stage of pregnancy. Thereafter she does only the lighter works. Besides the ban on hard manual work, there are a few other restrictions or taboos which are observed by the pregnant woman. These are noticed in all Savara inhabited villages.

"Besides unholy places like cremation grounds are not visited by pregnant women. The popular belief in this respect is that ghosts or evil spirits generally haunt or reside in such places and the baby in the womb may fall in victim to their malice and die consequently. If she has to travel to a distant place, a male member or some elderly woman always accompanies here.

"Some specific types of food like, prawn, crab, etc. are strictly forbidden for a pregnant woman. These are strictly forbidden on Monday and Friday. This restriction of taking food is called 'Paronkora". On these specific days, the women do not take non-vegetarian food like fish and meat, etc. particularly after five months of pregnancy.

"Some rites and rituals are performed by the pregnant Savara woman during pregnancy. Besides the restrictions, the guardians of the pregnant woman observe 'Manasik' or take vow to offer fruits, rice, or to sacrifice a goat to the local deity for the safety of the mother and the baby and a trouble-free delivery, Sometimes the pregnant woman throws a '*Singi*' (Heteropnenstis fossilis block) fish into a pond near the temple of the local deity. Such type of offerings however depend on the nature of the vow.

No ceremony is performed upto the four months of pregnancy. At the fifth month, a ceremony is performed which is called 'Sadh'. They also offer worship to God Bishnu. The worship is done by the priest. In this ceremony, different types of fruits, rice and vermilion are also offered to the God Siva and Goddess Kali. As this ceremony is held in the fifth month, so the expectant mother is fed with five kinds of sweets, five varieties of curries and rice. She also puts on a new red cloth at the time of taking such food. Such types of ceremonies are also performed at the seventh and ninth months of pregnancy. At the seventh month, seven types of sweets and seven kinds of curries are fed, and at ninth month, nine kinds of sweets and nine types of curries are given to her. The varieties of sweets and curries offered however, depend on the economic condition of the family concerned". The custom is related to the Savara caste in the eastern region.

Birth of a Girl Child more Welcome

A prominent anthropologist K.P. Bahadur writes, "In tribal society the birth of a girl is more welcomed than that of a boy, because the position is the reverse of the one existing in present day Hindu Society, and it is the girl who fetches the bride-price. A child is considered a gift of God therefore, barrenness is something not to be put up with, and a barren woman is usually divorced if the medicine man, excorcism, and worship to the gods are not able to remedy the condition. A Juang husband will worship the *sujna* tree if his wife turns out barren, and give her paste made of *sujna* flowers or *sujna* seeds to eat. Or he ties a sevenfold cotton string with seven knots round his wife's neck, believing this to be a kind of talisman which will procure conception.

"When it is known that a woman is pregnant, the members of the family show her all necessary consideration. Though in most of the tribes, the pregnant wife continues to perform household jobs and manual labour on fields and so forth, some of them spare the expectant mother from hard physical work at the sixth or seventh month of pregnancy. The Mundas, Hos, Gonds, Bhils and so forth, have this system.

"Taboos and restrictions in connection with birth are observed by almost all tribes in some form or the other. A pregnant Munda woman, for example, is not allowed to touch seed, for it is believed that should she do so the seed will not sprout. She must remain in the house at night, for if she ventures out, a witch *(churin)* will destroy the embryo. The Juangs do not allow their pregnant women to go to *devisthan.* She must not tie up anything, weave a mat, or plaster a house with mud. A pregnant Kuttia Khond woman of Orissa will never see a snake, and if she sees one by accident she believe that its evil spirit has entered into her, and has it exorcised by the medicine man."

The custom is prevalent among the Munda, Ho, Gonds, Bhils, Kuttia Khonds Tribals etc. in Bihar, Jharkhand, Orissa and West Bengal.

Infertility due to Supernatural Powers

As for the Mahali ideas about conception and conventional behaviour of parents during pregnancy of their daughters, They state without any hesitation that co-habitation between men and women results into conception, though sterility is attributed to some supernatural powers. They are not fully aware of the physiological processes through which conception takes place, but understand that the "Birji" or semen of a man entering into the woman's womb develops into a foetus. In Mahali opinion the Bongas or spirits are also responsible for the conception. They say, "A woman cannot conceive unless it is the will of the Bongas."

"Women only become fertile after they reach maturity. When the breasts of the women who have never conceived begin to sink or hang loose, the Mahalis think her to be barren. Their husbands sometimes consult the Ojhas or medicinemen to find out the causes of such barrenness. When the Ojha fails to determine the cause, he simply ascribes it to the will to the Bongas.

"...Mahalis consider that barrenness has increased appreciably compared with earlier days. They attribute this partly to the widespread practice of adultery. Their contention is that adulterous intercourse with so many men, spoils a woman's capacity for bearing child, when the wrath of the Bongas intermingle with this. There are various other supernatural influences which prevent conception, according to Mahali belief. These are witch-craft, curses of relatives and influences of dissatisfied Bongas and ancestors. They also believe that barrenness is moreover the effect of various magical rites and methods of unnatural and forced abortion, which women are said to employ in the case of unmarried motherhood.

"Among the Mahalis pregnancy often occurs before marriage, though hardly by regular intercourse, as may be called a 'marriage pattern'. But as illegitimacy of a child is a matter of social disapproval, when a girl becomes pregnant before marriage, she usually tries to induce her suitor to marry her without any loss of time. Pregnancy thus often provides the occasion for wedding.

"Conception is the primary stage of pregnancy. It is marked by physical changes in the mother and stoppage of her menstruation. The husband is little doubtful of its occurrence during the first month, since it sometimes happens that a woman misses her monthly menstruation cycle. But when in the third month he sees that his wife does not sleep apart, he is certain that she is carrying a child. In the meantime other signs of pregnancy become manifest. The old Mahali women say that when a woman becomes pregnant, her skin takes a new luster and glistens with a reddish brightness. Her body swells considerably and the contour becomes somewhat rounded, her breast becomes larger and firmer with prominent nipples having a darker shade and her belly bulges out prominently. The surest sign of pregnancy is a swollen abdomen from which they judge its course of advancement. A desire for choicest meals increase at this stage.

"There is no taboo in intercourse during pregnancy and a man continues to have sex relations with his wife at any rate during the first five or six months and sometimes even as late as the seventh month. Of course, there are some personal likings and dislikings regarding cohabitation during pregnancy. During pregnancy, intercourse is bad for the child as well as the mother. The child in the womb may be hurt or may die and as a result he may be crippled a man should cases intercourse at the advanced stage of pregnancy. Some women, however, dislike intercourse during pregnancy. A rigid prohibition on cohabitation commences after the child is born is observed for three to four months.

"The Mahali women is well aware that the pregnancy period generally lasts 10 months. The old people, especially, women can tell roughly the time when out of the womb the baby will be delivered. The relatives and parents of the pregnant women always make offerings to the deities and ancestral spirits at this time, offer prayers to the Bongas seeking their protection for the expectant mother and the child and for a trouble-free delivery. Besides, the pregnant women take vows to offer fruits, goats, fowls as sacrifice to the local deities for smooth delivery. As witch-craft is considered to be a real danger the husband always remains alert to protect his pregnant wife from witch-crafts. The contention of the Mahalis is that child bearing is safe so long as the witches could be kept at bay.

"The mother, on her part, observes a simple food taboo and refrains since it is customary, from going to some prohibitive places. But she ceases to observe such abstinence as soon as the child is born. The pregnancy taboos are considered important obligations among the Mahalis. Many of these taboos are found among other tribes of the locality and some regional Hindu castes, as such, some of these proscriptions may be considered as regional beliefs."

However, these are enforced almost in all the Mahali areas, as below:

(i) Unholy places like a burial or cremation ground should not be treaded upon by a pregnant woman. The popular belief is that the malevolent ghosts or evil spirits usually dwell in such places and the embryo in the womb may fall a victim to them and consequently die, if this is done. The smoke of the cremation ground is considered harmful and may cause a painful delivery. If a pregnant woman has to go to a distant place, a male member or an elderly woman of the family must accompany her. Fish caught in a basket-trap or fish coming out against the current of a river should not be eaten by a pregnant woman. The prevailing believe is that if a pregnant woman eats such fish, the embryo in the womb would become panicky and lingering pains like that suffered by those fishes in the trap and may affect her and the delivery may become difficult, as the child may move in opposite direction like the fish going against the river current. The Lodhas of the region have the similar belief. Bhowmick, P.K., *The Lodhas of West Bengal,* Calcutta, 1963. Fish caught by hook are also forbidden at this stage, lest the embryo in the womb should die of similar pain or of bleeding in its mouth, like the fish caught by the hook. A pregnant woman should not be allowed to sew torn pieces of clothes and should not pass the thread through the eye of a needle as the embryo may be born with crooked hands and blind eyes to such action of its mother. A pregnant woman is woman is forbidden from going to catch fish or where a fish-trap is set up, the common belief being that her presence would drive away the fishes. She also should not go to the corn-field as her presence may spoil the crops. The pregnant woman is not allowed to prepare cakes, lest her baby should be born with a cleft-lip, like the fissure which occurs during preparation of cakes. Moreover, she should not take a jack-fruit or wood-apple or pineapple. The prevalent Mahali belief is that if she takes these fruits, the child will suffer from similar cruption on its body, as the crests of these fruits bear.

According to Syamal Kant Sengupta "Other special behaviours of woman at this stage lack any ritual significance. They do not tie their clothes strongly at the waist during pregnancy, lest it may harm the child in the womb. A pregnant woman avoids any strenuous and heavier forms of labour, for instance, she does not go to the paddy fields to work as a labourer, or carry bamboo for basket-making, or earthen pitcher of drinking water from a distance, etc. But she continues to perform her household duties. She does so even within a few days of her delivery. It was a common sight to the author in the Mahali villages that woman in an advanced stage of pregnancy were grinding and thrashing corn, cooking and carrying water from the pond close to their huts. In practice, it is not until the child is born the Mahalis impose compulsory rest for the mother by confining her within the hut. A few informants told the author that some women become weak and crazy shortly after conception, though they soon pick up physically again and perform the daily routine of works as usual. However, they need the best and nutritious food during this period and their husbands try their best to procure it.

"After parturition, the women are given some kind of food to augment the breast milk. Some old women know the plants and vegetables which are taken to increase women's breast milk, for instance, the extract of Kurthi pulses *(Dolichos biflorus)* and boiled Kata note *(Amaranthus spinosa)* etc.

"The husbands treat their wives with better and urgent consideration during the pregnancy than at other times. Relatives and friends of the pregnant woman also take keen interest in her physical condition and news of her pregnancy spreads soon outside. In this way, the expectant mother gets special attention and help for her afflicted conditions. As soon as the child is delivered, the mother and the baby are confined into a room for protection from evil spirits which are hovering round this vicinity. The customs and rituals are practised among the Mahalis in the Eastern region.

Ceremonies, Rites and Rituals Related to Birth

Amal Kumar Das and Manis Kumar Raha writes, 'The Rabhas believe that child remains within the womb of the mother for 10 months and 10 days whereafter the child is born. At the time of child birth, generally the expectant mother remains at her husband's house or husband's father's house. For the birth generally no separate lying-in-room is erected. The main sleeping room or any other room is used as lying-in-room a bed on the floor is prepared for the pregnant woman. During winter months straw or grass is spread over the floor covered with a *Kantha* (rug made of old torn pieces of cloth) and a *chaddar* (bed-sheet) or a piece of cloth. No decoration is made inside or outside the room nor any picture is hung.

"From the day of birth till the completion and final purification (which usually takes places after a month, i.e., 30 days) no male member, even the husband, is allowed to sleep in that room. No outsider nor any stranger is also allowed to enter the room due to the fear of evil spirits or evil-eye or evil touch. For the treatment of the pregnant woman, severing the umbilical cord and also for other various parturition rites a *Dhaini* (midwife) employed. The *Dhaini* is either elderly and experienced Rabha woman or she belongs to some Hindu castes like Hari or Ghasi.

"When the labour pain starts, she is removed to the lying-in-room and *Dhaini* is called. Generally, the believe, the labour pain starts at the tenth month when the pregnancy is fully matured, but sometimes the pain starts even before the full maturity is gained at the 8th or 9th month. They also believe that if the child is born at this pre-matured stage, the child becomes sickly and less vigorous.

"On coming to treat the expectant mother the *Dhaini* first of all examines the patient to get an idea of her condition and probable time of delivery, by feeling the position of the baby in the womb. Sometimes the *Dhaini* understands the time of delivery by performing some magical rite. She pours some drops of mustard oil on the navel of the pregnant mother, and if the oil flows downwards, i.e., towards the vagina or thigh, then it is believed that the delivery will be finished quickly.

"Further by another magical means by *Dhaini* also comes to know whether the delivery will be quick and safe or not. This magical rite is performed in the following way:-The *Dhaini* takes a pitcher of water in which she revolves anti-clockwise a leaf for a number of times keeping that leaf by index fore-finger and the thumb. In each rotation she mutters incantation and also blows a air from her mouth. After this she gives the expectant mother that water to drink. This magical rite is known as *Jal Kasa* and the behind this is that this sanctified water will hasten a safe delivery.

"Before birth the *Dhaini* worships *Solomatrika,* deity for the child's welfare. For this *Puja* she requires some flowers (which she plucks), some plantain leaves, incense, sacred water containing some Basil leaves. She then sits on the doorway inside the room and keeps the flowers on the plantain leaves and the cup containing the sacred water by the side of the leaves. The incense sticks are kept burning. After sprinkling the sacred water on the flowers, she offers these flowers to the deity with incantations for safe, painless and quick delivery. After the puja the *Dhaini* gives her patient a little sacred water to drink and also keeps some flowers of the *puja* on her bed. After child-birth all the articles used in the *puja,* even the flowers in the patient's bed, are thrown away.

"Sometimes, when the pregnant woman suffers from acute labour pain, a *Roja* (exorcist) is called for soothing this pain. The *Roja* first of all, observes the patient keenly and then sitting by the side of the pregnant woman within the room, makes some vow *(Bai Sakao)* to the Goddess *Solomatrika* that if the deity concerned cures her of acute labour pain, the deity will be worshipped with such and such thing (the vow) on an appointed day after the easy and safe delivery. Sometimes even for protracted labour (and also for acute pain) the *Roja* gives for rubbing the belly of the pregnant woman, some luke-warm mustard oil sanctified by magical formulae or incantations for easy and quick delivery. Sometimes for the said reasons juice of the root of some tree is given to the patient to take or the root is tied to some parts of the body of the pregnant woman by means of a thread or a piece of cloth to act as an amulet.

"When the delivery is about to take place, the pregnant woman remains in kneeling or squatting position till the placenta (after birth) comes out. The child is allowed to be on the ground first in order to get the blessings of Mother Earth. As stated earlier delivery is conducted by the *Dhaini* (midwife). Though they do not have special training in midwifery still they are considered as traditional-professional midwives. Inspite of their lower position in social hierarchy, they are not hated even by the upper caste people for their profession. For this midwifery work a *Dhaini* gets Rs. 1 to Rs. 2 and sometimes one *Sari* and one or two kgs. of rice. At present with the opening of Health Centres, some enlightened and well-to-do Rabhas send their wives there for safe delivery and scientific treatment. They have also learnt of the safety and security in this scientific method of delivery applied in the Health Centres or hospitals or by trained midwife or nurse.

"During child birth only the elderly female-folk (generally married or widowed) are allowed to enter within the lying-in-room. But no male persons not even the husband, is permitted to be present in the room at that time.

Immediately after child-birth the midwife severs the umbilical cord by means of a sharp-edged bamboo-strip. After cutting the cord, the cut-end (navel of the child) is sprinkled with ashes of burnt plantain bark and the baby is placed on a bed made of torn cloth. During winter or rainy season the bed is made of straw on which some torn pieces of cloth are placed. The placenta is put into a cup made of the bark of plantain tree *(Kalar-donga)*. The baby is then washed with water. During summer cold water, and during winter luke-warm water is used. In the same way the mother is also treated. Then both are allowed to take rest. Afterwards the placenta which was kept within a plantain-bark cup *(Kalar-donga)* is buried under the earth within the room or sometimes just outside the room. If it be a still birth, the dead child and also the placenta is buried together a little away from the lying-in-room, just outside the boundary of the homestead. Nothing, in particular, is done in connection with twins or other multiple births. No infanticide is also heard of.

"After birth generally no treatment is done to the mother and the new-born except that if the mother suffers from eclaimpsia or any other illness the village quack is called who treats the mother. If the child does not cry after birth the *Dhaini* shakes it or gives it a gentle slap or blow through the mouth of the baby. If the mother has any bodily pain, she is generally given hot fomentation by the *Dhaini* or any other elderly woman.

"After birth the mother is generally given no food for that day. From the day after birth, she is generally supplied with stew of magur *(Calrius batrachus)* fish and hot curry of certain vegetable *(Asani sak).* They believe that this would cure body pain and also hasten the flow of milk in the mother's breast. Sometimes stew of *Musur* pulse is also given for 2 or 3 days. After 2 or 3 days rice, potato curry and pulse stew are given. But chilli, sweet cucumber, egg, inflorescence of plantain and meat are never given to a mother. At the same time she is not allowed to work hard or walk much. She is not permitted to enter into the kitchen or the place of worship. She is prohibited from cooking or worshipping or going to any house with or without occasion. She is not allowed to attend any religious festival taking place in the village or outside. This is also observed by other members of the family. No socio-religious ceremony can take place in this family unless the pollution period is over."

The Rabhas observe the birth related pollution period for 30 days by all the members of the family and sept. The writers add further, "The day when the pollution period ends, they observe *Chua Kamao* or purification ceremony. In the morning of this day the barber *(Napit)* is called for shaving ceremony. The barber shaves the head of the new born and also pairs off the nails of the mother. Other male members cut their hair, shave their beards and moustache and pair off their nails. When the shaving ceremony is over all the members of the family including the mother and the new born go to the nearest water source usually to some pond or spring or stream for purification by bathing. In the meantime the house is cleaned by a paste of cow dung and water by other female members of the family or some female relatives.

"After their return from bathing, the *Adhikari* is called for worshipping the deity *Balaram.* The arrangements are all made ready. Flowers, burning incense sticks, *Atap* rice, *Malbhag,* banana, milk, sugar, clarified butter, honey, Basil leaves, *Durba* grass, seat and napkin are all kept ready near the *Tulsi Mancha* (sacred Basil altar.)

"The Adhikari sits by the side of this altar facing eastward. The mother with her child also sits there. All others assemble nearby. The *Adhikari* then starts worshipping the deity. One after another he offers different articles to the deity muttering incantations each time. Then he revolves the incense sticks before the Basil plant for three times. In this way when the *puja* is over, he puts mark of the mud of the Basil altar *(Tulsi-mancha)* on the forehead of the child (if the child is male) or the mark of vermillion (in case of a female child). Afterwards he blesses the child with paddy and *Durba* grass and puts a flower of the puja on the ear of the child. The *Prosad* is then distributed to all the assembled persons who take the same with great devotion. Only the mother of the child does not take the *Prosad* as she is the convenor of the *puja*. In the evening a feast is given to all the invitees. The main items of the feast is either curd and chapped rice *(Chida)* or rice, pulse and vegetable, *Chakat* (rice beer) or tea being the common item. During this ceremony generally no sacrifice is made. The belief behind this is that the Rabhas do not prefer to kill an animal in the day of birth which act, they believe, will bring misfortune to the child.

"For their services in this ceremony the barber gets Rs. 2 in case of a male child, Re. 1 in case of a female child. Sometimes a well-to-do family gives the barber a *Dhuti* if there is a male child. The *Adhikari* gets 0.50 P. and some amount of uncooked rice, pulse, vegetables, etc. The *Dhaini* gets Re. 1 to Rs. 2 and sometimes one *Sari,*" they add. The custom is practiced among the Rabha Tribals of West Bengal, Orissa and Bihar.

Making Vows to make Sacrifices

Mr. J. Troisi writes in his book *Tribal Religion: Religious Believes and Practices among the Santals*, thus, "The Santals believe that a birth is rarely attended with any difficulty. In case of a difficult delivery, an *ojha* is called upon to divinise whether a *bonga* is present. If this is asserted, a vow is taken to make the proper sacrifices in the case of a speedy delivery. Midwives are engaged for the delivery. Though there are two Santal midwives in Pangro, certain households call upon a midwife from a neighbouring village. She is a Dom by caste. Several married women of the village, especially the older ones, gather in the house where the birth is to take place, to give courage to the mother, as they say. No men are allowed in the house as their presence is believed to hinder delivery.

"When the child is born, the umbilical cord is severed by the midwife using a sharp iron arrow. The placenta and the after-birth are then buried near the main door of the room where the delivery had taken place. The Santals assert that the reason for burying the afterbirth is because should it be eaten by a dog or any other animal, the mother will become sick and die. They also believe that if the afterbirth is buried deep in the ground, the difference in age between the present child and the next will be long. If it is, however, buried near the surface, another birth may be expected after a short time. It is also interesting to note that the Santals do not talk of their 'birthplace' but refer to it as 'the village where their afterbirth was buried. As soon as the child is born, the women present cry out the news to the husband who, taking a large stick, repeatedly beats the roof of the house so as to drive any lurking *bhuts* or *curins.* When the other villagers hear that a birth has taken place in their village, they ask 'Dipil se bharia?' which means,

'Does it carry on the shoulder (a boy) does it carry on the head (a girl)'.

"When a child is born, the house is considered ritually unclean. This ritual uncleanness is shared by the whole village. The *bangas* of the sacred grove are said to become defiled. No festival or any *bonga* worship is held in the village, and nobody drinks or dines in the house where the child has been born, till the purification ceremony is observed. One ceremony performed on the day of birth, is meant to protect the mother and the child. This ceremony is known as *Met Halan* which literally means 'lifting the eye'. The mother and the midwife sit facing each other on the floor of the house. The mother then fills a leaf cup with rice-beer and gives it to the midwife who throws away its contents on her left side. This is repeated three times and is believed to render both the child and the mother immune from any imminent danger.

"The cleansing ceremony after birth, is called *Janam Chatiar. Janam* means 'birth' and *chatiar* is a word connected with the Hindi word *chut* which means 'polluting'. This ceremony may be said to have a three-fold function: (i) it purifies the house and the village from the defilement caused by the birth of a child; (ii) it gives a child a name, thus formally admitting it into its father's clan and subclan, also giving it the protection of its father's spirits; (iii) it incorporates the child into the tribe.

"...Normally the *Janam Chatiar* ceremony is held on the third day after the birth of a girl and on the fifth day after the birth of a boy. Since, until this purifying ceremony is performed, the whole village remains polluted and no festivals, weddings or sacrifices can take place, the time rule mentioned is abruptly rescinded and the ceremony is anticipated if a festivals is imminent. This is also the case if a birth occurs on the eve of a wedding or on the day before a new moon. Even when postponed, the celebration must always be performed on any uneven day after the birth. The reason for the latter is that the Santals believe it is not propitious to name a child in a different month from that in which it is born. Misfortune may befall the child especially after his or her marriage.

"Blood relatives on the father's side are invited for the ceremony. They generally bring gifts of bead necklaces, cloth, bangles (in the case of girl), rice, etc., for the newborn child. The villagers also gather in the courtyard. Two essential elements in the removal of the defilement are shaving and bathing. (Shaving of the child and its father symbolises the passing of the child from one stage to another in his life-cycle). The barber shaves the male members of the villages starting with the village priest and ending with the child's father. Thereupon, the newborn child is brought out in the courtyard by the mid-wife. The barber then cuts some locks from the child's hair, which he puts in a leaf-cup. He pours some oil in the leaf-cup and gives it to the midwife who rubs the child's head with oil mixed with turmeric. Then the men go to the water tank to bathe. While they are away, the midwife winds two pieces of cotton thread around the arrow with which she had cut the child's umbilical cord, and collects the child's hair in a small bundle. On the return of the menfolk from their purificatory bath, the midwife, carrying the child, takes the mother and all the women present to bathe. Reaching the spot, she takes one of the strings from around the arrow and ties the bundle of hair. After invoking *Maran Buru* and the ancestral spirits of the child's father to take care of the child, letting it prosper in life and free from any disease, she lets the bundle float on the water.

"When everyone has returned to the child's house, the child's mother is made to sit down in the veranda with the baby in her lap. The midwife takes the other string wound around the arrow, soaks it in oil and turmeric and ties it round the child's waist as loin string (dora). She mixes some cowdung with water and lets it trickle into the left hand of the child's mother, who dabs it on her head and also sips a little. This concoction is credited with beneficent powers with the aid of which the mischievous influences of evil powers may be neutralized. The midwife, then, takes the child and entering into the house, puts it on the *parkom* (stringed bed) on which the mother lay when she had her labour pains. Making a mixture of *adwa coale* flour and water, the midwife sprinkles some of it on the four legs of the *parkom,* and on the child. She then brings the child out in the courtyard and sprinkles the mother and the assembled people. Once this is over, the midwife, taking the child in her arms, goes round the courtyard formally announcing the child's name."

Isolation of the expectant mother

The child is considered as supernaturally sent by the tribal deity *(Bonga).* They indicate it a direct relation with the supernatural world. With the recognition of pregnancy, a woman is gradually isolated from the rest of the villagers. In the initial stage of pregnancy, the isolation is not strictly maintained by the woman concerned or the village woman but in the advanced stage from the ninth month onwards she is isolated in the house even from the sacred place *Jaher.* She is not allowed to partake the food offered to the deities as she is thought to be polluted by the deities from this month onward. With the beginning of the labour pain she is separated from the rest of the members family house and made to stay in the inner part of the house, where the ancestral souls are kept (*Bhitar Orak*) or at a cowshed. After child birth, along with mother and the child, the entire village is deemed to become polluted. Restrictions observed during pregnancy as abstention of giving something from one boundary to the other, killing of any creature, from going outside of the house alone at noon or at night, has some supernatural value. As non-observance of these may cause harm to the child in the womb of the pregnant mother by the malevolent spirit *(Hoy Hisit).* Buddhadeb Choudhury writes, "Cutting of umbilical chord by mid-wife with an arrow-head and the use of a dried tail of *Calotes versicolour* (Ray Kakara) as its tongue has some magical value. The new-born baby is placed in the sun at the first opportunity after the birth is a custom to them through which they show the new born to their deities for blessing. As birth of a child pollutes the whole village and to eradicate the pollution, the males and the females take bath in the first settlers tank *(Bonga Pokhri)* with turmeric paste and mustard oil, served to them by the mid-wife on *Sal leaves.* After this bathing ceremony, rite of *Holong dak irichi* (ceremonial spreading of the mixture of *adwa* Sundried rice dust and water) incorporates the new born and the mother thereof within the members of the family which is recognized socially by the presence of the villagers. This rite is followed by the rite of *neem dak mandi* (ceremonial eating of the rice cooked with neem leaves) incorporates the new born and the mother among the villagers and during this time the parents of the new born are socially known to the villagers.

"On the third day of birth, the head of the family invites the *Majhi,* priest *(Naike),* assistant headman *(Paranik)* incharge of the youth messenger *(Godeth)* and offers them *Handi* (liquor) and proposes a name for the baby to be recognised by the gathering. Date of first hair cutting ceremony *(Hoyo ruar)* and name giving ceremony *(Chatiar)* may be performed on the same day. The midwife shaves the headhair of the child, takes it in *Phuruk* (vessel of Sal leave) and immerse in the water of *Bonga-Pokhri.* This immersion of the hair in the pond of the first-settlers is to bind themselves to each other supernaturally. This is followed by the rite *Bonga-Tala* ceremonial incorporation of the new born and the mother amongst the deities namely the *Marang Buru, Jaher era, Moreka-Turuiko, Puraudhul* etc. When the priest offers rice brew *(Handi)* to them which incorporates the new-born and the mother amongst the deities and lastly incorporates the whole village with the supernatural world. After *Bonga-Tola,* the assembled persons are offered cooked food which ends the name-giving ceremony (*Chatiar).* Till the performance of this ceremony, an individual is not allowed to go to the *Jaher.*" The custom is prevalent among the Santals in West Bengal.

Ceremony of *Sutamdaram*

Buddhadeb Chaudhury further writes, "Among the Mundas of the village studied a child is essential towards the fruitfulness of the marriage and completion of the family unit. Period of pollution after birth of a child and the purificatory rites indicate the extent of supernatural control on the societal and material affairs.

"The child is identified in the society by a name where the supernatural is invoked again. Choice of the name is not however, wider as it is restricted within the name of some of its agnates dead or alive. The bond of kinship thus extends to the decesed's family members. In the case of living, the relative enters into a new mode of relation with special rights and duties thereby intensifying the existing tie of the relationship. A tendency of giving other names is noticed, but still apologetically.

"In the case of the first pregnancy a ceremony called *sutamdaram* is performed in the 5th month. It is performed normally in the house of the husband. The father of the pregnant woman comes and takes an active part in the performance. He worships the god Dharma and prays for the prosperity of the coming child's cognates.

"For childbirth, a portion of the room or the verandah is covered up. A total period of pollution for 9 days is observed. During this period there are certain restrictions on the food of the woman. A midwife belonging to another community is called for cutting the umbilical cord of the newborn and for nursing the baby and its mother during the days of pollution. She lives in a neighbouring village. It is during the period of pollution only that the mother of the newborn and the midwife can touch the child. Relatives as well as neighbours can visit the house of the new-born but they do not take food there. The members of the family do not take fish, meat or eggs till the pollution is over. During this period all agricultural activities and ceremonies such as marriage or propitiation of deities etc. are prohibited in the house. Agricultural implements are not even touched.

"The purificatory ceremony is known as *Norta.* It is performed on the 9th day of the birth of the child. Besides the members of the parent's family, it is also attended by the parents of the mother and her maternal uncle etc. A few village elders are also invited to the ceremony. The Washerman and Barber play a vital role in the ceremony. They come from neighbouring Hindu village. The midwife is invited at the ceremony. The washerman washes the clothing of the members of the child's father's family and some of the lineage members. The barber pares the nails of the baby and the mother and shaves the male members of the family. The midwife washes the clothing of the child and its mother. The mother and the child now take their purificatory bath. The ceremony ends with a feast when flattened rice, puffed rice, some curry and rice beer *(handia)* are served to the invitee by the child's father. Midwife gets one seer of paddy for attending the delivery, half a seer for nursing the child and for the *Norta* in addition to five seers of paddy and one rupee in cash. She is also presented with the sari worn by the mother during childbirth. The washerman and the barber get a rupee each and five seers of paddy as their remuneration. Adds Mr. Chaudhury.

If the baby is born in the agricultural season, all agricultural, activities are prohibited to the members of the family. Then, the purificatory ceremony is held just after three days of the child birth called as soj. The ceremony is pertinent to the community of the Mundas.

Sweeperess conducting as Midwife

About the conduct of delivery and other birth related customs, rites and rituals Mr. Himangsu Mohan Roy writes, "When the pregnant woman feels the delivery pain, generally some elderly and experienced woman of the family or the community nurse caress her, and a Hadi (sweeper untouchable) woman serves as 'Dhai' or midwife. There is however no scope for setting apart a confinement room, because the majority of the Savaras have got a single-room small hut without any additional space to arrange for this purpose. However, a formal partition or screening is made within the hut with mats in one corner of the room to provide privacy. The midwife rubs mustard oil on the abdomen of the parturient woman, which is supposed to be helpful for smooth delivery, After delivery the midwife, at first, cleans the spot where the delivery has taken place and then she cuts the umbilical cord of the baby by a sterilised bamboo strip. Then she puts the placenta into a new earthen pot and then buries it under the floor of the room. The Savaras believe that if the placenta is buried outside or thrown away and thus it is eaten by animals, the new-born child will be harmed and even it may die. After delivery, the body of the baby is cleaned by a piece of cloth or napkin dipped into luke-warm water and then anointed with oil and turmeric paste by the midwife.

"A female barber is called to pair off the nails of both the mother and the child after delivery. The female washerman is also called on this occasion. She takes away all the dirty and unclean clothes and returns these for use after washing. Then the mother is also cleaned with a piece of cloth, but she is not given a full bath. Both the mother and the child are kept warm by applying dry compress. No other measure is taken or ritual is observed on the day of delivery. But on the day of delivery the diet of the mother is somewhat changed. She takes boiled rice, fried 'Maurala' fish, fried plaintain and potato, etc. Roots of plantain, inflorescence of maize and roots of 'tiki' are boiled with water and the boiled water is taken upto three days for quick drying up and recovery.

"The period of pollution lasts for nine days when the whole family is considered ritually unclean and debarred from participating in social and religious ceremonies. During this period, no worship is performed in the house. Sometimes the father of the child does not shave his head. However, there is no restriction to taking any item of food during the pollution period for the father as well as for other family members.

"On the 9th day, the purification ceremony is observed in the morning, when all articles of use in the house are washed and the floors of the hut are plastered with a paste of cowdung and water. The female barber comes on that day and cuts the nails of the mother and the child, and the female washerman washes all the used clothes for ritual purification. On the 21st day, the final purification ceremony is observed in the morning. On that day the same types of purification rituals are observed as on the ninth day. The speciality is that, on this day, all the members of the family and the attending barber and washerman rub turmeric paste and oil on their body and take bath in a tank. The new-born child and the mother also take bath in the pond. The earthen cooking pots are thrown outside and new pots are used for cooking. After this ceremony all the members of the family becomes ritually purified.

"The midwife gets five to ten rupees, a brass pot and a new piece of cloth for her services. The woman barber gets 1 kg rice and one rupee in cash thrice, once for the first day of delivery, next on the 9th day and lastly on the 21st day. The washer-women is also paid similarly for her services.

"The first rice-feeding ceremony is observed after six-months. Any fullmoon day is selected for the ceremony. To observe this ceremonial day, a barber is called to shave the baby and a female washerman washes all the used clothes before this day. The village priest (same priest of Hindu castes and of the Mahishya community) also attends and offers Bhog or sacred offering to the goddess Sasthi. Sometimes the priest brings his own family deity for such worship."

For the preparation of this sacred offering, they bring Atap rice (sun-dried rice), Molasses, and different types of fruits like plantain, cucumber, coconut, etc.

On the day fixed for the ceremony, early in the morning after taking bath, the priest came to house and collect all the articles necessary for conduct of worship. After arranging them properly, he placed an earthen pot full of water with a mango-twig on its mouth at the place of worship. He then worshipped godess *Sasthi*. The baby was taken to the place of worship and the priest rubbed vermillion and turmeric paste on its forehead. Then, some jaggery was put in a new earthen pot. The midwife took the baby on her lap and a small quantity of '*Panchamrita*' (five ingredients like, milk, honey, sugar clarified butter and curd offered as oblation to the deity) smeared on the lips of the baby and then on its head and body. Then she was fed a small quantity of jaggery with a coin. Thereafter, all the relatives share the jaggery with the coin and touched it into the mouth of the baby. Thus the first rice feeding ceremony was performed. The Brahman priest was paid rupees five in cash, one new napkin and 1.5 kg of sun-dried rice. He was also given a sumptuous beast on the occasion by the parents of the baby. The baby's father also gave a feast to the villagers to celebrate the occasion. Giving of such feast, however, depends on the economic condition of the family concerned. The birth ceremony is related to the Savara Snake-charmers' community.

Janam Chatiar Ceremony

"The Santals in Bihar and Jharkhand believe that after ten months the women give birth. When the labour pain begins the pregnant woman is confined in a room, which is generally a corner of the house or a portion of the verandah separated with bamboo and leaves. Mr. P.C. Biswas states, "At birth, an experienced elderly woman of the village or of the adjoining village officiates as midwife. No one is allowed to remain there except one or two female relatives of the pregnant woman. After birth, the umbilical cord is cut by the midwife with an arrow by placing a coin beneath it, which is 'afterwards taken by the midwife'. The placenta is then buried in a pit in one corner of the courtyard of the house. Immediately a birth is announced there is a gathering of friends and relations for congratulating the parents. After the birth of a child, the house and the village is considered polluted. So the Santals perform the *Janam Chatiar* ceremony, until this is done it is considered unpropituous to engage in any shikar or hunting expedition or religious ceremonies. The usual day for this ceremony is on the fifth day in the case of a male child and on the third day in the case of a female child. All the male members of the village come to the house of birth, first the village officials are shaved then all the other men present and then the father of the child. Then the midwife brings the child near the barber to cut a few locks of hair from the different parts of the head of the child, which are put in a leaf cup. The midwife then ties two threads to the arrow with which the umbilical cord was cut. All the village officials and other male members go to have their bath in a nearby streamlet. Then the midwife carries the child and together with the mother and the women of the village goes to the bathing place. There, the midwife throws the locks of hair and one of the threads in the water. After bathing they come back to the house. The midwife brings with her the second thread and the arrow, this thread is then smeared with turmeric and tied round the waist of the child.

"When the purification has been completed, the men, women and children of the village who have assembled at the house receive each a leaf cup full of rice water with which the leaves of Nim tree (*Melia azadirachta*) have been mixed. After this they all take a draught of their home-brewed liquor and depart.

"On the fifth day the child is given its name. Should it happen to be a son and heir he takes the name of his grandfather; should he be the second son born, he takes the name of his maternal grandfather: and thus the paternal grandfather's brother for the third boy, the maternal grandfather's brother for the fourth boy and so on. The same procedure is followed for girls, the feminine relations being in the same order from the female side.

Chacho Chhatiar

It is a very important Santal ceremony which enables the individual to take his place in Santal society and participate in its rights, rules and ceremonies. Without this ritual no Santal can be married or cremated; if anybody dies without conducting this ceremony he is otherwise buried. There is no fixed age for the ceremony though it must precede marriage. Generally the Santal parents perform this ceremony for several children in a joint observance.

Mr. O'Malley gives a full description of this ceremony in the District Gazetteer [L.S.S. O'Malley—*Bengal District Gazetters* (Santal Parganas) pp. 132-133]. in the following words. "The father brews handi and provides oil and turmeric for the villagers. When the handi is ready he calls the manjhi and paranik in the morning and gives them a drink. They ask him what handi it is, and, after drinking, the headman bids the godet call the villagers together. When they have come the girls of the village anoint the naeke and his wife, who sit on a mat, with oil and turmeric; next the kudam naeke and his wife, then the manjhi and his wife and all the officials in the same order as at the janam chhatiar: last of all, all the women are anointed. The handi is now served in leaf cups to the manjhi and paranik and then to the other people ; after which all are ready for further proceedings. They ask how many children the handi is for, and for each child four small leaf cups are given to all those present. Then they ask the father: 'How many iri (*Panicum crus-yalli*) and how many ebra (*Setaria Italica*) ears have ripened for you?' This is a figurative expression for 'How many boys and girls have you?' On receiving an answer they ask again, 'Where is the land?' The father tells them where the namesakes of the children live, whereupon they call for 'namesake handi' *i.e.,* beer which the namesakes present have brought with them. The people then sing a special song and dance and drink.

"A guru, who in a way officiates for the father of the family, now starts the binti, *i.e.,* a mythical historical recitation. He begins with the creation of the earth and relates the Santal history of mankind, their wanderings, etc., according to tradition, and recounts how their ancestors spread abroad, some of them coming to Sikhar, where the first pargana was Hikim, who said to the people: 'Let us settle here ; we have found primeval forest and virgin soil'. The ancestors said, 'Let us help him; we will burn and clear jungle, we will live and prosper'. Then they came to their present abode and married, cleared jungle and multiplied. Thereupon the guru on behalf of the family enters into a colloquy with the people, in which inter alia he says, 'We implore you to let us be with you to brew and drink beer, to fetch water, to pin leaves together on the day of marriage, the day of chhatiar, the day of cremation. We were like crows, we have become white like paddy birds. You, villagers, be our witnesses'. This ends the formal part of the proceedings.

"The festival is concluded by further drinking and singing of chhatiar and other songs. It will be seen that there is no special or formal act done by the village people. They are invited for the occasion ; the father (or his representative) implores the community to recognize the young ones as participators at the three great social occasions, and the people acknowledge this by drinking handi, the Santal mode of ratification. There is no kind of sacrifice at either janam or chacho chhatiar."

Mr. Biswas states further, "Among the Santals to adopt a child is of rare occurrence. Dr. Campbell says they do not practise adoption. Rev. P.O. Bodding is of the opinion that adoption is present among the Santals. I have also heard of one or two instances of adoption in the Damin area of the Santhal Parganas.

"If a man takes a second wife and this woman has a boy by a former husband, the man may adopt this boy. He proceeds in the following way: He first informs the village headman, then calls the nearest male relatives of the boy whose consent is necessary. If they agree they say so in the presence of the headman and the villagers of the village where the man, who will adopt the boy, lives. Then the male relatives of the boy renounce him and declare him henceforth to belong to the new father; it is also declared that the boy shall have no right of inheritance in the property of his natural father. When all this has been done the adopting father fixes a date for the formal adoption of the boy. The villagers of that village on that day behave as at *Janam Chhatiar* (name-giving ceremony of the Santal child). They shave and drink handi (rice beer). The usual procedure in a Janam Chhatiar is that the officiating midwife tells the assembled people the name of the new-born child; here she does not tell the name of the boy but the sept or sub-sept of the adopting father; henceforth that becomes the sept of the boy. Thereupon they leave the boy to eat the flesh of animals sacrificed to the tribal deities. Henceforward the boy becomes their own." The ceremony, customs, rites and rituals are related to the Santals.

Burying placenta in Hut

According to Dikshit Sinha, "The umbilical cord is cut by means of an arrowhead by any elderly woman of the hamlet. If the woman is a non-relative she will have to be paid ten kilogrammes of paddy. The placenta is disposed off by depositing it in a hole dug underneath the caves of the hut. The pollution period is observed for three, five, seven, or, nine days. The length of the period depends on the ability of the new mother. On the appointed day the newborn child's father gets up early in the morning when nobody in the hamlet gets up and goes to a natural pond and brings potful of water and keeps it on the *tulsi pinra.* His wife collects the ritual dust of the pollution floor along with sundried rice, vermilion, a little earthen pot and some branches of *vela (Semocarpus anacardium)* and throws these under a thicket. With this it is thought that the *Painsa-burhi* and *Painsa-burha* are conducted out of the hut. In the morning the *tulsi pinra* is smeared with mud water and then one or two kg. of paddy is poured on the *tulsi pinra* and the pot is placed on it. Then in the water of the pot three, five, or seven pairs of boiled and sundried grains of rice are deposited for sometime. These are taken out after a while and smeared with turmeric paste and left to dry. A little of this turmeric is also diluted in the water of the pot and three vermilion and black *(kajal)* dots are applied outside the pot. Then one dried grain of rice is carefully placed in the pot's water. If the grain subsides in the water then it is taken as a tale-tell mark of an omen that the child will not live. If the rice floats then it is regarded as a sign that the child will live and grow up. After this one fowl is sacrificed in the name of *Painsa-burhi* and *Painsa-burha.* The child is bathed in the water of the pot and its mother takes her bath in the pond. The lineage members as well as all the members of the hamlet take bath. The ceremony held to observe the pollution period's end is called an *naata.* In the past it was customary to host a feast but now-a-days this is not followed."

The ceremony is performed among the Hill Kharias; community.

Entire family under ritual pollution

About the tribal birth ceremonies in different groups, Mr. K.P. Bahadu states in his book caste, tribe *Culture of India Bengal, Bihar and Orissa,* "The naming of the child provides another occasion for ceremonies and also the inevitable taboos and restrictions. Thus when a child is born the entire family of the Munda household observe the ritual pollution which lasts from five to eight days. After this period the child is named. The Kharias, too, have a pollution period seven to nine days. The Hos not only observe a pollution period (six to eight days) but in addition keep the mother and father confined to a room, for it is believed that if they cast their eyes on the child he will die. The naming ceremony is performed on different days by different tribes. The Oraons perform it at the expiry of the pollution period, the Hos on any day between the twenty-first and thirtieth after birth. The Kharias are quick about it, and perform the ceremony in the morning following the day of birth. The birth customs prevailing among the tribes included in this study follows.

"Among the Bhuiyas the period of uncleanliness of mother and child is seven days after the birth. The child's head is then shaved and a name given. The name of the grandfather is given to the eldest son, the name of the great grandfather to the second son, and then the names of the collateral branches .according to seniority.

"Among the Hos, after the birth of the child both the mother and father are considered unclean *(bisi)* for eight days. During this period all the members of the household except the husband and the wife are sent out of the house, and the husband has to do all the cooking and other arrangements. If the child-birth has been difficult, it is supposed that some evil spirits are behind it and the soccerer finds out its name, after which a sacrifice is made to appease him.

"After the eight day segregation period the members of the family return. There is a big feast at which friends are invited, and the child is named with a brief ceremony. The first born son is usually given the name of the grandfather, but this is only after ascertaining whether it is suitable. The suitability is determined by throwing a grain of *urd* (a pulse) into a vessel containing water. If the grain floats the name is adopted, but if it sinks it is abandoned.

"The pregnant *Kandh* women visits her father's house accompanied by her husband about a month before her confinement. The woman's father gives toys for the baby to come, like a small bow and arrow, a winnowing fan and a small basket. These are kept in the house till the child is born. The actual-birth is not accompanied by any ceremonies, but there is the usual segregation and period of uncleanliness. The husband and his pregnant wife go to a room separate from house a few days before confinement. There the husband cooks the food and eats with his wife. If it is the first delivery he also sacrifices a pig and offers the cooked meat along with cooked and uncooked rice and libations of strong wine to the ancestor so that no ill may be fall the child. No one is allowed to enter the room during this period and if he does so he renders himself unclean. After the birth the earthen cooking pots which were in use are broken and people are allowed to enter the room. But they are forbidden to eat with the parents of the child till twelve more days have elapsed. After this the pots are broken again, and a feast given to the neighbours. When the child is two or three years old the hair of his head is shaved off and a ceremony held calling on the ancestors to protect the child against skin disease, scald and itch.

"The Mundas have elaborate birth ceremonies. They believe that Garasi Bonga, a god, watches the well-being of the pregnant woman. To ensure that he looks after them well, a gray or red fowl is set apart by the family head, and a jar of rice beer brewed as soon as the signs of pregnancy are observed in the woman. Prayers are offered to Garasi Bonga by the near relations and the fowl which has been ear marked is sacrificed followed by feasting and drinking. The period of uncleanliness of the mother is eight days and during this period no member of the caste is allowed to enter the room when the child is born. On the eighth day after the birth of the child the purificatory ceremonies are performed. The baby and his mother and the near relatives get their nails cut. The mother goes to bathe in a stream, accompanied by women of the household. The unclean mat on which the baby slept is burnt. On return, water is sprinkled all over the house from a brass vessel into which a piece of copper and basil leaves have been dropped. Rice beer is also sprinkled similarly. The house is thus purified, and the head of the family worships the household deity and everyone has a drink of rice beer to celebrate."

Calling spirit-finder to facilitate delivery

At the time of delivery, generally a Hadi (sweeper) woman, professionally called belonging to an untouchable caste, is rarely asked to render her service as the midwife. In case of prolonged labour pains or difficult birth, a *Gunni* or *Ojha* or spirit-finder and rarely the local doctor is called by the Mahalis. The period of labour pains appear to vary considerably in different cases. Some women have a quick delivery; while others struggle for one or two days in excruciating labour pain. Then medicinemen are also approached for conducing a safe, easy and smooth delivery. There is practically no arrangement for setting apart a confinement-room because a vast majority of poverty-stricken Mahalis own a small single room hut without any additional space to allot for confinement. But in some cases, a few Mahalis have two or more rooms in their hut, one of which is spared for purpose of delivery.

In a particular delivery case, a Hadi (sweeper) midwife was called in from a neighbouring village to attend the expectant mother, when she began to feel the intensity of labour pangs. A thick sheet of basketry (Chanch) and a brass pot filled with water were kept near the women in labour. Some elderly women of the village were also called to help her before the midwife came. When the pain became very acute, she gave out a loud cry and a sheet of basketry was spread out on the floor of the hut and she laid on it. The unmarried girls were bade to go out of the room. The popular Mahali belief is that if unmarried girls see the child-birth, they will be either barren or give birth to still-born children. Syamkanti Sengupta writes, "The reason of such belief could not be ascertained by the author it may be due to the fact that unmarried girls will be obsessed for the painful conditions of child birth and consequently it will affect their maritial relations. In the meantime the midwife massaged some cocoanut oil on the abdomen of the woman in labour pain to soften it and to cool the skin." But if the birth delayed further and she suffered acute pain.

She adds further, "The parents of the said woman took vows to offer fruits and fowls and sacrifices to the deities, Dharam (God of righteousness) and Garam (tutelary deity of the village) for the safety of the baby and the mother and for a trouble-free delivery. Lastly they called in a spirit-finder (Gunni), Subal Mandi, of the village belonging to the same community as they thought that the expectant mother was possessed by the spirit. The spirit-finder made a sort of performance known to the Mahalis as 'Sunumjnail' or 'Telpanja' *i.e.* oil divination to ascertain the causes of the possession."

Later, the spirit-finder, at first took some mustard oil in a leaf-cup in which the suffering woman dipped the left little finger. Then shaman took some vermilion from the woman's parents and put three vermilion marks on the ground in a cleaned corner of the courtyard in the name of *Dharam, Garam* and *Orak bonga* (family deity) of the parents. Next he took three jack-fruit leaves and put a drop of mustard oil on each in the name of *Dharam, Garam* and *Orak bonga*, stitched all with thorns and put them on the ground over the vermilion mark, made in the name of *Dharam, Garam* and *Orak bonga*. Then he invoked the deities and opened up the leaves after a few minutes. The oil drops put in the leaves, in the name of *Dharam* and *Garam* were remained intact whereas it spread on the surface of the leaf put in the name of *Orak bonga*.

Then, the Shaman asked the parents to sacrifice a fowl in the name of the Orak bonga. The fowl was not available at that time. So the woman's husband took a vow to offer a fowl to Orak bonga after which, incidentally, she gave birth to a son. The Shaman was given Rs. 2.00 for his service.

Sengupta writes further, "As soon as the child was born, the news was spread by the striking of a brass plate which the elder sister-in-law of the young mother struck with a stick. The mid-wife of Hadi (Sweeper) caste of Katabuni village cut the umbilical cord with a blade. The midwife of the own community in two other cases in another village Kotai was found to cut the umbilical cord with a sharpened piece of shell and in one case in Jayrampur, it was seen that the midwife of the Mahali community cut the umbilical cord with a sharp strip of a bamboo and instead of barber the nails of the baby were paired off by this midwife. Umbilical cord is cut by the midwife with an arrow by placing a coin beneath it which is afterwards taken by the midwife among the Santals Biswas, P.C. *The Santals of Santal Parganas*, Delhi, 956, p. 90. Among the Mahadev Kolis the umbilical cord is cut with a sickle. Some midwives keep a special small-size sickle for this purpose. Before use, the sickle is worshipped with an offering of turmeric and vermilion powders, some rice. Ghurye, G.S. *The Mahadev Kolis*, Bombay, 1957, p. 70. But among the Mahalis no custom of such worship prevails.

"The midwife instructed the woman to contract the muscles in the region of uterus so that the expulsion of the placenta may become easy and quick that happened in this case. The placenta was taken by the midwife with a stick and buried under the heap of cowdung, which was stacked at one corner of the courtyard. Then she took the child and washed it with a cloth dipped in hot water, outside the room. The baby was laid on a bed prepared for it on a mat over which several pieces of folded clothes, each one cubit either way in measure, were kept in the pattern of a small quilt. No efforts were spared to make the bed soft and suitable.

"After this she took an aluminium cup and squeezed some milk out of the mother's breasts and cast it off. This milk was thick. It is the general belief of the Mahalis that if the new born baby takes this thick milk, he will suffer from diarrhoea. The milk thus squeezed was poured into a nearby pond by the midwife to avoid the eyes of the evil spirits. The midwife was given Re. 1.00 and 1 kg. rice for her services. The whole set of earthen cooking utensils of the family were cast away, as an associated rite of pollution period. The broomstick which was used to sweep the room and the thick sheet of basketry on which the baby was born, were also thrown away. One receptacle for collyrium, prepared with mustard oil and lamp-black was kept on the bed of the child to avoid evil eye. On this day the young mother took nothing but a little hot water. The baby was fed with mother's milk from the third day. Before that whenever the baby cried hot water was given to the baby.

"On the second day, the mother took some local Kurthi pulses (*Dolichos biflorus*) boiled in water without salt and also a few pieces of garlic these being given by her sister-in-law. She drank some hot water. These pulses are believed to produce sufficient milk in the mother's breasts and help in quick recovery from weakness. So after parturition, the Mahalis prescribed

Kurthi pulses for the mother. The confinement room was considered as impure and nobody usually was allowed to enter, family members slept outside in the verandah. Relatives and villagers looked into the room from outside, through the door. It was said that if one enters the confinement room, one would require bath for purification.

"The midwife came on the second day to wash the mother and the baby with hot water. She also had her bath for purifying herself after this. Then she powdered some sundried rice by a mortar and pestle and then mixed it with water and standing outside the room near the door sprinkled it in the room where the mother and the baby were confined. After sprinkling this she came outside and washed her hands and feet. It is likely to be an imperfect and crude imitation of a customary and sacred preparations followed in all Hindu families of higher castes. On all religious occasion or social festivals grounded on some sort of religion, the venue and the space around it are decorated and painted with the powder of sundried rice mixed in water. It is an aesthetic means to create an atmosphere of holiness. The child birth also is regarded as something like holy creation; and as such the occasion becomes the part of the religious observations.

"On the third day of the birth, in the morning at 8/9 A.M., the mother took Kurthi pulses boiled in water and a little hot water. She also had the same food at 3/4 P.M. along with a few pieces of garlic. On this day, the midwife gave the mother a little mustard oil and some turmeric paste to rub on her body and hot water was served to her for sponging, which she did inside the hut. She was not allowed to move about.

"On the fourth day, she took bath and ate hot boiled rice with garlic only. Upto nineth day she had to maintain these restrictions on food. On the 10th day, a purificatory rite was performed by the husband. On that day Garam, the tutelary village deity was propitiated with rice beer according to the custom. Some of it was then given to Naeke or village priest who before drinking offered a little from it to Dharam (God of righteousness) and Garam (tutelary deity of the village) invoking their blessings for the baby and the mother. Ten betel-leaves were given to Naeke as his royalty.

"The midwife came on the 10th day. She took meal in the house which was prepared by the mother on that day, and after meal, she again sprinkled in the room and outside some rice powder mixed with water. On that day the midwife was given a new cloth. The mother was allowed to cook from this day.

"The name-giving ceremony and purificatory rites of the child were performed again on the 21st day. This ceremony was known as *Ekusia Ghar.*

A barber, Maheswar Paramanik, was called in to pare-off the nails of the mother and the baby.

"On the 21st day, the villagers were invited. The number of invitees varies from case to case as it depends on the economic condition of the family. All relatives and friends assembled in the house with gourds, brinjals and other vegetables as gifts and rice for preparing rice beer etc, when they came on that particular day, the name of the child was given. The name of the father's father was given to the child. Usually name of the father's father or father's uncle, is preferred. A female child gets the name of the father's mother, father's grandmother or the father's sister.

"On that day of *Ekusia* in the particular case in front of the hut, a small part of the courtyard was washed with cowdung solution and the grandfather of the baby presented a small shirt, a wooden bead necklace, a red thread for waist, a coarse towel and two iron-bangles to the child. Paddy was sprinkled over the place, smeared with cow-dung and sal (*Shorea robusta*) leaves were spread over it. On the sal leaves the coarse towel was spread, on which the baby was laid. After this the grandfather dressed him with the wooden bead necklace, red thread and the shirt, and put the iron-bangles around its wrists. These iron-bangles are supposed to protect the child from the evil eye. Among the Kols, the wood of Nim tree (*Melia azadirachta*), a valuable charm against evil spirits, is tied in the arm of the baby. Griffiths, W.G. *The Kol Tribe of Central India*, Calcutta, 1946, p. 60.

"Afterwards, ...the headman of the village and his wife came there with oil in two small brass pots. The child was laid on a mat, with his head in the east. Father's father of the baby sat near the head of the child and kept the brass pots with oil in front of him. Then he bent forward a little and dipped the tips of his forelock in the brass pot and brought his head near the child so that a few drops from his hair fall on the head. He did this from the two brass pots in turn. Then he stood and touched the forehead of the child and his navel with the first finger of his right leg and crossed over him. Again he did the same thing and came over to his former position. He then gave a fifty paise to the child. Similar things were also done by the child's father's mother. Later child's father's, elder uncle and elder uncle's wife repeated these rites.

"After this, almost all, those assembled in this ceremony, gave a few paise according to their means to the child as presentation. Later the child was taken inside the room by his mother. After this, dance and songs were arranged which provided special interest. The invitees, participated in this merry-making with their musical instruments like Tamak (flat drums), Tumda (conical drums), Regra (flat small drums) etc. In the end, all the participants were given rice-beer (Hanria) by the father of the child."

"Manjhi and his wife then applied oil mark on the forehead of each male and female guest present there and gave to the baby boy. Again all of them drank rice-beer and performed dances which continued for the entire night till the next morning. Like the Kols among the more Hinduised and better off Mahalis, the name is given by degraded Brahman priest. The priest is called upon to select the child's name and does this from a list of names in his possession which are considered auspicious for the children born at certain season and according to the Zodiac sign.

Sengupta writes further, "The birth of a child is surrounded by dangerous possibilities according to the Mahali belief. Magical art could help to control this. They further believe that the ancestors, evil spirits and Bongas control conception and the Gunni or diviner or sooth-sayer could communicate with them and regulate their activities. Native medicinemen or Ojhas, specialized in the treatment of pregnancy and birth, are rewarded on the basis of their performance. A Mahali makes his choice and adjustments in the light of his economic capacities. He employs a midwife to assist in delivery cases. Occasionally many Mahalis give a feast to their relatives on the occasion of the 21st day's purificatory ceremony. Some of them often procure medicines and charms. These mean that they observe a considerably expensive ritual. The primary need is simple. The safe birth of the baby is expected by all. Some conventional restrictions are put upon food consumption of the pregnant woman at this time. In the first place, a pregnant woman develops a keen desire for some special foods. In the second place, certain foods are prohibited for her or are avoided as a general practice to ensure the safety of the baby and the mother. The Mahlis prescribe after birth a special food like the extract of Kurthi pulses and boiled Katanote (*Amaranthus spinosa*) for quick recovery of the mother. Among the Kols a special drink are said to be made of ginger root (*Cleome viseosa*) molasses and certain jungle roots boiled together is given to a woman after parturition, three times a day until she is stronger. Grifiths, W.G. *op cit.* p. 59.

"The appointment of a midwife is the practical part of the preparation for any birth among the Mahalis and is supplemented by the calling of other specialists, if it is necessary. Very often as seen especially among the poorer families, an elderly female relative serves as the midwife. It is clear from this that there is a nucleus of a specialised profession among the elderly women of different families. Their services are always paid for. The sooth-sayer is one of the specialists in this respect. A few of them, have the reputation of being capable of dealing with special complications, while others possess the secrets of occult medicines, which they administer or prescribe on considerable payment. A large part of their knowledge hardly of any practical medical aspect. It concerns magical measures, necessarv to ward off surrounding-dangers and to enable the mother to face the crisis with confidence. The birth may be difficult or delayed for the anger of ancestors or Bongas. The husband and the parents of the woman often take a vow of sacrificing a goat or a fowl to the deity for safe delivery. Sometimes, influence of evil spirits makes the birth difficult as they believe, when magical treatment is arranged along with the normal medical treatment. The Tharus also observe precautions to protect the pregnant woman and her child from the dangers of evil spirits and to avert dangers due to physical phenomena and evil eyes of certain persons every pregnant woman wear many amulets made by a *Bharara* (medicinemen) who by his magical powers can protect the child in the mother's womb both from evil spirit and evil eyes, Srivastava, S.K. *The Tharus—A study of culture dynamics*, Agra, 1958, p. 122. As regards the Mahadev Kolis, Ghurye writes, "when parturition is delayed so as to cause anxiety and the case is feared to be serious, the help of a Bhaghat (medicinemen) is solicited. In addition to the esoteric charms of the 'Bhaghat' there are herbal prescriptions which are believed to be efficacious in serious cases." Ghurye, G.S. *The Mahadev Kolis*, Bombay, 1957, p. 70. The Tharus too, employ Bharara (medicinemen) in case of delayed birth. Among the more primitive Kols difficult labour is ascribed to evil spirits; the more advanced ones speak of it as a punishment due from Bhagwan for some bad Karma. Srivastava, S.K. op. cit. p. 127. More Hinduised Mahalis too, think that the difficult and delayed birth is owing to the bad Karma (deed).

"Following the birth, there is a period of careful dieting and abstention from work on the part of the mother .for a period, which generally depend on the economic resources of the Mahali families. At this stage, a feast in *Ekusia Ghar* is generally given to the relatives and neighbours, which is associated with the rituals. It comprises of name-giving to the baby and thanks-giving on the occasion, to the deities for their blessings to add another member to the family. It brings together the well wishers whose affection and blessings for the welfare of the child are thus expressed. The occasion provides a feast and drinking of plenty of rice beer. The mother also participates in the feast."

However, different types of services are rendered and funds expensed in such feasts depend on the means of individuals and the general cultural patterns. In one case, the women suffered from labour pain for two long days and her husband called the Mahali spirit-finder of the village to ascertain the causes of her prolonged labour pang and was told that it was due to the wrath of goddess Sitala. The women's husband paid the spiritfinder's fees and took the vow to offer a goat to the goddess. A midwife, and also a Barber both of the same village were called in to render their services. In the second case, the Mahali medicineman of the village was called in to ensure trouble-free delivery. He performed oil divination to ascertain, whether she was possessed by any evil spirit. The woman's husband took the vow to offer a goat to Orak Bonga according to the instruction of the spirit-finder for trouble-free delivery of his wife. A midwife of Hadi caste was called in. No barber was sent for, as the grandmother of the child trimmed the nails of the baby and the mother. In the case, it was her second issue. The Mahali tribal medicineman was sent for, to relieve the expectant mother of her sustaining labour pain. A Mahali widwife of the same village was called in but the barber's services were not needed as the midwife cut the nails of the baby and the mother on the 10th and the 21st day. The woman had to take medicine worth Rs. 2/- purchased from the local doctor.

The Mahali tribals claim that amongst them patterns of training of children differ greatly in different cases. But in fact, this difference could be hardly found. On the contrary, there is a remarkable similarity in these patterns of training in all the villages inhabited by the Mahalis. But the caste Hindus comment to the Mahalis that "their children are dirty, they sleep on the floor, they are fed with stale rice and leafy vegetables collected from unclean areas and often eaten with rice beer." But these claims are not correct and could not be so easily generalised about the Mahalis. Nevertheless the occasional variations in child training depend on individual situation and preferences. The general attitude towards children is strongly influenced by the local food situation and the toddlers are always considered a heavy economic burden. But when they come of age, the children become financially productive. The amount of attention a mother gives to her new born baby depends little upon the economic situation of the family, but much upon her individual attitude towards the child. A first child does not necessarily receive more attention than a third or the fourth. Even a woman who has to weave bamboo-baskets in order to support her family finds plenty of time to take care and bestow love of her baby. But they are found to be frequently negligent in this matter. Of course pressure of work, illness and fatigue make the young mothers little careless for paying more attention to their infants. Sengupta writes, "The author observed several mothers using both hands in weaving baskets while nursing their four or five months' old babies, clinging with the greatest effort to their breasts.

"About two weeks after the birth, the baby is given a little spoonful of sweetened rice water. In about four or five months, they are given occasional spoonful of rice soup and in about six or seven months, they are given a little rice broth. In the eighth month, many infants eat solid food like little boiled potatoes, brinjals and rice. But meat is given only after a year. Infants of eight months, can take with their own hand solid food that their mothers put into their hands instead of feeding them.

"Baby is weaned early. Besides, in case of new pregnancy, there are several other reasons for which a baby has to be weaned. The mother might feel weak or fall ill. She might be obliged to work hard, for fear of being for-saken by the child's father. Infants are always weaned quite suddenly by rubbing lemon juice, and neem juice on the nipples. During the first three months, babies cry very little and sleep most of the time, but if they do cry, they are usually suckled immediately. A baby is bathed only about two or three times a week. During the first two or three weeks, the water is made slightly warm. A baby is never cared for, by only one person, but always by a number of inmates, such as aunts, grandmothers, elder siblings and neighbours. During the second month, the baby is frequently carried outside the house and is taken to the houses of relatives. Such outings become more frequent after the third month, especially to visit the paternal and maternal grand-parents. On these occasions, the baby is not always carried by his own mother, but by the women of the villages of all ages, related or unrelated. Men rarely carry a baby on the street or for a visit to the house of a relative.

"Many mothers touch the baby only while nursing him, putting him to .sleep afterwards, while other adults or children, are in charge of other aspects of its care. Therefore, the infants begin to learn to distinguish, in about seventh month, between his own mother as a source of food, and other fondling women as sources of attention, affection and comfort. Many mothers often said to the author, 'my child draws my attention when he is hungry.' If the baby has an elder sibling the mother usually puts the child in charge of him or her. It is a common practice in the Mahali society that upto four or five months after the birth, the baby is taken care of and carried mostly by the elder child, and brought back to the mother for breast feeding. A father whose first children are girls, shows a certain amount of pride on his first son and occasionally carries him during visits to the houses of the neighbours. But he rarely takes care of the baby and feeds him.

"Teething of infants begins in about eighth month from the birth, but in many cases, this happens in the twelfth month or a bit later. During this period they become restive and sleepless and often cry aloud seeking more attention and care.

"Within about two-weeks of the birth, the mother-occasionally ties to the baby's wrist or around its neck, a cotton string with one or two seeds of myrobalan or wooden beads as a charm against the evil eye. Sometimes, carelessness, ignorance and pressure of domestic work or participation in the work of the field are enforced on the convalescing mother by the father. So pressing economic needs often compel the woman to neglect her infant's health to such an extent that serious disease and even death in some cases, occur as a result. The author witnessed several cases like this during his study. In one case, 'Y' wife of Mr. 'X' was compelled to help her husband in basketry and in agricultural operations for the most part of the day and so had little time to look after her 10-month old son. Often she had to go to the neighbouring market to sell products like small baskets, winnowing fans, etc. As a result her son remained uncared for, had an attack of pneumonia and died within a short time. Public opinion in the Mahali society scarcely takes any serious note of such occurrences and in most cases it ends into a mere gossip or criticism within a short time.

Daka-jam Parab or First Rice-eating Ceremony

"This ceremony was witnessed by the author when child of Mrs. 'B' was ceremonially fed with rice for the first time. This ceremony is not obligatory among the Mahalis. Those who are economically better off, perform this ceremony. It has been mentioned earlier that children generally live on breast milk till they are six months old. At the end of six months, the day for feeding rice in this particular case was fixed on a Thursday, all Thursdays being considered auspicious. A barber of a low Hindu caste attended this ceremony to pare off the nails of the child and to cut his hair. The village Naeke or priest of the Mahali community also attended this ceremony and secured the necessary articles to prepare porridge i.e., rice boiled in milk with molasses as the sacred offering for the deity. The porridge was prepared in a new earthen pot. Early in the morning Naeke took bath and cooked the porridge, wearing a clean cloth. He then went to Jahersthan or sacred grove of the village and offered the porridge to the deities Dharam and Garam and uttered some sacred formulae in his own language, praying for a long and trouble-free life for the baby. Some of the family members were also present at that time. The priest took a little of the consecrated food and handed it over to the baby's father.

"In the meantime, the barber caste Hindu completed shaving of the baby's head. He was given Rs. 21 for his services. The female relatives such as child's mother's sister, father's brother's wife and three married women of the village then rubbed a little turmeric paste and mustard oil on the body of the baby. Then the baby was bathed. The baby was dressed with a new shirt and a red thread round the waist. After completion of this, the maternal uncle of the baby then put a little porridge from the offerings made to Garam and Dharam earlier, into the baby's mouth twice. At that time the womenfolk blew conch-shells several times. After this, the relatives and a few villagers were entertained with a feast and rice beer.

"This is the usual pattern of the first rice eating ceremony. Variation of this pattern is only found in case of employing the barber to shave the head of the baby. In Jayrampur in the case of the first rice feeding ceremony... the barber was not called in, to attend... , one of the neighbour shaved the head of the baby. He got Rs. 2 for this. Sometimes formal presentations are made to the baby. In Ganjipur at the first rice feeding ceremony (of a girl) the woman's brother... gave a new red garment to the baby."

"About *dai* or the quack midwife in the eastern region of Bengal, Orissa and Bihar, Sir Herbert Risley writes thus, " Dai, a midwife, usually a Mahomedan or a Hindu of the Chamar caste. Among Hindus of all other castes there is a strong prejudice against cutting the navel cord, and a common term of abuse applied to a midwife is *narkátá* or cord-cutter. The male relatives of these women are usually tailors or musicians; while in villages they often work as weavers, and sometimes sell betel-leaves."

"In Dacca," says Dr. Wise, who had special opportunities for learning the truth on this subject, "the midwives are invariably ignorant and generally consequential, while, being few in number, they are very independent, extorting money in proportion to the anxieties of their patients. A midwife forms an important part of a household, and no family of note is without one. Like the Purohit and barber, the Dai is a privileged person, and has freedom of access to the female apartments at any hour. Her post is usually hereditary, but, if childless, the Dai adopts a young woman and educates her in the mysteries of the profession. Mahomedan ladies have no objection to be attended by a Hindu or Christian woman, but one of their own creed is preferred. The poorer classes attend on each other, and only in cases of difficulty is the European doctor, or the professional *accoucheuse,* called in. Parturition is in most instances easy, and the poor have seldom any need of skilled attendance; but among the listless inmates of zananas, who never lead a healthy or invigorating life, labour is often tedious and exhausting.

"When a woman, either Hindu or Mahomedan, approaches the term of her pregnancy, an outhouse, or detached room, is prepared for her, to which, when labour begins, she retires with the Dai and a servant. This den, to which the highest as well as the lowest is condemned, is known as the *Asaucha-ghar,* or *Chhathi-ghar.* The duty of the midwife is to rub and roll about the patient so as to increase the pains, and when the child is born to cut the cord with a piece of bamboo (tarla-ka-chhalti), and to give immediate warning for the 'Azan,' or call to prayers.

"Of the mechanism of parturition, of the dangers to be avoided and provided against, midwives are profoundly ignorant; a woman being satisfied if she is attended by the family Dai, or by the pupil of the Dai; who aided her mother or sister under similar circumstances. Being obliged to observe many customs, without the due performance of which her own and her child's life would be endangered, the mother resigns herself to the hands of the midwife, assured that all will go wall. To cause the uterus to contract they use an embrocation of the juice of the Nag-dauna leaf *(Artimisia vulgaris)* with spirit. When it is wished to stay the flow of milk, the dried bark of the Pani-kudu *(Cucurbita)* mixed with pease-meal *(Ervum hirsutum)* and rubbed up in water is used as a plaster.

"The midwife is expected to pay frequent visits until all danger has passed; but should the lady be rich, she is not allowed to leave the house for days. It devolves on her to anoint the infant daily, for in India babies are not bathed daily. Lampblack must be smeared along the eyelashes, and a mash of warm aromatics (ghutti) given daily. For two days after birth the mother is only allowed to take turmeric, molasses, and infusion of ajwain, while on the third and up to the fortieth day she may eat pulse (masur) and rice.

"After the birth of a child many strange rites are performed. A bonfire (alawa) is kept smouldering at the door of the Chhathighar for six days in the hot, for twenty-one in the cold season, and an oil lamp, placed within the room, must never be permitted to go out, on attendant being always on the watch to trim it, as darkness favours the entrance of evil spirits. A horse-shoe is placed beneath the bedding, as iron is most distasteful to all kinds of devils; and an earthen vessel, on which the name of God is written, is hung over the door. No one can leave the room before midday, and on no account must the baby's clothes be washed or dried anywhere but inside the room. If the husband or doctor, has to visit the mother, his clothes are fumigated with the smoke of mustard seed thrown on the fire, and when the visitor leaves any food, milk, or drinking water standing in the room must be flung away. For six days the Hindu mother is confined in this den, her Muhammadan sister remaining for ten.

"On the sixth or Chhathi day the barber and washerman are sent for; the former cutting the hair and paring the nails of the infant, the latter taking away the puerperal garments. It is from performing this menial work that the Dhoba belongs to a very unclean class.

"On the twenty-first or ikkisi day the barber and washerman again attend, when similar duties are discharged.

"On the fortieth day after the birth of a boy impurity ceases, as among the Jews, but several rites must be first of all performed. There is the "Kua-Jhankna," or peeping into the well, which is identical with the worship of Subhachani among Hindus, after which the mother resumes her household duties.

"If a child be stillborn, the mother is given an infusion of bamboo leaves in which a copper coin, has been soaked. The draught is believed to decompose the poison which caused the death of the child. Should a woman give birth to several stillborn children in succession, the popular belief is that the same child reappears on each occasion, when, to frustrate the designs of the ovil spirit that has taken possession of the child, the nose, or a portion of an ear, is out off, and the body is cast away on a dunghill.

"Dais have many secret remedies which they puff with unblushing assurance. Several are innocuous, a few useful, but in all cases they consist of so many and such heterogeneous substances that their action must be extremely doubtful. Their favourite remedy is called Masturi, or Battisa, from its being composed of thirty-two ingredients. Among other things it contains syrup, galls, litharge, sandal-wood, rock salt, and *gokhru (Tribulus lanuginosus),* and is applied on balls of cotton soaked in Champa oil in all diseases peculiar to women.

Naming Ceremony

About the name-giving ceremony of the Rabhas, Mr. Amal Kumar Das and Manis Kumar Raha writes, "When the age of the child is between one and two months, the father of the child gets busy to celebrate the name-giving ceremony. One day he goes to the Brahmin or *Adhikari* and requests him to select an auspicious day for performing this ceremony. The Brahmin or *Adhikari* after consulting a *Panji* (almanac) selects a suitable day for the name-giving ceremony. Name is also given at the time of *Chua Kamao* ceremony.

"On the selected day some of the relatives of the parents of the child and also some neighbouring villagers attend the ceremony. Generally the child's mother's father or mother's brother performs the ceremony. In the morning of the day he first of all takes a bath and wears a clean and new *Dhuti.* The child is also given a wash. Then he prepares a *Donga* (cup) by the bark of the plantain. Within this *Donga* some water is poured. Then he takes the child on his lap and drops a rice grain in the *Donga* uttering the name to be selected. If the rice floats, then this name is considered to be selected for the child. If the rice grain sinks down, another grain is taken, another name is selected and the same procedure is repeated. This process is continued until a rice floats and a name for the child is selected. Such name which is not present among the near relations is generally selected for the child. Sometimes the name of the day, month, village, particular bird, animal or flower or deities is given to the child. The name thus given, becomes the original name of the child, and at the same time the child possesses another nickname. The name-giving ceremony does not take place in the months of *Jaistha* (May-June), *Vadro* (August-September), *Pous* (December-January), and *Chaitra* (March-April), and a day like Friday and Saturday as these are considered as inauspicious months and days. On the same ground new-moon day and last day of the month *(Sankranti)* are avoided."

After the naming ceremony a feast of rice, meat curry and rice-beer is given to the assembled guests by the parents of the new born baby.

The writers notes further, "When the child grows up a little (in case of male child it is 9 months and in case of female child it is 7 months), the 'first feeding of rice' ceremony takes place. This ceremony usually takes place in the house of the child's father. For this purpose the father of the child goes to the Brahmin or *Adhikari* for a suitable date. The Brahmin or *Adhikari* after consulting the almanac, selects an auspicious day for the ceremony. Restrictions on months and days are same as those of the name-giving ceremony.

"In the morning of the day of the ceremony the priest after taking a bath and wearing a new *Dhuti* comes to perform the *puja.* The child is then bathed and dressed with new clothings. He is then allowed to sit on the lap of its father or mother's brother facing eastward because in the east *Narayan* and *Balaram,* the two important deities who are also believed as brothers, reside. In front of the child a plate containing a book, a pen of reed, paddy, *durba* grass, *Kajal* (black paint used to decorate eyes) and a lighted !amp is kept. A cup containing *Payes* (rice boiled with milk and sweet) is also kept. When all of these are ready, the priest performs the *Balaram puja* in the same way as is done in connection with child birth. After the end of the *puja* the mother's brother of the child takes a little of the *Payes* and feeds the child thrice. Throughout the feeding ceremony musical instruments are played and women utter *Ulu-Ulu* sound (sound done by the typical movement of the tongue, and this sound is considered sacred by the Hindus)."

Later a feast is given to the guests, kins, relatives and villagers who give some gifts to this baby according to their means. At this time whether they can give any gifts or not, all of them bless the child for its welfare. From this date with the end of this ceremony, the child takes boiled rice and other cooked food. Prior to this ceremony the child cannot be given any cooked food. As rice is the staple food of the Rabhas it cannot be given to a new-born child unless it is first touched by the family clan, or village deities. Once this *Prosad* or the sanctified food which was offered to the deity and considered as being tasted by the baby, deity, is taken by the baby, it acquired the right of taking any and every type of food. The ceremony, rites and rituals are performed among the Rabhas.

Janam Chatiar Ceremony

The name-giving among the Santals of Bengal is an essential part of the *Janam Chatiar* ceremony, for giving of a name to a baby formally admits it into its father's clan and sub-clan. In so doing, the child is given the protection of its father's *bangas*. In giving it a name, the father removes all traces of illegitimacy, if any, recognising the child as his own. The child thus acquired a definite status in the village tribal community, and the kinsfolk. It is considered to be a Santal. The name-giving also emphasizes the social obligations of the household to its new addition.

"Culshaw remarks that in the area around Sarenga, a village in Bankura district in West Bengal, this name-giving ceremony is sometimes performed on a separate day from that on which the shaving and the bathing take place. According to Mr. J. Troisi, "The name is chosen by the parents of the child. In assigning a name, however, they follow a traditional formula. Provided the marriage is not in the *ghar jawae* or *ghardi jawae* from, the first-born son is named after his paternal grandfather's the second after his maternal grandfather's the third receives the name of his paternal grandfather's eldest brother, while the name of the maternal grandfather's eldest brother is given to the fourth son. Other male offspring, if any, consecutively receive the name of their paternal grandfather's brothers and maternal grandmother's brothers. Daughters receive the name of the equivalent female relatives in the same order. In the case of the father being a *ghar jawae* or *ghardi jawae*, the naming order is reversed, that is, names on the maternal side come first. If the child's mother had taken any medicine, either from the *raranic* or *ojha*, or visited any Hindu shrine, so as to become pregnant, then the child receives the name of the man from whom medicine or advice has been obtained. By following these traditionally established practices in naming their children, the Santals perpetuate the memories of their ancestors. In the case of twins, the names are drawn from Hindu mythology. Thus, if both the twins are male, they are named Ram and Lakhon, and if female, Chita and Khapra. If one is male and the other female, they are named Ram and Chita. Other names for male twins are: Sidhu and Kanhu; Bhim and Arjun; and Bharat and Chatur. In the case of female twins, they are named: Hisi and Dhumni; Dargi and Pargi.

"It is interesting to note that most Santals are given two names. One is called *mul* or *bhitri nutum* which literally means 'inner' or 'private' name, and the other is called *bahna* or *cetan nutum* which, literally means 'upper' or 'outer' name. The *bhitri nutum* of the child must correspond to that of the relative after whom it is called. The *cetan nutum* is a kind of nickname. These nicknames, given in early childhood, are often replaced by others as the child grows up. This second name is important, because, on the whole, the Santals are reluctant to call someone by his real name fearing it may cause him harm. . . a name is said to be an integral part of its owner and consequently presents a very potent means to the sorcerer for his magical operations. The second name is also necessary as a result of the prohibition which the Santals attach to the use of the *bhitri nutum* by certain categories. Thus, if a boy has been named after one of his grandfathers, then all those who, due to kinship relations are prohibited from pronouncing the grandfather's name, like the grandmother, are equally prohibited from applying that name to anyone else. Brothers and sisters-in-law, husbands and wives are also prohibited from mentioning each other's names. Besides, to avoid confusion, the child is not called by its grandfather's name, while the latter is still alive.

"The conclusion of the ceremony is marked by the drinking effect. The household head offers some of the gruel to *Maran Buru* and the ancestor spirits, invoking them to give the baby a long and healthy life. All the people present are then offered *nim dak mandi,* after which everyone returns to his house. If the family can afford to do so, they give a meal to all the relatives. With the end of the ceremony, the village *bongas* are purified and the village and the house where the birth has taken place are cleansed.

"Three factors stand out as being of prime importance in the *Janam Chatiar* ceremony: (i) The religious role of the father who provides the child with *abge* and *orak bongas* (subclan and household spirits); (ii) The intimate connection between the removing of the childbirth pollution and the admission of the child into the tribe and the *bongas; (iii)* The Santals' reluctance to lose one of their progeny. Because of these three factors the illegitimate child is almost unknown in the Santal community. The ingenuity of the Santals has evolved a system whereby all children of Santal parentage are legitimated. Campbell, A., 'Rules of Succession and Partition of Property as observed by the Santals', *Journal of the Bihar* and *Orissa Research Society,* Patna 1(1) Mar. 1915, pp. 21-5. If a child is born to a Santal girl from a man of another tribe, or vice-versa, both the child and its Santal parent are outcasted for life.

"When a child is born to a Santal girl out of wedlock, the .girl's father and household are semi-outcasted *(Pante-Begar)* and they can only return to the tribe by arranging a father for the child. This can be done in two ways. First, if a person is proved to be the *genitor,* whether he accepts the paternity or not, he either has to marry the girl or pay for a 'bought husband'. Second, if the village cannot prove who the real father is, then a substitute father is arranged. In both instances, the *Nim Dak Mandi* ceremony removes all traces of illegitimacy and the child takes the *bongas* of his father." adds Mr. J. Troisi.

Ceremony of Eksia

In a ceremony called *Ekshia* the child is given a name. It is performed on the tenth day after birth either by the maternal grand mother or maternal aunt and is attended by the female members of the family. In the morning the woman takes the infant in her lap and sits in the cleansed open courtyard. She places a brass pot full of water before her. She drops three gains of paddy in the name of the gods *Dharma, Goram* and in the name of one of the paternal uncles or grandfathers in the case of male issue and the name of paternal grandmother or paternal aunt in the case of a female one. She eagerly awaits till the three grains of paddy meet together. If the grains do not meet, the process is repeated with other names of the persons of the said relatives till the paddy grains meet together. The person after whom the child is named, if alive, henceforth enters into a special friendly relation called as *Mita* or *Sakhi*, with the new born and has to render certain special ceremonial duties till his death.

In two cases it was observed that after this ceremonial name-giving ritual the infant is given another name. If the child is born on Sunday, he may be called *Rabi* (Sun), or based on any other day of the week.

The ear-boring ceremony (*Tukur lutui*) is performed between the first and third year age preferably in the month of Magh (Jan.-Feb.). One of the villagers expert in ear-boring performs the ritual. On the appointed day, the child is bathed and made to a new set of clothes and is made to sit on an wooden seat in the open courtyard while facing east. After perforation of ear, a chicken is sacrificed and a few drops of blood of the sacrificed fowl are put on the injured ear-lobe. Food and drink (rice-beer) are offered to the invitees. The *Mita* or the person after whom the child is ceremonially named, if alive, has some special functions to perform on this occasion. The ceremony and rituals are observed by the Mundas.

According to K.P. Bahadur, the Munda name giving ceremony is celebrated differently of different places, still, it marks similarity in its observance. "The selection of the name baby is made in an interesting manner. A grain of rice is dropped into a vessel of water. Then another grain is dropped and the name of some ancestor or relative uttered. If the second grain meets the first one, the baby is named after the relative. If it does not, another grain is dropped to the name of another ancestor. The process is repeated till the two grains join, and the name of the ancestor associated with the particular grain is given. This is the signal for more rejoicing and further consumption of the choice rice beer. The mother of the baby goes to the village spring and puts a mark of vermilion with the fingers of her left hand on the wooden enclosures encircling it. A girdle of thread is wound round the baby's waist.

"The ear of the baby is pierced in the first second or third year. The relation after whom the baby has been named comes on this occasion with present of rice, salt, mustard oil, rice-beer, bead necklaces, a new piece of cloth and a got. A figure is drawn in the courtyard with rice and flour dough. Paddy grains are cast on this, and a wooden *pirah* placed for the relation to sit. He rubs mustard oil on his head as well as on the head of the child. Barbers are called and they pierce the child's ears using a sharp copper or silver rod. A black fowl is sacrificed and the blood sprinkled over the figure drawn on the ground. There is feasting and drinking, and a prayer to Sing-Bonga to protect the child," adds Bahadur.

General Muslim Birth Customs

The customs, rites and rituals related to the Muslims life-cycle are common to all Muslims in India, except only a few minor variations, due to being influenced by the Islamic customs and observances. Mr. Ja'far Sarif describes the custom related to the birth ceremony. Thus, "Though the desire for male offspring does not influence Musalmans to the same extent as Hindus, who believe that it is only a son who can perform the funeral rites which admit the spirit of his father into the company of his sainted ancestors, still among Musalmans the craving for a male heir is often intense. Among the Brahuis, 'in the wide world there is naught man and wife set their hearts on more than the birth of a son. For who would be content to quit this world and leave no son behind? As for a daughter, a daughter is little more than a gift to your neighbour'. The Arabs objected to the birth of a girl. 'And they ascribe daughters unto God. Glory be to Him! But they desire them not for themselves' (*Koran*, xvi. 59). There is, however, no evidence of infanticide among them, a common custom among certain Hindu castes (*Census Report*, India, 1911, i. 215 ff.). The custom among the Gakkhars of the Panjab hills seems to be sporadic or of foreign origin (Ferishta, i. 183). Hence many devices are employed to relieve barrenness. In Gujarat, some 'Amils, or exorcists give their applicants cardamoms, or cloves, or pieces of candied sugar, on which the mystic and powerful Names of God being blown, they are supposed to possess the virtue of casting out the spirit of barrenness, since, as a rule, barrenness is due to spirit-possession. Others direct strands of thread to be worn round the abdomen or the neck; others, again, simply write or trace some name or charm of words with the tip of the finger over the womb of the women or the loins of the man. An exorcist or 'Amil has also to help after conception with the object that the issue may be male. He gives charms to be washed in water for a monthly bath. Some dead Saints have a reputation as child-givers. To tie knots on bits of string or ribbon to a post or pillar supporting the canopy over a Saint's tomb is considered by barren women one of the surest means of obtaining issue'. *BG*. ix, part 2, 147 f. Such tombs are known in the Panjab as *Khanaqah*, the original meaning of which is a convent' (Rose, i. 519). The tomb of Shaikh Salim Chishti at Fatehpur Sikri, by whose intercession Akbar believed that he had been blessed with a son, is even at the present day visited by childless Hindu and Musalman women who tie threads or rags on the lovely screen which surrounds it. Smith, Akbar the Great Mogul, 104 ff. Miniature cradies are often hung at shrines as a charm for children, a Bedouin practice. A.H. Layard, *Discoveries in the Ruins of Nineveh and Babylon*, 309. A tree in the enclosure of the Saint Shaikh 'Alam at Ahmadabad yields a peculiar acorn-like fruit which is much valued by childless women. If the birth of a child follows the eating of the fruit, the man or woman who used it should for a term of years at every anniversary of the death of the Saint come and water the roots of the tree with milk. The leaves of a tree near the grave of Miran Sahib at Anjha have the same effect. The Baloch, when a woman desires a child, hold a staff against a wall and make the woman pass three times beneath it, or she is sent to visit shrines, particularly that of Shah Wasawa, where she embraces a tree which overhangs his tomb. Other approved methods are : to give the woman a charm or magic diagram which is either washed in rose water and drunk, or worn round the neck ; to bathe in water drawn from seven wells on the night of the Divali or Hindu Feast of Lights, when spirits are abroad ; to scare the evil spirit which besets the woman by abusing her ; to castigate her with a charmed chain ; to write on a piece of bread a series of numbers which make up seventy-three, and give it to a black dog ; to burn down the hut of a neighbour to remove the taboo. The Brahui with the same object circumcise the woman, but if the fault is supposed to lie with her husband and a physician fails to remedy it, a Mulla provides a charm or amulet, and if this fails the blame is laid on the Jinn.

"When conception is announced, the expectant mother is subjected to various taboos, and she takes various precautions to avoid the attacks of evil spirits. All her carvings for food must be indulged, such as that for eating earth, which is supposed to check vomiting. If such things are denied to her, the result will be a miscarriage. In Gujarat she wears silk threads round her waist, each thread bearing a knot for each month of her pregnancy. At the ninth month these are unwound, incense is burned over them, and they are thrown into water. The Divali or Hindu feast of lights is a specially dangerous time, because evil spirits are likely to be about. She must not enter a shed used at marriage or other festivities ; she must not be present at death or other family rites. She, her husband, and her relatives must not eat anything during an eclipse, because these are supposed to be caused by evil spirits attacking the sun or moon. If anything folded, like betel, is cut at this time, the child will be born with folded ears or will suffer from hare-lip, and if any one smokes, the child will have a weak chest which causes gurgling like that of a tobacco pipe. During an eclipse the friends should pray and read the Koran, lay grain on a bed and give it to friends. During pregnancy the woman should not wear new clothes or ornaments, use eye collyrium, stain her hands or feet with henna, or colour her teeth, because such things attract the Evil Eye. She must not touch a coconut or any underground root because such things resist the gatherer, must be dug up with force, and thus delivery may be impeded. Many of these taboos are identical with those of the Hindus or have been borrowed from them.

"The sex of the expected child may be foretold by an examination of the woman by a committee of midwives. Among the Baloch a house snake is killed and the woman steps over its body, and then it is thrown in the air in the hope that it will fall on its back, but if it falls on its belly the birth of a daughter is certain. In Baroda a few drops of milk are squeezed from the woman's breasts, and if the milk is thin the birth of a boy is anticipated. *Census Report*, 1911, i. 178. Cf. Russell, ii. 27; A.L.K. Anantha Krishna Iyer, ii. 372.

"In the Deccan before the announcement of the first pregnancy the woman's lap and that of her husband are filled with fruits of various kinds, her mother sends clothes and the friends are feasted. The Satmasa, Satwansa or Satwasa, the rite in the seventh month which has been borrowed from the Hindus, is the most important. The woman is invited by her parents, who give her new clothes, perfume her with rose-water and sandalwood, invite a few friends to a party, sit up with her all night, and scare evil spirits by music and festivity. They press a little of her milk on a yellow cloth, and if a white stain is left they expect a girl, if it leaves a yellow mark a boy. At the Naumasa, or ninth month, the friends assemble, and the woman is allowed to wear the new clothes and jewellery which up to this time she has discarded. Then comes the Sahnak or pot rite of Bibi Fatima. Food is cooked in little pots, over which the Fatiha or first chapter of the Koran is read in the name of Fatima, daughter of the Prophet, and the food is given to some women who are selected on account of their virtue. Fatiha, 'the opener', the Paternoster prefixed to the Koran, was probably composed late in the Prophet's career, as it contains polemical references to Jews and Christians ('those who have incurred anger and go astry'), because his hostility to the Jews did not begin till after his migration, and that towards Christians some years later. Birth in the eighth month is unlucky, and it is attributed to a cat entering her room. Hence eight is never used in counting a child's age, being called *anginnat*, 'uncounted' (Rose, i. 738 f.). Vigil, as before, is kept with rejoicings. In Gujarat slaked lime is served with the food as a sort of ordeal, because it is supposed not to burn the mouth of a chaste woman. The glance of no male, not even that of a boy, must fall on the food thus served. In north India such rites are done four months and five days after the announcement of pregnancy, usually only in the case of the first child, and also at the ninth month. The woman's nails are cut and the parings are put in a silver box which is given to the barber's wife. The woman who dresses her must be one who enjoys the fullest married happiness. Among the Brahuis, on the new moon of the seventh month seven kinds of grain are cooked and distributed among the kin, who must send a gift in return. After the rite they keep vigil.

"It is a general custom that the first child should be born at the house of the mother's parents. A separate room is arranged, and a fire is kept burning in it to defend the mother and child from the Jinn and the Evil Eye. As among Hindus, many charms are used to aid delivery. A line of boys fetch water from the well, and the speed with which the vessel is passed from hand to hand helps delivery, or a lump of clay from a potter's wheel, which has thus acquired the quality of swiftness, is mixed with water and given to her to drink. A square rupee of Akbar, which bears the Emperor's name with that of the four Companions of the Prophet, is dipped in water which is given to her, but no British or other secular coin can be used in this way. By way of sympathetic magic, delivery is added by giving the schoolboy a holiday, or the girdle of some holy man is dipped in water which she drinks. In the act of delivery she lies on a quilt spread on the ground, with her head north and her feet south, for in case she dies in childbirth this is the position in which Musalmans are buried, with the face towards Mecca. Or she squats on the ground holding a bed while the midwife rubs her back and presses a broom against her abdomen. Among the Brahui she lies on sand, and they say that a boy is born with his head towards the ground, a girl facing her mother. In labour she is assisted by a midwife, known as Dai, Janai or Chamarin, who is so ignorant and careless about sanitary precautions that any but an ordinary presentation is fatal to the mother. In cases of protracted labour, alms are given to the poor, prayers are said, an amulet is hung on the thigh of the patient, water in which the beard of some holy man has been dipped is administered to her, a charmed potsherd is laid on her abdomen. Among the Pathans the midwife brings water to the husband, who washes his hands and feet, and the water is given to the woman to drink.

"Immediately after delivery she is made to swallow a small copper coin or a bit of copper to help to expel the placenta. The midwife calls for a piece of sharpened silver, which she claims as her perquisite after she has severed the cord with it. She then puts the cord into a pot with a copper coin and betel leaf, and buries it in a corner of the room or in a cool place where the water-pots are kept, so that the cool damp may cause it to grow and so benefit the child. If a knife is used to cut the cord it must not be put to any other purpose, but it is left near the patient till the fortieth day, when Kajal or lampblack is collected on it and applied to the eyes of the child. In the Panjab the pot containing the cord is buried inside the house, and betel leaf, silver, turmeric, and charcoal are thrown on it to repel evil spirits, while a fire is lighted over it for six days till it is supposed to be consumed. The Brahui bury the cord in a place where no dog can find it, for if it chances to be eaten by a dog the baby grows restless and becomes a squaller. The Baloch think that if a dog or cat gets hold of the cord the mother's milk will dry up, so they bury it in the house and cover it with rice and molasses, a precaution which leads to a second pregnancy. In the Imperial household they used to sever the cord with a thread and put it in a small bag which was kept under the child's pillow 'with certain superstitious writings'.

"As soon as the placenta is expelled, they give the woman some asafoetida to prevent her from catching cold. A handkerchief is tied on her head, a roller bound round her abdomen, and she is laid on a bed or on a sheet spread on the ground, in a warm room, which in rich families is enclosed with curtains, while beside the bed are laid a lemon, leaves of the Nim tree (*melia azadirachta*), a Katar or dirk, a knife or other weapon to keep off evil. They then give her a packet of betel leaves with some myrrh (*bol*) to chew. In Gujarat, when the child is born, the midwife, in order to deceive the spirits, if it is a boy, says that it is a girl or blind of an eye, but if it is a girl the fact is stated because a girl does not provoke jealousy and the Evil Eye. In north India, if it is a boy, the midwife cries 'A son, may you be lucky !'; if a girl 'May she be a blessing !' In the ease of a son the father discharges a gun from the housetop, as it is said to announce the birth, but really to scare evil spirits, and with the same object he strikes an iron griddle-plate three times with a stick. The midwife washes the baby in water mixed with Chana or gram flour, and the friends throw coins into the pot as her fee, while she also gets the clothes and bedding used by the patient. In the

Panjab the midwife washes the mother's breasts with water, using, as the Hindus do, some blades of holy grass as a brush, and this washing is done a second time by the baby's sister or some other woman of the family. Next day the midwife fastens a charm made of green leaves on the house door and the child is suckled.

"In south India the drink given to the mother for forty days is water boiled in which a red hot horseshoe or other piece of iron has been slaked. In some places, as in Persia, she gets nothing to eat or drink for the first three days. Some give Achhwani or Achwani, a caudle, so called because it consists of dill (*ajwain, ligusticum ajowan*), sugar and flour. This is followed by vegetables and wheaten flour, sugar and butter boiled into a paste, and then a wheatern dumpling (*thali, thuli*). Many people give her Sathaura or Sonthaura, so called because it is made of dry ginger (*sonth*), boiled with soft sugar and butter. After this she is allowed old rice seasoned with black pepper. By the tenth or twelfth day she resumes her ordinary food. In the Panjab she is fed with pieces of bread soaked in butter and sugar, which is said to promote the flow of milk and is used as long as she is suckiing. Soon after birth the midwife gives the baby Ghutti, 'a gulp or draught', a cleansing medicine made of aloes, spices, and borax, or honey water is given and next day an infusion of dill, beans, and a light sweetmeat. In Gujarat the Ghutti consists of aniseed, myrobolans, dried rose leaves, senna, and droppings of mice or goats.

"Whenever the child is bathed or taken out of the house the knife used to cut the cord is taken with it as a protective, and when the child is brought back the knife is replaced beside the mother, and it is used on the Chilla or fortieth day in sacrificing a sheep or a cock. In some families the mother does not oil or comb her hair for forty days after her delivery, but wears a handkerchief on her head, and some people during that time do not allow her to leave her room except to bathe on the Chhathi or sixth day and on the Chilla or fortieth, or for the purpose of counting the stars as described later on. During this time when a stranger enters the house he or she throws some Sipand or Ispand (*peganum harmala*) on the fire to disperse any evil that may have come with them. Some place an iron plate on which lampblack is collected and a broom beside the door until the fortieth day. Great care is taken that no dog or cat enters, and even the name of a cat is not mentioned. But Muhammad said 'Cats are not impure; they keep watch around us'.

"After the child is washed and swaddled he is presented to the friends. The Azan or Bang, the call to prayer, is uttered into his right ear and the Kalima or Creed in his left. This is generally done by the preacher or Khatib, or by a boy who gets a reward for saying 'Allahu akbar !' 'God is very great

!' Among rich people a Mashaikh, or venerable man, or the Murshid, or family guide, dips his finger in honey or chews a date or a grape and puts it into the child's mouth before he is put to the breast, in order that the wisdom of the sage may be imparted to him. The Fatiha is then said, and sugar and betel are distributed. When the friends hear of the birth they come to the house each of them carrying a blade or two of green grass, which the leader sticks in the father's hair. In return for congratulations he gives them a Got or present which is spent on an entertainment in one of their houses or in a neighbouring garden.

"The custom of moulding the child's head prevails on the north-west frontier. The Brahui shape by pressure the head and features of the child, measure the mouth, and if it is bigger than the space of a finger joint they press it into shape with a ring, rub the lips to make them thin and press the nose. In the case of a girl they press back any Bhaunri or lock of hair which projects in front, and at the same time the body and feet are anointed and brought into the proper shape. In the Bahawalpur State they mould the head in a deep cup-shaped earthen pot in order to make the back of the skull round.

"There are four kinds of Dai or nurses: the midwife, Dai, Daijanai, or Chamarin, wife of a man of the Chamar caste, workers in leather; Dai-dudh-pilai or Anna, a wet nurse; Dai-khilai, Chhochha, the dry nurse or nursery-maid; Daiasil, Mama, Aya, a ladies' maid. The Mughal name for a nurse or foster-mother was Anaga or Anka, for as foster-father Koka or Kukaltash, a nurse's husband and her male relations Atka. The poorer orders usually take nurses from the lower orders. Musalman children are generally nursed till they are two and a half years old, which according to the Law is the time during which the nurse is treated as a foster-mother; but if the child is nursed by another woman during that time she is not regarded as his proper foster-mother, and it is not unusual to see children three and four years old hanging about their mother's breasts. Ladies scarcely ever nurse their own children, as they consider nursing to be weakening and injurious to the figure.

"The child is bathed morning and evening and fumigated with the smoke of Ispand (*paganum harmala*) and lignum aloes, and they tie round its neck patchouli leaves (*pogostemon heyneanus*) and asafoetida to prevent the shadow of strangers falling upon it. Whenever the child is bathed they take some red or yellow dye made of quicklime and turmeric and add to it a few bits of charcoal, all of which the nurse waves three times over the child and then throws it away, or she merely takes some water in a vessel, waves it over the child, and then pours it on her own feet, signifying 'May all the child's misfortunes fail on me !' So people say 'All the child's troubles have beset the midwife'.

"The naming of children is often done on the day of birth or on that day week. Generally the former day is chosen because until the child is named the mother in some families does not receive even a drink of water, much less betel, perfumes, or other luxuries. After the naming the Fatiha is said over sweetmeats and these are sent accompanied by music to absent friends. This is the business of the midwife, who receives gifts in return. In Gujarat the mother, according to Hindu custom, is led to a window and made to count seven stars.

"The children of Musalmans belong to the tribe of the father, and consequently if the boy be a Sayyid's son the first word of his name will be Sayyid or Mir, as Sayyid 'Ali or Mir Ahmad. But these honorific titles are often dropped in after life, and so it becomes necessary to ask the tribe to which a man belongs. The original rule of the Law runs 'Call your children after the Prophet': and the names God loves best are 'Abdu-l-lah, 'servant of God', 'Abdu-I-rahman, 'servant of the Compassionate', Harith or 'husbandman', Humam 'diligent'; while the worst are Harb, 'war', and Murra, 'bitterness'. But these rules do not apply to modern Indo-Musalmans.

"If he be the son of a Shaikh, then at the beginning or end of his name is added one of the following designations : Khwaja, 'lord', Ghulam, 'servant'. Muhammad, the Prophet, Din, 'religion', 'Ali, son-in-law of the Prophet, Bakhsh, 'given', 'Abd,' 'servant'; as Khwaja Yusuf, Ghulam Nabi, Muhammad Husain, Shamsu-d-din, Hasan Bakhsh, Raza 'Ali, Shaikh Muhammad, 'Abdu-l-qadir. These names, however, do not always indicate a Shaikh, since Sayyids often use the same names.

"If he be the son of a Mughal, his name begins or ends with the titles Mirza, Mirza, Amirzada. 'son of an Amir or lord', or Aga, Agha, 'chief, as for instance, Mirza Ahmad Ismail Beg, Aga or Agha Ja'far. In the royal family of Persia the title Mirza is placed after the name instead of before it. The title Mirza seems to have been adopted because the mother was a Sayyid, the males of which group have the title Mir even if the father was a Mughal. In the case of Pathans the title Khan, 'lord, master'. or Khan Sahib is invariably used at the end of the name, as Bahadur Khan, 'valiant lord'. We frequently however, find Shaikhs and Sayyids with the title Khan attached to their names, as Ghulam Ahmad Khan; but in such cases it is bestowed upon them by their masters as an honorary title.

"The following are exceptions to these rules. Should the father be a Shaikh and the mother a Sayyid the word Sharif, 'eminent', is usually added to the beginning or end of the child's name, as Ja'far Sharif or Sharif Ja'far. It is customary with some people to add this appellation to all the names of the family, as Ja'far Sharif, son of 'Ali Sharif, son of Sharif Hamid.

In most cases, however, when the mother is a Sayyidani and the father a Shaikh, they leave out the word Sharif, call themselves Shaikh Ahmad, or some equivalent name, and belong to the Shaikh group. In other places, again, they add the word Khwaja, 'nobleman'. When the father is a Mughal and the mother a Sayyidani their offspring get the name of Khwajazada, 'son of a nobleman', and the title Khwaja is often given to spiritual guides, like the Pir or Murshid. Others, again, of all the four groups add to their names the titles Sahib, 'master', Miyan, 'sir', Jan, 'life' as, for example, Daud Sahib, 'Ammu Jan. This, however, is not the established practice in any group, but parents are accustomed to call their children by these familiar names out of affection, so that when they grow to manhood these names become established and the real names are often forgotten.

"The following names are added to the beginning or end of the full titles of girls. Among Sayyids women are called Begam, 'lady', Bi, Bibi, 'mistress', Nissa, 'woman', Shah, 'queen'. To the names of Shaikh girls they add only the titles Ma, 'mother', Bi or Bibi, except in the case of children of rank who get the title Begam. This is also the rule with Mughals and Pathans. Mughal women use the title Khanam, 'lady', added to the end of their names, but illegitimate daughters receive the title Bai, 'lady'. Rich people sometimes adopt the daughters of other people who are called Gayan, 'singers' and the word Bai is added to their names, but when they make favourites of such girls they are called Begam. In the old days, slave girls with whom their masters cohabited were first called Bibi, then Bai, Khanam or Begam. There are two kinds of Musalman dancing-girls, Natni and Kanchani, the latter being usually a Hindu, while Kasbi or Harjai is the usual term for a prostitute. The former sometimes receive the titles Bai or Kunwar, the latter Bakhsh.

"It is not customary among Musalmans to give their own names to their children. The modes of naming are as follows: First the child is named after some member of the family, as the grandfather on either side, or after the tutelary Saint of the family. In north India the name should never be that of an ancestor within two or three generations; indeed it is contrary to rule to give the child the name of a relation or member of the family. We must also distinguish the 'Alam, or individual name; Kunyat, that of relationship; Laqab, honorary; the 'Alamat, or royal title; the 'Anwan, that of honour; Ansab, that implying denomination, and Takhallus, the nom de plume. Secondly, at an auspicious time which is fixed from the table given below, eight or ten learned men meet and fix upon the first letter of any page of the Koran opened at random (*fal*) as that which should begin the name. The name is often fixed by astrological considerations. Thus Akbar was named immediately after his birth Badru-d-din 'full moon of religion', because he was born on the full moon of the month Sha'ban. But his relations, with the object of protecting him from Black Magic, and to frustrate the calculations of hostile astrologers, selected a new official birthday, the fifth of the month Rajab. His former name being thus inappropriate, he was renamed Jalalu-d-din 'the splendour of religion'. Thirdly a few tickets on which different names are inscribed are rolled up, laid on a plate or put into a cup which is covered with a handkerchief, and the contents are shaken about and scattered on the floor. Any little child present is desired to pick up one of them and the name inscribed on it is selected. Fourthly, some people choose a name from among those which begin with the letter found at the beginning or end of the name of the planet under which the child was born. The following are the rules: The planets, seven in number, Shams, the Sun, Qamar, the Moon, Zuhal, Kaiwan, Saturn, Zohra, Venus, 'Utarid, Mercury, Mirrikh, Mars, Mushtari. Jupiter, are supposed to preside over the twenty-four hours of day and night.

"...The planets exercise many influences, favourable and unfavourable, on the human race, of which a few examples may be given. The Dispositions of the Sun: One born under the dominance of the Sun, male or female, will be wealthy, sensible, passionate, easily irritated, generous, he will acquire much property, his word will be much respected, he will prefer black and red clothes, be amorous, addicted to drinking, a scoffer, little famed for pious works, annually indisposed, his birth will be inauspicious to his parents, he will live long and outlive them both. The Dispositions of Venus: he will be fond of music and singing, and still more of dress and sweets, partial to sweet and dainty dishes, amorous, beautiful, accomplished, amiable, endeavouring to appear neat and well dressed, constantly trying to enrich himself at the expense of others, unwilling to disclose his own secrets, never without perfumes, harmonious in voice and a good singer, a pleasant speaker of agreeable conversation, eloquent and charming to many, and he will support not only his parents but also his brothers and sisters. The Dispositions of Mercury: a man of wisdom and learning, a good scribe, versed in many sciences, a clever painter, blessed with a good memory, nay even a Hafiz, who knows the whole Koran by rote, (Aurangzeb and some ladies of the Mughal royal family knew the whole Koran by heart (Jadunath Sarkar, *Life of Aurangzib*, i. 8) a poet, wealthy, master of arts, his society and friendship profitable to many, never solitary, but surrounded by people obedient to his will, an arithmetician, of uncommon penetration, useful to any one to whom he is well disposed, but if he dislikes a person he will avoid even the sight of him. The Dispositions of the Moon: he will be a gambler, good-looking, a drunkard, a great traveller, addicted to falsehood, a gabbler, famous in the assemblies of the great, subject every half year to diseases due to debility and cold, dreading water, in danger of his life while travelling, a blessing to his parents and friends. The Dispositions of Saturn: of a swarthy, dark complexion, long lived, of thin habit of body, black eyes, a flatterer, of a bilious temperament, loud voiced, courageous and a brave soldier, good looking, of a hasty disposition, perverse, tyrannical, fond of chastising, unkind, liberal, capricious, detesting flattery, pure in mind, without malice, very forgetful. The Dispositions of Jupiter: his daily food will be ever abundant; he will be good-looking, a Hafiz, a man of science, a judge, learned, a governor, a monarch, a Nawwab, distinguished in science and politics; he will have many enemies, but will always overcome them; none will be able to injure him ; in handicraft, drawing and penmanship he will be unrivalled; sensible, a counsellor, charitable, firm in mind, of a delicate constitution, high-spirited, and extremely persevering in all undertakings. The Dispositions of Mars: he will be tyrannical, of a ruddy complexion, a quick talker, kind, easily irritated, fond of white dress and perfumes, skilled in many arts and sciences, earnest in the search of knowledge, inclined to deprive another of his money and to hoard it himself, most ambitious.

"The name of the child is selected from the following list. If a boy is born on the day or night of Sunday he is named Ibrahim, Abraham, Sulaiman, Solomon, Daud, David, Musa, Moses, 'Ayub, Job, Hashim, 'bread-breaker', Imran, 'long-lived'. If it be a girl she is called Halima, 'gentle', Habiba, 'friend', Zainab, 'fragrance', Khadija, 'aborter'. If on a Monday, a boy is named Muhammad, 'greatly praised', Ahmad, 'most praised', Mahmud, 'praised', Qasim, divided', Qadir, 'powerful'. If it be a girl she is called Fatima 'weaner', Amma, 'security', Hamida, 'praised', Rafi'a, 'exalted', Ruqia, 'enchanting', Zarina, 'golden'. If on a Tuesday, a boy is named Isma'il, Ishmael, Ishaq, Isaac, Abu Bakr, 'father of the maiden', Ilias, Elias, Yasin, Pharaoh, while a girl is called Hanifa, 'a sincere Muslim', 'Ayisha, 'life', wife of the Prophet, Sharifa, 'praised', Sakina, Hebrew Shekinah, 'that which dwells'. If on a Wednesday, a boy is named 'Usman, 'serpent', 'Ali, 'exalted', Harun, Aaron, Hasan, 'beautiful', Husain, 'little beauty', 'Umar, 'bought'. If a girl Rabi'i, 'vernal', 'Aziza, 'excellent', Jamila, 'beautiful', Fazila, 'excellent', Najm, 'star', Khurshed, 'sun', Sitara, 'star'. If on Thursday, a son is called Yusuf, Joseph, Hamid, 'praised'. Mustafa, Murtaza, 'the chosen', Sajjad, 'bowing in adoration', Baqir, 'learned', 'Askari', 'soldier', Raza, 'content', Ja'far, 'a stream', Muhammad Ghaus 'an ardent Saint'. If a girl, Maryam, Mary, Asya, 'running water', Zulaikha', 'she that slipped', the wife of Potiphar, Kharian, 'happy', Wajida, 'finder', Wasila, 'beloved', Ghafur, 'for-giving', Ma'rut, 'celebrated'. If on a Friday a son 'Isa, Jesus, Anwar, 'resplendent', Nur, 'bright', Haidar, 'lion', Akram, 'honour', Adam, Adam, Sultan 'monarch', Habibullah, 'a friend of God', Hafizu-llah, 'protected by God', Karimullah, 'blessed of God', Rahmatu-llah, 'mercy of God', 'Alimu-llah, 'learned in God',

Qudratu-llah, 'power of God', 'Abdu-llah, 'servant of God'. If a girl, Mah, 'beloved', Zohra, Venus, Mahbuba, 'beloved', Amira, 'princess', Ratan, 'jewel', Banu, 'lady', Khatun, 'lady', Niss, 'woman', 'Hawwa', 'Eve', 'Arifa', 'pious', Mama, 'mother'. If born on a Saturday, a boy is named 'Abdu-l-qadir, 'servant of the Almighty', 'Abdu-l-karim, 'servant of the All Gracious', 'Abdu-l-razzaq,' servant of the Bread Giver', 'Abdu-l-wahhab, 'servant of the All Bountiful', 'Abdu-l-shakur, 'servant of the Rewarder', 'Abdu-l-latif, 'servant of the All Gracious', Shamsu-d-din, 'Sun of the Faith', Nizamu-d-din, 'ruler of the Faith', Siraju-d-din, 'Sun of the Faith', Muharram, 'the tabooed, honoured', Siddiq, 'he who speaks the truth'. If it is a girl, she is called Nazuk, 'delicate', Ma'mula, 'customary', Latifa, 'the gentle', Bilqis, Queen of Sheba. (The interpretation of some of these names is uncertain. The lists in Sir R. Temple, *Proper Names of Panjabis*, have generally been followed.)

"Opprobrious names, implying degradation, disgust, impurity, are often given by low-class Musalmans to their children as a means of baffling the Evil Eye or the danger from exaggerated praise. Such are Nathu, 'nose-bored', Dukhi, 'afflicted', Gharib, 'poor', Bhikhi, 'beggar', Kaki, 'crow', Kubra, 'hunchback'."

Ceremonies and Rites after Birth

Mr. Ja'far Sarif continues, Patti, the parting of the mother's hair on both sides of the head, performed on the third day after the birth, a line being left in the middle, is probably a magical method of freeing the woman from any internal obstruction. The parting of the hair of a pregnant woman is probably intended to secure easy delivery, but in other cases it may be a fertility charm, on the analogy of the plough passing through the furrow. It may be compared with the Hindu rite of Simantonnayana (*ERE*. iii. 471, ii. 650 ; Monier-Williams, *Brahmanism and Hinduism*, 4th ed., 357). The women assemble, perform the rite, dress mother and child in red, tie a handkerchief over the woman's head, hold a red canopy over their heads and apply lampblack and soot to the eyes of mother and child. They fill the mother's lap with cakes spiced with ginger (*sonthana*) and with betel. The guests apply turmeric to the mother's face, deposit their parting gifts (*raktani, rukhsatana*) and depart. Among the Shi'as of Lucknow on the fourth day the friends are invited to share in the family joy and there is a noisy feast.

"From the birth till the sixth day there is as much festivity as the family can afford. Chhathi, or the sixth day rite, should be done on that day, but it takes place more generally on the seventh or ninth. When many deaths have occurred in the house, in order to change the luck, they perform it on the third. The selection of the sixth is due to the fact that the occurrence of puerperal fever in the mother and tetanus in the child, the latter being due to infection during the sloughing of navel-cord and the lack of sanitary precautions, is generally noticed on the sixth or seventh day, and these maladies are naturally attributed to the dangerous spirit of the sixth, Chhathi or Satvai. The midwife smears the house floor with yellow or white clay or cowdung, and the women friends, men taking no part in the rite, send to the mother soap-pods (*sikakai, ritha, acacia concinna),* used for cleansing the hair, gingeli or sesamum oil used in anointing the body before the Chiksa or perfumed powder is applied, with some lampblack, betel, and caudle. After the child has been bathed, a shirt (*kurta*) made of any old article of dress worn by some ancient worthy is put on the child, in place of the pinafore worn up to that time, in order that he may reach old age. Should the midwife be an old woman she makes the shirt out of her own clothes. The first clothes of Akbar were made out of the garments of the holy man, Sayyid 'Ali Shirazi. On that day it is the custom to wear borrowed *(prada, parad)* clothes, which are provided by the washerman.

"Then the mother sits on a bed and she is bathed with a decoction of aromatic herbs and leaves, a gift is given to the midwife, the liver *(kaleji)* of a sheep is served with rice and pulse, a portion is sent to absent friends, and the night is spent in amusement. This rite is done for all children, not for the first alone. From the evening meal a plateful is laid aside with the object that when the child grows up he may not covet every kind of food he sees. Should he prove to be greedy, people say that his dish *(bhanda)* was not properly filled. In the centre of the dish a four-wicked lamp made of flour paste is sometimes lighted, friends drop a coin or two into it, and it is kept burning all night. This food is called 'the dish of the sixth' *(chhathi ka bhanda)* or 'the vigil' *(ratjaga),* or by the vulgar 'Mother Sixth' (*Chhathi Ma*), because they suppose that Mother Sixth, the spirit which writes the fate of people, comes on that night und writes the child's destiny. Lower-class people keep the Chhathi rite, but the higher classes substitute the 'Aqiqa for it.

"In north India on the Chhathi day female friends assemble, the mother bathes in warm water, and presents (*chhuchak*, a term also applied to the gifts which she receives after she visits her parents when the impurity period ends) are sent by her relations. When mother and child are dressed they come out of the delivery room *(zachha* or *zacha-khana),* she holding a Koran in her hands and keeping her eyes shut. When she comes out she opens her eyes and looks seven times at the sky. While she is out of the room a little boy is made to sit on her bed for a moment, a magical device to secure another boy, and before he goes out he demands a present. Then food made of seven kinds of grain (*satnaja*), often used in magic, is laid before the mother, but before she eats, seven women whose husbands are alive each take a mouthful from the dish. The wives of the family barber and gardener make wreaths of green leaves, which are hung on the houses of relations who give them a present. In the Panjab during the first six days after the delivery the mother is never left alone. This, it is said, is done to prevent her from overlaying the child, but more probably to protect her from evil spirits, and a lamp is kept burning for the same reason all the time. Behmata or Bidhimata, 'Mother Fate', is here the goddess who records the child's destiny at birth. It is a deadly sin to refuse fire to her when she asks for it, and a story is told of a Faqir who did so and was turned into a glow-worm, which ever carries fire behind it in its tail. The Brahui, as soon as a child is born, paint a mark in indigo on all the four walls of the house, so that no spirit may enter, while some strew leaves of the *pipal* or sacred fig tree about the house to keep off witches, and thrust a knife into the ground near the child's head. This must remain there for forty days, and if the mother happens during that time to go out of doors she must carry it with her as a protective.

"As among the Semites, the impurity of the mother lasts for forty days. During that time she is not allowed to pray, touch the Koran, or enter a mosque. These taboos originally lasted as long as any issue of blood continued. In the Panjab she sits while she nurses her child, lest its nose may become deformed by pressing against her breasts. In south India on the fortieth as well as on the sixth, twelfth, and thirteenth days her friends bring gifts for the child, in particular amulets (*ta'wiz*) of gold or silver with verses of the Koran engraved on them which are hung over one shoulder, crossing the back and chest and reaching below the hip on the other side. This gift-giving in north India is usually done on the sixth day. In the Panjab among people who do not seclude their women, when the child is one month and ten days old, the mother bathes, is dressed in new clothes, puts on her head a couple of jars filled with boiled grain, goes to the well and offers the food to the water Saint, Khwaja Khizr, after which she fills the jars with water and goes home. In Gujarat little boats made of grass are taken to the nearest water and set afloat in the name of the Saint. In south India the fortieth day is spent in amusements. Hijras or eunuchs are paid to sing and dance, and they go about the town shouting 'Where is a son born?' If the child is a daughter they get little or nothing. If they are not paid they load the father with curses. In the evening male friends are feasted. The Fatiha is said over food in the name of Muhammad Mustafa the Chosen One—on whom be the Peace!—and it is then served to the guests. Some people take the mother and baby into the open air and make her count a few stars, after which a couple of arrows used to be shot into the air.

"According to the Traditions the birth sacrifice is combined with the first shaving, the hair being left on the child's head till the seventh, fourteenth, twenty-first, twenty-eighth, or thirty-fifth day after birth, when it is shaved and its weight in silver is given in aims, as the Prophet did when a son was born to him in his old age. In south India either on the sixth, fortieth, or other convenient day the 'Aqiqa' rite is done, two he-goats for a boy and one for a girl being sacrificed. ('*Aqiqa* properly means the hair of the new-born infant, but the term is applied by Metonymy to the shaving sacrifice. The victim must be above a year old, perfect and without blemish (*sahihu-l-a'za*), not blind of one or both eyes, or lame, and it must be so carefully skinned that no flesh remains on the hide, and the meat must be so cut up that no bone is broken. As it is difficult to separate the flesh from the smaller bones, they are boiled and dressed with the flesh, the guests are enjoined to chew and swallow the smaller bones, and the meat is carefully removed from the larger bones without injuring them. The meat is well boiled, and served with various kinds of bread. With the offering the benediction is said: 'O Almighty God ! I offer in the stead of my son, life for life, blood for blood, head for head, bone for bone, hair for hair, and skin for skin. In the name of God I sacrifice this he-goat'. It is held meritorious to distribute the meat to friends, but the person on whose account the offering is being made, his parents and his grand-parents, are forbidden to eat it. The bones, boiled or unboiled, skin, feet, and head are buried in the earth, and no one is allowed to use them. In Gujarat the 'Aqiqa is done on the seventh, fourteenth, or twenty-first day after birth, and the rite consists of two parts, the shaving of the child's head and the offering of the goats. The barber passes his razor over the child's head and draws a knife across the goats' throats with the invocation as recorded above. The parings of the child's hair and nails are laid on a flat half-baked cake and are thrown into a river. The bones are buried, the flesh and skin divided into three parts, one given in charity, one to friends, while the rest is eaten by the relatives, the parents and grand-parents being forbidden to share in it.

"In south India the Mundan or shaving follows the 'Aqiqa on some day after. Though most people combine these two rites, the poor observe only the latter, and the very poor combine the shaving with the ceremonies on the sixth and fortieth days. Those who can afford it have the shaving done with a silver-mounted razor and use a silver cup to hold the water, both being the perquisite of the barber, who receives other gifts. After the head is shaved, the rich rub it with saffron, the poor with sandalwood. The weight of the hair in silver is given to Faqirs, and the hair is tied up in cloth, buried or thrown into water. The rich, when disposing of the hair, make an offering to Khwaja Khizr and let the hair float away in a stream. Some leave a lock *(chonti)* uncut in the name of a Saint, and great care is taken that nothing pollutes it. Some postpone the shaving till it can be done at the Dargah or shrine of the Saint. In Sind when the hair is shaved it is put with the bones of the victim offered at the 'Aqiqa rite and buried in a cemetery or at the threshold of the house, the common belief being that at the Day of Resurrection the contents of the skin will rise in the form of a horse and will carry the soul of the child over the bridge of death, Al-Sirat, into Paradise. The Baloch perform the first tons ure prior to circumcision at the shrine of the Saint Sakhi Sarwar, the weight of the hair in silver being given to the Mujawir or attendants of the shrine.

"On the fortieth day, or before, the child is rocked in a swinging cradle *(gahwara),* a piece of magic to make the child grow taller as the swing goes higher. This is done in the evening, and women friends rub the legs of the cradle with sandalwood and decorate them with red thread. They put a coco-nut at each corner of the cradle with some gram cakes and betel laid on the ground, and while they sing a lullaby they scramble for the food. Then they sit up all night and amuse themselves with singing and dancing.

"When the child is about four months old it often claps its hands, and it is said to be making sweetmeat balls *(laddu bandhna).* These are provided, relations are invited, the Fatiha is said over them in the name of the Prophet—on whom be the Peace !—and the party eat them.

"When the child is seven months old, friends are invited, the Fatiha is said over a hasty pudding *(firni)* in the name of Muhammad Murtaza—on whom be the Peace ! They take with the forefinger a little pudding, rub it on the child's tongue and make him taste it. This may be regarded as the weaning, but according to the Traditions the child should be suckled for two and a half years, a period often extended to three or four. In Gujurat this rite is known as Botan *(bota,* 'a bit of meat') or Namakchashi, 'salt-tasting', for the father gives the child some rice and milk on a rupee and a bit of meat to suck. The Brahui wean a boy after a year and a half, a girl after two. They put seven dates in a pot and bid the child take as many as it pleases, the number marking the number of days it will trouble its mother for milk.

"The teething is called Dant nikalna, or Dant ghungni, because when the first tooth appears they make a mess of stirabout *(ghungni)* of grain boiled with sugar. After saying the Fatiha over this it is distributed. In north India the fate of the child is supposed to be bound up with that of its maternal uncle who officiates at the rite. A child who first shows a tooth in the upper jaw is unlucky. To avoid trouble, rice, copper coins, a piece of cloth, and four iron nails are put on a tray which is carried outside the limits of the village. The uncle drives the nails into the ground in the form of a square, and touching the child's tooth with the tray, leaves it within the square. The child is carried by his aunt, sister of his maternal uncle, who sits veiled and is not allowed to see what her brother is doing, while after the rite he goes home in silence.

"A rite is done when the child begins to close its fists *(mutthi bandhna)* and to crawl *(rengna)*. Parched rice *(murmura)* is made into balls which are given to friends, and the night is spent in singing and dancing. Among the Brahui, when a child begins to toddle they throw a little loaf among the assembled friends, and the child is told to pick it up. When he does this a bit of it is given to each guest, and there is a feast. In the case of Akbar the Turki custom was observed, that when a child begins to crawl, the father, grandfather, or whoever represents him takes off his turban and strikes the child with it so as to make him fall. This is said to be as good as the herb of grace *(ispand, sipand, Lawsonia inermis)* to protect him from the Evil Eye.

"When a girl is a year or two old her ears are bored. This is done by the goldsmith or barber, into whose lap two coconut kernels *(khopra)* are put, and his neck is smeared with sandal-wood. By degrees other holes are bored along the whole edge of the ear, and even in the centre part, till by the time the girl is two or three years old she has thirteen holes in the right and twelve in the left. Some people bore a hole in each lobe, in the part projecting over the orifice, one above it and a few others here and there, but in the Deccan most people think it vulgar to bore holes uniformly all round the edge, as that is the custom of the lower castes." adds Mr. Sarif.

References

1. Sachchidananda, *Profiles of Tribal Culture in Bihar*, Firma KLM, Calcutta, 1965.
2. Risley, Sir Herbert, *The Tribes and Castes of Bengal: Ethnographic Glossary,* Firma KLM, Calcutta 1998, originally published Bengal Secretariat Press, Calcutta, 1891.
3. Sengupta, Syamalkanti, *The Social Profiles of the Mahalis*, Firma KLM, Calcutta, 1980.
4. Chaudhury, Buddhadeb (ed)., *Tribal transformation in India; Religion, Ritual and Festivals*, Vol. V, Inter-India Publications, New Delhi, 1992.
5. Ray, Himansu, Mohan, *Savara–The Snake-charmer*, Institute of social Research and Applied Anthropology, Calcutta, 1986.
6. Sinha, Dikshit, *The Hill Kharia of Purulia*, Anthropological Survey of India, Calcutta, 1984.
7. Biswas, P.C., *Santals of the Santal Parganas*, Bharatiya Adimjati Sevak Sangh, Delhi, 1956.

8. Das, Amal Kumar and Raha, Manis Kumar, *The Rabhas of West Bengal*, Scheduled Castes and Tribes Welfare Department of West Bengal, Calcutta, 1967.
9. Troisi, J., *Tribal Religion : Religious Beliefs and Practices among the Santals*, Manohar, New Delhi, 1978.
10. Vidyarthi, L.P., *The Maler*, Bookland Pvt. Ltd., Calcutta, 1963.
11. Bhowmick, P.K., *The Lodhas of West Bengal*, Calcutta, 1963.
12. L.S.S. O'Malley, *Bengal District Gazetteers* (Santal Paraganas), Government Press, Calcutta.
13. Ghurye, G.S., *The Mahadev Kolis*, Popular Book Depot, Bombay, 1957.
14. Sarif, Ja'far, *Islam in India*, edited by William Crooke), Oriental Books, reprint corp., New Delhi, 1972, first published, 1921.
15. Singh, K.S. (Gen. ed.), *People of India : West Bengal*, Seagull Books, Calcutta, 2008.
16. Singh, K.S. (Gen. ed.), *People of India : Bihar*, Seagull Books, Calcutta, 2008.

2
Puberty

A man has to complete the cycle of growth from his infancy to adulthood and he has to make adjustment with the customs, rules and values prescribed by his society. In the beginning, the man must have been a son first and a father later, and the two roles are physiologically, psychologically and socially in a great contrast. Physiologically, he must first, have been dependant upon others for his very survival and later he must provide the same kind of security for his off-springs. Socially, he must first have struggled against his elders for satisfying his raw and uninhibited sexual urges during his premarital adolescent days, and later he must have put impediments to his younger ones for such satisfaction. In other words the age and status factors of a culture further put a premium to the social adjustment of the individuals.

No Ceremony, Rite or Ritual relating to Male Puberty

During the third year, the mother remains to be fully responsible for observing that he eats and sleeps in time and keeps at least moderately clean. In about three years most children go out of the house to empty bowels. Boys go naked until they reach four or five years of age, but girls are made to wear little clothes by the end of the second year and by the end of the third year, they are taught to keep themselves clean lest people should think badly of their mothers. Disease is endured with a sense of fatalism in the most children's cases and little or nothing is done to cure it. Home treatments are sometimes prepared and a mother occasionally makes a vow to the local deities promising sacrifice of a fowl for the child's cure. Expensive medicines of local doctors are rarely given to a child except in difficult cases. Local occultists specialists (Ojhas or Medicinemen) are generally consulted to treat ailments. Syamalkant Sengupta writes, "The author witnessed a very few cases during his study, when a sick child was taken to a trained physician of the locality for treatment.

"Respectful behaviour towards adults is taught to a child from early age. At the age of two years a child is expected to learn to respect an adult.

The need for such behaviour is not explained to the child but is taught by scolding and cautioning it each time, if does not behave respectfully with the elders. If a small child accompanies its parents to the fields or market, it is always given something to carry when returning to the village, may be fruit or a stick of firewood or a small bag with tubers.

"At about five years of age, the two sexes are separated at play, both boys and girls forming their own play groups. Little effort is made to teach children to tell the truth. Sometimes they are scolded for it but otherwise lying is thought to be a natural tendency which cannot be checked altogether. Stealing however is severely punished, particularly if a child steals something belonging to a member of another household. In the latter case the child is scolded as a part of training and also to avoid the possible consequences which might lead to create ill-feeling between two families.

"The complete lack of privacy and the indifference with which all biological function are treated by the adults cause children at a very early age, to become acquainted with the facts of adult life. Pregnancy, birth, menstruation, death, violence and drunkenness, all usually take place before the eyes of the children and little or no effort is made to hide these from them. The only exception is in the case of coitus, it being considered improper that a child should be aware of it.

"The boys or girls of ages between 3-7 usually pierce their ears. This rite generally occurs among the Mahalis in the months of Magh (January-February) and Phalgun (February-March). This ceremony is performed, as they believe, for three reasons: first it averts evil eye and saves the child from accidental death, secondly the Mahalis wear ornaments from their late childhood irrespective of their sex, men wearing light ear ornaments of copper, iron etc. and women wearing heavy ornaments of silver, iron etc. and thirdly the neighbours and relatives are entertained to get their blessings for the child."

This rite has three phases: (a) ceremonial bathing and wearing of new clothes; (b) piercing of the ears with a slender copper pin purchased from the market and, (c) entertaining the guests, relatives and villagers. Usually, the elderly woman of the family or of the neighbourhood pierce the ears of the first child with aid of a copper string. The villagers are given a feast at the time of piercing of the ears of the first son or daughter.

Boys often start smoking at about eight or nine years in secret. Rice-beer is not permitted to children but on festive occasions, a seven or eight-year old boy may enjoy a sip of rice-beer when offered to him. As boys and girls are usually separated during games, there is hardly any sex awareness at this age. Boys of eight or ten years sometimes show a certain tendency to transvestism, through putting on their sister's dresses and in company with girls, engaging in mimic female activities for a few hours. Girls of similar age too often put on male clothes. The grown-up children take an active part in family economics.

As common in rest of the human societies, in *Mahalis* too, adolescence appears as a continuous, unregulated growth in which the various steps and phases, are hardly distinguishable from one another.

Mr. Sengupta writes, "Till the age of ten or eleven, the boys and girls show little difference in their daily life. They eat and sleep together in the same hut, but in their work they follow different courses, typical of their sex; girls help their mothers to fetch water, firewood or cook meals and boys begin to tend livestock and assist, their fathers in agricultural fields. In bamboo work, both the boys and girls help their parents. With the attainment of puberty and the swelling of the girls' breasts and broken voices of the boys, the mode of their living are changed in two distinct ways.

The girls spend their days as before in their parents' house with their parents and eat at home and are kept separated from their brothers. In case of scarcity of space for such separation in the hut, the girls are occasionally sent to spend the night in the house of an old widow of the village. At the first menstruation, which on an average, starts at the age of 13 to 15, no special rites or avoidance are observed. The elderly women relatives or the mother teach them the necessary precautions during this period.

"With marriage and motherhood, the life of a woman finds its final pattern. The years that follow bring no more changes either in status or in the mode of life, in most cases. The life of a youngman in Mahali society runs through an equally smooth and uneventful course with no rites and ceremonies to mark the various stages of maturity and no tribal sports, no tests of manhood are required to be observed.

"A most important aspect of the childhood is formal schooling. About 13.58% of all Mahalis have attended school (men = 8.66% and women = 4.92%). The illiteracy is 91.34% in men and 95.08% in women. Few people amongst the Mahalis are able to write more than their names and still fewer can read a Bengali newspaper. Those who can read the regional language, read it very faulteringly and very few of them continue studies beyond the elementary or primary school stage. School attendance on the part of the Mahalis is not regular, because it depends on many personal factors. The records kept by the author shows that on an average a Mahali child misses two-thirds of the school days and 'wastage and stagnation' are common affair." Adds Sengupta.

Ceremony of *Caco Chatiar*

The adolescence of a child in the community of Santals is marked by a purificatory rite called *Caco Chatiar.* Mr. J. Troisi writes, "Though the word *caco* literally means 'a toddler', the ceremony is not performed until the child has grown up. In fact, there is no fixed time when the *Caco Chatiar* is to be held as long as it is observed before marriage. While the *Janam Chatiar* ceremony admits a child 'to the outer fringes of the tribe', the *Caco Chatiar* ceremony is believed to give an individual all the responsibilities and privileges of a full-fledged member of the tribe. Through this ceremony, an individual enters into a new relationship with the *bongas* whom he can now approach with sacrificial offerings and also share in the sacrificial meal.

"In Pangro and the neighbouring Santal villages, the performance of this ceremony is of an extremely casual nature. It is, however, considered important by Santals because of the dire consequences that would follow if it is not observed. Thus, no Santal boy can get married unless he has undergone this ceremony. The ceremony used to be rather expensive since the whole village had to be feasted. It has, therefore, now become customary for a family to wait until the ceremony can be performed for several children at the same time.

"On the day appointed by the headman, the villagers are summoned by the *godet* to the house where the ceremony is to take place. When all have assembled, the midwife, who had presided at the birth of the children, or, if this is not possible, anyother elderly village woman, bathes the children to be initiated by pouring water over them. Then three girls from the village anoint all those present with oil and turmeric, starting with the priest and his wife. Rice-beer, brewed for the occasion, is served to all present, after which they sing and dance in honour of the household in whose honour the ceremony is to be performed. An old man of the village, then recites the Santali account of creation, the wanderings of the Santal ancestors and how they came to occupy the present habitat in the village, making allusions to the household which has sponsored the ceremony. This is an essential aspect of the ceremony since it is considered very important for a Santal young man to be instructed in the tribal tradition and made to realise what being accepted as an adult Santal implies. The recitation also serves to transmit the Santal tribal lore, ensuring a certain continuity in the tradition.

"After serving rice-beer to all, the *jogmanjhi* of the village, stresses that by participating in the drinking of rice-beer, the village community has expressed its acceptance of these young persons as full participants in the village affairs. If the family can afford the expense, a meal is given to all those present. Otherwise, it is considered sufficient to feed the relatives and the village officials. Through this ceremony, the initiated persons are, as it were, reborn in society. The rebirth is signified by the presence of the midwife. No sacrifices are offered and the people's part consists mainly in approving the proceedings by drinking rice-beer.

"The universal custom, among the Santals, of cicatrization of boys and the tattooing among girls, has been connected by Hunter with the ceremony of initiation. There is, however, no evidence of such connection in the past and it certainly does not exist now. In fact, there is no ceremony to accompany this custom and Santal boys usually brand themselves when they are herding their cattle in the fields. A rag is rolled like a cigar to a thickness of about an inch and set alight. Each boy then presses the burning rag on to the skin of his left arm, midway between the wrist and the elbow. When the skin is burnt out, ashes are pressed on the scar. The branded marks remain for life. Each boy can brand himself as often as he wishes, though the scars must always be odd in number. Odd numbers are considered as ominous signs. They are said to signify life, *jion,* while even numbers mean death, *moron.* The term for each mark is known as *sika.* The Santal believes that the *sika* is an indication of his Santal identity. It is very important to show these marks to the guardians of the next world, for otherwise, huge worms in the form of *tumdaks,* will sit on his lap and slowly torment him till they eat him up. An individual is proud of his scars which are also considered as a mark of his endurance.

"A similar belief leads the girls to be tattooed. There seems to be no special connection between the designs tattooed, called *khoda,* and the Santal traditional history, as is the case among the Kharias. There is also no specific time when the girls are tattooed. The custom is that a girl must have her left arm, shoulder and breast tattooed prior to her marriage. A girl without these tattoo marks will not be accepted by her mother-in-law as a daughter of the house. After marriage, a woman gets her right arm, shoulder and breast tattooed. In Pangro, the work of tattooing is usually done during the cold season by a Karmakar woman from another village, who visits Pangro for this purpose. As in the case of Santal boys, if a woman dies before being tattooed, *Jom Raja* (the *bonga* of death) will consider her to be impure and will send her straight to the underworld.

"The Santals consider cicatrization of boys and tattooing of girls as having a social and religious importance. Through these magico-religious customs, the Santals protect themselves against any calamities at the hands of the malignant spirits in their future life. Commenting on a similar custom to be found among the Andaman Islanders, Radcliffe-Brown remarks that this custom marks a special relation between the adult Andaman Islander and that system of powers on which the welfare of the society and of the individual depends, adds Mr. Troisi.

Rearing of Child by Parents

"Following their formulation about child rearing in which six aspects of child training were delineated (obedience, responsibility, nurturance, achievement training, self-reliance, general independence) Barry, Bacon and Child (1959) examined the relationship between child rearing and subsistence economy. They found that child training practices and subsistence economy mutually affect each other during a continued process of cultural adjustment and evolution. They pointed out that generally societies which have food surplus put strong pressure on their children to be responsible, obedient and compliant whereas societies which have low accumulation of food orient their children to become self-reliant, independent and assertive. They write :

> 'Child training tends to be a suitable adaptation to subsistence economy. Pressure toward obedience and responsibility should tend to make children into the obedient and responsible adults who can best ensure the continuing welfare of a society with a high accumulation economy whose food supply must be protected and developed gradually throughout the year. Pressure toward self-reliance and achievement should shape children into venturesome, independent adults who can take initiative in wresting food daily from nature, and thus ensure survival in societies with a low accumulation economy *(ibid* 1959).'

"Among the Hill Kharia it is found that self-reliance is greatly emphasized. But achievement which Barry *et al.* reported as highly valued in hunting and gathering societies these days do not find much of an emphasis. We found that knowledge about the ecology which was necessary at one time for survival is not placed highly in the achievement scale. The technological base too has eroded. Even the highly prized character of manliness too is not emphasized. This is exemplified in the attenuation of the symbolic ceremony of groom selection. The food situation is so erratic and uncertain that the character of venturesomeness which Barry *et al,* talked of remain at a very low ebb. Behaviourial assertiveness in their own community and in relation to the peasants is often unhelpful. Instead the character of withdrawal is found to be much more valuable as an adaptive behaviourial trait.

"Among the Hill Kharia both husband and wife take part in child rearing. But toilet training is provided by the mother. Once a child passes the toddler's stage and starts playing with the peer group or follows his older siblings he remains with them for most of the time. No seggregation is made regarding the sex of young children. Girls are slowly inducted into household chores depending upon the presence or absence of her elder sisters. Burdened with their responsibility the girls are less free to explore the surroundings. They, however, accompany their mothers to the forest and thus learn the technique of food gathering. Boys, in contrast, are free to roam about and explore the surroundings and are even encouraged to find food for themselves. In this they receive instructions from their fathers. In their quest for birds, or birds' eggs, squirrel, etc., they receive a spontaneous training and gather valuable knowledge about the economic aspect of their life. But one aspect of life which is receiving less and less attention is imparting detailed knowledge about the forest. Informants pointed out that as most of the valuable plants have disappeared from the locality they find it difficult to transmit even the meager knowledge that they now possess about the forest to their children. Now-a-days after attaining the age of 8-10 years another phase of socialization begins for boys. This phase of adapting to the agricultural activities last till they get married. Girls of about the same age also start earning for the family as agricultural labourers. They take part in transplanting and harvesting paddy.

"Another aspect of children's socialization that needs particular emphasis is 'learning to live with hunger'. Children are allowed to suckle their mothers' breast as long as possible. But once they stop suckling their mothers, lest they are ridiculed, they are taught to endure hunger. They are encouraged to gather food for themselves so that they learn the value of food and difficulty involved in gathering food. I found quite often children frustrated in finding food for themselves and remaining unfed by their parents sitting before their door steps and crying silently from the pain of hunger. Sometimes they fall asleep while crying for food. This early training to endure hunger and to depend on themselves, at least partially, for acquiring food leads to the development of individuality among the Hill Kharia. From 8 years boys are sent to peasants' households, first as cow and goat herders and then as domestic-cum-agricultural servant *(Bagal).* Therefore, development of peer group relation and learning to experiment with group life ceases from this time. This is, perhaps, another reason why individuality develops among the Hill Kharia.

"Association between parents and children occurs for a very restricted period. Because all able-bodied persons have to work for procuring food rarely can a free person be found in the hamlet who can look after children when their parents are away for work. Therefore, as soon as children reach a stage when they can play about themselves they are left alone in the company of older siblings. This situation places additional burden on older siblings who must look after their younger siblings. But as has been pointed out earlier, anxiety for food and hunger keeps them busy in procuring whatever little food they can for themselves. This leaves little respite or leisure time to them to devote special attention to their younger siblings. Consequently, the Hill Kharia children follow their older siblings and by imitating their siblings learn to forage for food since much of their play time is consumed by quest for food.

"Adult males or females on the other hand do not show any interest for other people's children. On a hot summer afternoon in 1976 I was talking with Rathu Sabar. 5 boys aged between 3-6 of the hamlet came running to him. Among them was his youngest son, Baja, who asked him to mend his broken bow. Rathu immediately set about the task. It took him nearly 15 minutes to mend the bow. Other boys gathered round him watching the mending with interest. Among them Nabin. Rathu's elder brother's grandson asked him to make a new bow for him because his bow was broken beyond repair. Rathu brusquely showed him off saying that he had no time.

"From the above description it is apparent that the Hill Kharia place great emphasis on the future members' ability to look after themselves and endure hunger as far as possible. Experience to confront hunger and the realities of life around them from an early age perhaps makes the Hill Kharia aware of the value of individuality and withdrawing from group life as far as possible. Adds Pikshit Sinha.

Joining Bachelor's Dormitory

On this queer institution, Sir Herbert Rishley writes, "In matter of domestic economy the Oraons are a slovenly race, and their badly-built mud huts afford no sufficient accommodation for the unmarried members of the family. In the older Oraon villages this difficulty is provided for by a house called the dhumkuria, in which all the bachelors must sleep under penalty of a fine. Where the girls sleep is, says Colonel Dalton, 'somewhat of a mystery.' In some villages a separate building, under the charge of an elderly woman, is maintained for their use; and more commonly they are distributed among the widows of the village. 'But however billeted, it is well known that they often find their way to the bachelors' hall, and in some villages actually sleep there.'

"This curious institution is not peculiar to the Oraons. We meet with it among the Juangs, the Hill Bhuiyas of Keonjhur and Bonai, and the Jhumia Maghs of the Chittagong Hill Tracts. The Oraon system, though already looked upon as an ancient custom, and apparently tending to disuse in newly-formed villages, is still very elaborate. 'The Dhumkuria fraternity are under the severest penalties bound down to secrecy in regard to all that takes place in their dormitory; and even girls are punished if they dare to tell tales. They are not allowed to join in the dances till the offence is condoned. They have a regular system of fagging in this curious institution. The small boys serve those of larger growth, shampoo their limbs, and comb their hair, etc., and they are sometimes subjected to severe discipline to *make men* of them.' It is difficult not to see in this a survival of more primitive modes of life, possibly even of the initiatory ceremonies to which many tribes of savages attach so much importance." Adds Sir Risley.

Joining Dhumkuria or Youth Dormitory

The custom of the youth dormitory in the central, eastern and north-eastern has engaged the attention of anthropologists ever since the publication of accounts of such organisation among the Naga and the Oraon. Towards the close of the 19th century, Peal (1893) drew attention to the fact that, from Bhutan to New Zealand and from Marquesas to Niger, the institution of youth dormitories existed and was distinguished by certain common features, viz. the existence of a recognized building for unmarried young men and girls to sleep sometimes separately and sometimes together, complete sexual licence between the sexes before marriage, and the bar on the entry of married women into the dormitory. The Oraon youth dormitory or Dhumkuria has been described by E.T. Dalton (1872), Father P. Dehon (1905 and S.C. Roy (1915). The description given by S.C. Roy is the most elaborate. From reading his account one gathers the impression that the youth dormitory occurs in all Oraon villages and the customs associated with it are universal for the Oraon settlements. It also seems that all the dormitories during Roy's time were equally active and performed all the functions described by him. Verrier Elwin visited some Oraon youth dormitories in 1940 and has given a short account of them in 'The Muria and their Ghotul' (1947). He noticed a great many changes from the description given by S.C. Roy. To measure the change that has come over the Oraon youth dormitory it will be useful to recall in brief its chief features as described by S.C. Roy.

According to Mr. S.C. Roy, the only indigenous institution for the training of youth which the Oraon possessed was the Dhumkuria. "It must have been an effective economic organisation for purposes of food quest, a useful seminary for the training of young men in their social and other duties and an institution for magico-religious observances calculated to secure success in hunting and to augment the procreative power of young men so as to increase the number of hunters in the tribe." The youth dormitory building, where it existed consisted of a house with four mudwalls, one doorway and no windows. It was generally situated in a prominent part of the village. In most cases this building overlooked a beautifully kept dancing ground, sometimes surrounded by stone seats. The youths slept on palm-leaf mats, annually presented to them by the maidens of village. Bundles of straw were used as head rests. In winter, logs of wood were kept burning in one corner of the hall to keep it warm. The interior was kept fairly clean and tidy though the surroundings were insanitary. Adjoining the hall, and sometimes inside it, there was a stinking drain in which people urinated. In the hall were also kept flag poles, musical instruments like *nagara, dholak, narsingha,* and *jhanjh.* Besides these there were wooden replicas of certain totem animals like elephants, horses, tortoises and fish, states S.C. Roy.

Boys were admitted to the dormitory, or *Jokherpa* as it is called by the Oraon, at the age of eleven or twelve. Roy holds that the age of admission was originally higher but a reduction in the marriageable age of boys and girls due to Hindu influence has led to a reduction in it. The youth divided into three classes or grades called 'tur' viz. *Puna Jokhar* or novices *Majh Turia Jokhar* or members of the intermediate class and *Koha Jokhar* or the oldest members. Membership of the first two grades lasted three years each; in the last grades youths continued till marriage or till they had issues of their own. Supervision of the dormitory was vested in the hands of the Dhangar Mahto who was associated in his work by the Dhangar Kotwar. The Dhangar Mahto instructed the boys in social and religious duties while the Kotwar had to attend to the big tribal meets called Jatras and dances and to see that the boys were well equipped for them. He also collected flowers for the purpose and compelled disobedient boys to attend Jatra and dances. A pated straw whip was the insignia of his office. The Dhumkuria officers were elected for three years. These officers gave Oraon youth an early opportunity for exercise of responsibility and developing qualities of initiative and leadership.

Girls had their own dormitory called as the *Pel-erpa* though even in Roy's days it was not an independent structure. It was not a public building and its existence was not made public to outsiders. Its location was known only to its inmates and to those of *Jokherpa.* An elderly male Oraon called as *Pelo Kotwar* was put in charge and under him there was a senior girl known as the *Borka Dhangrin* who directed and controlled the inmates on the spot. In this dormitory there were also three grades analogous to those in the boy's dormitory.

S.C. Roy reports that new boys were admitted to the youth's dormitory once in three years on the new day of the moon in the month of Magh. The older boys decided as to which of the younger boys would be admitted. What happens to the boys left out has not been reported. Nor do we get any idea of the criteria of admission to the dormitory. The parents of the boy admitted had to pay some sort of a fee in the form of Karanj seeds which were later crushed into oil for lighting lamp in the dormitory. The scale of contribution was graduated according to the income of the parents. Boys of the youngest grade had to collect fuel for heating the dormitory during winter. They had to massage the bodies of their older colleagues as well as of other guests who came to stay in the dormitory. They had also to run errands for the senior inmates. Discipline was rigorously imposed and the lot of the new entrants could not be envied as they were bullied and punished by their senior's for any offence however minor. The most important function of the Dhumkuria youths was the performance of religious and magical rituals to secure success in hunting and to ensure the multiplication of male children.

From the day following their admission into the *Dhumkuria*, the boys were given instructions in their social and religious duties. Before they embarked on ceremonial hunting expeditions, the youths worshiped goddess Chandi. The youths of the dormitory had to make all arrangements for the huntings, which were joined not only by members of one village, but by most of the youths of the neighbouring villages. In this way they imbibed team spirit and learned to work as incorporate entity for the common good. S.C. Roy thinks that through appropriate magical rites Goddess Chandi may be made to impart sufficient strength to the procreative powers of the young men so as to enable them to indefinitely increase the number of huntsmen in the tribe. Such propitiation of this goddess was performed shortly after the Sarhul festival. Procreative vigour may be acquired from such powerful natural objects as the *Sal* tree. Twice in the year, once about a week before the Phagu festival and about a week before the Sarhul festival, the head of the *Dhumkuria* led the boys to a suitable place at some distance from their village where a curious ceremony was performed. According to Roy, the saliva of an efficient young man and the contact with the powerful Sal saplings and the sal stick are evidently supposed to promote fecundity.

In the wedding feast's or any other feasts in the village, the *Dhumkuria* youths had to dress the animal and fowls for the occasion and act as cooks as well as look after the guests. If a villager or guest was in need of service of labourers for thatching house or some other work he made request to the head of the Dhumkuria and struck a bargain with him, services rendered thus were known as *Pacha* services. The ways received were generally spent on the purchase of some musical instruments or other requisites specially for making flags. The Dhumkuria youths were privileged to gather once a year, fruit from all Karanj tree of the village. They enjoyed the similar liberty in regard to Mahua tree of the village. The Mahua flowers were stored by the head of the *Dhumkuria* and later they were sent for distillation. The beer thus produced was used on the occasion of inter-village gatherings. Sachehidananda notes, "An interesting magical ceremony, that the Oraon bachelors had to perform, was the driving away of the spirit that causes cattle disease. When such a disease appeared in a village, a day was fixed for driving away that spirit. At about mid-night the bachelors gathered in the dancing ground, stripped themselves completely naked and each took up cudgel in his hand. A village cow-herd with a wooden bell suspended by his neck was chased by the youths with shouts resembling the bellowing of cattle, when the latter was chased out of the bounds of the village he quickly dropped the cow-bell and beat a hasty retreat. Thus the disease was driven away from one village to the bounds of another village. The practice continued till the disease spirit was driven away from the entire neighbourhood.

"In December every year, a day or two before the annual Harbori (bone burial) day, youths of all categories went out in one body with their nets, dogs, drums, flags etc. to ceremonially drive away and if possible catch birds that eat up paddy grains. The youths of a Dhumkuria had also got the responsibility to polish the Mandarsalas (two or more clay menhir's resembling small pyramids). This structure existed in those villages in which Jatra was held. The day after the Poosh Jatra in some villages youths of the Dhumkuria used to entertain all the villagers to feast. On this occasion the elders discussed important affairs concerning the village.

"Dhumkuria youths had an important part to play in creating goodwill between villages in the neighbourhood. They generally went out in batches and pay ceremonial visits to Dhumkuria in other villages. At the sound of a drum, the youths of other villages came out to welcome their guests and after exchange of greetings they danced together and fraternised with each other. They also entered into Sangi form of friendship. Next day they were feasted and at the time of their departure the flag or other emblem was handed over by the headman of the Dhumkuria to the leader of the guest party. This inter-village fraternisation of youth is called *Bhaiyari.*

"Like the youths, the maidens of the girls dormitory had also certain privileges and duties. They wove palm leaf mats for themselves as well as for bachelors' dormitory. Besides this they had their own rituals which they performed in secrecy. On the occasion of a marriage in a village, the maidens took part in making arrangements for the feast. The maidens may also be hired out for sowing, transplanting or harvesting. Evidently even in the time of Sarat Chandra Roy, the maidens' dormitory was not a very active institution and could not compare with the youth dormitory in the efficiency of its organisation or the performances of its manifold functions.

"For both the youths and the maidens the songs and dances appear to be the chief items in the ordinary programme of their night business. In summer and winter night, young people of both the sexes may be seen dancing in the village Akhara from evening till mid-night. On the occasion of important religious festivals like Phagu, Sohrai and Karam, dancing might continue night and day. The Dhangar Kotwar looked after the training of the youths of the lowest grade in the various styles of dancing and singing. Similarly the Barka Dhangrin took care to see that the young girls imitate the elder girls correctly in the various steps of dances of different tunes of the songs. Dances for various occasions, seasons and festivals differed in technique and quality. Besides providing entertainment to the youths, maidens and the spectators, the daily programme of dance was interpreted by Roy to bring happiness, prosperity and stimulation of the healthful forces of nature so that the earth may be fruitful and the Oraon may be blessed with abundance of animals and vegetable food and the fertility of man and the rest of creation may increase. The dances and Jatra gathering may be said to be instrumental in fostering the tribal solidarity of the Oraon." Adds Mr. Sachchidananda.

S.C. Roy however, does not give any definite data regarding the relations between the boys and the girls dormitories. He presumed that there would naturally be many attachments between boys and girls in every village, though he adds that, according to Oraon customs and rule, no girl may enter the youths dormitory and if the girls break this rule, the boys would temporarily lose their sight. E.T. Dalton writing in 1872 said that girls often found their way to the boys dormitory and in some villages actually slept there. After the dance it was not unusual for boys and girls to pair off. Father P. Dehon hated the dormitory because to him it was another name for promiscuity. The youngest boys of the Dhumkuria are sent by their older colleagues to summon the latters' sweet hearts from the girls dormitory. Roy even believed that girls might be dragged by force and they may not resist. Generally the dormitory's youths were expected to have favourites amongst the maidens. The wishes of the boys generally signified by his wearing particular flowers or any other thing which particular girl habitually wore. Illicit companionship of a boy and girl went on till one of them was married off and sometimes until a child had been born to either of them. However, such ilicit liaison seldom led to marriage.

Later, Verrier Elwin visited some *Dhumkurias* in Oraon villages in the eastern part of Ranchi district in 1940. In the villages the dormitory was housed in a well kept hut with a door but no windows. In Barambe he found well decorated pillars and beams in the dormitory. Stone pillars were found in Kota. In most of the dormitories he found village emblems wooden images of elephants, horses, crocodiles and fish which are taken out on the occasion of fairs and festivals. The preservation of these semi-sacred objects in the

Dhumkuria was believed by Elwin to be the 'surest sign of the vitality of the institution.' The ceremonies stated by S. C. Roy prescribed for admission were not maintained everywhere. In one place Elwin was told that boys were admitted every year at the Sarhul festival when they had to bring certain offerings. Instead of meeting the Dhumkuria contribution in the form of Karanji, parents had to supply a lamp, a small earthen pot and enough oil to light the dormitory for a fortnight. In Mandar, Verrier Elwin was told that if a girl entered a youth dormitory she herself would get night blindness. W. G. Archer who was for a long time posted as Sub-Divisional Officer in Gumla Sub-Division, a predominantly Oraon area, did not find any Dhumkuria when he was working there in about 1940. In Jashpur, an area adjoining Gumla in Madhya Pradesh the Dhumkuria, was still surviving at that time though the public building had disappeared.

Mr. Sachchidananda writes (1965: 66), "During the past one year a number of Oraon villages were visited and the working of dormitories therein was observed. The facts revealed in this investigation showed that the Dhumkuria is no longer a distinguishing feature of all Oraon villages. It does not exist at all in the Gumla Sub-division in the form it is described by Sri S. C. Roy. In Khapia a joint dormitory for youths and maidens is found. It is known as *Jokh-Pelo Erpa.* It was not an independent building. In Chota Khapia it was located in the house of a widow and in Bara Khapia in another private house. Sleeping for youths and maidens in the dormitory is not compulsory and only those sleep there whose parents are indulgent enough to allow them to do so. A twelve year boy reported that he was forbidden by his parents to sleep in the dormitory though he was allowed to go to the dancing ground or the Akhra. In Chiri, 40 miles from Ranchi on the Ranchi-Lohardaga Road and the villages round about people had not even heard of the Dhumkuria though everywhere the Akhra exists. In Arangloya, three miles off the Ghaghra-Neterhat Road nobody had any knowledge of what a Dhumkuria is. This village is entirely composed of Oraons who are Bhagats. In Silpahari, a Christian village two miles from Chainpur, a Dhumkuria existed till three years back. There were separate houses for boys and girls. Christian songs and prayers were sung there. Village elders closed this institution due to the affair of Telesphore and Christine. But for the last six months the youths have started sleeping in another house where they play cards, sing songs or religious hymns. Hockey sticks are kept there.

"The most artistic Dhumkuria buildings were found in Barambe, Rani-Khatanga and Tangarbansli. In the first village there are two youth dormitories, one with a very artistic carved door and interior. This was the one which may have been visited by Elwin. It contained a number of flag poles, a few musical instruments and one village emblem, a wooden image of an elephant. In Rani-Khatanga also we find the sacred elephant which is taken to the Jatra with pomp and ceremony. In Mandar there was one big drum and three flutes. In one corner there was an oil crushing mechanism for crushing Karanj. It is no longer used now as a Kerosene lamp. On either side of the entrance of this dormitory is a small opening measuring 2 ft. by 1½ ft. which serves as window. There are three more windows in the building. There is a window in Tangarbansli and also in Barahiya Rol. In the latter case it has been opened by the Community Project authorities. The floor of the Dhumkuria is regularly polished with cow dung except in Barahiya Rol where the Project authorities have cemented it. In all other dormitories we found a slight depression in the floor which is used as a fire place to keep the hall warm in winter nights. Big logs of woods which are to be used as fuel are kept either in the building itself or in the verandah adjoining it. The youths sleep on palm leaf mats which were either spread on the floor or rolled up on one side.

"Rules of membership have become lax. In Barambe Ahir and Lohra youths were also found sleeping in the Dhumkuria though in most cases only non-Christian Oraon youths are allowed to do so. In Rani Khatanga the total membership was 45 and the age range was 8 to 22. In addition to regular members known as Dhangars other people such as widowers, issueless married males, youngmen whose wives were on a visit to their parents, visitors from other villages and minor Government Officials also frequent at the Dhumkuria. Admission into the Dhumkuria takes place once in every three years just after the Karam festival. The Dhangar Mahto announces the names of the boys who are to be admitted. Late at night, the youths of the seniormost age group visit all the houses from which a boy is to be admitted and place in front of every entrance a plough. When the parents of the young boys wake up in the morning they understand that the time for their admission has come. Youths of the lowest age grade collect eggs, oil and other eatables from the village and the newly admitted boys are feasted. The seniormost youths lecture to them about their new responsibilities and privileges. The initiates are taken round the village and its organisation is explained to them.

"The system of age grades in some of the Dhumkuria under observation is not maintained specially due to the fact that admission of members is not made regularly or properly. In Mandar it was observed that membership of the first two grades is decreasing fast. In Khapia though there is a Dhumkuria there is no system of age grades. In Rani Khatanga and Tanger Bansali however, three distinct age grades were observed. This conforms to the classifications mentioned by earlier observers. The first to arrive at the Dhumkuria in the evening are the members of the lowest age grade. They clean and sweep floor, spread mats and light the lamp. They then go back to their homes and return after meals. By this time members of the other age grades start arriving. During the rainy season and winter the members of the juniormost grade light the fire. It is the members of the intermediate grade who massage the bodies of the senior members. At Mandar I found that young boys do not like massaging the bodies of the older members. For negligence of this particular duty they are taken to task by the elders and this is one of the reasons why membership of the junior grades of the Dhumkuria is going down. It is at the time of the massage when the boys discuss the village affairs. After the massage all the inmates of the Dhumkuria go out to Akhra and the drums are sounded. This is a signal for inviting the girls for the dance. As soon as a good number of people arrive dancing begins and youths and maidens continue to join even after the dance is begun. After the dance which generally lasts till the mid-night, the boys and girls disperse, to their respective dormitories. Now-a-days dancing does not take place daily but on the alternate days except during the time they are having their festivals. After the dance they retire to sleep. The Dhumkuria building is also used in the day specially in the afternoon, if any youth wants to take a short nap.

"No formal relation exists between the boys and girls dormitories except for the making of palm-leaf mats by the maidens for the youth dormitories. Girls do not visit boys in their dormitory but the members of the seniormost grade of the youth dormitory take out the girls of their choice from the, girls' dormitory. For this they used the services of boys of the youngest age grade. It was also observed that secret meetings between youths and maidens at night was not secret and it was viewed kindly by the parents and elders in the village. Only in case the girl becomes pregnant the matter comes to the head and the defaulting families have to pay a fine. Nothing could be easier than a marriage between the defaulting couple if they belong to two different clans but in case they belong to the same clan they could under no circumstances be allowed to marry.

"In one of the youth dormitories the investigator was told that the Dhumkuria trained its inmates to keep the interest of the community undermost in their minds. In Malti, Mandar, Barambe, Rani Khatanga, and Tangarbansli *Pacha* service still continues. The money received is deposited with the Dhangar Mahto who utilises it for the benefit of the Dhumkuria. The members of the highest age grade provide the much needed leadership to the boys of the two other age grade. In Jatra and festivals the senior members see that the young boys take part in the dance and act as a well disciplined group. It seems that at present the only important function of the Dhumkuria is to arrange for the instruction of generation of Oraon boys and girls in the intricacies of different kinds of songs and dance. In Mandar, however; the election of the Dhangar Mahto and Kotwar had not taken place for the last five or six years. Two middle aged persons were holding offices of the Mahto and Kotwar respectively. Discipline had become lax and nobody is particular about the wearing of ceremonial dress at the time of dance. No hunting expeditions are now organised and the greed of money has upset whole idea of co-operation. Other functions which have been mentioned by S. C. Roy have now become obsolete. Even if attendance in the dance is not satisfactory no one takes care.

"The same is the case with the women's dormitory. Even in S.C. Roy's account this dormitory seems to have been rather weak in organisation as compared to its male counterpart. *Pacha* service is maintained in some villages for the girls also. They continue to help in wedding feasts." he adds.

Mr. Sachchidananda states further, "From the above account it becomes evident that the institution of the youths dormitory among the Oraon is in a process of decay and disintegration. The first stage was when the Dhumkuria lost its own building for some reason or the other youths began to sleep in a part of somebody's empty house. In village Belangi, the Dhumkuria has been in disuse for the last two or three years. Last year its roof was blown away by wind and its pillars and other things have been eaten by white-ants. Some other building material was taken away by the villagers for being used as fuel. On inquiry it was found that the Dhumkuria was not repaired due to the existence of feuds in the village. The two sections of this village have been bitterly critical of each other's activities and even though one of them wants to repair the Dhumkuria, the other party is bent upon hindering it. Some of the people interviewed considered the decay of the Dhumkuria, to be bad as henceforth guests of the village have no place to stay in, and nobody would be able to look after their comforts. Nor would needy people be helped during the time of marriage and the agricultural season.

"Two important reasons for the decay of the Dhumkuria has been the propaganda carried on by the Church and Social Welfare Workers. It has already been hinted above that as soon as an Oraon is converted, he ceases to attend the Dhumkuria and even if he wishes to continue as a member, he would not be admitted therein. In village Malti the Christian youths have built a separate Dhumkuria which has got the same type of organisation as the traditional one and Christian youths participate in all communal activities of the village except in the rituals. They have a separate *Pacha* service as they have their own exceptional case because among most converted Oraons, the Dhumkuria is not found at all. The Missionaries considered it to be a by-name for immorality and the converts were forbidden to have anything to do with the Dhumkuria. The establishment of schools in villages also seems to have adversely affected the Dhumkuria. In many villages the author was told that the dormitories were doing immense harm to their morality. Young girls after marriage did not like to leave their parents' village and even if they go there they continually keep running off. This phenomenon is related by many school-going Oraons, to the lure of the village dormitory and dancing ground. It is believed that dancing leads to romance and every marriageable girl is involved in some romance in their parental village. The freedom to dance does not exist for newly married bride in her husband's village but so long as she remains with her parents she can continue to attend her own dormitory and *Akhra.* In villages where schools have been established, most of the children going to school do not go to the Dhumkuria, as they do not get much time to do their home work if they go there. In Rani Khatanga parents do not send their sons to Dhumkuria and even paid fine for absence as they were all school-going boys. Young school-going children do not want to run errands for uneducated senior boys and the task of massaging somebody else's leg is greatly hated. Even in those villages where the Dhumkuria exists the elders admit the continual decline in strength. Night schools opened as in Social Education Centres have become a serious rival of the Dhumkuria.

"It is evident that the function of the Dhumkuria as the only mechanism for the instruction of tribal youth cannot be maintained now. Schools are being opened in almost all the villages and these must take up some of the functions of the Dhumkuria. Whenever the Dhumkuria exists it has three important functions *(a)* as a sleeping house, *(b)* as a school of dancing and music and *(c)* as providing a co-operative labour unit by requisition of any needy member of the village. It is highly desirable that efforts should be made to retain the last two functions of youth dormitory even if its use as a sleeping house may, in the long run, be given up. To my mind, whenever the institution exists it may be used as a Social Education Centre and the latter should, under no circumstances, act as rival of the traditional tribal institution. It may, therefore, be advisable to start Social Education Centres in the building of Dhumkuria where they exist and it might function as a literary wing to the traditional institution. Likewise, the Dhumkuria may come in handy for extension workers, anxious to organise youth clubs." He adds.

K.P. Bahadur states, "The Oraon villages are generally located on the highest piece of land available and as close as possible to a spring or a well. The huts are huddled together along tortuous lanes which become muddy and dirty in the rainy season because of lack of drainage. The houses are built in groups of three or four facing each other forming a small courtyard. Cattle are also housed in the huts, though pigs have separate dwellings.

The wells of the huts are of the red laterite soil which is found in the area and which fixes firmly so that the walls are quite strong. The houses are thatched with grass and earthen tiles made by the Hindu potter class.

"Every village has its dancing ground known as *akhara* (first 'a' as in car) and the *dhumkuria* or bachelor's dormitory. The *akhara* are situated in front of the bachelor's dormitories and, apart from being a place from where young men as field labourers can be got it has become quite an important institution as the *majangs* of the Juangs, the *morungs* of the Nagas and the *ghotuls* of the Murias of Madhya Pradesh; but because of the *dhumkuria* having gained a bad name for sexual relationships between the boys and the girls, and also because of the ingress of modernity the system is falling into disuse.

"An Oraon bachelor is made a member of the dormitory and retains the membership for three years or more or till his marriage. The girls, too, have their separate dormitory known as the *pelerpa* which is under the charge of an elderly Oraon called *Petro-kotwar.* The officers who manage the *dhumkuria* are elected by the members every three years. They performed more or less the function of schools in which discipline was created and the members learned how to live a corporate life. But with time the institution became also a place where young men found opportunity to carry on liaisons with their beloved sweethearts. *Colonel Dalton* has given an interesting account of institutions of the *dhumkuria* and the *akhara:*

"In all the older Oraon villages, when there is any conservation of ancient customs, there is a house called the Dhumkuria, in which all the bachelors in the village must, when not absent from it, sleep under penalty of a fine. Precisely similar institutions are met with amongst the Hill Bhuiyas of Keonjhur and Bonai, and, from the notes left by the late Reverend S. Hislop, I find, they are common to other Dravidian tribes. I have already observed that the domiciles of the Oraons have insufficient accommodation for a family, so that separate quarters for the young men are a necessity. The same remark applies to young unmarried women, and it is a fact that they do not sleep in the house with their parents. Where they do sleep is somewhat of a mystery. They are generally frank enough when questioned about their habits, but on this subject there is always a certain amount of reticence, and I have seen girls quietly withdraw when it was mooted. I am told that in some villages a separate building is provided for them like the Dhumkuria, in which they consort under the guardianship of an elderly *duenna*, but I believe the more common practice is to distribute them amongst the houses of the widows, and this is what the girls themselves assert if they answer at all when the question is asked, but however billeted, it is well known that they often find their way into the bachelor's hall, and in some villages actually sleep there.

I not long ago saw a Dhumkuria in a Sirguja village in which the boys and girls all slept every night. They themselves admit the fact, the elders of the village confirmed it, and appeared to think that there was no impropriety in the arrangement. That it leads to promiscuous intercourse is most indignantly denied, and it may be there is safety in the multitude, but it must sadly blunt all innate feelings of delicacy. Yet the young Oraon girls are modest in demeanour, their manner gentle, language entirely free from obscenity, and whilst hardly ever failing to present their husbands with a pledge of love in due after marriage, instances of illegitimate births are rare, though the often remain unmarried for some years after reaching maturity. Long and strong attachments between young couples are common. Dhumkuria lads are no doubt great flirts, but each has a special favourite among the young girls of his acquaintance, and the girls well known to whose touch or pressure in the dance each maiden's heart is especially responsive. Liaisons between boys and girls of the same village seldom end in marriage. It is considered more respectable to bring home a bride from distance but it does not follow from this that there is no preliminary love-making. Maidens of one village go frequently on visits to their friends in another and stay several days, and sisters can always arrange to have for visitors the girls whom their brothers are best pleased to see. It is singular that in matters of the affections, the feelings of these semisavages should be more in unison with the sentiments and customs of the highly organised western nations than with the methodical and unromantic heart schooling of their Aryan fellow country men.

"The Dhumkuria fraternity are under the severest penalties bound down to secrecy in regard to all that takes place in their dormitory; and even girls are punished if they dare to tell tales. They are not allowed to join in the dances till the offence is condoned. They have a regular system of fagging in this curious institution. The small boys serve those of larger growth shampoo their limbs, and comb their hair etc., and they are sometimes subjected to severe discipline to *make men* of them.'

'Immediately in front of the Dhumkuria is the dancing arena, called "Akhara", an open circus about forty feet in diameter with a stone or a post marking its centre. It is surrounded by seats for tired dancers or non-dancing spectators' and shaded by five old tamarind trees that give a picturesque effect to the animated scene, and afford in their gigantic stems convenient screens for moonlight or starlight flirtations. During the festive season of the years, dancing at the Akhara commences shortly after dark every night, and, if the supply of the home brew holds out, is often kept up till sunrise. Very rakish do the dancers appear in the early morning after a night so spent. On some occasions the circus is laid down with red earth which pulverises under the many twinkling feet and rises in a lurid cloud about the dancers, till the garments, the dusky skins, and the black hair of the performers become all of brick-dust hue; ordinarily on the party breaking up at dawn, they proceed from the Akhara to their usual avocations and work as cheerfully and vigorously as if their night had been passed in sound sleep. This says much for the wholesomeness of the beverage that supplies them with staying power." (E.T. Dalton *Descriptive Ethnology of Bengal,* 1972, pp. 247-49).

Mr. Sarat Chandra Roy writes again, "the *Dhumkuria* was housed in a separate building standing in a prominent part of the village. It consisted of a big hall in front of which was the village dancing ground, usually flanked by big trees. In the *Dhumkuria* mats were used for sleeping, and flag poles as well as certain emblems, wooden animals, figures of elephants, horses, fish, crocodiles etc., were kept there. Musical instruments were also placed there. Logs of wood were placed just outside the *Dhumkuria.*

The *Dhumkuria* was a school of social training from which the tribal youth learnt not only the tribal lore, but imbibed all the qualities which would make him a useful member of the Oraon community. A boy was sent to the *Dhumkuria* at 11 or 12 years of age. The admission took place once every three years, the older boys in consultation determined which boy of the village they would admit. Roy details several ceremonies by which the boys were admitted. During the period of their stay in the *Dhumkuria,* their parents made contributions of *Karanj* fruits from which oil is extracted to light the house. The contribution was on a graduated scale according to the status of the parents.

The boys were divided into three age-groups, each having clearly defined duties. The boys remained in each of the first two groups for a period of three years and continued to live in the Dhumkuria in the third group till marriage. The supervision and control of the *Dhumkuria* community rested in the hands of a senior boy who was styled as its *Mahto.* His assistant was called the *Dhangar Kotwar.* The appointment of these *Dhumkuria* officers was made after an elaborate ceremony in consultation with the village headman and the elders. On assuming office these youthful officers listened to an oration from the outgoing *Mahto* describing the duties pertaining to these offices. The *Dhangar Mahto* instructed the boys in their social and religious duties and the *Kotwar* attended to the arrangements of the Jatras and dances and saw to that the boys were properly decked with the flowers and finery for those occasions. Strict discipline was enforced in this respect. A boy refusing to massage the legs of the senior members of the *Dhumkuria* was severely taken to task. Among other duties of the junior members were collection of firewood for the *Dhumkuria* and running errands for the older members.

The *Dhumkuria* boys acted as a corporate body and helped in the preparation for weddings or any other feasts in the village. They acted as cooks and looked after the comforts of the visitors who were generally housed in the *Dhumkuria* building. A villager who needed the services of workmen for agricultural operations or for thatching the house struck a bargain with the *Dhangar Mahto.* The wages collectively received were spent on the purchase of musical instruments. The young man also acted as a messenger for the meeting of the *Parha Panchayats.* In December every year on a fixed date, the boys set out on a ceremonial expedition to catch and drive away birds which injure the paddy crops. As they passed through the fields they were entitled to gather some paddy from the fields. The proceeds from the sale of this paddy went to the funds of the *Dhumkuria.* On another fixed date in the year, the youth of the *Dhumkuria* entertained all the village elders to a feast where the elders discussd important affairs connected with the village. The *Dhumkuria* youths had an important role in cementing inter-village alliance of friendship. They visited other villages in a body and similarly received youths from other villages. They exchanged greetings, feasted and danced together and individual boys entered into ceremonial friendship pacts with the members of the *Dhumkuria* of other villages.

According to Mr. Sarat Chandra Roy, the Oraon had a separate dormitory for the girls. This was not a public building and its location was not supposed to be known to anybody, but its inmates and to those of the bachelors' dormitory. It functioned under the supervision of a *Pelo Kotwar* who was an elderly woman, but inside the girl's dormitory, the most intelligent girl became the monitor. Here also there was the division into the three age-groups. One of the functions of these girls was to weave palm leaf mats which were presented to the boy's dormitory. At weddings or other feasts, the services of the girls were requisitioned on token payment. They were very useful during marriage ceremonies and the harvesting season.

The most important function of the youth dormitory was to train the young men and women in singing and dancing. Every evening after early meals boys and girls used to dance in front of the dormitory. Various styles of singing and dancing were in vogue and it was the duty of the head of both the dormitories to see that their wards were well up to the standard. Before or after dancing, members of the dormitories used to indulge in story-telling, solution of riddles and puzzles etc. At the end of the programme, the girls left for their own dormitory.

Mr. Sachchidananda writes, "From the account given it appears that the *Dhumkuria* was a living force among the Oraon in Roy's time. Recent work in the field has, however, brought out that the *Dhumkuria* probably never existed in all the Oraon areas even in the days of S.C. Roy. This wrong impression has been created due to the fact that he has not mentioned the locale of his enquiry in his ethnography of the Oraons. It cannot, therefore, be said for certain in how many areas the *Dhumkuria* never existed and in how many more it has totally disappeared. In seven Oraon centres where work was conducted under the auspices of this study, the *Dhumkuria* in its proper form existed in only two centres. In two centres its name and functions were unknown to even older people in the villages. In two other centres the youth dormitory did not exist in its institutionalised form—in the form of the *Dhumkuria* as described by S. C. Roy. True, there was in each of these two villages one room in a bigger hut where some of the youths of the village slept and had occasional dancing, but this would not be called a *Dhumkuria* in the proper sense of the term. Fresh efforts are, therefore, necessary for knowing the exact area in which the *Dhumkuria* existed for a long time and the forms it has taken during the recent past.

"In Chiri and in the villages round about it, which are only forty miles from Ranchi and in the thick of the Oraon area, people had no knowledge of the existence of a youth dormitory. Even after detailed enquiry and continued rapport with the people its existence was denied. It cannot, therefore, be said that its presence or existence in the recent past was not revealed to the investigators. The *Akhra* which is the dancing ground for the village youths was, however, found in all the villages. In Arangloya, a village inhabited by Bhagat Oraons, there is not even a shred of evidence to support the fact of existence of the *Dhumkuria* in the recent past. There is no common place where the youths or the maidens sleep either together or separately.

"In Khapiya which is a traditional Oraon village there is no separate dormitory for boys or girls. There is a common house for boys and girls known as *Jonkh-Pelo Erpa.* This is located in the house of a private person. Boys and girls freely mix in the *Akhra* and sleep in this house. Strict parents do not allow their children to spend the night in the dormitory. This house cannot be said to be a *Dhumkuria* in the true sense of the term as a common sleeping house for the youths and maidens. Even an exception is not mentioned in S. C. Roy's book. He clearly says that among the Oraon there are separate houses for youths and maidens and whereas the youth house is a public building, the existence of the maiden's house is known only to their occupants and to the youths. Visits by the youths to the maidens' dormitory or *vice-versa* is prohibited by tribal custom. The person who is guilty of such an offence is supposed to be affected with blindness. So the combined dormitory is not a true dormitory at all. Besides, this dormitory is not an organisation and is not recognised by the people of the village as being a fit place for their children to spend their night. Moreover, this dormitory does not perform any of the magical rites, rituals and other social duties assigned to dormitories as are described by Roy. They do not supply co-operative labour in *Pachcha* service as is the practice among the dormitories proper. Thus the youth dormitory in Khapiya is not a traditional Oraon organisation of the youth dormitory, but just an arrangement of the youth of the village for convenience and pleasure.

"In the Christian village of Silphari the dormitory was under a ban by the village elders. Youths of the village used to sleep in a vacant hut where they played cards, sang songs and played on the *Mandar* or the drum. Some musical instruments and religious books were also kept in the dormitory. There was no fixed time at which youths collected at this place. Nobody interfered with this arrangement until it was found that a prominent member of the dormitory was responsible for the pregnancy of a girl of the same village. The elders became so angry at this that the youths were asked to disband the dormitory at once and directed to sleep in their respective houses. Instances have been found where parents finding their sons and daughters visiting the dormitory under ban have resorted to violence to bring them back to their own houses at night. This dormitory also, therefore, is not of the kind that is mentioned by Roy in his books. It seems to be an organisation of local growth.

"In Mandar there is a *Dhumkuria* where generally about twenty youths sleep. There is no rule that a young man of a particular age-group can only sleep in the *Dhumkuria.* There are two or three old men who regularly sleep there.

"The *Dhumkuria* lies in the centre of the village which is by the side of the *Akhra.* It has a long single room with one window and one entrance. There is no door in the entrance. Its walls are painted. The surroundings are not clean. In former days, however, the inmates contributed *Karanj* oilseeds from which oil was extracted. This was used for the lamp in the *Dhumkuria.* Now the boys contribute the oil themselves by buying it from the market. Boys are taken into the *Dhumkuria* at the interval of three years just after the appearance of the new moon in the month of *Magh.* But people's interest in this institution is on the wane and so admission of new members is not done regularly or properly. Most of the children who go to school do not want to attend the *Dhumkuria.* They fear that they would have to massage the legs of the older members. Since the membership is not taken seriously, anybody can sleep there whether he is a member or not.

"The *Dhangar Mahto* is the head of the dormitory and nothing can be done without his permission. The *Kotwar's* duty is to see that the boys attend and dance at the *Jatra* and that they are properly dressed in their ceremonial dress. Formerly the *Kotwar* strictly attended to his duty but now-a-days nothing is done properly. The election of *Dhangar Mahto* and *Kotiwar* has not taken place for the last five or six years so the old incumbents are still holding office. As a matter of fact, one who is very much interested in the institution begins to function as the *Mahto* or *Kotwar.* It is the duty of the village headman to select a *Dhangar Mahto* and *Kotwar* from amongst the members of the highest grade. At present Mangra (44) and Nawra (37) are holding the offices of the *Mahto* and *Kotwar* respectively.

"Formerly there was a feeling of fraternity among all the members of the *Dhumkuria* and they regarded this as a primary group. Many magical, religious, social or economic functions were assigned to them and they always worked as a single unit. Now-a-days the organisation of this unit has collapsed. During *Jatra* the boys carried the flags of their institutions and maintained the tradition of dances and songs. But now-a-days no hunting expedition is organised. Formerly strict disciplinary action was taken for non-co-operation in the work of the village, but these days no discipline exists in the *Dhumkuria.* The co-operation which the members of the *Dhumkuria* rendered at the time of a marriage, or repairs to the roof of a house, or tree planting or reaping of paddy is no longer to be found. Greed of money has upset the whole idea of co-operation. During General Elections the *Dhumkuria* was used by a political party to train the villagers to vote for it. The *Dhangars* were engaged to canvass for the party candidates.

"Formerly there were three grades in the *Dhumkuria.* The highest responsibility lay on the senior members. As a matter of fact the members of the other two grades received training. Day by day membership of the first two groups is declining. *Dhumkuria* discipline is not so severe now as in the past. One informant said: 'In my days beating was an everyday affair and even its memory is painful. Even now the younger boys are severely beaten by the senior members for dereliction of duty. This makes the younger people to avoid visits to the *Dhumkuria,* while the older youths are intent upon bringing them in.'

"The existence and situation of the girls' dormitory is known only to the members of the *Dhumkuria.* The latter are very hesitant in giving any information about the girls' dormitory. Tradition forbids a boy to visit the girls' dormitory or *vice-versa.* This prohibition is, however, not strictly observed. The girls' dormitory is not a permanent house and is not a public building. Its location is changed every six or seven months as any house which is vacant is occupied by the girls for sleeping. The making of mats by the inmates of the girls dormitory for the use in the boys' dormitory still continues.

"In Barhiya Rol the girls' dormitory is situated in a private house. The number of girls using it is small. There are two rooms one small and the other big. The small one is used for sleeping, while the bigger one is sometimes used for meeting lovers. In most cases sexual congress takes place outside the four walls of a house. It is only in winter and the rainy season that the bigger room is used. Sometimes girls also visit the *Dhumkuria* though this is forbidden by tradition.

"In Belangi the *Dhumkuria* has ceased to exist for the last two or three years. The reason for the decay of the *Dhumkuria* was the long standing feud between two factions in the village. Three years ago the *Dhumkuria* was the place where a fight broke out between the two factions and it was considered dangerous to visit the *Dhumkuria.* The building is now in a state of decay and people are not caring to get it repaired. Their interest in the institution has ceased. Some people are happy that due to this factor the Dhumkuria has stopped working. They think that it is only due to the Dhumkuria that the children do not attend school. Children who are at school seldom attend the *Dhumkuria* or even attend the dance of the *Akhra.* It is believed that the *Dhumkuria* is the sole source of sexual immorality. An Oraon who had read up to the middle standard said: '*Akhra* and *Dhumkuria* have ruined the purity of our society. They are not at all beneficial for us. They do immense harm to the chastity of our girls who are so much involved in love affairs in their parental village that after marriage they refuse to live with their husbands. If the girl is taken away forcibly by her husband, she will take the first opportunity to run away'.

"Traditional Oraon youths do not want the boys to attend the night schools, because they are deprived of the amenity of getting their legs massaged in the dormitory. Younger members are used by the elders to run errands for them specially calling the latter's girl friends from the girls' dormitory. For these two reasons the traditionalists want the *Dhumkuria* to continue.

"In the traditional Munda village of Serengdih, men have a dominating position. They are so jealous and suspicious of women that the latter are discriminated and prevented from stepping into ritual and political spheres. They have no voice in the *Panchayats.* They cannot appear before the *Panchayat* unless they are summoned or their presence is considered necessary. There is no freedom of movement for women except on the occasion of women hunts. Women are not allowed to go to the *Sarna* where worship of the deities is strictly confined to menfolk only. Women cannot even worship household deities. The *Pahan* said: 'Women cannot go to the *Ading* (place reserved for dead ancestors in a house) to worship the *Bonga* and if they do so, they would become witches. When the *Bonga* is propitiated by women, she is soon taken possession of by the spirit'.

"The mode of greeting also betrays the inferiority of women. When a woman greets a man she will kneel down with both her hands on the head and utter the word *'Johar,'* in a whisper. Men will only fold their hands and slightly bend in response to this greeting. Due to the impact of Hinduism, the Munda have taken to worshipping many gods and goddesses. Munda women are not allowed to worship gods and goddesses such as *Kalidevi, Mahadevi, Saraswati* etc. Another *Pahan* said that a woman might go to the *Ading* in the absence of men and may offer vermilion to the deity, but could not offer any sacrifice. In this village polygamy is a common affair. Even as far before as seven generations polygamy was practised. There are many persons with more than one wife, but in no case does the number of wives exceed two. The younger generation, however, is not interested in having more than one wife. None below the age of forty has more than one wife living.

"In Selda it is the man who played the most important role in the family. However, the relation between man and woman is always that of co-operation and mutual obligation. Women work in the field as well as in the house. At the time of settling a marriage the wife is always consulted. In domestic ceremonial it is the women who lead, but in the *Panchayat* and in the worship of *Bonga,* women have no place. The older people think that a woman should confine herself to the kitchen and other household work. Younger men hold that men and women are more or less equal in society. Among the Christian Oraon of Silphari, in church prayers and other religious affairs men and women take equal part. In Khapiya parents complained that they do not have a free hand now in the selection of marriage partners for their sons and daughters. It is the latter's wishes which are predominant.

In Belangi though the wife is considered subordinate to her husband, she is his economic partner in the fullest sense of the term. Women collect fuel from the jungle or dried leaves of trees from the uplands. Besides they work in the home, cooking, washing and looking after children. They help the menfolk in such agricultural occupations as sowing, harvesting, transplanting, husking etc. They also take the surplus produce of the home to the nearby markets for sale.

"The changing pattern of a woman's role can be had from the following observations of an enlightened Christian Oraon woman from Mandar: 'Our society is changing fast mainly because of the changing economic relations. Formerly women used to help men in the fields, but now the situation is different. Every woman can earn something for her family failing which we cannot have the amenities of modern life. Now we cannot do without lanterns. Some of us are attracted towards fine *Saris.* These fresh needs compel us to supplement the income of our husbands. I never take part in any ceremonial dance. Sometimes I wish to dance, but as I do not know it, it is not possible. Whenever I go to Ranchi, I go to the pictures. As a matter of fact I love to go to the pictures'.

However, different writers gave varying descriptions of the bachelors dormitories in the tribal Bihar and Jharkhand. Most of the details about them had been under wrap due to the element of indignity being involved. A few investigators and writers assailed and ridiculed this custom, whereas others appear to act like apologists. Here, Mr. J. Troisi describes the Oraon dormitory stating thus: "In a tribal village the tribal community is divided into two classes. The *Khutkattidars* or the *Bhuinhars* are the descendants of the first settlers of the village. The other class consists of people who are generally their affinal relatives. When the *Khutkatti* tenure was intact the members of the first community considered themselves owners of village lands and the second group was regarded a *Parja* or the subject community. They were not considered socially inferior to the owners and were admitted to all social, religious and economic activities of the village. The only privilege that the dominant clan enjoyed was that the secular and religious headmen of the village were drawn from their ranks. Now that the *Khutkatti* tenure has almost been destroyed, any distinction between the descendants of the original settlers and later arrivals tends to be wiped out.

"While in other tribes there is no social stratification in respect of the clans, among the Dudh and Dhelki Kharia, two clans, Muru and Samad are considered superior to others. Among the Ho, Kodankel and Bage clans are considered lower than others. But these facts do not affect the social unity of the village and in all social functions all clans of the village participate to the fullest possible extent.

"The *Akhara* and the youth dormitory are the places where the social unity of the village is much in evidence. At the *Akhara,* members of different social groups in the village mingle with each other. They are so adept in dancing that it is difficult to distinguish between the tribal and the long-resident Hindu castes in the *Akhara.* Sometimes the tribal Christian converts do not dance with others in the *Akhara.* They dance separately on occasions prescribed for them by the church authorities. In Silphari, an Oraon village, dancing takes place only on occasions such as Easter Sunday, Ascension, harvesting, Christmas and All Saints Day.

"In the social life of some of the Bihar tribes, notably the Oraon, the youth dormitory is an important institution and an integral part of the village organisation. There are separate dormitories for youths and maidens known as *Jonkh-erpa* and *Pelo-erpa* respectively. The youth's dormitory is popularly known as the *Dhumkuria.* While the men's dormitory is a public building, the maiden's dormitory. is a secret place which is supposed to be known only to its inmates or to the youths of the village. In village Khapia, however, there is common house for boys and girls known as *Jonkh-Pelo-erpa.* It is situated in the house of a private person. Boys and girls sleep together in this house. This is an exceptional case because in no other village has a common dormitory for boys and girls been found; nor does it find a mention in earlier works on the Oraon youth dormitories (Dehon, 1905 and Roy, 1915). This dormitory does not enjoy any social recognition. It does not perform any of the magical rites and rituals and other social duties assigned to the dormitories among the Oraon. It may be that the youth dormitory in Khapia is not the traditional youth organisation but just an arrangement of the youth of the village for convenience and pleasure.

"The *Dhumkuria* building is situated at a prominent place in the village. It consists of a rectangular hall. In the *Dhumkuria* in Barambe, decorated pillars and beams are found. Certain musical instruments are kept in the dormitory as well as emblems, wooden animals, figures of elephants, horses, fish, crocodile and such semi-sacred objects. In Ranikhatanga, we find the sacred elephant which is taken to fairs and festivals with pomp and ceremony. In Mandar, a big drum and three flutes were found in the *Dhumkuria.* In one corner of it there is an oil press for extracting oil from Karanj kernels. It is no longer in use now as a kerosene lamp has replaced the earthen lamp which used to burn with Karanj oil. Very few dormitories have windows. The windows in Tangarbansali and Barhiya Rol have recently been opened at the behest of the community development authorities. The floor of the dormitory is regularly polished with cowdung. In Barahiya Rol with the help of community development authorities the floor has been cemented. In most dormitories we find a slight depression in the floor which is used as a fire place. Fire is made to keep the hall warm on winter nights. Big logs of wood which are used as fuel are kept either in the building itself or in the veranda adjoining it. The youths sleep on palm leaf mats which are either spread on the floor or rolled up on one side. The *Dhumkuria* where it exists, is an active institution.

"The *Dhumkuria* is a school of social training from which the tribal youth learns not only the tribal lore but imbibes all the qualities which will make him a useful member of the tribal community. The boy is taken to the *Dhumkuria* at about eight or nine years of age. Formerly boys were admitted every third year, the older boys in consultation with the village headman determining which boys of the village, they will take over. Roy... details several ceremonies by which boys were admitted to the *Dhumkuria,* but most of them are not observed any longer. While in some villages non-Oraon boys are not taken, in others, they are freely taken in the *Dhumkuria.* In Barambe, Kota, Katu, Lahna, Purio, Katchacho and Karkara, non-Oraons can become members of the Dhumkuria if they so wish. Rules of membership have become lax. The age range is eight to twentytwo. Generally youths must leave the dormitory on marriage but they continue to sleep there till they get children of their own. Other people like widowers, issueless married males or youngmen whose wives were not with them, visitors from other villages and minor government officials also frequent the *Dhumkuria.*

"Admission to the *Dhumkuria* takes place just after the *Karam* festival in September. The *Dhangar Mahto,* the head of the *Dhumkuria* announces the names of the boys who are to be admitted. Late at night, the youths of the seniormost age grade visit all the houses from which a boy is to be admitted and place at every entrance a plough. When the parents of the young boys wake up in the morning, they understand that the time for their admission has come. Youths of the lowest age grade collect eggs, oil and other eatables from the village and the newly admitted boys are feasted. The seniormost youths talk to them about their new responsibilities and privileges.

"Traditionally, the boys are divided into three age grades, each grade having clearly defined duties. The boys are expected to remain in each of the first two grades for a period of three years and continue to live in the *Dhumkuria* in the third grade till marriage. The system of age grades in *Dhumkuria* is not maintained strictly due to the fact that admissions are not made regularly or properly. In Mandar, it was observed that membership of the first two grades is decreasing fast. In Khapia there are no age grades. In Rani Khatanga the three grades are found. The first to arrive at the *Dhumkuria* in the evening are the members of the lowest age grade. They clean and sweep the floor, spread mats and light the lamp. They then go back home and return after meals. By this time members of the other age grades start arriving. During the rains and in winter, members of the juniormost grade light the fire. Members of the intermediate grade massage the bodies of senior members. Young boys hate doing this job. For negligence of this duty they are taken to task by the elders and this is one of the reasons why the membership of the junior grades of the *Dhumkuria* is going down. It is at the time of the massage that the boys discuss village affairs. After the massage, all the inmates of the *Dhumkuria* go out to the *Akkra* and drums are sounded. This is the signal for inviting the girls for a dance. As soon as a good number of people arrive, dancing begins. Youths and maidens continue to join even after the dance has begun. After the dance which usually lasts till midnight, the boys and girls disperse to their respective dormitories.

"The most important function of the *Dhumkuria* youths is the performance of magical and religious rituals to secure success in hunting and to ensure the multiplication of male children. For the day of their admission to the *Dhumkuria,* the boys are given instruction in their social and religious duties. Before they embark on ceremonial hunting expeditions, the youths worship the goddess *Chandi.* The youths of the dormitory have to make all arrangements for the hunts which are joined not only by members of one village but by most of the youths of the entire neighbourhood. In this way they imbibe team spirit and learn work as a corporate unit for the common good. After the *Sarhul* festival the goddess *Chandi* is again worshipped. Procreative vigour is sought to be acquired from the worship of such natural object as the Sal tree.

"In a wedding or some other feast in a village the members of the *Dhumkuria* dress the animals and fowls for the occasion, act as cooks and also look after the guests. If a villager is in need of the services of labourers for thatching a house or agricultural work, he applies to the head of the *Dhumkuria* and strikes a bargain with him. Services rendered in this way are known as *Pacha* services. The wages received are generally spent on the purchase of musical instruments or some other requisites specially for making flags. In Malti, Mandar, Barambe, Rani Khatanga and Tangarbansli, *Pacha* service is still prevalent. The money received is deposited with the *Dhangar Mahto* who utilizes it for the benefit of the *Dhumkuria.*

"The *Dhumkuria* youths are privileged to gather once a year, fruit from all Karanj trees in the village. They enjoy a similar licence in regard to Mahua trees. The Mahua flowers are stored by the head of the *Dhumkuria* and later they are sent for distillation. The beer thus produced is used on the occasion of inter-village gatherings. An interesting magical ceremony that the Oraon bachelors have to perform is driving away of the spirit that causes cattle disease. When such a disease appears in a village, a day is fixed for the driving away of that spirit. At about mid-night the bachelors gather on the dancing ground, strip themselves completely naked and each takes a cudgel in his hand. The village cowherd with a wooden bell suspended from his neck is chased by the youths with shouts resembling the bellowing of cattle. When the former is chased out of the village, he quickly drops the cowbell and beats a hasty retreat. Thus the disease is thought to be driven away from one village to the bounds of another village. This practice continues from village to village until the disease spirit is driven from the entire neighbourhood.

"The *Dhumkuria* youths have an important part to play in creating goodwill between villages in the neighbourhood. They generally go out in batches to pay ceremonial visits to the *Dhumkuria* in other villages. At the sound of the drum, the youths of other villages come out to welcome their guests and after exchange of greetings dance together and fraternise with each other. At this time they enter into *Sangi* friendship pacts. The day following, they are feasted and at the time of their departure the flag or other emblem is handed over by the head man of the *Dhumkuria* to the leader of the visiting party.

"The management of the dormitory is in the hands of the *Dhangar Mahto* who is assisted in his work by the *Dhangar Koiwar.* The *Dhangar Mahto* instructs the boys in social and ritual duties while the *Kotwar* has to attend to the big tribal meets called *Jatra* and dances and to see that the boys are well-equipped for the purpose. He collects flowers and compels disobedient boys to attend *Jatra* and dance. A plaited straw whip is the insignia of his office. The *Dhumkuria* officers were traditionally elected for three years. In most places, however, the election has not taken place for many years. As a matter of fact, one who is very much interested in the institution begins to function as the *Mahto* or the *Kotwar.* The recognition of the village officials is formally given later on. In one village, the *Mahto* was aged forty-four and the *Kotwar* thirty-seven. *Dhumkuria* discipline, like its entire organization, has suffered very much in recent years. The *Dhumkuria* posts are meant to give training to promising youths in leadership, initiative and organization.

"Like the youths, the maidens of the girl's dormitory have certain rights and duties. They weave palm leaf mats for themselves as well as for the bachelors' dormitory. Besides this, they have their own rituals which they perform secretly. On the occasion of a marriage in a village, the maidens take part in making arrangements for a feast. The maidens may also be hired out for sowing, transplanting or harvesting. The maiden's dormitory is now in an advanced state of decay and functions only informally. The *Dhumkuria,* where it exists, is a great binding force for the youth of the village. Sometimes it acts on behalf of the entire village community. The village is interested in it because it is the channel through which the culture of the tribe as expressed in dance, song, riddle, proverbs etc., is transmitted from generation to generation.

Modern influences on Dhumkuria

"Though modern influences are making serious inroads in the economic unity of the village, there are many occasions on which it is amply demonstrated. One such occasion is the communal village hunt organized among the different tribes at various times in the year. The Oraon call these large hunting expeditions, *Sendra.* All these hunts are the concern not only of individual hunters working with their families but necessitates the co-operation of the entire village. The date for such hunts is fixed by the elders of the village. As the hunt lasts several days and needs elaborate preparation and organization, a leader is selected by the process of divination. Before starting, the goddess *Chandi* is propitiated by the newly chosen leader known as the *Chandi Pahan.* Hunting implements and nets from the entire village are pooled together. Each family of the village is expected to send one man for this expedition. As a rule, the kill is divided equally between the different families. The man who shoots the game receives an additional share. Dogs and boys accompanying the party receive half a share each.

"Among the Ho fishing is generally done in groups. The owner of a pond fixes a day on which fishing is to be done. This information is widely circulated. Groups of villagers from surrounding area gather the night before with their nets, bags and other fishing implements. The owner of the pond propitiates the *Nage Bonga* or the river spirit. The village priest offers a sacrifice to the same deity. Although people from several villages come for the same purpose, each village keeps together while fishing, so that the catch of each of the groups is distinct. There is a spirit of rivalry between people belonging to different villages. Thus for fishing the village forms a unit. When each village takes its catch home, it is distributed there in accordance with the usual rules.

"In agricultural operations, the spirit of co-operation evident in the village, is remarkable. Sowing does not begin until, on a day fixed by the elders, the village deities are propitiated by the village priest. Weeding and transplanting is done jointly by all the village women working together in different fields by turns. The monotonous work is enlivened by sweet songs sung in chorus by them.

Most of the agricultural labour required in a village is supplied locally. Generally the tribals are subsistence cultivators and members of a family can look after their agriculture without any outside help. There are some who have got more lands than they can cultivate. Such people maintain agricultural labour all the year round. The labourer is engaged in the month of *Magh* (January). He is paid either in cash or in kind and is housed and fed by his employer. From the day the labourer is engaged, he becomes a member of the employer's household and takes part in the life of the family. There is no difference in status between the employer and his *Dhangar* or agricultural labourer and the latter can even marry his employer's daughter or sister if their clans are different," He adds. For Muria's Ghotul see *Puberty* in the Volume on Central region.

Ceremony of *Upanayana*

Among the high-caste Hindus including Brahmans, Kshatriyas and Vaishyas etc., son's puberty was marked by the ritual and ceremony of wearing the sacred thread or upanayana. Brahmans specially attached significance to the ceremony as a young son could become entitled to his academic career and the study of sacred taxts like Vedas and Upanishads only after his investiture with the sacred threads. Here R.V. Russel and Hira Lal describe the ceremony thus : "Secular Brahmans now, however, greatly abridge the length of their prayers, and an hour or an hour and a half in the morning suffices for the daily bath and purification, the worship of the household deities and the morning meal.

"Brahman boys are invested with the sacred thread between the ages of five and nine. The ceremony is called Upanayana or the introduction to knowledge, since by it the boy acquires the right to read the sacred books. Until this ceremony he is not really a Brahman, and is not bound to observe the caste rules and restrictions. By its performance he becomes Dvija or twice-born, and the highest importance is attached to the change or initiation. He may then begin to acquire divine knowledge, and perhaps in past times it was thought that he obtained the divine character belonging to a Brahman. The sacred thread is made of three strands of cotton, which should be obtained from the cotton tree growing wild. Sometimes a tree is grown in the yard of the house for the provision of the threads. It has several knots in it, to which great importance is attached, the number of knots being different for a Brahman, a Kshatriya and a Vaishya, the three twice-born castes. The thread hangs from the left shoulder, falling on to the right hip. Sometimes, when a man is married, he wears a double thread of six strands, the second being for his wife; and after his father dies a treble one of nine strands. At the investiture the boy's nails are cut and his hair is shaved, and he performs the *hom* or fire sacrifice for the first time. He then acquires the status of a Brahmachari or disciple, and in former times he would proceed to some religious centre and begin to study the sacred books. The idea of this is preserved by a symbolic ritual. Some Brahmans shave the boy's head, completely, make a girdle of *kusha* or *munj* grass round his waist, provide him with a begging-bowl and tongs and the skin of an antelope to sit on and make him go and beg from four houses. Among others the boy gets on to a wooden horse and announces his intention of going off to Benares to study. His mother then sits on the edge of a well and threatens to throw herself in if he will not change his mind, or the maternal uncle promises to give the boy his daughter in marriage. Then the boy relinquishes his intention and agrees to stay at home. The sacred thread must always be passed through the hand before saying the Gayatri text in praise of the sun, the most sacred Brahmanical text. The sacred thread is changed once a year on the day of Rakshabandhan; the Brahman and all his family change it together. The word Rakshabandhan means binding or tying up the devils, and it would thus appear that the sacred thread and the knots in it may have been originally intended to some extent to be a protection against evil spirits. It is also changed on the occasion of a birth or death in the family, or of an eclipse, or if it breaks. The old threads are torn up or sewn into clothes by the very poor in the Maratha districts. It is said that the Brahmans are afraid that the Kunbis will get hold of their old threads, and if they do get one they will fold it into four strings, holding a lamp in the middle, and wave it over any one who is sick. The Brahmans think that if this is done all the accumulated virtue which they have obtained by many repetitions of the Gayatri or sacred prayer will be transferred to the sick Kunbi. Many castes now wear the sacred thread who have no proper claim to do so, especially those who have become landholders and aspire to the status of Rajputs.

"The Brahman is of course supreme in Hindu society. He never bows his head in salutation to any one who is not a Brahman, and acknowledges with a benediction the greetings of all other classes. No member of another caste, Dr. Bhattacharya states, can, consistently with Hindu etiquette and religious beliefs, refuse altogether to bow to a Brahman. "The more orthodox Sudras carry their veneration for the priestly caste to such an extent that they will not cross the shadow of a Brahman, and it is not unusual for them to be under a vow not to eat any food in the morning before drinking Brahman nectar,' *Bipracharanamrita*, or water in which the toe of a Brahman has been dipped. On the other hand, the pride of the Brahman is such that he does not bow even to the images of the gods in a Sudra's house. When a Brahman invites a Sudra the latter is usually asked to partake of the host's *prasada* or favour in the shape of the leavings of his plate. Orthodox Sudras actually take offence if invited by the use of any other formula. No Sudra is allowed to eat in the same room or at the same time with Brahmans." Hindu Castes and Sects, pp. 19-21.

References

1. Bahadur, K.P., Castes, Tribes and Culture of India: Bengal, Bihar and Orissa, ESS ESS Publications, New Delhi, 1977.
2. Sinha, Dikshit, The Hill Kharia of Purulia, Anthropological Survey of India, Calcutta, 1984.
3. Sachchidananda, Profiles of Tribal Culture in Bihar, Firma KLM, Calcutta, 1965.

4. Sarkar, Amitabha and Dasgupta, Samira, Spectrum of Tribal Bastar, Agam Kale Prakashan, Delhi, 1996.
5. Raychaudhuri, Tarak Chand and Ray Chaudhuri, Bikash, the Brahmans of Bengal, Anthropological Survey of India, Calcutta, 1981.
6. Russel, R.V. and Lal, Hira, The Tribes and Castes of the Central Provinces of India, Low Price Publications, Delhi (reprint) 1997, originally published MacMillan and Co., London, 1916.
7. Ghuryre, G.S., The *Mahadev Kolis*, Popular Book Depot, Bombay, 1957.
8. Sengupta, Syamalkanti, the Social Profiles of the Mahalis, Firma KLM, Calcutta, 1970.
9. Sachchidananda, the Tribal village in Bihar : A Study in Unity and Extension, Munshiram Manoharlal, Delhi, 1968.
10. Risley, Sir H.H., The Tribes and Castes of Bengal: Ethnographic Glossary, Firma KLM, Calcutta, 1998, originally published : Bengal Secretariat Press, Calcutta, 1891.
11. Dalton, E.T., Descriptive Ethnology of Bengal, Office of Superintendent of Government Press, Calcutta, 1872, reprint Firma KLM, Calcutta, 1960.
12. Sarif, Ja'far, *Islam in India* (edited by W. Crooke), Oriental Books, reprint Corp., New Delhi, 1972, originally published 1921.

3

Betrothal

Observing by the complexity of the rites, rituals and ceremonies and the long period of time during which the complete procedure for contracting a marital alliance is gone through, it is evident that marriage is the most important stage in tribal life-cycle. It is considered indispensable for every man and woman, whose tribe members cannot comprehend how a normal man or woman can remain unmarried. Bachelors and spinsters are looked upon by the people in society as unhappy wretches. As a result of this view unmarried people are very rarely found in the tribal society.

The general custom prevalent among the Santals and other tribals is to contract monogamous marital unions. Polygamy is not favoured unless the wife is barren, in which case, the husband can either divorce his wife or take a second wife with the former wife's consent. Otherwise, Santal opinion is against polygamy. Sandals contemplate that only a fool can live happily with more than one wife for, as the proverb goes, 'A co-wife pricks like spear grass'. Adult marriage is normally the accepted custom among all the Santals. It is considered more appropriate for the bride to the younger than the bridegroom. The average marriage age of a boy is 20 and that of a girl 16. To protect their tribal solidarity, the Santals have very stringent marriage laws.

A Santal tribal cannot marry a non-Santal or a woman of his own clan. The former match is considered as a threat to the tribe's existence and integrity, while the latter is considered an incestuous relationship. Formerly, a Santal was barred from marrying into his mother's subclan. The only forbidden degree of consanguinity in marital relation to marriage are brothers and sisters, cross-cousins or children of siblings of the opposite sex, and parallel cousins or children of siblings of the same sex. However, the Santals consider relationship up to three generations as a bar to marriage. Though senior levirate and sororate are prohibited, there have no restriction on junior levirate and sororate. Thus, a Santal, on the death of his wife, may marry the deceased woman's younger, but not elder sister. Similarly, on the death of her husband, a woman, may marry his younger but not elder brother. Sometimes levirate marriage is practised to keep the family property intact.

Among the Santals after marriage the residence is normally patrilocal. The bride goes to live in her father-in-law's house. It is only in the *ghardi jawae* or *ghar jawae* types of marriage, that this custom is reversed when a man goes to live in his in-laws' house. If the house is not big enough to shelter more than one married son and his family, then some build their own house, usually close to their father's house. There also exists a certain social reluctance towards intra-village marriage, as a proverb says, 'A hen and a bride from the same village run to their homes'.

Free Pre-marital Licence to Girls

Among the tribals, generally the grown-up children forge ceremonial friendship and blood brotherhoods. No marriage is allowed between the families of two ceremonial friends. At adolescence boys and girls have regular training in dance and songs organised in the village 'Akhara'. Premarital mixing between the sexes is allowed among the tribals. Very few of such friendships end in marriage because marriage in the same village, even though the parties belong to different clans is not regarded with favour.

Mr. Sachchidananda writes, "The importance of marriage is realised by all tribals. Without marriage no person can become a full member of the tribe. Even most of the deities are reported to have consorts. Adult marriage is the rule, though in some parts, due to Hindu influence, the age of marriage has gone down. In the choice of the mate the boy and girl have a free hand, but a marriage arranged by parents is considered to be ideal. Marriage by capture is now rare. '*Raji-Khushi*' marriage is one in which the boy and girl take the initiative. Bride price is not insisted upon in this marriage. Sometimes, a disappointed woman may intrude into the house of her beloved and refuse to go away. Poor people who have no money to pay as bride-price have to serve the girl's father for a certain period. Widow-remarriage or the marriage of a divorced woman is called 'Sagai' and only half bride-price is chargeable. The most prevalent form of marriage called '*Diku-Andi*' is a poor imitation of lower-class Hindu marriage. Marriage is arranged by go-betweens. The rate of bride-price is different among various tribes. Among the Munda Rs. 12/- and two heads of cattle is the traditional bride-price. Among the Ho it has risen so high that several girls do not find husbands who can pay such high bride-price. On the day fixed for marriage a small party consisting of the boy's male and female, relatives and friends goes to the girl's village where elaborate ceremonies together with much eating and drinking of rice-beer follow. The girl is brought to her husband's house where she is ceremonially adopted into her husband's clan. The bride visits her parents off and on. Parent's home is her ultimate refuse in case of quarrel with her husband or that of widowhood. Marriage creates a fresh network of relationships for both man and woman, but the latter has to adjust herself in the husband's family. Lack of adjustment leads to partition in the home and break-up of the family. Divorce is allowed to both parties on grounds of infidelity, theft, witchcraft etc. As it may lead to returning the bride-price, the approval of the village for divorce is necessary.

"The place of elders in tribal life is high. They are considered repositories of tribal tradition and experience. In village affairs their voice is important, specially in the Panchayat. But people who are senile have no status whatsoever. They eke out miserable existence toiling with their failing powers. Even though neglected, old men and women spend most of their time in looking after their grand-children in which task they derive great happiness and satisfaction. Old men feel out of tune with changing society and comment adversely upon the ways of youth. Only during festivals they lose all reserve and indulge freely in the dances, enjoyment and merry-making that mark those occasions." He adds.

Rule of Gotra Exogamy

Sir Risley wrote about the Agrawala rule of exogamy, "All the sections are strictly, exogamous, but the rule of unilateral exogamy is supplemented by provisions forbidding marriage with certain classes of relations. Thus a man may not marry a woman—*(a)* belonging to his own *gotra; (b)* descended from his own paternal or maternal grandfather, great-grandfather, or great-great-grandfather; (c) descended from his own paternal or maternal aunt; *(d)* belonging to the grand-maternal family *(nanihal)* of his own father or mother. He may marry the younger sister of his deceased wife, but not the elder sister, nor may he marry two sisters at the same time. As is usual in such cases, the classes of relations barred are not mutually exclusive. All the agnatic descendants of a man's three nearest male ascendants are necessarily members of his own *gotra,* and therefore come within class *(a)* as well as class (*b*) Again, the paternal and maternal aunt and their descendants are included among the descendants of the paternal and maternal grandfathers, while some of the members of the *nanihal* must also come under class *(c)* The *gotra* rule is undoubtedly the oldest; and it seems probable that the other prohibited classes may have been added from time to time as experience and the growing sense of the true nature of kinship demonstrated the incompleteness of the primitive rule of exogamy.

"It is certainly remarkable that a caste so widely diffused as the Agarwals should not have broken up into endogamous divisions, based upon differences of locality, of the type so common in Bengal. In the North-West

Provinces, indeed, it is stated that the Pachhainya or Western branch of the caste cannot intermarry with the Purbiya or Eastern Agarwals. Members of these groups, however, may eat together, and the prohibition on intermarriage is said to have arisen from a comparatively recent quarrel, which is now likely to be made up. In Bihar the tendency is to ignore these distinctions and to represent restrictions on intermarriage between Purbiyas and Pachhainyas as matters of family prejudice rather than of caste custom. This, however, may be due to the fact that most of the Bihar Agarwals belong to the Purbiya branch, and are regarded as socially inferior to the Pachhainyas. Both inter-marriage and community of food are prohibited to the Dasa sub-caste, who are illegitimate descendants of an Agarwal named Basu, and to the Biradari Raja, or Bisa, who are said to be descended from one Ratan Chand, who was made a Raja by the Emperor Farokhsir in the early part of last century." The custom is pertinent to the community of Agrawals.

Corpus Archaic Rituals

The function of match-making, writes Mr. Risley, is often confined to heads of families or villages, priests, genealogists, match-makers, and such-like persons whose business it is to look after the matrimonial arrangements of the tribe. For this reason they form not only the most archaic, but also the most durable portion of the body of custom which a given tribe or caste observes, and are the least liable to be modified or destroyed by the operation of fiction and of the inveterate tendency to imitate the institutions of groups supposed to be socially superior, which has done and is constantly doing so much to force all tribal observances into conformity with the standard Brahmanical pattern.

"The Kandhs of the Orissa Kandhmals are divided into fifty *gochis* or exogamous septs, each of which bears the name of a *mula* or village, believes all its members to be descended from a common ancestor, and as a rule dwells as a body of blood relations in the commune *muta* or group of villages after which it is called. The Kandh *gochi* appears therefore to represent the nearest approach that has yet been discovered to the "local exogamous tribe," supposed by Mr. McLennan to be the primary unit of human society. Each *gochi* is further split up into sub-septs called *klambus.* Each dwelling in one of the villages making up the *muta* or commune. Of these I have not yet been able to obtain a complete list.

"The sub-sept, like the sept, traces its origin to a single ancestor, but he is a personage of more recent date than the progenitor of the sept. The relations included in the former are comparatively near, while the connexion between members of the *gochi* is much more remote, and in the modern sense of the word they can hardly be called relations at all. The sub-sept seems in fact to be a sort of joint-family expanded to form a village community, the members of which are invited to marriages, festivals and similar domestic ceremonies to which it would be impossible to bring together the larger group. On occasions of special importance, when, for example, a *casus belli* is thought to have arisen between a sept and its neighbours, the whole *gochi* is summoned to meet in council and consider the question laid before it." Adds Mr. Risley.

Sexual Escapades with Outsiders Punishable

Any tribal man and woman who indulges in sexual intercourse with a non-Santal, the worst kind of offence, or with a person of the same clan is duly punished by the tribal council. According to various authors, *Bitlaha* custom was analogous to a hunt, in which the culprits were the hunted and the villagers were the hunters. The lewd songs and actions demonstrated the bestitality of the culprits. As Mr. W.G. Archer points out, 'It is the exposure to collective shame that is the essence of the ritual and which makes it far more dreaded than physical torture or confinement in a jail'. In certain cases of permanent excommunication the offenders suffer social death—they ceases to exist for the community as such. They are not allowed by the tribal people to take food with others, get water from the village well, join in any festival, hunt or village council, or give their children in marriage within the Santal community. In the case of sickness or death, nobody visits them. Anyone having any link with an excommunicated person was considered liable to being punished. So great was this punishment, that it could only be given by the Santal supreme council or court of appeal called as the *Lo Bir*. But nowadays, the incidence of *Bitlaha* is declining. The Government has stopped recognising this form of ostracism. At village, Pangro, nobody remembers any such event. This, however, does not mean that the Santals are becoming lax regarding their custom of tribal endogamy or clan exogamy. The participants of the All-India Santal Social Assembly which took place at Asansol in West Bengal since 13 to 16 April 1978, voiced the threat to their tribal integrity in inter-community marriages. Nowadays, heavy fines are imposed on the offenders of the rule of exogamy and endogamy.

Betrothal in Dhamkuria

The Oraons, generally, have the institution of dormitories called *dhumkurias*, which provide the opportunity of young people to come together and take part in the numerous gatherings. Although these are not strictly festivals, the customs of the male and female dormitories are of peculiar interest as most of them have a collective significance, and point to many observances of a magical and religious rites. Every new entrant of the dormitory has to get three earthen jugs.

On the night after his admission each newly admitted boy goes stark naked with his jug to some adjacent village to fill it with water along with mud. He puts a *sal* and mango leaves in it which as not borne fruit. He then hides the jugs. These jugs are periodically examined by the head of the dormitory to see if these are full of water and whether some dead insect or animal is found in it. If this is so, it is considered that the lad would become an expert huntsman. The contents of the jug is offered to the Chandi spirit through pouring the water and other things in it over the sacred Chandistone. The members of the *dhumkuria* also practice the spring hunt (*phagu-sendra*) held in March and the summer hunt (*bisu shikar*) in April-May. These hunts are preceded by a ceremony in which a priest in charge of this rite goes out completely naked at mid-night, to bathe in the village spring, take a gourdful of water to offer it to the Chandi-stone. He also puts three parallel vermilion marks on the stone. He is accompanied by boys from the dormitory walking at some distance behind him. After having carried out the ceremony, the priest returns to the dormitory and puts on his clothes. Mr. K.P. Bahadur writes, "A curious feature of the summer hunt is that for the period the men are away hunting, the Oraon women of the village behave as though they were men. They wear men's clothes, address each other as men do, and behave as men would to all the people of the village and to strangers. During this period they are free to use filthy language and abuse anyone they like without check. They also dance till late in the night, all dressed as men. If any woman refuses to join in, they pour water over her, poke at her with lathis, and drag her by force to the dancing ground (*akhara*)."

S.C. Roy writes in the Oraons of Chota Nagpur, thus, "Besides the hunt ceremonies, the Munda lads have ceremonies for fecundation in which Chandi is worshipped to give more progeny. This is done shortly after the *sarhul* festival (to celebrate the symbolic marriage of mother-earth with the sun). While the girls and lads dance in the *akhara*, young bachelors rob the women of their ear ornament called *bindios*. They take these and after sacrificing a blank fowl consign the *bindios* and the blood of the fowl into a hole dug by them. The bachelors then urinate into this hole, and fill it up, and pelt it with clods.

"Twice a year once in March and once in April-May another rite is observed for increasing progeny. The boys of the dormitory are led by the head to a place away from the village *abadi*, each pair of them carrying on their shoulders a wooden pole from which is slung a net with a basket in it. The head of the dormitory carries a new and thin stick of *sal* and a *sal* sapling in which a slit has been made resembling the vagina.

"When they have reached a suitable spot in a jungle or on some waste upland, the boys fill their basket with red ferruginuous earth (*panjri khajj* or *lalmati*). When their baskets are filled to the brim, the boys besmear one another all over the body with red earth. The *dhumkuria mahato* (head) has in the meanwhile planted the *sal* sapling firmly on the ground. The boys of the two upper grades now spit into the slit in the sapling. The boys of the lowest grade have now to strip themselves absolutely naked, and each boy in turn has to insert his organ into the saliva-filled slit. All the time the boy *mahato* stands beside *thesal* sapling with the new sal wood stick in his hands. And as each boy is about to step back after performing the magic operation, the *mahato* strikes the boy on his thigh a little below the groin with the *sal*-stick. (SC Roy, the Oraons of Chota Nagpur, 1915, pp. 242-3).

"These rites show the inclination of the Mundas for increasing their numbers. In matters of sexual morality, they maintain decorum in the sense that each boy selects his own favourite sweetheart, and for the first three years of their stay in the dormitory a boy is not permitted to have intimacy with a girl. But the older boys do have such intimacy." In fact as Mr. Roy writes, "they employ the freshers to procure their girls, from the girl's dormitory. If a freshman refuses or shows his disinclination the older boys press his legs with wooden pincers till the pain makes him agree. When the girls are brought, the boys each take a girl of their choice and enjoy her in some secluded spot or in a hay-stack. If a girl shows disinclination to come to the boy's dormitory she is forcefully brought by a number of young boys and if she refuses to go then with any boy to have sex with him, a number of boys violate her one after the other till she begs for mercy and speaks out the name of the boy with whom she is willing to disport." (*op. cit.* p. 246).

"The girls have their devices for preventing conception while having sexual relations in this manner with the boys, though these devices often do not work and they have to take recourse to abortion. To prevent conception, an Oraon maiden either reverses her loin-cloth for the nonce by wearing it with its front side to the back or ties to his loin-cloth just above the abdomen, the false plait of hair sometimes worn as a coiffure. When, notwithstanding such precautions inconvenient consequences follow such pre-marital connection, the girl is given a glass or two *phuli* or *wahua*-liquor to drink, and this, it is said, generally serves to cause abortion." (*op. cit.*, p. 248).

K.P. Bahadur writes, "As the lads of the *dhumkuria* have certain duties to perform even so the girls of the maidens dormitories called *pel-erpa,* have their tasks and ceremonial rites. During the first three years of her stay each Oraọn maiden makes a strip of palm-leaf mat. All these strips are stitched together by the boys to whom they are passed over and the huge mat thus made serves as a bed for the bachelors. In another rite they present the lads of the *dhumkuria,* barley shoots. In August the maidens litter the floor of their dormitory with a layer of sand. On this they scatter barley-seeds. They sprinkle water over the seeds and sit up late at night watching the seeds germinate, singing songs all the while. When the shoots sprout they distribute these to the young men at the *akhara* and the girls and the youths then dance together."

The tribal attitude to sex and marriage is surprisingly unfettered and liberal. In most tribes, pre-marital sex is not suppressed or frowned upon; in fact premarital sex is condoned. For example, about the Kandhs Mr. Risley records Kandh girls are usually married, when of full age in most cases to men of their own choice, and after a regular process of courtship. Considerable license is allowed to the young men and maidens of the tribe, and sexual intercourse before marriage is tacitly recognised.' H.H. Risely, *The Tribes and Castes of Bengal,* 1891, Vol. I, p. 401. At the same time the young men of the tribals do not, like those of our age, forget their obligations and responsibilities. If a galvinating lover gets involved with a girl so much as to burden her with child the liason ends in marriage. In spite of the freedom given to the Kandh girls, aforesaid noted, infidelity is rare. The young men and women dance and sing in the moonlight. Occasionally, they pair off and the bud of love blossoms. They have no inhibitions. They make love in natural surroundings, in deep woods and besides running streams, and their elders leave them alone, perhaps sighing at old remembrances and thinking of the days when they, too', like these lovelorn lads and lasses made love without inhibition under the moon's light. Women, amongst most of these tribals are held in high esteem, and in this too, the tribals show a surprisingly modern attitude.

About the Ho wife, for example, Dr. Hayes records, "A Kol or Ho makes a regular companion of his wife. She is consulted in all difficulties, and receives the fullest consideration due to her sex." There is, of course, the value of women as workers in fields and at other jobs, but this cannot be the only reason for such consideration. The status of women was high because they were considered equal partners in various aspects of home and social life. In marriage it was the bridegroom who had to pay the bride-price, not the girl's father who eked out a dowry. The ceremonial part of marriage is simple and mostly inexpensive. Remnants of antiquated customs remain among the Hos in which after the bride has remained for three days with her husband, she runs away, and her husband has to seek her and carry her away to his house by force. In divorce and widow remarriage, the tribals again show a liberal attitude. In the majority of tribes in the eastern zone this right this is permitted and divorce may be had on valid grounds, sometimes on the payment of a small fine. Polygamy is permitted, but due to the bride-price and the expense of maintenance of more wives than one, it is seldom practised, only if the first wife is barren.

Totemistic Clans

Sir H.H. Risley writes, "In the district of Bankura, where the original structure of the caste seems to have been singularly well preserved, we find the Bagdis divided into the following sub-castes:—(1) Tentulia, bearing the titles Bagh, Santra, Rai, Khan, Puila; (2) Kasaikulia, with the titles manjhi, Masalchi, Palankhai, Pherka; (3) Dulla, with titles Sardar and Dhara; (4) Ujha or Oja; (5) Machhua, Mcchhua, or Mecho; (6) Gulimanjhi; (7) Dandamanjhi; (8) Kusmetia, Kusmatia, or Kusputra; (9) Mallametia, Matia, or Matial. Within these again are a number of exogamous sections, among which may be mentioned *Kasbak*, the heron; *Ponkrishi,* the jungle cock; *Salrishi* or Salmach, the sal fish; *Patrishi,* the bean; and *Kachchhap,* the tortoise. The totem is taboo to the members of the section; that is to say, a Kasbak Bagdi may not kill or eat a heron; a Patrishi, like the Pythagoreans according to Lucian, may not touch a bean.

"A Bagdi cannot marry outside the sub-caste, nor inside the section to which he belongs. Thus a Tentulia must marry a Tentulia, but a man of the Salrishi section, to whatever sub-caste he may belong, cannot marry a woman of that section. The section names go by the male side, and the rule prohibiting marriage within the section requires therefore to be helped out by a separate set of rules, which to some extent overlap the rule of exogamy. Marriage with any person descended in a direct line from the same parents is forbidden as long as any relationship can be traced. To simplify the calculation of collateral relationship, the formula 'Paternal uncle, maternal uncle, paternal aunt, maternal aunt—these four relationships are to be avoided in marriage,' is in use. Ordinarily the prohibition extends only to three generations in the descending line; but if *bhaiyadi* or mutual recognition of relationship is kept up, intermarriage is barred for five or, as some say, seven generations. In counting generations the person under consideration is included.

"In the more eastern districts the organization of the caste seems to be less elaborate, and has clearly been affected by closer contact with Hinduism, inducing the adoption of Brahmanical customs. In the 24-Parganas only five sub-castes are found—Tentulia, Kusmetia, Trayodas, Manjhi, Noda; while the sections are reduced to three—Kasyapa, Raucho, and Dasya—the members of which profess to be descended from Vedic Rishis, and have abandoned the totemistic observances which are common further west. Traces of totemism, however, still survive in the names of sub-castes.

Tentulias admit that they are called after the tamarind, tree, and Kusmetias that they take their name from the kusa grass, but neither show any reverence for the plants in question. The system of exogamy has also been developed in the direction of closer conformity with the usages of the higher castes. The mother's section is excluded in addition to the father's, and marriage with *Sapindas* is prohibited. The custom is related to the Bagdi community in Bihar, Orissa and parts of Jharkhand.

Exogamous and Endogamous groups for Marriage

Sir Risley records, "An examination of the sections or exogenous groups into which the Babhans are divided appears, however, to tell strongly against the hypothesis that they are degraded Brahmans. These groups are usually the oldest and most durable element in the internal organization of a caste or tribe, and may therefore be expected to offer the clearest indications as to its origin. Now we find among the Babhans section-names of two distinct types—the one *territorial*, referring either to some very early settlement of the section, or to the birthplace of its founder, and the other *eponymous*, the eponym being in most cases a Vedic *rishi* or inspired saint. The names of the former class correspond to or closely resemble those current among Rajputs; the names of the latter are those of the standard Brahmanical *gotras*. Where the matrimonial prohibitions based on these two classes of sections conflict, as must obviously often happen where every member of the caste necessarily belongs to both sets, the authority of the territorial class overrides that of the eponymous or Brahmanical class. Suppose, for instance, that a man of the Karanch territorial section and of the Sandhilya eponymous section wishes to marry a woman of the Sakarwar territoria section, the fact that she also belongs to the Sandilya eponymous section will not operate as a bar to the marriage. Whatever may be the theory of the purohits of the caste, the Brahmanical *gotra* is disregarded in practice, and doubtful cases are decided in accordance with the *mul* or territorial section to which the parties belong. This circumstance seems to indicate that the *territorial* sections are the older of the *two,* and are probably the original sections of the caste; while the eponymous sections have been borrowed from the Brahmans in comparatively recent times. It would follow that the Babhans are an offshoot, not from the Brahmans, but from the Rajput. If Babhans had originally been Brahmans, they would at the time of their separation from the parent caste have been already fitted up with a complete set of Brahmanical *gotras,* and it is difficult to imagine any reason which could have induced them to borrow a strange and much more elaborate set of sections from a tribe of inferior status, and to relegate their own sections to an entirely subordinate position. Territorial sections, moreover, do not lend themselves to the process of borrowing. They are as a rule exceedingly numerous; the meanings of their name are obscure and difficult to trace; and, with the exception of a few names borne by famous Rajput clan, they are wanting in the note of social distinction. The Brahmanical *gotras*, on the other hand, form a clearly-defined and not inconveniently-numerous group to which well-known and honourable traditions attach; they can be borrowed *en masse* without any particular trouble; and the influence of Brahman *prohits* is sufficient to diffuse them throughout any caste which affects a high standard of ceremonial purity and wishes to rise in the social scale. Numerous examples of the process of borrowing the Brahmanical eponymous *gotras* can be found among most of the lower castes at the present day: I know of no instance of a caste adopting sections of another type. To take a familiar illustration: it is as unlikely that a rising caste would borrow territorial sections when the Brahmanical *gotras* were to be had for the asking, as it is that an English manufacturer who has got on in the world and is about to change his name would select Billing, Wace, or one of the earlier English patronymics instead of some more high-sounding name which may have come in with the conquest. Kasyapa, Sandilya, and the other Brahmanical section names do for the rising castes of Bengal what Vavasour, Bracy, and Montresor are supposed to do for the wealthy *parvenu* in England.

"It should be added here that alongside of the clearly territorial section names we find a few names of another type, such as Baghauchhia, Belauria, Kastuar, which are said to have reference to the tiger, the *bel* tree *(eagle marmelos),* and the *kas* grass, and Hararia, Kodaria, Bhusbarat, Domkatar (foundling, spade-wielder, husk-picker, Dom's knife), which seem to be nicknames of the same kind as we meet among some of the Himalayan tribes. In the absence of evidence that the members of the first three sections regard with veneration the animal and plants whose name's they bear, we are hardly justified in pronouncing the names to be survivals from the totemistic stage. Some suggestion of inferiority does, however, seem to attach to the last four sections. . . .For the purpose of controlling connubial arrangements, both of these classes seem to possess the same value as the territorial section, so that the argument stated above is not affected.

"The considerations set forth above appear to me to render it highly probable that the Babhans are a branch of the Rajputs. It must, however, be admitted that evidence in favour of a Brahmanical origin is not wanting. Mr. Sherring lays stress on the fact that the Bhuinhars of Benares 'call themselves Brahmans; have the *gotras*, titles, and family names of Brahmans, and practise for the most part the usages of Brahmans.' In Behar, though the claim to be Brahmans is not invariably put forward, Brahmanical titles, such as Misr, Panre, and Tewari, are used along with the Rajput titles of Singh,

Rai, and Thakur. In Shahabad and in parts of the North-Western Provinces members of other castes accord to a Babhan the salutation *pranam* ordinarily reserved for Brahmans; while the Babhan responds with the benediction *asirbad.* Further south, however, this practice is unknown; and in Patna a Bubhan would give the first greeting to a Kayasth, thereby implicitly recognizing the superior status of that caste in the social system.

"Like the Rajputs, the Babhans exclude the section of both father and mother, or, in other words, forbid a man to marry a woman who belongs to the same section as he himself or his mother. The operation of this rule is further extended by the manner in which it is applied. Account is taken, not merely of the section to which the proposed bride herself belongs (*i.e.,* her father's section), but also of her mother's section; so that the marriage will be barred if the bride's mother belonged to the same section as the bridegroom's mother, though of course neither bride nor bridegroom can be members of that section. In respect of prohibited degrees, they follow the rules current among the Kayasths and explained in the article on that caste.

"Among the Babhans of Benar, as among the Rajputs, no endogamous divisions exist, and they also intermarry on terms of equality with the Babhans of the North-Western Provinces. Some sections, however, are reckoned interior to the rest, notably the Hararia, Kodaria, and Bhusbarat mentioned above, regarding whom there is a saying in Behar :

'Hararia, Kodaria, Bhusbarat mare, to Tirhut ka pap hare'.

In the north of Manbhum the Rampai and Domkatar sections are in such low repute that members of the other sections will not give their daughters in marriage to Rampai or Domkatar men, although they have no objection to taking wives from those sections themselves. Consequently in that part of the country Rampai and Domkatar Babhans can only get wives from each other, though their women can obtain husbands from all sections except their own. If the restrictions were carried a step further, and Babhans belonging to other sections interdicted from taking Rampai and Domkatar women to wife, those sections would be wholly cut off from the *jus connubii,* and would in fact, if not in name, have hardened into a sub-caste. I have no evidence to show that this is at all likely to take place—the Manbhum practice indeed appears to be quite exceptional—but the point deserves notice as tending to throw light on the obscure problem of the formation of sub-castes.'

Rules of Caste Divisions

About the Brahman custom of caste divisions, Sir Risley notes, ". . .

two classes or grades of sacerdotal virtue were formed :—(1) the Kulin, being those who had observed the entire nine counsels of perfection; (2) the Srotriya, who, though regular students of the Vedas, had lost *avritti* by intermarrying with families of inferior birth. The Srotriya were again subdivided into Siddha or perfect, Sadhya or capable of attaining purity, and Kashta or difficult. The last-named group was also called Ari or enemy, because a Kulin marrying a daughter of that group was disgraced.

"The relations of these three classes in respect of marriage were regulated by the principle laid down in the Institutes of Manu for members of the three twice-born castes, a principle for which Mr. Denzil Ibbetson has adopted the convenient and expressive name of *hypergamy*. The rule was that a man of the Kulin class could marry a woman of his own class or of the two higher Srotriya classes; a Siddha Srotriya could marry in his own group or in the Sadhya Srotriya group; while the Sadhya and Kasta Srotriyas might take wives only within the limits of their own classes. Conversely, women of the Sadhya Srotriya class could marry in their own class or the two classes above them; Siddha Srotriya women in their own class or in the Kulin class; while Kulin women at one end of the scale and Kashta women at the other were restricted in their choice of husbands to the Kulin and Kashta groups. Unequal or irregular marriages involved loss of reputation and forfeiture of rank. On the other hand, the marriage of girl into a good Kulin house conferred a sort of reflected honour on her own family, and in course of time this idea was developed into the doctrine known as *kula-gotra*, where by the reputation of a family depended upon the character of the marriages made by its female members.

"This singular and artificial organization deranged the natural balance of the sexes, and set up a vigorous competition for husbands among the women of the higher groups. The Bansajas are those Kulins who lost their distinction on account of misconduct, *i.e.,* their want of charity, discipline, and due observance of marriage law, three qualities which in later times constituted Kulinism.

"The growth of the Bansaja class introduced a further element of complication. In the struggle for husbands, Kulin girls who had no brothers or whose mothers were widows were often given to the sons of Bansaja parents; but families resorting to this device were excluded from the recognised cadre. Thus the brothers of a girl who married beneath her at once became Bansaja, but this degradation did not extend to her uncles. If an original Kulin married a Bansaja maiden, he himself became a Swakrita Bhanga or broken Brahman. His descendants in the second generation were known as Dwipurusha, in the third as Tripurusha, and in the fourth as

Chaturthapurusha. After this stage special designations were dropped, and the branch was merged in the Bansaja class. Although in theory these lower branches were completely cut off from the original hierarchy formed by Ballal Sen, natural instincts could not be wholly eradicated from a number of closely related families, and girls of the Bhanga and Bansaja groups used to marry their cousins of the elder branch. It might perhaps have been expected that these groups would have been admitted to the same privileges as the Srotriya, but this was not the case.

"The invasion of Bengal by the Muhammadans in 1203 and the instant collapse of the Hindu kingdom was not without its effect upon the matrimonial organization of the Rarhi Brahmans. Ballal Sen's reforms had been imposed upon the caste by the order of a Hindu ruler, and their observance depended upon the maintenance of his supervising authority. When this check was removed, the system could no longer hold together, and soon showed signs of breaking up completely. Artificial restrictions had been introduced; the natural balance of the sexes had been disturbed, and a disastrous competition for husbands had set in among the three original groups. New and inferior groups had sprung up, and their natural ambitions still further swelled the demand for Kulin husbands. The pressure of necessity soon showed itself too strong for the rules. Poor Kulins sold their family rank and honour for the bridegroom-price, which had taken the place of the bride-price of earlier times; they added to the number of their wives without regard to the respectability of the families from which they came; and they raised their prices as the supply of suitable husbands diminished and competition ran higher for a Kulin bride-groom.

"The reforms undertaken in the fourteenth century by Devi Vara, a ghatak or genealogist of Jessore, extended only to the Kulins. These were divided into three grades—(i) Swabhava or original Kulins, (ii) Bhanga, (iii) Bansaja. The Swabhava grade was further subdivided into 36 *mels* or endogamous groups each bearing the name of the original ancestor of the clan or of his village. The names of the *mels* are as follows:—Phuliya, Khardaha, Sarvvanandi, Ballabhi, Surai, Acharya Sekhari, Pandit Ratni, Bangala, Gopala Ghataki, Chayanarendri, Pramadani, Dasaratha Ghataki, Subharjakhani, Nariya, Raya, Bhattaraghvi, Dehati, Chayi, Vijaya Pandit, Chadai, Madhai, Bidyadhari, Parihal, Sri Bangabhatti, Maladkara Khani, Kakumvi, Hari Majumdari, Sri Bandhani, Bhairava Ghataki, Achambita, Dharadhari, Vale, Baghava Ghosali, Sungo Sarvvanandi, Sadananda Khani, Chandravati. This restriction of the marriages of Kulins to their own *mel* was the leading feature of Devi Vara's reform. Its principle was adopted and extended, it is believed, by the Kulins themselves, in the singular arrangement known as Palti-Prakriti, or preservation of the type, by which families of equal rank were formed into triple groups as it were, for matrimonial purposes, and bound to observe a sort of reciprocity. Thus Mukhuti families were bound to marry their sons to the daughters of the Chatterji and Banerji families, and *vice versa.* All kinds of complications are said to have arisen from this understanding. If for example, the Mukhuti had only one marriageable son and the Chatterji or Banerji ten daughters approaching puberty, the former must marry all ten or all must remain spinsters. Meantime the rush of competition for Kulin husbands on the part of Bhanga, Bansaja, and Srotriya classes was as strong as before, while the proportionate number of pure Kulins had been reduced by the loss of those who had become Bhangas and Bansajas. In order to dispose of the surplus of women in the higher groups polygamy was introduced, and was resorted to on a very large scale. It was popular with the Kulins because it enabled them to make a handsome income by the accident of their birth; and it was accepted by the parents of the girls concerned as offering the only means of complying with the requirements of the Hindu religion. Tempted by a *pan* or premium, which often reached the sum of two thousand rupees, Swabhava Kulins made light of their *kul* and its obligations, and married Bansaja girls, whom they left after the ceremony to be taken care of by their parents. Matrimony became a sort of profession, and the honour of marrying a daughter to a Bhanga Kulin is said to have been so highly valued in Eastern Bengal that as soon as a boy was ten year old his friends began to discuss his matrimonial prospects, and before he was twenty he had become the husband of many wives of ages varying from five to fifty.

"With the spread of education among the upper classes of Bengal an advance in social morality has been made and the grosser forms of polygamy have fallen into disrepute. But the artificial organisation of the caste still presses hard on a Kulin father who is unlucky enough to have a large family of daughters. These must be married before they attain puberty, or disgrace will fall on the family, and three generations of ancestors will be dishonoured. But a Kulin bridegroom can only be obtained by paying a heavy premium, many of the *mels* instituted by Devi Vara have died out, and in such cases, reciprocal marriage being no longer possible, the son of a family left without a corresponding *mel* must marry the only daughter of a widow; while the daughter of a Kulin widow, for whom no husband of equal birth can be procured, may be married to a Srotriya, and a premium accepted without endangering the family prestige. According to Dr. Wise, a Kulin father in Eastern Bengal could only preserve his kul intact in one of three ways:—By giving her to a Kulin of equal rank; by making an effigy (*kusa-kanya*) of her with *kusa* grass and giving it in symbolical marriage to a Kulin; by saying to a Kulin in the presence of ghatak witnesses:—'I would give my daughter, if

I had one, to you,' and putting on his forehead the tilak or distinguishing mark which a married woman wears." Adds Mr. Risley. The customs and rituals are practised among the Brahmans, mainly in West Bengal.

Dying without Marriage and Family being a Disgrace

To a Hill Kharia tribal in Bihar and West Bengal to die before marriage and without a family means to die without attaining the full stature of manhood in complete disgrace. Of all their rituals, the marriage rituals are most elaborate. It has two clearly delineable aspects social-ceremonial and ritual. The ceremonial aspect begin right from the process of spouse selection which points out the value the Hill Kharia place on the role of women in family life. Among them it is customary for the bridegroom's relatives to make the first move. After preliminary contact has been established through ago-between (*raibaysha*) bridegroom's party would come to the bride's house. The negotiation is conducted in an indirect manner. The bridal party's initiating negotiations would ask of the bridegroom's party thus: "So many decades have elapsed but we have not seen so many people coming together. What for have you come?" The bridegroom's party answers, "One bird has been causing a great deal of destruction in our hamlet, killing fowl spoiling *bajra* and maize. We have news that the bird has come to your village. The bride's party would then reply, "Yes, there are some birds in the trees yonder. But what kind of bird are you looking for—*mayurchanda, bheladagi* or *banshtia*?" The three birds named represent three different age groups of girls. *Mayurchanda* refers to a bride whose age falls between 18-22, *bheladagi* 14-18 and *banshtia* 10-14. The bridegroom's party would answer according to the age of the bride they are looking for. The bride's party then would point out that the bird has been reared by them and that they cannot accede to their request of taking the bird away without any price. The bridegroom's party would then seek to know the bride price. The bride's party would give hundred maize seeds as their price. This transaction occurs through *raibaysha*. After hearing the price, the two parties would then come closer and the bridegroom's party would take out a few maize seeds and place 10 seeds as their price. After the seeds pass hands for three times and the amount of seeds increases to 50 it would stop and the bridegroom's party would ask the bride's party if they are satisfied, and they will answer in the negative. Then the negotiation is carried out in terms of rupees instead of seeds in a symbolic manner and a bargain is hammered out. Now-a-days the usual bride-price ranges from Rupees 20 to 40. Then the bride's party places a small quantity of rice, oil, etc., on a *sal* plate and request the bridegroom's party stating that they have collected a few fruits which they may kindly cook and eat. The bridegroom's party would say, "No, we are tired. We will eat whatever you prepare." The bride's party would say that they have not taken bath for days on end, therefore, the food may not be to their liking. The bridegroom's party would say that they would not mind. Whatever and in howsoever way they would cook food they would eat. After this it is customary for the groom to undergo a test of ability to demonstrate whether he is capable of looking after his wife. The custom is practised among the Hill Kharia of Purulia.

Betrothal in Mother's Sib Permitted

A known anthropologist Mr. P.C. Biswas writes about the Santal betrothed customs, thus, "Certain relatives by marriage, who may be grouped together under the three categories of *bahonharea ajhmurea,* and husband and wife, avoid mentioning each other's name. This rule is stretched to include, within the sphere of avoidance, the name of any person, place, plant, or animal bearing the same name as the one to be avoided. When a reference to such names has to be made, many ways of circumventing the taboo are employed, as, for instance, where a person is called father or mother of so and so. Violations of this rule are believed to be punished in the next world as well as this one.

"In addition to the family, the other important units of Santal social life in Birbhum are the *paris* or sib, the *khut* or sub-sib, and the village community, as in the traditional pattern. The sibs represented at Kuotola are Murmu, Hemroo, Hasdak', Merndi, Kisku, Baske, Tudu and Soraen. A few members of the other three sibs, Besra, Pauria, and Corae, are found in the adjoining village of Balipara. The number of families belonging to each of the eight sibs represented at Kuotola is as follows: The first four sibs claim 8, 4, 4 and 3 families respectively, while the last four have one each. The members of all these sibs enjoy the same social status, since there is no sib hierarchy. The patrilineal and patrilocal character of the sib and sub-sib are retained intact. Any sex relation between members of the same sib is regarded as an incest and tabooed.

"Though marriage with the mother's sib is permitted, this does not hold for those belonging to her *khut* or sub-sib, since the ties with mother's *khut* are held to be too close. Other than this, however, a person may marry into any other sib than his own. However, because the Besra and Corae sibs are regarded as inferior in social status to the others, there is an unwillingness to marry into them. This is more evident when it comes to men of other sibs marrying women belonging to them than it does where it is a question of permitting girls of other sibs to marry Besra and Corae men. The reason for this is because girls, on marriage, no longer belong to the sibs of their fathers, but adopt those of their husbands. Therefore, the action of the son is more important than that of the daughter in preserving social status.

"Of the seven traditional forms of Santal marriage, three are found at Kuotola and other villages in Birbhum. These are *kirin bahu bapla* or 'bought bride' marriage, *sanga, i.e.,* marriage between a widower or a divorced man and a widow or a divorced woman, and *ghardi jawae bapla* in which the father-in-law secures a 'house bridegroom'. The first form, contracted between unmarried young men and women, is the most common and respectable. The last form of marriage is present, but rare...

"*Kirin bahu bapla* is also called *bapla biha* by the Santal of Kuotola. The word *biha* comes from the Bengali word for marriage, *bibaha.* As the Santali word *bapla* also means marriage, *bapla biha* may be translated as "marriage par excellence". The average age for *kirin bahu bapla* is 20 for young men and 15 for young women. It is normally arranged by parents with the help of a *raebaric*' or match-maker. There is no professional class of match-makers, but friends and relatives usually act in this capacity. In every type of marriage, the consent of the principals is essential. If both live in the same village, it is easy to find out whether they like each other or not. But if they belong to different villages, the intermediary arranges a day when the parents and relatives of the two meet in an open field. They are introduced and salute each other. It is on this occasion that the principals get an opportunity to see one another from a distance, and coming to a decision about the proposed match.

"In arranging a marriage, the parents of the bridegroom pay bride-wealth to the parents of the bride. Bride-wealth consists of a cash amount known as *pan,* plus certain payments in kind, such as cloth and cattle. Three or four *sarees* or cotton cloths are given to the bride's mother and her other female relatives, and a male calf is given to the bride's elder brother.

"The amount of money that passes as bride-wealth increased after 1942 at Kuotola and neighbouring Santal villages; Rs. 12 or $4.80 sufficed until that time. Then, suddenly, the Santal of a village named Paruldanga demanded from a young man of Kuotola Rs. 14 or $5.60 for one of their girls, their reason being that prices were rising as a result of the war. There was much resistance to this demand on the part of Kuotola, but as the young man and his parents were anxious to make a match with this particular young woman, they eventually accepted it. Once the people of Kuotola were forced to accede to this increased rate, they began to demand the same amount from other villagers who sought their daughters in marriage. Other villages followed, so that in 1943 the sum of Rs. 14 had come to be fixed as the amount of *pon* for this area.

"In marriage involving a widow or a divorced woman, the money that passed was Rs. 7½ or $3.00 until about 1925. Then the amount was raised to

Rs. 12, the same as that for a *kirin bahu bapla.* When in 1942 the amount demanded for the latter form of marriage was increased, that for *sanga* marriage increased in like amount. The reason put forward for this was that a widow or a divorcee is usually grown, and consequently capable of doing more work than young women given in the *Kirin bahu bapla* type of marriage, where the bride is to be married for the first time.

"If a divorced man wishes to marry an unmarried young woman, he has to give Rs. 19 or $7.60,—that is, Rs. 5 more than that given by an unmarried young man. But in contracting such a marriage a widower has to give a still higher amount, Rs. 23 or $9-20. This is due to the belief that an unmarried young woman takes a risk of premature death in marrying a man whose first wife has died. Obviously, a greater pecuniary inducement becomes necessary to obtain the consent of her family to place her in this situation.

"Divorce may be had at the desire of either party to a marriage. If the wife decides to leave the husband, but without any fault on his part, the amount of *pan* (Rs. 14) and one male calf has to be returned. If the decision for divorce comes from the husband, he has to pay his wife Rs. 5, one cotton cloth, and a bell-metal dish, in addition to forfeiting his claim to a refund of the *pan.* The compensatory payments made by one party to the other on divorce are called *chadaodi.*

"It has been mentioned before that a divorced man or a widower, marrying an unmarried girl, has to pay a higher *pan* than usual. But if a wife decides to divorce such a husband, she is required to repay only Rs. 14, the usual amount of *pan* in the *kirin bahu bapla* type of marriage. Divorced men and widowers who have married or intend to marry such young women have come to regard this as unfair, however, and feel that in case of a divorce they should recover the full amount of *pan* paid by them. They have, therefore, begun to demand an increase in the amount of compensatory payment they are to recover on divorce. This matter is frequently discussed when the Santal of Kuotola and other villages in the region meet at the liquor shop at Bandhgora. The question, however, has not been resolved.

"The most common cause of divorce is adultery, but adultery does not necessarily lead to a divorce. After certain compensatory payments are made by the adulteror, husband and wife may be reconciled, and resume living together. Repeated offences on the part of one party, however, generally cause the other to have recourse to divorce. Unwillingness of one party to cohabit with the other is also recognised as grounds for divorce. For a woman to be suspected of witchcraft is not held a valid reason for divorce...

"All divorce cases are adjudged before the village *panchayat* or council which constitutes itself a kind of court to investigate all aspects of the situation. When guilt has been established, it is the duty of the *panchayat* to see that the customary payments are made. The marriage is ended by a rite called *sakam orec'* or "breaking off relations". In this ceremony, the Santal High God, *Sin Bonga,* the "national" deities, and ancestors are invoked; and the party wanting divorce tears off *sal* leaves to symbolize the breaking of relations.

"For married people, men as well as women, chastity and conjugal fidelity are socially prescribed. Adultery is always penalized. To have sex relations with a married woman is considered worse than with an unmarried one." This is reflected in the penalty exacted in the two different types of cases by the tribal council. The customs are related to the Santal tribels in the region.

Sept name Descending in Patritive

About the Chakma betrothal customs, Mr. H. Risley records, "I have been unable to obtain a list of the septs of the Doingnaks. It will be observed that many of the septs are of the same type as those found among the Limbus and Tibetans; that is, the names record some curious adventure or personal peculiarity of the supposed ancestor of the sept. Others, again, are territorial; only, instead of taking their names from a village or a tract of country, they follow the names of rivers. The sept name descends in the male line, and the rule of exogamy based upon it is unilateral; that is, while a man is forbidden to marry a woman belonging to his own sept, there is nothing, so far as the rule of exogamy goes, to prevent him from marrying a woman belonging to his mother's sept. The prohibition arising from the sept name is therefore supplemented by forbidding men to marry the following relatives and their descendants sister's :—Step-mother, mother's sister, sister, sister's daughter, mother's brother's daughter, father's sister's daughter, wife's elder sister. After his wife's death a man may marry her younger sister.

"Among the Chakmas, as perhaps among the Greeks and Romans in the beginning of their history, the sept is the unit of the tribal organization for certain public purposes, each sept is presided over by an hereditary dewan (among the Tungjainiy-as called ahun), who represents the family of the founder. This officer collects the poll-tax, keeps a certain proportion himself, and pays the remainder with a yearly offering of first fruits to the Chief of the tribe. When a wild animal fit for food is killed, he has a right to a share in the carcass. He also decided the disputes, mostly matrimonial or more or less connected with women, which make up most of the litigation within the tribe, and divides the fines with the Chief. Where the sept is large and scattered, the dewan has subordinate headmen (*kheja*) to assist him. These are exempt from poll-tax and *begani* or compulsory labour, but must make to the dewan a yearly offering of one measure of rice, one bamboo vessel (*chunga*) of spirits, and a fowl." Adds Mr. Risley. The betrothal custom pertains to the Chakmas.

Hypergamy being a Popular Custom

About the popular custom of hypergamy in Bengal Sir Herbert Risley records, "The Barendra Brahmans claim to be descended from the five Kanaujiya Brahmans imported by Adisura by their original or Hindustani wives. General tradition, however, rejects the latter portion of the claim, and holds that the Barendra are the offspring, not of the original wives, but of Bengali women whom the Kanaujiyas married after their settlement in Bengal. The sub-caste takes its name from the tract of country known as Barendra lying north of the river Padma between the Karatoya and Mahananda rivers, and corresponding roughly to the districts of Pabna, Rajshahi, and Bogra. Ballal Sen reorganised the Barendra at the same time as the Rarhi Brahmans, and divided them into three hypergamous classes: (1) Kulin, (2) Suddha or pure Srotriya, (3) Kashta or bad Srotriya. The first class was sub-divided into eight *gains* or communes: Bhadra, Bhadri, Bhima, Lahari, Maitra, Rudra-Vagisi, Sadhu-Vagisi, and Santamani or Sandilya; the second into seven groups of the same kind; Atharthi, Bhattasali, Champati, Kamadevta, Karanjan, Nandanavasi, and Navsi; and the third into eightyfour families, the names of which need not be enumerated here. In addition to the *gains* we find among the Kulins a further division into eight *pati* or social grades: Atub-Kahni, Baini, Bosnah, Janail, Kutb-Kahni, Nirabhil, Panchuria, Rahala. The object of this grouping is not very clear. Every *gain* belongs to a *pati*, but the *pati* is not always identical with the *gain*, for members of the same *gain* sometimes marry into different *patis*. The *gains* appear to be in theory endogamous. The system of reciprocal marriage (palti-prakriti) which prevails among Rarhi Brahmans is unknown in the Barendra group. The rules governing the three main classes permit a Kulin to marry a Suddha-Srotriya girl, and the children of such a marriage rank as Kulins. Should he marry a Kashta-Srotriya, he loses his kul and becomes a Kap, an irregular group occupying much the same position as the Bansaja among Rarhi Brahmans. If a Barendra Kulin marries the daughter of a Kap, he himself is degraded to the group to which his wife belongs, but his children hold somewhat higher rank, and are deemed eligible for marriage to Kulins. No Kulin girl may marry below her own class. If a suitable husband cannot be found, she goes through the form of symbolical marriage to a figure of *kusa* grass, and has red lead smeared upon her forehead to show that she is really a wife. The *gotras* of the Barendra sub-caste are the same as those of the Rarhi, viz., Bharadwaja, Kasyapa, Sandilya, Savarna and Vatsya. Their commonest titles are Bhattacharya, Bhumik, Chakravartti, Chaudhari, Majumdar, Parihal, and Sikhdar.

"Concerning the origin of the Vaidik Brahmans some differences of opinion exist. All agree in honouring them for their adherence to Vedic rites, their zeal for Vedic studies, their social independence, and their rejection of polygamy. From the fact that some of the most important settlements of the sub-caste are found in the outlying districts of Orissa and Sylhet, some authorities have been led to describe them as descendants of the original Brahmans of Bengal who refused to accept the reforms of Ballal Sen, and took refuge in regions beyond his jurisdiction. Genealogists of rival sub-castes maintain that Ballal Sen excluded them from his scheme on the ground that they did not come up to his standard of purity of descent. Buchanan mentions a tradition lingering among the Vaidik Brahmans of Dinajpur that they had been introduced into that district by Advaita Subuddhi Narayana, Raja of Sylhet." Adds Mr. Risley. The customs belong to the Brahmans in Bengal.

Custom Relating to Sex, Marriage under Transition

In the customs of sex and marriage a considerable change has come over among the Mundas and the Oraons. Even before the puberty, children get some idea of sex from the parents who sleep along with the children in the same room. There is practically no space to ensure any degree of privacy. In some areas certain games are in vogue which are clear imitations of the sexual act. On puberty though the boys and girls are given different responsibilities and there is a strict division of labour, yet there is no bar to mixing or sexual segregation and the young boys and girls meet in the house, field, forest and weekly markets frequently. In areas where the *Dhumkuria* stands younger members get regular sex training from the older members, who are used as agents by the elder boys for running errands to their sweet-hearts. The general atmosphere in the *Dhumkuria* and *Akhra* stimulates the sexual urge. Parents feel no hesitation in talking about sexual matters before their grown-up sons and daughters, with no prudery in their attitude to sex. The entire subject of sex which remains under wrap in modern society is like an open book among them.

Pre-martial sex is allowed in their society. Parents take the sexual affairs of their children as a matter of course. There is no talk of girls' virginity, to be esteemed, or is its preservation considered important. Pre-marital chastity is not insisted either on at the time of settling a marriage. Young boys are expected to have sweet-hearts, but they must avoid girls from of their own clan and sept as their sex relations are considered incestuous. They should also avoid members of their own village and people from a different tribe or caste. When the intimacy grows into sexual meetings, the lovers go behind the scene. Usually the Akhara is the place from where the girl learns to fall into the arms of lover. During '*Karam*' and other *Jarta* young boys and girls go to neighbouring village to dance for the entire night. On the way sometimes, to and from the dance, the boys and girls find opportunity to meet at some secret place and indulge in sex. Wherever the *Dhumkuria* exists in the Oraon region and the '*Giti Ora*' (Sleeping house for the youth among the Munda). In the Munda area, boys slip in stealthily to the place where the girls sleep pretending to ask for lime and tobacco from their sweet-hearts.

At night they go out as sexual meetings are not possible inside the house itself. The weekly market is also a place where tribal lovers meet, where most of the marriages are settled and most of the love affairs begin. Young boys and girls are found busy decorating their persons as for a festival. In the afternoon they proceed to the market and on the way back after dusk, they fix a place where to meet. In the course of their work in field many pre-marital affairs between boys and girls start. It could not be ascertained as to how many of these affairs ultimately led to marriage. If, however, the partners are well-suited and do not belong to the same-sept or clan or the same village, there is no bar to their marriage. Even when the girls come back very late on market days, their parents do not question them at all. Sometimes a boy is encouraged by his parents to indulge in pre-marital sexual relations so that he may easily win over a bride for himself, thus saving the father from paying a high bride-price.

In this connection Mr. Sachchidananda writes, "The change that has taken place in this aspect is that youths and maidens are not maintaining the reserve and restraint that is expected of them while having affairs with members of their own clan or village. In the old days they feared the authority of their parents. For any such sexual lapses the father and the *Panchayat* of the village usually came upon the offenders with a heavy hand. Now this strictness is not always observed. In Barhiya Rol five cases of such marriages have been found in which young men had married girls from their own village. Such a marriage is called '*Dhuka-Dhuki.*' In this list there was only one case of intra-clan marriage. Both the partners belonged to the *Kachhap* clan. When the young man married a girl of his own clan, all the villagers including his brother and the girl's parents strongly opposed it and even threatened to boycott them from society, but they refused to get separated. Ultimately the *Panchayat* of the village levied a fine of Rs. 140 on the young man which was paid to the girl's father. The girl's father has cut off all connection with her and they are not even on talking terms.

"In Birhu among the Christian Munda two cases of illegal marriages were discovered. In one case the man and the bride belonged to two endogamous branches of the Munda tribe. The man belonged to Kompat Munda group and the girl to Mahli Munda group. They fell in love but could not get married. The man did not dare bring the girl to his village and she was kept in a *Dharamsala* in a nearby town and then in a hut erected for her outside the village. For a long time the girl slept at the house of her lover, but left it before day-break. She put on masculine dress to disguise herself. After undergoing these hardships her lover brought her to his own home transgressing the social code.

"At the same time another affair had developed in which both the partners belonged to different Munda groups. One belonged to the Munda community and the other to the *Mahil* Munda groups. The man did not have to pay anything to please the *Panchayat*. He was not even called upon to pay a fine to the *Panchayat*. Both being in Government service and consequently influential, were accepted by the villagers. After keeping indifferent for sometime the villagers went to join the feasts given by them on ceremonial occasions."

Many cases were also discovered among the Oraons converted to Christianity where marriage had taken place within the same clan. Among animist Oraon also a number of breaches of clan exogamy were discovered. Among Christians it is not considered an offence, but amongst others it is a serious crime as well as a sin. In the three cases of intra-clan marriage at Mandar village, all of them have not paid the fine as the meeting of the *Panchayat* has not been called so far to consider these cases as opposed to the former days when an immediate action used to be taken.

At village, Arangloya inhabited predominately by Bhagat Oraon the scope of free sexual relationships between young men and women is restricted to a great extent. Young boys and girls sometimes sleep in somebody's vacant house, though the institution of youth dormitory is not to be found there. The scope of premarital and extra-marital relations is not as great as it is among the animist Oraons. Because, the Bhagats are a religious-minded people and put a heavy premium on morality, they have no provision of *Akhara* dancing and so there is a lack of opportunity for the sexual activity and the girls among the Bhagats go to their husband's home soon after the marriage.

According to Mr. Sachchidanand, "In those marriages were the boy's parents try to find girls as suitable mates for their sons the nature, disposition and ability of the girl to do household work are taken into consideration. She must also be healthy. Now-a-days young men who have been educated in schools want educated brides. Colour of the skin is also taken into consideration. Beauty and education are the primary requirements of the groom.

"Many kinds of marriages are prevalent among the Munda and the Oraon. Only one example of marriage by purchase was reported from Barhiya Rol. The largest number of '*Dhuku*' or Intrusion marriages which took place in a village to which the two parties belonged is reported from village Barhiya Rol. An intrusion marriage is one in which a woman enters the house of the man she loves and insists on living there as his wife even against the wishes of all members of his family. Recourse to such a kind of marriage is only taken by widows and divorcees. Out of 78 marriages, 13 were of this type.

In Belangi, nine such marriage was reported. It was from Jojohatu. *Rajikhusi* marriage or that which is settled by the boys and girls and in which later on the stamp of recognition is accorded by the parents has been reported from almost all the Oraon villages. Their number, however, is on the whole small. There are only four cases of such marriages in Mandar and one or two cases in other Oraon villages. In Jojohatu, however, we find such marriages widely prevalent. Thirty cases out of ninety-seven were of this kind. By far the largest number of marriages is of the arranged type, where parents take the initiative and the formal consent of boys and girls is taken at a later stage. In Birhu all the marriages were of the arranged type. In Selda eighty marriages were arranged as against one *Rajikhusi*. In Koenara ninety-four were of the arranged type and only three of the *Rajikhusi.* The same pattern is found among the Oraons." Adds Mr. Sachchidananda.

Among the Munda, a vast majority of boys marry after the age of 21. In Serengdih, 95% of the boys marry after they are 21, closely followed by the boys at Selda with 82%. In Birhu, however, 40% marriages of boys were in the age 16 to 20. In the same age group the corresponding figure for Koenara village is 30.4%. Munda girls at Serengdih marry after 21; 85.7% of the girls in Serngdih fall in this group. At Selda, however, 65.6% of the girls marry between the ages of 16 to 20. In Birhu and in Koenara, the corresponding figures are 61.8% and 53.9%. A vast number of girls married at the age 11 to 15 is from Jojohatu. At Koenara, the girls who married between the ages 11 to 15 are 20%. Among the Oraon, the majority of boys unmarried before 21.

Equating Sex with Hunger

A noted anthropologist, L.P. Vidyarthi notes about the Maler customs, "The popular term for sex among the Maler is *Bhookh* (hunger). To him sex is as inevitable, natural and common place as hunger. As hunger is to be satisfied by exploiting forest, so sex is also to be satisfied by meeting with the opposite sex. Consequently, it is neither much inhibited by attitudes of modesty and decorum nor much enhanced by ideals of beauty and charm. The society, though has put certain restriction on free mixing of the two sexes but the forest type of habitat and the quest for food conspire to undo them. The girl goes to the jungle for collecting fruits, flowers and above all fuels for her hearth and then water from the spring. The boy of the village spends most of his time in grazing goats and cattle and then moving in search of games (birds), wood and fruits etc. Away from the eyes of the elders and in the privacy of the forest they get suitable setting for sexual mixing. Absence of totemic clan and prevalence of village endogamy further put the boys and girls of the village free to enter into sexual relations with the hope to end them in marriage.

"Though society has tried to provide mechanism for controlling pre-marital sexual relations by ordeals like *saveli* (licking of Red Hot Iron) and oaths of salt-licking *(Nimak Chataua),* a youth has found out devices to counteract their effects and owing to this the fear of the ordeal and oath sanctioned by the society has also been considerably reduced. In general, then, the Maler youth enjoys some freedom in the matter of sex.

"The institution of youth dormitory further provides a socially safe place for both training and enjoyment of pre-marital sexual relations. Following the death of the spouse, a widow or widower may resume sex-relations with another spouse after the celebration of the annual Taddi festival. Frequency of divorce is another dimension of the Maler social life for understanding their sexual laxity. Their biographies, both of the male and the female, are full with examples which lead one to infer that chastity is not a virtue among the Maler society and this culture does not provide adequate mechanism, and taboos to check free mixing.

"When a boy or girl grows up and 'attains the capacity to understand sexual mating' the Maler parents encourage their sons and daughters to sleep in the village youth dormitory. This arrangement leaves the Maler couple to mix freely in his single roomed hut. The young boys and girls, on the other hand, gradually learn to be 'at home' with their play mates. Normally a boy or girl above the age of five or six becomes a member of *Koddada* or *Kod-Beha Adda* (youth Dormitory) where all the unmarried youths of the village sleep together under the same roof in the night. The boy and girl are not formally admitted to the Koddada after any celebration. He or she picks up the habit of going to the sleeping hut along with his or her playmates. Javra Paharia in his biography tells us about his informal initiation to the Koddada: In my childhood one day Surja, son of Tutu Mesa told me to sleep in the house of Gwali. This house is known as Koddada." In Gwali's House I began to sleep with my playmates Surja, Mesa, Rama, and other elderly boys of the village. There were some girls who slept in that house. They were Surji, Mesi, Rami, Magi, Konari and Tapari etc. While young I had seen with my own eyes the mating of Surja with Surji, Mesa with Jawari.

"When a junior boy or girl starts sleeping in the *Koddada* he learns not only riddles, puzzles, folk-songs and folk-tales from the senior inmates, but also learns by immitation, about the love and sex affairs. He learns to come in closer contact with the girl inmates, he observes the processes of wooing and gathers courage like his senior partners to indulge in courtship with the girls.

"The same informant, Javra Paharia, who was initiated to sleep in the Koddada and who saw the sexual affairs of his senior inmates became trained to act like the other members of the Koddada, and also picked up the same process of wooing. He narrates 'I had also sexual relation with Rami, Massi and Javri in the Koddada. Once Mesi went into the jungle alone and was cutting the wood. Fortunately I was passing through that way. I went to her and revealed my wish. She smiled at me. I then kissed her and caught her in my arms for five minutes. She then became very passionate, and showed the sign for taking her into the deeper forests for co-habitation'. Javra made another interesting statement regarding his experience in the village Koddada 'once again I was sleeping in Gwali's house at night. A girl named Kani placed my left hand on her breast. As soon as I woke up, I became very afraid of the other boys sleeping by my sides. At last both of us came out from the back door of the house and satisfied our sexual urge. Before her marriage I actively met with her more than twenty times in the forests'.

"Another informant Dharma Rama in his biography tells us how he was initiated to sexual acts in Koddada and how he came in contact with many girls of the youth dormitory.' 'I came in active contact with many girls in my pre-marital period. In Koddada I came to know about this habit. First of all I deeply fell in love with one Chandi. In addition to Chandi, I had many times co-habitation with Sanlango, Surji, in or around the Koddada and then in the forest.'

"Once the sex and its pleasure becomes known to a Maler youth, and once he gets the least resistance from the side of a girl, he does not feel much hesitation in contacting her for such acts specially in the deep forests away from the village. The forest as mentioned elsewhere in details is always visited by the girl for fetching fuel, flower, and raw materials for rope, especially *gungu,* and the boys mostly spend their time in the forest for grazing cattle. Owing to this, they get frequent chances to mix and enter into active contact with each other. The inmates of the Koddada, as a matter of fact, many time, fix-up engagements for meeting in the jungle and both the boys and the girls, as arranged in advance, go in the deep forest in group of two or three, and separate there in pairs. The parents and other elderly persons related to the girls think that they are quite safe while they go in the company of their friends. Several such incidents of pre-marital mating in the forest have been recorded in the biographies, Javra (21 years) says, 'Once at the age of 14 years I was going to Khallu field for watching the crops. In the meantime Surji daughter of D. Rama was coming with fuel on her head. I went to her and caught hold of her in my arms. But unfortunately at that very moment an old women 'Chandi' saw us from a distance. I could not proceed further. However, she did not disclose the matter to the villagers and I could easily escape the anger of the village elders'.

"Surja L. narrating about his pre-marital sexual relationship accepts that sex instincts dominated over him and since his very childhood he had been in a very close relationship with many girls. He gives very vivid description about his affairs with many girls. Following extract from his biography tells us how the forest provides a place for co-habitation for the adolescents of a Maler village.' "... next time when I was going to cut the wood from the forest, Kani a girl of 16 years, daughter of Mesa was coming alone with the bundle of wood on her head. I stopped her and kept my proposal for active contact. First, she refused the proposal, but I suggested repeatedly, and in the end she became ready and I succeeded in my affairs."

"Apart from providing temporary place for such mating the forests, at times, proves a very suitable place for the romantic Paharia boys and girls to escape from the village for a longer period. In the forests there are wild fruits, roots, flowers and leaves which can sustain such Maler lovers for some days, though such incident is very few. At Benderi we came across such an incident when Surja was forced by his beloved Chamri to escape from the village to the forest." Adds Mr. Vidyarthi.

As the boy or girl advances in adolescence, the nature of sexual activity becomes more serious. It ceases to be mere adolescents' play and assumes a prominent place among the life's main interests. What was before an unstable relation culminating in sexual acts becomes now an absorbing passion and a matter for serious endeavour which may ultimately result in marital alliance. Many young people developing such serious relationship with some girl which, if not ending in marriage makes his life miserable through ill-success in love. A boy or girl after passing through many passionate sexual experiences ultimately begin to think of marriage. The initiative for marriage may come either from the boy who communicates his wishes about a particular girl to his parents or the parents of the boy themselves initiate about the marriage of the sons to bring their sexual life in order.

Among the Malars the marriage of the son and the daughter is settled by the parents after oblaining consents of both the would-be bride and bridegroom. Generally parents give a free hand to their sons in selecting their wives and formally accept their choice, communicated through some of their friends and relatives. To a Maler, sex is not a very secret and private concern. They discuss the affairs of their sons and daughters openly as well and while making decision for their marriages, they consult them freely. Both the parents and the unmarried boys and girls have very wide choice in the selection of a suitable spouse. They can choose their spouses even in their own village without any consideration of clan exogamy which is non-existent in the Maler society. That is why, girls of them same and neighbouring villages, except the close kins are considered to be the potential wives.

Moreover, the customs of polygyny, remarriage of a divorced male and female and then remarriage of the widow and the widower further qualify all the Maler male and female to compete for marriage. Due to this, wide choice almost everybody in the Maler society has a married companion. Moreover, it is very difficult to get a single Maler adult, male or female who has been married only once. But, most of the males and the females of the villages have been married at least twice. In some cases the incidence of marriage in the life of a male Maler is as high as seven and in case of a female four.

Generally, the Maler practise adult marriage in the age of 18 to 25 for the boys, and 15 to 18 for the girls. But some cases of female child marriage are also found. Early marriage can be found only among the rich families who can afford to maintain her. In general, however, the girls are married at the age when they can perform all sorts of household work and can help their husbands in agriculture and other works. The boys also are married when able to earn sustenance of their family. But in case of widow's or widower's remarriage, the age does not seem to be an important consideration, several cases widow and widower even upto the age of 45 have been remarried. In cases of the male, an age even higher than this, is not a disqualification.

A marriage among them is fixed by the respective father with the help of a *sittodar* or a match-maker. When a boy attains the marriageable age his parents remain on look out for some suitable girl. They may select a girl of their choice from their own village or from the neighbouring villages. Generally, Bandna festival provides an ideal occasion for parents on look out of suitable girls. When such a girl of choice who can be an economic asset as well as who is good to look at, is selected, the match-maker called as sittodar is appointed and he contacts the girl's father to establish this marital relationship. The girl's father also appoints a *sittodar* and to finalise the marriage on behalf of the two parties. The sittodar of the boy's side firstly obtains consent of the boy regarding a particular girl and takes a towel with some money (varying from one to four rupees) and goes to the girl's place. There he discusses the matter with girl's father and offers the towel to him. The *sittodar* of the girl's side takes this towel and further offers it to the girl telling her all the relevant things and if she accepts the towel, it is supposed that the relationship is acceptable to her. The towel passes from her to elder brothers and then again back to the *sittodar*. If the father or girl or the brother does not accept the towel, it means the relationship is not acceptable to them. Finally, if the relationship is accepted the towel along with the money goes to the bride's brother. When the consent is given the *sittodars* also settle the bride-price. The Maler pays bride-price to the girl's father in shape of both cash and kind. The cash payment is known as *Banda Taka* in *Malto* or *Paun* in Santhali; and the payment in kind is known as *Bandi*. The bride-price normally varies from Rs. 20 to Rs. 120, the average being Rs. 40.

The bride-price was relaxed when a man would come to live with his father-in-law as *Gharjamai* and would help him in all agricultural and domestic matters. Usually, in addition to the cash, the ornaments made of brass, necklace made of beeds, a few pieces of clothes and at least a pig are also given in bride-price. Such objects given in kind are known as Bandi. The amount paid in bride-price by the boy's father to the girl's father, depends upon the financial position of both the sides. If the boy is himself smart and of suitable age, he may expect suitable wife, both active and beautiful by paying less bride-price. In case he is in an advanced age and likes to marry for the second or third time with a virgin girl, he has to pay a high bride-price. Normally, while finalising the bride-price the quality of the girl as an economic partner gets the first priority, beauty comes next. The girl's father expects high bride-price if the girl is being married for the first time, if the girl is known for her hard work, if she is beautiful brides being good at singing and dancing. Her price goes down as she advances in age and is either divorcee or widow. Taking these things into consideration the *sittodar* fix up the bride-price after some higgling and finally the bride-price is fixed up.

At Benderi, Deopahar and Tetuli, the bride-price has gone fairly high in comparison to the previous times. This has created some problems in Maler villages. The lack of enough money to pay the *Banda-Taka* (bride-price) and *Bandi* (gifts to the bride's party) makes some youth unable to get suitable wife. In many cases the youth has to take loan from the wolfish money-lenders or has to work in the house of the bride's father for sake of compensation. In some cases the bride-price or part of the bride-price is paid after the marriage is performed. There, youth is stimulated to work very hard on his Khallu or bagri land to raise money to pay bride price, and thus marries a girl of his choice. In order to avoid bride-price, in many cases the prospective husband has come to live with his wife's father as *Gharjamai*. Such *Gharjamais* occupy low esteem in his wife's village as he is supposed to have left his father for the sake of his wife.

The trend of increased bride-price has also given rise to the marriages by mutual consents between the desparate lovers. In such cases the parents have been completely disregarded. The extent of polygynous marriage is on decline owing to the increase in bride-price. Several Maler adults desiring to have more wives found the economic stringency standing, in their ways. When the matter regarding bride-price is finalised a date for marriage is fixed to suit the conveniences of both the parties, mostly in the months when they are free from agricultural operations, and have relatively adequate resources to meet the expenses of the marriage feast. Such a suitable season for marriage is fixed after their harvesting season in the month of February, March and April. The *Barat* Party (*Bariatar* in Malto) consisting of male and female relatives, friends, and Maler dancers from the bridegroom's village proceeds to the bride's village to reach there in the evening. The invitees accompanying a Barat party vary from 10 to 200 in number.

When both the parties belong to the same village, every thing is arranged conveniently the village by the *sittodars* of both the parties. On the appointed day, the bridegroom's party goes to the bride's house and the other formalities of marriage are performed in the usual traditional manner. Here also the dancing parties are divided into two and they dance together on a competitive level till one of the parties accepts its defeat. When the bride-groom's party reaches the bride's village, the latter gives feast to the bride-groom's party. The next morning, the pig which is received as Bandi from the bridegroom's father is sacrificed. The meat is preferably cooked by the bride's mother's mother and in her absence the mother cooks it. *Jagu*, a preparation of maize is also cooked in sufficient quantity. Sufficiently ahead in time, Taddi, the millet beverage is prepared for the marriage day. The rich Maler persons also distil wine from local *Mahua* flower. Some of them also fetch distilled liquor from the shop. Both the members of the bridegroom's (*Bariatar*) and the bride's (*Ketanolalur*) parties eat, drink and dance to their hearts' content, on the occasion.

Marriage with one or More Man and Women Allowed

Marital alliance between one or more men with one or more women is sanctioned by the Savara society. Marriage is an important institution of every society and the basis of nuclear family and a new relationship is established between the two families through marriage. After marriage economic partnership is also constituted between the husband and the wife. Marriage in India does not concerns merely two individuals—but it makes two families formally united. The ceremony brings together a large circle of kinsfolk contributing to social solidarity. The bride and the bridegroom receive many presents on the occasion which help them to set up a new home. The Savara's is a patriarchal society; after marriage the bride goes to live in her husband's house. The marriage is performed through certain prescribed rituals and customs.

The Savaras do not perform any ceremony or perform any puberty rite for either sex. The first '*Masik*' or *menstruation* of a Savara girl is however, an important event as it is considered indicative of her coming to age and capacity for procreation. But the castemen do not observe any ritual in connection with the first menstruation. A menstruating woman is considered ritually unclean and certain restrictions and prohibitions are imposed on her inside the house. During the period she is not allowed to do her household chores in kitchen or take part in any socio-religious functions. During the period she does not take bath, but there is no restriction on diet. After the period is over, she takes bath after massaging her body with mustard oil.

Pre-marital sex or extra-marital sex even after marriage relation is not uncommon among them. When a case of pre-marital sexual relation comes to the notice to the caste elders, they bring this to the notice of the parents of the boy and the girl concerned and see to it that they are married together. But if they do not agree to marry, the offenders are subjected to severe beating as well as heavy fine. Sometimes in case of married couples, if any clandestine relation is revealed, it results into dissolution of marriage. Illicit liaisons of a Savara female with a non-Savara male is considered to be a very serious offence. Then they are compelled to marry together under the strict Savara regulations and live in the Savara society. Illegitimate children, though sometimes subjected to whispering calumny, do not suffer from any social disabilities in their day to day life. Sometimes pre-marital courtship leads to sexual intercourse and impregnation the girl. Such pre-marital intercourse is not tolerated even when the boy and the girl belong to the same community; in case of such pregnancy the boy is compelled to marry the girl. However, such a girl is easily married, because by pregnancy she has given the proof of her fertility, and the children of illicit union do not suffer any social stigma.

The Savaras have a tendency to marry off their daughters at an early age. Adult marriage is a recent trend which has originated as a result of their cultural contacts with the neighbouring Hindu castes, as corroborated by the data on age of marriage collected; the wives in most cases, are 5-10 years younger than their husbands.

Both child and adult marriage are in vogue among the Savaras. Child marriage had been traditional among the Savaras. But due to contact with Hindu neighbours in recent times, adult marriage has become the general rule among them now. In adult marriage, the bridegroom's parents take initiative in starting marriage negotiations. Sometimes, the parents on both sides allow their sons and daughters to choose their parents and convey their choice to them for their formal approval. They may also start their love affairs with a spouse of their liking with the blessing of their parents. A period of courtship precedes the marriage. The usual age of marriage for the boy is between 16 to 22 years and that of the girls to 10 to 16 years.

To celebrate the marriage within the village is the general tendency of the Savaras. Among the Savaras partners in marriage are generally chosen not for from their homes. They always prefer a match of the same village. Generally, the Savaras want to make marital alliance within the village to form a nearest kin-group, as such affinal kins always offer liberal co-operation and assistance in the family pursuits. If not the village itself they try to establish marriage relationship in a neighbouring village. The present-day Savara village is a network of relationship where all the inhabitants are related to each other either through blood or by marriage.

In the Savara society, divorce is freely practised on the ground of wife's barrenness or adultery. Serious misconduct by either male or female spouses forms a valid ground for divorce. No formal intimation is required for a divorce. A wife cannot formally divorce her husband, but she can refuse to live with him on the ground, that the wife is illtreated by the husband or the husband's parents. Another cause of divorce is that a bride of tender age being immature, cannot satisfy her husband in sex. When a divorced woman marries another man, the latter is not required to pay compensation to the first husband. The remarriage contract is called '*Sanga*'. It costs less and no ostentations rites of the usual marriage ceremony are performed. Divorce cases are found in most of the villages. But in almost all cases, they were found to remarry.

Moreover, all the Savaras prefer usual betrothal by negotiation, but their society permits other types of marriages and the widow remarriage. Because they believe that, if these types of marriage are strictly prohibited, naturally illicit sexual intercourse will increase steeply and vitiate the society. The custom are peculiar to the Savara community.

Custom of Ardi

Among the Mundas, adult marriage is the custom among the Mundas. In Mundari the term for marriage is *Ardi*. Traditionally their marriage is by negotiation. *Ardi* means the marriage of an unmarried girl with an unmarried boy. The marriage of an unmarried girl with at widower, or a divorced girl or widow with a widower or a divorced man is known as *Dwajbor Ardi*. Marriage of a divorced man is called as *Songa Ardi*. The betrothal and marriage is negotiated by a person, *Dutamdar*, who is a friend or a relative. A Brahman priest predicts the future of the newly engaged couple, which is further confirmed by performing a native divination (*Tupchauli*) performed by the family women. The date of marriage is finally fixed after the Brahmin priest's approval. Two days prior to the marriage, a rite known as *Dangua biruar* is performed by the Munda priest to ward-off the evil eye, evil influence of ghosts and hostile deities. This rite is performed in both the bridegroom's and the bride's house. Oblation etc. in the sacred fire, tying the bride's cloth with that of the bridegroom's etc. are performed by the Brahman priest. In the case of re-marriage of the Mundas neither the village priest nor the Brahman priest has any function to perform. Generally the Munda re-marriages are not elaborate.

Examining Lineage of Female Ancestors

For the betrothal, the lineage is examined of the female ancestors, so that if, for example, the *mul* of the proposed bride's maternal grandmother should happen to have been the same as that of the proposed bridegroom's paternal grandmother, no marriage could take place between the parties, although the *mul* of the bride herself might not correspond with any of those prohibited to the bridegroom.

Elaborate as the system is, Sir Risley writes, shows that "the prohibitions of intermarriage bared on the *mul* or section required to be supplemented by the standard formula: *Chachera, mamera, phuphera, masera, ye char nata bachake shadi hota hai* ("The line of paternal uncle, maternal uncle, paternal aunt, maternal aunt,—these four relationships are to be avoided in marriage"). To a certain extent this rule overlaps the rule of exogamy reckoned from the *mul*. Thus in the first generation the whole of the paternal uncle's descendants, both male and female, would be excluded by the rule prohibiting marriage within the section. In the second and subsequent generation agnates would be barred, but descendants through females would not, for the paternal uncle's daughters having necessary married out of the section, their children would belong to some other section, and their second cousins would be able to marry. On the other hand, the rule of exogamy, if it stood alone, would permit the marriage of first cousins in three out of four possible cases. A reference to the table will show how this conclusion is arrived at; for Propositus belonging himself to section *A* might, so far as the rule of exogamy is concerned, marry the daughters of his paternal and maternal aunts, who would not belong to any of the *muls* barred for him. The rule defining the prohibited degrees is usually calculated to four generations in the descending line."

Sir Risley writes further, "The character of the exogamous sub-divisions of the Goalas and of the rules by which intermarriage is regulated differs markedly in different parts of the country. In Bengal the caste recognises six *gotras*, borrowed from the Brahmanical system, and forbids a man to marry a girl who belongs to the same *gotra* as himself. The *gotra* of the mother, or, to speak precisely, of the maternal grandfather, is not excluded. The intermarriage of *sapindas* is also prohibited, though the rules on this point observed by the Goalas are hardly so elaborate as those followed by the higher castes. In Behar the Brahmanical *gotras* are unknown, and marriage among the Goalas is regulated by a very large number of *muls* or exogamous groups of the territorial type, the names of which are given in the appendix. In some places where the existing *muls* have been found inconveniently large, and marriage has been rendered unduly difficult, certain *muls* have broken up into *purukhs* or sub-sections. Where this has taken place, a man may marry within the *mul*, but not within the *purukh*, the smaller and more convenient group taking the place of the larger one. Some difference of opinion prevails concerning the precise manner in which the rule of exogamy is worked, and the subject is one of such extreme intricacy that it would be unreasonable to look for uniformity of practice everywhere. The Satmulia or Kishnaut Goalas in Bhagalpur forbid a man to marry a woman belonging to the following sections or *muls*:—

(a) His own *mul*.

(b) His mother's *mul*.

(c) His maternal grandmother's *mul*.

(d) His maternal great-grandmother's *mul*.

(e) His paternal grandmother's *mul*.

(f) His paternal great-grandmother's *mul*.

(g) His paternal great-great-grandmother's *mul*.

"To these the Naomulia add—

(h) The *mul* of his paternal grandmother's mother.

(i) The *mul* of his paternal great-grandmother's mother. The custom pertains to the Gopala community.

Adoption of Hindu Customs

Sir Herbert Risley records about their transition to Hindu customs, "The

Kandhs of the Orissa Kandhmals, with whom alone we are now concerned, are supposed to have entered the Kandhmals from the south about 250 years ago, driving out the feeble and unwarlike Kurums or Kurmis who appear to have been the original occupants of these tracts. They are divided into two classes—(1) Uriya Kandh, (2) Malua or Arria Kandh. The former are Kandhs who from social intercourse with the Uriyas have abandoned many Kandh usages and adopted Hindu customs in their place; while the Malua or hill Kandhs still adhere strictly to the original observances of the tribe. Within the limits of the Kandhmals these two groups have not yet become strictly endogamous, and owing perhaps to the sparseness of the population of these tracts, intermarriages still take place between them. But the Malua Kandhs already refuse to intermarry with the Uriya Kandhs of Bod Proper and Gumsur, whom they regard as having lowered themselves by taking to Hindu practices; and it seems probable that in course of time an equally complete separation will be brought about between the Uriya and Malua Kandhs of the Kandhmals."

About the Kandh customs, rites and rituals, he further adds: "In close contact with the Kandhs and dwelling in the same villages with them, we find three castes bearing names which seem to indicate some sort of connexion with the tribe. These are the Kui-Kumharenju or Kandh-Kumhars, the Kui-Loharenju or Kandh-Lohars, and the Kui-Gonernju or Kandh-Gonds. Although these castes have adopted the religion, customs and dress of the Kandhs, they are still not recognised as members of the Kandh community, and Kandhs will not intermarry or eat with them. It is possible therefore that there may be no tie of blood between them and the Kandhs, and that their imitation of Kandh observances is due merely to their having been long settled in the Kandh country and having forgotten their own rites. On the other hand, if we compare these names with the similar combinations found among the Mundas, Oraons, and other tribes of Chota Nagpur, it is difficult to avoid the conclusion that the castes in question must have arisen from inter-marriages between women of the Kandh tribe and Hindu artisans who had settled in Kandh villages.

"Ethnologists have long been aware that the custom of exogamy is rigorously observed among the Kandhs. In his *Essay on Primitive Marriage*, first published in 1865, the late Mr. J. F. Melennan refers to Major Maepherson's *Account of the Religion of the Khonds in Orissa* for 'the distinct statement that among the Khonds inter-marriage between persons of the same tribe, however large or scattered, is considered incestuous and punishable by death.' Notwithstanding the stringency of the rule, and although owing to the prevalence among them of human sacrifices and infanticide, the Kandhs have been under the close observation of British officers ever since 1837, I have had the greatest difficulty in ascertaining the precise form of exogamy practiced by them, and indeed in getting any information at all on the subject. In reply to repeated inquiries addressed to several different correspondents well acquainted with the tribe and engaged in official work among them, I have been assured that the Kandhs have no exogamous sub-divisions at all, and that their matrimonial arrangements are regulated, so far as the avoidance of consanguineous marriages is concerned, by the comparatively modern system of calculating prohibited degrees from a common ancestor. The facts now recorded, which I regret to say are still incomplete, reached me only a few days before the completion of these volumes. They were ascertained for me in a special inquiry conducted at my request by Mr. James Taylor, Tahsildar of the Kandhmals, whose intelligence in carrying out my instructions I am glad to have this opportunity of acknowledging. That the facts should have been ascertained with difficulty, and that they should have escaped the notice of so many observers, is quite in keeping with my experience in other parts of Bengal. The rules which govern the custom of exogamy, and the caste or tribal divisions by means of which that custom is worked, concern the inner life of the people, and leave no trace on their relation with the outside world. They are a sort of shibboleth, understood only by members of the tribe itself." Adds Mr. Risley. The custom pertains to the Savage tribe of Kandhs.

Practice of Exogamy and Hypergamy

Sir Risley writes about the Rajput custom relating betrothal, "The original septs of the Rajput tribe appear to be for the most part of the territorial type, that is to say, their names seem to denote the tract of country in which the sept or its founder had their earliest habitat. Sesodia and Bhadauira may be taken as examples of this type. Other names again, such as Jadubansi, clearly refer to descent from particular families or stocks. ....The Rajputs of Behar also recognise the Brahmanical *gotras*, and the tendency is for the latter series to supplant and take the place of the latter. Usually where the original sept names are still held to govern intermarriage, the rule is that a man may not marry a woman who belongs to the same sept as his father or his mother, and the prohibition is often extended to the septs, of the paternal and maternal grandmothers. Notwithstanding this rule a case has been brought to my notice in which the son of a Salanki Rajput of Behar married a woman of the Chandel sept, although his father had married into the same sept. At the time of the betrothal a question was raised as to the correctness of the procedure, and the Brahmans held that, as the son's betrothal, though of the same *tribal sept* as his mother, belonged to a different Brahmanical *gotra*, the rule of exogamy would not be infringed by the marriage. The standard formula for reckoning prohibited degrees is also recognised by the Behar Rajputs, who in theory considered it binding down to seven generations on the father's and five on the mother's side. A man may marry two sisters, but he must take them in the order of age, and he cannot marry the elder sister if he is already married to the younger.

"In theory, as has been already stated, the whole body of Rajputs constitutes a single tribe divided into a very large number of septs or clans of descent, each of which is supposed to be descended from a common ancestor. Marriage within the sept is of course interdicted to its member, and in theory a Rajput belonging to any given sept has the whole community to choose from in seeking a bride for his son or a bridegroom for his daughter. In fact, however, the field of selection is greatly restricted by the operation of the laws of isogamy and hypergamy, the nature of which has been explained in the Introductory Essay. In a society so organised as to give the fullest play to the idea of purity of descent and the tradition of ceremonial orthodoxy, it must neither be that offences should come, and should be deemed to affect not only the offender himself and his family in the narrower sense, but the entire sept to which he belongs, which is conceived as an enlarged family. Thus in course of time is developed an infinite series of social distinctions giving rise to complicated and burdensome obligations in respect of marriage. In the case of the Rajputs these distinctions have not led to the formation of endogamous groups, as commonly happens among other castes, nor have they hardened into fixed hypergamous groupings, such as are exemplified by the Kulinism of Bengal. But running through the entire series of septs we find the usages of isogamy and hypergamy which have exercised and continue to exercise a profound influence on Rajput society. Isogamy or the law of equal marriage is defined by Mr. Ibbetson as the rule which arranges the septs of a given locality in a scale of social standing, and forbids a father to give his daughter to a man of any sept which stands lower than his own. Report on the Census of the Punjab, p. 356. Hypergamy or the law of superior marriage is the rule which compels him to wed his daughter with a member of a sept which shall be actually superior in rank to his own. In both cases a man usually does not seruple to take his wife, or at any rate his second wife, from a sept of inferior standing. It will be readily seen how the working of these rules must have given rise to all sorts of reciprocal obligations as between septs, and must have restricted the number of available husbands in any particular locality. The men of a higher sept can take their wives from a lower sept, while a corresponding privilege is denied to the women of the higher sept. Hence results a surplus of women in the higher septs and competition for husbands sets in, leading to the payment of a high price for bridegrooms, and enormously increases the expense of getting a daughter married. Under these circumstances poor families are under a strong temptation to get rid of their female infants by poison or intention neglect in order to be saved the expense of finding them suitable husbands or the disgrace of being compelled to marry them to men of lower degree." Adds Mr. Risley. The custom is pertinent to the community Rajputs.

Borrowing of Brahmanical Gotras

Sir Risley records, "The exogamous sections of the caste are very numerous. In_Behar they seem to be *territorial* or *titular;* while in Bankura the names are *totemistics,* and the members of particular sections refrain from injuring the animals after which they are called. In Central Bengal traces of totemism may perhaps be found, but the tendency is to borrow the Brahmanical *gotras,* while in the eastern districts all exogamous groups seem to have disappeared, and marriages are, regulated by the more modern system of counting prohibited degrees down to and including the fifth generation in descent from a common ancestor. The Magahiya Doms of Behar affect to observe a very elaborate method of working the rule of exogamy. They lay down that a man may not marry a woman belonging to the name section as his own (1) father, (2) paternal grandmother, (3) paternal great-grandmothers, (4) paternal great-great-grand-mothers, (5) mother, (6) maternal grandmother, (7) maternal great-grandmothers. In applying the rule to a particular case, all the sections, on both sides are taken into account in the manner described in the article on Bais, so that a marriage would be barred if one of the great-grandmothers of the proposed bride happened to have belonged to the same section as one of the great-great-grand-mothers of the proposed bridegroom, even though the parties themselves belonged to different *muls.* This mode of calculation appears to be confined to Behar; and in Bengal wherever sections exist, the only rule observed is that a man may not marry a woman of the same section as himself. The standard formula for reckoning prohibited degrees is in general use. In Bankura it is ordinarily calculated to three generations in the descending line; but where *bhaiadi,* or mutual recognition of relationship, has been kept up between two families, the prohibition extends to five generations. The Doms of the 24-Parganas affect to prohibit marriage between *sapindas,* but this is a palpable imitation of the customs of the higher castes. Members of other castes may be received into the Dom community by paying a fee to the panchayat and giving a feast to the Doms of the neighbourhood. At this feast the proselyto is required to wait upon his new associates and to eat with them. He must also have his head shaved and undergo a sort of baptism with water at the hands of the caste panchayat in token of his adoption of the Dom religion. Instances of men of other castes thus joining themselves to the Doms are very rare, and occur only when a man has been ejected from his own caste for living with a Dom woman. Some say, however, that in these cases the proselyto, though ordinarily spoken of as a Dom, is not admitted to complete equality with the original members of the caste. His children, however, will be Doms of the same sub-caste as their mother." The custom is related to the Doms in the eastern zone.

Marriage is enjoined upon and celibacy Condemned

About the marriage and betrothal customs of Muslims, Mr. Ja'far Sarif writes, "Marriage is enjoined on every Musalman, and celibacy was condemmed by the Prophet, but it is often enforced by poverty or other causes. The proportions of the married and unmarried among Musalmans differ from those of the Hindus. Among Musalmans 'the proportion of the unmarried is larger and that of the married and widowed smaller. Of every 100 males 53 are unmarried, 43 married, and 4 widowed, while of the same number of females 38 are unmarried, 47 married, and 15 widowed. The difference is most notable amongst the young of both sexes. Under the age of 5 the proportion of Muhammadan girls who are married is not much more than a quarter of the corresponding figure for Hindus, and between 5 and 10 it is only a half. It is not till the age period 15-20 that an equality between the proportions is reached, while above that age the relative number of females who are married is greater amongst Muhammadans than amongst Hindus. The Muhammadans have fewer widows at all ages, but the difference is most marked in the prime of life. This is owing to the fact that women who lose their first husbands while still capable of bearing children have less difficulty than their Hindu sisters in marrying a second time. A prejudice against widow marriage exists, however, amongst many classes of Muhammadans, especially those who are descended from local converts'. (*Census Report*, India, 1911, i. 266).

"The prohibited degrees include: consanguinity—mother, grandmother, sister, niece, aunt, &c. ; affinity—mother-in-law, step-daughters, grand-daughters, &c. ; fosterage ; with the wife's sister during the lifetime of the wife, unless she is divorced ; of the wife of another until the period of probation (*'iddat*) has expired, three months after divorce, four months ten days after widowhood ; with polytheists, who do not include Jews or Christians.

'It is considered desirable that a man should take as his first wife a virgin bride of the same social standing as himself, and preferably of the same division or tribe. As regards subsequent wives there is no restriction whatever. There are no exogamous groups; the marriage of persons more nearly related is forbidden, but that of first cousins, whether the children of brothers or sisters, is considered very suitable; failing them, an alliance is preferred with some family with which there have already been marriage relations ; it is sometimes said that the object of cousin marriage is to keep the family as free as possible from foreign blood, and to retain in the family the property inherited by the young couple'.

"Marriage is usually by dower or settlement (*mahr, saaqa, nuhl*), the latter 'not the exchange or consideration given by the man to the woman for entering into the contract, but imposed by law on the husband as a token of respect for its subject, the woman'. Marriage by purchase is not common, but Khojas in Gujarat practice the customs, the father of the bridegroom paying 5¼ rupees to the father of the bride, the amount being given over to the Jama'atkhana or assembly lodge of the caste, and it is the rule among the Arabs. In some cases, as among the Brahui, the wives of two brothers being pregnant promise to wed son to daughter, if such be born. Temporary marriage (*muta', sigha, nikah-i-muwaqqat*), contracted for a limited period, are recognized by Shi'as, a practice which has done much to demoralize the community. They were forbidden, but subsequently in part sanctioned by the Prophet. (Firoz Shah Bahmani (A.D. 1397-1422) raised a controversy on the subject, the Sunni divines denying its legality, the Shi'as maintaining that it was allowed in the time of the Prophet and of his first Khalifa, and that, though it was abrogated by the second Khalifa, it was still legal. The king accepted the reasoning of the Shi'as, and received into his harem three hundred women in one day. (Farishta, ii, 364 F). The term marriage by capture has sometimes been rather loosely applied to those cases where a real or pretended opposition is made by the friends of the bride when the bridegroom comes to fetch her home. Instances of this practice are found among Pathans, Khattaks, and Waziris ; among the last named tribe swords are brandished and injury occasionally results, and in the Delhi royal family it was the rule to make a mock resistance when the bridegroom came to take his bride home. The custom seems to be occasionally based upon the belief that a mock fight is a means of repelling evil spirits.

"When a man wishes to marry, he sends for three or four women who act as go-betweens, whom he deputes to search for a bride, beautiful, eligible, clever, accomplished, rich ; and he promises a reward in case they are successful. Special regard is paid to birth, position, and individual eligibility. Widows are to be avoided, and four points are to be sought : her stature should be less than that of her husband ; she should be younger; possess less property ; be inferior in rank and station. The best complexion is dark with black hair, indicating modesty and virtue ; a red pallid skin is to be avoided as it indicates a choleric, sensual temperament. These match-makers go about selling trifles and gossiping in families, by which means they come to know the girls and are able to report about them. If the girl belongs to the family of a friend or acquaintance go-betweens are not required, the negotiations being conducted by the senior ladies of both houses.

"According to the Law a boy should be married at puberty, a girl at the age of twelve. In Sind it is fixed at fifteen for males and twelve for girls ; in Gujarat between sixteen and twenty-two for men, ten to fifteen for girls ; in north India eighteen for youths, thirteen or fourteen for girls. Akbar forbade boys under sixteen and girls under fourteen to marry. "When the family connexions, pedigree, religion, and customs are found to correspond, and the parties consent to the union, astrologers are consulted to predict their destiny, good or bad. For this purpose a few persons in company with astrologers and Mullas, or men of understanding, meet and have the horoscopes of the pair cast. For instance, if a person's name begins with any of the following seven letters of the Arabic alphabet, the elements of his temperament will be as follows : Earth, *be, waw, ye, swad, te, zwad, nun* ; Water, *zal, he, lam, 'ain, re, khe, ghain* ; Air, *jim, ze, qaf, se, zae* ; Fire, *alif, he, toe, sin, dal.* Other astrologers refer to the following table to ascertain by the initial of the person's name his constitutional peculiarities."

"In order to ascertain the fate of the couple, the following plan is adopted : In the first place, it must be ascertained… to which of the elements, Fire, Air, Earth, Water, the initials of the parties correspond, and if these elements agree it is concluded they will harmonize. Thus, if a man's name be Ja'far, his initial being *J,* and his temperament Earth, and the girl's name be Banu Bibi, her initial being *B* and her temperament also Earth, these agreeing, it is held that they will live happily together. In detail, if the temperament of both be Earth, they will for the most part agree, but not always. If it be Water, they will agree for a time, but their love will soon decrease. If it be Air, they will be inclined to quarrel, but will be ready to make up their differences. If Fire, though quarrels will occur between them, they will not last long. If the temperament of a husband be Earth, and that of his wife Water they will agree and live amicably, the women being obedient to her lord. If the husband's be Water, and that of his wife Earth, they will agree, but the wife will rule the house. If the man's be Earth, and that of the girl Air, they will often quarrel, but they will settle their differences, and the wife will rule her husband. If the man's be Earth, and the girl's Fire, there will be little love between them, and the wife will rule her husband. If the man's be Fire, and the girl's Air, they will not be very affectionate, but if they are they will be very happy, and the man, will be subject to his wife. If the man's be Air, and the girl's Water, the result will be the same, but the husband will rule his wife. If the man's be Water, and the girl's Fire, it will be difficult for them to agree, and the husband will rule his wife. If the man's be Air, and the girl's

Fire, the result will be the same, but the wife will rule her husband. If the man's be Fire, and the girl's Air, they will love each other, and the husband will rule, but he will treat her kindly.

"Omens by consultation of a verse taken by random from the Koran or the works of the poet Hafiz, known as Fal, and Istikhara, or attempts to ascertain the will of the Deity by praying for a dream, are also used. The father of the youth, when a proposal is made by the friends of a girl will write 'To be' and 'Not to be' on several slips of paper, which he puts under his prayer-carpet, and after prayers he takes out one of them by random and then a second. If both are favourable the offer will be accepted.

"In the Deccan and south India when the astrologer reports that the prospects are good, some women of the youth's family visit the girl's house and say that they are come to eat sweet stew *(mitha pulao)* and sugared rice *(shakar-bhat)*. If the other side are well disposed they give a pleasant answer, if not the matter comes to an end. The women never settle the business at the first interview, but after a few visits, if all goes well, a date is fixed for the 'distribution of betel standing' *(khare pan),* the 'sugar bringing' *(shakarana)* or the 'asking' *(mangni)*. These three customs are not always done. The first being less expensive is preferred by the poor, the second by the middle classes, while the last is the most expensive because valuable presents must be given. It is the custom not to offer any food or drink, betel, tobacco, or even water to connexions on the other side until they have eaten something sweet, which they do on the 'sugar-bringing' day, or afterwards at a special entertainment, the sweets being supposed to bring affection and good luck.

"Many observances are included in the betrothal. In the Deccan there is, first, the rite of 'distributing betel standing'. Some friends of the youth go to the bride's house and distribute packets of betel-leaves, each receiving one in return. No presents are given, and the women call this rite the 'taking up of the betel' *(pan uthana)*. Betel is supposed to possess mystic powers, swearing on it is equivalent to an oath on the Koran, and Rajputs were in the habit of eating betel as a solemn pledge of loyalty before a battle. This, however, is not a part of the Law, but an innovation introduced by Indian Musalmans. The violation of such an agreement often leads to a quarrel, but if anything is found objectionable in the pedigree or character of one of the couple, the Qazi or law-officer may pronounce the betrothal void.

"In the 'sugar-bringing' rite the youth sends to the girl certain articles of dress, bangles, perfumes, and flowers. The first relation of the girl who meets the party receives the 'contract betel' *(qaul bird),* and then her friends make the following announcement : 'A son of B is betrothed to C daughter of D. Declare before the friends whether you do or do not agree to the marriage'. He replies 'I assent', and the question and answer are repeated three times. Then they recite the 'prayer of good will' *(niyat khair ka Fatiha)*; that is the first chapter of the Koran followed by the one hundred and tenth : 'When the help of God and the victory arrive and thou seest men entering the religion of God in troops, then utter the praise of thy Lord, for He loveth to turn in mercy'. These rites are performed by the Qazi or law-officer, the Khatib or preacher, the Naib-i-Qazi, or assistant law-officer, by a Mashaikh, or reverend man, or by a Mulla or Maulavi, doctors of the Law. In some cases the engagement by giving betel is dispensed with, and only the Fatiha is said, he who recites it naming the couple and saying 'Hereby I betioth you'. The betel and sugar are then divided and the gifts sent by the bridegroom are given to the bride, who sits; modestly, her head bent to the ground, her eyes closed and her face covered. Then the lady friends of the bridegroom anoint her head with perfumed oil, tie up her hair with a red string sent by the bridegroom, and adorn her with the jewels. An old woman of the family puts one hand behind her neck and the other under her chin and holds up her face to view. Each lady takes a look at her, and gives her a ring or some money, at the same time drawing her own hands over her head and cracking her fingers on her own temples so as to take away any ill luck on her own head *(balaen lend, tasaddud)*. This rite is known as the 'sugar-eating' *(shakarkhori),* the 'betrothal' *(nisbat),* the 'asking' *(mangni),* the 'sherbet-drinking' *(sharbatkhori),* and the 'green creeper' *(hari bel).*

"In some places, however, the 'asking' forms a special rite, when presents *(charhauwa, charhawa)* are given to the bride. The youth goes to her house with music and carries on trays various gifts. This procession starts in the afternoon and halts every now and then while the dancing-girls sing. If he lives at a distance the gifts are sent in his absence with the same ceremony. When the party arrives at the house they rest for a while and the 'betel of the contract' *(qaul bira)* is distributed. The trays with the gifts are sent to the bride's a room and the guests add something as they are being sent. If the bridegroom is present he receives a gift of clothes of the marriage colours, yellow, red, or green, for black symbolizes mourning and white that of the burial shroud. In Gujarat on the betrothal day the kindred on both sides meet, gifts are carried in procession, and sherbet is served at the bride's house. In north India this interchange of gifts between bride and bridegroom is called Sachaq.

"Some ten or fifteen days after the 'asking', the bride's people return the trays or pots in which the bridegroom's gifts were sent, filled with cakes which he shares with his friends.

"In the Deccan the rite of 'threshold treading' *(dahliz khundlana)* follows. This is done in case after the betrothal it is necessary to postpone the wedding. The bridegroom sends cooked food to the bride accompanied with music, and he receives the 'salutation gift' *(salami),* after which he salutes his mother-in-law. The reason of this custom is that it is unusual for the bridegroom to go to the bride's house or eat there until after the consummation of the marriage, but after this rite he becomes a member of the family and may eat any dish seasoned with salt at the house of his betrothed.

"In some places a day or two after the betrothal the bridegroom sends food and a betel-box *(pandan)* to the bride, who returns the compliment a day or two after. This is called the 'salt-tasting' *(namakchashi).* After this he may dispense with the rule to eat only sweets at her house, and he may eat food seasoned with salt or acid condiments. Various other gifts are also sent by the betrothed man to his fiancee. Thus at the Muharram festival he sends a necklace *(anti)* of coloured thread, perfumed powder *(abir),* a conserve *(sukhmukh)* made of betel nut, melon seeds, fine-cut coconut kernels, coffee, and cardamoms. At the Akhiri-char-shamba he sends cakes and sweets at Sha'ban food and fireworks; at Ramazan vermicelli *(siwaiyan)* and sweets; at the 'Id-i-qurbani a sheep and some money. During an eclipse the girl sends to him offerings of intercession *(sadqa)* with a goat or kid, which must be tied to the leg of his bed till the eclipse is over.

"Among respectable people the betrothed couple are kept apart till marriage. But among some Musalmans on the north and west frontier betrothal is deemed to be equivalent to marriage and the pair cohabit. In Sind 'after betrothal the prudent parents do all they can to prevent the parties meeting; both, however, are permitted to visit one another's relations of the same sex. Among the upper classes any *pregustatio matrimonii* is considered disgraceful. It is not, however, difficult here, as elsewhere, to persuade the betrothed female to grant favours which, under other circumstances, she would refuse ; consequently accidents are not of rare occurrence. It is the same in Afghanistan and other parts of Central Asia, where the mother of the betrothed not infrequently connives at what is called 'the game of the betrothed' *(namzadbazi),* or visiting the future bride unknown to her father. In Sind the lower classes, such as the Mohana and others, think they have a right to intrigue with their future brides ; some of them will go so far as to consider the mother-in-law a substitute for the daughter until the latter is of age to be married'. In Bannu the betrothed youth secretly visits his fiancee, and if he is detected he is detained for three days, and each night the unmarried girls pull him about till he is glad to escape.

Betrothal an Important Ritual

The ritual of betrothal was considered an important ritual in the Chinese wedding ceremony, but, now, its importance has diminished, though a few families still celebrate it. On the day of betrothal, the intended groom's mother sends two, or four, rings and a pair of embroidered pockets to the newly betrothed girl. Earlier, horoscopes were matched and compared for all betrothal, but this is not a strict necessity now. When the wedding day is fixed, a marriage agreement is written out and signed by both parties, to be retained as a marriage certificate and is considered binding. The customs pertain to the Chinese people in Calcutta and 24 Parganas district of West Bengal.

Ceremony of *Bagdan* among Christians

The ceremony of *Bagdan* or engagement is an important part of Christian marriage, and a prayer is held in the brides house, where a church priest is present. Here the bride and bridegroom agree to marry in the presence of relatives and the priest, and the wedding rings are exchanged. After the engagement, parents of both partners inform the church. The priests then examine the legal aspects of the marriage the age of the bride and bridegroom, their relation to each other and whether they have been baptized. The custom is related to the Christians in West Bengal.

Custom of Exchanging Wedding Ring

Before the marriage date is fixed, the boy and the girl get engaged to each other. The boy puts a ring on the girl's finger. The engagement takes place either in the Church or at the girl's residence. The betrothal customs is related to the Anglo-Indians in Bihar.

Betrothal and Marriage as per Church Rules

Their childhood rite is baptism (christening) of a child. Within seven days or sometimes within six months, they go to the church and after giving a holy bath to the child the priest performs baptism. During this ceremony, the baby is also named. Marriages are performed in the church by priests. Women wear wedding dresses *i.e.,* white gown and veil for marriage. The rituals are prevalent among the Armenians in West Bengal.

References

1. Sachchidananda, Profiles of Tribal Culture in Bihar, Firma KLM, Calcutta, 1965.
2. Risley, Sir H.H., The Tribes and Castes of Bengal: Ethnographic Glossary, Firma KLM Calcutta, 1998, Ist edition, Bengal Secretariat Press, Calcutta, 1891.

3. Bahadur, K.P., Caste, Tribe and Culture of India: Bengal, Bihar and Orissa, ESS ESS Publications, Delhi, 1977.
4. Ray, Himanshu Mohan, Savara—The Snake Charmars, Institute of Social Research and Applied Anthropology, Calcutta 1986.
5. Sinha, Dikshit, The Hill Kharia of Purulia, Anthropological Survey of India, Calcutta, 1984.
6. Biswas, P.C., *Santals of Santal Parganas*, Bharatiya Adimjati Sewak Sangh, Delhi, 1956.
7. Vidyarthi, L.P., *The Maler*, Bookland Pvt. Ltd., Calcutta, 1963.
8. Triosi, J., *Tribal Religion : Religions Beliefs and Practices Among the Santals*, Manohar, New Delhi, 1978.
9. Ibbetson, Sir, *Report on the Census of the Punjab*, Government Press, Lahore.
10. Sarif, Ja'far, Islam in India (ed. W. Crooke), Oriental Books reprint Corp., New Delhi, 1972, First published, 1921.
11. Singh, K.S., (Gen. ed.), *People of India* : *West Bengal*, Seagull Books, Calcutta, 2008.
12. Singh, K.S., (Gen. ed.), *People of India* : *Bihar*, Seagull Books, Calcutta, 2008.

4

Marriage Ceremony

Customs of Adhibas

In West Bengal, main Bengali marriage ceremony beings with the ritual of '*Adhibas*'. It is a gathering held in both the homes of the bride and the bridegroom on the evening before or on the day of the marriage. The elderly women of the family take active part in it. The '*baran dala*' or '*koola*' *i.e.,* a container made of bamboo, is decorated with lines drawn with vermilion. The ingredients of the '*baran dala*' are paddy, grass, sandal, turmeric, flowers, fruits, curd, ghee, gold, silver, copper, conch shell, '*chamor*' and cloth. The 'baran dala' also consists of seven beetle leaves, seven supari (bettle nuts) and seven 'kauri' (shell) at the bride's place, while the numbers increase to nine at the groom's place.

In a different platter a 'Sri' with rice and Mashkalai (variety of whole black leguminous seed yielding gram) is made. With all these the elders bless the bride and the bridegroom. The (durba) grass mixed with oil and turmeric are tied on the left hand of the bride and the right hand of the bridegroom. In East Bengal, the *Adhibus 'tatta*' or marriage items for the bride, are sent to the bride from bridegroom's.

Custom of Dhadhimangal or Churakaran

Before the sunrise, on the day of the marriage, in houses of the bride and the bridegroom, their respective mothers, along with the other five women bless the bride and the bridegroom and treat them with curd and *chira* (crushed rice). The bride and the bridegroom and their parents have to undergo a fast till the marriage ceremony is over. If the *sampradan* is performed by someone else other than the father, he or she also has to fast through out the day. According to the Hindu traditions fasting is common on all occasions which is a wonderful process of cleansing the body and the soul.

Rite of Nandimookh or Briddhashraddha

In the morning of the day marriage, any male relative of both the bride and the bridegroom have to perform certain rituals to appease the souls of the long gone ancestors. They take a solemn vow before the commencement of the religious ceremony mentioning the purpose for which it is intended and offer prayers to Lord Ganesh and a Devi along with an auspicious symbol painted the inner wall of a room called as Basudhara.

Rite of Jal Soha

The rite is about the arrangement for the water to be used by the bride and the bridegroom to take a bath after the '*gaye holud*'. This water taken from the nearby reservoir is made to trickle from the urn all along the path, till the person carrying it reaches a temple. Here water is collected from a married woman who is given *lac dye* (alta) and *sindoor* (vermilion). From the temple, the married *female relative* goes around the neighbourhood to collect water. Later bride and the bridegroom in their houses are made to sit in amid of four banana plants arranged at the four corners of a square plot. The ritual '*Gaye Holud*' is performed and later are bathed with the water collected.

Ritual of Gaye Holud

This ritual is also called as '*Stri-Achar*'. According to the West Bengal custom, '*Gaye Holud Tatta*' is sent to the bride from the bridegroom's place. In this 'Tatta' or gift package the turmeric used by the bridegroom is sent. This turmeric paste along with the turmeric paste of the bride's place is applied on the bride and other relatives after the barber pares their nails. Then the bride and the bridegroom are bathed. The bride has to carry a '*kajol lata*' (corriliu container) while the bridegroom has to carry 'janti' (bettle nut racker).

Climbing Tree Alongwith Bride

The Hill Kharia bridegroom goes taking the prospective bride with him in the jungle accompanied by some relatives from each side. There a big tree with a honeycomb in it is selected. The prospective bridegroom then climbs up the tree carrying along with him the bride and also the instrument for breaking honeycomb. If he can successfully negotiate the tree and break the honeycomb then only his claim to the bride's hand is accepted.

However, this standard procedure has changed altogether in recent times. The ceremony of *panr basa* or bride selection has become less elaborate. The bridegroom's party now-a-days does not consist more than two men primarily because of the desire to curtail the expenditure that they would entail for the bride's parents. The ceremony of proving the bridegroom's competence has also been dispensed away with. On the marriage day the groom's party accompanied by the bridegroom's maternal uncle, either real or classificatory, arrive at the bride's village and are made to stay well away from the bride's hut. In an open space, preferably near the *tulis pinra*, a sacred shrine is established where various ritual elements symbolising the deity called *Marua* are placed. The deity is placed under a canopy called *chamra* which looks like a kind of sun-shade having four upright poles on which rests a *mahul* and *sal* leaves covered roof. Underneath canopy a few articles, including sacred grass (*durba*), sundered rice, paddy, a betel nut or a *haritaki*, a copper coin and vermilion, are tied together in a *sal* leaf and placed in a hole and covered with earth. Two branches, one of *mahul* and the other of *sidha* trees are planted by the side of the place. Two earthen pots filled with water of natural ponds are then placed between these branches. Below the earthen pots a little paddy, a few blades of *durba* grass are placed. Inside the pot one branch of mango or *mahul* is placed. The earthen pots are filled by the bride's grandmother or, in her absence, some other female relatives who are of the same generation. The grandmother accompanied by other village women goes to a pool singing marriage songs (*bihar geet*).

At the pool the two pots are worshipped by applying vermilion, and sundried rice. Then one pot is carried by the grandmother, another pot by any other women of the village not directly related to the bride. They bring the pots to the *Marua* and demand some paisa from the bride's parents. They are offered some eatables usually *chira* (flattened paddy) and *gur* (molasses). By the side of the *Marua*, bride's brother-in-law or *bahanai* digs up a long furrow, being spread in east-west direction. On the right of the furrow a banana tree is planted, On the left an arrow is placed and three small wooden planks are also placed horizontally to the furrow.

In the evening when the bridegroom's marriage party arrives, the bride is made to sit on a brass plate and is carried to the *Marua* by the people of the bridegroom's party. She is then made to sit by the side of the *Marua* facing east. The bridegroom, carried by his maternal uncle, circumbulates the *Marua* and the bride thrice, facing the west. The presiding deities of the *Marua*, the Dharam and *Kandni-randhni* (the presiding diety of the child) are also worshipped. She is then led to a poll by her maternal uncle for bathing. The bride comes back to the *Marua* where she embraces the banana plant thrice. She then sits on a mat and her brother-in-law (*bahanai*) encircles five or seven thread strands around the little toe of her left leg and left ear. After taking it out betel nut and a bangle are tied to this thread; this is the sacred thread of the Hill Kharia. Meanwhile, the anointed with mustard oil and turmeric paste. The bride's brother-in-law or grandfather slips the sacred thread on her neck and bangle on to her right forearm. Then the brother-in-law takes out some hair of her forehead and twists it into a lock. Through this fore-lock two drops of turmeric-mixed-oil is made to trickle down to her leg. The third drop of oil then is applied on her head. Then, the brother-in-law carries her inside the hut. The bridegroom's party then again carry her back to the *Marua* where she is given a leaf smeared with vermilion and mustard oil. The bridegroom snatches this leave off from her hand and keeps it by his side, then he removes the veil off his bride and applies vermilion on her forehead. Then both the bridegroom and bride stand up and sprinkle water on each other from the pot kept under the *chamra* by means of a mango twig.

The bridegroom's party then take the bride and the bridegroom inside a hut from where the bridal party again take them back to the *chamra*, thrice. Then the bride's younger sisters wash the feet of their sisters and brothers-in-law. For this ritual they are given a token money. The people accompanying the bridegroom's party are similarly treated by the bride's brother.

Thereafter bride and the bridegroom are entertained with *chira* and *gur* separately. The bridegroom at first refuses to partake of the food till his father-in-law promises to give him some presents. In the past it was customary to make a symbolic presentation of a mountain; the presiding deity of mountain was supposed to provide the couple with food and protection from evils. But now-a-days a *dhuti* is given as present or a token payment is made in lieu of it. Next day a *sal* leaf smeared with vermilion is kept on the *tulsi-pinra*. The villagers present there touch this leaf. This signifies a pledge to work together in this ceremony. Then the people form bride's home request the bridegroom's party to cook food for themselves which they decline saying that they will rather eat food cooked by them. Then all the items procured for feast are placed before the bridegroom's party for formal permission to prepare food. The bridegroom's party is then entertained with some *handia* (rice beer).

Next day the bride and bridegroom leave for bridegroom's village. Before departing two important rituals are held. First, the bride is made to sit on a plank on the threshold on her mother's lap flanked by on her left and right side by her father and husband respectively. Her father throws a little quantity (one *pua*) of rice on her *anchal* (one end of her *sari*). She is then asked by mother, "where are you going my darling?" She answers, "kamin khatte" (to work as labourer). Then she throws back the rice which are collected by bridegroom's party. The ceremony of getting the supernatural sanction for the match is called *khatabara*, performed just after the party come out of the hut on their way to bridegroom's village.

At the bridegroom's house they are made to stand under a similarly constructed *chamra* like that of the bride's village. There the bridegroom's mother ceremonially hugs her and ushers her inside the hut. Meanwhile the hamlet women sing marriage songs (*bihar geet)*. Next day the bridegroom takes the bride along with a bow and an arrow for a ceremonial bath. Other women of the hamlet accompany them to the nearby pond. After the bath, the bridegroom takes up the bow and shoots the arrow at dummy figures of animal in symbolic action of hunting. The bride walks up to the point where the arrow has fallen, washes the arrow-head by pouring water from a pot she carries and then again dips it into the pot and hands it over to her husband. She also places a little *gur* (molasses) in his mouth. This way, they reach the *chamra*. Here the bridegrooms slips an iron bangle in her left forearm. In the ceremony the bride washes feet of the people of her husband's parental generation. The bridegroom's relatives are then entertained with feast.

Next day the bride and bridegroom return to the bride's village where he puts an end to the marriage ceremony by breaking the *chamra* and throwing it in the pond. His brother-in-law offers a mock resistance and yields after he is placated on being paid a token amount of cash. As soon as the bridegroom comes back to bride's village he sits under the *chamra* and bride's maternal uncle touches his forehead with a betel nut and gives it to the bridegroom. The bridegroom returns it to him. The maternal uncle then touches his forehead with mango leaves. After this the women accompanying the bridegroom anoint the bride with turmeric paste and present the bride and her mother with a *sari* each and a *dhuti* to the bride's maternal uncle. They then place a plate and spread a *dhuti* over it. The bride then sits on it and is carried out of the hut. The couple then start for the bridegroom's village.

However, changes in the ceremony like in the *panr basa* or procedure to test the capability of the bridegroom, etc, are striking. This reduction in the elaborate customary practices may be due to the poverty. The procedure of bride selection has been curtailed because it necessitated expenditure. But perhaps, the ceremony to test the bridegroom's capability has been given up because people no longer place an emphasis on hunting. One noticeable aspect of marriage is the occurrence of divorce for denial of food. But the most noticeable change in marriage ceremony is in the ceremonial feast; and even the circle of kin taking part in marriage has become restricted. The marriage customs pertain to the Hill Kharia tribals of Purulia in West Bengal.

Rite of Rukhsati

About the marriage customs of Agrawals, Sir Risley records, "Agrawals usually marry their daughter after they have reached their ninth year, but if no suitable match offers in infancy, it often happens that a girl is not married until she is grown up. In the latter case she goes to live with her husband at once. When married as an infant, the final ceremony (*rukhsati*), by which she is made over to her husband, may take place one year, three years, or five years after the regular marriage ceremony. That is to say, if the husband does not claim his wife at the expiration of one year, he must wait three; and if he does not come forward then, he must wait five years. This custom prevails among most of the higher castes in Northern India, and is believed to rest upon some obscure superstition regarding lucky numbers. Whatever may be the origin of the practice, it contrasts favourably with the custom in force among many families of the higher castes in Lower Bengal, in so far as it tends on the whole to defer child-bearing to years of comparative maturity.

"Polygamy is prohibited on pain of expulsion from caste, unless the first wife is barren. The Agarwals of Saharanpur, however, disregard the rule, and are nevertheless admitted to inter-marriage with the Jain Agarwals of Delhi. A widower may marry again: a widow may not. Divorce is not recognised. If a woman goes wrong, she is turned out of the caste, and must either join some religious sect of dubious morality or become a regular prostitute."

Custom of Child Marriage

Sir H.H. Risley writes in his ethnography *The Tribes and Castes of Bengal* thus, "All Babhans who can afford to do so marry their daughters as infants, the bride's age being often no more than four or five years. The same rule holds good for boys, only they are married comparatively later in life, and a son unmarried at the age of puberty does not bring the same sort of reproach on the family as a daughter is supposed to do. Instances, however, are not wanting where for special reasons the daughters of wealthy families have been married after they were grown up, as was the case with the late Maharani of Tikari; and it seems to be clear that even the most orthodox members of the caste do not take the extreme sacerdotal view of the necessity of infant marriage. Ordinarily a price is paid for a bridegroom, but the purchase of brides is by no means uncommon. A man may marry two sisters, and the number of wives he may have is subject to no limit except his ability to maintain them. Some say, however, that a second wife is only permissible if the first proves barren, is convicted of unchastity, or suffers from an incurable disease. Whatever may be the rule on the subject, it is rare to find a man with more than two wives. Widows are not allowed to marry again. Divorce is unknown : a faithless wife is simply turned out of the caste and left to shift for herself by becoming a prostitute, turning Mahomedan, or joining some of the less reputable religious sects.

"The marriage ceremony of the Babhans does not appear to differ materially from the standard type of a Behar marriage, which has been very fully described by Mr. Grierson at page 362 of *Behar Peasant Life*. It should perhaps be noted that a Babhan *marhwa* or marriage shed had six posts, not four, and that the bride is held throughout the ceremony by a woman of the Kahar caste. I may further observe that whereas according to Hindu law the completion of the seventh step by the bride renders the marriage final and irrevocable, a number of Babhans in Patna assured me with much particularity of statement that in their opinion *sindurdan*, or the smearing of vermilion on the parting of the bride's hair, formed the binding portion of the ceremony—not the circumambulation of the sacrifical fire (*bhanwar* or *bedi ghumaeh*), which in Behar takes the place of the Vedic *saptapadi*. My informants emphasized their statement by adding that if the bridegroom were to die after *bhanwar* and before *sindurdan*, the bride would not be deemed a widow, and would be permitted to marry another man." Adds Mr. Risley. The customs and rituals are peculiar to Babhans of the eastern regions.

Mock Marriage with Mahua tree

Sir Herbert Risley writes, "In Bankura Manbhum, and the north of Orissa, where the example of the aboriginal races is prominent, Bagdis practise both infant and adult marriage indifferently. In the cost of girls who are not married in fancy, sexual license before marriage is virtually tolerated, it being understood that if a girl becomes pregnant she will find some one to marry her. Further east, infant-marriage is the rule and adult the exception, while the Bagdis of the 24-Parganas, Jessore, an Nadiya pretend entire ignorance of the custom of adult-marriage. Polygamy is permitted. In theory, a man may marry as many wives as he can afford to maintain: practically, however, the standard of living of the caste limits him to two. He may also marry two sisters at the same time.

"Among a mass of ritual borrowed from the Brahmanical system, the marriage ceremony (*bibaha* or *byah* as opposed to *sanga*) of the Bagdis of Western Bengal has preserved some interesting usages, which appear to belong to a different, and perhaps more primitive, order of symbolism. Early on the wedding morning, before the bridegroom starts in procession for the bride's house, he goes through a mock marriage to a *mahua* tree (Bassia Intifodia). He embraces the tree and bedaubs it with vermilion; his right wrist is bound to it with thread, and after he is released from the tree this same thread is used to attach a bunch of *mahua* leaves to his wrist The *barat* or procession of the bridegroom's party is usually timed so as to reach the bride's house about sunset. On arrival, the inner courtyard of the house is defended by the bride's friends, and a mimic conflict takes place, which ends in the victory of the *barat*. Symbolic capture having been thus effected, the bridegroom himself is seated with his face to the east on a wooden stool (*pira*) placed under a bower of *sal* leaves, having pots of oil, grain, and turmeric at the four corners, and a small pool of water in the centre. When the bride enters, she marches seven times round the bower, keeping it always on her right hand, and seats herself opposite to the bridegroom, the pool of water being between the pair. The right hands of the bride, the bridegroom, and the bride's eldest relative are tied together with thread by the officiating Brahman, who at the same time recites sacred texts (*mantras*), the purport of which is that the bride has been given by her people to the bridegroom and has been accepted by him. The priest then claims his fee, and, after receiving it, unties the thread and knots together the scarves worn by the married couple. This part of the ceremony is called *gotrantar*, 'the change of *gotra*,' and is supposed to transfer the bride from her own section or exogamous groups into that of her husband. It is followed by *sindurdan*, when the bridegroom takes a small cup of vermilion in his left hand and with his right hand smears the colour on the parting of the bride's hair. By the Bagdis, as by most of the aboriginal tribes of Western Bengal, *sindurdan* is deemed to be the essential and binding portion of the marriage ceremony, and they know nothing of the "seven steps" of the Brahmanical rite. Garlands of flowers are then exchanged by the parties, and the rest of the night is spent in feasting, the married couple leaving for the bridegroom's house early next morning. The knotted scarves are not untied until the fourth day after the wedding.

"All sub-castes, except the Tenthulia Bagdis, allow widows to marry again by the ceremony known as Sanija—a maimed rite, at which no Brahman officiates, no *mantras* or Vedic texts are recited, and the sacred fire, which from the days of the Rig-Veda has formed the distinguishing feature of the marriage ritual, is not kindled. Among the Bagdis of the Tributary States of Orissa, I am informed that Brahmans do attend at the Sanga ceremony for the purpose of chanting mantras and sanctifying by their touch the new cloth and iron bracelet which the bridegroom present to the bride. In the Sanga ceremony as practised by the Bagdis of Central Bengal, the bride and bridegroom sit face to face on a mat, and each daubs the other's forehead with a paste of powdered turmeric and water. A sheet (*chadar*) is then thrown over the heads of the pair, so as to cover them entirely, and under this the bridegroom puts an iron bracelet (*lohar kharu*) on the left wrist of the bride. The proceedings are finished by a feast to the caste brethren of the village. If the newly-married couple are too poor to afford a feast, they pay a fee of Re. 1-4. A widow may marry her late husband's younger brother, but she is not compelled to do so.

"In the matter of divorce, the practice of the caste seems to vary in different parts of Bengal. Hinduised Bagdis follow the example of the higher castes in denying that such a thing is possible. The general opinion, however, seems to be that a wife may be divorced for barrenness, unchastity, or disobedience, duly proved to the satisfaction of a council of elders of the caste. When the council have given their assent, the husband closes the proceedings by the symbolical act of breaking a straw in two, or by taking away the iron bracelet which every married woman wears on her left wrist. A divorced wife is entitled to claim maintenance from her late husband for a period of six months after the divorce. She may marry again by the *Sanga* form, and in some districts such marriages are exceedingly common. Cases, indeed, have come to my notice in which a wife has taken steps to get a divorce with the avowed object of marrying another man. As a rule, however, the initiative is supposed to be taken by the husband." Adds Mr. Risley.

He further adds, "Like Bauris, all sub-castes of Bagdis, except the Tentulia, admit into their circle member of any caste higher than themselves in social standing. No regular ceremony is appointed for such occasions: the new member merely pays to the caste panchayat a sum of money, varying from Rs. 10 to Rs. 15, to be spent on a feast, in which for the first time he openly eats with his adopted caste brethren. When admitted into the Dulia sub-caste, he is made to take the palanquin or his shoulder to signify his acceptance of the characteristic occupation of the body to which he has joined himself. The origin of this singular practice, which is entirely out of accord with the spirit of the caste system at the present day, is apparently to be sought in the lax views of the Bagdis and Bauris on the subject of sexual morality. In every other caste a woman who has an intrigue with an outsider is punished by expulsion from the caste; but Bagdis and Bauris not only allow their women to live openly with men of other castes, but receive those men into their own community when, as frequently happens, they are outcasted by there own people for eating rice cooked by their mistresses." The marriage customs and rites are observed by the Bagdi community.

Practice of Child Marriage

"Bhats usually marry their daughters between the ages of nine and twelve; but in exceptional cases, where a girl's parents are poor, it may happen that she is not married until after the age of puberty. The marriage ceremony is of the orthodox type, and *kanyadan,* or the presentation of the bridge to the bridegroom and his acceptance of the gift, is reckoned to be the essential and binding portion of the ritual. Polygamy is not supposed to be allowed, but a man may take a second wife if the first is barren or suffers from an incurable disease. Widows are not allowed to marry again, nor is divorce recognised. An adulterous wife is turned out of the caste and cases thenceforth to be a member of respectable society." The custom is related to the Bhats.

"Among the Bhuiyas of the Tributary States, a girl rarely marries before she is fully grown up. Great freedom of courtship is allowed, and "slips of morality, so long as they are confined to the tribe, are not much headed." Colonel Dalton describes a curious and graceful custom by which the young men of one village pay a visit of courtship to the maidens of another, offering presents and receiving a meal, after which they spend the night in dancing and singing. He also mentions the fact that the bachelors always sleep together in a large house set apart for that purpose, and that in some villages the girls also have a house to themselves, where they spend the night with no one to look after them. In Singbhum these Arcadian habits seem to have died out, and infant-marriage, though by no means universal, is said to be gaining ground among the tribe. Khandaits, Tikaits, Ghatwals, and for the most part all landholding Bhuiyas in Hindu surroundings, marry their daughters as infants when they can get husbands for them. The two latter groups, however, are comparatively small, and their members are put to some difficulty in finding husbands within their own class; so that with them, as with the pseudo-Rajputs of Chota Nagpur, girls often remain unmarried until they have long passed the age of puberty. Musahars, on the other hand, still hold to adult-marriage.

"Polygamy is allowed, and, in theory at least, a man may have as many wives as he can maintain. Few, however, can afford the luxury of more than one, and custom does not favour the taking of a second wife except when the first is barren. A widow may marry again by the *sagai* form, and it is usual, though not compulsory, for her to marry her late husband's younger brother. If she marries an outsider, her children by her late husband belong as of right to his family, though children at the breast are usually left in her charge till they are big enough to be independent of their mother. Marriage with an elder brother is strictly forbidden.

"Divorce is permitted, with the sanction of the *panchayat* of the tribe, if the wife be proved unchaste, if the husband neglect to maintain her, or if either party suffer from an incurable disease, such as leprosy or impotence. A divorced woman may marry again by the *sagai* form, unless she has been guilty of a *liaison* with a man of a lower caste, in which case any Bhuiya who married her would render himself liable to expulsion from the community. An intrigue within the tribe or with a man of respectable caste admits of being condoned by a fine, and does not operate as a bar to remarriage.

The custom is related to the Bhuiyas of the eastern region.

Free Sexual Licence to Girls

The exogamous divisions of the Bhumis tribe are totemistic, and closely resemble those met with among the Mundas. The rule of exogamy is simple. Sir Risley records, "A man may not marry a woman of his own sept, nor a woman who comes within the standard formula for reckoning prohibited degrees, calculated as a rule to three generation in the descending line, but sometimes extended to five where *bhaiyadi* or mutual recognition of kinship has been maintained between the families.

"The aboriginal usage of adult-marriage still holds its ground among the Bhumij, though the wealthier members of the tribe prefer to marry their daughters as infants. The extreme view of the urgent necessity of early marriage is unknown among them, and it is thought no shame for a man to have a grown-up daughter unmarried in his house. Sexual intercourse before marriage is more or less recognised, it being understood that if a girl becomes pregnant arrangements will at once be made to marry her to the father of her child. Brides are bought for a price ranging usually from Rs. 3 to Rs. 12, and the wedding may take place, according to arrangement, at the house of either party. When, as is more usual, it is celebrated at the bride's house, a square space (*marwa*) is prepared in the courtyard (*angan*) by daubing the ground with rice-water. In the centre of this space branches of *mahua* and *sidha* trees are planted, bound together with five cowrie shells (*Cyproea mcneta*) and five pieces of turmeric, and at the corners are set four earthen water-vessels connected by a cotton thread, which marks the boundary of the square. Each vessel is half filled with pulse, and covered with a concave lid, in which a small lamp burns. On the arrival of the bridegroom with his following of friends, he is led at once to the *marwa* and made to sit on a bit of board (*pira*). The bride is then brought in and given a similar seat on his left hand. A sort of mimic resistance to the introduction of the bride is often offered by her more distant female relatives and friends, who receive trifling presents for allowing her to pass.

"After the bride has taken her seat and certain *mantras* or mystic formula have been pronounced by the priest, usually a Bengal Brahman, the bridegroom proceeds to light the lamps at the corners of the square. As fast as each lamp is lighted the bride blows it out, and this is repeated three, five, or seven times, as the case may be. The couple then return to their seats, and the bride is formally given to the bridegroom, appropriate *mantras* being recited at the time, and their right hands being joined together by the officiating priest. Last of all, the bridegroom smears vermilion on the bride's forehead, and his clothes are knotted to hers, the knot being kept intact for three, four, five seven, or ten days, according to the custom of the family. At the end of that time they must rub themselves with turmeric and bathe, and the knot is solemnly untied in the presence of the bridegroom's relations. No priest is present on this occasion.

"The Bhumij recognise polygamy, and in theory at least impose no limitation on the number of wives a man may have. The tribe, however, are for the most part poor, and their meagre standard of living proves an effectual bar to excessive indulgence in the luxury of polygamy. When a man has no children by his first wife, he usually marries again if he can afford to do so; and it frequently happens that the second wife is a young widow, whom he marries by the *sanga* ritual, paying a nominal bride-price and incurring far less expenditure than would be necessary in the event of his marrying a virgin. Widow-marriage is freely permitted by the *sanga* ritual, in which a widow smears on the bride's forehead vermilion which the bridegroom has previously touched with his great toe. It is deemed right for a widow to marry her late husband's younger brother or cousin, if such an arrangement be feasible; and in the event of her marrying an outsider, she forfeits all claim to a share in her late husband's property and to the custody of any children she may have had by him. Traces of the growth of a sentiment adverse to the practice of widow-marriages may perhaps be discerned in the fact that the children of widows by their second husbands experience some difficulty in getting married, and tend rather to form a class by themselves.

"The Bhumij of Manbhum allow divorce only when a woman has been guilty of adultery. A council of relations is called, who hear the evidence and determine whether the charge has been proved. If their finding is against the woman, her husband solemnly draws from her wrist the iron ring, which is the visible sign of wedlock. Water is then poured on a *sal* leaf, and the husband tears the wet leaf in two to symbolise separation. This ceremony is called *pat pani chira*, 'the wet leaf rent,' and besides making the divorce absolute, relieves the husband from any claim by the wife for maintenance. He is himself socially impure after the ceremony until he has shaved and performed certain expiatory rites, the most important of which appears to be giving a feast to the relatives who came together to adjudicate on the case. A woman has no right to divorce her husband; and if neglected or ill-treated her only remedy is to run away with another man. Divorced wives may marry again by the *sanga* ritual, but their offspring by their second husbands are at the same social disadvantage in respect of marriage as has been noticed above in referring to the children of widows. In both cases the sentiment is unquestionably due to the influence of Hinduism in modifying the original usages of the tribe.

"In matters of inheritance and succession the tribe usually affect to follow the school of Hindu law in vogue in their neighbourhood, and hardly any vestiges of special tribal custom can now be traced. Almost all Bhumij, however, give the eldest son an extra share (*jethangs* or *bara angs*) when the property is divided; and the *ghatuali* members of the tribe follow the local custom of primogeniture, the younger sons being provided for by small maintenance grants. If a man leaves no children,his widow takes a life-interest on the property." Adds Mr. Risley. The customs are deserved by the Bhumij community.

Initiative coming from Boy's Side

Among the Christian Oraon the girl's parents have to wait for an inititative from the boys' side. As a result, some girls remain unmarried even though they have crossed their twenties. Some enlightened parents have given full freedom to their children in the choice for their spouses. During the progress of negotiation when people go to visit the other party, the omens are taken. If a jackal crosses the path of the visitors of the cattle die, they consider it very inauspicious and further negotiations are stopped. Even though the actual marriage is performed at the Church, negotiations between the prospective in-laws remain completely in accordance with the traditional Oraon marriage customs. The clan is exogamous, but in case of a love marriage it may even take place even within the clan. It is, however, condemned by the Church. Marriage between boy and girl belonging to the same village may take place if they belong to different clans, yet it is not considered proper. In cases of marriage between Christians and non-Christians, if the girl is a non-Christian, she must first be converted to the Christianity. In case of marriage between a non-Christian boy and a Christian girl, it can take place with the special permission from the Archbishop of Chotanagpur proviso the children would accept the religion of the mother. Though in theory all Christian may inter-marry, tribal endogamy is the rule. The Roman Catholic Church does not permit marriage between its adherents and Christian of other denominations.

Among Christian Oraons also a bride-price has to be given and this is known as '*Dali-Dhiba*' which varies from Rs. 3/- to Rs. 5. Among the Christian Oraon no case was found of a woman fleeing to her father's place. Among the Christian Munda of Birhu, the social aspect of marriage is kept distinct from the religion. The marriage ceremony is held at the Church, followed by a social ceremonial at the house of the bride and the bridegroom without which a marriage is not deemed complete.

After the marriage, a procession is taken out complete with music, friends, relatives and co-villagers of both sexes of the bridegroom. The joyous party is received in the courtyard of the bride's house ceremonially by bride's relatives. The family women sprinkle water with a mango twig over the bridegroom. The parents of the bridegroom and the bride sprinkle water on each other. Young girls then wash bridegroom's feet for which he pays them a small sum. After that a dance is arranged lasting throughout the whole night. Then the bridegroom and his party are taken to the '*Marwa*' which is a rectangular shed made of *sal* saplings and thatched with green leaves and twigs. There the bridegroom's party usually meets the villagers of the bride's side and jokes are exchanged between them. Thereafter the assembled people say their prayers and give presents to the bride and the bridegroom. This is followed by a sumptuous feast to all the guests and relatives. The last ceremony is that of making over of the bride to the bridegroom. Then the two parties bid farewell to each other and the girl goes to the father-in-law's house. On arrival at her new house the bride is ceremonially received by having her feet washed and anointed with mustard oil. A big feast is held to celebrate the arrival of the bride in which all relatives and villagers participate.

Certain changes have occurred in the marriage ceremonial among the unconverted Munda also. Though a *Mandap* (a rectangular shed erected for the marriage ceremony) is necessary for a marriage, the bridegroom had done away with it for fear of witch-craft. A room was a better place for the marriage ceremony, instead of Mandap.

As a recent trend among the Mundas, a barber is invited from the nearby town to officiate at a marriage. Previously Brahmins were invited but they proved to be very greedy and demanded high fees for conduct of rituals. For this reason they do not call the Brahmins at all. Previously, the Pahan used to perform the ceremony. Even in the traditional village of Selda, the marriage ceremonial has changed. There are two forms of marriage: '*Arandi*' and '*Diku Arandi.*' The first form of marriage is in the traditional and the other form is borrowed from the Hindus. In the '*Diku*' form of ceremony the Brahmins are called to officiate the marriage. A few cases of marriage by simulated capture were also practised. Many cases of *Rajikhusi* or love marriage also exist.

In these cases, a boy and a girl loving each other may decide to marry inspite of the adverse wishes of their parents. The couple may elope and stay away from the village till such time as their parents relent. Later on a nominal '*gonong*' or bride price is paid to the bride's father. Instances of intrusion marriage were also found among the Mundas. Earlier Rs. 6 in cash two heads of cattle and three pieces of cloth comprised the customary bride price, but recently it has been raised to Rs. 12 in cash, two heads of cattle and five pieces of cloth. In the traditional marriage the parents of the boy and girl settle in provisionally, but before finally performing it, the boy and the girl are consulted. In Arangloya ceremony a marriage is celebrated generally two or three years after the betrothal. The Bhagats give away their daughters in marriage at a younger age than the traditional Oraon. Marriages is permitted between the Bishnu Bhagats and the Danha Bhagats. They also marry traditional Oraon and *Danha Bhagats*, provided the latter is a member of the Congress party. They hesitate, however, to give their girls to such families; they might bring girl of such a family to their own house and get her married. The period for which her marriage is kept pending or under probation, might extend to even three months. Once, a non-Bhagat girl was brought and purified by worship and concoction of milk, tulsi leaves, turmeric and water in which copper, gold and silver had been put in a rite called '*Udhar.*' *Bishnu Bhagats* may sometimes go to the house of a non-converted Oraon or *Danha Bhagats* as members of a *Barat* party. *Bishnu Bhagats* have no objection to accepting water or a meal cooked by a young and unmarried boy or girl from among the unconverted Oraons. However, *Danha Bhagats* and *Tana Bhagats* do not take food. During their marriage ceremony they sing songs, *kirtans* and *bhajans* and, in between different rituals, shout slogans such as *Mahatma Gandhi Ki Jai*, *Jawaharlal Ki Jai, Rajendra Prasad Ki Jai*, etc.

In a marriage ceremony at Chiri, petromax lamps, loudspeakers and an English band were being used. A ritual in the marriage ceremony of the Oraon of this place is remnant of capture. When the girl's party comes close, a show of fight is feinted and both parties come to a clash, three times. In such mock clashes many persons fall down and pretend to show that they are wounded. Thereafter the parents of the boy and the girl meet and all rejoice. In some marriage forms a Hindu Brahman is called to bless the couple. In the marriage ceremonial it was found that there was much in common between it and that prevailing among the Hindus. Even the names of the rituals seem to be borrowed from the high caste Hindus. Sometimes ago, it was customary to give one pig and one filly-goat to the marriage party when it visited the bride's village, but now people have given up this practice as it is costly. Sometimes even the best of hosts cannot manage the quantity of meat demanded by their guests; except on the occasion of marriage, pork is avoided.

Jumble of Complex Rituals and Rites

Sir Herbert Risley writes, "The marriage ceremonies of the Bengal Brahmans comprise five important stages, viz.—

"1. *Purba-bibdha*, consisting of—(1) The anointment, called *tel halud.* After preliminaries have been settled, and the *patra karan*, or formal intimation of the consent of the parties, or rather of their guardians on both sides, has been drawn up, an auspicious day is fixed for anointing both the bridegroom and the bride with turmeric. The process must be undergone by both on the same day—the bride a little while after the bridegroom, each in their own house, usually a part of the turmeric prepared for the bridegroom is sent by his guardian for the use of the bride, but if the couple live at a distance, this is not deemed essential. In any case the time at which the ceremony should be performed is fixed by letter. Those who can afford to do so distribute oil and turmeric among their neighbours on this occasion.

"2. The entertainment, *thubara* or *ayubriddhanna*. From the day of the anointment until the day of the marriage the betrothed couple are daily entertained by their friends and neighbours, a piece of new cloth being presented at the same time. Presents of sweetmeats and cloth are sent to their house by friends, and well-to-do people with a large circle of acquaintances often prolong the interval between the anointing with turmeric and the wedding from two or three days to a month. The rule is that after the anointing the first entertainment is given by the parents, and after that neither the bride nor the bridegroom should again eat in their own homes until they are married.

"3. The divine invocation or *adhibas*. On the night before the wedding some married ladies, the neighbours and relations of the bride and bridegroom are entertained with a repast, and given presents of betel leaves and areca nuts. This is supposed to render the occasion auspicious, and to draw down the blessing of the gods through the goodwill of the ladies entertained, who are looked upon as a sort of fairy god-mothers.

"4. The propitiation of ancestors, *Nandimukh or briddhi sraddh*, is an ordinary *sraddh* performed at noon on the wedding day in order to procure the blessing of the deceased ancestors on the couple. Four ancestors on the father's and three on the mother's side of both parties are thus invoked: if the father and grandfather of the intended bride or bridegroom be living, then only their two immediate (deceased) predecessors, and if only the father be living, then his three immediate predecessors only. The *sraddh* is performed by the father, or in his absence by the brother, or failing him again by a *gyati* (agnate) of the bride or the bridegroom as the case may be. If a *ghati* be not procurable, then the family priest may officiate.

"5. The bridal procession (*bar-jatri*). In the evening or, if he lives at a distance, earlier, the bridegroom goes in procession accompanied by a *kolbar*, or best man, who is usually his younger brother, and by a number of his relations, friends and neighbours to the house of the bride, where he is received as in a *durbar*, his approach being welcomed by the cry of *ulu-ulu* from the females of the bride's family. He sits on a *masnad* set apart for him in the centre of the hall, and there surrounded by those who accompanied him and by the bride's people (*kanyajatri*), he awaits the moment fixed by the astrologers as auspicious for the performance of the actual ceremony.

"6. *Jamata-baran,* or the bridegroom's welcome by the bride's father. When the proper time has come, the bridegroom is taken by the bride's father into the inner apartments of the house, and is made to stand on a piece of board painted with pounded or powdered rice stirred up with water. The bride's father then offers him water for washing his feet *(padya argha)* and also *modhuparkya,* a concoction of honey, in a small copper cup. These the bridegroom touches in token of acceptance.

"7. *Stri-achar,* or woman's usage, commences with the welcome given to the bridegroom by the bride's mother by pouring some curds on his feet. This is followed by—

"*(a)Satusi* or the seven lights of Hymen. Seven married ladies (including the bride's mother or, if she be a widow, one of the bride's aunts) in their best attire, each with a small torch made of *chita* twig and cotton steeped in oil, go round the bridegroom in procession, led by the bride's mother, who carries on her head a *kula,* or flat bamboo basket, on which are placed 21 small lights made of *dhatura* fruits. As they go round, they sprinkle libations of water, one of them blows a shell trumpet, and all vociferate the hymeneal cry of *ulu-ulu.* After going seven times round the bridegroom, the lights are thrown one by one over his head, so that they fall behind him. The *kula* is then picked up and placed in front of the bridegroom, and the bride's mother takes her stand upon it and touches *(baran)* the forehead of the bridegroom with water, paddy and *durba* grass, betel and areca nut, white mustard seed, curds, white sandal paste, vermilion, a looking-glass, a comb, a bit of clay from the bed of the Ganges, a yak's tail, shells, a cluster of plantains, and certain other odds and ends, while the rest of the women keep up the cry of *ulu-ulu.* The bridegroom's height is measured with a thin thread which the bride's mother eats in a bit of plantain. She then places a weaver's shuttle *(maku)* between his folded hands and ties them together with thread, and calls upon him, now that he has been bound hand and foot, to bleat once like a sheep to signify his humility and subjection. Last of all, she touches his breast with a padlock and turns the key, whereby the door of speech is closed to the passage of hard words against the bride.

"*(b) Satpak,* or the seven rounds of the bride. The bride is now brought out attired in a red silk cloth, and seated on a painted board is carried by two men seven times round the bridegroom, who remains standing and then placed in front of him. As they face each other, a cloth or cover is thrown over them, and their natural shyness being thus for the moment hidden, they are supposed to snatch the *subhadrishti* or auspicious glance, which will secure their mutual happiness during their married life. Then follows—

"*(c) Malyadan,* or the exchange of garlands, when the bride and bridegroom give each other garlands of flowers.

"II. *Sampradan,* or the gift and acceptance. The bride and bridegroom are next brought to a place set apart in the outer apartment or courtyard of the house, where the bride's party and the bridegroom's party can witness the formal gift of the bride and her formal acceptance by the bridegroom. The bride's father or guardian repeats the *mantras* recited by the family priest, and the bridegroom accepts the gift in these words:—'Who gave her? To whom did he give her? Love gave her. To love he gave har. Love is the giver. Love is the taker. Love pervades the ocean. With love I accept her. Love ! may this be thine.'

"At the same time wedding presents *(dan* or *dan samagri)* are given to the bridegroom, and after this the father or guardian is required to bear witness to the contract entered into by the bridegroom by accepting the bride, and as a token of his assent to the marriage accepts a present of five *haritaki* fruits and a piece of cloth. This present is called the *parihar.*

"III. *Basara* or the bridal wake. The bridegroom is next conducted along with the bride to a room in the inner apartment of the house, a corner of his *chadar* being tied to a corner of her cloth. The pair are there received by a bevy of young ladies, who make it their business to tease the bridegroom and try to keep him awake for the rest of the night.

"IV. *Kusandika* includes the *saptapadi gaman,* or pacing of the seven steps, which may be deemed the essential and binding portion of the marriage ritual observed by the higher castes. A sacred fire is prepared and worshipped with oblations of ghi. On the north side of the fire seven points are marked off, and the bride setting her face westward walks along these points, placing her foot on each in turn. As she walks, her husband follows close behind her, touching her heel with his toe and reciting at each step *mantras* or sacred texts.

"*Saptapadi gaman* is followed by *gotra paribarttan,* or the changing of the bride's *gotra* for that of the bridegroom, and the *sindurdan,* or the smearing of vermilion on the bride's forehead and the parting of her hair. The latter ceremony is performed by the husband with his own hand.

"Properly speaking, *kusandika* ought to take place on the day following the marriage, but Tuesdays and Saturdays are considered unlucky days for the ceremony; and if the day after the Wedding is Tuesday or Saturday, *kusandika* is deferred till the day following that. It is usually performed at the house of the bridegroom, but if he lives a long way off, the ceremony is performed at the bride's father's house. The marriage proper ends with *kusandika*, but certain minor ceremonies follow which may be briefly mentioned here.

"V. The concluding ceremonies—

(a) Phul-sajya or the bed of flowers. On the third night after the marriage, the married couple are laid together in a bed decorated with flowers.

(b) Ashta-mangala. On the eighth day the pair are made to enact with toys and cowrie shells a sort of pantomimic drama of their married life, playing the part of a faithful husband and wife, and affecting to bear with resignation the vicissitude of fortunes.

"*(c) Baubhat* or *Paka-sparsa.* All the *gyatis,* relations and friends of the bridegroom are entertained at his house. Their acceptance of the invitation is deemed an admission on their part that the marriage has been duly performed, and that the ceremonial purity of the bridegroom has in no wise been affected. In token of their recognition of this fact, they are supposed to eat rice prepared by the bride herself.

"After the *Paka-sparsa* ceremony, the bride is sent back to her father's house until she attains puberty. When this time arrives it is the custom of some families to perform the ceremony known as *garbhadhan* (purification of the womb) or *punarbibaha.* This rite, to which some Hindu writers have attributed a sort of sacramental character, seems to be closely analogous to the practices observed by a number of savage races on a similar occasion. The idea seems to be, as Mr. J. G. Frazer has pointed out, that dangerous influences emanate from a girl when passing through this physical change, and it is considered necessary to seclude her from the rest of the community, and subject her to a sort of penance which varies greatly in severity. Thus the Macusi tribe of British Guiana hang a girl in this state in a hammock at the top of the hut, and make her fast rigorously so long as the symptoms are at their height. When she gets well the pots and drinking vessels which she has used are broken; and after her first bath she must submit to be beaten by her mother with thin rode without uttering a cry. Another tribe, instead of beating; girls who have just recovered from this state, expose them to certain large ants whose bite is very painful. The usage followed by the Rarhi Brahmans of Bengal is less severe, but of the same general character as the savage observances. Like the Australian blacks and the African Bushmen, they require a girl to live alone, and do not allow her to see the face of any male. During three days she is shut up in a dark room and is made to undergo certain penances. She must lead the life of a Brahmachari, that is, she must live upon *atap* rice and ghee, fish and flesh being strictly interdicted, and she may not eat any sweetmeats. Where this ceremony is observed, it is held to be a necessary preliminary to the commencement of marital intercourse. By a recent change in the law it has been made criminal to have intercourse with a girl under twelve years of age." Adds Mr. Risley. The customs are peculiar to the Bengal Brahman who are akin to Orissa Brahmans also.

Child Marriage being Unknown

Mr. Risley writes, "I quote at length Major Lewin's graphic and sympathetic description of the marriage customs of the Chakmas *Hill Tracts of Chittagong*, pp. 70 et seq. :—

> 'Child-marriage among the Chakmas, or indeed among the hill people in general, are unknown. There is no fixed time for getting married. Some of the young men indeed do not marry until they reach the age of 24 or 25; after that age, however, it is rare to see a man unmarried. Marriage is after this fashion: Father, mother, and son first look about them and fix upon a bride. This indispensable preliminary accomplished, the parents go to the house where their intended daughter-in-law resides. They take with them a bottle of spirits (this is an absolute necessary in every hill palaver). The matter will at first be opened cautiously. The lad's father will say, 'That is a fine tree growing near young house; I would fain plant in its shadow.' Should all go well, they retire after mutual civilities. Both in going and coming omens are carefully observed, and many a promising match has been put a stop to by unfavourable auguries. A man or woman carrying fowls, water, fruit, or milk, if passed on the right hand, is a good omen and pleasant to meet with; but it is unfavourable to see a kite or a vulture, or to see one crow all by himself croaking on the left hand. If they are unfortunate enough to come upon the dead body of any animal on their road, they will go no further, but at once return home and stop all proceedings. Old people quote numerous stories to show that the disregard of unfavourable omen has in former times been productive of the most ruinous consequences.

"By the time a second visit is due the relatives on both sides have been consulted; and if all has progressed satisfactorily and there are no dissentient voices, they go accompanied by some of the girls of the village, taking with them presents of curds and *birni* grain, and *jogra*; a sweet fermented liquor made from rice. Then a day is settled (after the harvest is a favourite time), and a ring of betrothal is given to the bride. Now, also, is arranged what price the young man is to pay for his wife; for the Chakmas, in contradistinction to all our other tribes, buy their wives. The ordinary price is Rs. 100 to Rs. 150. On the marriage day a large stock of provisions is laid in by both houses. A procession of men and women start from the bridegroom's village with drums and music to fetch home the bride. The parents of the bridegroom present their intended daughter with her marriage dress. No ceremony, however, is performed; and the bride, after a short interval, is taken away, accompanied by all her relatives, to her new home.

'On arriving all enter the house, and the bride and the bridegroom sit down together at a small table—the bride on the left hand of her husband. On the table are eggs, sweetmeats, rice, and plantains, all laid out on leaf platters. The best man (*sowalla*) sits behind the bridegroom, and the bride has a representative bride-maid (*sowalli*) behind her. These two then bind around the couple a muslin scarf, asking. 'Are all willing, and shall this be accomplished.' Then all cry out, 'Bind them, Bind them,' so they are bound. The married pair have now to eat together the wife feeding the husband and the husband the wife; and as at this stage of the ceremony a great deal of bashfulness is evinced, the bridesmaid and best man raise the hands of their respective charges to and from each other's mouths, to the intense enjoyment and hilarity of every one present. After they have thus eaten and drunken, an elder of the village sprinkles them with river-water, pronounces them man and wife, and says a charm used for fruitfulness. The couple then retire, and the guests keep it up until an early hour on the following morning. The next day, at the morning meal, the newly married come hand in hand salute the elders of the families. The father of the bride generally improves this occasion by addressing a short lecture to his son-in-law on the subject of marital duties. 'Take her,' he says; 'I have given her to you; but she is young and not acquainted with her household duties. If therefore at any time you come back from the *jhum* and find the rice burnt, or anything else wrong, teach her: do not beat her. But at the end of three years, if she still continues ignorant, then beat her, but do not take her life; for if you do, I shall demand the price of blood at your hands, but for beating her I shall not hold you responsible or interfere.'

"All marriages, however, do not go on in this happy fashion: it often happens that the lad and the lass have made up their minds to couple, but the parents will not hear of the match. In such a case the lovers generally elope together; but should the girl's parents be very much set against the match, they have the right to demand back and take their daughter from the hands of her lover. If, notwithstanding this opposition, the lovers' intentions still remain unaltered and they elope a second time, no one has then the right to interfere with them. The young husband makes a present to his father-in-law according to his means, gives a feast to his new relatives, and is formally admitted into kinship.' Adds Mr. Lewin.

"Sexual indiscretions before marriage are not severely dealt with, and usually end in marriage. But a man who carries off a young girl against her will is fined Rs. 60, and "also receives a good beating from the lads of the village to which a girl belongs." Incest is punished by a fine of Rs. 50 and corporal punishment. Once married, the Chakma women are said to be good and faithful wives, and it is unusual for the village council to be called upon to exercise its power of granting a divorce. Such cases, however, do occur occasionally. The offender has to repay to the husband the bride-price and the expenses incurred in the marriage, and in addition a fine of Rs. 50 or Rs. 60, which is divided between the dewan or ahun of the sept and the Chief of the tribe. Divorced women can marry again.

"A widow is allowed to marry a second time. She may marry her husband's younger brother, but is not obliged to do so. The ceremony is simple, consisting mainly of a feast." Adds Mr. Risley. The customs, rites and rituals are practised among the Buddhist Chakmas.

No Marriage of two Sisters to the same Man Allowed

Sir Herbert Risley writes, about the Chamar marriage, "Like the Doms, and unlike most other castes, Chamars forbid the marriage of two sisters to the same husband. In the marriage ceremony an elder of the caste presides, but a Brahman is usually consulted to fix an auspicious day for the event. The father of the bride receives a sum of money for his daughter, but this is usually insufficient to meet the expenses of the wedding. During the marriage service the bridegroom sits on the knee of the bride's father, and the bridegroom's father receives a few ornaments and a cup of spirits, after which each of the guests is offered a cup. No *marua* or wedding bower is made, but a barber prepares and whitewashes a space (*chauk*), within which the couple sit. He also stains the feet of the bride and bridegroom with cotton soaked in lac dye (*alta*), and is responsible that all the relatives and friends are invited to the marriage. The caste elder, who officiates as priest, binds mango leaves on the wrists of the wedded pair, and chants *mantras* or mystic verses; while the bridegroom performs *sindurdan* by smearing vermilion on the bride's forehead and the parting of her hair. This is deemed the valid and binding portion of the ceremony. Widows are permitted to marry again. Usually when an elder brother dies childless the younger brother must marry the widow within a year or eighteen months, unless they mutually agree not to do so, in which case she returns to her father's house, where she is free to remarry with any one. If there are children by the first marriage, it is deemed the more incumbent on the widow to marry the younger brother; but even in this case she is not compelled to do so. The custody of the children, however, remains with their paternal uncle, and the widow forfeits all claim to share in her late husband's estate. On her remarriage the family of her first husband cannot claim any compensation for the bride-price which they paid for her on her marriage. Before a widow marries again her relatives go through the form of consulting the panchayat, with the object, it is said, of deciding whether the marriage is well-timed or not. Divorce is permitted with the sanction of the panchayat of the caste. Divorced wives may marry again." The customs, rites and rituals are pertinent to the Chamar community.

Both Infant and Adult Marriages Prevalent

Sir Risley writes, "Cheros profess to marry their daughters as infants, but it seems doubtful whether this practice has yet become fully established among them. The poorer members of the caste, particularly the totemistic Cheros of Chota Nagpur, have not yet completely cut themselves loose from the non-Aryan custom of adult-marriage; while the landholding Cheros find the same difficulties in getting husbands for their daughters which hamper all pseudo-Rajput families in the earlier stages of their promotion to the lower grades of the great Rajput group. The marriage service conforms on the whole to the orthodox pattern, but retains a few peculiar practices which may perhaps belong to a more ancient ritual. At the close of the *bhanwar* ceremony, when the couple march round an earthen vessel set up under the bridal canopy of boughs, the bridegroom, stooping, touches the toe of the bride and swears to be faithful to her through life. Again, after the binding rite of *sindurdan* has been completed, the bridegroom's elder brother washes the feet of the bride, lays the wedding jewellery in her joined hands, and then, taking the *patmauri* from the *maur* or pith head-dress worn by the bridegroom, places it on the bride's head. The practice known as *amlo* also deserves notice. This is performed by the bridegroom's mother before the bridal procession (*barat*) starts for the bride's house, and by the bride's mother after the procession has arrived. It consists of putting a mango leaf into the mouth and then bursting out into tears and loud lamentation: the maternal uncle of the bride or bridegroom meanwhile pours water on the leaf.

"Polygamy is permitted, but is not very common. There is said to be no theoretical limit to the number of wives a man may have. Widows may marry again, and among the less Hinduised members of the caste they usually do so. Widow-marriage, however, is regarded with disfavour by the wealthier Cheros, who affect orthodoxy, and within a generation or so we may expect that the practice will be abandoned. Where it is still recognised, the widow is expected, on grounds of family convenience, to marry her late husband's younger brother or cousin. She may, however, marry any one else provided that she does not infringe the prohibited degrees which were binding on her before her marriage, and does not select a man whose sister could not have been taken in marriage by her late husband. Divorce is not allowed. A woman found in adultery is turned out of the caste, and can under no circumstances marry again." Adds Mr. Risley. The marriage customs and rites are observed by the Cheros.

Dhoba Customs all Brahmanical

Sir Herbert Risley records, "The sections of the Bengal Dhobas present no points of special interest. All of them have been borrowed from the Brahmanical system, and are not taken into account in arranging marriages. There is, indeed, usually only one *gotra* current in each local community, and that seems to be retained mainly from the force of customs as a badge of social distinction. The prohibited degrees are the same as in other castes of about the same position in society.

"Bengal Dhobas, including the Manbhum members of the caste, marry their daughters as infants, at the age of from seven to nine years. Boys are usually married between eleven and fifteen, but the sons of poor men, who cannot afford to pay the bride-price (*pan*), often remain unmarried till five-and-twenty, by which time a man has probably earned enough to secure a wife for himself. The marriage ceremony is the same as is observed by most of the lower castes. The carrying of the bride seven times round the bridegroom is regarded as its binding portion. Polygamy is fully recognised in the case of well-to-do men whose first wives are barren; for others it is allowed, but is not considered quite respectable. Widows may not marry a second time. Divorce is not allowed but when a husband casts off his wife for adultery a reference is usually made to the panchayat and a purificatory ceremony (*prayaschitta*), such as is described in the article on Chasadhoba, is gone through by the husband. Women thus cast off cannot marry again.

"Among the Dhobas of Eastern Bengal some curious usages prevail in respect of marriage. Every *samaj* or local assemblage of the Ramer-Dhoba sub-caste is headed by three officials, known in order of rank as the Naik, the Paramanik, and the Barik. The rest of the assemblage or community are known by the general name Samajik. For marriages between equals, that is between persons both of whom belong to the same class, whether official or Samajik, the bride-price is fixed at Rs. 50. But where the parties do not belong to the same class, the bride-price varies above or below this sum in relation to the rank of the bride and bridegroom. Thus a Samajik marrying the daughter of a Barik, Paramanik, or Naik will pay Rs. 51, Rs. 52, Rs. 53, as the case may be; while a Naik marrying in the classes below him pays Rs. 49, Rs. 48, or Rs. 47, according to the rank of the bride. A somewhat less elaborate system exists in the Sitar-Dhoba sub-caste. There the headman of the Samaj is called Pradhan, and the second Paramanik, but there is no third official. The amount of *pan* varies with the rank of the bride, but neither the normal amount nor the scale of variation is fixed by custom. In Murshedabad and other districts of Central Bengal the Samaj of the Dhoba caste is presided over by three officials—Paramanik, Barik, and Mandal, who are consulted when a marriage is under consideration, and who decide any questions regarding affinity which may arise.

"The Dhobas of Orissa differ in several important particulars from the Dhobas of Bengal. In the first place they have among their *gotras* the distinctly totemistic group Nagasa, the members of which revere the snake as their common progenitor, and observe the primitive rule of exogamy, which forbids a man to marry a woman who bears the same totem as himself. Prohibited degrees of course are recognised, but the form in which they are stated shows them to be later amplifications of a more archaic method of preventing marriages between persons of near kin.

"Again, adult as well as infant marriages are sanctioned, and there are no limits to polygamy. A man may take as many wives as he likes or can afford to maintain. Widows may marry again under much the same conditions as are recognised by the non-Aryan races of Chota Nagpur. The ritual observed is *sanga*. When such a marriage is under consideration, the widow appears before a caste council and solemnly cuts an areca nut (*supari*) into two pieces. This is supposed to symbolize her complete severance from the family of her late husband. The actual ceremony gone through on the day of the *sanga* is of the simplest character. The bridegroom decks the bride with new ornaments, denoting that she has put off the unadorned state of widowhood, and a feast is given to the members of the caste, their presence at which is deemed to ratify the marriage. While permitting widows to remarry, the Orissa Dhobas do not extend this privilege to divorced women. In dealing with women taken in adultery, the main point is whether the paramour is a member of the caste or not. If he is, I gather that the moral sense of the community is satisfied by the imposition of some slight penance, and that the husband by no means invariably insists on getting rid of his wife. A *liaison* with an outsider, however, admits of no atonement, and the offending woman is simply turned out of the caste.

"The religion of the Dhoba caste, whether in Bengal or in Orissa, exhibits no points of special interest. Most Dhobas belong to the Vaishnava sect, and a few only are Saktas. Like many other serving castes, they pay especial reverence to Viswakarma. They employ Brahmans for religious and ceremonial purposes, but the Dhoba Brahman, as he is usually called, ranks very low, and is down upon by those members of the priestly order who serve the higher castes. In the disposal of the dead and the subsequent propitiatory ceremonies they follow the standard customs of lower class Hindus. It deserves notice that the Dhobas of Orissa bury children up to five years of age face downwards—a practice which in Upper India is confined to members of the sweeper caste.

"The necessities of Hindu society give rise to a very steady demand for the services of the Dhoba, and for this reason a comparatively small proportion of the caste have abandoned their distinctive occupation in favour of agriculture. The village Dhoba, however, besides receiving customary presents at all village festivals, often holds *chakaran* land in recognition of the services rendered by him to the community. In Eastern Bengal, according to Dr. Wise, the presence of the Dhoba is deemed indispensable at the marriages of the higher classes, as on the bridal morn he sprinkles the bride and bridegroom with water collected in the palms of his hands from the grooves..." The customs are practised by Dhoba caste in West Bengal and Orissa.

Custom of small Bride-price

"In Central and Eastern Bengal Doms, following the example of the higher castes, nearly always marry their daughters as infants, and regard it as wrong for a girl over ten years of age to remain unmarried in her father's house. A small bride-price *(pan),* varying from Rs. 5 to Rs. 10, is paid to the parents of the girl. In Behar and Western Bengal adult-marriage still holds its ground for those who cannot afford the more fashionable practice, and sexual intercourse before marriage is said to be tolerated. Among the Doms of the Dacca district the marriage service is peculiar. The guests being assembled on a propitious day fixed by a Brahman, the bridegroom's father takes his son on his knee, and, sitting down in the centre of the "Marcoha" opposite the bride's father, who is holding his daughter in a similar posture, repeats the names of his ancestors for seven generations, while the bride's father runs over his for three. They then call God to witness the ceremony, and the bridegroom's father addressing the other asks him, 'Have you lost your daughter?' The answer being in the affirmative, a similar interrogation and reply from the opposite party terminates the service. The boy-bridegroom then advances, smears the bride's forehead with *sindur* or red lead —the symbol of married life—takes her upon his knee, and finally carries her within doors. Like all aboriginal races, Doms are very fond of gaudy colours; the bridal dress consisting of yellow or red garments for the female, and a yellow cloth with a red turban for the male.

"In the 24-Parganas a more Hinduised ritual is in vogue. The marriage takes place on a raised earthen platform *(bedi),* to which a branch of a banian-tree is fixed. An earthen vessel full of Ganges water is placed in the centre.

On this vessel the bride and bride-groom lay their hands, one above the other, and the ceremony is completed by exchanging garlands of flowers. The Dom priest, Dharma-Pandit, presides and mutters words which purport to be sacred texts, and the actual marriage service is preceded by offerings to ancestors and the worship of Suryu, Ganesa, Durga, Mahadeva, and, Anti Kuldevata. Further west again, in the districts of Bankura and Manbhum, the ritual appears to differ little from that already described in the article on the Bagdi caste. There is, however, no marriage with a tree and no symbolic capture of the bride, as in the case of the Bagdis; while in the joining of the hands which precedes *sindurdan,* the bride presents her right hand if she is given away by a male, and her left if by a female relative. On the night before the wedding the ceremony of *adhibas* is performed in the houses of both parties by anointing the body with turmeric and oil and tying a thread soaked in this mixture and knotted with a few blades of *durva* grass on the right wrist of the bridegroom and the left wrist of the bride. The ritual followed in Behar is of the simplest character, consisting mainly of *sindurdan,* which is often performed in the open air under a tree. The wealthier Doms, however, erect a wedding canopy *(marwa),* and generally copy the Hindu ceremony with more or less accuracy of detail.

"Polygamy is everywhere permitted, and poverty forms the only restriction on the number of wives a man may have. The standard of living however is low, and it is unusual to find a Dom with more than two wives, and most men content themselves with one. A widow may marry again, and in Behar it is deemed right for her to marry her late husband's younger brother; but in Bengal this idea does not seem to prevail, and a widow may marry any one she pleases provided that she does not infringe the prohibited degrees binding on her before her first marriage. The ritual (*sanga* or *sagai*) observed at the marriage of a widow consists mainly of *sidurdan* and the present of new cloth. A *pan* is rarely paid, and never exceeds a rupee or two. In Murshedabad there is no *sindurdan*, and a formal declaration of consent before representatives of the caste is all that is required. Considerable license of divorce is admitted, and in some districts at any rate the right can be exercised by either husband or wife; so that a woman, by divesting herself of the iron bracelet given to her at marriage, can rid herself of a husband who ill-treats her or is too poor to maintain her properly. Dom women have a reputation for being rather masterful, and many of them are conspicuous for their powerful physique. It may be by virtue of their characteristic that they have established a right very rarely conceded to women in Bengal. A husband, on the other hand, can divorce his wife for infidelity or persistent ill-temper. In either case the action of the individual requires the confirmation of the panchayat, which however is usually given as a matter of course, and is expressed in Bhagalpur by solemnly pronouncing the pithy monosyllable *jao*. In North Bhagalpur the husband takes in his hand a bundle of rice straw and cuts it in half before the assemblage as a symbol of separation. Divorced wives may marry again by the same ritual as widows. Their children remain in the charge of their first husband. In Monghyr the second husband must give the panchayat a pig to form the basis of a feast, and if convicted of having seduced the woman away from her first husband must pay the latter Rs. 9 as compensation. A husband, again, who divorces his wife has to pay a fee of 10 annas to the panchayat for their trouble in deciding the case.

"Most of the sub-castes seem to have a fairly complete organisation for deciding social questions. The system of panchayats is everywhere in full force, and in Behar these are presided over by hereditary headmen, variously called *sardar, pradhan, manjhan, marar, gorait*, or *kabiraj*, each of whom bears rule in a definite local jurisdiction, and has under him a *chharidar* or rod-bearer to call together the panchayat and to see that its orders are carried out." adds Mr. Risley. The marriage customs are pertinent to the Doms of the region.

Both Infant and Adult Marriages Prevalent

Sir Risley records, 'Gorait marry their daughters both as infants and as adults, but the former practice is deemed the more respectable, and is followed by all who can afford it. After the bride has been selected, the parents of the bridegroom go to her parents' house to see her. On this occasion a feast is given by the bride's people, at which the liquor—an essential element in all non-Aryan rejoicings—is provided by the father of the bridegroom, and four annas, eight annas, or one rupee is presented to the bride as *muh-dekhi*, or fee for the privilege of seeing her face. On the next day the girl's parents visit the boy, and are entertained wholly at his father's expense. Lastly, if both parties are satisfied with this mutual inspection, the boy's people go to the bride's house and present to her a new *sari*, a he-goat, and Rs. 3 to buy ornaments with. These constitute the bride-price (*dali*).

"On the day before the wedding the bridegroom's party march in procession to the bride's house and stop there for the night. Next morning the fathers of the bride and bridegroom shake hands and embrace one another *(samdhi milan)*. Then, in the presence of some elders of the caste, the headman of the village and the priest of the rural gods *(pahn)*, who are received with great ceremony, the marriage is completed by the bride and bridegroom smearing vermilion on each other's foreheads *(sindurdan)*, while the elders solemnly exhort them to work hard, eat, drink, and prosper and not get divorced. This meagre ceremony takes place in a bamboo marriage shed *(marhwa)* erected in the courtyard. Brahmans are not called in, and the village barber takes no part in the ceremony. On the evening of the same day the bridegroom's party take the bride and bridegroom, both seated in the same palanquin, to the latter's house, where *sindurdan* is again performed. On that night the bridegroom, if he has attained puberty, sleeps with the bride. After three days the couple go to the bride's house and stay there nine days, returning finally to their own home on the tenth day.

"Polygamy is permitted, and there is no rule limiting the number of wives. A widow may marry again, and her choice is not fettered by the obligation to marry her late husband's younger brother. The ritual used at the marriage differs from that in use at the marriage of a virgin in that no *marhwa* is constructed and the money portion of the bride-price is only Re. 1. *Sindurdan* is performed in the presence of the widow's relatives, but there is no marriage procession, and the bride is taken home without any display. According to some authorities if the widow elects to live on with her brother-in-law, it is sufficient to announce this intention to the relatives, and no ceremony of any kind is required.

"A divorce *(chhora-chhuri)* maybe granted by the caste council (panchayat) if the wife is proved to bo unchaste, or if she frequently runs away to her father's house without the permission of her husband. Proceedings may also be initiated by the wife on the ground that her husband is too old for her or is an habitual drunkard. Divorced women may marry again by *sagai.*" Adds Mr. Risley. The marriage customs, rites and rituals are observed among the Goraits.

Custom of High Bride-price taking its Toll

Colonel E.T. Dalton writes about the customs and practices, "Owing to the high price placed on daughters by their fathers, the large number of adult unmarried girls seen in every considerable village in the Kolhan is a very peculiar feature in the social state of the community. In no other country in India are spinsters found so advanced in years. In many of the best families grey-headed old maids may be seen, whose charms were insufficient to warrant the large addition to the usual price, called *pan,* imposed in consideration of the high connection that the union would confer. The *pan* is calculated, and for the most part paid, in cattle, indicating that the custom dates from a time when, there was no current coin; and fathers of *manki* dignity demand from forty to fifty head of cattle for each of their girls. Dr. Hayes, finding that in consequence of this practice the number of marriages was annually diminishing and immoral intimacy between the sexes increasing, convened in 1868 a meeting of representative man for the express purpose of discussing this question; and after a long debate it was unanimously agreed that a reduction should be made. It was resolved that in future a *pan* was not to exceed ten head of cattle; and that if one pair of oxen, one cow, and seven rupees were given, it should be received as an equivalent for the ten head. For the poorer classes it was fixed at seven rupees. Even thus modified the *pan* in Singbhum is higher than it is in Chota Nagpur for the multitude. The *mankis* and headmen of the latter country, conforming to the Hindu customs, have given up exacting it. In olden times young men counteracted the machinations of avaricious parents against the course of true love by forcibly carrying off the girl, and still at times evade extortion by running away with her. Then the parents have to submit to such terms as arbitrators think fair. This abduction it was necessary to put a stop to, and elopements are not considered respectable; so, until the conference, prices had a tendency to rise rather than fall. The old generation of *mankis* vehemently opposed any reduction. The second generation, since the accession of the British, are now in the ascendant, and they entertained more enlightened views; but, notwithstanding the compact, I have not yet heard of a marriage in high life in which the reduced *pan* has been accepted. It is certainly not from any yearning for celibacy that the marriage of Singbhum maidens is so long postponed. The girls will tell you frankly that they do all they can to please the young men, and I have often heard them pathetically bewailing their want of success. They make themselves as attractive as they can, flirt in the most demonstrative manner, and are not too coy to receive in public attentions from those they admire. They may be often seen in well-assorted pairs returning from market with arms interlaced, and looking at each other as lovingly as if they were so many groups of Cupids and Psyches; but with all this the '*men will not propose.*' Tell a maiden you think her nice looking, she is sure to reply, 'Oh yes, I am; but what is the use of it? The young men of my acquaintance don't see it.' Even when a youth has fully made up his mind to marry, it may happen that fate is against the happiness of the young couple: bad omens are seen that cause the match to be postponed or broken off; or papa cannot, or will not, pay the price demanded. When a young man has made his choice, he communicates the fact to his parents; and a deputation of the friends of the family is sent to the girl's house to ascertain all that should be known regarding her family, age, appearance, and means. If the information obtained and the result of the inspection be satisfactory, and the omens observed on the road have been propitious, an offering is made on the part of the young man; and if it be received, the deputation are invited to stay, and are feasted. The report of the deputation being favourable, a day is fixed for a meeting between the parents, and the terrible question of the *pan* discussed. At this point many matches are broken off in consequence of greed on one side or stinginess on the other. The amount agreed on has to be paid before the day can be fixed for the marriage; and when delivery of the cattle is made a pot of her has to be groom from the bride's side for each animal. At last if all this is got over, the appointed day arrives, and the bride is escorted to the village for her intended by all her young female friends, with music and dancing. The young men and girls of the village, and those invited from neighbouring villages, form a cortege for the bridegroom. they go out and meet the bride's party, and, after a dance in the grove, in which the bride and bridegroom take part, mounted on the hipe of two of their female friends, they enter the village together, where there is a great feast, a great consumption of the rice-beer, and much more dancing and singing. Ceremony there is none; but the turning point in the rite is when the bride and groom pledge each other. A cup of beer is given to each; the groom pours some of the contents of his cup into the bride's cup, and she returns the compliment. Drinking the liquor thus blended they become of one *kili,* that is, the bride is admitted into her husband's tribe, and they become one. This has, I believe, succeeded an older custom of drinking from the same cup. After remaining with her husband for three days only, it is the correct thing for the wife to run away from him and tell all her friends that she loves him not, and will see him no more. This is perhaps reperation to the dignity of the sex, injured by the bride's going to the bridegroom's house to be married, instead of being sought for and taken as a wife from her own. So it is correct for the husband to show great anxiety for the loss of his wife and diligently seek her; and when he finds her, he carries her off by main force. I have seen a young wife thus found and claimed and borne away, screeching and struggling, in the arms of her husband from the midst of a crowded *bazaar.* No one interferes on these occasions, and no one assists. If the husband cannot manage the business himself, he must leave her alone. After this little escapade the wife at once settles down, assumes her place as the well-contented mistress of the household, and, as a rule, in no country in the world are wives better treated. Dr. Hayes says:—'A Kol or Ho makes a regular companion of his wife. She is consulted in all difficulties, and receives the fullest consideration due to her sex.' Indeed, it is not uncommon in the Kolhan to see husbands so subject to the influence of their wives that they may be regarded as henpecked. Instances of infidelity in wives are very rare. I never heard of one, but I suppose such things occur, as there is a regulated penalty. The unfaithful wife is discarded, and the seducer must pay to the husband the entire value of the *pan.*" Adds Mr. Dalton. The custom is peculiar to the Ho tribal group in Bihar, Jharkhand and on borders of West Bengal.

No Disgrace Attached to Adult Marriage

Sir Risley records about the Kaibarttas marriage, thus, "Like most orthodox Hindus, the Kaibarttas of Bengal perform the ceremonial marriage of their daughters before they attain puberty, and sometimes when they are only three years old. The girls, however, do not go to live with their husbands until they are fully grown up. Complaints, indeed, are not uncommon of a girl being kept at home by her people to assist in household work long after the time when she was physically capable of entering upon married life. In the case of males marriage is often delayed by inability to pay the *pan* or bride-price for a suitable maiden, which runs rather high among respectable Kaibarttas, and may amount to as much as Rs. 200 or Rs. 300. Polygamy is permitted in this sense and to the extent in which it is permitted to orthodox Hindus; but in practice it is very rarely resorted to. Widows may not marry a second husband. Divorce is permitted on the ground of adultery, but divorced wives are not allowed to marry again.

"The Kaibarttas of Orissa depart in certain material points from the orthodox standard in matters concerning marriage. Infant-marriage is allowed to be the more excellent way, and most parents endeavour to follow it; but no disgrace attaches to the marriage of a girl after puberty. The widow is allowed to marry again, and is expected to marry her late husband's younger brother. The ceremony is a simple one. a feast is given to the members of the caste, and a bracelet is put on the right wrist of the bride. Divorce may be effected by a *chhadapatra* or letter of divorce written in the presence of the headman and a few of the leading members of the caste. Divorced wives are allowed to marry again.

"In connection with the recognition of widow-marriage in Orissa, I may mention the tradition current in the Contai subdivision of Midnapur that in the Amli year 1223 a famine occurred in those parts and some widows took to themselves second husbands. The chief Kaibartta Raja is said to have put a stop to the practice. Can we argue from this that widow-marriage, still current among the Kaibarttas of Orissa, survived among the Kaibrattas of Bengal down to 1223?" adds Mr. Risley. The marriage customs are practised among the Kaibarttas.

Bridegroom should be Taller than Bride

Sir H. Risley records, "The Kamars of Bengal marry their daughters as infants, between the ages of five and ten years. The usual maximum limit of age in Behar is twelve for a girl and fifteen for a boy; but it is essential that the bridegroom should be taller than the bride, and this point is ascertained by actual measurement. In Bengal, however, the marriage of a son is sometimes delayed till he is twenty-five or so by reason of the necessity of paying a *pan* or bride-price in order to obtain a wife. Among the Kamars of Chota Nagpur adult marriage still holds its ground even for girls, though it is considered more proper for them to be married before attaining puberty. The Kamars of Midnapur, though regarding infant-marriage as essential, do not permit consummation to take place immediately after the ceremony, but keep their girls at home until they have reached puberty and may fairly be deemed *apta viro*. Another custom prevalent in that district is *kaparparana*, or presenting a piece of cloth and certain spices to the bride elect before the marriage. The acceptance of this cloth is held finally to bind the bride's family to keep faith with the bridegroom, so that if the girl were afterwards given to another man her father would run the risk of being turned out of the caste. In Bengal the marriage ceremony is of the standard type, while in Behar it closely resembles that described in the article on the Kewat caste. One curious practice, known as *ghaskati*, or cutting grass, is peculiar to Kamars. On the day after the marriage the wedded pair, followed by a number of women singing, are taken outside the house, and the bridegroom is given a sickle, with which he cuts a handful of grass. After this a maid-servant or one of the female members of the bride's household plants a stick in the ground at some distance off, and the bridegroom and his brother-in-law race for the stick, which the winner pulls up. In this contest it is an understood thing that the bridegroom must be allowed to win, and if the bride's brother seems to be getting the best of it he is headed back by the bridegroom's friends, so as to let the latter come in first. Polygamy is permitted in Bengal and Chota Nagpur, but is strongly disapproved of in Behar, where the rule is that a man may only take a second wife in the event of the first being barren or suffering from an incurable disease. Widow-marriage is forbidden in Bengal and Behar, but is still practised in Chota Nagpur by the Magahiya Kamars, who probably left Behar before the Kamars of that province had taken to orthodox ways. Divorce is recognised only in Singbhum and the Santal Parganas, where a *sal* leaf is torn in two before the panchayat as a symbol of separation, and divorced wives are allowed to marry again. In other districts a faithless wife is turned out of the caste, and either becomes a regular prostitute or joins some religious sect of dubious morality. Such measures, however, are only resorted to in extreme cases, and intrigues within the caste are usually condoned by the husband.

"The majority of the Kamars in Bengal are Vaishnavas, but a few follow the Sakta ritual. Their favourite deity is Viswakarma, who is worshipped on the last day of Bhadra with offerings of sweetmeats, parched rice, fruits, molasses, flowers, sandal-wood paste, Ganges water, cloth, silver ornaments, etc. At the same time they worship the hammer, anvil, and other tools used in their handicraft. In Behar they reverence as minor gods Hanuman. Bandi, Goraiya, Kali, Jawala Mukhi, Jalpa, Bhairab, and two Mahomedan saints—Miran or Shaikh Sadu and Saiyad. Cocks, *khir*, and *puri* are offered to the latter, and afterwards given away to poor Mahomedans. In Bengal the women perform the Ananta, Savitri, Sasthi, and Panchami *bratas*, and Nistarini, and

Mangal Chandi are worshipped by the women and children with offerings of sweetmeats, milk, fruit, etc. For the service of the greater gods and in the performance of *bratas* the caste employ Brahmans, who are received on equal terms by other members of the sacred order."

The marriage customs, rites and ritual are practised by the Kamar community.

Courtship Permitted in the Community

"A man may not marry a woman of his own *thar* or section, nor of the section to which his mother belonged before her marriage. Girls marry after they are grown up, and courtship is more or less recognised. Sexual intercourse before marriage is said not to be tolerated; but in fact the morals of the Kami girls are not stricter than those of the young women of other castes in the hills. The marriage ceremony appears to have been borrowed from the Hindu system. It takes place at night. The bride and bridegroom stand facing each other on either side of an earthen vessel containing what is supposed to be a sacred fire. Round this they walk seven times, keeping the fire always on the right hand. The bride then takes her stand by the bridegroom and places her hands on his, while her parents, who conduct the ceremony, lay on the joined hands of the couple some *kusa* grass, some leaves of the bel and *tulsi*, and a piece of copper, muttering at the same time some gibberish which purports to be Sanskrit sacred texts. The rite is completed by the bridegroom smearing some red lead on the bride's forehead and the parting of her hair and putting a necklace (*poti*) of white beads round her neck." Records Sir Risley.

He adds further, "Polygamy is permitted, and in theory at least a man may have as many wives as he can afford to maintain. Poverty, however, and the great liberty which is accorded to women in the hills, tend in practice to limit the number to two. Polyandry is unknown. A widow may marry again, and is restricted by no rules in her choice of a second husband, except that she may not marry her late husband's elder brother or elder cousin, and must observe the prohibited degrees which were binding on her before she married. The ceremony is of a simpler character than at the marriage of a virgin. No fire is kindled, nor are texts recited: the bridegroom merely puts vermilion on the bride's forehead and gives her a necklace, the proceedings being completed by a feast, at which the relations of both parties are present.

"The utmost license of divorce prevails. A husband can get rid of his wife whenever he pleases by going through the symbolic form of cutting in two a kind of fruit (*pang-ro*) with a bit of wood called *sinko*. In reference to this ceremony, which prevails among several other castes, divorce is commonly spoken of in the hills as *sinko-pangro*. Wives are supposed to have somewhat less extensive powers of divorce, and the theory is that they can only divorce their husbands on the ground of positive ill-treatment. In fact, however, a woman who is tired of her husband goes off with any man who will take her, and by the custom of the caste the husband has only the right to demand from his rival the bride-price originally paid for the woman. Divorced wives marry again by the same ceremony that is used at the marriage of a widow.

"Kamis admit into their caste members of any caste higher in rank than their own. No ceremony is performed on such occasions, and the consent of the panchayat of the caste is all that is required to confer the privilege of membership. Instances of such changes of caste taking place do not, however, very frequently occur. The usual cause is that a man of a higher caste has taken a Kami girl as a mistress, and has got into trouble with his own people for eating with a woman of lower rank.

"The caste know nothing of Hindu law, and profess to be guided in matters of inheritance and succession by a tribal custom of their own. This, however, presents no features of special interest. Sons take equal shares in the property. Failing sons, brothers and brothers' sons inherit. If no male relatives survive, daughters and daughters' sons succeed.

"Kamis pose as orthodox Hindus, worshipping Kali and regarding Viswakarma as their tutelary deity."

Free Courtship Permitted

Sir Rilsey writes, "Lepcha girls usually marry between the ages of sixteen and eighteen. Men marry later owing to the difficulty of getting together the bride-price, which ranges from Rs. 40 to Rs. 100 according to the rank of the parties. The freest courtship is permitted, and sexual license before marriage is tolerated. If a girl becomes pregnant, the man is expected either to marry her or to pay some compensation to her parents for the reduction in value which she has undergone. Formal proposals of marriage are usually made to the bride's parents by *pibus* or go-betweens acting on behalf of the lover. If the proposal is accepted, the *pibus* go to the bride's house with Rs. 5 as earnest-money, and ten seers of *marua* beer and a Tibetan scarf. An auspicious day for the marriage is then fixed by the Lamas. The ceremony, performed first at the bride's and then at the bridegroom's house, is of a very simple character. Bride and bridegroom sit side by side on a carpet, and the Lama ties a silk scarf round the neck of each and then changes the scarves, so that the bride wears the bridegroom's and *vice versa.* Rice is sprinkled over their heads, they eat together, and drink *marua* beer out of the same cup. The proceedings end with a feast. The married couple spend three days in the husband's house, and then usually go on a month's visit to the bride's parents.

"When a man is too poor to pay the bride-price, he is often allowed to marry, as it were, on credit; but the bride does not leave her father's house, and the husband goes to live with her and work for his father-in-law until the full amount has been made up.

"Polyandry, though comparatively rare, is not entirely unknown among the Lepchas. As might be expected, the Tibetan form of the custom is followed, and the younger brothers share the favours of the eldest brother's wife. Polygamy is permitted, but is not practised on a large scale.

"A widow may marry again, and is subject to no express restrictions in her choice of a second husband. It is considered, however, proper for her to marry her late husband's younger brother, and if she marries an outsider, this brother-in-law usually keeps the children and in any case may claim repayment of the bride-price. The full ceremony may be employed at the marriage of a widow, but the parties usually content themselves with the mere announcement by a Lama that they have become man and wife.

"If a married couple cannot agree, arbitrators (*pibus*) are appointed to attempt to adjust their differences. If they fail after two or three attempts, a formal divorce is effected with the concurrence of the Lama who married the pair. The wife returns to her father's house, and her husband pays some compensation to her parents. When a woman is taken in adultery, a panchayat considers the case and determines the amount of fine (*gysh*) to be paid to her husband by the paramour. The amount of the fine is not fixed by custom, nor does it bear any stated proportion to the bride-price. Where adultery is proved, the husband has a right to divorce his wife without paying comensation to her parents, and to take away her ornaments. Physical chastisement is never inflicted, nor is the right of divorce invariably exercised. Divorced wives may marry again by the same ceremony as is in use at the marriage of a virgin." The custom is practised by the Buddhist tribe of Lepchas in West Bengal as well as in Sikkim.

Girls Married to Men of their Choice

"A Kandh may not marry a woman of his own *gochi,* even though she belong to a different *klambu* from himself. Both *gochi* and *klambu* go by the father's side, and I can find no traces of female kinship having ever been recognised by the Kandhs. The use of the division into *klambus* can best be illustrated by an actual example. Let us suppose that a man of the Besringia *gochi* and Besera *klambu* marries a woman of the Kutrengia *gochi* and Bisunga *klambu.* Their son would belong to the same *gochi* and *klambu* as his father, and would be precluded from marrying a woman of the *klambu* to which his mother belonged, but might marry into any of the other four *klambus* of the Kutrengia *gochi.* This prohibition holds good for three generations in the descending line, and many Kandhs prefer to extend it to the fourth. They take, in fact, as Mr. Taylor pertinently remarks, much the same view of it as many Europeans take of inter-marriage between first cousins. It will be seen from this that the rule forbidding marriage within the mother's *klambu* serves for the Kandhs much the same purpose as is ordinarily effected by the standard formula for reckoning prohibited degrees. This formula is unknown to the Kandhs of the Kandhmals, and their arrangements for guarding against consanguineous marriages consist solely of the simple rules regarding the *gochi* and the *klambu* which have been explained above. A similar system exists among the Santals, but the septs and sub-septs are not *localised* as they are among the Kandhs, and the prohibition of marriage within the mother's sub-sept is not so stringently enforced." Writes Sir Risley in the Tribes and Castes of Bengal.

He further adds, "Kandh girls are usually married when of full age in most cases to men of their own choice, and after a regular process of courtship considerable license is allowed to the young men and maidens of the tribe, and sexual intercourse before marriage is tacitly recognised. Infidelity after marriage is said to be rare; the adulterer if found out atones for his fault by paying an indemnity to the husband. Until this has been done, the woman is excluded from social intercourse with her neighbours. Widows and divorced wives may marry again. A bride-price is paid to the father. The widow's choice of a second husband is in theory unfettered; but it is considered the right thing for her to marry her late husband's younger brother. In the event of her marrying an outsider, she retains the charge of her children until the girls attain puberty and the boys are old enough to hold the plough. In any case she has no rights over her late husband's property, which goes to his children, or failing them to his brother.

"When a Kandh youth is of an age to marry, his parents find out who he has fallen in love with, and 'send a go-between, usually a man of the Pan caste, to ascertain the views of the girl's parents, and to approach the delicate question of the price to be paid for the bride. If these preliminary negotiations are successful, a deputation of the boy's relations go soon afterwards to the girl's house, and a general drinking bout is held, at which the amount of the bride-price is definitely fixed. The price is reckoned in *pots* or lives, a term of somewhat vague connotation, which includes buffaloes cows, goats, brass plates and cooking vessels, ornaments and things in general. Its amount varies with the wealth of the bride's father, to whom it is paid. It may extend to as many as forty *pots*, and the payment may be spread over two or three years. Soon after the relations have reported the result of their negotiations, the bridegroom pays a visit to his future father-in-law's house, bringing with him the first instalment of the bride-price. The formal betrothal is then effected by the bridegroom putting a necklace round the girl's neck while she pours oil over his head.

"On the day before the wedding the bridegroom and his male relations go in procession to the bride's house, where they spend that evening and the next morning in feasting. The essential and binding portion of the marriage ceremony, in which the bride's father officiates as priest, is said to consist of his taking the right hands of the couple and spitting on the palm of each. The effect of this in the case of the bride is to remove her from her original sept, and to preclude her from re-entering her father's. The married couple are carried off of the backs of the bridegroom's friends to his house, where the marriage is consummated. On the next day a feast is made, and the girl sits on a couch surrounded by the women of the village and pretends to weep. After this has gone on for some time she and her husband are seized by his friends and carried about in triumph. A short dance follows, and both are replaced on the couch. Thou the bride's male relations take hold of the bride and run away with her, hotly pursued by the girls of the village who pummel the men soundly, recapture the bride, and bring her back to her husband. After this the bride's relations return to their own village. On the day after the marriage the bride and bridegroom, taking with them an old man to officiate as priest, go a little way outside the village and worship Dharma Pennu with offerings of fowls, eggs, rice and strong drink in order to secure a happy life and male offspring. A high standard of conjugal fidelity is observed among the Kandhs, and husbands usually treat their wives kindly. Polygamy as a practice is unknown. If a woman proves barren, the husband may take a second wife; but in such cases the two wives have separate houses and enjoy equal privileges." The customs pertain to the Kandh tribals in the eastern region of India.

The septs of the three sub-tribes are as Lewin has pointed out, appear to be the names of the rivers on which the original settlements of the sept were situated. The Maghs observe the simple rule that a man may not marry a woman of his own sept, supplemented by a table of prohibited degrees, which does not differ materially from that arrived at by the standard formula already often referred to. Sir Risley records, "In applying these prohibitions, however, there seems to be some laxity where descent is traced through females, for I am informed that a man may marry the daughters of his father's sister and of his mother's brother—a connexion which would not ordinarily be allowed.

"The Maramagri marry their daughters either as infants or as adults, and there is some tendency among them to regard the former usage as more respectable from the social point of view. Marmas and Thongchas adhere to the more primitive custom of adult-marriage, and more or less expressly tolerate sexual intercourse as one of the necessary incidents of pre-matrimonial courtship. Their marriage ceremony, says Lewin, *Hill Tracts of Chittagon*, p. 49. 'is distinctive and uncommon. On a young man attaining a marriageable age, that is, about 17 to 18, his parents look about for some young girl who would be a good wife to him unless, as is more often the case, he has fixed upon a partner for himself. Having determined upon a suitable match, a male relative of the family is sent off to the girl's parents to arrange matters. On arriving at their village he proceeds to the house, and before going up the house ladder he gives the usual salutation, with both hands joined and raised to the forehead. '*Ogatsa*,' he says, 'a boat has come to your landing place; will you bind it or loose it?' A favourable response is given, and he then goes up into the house. On seating himself he asks, 'Are the supports of the house firm ?' If the answer is, 'They are firm,' it is favourable, and matters may then be more fully entered into. The affair is taken into consideration, and he returns to his own village to report good progress to the bridegroom's parent, and to request them to fix a day for taking the omens. On the appointed day the parents meet, the young people being supposed to know nothing of all this. A fowl is killed by the fathers, its tongue taken out, and, according to certain marks thereon, the matter is pronounced good or bad. The bridegroom's parents sleep for the night at the house of the intended bride, and all parties look anxiously for dreams by which to foretell the happiness or the reverse of the union. On going away, should everything be propitious, their intended daughter kneels at their feet for a blessing, and they present her with a new petticoat and a silver ring. Learned persons are then called in, who, by consulting the stars and easting the nativity of the parties, determine a favourable day and hour when the ceremony shall be undertaken. Meantime the parents on both sides prepare pigs and spirits, rice and spices, unlimited, for the marriage feast. They also send round to all their kith and kin a fowl and a letter giving notice of the intended marriage; in some places a pice or copper coin is substituted for the fowl. On the auspicious day, and at the hour appointed, the bridegroom and all his relatives set out for the bride's house, dressed in the gayest colours, both men and women, with drums beating before them. On arriving at the entrance of the village the female relatives of the bride bar the approach with a bamboo. Across this barrier the bridegroom has to drink a loving cup of fraternity, generally spirits. Should the females on the bride's side muster strong, the road will probably be barred five or six times before the entry into the village is fairly made. The bridegroom, however, does not drink all that is given him, but after taking the liquor in his mouth he is allowed to eject it again upon the ground.

"In the village, on some open turfy spot, a number of bamboo booths have been erected, adorned with flowers and green boughs, and filled with materials for feasting. Here also sit an opposition party of drummers, and mighty is the row as the bridegroom's party defiles on to this spot. A separate and specially beautified booth has been erected for the young lover and his parents, and here they sit in state and receive visits from all the village. The bride in like manner, surrounded by her near relatives, sits in her father's house. The boys of the village, irrepressible as is the wont of that species, make raids upon both parties, for the purpose of chaffing and getting alternate feasts of comestibles. They also organize an amateur band of music, and serenade the bride towards evening with fiddles and flutes. Of course, all the girls of the village are congregated at the bride's father's house, and, as license and riot are the order of the day, the fun here grows fast and furious. Towards nightfall the bridegroom ascends to his bride's house amid a tempest of cheers and a hailstorm of drums. After this outburst a temporary bill ensues to permit of the ceremony being performed. The bride is brought forth from an inner chamber in the arms of the women. On the floor of the house are placed water in jars, rice, and mango leaves. Round there a new-spun cotton-thread is wound and carried again round the two contracting parties as they stand opposite to each other. The 'poongyee,' or priest, now comes forward; he recites some prayers in a language that is not understood even by himself (probably Pali), and then taking cooked rice, a handful in each hand, he crosses and recrosses his arms, giving seven alternate mouthfuls to the bride and bridegroom; after this he takes their hands and crooks the little finger of the bridegroom's right hand into the little finger of the bride's left. The ceremony is then concluded by more unintelligible mutterings. The bridegroom now takes the bride by the hand, and together they make the circuit of the room, saluting lowly the elder relatives of both families. They then sit down—the bride to the left of her husband, and their clothes are tied together. The wedding guests then come forward and place at their feet, each according to his or her means, some presents of clothes or household furniture. After this a saturnalia ensues, of dancing, drinking, fighting, and love-making. The bride and bridegroom are expected to sit up all night. I should add that the happy man does not consummate his marriage until he and his wife (sleeping apart) have for seven days eaten together seven times a day."

Sir Risley adds, "The bride-price among Thongchas and Marmas is said to be about Rs. 30. With the Maramngris, who as a class are wealthier, the average amount paid for a wife is Rs. 60, which may rise to Rs. 80 if the bridegroom is of inferior status, as, for example, in the event of a Bhuiya Magh marrying the daughter of a Bajbansi Magh. The ceremony in use among the Maramagris is of the same general character as that described above, the essential portion being the crooking together of the little fingers of the bridegroom's left hand and the bride's right, while the priest pours water over the hands thus joined. This is followed by *sindurdan* or smearing vermilion on the bride's forehead—a form which appears to have been borrowed from the Hindus. The Marma ritual is still more like that of the Thongchas, and does not include *sindurdan.* In the course of the wedding the bride and bridegroom eat some curry and rice from the same dish, and what they leave is kept in a covered earthen vessel for seven days, during which time the married couple may not leave the village or cross running water. On the eighth the vessel is opened, and if maggots are found in the food it is deemed an excellent omen, showing that the marriage will be a fruitful one.

"Polygamy is recognised: a man may have as many wives as he can afford to maintain. The first wife, however, is regarded as the highest in rank, and takes precedence of all subsequent wives, who are expected to treat her with special consideration.

"In all the sub-tribes widows are allowed to marry again, and are fettered by no restrictions in their choice of a second husband. No special ritual is ordained for this purpose, and as a rule the parties simply go and live together as man and wife. Divorce is permitted with the sanction of the tribal panchayat, on the ground of adultery or inability to live happily together. A written agreement is usually drawn up, and sometimes, when the authority of the panchayat is deemed insufficient, this 'writing of divorcement' is laid before the Magistrate of the district. Among the Thongchas the parties give one another flowers, and after bathing go off in different directions, exchanging all kinds of abusive epithets. Divorced wives may marry again by the ritual in use for the remarriage of widows.

"All Maghs are Buddhists of the Southern school, and regard the northern Buddhists of Tibet as wholly unorthodox. The wilder sections of the Thongchas, however, retain some vestiges of an earlier animistic faith, which bids them sacrifice cattle, gouts, and swine, and make offerings of rice, fruits, and flowers to the spirits of hill and river. Among the Maramagris, on the other hand, the tendency is to follow after modern Hinduism, particularly in its Tantric developments, and to add the gross worship of Siva and Durga to the simple observances prescribed by their own communion. It thus comes to pass that while the Buddhist *Phungyis* or *Raolis* are the recognised priest of all the tribes, considerable respect is shown to Brahimans, who are frequently employed to determine auspicious days for particular actions, and to assist in the worship of the Hindu gods. Among the Thongchas old women often devote themselves to the service of religion, and although not charged with special ceremonial functions, are regarded as in some sense priestesses, and are called by the distinctive name *lerdama.*" The customs are practised among the Buddhist Maghs in the eastern region.

Custom of Eloping with Suitors

"Among the Agnia-Mech the usual age for marriage is twelve years for females and sixteen for males, though here, as elsewhere, the influence of Hinduism shows itself in the desire on the part of well-to-do people to get their daughters married at a still earlier age. For the most part, however, the earlier usage of free courtship still holds its ground, and the consent of the parents is sought only after the young people have arranged matters between themselves. Even then, if objections are raised, the girl often solves the difficulty by going off with her lover and thus compelling her parents to take steps to get her married. The same system prevails among the Jati-Mech, but with them the age for marriage ranges from sixteen to twenty for both males and females, and it is not uncommon to find a woman married to a man younger than herself. The bride-price, called *mothom theka* by Agnia and *chumna* or *sodha* by the Jati-Mech, is supposed to be fixed with preference to the beauty and accomplishments, and may rise in the Agnia sub-tribe as high as Rs. 120 or even more. Among the Jati-Mech it is supposed to be fixed at Rs. 63, but this amount may be, and usually is, reduced by haggling.

"In both sub-tribes the marriage ceremony is exceedingly simple. Among the Agnia-Mech the essential and binding portion of the rite is the formal washing of the bride's feet in the presence of the friends and relatives of both parties with water poured from a bamboo water-vessel *(chunga).* This being done, she enters a room where the bridegroom is awaiting her, and consummation is supposed to take place at once. When she comes out a cock and a hen are sacrificed and two betel leaves and areca nuts offered to Siva, the latter articles being afterwards eaten by the wedded pair. Feasting then commences by the bride serving first the bridegroom, aud after him the other guests, with meat and boiled rice. The Jati-Mech do not wash the bride's feet, but make the pair exchange betel leaves and areca nuts. This is held to be the essential rite, and is followed by the sacrifice of a cook and hen to Siva. Some of my correspondents distinguish three modes or forms of marriage: thus—(1) the ordinary marriage, in which the parents' consent is obtained before the girl goes to her husband; (2) the *dakua* marriage, in which the bride elopes or is carried off, and may be reclaimed by her parents if the bride-price is not paid; (3) the *ghar sundi* marriage, when a girl takes a fancy to a man, goes to his house of her own accord, and sits as a suppliant by the symbol of the *ghar-devi,* which stands in the corner of the chief room. In such cases, after refusing the girl as a matters, of form, the man is bound ultimately to yield to her importunity. Clearly, however, these are not so much forms of marriage us modes of proposing marriage—Sir Risley.

"A widow may marry again, but if she has children it is deemed more respectable for her to live as a widow with her late husband's relatives, to whom in any case her children belong. If, however, she determines to contract a second marriage, she may not marry any relative, whether elder or younger, of her deceased, husband, but must return to her parents' house and get married from there by an informal ceremony called *nika,* in which the bridegroom makes with his little finger a single spot of vermilion on the bride's forehead. Fowls are sacrificed as in the regular form, but the bride's feet are not washed, nor does she exchange betel leaves and areca nuts with the bridegroom. The bride-price for a woman marrying a second time is reduced to one-half of the original amount, and if she marries a third time to one-fourth. In the presumably rare case of a woman marrying for the fourth time, no bride-price at all is paid. A remarried widow is deemed to be socially the inferior of a woman married as a virgin, and is not entitled to serve boiled rice to the guests assembled on any public or ceremonial occasion. Divorce may be effected, with the sanction of the panchayat, at the wish of the parties or on the ground of the wife's adultery. In the latter case the seducer is liable to repay the bride-price to the injured husband, and cannot marry the woman until he has done so. Divorced wives can only be remarried by the curtained ceremony in use at the latter. Their children also belong to the father. It would seem at first sight that the unrestricted courtship permitted by the Mech can hardly promote a high standard of female chastity, and in fact sexual intercourse before marriage, though not expressly recognised, is virtually tolerated, it being understood that if a girl becomes pregnant her lover will at once come forward and marry her. Regarding married women, however, a different order of ideas prevails, and as soon as a girl has finally pitched upon a husband, she is required to be strictly faithful to him. A curious usage, to which parallels may be found in European folklore, deserves notice in this connection. In the courtyard of every Mech house a sij plant (*Euphorbia Indica*) is carefully tended as the abode of the god Siva and as the emblem of conjugal fidelity. Should the leaves of the plant wither, this is supposed to show that something is wrong with one of the women of the household. Rice is deposited under the tree, and on the next day a panchayat is called, before which all the women are summoned and a handful of rice is given to each to chew. She who fails to masticate her portion is held guilty of unchastity, and if married is at once turned out of the house. If it is an unmarried girl who breaks down in the chewing ordeal, she is called upon to disclose the name of her paramour, so that arrangements may be made to get her married at once.

"The religion of the Mech, like that of the Dhimal, is still in an early stage of transition from animism to Hinduism. They describe themselves as Hindus of the Saiva sect, and worship Siva under the name of Batho, and his consort Kali as Bali Khungri. To the former the Agnia-Mech sacrifice buffaloes, goats, and pigeons; while his wife has to put up with the less respectable offerings of pigs, fowls, and goats, which the Jati-Mech offer indifferently to either. The Jati-Mech also reverence as a household goddess (*ghar-devi*), a nameless personge, supposed to be the mother of Siva, who is represented by a lump of sun-dried clay set in the corner of the chief room. Pigs, fowls, plantains and parched rice are offered to her on any day in the week except Sunday, Tuesday, or Wednesday. Among their other deities may be mentioned Tsimising, Tista Burhi (Buchanan's 'old lady of the Tista'), Mahesh Thakur, Sonnisi and Mabakal. They have no Brahmans, and priests (*dhami* or *ojha*) chosen from among the tribe to serve them for religious and ceremonial purposes." The customs are observed among the Mech people in the region.

Free Courtship Allowed

"Free courtship is allowed, and girls are married, when of full age, to men of their own choice. Sexual intercourse before marriage is not recognised in theory, but if an unmarried girl becomes pregnant a sacrifice is offered to atone for the indiscretion, and arrangements are made to get her married without delay." Records Sir Risley in his ethnographic account.

He adds further, "Marriage brokers (*sithu*) are employed to conduct the preliminary negotiations, and to settle the difficult question of the bride-price. When this has been satisfactorily arranged, an auspicious day is fixed, when the bridegroom goes with his friends to the bride's house, taking with him a goat to furnish forth the wedding feast, and the bride-price, a portion of which is sometimes paid before-hand through the *sithu*. The parties are made to sit opposite each other, the bridegroom facing east and the bride west, while her girl friends comb and oil her hair. Then the father take the bride by the hand and gives her to the bridegroom, pointing out that she is not halt, maimed or blind, and enjoining him to treat her kindly. This done, the *sithu* takes the bridegroom's right hand, dips the little finger in *sindur*, and makes five dots with it on the girl's fore-head afterwards using her finger to perform the same office for the bridegroom. Guns are fired to mark the completion of this essential rite, and the married couple then eat together out of the same dish in symbol of their union. The proceedings are concluded by a feast.

"Divorce is permitted with the sanction of the leading men of the village. If the husband demands a divorce on the ground that his wife is barren, that she has committed adultery, or that she is incurably lazy, he is entitled to claim a refund of the bride-price which he paid for her in the first instance. He forfeits this right if the reasons which he gives are deemed to be frivolous and insufficient. If the wife claims a divorce on whatever grounds, her family must refund the bride-price. The ritual observed consists in tearing a *sal* leaf of breaking small branch or a piece of string in token of separation and pouring a vessel of water over the woman's head. Divorced women may marry again." The custom is practised in the Male Community.

Sexual Licence Among Girls Tolerated

Sir Herbert Risley records, "Girls are married after they attain maturity, and sexual license before marriage is tolerated on the understanding that if a girl becomes pregnant, the father of her child shall at once be called upon to marry her. The marriage ceremony is of the Hindu type, *sindurdan,* or the smearing of vermilion on the bride's forehead, being its binding portion. Brahmans usually officiate, but this is not essential. A man may marry two or three wives, the only limit in practice being his ability to maintain them. A widow may not marry again by the standard ritual *(byah)* appointed for the wedding of a spinster, but a man may take her to live with him, and she is counted as his wife. Her children by her second husband are considered legitimate; they rank as Mangars (instead of belonging to a special category like the offspring of Brahman widows in Nepal), and they share in their father's property on equal terms with the children of a wife married in the regular form. Moreover, if any one runs away with a widow, he has to pay damages to the man she is living with just as if she were his regular wife. In Nepal husbands are entitled to wreak summary vengeance on the seducers of their wives. An adulterer taken in the act is killed offhand, and the faithless wife has her nose cut off. In such cases the question of divorce clearly does not arise. But in British territory, and I believe frequently in Nepal itself, disagreements of this sort are settled without resort to bloodshed. The wife goes off with her paramour, and the husband claims from the latter as damages the amount of the bride-price which he paid for the woman in the first instance. The panchayat enforces his claim, and justice is hold to have been satisfied.

"The religion of the Mangars may best be described as lax Hinduism tempered by survivals of an earlier animistic cult. Satya Narain is one of their favourite deities. Sansari and Aitabareh are also worshipped with offerings of goats, fowls and pigeons. Upadhya Brahmins assist at the cult of Satya Narain and of the recognised Hindu gods; but Sansari and Aitabareh are worshipped by the heads of households without the assistance priests. Brahmans are not held to be degraded by serving as priests in Mangar families."

The customs, rites and rituals are related to the Manger Community.

Pre-marital Licence Recognised

Sir Risley records, "A Munda may not marry a woman of his own sept. The sept-name goes by the father's side, and inter-marriage with persons nearly related through the mother is guarded against by reckoning prohibited degrees in the manner common in Behar. Adult marriage is still in fashion, and sexual intercourse before marriage is tacitly recognised, but in all respectable families matches are made by the parents, and the parties themselves have very little to say in the matter. The bride-price varies from Rs. 4 to Rs. 20. *Sindurdan*, or the smearing of vermilion on the bride's forehead by the bridebroom and on the bridegroom's forehead by the bride, is the essential and binding portion. The practice described by Colonel Dalton of marrying the bride to a *mahua* tree and the bridegroom to a mango seems now to have been abandoned. Traces still survive among the Mundas of a form of marriage, resembling the Santali *nir bolok*. It is called *dhuko era*, meaning a bride who has entered the household of her own accord. The children of a woman thus married seem to have an inferior status in respect of their rights to inherit the landed property of their father. The late Babu Rakhal Das Haldar, Manager of the estate of the Maharaja of Chota Nagpur, gave me an illustration of this fact. Some years ago the *munda* or headman of one of the villages of the Government estate of Barkagarh died, leaving an only son by a *dhuko era* wife, and a question was raised as to the latter's right to succeed. Under Colonel Dalton's orders, a number of headmen of villages were called together, and their opinions were taken. No decided results, however, could be arrived at. Some thought the son should get the whole property. Others proposed to exclude him altogether, and a third party considered him entitled to maintenance. Eventually the question was compromised by admitting the son's right to one-fourth of the land and the whole of the personal property. The case is a curious comment on the uncertainty of tribal custom. Widows may marry again by the ritual known as *sagai*, in which *sindurdan* is performed with the left hand. Divorce is allowed at the instance of either party, and divorced women are permitted to marry again. In cases of adultery the seducer is required to pay to the husband the full amount of the bride-price." The marriage custom and rites are pertinent to the Munda tribals.

Pre-marital Sexual Liaison Tolerated

"On the north of the Ganges, Tirhutia, Musahars are said to practise infant-marriage; while in Shahabad girls are usually not married until they have passed the age of puberty, and sexual intercourse before marriage is said to be tolerated. A bride-price of Rs. 2 is paid for a virgin, but the tender is reduced to half if there are reasons to doubt her integrity. The marriage ceremony is based on the Hindu model, and does not differ materially from that in vogue among other low castes in Behar. The well-known formula—

Ganga ka pani samundar ki sank

Bar Kanya jag jag anand

(May Ganges water and sea-shell betide

Enduring bliss to bridegroom and to bride)

is recited by one of the elders present, and water and rice are sprinkled on the bridegroom's head. The bride is then lifted by her mother, and the bridegroom marks her forehead five times with vermilion. Consummation follows at once, and the married couple usually leave for the bridegroom's house next day." Writes Sir Risley.

He adds further, "Polygamy is said to be unknown. The remarriage of widows by the *sagai* form is permitted, and is not feltered by the common condition requiring the widow to marry her late husband's younger brother. Divorce is allowed, with the sanction of the caste panchayat, for infidelity on the part of the wife. The husband breaks in two a piece of dried grass (*khar*) in the presence of the panchayat, and formally renounces his wife by saying that in future he will look upon her as his mother. Divorced women may marry again by the ritual appointed in the case of widows." The marriage customs are observed by community of Mushahars.

Field-mice —The Best Present by Suitors

In 1872, when Colonel Dalton published his account of the Oraons, infant-marriage is said to have been entirely unknown among the tribe. A few of the wealthier men, who affect to imitate Hindu customs, had taken to this practice, and marry their daughters before they have attained puberty. Sir Risley writes, "Among the mass of the people however, girls marry after they are grown up, and the freest courtship prevails at dances, festivals, and social gatherings of various kinds. Young men woo their sweethearts with offerings of flowers for the hair and presents of giled field-mice, 'which the Oraons declare to be the most delicate of food." Sexual intercourse before marriage is tacitly recognised, and is so generally practised that in the opinon of the best observers on Oraon girl is a virgin at the time of her marriage. To call this state of things immoral is to apply a modern conception to primitive habits of life. Within the tribe indeed the idea of sexual morality seems hardly to exist, and the unmarried Oraons are not far removed from the condition of modified promiscuity which prevails among many of the Australian tribes. Provided that the exogamous circle defined by the totem is respected, an unmarried woman may bestow her favours on whom she will. If, however, she becomes pregnant, arrangements are made to get her married without delay, and she is then expected to lead a virtuous life. Prostitution is unknown. Intrigues beyond the limits of the tribe are uncommon, and are punished by summary expulsion."

Colonel E.T. Dalton gives the following account of the Oraon marriage custom and ceremony: "When a young man makes up his mind to marry, his parents or guardians go through a form of selection for him; but it is always a girl that he has already selected for himself, and between whom and him there is a perfect understanding. The parents, however, have to arrange all preliminaries, including the price of the damsel, which is sometimes as low as Rs. 4 (8s.) In the visits that are inter-changed by the negotiators, omens are carefully observed by the Oraons, as by the Mundas, and there are, consequently, similar difficulties to overcome; but when all is settled, the bridegroom proceeds with a large party of his friends, male female, to the bride's house. Most of the males have warlike weapons, real or sham, and as they approach the village of the bride's family the young men from thence emerge, also armed, as if to repel the invasion, and a mimic fight ensues, which, like a dissolving view, blends pleasantly into a dance. In this the bride and bridegroom join, each riding on the hips of one of their friends. A bower is constructed in front of the residence of the bride's father, into which the bride and bridegroom are carried by women, and made to stand on a curry-stone, under which is placed a sheaf of corn, resting on a plough yoke. Here the mystery of the *sindurdan* is performed; but the operation is carefully screened from view, first by cloths thrown over the young couple, secondly by a circle of their male friends, some of whom hold up a screen cloth, while others keep guard with weapons upraised and look very fierce, as if they had been told off to cut down intruders, and were quite prepared to do so. In Oraon marriages the bridegroom stands on the curry-stone behind the bride, but in order that this may not be deemed a concession to the female, his toes are so placed as to tread on her heels. The old women under the cloth are very particular about this, as if they were specially interested in providing that the heel of the woman should be properly bruised. Thus poised the map stretches over the girl's head and daubs her forehead and crown with the red powder *sindur;* and if the girl is allowed to return the compliment (it is a controverted point whether she should do so or not), she performs the ceremony without turning her head, reaching back over her own shoulder and just touching his brow. When this is accomplished, a gun is fired; and then, by some arrangement, vessels full of water, placed over the bower, are capsized, and the young couple and those who stand near them receive a drenching shower-bath. They now retire into an apartment prepared for them, ostensibly to change their clothes, but they do not emerge for some time, and when they appear they are saluted as man and wife. Dancing is kept up during their retirement, one of the performers executing a *pas seul* with a basket on her head, which is said to contain the trousseau. The Oraons have no prescribed wedding garments. They do not follow the Hindu custom of using saffron-coloured robes on such occasions. The bride is attired in ordinary habiliments, and no special pains are taken to make her lovely for the occasion. The bridegroom is better dressed than usual. He wears a long coat and a turban. Nor have the Oraons any special days or seasons for marriages. The ceremony may take place in any month of the year, but, with all natives, the hot, dry months are generally selected if possible. There is then not much work on hand; granaries are full, and they prefer those months for marching and camping out."

Sir Risley adds, "Polygamy is permitted, and in theory at least there is no limit to the number of wives a man may have. This luxury, however, is but little sought after. Oraons are usually too poor to maintain many wives, and the majority content themselves with one. Widows may marry again, and are subject to no restrictions in selecting their second husband. In such marriages the fall ceremony is not performed: it is deemed sufficient for the female relatives of the bridegroom to smear, vermilion on the bride's forehead and the parting of her hair. Sometimes even this meagre form is omitted, and a valid marriage is constituted by the mere fact of the parties living together. Notwithstanding this laxity of formal observance, the children of a widow are recognised as holding equal rank with those of a woman married by the full ritual used in a first marriage. Divorce is readily effected at the will of either husband or wife. The consent of the panchayat is not required, nor is the intention to separate attested by any particular form. A husband turns away his wife, or a wife runs off from her husband, and the fact in either case is accepted as constituting a valid divorce. If a woman has children, her husband may be compelled to contribute to their maintenance if he divorces the mother on any other ground than adultery. Similarly, when a wife deserts her husband, not on account of ill-treatment, but merely because she takes a fancy to another man, her parents may be called upon to repay the bride-price which they received at her marriage. Divorced wives may marry again on the same terms and by the same form as widows." The customs relating to marriage are practised by the Oraon tribals.

Initiative Coming from Girl's Side

Sir Risley records marriage customs related to Rajputs, thus: "The demand being for husbands, not for wives, it follows that the negotiations leading to marriage are opened by the father or guardian of the girl, who sends his family priest and family barber to the boy's house to make inquiries and to answer any questions that may be asked. Some-time professional match-maker, *agua* or *ghatak,* is employed. In any case these preliminary negotiations are known as *aguai* or *bartuhari.* If these results are satisfactory, and the girl's family find that their offers are likely to be accepted, the same emissaries pay a second visit to the boy's house, accompanied by the girl's father, and bringing with them her horoscope, which is compared by the Brahmans of the two families with the horoscope of the boy in order to ascertain whether the match is likely to be auspicious. When this point has been satisfactorily settled, the question of the bridegroom-price *(tilak* and *dahej)* to be paid by the girl's family is discussed, and a certain proportion of it, usually half, is paid on the spot by way of clinching the bargain. This is called *bar chhenka* or *phaidan,* and by receiving it the boy's people are deemed to bind themselves to marry him to no other woman. Sometimes the father of the boy also pays a small sum *(sagun)* as earnest money to the family of the girl. This practice, however, is said to be unusual, and is only resorted to when it is thought that the girl's family may be disposed to evade fulfilment of their obligations. The first instalment of the *tilak,* or bridegroom-price is paid by one of the girl's relations to the boy himself in the presence of the family Brahman. At the same time a cocoanut is presented to him and a mark *(tilak)* is made with curds on his forehead. Both the gift and the mark are supposed to bring good luck. The balance of the bridegroom-price in paid in two equal instalments later on—one before and one after the marriage. On the occasion of paying the first instalment of *tilak,* presents are made to the Brahmans and barbers who have taken part in the proceedings, and a date is fixed for the celebration of the marriage, an interval of fifteen days being usually allowed.

"A few days before the wedding *dhanbatti* takes place, a barber is sent from the girl's house to the boy's with a present of unhusked rice. The boy's guardian takes this, mixes with it some rice of his own, and has the mixture parched. Two days before the wedding the women of the family scatter this parched rice about in the courtyard, singing songs which are supposed to bring good luck. On the next day, that is the day before the wedding, the rite of *ghidhari* is performed in the houses of the bride and bridegroom separately. The parents and nearest relations of the latter put on yellow clothes, and in the presence of the family priests worship Ganesa, the deity, who presides over success in life. The bridegroom is then smeared with oil, turmeric and *ghi,* offerings are made to the family gods, and the hair of the bridegroom's mother or his nearest female relative is anointed with oil. The same ceremony is gone through in the house of the bride, the only difference being that her family cloth themselves in red for the occasion. On the day of the marriage, hut before the wedding procession is arranged, the ceremony of *belonki mangna* is often, though not necessarily, performed. The parents of the betrothed couple distribute cakes to the neighbours, demanding in return small presents of money *(belonki).*

"The marriage procession is formed at the house of the bridegroom, and makes a somewhat noisy progress to the house of the bride. There the entire party is entertained. The bride and bridegroom are seated under a *marwa* or wedding canopy, and after the recital of appropriate *mantras* or texts, the family priest of the bride's household fills the bridegroom's right hand with *sindur;* and makes a mark with it on the bride's forehead, the women of the family meanwhile singing songs to celebrate the event. Among the Rajputs of Tirhut this is deemed the binding portion of the ritual, and the practice of walking round the sacred fire, usually considered essential in the marriage of the higher castes, is said to be unknown. The married couple then leave the *marwa* and go to the *kohbar* or house, where the family deity has been placed for the occasion. They worship and make offerings to him, and this concludes the marriage. The bridegroom then returns to the *janwasa* or lodgings reserved for his party, while the bride remains in her own house. Early next morning they are brought out and each is made to chew betel with which has been mixed a tiny drop of blood drawn from the other's little finger. This usage in which we may trace an interesting survival of primitive ideas is called *sineh jorua,* the joining of love. When it is over the bride is taken to her husband's house where she remains. On the fourth day after her arrival home and her husband stand together on a yoke such an is used for oxen, and a washerwoman pours water over them. This symbolical washing is supposed to be the first occasion on which the couple see each other by daylight after marriage. Among the Rajputs of North-Western India, and in some parts of Behar, the bride and bridegroom do not live together until after a second ceremony (called *gauna,* or with reference to the bride's 'going' to her husband's house) has been performed, which may take place one, three, five or even seven yours after the marriage, and is fixed with reference to the physical development of the bride. In Tirhut, however, the custom of premature consummation, mentioned by Buchanan as prevalent among the Rajputs of Behar, seems to have been introduced, and it is said to be unusual for a bride to be kept at home until she attains puberty. Another custom connected with marriage, which students of comparative ethnography will also recognise as a survival of more primitive ideas, may be referred to here. In Rajput families of Tirhut it is considered contrary to etiquette for a young married couple to see each other by day so long as the husband's parents are alive, and in particular they must avoid being seen together by the husband's parents, and must not speak to one another in their presence. It is of course extremely difficult to ascertain how far a rule of this sort is actually observed but I am assured that young married couples are very careful to avoid infringing it, although as they grow older their solicitude on this point is apt to wear off.

"The remarriage of widows is strictly forbidden among the Rajputs of Behar. Divorce is also prohibited, and when a woman is taken in adultery, she is summarily expelled from the caste, and either becomes a prostitute or joins herself to some religious sect of more or less dubious morality. In certain cases, however, where a married couple find themselves unable to live in harmony together, a separation is arrived at by mutual consent, each agreeing to look upon the other as a parent. In such cases the wife returns to her father's house, and the husband marries again. This is not however, looked upon as a divorce." The customs, rites and rituals pertain to the community of Rajputs.

A Liaison Outside the Caste not Allowed

"Rajwars marry their daughters either as infants or as adults. In the later case sexual intercourse before marriage is condoned, as with the Mundas and Oraons, provided that the lover marries the girl. An intrigue with a man of another caste would of course be punished by summary excommunication. The marriage closely resembles that in use among the Kurmis, *sindurdan* being the binding portion. Polygamy is permitted. A man may have as many wives as he can afford to maintain. A widow may marry a second time by the *sanga* form. She is not bound to marry her late husband's younger brother. Some Rajwars of Gya and Shahabad assured me that only childless widows might marry again, and that the privilege was under no circumstances extended to a widow with children. This looks like a first step towards the introduction of further restrictions, but I doubt whether my informants were correct in their statement; or, if they were, whether the modified usage extended beyond a small number of families. Divorce is allowed for adultery or incompatibility of temper, and divorced wives may marry again" writes Sir Risley. The marriage custom is practised among the Rajwars of the eastern region.

Polygamy Allowed

Sir H.H. Risley writes, "Girls are married either as infants or adults, usually between the ages of eight and eighteen. Sexual license before marriage is not openly recognised, as it is among the aborigines of Chota Nagpur; but I am informed that grown-up girls enjoy considerable liberty in this respect, it being understood that in case of pregnancy a husband will be at once forthcoming. In theory polygamy is allowed without any restriction being laid on the number of wives or any antecedent condition being insisted on, such as that the first wife must be barren or be inflicted with an incurable disease in order to entitle her husband to take another wife. In actual life, however, it is unusual to find a man with more than three or four wives. One simple reason for this is that few men can afford to keep many wives or have house-room to accommodate them, as by universal custom each wife must have a separate room.

"A widow is allowed to marry again by the *sagai* form, and it is considered right for her to marry her late husband's younger brother. Under no circumstances can she marry the elder brother. If she marries an outsider, her late husband's brother, father, or uncle have the right to the custody of all her children, both male and female. In any case she acquires no rights in her late husband's property, the whole of which passes to his eldest son, subject to certain obligations to provide, by way of maintenance, for younger brothers. If a widow marriage her late husband's younger brother, her children by him are not deemed the children of her first husband, nor have they any rights in respect of his property.

"The ritual used at the marriage of a widow is very simple. Five married women whose husbands are living take a *sari*, a pair of bracelets, and a little vermilion *(sindur)* to the bridegroom and get him to touch each article. They then return to the bride, attire her in the sort and bracelets, and daub the vermilion on her forehead. As in the case of a regular marriage, the proceedings conclude with a feast to the friends and relatives of the newly-married couple.

"A woman may be divorced for adultery or for eating with a member of another caste. For lighter offences than these, separation is the only punishment awarded; and in that case the husband is bound to maintain, his wife. A divorced woman may not marry again. If she lives with a man, she ranks as a concubine and her children are illegitimate.

"The ceremony performed at the marriage of a virgin bride contains several features of a primitive and non-Aryan character. In the first instance, both parties go through the form of marriage to a mango tree *(amba biha)*.

The essential and binding portions of the ritual are the knotting together of the clothes of the bride and bridegroom and *sindurdan,* which is effected by smearing on the bride's forehead a drop of blood drawn from the little finger of the bridegroom, and *vice versa.* Sakadwipi Brahmans officiate, and offerings are made to Gauri and Ganesa.

"Marriages are arranged by the parents or guardians of the parties, who have no freedom of choice in the matter. Professional marriage-brokers are unknown. The first offer is made by the father of the bridegroom, and a bride-price (*dali taka*), varying according to the means of the bridegroom's parents, is paid to the parents of the bride, by whom it is retained. No portion of the bride-price becomes the special property of the bride." The customs is popular among the Rautias.

Both infant and adult-marriage are in force, and sexual intercourse before marriage is said to be tolerated by the Chitwania Tharus. The traditional amount of the bride-price is supposed to be Rs. 9, but this is liable to vary according to the circumstances of the family. The marriage ceremony is modelled on the ritual in vogue among the lower Hindu castes. Slight traces of the form of capture may perhaps be discerned in it, but these are not very marked among the Tharus of Behar. Brahmans officiate of priests, and the brother-in-law (*ganjua*) of the bride usually takes a prominent part in the proceedings. In the Mardania and Chitwania sub-tribes the bridegroom's party, instead of being entertained by the bride's people, are expected to feast the latter for three days before the bride is produced. No second ceremony (*gauna*) is performed when the bride goes finally to live with her husband. When she is married as an adult, she goes to her husband at once. And in all cases I understand it is deemed proper for her to spend one night at her husband's house immediately after marriage. On the occasion of this visit she and the relations who accompany her are entertained at a feast called *dulhi bhatawan*, 'giving rice to the bride,' which celebrates her formal admission into the sept to which her husband belongs. If she is still an infant, she is taken back next day to her parent's house by her brother-in-law, and remains there until she has attained sexual maturity.

Polygamy is permitted, and there appears to be no definite role limiting the number of wives a man may have. Widows may marry again, and are subject to no special restrictions in their selection of a second husband. Divorce is allowed, and appears to be extremely common. The bond of wedlock is held in light esteem among the Tharus, who countenance a degree of sexual laxity analogous to that which prevails among many of the Nepalese castes, and generally among the sub-Himalayan races. Divorced women may marry again by the same ceremony as widows, and. both classes are distinguished by the designation *urari,* or 'selected,' from women who were married as virgins by the full ritual. The social status of an *urari* wife is respectable, though slightly inferior to that of a *byahi* wife. Even this position, however, is not accorded to her unless she is married with the consent of the relatives of her second husband, which is signified by the ceremony of *bhatana,* or formally admitting her to the *jus cibi* of the household. Unless this is done she is called a *suraitin,* or concubine, and her husband cannot take water or cooked food from her hands without endangering his own standing in the family. *Bhatana* is also necessary when any one has been debarred from social intercourse for an offence against the customs of the tribe. There seema to be some difference of practice among the Tharu sub-tribes in respect of the admission of women from a different sub-tribe. Some groups receive women from any other group, others only from certain specified groups, while Rautars decline to admit any outsiders to the privilege of *bhatana,* although they allow a woman of another sub-tribe to be kept by a Rautar man as a *suraitin.* Such women, however, have no rights as members of the family, and their child belong to their mother's sub-tribe. The marriage customs are practised among the Tharus.

Widow Remarriage Allowed

Sir Risley records in his ethnographic accounts, "Baistams profess to marry their daughters as infants, and this may be taken to be the rule of the caste, although in many instances it is departed from, as might be expected in a community comprising so many heterogeneous elements. Sexual intercourse before marriage is not visited by any social penalties, nor are girls who have led an immoral life turned out of the caste. Only before they can be formally married, they must again pass through the ceremony of initiation. The standard Hindu ritual is not observed in marriage. A guru or gosain presents to Chaitanya flowers and sandal wood paste, and lays before him offerings of *malsabhog,* a compound of rice, fruits and other articles. Hymns *(sankirtan)* in honour of Krishna and Chaitanya are then sung to an accompaniment of the *mridanga,* an elongated drum, tapering towards the ends, and the *kartal* or brass cymbal. The guardian of the girl takes her right hand in his and gives it to the bridegroom, and the couple exchange, small garlands of flowers and necklaces of beads. Sunkirtan is sung once more, and the ceremony is over. Its essential and binding portion is the exchange of flowers or beads, technically known as *kanthi-badal.* Widows may marry again *(sanga),* and are in no way restricted in the selection of their second husband, except that they may not marry within the prohibited degrees originally forbidden to them. The ritual is the same as that described above, except that no one gives away the bride. For a widow, as for a virgin, *kanthi-badal* is held to be the binding portion of the ceremony. Divorce is permitted at the option of either party, and divorced persons of either sex may marry again." Adds Sir Risley. The marriage customs, rites and rituals are practised among the Baistam Vaishnavas.

Informing Church about Wedding Date

Among the Chinese people, after the wedding day is fixed, the bridegroom's parents send various gifts to the bride, such as flowers, powder, jewellery, sweets, cakes and tea, besides the silk garments she will wear at the wedding. The Chinese Christians celebrate this occasion as a formal engagement, when the Church has to be informed about the engagement and wedding date. A notice put up in the Church must declare the intended marriage between the two persons for three consecutive Sundays during the Mass. The intended marriage can be dissolved if there comes any objection from anyone in the society.

The Chinese weddings are held at the bridegroom's house. The bridegroom or, in some cases a female relative goes to fetch the bride. They take with them the red silk bridal robe with floral designs. When the bride arrives at the bridegroom's house, a string of fire-crackers is set off to scare away any evil spirits hovering arowed the place. In the house, both bride and bridegroom worship the deities. Before meeting guests, the couple bow before the household deities, ancestral tablets and the bridegroom's parents. The bridegrooms parents hold a feast on this day. On the third day after the wedding, the bride returns to the house of her father, who holds another feast. The Chinese Christian sub-groups get married by a priest in Church and the couple have to register their marriage.

Custom of Announcing Banno of Banns

The intent of marriage is then announced for three consecutive Sundays during the Mass. After Sunday Mass, in a process known as *banno*. The proof of this announcement is presented to both bride and the bridegroom. The priest from the bride's church then sets in motion the arrangements for the wedding. There are certain rituals in a Bengali Christian wedding which, more or less, conform to local Hindu customs. *Aiburo-bhat* and *gayehalud* are two of them. The Christian brides have their wedding dresses gifted by their in-laws, and so do bridegrooms. Keeping local customs in mind, a Christian marriage is held over three days *biye* (the actual wedding ritual), *bashi-biye* (rituals on the next day) and *boubhat*, or *phulsajjya* (consummation). At all Christian marriage, couples have to sign a contract at the church after the religious ceremony. The bride goes to her in-laws house on the second day and consummation of marriage takes place on the third at the bridegrooms house. The bride's parents hold a feast on the wedding day and the grooms at *boubhat*. The marriage customs, rites and rituals are practised among the Christians.

Anglo-Indians Marrying with Europeans as well as Indians

The Anglo-Indians are stratified on class lines as rich, middleclass or poor, being are either Catholics or Protestants, depending on their Church affiliation. The Protestants are further divided into different denominations. They are aware of the Hindu Varna system. Though the Anglo Indians intermarry with the Europeans as well as with the Indians, the community in general, tends to be endogamous. Marriages are performed in accordance with the Church laws keeping in view the prohibited degrees of match-making. They practise adult marriage. Mutual consent is the general norm for acquiring mates, though negotiations are also prevalent. Wedding ring is their symbol of marriage. The custom of dowry or bride-price is absent.

Either party can divorce, with judicial approval, for adultery, or maladjustment. Compensation is given to the aggrieved party. After divorce, children stay with their father. Widow re-marriage is permissible. Remarriage of a widower, as well as male or female divorcee is permitted. Usually, they live in a nuclear and patrilocal family. Children get an equal share, in the father's property. Succession is held by the eldest son. The women have a role in the economic and socio-religious activities. The status of an Anglo Indian woman is equal to that of man. They can inherit property, and have role in the management of the family.

The marriage takes place in the Church. The local priest conducts the ritual of the marriage ceremony. Dress and customs are of the European model. They take certain vows about their duties and responsibilities to each other. After that they exchange rings. The marriage ceremony ends with the signatures of the bride and the bride-groom, on the certificate along with three witnesses. The customs are practised by the Anglo-Indians in the Eastern region.

Dress and customs of the Anglo-Indians are of European model. Selection of a life partner is considered a personal matter of the individual concerned. Marriage through courtship is the norm. Divorce is made through the court and marriage of a divorcee in West Bengal is generally a civil marriage. After marriage the couple set up their own home. Family is nuclear and kinship patterns as well as the terminology are both English. The status of an Anglo-Indian woman in relation to man is that of an equal. They have never been in seclusion like the Indian women. They have a long tradition of being working women and office-goers. Many of them are bread-winners today. They can inherit property and have a role in family management.

Being Christians their rites of passage are in accordance with the church practises. These are christening, confirmation, engagement, marriage and burial. Before independence the Anglo-Indians were recruited in specific branches of the government, such as railway, post and telegraph etc., in various capacities according to their education and aptitude. After independence with the end of job reservations, the economic structure of the community has been seriously disrupted. Those with requisite educational qualifications still find employment in private firms, but the larger group who are literate but without diplomas or degrees face a hard life. They took up jobs as waiters, stewards or musicians in hotels or in the race course as jockeys etc.

However, there is still a great demand for Anglo-Indian women for posts of secretaries, stenographers, teachers, singers, typists, receptionists, and dancers in hotels. Some members of the Anglo-Indian community have excelled themselves in many other fields; like in the armed forces, merchant navy and sports etc. The main sphere of contact between the Anglo-Indians and the other communities of the cities are the market, neighbourhood, school, college and place of work. The upper class Anglo-Indians come fairly close to the cosmopolitan upper class Indians through clubs. In Calcutta and rest of West Bengal the Anglo-Indians and the Muslims seem to share a common neighbourhood. The greatest social distance appears to be with the Bengali Hindus. The major contribution of the Anglo-Indians have been in the sphere of entertainments, games, western music and dance, spoken English, fashion parade and propagation of western manners. The leaders of the community highlight their excellence in the above spheres. In the past Anglo-Indian women had a major contribution in the nursing services. Though the older generation of Anglo-Indians fell a strong nostalgia for the British days, the younger generation of the educated elite families look at their present status and conditions from a more realistic point of view and they try to assess the strength and weakness of the community as a whole, their major problems and how best these can be solved.

They emphasise their Indian identity and plead for attaching greater importance to the education of their children and learn learning regional languages so that they are able to find employment. But in spite of everything emigration continues. One of the main reasons for emigration, is economic. Even with a minimum educational qualification or being just literate one can earn decent living in the western countries. There is neither dearth of jobs nor any stigma attached with manual labour. In India they stand no chance in the competition for jobs with Indian competitors who are matriculates if not graduates by the hundreds. Nor have they the necessary network of kinship and friendship with the higher-ups and gain any preference in jobs. Manual labour is neither acceptable socially nor remunerative according to their expectations as in the UK, USA or elsewhere in the west. Another reason given by the Anglo-Indian leaders is that very few are interested in being integrated with the Indian masses or learning the local languages. It is difficult for them to find suitable marriage partners, particularly for the girls within the community here. Being essentially an urban community, the Anglo-Indians enjoy the modern amenities of life available in the major urban centres of West Bengal and in the metropolis of Calcutta.

Acquiring Mates for Marriage through Courtship

The community of Armenians has no social segmentation, except the two economic class categories *i.e.,* rich and poor. They use many surnames among which a few are Basil, Arathoon, Grigory, Poladian, Sukias etc. They are westernized in their habits, manners, and culture.

Endogamy at community level is the marriage rule for the Armenians. But there is no bar to marry outside their community. There is no fixed age for marriage both for men and women. Generally marriages take place between the ages of 18 and 22 years both for men and women. Courtship is the primary mode for acquiring one's mate. Monogamy is the form of their marriage. Nowadays their marriage symbol is gold ring or diamond ring. Previously they also had another marriage symbol like the *mangal sutra* of the south Indian people calling it red and green threads.

On the wedding day the church priest used to tie it on the hand of the bride, but this custom is not in vogue now. Residence is patrilocal after marriage, but some couples also go for neolocal residence. Divorce is prohibited among them, except for one or two reasons. If there is madness or serious incurable disease, or if any partner leaves the other for seven years or so and if any partner changes religions, then the church priest approves the proceedings of divorce. Otherwise divorce is sought with the help of the court. Children are left under the care of his mother or father as the church or court decides. Remarriage is also allowed for both men and women. The change that has occurred is that previously teenage was preferred for marriage, but at present marriages are taking place at a later age. Armenian families are generally nuclear, but a few vertically extended families also exist. Interpersonal relations are very cordial and close-knit among the members of the family. They follow the rule of inheritance prevalent in the country, *i.e.,* they are now following the rule of equigeniture. Succession to family headship goes down from father to son. Inter-family linkages are also very cordial. The Armenians maintain a telephone connection and goes to clubs or the church to keep up social contact.

Their women get equal shares of their father's property. Their women are educated on a par with their male counterparts. Hence many of them are service holders, teachers, hotel owners etc. Many of the women are also just housewives. Normally the wife is expected to manage the household and jobs. The Armenian men respect the part played but the Armenian women. The Armenian women also contribute their earnings for family's expenditure.

Among the Armenians, a marriage feast is also given in their respective homes separately or jointly.

As the community is highly educated there are mainly service holders and businessmen. When they landed in India they were mainly a trading community. They were in the business of lac, spices, clothes and food etc. They own many hotels and restaurants in West Bengal. But today Armenians from India are dispersed all over the world and engaged in various services. Armenians of Calcutta are owners of hotels and shops, teachers, writers, students, and service holders. Some work in Church, graveyard, and Sir Catchick Paul Chater Home. They were a rich trading community from the past. Utilizing their purplus funds, they were able to build various educational institutions or schools, for the education for their children. Thousands of their people donate to their occupations are primary in nature. The church sometimes decides their cases in small matters. For serious cases they have to move the courts.

Marriage Essential for Muslims

The Bohras consider marriage as an essential social institution under the Islamic law. Both parallel and cross-cousins are considered the most eligible marriage partner. Second cousins are also taken into consideration. A man cannot marry his foster-mother, or foster-sister, if the foster brother and sister were nursed by the same woman. Sororate marriage is permitted when the wife is dead and if her parents are actually persuaded to give their second daughter in marriage. In an adult marriage, a mate is acquired through mutual consent and negotiations. Monogamy is the accepted form of marriage, though they can, and do, enter into polygynous union. Levirate is not restricted, but does not follow a set pattern. There is no marriage symbol for the Bohra women. *Meher* (a sum of money payable to the bride by her husband at the time of marriage) is a must. If it is not handed over at the time of marriage, it can be paid in future, but the amount varies widely. A nominal amount of Rs. 150 has been fixed by the Dawoodi Bohras and Rs. 127.50 by the Sunni Bohras. A newly married couple live in the patrilocal residence after marriage, their family being patriarchal and patrilineal. A man can divorce his wife for adultery, adjustment problems, or insanity, upon social and judicial approval. Compensation is paid to the aggrieved party. But a divorced woman can claim her *meher*. It is usually difficult for a woman to seek divorce. Children are maintained either by the father or mother.

In the Bohra community, no stigma attached to widow remarriage. If a widow has children, she may prefer to remain a widow, since the children may suffer at her new husband's house if she remarries, or if she leaves them in her dead husband's house, where they may not get proper care. However, remarriage for a widower is easier but a female divorcee rarely gets to marry a bachelor. If she has well-off parents or brothers with whom she can afford to spend her days in comfort, she lives without looking for a second husband. There are however a few nuclear families. A young, married woman maintains a relationship of distance with her father-in-law and husband's elder brother. She normally covers her head with a scarf. But this custom become irrelevant in case of cousin marriage where a woman's father-in-law is also either her maternal or paternal uncle, with whom she may already have a warm relationship. She is free to converse with her son-in-law. Mixed, extended families are predominant, which is well-suited to a business-oriented community. All business enterprise are looked after by members of their kins extended families have a functional utility.

A Bohra woman can meet her consanguineal and affinal relatives. Any relationship of avoidance is termed *purdah*, which prevents a woman from interacting with—or even being seen by—certain men who are not her kin. The observance of *purdah* varies widely, but does not prevent women from engaging in economic activities outside the home. In a Bohra family finances are mainly handled by the man. Though a woman contributes to the family income, the entire management is controlled by men. The ideal relationship between a woman and her husband's younger siblings and between a man and his wife's younger siblings is one of warmth and joking.

Bohra women are not prevented from taking part in economic activities. They take up jobs of teachers, or doctors. Dawoodi Bohra women in Calcutta have their own organization, such as the Bunayyatul Edizahabi, for providing service in *jamans* (community feasts) and for *karzan basanat* (giving loans without interest) for household articles. Women take part in religious activities, too. Dawoodi Bohra women have their own apartment in the community *masjid* in which they gather for *namaaz* (prayer). There is the Saifee Women's Association to look after *masjid* arrangements and for running cooking classes. There is another organization for *Dawoodi Bohra women*, namely the Saifee *Golden Jubilee Home Industries* (guild) for promoting home industries among women. Profits earned from this are donated towards *masjid's* maintenance.

The Bohras follow Islamic rules of inheritance, which also gives daughters the right to inherit property. Women however inherit smaller shares than men do. The eldest son succeeds to the post of family head in a Bohra family. Generally women in neither group have any political role, or find a place in the mechanism of social control.

After delivery of a child a Bohra woman is not permitted to pray, to touch the *Koran*, or to enter a mosque for forty days. When this pollution period ends she is bathed and dressed in new clothes, while relatives bring new clothes for the baby, too. *Chatti* (naming ceremony) is observed on the sixth day after birth. The paternal aunt conducts the ceremony. *Aqiqa* is performed within twenty-one days after birth. On the occasions two goats are sacrificed if the newborn is a boy and one if it is a girl. The child's hair is also shaved for the first time. A boy is usually circumcised at age six or seven, in some cases only a few days after birth.

Among the Dawoodi Bohras, there is an oath-taking ceremony known as *misag*, administered to every adult including women. Through this he or she affirms his or her loyalty to the *imam* and the Dai-ul-Mutlaq and swears to refrain from any act prejudicial to his interests. Since Bohra marriages usually take place within relations, the formal negotiations and settlement of marriage is a relatively simple affair.

The Dawoodi Bohras inform the local community leader, the *Amil*, and their religious chief, the *Dai*, of the marriage proposal. The Bohras follow the lunar calendar and the wedding date is fixed in its accordance. The *mangni* or engagement is performed by sending clothes and ornaments to the girl. *Pithi* (smearing of turmeric paste mixed with oil) is held two or three days before marriage. *Katho* (kind of a sweet made from wheat and sugar) is made by the *mami* (wife of the bride's maternal uncle) and *fufi* (father's sister) and then sent to the groom's house before the wedding. Another ritual, *mosalu*, refers to the gifts given by bride's brothers and bridegroom's mother. *Mehendi* paste (red henna) is applied on the bride's hands and feet on wedding day. The most essential ceremony of a Bohra wedding is *nikah* that takes place at the bride's residence. The Imam or the *Amil* presides over *Nikah* ceremony after the bride gives her consent, in presence of two witnesses to the marriage. Some verses and *dua* (prayers) are recited in Urdu. The bridegroom has to sign a marriage register kept by the Imam, where the girl also puts her signature after giving her consent. If the *nikah* (wedding) is solemnised at night, the reception may be arranged on any other day. The *ruksati* ceremony—also a part of the wedding ritual—is held last. In the ceremony, the bride goes to her new residence with her bridegroom and stays there for one night. The next morning, she returns to her parents' house ceremonially and stays for a day. The bridegroom's sister and a few members of his family then go to the house of the bride's parents and bring back the bride to the husband's residence, where she spends four days. After four days, she comes back again to her parents' house, and after a few days, she returns finally to her husband's house, escorted by members of her family. There is a custom of *saifi-rasam*, or *samuho-nikah* (mass-marriage), prevalent among the Dawoodi Bohras. When the Dai-ul-Mutlaq visits the city, several *nikahs* are performed at a time at their mosque. The main objective of this custom is to curtail unwanted expenses and the wanton splurge of money by the rich. After the *nikah* is completed, a feast is organised for the rich and the poor. The expenses for the feast are paid from the *masjid* fund.

References

1. Risley, Sir Herbert, *The Tribes and Castes of Bengal: Ethnographic Glossary*, Firma KLM, Calcutta, 1998, Originally Published, Bengal Secretariat Press, Calcutta, 1891.
2. Bahadur, K.P., *Castes, Tribes and Culture of India: Bengal, Bihar and Orissa*, Ess Ess Publications, Delhi, 1977.
3. Chaudhury, Buddhadeb (ed). *Tribal transformation in India: Religion, Rituals and Festivals*, Vol. V, Inter-India Publications, New Delhi, 1992.
4. Sinha, Dikshit, *The Hill Kharia of Purulia*, Anthropological Survey of India, Calcutta, 1984.
5. P. Sachchidananda, *Profiles of Tribal Culture in Bihar*, Firma KLM, Calcutta, 1965.
6. Dalton, Colonel E.T., Descriptive Ethnology of Bengal Government Press, Calcutta, 1872.
7. Sherring, MA, Hindu Tribes and Castes, Thaker Spink and Co., Calcutta, 1879.

5

Death Rituals : Cremation

By way of the disposal of the dead, most of Hindus in the eastern region practise cremation, except the death of child, dying small pox etc. As for the animist tribal they traditionally practised burial, but after coming into contact with neighbouring Hindu, they have switched to cremation. However, poor persons among them face difficulty, due to rite of cremation being costly for which sometimes they have to borrow from moneylenders.

Shradhar Ceremony

"Babhans burn their dead and perform the *sraddh* ceremony on the eleventh day after death in the fashion described by Mr. Grierson (*Behar Peasant Life*, p. 391). Bairagi Babhans are buried. In case of extreme poverty the corpse is thrown into a river after the nearest relative has touched the mouth with a burning torch. At the *Sraddh* ceremony, as in all other acts of domestic worship for which the services of a *purohit* are required, Kannaujia Brahmans officiate without thereby incurring any degradation in comparison with the Brahmans who serve the higher castes. In some parts of Eastern Behar Maithil Brahmans are employed by the Babhans. These rank below Kannaujias, and are looked down upon by the Brotriya Brahmans, not because they serve in Babhans' houses, but because their own origin is believed to be of doubtful purity." The custom is prevalent among the Babhans.

Burning the Dead

Bagdis burn their dead and throw the ashes into a stream or tank. The bodies of persons who die of small-pox or cholera are either buried or exposed. Infants under three years are buried. In parts of Orissa the universal practise is to bury the dead on the left side with the head towards the north. The *sraddh* ceremony is performed a month after death under the supervision of a Brahman and in general conformity with the standard Hindu ritual. The custom is practised among the Bagdis.

Cremation of the Dead

"The dead are burned and the ashes left at the burning ground until the next day. The relatives then go to the spot and burn over the ashes a cloth and some rice, at the same time calling upon the dead man to keep quiet and employ his spare time in ploughing or in gathering the leaves used for plates, and not to transform himself into a tiger and become a nuisance to his friends. A fowl is also killed and a portion of the flesh laid close to the ashes. Having thus done their best to provide for the comfort of the deceased in the next world, and to induce him to refrain from giving trouble to the living, the mourners return home and solace themselves with a drinking-bout. Relations who live in other villages are expected to pay visits of condolence to the dead man's house, and to bring with them a sufficient quantity of liquor" writes Sir Risley. The customs is related to the Kanth community.

Cremation or Immersion in Stream

Sir Risley writes, "The dead among the Kamis are burned, thrown into a river, or buried, as may be found convenient at the time. The two former methods are considered the most respectable. Persons who affect special orthodoxy take the ashes of their dead to the Ganges, but such cases are comparatively rare. The funeral ceremony is a curious one. After the corpse has been disposed of, the mourners have their heads and faces entirely shaved, including the eyebrows. They put off their ordinary clothes and dress themselves in a waistcloth and a blanket, a bit of white linen being tied over the forehead. In this dress they stay at home for ten days, during which time they take only one meal a day, abstain from meat, salt, and oil, do not receive or pay visits, and, as far as may be, avoid conversing with their fellows. On the eleventh day a feast is prepared for the relatives of the deceased; but before they can partake of it a small portion of every dish must be put on a leaf-plate and taken out into the jungle for the spirit of the dead man, and carefully watched until a fly or other insect settles on it. The watcher then covers up the plate with a slab of stone, eats his own food, which he brings with him to the place, and returns to tell the relatives that the dead man's spirit has received the offering set for him. The feast can then begin. The watcher is a member of the caste, who is paid for his services as if he were a Brahman. No ceremonies are performed for the benefit of ancestors in general, childless ancestors, or men who have died a violent death."

Showing a Great Reverence for the Dead

Mr. E.T. Dalton records, "The funeral ceremonies of the Hos are deserving of special notice, as they show great reverence for the dead; and the variety and singularity of the rites performed may materially aid us in tracing the connection of the people we are describing. In my account of the Khasias I have already drawn attention to the similarity between their funeral ceremonies and those of the Hos. The funeral rites of the Hos and Qaroa have also many points of resemblance. On the death of a respectable Ho a very substantial coffin is constructed and placed on faggots of firewood. The body, carefully washed and anointed with oil and turmeric, is reverently laid in the coffin; all the clothes, ornaments, and agricultural implements that the deceased was in the habit of using are placed with it and also any money that he had about him when he died. Then the lid of the coffin is put on, and faggots placed around and above it, and the whole is burned. The cremation takes place in front of the house of the deceased. Next morning water is thrown on the ashes, search made for bones, and a few of the larger fragments are carefully preserved, whilst the remainder, with the ashes, are buried. The selected bones are placed in a vessel of earthenware,—we may call it an urn,—and hung up in the apartment of the chief mourner, generally the mother or widow, that she may have them continually in view, and occasionally weep over them. Thus, they remain till the very extensive arrangements necessary for their final disposal are effected. A large tombstone has to be procured, and it is sometimes so ponderous that the men of several villages are employed to move it. Some wealthy men, knowing that their successors may not have the same influence that they possess, select during their lifetime a suitable monument to commemorate their worth, and have it moved to a handy position to be used when they die. When required for use it is brought to the family burial place, which with the Hos is close to the houses, and near it a deep round hole is dug for the reception of the cinerary urn. When all is ready a funeral party collect in front of the deceased's house—three or four men with very deep-toned drums, and a group of about eight young girls. The chief mourner comes forth, carrying the bones exposed on a decorated tray, and a procession is formed. The chief mourner, with the tray, leads; the girls form in two rows, those in front carrying empty and partly broken pitchers and battered brass vessels; and the men, with drums, bring up the rear. The procession advances with a very ghostly dancing movement, slow and solemn as a minute in time to the beat of the deep-toned drums, not straightforward, but mysteriously gliding,—now right, now left, now marking time, all in the same mournful cadence—a sad dead march. The chief mourner carries the tray, generally on her head; but at regular intervals she slowly lowers it, and as she does so the girls also gently lower and mournfully reverse the pitchers and brass vessels, and, looking up for the moment with eyes full of tears, seem to say, 'Ah! see! they are empty.' In this manner the remains are taken to the house of every friend and relative of the deceased within a circle of a few miles, and to every house in the village. As the procession approaches each habitation, in the weird-like manner described, the inmates all come out and the tray having been placed on the ground at their door, they kneel over it and mourn, shedding tears on the remains as their last tribute of affection to their deceased friend. The bones are also thus conveyed to all his favourite haunts,—to the fields he cultivated, to the grove he planted, to the tank he excavated, to the threshing-floor where he worked with his people, to the *akhra* or dancing arena where he made merry with them,—and each spot which is hallowed with reminiscences of the deceased draws forth fresh tears from the mourners. In truth, there is a reality in their sadness that would put to shame the efforts of our undertakers and the purchased gravity of the best mutes; and it is far less noisy and more sincere than the Irish 'keening.' When this part of the ceremony is completed the procession returns to the village, and, slowly gyrating round the great slab, gradually approaches its goal. At last it stops; a quantity of rice, cooked and uncooked, and other food is now cast into the grave, and the charred fragments of bone transferred from the tray to a new earthen vessel placed over it. The hole is then filled up and covered with the large slab, which effectually closes it against desecration. The slab, however, does not rest on the ground, but on smaller stones, which raise it a little. With the Mundas, as among the Khasias, these slabs may cover the graves of several members of a family; but the ghost of a Ho likes to have his grave all to himself. A collection of these massive gravestones indelibly marks the site of every Ho or Mundari village; and they may now be found so marking sites in parts of the country where there have been no Kols for ages. But in addition to the slab on the tomb, a megalithic monument is set up to the memory of the deceased in some conspicuous spot outside the village. The pillars vary in height from five or six to fifteen feet, and apparently fragments of rock of the most fantastic shape are most favoured. Close to the station of Chaibasa, on the road to Keunjhar, may be seen a group of cenotaphs of unusual size,—one eleven feet two inches, another thirteen feet, and a third fourteen feet above the earth; and many others of smaller dimensions. The groups of such stones that have come under my observation in the Munda and Ho country are always in line. The circular arrangement, so common elsewhere, I have not seen." Adds Mr. Dalton. The custom is related to the Ho community in the region.

Death due to Anger of Deity

In General, the tribal people consider death to be due to the anger of some gods and deities, and often the consequence of the ill-effect of socerers and witches. When death occurs they have a series of ritual at different stage which include.

Rituals at the house of the deceased: when death occurs there is often some way of proclaiming the event to the villagers. Some tribes place an axe on the roof, or some tiles are taken out. Messengers are sent to inform the villagers. The Hos lament loudly and sound a horn. A coffin is made, and the tribal priest scatters rice grains from the room in which death has taken place on the courtyard, all the time chanting mantras. Generally the women bring out the corpse; and utensils, pots, ornament and so forth, are placed by its side. Grains of rice and pulse are placed on the palm of the deceased, and some seeds are also thrown which are later gathered and are believed to bring a good harvest if sown in the fields. The Oraons wrap up the corpse in a white shroud and if a woman whose husband is living has died a paste of oil and vermilion is applied. Boiled rice and milk is put in the mouth of the dead. A basket and earthen jar are kept by the side of the body and visiting friends and relations drop paddy into them. The Birhors give a little water to the person who is near death, and then leave him alone, keeping the door wide open so that the soul may have a clear passage to escape. The family members lament loudly so that the rumble made by the escaping soul is drowned in the noise.

Generally the tribal methods are cremation for some, and burial for others like children, victims of diseases of small pox, and cholera and snake bite and so forth. The Mundas have both methods depending on the period of the year in which the death occurs. The Oraons and Hos, too, adopt both methods, and also build monoliths. The Saurias and the Paharias bury the corpse and expose victims of epidemics in nearby jungles to the wild animals.

Among them, a mourning period is observed, three to nine days for the Mundas, two days the Kharias' seven days for the Birhors and twelve for Juang tribals. During this period men do not shave, and sometimes abstain from oiling their hair, and have some ritualistic restrictions on diet and work. Sacrifice to the ancestors and feasting the member of the community, are the common observances. It is said that without a feast funeral rites are incomplete. The tribal people give a great reverence to their ancestors, and consider that they have a decisive influence on the lives of those they have left behind, and on the events taking place in their lives. The ancestor worship thus is generally an essential ritual. Once a year ancestors are worshipped by offering sacrifices, and prayers by the village priests, and by oblations of rice, wheat cakes, cooked food, meat, wine etc. The ancestor worship is an obligatory act and, despite the heavy expenses it entails, every tribal man and family tries to carry it out.

In sum, the funeral ceremonies of the individual tribes are as follow: The Bagdis cremate their dead and throw the ashes in a running stream or tank. But if a persons dying of epidemics like smallpox or cholera, burial is resorted to. In Orissa there are certain areas where burial is the traditional custom and the deceased is buried with the head towards the north. The *sraddha* ceremony is performed a month after, according to Hindu rites, under the supervision of a tribal priest cum-sorcerer. The Juangs cremate their dead. The corpse is laid on the pyre with the head to the south. The ashes may be abandoned on the spot of cremation, or they may be thrown into a running stream. A propitiatory ceremony is held a few days later in which the maternal uncle of the deceased act as priest. Offerings are made to the ancestors when the autumn rice crop is harvested.

When a Bhumij dies his corpse is laid with the head towards south on the funeral pyre. The male relations set it alight. When the fire is burning well they go back and the wife, sister, of other female relation comes and takes their place, carrying with them an earthen vessel full of water. The widow sprinkles water on the pyre when it has burned out, and picking out the bones left puts them in the vessel. Some of these bones are interred under a *tulsi* (basil) plant in the courtyard of the deceased's house, and the rest, along with the vessel, are taken to the family cemetery and placed in a dug up hole. The inside is supported by three stones, and the earth is then filled in. A large flat stone is placed on the top and a fowl is sacrificed on it. Then, a feast of the rice, pulse and vegetables; is organised which the more distant relations of the dead man prepare. The spirits of ancestors spirits whose bones are alrealy buried are formally informed by the mourners that so and so has come to join their rank, and they are instructed to rest all together and not quarrel!

The *shraddh* and the *panda-dan* ceremonies are similar to the Hindus, but the Shelo Bhumij have a peculiar custom of appeasing the departed spirit. On the eleventh day after death, the chief mourner strikes a drinking vessel made of bell metal with a stick, while another relative of the deceased calls out loudly the name of the deceased. Thereupon a third man who is supposed to deputise for the dead one's spirit is asked what he wants to eat. He mentions various kinds of foods, which are placed before him, and after eating them he goes away, carrying with him, as is believed, the spirit of the dead man. Among the Koch or Rajbansis cremation is usually practised. Children, lepers, and persons dying of small pox, cholera and snake-bite are buried. Some put up a small white flag or muslin canopy over the grave. Others put a water pot and twig of the *tulsi*. The ceremonies of *sraddh* etc. are the usual ones which are adopted by Hindus. The Mahilis of north Manbhum bury their dead with their face downwards, but the Patar Mahilis and the Santhal Pargana cremate the corpse and bury the ashes and bones nearby. Offerings of milk, ghee, and rice are made at the burial place. Similar offerings are made in Chait and Kartik for the propitiation of all the departed ancestors.

Colonel E.T. Dalton gives a description of the funeral ceremony of the Oraons as follows: "Where a death occurs in an Oraon family it is made known to the village by the loud lamentations of the women, who loosen their hair, a demonstration of grief which appears to prevail in countries, and cry vigorously. They lay out the body on the common cot, called '*charpai*' and after washing it carefully, convey it to the appointed burning place, covered with a new cloth, and escorted by all the villages, male and female who are not, for some reason, unable to attend. In some families the funeral procession proceeds with music, but others dislike the custom, and nothing is heard but the cries of the women. Arrived at the place where the funeral pile has been prepared, the body is again washed, and the nearest relations of the deceased make offerings of rice, and put rice into the mouth of the corpse, and put some rice or other coin. The body is placed on the pile and anointed, and further offerings of rice are made, and the pile is ignited by a father or mother, a wife or a husband. When the body has been consumed, notice is given in the village and there is another collection of friends and relatives to collect the charred bones which remain. These are placed in a new earthen vessel, and ceremoniously taken to the village, and as the procession returns, parched rice is dropped on the road to mark the route selected. The cinerary urn is suspended to a post erected in front of the deceased's residence, the guests are feasted and the party breaks up.

"In the month of December or January next ensuing, the friends and relations are all again collected to witness the disposal of the bones in the place that, from the first establishment of the community, has been appropriated for the purpose. This is a point on which the Oraons are exceedingly tenacious; and even when one of them dies far from his home, his relations will, if possible sooner or later, recover the fragments of his bones, and bear them back to the village, to be deposited with the ashes of his ancestors. The burial ground is always near a river, stream, or tank. As the procession proceeds with music to this place, offerings of rice are continually thrown over the cinerary urn till it is deposited in the grave prepared for it, and a large flat stone placed above. Then all must bathe, and after paying the musicians the party returns to the village. The money that was placed in the mouth of the corpse and afterwards saved from the ashes is the fee of the musicians. The persons who carried the bones to the grave have to undergo purification by incense and the sprinkling of water. It is to be observed that this ceremony occurs in each village but once a year, and on the appointed day the ashes of all who have died during the year are simultaneously relegated to their final resting place. No marriage can take place in a village whilst the bones of the dead are retained there. The most ardent lovers must patiently await the day of *hadbari* or sepulture.' Dalton, *Descriptive Ethnology of Bengal*, 1872, p. 261-2.

SC Roy describes, "Among the Mundas the corpse is usually burnt and the bones collected for ceremonial interment. In some villages, however, burial is the custom, and in this case, too, after a certain period the bones are taken out and deposited under the family burial stone, or a little of the earth of the burial place is used for this purpose.

"After the dead body has been burnt up the bones are collected, after water has been poured on the spot by some female relation. A small effigy of the deceased is made of tender grass shoots and a figure is drawn on the ground with parched rice to represent the deceased. The effigy is placed over the figure. Some *kitcheri* (boiled rice and pulse) is placed in two *pipar* leaves and these are swayed too and fro three times. The effigy, parched rice, and bones are then all put into an earthen pot and covered with a piece of cloth. The pot is hung on a tree near the dead man's house. The mourners bathe and sprinkle themselves with water in which *tulsi* leaves have been dipped.

"The beards of the near relations of the dead man are shaved and their nails pared. After bathing again, these relations plant saplings where the bier of the dead man was put down on the way to the cremation ground. These saplings are planted so as to form a six-pointed star. One of the relations presents offerings of rice mixed with powdered turmeric to the spirit of the dead man. Meanwhile a small straw structure covering an earthen vessel which has been prepared from before, is sent afire and the kinsmen of the deceased call out his name thrice and say, 'Come, so and so, your house is burning.' The party then return home, where yet another ceremony is held.

"In the meanwhile, the female members of the deceased family have placed just inside the door of the house a few leaf-cups filled respectively with boiled rice, boiled vegetables, cooked pulse, and chicken curry,—all covered over with a *sup* or winnowing fan. They also strew ashes on the floor of the house. The door of the house is fastened from inside, and the inmates maintain dead silence from the moment they catch the first sound of the ploughshares striking against each other. On their arrival at the house, one of the party knocks at the door. On being questioned by the inmates of the house from within as to who they are, they all reply in one voice, 'We take away sorrow and bring happiness.' Then the door is opened, and the party enter the house. The man carrying a stool in his hands goes with it to the *ading* and leaves it there. He then comes out of the *ading* and scrutinises the ashes and the leaf-cups to discover if the ashes have been disturbed and any portion of the rice has been taken by the spirit of the deceased. For, the Mundas believe that the spirit of a dead man will come and take a portion of the rice thus laid out for it, and as a sign of its having partaken of the offering, leave a grain or two of the rice on the ground and leave the mark of its footsteps on the ashes. If no such marks of the return of the shade to its former house are discovered, the ceremony is repeated. Last of all, a member of the family enters the *ading*, offers libations of rice-beer to the spirits of departed ancestors and prays to them that the deceased may enter into, "your fraternity, your caste, and your *kili* (sept)." A feast to the assembled relatives concluded the day's functions. S.C. Roy, *The Mundas and Their Country*, 1912, Calcutta, pp. 463-65.

Then, the ceremony of *jang-topa* is conducted in which the bones of the deceased Mundas are ceremonially deposited in the family burial ground after the harvesting of the winter rice. The bones are deposited under a stone slab on which rice-flour is sprinkled. The stone is anointed with oil, and three, five, or seven vermilion marks placed on them. Having interred the bones, the relations go to bathe, all sit down to a feast, describes Mr. Roy.

Cutting up Corpse into Pieces and Immersing

According to Dr. Wise it is universally believed in Bengal that_Doms do not bury or burn their dead, but dismember the corpse at night, like the inhabitants of Tibet, placing the pieces in a pot and sinking them in the nearest river or reservoir. This horrid idea probably originated from the old Hindu law which compelled the Doms to bury their dead at night The Doms of Dacca say that the dead are cast into a river, while the bodies of the rich or influential are buried. When the funeral is ended each man bathes, and successively touches a piece of iron, a stone, and a lump of dry cowdung, afterwards making offerings of rice and spirits to the manes of the deceased, while the relatives abstain from flesh and fish for nine days. On the tenth day a swine is slaughtered, and its flesh cooked and eaten, after which quantities of raw spirits are drunk until everybody is intoxicated. In Western Bengal and Behar the usual practise is to burn the dead and present offerings to the spirit of the deceased on the eleventh day, or, as some say, on the thirteenth. Before going to the place of cremation the Behar Doms worship Masan, a demon who is supposed to torment the dead if not duly propitiated. Burial is occasionally resorted to, but is not common, except in the case of persons who die of cholera or small-pox and children under three years of age. In these cases the body is laid in the grave face downward with the head pointing to the north. The custom is peculiar to the Doms in the eastern region.

Cremation of the Deceased

In Behar the dead are burned in the ordinary fashion, and *sraddh* performed on the tenth or, according to some, the thirteenth day after death. Libations of water (*tarpan*) and balls of rice (*pinda*) are offered to the spirit of ancestors in general in the month of Aswin. In Eastern Bengal Chamars usually bury their dead, and if the husband is buried his widow will be laid beside him if she had been taught the same *mantra*, otherwise her body is burned. Sants of the Sri-Narayani sect are objects of special reverence, and whenever one dies in a strange place the Sants on the spot subscribe and bury him. The funeral procession is impressive, but very noisy. The corpse, wrapped in a sheet with a roll of cloth wound round the head, is deposited on a covered litter. Red flags flutter from the four corners, and a white cloth acts as a pall. With discordant music the body is carried to the grave, dug in some waste place, where it is laid flat, not sitting, as with the Jugis. The rituals are prevalent among the Chamars of the region.

Burning the Dead

Sir Herbert Risley states, "Chakmas burn their dead. The body of a man is burned with the head to the west on a pyre composed of five layers of wood: that of a woman on a pyre of seven layers, the head being turned to the east. The ashes are thrown into the river. A bamboo post, or some other portion of a dead man's house, is usually burned with him—probably in order to provide him with shelter in the next world. At the burning place the relatives set up a pole with a streamer of coarse cloth. Infants and persons who die of small-pox or cholera or by a violent death are buried. If a man is supposed to have died from witchcraft, his body when half-burned is split in two down the chest—a practise curiously analogous to the ancient treatment of suicides in Europe. Seven days after death priests are sent for to read prayers for the dead, and the relatives give alms. It is optional to repeat this ceremony at the end of a month. At the end of the year, or at the festival of *navanha* (eating of new rice), rice cooked with various kinds of curry, meat, honey, wine, are offered to departed ancestors in a separate room and afterwards thrown into a river. Should a flea, or, better still, a number of fleas, be attracted by the repast, this is looked upon as a sign that the dead are pleased with the offerings laid before them." The customs, rites and rituals are practised among the Chakmas.

Employing Brahmans to Conduct Rituals

Sir Risley describes, "For religious and ceremonial purposes Rajputs employ Brahmans, who are received on equal terms by other members of the sacred order. The dead are burned and the ashes thrown into the Ganges or ones of its tributaries. *Sraddh* is performed on the thirteenth day after death, and on the fourteenth a feast is given to the Brahmans of the neighbourhood. It is followed by the *barki sraddh* on the first anniversary of the death, when the members of the dead man's family shave their heads and faces, and present a *pinda* to the deceased, while the Brahmans recite mantras. Then the priests and the members of the family partake of a feast. It is said to be a tradition that the expenditure on this ceremony must not exceed half of that incurred on the original *sraddh.* After the *barkhi* the *tarpan* or *nittarpan,* a daily offering of water is presented regularly by all the sons of the deceased, and particularly by the eldest. This practice, however, is observed only by highly-educated Rajputs, who know their religious obligations in this matter. On the first fifteen days of Asin the *pitri paksh* or ancestors' fortnight is observed with offerings of water to all deceased ancestors. If a man dies sonless, leaving a wife and daughter, the *sraddh* and the *barki* are performed by one of them, the other ceremonies being omitted. Failing these the nearest agnate *gotia* will take upon himself these pious duties. In the event of a man dying away from his people and being burned or buried without the proper rites, his body is burned in effigy by his relatives, and the other ceremonies are performed in the usual fashion. When a man has died a sudden or violent death, it is thought right for his son to make a pilgrimage to Gya and perform the *sraddh* ceremony there in order to secure the repose of his soul." The customs and rituals are observed by the Rajput of the region.

Cremating the Dead

"The dead are usually disposed of by burning, except in the case of Kabirpanthi Rautias, who are buried standing upright and facing to the north. In the former case the corpse, covered with a new cloth, is taken to the place of cremation *(masan)* and there sleeping, bathed, and clothed in a new waistcloth and sheet. If the body be that of a woman whose husband is alive, it is bathed, anointed with oil, and dressed in a new *sari.* In the case of a widow the oiling is omitted. The corpse is then placed on the funeral pile with the head to the north, and the chief mourner, lighting a torch made of five dry twigs of a *bel* tree tied to the end of a bit of wood and soaked in *ghi,* walks round the pile seven times, applies the torch to the mouth of the deceased, and then sets fire to the pile. Before doing so however, he takes a portion of the sheet in which the corpse is dressed and wraps up in it a knife or a piece of iron. This piece of cloth must be kept for ten days. After the body has been consumed, the ashes are collected in a new earthen vessel *(ghanti).* On returning home the mourners wash their feet with water previously placed for them outside the house. Inside the courtyard a shallow brass dish *(thali)* is laid ready with leaves of the *tulsi (Ocymum sanctum)* and *kareli (Momordica charantia),* one pice, and a vessel of water. Some person, not a member of the family, pours a little water into the hand of each mourner, who drinks it off. For ten days after the cremation the ashes of the deceased *(santh)* are hung up in the vessel in which they were placed. During this time the chief mourner must make daily libations to the ashes, and must keep on his person the piece of sheet and the iron already referred to. He may not change his clothes, sleep on a bed, or eat salt, and he can only take one meal a day, which he must cook himself. At the end of this time the ashes are either buried at the *masna,* or, where the family are wealthy enough. to undertake the journey, are kept for transport to Benares or Gya. On the tenth day he and the other relatives bathe, shave, anoint themselves with a mixture of oil and oil-cake, and put on clean clothes. The chief mourner also offers to the deceased ten cakes *(pinda)* made of rice, milk, linseed, barley, and honey. On the eleventh day the regular *sraddh* ceremony is performed with the assistance of a Kanaujia, or, failing him, of a Sakadwipi Brahman who mutters unintelligible nonsense, supposed to be Vedic texts, and the Kantaha or Mahabrahman is fed and receives presents. On the twelfth day Sakadwipi Brahmans and friends of different castes are entertained, and one *pinda* is offered in order that the deceased may be united to the company of ancestors. On the thirteenth day relatives are fed and final purification is obtained. The anniversary of the death is celebrated only once *(barkhi sraddh).* While this is going on no marriage can take place in the family; and in order to avoid this inconvenience the *barkhi sraddh* is often performed some months before a year has elapsed from the time of death. Offerings to ancestors in general (*tarpan*) are made through the agency of Brahmans on the 15th of the dark half of Asin (end of September), and by the people themselves at the Nawa Khani, Jitia, and Phagua festivals. Childless relatives, lepers, persons who die a violent death, and women who die in child-birth, get only one *pinda*, and are not counted as ancestors. Lepers are usually buried." adds Sir Risley. The customs are peculiar to the Rautia community of the region.

Making Residence for the Soul of the Deceased

When a Santal is dying the family members generally keep the doors open, as they prefer to have the spirit of the deceased wandering about outside the house than taking permanent dwelling inside. This is probably one of the reasons why the Manjhisthan is built by the Santals, as it affords a residence to the manes of the deceased; although Manjhisthan is build before the house of the village headman yet it seems that the spirits of all deceased villagers are commonly considered to congregate there.

Mr. P.C. Biswas describes the Santal funeral rites, "After death, the body is carried on a bedstead by the relatives and villagers who cover the body with a new shroud. When they reach a cross road some parched rice and cotton seeds are scattered about as a charm against the malignant spirits that might throw obstacles in the way. On that cross road they wait for an hour and the women and relations lament over the deceased. They carry the dead body to the bank of a streamlet nearby. The clothes, brass utensils and weapons of the departed are brought with the dead body. These things are sold at half price near the pyre. The pyre is prepared with the wood which is brought from the jungle nearby. Before placing the dead body on the pyre, the hair of the deceased with his face averted and walking backwards inserts a piece of grass between the lips of the dead man and places a silver coin in his hand. The dead body with the bed-stead is placed on the funeral pyre and a small chip is taken off the collar-bone and deposited in a new pot and the hair then applies fire to the dead body by placing a piece of burning wood on the face of the corpse. Before setting fire to the body it is covered with a branch and four pieces of wood are put on it. A fowl is taken round the pyre thrice and is finally nailed to the south-west corner pole. After the heir has placed a piece of burning wood on the dead man's face, all the relatives and others present throw a log on the pyre and proceed to kindle it. The people sit at a distance and watch the body being consumed. The pot in which the bit of the collar-bone is kept, is then buried outside the village. Then they shave and bathe and before they enter the village smear themselves with sal resin. The men who carried the dead man and also those who accompanied the dead to the cremation ground drink handi bought with the money realised from the dead man's articles. Coming back after cremating the body they hang a pot of leaves in the room where the man had breathed his last. In a cup they put some boiled rice and above the rice they place another pot containing fried fish. If the next morning some boiled rice can be seen on the fish then they think the spirit of the departed came and partook of a portion of the rice. But if no rice can be seen then they think that the spirit did not come. In this case they believe that something of the departed is left with them, that is why the spirit did not come.

"After five days there is a ceremony called Tel nahan. All the villagers assemble at the dead man's house and shave. Then they go and bathe, the men in one place, the women in another. The men take with them a little earth (used as soap), oilcake, oil, three sal twigs (used as tooth-brushes) and a couple of leaves. The villagers put these at the edge of the water on three separate leaves, and offer all with the left hand first to the dead, then to Pilchu Haram and Pilchu Burhi (first man and woman). The last two are invoked to take the dead man under their care. The Santals keep a little bone to throw in the water of the Damodar river. There is no fixed time for taking the bones to that river. It is the custom of the Santals to wait until a sufficient number of their relatives have died. Along the river there are several ghats where the relative who has brought the bones offers earth and tooth-brushes to the departed and to Pilchu Haram and Burhi after throwing the bones, etc., into the river. He goes into deep water and facing East dives and while under the water he lets the bones go. The last function is known as Chandan. On the floor of the room where the man breathed his last the eldest son puts a quantity of adwa rice on a plate of Sal-leaves. Then a he-goat is cut by holding the neck over this rice and the blood which falls is mixed with the rice properly. All the members of the house take a little of it taking the name of the departed. Then a great feast is given by the sons of the departed in which all the relatives and villagers join. When this is over the mourners resume their ordinary life, but till then they can neither sacrifice nor use vermilion, nor can marriage or any other ceremony take place in the village.

"When a little child or a pregnant woman dies the Santals bury the corpse. After the death the female relatives and villagers, taking a little mustard oil and turmeric (powdered), rub it on dead body covering it with a new cloth, all utensils and other objects of the departed being carried to the burial ground. When they reach the destination they place the bedstead in such a way that the head of the dead body points towards the South. A branch of the Mowah tree is put on the bed near the head. The pit is made North to South. All those who accompany the dead do not forget to take a pot with water from the house of the departed and a rupee. They then, taking a little water from the pit and the rupee touch the hands, feet and mouth of the corpse. They place the body within the grave; all those who are present there take a little earth and put it on the mouth of the dead uttering the following words :

Ma taba khan tahi khanad ala khanem bagarana

Onata nsa sanam ko hasala amam kana

Alaho Jaman bis badala tahen ma

(You have been separated from us that is why I am giving a little earth to you. Please see that we may remain in good health.)

"Then they cover the grave with earth. The relatives take a little earth from the burial ground and a nail from the dead body, they then throw these into the Damodar river. In the case of the pregnant woman they insert an iron nail in the sole of the foot. The reason of this is that Churinbhut may not come out from the grave." Adds Mr. Biswas. An analysis of Santal religion is as difficult as it is necessary for the history of succession of religious ideas. If there is any culture which still carries on the impress of the underlying philosophic speculation and order of thought that was widespread in India prior to the rise of the Dravidian culture, it was very likely the belief and social order of the Pre-Dravidian Santals. In the evolution of religious ideas, the Santals figure prominently. Thus Clodd cites them as an example of beliefs proceeding animism, saying:

"This is very interesting considering the sway of the ideas of impersonal universal spirit or *mana* so widely prevalent amongst the Austric speaking people of which the Santals are a western peripheral branch. It is a subject for future enquiry, whether there had been any influence of Vedic or Upanishadic speculations of the universal supreme energy carried by these people in the migration eastward. There is a calling back of the shade of the departed common amongst those pre-Dravidian tribes of Chota Nagpur which recalls the Vedic passages (*Rigveda, Mandal* 10)."

Disposal of Dead as per Cause of Death

So disposal of the dead is an important life-cycle ritual among the Savaras of West Bengal. Sometimes they cremate or bury dead which are both reported to be their traditional modes of disposal of the dead. Cremation is, however, more expensive than the burial. Thus, their method of disposal is determined according to the nature of death, like caused by snake-bite, drowning or epidemics or delivery, or it may be a natural death due to the old age. However, generally babies and small children are buried. In case of death caused by cholera and small-pox, the Savaras usually abandon the body either in some desolate place, or sometimes bury it.

Among them, one may die of any disease or of old age in the normal way. If anybody suffers from any disease, at first the sons or near kins try to cure him by applying medicinal herbs, leaves or roots, after consulting the medicineman or the witch-doctor. In case of no improvement, the local medical practitioner is called. When all types of treatments fail a man dies at last. On the approach of death, at first the eldest son in case of father, and the youngest son in case of mother, and then the other kin-groups pour last drop of water into the mouth of the dying man, before the patient breaths his last.

Mr. Himanshu Mohan Roy describes the Savara customs, "The dead person is laid upon a mat or bedding and his mouth is tied with a piece of cloth. Then the deadbody is covered with a new cloth. If a new cloth is not available then it is covered by an old cloth. Within a short time all the relatives and other villagers assemble in the house of the deceased. The deadbody is not turned either towards left or right. A sickle is placed near the head of the dead person to protect the body from being possessed by spirit. Then some elderly women of the neighbourhood or relatives prepare turmeric paste. A little mustard oil is mixed with it. Then the deadbody is smeared with this oil and turmeric paste.

"In the meantime, a few villagers prepare a bier made of bamboos. It is prepared with two long horizontal bamboo poles placed parallel to each other at a distance of approximately 2.5 ft. and some small bamboo strips are then tied to these poles with ropes at regular intervals. Then a mat is spread on the bier. In the meantime the villagers collect some firewood for burning the body. In case of father, the eldest son or in case of mother, the youngest son worships the firewood with a nut and vermilion. Then a piece of firewood is carried to the cremation ground by the eldest son, in case of father, or by the youngest son in case of mother. Then all the pieces of firewood are carried to the cremation ground by others attending the funeral.

"The deadbody is then placed on the bier with the head placed northwards. The sickle is also placed by the side of the head and the corpse is tied with the bier by straw ropes. Then the bier is taken to the cremation ground on shoulder by the sons or brothers or near relatives. Other villagers follow them shouting 'Haribol' (a form of invocation of Lord Hari) at frequent intervals. They also take a hoe, an earthen vessel, a bunch of 'Jun' (*Ichamum angustfolium*) grass with them. After disposal of the deadbody the female members clean the floor and the courtyard of the house where the deceased was laid with the paste of cowdung and water. They also sprinkle cowdung solution around the boundary-walls of the house."

Mr. Roy states further, "The cremation ground is generally selected by the Savaras a little distance from the village by the side of a pond. Such types of ponds are not used by the people for other purposes. When the party reach the cremation ground, the bier is kept on the ground and the head of the deceased placed northwards. Someone remains touching the deadbody to protect it from being possessed by spirits. Then the eldest son strikes the hoe at a particular place and digs a pit measuring 5 feet long, 2 feet wide and 6 inches deep, the chief mourner himself giving only one stroke and the others attending the funeral party fully digging it up.

"Then firewood are arranged in a pile of about 3 feet high. At first 2 logs, 3 feet in length, are placed in the north-south direction, leaving a space of about 2 feet between them. Across them the other logs are placed then. Such layers are formed alternatively upto a height of 3-4 feet, which is called '*Shaw*' (burning place). Then the deadbody is brought from the bier and held in a upright position. In case of father, the eldest son and in case of mother, the youngest son pours water on the head of the deadbody for bathing. Then a piece of new cloth is tied around its waist. After that the deadbody is placed on the pyre with the head placed towards the north and the face upwards.

"In case of father, the eldest son touches fire at the mouth of the deadbody which is called '*Mukhagni*' by '*Jun*' (a kind of grass) after spraying clarified butter on it, and in case of mother, the youngest son does so. At the end of burning when the head bursts out, two small pieces of the charred bones are collected and put in a new earthen pot covered by another earthen pot as lid. After the body is burnt completely, the party pour water on the pyre to put it off, shouting '*Haribol*' thrice. Then the party and other relatives of the dead go to the nearest pond for bathing. One of them floats the pot containing the fragments of the charred bones on the water of the pond after covering it with thorns to protect the contents from being eaten up by crows or other animals. Then they go into the depth of it and take bath. But the '*Agnikarta*' who applies fire at the mouth of the dead wears a piece of coarse new loin-cloth around the throat with a key tied to it to protect him from evil spirits. Then they return home and take fried rice with sweets.

"After three or four days, the '*Choturtha*' ceremony is observed. In case of death of father, the eldest son observes this after three days, and in case of mother, the youngest son observes it after four days. On these days the '*Agnikarta*' takes only fruits. After these days any of the nearest relatives sends a '*Sidha*' *i.e.* rice, vegetables, etc. in a new earthen pitcher or in a '*Dhama*' (basket made of cane) to the house of the deceased. These food articles are cooked without oil and turmeric. A small portion of this cooked food is then taken on a plantain leaf and floated in a pond as offering to the spirit of the dead. Then a portion of the fragment of the bones collected from the cremation ground is buried just in front of the house. They think that the spirit of the dead is not separated from the family. Another portion is thrown into the Ganges or the nearest river, which is called '*Asthi Dewa*'. After this ceremony they take all kinds of food excepting fish or meat or egg till the pollution period is over."

Mr. Roy describes further, "The '*Agnikarta*' offers fruits daily in front of the buried fragment of charred bone before taking meal. He takes rice and boiled vegetables without oil and clarified butter once a day. At the time of taking food, no sound or noise is made at that place. He also takes the food silently. After taking food he goes to the pond straightway to take bath without rubbing oil on the body and comes back with the wet cloth. This is rinsed and dried on the body as he wears only a piece of cloth. In this way he has to spend nine days. The pollution period lasts for ten days irrespective of sex and age of the deceased.

"On the last day of mourning, *i.e.* on the tenth day, they perform certain ceremonies. Early in the morning, the female members of the house of the deceased clean the house and the courtyard with cowdung solution. The earthen pots which are used during the pollution period for cooking, are thrown away into the jungle. They do not take food for the whole day but the relatives who come to the house of the deceased take food.

"In the afternoon all the members of the deceased's family assemble on the bank of the pond for performing the ritual termination of pollution. The Brahman priest, barber and washerman also participate in it. The barber shaves the head of the sons, grandsons, un-adult grand daughters, nephews, etc. of the deceased. The other members cut their nail and hair. Then all of them take bath by smearing oil on the head and the body. At last the '*Agnikarta*' takes bath.

"Then 'Pinda' or rice balls are prepared. First of all the Brahman priest takes some unboiled rice, milk and water in a new earthen pot and boils these together. He kindles a fire by two-and-half handful of straw in a temporary oven. Then it is prepared full boiled. After preparation the pot is over-turned on a plantain leaf and mixed up with 'Panchamrita' (milk, curd, clarified butter and honey). This 'Pinda' is divided into twelve equal portions. The '*Agnikarta*' sits in front of the Brahman priest. He takes these rice balls one by one and the priest reads out to him the incantations for offering these to the spirit of the dead. Then he throws all these rice balls into the water and takes a dipping bath. While consigning these rice balls he utters the incantations twelve times. Then all the members proceed towards the house. The 'Agnikarta' does not take any food this day. He takes only a spoonful of ghee and the other members eat rice prepared in a new earthen pot. This rice is called Gheto Bhat'. On this day, the near relatives come to the deceased's house with some offerings like cloth and sweets." adds Mr. Roy.

The *Sraddh* ceremony is conducted on the eleventh day. All the offerings are made by the '*Agnikarta*' or the chief mourner which include one kg *Atap* (unboiled) rice, fruits, honey, *batasa* (puffed sugar-cake), vermilion and turmeric. All these things are offered in the name of the deceased. Then a fish is roasted on fire, and eaten in a small quantity by all the persons under pollution. The ritual is called '*Anschakha*'.

On the day a feast is given to the villagers and to those who participate in the funeral as part of the custom. At first the priest and other Brahmans (if possible) are fed, then other persons and guests partake in this feast. The priest gets 'Dakshmina' or as personal gift also. Then the 'Agnikarta' or the chief mourner gets formal permission to take food.

On the night of the eleventh day, a new hearth is prepared in the courtyard by the family of the deceased. Some measure of rice, vegetables, fish or meat are boiled together in a new earthen pot. The rice is also mixed with 'neem-leaf' (margosa leaf). Then the earthen pot with cooked food is spilled in the cremation ground where the dead was burnt; the ritual is called '*Sasan Bhat*' (cremation rice). They consider that the spirit of the deceased will take it and the taste is made bitter, since separation by death always creates bitterness. Then all the family members and relatives take food.

On the twelfth day, the family members put oil and grounded turmeric ritually on the foot of the priest, which is called '*Niam Bhanga*'. From this day all the ritualistic pollutions are considered to be removed and the family members lead a normal life.

Piercing Fowl through Eyes on Pyre

About the Santal funeral custom in West Bengal Buddhadeb Chaudhury writes, "Immediately after death, a mixture of turmeric paste and mustard oil is anointed at the feet of the deceased which indicates the ceremonial separation of the deceased from the villagers. On the way to cremation ground the corpse is taken at *Dobati* (near the entrance of the village where no huts are present) anointed again with turmeric paste and oil showing a separation from village both physically and supernaturally. When the corpse is on fire, a hen is sacrificed by piercing its eyes with a stick posted within the fire, which puts the belief that the soul of the offered hen accompany the soul of the dead in his future. Fried paddy are spread over the fire. The forehead bone *(Tang-boha)* removed from the dead body, kept in an earthern pot with a lid having a hole in its middle through which a stick is passed so that it guides the soul substance for its easy movement within the earthern pot. Short-lived materials used by the funeral party are not taken back into the village. The funeral party as they become polluted take bath firstly and the smoke produced by burning sal leaves spread over their body allow themselves to enter into the village as the village is supernaturally holy to them. They are offered one part of rice and cooked curry at the deceased's house by the head of the family. Whereas the other part kept in a vessel made by sal leaves is taken at *Dobati* where a shed *(Umul Khar)* is constructed. The food is offered there in the name of the deceased's soul under the shed in two parts of which one part is taken back at home and hanged just over the place where the death occurs. The shed is burnt before leaving the *Dobati.* It is followed by *Umul Khar* ceremony when the villagers including relatives both affinal and distant use to touch mustard oil at each other's forehead and touch the offered food at their mouth. This is to bring back the soul of the deceased in the domicile socially recognised by the presence of the villagers. Burning of the shed at *Dobati* indicates ceremonial destruction of the deceased's dwelling place while living and thereby separation of the soul from the villagers in the super-natural world for some time. And as soon as the stick, at the two ends of which legs and feathers of the offered hen are tied is thrown over the main room of the deceased's domicile, the soul of the dead is separated from the stick and comes down into the room.

"On the fifth day the performance of the rite of *Tel Nahan* purifies the family members of the deceased. During this time the chief mourner takes soapy earth *(Narak Hasa)* a product of Mahua seed *(Kudi Kare),* three thin Sal sticks *(Datan)* and mustard oil in the bank of the tank to offer firstly to the deceased, secondly to the *Pilchu Haram* and *Pilchu Budi* and lastly to the deity *Marang buru* and finally used by the corpse-carriers. Till the performance of *Tel-Nahan* rite, the deceased's family as well as the villagers with the supernatural world are polluted, but with the use of the *Narak hase* (soapy earth), *kuidi Kara* (a product of mahua seed), mustard oil and *Datan* (Sal stick) and bathing in the first settler's tank make them free from the pollution. This rite is followed by *Room Dakao* rite when three experts in possession are taken at the place where the death occurs who become possessed by the soul of the deceased by the soul of the dead ancestors *(Purudhul)* and by the soul of the *Marang buru.* The deceased's soul possessed person says anything it desires when asked by its family members and is offered Handi, water etc. Through this the soul of the deceased is introduced to the supernatural world by the members of the deceased's family at the presence of *Purudhul* and *Marang buru.* Immediately after *Room Dakao* hens are sacrificed at *Marang buru* and this ceremonial eating of food at the domicile of the deceased indicates a ritual permission for taking flesh and fish etc. Rite of *Tel-Nahan* leads to the rite of *Naite-idi* which is performed within a few months when the separated forehead bone of the deceased is immersed in the river Damodar. During this ceremonial immersion of *Tang baha, Bonga Tala* is performed when *Marang buru* and *purudhul* are remembered. Thus worshipping of the soul of the deceased with the deity on the bank of the rivers Damodar is only a technique of *Bonga Tala* through which the villagers safely hand over the soul of deceased to the deities who was sent by them. Perhaps, it is the duty of the members of deceased's family to place the soul of deceased safely amongst the deities.

"Besides, at the death of a child after birth not only the members of the family, but also the mid-wife is polluted till the end of the rite *More Maha* (Held on the fifth day after death when *Marang buru* is remembered) during which they have to pass through certain restrictions. Moreover, another rite may also be performed known as *Bhandan* ceremony and ceremonial cutting of hair and nail, shaving and bathing in the first settler's tank to be free from pollution, recognised by the presence of the villagers and kins of both affinal and distant; here *Marang buru*, *Purudhul* and the soul of deceased are called back through expert possessioners. This rite it generally performed either within a few months of death or after few years of death. Thus, on the whole, pollution involved due to death of an individual affects a village life more in social, economic and religious spheres. It pollutes not only the deceased's family members, the relatives and the funeral party, but the supernatural world also, which figures prominently at the rite of *Tel-Nahan.* The period of pollution varies greatly from the funeral party to the deities, *e.g.* the funeral party for a few hours, the deceased's family till the performance of the rite of *Bhandhani* and the supernatural world till the performance of the rite of *Tel Nahan.*

"The Souls of the dead ancestors are kept at *Bhitar orak,* the sacred and secret place in the main room, where they are propitiated at times with *Handi* in *Phuruk* (vessel of Sal leaves) and *prosad* as cooked food. Besides, if any diseases or want appear in the family they ask the remedy and request them to take away evil element from the family, as they believe that such evil affect may be caused due to the anger of the ancestral souls over them. Thus, happy life in a family is purely controlled by superhuman powers, always kept among themselves.

"Calling back of the soul of a deceased after its death is purely obligatory towards a deceased, which is to be kept at the *Bhitar orak,* though the rite, *Umul Khar,* discussed earlier. But *Room Dakao* is another form of calling back of soul mainly performed to know the cause of death, disease, abstention of seasonal rain and sometimes to neutralize pollution from the village etc. For example, the *Sendra Bonga* is remembered through its possession by an expert to know the cause of illness; the soul of the *Bhairab Haram* is remembered through its possession by an expert to know the cause of no-rainfall. Thus rite of *Room Dakao* involves certain duties due to some social obligation to them and failure to observe any duty bring want, disease or even death. One thing should be mentioned here in this context. *Handi* (rice-brew) is essential to propitiate the souls of dead ancestors and the deities. Thus it may be regarded as a means to make easy the link between the villagers and the supernatural world." adds Mr. Chaudhury.

Moreover, the souls of the dead ancestors are mainly propitiated by the *Naike* of the village, though any head of the family may worship or propitiate them. The Chief communal ceremony *Baha*, the three-day long communal festival of the Santhal of Kamarbandi takes place in *Phagun* (February-March) when Sal (*Shorea robusta*) and Mahua (*Madhuca indica*) flowers appear in the forest. The festival happens at the *Jaher*. With the appearance of the Sal and Mahua flowers, the tribals inform the headman (*Majhi*) of the village who consults with the other leaders of the village to fix the date of performance and rate of subscription. During this time till the end of the festival the villagers become isolated from the plants as they are threatened to be polluted (*Chut*) for plucking any flower or breaking any twig from any tree. Thus like the villagers, the village priest also becomes isolated from the villagers, from his family members or even from his wife as he has to follow certain taboos during period till the end of the *Baha*.

Though he becomes isolated, but is not left alone at his work as accompanied by the villagers, by the manes ancestors, the souls of the first headman and priest and even by the deities. This isolation comes to an end with the end of the *Baha*.

Baha is the ony festival when all the deities of the villagers like *Jaher era, Marang buru, Turuiko, Sendra Bonga, Koreko, Dharama, Janthar, Sima Bonga, Bhangal (Baram Than) Kuchla Janthar, Madhugiria, Bhairab Haram, Majhi Haram, Naike Haram, Bonga Pokhri, Disom Bonga,* and *Lewersin Titirsin* etc. are worshipped.

Though the first headman and the priest, *Majhi Haram* and *Naike Haram* were human beings yet they are worshipped along with the tribal deities.

Before the performance, the unmarried boys clean the *Jaher*, *Bhairab Than* and *Akhara* where four sheds are constructed. The *godeth* cleans the material used in the propitiation. The priest puts vermillion marks on each sites and material. In the evening the villagers assemble on the courtyard of the priest where they sing after the first headman and priest. Meanwhile, as they believe, the propitiated spirits came down to them through selected oracles. When it ends, they gather at the *Akhara* to dance and sing till next morning. On the 2nd day morning, they again gather at the *Akhara* with musical instruments and proceed towards the *Jaher* headed by the priest, who propitiates the *Bongas* there while others dance and sing. The priest worship *Jaher era* first and all the other deities and the souls. The villagers again assemble in the afternoon at the *Jaher* to dance and sing when the oracles again become possessed, but they do not perform any memorable activity. In the evening the deities take the symbolic materials through oracles and come back to the village with the dancing party headed by the *Naike*. The villagers wash the feet of the *Naike* who offers them Sal and Mahua flowers used during propitiation. After this, all the villagers assemble at the *Akhara* and dance to enjoy there till the morning.

On the third day the villagers sprinkle water on each other and enjoy themselves which ends the *Baha* festival. Considering the whole festival it is evident that the total social function of the festival is to cohere the villagers with their deities, souls of the dead ancestors and the souls of the first headman and priest being accompanied with whom the villagers pass some time during the festival. The customs are related to the Santals in West Bengal.

Death due to Anger of Malevolent Spirits

The Rabhas in West Bengal, believe that human being dies mainly due to the anger of malevolent spirits. But now-a-days the Rabhas think that death is generally due to old age, diseases, accident or some such causes. But these educated Rabhas decline to believe the spirit's anger only. Some also make the fate responsible. They say that man dies as his longevity finishes. The common uneducated Rabhas still believe that due to spirit action human beings fall ill and die.

Amal Kumar Das and Manis Kumar Raha describe the Rabha cremation and other funeral ceremony, "When a man dies, the family members specially the women and children wail loudly. Whether a person is dead or not it is understood by the cessation of breath, pulse and movement of the body, fixation of eye-ball and fall of body temperature, etc. The medicine man or some experienced and aged persons are asked to confirm the death.

"After the expiry of sufficient time they arrange for the disposal of the dead body. (On query, some Rabhas stated that they wait a certain period after the death of a person only to be sure of his death). Cremation is the general rule of disposal of the dead in the Rabha society of West Bengal, though burial is also prac-tised. Friend-Pereira also noticed the prevalence of cremation among the Rabhas of Assam.

"In the first stage for the preparation of the disposal of the dead among the Rabhas of West Bengal, relatives who live in the village or in the neighbouring villages are informed, generally by the family members or by the neighbours of the dead. In the meantime in the house, someone of the family cleans some portion of the land near the altar of *Tulsi* (sacred Basil) with cow-dung paste and water. Some male-folk then prepares *Moirsangrang* (funeral bier) by means of bamboo. To prepare a bier, first of all two long poles of bamboo about 8 ft. to 10 ft. each are placed parallelly, keeping a distance of 2.5 ft. to 3.5 ft between them. On these two poles, some odd number of bamboo splits (5, 7 or 9 in number) are placed. These bamboo splits are tied with the bamboo poles by means of bamboo string winding round the split and the poles without giving any knot. Knot must not be given in tying the splits with the poles. When the bier is ready, it is kept north-south direction before the *Tulsi mancha* (altar in which the sacred Basil plant has been planted) which was cleaned with cow-dung mixture. Meanwhile the dead body is dressed with a sheet of new white cloth which is about 7ft. to 12 ft. in length.

"If the dead is male by sex he is usually dressed by males and if female by the females. But if the dead is married one, the dressing is done by the respective spouse *i.e.* if the husband dies then the wife dresses the body and *vice versa.* When the dressing is complete another sheet of new cloth about 6 ft. in length is placed on the bier. Then two or three persons hold the dead body and place it on the bier where the body is further covered with another piece of cloth of previous size.

"When all these activities are completed, four persons preferably the kins of the dead, take the bier on their shoulder and start for the cemetry. But before they leave the house of the dead, they with the dead body on the bier, revolve round the courtyard or the front of the house anti-clockwise seven times uttering '*Horibol*' (calling the name of the Lord Hari). The dead body is followed by a number of persons including the relatives, friends and neighbours of the dead. If the husband dies the wife also accompanies the procession. The party takes with them several things such as a hoe, an earthen pot, a digging stick, a stool, a cup containing *Til* (a kind of oil seed), mustard seeds, etc., a bottle containing a little oil, a hand fan made of palmyra palm leaf or grass, sticks and lighted straw-rope *(Bhuti)* etc. The cremation ground is generally situated by the side of the nearby river or spring or canal. Reaching the cremation ground the bier-carriers keep the bier on the ground in the north-south direction. Then the eldest son (in his absence any other son in order of seniority, in absence, any senior male relative) keeps a pice on the ground where the cremation will take place in order to purchase the land symbolically from the supreme god. There after those who carried the bier or some other persons prepare the funeral pyre for the cremation of the dead body. One of them first of all dig a small pit, on four sides of which four pegs each about 1 to 2 ft. in height, are planted.

"On these four pegs wooden pieces are arranged in cross-rows. In this way three or four cross rows of wooden logs are made; and the funeral pyre points north-southward. Then those persons who carried the bier lift the body and place it on the pyre. (More Hinduised Rabhas revolve the dead body anti-clockwise round the pyre for seven times). Thereafter a female relative of the dead having some *Husuk* with him, gives *Julapinda.* Generally ElSi, YoSi, Mo, MoMo or any other female member of the dead's mother's line having dead's mother's clan, can perform this rite. They first of all pour a little water on the mouth of the dead and then a little *Chakat* every time chanting incantations. Now-a-days this burden is taken by the males in many Rabha houses. Then another few rows of wood are placed on the body, keeping only the mouth of the dead open. Then *Mukhe-agun,* (touching the mouth of the dead with fire) ceremony is performed. If the parents die then this rite is performed by the eldest son, in his absence the next son; in absense of the son, nearest male relative bearing his clan does the same. The person concerned then takes a bunch of jute sticks, lights it and then revolves the same round the pyre seven times anti-clockwise. At the completion of each round he touches the mouth of the dead with the fire turning his face on opposite direction. At the end of the seventh time he first of all lights the pyre with the fire. Others follow him. The dead body is then allowed to be consumed by the fire totally.

"The spot where once a body is cremated will not be used for cremating another body. Another place is generally selected for the purpose. When the cremation is complete, the person who performed the *Mukhe-agun* ceremony, first of all pours an earthen pitcher of water on the pyre. Then one after another the near kins, villagers, friends and others do the same. When the pouring of water is complete, a small pit is dug first by the side of the pyre in which the ashes, bones (if any), etc., are buried. Then four bamboo poles of about 8 to 10 ft. high are planted on four sides of the pyre. With the four free end of the pole a canopy of a piece of white cloth is held. On the middle of the ground under the canopy, that empty earthen pitcher is kept. In one side of the pyre a long bamboo stick is planted into which a flag is tied. With the pole of the canopy the umbrella, sandal, etc., of the dead person are also tied. Then on the spot seeds of mustard, *Til,* etc., are broadcast so that plants may grow out of these. Sometimes this area is also fenced.

"When all these are over they take purificatory bath and with the wet clothings all of them return back to the house of the deceased uttering "*Bala Hari*" "*Hari Bol*" (name of Lord Hari). Meanwhile the whole house is cleaned with a mixture of cowdung earth and water. As soon as they return and shout *Haribol* finally, someone in the house sprinkles sacred water of *Tulsi (Tulsijal)* for the final purification. Then they are supplied with *Chakat* or tea. After the drink the villagers, friends and distant relatives go back to their respective houses and change their dresses. The nearest kins wear the same dress which they wore at the time of cremation.

"The Rabhas observe *Chhua* (mourning) for a month. Generally the near kinsmen observe the *Chhua.* During this period they observe a number of restrictions such as the mourner do not take fish, meat, egg, onion, *Musuri* pulse etc. They do not wear any other clothing excepting what they wore after the time of cremation, nor they use shoe or sandal, oil, cosmetics etc. Generally they take meal once a day. The meal consists of cooked arua rice and vegetables, clarified butter, sweets, fruits etc. If the father dies the sons should not take banana (ripe or green) and in case of mother, milk.

"On the 10th day after cremation *Dasa* ceremony is observed. In the morning of this day the sons of the dead take bath and give up using the polluted clothings so long they have worn. After bath they wear new clothings. Then they all go to the very place where the dead body was cremated. On that spot a miniature hut is constructed where various rites and rituals take place. The *Dasa* ceremony has several rites of which *Chitakaram, Pindadan, Vairab-puja, Kheru,* etc. are important. At the time of *Chitakara* rite a small pyre is made on which a piece of bone of the dead which was collected at the time of the cremation, is kept. Then the sons put fire in the pyre by means of a bunch of jute stick. When this symbolic cremation is over, the bone is taken in a *Kalar-donga* and kept the same afterwards in the *Than* made there. Then *Pindadan* ceremony is observed. In this rite the son offers several articles to the departed souls. Thereafter the bone is buried in a pit there. After this ceremonial burial of the bone six *Pindas* made of *Atap* rice, pea, curd, milk clarified butter, honey, banana, etc., are offered. When the offering of bone is over the *Vairab puja* is celebrated. It is done by the priest who performs the *puja* by offering flowers, basil leaves, *Atap* rice, fruits etc.

"After *Dasa,* mourning period for another 20 days is observed. On the 29th day *i.e.* 19 days after Dasa the *Kheuri* or *Kaman* (final purification) ceremony is performed. This rite of purification *(Kheuri)* is done by means of shaving the hair, beard, moustache and also by paring off the nails. A *Napit* (barber) is called who does all these things. The relatives other than sons and also some other villagers who took active part in the funeral rites, generally cut their hair, shave beard and moustache and pare off nails. The sons shave their head completely and also shave their beard and moustache and pare off nails. Women-folk of the family cut nails only. Then after bath and wearing new clothings they become fresh.

"Next day *Kam* (obsequial) ceremony takes place. From the dawn the arrangements for this ritual starts. The home, courtyard, etc., are cleaned. The ceremony is conducted by the priest. Several articles such as utensils fruits, flowers, *Atap* rice, sweet etc., are required. The main item of this ceremony is to offer *Pindas* to the departed souls along with the hyme of *mantras*. When the *Kam* ceremony is over the priest is given his remuneration and also all the articles required in the ceremony."

Thereafter a feast consisting of curd, *Childa* (chapped rice), molasses and slat is given to all the assembled guests and relatives. This ends the funeral ceremony and from this day they lead their normal life, free of the ritual pollution.

Laying Corpse with Head to South

Sir Risley writes about the Bhumij cremation and other funeral rites, "The funeral rites of the Bhumij are characteristic, and lend strong support to the opinion that the tribe is merely a branch of the Mundas. On the death of a Bhumij his body is laid with the head to the south on a funeral pyre, which is kindled by his male relatives. When the pyre is well alight, the males go home, and the wife, sister, or other female relative of the deceased comes to the burning-place, carrying an earthen vessel of water. There she waits till the fire has burned down, quenches the ashes with water, and picks out and places in the vessel the fragments of bone left unconsumed. Some of these fragments are interred at the foot of a *tulsi* plant (*Ocymum sanctum*) in the courtyard of the dead man's house, others are taken in the vessel to the original cemetery of his family. The theory is that the bones should be taken to the village in which the ancestors of the deceased had the status of *bhuinhars* or first clearers of the soil; but this is not invariably acted up to and the rule is held to be sufficiently complied with if a man's bones are buried in a village where he or his ancestors have been settled for a tolerably long time. It deserves notice that the Tamarhia Bhumij of Midnapur transport the bones of their dead to the great Munda cemetery at Chokahatu, the place of mourning in pargana Tamarh of Lohardaga. No stronger proof could well be given of the identity of the Bhumij with the Mundas. The Desi Bhumij of Midnapur go to Kuchong, in Singbhum, and some of the Singbhum Bhumij to Suisa, in Bagmundi of Manbhum—Sir Risley. There a hole is dug and the vessel of bones placed inside, supported by three stones. The earth is then filled in, and a large flat stone laid over all, on which a fowl is sacrificed to ensure the repose of the dead. The spirits of those whose bones rest in the same place are solemnly informed that another has been added to their number, and are enjoined not to quarrel, but to abide peacefully in the land of the dead. The survivors then partake of a feast of rice, *dal*, and other vegetables prepared by the more distant relatives of the deceased. This strictly non-Aryan ritual has of late years been to some extent overlaid by observances borrowed from the regular Hindu *sraddh*. On the tenth day the mourners are shaved, and on the eleventh balls (*pinda*) of rice, sesamum, molasses, and plantain are offered to ancestors under the supervision of a Brahman, who receives such presents as the means of the family permit them to give. A more primitive mode of appeasing the departed spirit is met with among the Shelo Bhumij. On the eleventh day death the chief mourner beats a bell-metal drinking-vessel with a stick, while another relation, standing by his side, calls loudly on the name of the dead. After a while a third man, unconnected with the family, and often a laya, comes forward to perronate the deceased, by whose name he is addressed, and asked what he wants to eat. Acting thus as the dead man's proxy, he mentions various articles of food, which are put before him. After making a regular meal he goes away, and the spirit of the deceased is believed to go with him. The relatives then finish the food prepared for the occasion.

"Mention is made... of the custom by which the graves of the *bhuinhars,* or representatives of those who first cleared the soil and founded the village, are marked by an upright stone pillar in addition to the horizontal slab which covers the bones of an ordinary raiyat not descended with one of these pioneer families. Precisely the same distinction is made among the Bhumij *ghatuals* of Manbhum between village *sardars,* or holders of entire *ghatwal* tenures, and the *tabidars,* or rural constables, who make up the rank and file of the *ghatwali* force. The graves of the former are invariably distinguished by an upright monolith, sometimes bearing traces of rude attempts at ornamental shaping, while the tombs of the latter consist merely of a slab laid flush with the ground. This singular correspondence of funeral usage, coupled with the fact that many of the Manbhum *ghatwals* call themselves by the title *bhuinhar* or *bhuinya,* suggests the conjecture that the *ghatwali* tenures in the south of that district are a survival under different names and changed conditions of the ancient tribal holdings known in Lohardaga as *bhuinhari.* Personal service of various kinds is one of the oldest incidents of the *bhuinhari* tenure, and it is not difficult to see how in a border district like Manbhum the character of this service might gradually be changed in accordance with local necessities until it came to take the form of the petty police functions which the *ghatwals* perform, or are supposed to perform, at the present day. Their duties, it is true, are now discharged under the orders of Government, and not at the will of the zamindar." The customs, rites and rituals are observed among the Bhumij community.

Women giving out Loud Cries

The cremation and related funeral ceremonies of the Maghs are thus described by Mr. Lewin: "When a person has died, his relatives assemble. Some one of them sits down and commences to beat the funeral roll on the drum; the women weep and cry, and the men busy themselves, some in performing the last offices to the corpse, of washing, dressing, etc., while others go off to the woods and bring wood for the funeral pile, and bamboos with which to construct the bier. About 24 hours generally elapse from the time of death to that of cremation. In bearing the corpse from the house to the burning ground, if the deceased were a man of wealth or influence, the body may be borne on a wheeled car; all women also have this privilege; the plebs, however, are simply carried to the funeral pile on the shoulders of their relatives. The procession is after this fashion:—First come the priests, if there are any in the vicinity to attend; they march gravely at the head of the party, bearing on their shoulders their curved palm-leaf fans, clad in their ordinary saffron-coloured robes, and attended by their disciples. Next come relatives of the deceased, two and two, bearing food, clothes, etc., which have been offered as alms to the priests on behalf of the departed. Next is borne the bier, carried on bamboos by six men, and accompanied by as many drums as can be procured. Behind the coffin come the male relatives; and lastly, the procession is closed by the women of the village, clad in their best. The funeral pile is composed of four layers of wood for a woman, three for a man. The body is placed on the pile; the leading priest takes an end of the dead man's turban, and, holding it, repeats some passages of the law, four of the deceased's male relatives standing meanwhile at the four corners of the pile and sprinkling a few drops of water thereon. The nearest blood relative, male or female, of the dead man then fires the pile. When the fire is extinguished the ashes are scrupulously collected together and buried over the spot; a small conical mound of earth is heaped up, and a very long bamboo pole, with an equally lengthy flag, is erected over the grave. On returning from the place all parties bathe themselves. If it is the master of the house who has died, the ladder leading up to the house is thrown down, and they must effect an entrance by cutting a hole in the back wall and so creeping up. The relatives eat and drink, and each contributes according to his means to defray the expenses incurred. After seven days the priests reassemble at he house to read prayers for the dead."

Sir Risley adds, "In the case of priests and persons of high social position the corpse is dried or embalmed and kept for a year in a special coffin, while arrangements are being made for an elaborate funeral, which usually takes place on the 1st of Baisakh. A temporary pagoda is built of bamboo decorated with coloured paper and flags, and is set up in some open place faced by a row of bamboo cannon mounted on wheels, crammed to the muzzle with tightly-rammed powder and fitted with a long fuse. These cannon are presented by persons desirous of doing honour to the deceased, and it is deemed an act of great merit to send a cannon to the funeral of a Phungyi. On the arrival of the coffin a mimic conflict—a 'tug of war'—takes place over it, the women pulling it one way and the men the other. According to another account the contest is not between the men and the women, but between the unmarried and married persons of either sex. The coffin is then placed in the pagoda, and the bamboo cannon are discharged in order of the precedence of those who presented them. Last of all the pagoda and coffin are burned, and a long bamboo, carrying a triangular flag forty-five feet long, is set up on the place. A funeral offering *(kongmu)* of various kinds of food is placed on the ground on the eighth day, and this ceremony is repeated every year." The rituals and customs are practised by the Maghs in the eastern region.

Both Cremation and Burial in Vogue

Sir Risley describes, the Limbu funeral thus, "Both cremation and burial are in vogue among the Limbus, the latter being the more common, and probably the older, practise. The corpse is placed lying on its back with the head to the east. The grave is lined with stones, and a cairn, consisting of four tiers for man and three for a woman, erected on the top. The Phedangma attends at the funeral and delivers a brief address to the departed spirits on the general lot of mankind and the doom of birth and death, concluding with the command to go whither his fathers have gone and not to come back to trouble the living with dreams. Neither food nor clothes are placed in the grave, but sometimes a brass plate with a rupee in it is laid under the head of the corpse. For nine days after the funeral the sons of the deceased live on plain rice without any salt; and for a month or two the relatives wear flowers in their hair and avoid merry-makings. The special and characteristic sign of mourning is a piece of white rag tied round the head. There is no periodical ceremony for the propitiation of ancestors." The customs, rites and rituals are peculiar to the Limbu community.

References

1. Grierson, Sir, G.A., Behar Peasant Life, Superintendent Government Press.
2. Dalton, E.T., Descriptive Ethnography of Bengal, Government Press, Calcutta, 1872.
3. Roy, S.C., The Mundas and their Country, City Book Society, Calcutta, 1912.
4. Roy, S.S., The Oraon of Chotanagpur, the Brahmo Mission Press, Calcutta, 1915.

5. Sengupta, Syamalkanti, The Social Profiles of the Mahalis, Firma KLM, Calcutta, 1970.

6. Bahədur, K.P., *Castes, Tribes and Culture of India: Bengal, Bihar and Orissa*, ESS Publications, Delhi, 1977.

7. Chaudhury, Buddhadeb (ed.) *Tribal transformation in India: Religion Rituals and Festivals*, Vol. V. Inter-India Publications, New Delhi, 1992.

8. Biswas, P.C., Santals of the Santal Parganas, Bharatiya Adimjati Sevak Sangh, Delhi, 1956.

9. Das, Amal Kumar and Raha, Manis Kumar, The Rabhas of West Bengal: Scheduled Castes and Tribal Welfare Department, Government of West Bengal, Calcutta, 1967.

6

Death Rituals : Burial

The tribals and rest of Hindus distinguish between natural and unnatural death. The one occurring due to old age or chromic disease are considered the natural death. While the death caused by any wild animal, fall from tree, small pox, and epidemics etc. are considered unnatural. Both type of deaths have different form of funeral rites and rituals.

Custom of Burial

Although the world of the dead is regarded as a separate domain the Hill Kharia maintain and regard it as obligatory on their part to keep contact with their dead ancestors. The funeral rituals amply demonstrate this. After a person dies the body is carried to the burial place. There the body is placed in a grave with its head towards south. The Hill Kharia point out that the Kurmi Mahato place their body's head in northernly direction. Then a torch made up of branches of bel (*Aegle marmelos*) tree is lit and put on the mouth of the dead to burn. The eldest or youngest son usually conducts the ritual. In the absence of sons, daughters may also perform this funeral rites. After this the grave is filled up. Previously it was customary to deposit with the corpse food, new clothes and one or two implements. But now this custom is no longer practised.

Mr. Dikshit Sinha describes their funeral customs, rites and rituals in detail thus, "While coming back to the hamlet the *laya* (priest) performs a ritual called *kantaduari* at a junction of two roads. Here *laya* places a big stone in the middle of the junction and covers it with a few thorny twigs. All the persons accompanying the dead leap over the thorn. On reaching the hamlet they take bath. The idea behind the ritual of *kantaduari* is to prevent the spirit of the dead from coming back to the hamlet. Ten days after the burial *ghatsradha* is performed. During this ceremony the *laya* applies vermilion and sundried rice on the shoulders of the four persons who carried the dead body to the burial ground. Two small fowls are then allowed to feed on the rice and after that these are killed by striking with branch of *Kend.* This procedure is called as *khand kataya namano* or procedure to dispel the spirit of the dead from the shoulders of the four persons who carried it. Then all the inhabitants of the hamlet take bath after smearing their body with turmeric and oil. The son of the dead person then comes back to the hamlet and offers his sister's son a few roots and tubers, Rupees 1.25 and one and a half kg. of rice. This offer is made at the *tulsi pinra.* The *laya* is also presented with a new *dhuti.*

"After a year of the first burial the second part of the mortuary rite takes place. This is termed as *dothupa* or second burial. On the appointed day the *laya* brings one unused stone slab at the *nisangarah* or *muragarah* or (ossuary) and worships it by applying vermilion and sundried rice. Then he goes to the first burial ground and sacrifices one red fowl after making it to peck a few grains of sundried rice. Then it is struck by means of a *kend (Melanoxylon)* stick at its neck. If it does not die it is killed by twisting its neck. This is done to appease the spirit of the dead. Then the *laya* collects the little toe of the left leg and any bone of the skeletal remains of the dead body in a new earthen pot and covers it with a new piece of cloth. This is then carried to the *nisangarah* and placed in a hole and a new stone slab (dolmen) is horizontally placed over it. The sons of the dead persons then return to their hamlet where their wives wash the feet of their husbands and other elderly persons. On the same night sons go to the *nisangarah* with fresh cooked rice and place it in five *sal* leaf plates. By bringing their mouths close to the pot in which rice was cooked pray to their parent to come and take the food. This ceremony is called *naba daka.* In the case of unmarried person this ceremony is naturally not performed and the grave stone slab (menhir), in contrast to the married persons, is also placed perpendicular to the earthen pot containing mortal remains of the dead.

"... the second part of the mortuary ritual is now rarely observed by the Hill Kharia of Purulia. This has given rise to a new term *turukthupa* Kharia or the Kharia who do not practise the second mortuary ritual. Not only is the ritual of second burial skipped but also the customary feast usually hosted at the end of this ceremony is avoided.

"Thus we find that even at the level of preliterate tribal communities the economic constraint hampers the optimal operation of some institutions of the society. In all the three life crisis rituals the most affected part of the institutions is social participation of the kin. In both the ceremonies connected with death and birth the customary feasts are avoided. In marriage we find that the elaborate procedure of marriage negotiation has undergone marked abbreviation and participation of the kin is less." Adds Mr. Sinha.

The customs are practised among the Hill Kharia tribals of West Bengal.

Burying Knife along with Corpse

If the death is caused by small-pox the Mahali bury the bodies. A *Katu* (small cutter used for basketry) made of iron is kept on the bed of the deceased to protect the deceased from the possession of evil spirits. The Mahali belief is that iron keeps away the malevolent spirits. The female members of the bereaved family apply turmeric paste on the body of the deceased. A palm-leaf mat is spread upon the bier and the corpse is placed on the bier, keeping the head towards north.

Syamalkanti Sengupta describes the burial in detail thus, "The Mahalis have a separate burial ground. The funeral party reaches the burial ground after some time with frequent shouts of '*Haribol*' (a form of invocation of Lord Hari). The bier is placed on the burial ground, keeping the head of the deceased northward. The dead-body is held thereafter by hands by the deceased son, as it is their custom that the corpse after death, should not be left alone. The deadbody is placed in the burial pit after performing *mukhagni* rite i.e. putting fire in the mouth of the deceased by his sons. The deadbody is put into the pit with the head facing northward and the face facing the ground. Then the feet are turned upwards and placed over the back and so also the hands, over which the bamboo poles and bars are placed, untieing them from the bier. To protect the deadbody from the depredation of the jackals and dogs, some thorny branches of the wild Kul tree are placed over it. The earth placed over the burial is levelled then with pressure of the blade of the hoe. The earthen pitcher which they carried from the house of the deceased is then filled with water by the eldest son of the deceased and placed on the north of the grave. After that two bamboo splits are stuck by a person into the earth of the grave, one on the north and the other on the south and a piece of white cloth is then fixed upon this by the eldest son of the deceased. Thus the burial is over.

"At the end of the graveyard, one of them cuts a small channel with his hoe and puts a thorny branch of wild Kul tree there, and says addressing the dead—'You shall not cross this channel, this being the demarcation line between the dead and the living'.

"After bath in the pond, they embrace a Suth (*Fieas religiosa*) tree on their way back to the house. They do so thrice and after that proceed towards home. When they reach the village street in front of the deceased's house, a woman comes out with an earthen pot containing several burning wooden pieces. All of them bake their hands and feet on it and touch their warm hands on their breast and ears. After doing this, they enter the house of the deceased and sit on the courtyard and change their cloths thereafter.

"The womenfolk of the family 'as well as those neighbours who come to the deceased's house then go to take bath and take with them some oil and turmeric and apply this on their body before bath. The iron bangle of the deceased's wife is thrown into the water.

"On the second day, the eldest son of the deceased prepares some rice and cooks a little vegetable curry in a new earthen pot. No fish or meat is cooked by him. After cooking in the noon, he takes some rice, curry and water in three cups of sal leaves and goes to keep it on the village street. He keeps it there and bows down before the offering and invokes the soul (*Umul*) of the dead and requests him to take it and then returns home. The adult members then take their meal. The children are given meal just after the departure of the deceased's son for offering the food to the soul of his deceased father. Such offering is made for nine days. There offerings are supposed to be eaten up by some jackals or some other nocturnal animals. Throughout the mourning period the members of the deceased's family do not eat fish, meat or egg and do not use oil for any purpose. They do not wash their cloth with soap and rub oil on their body. Even they do not use a towel to rub their body. They have to observe the taboo of not cropping their hair or paring off their nails and are forbidden to use any comb during this period.

"Early in the morning of the tenth day the female members of the family throw away the old earthen pots which are purchased during the mourning period. Once again they cleanse the house and the courtyard with cowdung solution. After purification they take rice and other curries of their choice being cooked in new earthen pots.

"Feeding of 'Kandh Khatia' means the men who carry the corpse on their shoulder and help in burial. It is obligatory on the part of the chief mourner to feed them on the day of the *Sradh* ceremony even if others have to be left out for lack of means. Two separate earthen pots of big size are purchased from the market, one for preparing food for the members of the family and the other fop the invited guests. One new hearth is prepared in the courtyard and the female members of the family cook the food for the feast. The rest of the observances followed in this connection are similar to those observed in relation to cremation.

"In case of death of a pregnant woman, the body is disposed of, by burial. *Alta* or lac-dye is applied to her feet and the forehead is smeared with vermilion to indicate that her husband is still alive. Mustard oil and turmeric paste are applied on her. The deadbody is taken to the burial ground on a bier made of bamboos. A grave is dug by the funeral party. A sharp *Katu* is also taken by the deceased's husband to the burial ground.

"The hands and feet of the deceased are pricked with a few thorns of the wild palm. The Mahali conviction is that the woman who dies in pregnant condition bears a strong passion for material happiness and so she may haunt the house of her husband and do harm to the family members. To prevent this, the hands and feet of such women are pricked so that they cannot move about if in case they become ghosts. Their faces are turned towards the ground and the hands and feet are turned over the back. The clothes and the few ornaments that they wear, are not taken out.

"The deceased's husband puts the first lump of clod on the grave. The others who accompanies him, then fills it up together. Filling up half of the grave, they throw into it some thorny branches of wild palm and the twisted straw rope (*Budi*) which is used to carry fire to the burial ground, to apply fire in the mouth of the deceased by her husband. Then again clods are placed over the thorns till it is completely filled up after which it is levelled up with the ground.

"Ten days are observed as mourning period. On the tenth day, the usual ceremonies in connection with death are performed; the '*Khandh Khatias*' and a few other relatives are fed.

"Children below one year of age and in certain cases of ages ranging from 1 to 4 years, are buried according to the custom prevailing among the Mahalis. Three or five days are observed as pollution period after which the mourners pare off their nails, crop their hair and have a shave by the barber. A washerman is also called to take the used clothes of the mourners for washing. No *Sradh* is performed on such occasion. According to some Mahalis, in the case of accidental deaths, such as those from snake-bite, attack by an wild animal or death by drowning, the dead bodies are usually left undisposed (*Fica*) on the burial ground, or in a jungle. Persons dying of leprosy are usually buried."

Slight variations may be observed in different localities, in minor details of the ritual and beliefs relating to the customs of disposal of the dead. Many Hinduised traits are creeping in the ceremonies performed by the Mahalis in connection with funeral rites. Invocation or calling back of the soul of the deceased is thought to be ominous by the Mahalis in general, as is considered amongst the Hindus. The custom are related to the Mahali community in West Bengal.

Death caused by Malignant Spirits

Transition is coming in the tribal culture gradually with the change of times. Unlike the people of old generation, people of the modern generation have now begun to feel that gods and spirits cannot cure them. It is said that people have become dishonest and selfish, and so the deities have given up caring for them. One tribal wanted to get his wife treated as she was supposed to be barren. He tried the *Mati* or the tribal quack several times, but ultimately took her to the Ranchi Hospital for treatment. Similarly, one or two persons who were suffering from leprosy had been admitted to the Leper Asylum nearby. A sixty-year old *Mati* said that his practise had gone down considerably since the opening of the Government dispensary in the neighbourhood. In Mandar there is a very big and efficient Missionary hospital, but the tribals do not go to the hospital, unless they are critically ill. In cases of fever they take certain potions prepared from indigenous herbs. The younger generations, however, do not know many of these old remedies. Also due to indiscriminate cutting of the forests, herbs are not to be found in the immediate vicinity of settlements.

In cases of bleeding, leach bites, and blisters etc., people do not rush to doctors, because their indigenous drugs are quite effective. No magical or religious superstition is attached to diseases these days. In Silphari diseases are attributed to physiological causes. Only insanity is attributed to evil spirits. The village *Pracharak* who is Mission employee knows the use of indigenous medicines. The Mission maintains dispensaries at important centres and the villagers of Silphari take advantage of them whenever they are in need. Two villagers keep medicines chests, who said that they kept allopathic medicines for use in their own family, but other people had also benefit from them. One of these persons worked as a compounder of a doctor in Assam for sometimes. Besides keeping some patent medicines, he also uses some indigenous remedies. Many people in the village, however, do not take adequate care of themselves or of their children when they are ailing. Unless a person is bed-ridden for a long time no person cares to give him any medicine.

Generally with the onset of rains many parents get their children's head shaved. The reason given was that children playing in the rain would not catch a cold because they would be quickly acclimatised and water would not soak their hair. One tribal said that whenever any disease overtakes anybody, he advises him to fast for a day or two and the disease disappears of its own accord. Besides administering medicines in the church, prayer is also offered to God for the recovery of the ailing person. It was seen in some cases that a picture of Christ or Mary or a Cross or a Rosary was placed near the bed of the patient.

When a man falls terminally ill, a Parish priest or any other Catholic Missionary who is available is called for the last Sacrament. Sometimes a patient recovers after the administration of the last Sacrament. In Selda and Birhu, tribals have a great distrust of Allopathic medicines and the Government dispensaries. Very few people would like to go to the hospital even though it is not more than two and a half miles away. In case of serious diseases, the *Sokha* is sent for. Sometimes the patient gets well and sometimes he does not. But the faith in the *Sokha* remains undwindled. Besides offering prayers and chanting *mantras*, the *Sokha* also uses some herbal remedies. One reason for the distrust of Government hospitals in the fact that the tribals are harassed by the lower staff of the dispensaries for bribe and adequate care is not taken of them for lack of bribe.

The funeral customs rites and rituals of tribals have been profoundly influenced by Hinduism. If a tribal dies during the sowing season, he is buried. The mode of disposal of the dead also to some extent depends upon the economic status of the deceased. A person who dies of cholera or of small pox is not buried, but cremated. Mr. Sachchidananda writes about their funeral customs, "Ten days after death the *Daskarma* or funeral rites are performed. The relatives of the dead man have to collect his bones and ashes immediately after the corpse has been cremated. A pot is hung on a *Peepal* tree in the village and the man *who* lit the fire will offer water to it everyday for ten days after his bath and before taking his meal. This practise is a clear imitation of Hindu custom. The '*Gami*' (equivalent to *Sradh)* may be performed on the day of funeral or after ten days depending upon the ability and resources of the family concerned. People believe that the main thing within the body is the '*Pran*' or soul. They believe in rebirth and in the transmigration of souls. When it leaves the body, the man is dead. A man may be reborn as a man or as an animal. He is born a man only if he has done good deeds in his previous life.

"Budhu was the first man to initiate the idea that there should be no killing of animals for feast on the day after '*gami*'. This occurred to him after the death of his father-in-law. He told people that it did not look decent to shed blood in the funeral feast, as it appeared to him that by doing so they were taking the flesh of the dead person. Since then no killing takes place on such occasions.

"Strangely enough though the Bhagats have adopted many Hindu customs they still continue to bury their dead. The *Tana Bhagats* dig the grave in the north-south direction, while the *Bishnu Bhagats* dig the graves in the east-west direction. The dead body is laid on a piece of wood and is covered with a piece of cloth. On that day people go to the grave and sprinkle cow dung, milk and turmeric water on it. This is known as '*Sudhar karna*'. Among the *Tana Bhagats* shaving of the head and beard of the male members of the family of the deceased is essential. Hindu influence is obvious in this case.

"In Silphari, death and mourning customs are the same as in any Christian community. Devout Christians do not lament bitterly the death of their relatives and there is nothing like ceremonial mourning. The relatives of the dead feel satisfied if a Mission Father comes to the dying person and he is duly administered the last Sacrament. It is the general custom to bury the dead. At the door of the room where the dead body rests, a tile containing burning charcoal and a small cup containing some oil is kept. Persons who go to the funeral party take some oil and apply it on their hands, feet and head. Smearing with oil and putting of some earth in the grave by all the people assembled is an old custom which even the converts are following. This rite is not enjoined by religion. The funeral feast is held several weeks or even a year after the death of the person. It all depends upon the convenience of the relatives of the deceased. Some persons get their heads and beards shaved as it is considered to be a sign of mourning. This also is not required by Christianity.

"Among the Munda of Selda there is a belief that when a man's time is over he must die. After death heart and mind leave the body and mix with the air. In this village there are three *Sasan* or bone burial grounds belonging respectively to the Munda, Lohras and Ghasi. The heads and the beards of the mourners may be shaved after three, five, seven or nine days of the death of the person. A barber is employed for this purpose.

"In Koenara, if a person is thought to be on his death-bed and recovery seems impossible, prayers are offered. It is believed that it helps in his recovery. There are still people who believe that spirits cause death and if they are propitiated by prayers, the ailing man would survive. After death the body is not bathed and the clothes which the dead man wore are allowed to remain on his body. The body is covered with a shroud and put on a mat. The funeral bier is made out of sal wood or bamboo. Five or six pieces are placed horizontally and two pieces vertically. The people who assemble there carry the corpse to the burial ground by holding the vertical poles. Before lowering it into the grave prayers are offered. After burial, if the bier is made of sal wood, it is placed on the grave after cutting it according to size but if it is made of bamboo it is thrown away.

"The Munda erect memorial stones in the burial ground called *Sasan.* When a stone has to be put up in the memory of a departed person, information goes round the surrounding villages by beat of drum and large numbers of people gather with digging implements, bamboos, ropes etc. The stones have to be very big and, therefore, the man-power required is large. Against each memorial-stone one sheep is set aside to be slaughtered. After the stone is erected, a feast is held in which everybody partakes of the meat of the sheep as well as the rice-beer. On one particular day as many as two hundred and eighty-eight persons belonging to five villages took part in it. Such an example of co-operation is not found these days in an acculturated village.

"A case history of activities connected with the erection of a memorial stone was reported from Jojohatu as follows:—The *Bhandari* announced in the morning that people who would go to carry stones for Jugai Pahan would be given meat. The stones were to be carried from a place two furlongs from Jojohatu. About fifty persons collected with ropes, iron bars and wooden poles. They consisted of young persons and old from Jojohatu, Chandor and Salehatu. When the people gathered, two goats and two sheep were brought by Jugai, son of Lepa, for whom and for his two brothers Sugua and Dasai and their farther Lal the stones were to be erected. The people were first of all asked if they were satisfied with the animals reserved for the feast. The animals were inspected and it was given out that the animals were small and also few in number and so the share of each person would be very small. At this Jugai requested the people to accept the offer with folded hands as he was unable to arrange for anything more. Sukhram got up and humbly but firmly said that the offer could not be accepted. After a long wait Jugai said that he would give one more sheep. When the other sheep was brought people felt that even this was not sufficient, whereupon in the afternoon Jugai got another goat. After that people became willing to carry the stones. When the work was over the people gathered on the hillock and the meat was distributed. Those who had brought ropes, rods and cooked the meat, got one additional share each. Jugai spent in all Rs. 121 towards the cost of the feast." he adds.

Among the Munda of Koenara converted to Christianity memorial stones are placed on the graves at the time of Easter. These stones are carried by the family members of the deceased, but no particular ceremony is held. If a slab is very big and heavy, many people are employed to carry it to the grave. They are given feast for it. If the stones are erected to the memory of the members of a particular *Khunt* like *Pahan Khunt, Munda Khunt,* or *Mahto Khunt*, all the members of that *Khunt* are treated to a feast. The custom is peculiar to the Munda tribals in Bihar and Jharkhand.

Harassed by the Phenomenum of Death

The again mother and father are usually respected by the offsprings in the Maler society as they have taken all pains to rear their sons. They have fed them, and protected them from the malevolent spirits and have helped them in brining their wives. The mother enjoys better position than a young wife if the former is living with her son. When the mother and the father are living in a separate hut in the same village, the family members come to help each other when in need. In this way the old mother and father feel both emotional and economic security if they have grown up sons living in the same village. A Maler old mother or father, thus reach the dusk of their life and one day they meet the inevitable death. Though death is inevitable and a commonplace event it is looked upon as an event of great horror by the Maler society. For the Maler, death is a great mystery which is mainly caused due to evil influences of the *gossiyan* and their entire religious beliefs and practises, in the ultimate analysis revolve round this major event of life.

Mr. L.P. Vidyarthi discusses the funeral customs, rites and rituals of the Maler Society, thus, "If the basic needs of hunger and sex provide a configuration of the cultural behaviour to the Maler simple community, their experiences into death develop the state of mind, the *insidedness* of the Maler thinking. A Maler, from the very beginning of his life sees the incidence of death in his family, village, and in his circle of relations. He sees a long continued illness, or abrupt death of persons of different age and he feels perplexed to explain the cause of death. A Maler, in the forested and hilly environment, feels the existence of a number of spirits which may be accountable for the diseases, death and decline in the society. The Maler have developed a frame of reference regarding the good and bad incidents of life in terms of the spirits. They have a common term gossaiyan to make this reference to the spirit world...

"As is evident from the biographies, the gossaiyan is a powerful force which controls and influences the happenings in the Maler community. Death and disease in most of the cases are invariably interpreted as the act of gossaiyan. Many of our informants interpreted disease as good disease, meaning thereby that the man has died without any effect of the spirit, either evil or ancestral or directed by a witch. But most of the diseases were interpreted as caused by the above types of spirits and efforts were made by the village Demano and the village Guru (indigenous medicant) to detect the specific gossaiyan or spirit responsible for the disease or death as the case may be. In most of the cases, the Guru administers *Jharphook* (utterances) or apply forest herbs to cure the disease. Many of their gossaiyan are responsible (Bainbridge: 1906; 65-83) for inflicting different types of diseases on the Maler and in order to appease them the Maler worship and make suitable sacrifices.

"When the different gossaiyan are not satisfied, or when some specific gossaiyan becomes angry or when some evil spirits *(Bhute)* attack a person or when a witch directs her evil power and the Demano is not in a position to pacify them, the death of a near one's takes place. The death, thus, is caused by some supernatural power. The Maler further believe that the Jibe-Urkkeya (life's substance or the soul of the Dead) hover around the house till the periodical death ceremonies are not adequately performed. The Maler observe a series of rituals after the death of any of its member. In addition to the funeral and other periodical death rituals, the ancestors are worshipped by the Maler on all important economic and social occasions. The Maler have vague belief that the soul substance is not destroyed with the body and it continues to bring harm and happiness to its past family. This belief leads a Maler to observe a set of rituals and offer a series of sacrifices in the name of ancestor's worship. From the study of the beliefs and practises of the Maler religion, it appears to us that the death and ancestral worship go a long way in explaining the Maler religion and their conception to gossaiyan.

"According to the tradition of the Maler when a man or woman is dead, he or she may either be buried or cremated. At Benderi and Nirbhitta, the villagers exclusively stick to burial ceremony while at Garshingla the villagers observe exclusive cremation and at Tetuli some families buried the dead body (eleven families), while the other families (fifteen in numbers) practise the cremation ceremony. It appears that originally the Maler practised burial ceremony but under the influence of the Hindu, some of the Maler villages or a few families of those villagers have taken up the custom of cremation. In case of a person dying of Small Pox, the Maler never burn the dead body. In all the villages... except Tetuli and Garsingla, the dead body is left in one corner of the graveyard (Masani) surrounded with stones and strong bamboo enclosures to protect it from wild animals. At Garsingla and Tetuli, however, the dead body of a person dying of Small Pox is buried like the Hindu. Perhaps these villages have borrowed the Hindu custom for the disposal of such dead bodies along with the general cremation ceremony. When an infant is dead, it is usually kept in an earthen pot and buried in a corner of the *Masani* (burial grove).

"When any death occurs in the village, a man preferably the village *gurait* (messenger) climbs on the roof of the hut in which death has occurred and beats the drum loudly in a manner that may produce a note of alarm. Hearing the traditional types of drum beating, the villagers of the neighbouring villages come to know about the death, and leaving all works, assemble in front of the hut of the bereaved family. The *Gurait* also goes to inform about the death to the close maternal and paternal relatives of the dead man or woman in the villages falling within six to eight miles. When all the important relatives and the villagers assemble, the dead is taken to the graveyard.

"While the relatives of villages living usually within a radius of eight miles take time to assemble, the local relatives and elderly persons, prepare bier *(Ranthi)* of fresh bamboos brought from the grove of the dead man or woman or his or her relatives. The dead body is neatly bathed and is clothed in his or her best dresses. In case of woman, all her ornaments are put in the respective parts of the body. It was also reported that vermilion is applied on the forehead of the dead body which symbolises his or her marriage with the people of the other world. When the dead body is properly bathed and clothed, it is brought out of the hut and is placed on the bier. The ceremonial lamentation becomes more tense and loud as the body is raised for this procession, and all assembled there accompany the dead body to the graveyard. The menstruating women and their husbands, as also the pregnant women, however, take a special care not to join the funeral procession.

"The graveyard (Masani) is usually located at a distance of about a mile and at a place which is out of way from the village settlement so that it may not be visited by the Maler villages frequently. The Maler consider the Masani to be the abode of evil spirits especially of the *Mari Bhut.* It is their general belief that nobody can escape the Mari Bhut when he goes near the Masani and when he attacks a particular person, he is sure to suffer from Small Pox.

"The dead body is brought to the Masani. The women who accompany the dead body do not enter the burial place. They stay at a little distance away from the Masani and continue their ceremonial weeping while the adult males go to the Masani and make preparation for the burial of the dead body. While camping at Tetuli, we got a chance to observe the funeral rites of the Maler in the Masani. A ditch of five feet in length, three and a half feet in width and four feet in depth was dug, the surface of' the ditch was covered with green leaves and twigs of trees upon which the dead body of the woman was placed with her head facing west. Her belongings like a few pieces of clothes and ornaments were also placed with the body. In case of male, it was reported that his bows and arrows, umbrellas and weapons and such other personal belongings like flute etc. are also placed with the dead body so that they may not come for them in the hut and may use them in the other world. Along with these some quantity of maize and in some cases rice is also placed inside the burial with the belief that the deceased would need it for food.

"When the body is interned, heavy blocks of stones are placed on the loose earth to protect it from the depridation of wild beasts. An earthen pitcher full of water is also placed near the stones (by the side of the head) with the belief that the deceased would need it for drinking purposes. The bier is also broken and along with the cot of the dead person it is also placed on the grave. In case stones are not easily available in the neighbourhood, branches of trees are placed on the grave. At Malgo we observed them keeping branches of trees etc. When the internment of the dead body is complete, an egg or a cock is sacrificed in the name of the Masani Bhut and the people thus are ready to come back to the house of the deceased. While they come to a certain limit, they pass under an egg which is kept in hand by a near relative of the dead. It is believed by them if they pass under the egg (which in the end is offered to the Masani), no evil spirit including Masani Bhut will enter in the village with them. With the male members, the female members who continue to weep near the Masani also come back to the village.

"After returning home all the mourners who accompanied the dead to the Masani wash their hands and feet seven times taking water from the *Ukhli.* This purifies them further and now the members of the family collect all the other household belongings including the hunting and agricultural implements and spray water from the *Ukhli* to purify them. At this time, in some cases, a simple feast may be also given to those who helped the family in making the bier and digging the grave.

"This occasion, when all the villagers and the relatives of the deceased are there, the suspicion regarding the cause of death either owing to witchcraft or poison or by the anger of the gossaiyan are ascertained. Every claim and suspicion as regards the death must be put forward at this time, otherwise it will not be recognised by the people if announced later. The Guru administers *Telpatta* to ascertain the cause of death.

"The Maler family which has lost its member, continues to live in an atmosphere of bereavement and the spirit of the dead in the beginning invariably becomes a source of fear for them. The atmosphere of fear and impurity continues specially till the first feast is not given to the dead. The second feast and sacrifice takes place annually which further minimises the emotional tension and lifts many taboos imposed upon the chief mourner owing to death in the family. In the name of ancestors, again, occasional sacrifices are made from time to time, the description of which will follow here.

"After the funeral the first feast normally takes place on the fifth day but in many cases it may be postponed for another week or so on economic reasons. On this occasion a cow or a pig is sacrificed before the *Jhanda gossaiyan* located in one corner of the hut of the deceased family or in the 'Sacred Zone' of the village as the case may be. The chief mourner offers the food and drink firstly to the dead. The other invited members before feasting, place some food at the spot where the dead body was laid down. These things are placed in the *Saal* leaves and the relatives follow the traditions in making the offering. The deceased is invoked, and is requested to accept the food, and then the community feast follows. Normally, the feast is limited to the members of the village and the close relatives of the dead living in the neighbouring villages. While feasting, the invited members usually talk about the qualities of the deceased and console the chief mourner and other relatives of the dead.

"The death anniversary of every dead person except the infant is observed either singally or with other such bereaved families of the village. This day is marked with solemn sacrifices, observance of fast and bath and ultimately with feast, drink and dance. On this occasion invitations are sent to all relatives who normally live in neighbouring villages within a radius of ten miles. They invariably attend the death anniversary and bring with them offerings of maize or rice and *taddi.*

The actual celebration starts with the beating of drum by a ritualistically selected person. While the drumming is on, the Demano drinks *taddi* inside the house of the bereaved family. When he is completely drunk he comes out of the house, washes his feet and hands or takes full bath in the village spring, and then calls to the deceased waving straws in his hands. He calls the name of the dead, and ultimately he comes, and the Demano is possessed by his spirit. The Demano begins to speak as if the dead man is speaking. The spirit of the dead addresses his mother, and his father and such other close relatives and asks them to provide him with clothes, food and such other things. Everything desired by the spirit (the Demano) is given so that it may be appeased, and it may not send disease, death and unhappiness to the family.

"The possessed Demano eats the offered food carelessly and throws part of it on his head and shoulder. The people assembled there are all spell-bound, emotionally disturbed owing to the advent of the dead and with the fear of active spirit. On this situation, the villagers become very serious and consider the words of the Demano coming straight from the mouth of a dead ancestor. The dead on this occasion expresses all his wish to give happiness to some of his relatives and villagers and to bring disaster and even death to some. The opportunity is taken by the deceased relative to ask question concerning his death and other such matters. This continues for more than an hour and when the dead spirit is satisfied, the Demano says 'I am satisfied with your hospitality, I have eaten and drunk, and now I am going back to the *Bero Gossaiyan* (the Sun God)'. When the worship of the dead is complete, the feast follows. The invited guests share the food and drink and dance for the whole night. The whole festival is known as *Bhoje* and is mostly celebrated after the harvesting season. After the celebration of this festival, the persons who have lost their partners (widow or widower) are now free to remarry. This breaking of taboo, and sanction on the part of the widow or widower to select ones partner gives a touch of courtship and sexual enjoyment to this celebration. The *Bhoje* celebration, thus is also of great attraction to the unmarried boys and girls who take the opportunity in the night to mix freely and choose their partners for marriage or for free mixing and also for eventual marriage.

"There are several regional variations in the observance of the above *Bhoje* celebration. In many villages, for example at Benderi, we noted that the whole celebration is combined with *Pillai* or *Bandna* festival. The pillai festival lasts for four days when the various Gossaiyan specially *Chaal Nadu* and *Amte Gossaiyan* are worshipped on both the family and the village levels and, then the annual ancestor worship and finally the feasts also follow.

"The offerings to the dead are made on the second day of the Bandna festival when on the outskirt of the village, rice and chicken are served by the chief mourner and call the dead ones by name to eat them. Sacrifices of cow or pig are also made in the name of the ancestor. The sacrifice is made by any elderly member of the family but if his wife is in the menstruation period, any person related to him makes the sacrifice. Women are not allowed to participate in celebrations. Such males whose wives are in menstruation periods are also not considered pure to participate in the ancestral sacrifices and feasts.

"In the year 1956, while I had an occasion to attend the Bandna ceremony at Benderi, I noted that the bereaved families made sacrifices on small scale near the Masani individually. The worship is mainly attended by the near male relatives when the mourner himself (as narrated by Bhama) makes sacrifices of cooked rice, ground maize (Sattu), rice or maize beer, tobacco etc. After these sacrifices and worship on the family level, the Bandna festival is observed on the village level when cow and pig or some year, a buffalo purchased by subscription raised from each family of the village are sacrificed and then feast, drink and dance follow.

"Among all the sacrifices, the buffalo sacrifice known as *Mangarwin* (Manakh and arwin or Buffalo's Worshipping) or *Kara Puja* is considered to be the best of all sacrifices that the Maler can think of to satisfy their ancestors and appease the other Gossaiyan. This sacrifice the Maler would like to make every year but as it is an expensive affair, the buffalo sacrifice is normally celebrated on the village level once in three or five years by the Maler villages." Adds Mr. Vidyarthi. The burial customs, rites and rituals are related to the Maler community of tribals.

Burying under Floor of the House

Mr. Nesfield describes the funeral customs of the Tharu tribals, thus: "The burial rites of Tharus are of various kinds. Sepulture or earth-burial seems to have been the original custom; but the Hindu rite of cremation has now become common in many clans, except in the case of persons who have died of cholera or small-pox; and these are invariably buried in the earth. After cremation the ashes are scattered on the nearest river. Before, however, the corpse has been disposed of by either rite, it is usual to paint it with vermilion and expose it for one night on a mound outside the house. From this mound, as from a stronghold, the spirit of the dead is supposed to scare away wild animals from the corpse. Whether the body is buried or burnt, the ceremony is always performed on the southern side of the village—a notion probably borrowed from Hindus, who consider that the north is the region commonly frequented by divine spirits, and the south by human souls. The man who puts the first fire to the funeral pyre is considered to be unclean, from having brought himself within dangerous reach of the contagion of death. He is therefore kept at a distance for ten days after cremation, and compelled to live entirely alone.". . . . ."On the expiry of the tenth day (or the thirteenth, as some Tharus relate), the friends of the deceased meet at the house where he died, and after undergoing the ceremony of shaving they hold 'a feast of the dead.' The banquet prepared for this purpose consists of cooked flesh and wine, the scent and smoke of which are intended to refresh the departed soul: the solid parts—that is, the flesh and wine themselves—are consumed by the living."

"In certain rare cases the burial rite is performed in a manner; distinct from either of those already described. A man noted above his fellows for wisdom in counsel, bravery in the chase, or knowledge of the magical and medicinal arts, is buried under the floor of the house in which he was living before his spirit departed. The house thenceforth becomes a temple, and ceases to be used as a dwelling place for man. The soul of the dead becomes its occupant, and it lives there to bless those whom it has left behind. At periods of three or six months after the death, the friends and neighbours of the deceased assemble around his grave or temple and make an effigy in clay, parts of which are painted in various colours, intended to reproduce the appearance of resuscitated life. His worshippers fall down weeping and wailing before the image, and place offerings of cooked flesh and wine at its feet. Presently, at a given signal, as soon as the soul of the dead is believed to have been propitiated by the scent of roast meat and the fumes of wine, they commence to dance and sing with every demonstration of joy; and the proceedings of the day are closed with consuming the solid parts of the offerings."

Sir Risley adds, "The Tharus stand wholly outside of the Hindu caste organisation, and their social status cannot be defined by any of the ordinary standards. No orthodox Hindu will eat with a Tharu or take water from his hands, and by the higher castes his mere touch would be deemed pollution. This comparatively degraded position is, however, due in great measure to the nomadic habits of the tribe, and to the fact that they come very little into contact with settled Hindu communities. Tharus follow the forest; their typical village is a line of huts in the middle of a clearing, and their favourite mode of husbandry was until lately the *jhum* method of burning the jungle and planting a crop in the ashes. The scanty crops obtained in this fashion are eked out by hunting and fishing, by gathering forest fruits and vegetables, and by grazing cows and buffaloes. Avoiding the larger villages of the plains, they live their own life on the outskirts of Hindu civilization, and no place has as yet been allotted in the Hindu social system. 'Every little village,' says Mr. Nesfield, 'is a self-governing community. Disputes are decided by a council of elders; and this is sometimes presided over by a headman, who in the Tharu language was formerly called *barwaik,* but who is now dubbed even by themselves with the ordinary Hindi title of *chaudhari.* The office of headman is not hereditary. The man selected is one whose age, experience, and knowledge of the magical and medicinal arts entitle him to more respect than the rest; and he acquires the status of headman by tacit consent, and not by formal election. The decisions of the council or the headman are obeyed unreservedly, and there is no such thing known as a Tharu taking a fellow tribesman before a tribunal outside his own community. Litigation between Tharus and Hindus is equally unknown. Among themselves the Tharus are for the most part a peaceful and good-natured race, following without question, as if by a law of nature, the customs and maxims of their ancestors.' Notwithstanding their comparative isolation, their customs show many signs of the influence of Hindu example. Their religious observances tend unmistakeably towards Sivaism; their marriage ceremony is framed on a Hindu model; they revere the cow, and scrupulously abstain from eating beef. Their ultimate reception into the standard social system seems therefore merely to be a question of time. In other respects their practise in matters of food falls short of the orthodox standard. They eat pigs and fowls, and make no distinction between the clean and unclean species of fish. Field-rats they will cook when pressed for food, and the porcupine *(sahi)* is thought a delicacy, because his flesh resembles that of the pig. Mr. Nesfield mentions that when their stock of meat becomes larger than they can consume at once, they preserve it by cutting it into strips and drying it in the sun." The customs, rites and rituals pertain to the Tharu tribals spread from Uttarakhand, UP, Bihar and Nepal.

Burial of Corpse Fully Clothed in Sitting Position

About the burial of the Lepchas, Sir Risley records, "The dead are usually buried, fully clothed and in a sitting position, facing towards the east. Before burial the corpse is kept sitting in the house for two or three days with food before it. The grave is lined with stones and a round cairn built on the top surmounted by a flag. Among the Rong Lepchas an Ojha is called in about a month after death to perform a simple propitiatory rite, at which a cow or a goat is killed and much *marua* beer is drunk. This is sometimes repeated on the first anniversary of the death. The objects is put the dead man's spirit to rest, and to prevent him from plaguing the living with bad dreams. At harvest time offerings of rice, *marua* beer, and various kinds of food are presented by the head of the household for the benefit of ancestors in general.

"The higher classes of Khamba Lepchas burn their dead, pound the fragments of the bones which remain, and throw them into a river, not into a *jhora* or hill stream. The subsequent propitiatory ceremony is sometimes very elaborate, as in the case of the obsequies of the sister of the Sikkim Raja, described by Mr. J. Ware Edgar, C.S.I., in the following passage *Report of a Visit to Sikkim*, pp. 57-58.

"Before the figure [meant to represent the dead person, in this case the Sikkim Rajah's sister, who was a nun] was a table on which were different kinds of food; on another table at the side were various things which had belonged to the woman when alive; while on a third, 108 little brass lamps were arranged in rows. Long lines of monks in dark red robes and with very tall cups of bright crimson on their heads sat on carpets placed in the middle of the chapel and chanted litanies throughout each day of my stay at Toomlong.

"It chanced that I saw the conclusion, and learned the meaning of this ceremony at Pemiongehi, where the lay-figure of the nun was taken some days after I left Toomlong. There for three days the figure was seated before the altar, and the monks chanted the litanies for the departure of the soul of the dead nun. . . On the third day the relations, friends, and dependents of the deceased brought or sent gifts of food or clothing or money, which were all laid before the figure of the dead woman; while the head Lama, standing in front of his chair and turning towards the figure, stated the nature of each gift and the name of the donor. Towards evening the tea-cup of the nun was freshly filled with tea and her murwa jug with murwa, and all the monks solemnly drank tea with her. Then many people who had known and loved the nun when alive went up, and prostrating themselves before the figure, kissed the hem of the robe as a last farewell, while the monks chanted the litanies more zealously than ever, and the head Lama, who had left his chair and gone to one of the tables, went through some elaborate ceremonies the meaning of which I could not make out. At about nine o'clock the chanting ceased, and the Lama again standing in front of his chair made a long speech to the soul of the nun, in which he told her that all that could be done to make her journey to another world easy had been done, and that now she would have to go forth alone and unassisted to appear before the king and judge of the dead . . . When the Lama had finished his address, some of the monks took down the lay-figure and undressed it; while others formed a procession and conducted the soul of the nun into the darkness outside the monastery, with a discordant noise of conch-shells, thigh bone trumpets, Tibetan flutes, gongs, cymbals, tambourines, drums, and other most disagreeable but nameless instruments." The custom is related to the Buddhist Lepchas in West Bengal.

Resorting to Burial due to Poverty

Sir Risley notes, "Those who can afford a funeral pyre prefer to burn the dead, while the poorer members of the tribe bury, placing the corpse face upwards with the head pointing towards the south. In the latter case a small fire is kindled upon the grave, in which food and drink are burned for the benefit of the deceased. The Agnia-Mech perform a meagre propitiatory rite on the eighth day, and the Jati-Mech on the fourth day, after death. With both the important part of the proceedings is the feast which is given to the friends and relatives of the deceased. Some repeat the ceremony every year after the manner of the Hindus, but this is unusual." The funeral custom is practised by the Mech community.

Tying body to Stout Pole and Carrying it to Grave

Sir Risley notes, "The funeral ceremonies of the Mangars, which are the same as those of the Gurung and Sunuwars, are curious and interesting. Immediately after death the corpse is tied with three pieces of rope to a stout pole and carried to the grave. There it is stripped, dressed in new clothes, and laid on its back in the grave with the head pointing to the north. The forehead is smeared with sandal wood paste. One of the maternal relatives of the deceased, usually the maternal uncle, is then chosen to act as priest for the occasion, and to conduct the ritual appointed for the propitiation of the dead. First of all he puts in the mouth of the corpse some silver coins and some coral, which is greatly prized by the Himalayan races. Then he lights a wick soaked in clarified butter, touches the lips with fire, scatters some parched rice about the mouth, and lastly covers the face with a cloth called *pujunri.* Two bits of wood, about three feet long, are set up on either side of the grave. In the one are cut nine steps or notches forming a ladder for the spirit of the dead to ascend to heaven; on the other every one present at the funeral cuts a notch to show that he has been there. As the maternal uncle stops out of the grave, he bids a solemn farewell to the dead and calls upon him to ascend to heaven by the ladder that stands ready for him. When the earth has been filled in, the stick notched by the funeral party is taken away to a distance and broken in two pieces, lest by its means the dead man should do the survivors a mischief. The pole used to carry the corpse is also broken up, and the spades and ropes are left in the grave.

When the mourners return home, one of their party goes ahead and makes a barricade of thorn bushes across the road midway between the grave and the house of the deceased. On the top of the thorns he puts a big stone on which he takes his stand, holding a pot of burning incense in his left hand and some woollen thread in his right. One by one the mourners step on the stone and pass through the smoke of the incense to the other side of the thorny barrier. As they pass, each takes a piece of thread from the man who holds the incense and ties it round his neck. The object of this curious ceremony is to prevent the spirit of the dead from coming home with the mourners and establishing itself in its old haunts. Conceived of as a miniature man, it is believed to be unable to make its way on foot through the thorns, while the smell of the incense, to which all spirits are highly sensitive, prevents it from surmounting this obstacle on the shoulders of one of the mourners.

"Agriculture, trade and soldiering are the chief occupations of the Mangars, but no means of earning a livelihood comes amiss to them, provided that it does not involve doing things which are recognised as the proper business of the lower castes. They abstain from beef, but eat pork and domestic fowls, and indulge freely in strong drink. Before marriage a Mangar will eat any sort of food with a Gurung or Khas, but after he has been married, he can only take chupatties from these castes, and not take rice or dal. Mangars smoke in the same hookah with Gurungs, Khas and Brahmans." The customs, rites and rituals are related to the *Mangar* community.

Lying corpse on *Bhelak* Leaves

Sir Herbert Risley records, "As a rule the Male bury their dead, the corpse being laid on a layer of *bhelak* leaves with the head pointing towards the north. The bodies of those who died of snake-bite or have come to a violent end are exposed in the jungle. According to Colonel Dalton, the bodies of Demanos are dealt with in this fashion, on the ground that if they are buried in the village, their ghosts walk and cause annoyance to the living. On the fifth day after death a feast is given, to which all members of the family are invited. Six months or a year later a special ceremony is held for the purpose of appeasing the spirit of the dead man. The chief part is played by the Demano, who represents the deceased, and is dressed so as to personate him as closely as possible. In this character he demands clothes, ornaments, food and whatever the dead man was fond of in this life, the belief being that if they are given to the Demano, the spirit will in some unexplained fashion have the use of them in the world of the dead. When the Demano has got all that he asked for, he goes into a fit and remains insensible for some minutes, during which time he is supposed to be in communication with the spirit of the deceased. On his revival the company partake of a feast.

"The property left by the dead man cannot be divided until this second feast has taken place. According to Colonel Dalton, the eldest son takes half, and the remainder is equally divided among the agnates. Some say, however, that division among the sons takes place on a sort of diminishing scale according to order of birth, the eldest getting the largest share, the second less, and so on." The custom pertains to the *Male* community.

Death caused by Malevolent Bongas

The Santals do not subscribe to the idea of the possibility of a natural death. They are also say that death never occurs due to accident, but like other tribals, generally attribute death to the malignancy of certain *bongas*, impersonal powers and witchcraft. The Santals believe that these malignant spirits against whom an individual has to counteract throughout his life-time in jungle, put an end to his life.

Mr. J. Troisi writes about the Santals, "Their ideas about life in the future world (*hanapuri*) as opposed to this world (noapuri) are rather confused. One thing is certain—the belief in the survival of the soul after death... the Santals believe that, on the death of an individual, his social personality is not annihilated but rather transformed. *Vide* Du Toit, B.M., 'some Aspects of the Soul-Concept among the Bantu-Speaking Nguni Tribes of South Africa', *Anthropological Quarterly*, Washington, 33(3), July 1960, pp. 134-42; Firth, Raymond, *The Fate of the Soul: An Interpretation of Some Primitive Concepts*, Cambridge: Cambridge University Press, 1955. As some of the expressions used to denote the death of a person indicate, according to Santal belief, the soul, after leaving the body, becomes a *bonga* joining the abode of its deceased ancestors. We thus have expressions like, 'nitok doe hapramena', meaning, 'he has become a *bonga*'. This belief in the soul of a person becoming a *bonga* and joining the abode of his ancestors, predominates, as we shall see, in all the rituals and ceremonies connected with death. The Santals believe that one becomes a *hapram bonga* only after all the funerary rites have been performed in his honour. If a person dies an unnatural death, or in the case of a woman dying in pregnancy or childbirth, they do not achieve full spiritual status and their ghosts are believed to continue hovering around the world as *bhuts* or *curins.*

"Some of the current ideas about future life have a moral content. Thus, the Santals believe that their future life is determined by the good or bad deeds a person has committed in his earthly life. Ideas regarding punishment and reward show that the sufferer will be comforted, the good man rewarded, while the wicked man will be punished by *Jom Raja* who, along with *Hudar Raja,* is the regent of the nether world. If a person, during his life-time in *noapuri* has treated others unjustly, in *hanapuri* he is made to carry rotting meat on his head, wrestle with huge worms or sit immersed in excrement. Special tortures are also meted out to those who transgress the tribal code of morality and to those who, as we have seen, fail to show the traditional tribal marks, *sika* and *khoda,* on their bodies. On the other hand, he who leads an honest and kind life in *noapuri* will be rewarded in *hanapuri.*

"When a Santal dies, his house and village become polluted. The village is bereft of its protective *bongas* and the household is deprived of the care of its *orak bongas.* No marriages, festivals or any public worship can be performed within the village until the funerary rites have been performed. The pollution is due to the belief that death is a victory of the malignant agencies. It is an insult to the benevolent *bongas* whose major concern is the Santals' well-being. Through death, *the jaher bongas* of a village and the household *bongas* are polluted. Besides, as long as the funerary rites are not performed, the soul of the departed person still remains a menace to all the living members of his household. As a result, when a Santal dies, the family and village co-operate in performing the funerary rites.

"On a death occurring in a village, a loud chorus of lamentations and wailing is set up by the female relatives of the deceased. According to Durkheim, in the case of mourning, the social pressure is to bear witness, by significant actions, to the people's sorrow and perplexity. The people concerned have to show that they are not indifferent to what has happened. The family members must react to the loss of one of their members by renewing their collective sentiments. The sharing of similar emotions produces a sense of comfort compensating for the original loss. The *godet* is told and he, in turn, informs all the villagers, starting with the headman. All the deceased's relatives, living within a reasonable distance, are also apprised of the occurrence. The body is then prepared for burial. Though many authors like Bodding Culshaw Datta-Majumder; and Archer speak of cremation as the Santal way of disposing of a dead body, no cremation has taken place in Pangro since 1946. From information gathered from Santals in other parts of the district, burial seems to be the main way of disposing of a corpse in Santal Parganas. The reason often given is the difficulty in obtaining sufficient firewood.

According to these authors, burial was considered an exception and was resorted to in the case of children who die before puberty, men and women who die from certain contagious diseases such as leprosy, smallpox and tuberculosis, persons who die an unnatural death or without their *Caco Chatiar* ceremony, and by women who die in pregnancy or childbirth. It is anointed with oil and turmeric, dressed in new clothes and laid on a *parkom* (stringed bed) which is brought out into the courtyard. In the case of a woman whose husband is still alive, vermilion is put on her forehead by a female relative. A piece of cloth containing some money, a brass plate *(thari),* drinking vessel *(bati),* and other gifts donated by the family and near kinsmen as a token of mourning, are placed on the cot which is carried by four of the deceased male relatives or friends. Women do not go to the burial place.

"On reaching the outskirts of the village, a grave *(gadlak)* facing north to south, is dug deep in the ground by some of the villagers. The Santals do not have a specific burial ground. Bodies are generally buried in the deceased's agricultural land at some distance from village. Graves are not the places of cult and are not long remembered. All the ornaments are removed from the body and so are the gifts placed on the cot. These are taken by those present and sold, buying *handi* and *paura* in return. A cloth is laid in the grave and the body is carried around the grave three times. The chief mourner then puts some burning embers into the deceased's mouth. The body is lowered in the grave, its head facing the south. Branches are put into the slots prepared. These serve as a kind of canopy over which other branches are laid. The cot is broken and the wood is placed on top of the branches. The chief mourner, followed by the other relatives and villagers throws earth into the grave until it is filled. A mound of soil is raised on the grave around which some stones are also placed so as to keep away any stray animals. An earthenware water pot *(kandha)* and a winnowing fan containing some paddy are left beside the grave, which is purified by the sprinkling of cowdung mixed with water. The *hatak* filled with paddy signifies that the body is provided with food and, therefore, it does not have to return to its house in search of food. The mourners then go for their purificatory bath, after which they anoint themselves with oil and turmeric. The chief mourner has his head shaved completely. As in the case of *Janam Chatiar*, the shaving of the chief mourner's head expresses the transition of the deceased from one state to another.

"As a rule, the eldest son is the chief mourner in the case of the deceased being a man. If the deceased has no male children, then the right of placing the burning embers into the corpse's mouth, descends in this order on the following persons: father, brother, senior kinsman on the male side. In the case of a woman, it is the husband who performs this ritual. If she is a widow, her eldest son does this. When asked the meaning of this ritual of putting burning embers into the corpse's mouth, the spontaneous answer received was that this was a remnant of the times when dead bodies used to be cremated. On further probing, I was told that the one who applies the embers is looked upon as the deceased's successor in the management of his household affairs. It is he who meets the expenses of the funerary ceremonies.

"The next phase in the funerary ceremonies is known as *Tel Nahan* or 'oil washing'. It is also known as *Umul Ader* or 'bringing in the shadow'. The soul or spirit of a man is identified with his shadow which in turn is credited with a number of powers. This purification ceremony, performed on the fifth day after death, is said to be of great importance. Until it is performed, the dead person will remain in the clutches of the hostile agency which brought about his death and is thus a menace to his household and village. Through this ceremony, the villagers are safeguarded against such dangers while the deceased's soul is freed from its shackles. It now dwells inside the family's *bhitar*. The village *bongas* cease to be unclean, the village is purified and feasts and public worship can once more be performed. Though the deceased's immediate family members still remain, as they say, 'in the shadow', his other kinsmen are free to perform weddings and offer sacrifices.

"The *Tel Nahan* ceremony starts when the village men gather at the dead man's house. After all have been shaved, some male relatives of the deceased accompanied by other villagers go to the grave. Here, the chief mourner collects a handful of earth which he burns and puts into a new earthenware pot. On returning to the end of the village *kullhi,* where they are met by the womenfolk, the pot is smashed to pieces and the burnt earth is sprinkled with water and turmeric. The burnt handful of earth is said to be reminiscent of the *jan baha* which literally means 'flowers of bone' but which, in the context of cremation, meant a piece of the frontal portion of the skull and two bits from the collar bone. These bones used to be rescued from the funeral pyre and, after sometime, a special ceremony was observed in which these bones were immersed into the Damodar river *(Nai Gada)* or into any stream or pond. Then everyone goes for his purificatory bath, the chief mourner carrying the burnt earth on a leaf plate. After, taking a bath and rubbing themselves with oil given by the deceased's family, the chief mourner, surrounded by his male relatives and villagers, makes offerings of oil cakes and *sal* twigs to *Maran Buru, Pilcu Haram* and *Pilcu Budhi,* and to the departed soul. He implores *Maran Burn* to lodge the deceased's soul in the 'shadow of the house' till he reaches his final rest. He also invokes the departed spirit to accept his new temporary abode.

"Everyone then returns to the deceased's house for the *Umul Ader* ceremony. Here, two persons are said to become possessed, one by *Maran Bum* and the other by the spirit of the deceased. They are given water and rice-beer to drink. One of the deceased's relatives then asks the spirit of the dead person the cause of his death—whether he left of his own free-will or whether it was through some disease or through someone's hostility. Once the villagers are satisfied with the answers given, the two individuals impersonating the spirits resume their normal roles. The sacrificial animal is offered to the spirit of the deceased by the chief mourner. Each of the houses in the village, or in certain cases those who can afford to, provides a fowl for the purification of the village and to celebrate the departed spirit's release from the underworld. All these animals are slain with a blow on the back of the head. They are not beheaded as in other sacrifices. When the food is ready, the people present are served. They are also given rice-beer. The flesh from the animal's head is reserved for the chief mourner and his family. After everyone has had his fill, they return to their homes happy that their village has been purified.

"Though with the *Tel Nahan* ceremony, the departed spirit is said to have been released from the underworld, he has not yet reached his final abode. He is still, as it were, in transit. It is only with the *Bhandan* ceremony that he finally joins the realm of his ancestors. With this ceremony, the deceased's relatives bid the departed their last farewell and send him happy and honoured to his abode. All mourning comes to an end and the deceased's immediate family once more is free to sacrifice to their *bongas,* attend festivals, and celebrate marriages.

"As such, there is no specified time when this ceremony should be performed. It all depends on the economic situation of the deceased's relatives. Thus, in the case of Singrai Marndi, his relatives performed the

Bhandan ceremony a year after his death, while Lokhon Tudu's *Bhandan* was performed six months after. On the fixed date, all the villagers and deceased's relatives assemble in the deceased's house. Here the chief mourner's head is once more completely shaved, while the other villagers have their beards shaved. On returning from their purificatory bath, all are given *taben* and *khajari* to eat and rice-beer to drink. Three persons are possessed by the spirits of the dead person, the founder of the village and *Maran Buru* respectively. The dead man is made to re-identify himself. Then the three spirits are asked whether they were satisfied with all the ceremonies already performed in honour of the departed spirit. On giving their assent, the three men emerge from their roles and are given rice-beer.

"A goat is brought into the courtyard. After preparing the *khond,* the chief mourner offers the goat to the spirit of the dead person invoking him to protect his living relatives and keep away any harm or misfortune. The animal is then slain by the *jog manjhi* who strikes it with the buttend of an axe. The side on which the animal falls is retained by the deceased's family, while the other side is given to the villagers. Rice-beer libations are also made in the dead man's honour. Fowls are offered to each ancestor spirit of the family, mentioning each one by name. Rice-beer libations are also made in their honour. After each libation, all those present drink.

"Meanwhile, several relatives and fellow villagers bring goats and fowls to be offered in the name of the departed spirit. While offering these animals, the giver mentions his name saying, 'Take note, this animal is being offered to you by so and so'. When all the sacrifices are over, the flesh is dressed and cooked with rice. Besides the uncooked portion set aside for the dead man's family and relatives, two other portions are made. One is eaten by all those present, the villagers and the household members, the other portion is divided among the villagers who take their share back to their homes. Before the food is served, the chief mourner offers some of the food to the departed spirit invoking it to accept the food and to purify the household completely. The whole night is spent in feasting, dancing and singing.

"In this way, all the funerary ceremonies come to an end. The dead man's family is free to resume normal relations with the world of men and spirits. Judging by what has been said here, we can rightly apply Radcliffe-Brown's findings on burial customs among the Andaman Islanders to the Santal funerary rites. In both cases, the burial customs can be visualised and explained 'as a collective reaction against the attack on the collective feeling of solidarity constituted by the death of a member of the social group'. We can also say that the main object of the Santals' funerary rites is twofold: (*i*) to rid the living survivors of the death pollution and of the evil attentions of the departed spirit which is believed to haunt them until it is united with the ancestor spirits; and *(ii)* to release the departed spirit from the underworld and help it find final rest in its abode. According to Malinowski, funeral rites provide a useful catharsis of the emotions of those most closely affected. They are also an expression of the new adjustment of statutes and roles in a group after the death of a member. Ancestor worship ritually brings the spirit of the deceased back into the community reaffirming the connections between the dead and the survivors."

The Santals believe in their relation and dependence on their spirits. This intimate relationship is concretely manifested in the various funerary rituals performed. This relationship is expressed in the Santal seasonal rites and festivals, most of which are associated with their agricultural cycle. Through various rites and ceremonies Santal society seeks to bring the world of the bongas or spirits into relation with the individual in the critical junctures of his life. The main impact of Van Gennep's theory was on the study of the mechanism of rituals with special emphasis on the rites of passage. He rightly pointed out that the passage from one stage to another in an individual's life-cycle does not by itself explain the complex ceremonies which accompanied it. Each ritual has specific protective, propitiatory, purificatory and productive purposes. However, he has failed to clearly demonstrate the association of these rites with the social structure of the society in which they are performed. A later generation of social anthropologists like Durkheim, Radcliffe-Brown, Evans-Pritchard, Forde, Turner, Junod and others, were more concerned in analysing the social function of these rites rather than elaborating on their mechanism. Thus, Radcliffe-Brown in his analyses of the rites of passage performed by the Andaman Islanders shows how these rites deal with the 'social personality' of the individual.

Mr. Troisi discusses further, "Likewise, in the analytical description of the nature and function of the rites of passage prevalent in Santal society in Pangro, attention has been paid to the symbolic social values of the rituals and ceremonies performed. It has been shown how in their congregational aspect, these rites and ceremonies help to re-enact the community's relationship of dependence and fellowship with their spirits. In so doing, they reinforce the community's own solidarity and reaffirm its own values.

"As we have seen, the critical junctures in the life-cycle of an individual are replete with danger. The individual is himself in danger. He also passes this danger on to his family, village and tribe at large. Besides the individual, his family and village are also defiled. The village *bongas* are polluted. No festivals, marriages or public sacrifices, can be held unless the purificatory rituals are performed. In view of this, we can say that the main object of all the rites/and ceremonies attending birth, initiation, marriage and death, is twofold:—(*i*) to remove the pollution attendant on the individual's household and village, and to protect them against any calamities at the hands of the evil spirits and powers; *(ii)* to purify the individual himself, keep him away from any hostile agencies, and to ensure for him the security and care given by the benevolent spirits. Thus, the *Janam Chatiar* reveals an anxiety to integrate the new-born child into its father's clan, subclan and *bongas. Caco Chatiar* reveals an anxiety to integrate the initiated person into a new relationship with his *bongas.* Various marriage rituals manifest the anxiety for the future welfare of the married couple, guarding its luck, and warding off evil spirits and impersonal powers. The funerary rites help the departed spirit to liberate itself from the underworld and to finally join the abode of its ancestors.

"... these ceremonies serve as occasions for emphasising the relations of mutual harmony and dependence between the individual and his society and..., in so doing, village solidarity is strengthened. The whole Santal village community acts like one man. Their presence is required to give sanction to the proceedings. The person who conducts each ritual is merely the active representative of the community. The feasting, social reunion and rejoicing that mark their successful termination, make it clear that each rite of passage is a matter which concerns not only the individual who enters into it, but the whole community. The various gifts bestowed upon him, are a clear expression of the general goodwill towards him." The custom, rites and rituals are practised by the Santals.

Ancestral Spirits' (Hapramko Bongas) worship

Each Santal household worships the spirits of its ancestors called *Hapramko Bongas*. In addition to the household *bongas.* Among the Oraons, the spirits of the dead ancestors are venerated as a separate class of spirits. Ancestor worship is a strong factor in Santal social and household solidarity. Ancestor worship has played a very important part in the religion of ancient Greece and Rome. It is also a very important feature of traditional Chinese and Japanese societies. Cults of the same kind exist today in many parts of Africa and Asia. The degree of interaction between the dead and the living varies from culture to culture.

Mr. Troisi notes, "The term ancestor worship is sometimes used in a very wide sense to refer to any sort of rituals performed in honour of dead persons including tribal or national heroes and leaders. Here, I will be using the term in the way in which Radcliffe-Brown has used it, limiting the cult group to the 'members of a lineage with reference to the deceased members of the lineage' (Radcliffe-Brown). Ancestors are kin. In most cases they are senior kin and the living behave towards them as towards senior living kin.

The cause behind the ancestor worship is the notion that at the death of an individual, his social personality is not annihilated, but rather transformed. 'The belief in ancestor spirits', Malinowski points out 'is the result of the belief in immortality... which is the result of a deep emotional revelation, standardised by religion rather than a primitive philosophical tradition:' The Santals, like the most other primitive tribes, hold the belief in the survival of the soul after death. According to the original Santal belief the 'soul' after leaving the body, becomes a *bonga*. The phrases often used when one dies are 'nitok doe hapramena' meaning 'now he has become an ancestor (died)', or, simply, 'bongaenae', meaning 'he has become a *bonga*'. The word *hapram* is nowadays almost exclusively used when referring to the dead ancestor.

A deceased, however, becomes a *hapram bonga* only after his funerary rites have been performed. Mr. Troisi notes, "Those who die an unnatural death or without their *Caco Chatiar* ceremony, those who die from certain infectious diseases such as leprosy, smallpox, etc., and women who die in pregnancy or in childbirth, are not given full funerary rites. They do not achieve full spiritual status and their ghosts are believed to continue hovering around the world as *bhuts* or *curins.* With the *Tel Nahan* ceremony, performed five days after a person's death, the dead person is freed from the enemy that killed him but is not as yet admitted to the realm of the ancestors. He dallies in the household's *bhitar.* S.C. Roy (1972:26) reports how, among the Oraons, through the *Ekh-Mankhna* ceremony, the shade of a deceased person is said to be brought back to his former house to remain there till it is admitted into the community of the *Pach-balar* (the pre-deceased relatives) through the *Utur-Khila* ceremony. The Khonds of Orissa and the Gonds of the Central Provinces call back the shades of the dead to their old homes through similar ceremonies. It is only once the *Bhandan* ceremony is over that he finally joins his ancestors, along with whom he continues taking active interest in the household affairs. Ancestors are believed to 'live' with the living, assisting at births and weddings, and also in the settling of household problems. In this way, the living and dead of the same lineage stand in a close relationship with each other. The dead are said to be aware of the actions and even the thoughts of their living relatives. So long as they are remembered, ancestors continue influencing a household's affairs helping out in times of crises. It is almost a duty of the spirits of the departed to see to the welfare of their living relatives.

"Ancestor worship serves to keep the memory of the dead alive and welds the community of the living into one with those who have lived in the past. Their welfare is bound up with that of their living relatives. For one generation, at least, they must not be ignored and the conventional tributes must be given to them. Otherwise, though generally benevolent, they would visit the family with sickness and other misfortunes for they are very sensitive to neglect and would make the careless and the forgetful ill. Hence, as with other primitive tribes, the Santals have special rites of veneration for their ancestors. In all festivals, private or public, they are venerated and special offerings are made to them. Their blessings are invoked at every social ceremony. Whenever fresh *handi* is drunk, libations are poured out in their honour. Similarly, the Santals had a custom which is slowly being forgotten, according to which the woman of the house, while preparing the food, used to set aside some uncooked rice grains for the ancestors, making the meal a communion between the dead and the living. S.C. Roy reports similar customs among the orthodox Oraons. This supports Archer's statement that: whether it is a time of drinking rice-beer, eating a meal, celebrating a festival, a birth or a wedding or placating the *bongas* the recent dead must be given their small offering.

"During the *Sohrae,* fowls and rice-beer libations are offered by each family in honour of its ancestors. Since the Santals believe that their ancestors are still alive as spirits with human qualities and needs, they insist that in their sacrifices there must be the feeling that the ancestors 'are really there'. Thus, during the *Sohrae,* as many relatives as have died from the time of the grandfather and grandmother are each offered a fowi. Gausdal remarks, 'It is one hen for every one who has died; father, mother, uncle, aunt, brother, sister or children'. The name of each person is mentioned. If, due to the lack of fowls, sacrifices to the departed are not made during the *Sohrae,* then these sacrifices are performed during the *Baha* festival. Otherwise, only rice-beer libations are offered in their honour during the *Baha* and the *Erok* or Sowing festival.

"Sacrifices to the departed are an extension of filial piety. The eldest male member of the household acts as the officiating priest. If there is no male member of the household qualified to perform the sacrifice, then an agnate of the departed is asked to do so. On the day of the sacrifice the *bhitar* is cleansed and plastered with cowdung. The officiating person does not observe any specific taboos, except that he does not eat anything on the eve of the sacrifice and he takes a purificatory bath. The sacrificial rite is the same as for the *orak bongas,* with the following modifications. No vermilion is used; the sacrificed fowl is not beheaded but it is slain by a blow on the back of the head without any blood being sprinkled on the rice in the *khond.* The ancestral *bongas* are 'made to eat' of the sacrificial meal *(sura daka)* and to 'drink' of the *handi* together with the other living relatives present. In fact, leaf plates containing *sura daka* and leaf cups containing rice-beer are first offered to each of the ancestral spirits prior to anyone present starting to eat and drink.

"The social function of the ritual mentioned sacrifices offered to the ancestral spirits is now clear. Their solemnity and collective expression help to reaffirm and strengthen the solidarity of the family. As Radcliffe-Brown observed, they give stability to the social structure by giving solidarity and continuity to the lineage, past, present and future. The Santal is made to feel a certain dependence on his ancestors, who, in turn, watch over him with loving care as long as they are remembered and venerated. Otherwise, they will not only stop sending their blessings but will visit him with illness or other misfortunes. The motives involved in ancestor worship, though not always the same, are chiefly: (*i*) a desire to venerate the dead; *(ii)* a desire for their blessings and protection; *(iii)* a feeling of reverence due to them; (*iv*) a fear of incurring their wrath. In short, we can say that the feelings of the living towards their dead relatives are ambivalent, compounded of affection and fear. The family, represented by the living and the dead, continues to be a focus of powerful sentiments. It is, therefore, unfortunate that those Santals who become Christians are forbidden to make any animal offerings to their ancestors. As Culshaw remarks: 'the Christians are evidently aware of a void in the teaching that they have received in regard to it'."

The *jaher bongas* protect the entire Santals tribe, the *abge bongas* their *khut* members, the *orak bongas* their household members and the *hapram bongas* their patrilineace members. There is still another class of *bongas* whose function is their beneficence called as the *saket bongas* or the tutelary *bongas* of the *ojhas*, medicine-men who also act as exorcists and diviners. The *ojha*, one of the most respected persons in a Santal village, is believed to have special retained *bongas* through whose aid the forces of evil and sorceries are countered. The Santals do acknowledge natural causes of illness. Yet, if the disease assumes an unusual character and does not respond to various medicines taken, it is attributed to the displeasure of a *bonga* or to the presence of a malevolent deity. Similary, when a number of misfortunes occur within a short time in a house, the members suspect the presence of a malevolent spirit.

About the ancestor worship by the Santals Mr. Sachchidananda points out, "The Santhal call their ancestor spirit as Hapramko Bongas and their blessings are invoked at every social ceremony. Whenever fresh *handia* is drunk, libations are poured out in their honour. During the Sohrae, fowls and rice-beer libations are offered by each family in honour of its ancestors and the name of each person is mentioned. If due to lack of fowls, sacrifices to the departed are not made during the Sohrae, then these sacrifices are performed during the Baha festival. Otherwise, only rice-beer libations are offered in their honour during the Baha and the *Erok* or sowing festival. On the day of the sacrifice, the bhitar is cleared and plastered with cowdung. The officiating person does not observe any specific taboos, except that he does not eat anything on the eve of the sacrifice and he takes a purificatory bath.

"The Oraon call their ancestor spirit as Pach-balar. Although except the annual Harbora ceremony (a kind of all souls feast) there is no special religious festival at which offerings or sacrifices are made solely to the ancestor spirits, those spirits are invoked and offerings are made to them by their living relations at every feast and on every suitable occasion. Thus at the Sarhul, the Karma, and the Phagua festivals, the first loaves of rice-flour bread made at most Oraon houses are broken into pieces and offered to the Pach-balar spirits of the family by name—so far as their names are remembered. At the Jitia festival, rice-gruel is similarly offered to them on six leaf-plates, two for the spirits of dead ancestors and ancestresses, two for the spirits of dead children, one for the remaining deceased members of the clan. And at the two Nawakhani festivals of the year—once in the month of *Sraban* when the new *gondli* (panicum miliar) is first ceremonially eaten and again in *Bhadra* or *Aswin* when the new gora (upland rice) is first ceremonially eaten—a little of the gondli or gora rice, as the case may be, besides boiled rice and vegetables, has first to be similarly offered to the ancestor-spirits before their living relatives proceed to partake them. The Nawakhani is, in fact, a festival in honour of the Pach-balar.

"The Munda's Ora-Bongake (house-gods)—are the spirits of the deceased ancestors of each Munda family. The head of every Munda family worships these household deities at the ading or sacred tabernacle of his house. Their blessings are invoked at every social ceremony and religious festival.

"Burha-burhi and Mari Masan are the Kharia's ancestor spirits. These two are spirits of the Kharia pantheon who watch over the customary morals of their descendants in the land of the living and protect them from harm." he adds.

Before taking his rice meal, every adult Birhor sets aside on the ground a few grains of rice from his plate in a pious act in the names of his ancestor-spirits—*Haprom* or *Burha-Burhi* and, similarly, before drinking liquor he must sprinkle a few drops on the ground in their names. The Mua Puja is also widely practised among the Birjia and Korwa.

The tribes of Bihar believe the dead ancestors are the real benefactors of the families clan and the entire community to which they belong and that they are easily approachable by their living kinsmen. First fruits and grains from the field are offered to the chief ancestor-spirit by the Maler near the hearth (oven) and by the Mahlis at the outer caves of their huts or house. The *Chik-baraik* also practise ancestor-worship as according to them, ancestors are the real protectors and saviours. Hence they are worshipped at the time of crises be-falling them. According to the Maler and Mal Pahariya, death is not the complete negation of life, but is a resurrection which envisages life after death. Therefore they believe that their forefathers who were with them till yesteryears may be able to help them. Hence, they remember their ancestors on all occasions from birth to death. In a process the idea of ancestor worship has grown fully in their minds. On all occasions, birth, marriage, death, and at the harvesting of each crop, seasonwise and cropwise, a host of spirits along with the ancestors are worshipped and offered their due puja and sacrifices. The Gonds also worship their ancestors along with other household gods, deities and demons.

In fact, the manes of the ancestors are dreaded most in the tribal pantheon. To appease them and to gain their favour the tribes of Bihar, whether settled agriculturist or the slash and burn cultivators or artisans or hunters and food-collectors, offer their due worship and sacrifices to them on different important occasion of their life and culture. The milieu in which these tribes have been inhabiting since time immemorial, the fear of the spirits, both benevolent and malevolent, have organised the idea of seeking assistance from their dead-ancestors who are supposed to be their real benefactors.

Custom of Reciting *Kalima*

When you have to see somebody on death bed, continuously recite loudly the Islamic article of faith:

"*La-ilaha illal-alm Muham-madur Rasulullh.* (Kalima)

(There is no god except Allah and Muhammad is His Messenger).

The Holy Prophet has directed, "When you go to a man who is on death's door keep reciting the *Kalima.*" When somebody is in the agony of death, recite Surah Yasin from the Holy Quran. The Holy Prophet has instructed "Recite Surah Yasin by the side of those persons, who are having their last breath." And when the person has expired and till his dead body is bathed, the Holy Quran should not be recited near the dead body and those persons not clean and need washing, and the females in menses or passing after birth discharge, should refrain from going near the dead body.

On Hearing the News of Death you should Say, "Verily we belong to Allah and shall return to Him." The Holy Prophet has said that one who recites this verse will have three rewards from Allah: Firstly he gets Allah's blessings and peace from Him. Secondly, he becomes entitled to recompense for the search of truth, and thirdly he is indemnified for the loss he has suffered and gets a better replacement of the loss. As soon as one has breathed his/her last straighten his/her, body, arms and feet, close the eyes, and passing a bandage below his/her chin, knot at the head. The toes of the feet fastened together with a strip of cloth, and cover the body with a sheet. All those present should recite:

"*Bismillahe wa ala millate Rasul-ullah*". In the name of Allah and on the millat of the Holy Prophet of Allah. All concerned should be informed of the event. While lowering the body in the grave also recite this supplication. Only good deeds of the dead person should be recounted and not bad ones. The Holy Prophet has directed:

"Narrate only virtues of your dead persons and do not mention their evils." (Abu Daud)

He has also said: "When somebody dies and his four neighbours testify that he was a virtuous man then Allah says "I have accepted your testimony, and have forgiven him for those things which were not known to you." (Ibn Habban)

Once the companions of the Holy Prophet recounted the good deeds of a person in his presence. The Holy Prophet stated: "Gentlemen, since you are the witnesses of Allah on earth (on your testimony) this person has been allotted the Paradise (by Allah). When you call a dead person as good, Allah admits him into the Paradise, and whom you call bad, Allah sends him to the Hell." (Bukhari - Muslim)

The Holy Prophet (S.A.W.) has further said: "Whenever you pay a visit to a sickman or accompany a funeral procession, always have good words on your tongue, for the angels ditto you and say amen (it may be so).

Washing Entire Dead Body Without Loss of Time

For bathing prepare mild warm water with some strawberry leaves in it, if possible. Put the dead body on a neat wooden plank, remove his clothes and cover the lower part of his body with a sheet of cloth. Cover your hands with hand gloves or a piece of cloth. Then clean his private parts first, and see that the sheet continues to cover the same. Thereafter, perform the ablution of the dead body. In this you need not put water into the mouth and the ears. While giving a bath, plug the ears and nose so that water may not enter into the body through these holes. Then wash the head with soap or any other thing. Then tilt the body a little towards the left, and rush water on the right side from head to feet and repeat this process on the other side. Now remove the water-soaked sheet and replace it with a dry one. Lift the body from the plank and place it on a cot wrapped with coffin. The Holy Prophet has said, "Allah forgives forty grave sins of a person who has given bath to a dead person and kept secret of his or her shortcomings or defects; and one who has lowered the dead body into the pit is like a person who has provided a house to the dead person till the Resurrection." (Tibrani)

A medium quality cloth of white colour should be used for the shroud of a dead person. It should neither be too costly nor of a very low quality. For males there should be three pieces of the shrouds one sheet (or *outer garment),* one piece (or tahband) to cover his lower part, and a pieced to be used as shirt or *"Kafni"*. The sheet should be longer in length and a bit wider so as to fully cover the dead body and its ends may be tied covering the head and the feet.

For females, in addition to these three pieces, arrange a piece of cloth (Sarband) a little more than a meter in length and a little less than a meter in breadth, to cover the head and the hair; and another piece called seena band (chest cover) of sufficient length to provide additional covering from the arms-pit to the knee. The Holy Prophet has said: "Anybody who clothes a dead body with coffin, will get a dress of *Sundus* and *Istabraq* (a fine variety of silken cloth interwoven with silver and gold thread) in the Heaven." (Hakim)

The Holy Prophet has said: "Be quick in taking the funeral procession (to the graveyard)." Hadrat Ibn Masud enquired from the Holy Prophet "O Prophet of Allah at what speed we should march with the dead to the graveyard?" The Holy Prophet replied. "A little less than running. If the dead person was a virtuous man, he should be carried to his good end hastily. If he was not a good person, hasten to remove him from your surrounding." (Abu Daud)

Once the holy Prophet was accompanying a funeral procession. He noticed some persons riding. He reprimanded them and said: "You ought to feel ashamed, whereas angels are walking on foot you are riding on the back of animals." You may, however, use some means of transport while returning from the graveyard. The Holy Prophet accompanied the funeral procession of Abu Wahidi on foot and returned riding a horse.

When you see a funeral procession coming, stand up, and if you do not have time to accompany it, wait for some time till the procession has gone ahead. The Holy Prophet has said: "When you see a bier, stand up, and those who are accompanying it should not sit till it is placed (on the ground)."

You should make it a point to offer funeral prayers, and accompany the funeral procession to the graveyard and lend your shoulders to carry the bier to the graveyard. . . .

The grave should be dug according to the direction of Qibla, and the dead body should be lowered into the pit from the side of Qibla. If the body is not heavy, two persons would be enough to lower it, otherwise, three or four persons may have to be employed for the purpose. While lowering the body, turn its face towards the Qibla. After having laid the body untie the knots of the shroud.

If you get involved in some serious worries and calamities which may make your life quite miserable; even then you should not lose heart nor ever try to commit suicide, for this is not only sheer cowardice but misappropriation of Allah's trust and munificence and this is a sin as well. Under such circumstances have recourse to Allah and regularly recite this prayer; "O Allah, with Your knowledge of the Unseen and Your power over Your creatures, keep me alive, as long as You know it is good for me to live, and grant me death when You know, it is better for me to die." (Musnad Ahmad)

Whenever you see somebody in distress, recite the following invocation, Hadrat Abu Hurrayrah quotes the holy Prophet as having said that whosoever recites this supplication on seeing somebody in trouble, he by the Will of Allah, himself remains immune from trouble: "Thanks be to Allah Who has kept me safe from this ordeal in which you are involved, and has granted me supremacy over many of His creatures."

Observe Purdah to Bury a Female When lowering the body of a female in the grave, arrangements should be made for Purdah (Seclusion or keeping away women from the sight of strangers). While covering the pit with earth, start from the side of the head. Gather soft clay with both the hands and throw it on the grave three times. For the first time while throwing soil say:

Minha khalq-na-kum (We created you from this very earth;

While throwing the earth second time say:

Wa fiha nueedu hum (And We are returning you to the same),

And when throwing the same for the third time say:

Wa minha nukh-riju-kum taratan ukhra.

(And We shall raise you again from this earth).

Do not build the grave too high nor make it like a quadrangle. Only so much earth should be thrown over the grave, which has been excavated from the pit. When the grave has been filled with the earth some water may be sprinkled over it. After having finished the burial, stay for some time near the grave praying for the salvation of the deceased and recite verses from the Holy Quran for the repose of the departed soul. Other people should also be asked to join in the prayers for the deceased. The Holy Prophet used to pray for the dead person after his burial and also asked others. "This is the time for the reckoning of accounts. Pray to Allah for the stead-fastness of your brother, and beg for Allah's mercy for him." (*Abu Daud*)

In case of a death taking place among your relatives or neighbours, arrange to send cooked food for one or two times, to that house, as the bereaved family would be too much grieved and upset to think of preparing food. This is a token of sympathy and love with the grieved family. Give something according to your means in charity for the peace of the departed soul. But refrain from indulging in irreligious and unauthorised practises and rituals.

You should make it a point to invariably attend funeral prayers. Participation in funeral prayers is like beseeching Allah for the peace of the soul of the dead person, and this is an important right of the deceased. In case there is a danger that the prayer is likely to be missed if you have to perform ablution, then you should perform Tayammtim and join the prayer. The Holy Prophet's injunction in this regard is: "Offer funeral prayers, such a prayer may move you and soften your heart. A tender-hearted person remains under the shadow of Allah and he welcomes every good act." (*Mustadrak Hakim*)

And the Holy Prophet has also said," A dead body for which three rows of Muslims offer prayers will certainly go to heaven. (*Abu Daud*)

The Holy Prophet has further remarked "When a person participates in the funeral of another person, and offers funeral prayers for him, the former will get a recompense equivalent to one qayrat and one who takes part in the burial as well, will get recompense equal to two qayrat. Some one asked about the volume of two qayrat the Holy Prophet replied "they will be equal to two mountains." (*Bukhari-Muslim*)

The bier should be set in such a way that the head of the dead person should face North and the feet South; and the face mould be in the direction of *Qibla.* If you are leading a funeral prayer, stand in such a way that you may be facing the chest of the deceased. The number of rows of participants in a funeral service should be odd. If there are a few persons, only one row should be formed, otherwise set up more rows, but their number must be odd. Niyyat (Intention) When you begin funeral prayers, affirm in your heart (Niyyat) that you are praying for the salvation of the dead person from Allah. The Most Compassionate of the compassionates. Both the *Imam* and the followers should make this affirmation. In a funeral prayer the Imam and the congregation should recite the same supplication. The followers should not remain quite. The Imam may call the Takbir loudly and the followers should repeat them slowly.

In a funeral prayer four *Takbirs* (Allah-u-Akbar) are recited loudly. With the first Takbir raise your hands upto your ears and thereafter fold them, and recite the following sana (eulogy). "Allah! Thou art Pure and sublime alongwith their praise and laudation. Thy Name brings good and blessings; and Thy Greatness and Magnitude are highest, Great is Thy Praise, and there is no god but Thee." Now recite the second Takbir but do not raise your hands nor make any sign with your head. After the second Takbir the following Salat may be recited: "Allah! vouchsafe Thy compassion upon Muhammad and his descendents; just as Thou hadst mercy and Thou sent peace and blessed and hadst compassion on the descendents of Ibrahim. Verily Thou art praiseworthy, the Great." The third Takbir is to he said without raising of hinds and the prescribed prayers is to be recited for the dead.

If the body is of an adult man or woman, the following prayer, is to be offered after the third Takbin "Allah! forgive our living and dead; those present and those who are not present; our minors and elders; our males and females. Allah! those whom Thou keepest alive, may they be kept alive in the fold of Islam; and those whom Thou deems fit to send death, may they die in faith."

The following prayer is to be recited in case the body is that of a boy: "Allah make this male child a means for our salvation; and make him a means for our reward a store (for our reward) in Hereafter, and make him the intercessor whose intercession may be accepted. If the body is that of a minor girl, the prayer to be offered is given below: "Allah make this female child a means for our salvation, and make her a means for our reward store (for our reward) in Hereafter, and make the intercessor whose intercession may be accepted. Finally the fourth Takbir is to be said and the Salams are to be said in both directions (right and left).

While accompanying a funeral, we should always reflect upon our destiny and consider that just as you are going to bury some one today, so some day you too will be buried by others and a funeral procession will march for you. We should, for that while at least have time to reflect upon (our end) and the hereafter and purge ourselves of the base emotions of the world.

Accompany a bier to the graveyard, and participate in the burial of the deceased. Apart from this, you should visit graveyards quite often, as it revives the remembrance of the Hereafter, as well as helps us prepare ourselves for the journey of life after death. The Holy Prophet once accompanied a funeral procession to the graveyard, where he wept by the side of a grave so much that the ground became wet. Addressing the Companions, he said: "Brethren! prepare yourself for this day (of death)." (*Ibn Majah*)

On another occasion, sitting by the side of a grave, he said: "The grave daily declares in a very frightening tone: Children of Adam, have you forgotten me? I am the house of solitude; the place of isolation and nightmare; the abode of insects and worms; and shortness and ordeals, (for you) except for those blessed ones for whom Allah make me broad and wide. For all men I am a source of torture". And he (S.A.W.) further said: "Either grave is a pit among the pits or the Gardens or the Paradise." (*Tibrani*)

A visit to the graveyard should infuse into you the.imagery of life after death. While entering a graveyard, the following prayer may be recited: "Peace be upon you, O Obedient faithfuls, the dwellers of this place, God willing, soon we shall join you. We Pray to Allah for you and ourselves, that He may keep us safe." A graveyard is not a place where you may indulge in irresponsible and loose talks; cut jokes, laugh and chit chat on worldly matters. The grave is the gateway to the Hereafter on seeing which you should feel overwhelmed with the feelings remorse and repentance, which may bring tears in your eyes. The Holy Prophet has said: "I had asked you not to visit the graveyard to save you from shirk. If you now like, can go (to see the graves) since graves revive the memories of the Hereafter.

The Holy Prophet has specifically prohibited from making graves as permanent structures or decorating them. When the Holy Prophet was near the end of his worldly life, and felt much pain and uneasiness so much so that at times he covered his face with his sheet and then uncovered his face alternately. In this state of pain and restlessness Hadrat Aishah heard him saying "Allah's curse be upon the Jews and Christian who had converted the graves of their Prophets into places of worship."

You should go to the graveyard and pray to Allah for salvation of the dead. According to Hadrat Sufyan, "Just as the living persons are in need of food and water, so the dead are in great need of prayers." According to a tradition, when Allah elevates the status of a virtuous servant in the Paradise by one degree he asks Allah, "O Lord, how did I get this elevation'?" And Allah answers: "Because of your son, who has been praying for thy salvation." (*Tibrani*)

According to Islamic injunctions, here are a few things That Need to be Done When Someone Dies :

- Notification of a person's death to friends and the public may well be through an announcement in the local press, provided that such an announcement does not praise or commend the dead person or demonstrate his esteem. Instead, the announcement would do better to ask others to pray for the dead person.
- Preparing the corpse for burial by washing and shrouding it is necessary. This should be carried out in an inexpensive way.
- Dead men are washed by men, dead women by women, except in the case of a married couple, where the survivor is allowed to wash the dead person.
- The dead person should be washed with water and, if available, lotus leaves, an odd number of times, three or five, or more if necessary, beginning with the right side and, for the last washing, camphor should be added to the solution. If the dead person is a woman, then her hair should be braided into three plaits and placed behind her back.
- Though shrouding the dead should be done with cloth of moderate quality, extravagance is not recommended and using a coffin is not allowed unless necessary for health reasons.
- The Shuhada' martyrs should be stripped of their jewelry and buried in their clothing without having the blood washed off.
- A Muslim who dies while performing pilgrimage or Umrah should be washed with water and lotus leaves, if available, and shrouded in the same two pieces of cloth with which he covered himself for the pilgrimage or Umrah. No perfume, in this case, should be put on the dead, neither should his head be covered.
- Anyone who has washed a dead body is recommended to bathe himself and anyone who has carried it is recommended to perform ablution.

- It is the duty of those who wash the dead not to mention to others whatever they may have noticed of the bodily imperfections of the dead person. Mentioning good things is allowed.

- It is recommended that, immediately after washing and shrouding it, the body not be kept long, but rather taken quickly, prayed over, and then buried.

- The funeral of a Muslim must be attended by other Muslims. Therefore, a Muslim should not be slow to participate in escorting the funeral, whether or not the dead person or his relatives are known to him directly.

- Escorting a funeral consists of two stages; the first lasts till the funeral prayer is offered, and the second till the dead person is buried. It is recommended, however, that those attending the first stage also wait until the second stage is completed.

- Prayer should be performed over every Muslim who dies, including infants. Taking the dead body into the mosque for the funeral prayers is not recommended. Prayers should be conducted in a place outside the mosque, e.g. in the courtyard.

- It is not proper that some people, especially relatives of the dead, do not take part in the funeral prayers, instead waiting on others to do so in their place.

- The pace of the procession should be neither too quick nor too slow.

- Those following and escorting a funeral on foot should walk either in front of or behind the bier, or on the right or left, keeping near it. Those riding, however, should keep behind.

- Following the funeral with incense or candles, mentioning God's name audibly or loudly, weeping aloud, or reading the Quran aloud, are forbidden when escorting a funeral.

- Speech should be kept short and light during the funeral procession.

- When a Muslim sees a funeral passing he may stand up.

- Conveying the deceased by car or other vehicle is not recommended, unless the cemetery is far away.

- It is recommended that those who carry a bier perform ablution afterwards. This will help to refresh and reorientate them physically and emotionally.

- Walking when following the funeral is better than riding, unless the cemetery is far away. However, on returning from the burial it is permissible to ride or walk.
- It is a matter of great importance that a special cemetery be devoted exclusively for the use of Muslims. Muslims may not be buried in the cemeteries of non-Muslims, nor vice versa.
- No person may be cremated, even if the dead person has specifically requested it. Such a request must not be fulfilled.
- The dead should be interred in the cemetery, except the Shuhada (those killed on the battlefield) who should be buried where they are martyred.
- The dead person should be buried in the locality where he died. It is undesirable that the body be taken back to the person's own country or moved to another city.
- The burial must take place as soon as possible after death, with the following exceptions :

  (a) At night.

  (b) From sunrise until the sun is about 4.5 degrees above the horizon (when it is fully risen).

  (c) At the zenith of the sun (when it is at the meridian) until it passes the meridian.

  (d) When the sun pales before sunset until it has set. Burying the dead during these times is forbidden unless there is an urgent necessity.
- Allocating a special cemetery for state leaders or for the rich is utterly forbidden. Islam rejects the class system in life and at death.
- When more than one person is to be buried in a single grave, *e.g.* in the case of war or a widespread epidemic, then that person who in life read the Quran the most should be buried first.
- The task of placing the dead person in the grave must be carried out by men only. The deceased's male relatives are actually expected to place him or her in the grave.
- It is not proper to hire others to wash, shroud or inter the deceased. It is expected that the person's relatives and family do these things. Islam attaches great importance to strong relations between family members in life and at death.

- The deceased is placed in the grave on his right side with his face towards the Qiblah.
- Whoever places the dead in the grave should say: *Bismillah wa ala millati rasoolillah* (In the name of God, by God's grace, and following the Sunnah of the Prophet). The corpse is lowered into the grave from the rear of the grave.
- Standing up in the cemetery until the body is put into the grave is not required. Except for those who place the deceased in the grave, the mourners may be seated.
- It is recommended that those standing around the grave, after the corpse has been lowered into it and before the covering has been placed over it, throw three handfuls of earth into the grave.
- It is an innovation to admonish the dead person after his death. Admonishing should be done during his dying.
- It is recommended to pray for the dead person.
- If the person died in debt it is the responsibility of his relatives to discharge the debt as soon as possible, provided that this is within their capacity.
- The deceased's last wishes should be fulfilled except if they contradict the teachings of Islam; if, for example, he instructed his survivors to give an extra sum of money to one of his heirs, as Islam already regulates the inheritance for this group of people.
- It is a Muslim's duty to offer condolences, comfort, and sympathy to the bereaved. To do so contributes to strengthening relationships within Muslim society. Therefore, mixing socially with the bereaved family for a period following the death is Islamic conduct, helping to get them back to normal life as quickly as possible.
- When offering condolences one's words should be chosen carefully. The right words should be used to convey sympathy and to encourage the bereaved to accept God's will.
- Islamic phrases of sympathy are, for instance: *Ghafarallahu limayyitikum* (May God forgive the deceased his sins) and *Inna lillahi ma akhadha wa lahw ma ata wa Kullu shayin indalw ila ajalin musamma* (What God has taken or given does indeed belong to Him and He has an appointed time for every thing).

- Comforting and encouraging (the bereaved is required for as long as the necessity remains. Thus, the bereaved should be visited from time to time.
- The bereaved family is not supposed to cook food for or serve visitors. On the contrary, friends, neighbours and relatives are advised to prepare food for them, for the loss of their loved one occupies the family's whole attention.
- Showing sympathy to the bereaved is good conduct, but it should be done without exaggeration. Speeches should be kept short and light; jokes, laughing and anything that may give offence should be avoided.
- All innovative practises following the death of a Muslim (such as holding a 'wake' on the fortieth day, etc.) must be avoided.
- Though mourning over the dead is allowed in Islam, great differences exist between the Islamic viewpoint on this and the practise of Muslims at the present time.
- Women have the right to mourn a deceased relative, for a period not exceeding three days. For widows the period of mourning may extend to four lunar months and ten days.
- No loss, however great, should be permitted to sour one's outlook. Endurance should be shown by the bereaved, who are recommended to praise God and say: *Inna lillahi wa-inna ilayhi rajiun* (We belong to Him, to Him do we return).
- Grief at the death of a relative or friend is normal. It is also normal and usual to see people weeping for the dead, and this is allowed in Islam. What is completely forbidden is to express grief by wailing, shrieking, beating the cheeks and tearing hair or clothes.
- When mourning a dead person, care must be taken to avoid phrases that contradict Islamic principles, *e.g.* 'What will become of me now?' or 'Now our supporter is gone.' This implies relying on human beings rather than on Allah.
- It is a Muslim's duty to advise those who wail for the dead in this way to stop doing so.
- Islam prescribes that a widow may not remarry during her period of mourning; it is considered impolite, therefore, to ask for a woman's hand during this period.

- A widow in mourning may not wear clothes of saffron colour, or wear jewelry, or dye her hair with henna or use antimony on her eyes.

Pollution Period Lasting for Forty Days

After a Bohra dies, the ritualistic pollution lasts forty days. The widow is strictly secluded for four months and thirteen days. During the mourning period she is not permitted to view herself in the mirror, or venture out. This period is known as *iddat*. Relatives and members of the family offer *taziat* (prayer) at the grave of the deceased. *Fateha* (sending of sweets by the family) also takes place. All these rites and rituals have regional variations and have now been curtailed to some extent. The funeral custom pertain to Bohra Muslims in West Bengal, Bihar and Orissa.

Common Type Muslim Burial

Common to the Muslim tradition, Abdals bury their dead. Before that, they dress the corpse in *kaphan-laphen* (clothes for burial) and carry them on a *mahapa* (bier) to the graveyard. A significant change in their life-cycle rituals is in the method of disposal of the deceased. Even a couple of generations ago, there were instances in which Abdals cremated their corpses on the bank of river, in what was known as *Gangadewa*. Abdals are now, gradually, becoming Islamized and, very soon, they will, perhaps, give up a few more specifically local Hindu customs still in vogue. The funeral custom and rituals belong to the Abdal Muslims.

Burial in Church Cemetery

The Chinese people bury their dead, but funeral and mourning customs vary within the community. After a person dies, the body is bathed and then clothed in a new apparel. The feet are bound together with a cord and the body is laid in a coffin, padded with quits. After these initial preparations, the church priests chant prayers to open the gates to heaven. Every day for the first year after the death, the family places food before a tablet for the deceased. Mourning customs are strict amongst them. The outer garment for men and women is coarse, unhemmed, white clothes. The period of deepest mourning varies among different Chinese communities, but for most, it is sixty days, during which a man may not shave or cut his hair. This is for the sons and unmarried daughters, paternal nephews and unmarried nieces, daughters-in-law and grandchildren of the deceased. In mourning, too, a mourner may not travel, unless it is absolutely necessary. Women must not visit temples shrines or monasteries. On the third day after the funeral the mourners visit the grave and offer food to the memory of the departed soul.

On the twenty-first day, food is offered before the tablet. On the thirty-fifth, paper imitations of gold and silver ingots are burned. On the forty-ninth, the same rituals as those on the twenty-first, are repeated by the bereaved family. On the sixtieth, as on previous occasions, food is offered, but on this day, a tablet with the name of the deceased engraved on it, is put on the table and worshipped. The Chinese Christians mourn a death for a hundred days, and a white tab marks the hands and head. But they do not worship any ancestoral deity. Of late most wedding and death rituals have been curtailed to suit modern needs. The mourning period has also been reduced. Weddings of Buddhist Chinese are performed in the temples and the pomp and expense for a wedding have greatly increased, too.

The Usual Christian Burial

The Christian bury their dead. On the third day after a person dies, members of the bereaved family visit the burial ground and offer prayers at grave of the deceased. Earlier, Christians mourned for forty days, but now this had been shortened to eleven days. During mourning, close relatives do not have non-vegetarian food. They pray for the soul of the departed person on the twelfth day in a mass conduct at the house of the deceased.

The Christians are buried in the church cemetery. Before burial, the dead body is taken to the Church and some prayers are offered by the local priest. Then the body is put in a coffin and lowered into the grave. The family members throw earth in the grave. The customs pertain to the Christians in Bihar and Orissa.

No Strict Predelivery Rituals

Among the Chinese Christians, there are no strict pre-delivery rituals. But when a woman wants a son she goes to the temple and prays to the Niang Niang Shen. She makes a vow to the goddess that if her prayer is heard, she would present new clothes and gifts to the goddess. Sometimes an expectant mother may keep a long sharp knife on her bed to frighten away evil spirits. At the time of childbirth the expectant mother prays to the goddess.

After birth, the newborn is not bathed until the third day, when friends and relatives bring gifts for the mother. Before the baby is bathed, a bunch of joss-sticks is lit and stuck in a bowl of uncooked rice. Eggs are put in some water. One if the child is a boy and two if it is a girl. Beside the bath, a dish full of tepid water, a spoon and equal number of red and white hard-boiled eggs are kept. While the baby is being bathed, each guest adds a spoonful of water to the bath and blesses the child. They put eggs into the bath, too. The white egg indicates a blessing for a long life and the red for abundant luck.

The Chinese word, meaning red, stands for abundant and red symbolizes joy. Each guest places a gift of jewellery or money in the bath. The deities, Kang Kung and Kang Mu are offered cakes. On the twelfth day after the child is born, meat dumplings made by the maternal grandmother are given to the mother to eat so that she may become stronger. When a baby is a month old, the naming ceremony takes place. This is a great occasion for a feast and gifts are brought for the baby. On the child's first birthday another feast is held and idols are worshipped by burning incense. On this day, the child is made to sit in a large basket. All sorts of articles are put into the basket. It is believed that whatever the child picks up indicates what he will later be in life. Baptism is compulsory for Chinese Christians. It is held in a Church when a boy, or girl, is twelve to thirteen years of age. Confirmation at eight, or nine, years of age is observed to strengthen ones Christianity. The customs, rites and observances are pertinent to the community of Chinese living in Calcutta.

Rite of *Sadh* in Seventh Month of Pregnancy

The Christians do observe certain pre- and post-delivery rituals and restrictions, though Christians have none. *Sadh* is held in the seventh and ninth months of pregnancy. In the seventh, the celebration takes place at the in-laws house, where the expectant mother is offered special dishes of her choice. Clothes and jewellery are gifted to her. Relatives and friends are invited to the feast. After the ceremony, the woman goes to her parents house, where she is not allowed to do any heavy work. They generally do not observe any post-delivery restriction or pollution. The first ceremony after childbirth is christening, which takes place within three months, or forty days, of birth. This is also their naming ceremony. In some cases, *annaprashan* is held in the seventh or eighth month. A child is baptized at age twelve or thirteen. The birth customs and rituals pertain to the Christians in West Bengal.

Rites, Rituals and Customs common to all Christians

Among the Anglo-Indians the rites and customs of christening, confirmation, engagement, marriage, and burials, are in accordance with the Church practises. There is no observation of pollution at birth. Generally, after one month of birth the child is christened in the church. At the time of christening, two god parents, one male and one female are present with the mutual consent of the child's parents the child is baptized in the Church.

The names of godparents are on the Baptism certificate and in the church records. The priest sprinkles holy water on the infant. The confirmation ceremony is observed for the girls and boys, normally at the end of adolescence. The Bishop confirms them by asking some questions regarding their religion. After being satisfied with the answer, the Bishop confirms them as communicant members of the Church. This is called the Holy Communion. From now onwards they can take bread and wine from the Altar. The customs pertain to Anglo-Indians in Bihar.

Rite of *Bismillah* or the Initiation

Mr. Ja'far Sarif writes about the Muslim-custom Bismillah, "The rite of initiation, Bi'smillah, 'pronouncing the name of God', is observed when a boy or girl has reached the age of four years four months and four days. In the case of girls the plaiting of the side locks *(palgundhan, pahlugundhan)* is done for the first time at this rite. Strings of black silk are plaited into the long hair, the braids or plaits must be uneven in number, and women swear by them as men do by their beards. During two or three days before the rite, the child is dressed from head to foot in yellow clothes, Chiksa or scented powder is rubbed on his body by women whose husbands are alive *(suhagan),* and he is seated in a room with a canopy over his head, and coloured clothes hung round to resemble a throne. Every morning and evening while he is being massaged, musicians play and the child is not allowed to walk about. This part of the rite is called in south India 'sitting in state' *(manja, manjha baithna).* The day before the ceremony the lady guests are invited by sending round cardamoms to their houses, and other friends by letter in the following form : 'To such a one, the obliger of friends greeting ! At this poor man's house his son (or daughter, as the case may be) is this evening to be taught to repeat the name of God *(Bi'smillah-khwani}*. I beg that you by joining the party will grace the assembly with your presence and joyfully partake of something. For by so doing you will afford me peculiar pleasure'. Then the men and women meet apart. The child having been well bathed in the afternoon, and all the perfumed paste removed from his body, his yellow dress is exchanged for better garments, red or white, made of various kinds of brocade or other stuffs. Gold or silver amulets, which some of the friends may have given, are hung on his neck, and he is perfumed. Garlands of flowers are hung round his neck and wrists and a wreath made of gold wire *(sehara, sehra)* over his forehead. Thus bedecked, he is seated in the presence of his family tutor or some Mashaikh or venerable personage. Near them are placed trays with sweetmeats, two of the largest balls having gold or silver paper pasted over them, with other gifts including a small gold or silver plate and a pen and inkstand intended as gifts for the tutor. He, after reciting the Fatiha over the food in the name of the Prophet—on whom be the Peace !—writes on a plate with his pen dipped in sandalwood the words 'In the name of God, the Merciful, the Compassionate !' and orders the child to lick it off. He lays the two ornamented sweet balls in the child's hands to tempt him to perform his task. It is also the rule to write the first chapter of the Koran on red paper, but those who can afford it write this on a gold or silver plate, and giving it to the boy or girl require him or her to repeat first the words 'In the name of God, the Merciful, the Compassionate !' and afterwards from the ninety-sixth chapter the opening words : 'Recite thou in the name of the Lord who created, created man from clots of blood ! Recite thou ! For thy Lord is most beneficent, who has taught the use of the pen, hath taught that thou knowest not !' This being the first sentence of the Koran revealed to the Prophet—on whom be the Blessing !—it is considered of high value, and is taught to children. In north India the words of the blessing are engraved on a small silver tablet which the child, after repeating the words, hands to the old man after whom he has said them. Presents are then made to the tutor, and the child rises from his seat, salutes his tutor, and the friends present who give him presents. Then the sweets over which the Fatiha has been said are placed on the Dastarkhwan or dining cloth, and with other food are served to the guests. Next day the lady guests are sent home in litters after the host has given them presents. After this the boy is sent to school. In Gujarat the boy is sent to visit the shrine of the family Saint, and when he returns the women surround him and each strives to be the first to take his troubles upon herself *(balaen lena)* by passing her hands over him from head to foot and then pressing against his temples her knuckles and fingertips till they crack. Among the Bannuchi some old women wave three red chillies several times round the head of a person troubled by evil spirits, each time saying, 'Herewith I draw off the eye, be it man's, woman's, or spirits.' Then each pepper-pod is put into the fire (Thorburn, 161). Cf. *ERE.* iii. 447. Compare the Hindu Arti, or waning rite (Manucci, iii. 340). When the Emperor Shahjahan was sick, his daughter liberated several slaves, made them walk round her father, and then sent them away to carry his infirmities with them (Ibid. i. 217. Mrs. Meer Hassan Ali, 215).

"The mode of sending invitations to guests to attend family rites is of great importance. In the Deccan and south India female guests receive invitations *(da'wat)* to attend these and other rites by the sending of cardamoms *(ilachi),* while men are generally invited by letter. When ladies are invited, some woman who is in the habit of going about the bazars and lanes of the town or city is employed as a messenger. She is decked in her best clothes, and, accompanied by musicians, she starts with a plate in her hand containing sandalwood, packets of betel-leaf and areca nut, with sugar candy and cardamoms wrapped in red paper, a packet for each guest. She approaches the lady with much respect, and making a salutation she delivers the message in these terms: ' Such and such a lady (naming her) sends her best compliments and embraces to you, and informs you that tomorrow there will be a little gaiety at her house. She wishes all her lady friends by their presence to grace and ornament with their feet the house of this poor person, and thereby to make it a garden of roses. So you must certainly come, and by remaining a couple of hours honour her humble abode by your company'. Should the lady accept the invitation, the bearer of the cardamoms rubs a little sandalwood paste on her neck, breast, and back, and puts her share of the sugar candy and cardamoms into her mouth, or these things are handed to her with the packet of betel-leaves. If the lady declines the invitation, sandalwood alone is applied, and a packet of betel without any of the cardamoms and sugar candy is handed to her. When the messenger has finished the round of visits and announced the names of those who have accepted the invitation of her employer, next day a litter *(doli),* accompanied by a maid-servant, is sent to fetch each guest. If the lady of the house be poor, she merely sends her own maid-servant to escort the guests to her house a little before daybreak.

"When they arrive the hostess advances to the gate to welcome them, takes them by the hand, and leading them into the house seats them on the carpet. On other less important occasions invitations are sent by a messenger, but she is not attended with music and does not carry sugar candy, cardamoms, or betel-leaf.

When guests attend such rites they are expected to bring presents *(neota, manja)* with them proportionate in value to the nature of the rite and their own means. At the Chhathi and Chilla rites, already described, the gifts consist generally of a necklace *(hansli),* ankle-rings *(kara),* a cap *(topi),* a sheet *(sari),* a bodice *(choli),* betel-leaves, areca nut, flowers, and sandalwood. At the Bi'smillah rite for children they bring a small gold or silver plate weighing eight annas, or half a rupee (a rupee = 1 *tola,* 179 grains), hung on a red thread together with sufficient velvet to make a bodice, betel, flowers, sandalwood, and sweetmeats. For a wedding the gift consists of a shawl, a piece of muslin, a sheet, a turban, a bodice, betel, some choice delicacy, cakes *(malida),* sweetmeats, or merely betel with plantains, and coconuts. The guests bring these things in person, or in the case of great people they are brought by the men guests with great pomp and state: Poor people give at least a velvet bodice, sweetmeats, betel, flowers, and sandalwood, according to their means. If they have brought no gift in kind they are expected to put a rupee or two or less into the hand of the child or of the mistress of the house.

The anniversary of the birthday is celebrated with great rejoicing, relatives being entertained, and the Fatiha said over the food in the name of the Prophet and Father Nuh or Noah—on whom be the Peace!—so that the child may attain the age of the patriarch. Then some old woman ties a knot in a red or yellow thread, known as the Salgirah or 'year knot', or by converts from Hinduism Janamganth or 'birth knot'. The mother keeps the string and produces it at each of the boy's birthdays. A girl's years are counted by a silver loop or ring being added yearly to her Gardani or silver neck-ring. The occasion is marked by feasting and rejoicings. The practise is believed to have been borrowed from the Hindus, and Akbar is said to have adopted it from the Hindu ladies of his Zanana. On his birthday Akbar was weighed against gold and other valuables, the proceeds of which were given to the poor, while in the time of Aurangzeb a yellow cord was used for princes and princesses." Jafar Sharif, remarks that on such occasions in southern India drinking is not uncommon; 'though in public women, as well as men, drink only water sherbet, or milk, it is not uncommon for them in private to take strong drink, although it is prohibited in the Koran excusing themselves by saying that there is no harm in the use of the juice of a fruit, meaning the grape'.

Custom of Khatna or Circumcision

About the custom of Khatna, Mr. Ja'far Sarif writes, "Circumcision (*Khatna, sunnat,* in Sind *sathra, toharu*) should be performed between the ages of seven and twelve or fourteen, but it is lawful to do it seven days after birth. Akbar prohibited the rite before the age of twelve, and it was then to be optional with the boy.

"On the appointed day friends are invited and entertained. For a few days before the rite the boy is rubbed with Haldi or turmeric and made to sit in state (known in south India as *manja baithna).* He is dressed in red or yellow clothes, decorated with flowers, and Missi or dentifrice is rubbed on his teeth, this being the only occasion on which males use it. He is then carried in procession round the town. Others postpone the dinner and the procession till after the operation. The boy is seated on a large new earthen pot inverted, or on a chair with a red handkerchief spread over it. A couple of hours before he has been dosed with the electuary known as Ma'jun, made from hemp and used as an anodyne. Some friends hold the boy firmly and the barber performs the operation with a sharp razor. When it is over the boy is told to call out three times 'Din', 'The Faith'. To divert his attention he is made to slap the operator for causing him so much pain. One of the relatives chews betel and squirts the red spittle on the wound to make him believe that there has been no flow of blood. While the operation is in progress the Brahui mother puts a handmill on her head, a kinswoman a Koran, and they stand facing west and praying till all is over ; in the Mari tribe the mother stands in the centre of a group of singing women having in her hands an upper millstone over which are sprinkled red earth and rice, and on these an iron ring, a green bead, and a piece of red cloth, all tied together with a red string apparently symbolical of virility. In Sind, while the mother holds a stone on her head, a male relation pours water upon it, and sometimes instead of the mother, the father stands with his feet in water and holds a Koran on his head. Care is taken of the severed foreskin, lest a witch may work evil magic by means of it. Pathans on the north-west frontier bury it in a damp part of the house where the water jars are kept, possibly in the hope that it may grow and increase the virility of the boy. In other parts of the Panjab it is buried, thrown on the house roof, or attached to it by a straw ; in Delhi it is tied with a peacock's feather to the boy's left foot, so that no evil shadow may fall upon him and injure him. Some Brahuis bury it under a green tree so that the lad may be fruitful in generation, or they bury it in damp earth, thinking to cool the burning pain of the wound.

"After the operation the barber applies a dressing, and the wound heals in the course of a week or so. While the rite is being done, some rice and other gifts are laid close by which are given to the barber, but if the boy was seated on a chair this is not given away. In Sind the father places the fee under the lad's right foot and the friends wave money, which the barber receives, over the boy's head, or he puts his brass saucer in the room and people drop money into it.

"Some people never have a boy circumcised alone, but always with another to make the number equal, because the operation involves taboo. Hence when they have one or three boys to undergo the rite, they get some poor woman's son to be circumcised with them. If they fail to find such a boy they substitute for him a Badhna, or water-pot with a spout, in the mouth of which a packet of betel is placed and cut by the barber. They think it favourable if the boy during the operation makes water, as this clears the urethra. They guard the boy against contact with dogs or cats and from other defilements, such as that of a woman in her courses. Ants are kept away, by spreading ashes round the bed, or by placing the legs of it in stone pots filled with water. They tie a peacock's feather, a copper ring *(chhalla)* with a blue thread to the wrist, neck, or ankle of the lad, and they burn Ispand or herb of grace as a protective.

"Female circumcision, or clitorodectomy, prevails among some tribes in the Panjab and on the north-west frontier and probably extends more widely, but from the nature of the case, it is difficult to procure evidence. Some Musalman Jatis remove the tip of the clitoris, not with the idea of promoting chastity; but as a religious act. The Brahui circumcise a woman to remove the curse of barrenness, and the custom prevails in the Bahawalpur State and among the Mari of Baluchistan. The authenticity of a tradition allowing it has been disputed. The custom seems to have spread eastwards from Egypt and the Sudan."

Mr. Sarif adds, "... a boy is given trousers at the age of three, a girl between two and four. On the falling of the first tooth the child's mouth is washed with salt and bitter oil, that the new tooth may be white and shapely. He is made to jump out of doors, shouting 'O crow ! Thy teeth are black ! Look, mine are bright ! O crow ! Thy teeth are crooked, mine aright !' (Hindus, when a child's teeth fall out, throw them on the house roof, which is infested by rats and mice, in the hope that the new teeth will be as white and shapely as those possessed by these animals.)

"After a boy or girl has finished the reading of the Koran from end to end, a propitious day is fixed, according to the system used in selecting names, for the purpose of making gifts to the tutor and exhibiting the child's skill in reading. The friends are invited, and the boy now able to read the Koran *(qur'an-khwan),* dressed in his best, is seated in the men's hall with the Koran in his hands. A robe of honour (*khil'at*) and other gifts are set out for the tutor, and the boy is made to read the first, part of the second, the thirty-sixth, and the fifty-fifth chapters. The tutor then recites the Fatiha over the food in the name of the Prophet—the Blessing !—and makes the boy breathe on it. After the blessing he says 'I forgive all the trouble I have undergone in teaching the sacred Koran, and I freely bestow on thee the knowledge which I have taught thee !' Then the food which has become sacred by having the whole contents of the Koran blown upon it is distributed, and the gifts are given to the tutor. (When Humayun was about to invade India, he sent for his son Akbar, read some verses of the Koran, and at the end of each verse blew upon the boy (Smith, *Akbar*, 28). For Christian examples of blowing upon a person as a means of communicating afilatus.)

"Besides this ceremony, at every feast, marriage, or dinner the tutor receives his dues. He is honoured, as a father, because a man is said to have four fathers : his natural father, his tutor, his father-in-law, and his Murshid or spiritual guide. Besides this, the Prophet has assured us that if any person in his daily prayers says the Du'a-i-ma'sur, or prayer for the remission of sins, for his parents and his tutor, the Almighty will hear and answer. For children who go to school the master usually writes the 'Idi or 'feast verse', or a blessing on the child, on paper sprinkled with gold dust *(zar-i-fishan),* and desires him to read it to his parents, who send an 'Idi, or feast gift, in return. Such presents are made at four festivals, the Akhiri-char-shamba, the Shab-i-barat, the Ramazan, and the Baqar 'Id. In Musalman schools in north India the pupils on the eve of the Friday holiday bring lamp-money *(charaghi, chiraghi)* for the teacher, a term also used for money spent in lighting a lamp on a Saint's tomb, or the percentage taken by the owner of a gambling-house.

"There are thirty sections *(juz, sipara)* in the Koran, and at the beginning and end of each of these it is usual to give a present to the tutor, this gift being known as Hadiya. Of these there are four principal occasions : at the end of a quarter, half, three quarters, or the whole Koran, of which the last is most important. Besides this, when a boy begins a new book it is usual to give a present, sweetmeats, betel, and money. The tutor recites the Fatiha over these, rubs sandalwood on the boy's neck and sometimes on his own, or taking them in his hand smells them, repeats the Durud or blessing, hears the lessons, and then gives a half-holiday. If the number of boys be great, and so it would be necessary to give a half-holiday for each, he puts off the Fatiha till a Thursday, the usual half-holiday, and deals with the gifts of two or more boys at the same time.

"In short, every opportunity is taken to compliment the tutor, for a blessing from his auspicious lips is as good as the reading of a hundred books, and if his curse rests on any one the reading of a hundred books will be of little profit; nay, he is equal to, if not greater than one's father or mother, inasmuch as he teaches the Law and the writings of God and His Messenger, and explains the doctrines of the Faith. While his natural parents nourish the body of their son with temporal food, he provides that which is spiritual."

About the coming of age of a girl or a boy Mr. Ja'far Sarif writes, "When a girl menstruates for the first time she is said to be 'grown up' *(baligh hona),* 'to have her head dirty for the first time' *(pahle sir maila hona),* owing to the prohibition against bathing during this period, or 'to mix with those who are grown up' *(baron men milna).* The illness at the lunar periods is expressed by 'the approach of the menses' *(haiz ana*), 'the arrival of the season for bathing' *(nihani ana),* 'the head becoming dirty' *(sir maila hona),* 'becoming unfit for prayers' *(benamazi ana),* or 'to become unclean' *(napak hana*). Among Musalman girls the time of puberty is from ten to fourteen, generally about twelve, and the function continues till the fortieth, or in some cases the forty-fifth year. Among women in south Gujarat a ceremony known as 'donning the scarf *(orhni urana)* is performed secretly when a girl reaches womanhood. Baloch mothers press their daughters' breasts and rub them with ashes and salt to prevent them from swelling or holding milk, and when menstruation occurs for the first time the mother takes three small stones', arranges them on the ground in the form of a triangle, and bids the girl leap over them thrice, in order that the menses may not last more than three days, the furthest limit being five or six days. At a girl's first menstruation in the Deccan seven or nine married women of the house and neighbourhood meet in the afternoon and each of them rubs a little perfumed powder *(chiksa)* on the girl's body, puts a couple of garlands of flowers round her neck and anoints her with fragrant oil *(phulel ka tel*). After this she is confined in a private room and the women go home after spending a little time in music. For seven days the girl is kept shut up in this room, she is not allowed to go out, to do any sort of work, or to bathe. During this time her diet consists of rice boiled with pulse *(khichari),* fish, flesh; salt, and acid foods being prohibited. On the seventh day she is bathed. The married women, as before, assemble in the morning, hold a red cloth over her head as a canopy, take a small water vessel with a spout *(badhni),* either plain or decorated with paint, fasten a packet of betel-leaves with a red thread to the neck of the pot, drop into it four or five fruits of the two kinds of myrobalan, and each woman pours water from it twice over the girl's head. Before the women do this their laps are filled with cakes and betel, and sandalwood is rubbed on their necks. On that evening a feast is given, and the girl is adorned with glass bangles and dressed in her best. They keep vigil during the night to guard against evil spirits. If the girl be already married and consummation has not yet taken place, which is more than probable as Musalmans object to infant marriage, her husband, leaving the party to enjoy themselves, takes his bride home and consummates the marriage. On this occasion he is usually given a present of clothes, and the pair are wreathed with flowers. But it is only the lower classes who make this public, and more respectable people do not announce the event.

"When a boy on arriving at his twelfth, thirteenth, fourteenth, or fifteenth year, or as some say at the age of eighteen, experiences a pollution octurna, he must conform to the duties of his religion as regards prayer, fasting, almsgiving, and pilgrimage. This is also the rule for girls. Previous to this period, that is, during childhood, all their good and evil deeds are laid to the charge of their parents, but after this they are responsible for their own actions. When the youth is overtaken with pollutio in somno he must perform the Ghusl or major ablution by bathing on the following morning, for until he has purified himself in this way it is unlawful for him to eat, pray, touch the Koran, or go to the mosque. These rules also extend to other ablutions, of which there are four : after pollutio nocturna *(ihtilam),* which was abrogated by Akbar ; after coitus *(jima')* ; after menses *(haiz)* ; after puerperinm *(nifas).* The period to which the first and second bathing may be deferred is nine or ten next morning ; the last should be deferred till the discharge has ceased, but some ignorant women have fixed it for the fortieth day after childbed. The bathing is done thus : After slightly wetting the body and reciting some short prayers appointed for this purpose, the boy gargles his throat three times, then he bathes, thoroughly wetting his whole boy and uttering the following sentences in Arabic : 'I desire by the ablution to purify my body for prayer and to remove all inward filth and corruption'. Some ignorant or vulgar people first throw three pots of water on the head, then three on the right shoulder, then three on the left, and having taken a little water in the hand, either after or without reciting the Durud or blessing, they sprinkle it on the clothes which are thus purified. In the complete ablution the water must be pure and not less than a certain quantity, and it must touch every part of the skin beginning with the right side of the person and ending with the left. Hence among Arabs a plunge bath is generally preferred." (Properly speaking, it should be done in running water, and hence Musulmans use a vessel with a spout (*badhna*) for the purpose.)

Custom of Human Sacrifice

Mr. ET Dalton describes the custom of human sacrifice practised by the savages, thus, "The *Meriah* sacrifices, as they were called, and Kondh female infanticide, may now be regarded as amongst the plague spots of the land which have been effectually cured and obliterated by the enlightened treatment and strong hand of the British Government. It seems to be admitted, not only that the practises have ceased, but the people have been actually weaned from the fears and superstitions which gave rise to them. Nevertheless, no account of the Kondhs would be complete without a description of the mysterious and awe-inspiring rites of a *Meriah* sacrifice, and a detail of the circumstances under which female infants were so unmercifully massacred.

"The Kondhs are strictly an agricultural people and the salient points of their religious belief all have reference to the fertilization of the earth.

"Ten or twelve days before the time appointed for a sacrifice, the hair of the victim selected, till then unshaved, is cut off, and the villagers, having bathed, go to the sacred grove with the priest, who there invokes the goddess, and proclaims to her that they are preparing for her the repast she loves best, and implores her favour in return. The festival itself lasts three days, and it is a time of unbridled license, drunken feasting and mad dances under excitement which the goddess is believed to inspire and which it would be impious to resist. On the second morning, the victim, who has been kept fasting from the preceding evening, is carefully washed, dressed in a new garment, and led forth from the village in solemn procession, with music and dancing, to the *Meriah* grove. This, as with the Oraons and other tribes, is a remnant of the old forest, kept sacred from the axe and haunted by ghosts and spirits. In the centre of the grove a post is set up sometimes between two plants of the 'Sankissar' shrub, to which the victim is bound in sitting posture by the priest. He is then anointed with oil, ghee, and turmeric, adorned with flowers and worshipped, and there is now great contention amongst the bystanders to obtain some relic of his sacred person, even a portion of the unguent with which he has been anointed. He is thus left all night, during which the licentious feasting of the previous night is resumed, and the air resounds with horrid revelry. At noon on the third morning these orgies terminate, and the assemblage proceeds with stunning shouts and pealing music to consummate the sacrifice.

"The victim must not die in bonds, and to prevent escape, of which there have been instances, the arms and legs are broken or stupefaction by opium is produced.

"The priest now offers prayers to the earth goddess for full granaries, increase of children, cattle, pigs, and poultry and for the decrease or disappearance of tigers and snakes; besides which, each individual of the assembled multitude gives expression to the wish that is at the moment uppermost in his thoughts. The priest then recites the tradition of the origin of the sacrifice and the necessity they were under of continuing it, and this, according to the author I am now chiefly quoting, is followed by a very long and somewhat sentimental, but at the same time argumentative, conversation between the priest and *meriah,* the object of the one being to show that the victim must calmly submit to suffering in a cause so great to the benefit of mankind, and that had nothing to complain of, as the Kondhs had purchased him for that special purpose; and of the other to prove that he had been cruelly decieved, that he had not been a party to his own sale, but believing that he had been purchased as a labourer, he had honesty worked for his employer."

Captain MacViccar, in a report dated the 6th April, 1851, thus detailed the mode of performing the sacrifice in Maji Deso, midway between Baud and Patna, "On the day of sacrifice, after the appointed ceremonies, the *meriah* is surrounded by the Kondhs, who beat him violently on the head with the heavy metal bangles, which they purchase at the fair, and wear on the occasion. If this does not destory life, an end is put to his sufferings by strangulation by means of a slit bamboo. Strips of flesh are then cut off the back and each recipient carries his portion to the stream which waters his fields, and there suspends it on a pole. The remains of the mangled carcass are then buried, and funeral obsequies are performed and repeated a year afterwards. This is apparently in imitation of the Hindu *shradh.*"

From all the description given above it would be apparent that the British Army Officers and civilians who recorded their knowledge of and encounter with, this custom and rite of human sacrifice, could not appreciate its sociological and anthropological significance. Worship of the Earth Mother is almost a universal phenomenon in all the primitive societies. It has been quite a task for anthropologists to classify and study the different forms of this worship, their origin, development and significance and how they are different from one culture to another. It is not proposed to go into any busthy discussion of the subject on which the literature is vast. This is only to emphasise the point that the sociological roots of human sacrifice and Earth worship were not understood initially by the 19th Century British Civilians and army officers. The American-Indian, for example, refuses to till the soil because he will not wound the body of his mother, the Earth. "It is a sin", he would say, "To wound our God, tear or scratch our common mother by working at agriculture" and adds "that you ask me to dig in the Earth? Am I to take a knife and plunge it into the breast of my mother? But then when I die, she will not gather me again into her bosom. You tell me to dig up and take away the stones. Must I mutilate her flesh so as to get at her bones? Then I can never again enter into her body and be born again". This is one extreme of the mythology of the primitive people relating to Earth Mother. Other Indian mythology speak of a remote age in which the "Earth-Mother produced human beings in the same manner as she now produces bushes of reeds". The birth of a child from the darkness of the womb to outside light is compared to the coming out from the darkness of earth's womb to the surface sunlight. In the primitive mind regeneration has always a significance at a return to the fundamentals and 'a repetition of the cosmogony'. Wheelwright has studied this aspect of the "Laborious journey from the darkness of the passing of the earth to the surface of the soil and into the light".

Paul Radin has thus described the experience of an Towa Shaman recounting the experience of reincarnation "Down there, I remained conscious all the time. One day I heard the sounds of little children outside, and other sounds too, and I decided to go out. Then it seemed to me that I went through a door, but in reality, I was just newly born from a woman. As soon as I had come out the cool air chilled me and I began to cry". This is supposed to be the call of Mother Earth and it seeks to connect the ontogenetic with the filogenetic. Buddhadeb Chaudhary points out, "The Kondh like most other primitive people always feels a mysterious sense of union with the earth. There is also something quite different: the mystical experience of autochthony; the profound feeling of having come from the soil, of having been born of Earth in the same way that the Earth, with her inexhaustible fecundity, gives birth to the rocks, rivers, trees and flowers. The rites of the Earth Mother are thus reiterations of the events which happened in *illo tempore* in mythical times. The rituals of the *Terra mater* refer man back to his primevel association with the Earth and the symbolic assumption of the organic link of man with Mother Earth. Human sacrifices were prevalent in many agrarian primitive cultures." Frazer has discussed them in detail in his *Spirits of the Corn and The Golden Bough.* Mircea Eliade has also documented many of these forms in *Patterns in Comparative Religion.* Here is the account of *meriah* sacrifice by J.G. Frazer:

"The *meriah* was a voluntary victim, bought by the community. He was allowed to live for years, he could marry and have children. A few days before the sacrifice the *meriah* was consecrated, that is, he was identified with the divinity to be sacrificed; the people danced around, and worshipped him. After this, they prayed to the Earth: 'O Goddess, we offer this sacrifice; give us good harvest, good seasons and good health.' And they added turning to the victim: 'We have bought thee and have not seized thee by force: now we sacrifice thee and may no sin be accounted to us. 'The ceremony also included an orgy lasting several days. Finally the *meriah* was drugged with opium, and, after they had strangled him, they cut him into pieces. Each of the villages received a fragment of his body which they buried in the fields. The remainder of the body was burnt, and the ashes strewn over the land.'

"The elaborate ritual accompanying the sacrifice, the wild rejoicings which preceded and followed indicate the intense involvement of the community in this ritual sacrifice. In the song the prayer for good crop, for peace and plenty is eloquent about the concern for community. This is reminiscent not only of the Vedic *slokas* where the Rain God, the Wind God, the Earth Goddess are invoked for conferring peace and prosperity on the community; their song is also comparable to the ritual invocation songs called *Bakhens* prevalent among the Santals where gods and goddesses are propitiated with requests for plenty of rains which will make the crop thrive and 'hundred grains grow from one seed. 'It is also worth noting that the Kondhs disclaim all sense of guilt in this matter of human sacrifice. After all it is meant for the gods. The gods have to be offered so many bribes and they offer a human being only as a 'small offering' so that no creepers will enmesh the head, no thorns will prick. And in any case the gods have made the sword and the axe and 'they eat the *Meria*'. The sacrifice is given so that the land will be happy, the gods will be happy. As mentioned earlier, the actual sacrifice of the victim was made in different ways. Sometimes the victim was dragged along the fields by the group who cut the flesh from his body till he died. Elsewhere, the victim was tied to a wooden elephant or large-sized peacock symbolising the Earth Goddess which revolved round a post and as it revolved, the people cut the flesh from his body. The method of putting the victim to death was made deliberately painful as the belief was that more tears he shed, the more abundant would be the supply of rain. The victim's blood was similarly supposed to cause the redness to turmeric. The victim who was ritually worshipped, dressed up in new clothes, taken in procession in the village and virtually treated as a god, was thus supposed to possess supernatural powers." Lord Alwin in his minutes of the year 1841 had observed: "In the religion of the *Kondhs* we find traces of the primitive elemental worship of the Vadas before it was overlaid by the superstructure which now almost conceals it from our eyes." It may not pertinent to mention here that human sacrifices before gods or goddesses prevailed in many parts of India. In Bastar area of Madhya Pradesh, Assam, and in Jeypore territory of Orissa, human beings were sometimes sacrificed before the image of *Kali,* the dark Goddess of death and Time. As Verrier Elwin mentions in his *Meria Murder and Suicide* (pp. 71-74), the Rajas and Gond chiefs of Bastar used to offer human sacrifice in honour of Danteswari, the tutelary goddess of Bastar. Danteswari was identified with Kili. It is reported that once the Raja of Bastar organised the most expensive sacrifice that had ever been heard of; on which occasion 27 adult males had been immolated.

Mr. Buddhadeb Chaudhary adds, "The Hindus call the *maria* victims as *Junna.* At Ramgiri in the Jeypore *taluk, 2 Junna* victims were sacrificed by the Hindus to propitiate a local goddess Goorboneshanni who was supposed to be at the bottom of a hole 18 inches square and 3 feet deep. In 1861 in Jeypore taluk, a girl of about 12 years of age was sacrificed at the shrine of another goddess Kanakadurga as cholera was spreading and taking many lives in the area. In May 1854 a female *junna* aged 10 years was sacrificed by the Rani of Jeypore in fulfilment of a vow for the restoration or health. In Mac Viccar's report there are also references to human sacrifices celebrated during Dusserah—the object in all cases was to pray for benefits and to ward off evils. Thus the Kondh rite of human sacrifice has to be seen in the broad cross-cultural perspective of the worship of Earth Goddess for the welfare of the community and to invoke their blessing for warding off diseases and death and to seek peace and prosperity for the group."

It is not that he despairs of life. If he did, he would not have survived the inclemencies of nature and the cruelties of his more clever neighbours. In fact his belief in divine justice, the cycles of life and an awareness of joy in little things keep him going. The life of the Kondhs is marked a cycle of festivals round the year. This adds flavour to his otherwise drab life. The general tone of songs is pessimistic brooding and meditative like the shadows cast by the densely-wooded hills over the cluster of huts that is his village.

The *Kondhs* and *Parajas* are among the most primitive and savage tribes not only in Orissa, but in the whole of India. They live primarily in the hills of Koraput and Phulbani districts. Still, the Kondhs were notorious in history for the *Meriah* sacrifice. In 1961 census their population in Orissa was about 8.2 lakhs and that of the *Parajas* 1.6 lakhs. In 1971 census Kondh population had gone up to a little above 9 lakhs. According to Macpherson, the world 'Kondh' is derived from the Telugu world '*Kanda*' meaning a hill. Traditionally, the *Kondhs* have been known for their simplicity and unique sense of hospitality. A guest in the village is treated with full honour and even when a *Kondh* family is starving, it would go out of its way to treat well the guest. In fact, an outsider becomes the guest of the entire village. The *Kondh* addiction to liquor and the rite of human sacrifice made the British officers think that the Kondhs were a barbaric people given to orgies, to drinking, debauchery and murder. However, this opinion was based upon a complete misunderstanding of the significance of the rite of human sacrifice and the nature of *Kondh* polity and their psychology. The *Kondhs* are an agricultural people. In most agricultural communities, the earth is worshipped as goddess. Dhartani is mother earth; she sustains life by yielding crops, allows the individual to play in her lap, dance, and romp about and at the end of the day, when weariness comes and the night closes in, she takes him back again to her fold. Dust returns to dust.

Thus, the Kondh feels indebted to Mother Earth and prays her to give him good crops and to make his society live in plenty and prosperity. This is the basic notion behind the worship of Earth Goddess and the *Meriah Puja* (Human Sacrifice.) There are different version of the observance of this human sacrifice in ancient times.

References

1. Furer-Haimandorf, Christophvon, The After Life in Indian Tribal Belief; *Journal of the Royal Anthropological Society*, London, 3 (1) January-June 1953, pp. 37-49.
2. Firth, Raymond, The Fate of the Soul : An Interpretation of some primitive concepts, Cambridge University Press, Cambridge, 1955.
3. Dalton, E.T., *Descriptive Ethnography of Bengal*, Government Press, Calcutta, 1872.
4. Roy, S.C., *The Mundas and their Country*, City Book Society, Calcutta, 1912.
5. Risley, Sir Herbert, *The Tribes and Castes of Bengal: Ethnographic Glossary*, Bengal Secretariat Press, Calcutta, 1891.

6. Sengupta, Syamalkanti, *The Social Profiles of the Mahalis*, Firma KLM, Calcutta, 1970.
7. Chaudhury Buddhadeb, (ed), *Tribal Transformation in India: Religion, Rituals and Festivels*, Vol. V, Inter-India Publications, New Delhi, 1992.
8. Sinha, Dikshit, *The Hill Kharia of Purulia*, Anthropological Survey of India, Calcutta, 1984.
9. Sachchidananda, *Profiles of Tribal Culture in Bihar*, Firma KLM, Calcutta, 1965.
10. Troise, J., *Tribal Religion: Religious Beliefs and Practises Among the Santals*, Manohar, New Delhi, 1978.
11. Singh, K.S. (Gen. ed.), *People of India : Bihar*, Seagul Books, Calcutta, 2008.
12. Singh, K.S. (Gen. ed.), *People of India : West Bengal*, Seagul Books, Calcutta, 2008.
13. Sarif, Ja'far, *Islam in India* (edited by W. Crooke), Oriental Books Reprint Corp; New Delhi, 1972, First Published 1921.

7

Social Customs

In the eastern region, social customs of castes, tribes and religious communities are varied and divergent, even the Hindu priestly class Brahmans has distinct sub-groups.

No Distinct Social Position of Babhans

Sir Risley points out about the Babhan social customs, "Owing probably to the controversy about their origin, the social standing of the Babhans is not altogether easy to determine precisely, and varies slightly in different parts of the area which they inhabit. In south-Eastern Behar they rank immediately below Kayasths, but in Shahabad, Saran, and the North-Western Provinces they appear to stand on much the same level as Rajputs. The fact that in Patna and Gya the Amashtha or Karan Kayasths will eat *kachchi* food which has been cooked by a Babhan, while the other sub-castes of Kayasths will not, may perhaps be a survival from times when Babhans occupied a higher position than they do at the present day. In Champaran, according to Mr. Beames, Babhans are not permitted to drink and smoke with Brahmans, 'and only under some restrictions with Rajputs'. Thus, a Rajput may eat rice with them only when it is without condiments; he may not eat bread, and he may drink water 'only from an earthen vessel, not from a brass *lota*."

He adds further, "the religion of the Babhan, like that of the ordinary high-caste Hindu, conforms in its details to the ritual of whatever recognised sect he happens to belong to. Representatives of all sects are found amongst the caste in much the same proportion as in the population at large. Vaishnavism, however, is said to have been only recently introduced among them, and in North Behar most Babhans are either Saivas or Saktas. No social consequences are involved by professing the tenets of any of the regular sects, and intermarriage between their members goes on freely within the limits of the caste. Besides the standard worship which a Babhan performs in virtue of belonging to a particular sect, all householders offer he goats and rams to Kali on the 24th or 25th of Kuar (September-October), sweetmeats, sandal-paste, flowers to Sitala on the 24th Chait (March-April), and sugared cakes to Hanuman on every Tuesday. On the 1st of Chait these three deities are propitiated with *pua* (wheat-flour and molasses cooked in oil), *bara* (cakes of urid fried in oil), and *kachwania* (round balls of rice-flour, sugar, and butter). These offerings are presented by the men of the family without the aid of a Brahman, and are afterwards divided among the members of the household. To the women is relegated the task of appeasing lower order of gods—Bandi Mai, Sokha, and Goraiya—with molasses and *pitha*, a sort of boiled pudding made of *sattu* or meal." The social customs are practised by the community of Babhans.

Eating Beef and Pork Causing Low Social Status

Sir Risley records, "Their social rank is very low. They are usually classed with Bauris and Bhaiyas as dwellers on the outskirts of Hinduism. Some Bagdis eat beef and pork, and all indulge freely in flesh of other kinds, and are greatly addicted to drink. Tentalia Bagdis, however, will not eat beef, and many members of this sub-caste have become Vaishnavas and abstain from all sorts of flesh. By abstaining from beef they consider themselves to be raised above the Bauri, Muchi, and Oraon, and the beef-eating members of their own caste.

"Dulia Bagdis eat tortoises. In Western Bengal the Bagdis eat and drink with the Mal; in Orissa they eat rice with the Lohar Manjhi and sweetmeats with the Bhuiya.

"Bagdis profess to follow the Hindu law of inheritance, but their legal business, as with most of the lower castes, is of a very simple character, and is generally disposed of by their own caste councils (panchayats) without the intervention of the Courts. In making a division of property the eldest son gets an extra share (*jeth-angs*), which seems to be intended to enable him to support the female members of the family, who remain under his care. A similar provision was recognised by early Hindu law, but it has since become obsolete, and entire equality of division is now the rule among all the higher castes, unless perhaps where some special family custom can be proved.

"Opinions differ regarding the original occupation of the caste. Some say fishing, others personal service, but the question clearly is not one on which we can hope to arrive at any definite conclusion. At the present day the Tentulia and Kasaikulia Bagdis work as masons, and also prepare the lime which is mixed with betel and areca nut. Dulia Bagdis carry palanquins or *dulis*, and, in common with the other sub-castes, earn their livelihood by fishing, making gunny-bags, weaving cotton, and preparing the red powder (*abir*) used in the Holi festival. The Bagdi fisherman uses the ordinary circular cast-net described in the article on Malo, but swings the net round his head before casting it—a practise which is supposed by the regular fishing castes of Bengal—Tiyar, Malo, and Kaibartta—to be peculiarly dishonourable. Most of the Bagdis are also to some extent engaged in agriculture, usually as *kurfa* or under-raiyats, and comparatively few have attained the more respectable position of occupancy tenants. In Western Bengal we find large number of them working as landless day-labourers, paid in cash or kind, or as nomadic cultivators, tiling other men's lands on the *bhag-jot* system, under which they are remunerated by a definite share of the produce—sometimes one—half, sometimes less, as may be arranged with their immediate landlord. I can recall no instance of a Bagdi holding a zemindari, or even a superior tenure, such as *patni* or *mukarari*, of any importance; but some of the Manbhum zemindars, who now claim to be Rajputs, are said by Colonel Dalton to be really Bagdis, and the conjecture is likely enough to be true. In the neighbouring district of Bankura, Bagdis must have been among the earliest settlers, if not the actual aborigines of that part of the country for at the present time there are 14 Bagdis holding the tenure of *sardar ghatudal*, 6 are *saduits*, 2 are are village *sardars*, 178 *tabidars*, and 117 *chakran chaukidars*. In Manbhum one Bagdi holds a village *sardar's* tenure, and four are employed as *tabidars*. In Central Bengal, Bagdis are frequently met with as chaukidars.

"The religion of the Bagdis is compounded of elements borrowed from orthodox Hinduism and survivals from the mingled Animism and Nature-worship which prevails among the aborigines of Western Bengal. Siva, Vishnu, Dharmaraj (Yama), Durga, the Saktis, and the myriad names of the modern Hindu Pantheon, are worshipped in a more or less intelligent fashion under the guidance of the degraded (*patit*) Brahmans who look after the spiritual welfare of the lower castes. Alongside of these greater gods we find the Santali goddess Gosain Era and Barpahar, the 'great mountain' god (Marang Buru) of the same tribe. According to the Bagdis themselves, their favourite and characteristic deity is Manasa, the sister of the Snake-king Vasuki, the wife of Jaratkaru and mother of Astika, whose intervention saved the snake race from destruction by Janmejaya.

"Manasa is worshipped by the caste with great pomp and circumstance. On the 5th and 20th of the four rainy months—Asar, Sraban, Bhadra, and

Aswin (middle of June to middle of October)—rams and he-goats are sacrificed, rice, sweetmeats, fruit, and flowers are offered; and on the Nagpanchami (5th of the light half of Sraban end of August) a four-armed effigy of the goddess, crowned by a tiara of snakes, grasping a cobra in each hand, and with her feet resting on a goose, is carried round the village with much discordant music, and finally thrown into a tank. The cult of Manasa is of course by no means confined to the Bagdis. In Eastern Bengal all castes, from the Brahman to the Chandal, adore her, and no class is more strict in attending to the details of her worship than the Kulin Brahmans of Bikrampur in Dacca. Bagdis, however, regard her with peculiar respect, and say that they alone among her votaries make images in her honour. Some add that the *puja* has the effect of securing the worshippers from snake-bite, which is naturally more frequent during the rains; and this notion finds a curious echo in the promise given by Vasuki to Astika in the Mahabharata, that those who call upon his name, be they Brahmans or common folk, shall be safe from the attacks of the snake race.

"On the last day of Bhadra (middle of September) the Bagdis of Manbhum and Bankura carry in procession the effigy of a female saint named Bhadu, who is said to have been the favourite daughter of a former Raja of Pachete, and to have died a virgin for the good of the people. The worship consists of songs and wild dances, in which men, women, and children take part. The story of its origin may well have some foundation in fact, it being notorious that the Rajas of Pachete, like most of the pseudo-Rajput families of Chota Nagpur, find great difficulty in arranging suitable alliances for their daughters, and often have to keep them at home unmarried until they have long passed the age of puberty. Regarded from this point of view, the legend adds one more to the numerous instances which may be cited in support of the theory propounded by Sir Alfred Lyall..." adds Sir Risley. The social customs are practised by the Bagdis in the eastern region.

Wearing of Sacred Thread

About the Bhat social customs, Sir Risley records, "In point of social precedence Bhats rank immediately below Kayasths. They wear the sacred thread (*janeo*), and Brahmans take water from their hands. Their own rules concerning diet are the same as are observed by the higher castes, and, like them, they will take water and certain sweetmeats from Kurmis, Kahars, and castes of corresponding status."

He states further, "In questions concerning the devolution of property, the caste are guided for the most part by the standard Hindu law recognised in the area where they live; that is to say, in Bengal they follow the Dayabhaga, and in Behar the Mitakshara Code. In one point, however, they observe a peculiar usage of their own. Where under the ordinary law a daughter's son would succeed, Bhat customs holds him to be excluded by the nearest male relative of the same section. It is the more remarkable that this custom should have survived, as the Bhats are not governed by panchayat or caste councils to the same extent as the lower castes, and thus lack the most effective machinery for preserving peculiar usages, which the courts tend on the whole to destroy."

Sir Risley adds further, "The religion of the Bhats of Behar differs little from that of the average middle-class Hindu. representatives of all the regular sects are found among their numbers, and the caste cannot be said to favour the tenets of any particular body. In Eastern Bengal, on the other hand, they are said to be mostly Sakti worshippers, and to be greatly addicted to intemperance. They employ Brahmans for religious and ceremonial purposes, who are received on equal terms by other members of the sacred order. Their minor gods are Bandi or Sanvardhir and Bariji, who are worshipped on the 22nd Sravan and the 24th Chait with offerings of be-goats, wheaten cakes, '*ilchauri* made of rice and molasses, coloured cloths, and vermilion. The eatable portion of the offerings is divided among the members of the household. The dead are burned, and the ceremony of *sraddh* is performed on the thirteenth day after death."

He adds, "The characteristic profession of the Bhats has an ancient and distinguished history. The literature of both Greece and India owes the preservation of its oldest treasures to the singers, who recited pomes in the households of the chief, and doubtless helped in some measure to shape the masterpieces which they handed down. Their place was one of marked distinction. In the days when writing was unknown, the man who could remember many verses was held in high honour by the tribal chief, who depended upon the memory of his bard for his personal amusement, for the record of his own and his ancestors' prowess, and for the maintenance of the genealogy which established the purity of his descent. The bard, like the herald, was not lightly to be slain, and even Odyssens, in the heat of his vengeance, spares the *aotoos* Phemius, 'who sang among the wooers of necessity.' *Odyssey xxii*, 331. Possibly the duties of bard and herald may often have been discharged by the same person. However this may be, it is curious to find that about the middle of the sixteenth century the person of a Bhat was deemed inviolable by highway robbers in Rajputana and Guzerat, so that a member of that caste could protect a caravan of traders from attack by threatening to kill himself if they were molested; while as late as 1775 many of them made their living by pledging themselves as hostages for the payment of revenue, the performance of treaties and bonds, and the general good behaviour of princes or private individuals. Yule, *Anglo-Indian Glossary,* S.V. Bhat.

"In most parts of modern India, except perhaps in Rajputana, the Bhats have fallen from their former state, and are now the cawdriest parody on the Homeric *aoioos*. Mr. Nesfield describes them as 'rapacious and conceited mendicants, too proud to work, but not too proud to beg.' Mr. Sherring says they 'are notorious for their rapacity as beggars, and are much dreaded by their employers on account of the power they have of distorting family history at public recitations if they choose to do so, and of subjecting any member to general ridicule.' Dr. Wise's notes contain a telling sketch of the Bhats of Eastern Bengal:—'In January they leave their homes, traveling to all parts of Eastern Bengal, and, being in great request, are fully engaged during the subsequent Hindu matrimonial season. Each company receives a fixed yearly sum from every Hindu household within a definite area, amounting usually to eight annas. In return they are expected to visit the house and recite Kavitas, or songs extolling the worth and renown of the family. Satirical songs are great favourites with Hindus, and none win more applause than those laying bare the foibles and well-intentioned vagaries of the English rule or the eccentricities and irascibility of some local magnate. Very few bards can sings extemporary songs, their effusions, usually composed by one and leaned off by heart by the others, being always metrical, often humorous, and generally seasoned with puns and equivocal words. Their sole occupation is the recital of verses, unaccompanied by instrumental music. They are met with everywhere when Hindu families celebrate a festival of domestic event, appearing on such occasions uninvited, and exacting by their noisy importunity a share of the food and charity that is being doled to the poor. Their shamelessness in this respect is incredible. During the Durga Puja they force their way into respectable houses and make such a horrid uproar by shouting and singing that the inmates gladly pay something to be rid of them. Should this persecution have no effect on the rich man inside, they by means of a brass *lota* and an iron rod madden the most phlegmatic Babu, who pays liberally for their departure. The Bengali Bhat is as a rule uneducated, and very few know Sanskrit.'

"At weddings in Behar it is one of the duties of the Bhat to march out several miles to meet the bridegroom's procession, bearing with him a letter of welcome from the bride's father, and to conduct them to the bride's house. For these services, and for reciting verses and making himself generally useful, he receives presents of money and clothes. In some Behar districts and in parts of Chota Nagpur Bhats hold small parcels of land, usually about three or four *bighas* in extent, rent-free under the tenure known as *bhatottar*. Such grants are mostly of rather ancient date, and are regarded with disfavour by the landholders of to-day, who look more to Government as the fountain of honour, and do not make much account of the Bhats. A few Bhats have risen to be zamindars or tenure holders, but the bulk of the caste are occupancy raiyats, cultivating by means of hired labourers and disdaining to touch the plough themselves." Adds Sir Risley. The customs are pertinent to the community of Bhats.

Animism and Nature Worship

Influence of Christianity, modern public education, industrialization, urbanization, communication development and Government efforts in all round development acted as factors of significant change in the tribal life and culture, which has resulted in and vanishing of their many customs and traditional institutions. They began to move away from traditional occupation to different business houses, public sector and Government offices. Thus forces of change and development that were initiated during the mid-19th century continues even today. Even to the extent that many educated and converted tribals forgot their age-old traditions like dance, music, drama; still the fear of unknown, mysterious world has got hold of them. They believe that they can not escape the wrath of malignant ghosts and spirits who haunt lonely places in villages. Many still learn the craft of Ojha or the Shamans.

Mr. P.O. Boding points out, "The Science of *ojha* or *ojha bidia* which includes a knowledge of incantations, sacrifices, medicines, and charms has to be learnt from an *ojha guru*. It is customary for young men of a village to go through the yearly course of training in *ojha* science, held by the village *ojha guru*, commencing from the last days of May to the end of September or the beginning of October. Students in these courses are of two kinds, amateurs and those who intend to be professionals. All students who go through this yearly course become *paisari*, but they are not thereby fit to practise as an *ojha*. Serious and competent students are selected from among the *paisari* for special training in divination and the art of getting possessed by spirits. After attending two or three years' courses, one or two principal students may succeed in becoming *kat khura*. Only a *kat khura* is considered fit to receive final *sid*, that is, formal initiation as a full-fledged ojha. *(The Santals and Disease,* pp. 45-63, *ibid.*, 45-63.)

The tribal priest or *Naike* and henceforth the previous generations of *Majhi*-family who attain some distinctions from the rest, in their tribal society. Though, the headman (*Majhi*) has no distinction at all with the other villagers on social and economic levels, except in the political and religious life. To show the reverence to the first settlers of the tribal settlements traditional songs in the name of the first settler are sung by the villagers, and the water of the tank dug by the first-settler (*Bonga-Pokhri*) is used only in the purificatory rites. The other places of religious significance in the village are *Majhi than* (near the dwelling of the first settler), the courtyard of the priest situated on the right side of the village main road where villagers celebrate Baha festival; Jaher at the North-east corner of the village, *Bhairab than* at the Southern corner of the Jaher, where there is the *Bhairab Haram*.

Besides, there are a number of deities propitiated by their names only are known according to the place where they are worshipped such as *Ganthar* at the eastern side, *Sendra Bonga* and *Disom Bonga* near Jaher, *Kuchla Janthar* at the southern part under a Kuchla tree, *Madhugiria* at the southern corner on the bank of a tank. At the north-east corner another site is seen where the members of the *Majhi* family propitiate their *Orak-Bonga* and *Sendra-Bonga*.

The cultural communication within the village is conducted by the village-messenger. But the most important media is the *Akhara*, an open ground at the middle of the village main road where they use to dance during festival or assemble for meeting or gossip regularly.

Buddhadeb Chaudhury points out, "The Santhals living in this village refer themselves as *Hor* who bear the surname Soren, Murmu, Hasdak, Hemborm etc. Village Headman (*Majhi*) and village Priest (*Naike*) are selected from the generations of the first headman and first priest respectively. Assistant to the headman (Paranik) village messenger (*Godeth*) are also present in the village. The Headman performs both administrative and religious functions whereas the priest has to look after the religious functions only.

"The communication of the village-santhals is presently widened as education is taking a shape in them slowly, but steadily. Moreover, though their main occupation is agriculture, but some of them are in service. Religious rites are associated with the Birth and Death of the Santhals of this village, but not such rite is found at marriage which is a social affair entirely."

Worshipping Supernatural Phenomenon

Traditionally, the supernatural powers are considered as benevolent, while some are held as evil. The villagers propitiate all these supernatural powers to lessen their wordly anxieties, fear or to protect themselves from the ill effect which may cause to them. However, all these collectively form the latent framework of the supernatural world. All of these goblins, and demi-gods are envisaged certain rights and duties.

Thakur, a male deity, is invisible and incharge of everything in the world and supernatural world. He is never worshipped, but is always remembered.

"*Marang Buru*, the male deity, messenger to *Thakur*, whose name was *Lita*, created this earth and transferred *Pkichu Haram* and *Pilchu Budi* over there. He taught them to prepare and use *Handi*. He introduced *Chut* (Pollution) in the world of human being for which once he had been turned out from the heaven. Then he was *Lita* which had been changed to *Marang Buru* (the great mountain) on his entry to the heaven. He is symbolised by *Kapi* (a type of axe). He is worshipped when any change in familial or village level like birth, death, festival (like Baha festival) take place in the village. He may be worshipped by the priest or any member of the village. *Jaher era,* the sister of *Marang buru* and *Dharma*, a female deity who is the incharge of the *Jaher*, symbolised with *Jonok* (broom stick), *Dala* (Basket) and *Ghunsi mala* (a type of necklace) is brought down over the earth is a medium, when she uses to pass some time with the villagers, during the *Baha* festival.

Dharma, the brother of *Marang buru* and *Jaher era*, is propitiated within or outside the *Jaher*, during *Baha* festival. *Moreko*, the five brothers, are propitiated with *Turuiko* within and outside the *Jaher* by the priest or any adult male. They have no special power on human life. *Chando Bonga* are two as *sin Chando* gives light in day time and *Ninda Chand* gives light at night. They are not worshipped but simply remembered.

"Besides, there are many other deities who are in general term known as *Abge* and *Orak Bonga*. There are twelve *Khuts* amongst the Santhals and each of these has different *Abge Bonga* and *Orak Bonga*. These *bongas* are worshipped by the head of family, within or outside the domicile boundary.

Influence of malevolent spirits like *Hoy Hisit Churin*, *Jugin* and *Dan* though rare, but not uncommon to them and *Kudam Naike* possesses the powers to control them. *Hoy Hisit* are unsatisfied souls, move in air have a grudge over the human being; they generally reside in open field, forest, in the bank of *Bandh* etc. They are invisible. *Churin*, female evil spirit, seen in the open field, forest, on the bank of bandh etc. is invisible and harmful to human beings. *Dan* is a type of evil spirit possessed man or woman who lives amongst the villagers and seen at night. Full moon or new moon are best time for their activity. They like to eat liver of human being. *Jugin* are also a type of female spirit, may be beneficial or harmful. They are symbolised with a basket and a broom stick at their hands. Sometimes it appears with this before a sick bed. *Jaher* is the only sacred place in the village, having a great value to the villagers as they use to propitiate or worship their deities in this place. The *Naike* of the village who as a custom worship the deities, though in the absence of the *Naike*, the headman of the village (*Majhi*) worship the deities. Thus the priest (*Naike*) is a supernaturally selected man who makes a connecting link between the villagers of Kamarabandi and the supernatural world towards its equilibrium.

Communal Festivals and Appearing *Bongas*

"In the month of Bhadra (July-August) Karam festival is performed in each family by the female members where a branch of Karam tree is worshipped. Both these worships are done for the prosperity of the family. In the month of Pous (January-February) regional cult *Tusu* is observed by the unmarried girls in each family). It is more a festival than a ceremony. All communal festivals are observed at the different public places in the village. At the entrance of the village there is the seat of *Kendua budi,* the female deity of the village. There are two seats of the goddess *Manasa* and deity of snakes, one below the trees other with in a hut. There are two seats of *Boram,* the deity of the woods, one under a banyan tree and the other near the village dancing around *(Akhara),* at the southwestern part of the village. Seat of Goram deota or the tutelary village deity is situated at the southern corner of the village below an old banyan tree. At the centre of the village there is the seat of the goddess *Sitala* (goddess presiding over diseases especially small pox).

"All the communal worships are performed by the Munda village priest *(Deheri).* Except in the *Karam* and *Tusu* the women are not allowed to propitiate any other individual or communal worships. In the month of Magh (January-February) *Goram, Boram* and *Sitala* are worshipped by the Deheri at their respective seats. He prays for prosperity, peace and good health of the villagers for the year.

"In the month of Falgun (February-March) *Uliana* worship is performed. This is particularly aimed at the protection of the village from all the wordly calamities. It is performed by the village priest along with a few village youth.

Early in the morning or before day-break or at night it is performed. The priest encircles the village boundary with the other fellows muttering incantations and sprinkling mustard seeds. He does so leaving a narrow passage and an outlet. Next he collects a few refused article like broomsticks etc. from the village, mutters incantations upon these and through the narrow passage left while encircling the village, under the shadow of darkness he goes to the boundary of any other neighbouring village and leaves those refuses there. While returning to the village he by uttering spells closes the narrow passage which remained open so long for the purpose. It is believed that all misfortunes and disease etc. of the village are transferred to the other village magically leaving this village trouble free for the year. To avoid the physical resistances of the other village the ceremony is performed in the dark.

"Communal propitiation of *Dhuria* is performed before first ploughing, *Kusna* before first sowing, *Ashari* before transplantation *and Kendua budi* before reaping in the month of *Baisakh* (March-April), Jaistha (April-May), Ashar (May-June) and Kartick (October-November) respectively. All these worships are performed by the Deheri at the seats of *Boram* and *Goram* and attended by the adults of the village. In the month of *Sravan* (June-July) and Aswin (September-October) *Manasa* the goddess of snakes is worshipped at her seats by the *Deheri.* He prays for the protection of the villages from snake bite. *Sohrai* or *Bandna* ceremony is performed in the month of *Kartik* (October-November) by each family head for the betterment of the domestic cattles. At the end of the ceremony the people assemble in a field where cows and bulls decorated by colourful spots on their body are teased in different manner by some of them and this is enjoyed by the others. *Manasa* is worshipped throughout the year on every Tuesday and Saturday by the village medicine man in his house." Adds Mr. Chaudhury. The social customs are related to the Santal tribals.

Magic and Sorcery-primitive Men's Science

Mr. J.G. Frazer understood religion as "a propitiation and conciliation of powers superior to man which are believed to direct and control the course of nature and of human life". Thus religion has two important aspects, belief in a supernatural power, and an endeavour to propitiate or please it. Benedict writes, "we cannot see the basis of religion in animal life and it is by no means obvious upon which of the specifically human endowments it is built up". According to Herbert Spencer, religion began with respect for the elder generations of one's family which ultimately became ancestor-worship. Tylor based his conclusions on the assumption of soul or *mana* which was separate from one's body. This was the basis of the concept of animism which was based on the belief in spirits and preliterate mentality, which did not distinguish between man and his outer surroundings. Durkheim thought that religion was the outcome of crowd exilement, which he thought was connected with totemism. Another basis of religion is the fear of the unknown and the unknowable. With crude and clumsy tools and implements, man was a poor sport at the hands of nature.

Thus the uncertainty of assured food supply made man conceive the presence of supernatural beings who with appropriate cajoling, and offerings helped him to get sufficient and assured food-supply. The nature of worship also varies. The primeval man considered vegetable and animal kingdoms in his environment as similar to man. Hence, the idea of totemic relation and inheritance gained ground among the ancient man. The totem animal is often believed to harbour the soul of an ancestor or of one of the mysterious or supernatural beings. The popular belief among the preliterate people is that the ancestors visit the living in the shape of animals or such other creatures. Like the animal worship, the worship of plants has close connection with the belief in souls animating trees and plants. This semblance brings man nearer and the soul of the plants and animals seem to be same as the soul to spirit animating man. The theory of re-incarnation as prevalent among the primeval man, therefore, refers not only to animals but also to trees and plants. Similarly, the worship of sacred groves became important among many a primeval people of the world.

As Karsten wrote, it is difficult to say whether the worshipped tree spirit is the very soul of the tree related to it in the same way as the human soul and body are related or whether it is another spirit which for some reason or other has taken up its abode there. Animism has been developed into fetishism, and as far as the tree-spirit is conceived as a personal being, into polytheism even. Special powers are often ascribed to these tree-gods or spirits. From the foregoing discussion it would be easy for us to understand how from the animistic ideas like these a socio-religious system like totemism has originated. Frazer considered that the concept of totemism originated on the conceptional theory based essentially on the preliterate notion of conception and child-birth, where there is complete ignorance of the physical processes of procreation and the role of male in it. Karsten further noted that "Totemism certainly assumes a peculiar primitive idea of conception but to understand it fully we ought not only to take into account the savage man's idea of conception, but his whole theory of generation and descent." As given in Frazer's theory of the origin of totemism, the spirit believed is only an ancestor who has been reborn in one of his descendants. Speaking generally from this point of view birth and death have not the same meaning for the preliterate people as among the literate and analytical mind. For the former these are the two temporary phases in one's life which are not absolute. With the birth of a child there is nothing new in their sense but a spirit already existing in human form has taken that form again which is nothing more than the forefather appearing again as a newborn in the same family. Hence, we come across even among the preliterate people of to-day 'the new-born being named after one of its forefathers. Similarly, death does not severe all one's connections with life but it is transition from one form to another. The worship of ancestors has developed among the preliterate people on this basis as the awe and fear of the malevolent spirits which haunt their regions have placed premium on the ancestors benign help and protection. Magic which was described by Frazer as "primitive man's science may be called as the precursor of religion." Magic has been divided into two parts, *homoeopathic* or *imitative* based on the principle of imitation, and *contagious* or *sympathetic* by Frazer. The magician or sorcerer wields his power to control the soul or the spirit and hence he is considered mysteriously powerful. The magician or sorcerer influences the people with awe and fear.

Air is Filled with Spirits – Bad and Good

About the supernatural beliefs and notions of the Hill Kharia, Mr. Dikshit Sinha writes, "The Hill Kharia describe the earth as a square table resting on the shoulders of four big turtles. Below the earth there is an interminable stream of water. Above, the earth is covered by air in which different spirits, both benevolent and malevolent *(Nada, Churgin,* etc.) float about. In the air there are also various bodies like the sun *(bera),* the moon *(chando)* and the stars *(tarai)* which are responsible for the division of day and night. There are six stars which are particularly identified and greatly relied upon for gauging the length of the night at different seasons *bhurka tarai* (Venus), *chor kheda,* (pole-star), *juha khata* (orion), *sanjha tarai* (Mercury), *dhudi bhaira* (Canis major) and *sat bhaira* (Ursa major).

"The supernatural world is conceived of as divided into various spheres, social and natural, each of which is controlled by a particular spirit. Thus, each family has its own ancestral spirits, *Burha* and *Burhi,* and the locality where a particular group lives has its own spirit too. This spirit varies in name and characters from locality to locality. When a man is away from the village for a long time or when a kin comes to the hamlet after a long interval a ritual called *satra* (when an anointed *sal* leaf is torn apart by two men holding it simultaneously from one end) is performed. If this is not performed the two guardian spirits of the place as well as the ancestral spirits might get annoyed and cause sickness or other harms to the host. The forest is ruled by a host of spirits but the supply of food is governed by the female spirit called *Bankunari.* The honey production is looked after by another spirit called *Sikari.* The formation of cloud is assigned to another spirit called *Lagbir,* storms to *Uranbir,* etc. The well-being of a child is looked after by *Kandnirandhni.* The *Painsa-burhi* and *Painsa-burha* influence the safety of the human embryo's full gestation in the womb.

"Although the supernatural world is thus segmented the chief of all spirits is thought to be *Dharam* which is conceived to be very powerful and permeates every corner of the earth. Apart from this, all the hills are thought to be symbols of particular spirits and the chief of all the hill spirits is thought to be *Barpahari.* Other deities and spirits particularly worshipped by the Hill Kharia are *Baghut, Vimli kanya* (the deity of lightning), *Rangahari* and *Bisaichandi.* Now-a-days some Hill Kharia also worship the Hindu goddess *Kali* particularly on the eve of dacoity or such other criminal activities."

Though the supernatural world of the Hill Kharia is full of spirits and goblins, the paucity of the festivals when these spirits are invoked for various reasons is striking. In contrast, the peasant's life is punctuated by as many as 11 festivals in a year. In Mayurbhanj Roy recorded various festivals in connection with shifting cultivation. The Hill Kharia of Purulia have only two major festivals *Magh puja* and *Sarul.* On the first day of *Magh* the Hill Kharia worship all their deities and spirits. Just as this festival coincides with peasants festival *akhan jatra* or first ploughing ceremony this is also called *akhan jatra.* On the occasion each family invokes its ancestral spirits who are thought to dwell at the *chulah sal* (oven) to come and partake of the food offered to them. A few coins are also offered to them which must not be spent for personal end, but should be kept aside and given away at the end of the year to any outsider not belonging to the tribe. Besides at the *tulsi pinra,* all the spirits and deities are worshipped. Each family, according to its financial capability offers fowl to the spirits. It was said that previously each spirit was offered one fowl. The *laya* also performs *puja* on behalf of the families residing at the hamlet.

Another *puja* performed by the Hill Kharia is *Sarul* or ceremonial offering of new fruits to the supernatural spirits. This is performed by individual families in the month of *Baisakh* (April-May) just after *gajan*. During *sarul* festivity the deities are worshipped with boiled *mahul* (*Basia latifolia*), green mango, *kul* (*Zizyphus*), five kinds of flowers, such as *sal*, *mango*, *palas* (*Butea frondosa*), *jamun* (*Eugenia sp.*), *mahul*, etc., offering them on a plate made from new *sal* leaves at the *tulsi pinra* to the spirits and deities.

According to Mr. Sachchidananda, the tribal religious performances reflect, to a significant extent the qualities people have attributed to the supernatural. Many supernatural powers to which the generic term god is applied are believed to be self-created. Deities are individually known, named, and personalised, they are recognizable by their given attributes. Their numbers within any given religious system may be large or small. Frequently, deities are called by several names, by different tribal communities. For example, the sun god is called as *Sing Bonga* by Santhal, Munda, Birhor, *Dharmes* by Oraon, *Dharam* by Kharia and *Bhagwan* by Korwa.

While the term god is best applied to those supernatural powers of supernatural origin that are individualised and personally known, the term spirits would refer to those that appear collectively. The spirit population is too numerous to be counted, and as a consequence, spirits are not usually named individually but referred to by category. Some spirits have their good effect on the society (benevolent) and some have bad (malevolent).

Mr. Sachchidananda describes, "Spirits are usually below gods in rank. When gods and spirits coexist in one religious system, as is often the case, the gods are the creators, the upholders of the universal order. Spirits are usually created by the gods. However, the power of creation is of less social importance than the power to intervene in everyday human affairs, the growing of the crops, health, and other matters directly concerning human welfare. When spirits are believed to be responsible for common aspects of daily life, they loom larger in man's consciousness, and rituals in their honour are more frequent. The social functions of spirits overlap with those of the gods. Spirits may aid or punish, be favourably or unfavourably inclined toward mankind, demand offerings and sacrifices, and be worshipped and invoked.

"The departmentalisation of gods is largely a function of economic and social stratification in human society. The *sing Bonga* (sun god) or *Dharmes* or *Bhagwan* or *Dharam* is worshipped by most of the agriculturist tribes of Bihar while *Chandi* (hunting deity) and *Bhagaut* deity (tiger-god) received much greater ritual attention than the agricultural. Although divine specialization usually takes place when social structure becomes more complex.

"The tribes of central India and those of Chotanagpur view the world as being inhabited by invisible supernatural beings and powers. According to tribal belief, the world is inhabited by a large number of spiritual beings of different kinds. The primitive people regard themselves as living, moving, and having their being in this world of supernatural entities. So intimate is the relationship between a tribal and these supernatural beings and powers that one can not fully analyse the tribal social structure unless one understands their religious universe. In course of time, the tribals have gradually evolved a system of beliefs and rituals so as to cope with the unknown supernatural world."

The religious practise of the tribes of Bihar may be said to be a of spiritism or animism. The religious activities of all the four cultural types as classified by LP Vidyarthi, (1985:76), in the tribal Bihar may be broadly divided into four separate groups: worships of nature and natural objects, worship of ancestors, worship of gods and deities and worship of gods and deities of Hindu and other pantheon.

The primitive tribes of Bihar are in different economic stages, and levels of culture. Hence the customs, rites, rituals and sacrifices are very much dependent on their economic and cultural levels specific to the tribes. Even today, some tribes are still in hunting and food-collecting stage like Korwa and Kora. A tribe still in the primitive stage of economic development, is the Birhors, who are a nomadic tribe, still live in deep forests and depend upon the forest produces for food as well as for habitation. The rites and rituals adopted by the Birhors are centred on the propitiation and conciliation of benevolent and malevolent spirits which abound their surroundings. The trees, the streams, earth and such other objects are considered by them to be the dwelling of these spirits which are to be propitiated to give them assured game supply and to keep the entire *Birhor tanda* in happiness. The customs, rites, rituals, festivals and ceremonies of this hunting, food collecting and nomadic tribe are very much like the religious activities of the agriculturist tribe. Even the settled Santhal, Oraon, Munda, Ho, Kharia (Dudh Kharia), Kharwar, Gond, Chero, Bathudi, Bedia, Bhumij, Gorait and Kisan, worship the natural phenomena, spirit, gnomes and spook, which they can imagine in their weird surroundings amid the forests.

As for the worship of the supreme being, village gods and deities, the most important of them have their origin in the natural surroundings around them. S.C. Roy opined that though there is general similarity in the religious systems of the tribes of Chotanagpur, what they really differ in, is the relative significance of the different classes of supernatural beings recognised in their respective pantheons.

Mr. Sachchidananda, describes, "The Santhal's supreme god is *Cando* which means the sun. Thakur or Jiu is also regarded as supreme deity among them. The Santhal use the terms Sin Cando for sun and *Ninda Cando* for moon. The *Dharmes* (Oraon), *Sing Bonga* (Munda), *Dharam* (Kharia), *Bhagwan* (Korwa) are the synonyms for denoting the supreme god-sun. Most of the tribes of Bihar regard sun as their supreme god. The tribals believe that sun or *Sing Bonga* is the creator and sustainer of the universe. He is considered to be a benevolent deity. In fact, *Sing Bonga* has no specific worship but is reverentially remembered on every important occasion such as marriage and death. The east, the direction of the rising sun, has great significance in tribal rituals and practises. Thus when worshipping their spirits, they always face the east. The east is associated with life. The tribal has no temple or sacred grove or other seat specially assigned to *Dharmes* or *Sing Bonga*, nor has he any special season for offering sacrifices to *Dharmes* or *Sing* Bonga, but the tribals offer the sacrifice of a white cock to Him at every important festival such as the Sarhul, Harihar Sim, Batauli, Sohrai etc. They sacrifice only white fowl to sun god as they identify his colour as white."

SC Roy states, "Maran buru is the chief of the Santhal bonga pantheon. He is also worshipped by the Bhumij, Birhor, Ho and Munda. The Ho consider Maran Buru as a minor deity. Among the Birhors he is reckoned as a household spirit.

Mr. Sachchidananda further adds, "Chala Pachcho, an old lady of the grove also known as Sarna Burhia is most popular in Oraon deities and receives sacrifices attended with the most elaborate ritual at the annual spring festival known as the Khaddi or Sarhul held in her honour. Among the Oraon, pat or pat Raja is the master of all village bhuts or spirits, whom it controls and keeps under check. Pat has its seat on the hill, and in Oraon villages under some bush or tree on the outskirt of the village. Darha Deswali is the most dreaded of the village spirits among the Oraon. It acts as the guard or gate-keeper of the village which it is believed to protect from the incursions of spirits from outside. It has its seat on a plot of upland known as

Darhatonka or Darha-tanr suitable on or near the boundary of every Oraon village. The whole or more generally, a portion of the land is left fallow. Chala Pachcho is represented by a stone at the sarna, the Darha spirit is represented by a wooden stake driven into the ground at the Darha-tonka, and the old stake is replaced by a new one at the interval of several years, when a buffalo is sacrificed, and the spirit is told to remain quite for a generation or so when it will again be offered buffalo meat. Like the Oraon, the Munda also have a presiding deity of the village—the Hatu Bongako (village gods).

"The Deos (village deity) of the Birjia tribe dwells on different hills or pats. When the iron smelting and the hunting were practised, the Birjias were worshipping kutsh and bhut (a spirit presiding over the smelting furnace) and the Gadi Dara Roedas (a spirit controlling the movement of the deer and the animals to be hunted in the forest).

"The Korwas Rakshel (village god) has its seat at sarna. Gohel is the god exclusively meant for Korwa. Gohel is worshipped only where lac is grown abundantly. It also lives at sarna and is worshipped for good yield of lac. They believe that if the Gohel is displeased with the people the yield of lac would be insufficient. Thus, before cutting the lac this god is most worshipped. Among the Birhors, Buru-Bongas or Ora-Bongas are the spirits of the different hills reputed to have formed the original homes of the different Birhor clans. They are generally identified with the hills themselves.

"Among the Santhals, the Jaher era—as the name implies, is said to be the lady of the sacred grove (jaherthan) over which she presides. The cult of the old lady as a tribal spirit is also prevalent among other tribes. Among the Oraons 'The Old Lady of the Grove' or Chala Pachcho, is the most popular deity known also as Sarna Burhia or Jhakra Burhia. She is considered as a sociable Oraon deity. The Mundas call her as Jaher Buri. The Birjia call this deity as Ghati Sarna and she is known as Devi-Mai among the Birhors.

"The Pargana Bonga and Abge Bonga (sub-clan bonga) reside in sarna or jaherthan. The deities of the sarna are often considered by the tribals as their national spirits since they are worshipped by all (villagers). Sacrifices are performed during the principal festivals, namely the Sohrae (Harvest festival), the Baham (flower festival), the sowing festival, eating of first fruit festival etc. while different gods and deities are propitiated by the village priest.

"A female deity popularly known as Chandi (Oraon, Munda, Birjia, Korwa, Birhor) and Rongo Ruji Bonga among the Santhals—is responsible for a successful hunting. This deity is worshipped so that no mishap occurs during the hunt. This deity is said to reside in the forest, where a special tree called *terel* (diaspyros tomentosa) is reserved for her among the Santhals. S.C. Roy (1928) pointed out that Oraon young unmarried men propitiate Chandi, a female spirit who is believed to bring success in hunting. She is also the spirit of Oraon bachelors and is represented by a roundish stone.

"In fact, among all the principal tribes of the Munda stock, we find the propitiation or worship of the ancestor-spirits and the Hill-spirits to be the common element of their religion. Thus the Munda have their Haran Horo-Ko (ancestor spirits) also called Ora Bongako (house spirits), and their Bum Bongako (hill spirits); the Ho have their Ham-Ho-Ko (ancestor spirits) and Oa haprom or Oa-ham (house ancestors), the Birhor have their Buru bongako (hill spirits) and Haprom (ancestor spirits), the Santhal have their Orak-bonga-ko or house gods (bearing such names of hills, as Baur Pahar, Bar Pahar etc.). The Bhumij, though now mostly Hinduised, have their Burns (hill gods) as well as ancestor spirits. Hill-Bhuiya have their pitrus or ancestor spirits and their pats or hill spirits.

In Bihar and Jharkhand, out of thirty-one scheduled tribes more than one-third have undergone different degrees of transition due to exposure to Hinduism. The Kharwar, Mal Paharia, Bhumij, Beida, Chero, Kisan, Binjhia Parhaiya, and Bathudi appear to be more Hinduised tribes, though Hindu influence is also visible on certain sections of other major and more important tribes like the Santhal, Oraon, Munda and Kharia etc. Hindu impact has worked on these tribal people through more than one sources.

Instead of Temples, Worshipping in Sacred Groves

Colonel Dalton has the following remarks on the religion of the Bhuiyas in the Tributary State of Bonai:—

"They have their own priests, called deoris, and their sacred groves, called 'deota sara', dedicated to four deities—Dasum Pat, Bamoni, Pat, Koisar Pat, and Boram. The three first are brethren, but there was some difference of opinion as to whether Bamoni was male or female. Boram is the sun, also worshipped under the name of Dharm Deota, as with the Oraons. The three minor deities are represented by stones in the sara, but Boram has no representation. Boram, as the first and greatest of gods and as the creator is invoked at the sowing season with the offering of a white cook. In cases of sickness goats are offered to Dasum Pat and his brethren. On such occasions the goat is given by the owner of the house in which the sick person resides. On other occasions the victim is provided by the community. The sacrifices are all offered at the foot of trees in the sara; only men partake of the meat. The deori gets the head."

Sir Herbert Risley remakrs on their social customs, "The Bhuiyas of Southern Lohardaga have advanced somewhat further on the path of orthodox Hinduism, but do not regularly employ Brahmans, except, at the marriage ceremony. On certain occasions, however, Brahmans are called in to recite *mantras*, and the tendency towards conformity with Hindu usage will doubtless go on spreading as the country is opened up by the gradual improvement of communications. Already Thakurani Mai, the 'bloodthirsty tutelary goddess' to whom, only twenty years ago, 1st May 1868. Dalton's *Ethnology*, p. 147, the Hills Bhuiyas of Keonjhar offered the head of the obnoxious Dewan of their chief, has been transformed, in Singbhum and Lohardaga, into the Hindu Durga, to whom a Bhuiya priest makes offerings of goats, sheep, etc., which are afterwards partaken of by the worshippers. Changes of this sort raise an impassable barrier against researches into the origin of things, so that vestiges of the earlier beliefs of the people must be sought rather among the gods of the village and of the family than among the recognised *di majores* of popular worship. Thus the communal ghosts *Darha, Kudra, Kudri, Dano, Pacheria, Haserwar, Pakahi,* with their ill-defined functions and general capacity for mischief and malevolence, are clearly a king to the host of evil spirits which people the world of the Munda and Oraon. To appease these ghosts by occasional offerings of fowls and rice, and thus to guarantee the community against the consequences of their ill-will, is the special function of the village Pahan, who levies small subscriptions for this sort of spiritual insurance. The tribal deities Rikhmun and Tulsibir belong to a different and less primitive type. Rikhmun,... is believed to be the original ancestor of the tribe; while Tulsibir was a restless and valorous Bhuiya, who made war upon the gods until they appeased his wrath by admitting him to divine honours. I venture the conjecture that both Rikhmun and Tulsibir are merely transmuted totems, in the hope that further enquiries among the more primitive Bhuiyas may bring out evidence on this point. Neither of these gods has special priests; their worship is conducted by any older of the tribe. Sheep, goats, pigs, sweetmeats, and wine are the usual offerings, which afterwards furnish a feast for the assembled votaries. Snakes are only worshipped by those families which have lost one of their members by snake-bite. A certain herb, known as *gandhari sag*, and used as condiment, must be worshipped once a year, and can only be eaten if this rule is complied with. The custom suggests that the herb must once have been a totem of the tribe, but this cannot be certainly ascertained to be the case."

The religious customs are performed among the Bhuiyas in Bihar and Jharkhand.

Religion Varying According to Social Status

Sir H. Risley remarks on Bhumij religious and social practises, "The religion of the Bhumij varies, within certain limits, according to the social position and territorial status of the individuals concerned. Zamindars and well-to-do tenure-holders employ Brahmans as their family priests, and offer sacrifices to Kali or Mahamaya. The mass of the people revere the sun under the names of Sing-Bonga and Dharm, as the giver of harvests to men and the cause of all changes of seasons affecting their agricultural fortunes. They also worship a host of minor gods, among whom the following deserve special mention: —(1) *Jahir-Buru*, worshipped in the sacred grove of the village (*jahir-than*) with offerings of goats, fowls, rice, and ghee at the Sarhul festival in the months of Baisakh (April-May) and Phalgun (January-February). The laya presides at the sacrifice, and the offerings are divided between him and the worshippers. Jahir-Buru is supposed to be capable of blasting the crops if not duly propitiated, and her worship is a necessary preliminary to the commencement of the agricultural operations of the year. (2) *Karakata*, (*Kara* 'buffalo,' and *Kata*- 'to cut') another agricultural deity, to whom buffaloes and goats are offered towards the commencement of the rains. The skin of the buffalo is taken by the worshippers; the horns form the perquisite of the laya; while the Doms, who make music at the sacrifice, are allowed to carry off the flesh. In the case of goats, the laya's share is one-third of the flesh. If Karakata is neglected, it is believed there will be a failure of the rains. The cult of this deity, however, is not so universal as that of Jahir-Buru. (3) *Baghut* or *Bagh-Bhut*, who protects his votaries from tigers, is worshipped in Kartick (October-November) on the night of the Amabasya or the day preceding, it. The offerings are goats, fowls, ghee, rice, etc, which may be presented either in the homestead or on the high land *(tanr)* close to the village. In the former case the head of the family officiates as priest; in the latter the laya's services are enlisted, and he can claim a share of the offerings. (4) *Gram-Deota* and *Deoshali*, gods of village life, who ward off sickness and watch over the supply of water for drinking and irrigation of the crops. They are propitiated in Ashar (July-August) with offerings of goats, fowls, and rice, at which layae preside. (5) *Buru*, a mountain deity associated with many different hills throughout the Bhumij country, and worshipped for recovery from sickness and general prosperity on the first or second Magh. The head of the family or a laya serves as priest. (6) *Kudra* and *Bisaychandi* are malignant ghosts of cannibalistic propensities, whom the layas propitiate in the interests of the community. Private individuals do not worship them. (7) *Panchbahini* and *Baradela* are local deities worshipped by the Bankura Bhumij in much the same fashion as Jahir-Buru, the chief difference being that the offerings to Panchbahini are she-goats and a kind of scent called *mathaghasha,* while only fowls are presented to Baradela.

"With the Bhumij, as with other non-Aryan tribes of Chota Nagpur, the Karam festival, Colonel Dalton's description... seems to be especially popular. The Bhumij of Bankura district celebrate this feast in the latter half of the month Bhadra, corresponding roughly to the first half of September. A branch of the karam-tree *(Naucba parvifolia)* is planted by the laya in the centre of the village dancing ground *(akhrạ).* At the foot of this branch is a vessel partly filled with earth, into which, on the first day of the festival, the unmarried girls of the village throw various kinds of seed grain. These are carefully tended and watered from time to time so as to germinate by the Sankranti, or last day of the month, when the girls give the sprouting blades to each other, and wear them in their hair at the dance, which usually lasts the whole of that night.

"The sacerdotal arrangements of the tribe have already been incidentally referred to. The upper classes employ Brahmans of their own, and ignore the cult of the earlier gods; while the mass of the tribe are guided in their regular observances by the teachings of the layas or priests of the forest gods, and only call in the assistance of Brahmans on the comparatively rare occasions when it is deemed necessary to propitiate one of the standard Hindu deities. But the Brahman who serves the Bhumij zamindar or tenure holder as a family priest takes a higher place in the local community of Brahmans than the casual Brahman who ministers to the spiritual needs of the ordinary cultivator. The former will call himself a Rarhi Kulin, and will be received on equal terms by all other members of the sacred order; while the latter belongs to a much lower class, and associates with the comparatively degraded Brahmans who work for Kurmis and Dhobas." The social customs, rites and rituals are prevalent among the Bhumij tribals.

He adds furthers, "The original occupation of the Manbhum Bhumij is believed by themselves to have been military service, and there can be little doubt that the bands of Chuars or plunderers, who repeatedly overran the Midnapur district towards the end of last century, were largely recruited from this tribe. The circumstance, however, that they took a more or less prominent part in a series of marauding attacks on an unarmed and unwarlike population affords no ground for a belief in the existence among them of any real military instinct; and in fact they are conspicuous for the dislike of' discipline, which is one of the prominent characteristics of the Kolarian races. For many years past agriculture has been the sole profession of all the sub-tribe except the iron-smelting Shelo. A few have engaged in petty trade, and some have emigrated to the tea districts of Assam. Their relations to the land are various.

The zamindars of Darabhum, Dhalbhum, Manbhum, Patkum, and Bagmundi probably belong to the Bhumij tribe, though they now call themselves Rajputs. Next to them rank the sardar ghatwals of the large service-tenures known in Manbhum as *tarafs.* Three of these admit themselves to be Bhumij, while the fourth, Manmohan Singh, of Taraf Satarakhani, now claims to be a Rajput, regardless of the fact that a few years ago his grandfather wrote himself down in public documents as Bhumij. I mention this instance as an illustration of the facility with which brevet rank as a self-made Rajput may be obtained. Manmohan Singh keeps a Brahman to support his pretensions, and professes to be very particular in all matters of ceremonial observance. His descendants will doubtless obtain unquestioning recognition as local Rajputs, and will intermarry with families who have undergone the same process of transformation as themselves. The great bulk of the Bhumij, who are simple cultivators and labourers, stand on a far lower social level than the landholding members of the tribe. They rank somewhat below the Kurmi, and members of the higher castes will not take water from their hands. In their turn the Bhumij, though eating fowls and drinking spirituous liquors, look down upon Bauris, Bagdis, Doras, and Ghasis as more unclean feeders than themselves."

Adoption of Hindu Customs and Rituals

Sir Risley describes, "The Chakmas profess to be Buddhists, but during the last generation or so their practise in matters of religion has been noticeably coloured by contact with the gross Hinduism of Eastern Bengal. This tendency was encouraged by the example of Raja Dharm Baksh Khan and his wife Kalindi Rani, who observed the Hindu festivals, consulted Hindu astrologers, kept a Chittagong Brahman to supervise the daily worship of the goddess Kali, and persuaded themselves that they were lineal representatives of the Kshatriya caste. Some years ago, however, a celebrated Phoongyee came over from Arakan after the Raja's death to endeavour to strengthen the cause of Buddhism and to take the Rani to task for her leanings towards idolatry. His efforts are said to have met with some success, and the Rani is believed to have formally proclaimed her adhesion to Buddhism.

"Lakhsmi is worshipped by the Tungjainya sub-tribe as the goddess of harvest in a small bamboo hut set apart for this purpose. She is represented by a rude block of stone with seven skeins of cotton bound seven times round it. The offerings are pigs and fowls, which are afterwards eaten by the votaries. Chakmas observe the same worship with a few differences of detail,...

"Vestiges of the primitive animism, which we may believe to have been the religion of the Chakmas before their conversion to Buddhism, still survive in the festival called *Shongbasa*, when *nats,* or the spirits of wood and stream, are worshipped, either by the votary himself or by an exorcist *(ojha* or *naichhura),* who is called in to perform the necessary ceremonies. The demons of cholera, fever, and other diseases are propitiated in a river-bed or in the thick jungle, where spirits delight to dwell, with offerings of goats, fowls, ducks, pigeons, and flowers. The regular priests have nothing to do with this ritual, which has been condemned as unorthodox.

"At a Chakma village," says Major Lewin, "I was present when sacrifice was thus offered up by the headman. The occasion was a thank-offering for the recovery of his wife from child-birth. The offering consisted of a suckling pig and a fowl. The altar was of bamboo, decorated with young plantain shoots and leaves. On this raised platform were placed small cups containing rice, vegetables, and a spirit distilled from rice. Round the whole from the house-mother's distaff had been spun a long white thread, which encircled the altar, and then, carried into the house, was held at its two ends by the good man's wife. The sacrifice commenced by a long invocation uttered by the husband, who stood the opposite to his altar, and between each snatch of his charm tatooed the small platform with his hill knife and uttered a long wailing cry. This was for the purpose of attracting the numerous wandering spirits who go up and down upon the earth and calling them to the feast. When a sufficient number of these invisible guests were believed to be assembled, he cut the throats of the victims with his *dao* and poured a libation of blood upon the altar and over the thread. The flesh of the things sacrificed was afterwards cooked and eaten at the household meal, of which I was invited to partake."

Sir Risley adds, "Of late years Bairagi Vaishnavas have taken to visiting the Hill tracts, and have made a few disciples among the Chakmas. The outward signs of conversion to Vaishbnavism are wearing a necklace of *tulsi* beads (*Ocymum sanctum*), which is used to repeat the mantra or mystic formula of the sect. Abstinence from animal food and strong drink is also enjoined. I understand, however, that very few Chakmas have been found to submit to this degree of austerity.

"Like the rest of Hill Tribes, the Chakmas live by *jhum* cultivation, which they carry on . . . In spite of the necessarily shifting character of their husbandry, they show remarkable attachment to the sites of their villages, and do not change these like most of the other tribes. Their bamboo houses, built upon high piles, are constructed with great care." The social customs are practised by the Chakmas.

Caste Elders Conducting Religious Ceremonies

"By far the most interesting feature of the Chamar caste," says Dr. Wise, "are their religious and social customs. They have no purohit; their religious ceremonies, like those of the Doms, being directed by one of the elders of the caste. But gurus, who give *mantras* to children, are found, and a Hindustani Brahman is often consulted regarding a lucky day for a wedding. Chamars have always exhibited a remarkable dislike to Brahmans and to the Hindu ritual. They nevertheless observe many rites popularly supposed to be of Hindu origin, but which are more probably survivals of the worship paid to the village gods for ages before the Aryan invasion. The large majority of Bengali Chamars profess the deistic Sri-Narayani creed. Sants, or professed devotees, are common among them, and the Mahant of that sect is always regarded as the religious head of the whole tribe. A few Dacca Chamars belong to the Kabir-Panth, but none have joined any of the Vaishnava sects."

Sir Risley adds, "The principal annual festival of the Chamars is the Sripanchami, celebrated on the fifth day of the lunar month of Magh (January-February), when they abstain from work for two days, spending them in alternate devotion at the Dhamghar, or conventicle of the Sri-Narayani sect, and in intoxication at home. The Dhamghar is usually a thatched house consisting of one large room with verandahs on all sides. At one end is a raised earthen platform, on which the open Grantha garlanded with flowers is laid, and before this each disciple makes obeisance as he enters. The Grantha or scriptures of the Sri-Narayani or Siva-Narayani sect are believed by them to have existed for eleven hundred and forty-five years, but to have been unintelligible until Sitala, an inspired Sannyasi, translated it in compliance with a divine command. The translation, consisting of several works in the Devanagari character, is the undoubted composition of the Rajput Sivanarayana of Ghazipur, who wrote it about A.D. 1735.

The most important of these works are the Guru-nyasa and Santa-vilasa. The former, compiled from the Puranas, gives an account of the ten Avatars of Vishnu, or Narayana, and is subdivided into fourteen chapters, of which the first six treat of the author, of faith, of the punishment of sinners, of virtue, of a future state, and of discipline. The later is a treatise on moral sentiments. The opening lines are,—'The love of God, and His knowledge is the only true understanding.'—Sir Risley. The congregation squats all round the room, the women in one corner, listening to a few musicians chanting religious hymns and smoking tobacco and ganja, indifferent to the heat, smoke, and stench of the crowded room. The Mahant, escorted by the Sants carrying their parwanas or certificated of membership, enters about 1 A.M., when the service begins. It is of the simplest form. The Mahant, after reading a few sentences in Nagali, unintelligible to most of his hearers, receives offerings of money and fruit. The congregation then disperses, but the majority seat themselves in the verandhas and drink spirits. If the physical endurance of the worshippers be not exhausted, similar services are held for several successive nights, but the ordinary one only lasts two nights.

"On the 'Nauami,' or ninth lunar day of Aswin (September-October), the day preceding the Dashara, the worship of Devi is observed, and offerings of swine, goats, and spirits made to the dread goddess. On this day the old Dravidian system of demonolatry, or Shamanism, is exhibited, when one of their number, working himself up into a frenzy, becomes possessed by the demon and reveals futurity. The Chamars place great value on the answers given, and very few are so contented with their lot in life as not to desire an insight into the future. A few days before the Dashara the Chamains perambulate the streets, playing and singing, with a pot of water in the left hand, a sprig of *nim* in the right, soliciting alms for the approaching Devi festival. Money or grain must be got by begging, for they believe the worship would be ineffectual if the offerings had to be paid for. Another of their festivals is the Ramanauami, or birth-day of Rama, held on the ninth lunar day of Chaitra (March-April), when they offer flowers, betel-nut, and sweetmeats to their ancestor, Ravi Das.

"When sickness or epidemic diseases invade their homes, the women fasten a piece of plantain leaf round their necks and go about begging. Should their wishes be fulfilled, a vow is taken to celebrate the worship of Devi, Sitala, or Jalka Devi, whichever goddess is supposed to cause the outbreak. The worship is held on a piece of ground marked off and smeared with cowdung. A fire being lighted, and *ghi* and spirits thrown on it, the worshipper makes obeisance, bowing his forehead to the ground and muttering certain incantations. A swine is then sacrificed, and the bones and offal being buried, the flesh is roosted and eaten, but no one must take home with him any scrap of the victim. Jalka Devi seems identical with the Rakshya Kali of Bengali villagers, and is said to have seven sisters, who are worshipped on special occasions.

"The Chamars of Behar are more orthodox in matters of religion than their brethren of Eastern Bengal, and appear to conform in the main to the popular Hinduism practised by their neighbours. Some of them indeed have advanced so far in this direction as to employ Maithil Brahmans for the worship of the regular Hindu gods, while others content themselves with priests of their own caste. In the Santal Parganas such priests go by the name of *puri,* and the story is that they are Kanaujia Brahmans, who were somehow degraded to be Chamars. Lokesari, Rakat Mala, Mansaram, Lala, Karu Dana, Masna, Mamia, and Jalpait aro the special minor gods of the caste, but Bandi, Goruiya, and Kali are also hold in reverence. Some hold that Ravi Das ranks highest of all, but he seems to be looked upon as a sort of deity, and not as the preacher of a deistic religion. The offerings to all of these gods consist of sheep, goats, milk, fruit, and sweetmeats, of which the members of the household afterwards partake. According to Mr. Nesfield, the caste also worship the *rapi,* or tanner's knife, at the Diwali festival. It is a curious circumstance, illustrating the queer reputation borne by the Chamars, that throughout Hindustan parents frighten naughty children by telling them that Nona Chamain will carry them off. This redoubtable old witch is said by the Chamars to have been the mother or grandmother of Ravi Das; but why she acquired such unenviable notoriety is unknown. In Bengal her name is never heard of, but a domestic bogey haunts each household. In one it is the Burhi, or old woman; in another, Bhuta, a ghost; in a third, Pretni, a witch; and in a fourth, Gala-Kata Kafir, literally, the 'infidel with his throat gashed.'

"By virtue of his occupation, his habits, and his traditional descent, the Chamar stands condemned to rank at the very bottom of the Hindu social system; and even the non-Aryan tribes who have of recent years sought admission into the Hindu communion are speedily promoted over his head. His ideas on the subject of diet are in keeping with his degraded position. He eats beef, pork, and fowls, all unclean to the average Hindu, and, like the gypsies of Europe, has no repugnance to cooking the flesh of animals which have died a natural death. Some say that they only eat cattle which have died a natural death, but this may be merely a device to avert the suspicion of killing cattle by poison, which naturally attaches to people who deal in hides and horns. Despised, however, as he is by all classes of orthodox Hindus, the Chamar is proud and punctilious on certain special points, never touching the leavings of a Brahman's meal, nor eating anything cooked by a Bengali Brahman, though he has no objection to take food from a Brahman of Hindustan. Chamars are, says Dr. Wise, inconceivably dirty in their habits, and offend others besides the Hindu by their neglect of all sanitary laws. Large droves of pigs are bred by them, and it is no uncommon sight to witness children and pigs wallowing together in the mire. Hides in various stages of preparation hang about their huts, yet, strange to say, the women are very prolific, and, except in a fisher settlement, nowhere are so many healthy-looking children to be seen as in a filthy Chamar village. Mr. Beames, however, mentions in a note to his edition of Sir Henry Elliot's *Glossary* that Chamars, from their dirty habits, are peculiarly liable to leprosy, and that the name of the Kori or Korhi sub-caste probably refers to this fact.

"Chamars are employed in tanning leather, making shoes and saddlery, and grooming horses. In Eastern Bengal the Chamra-farosh hire them to preserve hides, but there is such bitter enmity between them and the allied caste of Muchi or Rishi, that they are rarely engaged to skin animals, lest the perquisites of the latter group should seem to have been interfered with. To some extent the distinctions between the various sub-castes seem to be based upon differences of occupation. Thus the Dhusia sub-caste adhere to the original occupation of leather-dressing, and also make shoes and serve as musicians at wedding and other domestic festivities, their favourite instruments being the *dhol* or drum, the cymbals *(jhanjh),* the harp *(ektara),* and the tambourine *(khanjari).* Most of these occupations are also followed by the Dharh, who besides carry palanquins and eat the flesh of animals that have died a natural death, except only the horse. The Guria are cultivators; some few holding occupancy rights, and others being landless day-labourers, who wander about and work for hire at harvest time. The Jaiswara work as syces; the Dohar are cobblers, using only leather string, and not cotton thread, to mend rents; the Sikharia are cultivators and shoemakers; the Chamar Tanti work us weavers, and will not touch carrion; and the Sarki, many of whom have emigrated from Nepal into Chumparan, are both butchers and hide-dressers. Some Chamars burn lime, but this occupation has not become the badge of a sub-caste, though those who follow it call themselves Chunihara. In Behar the Chamar is a village functionary like the Chaukidar or Gorait. He holds a small portion of village land, and is invariably called to post up official notices, and to go round with his drum proclaiming public announcements.

"The Chamains, or female Chamars, says Dr. Wise, are distinguished throughout Bengal by their huge inelegant anklets *(pairi)* and bracelets *(bangri),* made of bell-metal. The former often weigh from eight to ten pounds, the latter from two to four, and both closely resemble the corresponding ornaments worn by Santal women. They also wear the *tikli,* or spangle, on the forehead, although in Bengal it is regarded as a tawdry ornament of the lowest and most immoral women. Chamains consider it a great attraction to have their bodies tattooed; consequently their chests, foreheads, arms, and legs are disfigured with patterns of fantastic shape. In Hindustan the Natni is the great tattooer; but as members of this caste are seldom met with in Eastern Bengal, the Chamains are often put to great straits, being frequently obliged to pay a visit to their original homes for the purpose of having the fashionable decoration indelibly stained on their bodies.

"Chamar women are ceremonially unclean for ten days subsequent to childbirth, when after bathing, casting away all old cooking utensils, and buying now ones, a feast, called *Barahiya,* is celebrated, upon which she resumes her usual household duties. They still observe the pleasing custom of *Bhaiphota* on the last day of the Hindu year, when sisters present their brothers with a new suit of clothes and sweetmeats, and make with a paste of red sandal wood a dot on their foreheads; a similar usage, known as *Bhratridritiya,* is practised by Bengalis on the second day after the new moon of Kartik.

"Chamains are the midwives of India, and are generally believed, though erroneously, to be skilled in all the mysteries of parturition. They have no scruples about cutting the navel string, as other Hindus have; but in the villages of the interior, where no Chamains reside, the females of the Bhuinmali, Chandal, and Ghulam Kayath castes act as midwives, and are equally unscrupulous. It is a proverbial saying among Hindus that a household becomes unclean if a Chamar woman has not attended at the birth of any child belonging to it." Add Sir Risley. The social customs are related to the Chamar caste.

Affecting ritual purity of High Hindu Castes

Sir Risley describes, "The religion of the Cheros is still in a state of transition, and they observe a sort of dual worship, which discloses unmistakable traces of their non-Aryan descent. For the worship of the Hindu gods they employ Kanaujia or Sakadwipi Brahmans, who are received on terms of equality by other members of the sacred order. Their spiritual guides (*gurus*) are either Brahmans or Gharbari Gosains. They also reverence animistic deities of the type known to the Kharias and Mundas—*Baghaut, Chenri, Darha, Dharti, Dukhnahi, Dwarpar*, and others, to whom goats, fowls, sweetmeats, and wine are offered in the month of Aghan so as to secure a good harvest. In these sacrifices Brahmans take no part, and they are conducted by a priest (*baiga*) belonging to one of the aboriginal races. Cheros also, like the Kols, observe triennial sacrifices. 'Every three years,' says Colonel Dalton, 'a buffalo and other animals are offered in the sacred grove of *sarna*, or on a rock near the village. They also have, like some of the Kols, a priest for each village, called *pahn*. He is always one of the impure tribes, a Bhuiya, or Kharwar, or a Parheya, and is also called *baiga*. He alone can offer this great sacrifice. No Brahmanical priests are allowed on these occasions to interfere. The deity honoured is the tutelary god of the village, sometimes called Duar Pahar, sometimes Dharti, sometimes Purgahaili, or Daknai, a female, or Dura, a sylvan god—the same perhaps as the Darha of the Kols. I found that the above were all worshipped in the village of Munka, in Palamau, which belongs to a typical Chero, Kunwar Bhikari Sinh.'

"The Cheros of Palamau affect the ceremonial purity characteristic of the higher castes of Hindus, and the connexion of their leading families with the land secures to them a fairly high social position. Many of them wear the sacred thread with which they are invested by a Brahman at the time of their marriage. Brahmans will take water from their hands, and eat anything but rice that has been cooked by them. They are held, in fact, in much the same estimation as any of the local Rajputs. In Chota Nagpur, on the other hand, the status of the caste is by no means so high, and the Bhogtas, while admitting the Cheros to be a sub-caste of their community, decline to eat with them, and regard them as socially their inferiors. Agriculture is supposed to be the original occupation of the caste, and in Palamau many of them still hold various kinds of *jagir* tenures. Some have taken to shopkeeping and petty trade, while others live by cartage, working on roads or in coal-mines, and by collecting *tasar* cocoons, catechu, and lac. For all this, says Mr. Forbes, 'the Cheros are a proud race, and exceedingly jealous of their national honour. They have never forgotten that they were once a great people, and that their descent was an honourable one. Only the very poorest among them will hold the plough, and none of them will carry earth upon their heads.'

No Conformity with a Unform Customs

Sir H. Risley mentions the Dors social customs, "The religion of the Doms varies greatly in different parts of the country, and may be described generally as a chaotic mixture of survivals from the elemental or animistic cults characteristic of the aboriginal races, and of observances borrowed in a haphazard fashion from whatever Hindu sect happens to be dominant in a particular locality. The composite and chaotic nature of their belief is due partly to the great ignorance of the caste, but mainly to the fact that as a rule they have no Brahmans, and thus are without any central authority or standard which would tend to mould their religious usages into conformity with a uniform standard. In Behar, for instance, the son of a deceased man's sister or of his female cousin officiates as priest at his funeral and recites appropriate *mantras,* receiving a fee for his services when the inheritance comes to be divided. Some Doms, indeed, assured me that the sister's son used formerly to get a share of the property, and that this rule had only recently fallen into disuse; but their statements did not seem to be definite enough to carry entire conviction, and I have met with no corroborative evidence bearing on the point. So also in marriage the sister's son, or occasionally the sister *(sawasin),* repeats *mantras,* and acts generally as priest. Failing either of these, the head of the household officiates. The possible significance of these facts in relation to the early history of the caste need not be elaborated hero. No other indications of an extinct custom of female kinship are now traceable, and the fact that in Western Bengal the eldest son gets an extra share *(jeth-angs)* on the division of an inheritance seems to show that kinship by males must have boon in force for a very long time past. In Bengal the sister's son exercises no priestly functions, these being usually discharged by a special class of Dom, known in Bankum as Degharia, and in other districts as Dharma-Pandit. Their office is hereditary, and they wear copper rings on their fingers as a mark of distinction. In Murshidabad, on the other hand, most Doms, with the exception of the Banukia sub-caste and some of the Ankurias, have the services of low Brahmans, who may perhaps be ranked as Barna-Brahmans. The same state of things appears to prevail in the north of Manbhum. In the Santal Parganas barbers minister to the spiritual wants of the caste.

"With such a motley array of amateur and professional priests, it is clearly out of the question to look for any unity of religious organization among the Doms. In *Bankura* and Western Bengal generally they seem on the whole to lean towards Vaishnavism, but in addition to Radha and Krishna they worship Dharam or Dharma-raj in form of a man with a fish's tail on the last day of Jaishtha with offerings of rise, molasses, plantain, and sugar, the object of which is said to be to obtain the blessing of the sun on the corps of the season. Every year in the month of Baisakh the members of the caste go into the jungle to offer sacrifices of goats, fruits, and sweetmeats to their ancestral deity Kalubir; and at the appointed season they join in the worship of the goddess Bhadu,...

At the time of the Durga Puja, Bajunia Doms worship the drum, which they regard as the symbol of their craft. This usage has clearly been borrowed from the artisan casts among the Hindus. In Central Bengal Kali appears to be their favourite goddess; and in Eastern Bengal many Doms follow the *Panth*, or path of Supat, Supan, or Sobhana Bhagat, who is there regarded as a guru rather than as the progenitor of the caste. Others, again, call themselves Haris Chandis, from Raja Haris Chandra, who was so generous that he gave away all his wealth in charity, and was reduced to such straits that he took service with a Dom, who treated him kindly. In return the Raja converted the whole tribe to his religion, which they have faithfully followed ever since. This is the form of the legend current among the Doms of Dacca. It will be observed that the Chandala of the Markandeya Purana has been turned into a Dom, and the pious king into a religious reformer. According to Dr. Wise, Haris Chandra is a well-known figure in the popular mythology of Bengal, and it is of him that natives tell the following story, strangely like that narrated in the xviiith chapter of the Koran regarding Moscs and Joshua. He and his Rani, wandering in the forest, almost starved, caught a fish and boiled it on a wood fire. She took it to the river to wash off the ashes, but on touching the water the fish revived and swam away. At the present day a fish called kalbosa (*Labco calbasu*), of black colour and yellow flesh, is identified with the historical one, and no low-caste Hindu will touch it. In Hindustan the following couplet is quoted concerning a similar disaster which befell the gambler nala, the moral being the same as that of the English proverb— Misfortunes never come singly:—

'Raja Nal par bihat pare,

Bhune machhle jal men tire.'

"The principal festival of the Doms in Eastern Bengal is the Sravannia Puja, observed in the month of that name, corresponding to July and August, when a pig is sacrificed and its blood caught in a cup. This cup of blood, along with one of milk and three of spirits, are offered to Narayan. Again, on a dark night of Bhadra (August) they offer a pot of milk, four of spirits, a fresh cocoanut, a pipe of tobacco, and a little Indian hemp to Hari Ram, after which swine are slaughtered and a feast celebrated. A curious custom followed by all castes throughout Bengal is associated with the Dom, and may perhaps be a survival from times when that caste were the recognised priests of the elemental deities worshipped by the non-Aryan races. Whenever an eclipse of the sun or moon occurs, every Hindu householder places at his door a few copper coins, which, though now claimed by the Acharji Brahman, were until recently regarded as the exclusive perquisite of the Dom.

"Similar confusion prevails in Behar under the *regime* of the sister's son, only with this difference, that the advance in the direction of Hinduism seems to be on the whole less conspicuous than in Bengal. Mahadeva, Kali, and the river Ganges receive, it is true, sparing and infrequent homage, but the working deities of the caste are Syam Singh, whom Rome hold to be the deified ancestor of all Doms, Bakat Mala, Ghihal or Gohil, Goraiya, Bandi, Lakeswar, Dihwar, Dak, and other ill-defined and primitive shapes, which have not yet gained admission into the orthodox pantheon. At Deodha, in Darbhanga, Syam Singh has been honoured with a special temple; but usually both he and the other gods mentioned above are represented by lumps of dried clay, set up in a round space smeared with cow-dung inside the house, under a tree, or at the village boundary. Before these lumps, formless as the creed of the worshipper who has moulded them, pigs are sacrificed and strong drink offered up at festivals, marriages, and when disease threatens the family or its live-stock. The circle of these *godlings,* as Mr. Ibbetson has excellently called them, is by no means an exclusive one, and a common custom shows how simply and readily their number may be added to. If a man dies of snake-bite, say the Magahiya Doms of the Gya district, we worship his spirit as a *Samperiya,* lest he should come back and give us bad dreams; we also worship the snake who bit him, lest the snake-god should serve us in like fashion. Any man therefore conspicuous enough by his doings in life or for the manner of his death to stand a chance of being dreamed of among a tolerably large circle is likely in course of time to take rank as a god. Judging, indeed, from the antecedents of the caste, Syam Singh himself may well have been nothing more than a successful dacoit, whose career on earth ended in some sudden or tragic fashion, and who lived in the dreams of his brethren long enough to gain a place in their rather disreputable pantheon. Systematic robbery is so far a recognised mode of life among the Magahiya Doms that it has impressed itself on their religion, and a distinct ritual is ordained for observance by those who go forth to commit a burglary. The object of veneration on these occasions is Sansari Mai, whom some hold to be a form of Kali, but who seems rather to be the earth-mother known to most primitive religions. No image, not even the usual lump of clay, is set up to represent the goddess: a circle one span and four fingers in diameter is drawn on the ground and smeared smooth with cowdung. Squatting in front of this the worshipper gashes his left arm with the curved Dom knife *(katari),* and daubs five streaks of blood with his finger in the centre of the circle, praying in a low voice that a dark night may aid his designs; that his booty may be ample; and that he and his gang may escape detection.

"Labra movet metuens andiri: pulchra Laverna,

Da mini fallere, da justo sanctoque videri,

Noctem peccatis et fraudibus objice nubem."

'By all classes of Hindus,' says Dr. Wise, the Dom is regarded with both disgust and fear, not only on account of his habits being abhorrent and abominable, but also because he is believed to have no humane or kindly feelings. To those, however, who view him as a human being, the Dom appears as an improvident and dissolute man, addicted to sensuality and intemperance, but often an affectionate husband and indulgent father. As no Hindu can approach a Dom, his peculiar customs are unknown, and are therefore said to be wicked and accursed. A tradition survives among the Dacca Doms, that in the days of the Nawabs their ancestors were brought from Patna for employment as executioners (jallad) and disposers of the dead—hateful duties, which they perform at the present day. On the paid establishment of each magistracy a Dom hangman is borne, who officiates whenever sentence of death is carried out. On these occasions he is assisted by his relatives, and as the bolt is drawn shouts of 'Dohai Maharani!' or 'Dohai Judge Sahib' are raised to exonerate them from all blame.

The peculiar functions which the caste performs at all Hindu funerals may be observed by all visitors to Benares, and are described by Mr. Sherring as follows:— "On the arrival of the dead body at the place of cremation, which in Benares is at the base of one of the steep stairs or *ghats,* called the Burning Ghat, leading down from the streets above to the bed of the river Ganges, the Dom supplies five logs of wood, which he lays in order upon the ground, the rest of the wood being given by the family of the deceased. When the pile is ready for burning, a handful of lighted straw is brought by the Dom, and is taken from him and applied by one of the chief members of the family to the wood. The Dom is the only person who can furnish the light for the purpose; and if from any circumstance the services of one cannot be obtained, great delay and inconvenience are apt to arise. The Dom exacts his fee for three things, namely, first, for the five logs; secondly, for the bunch of straw; and thirdly, for the light." Sir Risley adds his remarks, It should be added that the amount of the fee is not fixed, but depends upon the rank and circumstances of the deceased. In Eastern Bengal, according to Dr. Wise, the services of the Dom at the funeral pyre are not now absolutely essential. Of late years, at any rate in Dacca, household servants carry the corpse to the burning ghat, where the pyre constructed by them is lighted by the nearest relative.

"The degraded position forced upon all Doms by reason of the functions which some of them perform is on the whole acquiesced in by the entire caste, most of whom, however, follow the comparatively cleanly occupation of making baskets and mats. Taking food as the test of social status, it will be seen that Doms eat beef, pork, horse-flesh, fowls, ducks, field-rats, and the flesh of animals which have died a natural death. In Murshedabad and Eastern Bengal they profess to abstain from beef and hold themselves superior to Muchis and Bauris for so doing. In Assam buffalo meat is also forbidden. All of them, moreover, except the Bansphor and Chapariya sub-castes, will eat the leavings of men of other castes. To this last point one exception must be noted. No Dom will touch the leavings of a Dhobi, nor will he take water, sweetmeats, or any sort of food or drink from a mart of that caste. Some Doms say they will not eat the leavings of Dosadhs and Chamars, but this refinement is not general. The aversion with which the Dhobi is regarded is so pronounced that Doms of Behar have assured me that they would not take food from a Muhammadan who had his water fetched for him by a washerman of his own religion. The reason is obscure. Some people say the Dhobi is deemed impure because he washes women's clothes after childbirth; but this fact, though conclusive enough for the average Hindu, would not, I imagine, count for much with a Dom. Moreover, the Doms themselves say nothing of the kind, but tell a very singular story to account for their hatred of the Dhobis. Once upon a time, they say, Supat Bhakat, the ancestor of the Doms, was returning tired and hungry from a long journey. On his way he met a Dhobi going along with a donkey carrying a bundle of clothes, and asked him for food and drink. The Dhobi would give him nothing and abused him into the bargain, whereupon Supat Bhakat fell upon the Dhobi, drove him away with blows, killed his donkey, and cooked and ate it on the spot. After he had eaten he repented of what he had done, and seeing that it was all the Dhobi's fault declared him and his caste to be accursed for the Doms for over, so that a Dom should never take food from a Dhobi or eat in his house. The legend may perhaps be a distorted version of the breach of some primitive taboo in which Dhobis and donkeys somehow played a part. Doms will not touch a donkey, but the animal is not regarded by the caste in the light of a totem. In this connexion may mention the curious fact that the Ankuria and Bisdelia Doms of Birbhum will not hold a horse or kill a dog, nor will they use a *dao* with a wooden handle, explaining that their ancestors always worked with landleless *daos,* and that they are bound to adhere to the ancient custom. The prejudice against killing a dog seems at first sight to suggest some connexion with the Bauris; but it may equally arise from the fact that one of the duties of scavenging Doms in towns is to kill ownerless dogs.

"Doms believe their original profession to be the making of baskets and mats, and even the menial and scavenging sub-castes follow these occupations to some extent. About half of the caste are believed to have taken to agriculture, but none of these have risen above the rank of occupancy raiyats, and a large proportion are nomadic cultivators and landless day-labourers. In the south of Manbhum a small number of rent-free tenures, bearing the name *sibottar,* and supposed to be set apart for the worship of the god Siva, are now in the possession of Doms—a fact of which I can suggest no explanation. The Bajunia sub-caste are employed to make highly discordant music at marriages and festivals. His women-folk, however, only perform as musicians at the wedding of their own people, it being considered highly derogatory for them to do so for outsiders. At home the Domni manufactures baskets and rattles for children. A single wandering branch of the Magahiya sub-caste has earned for itself a reputation which has extended to the whole of that group. 'The Magahiya Doms of Champaran,' says Mr. Beames, 'are a race of professional thieves. They extend their operations into the contiguous districts of Nepal. They are rather dainty in their operations, and object to commit burglary by digging through the walls of houses: they always enter a house by the door; and if it is dark, they carry a light. Of course all this is merely done by way of bravado. Magahiyas never live long in one place. They move about constantly, pitching their ragged little reed tents or *sirkis* outside a village or on a grassy patch by the roadside, like our gipsies, till they have done all the plundering that offers itself in the neighbourhood, when the move off again.' The popular belief that all Magahiya Doms are habitual criminals is, however, a mistake Burglary is followed as a profession only by the wandering members of that sub-caste. The Magahiyas of Gya are peaceable basket-makers and cultivators, who regard thieving with as much horror as their neighbours, and know nothing of the Laverna cult of Sansari Mai, whom they identify with Jagadamba, the small-pox goddess, one of a group of seven sisters presiding over various diseases. There seems, indeed, reason to believe that the predatory habita of the gipsy Magahiyas of Champaran are due rather to force of circumstances than to an inborn criminal instinct; and the success of the measures introduced, for their reclamation by Mr. R. Henry while Magistrate of Champaran affords grounds for the hope that they may in course of time settle down as peaceable cultivators." Adds Mr. Risley. The social customs pertain to the Dom Community in the eastern region.

Eschewing Horse Meat

The Armenians in West Bengal are a non-vegetarian people who consume flesh of various animals, with a few exceptions such as horse meat. But they are completely vegetarian for forty days before Easter which is one of their major religious festivals, the period being called Lent. Indian Armenians take milk, *ghee* or butter, but they do not consume any meat during Lent. Their staple food is bread along with fish curry or meat curry. If they take anything more, they take fruit, salad, honey, nuts, and curd etc. In their country they received anybody with bread, salt, cheese and water. As Armenia is a cold country, these people are used to drinking cognac. They grow grapes in their Orchards. Their special dish is *polao* with a rounded omelette, prepared with chopped green onion plant. Both men and women smoke cigarettes and also take snuff.

The Armenians are the immigrant people who came to India for trade and commerce many centuries ago. It was Akbar who induced them to settle in his dominions, instead of roaming round the country. Earlier, Armenia was a separate country prior to coming under the socialist rule of Soviet Russia. They had come to Bengal for the trade purposes. Their earliest land settlement records in Bengal reveal that they were the founders of Calcutta. Prior to the arrival of Job Charnock, they had built various churches, *ghats*, buildings, schools, streets, and graveyards in Calcutta after their permanent settlement here. They were the first Christian people in the city and they are still very conservative as far as their religion is concerned. Today 200 to 300 Armenian people are living in India, majority of them lives in Calcutta, which includes the students who come to the Armenian College from abroad. They live in significant numbers in Bombay also.

The Armenians are a Christian people and their Christianity follows the rule of Eastern Church, *i.e.* an apostolic church. This Armenian Church has several features in common with the Syrian, Egyptian, Latin, Greek and Russian orthodox churches. The Armenians are the first Christian nation in the world and they are still very conservative in regard to their religious beliefs. There are many festivals and festive occasions in the Armenian Church calendar but the Armenians only follow the five major festivals through out the year. Their first festival is Christian's Day on the 6th of January which they celebrate with various food items. Easter is their biggest festival and they eat only vegetarian food for forty days before Good Friday. At present only a few of Armenians strictly observe full forty days Lent period. Their third festival is the transfiguration of Jesus Christ in the month of July performed on a Sunday. It may fall on any day of the month but they fix it on a Sunday. The fourth festival is the Assumption of the Blessed Virgin Mary on the 14th of August; fifth festival is exaltation of the Holy Cross. On all the festive occasions they assemble at the church and participate in prayers and celebrate the festivities. Their belief is that they are the apostolics which means founder of the Church of the Christian.

Their sacred centres for pilgrimage are their churches. In Bengal, except their church in Calcutta they visit sometimes the Church of Chinsurah or the Church of Saidabad. The priest of the church is their sacred specialist who solemnises their marriage, and conducts baptism of a new born etc. They have a socio-religious movement among themselves for retaining Christianity. The Armenians are also a very artistic people and from its beginning Armenia was a country of stone architecture and minars. The people of that country started their economic life from the stone sculpture and engraving. With these art objects they travelled across the world to start their business. They are also an art loving community. They have many world famous painters among them. Many large oil paintings were painted by Armenian artists in Nawab Sirajuddoulah's palace. The Armenian people also were famous for their craft of making carpets in their homeland. Armenian songs are mostly folk songs and dances are also mostly folk dance. They do not prefer solo performance of western dance, performed by a group of men and women. They have folk tales, inner meanings is impregnated with the lessons of life.

The Armenians has no traditional inter-community linkage with other locals at present. Previously they might have certain trade relationships because in earlier days they had to collect lac or thread or clothes from various communities in rural sides for running their trade. But at present they are in various services after getting sufficient education and at the same time after the end of British rule they wound up their trade and business from the remote or rural areas of the country. The Armenians do not follow any commensal restriction. They exchange food with members of any community who are their friends or customers. They also can establish marital relation with any community if they so decide, there is no bar on inter-community marriage among them, still they prefer to marry within their own community. The community has ritual based fathership and mothership. At the time of baptism of a child a man or a woman from among the relatives or friends acts the god-father or god-mother whose duty is to look after the spiritual welfare of the new born. They enjoy free access to temples, mosques, schools, colleges and roads, etc.

At present they are linked with various communities of India and abroad through modern inter-community linkage. In 1958 Dr. Suniti Kumar Chatterjee delivered a speech at the Armenian College on the occasion of prize giving ceremony. The speech was subsequently published by the principal of the Armenian college and all the persons among the Armenians know it and they showed a great respect towards Dr. Chatterjee and his family. In the Armenian college people from many communities are found to be serving as teachers and clerks. Armenians have no political or ethnic movement among them. The Armenians are highly literate and educated. They restrict their family size according to their choice, sometimes with one child and sometimes two to four children and they control child birth without using any family planning method.

Eating Live Fishes

The Bohra Muslims are non-vegetarian and eat beef, but not pork. They are allowed to eat live fishes after Zabah, a ritual slaughter of animals. Rice and wheat are staple food, along with pulses such as *gram, urad, tuar* and *masur*. They abstain from alcoholic drinks.

The Bohras are a Muslim community with a Gujarati origin. 'Bohra' is a Gujarati word, possibly meaning trader. So the Bohras are considered one of the early traders who originated from Gujarat. The Bohras have two sectarian sub-groups—the Ismaili Shia, popularly known as the Dawoodi Bohras who follow the Shia sect of Islam; and the Sunni Bohras, who follow Sunni sect. Both groups comprise several regional units, with minor variations, such as the Sidhupuris are from Sidhpur. Kathiawadis from Kathiawad, Surtis from Surat and Lunawadis from Lunawad. The Dawoodi Bohras are a homogeneous group belonging to a Hindu caste in Gujarat, before converting to Islam. The Sunni Bohras as their name suggests have the same origin, but differ only on account of sectarian affiliations to the wider section of Muslims. Group boundaries are strictly maintained through sect endogamy. The inner organizations of the sects deal with the ecclesiastical affairs of the members of their respective sects, as well as provide guidance to them in their social affairs.

The Bohras profess the faith of Islam. But the Dawoodi Bohras are the followers of the Shia sect, while the Surti Sunni Bohras follow the sect. The Ismaili group branched off from the main body of the Shia sect after the death of the sixth Imam. This group split into two further sub-groups after the death of 19th Imam the Nizarian and the Mustalian. Dawoodi Bohras belong to the Mustalian group.

When, the 21st Imam of the sect went into seclusion, the institution of the *Dai* was established. The Sunni Bohras believe in spiritualism, in *pirs*, and in the Chishtia Silsila order. There may be individual, or family, affiliations to the *pir*. The *Amil*, among the Dawoodi Bohras, and the Qazi work as their sacred specialists. There is no inherent impurity or inequality, of individuals within the fold of Islam and Bohra tenets. So restrictions on commensal relationship do not take any definite form, but they avoid accepting water or food from groups with a very low status, such as the Lal Begis (sweepers), still religious practises bring them together within the mosque. Such gatherings also take place on other social occasions. Traditionally they are not permitted to accept any victuals from the Hindus, but in an urban environment, there are many commercial establishments, where people—irrespective of caste, or religion—eat with each other. During the festival of *Milad*, the sweets distributed by them in their community may be made by Hindu confectioners. These are some forms of secular inter-community linkage which these people establish in the modern urban milieu. Both the groups have burial grounds of their own and the Dawoodi Bohras have their own *Saifee masjid* (mosque). The social customs are related to the Bohra Muslims.

Buddhist Chinese Eschew Meat

Most Chinese people in Calcutta except a few followers of Buddhism are non-vegetarian who eat all poultry products, including ducks and quails, besides beef and pork. Their staple food is rice, still they have food products made from wheat as snacks. Some Chinese dishes are called as *ba kav sui mai* (vegetables and prawn steamed inside a crust of flour), *tai pao* (pork ball in clear soup), *ham chin pung* (flour ball stuffed with meat), *too fu kok* (long strips of deep-fried flour), and the world renowned *chow*, or noodles. In fact, the Chinese people eat very little pulses, of which they have mainly gram, *tuar*, peas, beans and *masur*. The indigenous Chinese cooking medium is lard, but now most use groundnut and sunflower oil. However the Chinese prefer to have vegetables and fruits of their place of origin. They grow such fruits and vegetables as Chinese beans, cabbage, lettuce and parsnips in Tangra. They prefer to drink green tea prepared their way. Milk and milk products are not very popular among them, though now they consider it a nourishing drink mainly for the children and ailing old people. However, the Chinese food habits are gradually changing. The younger generation enjoys non-Chinese food and often eats out, while at home they have started having local vegetables and more of pulses.

The Chinese people in Calcutta are proud that they have no social divisions. The people feel they are in the middle ranks of the regional social hierarchy, and the other communities too think the same of them.

However, the Calcutta Chinese have two distinct religious groups — Buddhists and Christians. The Chinese Buddhists belong to the Mahayana sect. The cult of their ancestors is of great importance to the majority of the Chinese. Both Buddhists and Christians observe elaborate rites and rituals with regard to their dead ancestors when they visit cemeteries to observe the biannual ceremony of offering food and drinks to the dead ancestors. Besides visiting the clan graveyards, they also worship deities—at the family level, mainly *Supuko, Kuanti, Choi-Sun* (God of Wealth), *Nu-Fon* and *Thei-Kun.* The priests and functionaries of the Chinese Buddhist temples are, more or less, exclusively drawn from among the Chinese themselves. The Chinese Christians also have their separate Churches and priests.

Whereas the Calcutta Chinese celebrate Chinese New Year with great pomp. The Kitchen God is worshipped on the occasion. During the New Years festival many people visit different temples to burn incense and record their vows. Every day until the sixteenth, tablets of their ancestors are worshipped and incense burned before them. Five kinds of edibles are also offered to them. Other important festivals are the fifth moon and eighth moon festivals. The fifth moon festival is called by several names as *Twan-Yan-*

Chieh, or Dragon-Boat festival, *Li-Chun* (spring). *Ching-Ming* (Bright and Clear) and *Yi-Lan-Hwei* (Meeting at the *Yu-Lan River*). Most of these festivals are marked by special feasts. Both Buddhists and Christians celebrate them.

The Calcutta Chinese have folk-tales and folk-songs, sung at festivals. A folk-tale associated with the Dragon-Boat festival reveals the legend of Kuh-Yuan, who drowned himself in sheer disgust in the Mih-Lo River after being falsely implicated by one of the smaller princes of the state. Young Chinese boys and girls take especial interest mainly in Western music and dance, though at some traditional ethnic festivals they do take part in Chinese music and dance.

There are no Minor Deities

All members of this community follow Christianity, they have no minor deities. Their priests, who come from both Bengali and non-Bengali Christian communities, hold services, preach sermons from the church pulpit and perform the life-cycle rituals of the lay Christians. Their main festivals are Christmas, New Year and Easter. While Christmas and New Year are festivals of joy, Easter is a festival of sorrow. A Mass is held forty days before Easter, called as Ash Wednesday. Some have vegetarian food on Wednesday and Fridays during the period of Lent. Evening prayers are held every Wednesday and Friday till Easter. The Christians also take part in traditional Hindu festivals, such as Holi and Diwali. They have folk songs just the same as other Bengalis. They prefer folk-tales from the Bible, along with traditional ones. Though their interest runs to Western music and dance, some show interest in Indian classical music too. They have no restrictions on sharing water with other communities. Inter-community marriage take place in the community.

Progenies of Outcaste Europeans and Outcaste Indians

The Anglo Indians in the entire Eastern region are nonvegetarians who also eat beef and pork. Rice is their staple food besides wheat and pulses like gram and *moong*. Generally, their midday meal consists of rice, dal and spicy curries of meat and vegetables, followed by a dessert consisting fruit or sweet. Breakfast and dinner are of the continental type. They have no taboo on taking alcoholic drinks for either the men or women or the children. They also take coffee, milk and milk products.

Under Art. 366(2), the Constitution of India state "An Anglo- Indian means a person whose father or any of whose other male progenitor in the male line is or was of European descent but who is domiciled within the territory of India and is or was born within such territory of parents habitually resident therein and not established there for temporary purposes only". In course of times they have come to be known as the country-born, Indo-Britons, Eurasians and Anglo-Indians. There is a widespread belief that the Anglo-Indian community like some other mixed communities perhaps was the result of a haphazard process of miscegenation between outcaste Englishmen and outcaste Indian women. The Anglo-Indians were begotten in illicit sexual liaisons when the British soldiers came to India and cohabited with the low-caste Indian women by way of entertainment.

The historic Anglo-Indian settlement of McCluskiegunj, in the Ranchi district, Bihar (now in Jharkhand-ed.) was founded by the Late S.I. McCluskie, M.L.C. McCluskiegunj is an enchanting hamlet, with colonial style bungalows and cottages, farms and orchards, nestling between the Adivasi villages of Kouka and Lapra, in the heart of the Chotanagpur Plateau. Mr. McCluskie obtained a lease of approximately 10,000 acres of land from the Raja of Ratu for founding a colony for people of European descent *i.e.,* Anglo-Indians and domiciled Europeans. Besides McCluskiegunj, they are distributed in Bhagalpur, Darbhanga, Hazaribagh, Munger, Muzaffarpur, Patna, Ranchi, Saharsa, Sahebganj and Singhbhum districts. The Anglo-Indian population in Bihar according to the 1951 Census was only 4,596. They speak English and Hindi and use the Roman and the Devanagari scripts and listed as Anglo-Indians in the constitution.

The Anglo-Indians have their own association, known as the Anglo-Indian Association. The role of the association is to plan and implement welfare projects for the community. They profess Christianity. The Church is their major place of worship. They utilise the services of the Priest for baptism, confirmation, marriage and funeral rites. Christmas is their most important festival celebrated on December 24th and 25th to commemorate the birth of Jesus Christ. On Christmas Eve, scenes from the life of Christ are enacted. In tableaux, cribs are put in the Church, which people, particularly children flock to see. People attend the special Mass at church, exchange presents, and rejoices. Easter is observed by them to commemorate the resurrection of Jesus Christ prior to his death. Forty days before Easter they observe Lent, when most Anglo-Indians sacrifice something they like most for the purification of their spirit. Some give up smoking, drinking of alcohol and or meat. Those who observe a fast, take their meal only after sunset. Good-Friday is observed as the day of crucifixion.

The Anglo-Indians have folk-songs, folk-tales drawn from the English and other European repertoire and percussion, wind, string and valve musical instruments. They prefer western music. Both men and women participate in dancing. Inter-community relationships are maintained by participation in different rituals and ceremonies. The increasing opportunities at social, political and economic levels have accelerated the development of inter-community linkages in the local society. Through their educational institutions, the Anglo-Indians have played a vital role in forging inter-community linkages and imparting education to the students of different local communities who had so far remained steep in illiteracy, lack of education and ignorance.

Ornaments not a Means of Investment

About the Muslim custom of Jewellery, food drinks and intoxicants, Mr. Ja'far Sarif writes, "The jewellery worn by Musalmans presents great differences of type and fashion, but there is little that is really distinctive, both men and women often wearing patterns closely resembling those of the Hindus, this being particularly the case among the many converts from Hinduism to Islam, though, of course, the use of symbols or figures of Hindu deities are avoided. Musalmans as compared with Hindus do not invest so much of their savings in jewellery to be sold in times of need. In some parts of the country there is a prejudice against wearing gold on the feet. Some classes forbid their women to wear anything save gold above the feet, but silver may be used in the form of anklets or toe-rings, and if this is not procurable some cheaper substance like pewter or bell-metal is used. (*Census Report*, Central India, 1901, i. 208). In the time of the Prophet, when the type of daily life was simpler, the wearing of gold rings was prohibited. ((According to Ferishta, Husain Nizam Shah, King of Ahmadnagar (A.D. 1553-65), on one occasion, after prayers, observing that he was wearing a girdle of gold, recollected that it was unlawful to pray while wearing it, cast it off and repeated his prayers). Among Musalmans, as among Hindus, the primary intention in wearing jewellery is not for ornament, but to secure protection against the Evil Eye and the attacks of spirits. Hence comes the use of things supposed to possess spirit power, such as the wood or leaves of certain trees and plants, the hair or claws of tigers or parts of other animals. Men, as a rule, wear little jewellery except as amulets, but among the rich trading classes in western India, like the Bohras or Memans. the wearing of necklaces, wristlets, ear-rings, bangles, finger rings, collarettes, or gold chains is common.

"According to a Rabbinical legend adopted by Islam, Sarah, when she was jealous of Hagar, declared that she could not rest till her hands were stained with the blood of her rival. So Abraham pierced Hagar's 'ears and Sarah was thus able to stain her hands with the blood. Hence came the use of ear-rings. Musalman women usually wear these rings fixed all along the outer border of the ear, often four to eleven in each, the left having invariably one less than the right. The Traditions declare, 'Whoever likes to put into the nose or ear of his friend a ring of hell fire, let it be a gold ring ; wherefore be it on you to make your ornaments of silver'. But this law is now generally ignored, and many Musalman women wear a gold nose ring *(nath)* in the left nostril, and another *(bulaq)* in the central cartilage. Many women wear round their necks, strung with black thread, silver cases containing a verse from the Koran, some charm, or some animal or vegetable substance. 'Verily spells and tying round the necks of children the nails of tearing animals, and the thread which is tied round a woman's neck to make her husband love her, all these are of the polytheists'. Among Musalman women in southern India the ear is often dilated widely by the use of pegs or pledgets of cloth, each of a size larger than the last. Among Hindus and some Musalmans in the Central Provinces, if the flesh of the ear thus dilated happens to be torn by accident or in a scuffle, the woman is regarded as defiled and has to undergo special purification. In north India young children, otherwise naked, wear some protective hung from the waist to repel the Evil Eye. In the south little girls wear a 'fig-leaf' of silver with the same object, while little boys wear a conical, elongated object, both amulets having a phallic significance."

As for the food and drink habits, Mr. Ja'far Sarif writes, "Musalmans submit to few of the vexatious restrictions which the rules of caste impose upon Hindus, but their association with this people suggests taboos in the use of certain foods, some of which are of foreign origin and come from the early days of Islam. According to the *Kansu-l-daqaiq* and the *Shar-i-waqiat,* the flesh of certain animals is unlawful, that of others prohibited. The flesh of those that are cloven-footed, those that chew the cud, and are not beasts of prey, is lawful food, such as that of sheep and goats, deer, antelopes, the hare, the rabbit, the cow, bull, female and male buffalo, &c. Those that are neither cloven-footed nor chew the cud, like the jackass, &c., are unlawful. Others which though cloven-footed do not chew the cud, or those which have merely : canine teeth, are unlawful, such as the hog, wolf, jackal, tiger, bear, hyaena, and the like. 'That which dieth of itself, and blood and swine's flesh, and that over which any other name than that of God hath been invoked, is forbidden to you. But he that shall partake of them by constraint, without lust or wilfulness, no sin shall be upon him. Verily God is Indulgent Merciful'. Although the Imam 'Azam, Abu Hanifa of Kufa, has pronounced horseflesh unlawful, his disciples contradict this, and, therefore, some considering it improper *(makruh),* that is to say, things from which the Prophet abstained yet did not forbid to others, eat of it. But most people regard it as unlawful food. Of birds, all those that catch prey with their claws or tear it with their teeth, are unlawful, such as the sparrow-hawk *(shikra, micronisus badius),* the peregrine falcon *(bahri, falco peregrinus),* and the goshawk *(baz, astur palumbarius),* the kite, crow, vulture, bat, kingcrow, and other fruits, lemon grass *(cymbopogon nardus),* fenugreek, the leaves of which greatly improve a curry.

"The varieties of materials used in curries is very great: various kinds of meat, flour of different kinds of grain, and vegetables which it is unnecessary to describe in detail.

"Curry powder. The following is an excellent receipt for curry powder: Take of powdered turmeric 20 teaspoonfuls, red dried chillies or cayenne pepper 8 teaspoonfuls, coriander seed cummin, dried cassia leaves, of each 12 teaspoonfuls, and mix them together.

"Sweetmeats. The varieties of sweetmeats *(shirin, mithai)* are innumerable. One of the favourite kinds, Halwa, is made as follows : Fine wheat flour *(suji)* 2 lb., fried in 1 lb. butter, to which add 4 to 6 lb: syrup, 8 rupees' weight of coco-nut kernel, 1/3 rupee weight of spices, 1 stick cinnamon, 10 cloves, 10 cardamoms and a little aniseed, and mix over a fire. In Akbar's time Halwa was made of flour, sugar-candy, butter, 20 lb. of each, the whole providing 15 dishes.

"Sherbet (sharbat) is a solution of sugar in water or of sugar-candy in rose-water. If lime juice is added it is called Abshora. Another variety is made of the best Damascus plums in water, with lemon or orange juice and sugar. Other kinds are made from violets, honey, raisin juice, & c.

"Pickles *(achar).* To make mango pickle, take 300 green mangoes, split them in two, take out the stones and dry them in the sun for three days. Then take 4½ oz. of turmeric, $3^3/_{16}$ oz. garlic, 6 lb. salt, 1½ oz. mustard seed, and the same quantity of coriander seed toasted. Mix the spices together and lay the mixture in alternate layers with the mangoes. Add 9 oz. gingeli or sesamum oil, or as much as will cover them.

"Curds, curdled milk *(dahi).* 'Dahi differs from curd as prepared in Europe in being practically sour boiled milk, the fermenting agent being added when it is nearly cold. And the milk being boiled immediately as obtained from the cow contains all its fat or butter. In this form it is called Sara, and if kept hot may be accumulated for some days till sufficient has been collected to make Dahi. Whole-milk Dahi contains too much fat to be made into cheese.' It is, in fact, cream cheese'. The ferment used is a little stale Dahi, tamarind or lime juice." Mr. Sarif adds.

As for the intoxicants and stimulants, Mr. Ja'far Sarif writes, "Opum (*afyun, afim*) is the inspissated juice of the opium poppy *(papaver somniferum).* It is used in various forms by Musalmans, particularly by those living in cities, but in rural districts the habitual opium-eater, known as Afyunchi, Afimchi, Pinak, 'drinker', or Shahdmakkhi, 'honey bee', from his fondness for sweets, is rarely seen. Opium is taken in the form of pills, followed by a little sugar or sweetmeats, or dissolved in water, and, if it is impure, strained or mixed with saffron. This last, the liquid form, is called Kusumbha, 'saffron', and is commonly used by Rajputs. (Tod, *Annals of Rajasthan* (ed. 1920), i. 341, 541). It is often taken in moderate quantities to flavour tobacco and as a febrifuge and stimulant. Though much evil results from the excessive use of the drug, the demoralization said to be due to it has been much exaggerated. Very moderate consumers take about 1 Tola, 180 grains Troy, 11. 662 grammes per month, and the average consumption by an habitual opium-eater is believed to be about 5 Tola per mensem. In some cases it has been reported that as much as a Tola a day is taken boiled in milk. The worst forms of the drug are Chandu and Madak or Madad. Chandu is made by steeping opium in water till it becomes soft, when it is boiled and strained. It is thus reduced to syrup *(qiwam, qimam),* which is kept for use. The pipe *(bambu)* is cleaned with a wire *(girmit)* and the Chandu is heated in the flame of a lamp till it becomes soft, when a little is placed in the pipe-bowl *(dawat),* lighted and inhaled. Madak or Madad is made from the syrup of opium as above described, or more usually from the inspissated juice *(pasewa)* of the opium, which separates as it dries after being collected from the capsules, and this juice when collected on rags is known in northern India as Kafa. This syrup is mixed with chopped betel leaves, paper, acacia leaves, cardamoms or chopped coco fibre, and it is sold in balls. Chandu is smoked in a special pipe *(nigali),* but Madak in the ordinary tobacco bowl *(chilam, mahru).* A form of opium constantly mentioned by the older travellers is Post or Koknar, a decoction of opium capsules, which was administered by the Mughal Emperors to princes or other men of rank whom it was desired to reduce to idiocy or remove without scandal.

"Among the preparations of hemp, Bhang, also known as Siddhi, 'accomplishment', 'Sabzi, 'green leaves', Thandai, 'a cooling drink', Bijaya or Vijaya, 'conquering', Buti, 'sprig, flower', is the dried larger leaves of either or both the male and female plants, whether wild or cultivated, of *Cannabis saliva.* Charas is the resinous substance that appears spontaneously on the leaves, stems, inflorescence, and fruits of the hemp plant when cultivated in cold and dry regions. Ganja is the dried flowering tops of the cultivated female plants, which become coated with a resinous exudation from glandular hairs, very largely in consequence of their being deprived of the opportunity of forming seed. Bhang is prepared by mixing black pepper with the hemp and crushing the mixture on a stone slab *(sil)* with a roller *(batta).* This is infused in water, strained and drunk. Bhang butter *(bhang ghi)* is made by boiling Bhang in milk, skimming off the cream and turning it into butter ; it is used as an anaesthetic by native surgeons. In the Deccan the hemp leaves *(siddhi)* are washed in water to the amount of 3 drachms, to which are added 45 grains black pepper, cloves, nutmeg, and mace, of each 11¼ grains. This is tritrated with 8 oz. water, milk, juice of water-melons, or cucumber seed, strained and drunk. It is often drunk without the spices, which are believed to make it more intoxicating.

"In the case of Charas the exudation is collected by a man who covers himself with a blanket and runs through a hemp field, thus absorbing the gum with the dew adhering to the leaves. The blanket is then scraped, washed, and wrung. The products are made into an electuary of which five grains mixed with tobacco is smoked and proves speedily intoxicating. In Sind it is never eaten raw either for intoxication or as a medicine, but it is either smoked or eaten in the form of an electuary known as Ma'jun. Bhang is said to terrify the consumer, to make him speak in an animated way, and to keep him armed against any efforts to make him reveal confidential matters. Ganja is used by rubbing the leaves between the hands and smoking it with tobacco, but it is also smoked by itself. Ma'jun is an electuary taken internally by Musalmans, particularly by the most dissolute, as a nerve stimulant, intoxicant, and for the relief of pain. An overdose not infrequently causes mental derangement. In the popular belief it gives intoxication *(kaifa),* vigour *(quwwai),* and it is used as an aphrodisiac. The chief ingredients of this electuary are Ganja, milk, butter, poppy seeds, flowers of the Dhatura or thorn-apple, powder of Nux vomica and sugar. Another receipt is as follows : Take 2 quarts milk, put into it 2 lb. Ganja leaves and boil till the liquid is reduced to 3 lb. Take but the leaves and coagulate the milk by adding a little sour milk *(dahi).* Next day churn it and separate the butter, adding wild cloves, nutmeg, cloves, mace, saffron, of each 3 drachms, sugar-candy 15 drachms, and boil till it forms an electuary. Or, more simply, the leaves of the hemp are fried in butter and strained and the residue is drunk with some sugar, or the liquor is boiled with sugar until it acquires a consistence sufficiently thick to form cakes when it cools. In the north of India 6 lb. of Bhang are added to 4 lb. clarified butter and 70 lb. sugar. The Bhang is soaked for a night in water and next day the water is drained off. A little butter is melted in a pan, and the Bhang is mixed with it. Water is then added, and the mixture is boiled until the Bhang becomes soft, when it is strained and pounded into a paste. This is then boiled with the rest of the sugar and milk. It is allowed to harden by drying and cut into small pieces. Two squares are enough to cause intoxication to an ordinary person. People seldom become used to taking Ma'jun, and it is usually employed as a sexual stimulant and as an excitant to debauch. (Bill Atkinson, *Himalayan Gazetteer*, i. 765 f.)

"Tobacco is known in northern India as Tambaku, the Indian form of the Spanish tobacco, from the American name of the plant, thus showing its foreign origin. (Tobacco was introduced into northern India in 1604-5, and the historian, Asad Beg, gives a curious account of the first experiment of its use in Akbar's court. His Majesty, however, was advised not to use it (Elliot-Dowson, vi. 165 ff.; Smith, *Akbar*, 407 ff.). Doubtless to the Portuguese is due the credit of having conveyed both the plant and the knowledge of its properties to India and China (*Watt, Econ.* Prod. 796). In the Deccan it is called Gudaku or Guraku (*gur*, 'raw sugar', Telugu *aku,* 'leaf'). Most Musalmans smoke or chew tobacco, or use snuff, and women smoke and sometimes chew. In the Panjab Shi'as smoke tobacco in a clay bowl *(chilam),* but the Mullas of the Sunni Pathans discourage smoking and the use of Charas. Musalmans very generally use the Huqqa or pipe with a stand, while Hindus often prefer the small hand pipe made of a coconut bow', which can be handed from one man to another and carried while travelling. But the use of cigarettes is rapidly increasing. The right to use the caste or tribal pipe is carefully restricted, and exclusion from its use is a common form of social boycott *(huqqa pani band karna,* 'refusal to allow a man to smoke or drink water with his fellows'). In Lucknow, which is famous for its tobacco, it is made plain *(sada)* or fermented *(khamira).* In the former the dried leaf is pounded and mixed with its own weight of coarse sugar *(shira).* Khamira tobacco is made by adding to the leaves musk and spices. Chewing tobacco *(khaini, surati,* 'from Surat') is steeped when green in red ochre and dried. The following are approved receipts for pipe tobacco in the Deccan : 8 lb. tobacco leaves, 8 lb. treacle, 1 lb. preserved apples, or, as a substitute, preserved pine-apple or jujube *(ber, zizyphus jujuba),* 1 lb. raisins, 1 lb. conserve of roses *(gulqand).* These are well pounded together in a wooden mortar, put into an earthen pot, the mouth of which is made air-tight, and it is buried underground for three months before being used. If spiced tobacco be desired, they add Pegu cardamoms, cubebs, sandalwood, patchouli, and spikenard, 8 oz. of each, and mix them well together before the pot is buried. In the Panjab the spices comprise preserved apple conserve of roses, dried betel leaves, a kind of scented wood *(mushkbala),* sandalwood, wild jujube, and the pulp of the Amaltas *(cassia fistula).* Tobacco without spices is considered the most wholesome, and if it is duly fermented underground it becomes mellow and agreeable. A mild tobacco *(halka, phika)* is distinguished from the strong *(kaura)* by placing a little on the tongue and seeing if it causes irritation. If a mild tobacco is desired, wash the leaves a few times in cold water and then dry in the sun, then pound. Another receipt is as follows : Take of good tobacco 40 lb., raw palmyra sugar 40 lb., *nagarmotha (cyperus rotundus)* 6 drachms, twenty ripe plantains, 10 wood apples, 6 drachms cloves. Pound all separately, except the tobacco and sugar. Then mix with them 4 lb. tobacco and sugar ; make eight divisions of the remaining tobacco and sugar, grind one at a time well with the mass, add them all together and knead them well with the hands. Then bury the compound for a month in a dunghill.

"The common tobacco pipe *(huqqa, qaliyun)* consists of three parts : the bowl *(chilam)* containing the fire and the tobacco ; the stem with the 'snake' *(naicha)* on which the pipe-head is fixed ; the bowl containing water or rose-water. The pipe used by rich people is often a work of art. That used by middle and low-class people is of the same shape, but the bowl is of clay, the stem of wood, and a coconut shell serves as the water bowl.

"Snuff *(sunghni, nas)* is dry tobacco powdered and perfumed. In eastern Bengal it is rarely used except medicinally, being said to cure headaches by eliminating morbid humours from the brain. The best comes from Benares and Masulipatam.

"For lighting the tobacco specially prepared balls of charcoal *(gul)* are used. They are made of tamarind or Pipal *(ficus religiosa)* charcoal, mixed with acacia gum molasses, and rice gruel.

"The use of Betel *(pan)* is habitual among Indian Musalmans of both sexes. Betel leaf is the produce of a perennial creeper *(piper belle),* probably introduced into India from Java. It has been used from very early times and is chewed generally in a packet *(bira),* among the lower classes the leaf being generally mixed with areca nut *(areca catechu),* known as Supart, lime and Kath, a crystalline substance produced from the tree *Acacia catechu,* and by richer people with cardamoms, camphor, and other spices. 'It is somewhat astonishing that a narcotic stimulant so much used by all natives of India should have attracted so little attention in writings on medicine... But no European physician in India seems to have experimented on the value of the drug as a tonic, stomachic, and slight stimulant. Acting on the great reputation enjoyed by Pan all over the East, and on the remarks made on the drug by such early travellers as Marco Polo, Dutch botanists and physicians have used it experimentally, and have come to the conclusion that the chewing of betel leaves does promote health in the damp and miasmatic climate of that country'. The juice stains the teeth and mouth, and in popular belief it is an indispensable adjunct to a woman's beauty, and it is said to distinguish a man from a dog. The distribution of betel is a prominent act in the reception of visitors, when it is recognized as a sign of closing an interview, and at Darbars or public levees. The usual etiquette is that when given from the hand it implies the superiority of the donor, when presented in a silver or gold box it implies equality. The giving of betel, probably owing to its supposed spirit power as a stimulant, assumes a sacramental form. Among the Rajputs it was given before going into battle or on dangerous service," he adds.

References

1. Land Settlement Report of Santhal Parganas, Calcutta, Government Press, 1919.
2. Chaturvedi, M.D., Tour Notes on the Forests of Orissa, 1950.
3. Dalton, E.T., *Descriptive Ethnology of Bengal*, Office of the Superintendent of Government Printing Press, Calcutta, 1872.
4. Sherring, M.A., *Hindu Tribes and Castes*, Thaker Spink and Co., Calcutta 1879, reprint Cosmo Publications, Delhi, 1974.
5. Risley, Sir Herbert, *Tribes and Castes of Bengal: Ethnographic Glossary*, Bengal Secretariat Press, Calcutta, 1891, reprint, Firma KLM, Calcutta, 1998.
6. Bahadur, K.P., *Castes, Tribes and Culture of India, Bengal, Bihar and Orissa,* Ess Ess Publications, New Delhi, 1977.
7. Chaudhury, Buddhadeb, (ed.) *Tribal Transformation in India: Religion, Ritual and Festivals*, Inter-India Publications, New Delhi, 1992.
8. Sinha, Dikshit, *The Hill Kharia of Purulia*, Anthropological Survey of India, Calcutta, 1984.
9. Sachchidananda, *Profiles of Tribal Culture in Bihar*, Firma KLM, Calcutta, 1965.
10. Sarif, Ja'gar, *Islam in India* (edited by W. Crooke), Oriental Books, Reprint Corp; New Delhi, 1972, First Published 1921.
11. Singh, K.S. (Gen. ed.), *People of India : West Bengal*, Seagul Books, Calcutta, 2008.
12. Singh, K.S. (Gen. ed.), *People of India : Bihar*, Seagul Books, Calcutta, 2008.

Bibliography

Bahadur, K.P., Caste, Tribe and Culture of India: Bengal, Bihar and Orissa, ESS ESS Publications, Delhi, 1977.

Biswas, P.C., *Santals of Santal Parganas*, Bharatiya Adimjati Sewak Sangh, Delhi, 1956.

Chaturvedi, M.D., Tour Notes on the Forests of Orissa, 1950.

Chaudhury Buddhadeb, (ed), *Tribal Transformation in India: Religion, Rituals and Festivels*, Vol. V, Inter-India Publications, New Delhi, 1992.

Dalton, Colonel E.T., Descriptive Ethnology of Bengal Government Press, Calcutta, 1872.

Dalton, E.T., Descriptive Ethnology of Bengal, Office of Superintendent of Government Press, Calcutta, 1872, reprint Firma KLM, Calcutta, 1960.

Das, Amal Kumar and Raha, Manis Kumar, The Rabhas of West Bengal: Scheduled Castes and Tribal Welfare Department, Government of West Bengal, Calcutta, 1967.

Firth, Raymond, The Fate of the Soul : An Interpretation of some primitive concepts, Cambridge University Press, Cambridge, 1955.

Furer-Haimandorf, Christophvon, The After Life in Indian Tribal Belief; *Journal of the Royal Anthropological Society*, London, 3 (1) January-June 1953, pp. 37-49.

Ghuryre, G.S., The *Mahadev Kolis*, Popular Book Depot, Bombay, 1957.

Grierson, Sir, G.A., Behar Peasant Life, Superintendent Government Press.

Ibbetson, Sir, *Report on the Census of the Punjab*, Government Press, Lahore.

Land Settlement Report of Santhal Parganas, Calcutta, Government Press, 1919.

P. Sachchidananda, *Profiles of Tribal Culture in Bihar*, Firma KLM, Calcutta, 1965.

Ray, Himanshu Mohan, Savara—The Snake Charmars, Institute of Social Research and Applied Anthropology, Calcutta 1986.

Ray, Himansu, Mohan, *Savara–The Snake-charmer*, Institute of social Research and Applied Anthropology, Calcutta, 1986.

Raychaudhuri, Tarak Chand and Ray Chaudhuri, Bikash, the Brahmans of Bengal, Anthropological Survey of India, Calcutta, 1981.

Risley, Sir Herbert, *Tribes and Castes of Bengal: Ethnographic Glossary*, Bengal Secretariat Press, Calcutta, 1891, reprint, Firma KLM, Calcutta, 1998.

Roy, S.C., The Mundas and their Country, City Book Society, Calcutta, 1912.

Roy, S.S., The Oraon of Chotanagpur, the Brahmo Mission Press, Calcutta, 1915.

Russel, R.V. and Lal, Hira, The Tribes and Castes of the Central Provinces of India, Low Price Publications, Delhi (reprint) 1997, originally published MacMillan and Co., London, 1916.

Sachchidananda, *Profiles of Tribal Culture in Bihar*, Firma KLM, Calcutta, 1965.

Sachchidananda, the Tribal village in Bihar : A Study in Unity and Extension, Munshiram Manoharlal, Delhi, 1968.

Sarif, Ja'far, *Islam in India* (edited by W. Crooke), Oriental Books, reprint Corp., New Delhi, 1972, originally published 1921.

Sarkar, Amitabha and Dasgupta, Samira, Spectrum of Tribal Bastar, Agam Kale Prakashan, Delhi, 1996.

Sengupta, Syamalkanti, The Social Profiles of the Mahalis, Firma KLM, Calcutta, 1970.

Sherring, M.A., *Hindu Tribes and Castes*, Thaker Spink and Co., Calcutta 1879, reprint Cosmo Publications, Delhi, 1974.

Singh, K.S. (Gen. ed.), *People of India : Bihar*, Seagul Books, Calcutta, 2008.

Sinha, Dikshit, *The Hill Kharia of Purulia*, Anthropological Survey of India, Calcutta, 1984.

Triosi, J., *Tribal Religion : Religions Beliefs and Practices Among the Santals*, Manohar, New Delhi, 1978.

Vidyarthi, L.P., *The Maler*, Bookland Pvt. Ltd., Calcutta, 1963.

Index

O

P

R

S

T

U

CUSTOMS OF INDIA

CUSTOMS OF INDIA

(In Six Volumes)

Volume 6

North Eastern: Arunachal Pradesh, Assam, Manipur, Meghalaya, Mizoram, Nagaland, Sikkim, Tripura

Editor

Gopal Bhargava

ISHA

Customs of India

ISBN: 978-81-8205-524-7 (Set)
ISBN: 978-81-8205-530-8 (Vol. 6)

Published in 2012 in India by
Isha Books
B-69, New Gupta Colony
New DDA Market
Delhi - 110009

Laser Type Setting : Quick Media, Delhi
Printed at : G. Print Process, Delhi

Contents

List of Illustrations

4. Children dance in a festival.

Nagaland

1. Men and women performing dance in traditional dress.
2. Nagas traditional dance during a festival.
3. The Nagas dancing in traditional dress with their arms.
4. The Nagas men and women, in a festive mood after the festival.

Sikkim

1. A Person is dancing in Panglhabsol festival.
2. Alone Monk praying in the Monastery.
3. A man and woman in traditional dress in festive mood.
4. Women are dancing in Bumchu festival.

Tripura

1. Hozagiri dance in progress during festival.
2. Lebung Boomani A dance of Tripuri Community during festival.
3. Men and women are dancing in traditional dress during festival.
4. Garia a dance of Tripuri Community.

Preface

This painstakingly researched volume on the customs of India is a vast treasure trove of information on individual tribes and castes of the region. This volume showcases the primitive people of India prior to the arrival of British, advent of Christianity and in the later times of Post-independence. Each volume contains introduction on customs, Characteristics of the people of the states and region concerned and the general view of probable origin of the customs. Besides, each volume contains seven chapters, including : Conceiving and birth, puberty, betrothal, marriage ceremony, death rituals : cremation, death rituals ; Burial and Social customs. The book describes at length the ancient forms of customs, rites, rituals and usages as recorded by numerous British and Indian ethnographers, gazetteers; writers, surveyors of settlement report, monograph writers and anthropologists etc. Following independence of India in 1947, the entire scenario of social, economic life, customs, culture, rites and rituals belong to both tribal and non-tribal communities in the northeastern India had been in a constant transition. The region has been impinged upon by Indian and global influences and factors. All these new changes in the customs, rites and rituals had been incorporated into this work.

The entire mass of information and knowledge has been painstakingly researched, written and edited with the anthropological point of view that makes this work all the more valuable for the purpose of scholars, scientists, researchers, teachers and students in different disciplines.

Every detail of the information, collected, collated and formatted has gone through meticulous validations, checks and rechecks. In line with the evolution of the text, this work, too, will have to be updated and improved in the successive editions. In a country as vast and complex as India, there will always be a scope for improving this vast work of eminence through suggestions, deletions, and additions pointed out for rectifications. We invite the beneficiaries of this work to participate in its evolution.

This work contains the collected, collated, formatted and validated information on customs of India on a 'best and sincere effort' basis for presentation in a single comprehensive work. This work does not constitute an advisory for research, analysis or investment planning, nor, in general, any professional advice. The reader should seek the services of qualified professionals for such advice.

The information presented here is to be regarded as a 'first information service' on this work. The reader should make his/ her own deeper investigation of the information on any particular matter before making any decision or investment of any kind. The Editorial Board or the Publishers cannot be held responsible for loss, if any, incurred as a result of specific planning or decisions or investments made by the reader in pursuance of this work.

Our sincere thanks are due to the scholars, researchers, authors, Publication Division, Ministry of Culture, Census Commissioner, Settlement Reports, Ethnographers, Anthropological Survey of India, State Editor (Gazetteers), and others. We have studied the contents of a large number of published works, and drawn from them. The credit for producing and furnishing authentic information and knowledge goes to them. We have merely weaved, consolidated and formulated the contents of the mass of information collected from them.

Editor

INTRODUCTION

Customs and traditions pertaining to the North-eastern region comprising Arunachal Pradesh, Manipur, Assam, Meghalaya, Mizoram, Nagaland, Tripura and Sikkim are somewhat unique due to being inhabited by predominantly by the tribal people called by the British as savage and wild. From the very dawn of civilization, the region had remained cut off amid the dense forest and inhospitable tracts. Here is an introduction to their customs and tradition, and the impact of modern civilisation on them since the arrivals of the British rulers and Christian Missionaries, and later on the further improvements introduced by the Government of India of the independence, mainly in form of tremendous opportunities under the scheduled tribes status. The society of Assam consists of many heterogeneous races. Since the time immemorial Assam has been the meeting ground of diverse ethnic and cultural streams - principle migrants have been the Austro-Asiatics, the Dravidians, the Tibeto-Burman, the Mongoloid and Aryans. flowing in from different directions.

The ethnic origin of the Assamese varies from Mongoloid tribes to those of directly Aryan stock. The earliest inhabitants of Assam were probably of Austric people. They are termed as proto-Austroloid because they are said to have migrated from the Australian and some other islands of the Pacific Ocean to the Asiatic mainland. The Khasis and Jaintias seem to be the descendants of the proto-Austroloids inhabitants of ancient Assam. After the Austries, the Mongoloids had entered the region of Assam, the Bodo tribe appeared and established over the valley of Brahmaputra. The Kacharis also known as the Bodos were once very powerful people. In course of history, they are known to have ruled over the entire Assam. The other branches of this tribe are - Kacharis, Meches, Garos, Abors, Miris, Mishmis, Rabha, Tipra, Akas, Daflas, Kukis, Mikirs, Nagas, and Mizos.

On the arrival of Ahoms in the 13th century, the Kacharis and Chutias were ruling over a large part of eastern Assam. Thereafter, came the Aryans who settled in the Brahmaputra valley at an early period of history. Of course, among different races, the Aryans could establish their cultural supremacy over this country. The Austro-Asiatics are the earlier migrants who initially dwelt in the Brahmaputra valley and later on made their alternative homes in the neighbouring Hills. The Khasi and Jantias of Meghalaya are said to be their descendents; the Dravidians came next.

In general, the Mongoloids belong to the Tibeto-Burman family of the Indo-Chinese Group. The early waves brought in the forefather of the Kacharis. The Dimasa, the Bodos, the Rabhas, the Lalungs. Whereas, the Kochs have in them an admixture of Dravidians and Mongoloid stocks and are called the Rajbanshis in Golpara. The Chutias originally settled in the North-eastern tip in upper Assam and later on gave way to make room for the Ahoms who belong to the Shan sub-section of the Indo-Chinese family. The Miris and Karbis both belong to Tibeto-Burman races.

The state of Assam comprises 23 Schedule Tribes constituting 10.99% of the total population. Due mainly to the mixture of the Mongolian element in the society the caste system amongst the local Hindu is less rigid than in other parts of India.

In the modern times, in the Northeast, ethno-linguistic differences are just as important as religious, socio-economic or class based differences for development.

The density of population in Assam have been pointing at the rapid rate of increase leading to reduction in land-man ratio. The threat of influx by different communities, be it Bengali Muslims from Bangladesh, Bengali Hindus from erstwhile East Bengal or migrant tribes from other states like Orissa. West Bengal, Bihar, has always been the most sensitive issue among the local tribal and other people.

In Assam, the entire population was divided into two groups, the *Paiks* or *Kari-Paiks* and the Chamuas the latter being engaged in professions like gold-*smithy*, black smithy and tailoring. While each male was a member of Khel weaving and spinning was the business of all section of people irrespective of their being a *Paik*. The Khel was a guild for the performance of duties assigned to each member. Four adult males constituted a got, an indispensable part of *Khel*, which functioned under an assigned officer. Assamese society was divided into several territorial and vocational *Khels*. People belonging to different *Khels* were settled in each village and within their limits they gave some evidence of functioning democracy.

A principal Ahom officer with such subordinates as Hazarika, Saikia, and Bora, excercised superintendence over the Khels. In the closing years of the Ahom dynasty non-Ahom officers were also appointed to conduct supervision over the work of *Khels*. The village economy prospered under the Khel system. The Ahom rules had organized the entire population into groups for services of all kinds. Each individual rendering such service was entitled to a certain quantity of land for his maintenance. As a remuneration for rendering services to the state, each *Paik* was a holding called 'Bari' Land for a house and garden; besides two 'Puras' of land called 'Goamatti'. In the event, however, of his services not being required each Paik was liable to a capitation tax of two or three rupees.

All lands occupied by the Paiks were registered as Pyker lands, and were inalienable from the Paik. At the same time these land were not hereditary. *Mels* or estates were created for the financial support to the members of the royal family. It gave rise to three hereditary estates as *Charing*, *Tipan* and *Namrup*. Mels were also granted to the sons and other near relatives of a reigning monarch.

The people of Assam can be divided into three ethnic groups namely the tribal population, the non-tribal population and the scheduled castes. The Tribals consist of different ethno-cultural groups such as the Kacharis (Bodos). The Miris, the Deoris, the Rabhas, the Nagas, the Garos, and the Khasis etc. The non-tribal groups include Ahoms, the Kayashtas, the Kalitas, the Morans, the Muttaks, and the Chutias, etc. The scheduled castes includes the Basfors, Baniyas, the Dhobis, the Hiras, the Kaibartas and the Namasudras etc.

The new immigration was mostly from Bengal, Bangladesh, Bihar, Uttar Pradesh, Nepal and Rajasthan. Another group was known as 'Baganias' who were brought from Bengal, Bihar, Orissa, and Madhya Pradesh by the British tea planters during the British rule. Some of the early settlers as Assam were of Aryan and Dravidian stock. The original inhabitants were known as the *Kiratas* of divergent tribal groups as mentioned in the *Mahabharata*. The fusion of divergent cultures of the Aryan, the Dravidians, the Austrics and the Mongoloid races now constitutes the state's composite culture.

Currently, though there is no Australoid population as such in any part of Assam, but recent anthropological researches support that Australoid elements are discernible not only among many tribal groups but also in certain Hindu caste groups of Assam. Most of the ancient Australoid traits were absorbed by the Mongoloids and the Caucasoids in due course of time. Now, it is very difficult to say who came first between the Mongoloid and the Caucasoid but by physical appearance they have both retained their features as separate groups though it is very difficult, if not impossible to distinguish them on the basis of individuals. For example, the Ahoms who figure so prominently in the history of Assam were a Mongoloid people, so are the small Buddhist people of Khamti, Tai Phake, Khamyang, Aiton and Turung in Upper Assam. Among the Assamese castes, the Brahmans and the Kshatriyas find mention in the records of Hiuen Tsang and are considered to be people Caucasoid origin. Since time immemorial, Assam has been the happy meeting place of people belonging to different ethnic groups, communities and cultural entities. Even the Brahmaputra Valley is an area rich with the contribution of different such groups most of whom got assimilated in the composite Assamese identity. To the south, in the Barak valley, Bengali-speaking people along with tribal communities have distinct identity. Another important group which deserves special mention is that of the tea garden community. During the second half of the Nineteenth Century, when the British planters started tea cultivation on a large scale in Assam, they were faced with the problem of labour. Hence, they brought in people from Orissa and Bihar and from as far as Tamil Nadu and Kerala. These people ultimately settled down in the state, and successive generations not only intermingled among themselves, but also assimilated much of the Assamese culture and customs to develop a lifestyle of their own. Some of them left the lea estates and found other occupations in the local society.

The Assamese people of today are in fact, the result of assimilation and integration of people of different racial stocks who migrated to Assam in course of time. The entire non-tribal population of Assam can be said to be concentrated in the Brahmaputra and the Barak Valleys. Constituting the majority in the state and the dominant populace in almost all the urban areas, their lifestyle is considerably modern and closer to the mainstream of the nation. They are the people who speak the Assamese language. The Hindus who constitute a majority among the non-tribals are divided into castes and sub-castes along the same lines as in the rest of the country though caste barriers are not as rigid here. Thus, we have the Brahmins and the Kshatriyas, and the Vaishyas and the Sudras. However, a majority of the non-tribal population of today were tribals of the past, who underwent the transformation by adopting Hinduism and its way of life gradually rising in status in the Hindu caste system.

The Ahoms themselves were absorbed into their Hinduized or Hindu Assamese-speaking subjects towards the end of their long reign. The non-tribals can again be divided on basis of their religion amongst whom the Muslims constitute the second largest group followed by the Christians, Sikhs and the Buddhists.

On their part the tribals have been divided into the hills tribes and the plains tribes according to geography of their habitation. A majority of the tribals practice animism with some ingredients of Hinduism. A considerable part of the tribal population has also adopted Christianity and on the rare occasion, Islam. Each of its 23 different primitive tribes exhibit distinct and exquisite ways of life. There are tribes like the Bodo Kacharis, Karbis and Lalungs which are purely patriarchal, and the Khasis, Jaintias and Garos which are strictly matriarchal. The Dimasas who while having a patriarchal system of family structure also have a system of almost parallel male and female clans which accords exclusive rights to women and the matriarchal system.

A number of tribes such as the Hmars, Rengma Nagas and Garos have a social institution called the Youth Dormitory called in different names in which the young males live away from their families and undergo education and training. Dormitories also serve as the centres of social work and are in some cases entrusted with the security of the village. The Zeme Nagas have separate dormitories both for males and females.

In the society, there is a gradual development of liberalism in religious system. The indigenous groups practice Animism, Tantricism, Brahminism and Vaishnavism. They also were practicing Tantric forms of rituals, until the advent of the new Vaishnavite religion formed by Shrimanta Sankardeva (1449-1568). The pristine form of Hinduism rose only when the Aryans arrived in Assam. The present Hindu caste system had emerged in the local society with the immigration of outsiders. Neo-Vaishnavism entered during the 15th century and is the dominant faith of the Assamese people at present. This is an open society based on the principles of liberalism. It allows the idol worshippers of Durga, Kali, Saraswati, and others to follow the Vaishnava faith. The Muslims started coming in the 13th century and built mosques in Assam. Christianity began to grow in the state since the time of the British rule and spread out to all corners of the eastern regions quickly. Caste system has never taken firm roots in the Assamese social stratification.

The majority of Hindus, practice different disciplines of religion. Sakti temples such as the Kamakhya shrine at Guwahati and the Kechaikhati temple at Sadiya stands testimony to a past in which tantricism was the predominant form of Hindu worship. This was followed by its modified form Saktism, a primitive faith which like tantricism worshipped the female form of God.

The revival of Vaisnava of the Middle Ages popularized by the great Vaisnavite saint Srimanta Sankardeva (1449-1568) who developed and propagated *Eka-sarana-namadharma* (a faith of allegiance to one God) which was part of the neo-Vaisnavite movement in India and is characterized by absence of the bizarre rituals practiced by the Saktas and the principle of equality which prepudiated all caste barriers. The Vaisnava

Traditional monastic dance during the Torgya festival.

Folk dance performance with artificial wild animals.

Offering being distributed at the Myko Festival.

Men performing dance in traditional dress in a festival.

Bihu dance in Progress.

Men and Woman engaged in Bihu dance in traditional dress.

Bridge in Assam.

Huchori Performance by Assamese
Singers and dancers in Rogali Bihu Festival.

Ladies engaged in folk dance.

Dance performance in a festival in traditional dress.

Folk dance in progress.

Ritual Dance, known as Rasa Dance, being performed during Hooly festival.

Numerous processions, one after another, during Behadiankhalam festival.

A lady in traditional dress to participate in a festival.

The Jaintia youths spreading sand during Behadiankhalam festival.

Khasi dance.

Cheraw dance during chapchar kut festival.

Girls are in festive mood.

Sarlamkai dance during Chapchar Kut festival

Children dance in a festival.

F

Men and women performing dance in traditional dress.

Nagas traditional dance during a festival

The Nagas dancing in traditional dress with their arms

The Nagas men and women, in a festive mood after the festival.

A Person is dancing in Panglhabsol festival.

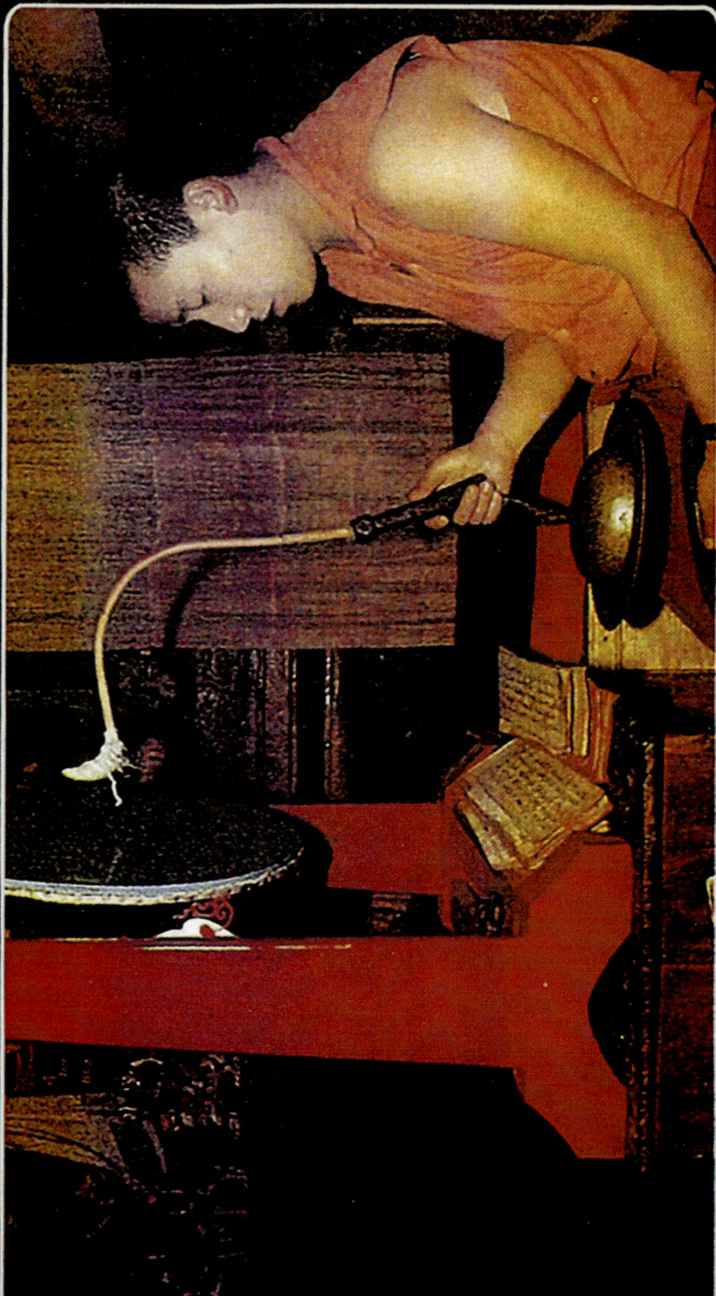

Alone Monk praying in the Monastery.

A man and woman in traditional dress in festive mood.

Women are dancing in Bumchu festival.

Hozagiri dance in progress during festival.

Boomani: A dance of Tripuri Community during festival

Men and women are dancing in traditional dress during festival.

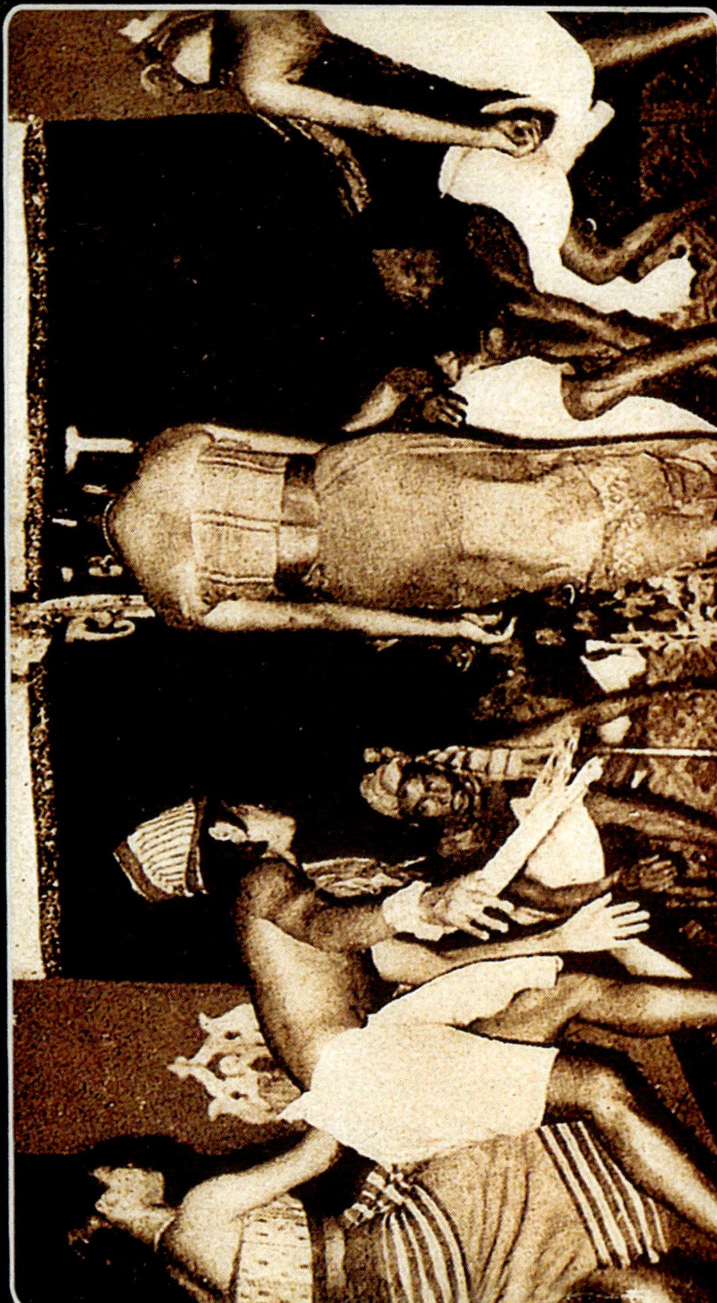

Garia a dance of Tripuri Community.

way Mahapurush Sri Sri Sankaradeva, as he is known in the State, composed hymns (*borgeet*), dance-dramas (*ankianaat*) and recitals, and with the help of his disciples, set up *sattras* (monasteries) and *namghars* (community prayer halls) for the propagation of the faith which soon gained a vast popularity in the regions of Assam, Manipur, Arunachal Pradesh and other states. Thus, Assam developed its own form of Vaisnavism which is today the predominant faith among the Hindus. So much so that *borgeets*, *ankianaats* and many other Vaisnavite art-forms and social customs and conventions are now considered to be integral parts of the Assamese culture. Saivaism which holds the procreative energy of males in reverence and is related to the worship of Lord Shiva as well as Saktaism are other forms of Hinduism still practiced in the State.

Christianity and Islam are the two other religions which have a considerable number of followers in Assam. The reformation movement by the Muslim missionary Shah Miran, known as *Ajan Fakir*, deserves special mention in this context. *Ajan Fakir* came to Assam from the Middle East about 200 years after the rise of Shankaradeva and found that the Muslims who had come and settled in the land as early as in the 13th Century A.D. were practicing a form of Islam somewhat distorted by elements of the local Hindu and tribal religion. Shah Miran, set out to reinforce Islamic ideals fundamentalism and religious practices, and composed religious songs (known as Jikirs and Jaris) in the spoken language, much in the same fashion as the *Borgeets* of Sankardeva. Very soon he gained popularity and gathered a large following and Zikirs and Jaris remain unique elements of Islam in Assam. There are scattered populations of Buddhists, Sikhs and Jains in different parts of the state notable among which are the Buddhists in the Khamti tribes and the Assamese Sikhs of Borkhola in the district of Nagaon.

Practice of Animism

However, among the tribals, all elements of the cult of fertility, head-hunting, human sacrifice, faith in reincarnation, ancestor worship and the rites connected with the dead, belief in heavenly bodies, magic and sorcery were indicated to their animistic belief. The existing ancient materials, though meager, explain these weird cults. It was definitely contributed to by the Austric and Tibeto-Burmans, and formed the basis of Tantricism in Assam and other neighbouring states which passed on into the Hindu and later into the Buddhist faiths. Much like the tribal communities, an Assamese household undergoes a period of pollution during childbirth, after the death of an inmate and during the menstruation of a woman member. Certain primitive rules are followed by the peoples concerned during the period of pollution. Even today, a person suffering from small pox puts his household under taboo. The worship of the goddess Sitala (smallpox) by the caste people has a parallel in the Assam, Meghalaya, Mizoram and Manipur tribal worship of snake. The stoppage of agricultural work on certain days by tribal communities is parallel with the Hindu restrictions on days like *Ekadasi* or *Sankranti*. In fact, most of the tribal agricultural rites lie at the foundation of the Assamese Hindu harvesting festival '*Bihu*' which in its origin was nothing but a combination of a solar cult and a cult of fertility, contributed alike by the Pre-Aryan and non-Aryan, such as Austric, Alpine and Tibeto-Burman races. In spite of the prevalence of so many Aryan and non-Aryan cults, there was much tolerance among their adherents. The temple ruins in the states indicate that at a single place, images of different deities were built on the same site. The best example is furnished by the shrines at Kamakhya (Guwahati) and Hajo (near Guwahati). Another important feature of the religious history of Assam is that many non-Aryan ruling families and tribes, particularly of the plains, were gradually brought within the fold of Hinduism and most of them had been bestowed with the divine ancestry. Thus, the Koch kings trace their origin from Siva and have gradually become completely Hinduised. The Kacharis were converted, and their rulers trace their origin from Bhima and Hidimba of the *Mahabharats*. The Chutiyas, who established their kingdom in the Sadiya region of upper Assam not later than the 13th century A.D., claimed their Hindu descent after conversion to Hinduism. The Ahoms who established their kingdom in upper Assam in the beginning of the 13th century A.D, traced their origin from Indra and within a short period of their settlement there, they adopted Hinduism.

Due to conversion and assimilation of the culture of the plains, the Hindu population increased, and this resulted in the fusion of different communities. Even though the inhabitants of both the hills and plains continued to profess different faith and the related customs, rites and rituals, the followers of all Hindu sects prospered equally well here. The rise of neo-Vaishnaism could not effectively wipe out the influence of the Tantric system. As per 1971 census, Hindus in Assam account for only 72.51 percent as against the all-India figures of 83 percent. The followers of Islam form 24.56 percent of the population. The religion next in numerical importance is Christianity, which constitutes 2.61 percent of the total population. Sikhism, Buddhism and Jainism together account for 0.32 percent of Assam's population. Shankardeva has left a deep impression on the culture, literature, religion and life style of the people of Assam. Sankardeva propagated Vaishnavism at a time when ritualism was gaining ground with occasional human sacrifices at the Shakta temples.

Customs of Arunachal Pradesh

The people of Arunachal are predominantly tribal in character and there are about 20 major tribes which are divided into a number of subtribes. The principla tribes are Adi, Apatani, Nishi, Tagin, Mismi, Khampti, Wancho, Tangsha, Noite, Singpho, Monpa, Sherdukpen and Aka. The major social and cultural events of the state are very much associated with the tribal life. They have many customs and traditions which link the state to the rest of the country and its ancient past. Even now the Brahmakund, which has hot springs, is visited by thousands of people every year in the winter month of *Pausha* for a bath. The waters of the spring were used for the coronation and anointment of the ancient Ahom kings of Assam. The Brahmakund is also called *Parashuram Kund* after the fiery sage who is said to have created a path in the mountains and, also the lake here.

The Adis are a major tribe inhabiting the West Siang district. The different sub-tribes of the Adis include Gallong, Janbe, Karka, Memba, Ashing, Bori, Bogum, Bagi, Pailibo, Minyong etc. Monship and Rashbeng, dormitories for boys and girls respectively, play an important role in the Adi society. Different sections of the Adis call these institutions by different names such as the Padams, and Dere etc. It is customary for boys and girls to become the members of their respective institutions when they attain the age of ten. They remain in their respective dormitories till their marriage. There is no restriction for the boys of different Monship to visit girls in their Rashbengs. In course of such visits if a boy and girl happen to get attracted to each other, negotiations are made between the boy's and the girl's parents. If approved by their parents, formal marriage take place according to their tribal custom. The bride after marriage usually continues to live with her parents till the birth of her first child. It is expected that groom in the mean time, would be able to construct a house of his own.

In the Adi society descent is traced through the father and the property devolves in the male line and the children belong to the fathers clan. If a child born in an extra-marital relation is a boy, he belongs to the father's clan and if it is a girl, she belongs to mother's clan. The elder son generally set up their separate households, even while the father is alive. They have equal shares in the parents property. They do not dispute with the youngest brother who stays with the parents and inherits the ancestral house and property by common consent. The widowed mother is considered a special responsibility of the eldest son but in practice, she prefers to live with the youngest son under the roof of her deceased husband's home.

All important decisions of tribal, social and communal matters as well as the disputes are tried and settled by the council called as *Kebang*. The various kebangs are Bane Kebang, Bango Kebang, Bogum Bokang Kebang and Atek Kebang. In Bane Kebang, all the male members of the village can partake and express their opinion freely. Bango kebang consists of the head Gams of the number of villages and it has one secretary and also some funds to manage. It mainly deals with inter-village disputes and development problems. Atek Kebang is for the settlement of particular cases of disputes. The *Bogum Bokang Kebang* is a federal organization—its jurisdiction extends to the whole district of Siang. The social customs and relations of inter-village, inter-bango disputes, political and economic changes affecting their life etc are settled in this Kebang. The Bogum Bokong adopt resolutions and recommends measures to the government for meeting them.

The *Akas* are inhabitants of the south-eastern part of Kameng district of the state. Their main concentration is in the Thrizine area. The name '*Aka*' is given to them by the plains people while they call themselves as 'Hrusso'. The word 'Aka' denotes 'painted' and their customs of painting the faces profusely, served as a distinctive mark. The Aka houses varies from medium to tall.

Consist a long structure on a raise platform, about six feet above the ground and divided into two compartments by a partition wall. The space between the raised platform and ground serves as a shed for pigs and goats of the household. The house is a work of bamboo and wood, bamboo sheets forming the floor, the wall and the roof and wooden logs serving as the main pillars over which the structure of the house is created. The roof is usually thatched and often supported by bamboo sheets. The four walls of the house are usually high.

The Aka women wear a number of silver ornaments as well as beads necklaces. The common silver ornaments are melu-a flat shaped ornament worn over the chest, rombin-the ear bulbs, gichlu-the earrings and gejjul-the wristlets. Wealthy women wear a fillet of silver chain-work called *lenchhi*. An ancestral necklace, called *aescheri* is worn invariably by women and often by men. It forms a necessary part of gift which a brides parents give at her marriage. Women tattoo their faces in a pattern of a straight line running from below the forehead to the chin where it bifurcates into two directions. No other part of the body are tattooed.

Aka society freely practices slavery. The slaves are known as *Khulo*. The *Khulo* have to till the soil, look after the palm and the jhum-field, the cattle and the household and do all such menial jobs as their masters may order them to do.

In Arunachal Pradesh, the social organization is concerned with communal activities, relations and behaviour. It can be seen through their social institutions like family, marriage, clan and the dormitory systems. The smallest unit of the society is the family consisting of father, mother, the spouses and their children. Mixed extended families are commonly found in most of the communities in Arunachal Pradesh. However, nuclear and vertically and horizontally extended families are also found. When a family breaks up, custom demands that either the youngest or the eldest son continues to live the parental house to support the family and his old parents. Sometimes, even after marriage, other sons stay on with the parents till they have two or three issues.

According to custom, in some cases, the delivery cannot take place in the father's house. All members of a family in the same household take their meals from a common hearth. The food is cooked by the mother, or by the wife of the eldest son if the mother is too old. All movable and immovable property such as cultivated land, bamboo groves, palm leaves, gardens, livestock, granaries, utensils and ornaments are held commonly by the family. The father who is the head of the family is only the titular owner of the property. The final authority over the property is invested in the father and is inherited by the eldest or youngest son, or by all sons equally after his death. The women have no claim over family property, except the articles given to them when they get married. Polyandrous families are prevalent among the Buddhist communities like the Monpas.

In the state almost all tribes have a number of clans denoted by local categories. Some of the communities have sub-clans, for example, the Tangsas which are not connected with totemic objects, but are ancestral clans. Each tribe traces its descent from a single ancestor, a semi-mythical figure. The subsidiary ancestors are the founders of distinct clans. The clan's function is to regulate the marriage system. Flouting clan endogamy is considered to be a heinous crime and traditionally punishable. The clans and sub-clans are exogamous. In the past, among the tribals the settlement pattern of the villages depended on the distribution of clans which are noticeable among the Singphos at present. The social organization of the Noctes is greatly influenced by the traditional chieftainship system. Two distinct classes are found among them—the chief and his kinsmen form one class, while the commoners form the other. Within these two main classes there are different clans.

Similarly, the social organization of the Wanchos is controlled by a traditional chieftainship system. There are four classes in their society (in descending order): Wangham (the chiefs), Wangsa (the small chiefs), Wangsu (the intermediate class) and Wangpan (the commoners).

The tribes are endogamous, but clan, phratry or moiety exogamy is practiced strictly. Intra-clan marriage is considered a serious crime. If any one violates this rule he or she will not only be excommunicated but also be exterminated by the society, except in the case of the Lisus.

Marriages are generally confined to the same or particular villages. Monogamy is the general rule, but polygynous marriages are prevalent among the tribal chiefs of the Noctes and Wanchos. Some cases of polyandrous marriages are found among the Monpas highlanders and some other sections of the Buddhist communities. Mostly negotiated and love marriages are practiced among the communities. There is no fixed age of marriage. Sororate and levirate marriages are also prevalent. Bride price is a common practice among the tribals and is generally paid in form of mithun, its horns and other simple articles. Marriage with the cross-cousin (specially mother's brothers' daughter) is preferred in many of the communities. Divorce is allowed on payment of a fine and both the spouses have the right to seek divorce among the Noctes, Wanchos and most of the Tangsa sub-groups, Adis and Mishmis it is not permissible among the Deoris, Tikhaks and Mukloms.

The communities allow a tremendous of freedom and licence to young boys and girls who can mix freely with each other provided they observe the rules of clan exogamy and avoid incest. The boys and girls of the different clans select their mates freely and meet each other generally in the place where young girls sleep. This unrestricted mixing helps them in selecting their life partners. The dormitory also provides a place to learn the art of tribal living in an informal manner. It gives an opportunity to young unmarried boys and girls for courtship prior to proposing for marriage. Among the Singphos, when the girl attains puberty she is segregated from the family. She is then provided with a separate room called *pinta-khak* in the house. The girl's dormitory or *pinta-khak* is always situated at the end of the house so that the girl and her suitors may enter without being noticed by any member of the family. Among the Noctes, the boy's dormitory is called *pang*, but the girl's dormitory is very rare, though not unheard of. The Wancho grown-up boys also sleep in dormitories called *morung*. There is no separate dormitory for the girls, but they sleep in the houses of widows who are not the blood relations. Each Wancho village has several *morungs* for boys. Among the sub-groups of the Tangsas, the Mukloms have a girls' dormitory. In the Adi society also the *moshup* (bachelors' dormitory) is a very important institution. It is not only a training centre for all practical purposes but also the centre and upholder of cultural traits. The institution is called by different names by the different sub-groups of the Adis. The Minyong tribals call it *dere*, the Padams term it *moshup* and among the Milangs and other allied groups the institution is known as *ngaptek*. The Boris and Ashings call it *bango*. Generally, the *moshup* is built in the centre of the village from where different approaches to it can be watched and guarded by the armed youths. The *moshup* is used as a sleeping house by all young men from the age of 10 till they take wives to their homes. There are a number of *merums* (fireplaces) in a *moshup*. Each *merum* is under the supervision of a senior boy who is responsible for the maintaining discipline in his *merum* and is empowered to punish any defaulter. The *moshup* is used for holding different types of meetings, especially those of the *kebang*. The dormitories are also used for feasts and festivals on different occasions. During some festivals, girls are allowed to dance inside the *moshup*. Like the Mukloms, the Adis have a dormitory for girls called *rasheng*, usually a small hut with only one square room with a fireplace in the centre. The adolescent and unmarried girls of the village sleep in their respective clan *rashengs*. These remain unoccupied during the day as the girls return to their parental houses early in the morning. Like the *moshups*, each *rasheng* is under the supervision of a senior and experienced girl and is the training institution for spinning, weaving, knitting, dancing, singing and discipline. Young boys from different *moshups* come and join the girls in the *rashengs* at night and mates are selected in the process. In Adi society marriage succeeds the selection of a life partner by the boys and the girls during their stay in the *moshup* and *rasheng*. Thus, *moshup* and *rasheng*, among other things, play an important role in matrimony.

Customs of Meghalaya

Meghalaya is the home of the Tribal communities especially the Khasis, Jaintias. Mikirs and Cacharis, who are said to have inhabited the mountainous region prior to the Christian era. These tribes migrated into the north-east who belonged to the Indo-Chinese linguistic stock, the Mon-Khmer and Tibeto-Burman. The Khasis came from the Khasis and Jaintias. The Tibeto-Burman sub-family were the Naga, Kukichin and Bodo. The Bodos were later sub-divided into small linguistic groups such as Chutiyas Dimasa, Garo, Kachari, Mechs, Lalung, Rabha, and Tippea. The British occupied the Garo Hills in 1872. The tribal district council was established. The tradition among the tribals was kingship. The earliest Jaintia Raja is said to have ruled from 1500 AD. They were influenced by the Hindu culture and customs. The British influence in Meghalaya extended with the improvement of the landscape, development of roads communication.

The state is dominated by three principal groups of tribals. The Garo in the east and west Garo hills, the Khasi-Pnar in the east and west Khasi hills and the Jaintia hills. They follow primarily a matrilineal system. The Khasi group belongs to the Mon-Khemar sub-family of the Austro group of migrants. The Garo groups is part of the greater Bodo Kacheri stock both by ethnic group and language. Their present location enabled them to maintain many of their traits and characteristics. A common cultural tradition of all these tribes is the matriarchal law of inheritance. In the matrilineal system, property and succession of family position passes from the mother to the youngest daughter. For long, the tribes practiced shifting cultivation but are gradually moving to more settled ways of life.

Khasi and Garo are the principal languages and, together with Jaintia and English, are the official languages. The Khasi, Garo and the Jaintia cultural traits and ethnic origins remain distinctive, mainly due to their long geographical isolation. The Khasi and Jaintia trace their ancestry to the Mongolian race. The Garo, on the other hand, belong to the Tibeto-Burman race and are also called Achik. They originally predominated in the Garo Hills. In 19th century, To British travelers the Garos appeared as bloodthirsty savages. Like the other Meghalayan tribes, the Garo lived in permanent villages with the headman or *nokma* as leader. The British moved into the area in the early 19th century, when Burmese incursions became more frequent and France emerged as a rival colonial power in Indochina. Since 1826 to 1836, all the small tribal principalities in the region were incorporated into British dominions. But the principalities and their tribals, resenting the loss of autonomy and intrusion of outsiders, frequently rebelled. A prominent feature of society in this region is the comparative freedom and licences that women enjoy albeit in different degrees, a trait more characteristic in the Mongoloid races of South-East Asia. Just as North-East Indian society can be classified as either Aryan-based or Mongoloid. Within the so-called Mongoloid communities, distinction must be made between those that are matrilineal as in Meghalaya, and those that are patrilineal as in the rest of the tribal areas of the north-east.

The practice of bride-price does not exist in a matrilineal society like that of the Garos and Khasi, Pnars presumably because of its incompatibility with a system in which the woman plays a more important and dominant role in the social system than the man. This is often exaggerated and women themselves would be the last to arrogate to themselves the role of matriarchs. To the uninitiated, the idea that they 'rule the roost' is a favourite one and others are led to believe that here, woman lay down the law for the rest of the family to follow. Women is accorded respect as one through whom the race or more precisely the clan is propagated, but due to her commitments as mother and housewife are a fulltime occupation. Responsibilities relating to regulation of the family are entrusted to menfolk. However, among the Garos, male blood relations or Mahari exercise control over affairs of the family and even in matters effecting women. In settlement of marriage, for instance, women are not consulted though male-in-laws often are. In relation to property though, it is inherited in female line. It is always managed by the male Mahari.

In the tribe of the Khasi-Pnar, household responsibilities are shared between woman's brother and husband. The father earns for his own wife and children but in matters affecting the clan or the family, such as the arrangement of marriages, management of ancestral property and performance of religious duties, it is the brother who makes the final decisions though generally in consultations with other members of the family. Thus there is a virtual three fold division of family responsibility-the mother looks after the hearth and home, the husband provides for the necessities of life of his wife and children and the brother attends to the business affairs that come before the family. A man does not forego membership in his own clan after marriage. His position in his wife's house is that of 'being in it, but not of it'. The impact of modernism and of other cultures has no doubt eroded the maternal uncle's authority but, by and large the convention is still honoured.

However, in Khasi society, the husband is isolated from his wife and children in such social matters. In non-Christian families, even in death, his bones must not lie with those of his wife and children. Only to be buried a separate ossuary with those of his maternal or blood relations. In well-organised families, the duties of the husband and those of the brother are clearly defined. Troubles, if and when they arise, are caused by intrusion of one into the sphere that properly belongs to the other. This isolation of the husband from the wife's family is carried to a greater extent among the Pnars, especially in the traditional families. Often the husband may only be at his wife's home during the night. By morning, he is out to return to his maternal home. There alone, he can act freely.

By and large in Meghalaya society, women enjoy great freedom and independence. Many of them look after their own interest and earn their livelihood with success. Although as a rule they have no direct say in communal matters, in their own families, they exert a good deal of influence. The custom of "*nok-na*" among Garos or Khadduh among Khasi-Pnars confers general advantage upon the community in that at least in theory it assures protection to every member of the family. The important features of Garo religious customs are animal and birds sacrifice and consumption of rice-beer. They offer animal sacrifice with the hope of curing diseases, for seeking protection from natural hazards and for a good harvest. It is through remembrance and offerings that they renew their relationship with the spirits. Sacrifices and offerings are made at the sacrificial altar. These altars are built of bamboo and leaves, but their form and structure differ according to the spirit to whom the offering is made. When the offering is made at the sacrificial altar, blood of the animal or bird is smeared on it. The village priest *kamal* performs the sacrifice in a ritually prescribed manner. Normally, the priest receives no reward for his work, but sometimes he receives food and drink for his services. Any member of the village, proficient in performing religious rites and rituals, can be engaged as a priest.

Generally, the religious beliefs of different groups of non-Christian Garos appear relatively uniform, but the ceremonies performed are varied. Christianisation of the Garo began only after the British advent in the Garo Hills during the mid-nineteenth century. American Baptist missionaries were the first to establish their Mission in the Garo Hills in 1864 the Roman Catholic Mission was set up at Tura in 1933, and the Seventh Day Adventist mission at Rajasimla, in 1954. The present day Garo have become Christians of one sect or the practice of traditional religious customs, rites and supplication of the spirits or gods and have adopted Christianity in its pristine form. They attend church services on Sunday and prayer meetings on the other days. Many of them also observe Sunday as the day of rest. The non-Christian Garos observe major festivals and rituals at different stages of the *jhum* cultivation cycle. Their agricultural season starts with the observance of *De'nbitsia* ceremony (*de'n* means cut *bilsia* means year). This marks the completion of the preparation of the new *jhum* fields. This ceremony is performed by the tribals in the *nokma* houses with sacrifice of a goat on the village altar. Afterwards, villagers join in the feast, beat gongs and some of them perform dances. *Wangala* is considered to be the most important of all the Garo. Festival held to propitiate *Misi sajong* the god of agriculture and other gods at the closing of the *Jhum* cycle, usually in

October and November. This is the most joyous celebration of the year, in which sacrifices are made for a good harvest. This celebration lasts for many days and is marked by the drinking of rice-beer, feasting, music, dancing and merry-making. A few other important agricultural ceremonies are also performed in some Garo villages. *Agalmaka* is celebrated after the burning of the *jhum* fields. *Mismua* is performed just before the paddy starts ripening. *Ahaia*, is held after the rice harvest has been completed. Music and dance form an integral part of the rites and rituals of the Garos. They perform different kinds of dances on festive occasions. Styles and forms of dance vary according to the nature of the festival. They have a variety of musical instruments, line drums (known as *dama, kram, nadil* and *nagara*), trumpets (called *adil* and *singga*) and flutes. Most of their musical instruments are made of forest products.

Mizo Customs

The origin of the Mizos, like those of many other tribes in the North Eastern India is shrouded in mystery. They are generally accepted as part of a great Mongoloid wave of migration from China and later moved out to India to their present habitat. Perhaps, the Mizos came from Shinlung or Chhinlungsan located on the banks of the river Yalung in China. They first settled in the Shan State and moved on to Kabaw Valley to Khampat and then to the Chin Hills in the middle of the 16th century. The earliest Mizos who migrated to India were called as Kukis, the second wave of immigrants were called New Kukis. The Lushais were the last of the Mizo tribes migrate to India.

The process of the consolidated of the British administration in tribal dominated area in Assam started in 1919 when Lushai Hills along with some other hill districts was declared a Backward Tract under government of India Act.

One of the beneficial result of Missionary activities under the British rule was the spread of education. The missionaries introduced the Roman script for the Mizo language and formal education in the public education system. The cumulative result is high percentage 95% which is considered to be highest in India. The Mizos area distinct community and the social unit was the village. Around it revolved the life of a Mizo. Mizo Village is usually founded on the top of a hill with the chief's house at the centre and the bachelor's dormitory called *Zawlbuk* prominently. In a way the focal point in the village was the *Zawlbuk* where all young bachelors of the village slept. *Zawlbuk* was the training ground, and indeed, the cradle wherein the Mizo youth was shaped into a responsibility adult member of the society.

However, the fabric of social life in the Mizo society has undergone tremendous changes over the years. Before the British moved into the hills, for all practical purposes the village and the clan formed units of Mizo society. The Mizo code of ethics or Dharma moved around "*Tlawmngaihna*", an untranslatable term meaning on the part of everyone to be hospitable, kind, unselfish and helpful to others. *Tlawmngaihna* to the Mizo stands for the compelling moral force which finds expression in self-sacrifice for the service of the others. The old belief, Pathian is still use in term God till today. The Mizos have been enchanted to their new-found faith of Christianity with so much dedication and submission that their entire social life and thought process been transformed and guided by the Christian Church Organisation and their sense of values has also undergone drastic changes.

The Mizos area close-knit society with no class distinction and no discrimination on grounds of sex. Ninety percent of them are cultivators and the village exists like a big family. Birth of a child, marriage in the village and death of a person in the village or a community feast arranged by a member of the village are important occasions in which the whole village is involved.

The Mizos are a *Mongloid* race who originally came from the Chin hills of neighbouring Myanmar (formerly Burma). *Mizo* is a generic term and means a man from the hills and denotes the Mizoram is essentially a mountaineous area. They are the people getting the best possible education but also the process of modernization has enveloped all aspects of life in the tribal Mizo society. But it still has its traditional dances and festivals which are preserved through the times. The dances are common to the Mizos, the Lakhers and Pawis, the main tribes in the state along with the Chakmas. Although modernity has its impact and many people are also aware of the harmful effects of smoking, the Mizos continue to be much attached to their smoking habit. Both men and women smoke although the pipes for the two are different. Unlike the *hukkah* in north India for men, where water is used for filtering tobacco smoke the pipes in Mizoram are designed that way for women while the men smoke tobacco directly from their pipes.

The Mizo marriages are generally arranged by parents. Among the Mizos there is yet another interesting custom of inheritance. The youngest son inherits all the movable and immovable property of the father. The elder sons are supposed to move out of the parental home after marriage. The youngest son has the responsibility of looking after the parents in their old age. There was no system of making a will in the Mizo society but in the Inheritance Act was passed by the Mizo district council in 1956 under which a will could be made by any property holder. This was not the case under the old custom but gradually it has been accepted by the society. The dead are buried and memorial stone are erected by the successors. Hymns and dirges are sung in the house of the bereaved for about a week. The Mizos are well advanced and have taken up occupations and services in neighbouring states and at the centre. They can thus be seen in sufficient numbers in places far and near their state. Wearing of hats is common and these are made of bamboo and cane look like country caps worn by cricket-players. The villagers carry an artistically designed and hand-woven shoulder bag in which they carry their tobacco pipe and other equipment. Weaving is an important occupations for the people in Mizoram as in the whole of north-east India and colourful shawls and warps are woven and worn with great care. There are a number of laudable persons among the Mizos who like the self-help and voluntary work which an individual is expected to contribute to the village for works of common benefit. In the way, common halls for the village community, water points and inter-village paths are builts. Helping someone in distress is an obligation on all the Mizos.

The custom of *Zawlbuk* was mostly prevalent in Lushai and Pawi villages. The Raltes did not have this system but adopted it after coming under influence of the Lushais. The Paites did not have *zawlbuk* as such, but young men would sleep in the verandah front porch of the houses of influential men of the village who would provide adequate sleeping platform for the purpose. They would help their host in construction and repairs of his house and also in his cultivation, who in return would occasionally give them a feast. However, the Lakhers did not have zawlbuk. The young men, however, did not sleep in their parents house. They would sleep in the house of the maidens whom they were courting.

Customs of Tlawmngaihna

The Mizos have an excellent custom called *Tlawmngaihna* by which one was duty bound to help others. Under this custom everyone in the society was required to be courteous and considerate and to help others always and every time, irrespective of one's inconvenience. Everyone would try to surpass others in unselfishness and cooperation. This was an excellent custom in the daily life of a Lushai. For example, while travelling together, if one of the party would fall sick, all would wait for him to recover and would then resume the journey together.

With the arrival of Christianity, the institution of *Zawlbuk* and the custom of *Tlawmngaihna* gradually died. The Christian in a village would not join a *Zawlbuk* and hence when the majority in a village become Christians, the *zawlbuk* in the village languished and ultimately become extinct. Similar was the fate of tlawmngaihna. When the people were turning away from their old beliefs, the customary network of duties and obligations was also stopped. New structures and institution like village churches, schools, medical centres and administrative centres etc, were coming up. The people started depending, individually and collectively, more on the church and the Government for guidance and help even in their daily need.

Customs of Bawi

In the Mizo hills, social system permitted was partly a type of slavery and partly a system of social security. Amongst the Lushais, this was the system of the *bawi*. Under this system a chieftain would have a number of dependants (*bawis*) who would remain with the chief, work for him and help him in all respects and in turn would get food and shelter from him. He could free himself from the obligation to the chieftain only under certain conditions, usually on giving a *mithun* or payment of certain amount. Apart from the *bawis*, there was another class of dependants consisting of the persons captured during raids. They were called *sals*. The victors in a raid would slaughter the adult warriors and old women of the defeated village. The marriageable women and children would be held captives and would be treated well in the captor's family.

However, the Lakher counterpart of the Lushai *bawi* was *Sei*. Unlike the Lushais among whom only the chiefs could have *pawis*, the Lakhen custom allowed anyone to keep one's captive as a *Sei*. A *Sei* was sometimes allowed to set up his own household. But the obligation was hereditary. A Sei could acquire property of his own, but his master could always take a share of the crops or animals of the *sei*.

With the British administration prohibiting raids by the Mizo chieftains, the custom of *tuklut bawi*, *sal* and *sei* ceased to have new entrants. The custom was of mutual assistance, help and obligation and not of slavery. The *bawi* was afterwards treated as a part of the family and could be adopted in the family by the *saphun* (adoption) ceremony.

The *bawi* custom gradually died out. The administration liberally allowed freedom of the *bawis* on usual cash payment. A *bawi* was allowed to leave at will and the chieftain only had the remedy to sue for the compensation.

As the Mizos have almost all become Christians, most of their ancient beliefs and practices, rites, rituals and sacrifices have disappeared. Most of their ancient institutions in the wake of new upsurges, as it is with Christians, have become extinct. Some of their arts of dance and music as social traditions have now been renewed. New substitutes for Christian festivals have also been started. For example, the Christmas festival prolonging to the New Year's week is now observed in the old community spirit, but now singing Christian tunes either translated or indigenous compositions have been more dominant. Prayers and services in the community are also held.

Other entertainment programmes are necessary for the observance on these joyous occasions. There are also the other cultural programmes and exhibitions being displayed occasionally. Community spirit and team undertakings appear to have their stronghold.

Customs of Manipur

The state of Manipur has an area of 8456 square miles of which the hills surrounding the valley at the centre is about nearly 7806 square miles. The valley is the habitat of the largest community known as the Meithei. Ethnically, culturally and linguistically the Meithei is an organized and consolidated community having distinctive traits in the region. They can be clearly distinguished from the other people living in the hills. The hill areas of Manipur are contiguous to Burma in the east and south-east, Assam in the west and Mizoram in the south-west. The land-route connecting Manipur valley with Burma, Cachar District (Assam) and Nagaland lie across these hills. Still very little inter-communication existed inside the hilly region, between the hills and the Manipur valley as well as between the hills and the people of neighbouring states. This is responsible for their isolation and the material backwardness.

In Manipur, the sons of the hills consist of 28 tribes. Among those the Thadou, the Tangkhul, the Kabui, the Mao, the Paite, the Hmar and the Kacha Naga form numerically sizeable tribes. Ethnically those 28 tribes of Manipur may be broadly classified into two groups (1) the Naga and (2) the non-Naga (Kuki-chin) stocks.

The important Naga tribes of Manipur include the Tangkhul, the Roungmei (Kabui), the Mao, the Kacha Naga (Liangmei), the Maram, the Maring, the Anal, the Monsang, the Lamgang, the Moyon, the Zemi and the Thangal. Besides, there are also some Angami and Sema Nagas. The Zemis Liangmeis (Kacha Nagas) and the Ruongmeis (the Kabui) who are the allied tribes. They dwell in the Tamenglong sub-division in the western hills of Manipur. The *Mao* (now called the *Paomata*), the Maram and the Thangals live in the northern sub-division of Mao and sadar hills bordering Nagaland. The Tangkhuls live in the Ukhrul sub-division in the south-west bordering Burma. The

Marings, the Moyon, the Monsang, the Lamgang and the Anals dwell in the Tengnoupal sub-division in the South-west bordering Burma. Originally the Moyon, the Monsang, the Lamgang changed their affiliation and are now included in the Naga-tribes. These tribes in addition to their Kuki-chin traits have assimilated some Naga characteristics in their ways of life. Thus they form a bridge between the Naga and the Kuki-chin tribes of Manipur.

Among the non-naga, Kuki-chin tribes of Manipur are:

Kuki-chin Tribes—The Aimol, the Chothe, the Chiru, the Kom, the Purum, the Gangte, the Paite, the Simte, the Thadou, the Vaiphei, the Hmar, the Zou, the Ralte and the Any Mizo. Ethnologically they belong to the Kuki-chin family who dwell in the Sadar Hills, Churachandpur, Jiribam and Tengnoupal sub-divisions of Manipur.

In Manipur, the Naga tribes have ethnic and cultural affinities with the people of Nagaland, whereas the Non-Naga tribes belonging to the Kuki-chin family have affinity with the Chins of Burma and the Mizos of the Mizoram territory. All these tribes belonging to both the stocks have their kith and kin scattered in Cachar, Assam valley and in upper Burma. Many tribal villages have sprang up in the Imphal valley also. The latest trend among the educated and well-to-do Naga-tribes is to build houses in Imphal to enjoy amenities of modern town life. The Kuki-chin tribes have their maximum concentration in Churachandpur which is also fast developing into a modern township, and in order of importance second only to Imphal, the capital of Manipur state.

In the state, the Nagas have varying physical features. The *Tangkhuls* are tall and muscular having some Caucasian traits. Some of the Maos, the Marams and the Thangals are of middle height, but the majority of them have short stature. They have close affinity with the Chakhesangs and the Angamis. The Zemis, the Liangmies and the Ruongmeis are short and muscular. The Liangemeis are rather athletic, while the Zemis are sturdy. The Marings, the Anals, the Moyons, the Monsangs nagar etc. have some Burmese features. Some of them are slim and short. Among the Nagas there is a wide variation in complexion ranging from dark brown to golden yellow. With some exceptions, the Aimols, the Chirus, the Koms, the Purums, the Chothes are on an average shorter than the Naga tribes. They are slim and dark. Other non-Naga tribes are sturdy, muscular and dark complexioned though brown features are also found. Oblique eye, prominent cheek-bone, snub-nose, broad forehead etc. make them distinct. Their chieftains are fairer than their followers.

The social, cultural and customery life of the hill-men is very much influenced by their geographical environment. They set up their villages on the top of slopes of high hills covered with forests. In selecting sites for their villages they must have been guided by two considerations: security and health. Frequent inter-tribal raids made them security conscious. Hill-tops are not easily accessible and they allow distant views which help in detecting enemy movements from the far off. These hill-tops with abundant sun-light and air are more hygienic than the damp, insect-ridden thickly wooded river valleys.

But the Kuk-chins being newcomers preferred the foot of the hills and the fertile valleys in the hills. Search for hunt and fertile soils have still kept them on the move. Hill-men depend much on their neighbouring dense forests. Each village has its forest owned collectively by the villagers which supplies them bamboo for their houses, fire-wood for their hearth and offers them a hunting ground for wild games. Hill-man is assured of his livelihood so long as he is in the forest. But life in the hills devoid of connecting roads with other parts of the country is bound to be insular and stagnant. Hill-men living in isolation for centuries in their tiny villages developed a fear complex even in respect of the hill-men of other villages. Inter-village ill-feelings and inter-tribal fueds which continued as an unpleasant characteristic of tribal life even down to the British period may be explained as the outcome of their insular attitude and fear complex for which the topography of their habitat is entirely responsible.

Naga Customs

The Nagas of Nagaland lead essentially a community life. In the agricultural field they go together, work together and come back together. Even when they have to go to the jungle to collect firewood or wild fruits tubers, roots and leaves they go several persons together. Thus in every sphere of life they work together. Village is their social unit. Within the village, khel based on clan is a sub-unit. Then comes family as a unit. If any untoward incident happens to any member of the family, rest of the family members consider it their own misfortune and share the consequences together. If a member of the *khel* is in dispute or feud with another person of another *khel*, the entire *khel* people will go in to support his own *khel* man provided it is not a criminal case, and try to rescue him from the perilous situation, if any. Similarly when a villager is involved in any serious trouble with people of other village, the entire village will go out in support of him. Thus everywhere they stand united on the basis of village, *khel* or family. And, of course, in the wider perspective they have got such unity of the tribe itself which we call bribalism. There are also community hunting and community fishing expeditions.

A Naga cultivated his land and that brings his sustenance and the other necessities of life. He is concerned with his day-to-day life and there was no thought of becoming richer or having a thought for future. His life revolved round on food and drink and, of course, sex was there. The Nagas used to eat meat to heart's content when it was available and were ready to go without it for several days when not available, rather than consuming it in small quantity and saving something for the days ahead. The life centred on 'present' only and there was less thought for future. It was not needed because it was presumed that the sons and daughters would be able to take care of themselves by cultivating *jhum* fields, as he himself had done. Therefore it was the time of 'living present' only and the philosophy of life was 'eat drink and be merry' when the sun shines.

Having gone to the field, generally *jhum*, the people work there the entire day taking rest at noon only. They take their mid-day meal in the field house. Often they carry cooked rice and curry from home and some times they cook meat and rice there also. The people like the field and it is the play ground of the people and the field house is the second home. This is of course true about *jhum* field, not terrace, because there is not much work in the terrace and moreover it is wet and so cannot be used as the playground. However, there are sometimes field houses in the terrace field also.

After the day's back-breaking work, the people come back home in the evening, little before sunset and sometimes, during heavy pressure of work, after sunset also. They carry home fire-wood and vegetables as well as wild leaves for pigs feed. On their way back, the women and children stay in front of the single file and men with spears and guns keep the rear. While going to fields the reverse thing happens, that is the armed men go in front and women and children keep the rear. It is all because of traditional precaution against enemy head hunters who may be lurking in the thick jungle and it still continues.

After arriving at home, they cook the evening meal and eat it and after that they are free for family talk and village gossip. This is the time when people visit friends and relatives within the village and the youngsters to the youths' dormitories. They also discuss village politics. Some of the important topics of their discussion are the ancient lores of heroism, head-hunting, inter-tribal and inter-village feuds etc. and in the modern days it is politics too. The people of Nagaland go to bed early—by 7 or 8 p.m. and get up early in the morning.

In olden days, '*morung* or bachelors' dormitory was the fortress of the village where all the unmarried youngmen of the village used to sleep in their respective *morung*, khel-wise, and it was the centre of all the village activity, but nowadays in the times of more policing and spread of education the institution, has fallen to disuse. *Morungs* are still there in numerous villages where it had been but it is only a house now and seldom youths sleep there. Where there was morung system, there was also a custom of unmarried girls gathering in a particular place. Morung system is there among the Konyak, Phom, Chang, Sangtam, Ao, Lotha etc tribes as well as it is found in some villages of the Angami, Chakhesang, Zeliangroung etc tribes but not in all their villages. Unmarried girls used to gather in the outer-room or porch of the house of a socially respectable person of the same *khel* to which the girls belonged to. The unmarried youths used to come there and sing and joke with the girls. Among the Konyak tribals, the youths used to slip away taking a girl each into the jungle and the girls used to come back late at night or early in the morning. It is still in practice. But all these practices are fading away due to education and spread of Christianity among them. In most of the morungs there is a logdrum which the people beat to announce any important thing.

In the modern times, education being considered essential, and every village having at least one primary school, the children do not go to the *jhum* field with their parents, but later, when the school is over by 10 or 11 a.m. Children going to middle or High School, of course, do not go to the field because they attend the school generally from 9 a.m. to 2 p.m. They go to field only on any holiday, other than Sunday, and that also reluctantly, because the modern school-going children are averse to physical work dubbing the agriculture as debaring. Notably that majority of the people being Christian, they do not go to field or do not undertake any hard work on Sundays.

A vast majority of the Christian converts of Nagaland belong to the denomination of American Baptist Mission though later there had come other denominations also such as Roman Catholic, Pentecostalist, Protestants, and Presbyterians Assembly of God etc. Recently, the Roman Catholics, have made a sound footing and they have started many schools, almost one in every administrative centre. After becoming Christians, the Naga people have given up some of their primitive tribal beliefs and practices but since old habits and traditions die hard some of them still persist or have modified to suit the Christian philosophy. One of them is the belief in spirit. Though in the villages, the belief in the spirit still continues, the educated Christians call it *satan*. Another is personification in animals, or wraith. It is believed that some people can assume the form of tiger and if that tiger is injured or has killed a persons who has taken the form of the tiger will get injured or killed as the case may be. This belief is common among the tribal Christians converts. Besides, there is the magic cure of illness. In some villages are found some medicine men or women who claim to cure the illness of a person by drawing out pebbles, pieces of bones, and chewed leaves etc. from the body of the sick person without leaving any mark where it came from. Apparently this is a magical cure and the village believe in it.

During the British rule, prior to establishing the Mission Centre at Impur by Rev. E.W. Clark, one Godhula, a committed Assamese Evangelist, went to Ao area and established his Evangelistical Centre at Malungyimchen and started working there in 1871. The first Ao convert was a person from Merenkong village and was baptized in 1851. The efforts of Shri Godhula bore fruits when nine Ao Nagas were subsequently converted and baptized at Sibsagar in Assam valley. Rev. E.W. Clark went to join Shri Godhula in 1876. Mrs. Clark also assisted them in every possible manner in the spread of Christianity. From then onward, conversion of the tribals picked up momentum and the primitive traditional customs such as drinking of rice beer, participation in religious sacrifices and rituals, and community sleeping at Morung etc. were given up. When Dr. S.W. Rivenburg joined Rev. Clark, educational work and medical relief were also supplemented to the evangelistic work. To co-ordinate all this work effectively, the Mission Centre was moved to Impur in 1894 which was more centrally located. The Ao Nagas accepted the new faith particularly finding that their belief in one 'Great Living Spirit' and also the end of the world by hell fire from heaven were in agreement with the Christian scripture. In 1891 the number of conversions shot up to 211 which further became 579 in 1901. A school was started to train Pastors and Evangelists with the arrival of Rev. S.A. Perrine in 1898. Later when Rev. and Mrs. Haggard and Mr. and Mrs. Dowd joined Impur Centre, the number of schools and students grew much larger. Inspite of the fact that intermittent village raids and feud persisted, the conversions progressed after the missionaries started functioning in a well-organised and co-ordinated manner. It was obviously clear that the American Christians started faring much better than their counterparts. This was possible because a better organized and regulated life-style replaced the traditional social system. This became an additional attraction to the Christian Faith.

Among the Angami Nagas, a missionary Rev. C.D. King started evangelizing since 1878 onward. He established his Centre and constructed a church at Kohima in 1883. Thereafter, he was joined by Dr. Rivenburg and the two started preaching the gospel in a planned manner. Rev. W.E. Witter came a little later, but he went to Wokha to work among the Lotha Nagas since 1885 onward. Mrs. Witter also assisted devotedly and effectively her missionary husband winning many souls to Jesus. Later on, Rev. M. Bronson established a Centre at Namsang village in the Konyak area as early as 1842.

Thus, the changed situation has led to the change of ideas. Since there has been tremendous development since 1957, the Nagas have developed the need for everything available on earth, from a wristwatch to a car and of course education is there. Therefore the Nagas have become money-minded and saving-oriented. Not only they want to earn more money by any means, fair or foul, but they also want to save it. They now want to accumulate it for all the modern needs, children's education as well as for himself, because now they cannot simply think of depending on unpredictable cultivation. This has brought the people more or less at par with the people of rest of the country in the matter of monetary economy. But still Naga people in the villages are found who are more concerned with the living at present rather than for unknown future.

Nagas also tend to consider everybody equal irrespective of official position, and that is why in the early days of administration the people used to address the officers also by name. But due to the official superiority of the officers it became embarrassing for them, and many of the officers were Nagas themselves. This embarrassing situation led the Naga people to change their ideas of equality and only from 1960s the Angamis decided to use the term 'Sir'. Other tribes also started it almost at the same time, and now they have accepted the inequality of official status of different people in the government and administration. The Nagas hold personal liberty above any other thing else. Nobody wants to be subordinate or take order from others. Nobody wants to be coerced by any body or coerce others. It is so much so that even the parents do not restrain the children from doing anything they want to do. They do not rebuke the children, let alone beating them. They would politely help and guide the children rather than to be rude. In recent times, there has been some change in this idea and the parents have taken to chiding or even beating the children for matters relating to going to school and study, but that too is about very minor children. Children of fifteen or so are allowed to think and do as they like. At this age, many boys and girls give up education because their parents are ineffectual in forcing them to go to school or undertake the study seriously. Girls of this age are allowed freedom of movement and choice of their life's partner. They are even provided with a separate room for their use, where it is possible, where they meet their suitors

The Nagas believe in free association of men and women and that is why marriage is a matter between the boy and the girl concerned and divorce is also common—none is forced or pressurized to live with any husband or wife against his or her will. Of course, divorce is not so easy among some tribes because of the monetary sting attached with it. During the earlier times, the practice of head-hunting it was a chivalry and sport among them. The person who hunts the head is acclaimed as hero and he was so much honoured and loved by the village girls that they used to offer themselves willingly to be enjoyed by him. On the other hand, the family or village from which the head is hunted, considered it merely as an accident. And of course they would surely think of retaliation if their strength permit. Though head-hunting was a sport, it could not be attempted on each and everybody, but only on the enemy village though irrespective of sex and age—any body, a man, woman or a child could be hunted. Whereas, killing of any man of one's own village is a serious offence and if any such incident happens, the aggrieved family may kill the offender with impunity. That is why in any case of accidental or otherwise killing of a person of one's own village, the killer escaped to the safety of another village. Even his close kins will also leave the village for the fear of retaliation. Tooth for tooth and blood for blood is the philosophy of life. But if the killer cannot be killed immediately or avenged quickly and the anger clams down, then heavy fine was collected as compensation from the offender. Even road accident is settled in this way nowadays. The rate of compensation in case of road accident of a fowl or a dog varies from tribe to tribe, and it is highest in Angami regions—seven times the price of the animal run over. People have become nowadays more reasonable, rational and tolerant and that is why the fine is often not exacted at this high rate, and sometimes even not all.

Accidental death such as due to falling from tree, or drowning is considered as devil's handi work. In such case the movable property of the deceased becomes *apotiya*, an Assamese term, which mean 'objectionable' and people do not touch it. Then it becomes difficult to find people to carry such a dead body for burial. Nowadays people becoming Christian such superstition is not so strong. Among the Angamis also such a death being considered as the handi work of the devil, the near relatives of the deceased physically challenge the devil with a spear in hand. He jumps round the dead shouting and inviting the devil for fight, to confront him rather than taking away the life in a stealthy way. It is so real as if he is actually fighting the devil there. In 1960 one Thinuovicha, a gazetted officer was captured and tied with a tree by the rebels in Phek district but in his efforts to escape he fell down the precipice and got serious injury and died later in Jorhat Hospital. When his body was brought back to Dimapur, his father with a spear in hand made such a show of shouting and jumping round the body that it appeared as if he was really fighting the devil there.

Among the Konyak tribals in case of a natural death the friends and relatives sit round the corpse and praise the works of the deceased during his life time. If he is under-aged then how he is brought up is described by the guardian. In case of a wealthy person all his wealth consisting of gongs *Burma Chonti*, clothes, and weapons etc., are displayed to the people.

In Nagaland, every Naga tribe believes in life in the next world and they respect the ancestors. Because of these two reasons often the grave of the dead is provided with cooked food and foodstuff and is decorated with flowers, and often a tomb stone is erected here for everyone, however big or small he or she is, however, richer the person better is the tombstone. In their outlook people are materialistic. They are more concerned with the life here than the life in the next world. They do not have the illusion of an eternal bliss after death, and going to heaven or hell according to good or bad deeds done in this world. They do not believe in austerity of life for satisfaction of God, or fasting for this or that thing.

The Nagas do not have any knowledge of astrology, neither they believe in the influence of any star or planet on the human life. That is why the dates of festivals and marriage etc. are fixed without any reference to planetary position or even phases of the moon. However, some modern educated Nagas are reading and believing in astrology—horoscope and palmistry, and often they wear various stones in their rings. There is no concept of sin and merit in Naga society. The concept of sin has been introduced by Christianity, but before that there was the sense of right and wrong, but not sin. Now the concept of sin, though new, has come to stay. There is no concept of *punya* (merit) and consequently there is no particular work which the people like to do to earn *punya*. Therefore almsgiving, helping the poor or distressed, non-injury to any animal etc. from the stand point of earning some *punya* is unknown among them.

But since the times of the British rule, and the arrival of Christianity, there remained very little in Nagaland that has not been affected by the changes brought about. It is unthinkable for them to dress now as they did a generation ago. There are only a few older people who regularly wear the traditional ornaments, beads, feathers, shells, brass, tiger's teeth, boar's tusk, cane and ivory put together with a truly artistic sense of form and colour. Otherwise, those who still own ornaments only wear them as costumes. Complete traditional outfits are mainly worn while taking part in the official celebrations or welcoming comities putting up a performance for VIPs. The treasured Hornbill feathers that people of wealth wore in the hair have now become even more precious because of the unavailability. Fake feathers made of white paper with a band of black paints across the top are used instead. Though most of the women still wear Mekhala's (sarongs) few men wear the aprons even in the villages. Pants or Shorts, however tattered, are preferred. Similarly, the women wear blouses.

In many ways the fears that the Naga Club expressed about being engulfed by an alien culture were prophetic. But even they may not have been aware of just how vulnerable they were. Nagaland has rapidly acquired all the worst traits of modern Indian and western culture. Politics has become notoriously corrupt. There have been little developments in the state though as a backward state it receives massive amounts of funds from the centre of development. The gap between the rich and the poor grows wider every day. Those without economic or political clout cannot progress beyond a certain point in their careers by virtue of merit alone. The villagers, still mostly illiterate are neglected. The average Naga villager just manages to get by with no alternatives than farming. All the work is still done by hand with the aid of crude agricultural implements. The crops are usually not sufficient and have to be supplemented by rice of very poor quality supplied by the Government at Fair Price outlets. Fewer and fewer young people want to till the land. Anyone with even a little education wants a desk job. Manual labour is looked down upon. Even villagers want government jobs for their children's, to spare them the hardships of a poor farmer's life. For most educated young people, even graduates, such goals are unthinkable.

When change has brought about so many social ills and so much disillusionment, Naga's are beginning to look to the past and the customs and traditions that Naga's grew up on. Young Naga leaders and students have begun movements to revive and preserve many past traditions that were given up or are dying out. It is the spirit of cooperation behind many of the old traditions that they hope to revive for the benefit of the community. It still exists in the villages but as more and more people seeks a life in modern towns, its gives way to individualism. It is also a move to strengthen ethnic pride in a culture that many Naga's had been taught by the missionaries to look upon as inferior. They were expected to model themselves after an alien culture; first that of the Christian Europe, then of mainstream India, rather than develop along their own customs. The results have had negative impact on every Naga.

When a Naga Christian dies, he is given a Christian burial but usually an object that he particularly cherished is put into the coffin just as a deceased's prized possessions were displayed on his funeral platform. Before burial, family members address words of farewell to the deceased with an emphasis on the statement that he should not grieve as he goes to the next world nor should he return to search for those he has left behind (Naga's believe that the dead returns to take with them members of their family). This wake is held in the traditional ways. Naga Christians do not see these traditions that belong to a pre-Christian era an in any way clashing with Christian way of living.

Many festivals, particularly the ones celebrated during springs and at the end of sowing and after harvests, are still celebrated, but without the traditional rites and rituals. It is during these festivals that the brewing and drinking of rice beer is tacitly permitted, otherwise strictly pro-prohibited by the Church; a decade ago Nagaland has been declared a dry state, yet alcoholic beverages still flows to the state from all places and people pay hefty sums just to drink them. Just as wealthy men would feed the whole village during feasts of merit in the past, today the Churches give feasts during Christmas and other important Christian events to the community.

Sikkim Customs

In Sikkim, communities, cultures, religions and customs of different hues intermingle freely to constitute a homogeneous blend. Hindu temples coexist along with Buddhist monasteries and there are even a few Christian churches, Muslim mosques and Sikh Gurdwaras. The predominant communities are the Bhutias, Lepchas, and the Nepalis. In urban areas many plainsmen - Marwaris, Biharis, Bengalis, South Indians, Punjabis have also settled and they are mostly engaged in business activities and government service. Because of development and construction works going on all over the state, a small part of the population consists of migrant labourers from the plains and Nepal. A few thousand Tibetan Refugees also have settled in Sikkim. The original inhabitants of Sikkim are said to be Lepchas. They existed much before the Bhutias and Nepalese migrated to the state. Before adopting Buddhism or Christianity as their religion, the earliest Lepcha settlers were believers in the bone faith or mune faith. This faith was basically based on spirits, benevolent and malevolent. They worshipped spirits of the mountains, rivers and forests which was but natural for a tribe that lived in the wild surroundings.

The Lepcha (Zongu) folklore is rich with stories. The Lepcha population is concentrated in the central part of the Sikkim. This is the area that encompasses the confluence of Lachen and Lachung rivers and Dickchu. Life in a Lepcha settlements is very simple. The male Lepcha wears a dress called a *pagi* made of cotton, which is stripped. The female Lepcha wear a two piece dress. The Lepchas speak the language *lepcha*, although this language is not much developed, but is rich in vocabulary related to the flora and fauna of Sikkim. The polyandry marriages are permitted amongst the Lepchas.

In the state, Bhutias are the people of Tibetan origin. They migrated to Sikkim perhaps after the 15th century. In Northern Sikkim, where they are in majority, they are known as the *Lachenpas* and *Lachungpas*. The language spoken by the Bhutias is Sikkimese. Bhutia villages are as large as those compared to those of Lepchas. The traditional dress of the male Bhutia is known as the '*Bakhu*' which is a loose cloak type garment with full sleeves. The female dress consists of a silken *Honju* which is a full sleeve blouse and a loose gown type garment. The women are very fond of heavy jewelry made of pure gold.

The Nepalese people migrated to Sikkim much after the Lepchas and Bhutias in large numbers and soon became a dominant community. The Nepalese now constitute more than 80 per cent of the total population. The Nepali settlers introduced the terraced system of cultivation. Cardamom was an important cash crop introduced by them. Except for the Sherpas and Tamangs who are Buddhists, the Nepalis' are orthodox Hindus with the usual cast system. The traditional male Nepali dress consists of long double breast garment flowing below the waist and a trouser known as *Daura Suruwal*. The female dress consists of a double breasted garment with strings to tie on both the sides at four places, which is shorter than the *Daura* and is called as *Chow Bandi Choli*. They also drape a shawl known as Majetro.

The inhabitants of Sikkim are warm, simple and friendly with a nature gaiety. The customs, rites and rituals of Sikkim are as diverse as the ethnic that inhabit the land; the 'Lepchas'—essentially children of the forest, the 'Bhutias' and the 'Nepalese'. The people of Sikkim love to celebrate festivals. Be it the chasing away of the evil spirit or the celebrations on the occasion of the new year, the Sikkimese people do it all with a clan. The population of Sikkim is 5 lakh 40 thousand, mainly consisting of the Nepalese, the Lepchas and the Bhutias. Of them, the Nepalese are the largest in number followed by the Bhutia and Lepcha communities. A small number of people from other parts of India have also settled in Sikkim. Despite such an ethnic diversity, a remarkable feature of Sikkimese society is the acceptance of different cultures, and their harmonious co-existence.

In Sikkim, the original inhabitants are the Lepchas who dwell in the central and northern areas; lower valleys are inhabited by Nepali migrants. Other ethnic groups are the Magars renowned as warriors and the Bhotias, who came to Sikkim from the Kham area of Tibet during the 13th century.

The Bhutias are the descendants of the early settlers from Tibet and Bhutan who accompanied the ancestors of the first Chogyal, Phuntsok Namgyal who belong to this ethnic group. The early Bhutias had three distinctive social groups the aristocracy, the quasi-aristocracy - those belonging to the leading Bhutia families who were land holders and were called Kazis - and the commoners. When the monarchy was abolished, these social distinctions also became extinct. The Nepalese community of Sikkim is itself a conglomeration of diverse ethnic groups which can be roughly consists the Magars, Murmis, Tamangs, Gurungs, Rais, Limbus, Damis, Kamis, Bahuns and the Chhetris etc. The Rais, Limbus, Tamangs, Magars, Murmis, and Gurungs have somewhat similar physical characteristics inasmuch as they are all Mongoloid. But each group has its own distinctive culture and customs. These ethnic groups have been known for their bravery and a large number of them have served as soldiers in the British and Indian armies. The major festival of the Hindu Nepalese in Sikkim include Dasain, Teohar, Makar Sankranti and Baisakhi. Sikkim is one of the most peaceful States in the country and the ethnic groups with their different languages, dialects, cultural background live in total harmony, symbolizing the essence of unity in diversity.

The central zone, inhabited by the Lepchas, roughly covers the stretch from the confluence of the river Teesta and the Lachung river to the junction of the Teesta and the Dikehee rivers. The *Rong-pas*, who are known as the Lepchas are the original inhabitants of Sikkim. Earlier it was believed that, the tribe had originated from southern Tibet. Their physical characteristics showed them to be a member of the Mongolian race. But later, it was supposed that they had come from the east, from the direction of Assam and Burma. The Lepchas are markedly Mongolian in features and differ from the Tibetans. It is also believed that the Lepchas have similarity with the tribes of Hangarang in the North West Frontier Province and with the mountain tribes of the Laree area in Ladakh. Other scholars claim that the Lepchas and the Khasias of Khasi-Jaintai area are two different branches of the same ethnic group. Though, at one time, the Lepchas had blood relation only with the Limbus at present no restriction is maintained in establishing matrimonial relations with other tribes. The Lepchas maintain no caste distinction, but claim that they belong to either of the five classes of Syang-Den, Mu, Ling-SingMu, Himu, Karthak Mu and Thikung Syalang. There are certain other classes based on the places of residence.

In the earlier times, polyandry was prevalent among the Lepchas. Marriage of wards is normally negotiated by the parents and after fulfilling certain condition, the marriage is celebrated with much pomp and feasting. The Lepchas are primarily animists. They acknowledge the existence of god and the bad spirits and do a lot to appease the malevolent one. Every class has a priest doctor, who is in fact an exorcist. The priest doctors may be either male or female. The male one is called *bon* and female one is called generally *monn*.

The Lepcha tribesmen are very intelligent, amiable and always cheerful. They are very modest, extremely hospitable people. They love sports and games and are sociable. They are innocent and good humoured. They are peace-loving people who avoid quarrels.

The Bhutias, who are mainly Buddhists, are quite distinct from the Lepchas. The Tibetan Bhutias entered Sikkim through Bhutan and settled in higher altitudes after driving the original inhabitants, the Lepchas into forests and lower valleys. They converted the indigenous Lepcha people to their Buddhism, established matrimonial relations with them and thereby paved the way for cultural and social assimilation of the two races. This gave rise to a new race. The matrimonial relation between the Tibetan nobles and Lepcha chiefs or *Jongpons* gave rise to a new affluent class of *Kazis*. The *Sherpas* are considered to have descended from the Bhutia-Lepcha cross stock. The Bhutias are mostly traders and Herdsman. But many of them are accustomed to cultivation now-a-days. The Bhutias are more assertive and industrious than the Lepchas. The Bhutiyas are not fond of isolation as the Lepchas. The Bhutia social structure is patriarchal. The practice of polyandry was very prevalent among them. But with the passage of time and spread of education this practice finds no favour with the young modern Bhutias. Normally, the Bhutias live in a joint family. Polyandry served to prevent the family and the property from being split up. There is no caste distinction among the Bhutias. The Bhutia women generally enjoy a great deal of independence and they are treated as equal to men. Marriage is normally arranged and settled by the parents. In marriage, maternal uncle and astrologer play an important role. Both man and woman can seek a divorce. If the matrimonial relation has to be severed, the man or the wife would refer the case to the village elders. At present the aggrieved parties go to the court of law also. Traditionally, the parties who apply for divorce has to pay a penalty and the actual expense incurred during marriage.

The Nepali community is composed of different sub-cultural groups, with considerable differences in physical characteristic and customs. Each tribe is sub-divided into many classes, which include: Limta, Gurung, Magar, Mewar, Rai, Tamang, etc. Of the caste Hindus, there are the Brahmins, Thakurs and Chettris etc. Among the low caste tradesman there are the Sarki, Kami and Damai etc. The Nepalese are spread throughout the east, south and west of Sikkim. They are mostly Hindus but some of them are Buddhists. They have terraced fields and also work on building roads. The Nepalis are good at trade and also work as Silversmiths.

The arrival of the Nepalese and their rapid increase in numbers has created a serious problem for the original inhabitants - the Lepchas and the Bhutias. The Nepalese are not only multiplying more rapidly in numbers but are also far ahead in education which enables them to get jobs in administration. While the Lepchas and Bhutias still prefer the traditional education in the monasteries, the Nepalese send their children to modern schools. The Lepchas and Bhutias are averse to cultivate waste land. Nepalese plant maize which grows in abundance and is their staple food. The Nepalese children work from the age of five and when they are ten years of age are able to earn more than they consume. The Nepali style of living is comparatively much economical. Their dress and diet are simple. They do not spend much on marriage and festival. Whereas, the Lepchas and Bhutias take rice with meat, if possible. Their dress is expensive. Above all, they have to support the Buddhist lamas, according to the religious custom, make occasional offerings, either in kind or cash to the 'gompa' and then pay a high fee to the lamas for the various services rendered by them.

The Limbu is sub-group of the Kirati tribe who have a tradition of inter-marriage with other tribes particularly with the Lepchas and in certain aspects their habits are similar to those of the Lepchas. They have also matrimonial relation with the *Rai* or *Khambas*. The Limbus call themselves Yakthamba. One of the sub-group came via Lhasa and is called the Lhasa gotra, while the other branch which came from Benaras is called the Kashi gotra. The Limbu have their own priests, known as '*Phedangba*' who conduct the religious ceremonies, and also deals in omen and forecasts in their own language, called the *Limbu Kura*. Limbu marriage is often conducted without the consent of the parents.

The Rai or Khambas are much in common with the Limbus who are Hindus. Men of their own tribe called the 'home' serve as their priest. But now-a-days, Brahmins are engaged to conduct rituals. They also engage *Bijuwas* or occasionally a *Phedangba* or a *Jhankri* to ward off evil spirits. Their marriage customs do not differ much from those of other *Kirati* tribes. The Rai people have a dialect of their own. They have artistic talents. They are mainly agriculturists. The Magars customs and religious ceremonies closely are similar to those of the Hindus. They have a language of their own called as *Magar kura* which is of Tibeto-Burmese group. There are seven classes of Magar who are all socially equal including Ale, Burathoki, Gharti, Pun, Rana, Roka and Thapa. Thapa is the largest class of the Magar. Inter-marriage is permissible among all the classes.

The Gurang are of Mongolian origin and they profess Hinduism. But earlier they in fact, used the services of the Lama instead of Brahmins for all priestly functions. Now-a-days, they engage Brahmins also. This tribe is divided into two groups: the *Char Jat* and *Sora Jat*. But the distinction is now disappearing. Marriage between the two sub-groups is now common. The Gurungs have their own languages which is called the Gurung Kura. The Gurungs in the urban areas now generally follow Hindu customs and rituals. The Tamangs claim their origin from four families: Bal, Yonjon, Moktan, Ghising. Their two main sub-divisions are Bara Tamang and Atharajat. Bara Tamang is socially superior. Tamangs have a similarity with the Gurangs. Their language is similar to Gurang Kura. The Tamangs are Lamaist Buddhists. The Mewar are originally agriculturists and masons, but in Sikkim many of them have taken to trade who are mostly Hindus.

Among the Gurkhas of Sikkim, the Brahmins have the highest social standing. Being the orthodox Hindus they would not normally have any matrimonial relations with other lower castes. But now social rigidity is fast disappearing. In the urban areas Brahmins are found marrying with non-Brahmins, taking up a variety of professions other than priesthood and mixing freely with other caste people. Next in social rank are the Thakurs who are entitled to wear sacred thread. Inter-marriage among certain class of Thakurs is permissible while marriage with members of other classes is restricted. The Chettris also wear sacred thread and have Brahmanical prejudices. Though inter-marriage with other castes is common, they prefer marriage only among their own class. In Sikkim, inter-marriage among these higher castes is not uncommon. Traditionally a Gurkha can possess any number of wives. A wife taken through formal ceremonial marriage is called a '*Behaite*' while others are called '*Lihaites*'.

Tripura Customs

Except the Garos and Khasis, all the Tripura tribes and communities are patriarchal and patrilineal. Father is the head of the family. Families of the same tribe living in a village constitute a *para* or *bari* and are very often named after the village chieftain. Sometimes, they are named after the *chharas*. Most of the tribes are strongly united through village organizations, cooperation and fellow feeling, collective worship of gods and goddesses, groups jhum cultivation etc. Among them love marriages, marriages by elopement with previous understanding and negotiated marriages are prevalent. *Jamaikhata* (marriage by service) is also in practice among the tribals. Both bride price and dowry are prevalent. Child marriage is on the wane. The tribes either cremate or bury their dead. The disposal of bones in water and ancestor worship are practiced by most of the tribes and communities.

In the state, there are four predominant religions—Hinduism, Islam, Buddhism and Christianity. Most of the tribal people have their own tribal customs and beliefs, but in the broader sense the tribal religion is a curious mix of Hinduism and folk religion. There are Buddhist tribes like the Maghs and Chakmas, and Christian like the Garos and Kukis. Vaishnavism is practiced by the Murasings. The people belonging to the broad group Halam claim that they speak Halam. The Magh community speaks the language of Burma. There are some other tribes like the Mundas and Bhils who do not seem to have a dialect of their own, and speak their neighbour's dialect for their daily life.

Among their festivals, the one that occupies the pride of place is the worship of *Choddo Devota* or *Chaudda Devata*

(Fourteen Gods). Next come *Ker* and *Garia Puja*, both traditional tribal festivals. Another important tribal festival is *Ganga Puja*. They observe two other important and popular festivals—*Durga Puja* and *Diwali*. The fairs of Tripura are mainly socio-religious in nature. Noteworth among them are *Baisakhi Mela, Pous, Sankranti Mela* at Trithamukh and *Mahamanipara Mela* at Belonia. The fairs at Unakoti (in the North Tripura district) and the temple of *Tripura Sundari* are also important. However, both tribal and non-tribal communities of Tripura have their own ways of running their societies. In case of non-tribals like the Brahmans and Kumbhakars, the customs are not followed strictly. This is mainly due to their scattered distribution. In fact, their involvement with codified laws has blurred their traditional customary laws. The Muslims however, differ from other non-tribals to some extent. Disputes over issues like marriage and divorce are still resolved by religious heads according to the religious beliefs and practices. The tribals have however retained their customary laws relatively well. They generally have two sets of mechanisms to maintain law and customs. One is at the village level, while the other is at the inter-village level. The tribals rarely approach the court to resolve disputes which are generally resolved on the basis of their traditional beliefs, ideas and customs.

1

Conceiving and Birth

Customs relating to conceiving and birth present a sharp contrast in the north-eastern region comprising the states of Sikkim, Assam, Nagaland, Mizoram, Meghalaya, Manipur, Tripura and Arunachal Pradesh. Here, the tribal as well as the non-tribal customs, religion, beliefs and practices vary widely. The tribal people are closely associated with certain amount of superstition in matters relating to the conceiving and birth customs and rituals in much the same way as their routine life which is run by some code of conduct. Thus, every aspect of tribal life functions within the ambit of their social system manifested in some form or other. In their habit of drinking, eating, religious and other ceremonial rites, the tribals move through a certain set pattern of behaviour which reflects their social behaviour. Such structural functions also regulate their social belief, behaviour and observances of certain restraints in the activities in social, economic, religious and political life. It is strongly believed that during pregnancy of woman there are certain things her husband is supposed to do and to restrain from, inasmuch as his wife is regulated in her activities. Such socially regulated activities of a man and his wife continue till a baby reaches a point of its age. Such restraint in activities of one's life is the basis of the belief that a man, wife and the child are the subject to all kinds of misfortune and accident in life during pregnancy and also after child-birth.

Custom of Avoiding Pupa

It is customary that a man must not quarrel with anybody, nor should he be in polemics during the pregnancy of his wife. It is said that a man is subject to misfortune and is prone to accidents. A pregnant woman must not take 'Pupa' or *Khoinuou* during pregnancy. It is believed that if a pregnant woman takes it, the child shivers like the fluttering wings of the bee when the former grows up. Eggs are not to be touched by a pregnant woman. The outer cover of an egg, containing the white liquid of an egg, is believed to have transformed into the membrane of the child in the womb. If, therefore, a woman touches the egg during pregnancy, she experiences problems during the child birth. The pregnant woman can, thus, eat cooked, boiled or fried eggs.

Moreover, a snake must not be killed by a woman during pregnancy. It is said that if a woman kills a snake during pregnancy, the tongue of the child will take the shape of the fang of a snake. A pregnant woman must not expose her waist to the fire for taking heat-treatment due to the fear of the womb being pasted to the waist. The womb, therefore, cannot come out easily during child birth and, in that case the woman dies. It is a taboo to hold a pregnant woman by hair due to anger during a quarrel between the husband and the wife, or for that matter, by anybody else, due to the fear that the child may be born prematurely, or there occurs an abortion.

The pestle used for rice pounding, called '*Suh*' must not be prepared and cut by the husband of the pregnant woman during the pregnancy. It is generally apprehended that in that case, the child (if it is a boy) may be born with circumcised penis. It is also said that such circumcised person is not liked by serpents (Gulpi) at all. The husband of a pregnant woman also must avoid cutting mouth of a bamboo water-container. The Kuki tribals in Manipur do not have any other type of water container. The only water container of indigeneous product is made of bamboo, popularly known as '*Gotui Thei*'. Its mouth is not cut evenly, but slantingly. Therefore, it is feared that if a man, whose wife is pregnant, cuts the mouth of the bamboo water-container, the mouth of the child will be slant, just like that of the container itself.

It is customary practice among the Kukis of Manipur that the '*Tucha*' of a person, who performs some kind of social function, is to clean and dress properly the intestine of the animal killed during such function, which is called '*Sa Gil Sah*'. In the social system of relationship a man among the Kukis is either a '*Tucha*' or '*Songgao*' in relation to someone necessarily through matrimonial alliance. Therefore, the husband of a pregnant woman must not attend to the dressing and cleaning of the intestine of any animal killed during the pregnancy of his wife. The popular superstition in this regard is too severe, even to utter about it. It is simply said, "not permitted". This, however, is due to the apprehension that dressing of intestine of an animal during pregnancy of one's wife represents doing the same to man's wife, which is a sign of the death of a man's wife during pregnancy.

The Kukis also believe that in much the same way as the waist of the mother is open for the birth of the child, everything connected with the acts of opening on the part of the pregnant woman should remain open as the pregnant woman feels the birth-pang for an easy delivery. Hence, the labour pain commences, a pregnant woman opens all her boxes, including her cane container or box, and basket type container made of cane, called '*Lel*' and '*Sinkhup*' etc. Normally, from the day a woman knows that she has conceived, she brews one big jar of '*Zu*' or rice- bear which becomes as old as nine or ten months. It produce very sweet odour and contain a high degree of intoxicating agent. This is to be prepared and offered either for drinking or sipping to those who attend to the woman on the day of delivering a child and also to the guests who come to offer greetings. This act is preceded by the opening of the cover of the jar of '*Zu*' which has so far been kept air-tight. She also throws open the gates of her poultry, piggery, and cattle-pen etc.

It is also apprehended that if a woman fords a stream during the menstruation period misfortune may befall her. Therefore, she is forbidden from crossing a stream. All these superstitions and taboos are based on practical knowledge and experiences by the tribal elders through ages, which at one time or the other came true in the past. As an instance of an incident may be cited: during the Second World War, when the Japanese overrun Changoubung village, all the villagers fled in fear of danger to life. But a pregnant woman, who was expecting an imminent delivery, could not move out and when the Japanese gendarmes came into the village, she was in unbearable labour pain. On seeing her condition, and knowing as he did, a

Japanese soldier grasped her hair and shook her head, as a result of which she gave birth to the baby immediately. The customs are related to the Kuki people of Manipur.

Custom of Avoiding Meat

Mr. C. De Beauvoir stocks recorded the conceiving and pregnancy customs of Sikkim, stating, "Virgin birth is only connected with folk-tales in Sikkim. There seem to be no legends of a son 'beautiful as a celestial' whose father was the Sun-god, like we read of in the Mahabharata. The woman who expects a child must not eat the flesh of any animal whose throat has been cut from the fifth month. If she does, the child will be born with a red mark round its neck and he will die. An animal must not either be eaten that has been killed in her presence. Should the woman by any mistake have eaten of an animal who was killed in this manner, the bones are kept until the child is born and are then rubbed on his throat. Distorted plantains that are twisted and out of shape must not be eaten by the woman or else it is believed the child's fingers and toes will resemble them. Should the basket she carries fall off her back when containing food, she may not eat any of the contents. She is also expected to lead a quiet homely life and not go out at night lest the child die. Women at that time go often to a river and protect themselves against evil spirits by sacrificing two fowls.

"The husband at that time may not ride, he must not touch a pony or even a saddle and bridle. Should he do so, it may be twelve months before the child is born and in that case the woman will be sure to die."

The custom pertains to the Lepcha Tribals of Sikkim.

Custom of Wearing Amulets

The Bhils originating from Madhya Pradesh and Rajasthan observe both pre-delivery and post-delivery rituals and taboos. Pregnancy is a period of anxiety. The would-be mother wears amulets, drinks *jalpara* or sanctified water, does not move about much and does only a little work which is not labourious. She is given *sadhbhakshan* on an auspicious day during the sixth month of pregnancy. The custom is related to the Bhils in Assam.

Ritual of Simontannyan Observed

A pre-birth ritual called *simontannyan* is conducted in the sixth month of a woman's first pregnancy. The ritual is conducted in her husband's house. Her parents send ceremoniously the utensils needed to cook *paramanna*, rice, milk, sweets, fish and five sorts of fruits. A *yajna* is performed, and the expectant mother and her husband attend the ritual together, wearing new garments. Another pre-birth ritual called *sadhbhakshan* is performed during the ninth month of pregnancy. This ritual is observed either in the husband's house, or in her paternal house. During *sadhbhakshan* the pregnant woman is given the sumptuous food she desires to eat and also gifted new garments.

The custom is practiced by the Acharyas in Assam.

Taboos During Pregnancy

The Dimasa tribals in Assam believe that the offsprings are like blessings of God. The tribals have some knowledge of biological paternity and recognize the definite role of father in procreation; such as sexual union is necessary for impregnation, but are not clear about role of sperm and egg. They call them male and female seeds. The Dimasa consider equity of responsibility of both the parents in begetting a child comparing a woman with the earth. As the seeds sown in the earth germinate as plants, so seeds of male when sown in a female womb take shape of a new baby.

The Dimasa tribals have their own 'rhythm' theory of conceiving and birth; according to which copulation between the third and the seventh day after menstruation in case of young girls and between the third and fourteenth day in case of elderly women leads to pregnancy. The young girls can conceive even before experiencing external menstruation, however the children born of such cases are supposed to die of thunder-bolt. The Dimasa know that women loose fertility with menopause in the old age.

Generally, cessation of menstruation indicates pregnancy. Still a pregnant woman is not debarred from her normal life. She takes care of the routine works until her confinement. In the advanced stage, however, she does not move outside the village, nor does she go to the forest or visit a cremation ground lest the evil spirits harm the embryo in the womb. She is also not allowed to attend any funeral. Fish without scale and tortoise meat are strictly prohibited to a pregnant woman even dreaming of these objects is considered as bad omen.

Husband of a pregnant woman propitiates Naisodi-nusodi by sacrificing a hen which can make the delivery safe and easy. Delivery of a baby always takes place inside the living quarters. In the Dimasa language birth of a baby is called *hagusujaba*. *Ha* means earth and *gusujaba* means polluted, that is, where a birth takes place the earth gets polluted.

The custom is practiced by the Dimasa tribals of Assam.

No Charms used for Pregnant Women

About the pregnancy customs of the Ao Nagas of Nagaland, Mr. JP Mills recorded, "An Ao longs to have children. Sons are most desired, but daughters too are welcome. From childhood till marriage all will bear their share of the work in the fields, and be, in fact, self-supporting, and afterwards they will help to support their aged parents at the last. No thoughts of heavy school bills and the choice of a career weigh upon the Ao father's mind; what few schools there are are free, and for a career there is the soil. No charms are used to promote fertility in women. A childless couple consult a "medicine-man," and either send an offering to their *tiya* in the sky or to the living parents of one of the couple whose disapproval is causing the marriage to the unblessed and fruitless. A woman must be especially careful of her food when pregnant and abstain scrupulously from all food forbidden to her. If she finds a tasty beetle in the fields she may not bring it up for supper tucked into her skirt at the waist, or her child will be born with a birthmark; she must bring it tied in a corner of her cloth so that it does not touch her. Nor may a pregnant woman kill a snake, lest her child have a tremulous tongue.[1] It is admitted, however, that the temptation to kill a poisonous snake on sight is so strong that this prohibition is often disregarded. But an expectant mother will never under any circumstances kill a slow-worm. If she does her child will be born blind. A woman may not eat tortoise or turtle at any time, and this food is also 'tabu' to a man while his wife is pregnant. Strictly speaking, at such a time neither of the parents ought to go near one of these creatures. In this connection two examples of the working of the Ao mind came to my notice. In Wamukan a baby girl, born with a deformity which was bound to prove fatal, was brought to me to look at. The father complained that some Merangkong men, while his wife was pregnant, had come up to Wamukan on their way back from the plains. While visiting a friend in another house, they had left in the outer room of his house a turtle they had been carrying. Since it had been brought into his house the father had wanted to eat it, but they had refused to part with it. Had he eaten it, he said, his child would not have been deformed. More recently one of my Ao interpreters, a most intelligent man, was very worried because his little daughter was slow in learning to walk. He was advised by a 'medicine-man' that it was because he had partaken of a tortoise of mine that had had to be killed shortly before the child's birth. He therefore hung a little bit of tortoise skin by a thread round her neck, and to its efficacy ascribed the fact that she soon learnt to walk. The line of argument in these cases is difficult to grasp. One would think at first sight that to eat the turtle or hang the tortoise skin round the child's neck would only make things worse. But the Ao apparently reasons that, having come under the influence of the evil thing, the best thing he can do is to bring it into more intimate contact and so into his power.

"When an expectant mother thinks that there are only two more months to elapse before the birth of her child, she tells her husband, and he must refrain from intercourse from that time on 'or the child in the womb will feel shame and die.' Intercourse is resumed three months after the birth, but may only take place when the baby is asleep. Intercourse is also never indulged in during the menstrual flow, but can be resumed again immediately it ceases." Mr. Mills added.

The custom pertains to the Ao Nagas of Nagaland.

Noting Dreams

According to a traditional belief; a pregnant woman must not eat the flesh of a cow or sow which was pregnant and died. Memi Nagas dreams do not eat goats either.

If either parent dreams of a spear or a cock, the child will be a boy; but if the dream is of a woman's iron walking rod or a hen, the child will be a girl. Boys are generally preferred by the tribals, and in order to get a son the parents must meditate on *Urame*. No attempt, however, at abortion is ever made.

The custom is prevalent among the Angami Nagas of Nagaland.

Performing Rituals to Ward off Evil Spirits

Pre-delivery rituals are performed to avoid future complications, but in case of certain problems a ritual becomes a must to ward off evil spirits. The method of animal sacrifice in the tribal ritual depends upon the financial condition of the person concerned, as well as on the severity of the case. The custom pertains to Adi-Ashing tribe of Arunachal Pradesh.

Restraining from Planting Bamboo and Banana

A pregnant woman may not perform hard work however she continues to work in the *Jhum* fields. It is taboo for her husband to plant bamboo saplings or banana trees. He is also restrained from joining in making the hearth (*pakum*) when a new house is constructed in the village. The pregnant woman may not eat double bananas or any creeping plants that bear fruit. They keep no special hut or place for the delivery. In this society women have a lower status. No woman is allowed to hold any office in the village Panchayat, who remain under the control of their father, and after marriage, their husband. The men remain concerned with work like lopping trees, constructing houses, and hunting, etc. Besides collecting fuel and water, weaving and cooking, women also participate in agricultural activities. The woman plays little role in conducting social functions or rituals. The custom is prevalent in the Aual tribe of Manipur.

Birth Customs: Giving Woman a Replica of Dorje

About the birth customs of Sikkimese people, Mr. C. De Beauvoir stocks recorded, "Although couvade existed formerly in the south of India, very few traces of the custom are to be found in Sikhim. In some cases I heard of a man going into seclusion for ten days before the birth of his child. During those days he lives in another room of the cottage, ignoring his wife completely, but he sees she has the best food and that she is well attended. This they say is an incentive to bring good-luck, and it is frequently mentioned in folk-tales.

"The *lamas* in the village give pregnant women a stone having the shape of a *dorje* (a thunderbolt) from which paste is made which they eat. It is supposed to facilitate child-birth."

"The following story was given at Tumun, (great superstition is attached to a thunderbolt, and a 'dorje' in brass, is the religious symbol of a *lama)*: 'Once upon a time, an orphan boy went over the hill and fell over a steep precipitous rock. It was twilight and he fell into a pig-sty landing on the back of a pig. Then it commenced to thunder so that he shook with fright. One report was so loud that it reverberated and sent the boy to the top of the mountain once more. So it is a Lapcha fable that a pig is the cause of thunder and we never laugh at it. A horse, dog, cow and goat must not be laughed at either. If they are it may cause thunder and lightning, and should a tree ever be struck, the form of a '*sa-dar*' is always found underneath it, though it is only made of stone. The '*sa-dar*' is the Demon of Lightning, and is always carved on a Buddhist altar, being eight feet high. It is represented as a dragon holding three precious stones *(norpu)* in his claws.)

"Should the husband be a *lama he* utters prayers for one night in the Tibetan language, while a '*mun*' is called in to make sacrifices to propitiate the evil demons. A cock or a hen is frequently offered, but should the demon be not appeased, he is called the *gyek-rum* and is turned into a god in order to conciliate, whilst a pig is also given him! The friend who is called in to help receives Rupee one and two yards of cloth. Frequently the woman goes into the wood to have a child, thus leaving everything to nature.

"The duration of uncleanness is one month. After then the position of the woman in the village improves considerably, the mother of a child having more authority.

"The child is visited by a *lama* after three days, who prepares a horoscope telling the parents how long the child will live, how often he will be ill, and whether he will be lucky or unlucky. He also names him, choosing the day of the week on which he is born. Thus a boy may be called *Posa* meaning *Friday,* whilst the parents choose the name *Potet.* The parents receive their name from the first child, and if the son were called

Posa-Potet the father would be *Posa-Potet-bo* (father), while the mother would be known as *Posa-Potet-mo,* the language being teknonymous.

"Directly the child is born butter is placed in his mouth and after one hour ground rice is given to him. It is considered unlucky for a child to be born with long hair or having teeth, as it means the father and mother will both die that year.

"Boys are weaned after three years, and girls after four. During teething the child is taken great care of, and the mother may not eat salt, drink '*chi,*' or have anything that has acid in it.

"When a child is very ill, a *Mun* is called in to sacrifice to the demons. When the child recovers it is said she has cured it. The demons are supposed to send disease, and the one who sends small-pox is known as the *rum-du.* Tetanus is believed to be caused by touching the image of a god, *e.g.,* the Buddha that is found on household altars.

"Deformed children are instantly killed, the mother in a case of that sort being well treated by her husband but badly by her neighbours. Insanity is said to be caused through a demon's presence in a child. The villagers say, '*Mung-suk* the demon has him.'

"If a child dies when he is under five years old, he is placed in a box under some stones on the mountain side as it is said he is too young to bear the weight of the earth. A little soil is put round the spot which is fenced round. After three days the place is visited, and the foot-marks on the soil noticed, which show the relatives if the child has re-incarnated into a human person again or another animal. If no marks are observed the relatives believe the child has gone to play with its ancestors in Heaven (the *rum-lyang).* If the child is a boy, he wears a pair of short knickers made from a species of nettle called the *sa-hrong.* This is first soaked and then dried with ashes over it making the pulpy substance fall off, and the fibre is used as thread. A girl wears a cloth of the same material fastened over her shoulder with a bamboo pin. A belt is also worn that is made from the bark of a fruit tree (the *kun-pot).* A cradle is never used, the baby sleeps on the floor wrapped in a blanket, and when carried is placed in the *kasok,* the pouch-like fold a woman makes with the end of her garment and that is tucked into her belt. When older, the child is carried on the back and fastened with a long piece of cloth. He never wears any head-dress.

"The Lapcha has few toys. Boys only play with leaves and mud. The girls play with a doll *(a-kup dim)* made from the leaves of a kind of lemon, the *kan-tu,* that are rolled together and tied in the centre with a piece of fibre. It is always feminine and rejoices in the name of "*maim*" which means a lady.

"A woman or a man will never touch a doll when they are expecting a child, as it is believed he might be dumb or sight-less. Boys when older make a small flute called a *pa-lit* which is also made from the bark of the fruit tree, *kun-pot.* Children's clothes are thrown away after their death in order to prevent unhappy reminders.

"A boy wears a lucky necklace which comes from Tibet as an amulet. It contains three beads only, one long black one and two coral. The girl wears an amulet having many beads, five long black ones and several coloured ones. She also wears a bracelet which a boy does not, but they both wear ear-rings even when they are very small, but a Lap-cha woman never has her nose pierced or wears anklets.

"The birth of a girl for the first child is considered very lucky, as a girl helps the parents much more than a boy, who plays the whole time.

"The *Rum* are supposed to take care of a child, and there are many demons who would harm him. The *sung-grong-mung* is the name of the demon who steals little children. If a baby sucks a thumb or big toe it is considered lucky, but should it suck nothing at all it is unlucky. Should a child cry it means he is unhappy, and he gives the parents no rest. Should he however play a great deal it is considered propitious.

"The Lapcha never practises circumcision. When illegitimate children are born, the mother is known to have thrown the corpse into a river at night, thus hiding her wrong from the villagers. Bad crops are said to be a result of some one behaving wrongly and a *Mun* is required to offer sacrifices.

"When a child is thrown into the river it is believed a demon takes him. I have not been able to find out whether infanticide is due to economic causes or not.

"Salt is never given to small children as it is said their bones will become soft." The customs are prevalent among the Lepchas of Sikkim.

Keeping the Umbilical Cord Uncut for Three-four Days

A renowned anthropologist S.H.M. Rizvi wrote about the child-birth in Arunachal Pradesh, stating, "Ramo families are generally small in size because of the high rate of infant mortality and short span of life. Child birth is assisted by an old and experienced lady of the family. Placenta and after birth are thrown at distant place and beyond the reach of animals. Umbilical cord remains unseparated for three to four days and after which it dries out itself. During this period the members of family observe a taboo and neither go out for work nor visit anyone outside the village. Childbirth generally is preferred at husband's house. Prenatal restrictions on diet is observed. The expectant mother is refrained from eating ripe fruits, excess quantity of chillies and sweet things. But no restriction is imposed on eating meat and drinking *O*. The child is breast fed. In case it is not sufficient the mother chews the food until it is a liquid or semi-liquid form and feeds the same to the newborn. In case of a normal delivery the family offers a feast and a name is given to the newborn. In case of any complication and difficult child birth they sacrifice animals and perform ritual accompanied with singing of *jajin*. There is no discriminatory treatment with regards to sex of the baby, thus, celebrations are similar in case of birth of a son or a daughter. But the urge for a son is universal since each Ramo desires to have atleast a son. The naming ceremony is locally referred to as *amin menam*. While selecting a name care is taken to avoid names of father/mother, uncle, uncle's wife, grand-father/mother, brother and sister. The divination is sought on the selected name by performing *peppi penam*. Some of the commonly found names are generally adjectives and related to physical appearance, looks, facial features and relative chronological position of the new born within his/her sibs. As for example, Tanya (for boy) a—Yanya (for girl) name is generally given to the last born since it signify that when he/she was born the parents were old or in middle age. If a boy is having a broad forehead or has scanty hair on his head he is named Talok (literally meaning baldy). Since Ramo vocabulary has limited and few names it is not surprising to find many persons bearing the same name. But to overcome this shortcoming they use clan and village name to identify the person and to avoid confusion specially during conversation. For example, Tuteng may be a common name but adding Koje or Komi with the name identifies the person with a particular clan and village. It may be noted here that high incidence of infant mortality may be due to the lack of medicare facilities including immunization facilities. Thus survival of children depends upon nature and chance factors coupled with performance of rituals to ensure a long life of a child.." Rizvi added.

The custom pertains to the Ramo group of Adi tribe in Arunachal Pradesh.

Throwing Away the After-birth Below the House

The tribal child-birth in a house is assisted by any elderly woman of the family. The after-birth or *neynam* is generally thrown away below the house. Naming ceremony or *ami-amin menam* is conducted after three or four days after birth. Names are generally selected through divinations. The child also gets an additional name on the basis of his facial features or circumstances under which it was born. For example, if the child had a red face it was called *moli*. If the child was thin he was called *tasen* (*yasen* for the girl). If a baby was born when the family was undergoing some difficulties he was named as *taluk* (*yaluk* for the girl). The custom pertains to the Pailibo group of Adi tribe in Arunachal Pradesh.

Out of the 66 communities in the state of Arunachal Pradesh, 63 are scheduled tribes. The Nepalis, Sonowal Kacharis, Tibetans and Chakmas are migrant people. Some of the communities are well known. The westernmost tribal group in Arunachal Pradesh is the Monpa, which as six sub-groups, including the But Monpa, Chug Monpa, Dirang Monpa, Kalatang Monpa, Lish Monpa and the Twang Monpa. The Tawang district is exclusively inhabited by the Tawang Monpas.

The rest of the Monpas, Sherdukpens, Akas, Khowas and Mijis inhabit the West Kameng district.

The Bangnis are the predominant community in the East Kameng district along with the Sulungs and some of the Mijis and Akas. The Nishis, Apatanis, Hill Miris, Tagins, Mikirs, Nas and Sulungs live in the Upper and Lower Subansiri districts. The 15 sub-groups of the Adis, namely, the Ashings, Bokars, Boris, Gallongs, Karkos, Komkars, Milangs, Minyongs, Padams, Pasis, Pailibos, Pangis, Ramos, Shimongs and Tangams along with the Membas, Khambas and Mishings/Miris are inhabitants of the East and West Siang districts. The Mishmis have three sub-groups—the Idu Mishmis, Digaru Mishmis and Miju Mishmis. The first sub-group lives in Dibang Valley along with some of the Adi communities. The other two sub-groups are distributed in the Lohit district where the Khamptis, Khamiyangs, Zakhrings/Meyors, Chakmas and Tibetans also inhabit. The Tangsas with 15 sub-groups, namely the Havis, Juglis, Kimsings, Lungchangs, Lungphis, Mukloms, Morangs, Mosangs, Ronrangs, Sangwals, Sankes, Tikhaks, Tonglims and Yongkuks live in the Changlang district. Changlang is home to the Singphos, Deoris, Lisus, Chakmas, Sonowal Kacharis and Nepalis as well.

The Tirap district is inhabited by the Noctes and Wanchos. Arunachal Pradesh consists broadly five cultural zones. From west to east these are: (i) The Mon cultural zone, which covers the Tawang and West Kameng districts and is inhabited mainly by the Monpas and Sherdukpens. The Akas, Mijis and Khowas also belong to this zone. (ii) To the east of the first zone lies the Nishi cultural zone encompassing the Bangnis of the East Kameng district, the Nishis of the Lower and Upper Subansiri districts and two unique communities—the Sulungs and Apatnis. Other groups living in the zone include the Nas, Tagins, Mikirs and Hill Miris. (iii) The Adi cultural zone extends from the eastern part of the Upper Subansiri district to the western boundary of the Dibang Valley district, covering all the Adi sub-groups as well as the Khambas, Membas and Mishings/ Miris. (iv) The Mishmi cultural zone, covering the districts of the Dibang Valley and Lohit, is predominated by the three sub-groups of the Mishmi community, and among them lives a small community—the Zakhrimgs/Meyors. Other communities in this zone are the Khamptis, Khamiyangs, Deoris, Chakmas and Tibetans who are settled in the plains bordering Assam. In the past, the Khampits and Khamiyangs have functioned as a liaison between the Mishmis and people of Assam. (v) The Nocte-Tangsa cultural zone is spread over the Tirap and Changlang districts. The major communities of this zone are the Noctes, Wanchos and Tangsas, with the Singphos, Sonowal Kacharis, Lisus and Nepalis being the small groups inhabiting this cultural zone.

Giving rice-beer to Midwives to Drink

The community a few aged and experienced women skilled as midwives, who render their services during childbirth, for which they are given ricebeer and some eatables. The umbilical cord is cut with a sharp piece of bamboo by the midwife. The afterbirth, and placenta, are wrapped in an old cloth and buried under the floor where the birth takes place. The day the child is born, the family performs *khiwnaghring* rite through sacrificing a hen and eating it along with ricebeer. After two months the family performs *ritun* in which a pig or a dog is slaughtered. The last ceremony after childbirth is *pathakal* in which animal sacrifice is followed with distribution of ricebeer. The tribal priest called as *dopu* presides during these occasions. He receives meat or (*sating*) and a cup of ricebeer in return.

The custom is popular among the Anal tribesmen in Manipur.

Beating of *Ulu* and *Dhenki*

"The birth of a child is immediately announced by the traditional method of making the sound of *ulu* and *dhenki* (husking pedal). This is done five times for a male baby and thrice for a female one. On the sixth day since the birth *Sasthi Puja* is celebrated. On the same evening the naming ceremony is observed and sweets are distributed. The post-birth pollution period comes to an end on the 21st day. The end is marked with *Surya Puja*, nail paring and *mundane. Annaprasan* (the first rice feed) is held when the child is six months old. *Upanayan* (sacred thread tying ceremony in the case of boys) is observed when the child attains seven years of age."

The custom is prevalent among the Bhil tribes people working in the tea gardens of Assam.

Performing of *Sasthi Puja*

In the evening on the sixth day after the birth *Sashti Puja* is performed. The articles needed for the observance are a *taga*, a *gamchha* (napkin), a *tulsi mala* (garland of tulsi wood), five *cowries* (shells), five ripe bananas, an earthen ink pot, a *bater dal* (twig of banyan tree) and a reed pen. The baby is named the same evening which involves lighting oil lamps. As a oil lamp is lit, each name is uttered. The name that gets selected is the one with the utterance of which the oil lamp burns the brightest. In case of a male child, a pollution lasts 21 days at the end of this period, the child's head is shaved by a barber, as part of a purificatory ceremony. The mother also gets her nails paired. In the case of a female child, birth pollution lasts 30 days, which is followed by the purificatory tonsuring of the head.

After the end of the pollution period, *Surya Darshan* and *Chandi Puja* are performed. *Chandi Puja* is performed in the room in which the birth took place and mother and the child stayed during the pollution period. The following articles are required for the *Puja: ghat* (earthen pot), *gamchha, narkel* (coconut), ghee, *madhu* (honey) *sabri kalas* (a variety of ripe bananas) and *aamkath* (mango wood). A *yajna* is performed during *Chandi Puja*. For *Surya Darshan* articles like a *ghat*, mango twig, *chall* (rice) and *paka kalas* (rice bananas) are required.

After *Chandi Puja* and *Surya Darshan* the birth pollution is considered to be removed; and the woman begins to attend to her usual family chores. *Annaprasan*, the first rice-eating ceremony, is performed in the sixth month in the case of a male child, and in the seventh in the case of a female child. On the occasion, the child is presented with garments, toys, utensils and sweets by the maternal uncle, or the maternal grandparents. The customs prevail among the Acharyas of Assam. The Acharyas profess Hinduism. Most of them belong to the Sakta sect. Their family deity is goddess *Lakshmi*, while the village deity is goddess *Kali*. The regional deities are

Chaturadash Devata and *Tripura Sundari*. The sacred centres which attract a large number of Acharya pilgrims include Chaturadash Devatar Bari, Matar Bari, Bari. No change of religion in the community was reported during the British rule. No significant change was noticed in the religious patterns or behaviour. However, the religious fairs have become very expensive. The custom is prevalent among the Acharyas of Assam.

After Birth, Woman Stops Cohabiting

"After the birth of a baby, the wife does not cohabit with her husband for one month. On the seventh, fourteenth or twenty first day after the birth, shaving of hair and paring of nails of the baby are done and the shaved hair and pared nails are buried. Donations of money or silver are given to the poor. *Aqiqa*, an important ritual, is usually performed on the seventh, fourteenth or twenty-first day after the birth. On this occasion, animals are sacrificed and the sacrificed meat it consumed by all. In the case of a male baby, two goats are sacrificed while in the case of a female, one goat is sacrificed. Naming of the chiled is done on any day after birth. The parents choose any one of the ninety-nine qualities of *Allah* for their child.

"The male child has to undergo *Khutna* or *Musalman* (circumcision) before he is ten years of age. On this occasion, a feast is arranged by the father."

The custom pertains to the Assamese Muslims.

Baby given Breast-milk of Surrogate Mother

The tribal midwife or *Hojaijik*, helps a pregnant woman in labour, who is helped by a *sengjaodi* or an assistant midwife in her work. Where an assistant midwife is not found an *anuma* or surrogate mother helps the tribal midwife. Any mother of a suckling baby can become a surrogate mother. It is the Dimasa custom that mothers of male and female children can become *anuma* of female and male babies respectively. As per the custom, a Dimasa can marry the son or daughter of her or his *anuma*, provided there is no incest relationship between them. Any way, the first breast milk is given to a new born baby by his or her surrogate mother. If no woman is available to be a surrogate mother, the midwife does all the work by herself. She also offers the first breast milk to the baby, provided of course she has breast milk at that time. When a child is born, the midwife performs worship at the nearby river, who also buries the placenta under the eaves of the house in the right side if the child is a male and in the left side if the child is a female. The Dimasa keep an axe under the bed of a new-born baby to protect the baby against *bangla* fever.

At a village of the North Cachar Hills called Semkhor further sex-linked customs were observed in which the umbilical chord of a male child was cut by putting it on the handle of an axe and that of a female child was cut by putting it on *thuri* (a part of a loom). In no other Dimasa village this custom was found to be observed. The period of seclusion for the new mother varies from two weeks to a month depending on the time it takes for the umbilical chord to get dry and fall. During the pollution period the mother cannot cook and fetch water for others. Nobody is allowed to touch her; all except the little children who touch her have to take a purificatory bath. During period of seclusion usually her mother, if she lives there, or in her absence her mother-in-law or any female relative does the household work on her behalf and also takes care of her. She needs care usually only for a day or two. After that the new mother gets recovered and then onwards does her own cooking.

Following birth, the father of the child cannot go out of the village for three days. The village as a whole also observes a period of pollution. No *gerba* or the village worship can take place during pollution period. When the village is too big, the entire village does not observe the pollution, but only the clan members observe the pollution. On the day when the umbilical chord of the baby falls both the mother and the father have a purificatory bath and the house and the household objects are cleaned. On the day the father shaves the head of the new born baby, or any other senior male member of the patriclan can serve the purpose. The mother or any other woman cannot conduct the shaving, particularly when the child is a boy. If they do, the boy will not be allowed to worship the Dimasa gods. Though the female child is mostly shaved by her mother, or even the father can also do the shaving. This ceremonial shaving is compulsory among the Dimasa known as *Khanaigusugarba*.

Usually, *daosathaiba* or a special ceremony for bringing the new born baby outside the house for the first time is performed the next day. Sometimes the ceremony is performed on some other day also as per to the convenience of parents. This special ceremony is called *nanadihangba*. The midwife brings the baby outside the house and shows him to fraternity and other village people invited for the occasion. The invitees shower blessings on the baby. Before the baby is brought outside the house, special care is taken to ward the evil spirits. The maternal uncle spits on the face of the baby after chewing sesame seeds, or any other male member of the mother's patriclan.

On the day of *nanadihangba*, or bringing the baby outside the hut, as observed at Semkhor, the father of the baby sacrificed a cock and a hen on the spot where the placenta was buried. These sacrifical animals were later given to the midwife and the surrogate mother. But this custom was not performed in any other Dimasa village, either of Mikir Hills or of North Cachar Hills. Then the surrogate mother facing east, plasters the front space of the door with and spreads a banana leaf there. The midwife then puts down the baby on that leaf, and lifts him three times. Thereafter, she sprinkles water on the right and mustard oil on the left carrying the baby in her lap. Then again facing east she counts from one to ten carrying an axe in her hand. The Dimasa could not explain the significance of this ritual. They claim, the axe is carried toward of the evil spirits. The midwife again repeats the counting turning once to the right and then to the left. Thereafter the midwife and the assistant midwife or the surrogate mother request the father of the baby to accept him. They say, 'We have brought gold and silver. Who is the father and who will take them?' Then the father takes the baby wrapping him with a new piece of cloth.

All the guests then bless the baby for a long and prosperous life. The maternal uncle and if his parents are alive blesses the child in a special way. He chews some rice and sesame seeds and spits on the baby's face. The sesame seeds, it is believed, will give him ling life and the rice will bring prosperity to him. In the absence of maternal uncle any other man of the mother's patriclan whose parents are alive can perform this ceremony. The midwife then is supplied with rice beer by the father with which she washes baby's hands. Thereafter she puts a little cooked rice and a drop of rice and a drop of rice beer into the mouth of the baby. In case of a male child only *akhi* or puffed rice is put into his mouth. It is considered that this enables the baby to learn to speak quickly. When the ceremony is over, the invitees are entertained with rice beer. Those who can afford, also supply food to the invitees. In other Dimasa village other than *Semkhor* these ceremonies are observed in brief. There the midwife simply brings out the baby and seeks blessings for him. In the case of special blessings by the maternal uncle, no strictness is observed whether his parents are alive or dead. No cock or hen is sacrificed there either. Though the chewing of sesame seeds and the ceremonial spitting on the face of the baby is performed this act is interpreted differently. The spitting does not stand for blessing, but to protect the baby from the evil spirits. However, the midwife and assistant midwife or the surrogate mother are entertained with food and drink and supplied with cloth for their services rendered. They are usually treated on the first rice eating ceremony of the baby. If the parents cannot afford to have a separate rice eating ceremony he pays the dues of the attendants on the day of *nanadihangba*, sometimes in cash also.

The first rice eating ceremony is sometimes performed between the sixth and twelfth month of the baby known as *bisingijiriba* performed by the midwife. At that time the name of the baby is also given usually chosen by the parents. Any suggestions from the relatives and guests are also considered.

Almost throughout the working day, the baby is kept tied on the mother's back. The new mother does not seem to have any difficulty in her work with the back-load of the baby. Everywhere, whether in jhum field, or river, or market, mothers are found carrying their babies in the same fashion. They are placed on the back in such a way that they can suckle the mother's breast easily without causing any impediment to their mothers. Sometimes, the baby is transferred to his father' back for a short while. Thus it is found among the Dimasa that one's early childhood is revolves around the parents only. When the baby grows a little the mother trains the child to walk and makes him eat the solid food. Till the age of four the child remains entirely dependent on parents. At that age children learn to defecate and to clean themselves without any help from parents. Then, they start becoming independent. In many Dimasa villages there are no latrines as such for excretion. The nearby forests are used by them for this purpose.

For the very infancy children accompany parents everywhere and nothing is purposely kept hidden from them. Gradually, a child begins to learn the sanctions and taboos of their tribal life. The Dimasa way of learning is rather an active and practical process.

From the fifth year onwards, children enter the world of their own. They form a group of their own age-mates. Till age of ten they don't have to share any family burden. They simply play around the village or collect edible fruits and tubers from jungle. They also catch fish in shallow streams and enjoy the delicacy of raw prawn. Venture for the swarm of butterfly is also a favourite pastime for them. They are found shooting birds with catapults. Parents seem to be indulgently liberal to them during the childhood. They neither ask them to work, or give any formal teaching. They discuss, even otherwise, confidential matters in presence of their children without any prejudice. The young boys spend their day in participating in games and sports. The following are a few Dimasa games:

Watab Kaba is a game of both Dimasa boys and girls who participate in it while having their bath. The children make a sound in the river water by pushing water from the opposite directions, a favourite game, specially among the unmarried young girls.

Hatai kaba is a game of small earthen balls. Only young boys take part in this game.

Roman nilaiba is of physical strength; boys usually participate in this game. But at the time of *busu* or a marriage ceremony, the youth and the adult members also participate in this game. Two persons hold the opposite ends of a bamboo and simply push each other by their shoulders. Sometimes they do not use bamboo, and simply push each other by their shoulders.

Balibathang is a male sport in which an equal number of boys stand on either side of a demarcating line on the ground. Then by holding his breath and causing a sound with indistinct melodious pronunciation of *balibathang-thing*, one of the members of a party crosses the demarcation line, and tries to touch a member of rival party and comes back. If he can come back successfully after touching a member of the opposite party in a single breath, that particular member of the party is eliminated. Then one member of the other party does the same. This process is repeated until all the members of one side are eliminated. The remaining party is declared the winner.

Panthao malao khawala young boys' game. A group of boys take part in this game. One of them acts a jackfruit tree, other member is the owner of the tree, yet other is a thief and the rest are jackfruits. The 'jackfruits' hang from the tree and the owner of the tree guards them against the thief. The thief comes stealthily and examines as to whether the jack fruits are ready for consumption. Sometimes he steals fruits successfully, and sometimes caught by the owner and beaten. The game is repeated until all the fruits are stolen away.

The life of young girls is different from that of the boys of the same age-group. The girls prefer to move along with their mother all the time, and help them in every domestic work. Often girls of about eight years accompany their mothers to market places with small loads fuelwood on their back. Young girls also fetch drinking water and small bundles of firewood. Thus the girls begin formal training at a comparatively young age, while the boys remain free of all responsibilities till their adolescence.

Giving a Temporary name Soon after Birth

As soon as a baby is born, a temporary name is given. The moment the sex of the child is determined by the attending persons to the mother, the child is given a temporary name, which may be changed later, if necessary. The baby named generally after one of its grandparents. If a child is not given a name immediately, the devils, called '*Thilha Ho*', give a name first to the child resulting in cutting short life of the child. The umbilical cord is cut with a fresh bamboo split called '*Nat-Go*', sharpened sufficiently for the purpose. It is said that as soon as the child is born, the grandparents or the father or whoever helps in the delivery must say: Here do I proclaim that I have cut the naval-cord of my grandchild or child or this child, no one else has the right to cut it.

This naming of the baby is called as *'Nao Min Chu'*. Such proclamation stems from a legend that long ago a man went out for hunting in dense forest when his wife was in an advanced stage of pregnancy. In the forest, it was too late for him to return home. So, the hunter spent the night under a huge tree. There was a hollow in a tree trunk. He managed to catch a wild hare or Buipi and carried it. In the trunk hollow lived a family of devils called *'Thilha'*. At the dead of night, when he was fast asleep, he was awakened by some voices drawing towards the tree trunk. As the voices reached there, they called out. The family of *'Thinla'* living in the trunk hollow responded. The voices asked the family that lived in the trunk whether they could join them, and go to a nearby village to cut the umbilical cord of a new-born baby. This invitation was politely refused by the *'Thilhas'* on the ground that there was a guest who had a dog with him this implied that there was a hunter with his cane basket wherein a *'Buipi'* was present. Hence, the devils in the hollow could not join them and the voice should proceed without them.

A few hours later, the voices returned from the village. The family of the devils living in the hollow asked as to the health and condition of the new born for whose birth and cutting the naval cord they went. They replied, 'The tiger king had cut the naval cord of the child ahead of us.' Then the female devil of the trunk inquired—"What was the time fixed by the tiger king". The reply was: 'The boy becomes a Youngman, get married with two wives. The two wives will one day quarrel, while pounding rice using the pestle or legs as battons freely. The boy then would think that the two wives of his ought to have separate rice pounder each. So, he would go to the jungle the next day to prepare one more rice pounder. While he works on the rice pounder, the tiger would have the naval cord of the boy cut.'

Now, the hunter thought that the subject-matter of discussion among the *'Thilhas'* must have concerned his own family, because he left his wife in her advance stage of pregnancy and whose labour-pain could have started at any time during the day. Being apprehensive, he could no longer sleep during the night. So, before the day-break he started for his house to reach there early. On arrival, when he heard that a son had born to him, he enquired about the timing of the delivery. He was told that the child was born last midnight. The time, he felt, exactly synchronized with the time the '*Thilhas*' were claimed to have been talking about cutting the naval cord of a new-born child. The hunter kept the matter to himself and did not divulge it to anyone throughout the life-time of his son. He observed the growth and the way of life of his son, keeping in mind the conversation of the '*Thilhas*' on that unforgettable night in the jungle. As the boy grew up to manhood, what his father heard years ago came true. His son married two wives and, as was predicted on that fateful night by the '*Thilhas*', the two wives quarreled one day over the rice-pounder.

To settle the dispute, their husband thought it better to provide both with one rice pounder each. Therefore, he went to the jungle to prepare one more rice-pounder. His father, knowing what fate awaited his son, followed him secretly into the jungle to protect him against his fate, according to the prediction of the '*Thilhas*'. As the son began to cut the wood, a tiger came and stood at a vantage point to pounce on the son at the first opportunity. While the tiger was hiding to kill the son, the father was ambushing the tiger to kill him and foil the danger. As the son struck his axe on the log for cutting the wood, he bent down. Likewise, as he alighted the axe from the wood, he straightened. This movement of bending and straightening made the tiger unable to adjust its target correctly, and as such, it took some time to jump on its pray. At last, as it jumped, the hunter-father also took a head-long jump on the leeping tiger and killed the big cat with a single shot. Meanwhile the son was unaware of what was happening around him. Having seen a dead tiger and his father, he could sense the happening and was grateful to his father for saving his life. Going to the carcass he cursed the dead tiger saying 'Had my father not killed you, you would have killed me. It is a petty that you have to be a dead tiger.' As he said this, he unconsciously rubbed tiger's whiskers up and down. While doing so, he received a deep cut in one of his fingers which brought him death ultimately. He could not be saved despite his father's attempt. The incident proved that destiny cannot be blotted. The hunter's son died just the way the '*Thilhas*' predicted. Henceforth, it was believed that the name of the new-born baby should be given as soon as the naval-cord of the child is severed from the mother.

The cover of the jar containing '*Zu*' prepared by the expectant mother is to be opened first, offered to the new mother as also to those who nursed her and those who come to greet the child. This is called '*Nao-Zu*' or wine or the child. Indeed, the wine helps the woman to restore her energy and to clear whatever was there to come out with the placenta. The wine is medically salubrious and is prescribed by the tribal Priest who propitiates with his usual rituals for the health of both the child and the mother. Soon after the liquor is drunk, the mother feels hungry. Earlier as soon as a women felt that she had conceived, she prepared '*Zu*' and kept it shelved for 9 or 10 months. On the day of delivery, the '*Zu*' is uncorked by the pregnant woman herself and taken. Besides, a cock or hen is killed as soon as the child is born. The chicken is then boiled and its soup is taken by the new mother. The meat is cooked and boiled well with some rice which is also eaten by the mother. This gives her strength and help her in quick recovery. The meat is also taken by those attending on her. Thus, the wine served on the occasion is continued to be sipped until its intoxicating element is exhausted, which might carry them for the entire night. As the child grows upto about five years, the head of a girl is shaved, except for a small patch at the back. It remains so till her puberty. On the other hand, a boy is also shaved with a tuft on top of his head which remains as he is grown up. Thereafter he grows his hair long in much the same manner as to that of a girl. This difference in hair cutting during childhood is just to distinguish a boy from a girl.

After the child birth, when the mother is able to undertake the daily chores at home and field, there are some prohibitions and taboos she is expected to observe, which include: Whenever the mother goes to the field, she bids farewell to her child saying, 'Be at home, my child, while I go to the field.' Otherwise, it is believed that the child's soul may follow her. For fear of the child's soul following her to the field, she is always supposed to say at returning home, thus: 'Come my child, let us go home'. If this is not said, and if the soul of the child happens to follow her, it cannot come back with its mother. And thus left alone in the field, the child's soul wanders about in the jungle in search of its mother. This results in illness and sufferance of the baby. The tribal priest then has to propitiate and call back the child's soul from the jungle. Similarly, when the mother of the child arrives home from the field with her load of firewood, in a basket or anything domestically useful, it is not simply thrown down on the ground. It is said that the soul of the child having followed the mother has come back from *jhum* and might be standing or playing around her. If, therefore, the load is suddenly put down without giving prior warning to the child's soul, of might hurt the child. Therefore, before putting down the heavy load the mother always say first - 'Be away, my child, I am putting down the firewood (or whatever load) on the ground.'

Likewise, certain other things are also to be observed by the father. If a father is to undertake touring along with a child, burnt-coal or smoked portion of the hearth is painted on its forehead before embarking out of the house. It is believed that such act of paining the child helps ward off the evil eye, illness and other misfortune. The same procedure is followed on the return journey also. This is to identify that child is being accompanied by the parents and grandparents, so that '*Thilhas*' might not cast their evil spell on it. Similarly, when a child is taken out in the evening after sunset or nightfall, ginger is applied on its forehead to avoid illness.

The custom belong to the Kukis of Manipur.

Killing of Dog or Pig at Birth

About the birth customs of Seema Nagas in Nagaland Mr. J.H. Hutton recorded, "When a male child is born its mother observes six days' *genna*, and five for a female child, but in the case of her first child, of whichever sex, the genna is ten days. A dog or pig is killed. Wild vegetables, flesh killed by wild animals, or any other 'bad meat' is forbidden to the household, which must live on food of its own provision. The members of the household may not work in their own fields or go to their granary, but may work in the fields of others. The mother herself must stay at home for the period of the genna and may not leave the precincts of the house except to defecate, and may not speak to any stranger. As soon as the child is born she eats a chicken of the same sex as the child.

"When the days of *genna* are completed the mother takes a child of the same sex as her infant, an empty basket, and a rain shield, and goes to the end of the village and says 'I am going to the fields,' and then returns to the house. The *genna* is then at an end.

"Should the father be out when the birth takes place he may not enter the house till the sun has set.

"The method of delivery (or at any rate one method) is for the mother to squat on her heels upon a cloth spread on the ground. A woman steadies her shoulders from behind, another doing the same from in front, while a third steadies and supports her knees.

"The after-birth is buried inside the house under the bed or in some other spot where no one is likely to tread. An old woman buries it and washes her hands and face thereafter, and, though eating in the house, eats separately for three days.

"Should the mother die in childbirth she is taken out by the back door and buried behind the house. The husband in such a case is genna for eleven days. All the dead woman's beads, ornaments, clothes, etc., are thrown away, and her husband's personal property is not touched by anyone 'for a year,' *i.e.,* until after the next harvest. Even then all utensils, etc., are got rid of as soon as they can be replaced, and no one will touch them except the aged. If the child lives and there is no woman of the household to take charge of it, it is given to some childless couple, who eventually take half the marriage price if it is a girl, and who bring it up as their own son if a boy, though in the latter case the boy does not change his clan for that of his foster-parents. If the child dies at the same time as its mother it is buried with her.

"A new-born child which dies is buried in the *akishekhoh,*

and is not buried with a cloth, but only with bamboo bark instead. Three days' genna only is observed for its death.

"Children are suckled for from one to three years, and it is not unusual to see a Sema mother suckling two children who may have more than a year's difference between them in the matter of age.

"On the third day after the child's birth the lobe of the ear is pierced by some clans, notably the Yepothomi and others to the north, and a wisp of cotton put into it, and at the same time a tiny basket is made and lined with leaf and six pebbles, and six bits of ash are put into it. When the mother takes a child and goes (nominally) to the fields to break the genna, the child carries this basket and its contents to the village well, where it throws them away. The child taken on this occasion may be a brother or a sister of the infant or near relative or merely a neighbour. Just before the boring of the ear the child is given a chicken of the same sex as itself. The mother may not eat of this chicken. The Asimi, Zumomi, and some other clans do not bore the ear at all on this occasion, and by those that do so only the lobe of the ear is bored then. In the case of boys the concha of the ear is pierced later, and usually somewhere about the age of puberty. If not done before marriage the concha of the ear cannot be pierced unless the genna for touching an enemy's corpse is done. Among the northern Semas two holes are made, one at the edge of the fossa of the antihelix and one in the concha, and become gradually enlarged by the insertion of thick wads of cotton wool until in the aged they are distended to an enormous size. In the case of girls all Semas alike bore the hole at the apex of the helix from below upwards. These holes are in addition to the hole in the lobe which every Sema has. A Sema accustomed to wear cotton in the holes in his ears cannot discontinue it without discomfort, largely owing to passage of air through the empty apertures, which interferes with his hearing.

"The distension of the ear sometimes causes even the outer edge to split, while to inflict an injury on a man by tearing his ear, whether the lobe or the concha, is a serious offence, as the torn ear will not hold ornaments. The torn ear, however, can be mended, as if tied up quickly and spliced with fresh chicken skin the parts grow together again.

"The Asimi, Zumomi, and other clans who do not always pierce the lobe of the ear on the third day have a regular occasion for doing so. Anyone who is so inclined and has a son of suitable age celebrates a genna called *anivu,* in which he kills a pig and provides a large quantity of rice liquor and gives a feast. Anyone in the village who has a son or daughter with ears unpierced may have them pierced on that day. For boys they make only one hole in the middle of the concha instead of two, and one in the lobe. The number and position of holes bored vary by locality rather than by clan, the southern Semas following the last-mentioned custom generally, while one or two villages like Iganumi, much influenced by Angamis, bore four small holes in the outer edge of the helix and one in the lobe, no others.

Giving Cold Water Bath to the New-born

The Lakhers perform *sakia* ceremony to beget children. The pregnant woman and her husband have to follow certain Taboos, like not participating in some sacrifices of animals, crossing a river or touching a corpse. While delivering, the expectant mother kneels down by the side of a bed and female relatives helped her in the delivery. Following birth, the baby would be given a cold water bath to wake it up and the mother a warm water bath. The baby would not be taken out the room for three days. On the fourth day the baby would be taken out in the village street and its earlobes are pierced for wearing earrings. On the ninth day for a girl and the ten days in case a male child, a fowl is sacrificed at the spot of the birth. After the ceremony, called *radeide*, the child was taken to pupa's house and pupa would give some meat or fowl and rice. On this day the baby's hair are cut and kept short till the child becomes eight or nine years old; thereafter the hair are kept uncut and tied in a knot for a boy or a bun for a girl. Two or three months after the birth, a ceremony called *nawhri* is performed to propitiate the child's *shri* or disease germ to keep it free from illness. A child is given two or three names to help God remember atleast one of the names. Usually, a male baby would get a name same as the grand father's and the girl, grandmother's.

The custom is prevalent among the Lakhar tribals of Mizoram.

Cutting Umbilical Cord in Five or Seven Strokes

Mr. Endle recorded the customs relating to the birth ceremony, rites and rituals. Thus, "In a Kachari village community there would seem to be no formally recognised midwives (*dhais*), any respectable and competent matron being at liberty to give attendance and assistance to the patient in such cases. In severing the umbilical cord no scissors, knife, or other implement of steel is ever used, nor is the severance effected at one stroke, but in a succession of slight cuts, *seven* such cuts being made in the case of a girl, and only *five* in that of a boy. The cutting instruments consist of thin hard strips of bamboo, shaped roughly into the form of a knife; and a separate bamboo knife must be used in making each slight cut, seven such knives being thus made use of for a female child and five for a male. It is not unusual for one of the bystanders to give a name to the newly-born child at the severing of the umbilical cord. The good matron who officiates as midwife receives no money payment for her services, but on the mother becoming convalescent a feast is given at the parent's expense, in which pork and other flesh meat is always present in abundance; and at this feast the officiating midwife is accorded the place of honour, as some recognition of the value of her kindly ministrations in her neighbour's hour of trial and need.

"For about a month or six weeks, (the period seems to vary within these limits) after giving birth to a child, the mother is held to be technically "unclean," and is subjected to certain social and religious limitations; *e.g.,* she may not approach the *dham* or domestic altar commonly found inside a Kachari's dwelling-house, and on which she is ordinarily in the habit of making offerings of eggs, chickens, in times of trouble. This period of *ceremonial* uncleanness is usually terminated by the use of the water of peace *(Santi-jal)*. The *deori* freely sprinkles the mother as well as the house and its contents with this holy water, after which she is fully at liberty to resume social intercourse with her neighbours," he added.

During Delivery Presence of Father Necessary

About the customs, rites and rituals relating birth, Mr. S.P. Mills recorded, "It is considered most important that if possible the father should be present at the birth of his child. Otherwise the delivery will be a difficult one. If the husband happens to be away when his wife's labour begins, and comes hurrying home when he hears the news, it is believed that the child 'waits for its father' and will not be born till he arrives. The woman is delivered in a squatting position, supported by her husband and her mother, unless the latter is of the husband's clan. If she is, she may not be present, for the husband would feel shame before her at such a time. The umbilical cord is held by the mother with her toe and cut by the father with a bamboo knife between the toe and the child. Six such knives are prepared by the father before the birth, one being thrown away if the child proves to be a daughter. The one used and the other five, or four as the case may be, are tied in a bundle and stuck into the thatch over the mother's bed in order to ward off evil spirits. The child is washed and the father touches it with his left hand, and with his right hand puts into its mouth a little masticated rice, saying: 'I have touched it before the *tsungrem*. No *tsungrem* can seize this child.' The after-birth is washed and disposed of as follows: The father places it in a basket lined with leaves, and some distance behind the house, but exactly in line with the hearth, makes a sort of pen rack about six feet high of crossed sticks and bamboos. For a boy he uses three sticks and three bamboos and for a girl two sticks and three bamboos. On this he places the basket, flanked with six (or five, if for a girl) imitation snares made of slips of bamboo. The object is said to be to frighten crows away. After putting the basket and snares in position the father walks away a few yards, and returns five times for a boy and four times for a girl. Ordinarily the after-birth is never looked at again, but it is believed that if maggots get at it the baby will cry. If a new-born child therefore gives the household sleepless nights the father goes and examines the after-birth and pours hot water on it to kill any maggots which may be there. When the navel cord drops off it is wrapped up by the mother with a tuft of the child's hair in a bit of rag and preserved in a basket in the house. When the child is six months or more old the mother goes and hides this little package in the jungle. Should the house be burnt by any chance while the cord is in it the father may not rebuild on the same site, though another man may. On the second day after birth the lobes of the child's ears are pierced with a sharp piece of bamboo, and a little tuft of hair is cut with a 'dao' and a mallet made of half a sword-bean seed. A mallet of seven such seeds is used by the Phom tribe for the ceremonial hair-cutting that the small boys undergo after first touching meat. The hair and mallet are kept in the house and can never be given away. The piercing of the ear is most important. It is done by the father, who thereby acknowledges the child as his. If he be dead it can be done by the mother or by the grandfather on either side. (In some villages the ear is always pierced by the grandfather if the father be young, on the ground that a young man will suffer from cataract if he does this). If the father of an illegitimate child be unknown the mother pierces its ears, but the child can never be admitted into any clan and must always bear the shame of its birth. It is for this reason that Ao women invariably bring maintenance cases before the child is born, and an order of this nature against a man is always to the effect that he must build a house in which the child can be born (for a girl cannot give birth to a child in her parents house; she would feel shame before her father), must pierce the child's ears, and must pay so much a month maintenance. The child is named by whoever pierces its ears at the time that this ceremony is performed... A household is 'genna' for six days after the birth of a boy and for live days after the birth of a girl. On the seventh (or sixth) day the parents wash at the village spring, and on the next day the husband offers a fowl and an egg in front of his field-house. This concludes the ceremonies.

"In cases of difficult delivery, baskets and any other closed receptacles there may be in the house are opened, and a fowl or a pig is offered outside the house to appease whatever evil spirit is responsible. Occasionally the woman's stomach is poulticed with cloths dipped in hot water.

"So terrible is the stigma on a child whom no one will acknowledge as his that in the old days mothers often preferred to do away with them. Sometimes abortion was practised. When the woman was well advanced in pregnancy an old woman was called in who, having caused the girl to starve for six days, felt for the head of the child and cither bit it or hit it a sharp blow with a smooth stone. More usually, however, the child was killed immediately after birth by the mother, who stamped on its neck. Abortion and infanticide are, of course, forbidden now, and there is also less temptation to practise them. In the old days it was chiefly slave-girls who got rid of their children—if they did bring a claim against a man there was no one to support their cause and no impartial tribunal to which they could bring it. Now any girl who comes to Court can get her claim decided one way or the other, and many a young buck, whom family influence and bribes would have got off in the old days, finds himself compelled to acknowledge his offspring whether he likes it or not. But illegitimate children are much disliked, for their existence is believed to prevent the birth of legitimate children. Usually, therefore, if the parties are unmarried they square matters by marrying before the child is born. After all, an Ao marriage often does not last very long, and if the couple find they are not as fond of one another as they thought they were, they can easily separate.

"Children born at or just before the dark of the moon are believed by their love of meat to show their resemblance to tigers and leopards, which are supposed always to be born at this time of the month. Triplets are unknown, and twins, which are rare, are disliked. Both are kept, but their birth is supposed to forebode the early death of one of the parents, (So some Sema (*vide The Sema Nagas,* p. 262); but most Sema, like the Angami, object to twins as weaker than single children and therefore less likely to survive, particularly as if one goes the other is likely to follow suit because they are twins), or at any rate of some near relation. Children are often not weaned till they are three years old, boys being suckled longer than girls as a rule. But from a very tender age they are given masticated rice. The process of feeding is a most curious one to watch. The mother sits with the child on her knee and chews little mouthfuls of boiled rice, which she shoots from her mouth into the child's. The child understands what is happening quite well and as it swallows each mouthful pouts its lips to receive the next dainty morsel, exactly as a young bird opens its mouth for the next worm. Women who are sisters or paternal first cousins often suckle each other's children, and should the mother die no one but a sister or paternal first cousin or the child's grandmother may perform this duty. A widower who can find no one to suckle his child has to keep it alive as best he can on masticated rice, eggs and soup. Strange though it may seem, many babies flourish quite well on this diet. For motherless twins it is the only possible diet, for no one may suckle them after the mother's death."

Breaking Strings of Beads

About the birth customs of the Angami people, Mr. J.H. Hutton records, "An Angami woman when about to deliver a child breaks the strings of beads that she is wearing, letting the beads fall about the floor, and throws off all her clothes except a single cloth wrapped round her body like a shawl. She delivers her child hanging by her hands to a head-band (for carrying loads), which is fastened to a beam in the house, her knees being clear of the ground. (The Kezami Angamis when a birth is about to take place put all eatables and drinkables outside the house. the Kacha Nagas do the same, but not the Tengima Angamis). The genna that follows is the same whichever the sex of the child. The mother is kept separate from the rest of the household, her bed being separated, and a separate hearth being built for her, though in the same room as the general hearth. Immediately after the delivery and before the cutting of the navel-string, she is fed on rice-beer, rice, and the flesh of a hen (never that of a cock) which has been touched by the child. (Among the Memi, at any rate, this is done by the mother herself with a bamboo knife. I think the Tengima bury the *placenta* in the house. Certainly the Memi do). For five days, for ten in the case of her first child, (It is after the birth of her first child that an Angami girl removes from her ears the white shells that she has worn from infancy. She gives them to her husband. Similar shells are worn by the Ao girl, who, however, parts with them when she is tattooed, a ceremony which takes place as soon as she is considered old enough to be married and usually after her betrothal, or what practically amounts to such.) the mother is fed exclusively on this food, a second hen being killed if the first is not enough, and during these five days her husband is *kenna,* and in some villages the whole household is *kenna*. The household is *kenna* in any case on the day of birth, as it is if any domestic animal gives birth to young.

"When the five days have expired the mother is allowed to go out, but by the back door of the house only, and if there is no back door one has to be made for the purpose. No one must see her going out, she goes out by stealth, taking all the cooking, eating, and drinking utensils of the household with her, and when no one is looking she throws them away behind the house. Her husband opens the back door for her and keeps a look-out to see that there is no one watching, but he must not look at his wife as she is coming out to throw the things away.

"The baby is washed with warm water on the day of its birth, and this washing is followed by the cutting of the navel cord, but it is not washed again till the five days' genna have expired. On the sixth day, after throwing away the cooking utensils, the mother takes any child of her husband's kindred and of the same sex as her baby and goes with this child to the village water-hole. The child draws water and gives it to the mother, who carries it back to the house and washes her baby with it without heating the water. The mother also on her way plucks two or three sprays of the plant called '*tsoheh,*' which she brings back with her. She puts a drop of water and then a twig of this plant on the babe's forehead and adjures it to become strong and hard like the *tsoheh* plant. At the same time she tears the twig in two. This ceremony she repeats on the right and on the left hand of the infant. On the eighth day she carries the child who accompanied her to the well to the house of one of her husband's kindred who is newly married and has suffered no misfortune. For this purpose the house of a married man whose children are all alive will also serve. The wife of this man places a little rice beer on the child's lips and gives the child a little rice and a little rice beer in a diminutive gourd, after which the mother of the newly-born baby again carries the child back to her house.

"The infant, when it grows up, stands in a particular relation to the newly-married man to whose house the child was taken. He or she must call him 'father' and his wife 'mother,' land neither must on any account behave aggressively toward the other.

"On the ninth day the father and the mother, taking the baby itself, go to the fields, and after pretending to do a little work they eat and drink and then return home. (In one version of the birth ceremonial given me it was the baby itself which was fed in the house of one of the husband's kindred, while it was a boy or girl from the husband's kindred who was taken out of the village to dig). Sometimes they do not even go to their fields, but go out of the village and dig some ground anywhere at all. When returning home they bring back two pieces of alder tree. This concludes all birth ceremonies.

"If the child be born dead, or die before the completion of the five days' genna, one day's *kenna* is observed, nothing more, and the child is buried inside the house. The father must be present when it is buried, and if he is away from home the burial of the body is put off until he returns. A case occurred in Jotsoma during the Abor expedition of 1912 in which the wife of a man who was with the expedition gave birth to a daughter which died. The body was kept unburied in the house for two months until the father returned to his family—and they living in the house all the time.

"If a woman die in childbirth or before the completion of the five days' genna, she is taken out, not by the door, but through a hole made in the side of the house, and buried with all her property. Her baby is taken out and buried with her, if it die as well. Should it live it would normally be brought up on rice pulp, but cases of gynecomastism seem to occur occasionally. (In Yampi, a Chang village, there is a noted warrior named Yenso, who is said to have breasts like a woman, while in Yuonyar there is an hermaphrodite named Chualan Abaja. Cases of the suckling of orphaned children by quite old women seem to occur from time to time among the Lhotas). There is at the time of writing a girl in Jotsoma whose mother died when she was an infant and who was suckled by her father Niselhu, also still living, who first let the child suck at his breast to comfort it, but after a time was able to give it milk. In the Lhota village of Longsa a girl named Pontselo, still living, is said to have been suckled by her father Chiathang from the time she was fifteen days old, when her mother died. Angami children are usually suckled until they are two or three years old. One may frequently see a woman with a baby and an older child, both of which she is suckling. Children whose father dies remain in the custody of the mother or her relations until weaned, after which the father's heirs have the custody of them.

"Infanticide used to be practised in the case of children born of unmarried girls. In such cases delivery had to take place in the jungle, and the child was killed; the Kezami women used further to pierce its feet all over with thorns to prevent its visiting and haunting the mother in her dreams. It was believed that if it was allowed to grow up the village would have no success in hunting or in war. Nowadays an unmarried girl who is pregnant is turned out of her parents house before delivery, and gives birth in the cow-house of someone else's porch or some similar place, and the presence of any second person at the time of delivery is *kenna*. Whether the mother performs any ceremony is not known.

"Twins are uncommon, but the occurrence of twins is not disliked (It is regarded as extremely fortunate by the Memi.), and if both are boys it is a matter for con-gratulation; their mother is under an obligation to give them flowers of the same variety and cloths of exactly the same pattern. Triplets are very rare indeed. One case is remembered to have occurred in Mozema, but all three died."

Mr. Hutton added further about the taboos and rituals in his book

The Angami Nagas: with some notes on neighbouring tribes, Thus, "After the birth the father may not eat green vegetables for one day, and must not go out at night for six or seven days.

"The ear-piercing is done by an old man, who gets a piece of wood for his trouble. Some day after the seventh the parents eat a fowl together and meditate on Urame; after this the child is given rice, gradually. The afterbirth is buried very carefully in a pot under the floor of the home, because should it be eaten by a dog or pig the child would die. On this day the mat on which the mother lay and her cooking pots are thrown outside the village. After a child has been named a garland of Kollaw grass is placed round its neck.

"Twins are thought *very lucky.* No work is done on the day twins are born. The event is thought to presage good fortune for the *Mohvu,* it is therefore not surprising that twins always are helped first when any food is being distributed.

"The body is buried under the spot on which the birth took place, if the child dies within five days of birth.

"When the child is two years old, several fowls are killed and his friends are regaled. There is no special ceremony when he first goes to sleep in the young men's house.

"Only the father may be present, if he cannot be there an old woman takes his place. The mother herself cuts the navel cord with a bamboo knife, and buries the afterbirth in the room alongside of the birthplace. The delivery takes place on the floor to left of the central hearth, as you enter the living room, and the mother remains there for five days. When the mother has buried the afterbirth an old woman brings in stones to make a now cooking place, and if the child be a boy six stones, to make two new fireplaces, as for five days the father and mother must have their food cooked separately and eat separately; and if the child be a boy a new cooking place must be made for the father also. As soon as the new fireplace has been made, water is warmed to give the child a bath, after which a cock or a hen, according to the sex of the infant, is killed by a boy, and cooked by the mother, who eats it all herself, except small portions given to *Urame.* Then if the parents are wealthy a pig and several fowls may be killed and a feast given. On the day of the birth the father must do no work. For five days the mother must not leave the house, even, for purposes of nature. On the fifth day the name is given. The father thinks of the name at the moment of birth, but should he subsequently dream of broken weapons, torn cloth, or killing animals, the name must be changed. A cock or a hen is killed and eaten by the mother, helped, if necessary, by an old woman. On the same day a bull is killed for *Urame* and the flesh divided among the villagers. (That is apparently only done for boys, and then only in certain circumstances.) Then the name is given as follows. An elderly male relative holds a spear in one hand and a piece of burning fir-wood in the other, and somehow also takes the child. He first stands on the birth-place, then he crosses to the other side of the house and announces the name. The mother now throws away the pots she has been using and the special fireplace is removed and the mother rejoins her husband on the family couch.

"On the sixth day the father and mother eat together, and then the mother takes the child just outside the village and then returns. On the seventh day the mother leaves the child in the house and goes and fetches water. Then she cooks rice and the flesh of some animal and places a little on the breast, mouth, and forehead of the child. The mother then takes her child, and with it a little dhan and a sickle to the house of another woman who has children living. The dhan and the sickle are left there and others brought in exchange. If after several girls have been born a son appears, the parents sometimes celebrate the event by killing a bull and feasting the villagers.

"This must be done within two months of birth. The parents must remain chaste for the remainder of the month, in which the piercing is done, so most of them perform it on the last day of the two months. Some time later, within a year or two, the *Ale-we* genna is celebrated. The father and mother keep apart for five days and the mother and child eat together. During these days the mother does no work. When the child is two or three he gives a feast to his little friends—this is called *Muchazue.* This terminates the ceremonies connected with birth and childhood." added Mr. Hutton.

The custom is practiced among the Angami tribals of Nagaland.

Father Abstains Touching Anybody

About the birth genna of Manipur, Mr. T.C. Hodson records in his book *The Naga Tribes of Manipur,* thus, "Household gennas are occasioned by events such as the birth of children, the birth of domesticated animals in the house, the first occasion of haircutting and ear-piercing, naming of children and finally the death of domesticated animals in the house. They affect all those who are normally inmates of the house and any others who are temporarily in the house, such as women acting as midwives. Their duration varies not only from tribe to tribe but from village to village.

"Among the Tangkhuls the husband may not go out of the village or do any work after the birth of a child for six days if the child be a boy or for five days when the child is a girl. So also strangers are forbidden to enter his home during this period lest harm should come to the child. For woman comes in to act as midwife, she too is genna. At Sanding one of the cloth-weaving villages the period of restriction lasts for one day only and we have the interesting information that the father may not touch any one for fear of harm coming to the newly born infant. At the village of Toloi the prohibition lasts for ten days and it is expressly stated that the mother may go out of the house the day after the child is born, but the father stays inside the whole time. Apparently the man may go to the front of the house, but not into any one else's house, and as the area of the house and its noontide shadow is held to be the domain of the house spirit, we may say that he must remain within the limits of the power of the deity who is *ex-officio* most concerned with their domestic life. The head of the household is the person who performs the rites incidental to the worship of the house spirit and the sacrifice of a fowl which is part of the genna is made by him. Now the birth genna includes the ceremony of naming the child which takes place on the last day of the birth genna and for the purposes of which the sacrifice of a fowl is necessary as the name is determined by omens. Zu is given to the women of the village.

"In the Mao group both parents are genna and at Jessami this lasts five days, while at Laiyi Liyai and Maikel it lasts for fifteen days at least in the case of all except the eldest child, when it is, or was, prolonged to thirty days. At Mao the genna for the first child is ten days and for the others five days.

"A cock is sacrificed for a boy and a hen for a girl, but whether the taking of omens is the main or a secondary purpose is not clear.

"At Maram they say that at one time this genna lasted for one month but is now observed for ten days only, during which neither parent may touch any other person nor may the woman eat any food except fish and salt. A fowl is sacrificed on the day of birth, but I do not know who eats it. At Uilong the woman goes out at the end of the genna to bathe accompanied by a village boy who must not have attained a marriageable age, and whose presence is necessary in case any evil spirit meet the woman.

"At Liyang village which I know is not a pure Quoireng village, the birth genna lasts for one month, during which the only food permitted to the parents is fish and fowl, meat of any other kind being most strictly forbidden. The same prohibition of meat is found among the Quoirengs who, with the exception of the village of Taron, keep the birth genna for a month. At Lemta and Maolong I was told that the fowl which is killed on the birth of a child may not be eaten by the father, who, at Taron, is kept without any food that day. The flesh of fowls is not regarded as meat. The Kabuis appear to have a birth genna for the first child and do not allow the father to eat, drink, or smoke that day. The Koms prolong the genna to one month for the birth of a son and for the birth of a daughter regard five days as sufficient for the father, who may do no work during the genna, and may not go far from the village, while exacting a month from the mother. The Chirus are genna for one month, though later information points to ten days as the period, and offer two jars of zu and two fowls to the house spirit. Some villages regard five days as long enough. If the navel cord and after-birth are buried by a person other than the father, that person shares the genna. Either a fowl or a pig or a fish are sacrificed to the house spirit.

"The Marrings also require a month's genna for the birth of a child, and sacrifice a fowl to the house spirit immediately the child is born. At the end of the genna there is a feast, that is, one or more fowls are killed, which are eaten by the men of the father's clan, each of whom, on entering the house, pours a drop or two of zu inside the threshold of the house, as an offering to the house spirit.

"Naming ceremonies either form part of or conclude the birth genna, and are an essential feature of this domestic genna. We may note that among the Quoirengs the fowl that is sacrificed is eaten by the youngsters and women, but not by the father.

"Among the Tangkhuls there does not seem to be any fixed time for ear-piercing, but it occasions a genna. The animal sacrificed varies according to the wealth of the parents. A rich man may kill a buffalo and a poor man a fowl. At Kalhang a hen is the usual offering. In most villages this genna lasts for one days, but at Kharasom it needs six days when a son is the victim and five for a girl.

"There is more variety among the Mao Nagas, for at Jessami the rite takes place three months after the birth of the child and for one day only, while at Liyai it takes place on the last day of the birth genna, and at Laiyi on the fifth day after the child is born, that is on the same day as the naming. At Liyai the parents may not eat salt on the day of the genna. At Mao and Maikel the ceremony is performed two months after birth, on the last day of the moon, for all other days are genna or forbidden. Both oil and pulse are forbidden to the parents, for serious illness would come to the child if they partook of these dainties. They are also forbidden marital intercourse on the night preceding this genna.

"At Maikel the hair of the child is cut one month after birth, and a cock is killed for a boy and hen for a girl.

"At Maran the hair is cut on the ninth day after birth and on the following day the ears are pierced, and on these days salt only may be eaten with the rice consumed by the parents.

"Among the Quoirengs the ear-piercing is performed in the cold weather and seems to take place during the Mangla tha, though in one village I was told that it was done five days after birth. The hair-cutting here requires a village genna.

"The Koms cut the hair of the children on the day of the name genna, while the Chirus postpone both it and ear-piercing for two months. The Marrings again delay the ear-piercing for perhaps as long as three years, but cut the hair on the last day of the birth genna."

The customs are practiced by the Naga tribes of Manipur.

Naming Ceremony

Village Elders Giving Name to New-born

"On the birth of a child, the name to be given is settled upon, not by the parents, but by the old men and women of the village, a big feast being held on the occasion.

"Subsequent to the birth of a child the father and mother drop their own names, and are addressed by that borne by their offspring, the terms of father and mother being affixed, thus 'So-and-so's father', 'So-and-so's mother'.

"Should a couple grow old and have no children, they are addressed as 'the father of no child' and 'the mother of no child' respectively."

The custom is prevalent among the Nagas of Cachar.

Conducting Shastric Rites

The ceremonies related to a new-born baby such as *namakaram, chudakaram* and *annaprasam* are performed by Brahmins according to the Shastric rites. Non-Brahmin Hindus hold only the ceremony of *annaprasam* when the baby is in its fifth, seventh or ninth month. The first morsel is put into its mouth by its maternal uncle. A feast is given to relatives, clansmen and congregational prayers are held.

Some Buddhists of Assam observe a kind of purification rite for both mother and child. The *Dowaniyas* do it with the help of a *Fungi* (priest) who performs religious functions. The Buddhist *Fakials* bring the baby outside to the elevated verandah of the houses built on poles only after seven days and bring down the baby to the ground only after a month, when old women tie black treated to its hands and legs to wish it well in life. Some Hindus also tie a black thread around the baby's waist to ward off effects of evil eyes. The naming ceremony of the Khasis is an interesting custom: an experienced elderly man of the tribe is invited to the house to act as a witness, and will go on uttering name after name; the priest will go on pouring wine, the name that coincide with the last drop of wine will be adopted. Amongst the Bodos a thread is tied at the base of intestinal canal and then the canal is cut above the knot with a sharp bamboo blade or with a knife or a razor.

No widow or widower or a barren person is allowed to perform this act. Then the baby is washed with tepid water. Nine *durba* grasse blades, a branch of *tulis* and a gold ring are tied in a bundle which is dipped into water from a river and sprinkled over the new-born baby and asked "O baby, what were you in your previous birth? Whatever you were, from this day you have become a Bodo". A cock is sacrificed to propitiate the Gods for the welfare of the baby. There is no other ceremony. The scar from the navel is put in a talisman and hung from the baby's neck. The mother has to entertain the *dhai* and others who helped her to a feast and rewards, if any; not to do so is considered a sin. There is no formal feeding of a Bodo baby. But when a boy is five years old, his maternal uncle comes and shaves off his head.

Sometimes in Bodo families where babies often die, a three-month old boy is married to his mother and a three-month-old girl to her father in the hope that it will give them a long lease of life. Again, sometimes a father without luck will put his new-born child into a basket, carry the burden ritually on his head and try to 'sell' the infant peddling from house to house in the village, every door he approached will express inability to 'buy' and direct him to the next door, thus 'unable to sell' the infant he will return to his home and make an atonement, by throwing a feast to the villagers.

Name given by the Community Priest

A name is given to the new born baby by the priest. Usually, a priest is drawn from the Bihari community. At such social and religious functions, the role of the maternal uncle is very important. The maternal uncle is the most important and respected person among the people of the Basphor community. No religious function of the community is performed without his presence. So, the people of the community consider the maternal uncle as equivalent to the priest. Hence, in most of the socio-religious functions of the community, they engage a maternal uncle instead of the priest. No major ritual is observed in connection with the Basphor name-giving ceremony. They simply decide on a name after consulting with the invitees and the priest.

The custom is related to the Basphor community of Assam.

Naming the Baby Immediately after Birth

The child is christened immediately after birth. Part of the name would include the order of the birth such as *mote* for the first-born, *kepu* for the second-born etc. Some part of the child's paternal grandmother's name, in case of a boy, and the paternal grandmother's name if it is also used. The piercing of ear-lobes (*anaivi*) is performed during the first year by family elder using a needle and thread, on the occasion a feast is arranged. Sweet-smelling brown rice (*cakhow*) must be served along with other eatables.

The custom prevails among the Anal tribes people of Manipur.

Naming the New-born Immediately Following Birth

A name is given to the child immediately after birth, either by the elders or relatives, to save the baby from the clutches of evil spirits.

The custom is related to the Adi (Ashing) tribe of Arunachal Pradesh.

Custom of Giving Ugly Names

About the naming ceremony of the Sema Nagas of Nagaland, Mr. J.H. Hutton records, thus: "In the Yepothomi and in the other clans who bore the lobe on the third day the child's name is usually given on the same day. It may be given by the parents or by anyone at all who has ideas on the subject. Omens as to its suitability are not taken, but the choice of a name, as among all Semas, except possibly the villages of the Lazemi group, is limited by the social standing and degree of prosperity of its parents. If an ambitious name is given to the child of poor parents people remark, '*Aho! oho!*' ('Oh! I say,' as one might put it), and most frequently the child dies. In any case it is a subject for ridicule, and probably receives a nickname much more opprobrious than a name that might in the first place have been suitably bestowed. Thus while a chief will give a child names implying prowess in war or prosperity in peace, the names given to a poor man's son denominate him an object of poverty, scorn, or aversion. Among chiefs' names we find such as 'Victor' *Gwovishe,* 'Challenger' *(Nikhui),* 'Preventer' *(Ka-Khiya,* one who holds the road and prevents the escape or onslaught of the enemy), 'Resorted to' *(Inato),* 'Enriched' *(Nikiye),* or in the case of girls 'Peace-maker' *(Sukhali),* 'Hostess' *(Khezeli).* As examples of the names of nobodies, we might take 'Eyesore' '*(Zunache),* 'Notorious debtor' *(Nachezu, Nachelho,* the debts being in paddy and this existence implying permanent poverty),

'Untouchable' *(Sholepu,* because of the filthiness of his habits,) 'Outcast' *(Yevetha),* and for girls 'Spurned' (*Mithili*), 'Gossiper' (*Pilheli*). Or, perhaps, "chatterbox," but the name has the implication that the chatter is of an unpleasant if not abusive description, and that the owner's tongue is without restraint—"Billingsgate" might almost pass as a translation.

"In the more southern villages of Zumomi and Asimi the name of a child is fixed upon when the genna for its birth expires, but it is not used and the child is spoken of as Kumtsa, Kumtsa = "Bitter," a very common name indeed, or Kakhu, or some such common name, the real name not being used till the child is some months old, an indication of the excessive susceptibility of new-born children to evil influences. Another instance of this is found in the superstition that the sand-lizard *(aniza)* informs the spirits *(teghami)* of the birth of male children, with the result that the spirits collect and destroy the new-born child. For this reason men kill the sand-lizard on sight. Women, on the other hand, always let it go scathless, as when a female child is born it remains *chini* and does not leave its hole. The women, moreover, sometimes make a fuss if men try to kill an *aniza* and endeavour to protect it.

Generally speaking, the Sema has the same disinclination to mention his own name that most Nagas have, though the feeling is fast weakening. It may have some connection with the notion that a man's soul answers to the name as well as his body.

"Before leaving the question of nomenclature it should be mentioned that the Sema never gives to the child the name of a living relation, though the names of dead ancestors are popular among those with a child to name. The explanation given is that, if the name of a living senior be given, the elder will die, as a substitute for him in this world has been provided. Possibly there is behind this some fear that such nomenclature would be tantamount to saddling one soul with two bodies, one of which, being useless, would die. The very strong objection which Semas have to having an animal named after them may be connected with the same idea. At the same time, they do not appear to have, at the present time, any belief at all that the dead are reincarnated in the living.

"In addressing one another, Semas are most punctilious in using a suitable appellation in speaking to or of any but intimates or inferiors. They use the terms of family relation when speaking to a senior or a stranger who is of their clan, calling them '*imu* (my elder brother) So-and-so,' '*Ini* (aunt) So-and-so,' '*Itukuzu* (my younger brother) So-and-so,' and so forth, according to their seniority. Similarly, members of a clan to which the speaker is related by marriage will be addressed as '*ichi*' (my brother-in-law) So-and-so,' etc. Equals who are not intimates or relations are addressed as '*ishou* (my friend) So-and-so,' inferiors (in age) who are not related are addressed as *apu* ('lad'), while the terms *ipu* and *iza* ('my father', 'my mother') are used for any very senior person or one to whom much respect is due owing to his position. Thus the writer was always addressed as *Ipu shaha* ('Father Sahib') until well enough known to become '*Ipu*' simply."

Naming Baby After the Day of Birth

About the custom of giving names to the newly born babies, Mr. J.P. Mills records in *The Ao Nagas,* Thus: "The day after a child is born it is called by some name, and ordinarily that name will be formally bestowed upon it next day, when its ears are pierced. Should it cry much, however, during the first day, another name is chosen and bestowed when its ears are pierced, for the first name clearly did not agree with it. The name chosen must be that of a dead ancestor; a living relation's name cannot be selected; nor would a father give to another child the name of a former child which had died young. If a man is killed in war none of his descendants may take his name unless the disgrace has been wiped out by the taking of a head in exchange. If a man dies 'apotia' his name is never again taken by any descendant, and however wealthy he may have been his name is never included in the lists of rich ancestors recited at mithan sacrifices. Save when an unpleasant name is given for a special reason, an Ao invariably has a high-sounding name. This does not mean that they are a particularly bombastic race; the reason is that their names resemble titles, great men in the past by displays of wealth and valour having earned for their descendants the right to use certain names. Thus the mildest of youths may be called Rokritangba ('taker of three-score heads') or a man who has never been on a raid in his life Litimmangyang ('taker of a head in exchange from Litim'). Certain terminations are common. For instance, *niken* means 'envied' *(e.g.* Mangyangniken— 'envied for taking a head in exchange,' or Rongsenniken— 'envied for his riches'); *wati* means 'rich in' *(e.g.* Subungwati— 'rich in mithan sacrifices,' or Rongsenwati— 'rich in wealth'); *lamba* means 'rich in,' 'copious giver' *(e.g.* Subunglamba— 'generous giver at mithan sacrifices,' or Chongsilamba— "generous giver at feasts of peace-making," or Sakulamba—"rich in heads"). Other typical men's names are Mendangchiba ("great ambusher"), Lanukamzak ("saviour of the boys," *i.e.* withstood the enemy, and so saved the lives of the village boys), Yimtitangzak (C) or Yimtitonglak (M) ("defender of the village"), Yimnasusu ("village rearguard") Repanokten ("killer of a pair") and Pongrichiba ("leader of a band"). Women's names are earned and bestowed on the same principle. Typical examples are Tunikshila ("envied one"), Latunglamla ("rich in slaves"), Temchen-chila ("chief among the rich"), Mangyangsangla ("receiver of praise at the taking of a head in exchange") or Pangchonglila ("pleased at purchases," *i.e.* of mithan or slaves). A common name for the daughter of Christian parents is Yimcharenla ("prosperity of Christianity"), though the belief in *aren* (see p. 112, *supra)* has nothing whatever to do with Christianity.

"If a young child be weakly and always ailing the "medicine-man," on being consulted, pronounces it to be a case of *tening mokok* ("name unable"); that is to say, the child's name is too great for it. A little pig is then chosen and some of the child's spittle is smeared on it, six times for a boy and five times for a girl. The animal is then fattened up and sacrificed—among the Mongsen by the senior clan priest, and among the Chongli by the grandfather—with the words: "This child is ill and cannot carry its name. Let wind and water bear away its illness. Let it grow up like a cane-shoot and like a bamboo-shoot." Fowls are then sacrificed with a similar prayer. If this ceremony is unsuccessful a new, opprobrious name (usually some combination of *likok,* "bitter berry") is given to the child. A similar name is also given to a child born after several children have died in infancy, in the hope that the *tiya* will not think it worth its while to take away a child with such an objectionable name.

"In the Chongli and Mongsen groups a man usually has one name only, but in the Changki group many have two. Neither is really secret, but one is only used in the village and is not ordinarily revealed to strangers. No one is forbidden to utter his own name. In the Changki group great friends often address each other as 'the father of So-and-so,' instead of using each other's names, or a man may sometimes be called 'the son of So-and-so'."

The custom is related to the Ao Nagas of Nagaland.

Naming Children After Day and Month

About the naming custom Mr. Endle records: "There does not seem to be any special principle underlying the giving of names to children, nor do such names as a rule resemble those of their fathers. Like some of the lower castes among their Hindu neighbours, children often take the name of the day or the month in which they were born. Hence we often find such names as Deobar, Mangal, Budhu, as also Maghua, Phaguna (names of months), etc., in use among the Kacharis. Other names are obviously adopted from the Hindus, *e.g.,* Ganga Ram, Sati Ram, etc. Others, again, were probably given by the mother in infancy expressive of some peculiarity in the new-born child's mental or physical temperament. Of this type, probably, is a very common name, 'Khangkhoa,' *i.e.,* the 'voracious one,' the 'great eater.' Another illustration is the name Gab-gra, *i.e.,* the weeper, the crier, etc. In short, any unusually prominent physical peculiarity is often seized upon to become the name by which the child is known throughout his whole after-life."

The custom is particularly practiced by the Cacharis of Assam.

No Naming Ceremony Performed

About the naming custom prevalent among the Angamis, Mr. J.H. Hutton records, thus: "The Angamis have no ear-piercing ceremony, the ears of girls being pierced when they are from six to twelve months old, and those of boys as soon as they can speak. Also, in the case of the majority of them, no naming ceremony is performed. A ceremony, however, is sometimes performed on the fifth day after birth, when the omens are taken in the usual way by slicing pieces from a stick of the shrub called *chiese,* and dropping two pieces parallel, and other two on the top of them. If the second two stay on without falling off, the name suggested is chosen. A child is called at first "*Kechibu*" or "*Kechino*" according to sex, until someone, usually one of its parents, gives it a name. The husband's relations are sometimes, but not necessarily, consulted.

The Aos take the similar omen with the fire-stick, when they take one at all.

This name is, with the Angamis, a name of abstract significance suggesting the presence of good qualities or good fortune, such as Kevise, 'arriving at a good time,' Vinile, 'keep good', Viyale, 'let your share be good,' Rhichale, 'long living' (or 'long let him live'), Visanyu, 'want more good,' Zelucha, which might be rendered 'Companion on the Long Road.' This rendering is perhaps a little fanciful. An English-speaking Angami translated it to me as meaning "long comfortation," but this does not give the full idea either. The word contains the ideas of companionship, consolation, and road, duration, or distance, and was given because his parents had lost two or three sons born to them previously and hoped to be comforted by Zelucha into their old age. The root *vi* ('good') is particularly common, as in Vibile, Visopra, Visatsu, Viponyu, and a host of others. There are, however, certain circumstances under which a child is given a second name. Should he be born under conditions of unusual distress or affliction his mother will give him a suitable name of precisely an opposite nature to that of the names mentioned. This name is in some villages kept secret and told to no one but the child himself when he is old enough, and the very existence of such a second name and of the practice of giving one is stoutly denied. In other villages the second name, though not a secret, is not generally known and is not used. The Angami has an objection, still strong in some places, although not insurmountable and now rapidly dying out, to mentioning his own name himself. If he does so he is liable to be mocked at by his fellows as an '*huthu,*' *i.e.* an owl that is always calling out its own name, while every Angami is averse to mentioning the name of his wife. In the case of a newly-married man nothing will induce him to do so. Women likewise are very reluctant to mention their own names.

"When about four to six years old a boy leaves his mother's side (till then he may sleep on his mother's bed) and goes to his father's side of the house. This takes place at the Sekrengi genna, when the child strangles a fowl according to custom. From that time forward he definitely belongs to the male community and no longer remains with the women at gennas, when the sexes are separated. In the Kohima group he is no longer allowed to sleep in the same room as his parents. There is no ceremony on attaining puberty or on assuming man's clothes.

"Bad language must be avoided while a child's first cloth is being woven, as if bad language is used under such circumstances the child that wears it will be affected for the worse." adds Mr. Hutton. The customs are peculiar to the Angami Nagas of Nagaland.

REFERENCES

1. Hutton, J.H., The Angami Nagas: with some notes on neighbouring tribes, Oxford University Press, Bombay 1969, (first Published 1921).
2. Endle, The Kacharis, Cosmo Publications, New Delhi (rpt) 1987, Originally Published 1911.
3. Danda, Dipali, G, Among the Dimasa of Assam: An Ethnographic Study, Sterling Publishers, New Delhi 1978.
4. Hutton, J.H., The Sema Nagas, Oxford University Press, Bombay 1968 first Published 1921.
5. Roy, Jyotirmoy, History of Manipur, East Light House, Calcutta 1973 (rpt) first Published May 1958.
6. Hodson, T.C., The Naga Tribes of Manipur, BR Publishing Corp., New Delhi (rpt) 1974, Originally Published 1911.
7. Mills. J.P., The Ao Nagas, Oxford University Press, Bombay 1973 (rpt) Originally Published 1926, Macmillan and Co., London.
8. Stocks, C. De Beauvoir, Sikkim; Customs and Folklore, Cosmo Publications, New Delhi (rept) 1975.
9. Gangte, Thangkhomang, The Kukis of Manipur, A Historical Analysis, Gyan Publishing House, New Delhi 1993.
10. Rizvi, S.H.M. and Roy, Shibani, The Adi Tribes of Arunachal Pradesh, BR Publications, New Delhi 2006.
11. Singh, K.S. (Gen. ed.) People of India: Arunachal Pradesh, Seagull Book, Calcutta 1995.

2

Puberty

Puberty customs in the region are varied in different tribes and non-tribal communities - ranging from being elaborate to almost non-existant among the primitive groups. However, the customs, rites and rituals had undergone a vast change in the region with the arrival of the British, followed by the Christian Missionaries. Some communities and social groups in the region also came under influence of Brahmanic impact emanating from West Bengal. The first impact of Christianity was on the religious beliefs, customs and usages of the people of Assam, Manipur, Mizoram, Arunachal Pradesh Sikkim, Nagaland etc. With the spread of Christianity, belief in all multifarious spirits and in the efficacy of propitiation through sacrifices and rituals was replaced by the new faith. But belief among the Mizos in *Pathian* continued with a new connotation as God of Christianity. The sacrifices were replaced by Christian prayers. The transformation is now almost complete. The old animistic rituals are seldom to be found in Northeast region today. Only through the revivalist movements, some of the Mizo and Naga etc. culture, like traditional music, dances and drum beats, has come to be incorporated in the accepted code of religious behaviour in the newly converted Christian society.

No Puberty Rites for Girls

In the Northeast region, Assam is one of the most developed state in civilization, culture and customary usages under impact of Brahmanism emanating from West Bengal, where the puberty rites and customs are pan-Indian elaborate and sometimes even complex. Whereas, in the most primitive social groups inhabiting the far-flung areas, those are almost non-existant. In these places, the puberty among girls is marked by the first menstruation at the early age of twelve or so. However, there are no formal rituals or ceremonies to mark her entry into the age in which she becomes ripe for motherhood. A girl is not embarrassed at sighting the blood of her first menses, because she has already learnt secretly what it means. A menstruating woman here is not surrounded by many pollution related taboos; consequently, though she may feel a little awkward, she has very few practical inconveniences. She must not have sexual intercourse with her husband for five nights and should not eat meat of wild boar. But these apart, she has nothing to avoid and leads a normal life. She can cook in the family kitchen and do other household work, brew beer and go to *jhums*. There is no pollution related taboo on touching people, nor on eating with others. The pubic cloth is unknown to them, so the skirt that a woman puts on below the main garment serves as the sanitary towel.

She may bleed on the way *jhum* and wipe, herself with green leaves, and even if she is careless in throwing the stained leaves away, no harm will come to her from the *Wiyus*. Nor is a man embarrassed at finding a trail of blood on the track, or at accidentally coming in contact with the blood of a woman working in jhums. The dread of the menstrual blood which is considered so polluting among some tribes of central India is absent here. The sixth day after her period commences, she washes her hair, hands and thighs, in a secluded corner slightly away from the house, or sometimes in a small flowing stream. She does not wash herself or her skirt in big rivers for fear of offending the water *Wiyus*.

As she grows older, menstruation is taken as a routine matter that occurs every month and which ends only when a woman has become old. Marriage among them is not normally preceded by love, yet wooing often results in a happy union rather than ending up in frustration. Obviously, a girl whose bride-price is already being paid in instalments, is supposed to act with prudence and is usually guarded against the overtures from other young men. Yet there are times when the heart wins over the conflicting claims of the mind, forgetting about the consequences. However, the love among these simple people is merely an outburst of carnal passion. The carnal aspect is not minimized, still love rests on deeper levels of heart. Generally, the young lover's ambition is to get married and establish a happy home. The exchange of gifts is a recognized way of showing love and attachment. The lover, for example, may give his beloved some fine beads and she, in turn, may offer him the finest rice-beer. Seclusion is the essence of romance but, whereas many a lover may confess that he has fondled his girl, rarely will he reveal that he has gone beyond that. The love situation gradually becomes known to the parents. If the bride-price is paid to the girl's parents, she can get married and live with her suitor in the new social status of a wife.

Institution of Morung

As soon as a child reaches the age of eight or ten, he or she starts covering the private parts with a little piece of cloths and cane, or any crupper belt. At the time they also start going to youths' dormitory to sleep instead of sleeping at parental house. The *Morung* was to the Nagas and other tribals in the north-east what the 'Hebrew University is to the Jews'. It was a unique institution used by many tribes, while some other tribes used other forums or institutions in lieu of a learning institution. Morung is where all the young male members of the village conscripted themselves as members up to a certain age-groups to train and educate themselves in all round customary usages and practices and to be groomed to a standard community member to the fitness of the contemporary society. *Morung* also served as incessant 'Watch Tower' to detect the incoming enemy's raid and for other village security. The safety and prestige of the village were in the vigilance of tribal *Morung*. All male members of the village were trained here in all disciplines. The old glory and good job done in the past is attributed to the institution of *Morung* life.

Morung in Mizoram

Like the institution of despotic chieftainship, most of the Mizo tribes have a system of bachelor's dormitory where the young men learn the customs of the tribes and get indoctrinated into norms of social behaviour. The Lushais had in every village a bachelor's dormitory, called *zawlbuk*. The *Zawlbuk* would be situated at prime location in the village, generally opposite the chieftain house. The hall of the *zawlbuk* would be big enough to accommodate all the young men of the village. The hearth in the centre of the hall would always have a smouldering fire to keep off the cold. Every evening, after the day's work, the young men would gather in the Zawlbuk and would have common pastimes and entertainments like wrestling, singing songs, telling stories, and training in arms etc. Later in the evening, the young men would go round the village in *nula rim*, to court young girls. Late in the night they would return to the *Zawlbuk* which had many raised sleeping platforms. Usually travellers halting at a village for the night would stay at the *zawlbuk*. The chieftain also used the hall of the *zawlbuk* to hold meetings of the village councils as this would be the only common hall and the biggest hall available in the village. All the young men of the village would be available in the *zawlbuk* for emergencies and common work for the village. Along with the spirit of co-operation, completion would also be encouraged.

The most industrious young men and the best hunter among them would be rewarded with special cups of zutaima zuns given to the former and huai zuno to the latter. Boys, naupangs, till they attained puberty would live with their parents, but they were required to do odd jobs for the young men of the *zawlbuk* like collecting firewood and helping in the digging of graves for the community deads by carrying bamboos and stones. Once they attained puberty, they would be elevated to the full membership of *zawlbuk*. The *naupangs* or the young trainees were commanded by a captain called *hotu*. There would be a number of *hotus* in the village - one for each *veng* or part of a village. They would ensure complete control by the *Zawlbuk* over all the boys in the village.

Every morning there would be roll calls to ensure attendance of all boys and young men in the *zawlbuk*. The leader of the young men of the *zawlbuk*, called *tlangval upa*, would assign work among the inmates of the *zawlbuk* and enforce discipline amongst them. A review would be done to see that the boys had done their work as allotted to them. The defaulters would be allotted extra work by way of punishment. *Zawlbuk* had a strict system of discipline. There was an interesting system of punishment for the recalcitrant young members. If the father of a boy would admonish or assault a *hotu* for ill treatment of his son, all the *tlangvals* would gather at the house of the offending man and vigorously shake the house to make it nearly tumble down. This treatment would serve as sufficiently deterrent for others opponents not to interfere in enforcement of discipline by the *hotus*. Only the chieftain of the village had some control over the *zawlbuk*. He could throw a stone on the roof of the *zawlbuk* signaling the young men to quiet down if they made too much noise at night. Theft of any article from the *zawlbuk* would attract fine of forty rupees, irrespective of the value of the article.

The institution of *zawlbuk* was mostly prevalent in Lushai and Pawi villages. The Raltes did not have this system, but adopted it after coming under influence of the Lushais. Paites did not have *zawlbuk* as such, but young men would sleep in the verandah or front porch of the houses of influential men of the village who would provide adequate sleeping platform to them for the purpose. They would help their host in construction and repairs of his house and also in his *jhum* cultivation, who in return would frequently give them a feast. The Lakhers did not have *zawlbuk*. The young men, however, did not sleep in the parents house. They would sleep in the house of the maidens whom they were courting. Beside the *zawlbuk*, there was an excellent custom called *tlawngaihna* by which one was duty bound to extend cooperation to others. Under this custom everyone of the social group was required to be courteous and considerate and to help others always and every time, irrespective of one's inconvenience. Everyone of the community would try to surpass others in unselfishness and cooperation. This was an excellent custom in the daily life of a Lushai like the other Mizos. For example while travelling together, if one of the party would fall sick, all would wait for him to recover and would then resume the journey together. With the arrival of Christianity the institution of *Zawlbuk* and the custom of *tlawmngaihna* gradually dies. The Christian in a village would not join a *Zawlbuk* and hence when the majority in a village become Christians, the *zawlbuk* in the village languished and ultimately become extinct. Similar was the fate of *tlawmngaihna*. When the people were turning away from their old beliefs, the customary network of duties and cooperation was also snapped. New buildings and institutions like village churches, schools, medical centres and administrative centres etc, were coming up. The Mizo people started depending, individually and collectively, more on the church and the state Government for guidance and help.

The custom is prevalent among the tribes of Mizoram.

Bachelors' Dormitory in Nagaland

McCulloch noticed in Nagaland the institution of the dormitory of both boys and girls. He described them as 'Clubs'. He writes, "According as the village is large or small, the (boys) assemble in one or several houses which to them for the time became their house. These clubs are ruled despotically by the seniors among them, who exalt their juniors with unsparing hand service of all kinds. Young women have their places of resort and between them and youngmen: intercourse is unlimited without leading to immorality which is the exception".

The custom is related to the Zeliangrong Nagas of Nagaland.

Sexual Licence to Naga Girls

In the census of India 1901 (Vol. I, p. 229) it was stated that among the Lusheis, 'until a girl is married, she may indulge in as many intrigues as she likes, but should she become pregnant, her lover must pay a *metna* to her father... If a man is willing at once to marry a girl whom he has seduced, he is not expected to pay more than the usual marriage price.'

Campbell, in writing of the Lusheis, (J.A.I. III p. 61) states that "intercourse between the unmarried of both sexes is unchecked, but not so after marriage." This custom is also followed by the hill tribes of North Arracan. "Till marriage the intercourse between the sexes is unrestrained, and it is considered rather a good thing to marry a girl in the family-way, even though by another man... Not to be sought after by the young men is considered a reproach. After marriage, however... conjugal fidelity is generally respected." (J.A.I. p. 236)

'Among the Angami Nagas... girls consider short hair, the symbol of virginity, a disgrace and are anxious to become entitled to wear it long. Men are desirous to have proof that their wives will not be barren. Chastity begins with marriage.' The Rev. Joseph E. Tanquist, in an unpublished manuscript, refers to this practice. 'Rather loose morals,' he writes, 'are said to obtain up to the time of marriage. After that time both husband and wife, between whom equality practically exists, jealously require proper conduct from one another.'

'The Angami woman before marriage,' writes Hutton, "is given a very great deal of liberty, though the extent to which she takes advantage of this has possibly been exaggerated. Mr. Davis, speaking not of Angamis in particular, but of Nagas generally, says: 'I should say it way very rare for a girl not to have at least one lover.' Customs, however, differ in this respect in a very great degree between different tribes. While the Ao girl is bound to admit men to the girls' house at night, chastity before marriage prevails among the Semas, where the marriage price of a girl is reduced at least 50 per cent, by the fact of her having an intrigue. The Angamis would seem to fall somewhere between the Ao and the Semas, for while separate girls' houses do not exist in Angami (Tengima) villages, though they are found in Memi villages, girls are not looked after with the same jealousy as that with which a Sema girl is watched until her marriage." Among the Banpara Nagas considerable looseness between the sexes is customary. (J.A.I. Vol. XXII p. 259)

Among the Changes, "unmarried girls" states Hutton, "are not expected to be chaste. They sleep in the outer room of the house, into which the young men force their way at night, the girls defending themselves with sticks and firebrands. Intrigues of this sort are, however, usually followed by marriage with the lover. Strangers are never admitted in this way." The Ao Nagas are addicted to this practice. Hutton also makes a statement concerning this tribe. "The Aos," he states, (The Angami Nagas, p. 374) "are notorious for the unchastity of their women... From a tender age girls are free to do as they like before marriage, and are thus with difficulty prevented from doing so afterwards."

Informal Teaching in Dormitory

About the Ao Naga system about *Morung*, Mr. J.P. Mills recorded, in this book the Ao Nagas, thus: "The organization of the village is based on two main principles. First the whole village is divided into age-groups *(yingar* C; *yengar* M), to which the various communal duties are assigned. Secondly the control of affairs lies with a council, whose method of election and tenure of office vary in the different language groups. There is nothing corresponding to an hereditary chieftainship. The system of age-groups is in brief as follows: Every three years a new group of boys born within the same three years enters the 'morung.' It is these groups that I have termed age-groups. A boy remains in his original age-group till he dies, each group taking its name from some prominent member. Girls also have their age-groups, but the system does not play a very prominent part in female life. Boys on first entering the 'morung' have certain menial duties to perform, till, in three years' time, a new age-group takes their place and the fags of yesterday blossom into bloods for the next three years of 'morung' life. After his time in the 'morung' is over a man settles down and marries, and probably in time becomes a councillor. His term of office over, he very likely becomes a priest till he dies. But all through his life he remains a member of his original age-group. For instance, when pigs are being ringed each age-group is assigned a particular portion of the fence to make; or when village paths are being cleared each group is given a stretch. From the cradle to the grave a man is part of a machine. Only on these lines could a village of perhaps two thousand souls, without king or chief, be run.

"The Changki organization illustrates the working of the age-group system particularly clearly. Every three years a new group of boys, of ages ranging from about twelve to fourteen, enters the 'morung.' These are called *noza-barihori* ('unripe gang'). They must sleep in the 'morung' and work like slaves for the elder boys. In three years a new group takes their place and they become *tukapbahori* ('ripening gang'). They now make the new-comers work for them just as hard as they worked. They need not sleep in the 'morung' if they do not want to, and may marry towards the end of their time. Their duty is to carry messages and work in general for the village. After three years of this they become *chuchenbahori* ('morung leaders gang'). The 'morung' is under their control, and in the old days youths first went on raids when they reached this stage. Then, after another three years, they become *okchangshamicharihori* ('pig's leg eaters'). The name indicates that they get the legs of pigs killed at 'morung' feasts. Their duties are much the same as for the previous three years. For the next three years they are *kidong mabang* ('clan leaders'). On entering this period they have no more to do with the 'morung' they have left their youth behind them and are villagers of standing. After this they become *khonri* ('load carriers') for three years. They supply men to carry loads containing sacrificial pigs, fowls and so on at ceremonies, and receive small shares of the councillors meat. At the end of this period they become councillors *(tatari)* for three years, and, with the advice of yet older groups, run the village. After this short term of office, during which they get the biggest shares of meat, they become *maozamba telakba*—assistant councillors. They still obtain shares of meat, but only very small ones. Finally, after three years as assistant councillors, they become *maozamba temamba.* A few of this last group pass on to be priests *(patir),* but for most men this is the last stage. They represent the age and experience of the village and the *tatari* are expected to ask their advice on any matter of importance.

"In the Chongli and Mongsen system fewer groups are recognized. The Chongli custom is as follows. New entrants into the 'morung' are called *songpur* and have to work for the older boys for three years. They then become *sangmen* for another three years. While in this group they can carry food for raiders, but are considered too young to take part in the fighting. After this a boy becomes an *achuzen,* a class which includes all young unmarried men. These provide the chief fighting force. After marriage men are simply called *arichungr* ('morung men'). They cease to sleep in the 'morung,' but remain connected with it till they are about thirty. That is to say, they help at repairing it and subscribe to and share in 'morung' feasts. After that, if they frequent it, it is only as guests.

"In the Mongsen language-group the youngest class of boys is called *songyur.* These, in turn, after three years blossom into *tunabang.* As soon as one of this class marries he joins the class called *pur,* in which he remains for four or five years, before he enters the *chuyenr* group. These latter are often spoken of simply as *arichunungr* ('morung' men), and in this group a man remains until some member of his age-group has a son old enough to enter the 'morung.' The cycle of age-groups is then complete and members of that *yengar* have no more to do with the 'morung.'

"A man does not usually speak of himself as belonging to such and such a 'khel' of a village, but to such and such a 'morung,' of which a 'khel' may contain two or three. They are organized on the clan system, boys of one, or perhaps two, clans occupying the same 'morung.' Should most of a boy's friends happen to be members of another clan he may leave the rest of his clan and join his friends 'morung,' but he is supposed to help his ancestral 'morung' when necessary, though he cannot be fined for not doing so. New boys enter the 'morung' in the autumn, at the time when the village fences are renewed. Of the two hearths in the 'morung' the new boys use the inner one for their first period of three years, the one nearer the door being reserved for the senior classes. Men who are now middle-aged say that when they first entered the 'morung' they were very severely disciplined, not to say bullied. They were, for instance, held over the fire and compelled to endure the heat without a cry. Or they were made to show their pluck by being sent alone on a dark night to fetch a bamboo from a certain clump. The boy sent was allowed no torch or weapon, and had to gnaw the bamboo through with his teeth or hack it off with a sharp stone. Or, again, a boy would be sent to leave a torch at some particular spot far away in the jungle and come back alone in the dark without a light. In the morning the older boys would go and see if the burnt remains of the torch were in the proper place. Nowadays boys have an easier time, but a considerable number of duties falls to their lot, and for the first three years a boy's life is very like that of a fag at an English Public School. Boys of the lowest class must keep a supply of torches in the 'morung' for travellers passing through the village late in the evening; they have to massage the bigger boys' legs when they come in tired from the fields. The same duty falls to the lot of the younger members of the *Dhumkuria* of the Oraons, which is virtually the same institution as the Ao 'morung' system, and, like it, is worked on a three-year age-group basis; they are, responsible for the wood and water needed for cooking. So, too, the boys of the Lushei *zawlbuk*, another instance of the same institution (Shakespear, *Lushei Kuki Clans*, p. 22); they must make pipes and sharpen 'daos' for their seniors. In fact, for three years they have to do what they are told, and do it quickly—a most excellent system. When the junior grade, at the end of three years, moves up to make room for a younger group every member of it must contribute three good logs of wood, as a sort of entrance fee into the next grade. These are piled up by the door and used as firewood.

"No one who is no longer a member of a 'morung' can interfere with its internal affairs, and anyone attempting to do so can be fined. A 'morung' is a microcosm of the village and has its own council, reminding one strongly again of a Public School with its prefects. A typical Chongli council would be composed as follows: one *Ungr* (head), one *Tonglu* (assistant head), fourteen *Tatar* (councillors), two *Tingyar* (works overseers), who see that repairs, etc., are properly carried out, and two *Yibutir* ('madhu' carriers), who must see that every guest has food and drink when the 'morung' entertains other men of the village on such occasions as the *Moatsu* festival. This council, which consists of senior boys, settles all disputes and quarrels arising in the 'morung' and inflicts and eats fines of pork, the parents of the boys at fault having to pay, of course.

"The most striking feature of the Chongli system is that at the end of every generation all the councillors of a 'khel' vacate office and a new body takes their place. Every Chongli village has a standardized generation of so many years, usually between twenty-five and thirty. When the time comes to vacate office there is almost always a violent quarrel. The office holders, reluctant to relinquish their power and shares of meat, argue that their time is not up yet, while the younger generation are eager to take their place. It must have often happened in the past that the old men were able to put up a stout fight and prolong their period of office, or that the young men have been able to oust their elders before their time was up, for might is often right in Naga life. I remember a case in point occurring at Mongsenyimti. The 'generation' period used to be 30 years. In the course of a quarrel as to when the existing *tatar* were to vacate office, the successors were backed by the village and it was emphatically decided that the real period was not 30, but 25 years, in order to get the old men out. What will happen when the 25 years expire and the present holders find that they preferred to eat their cake in 1917 rather than keep it for 1942 remains to be seen. This would account for the local differences in the length of a generation. In Longmisa, for instance, one 'khel' changes its council every six years, a result, as is acknowledged, of continual pressure by the younger men. The Chongli recognize a cycle of five generations.

About the Bachelors' dormitory of the Tangkhul Nagas Mr. M. Horam stated, "Villages were often isolated from one another, at least from the known enemy villages. There were very few, if any trade relations except when all hostilities were suspended during the festival of Luira. Some villages lived in a constant state of feud even though the original quarrel would be centuries old. This may, to a certain extent, account for the great divergence of dialect from one village to the next within the same tribe. Most villages were perched on hill-tops both for reasons of security and for a vantage view of the surrounding valleys. Even though heads are very safe today, villages have not shifted from their ancient sites. This poses communication problems, but the Tangkhul loves his land above all benefits that civilization may have to offer. From the point of view of health, the choice of the village site is excellent. The entrance to many a village is still via the passage where the strong village gate must have been in the past.

"The size of a Tangkhul village depends on the number of households it has. The smallest village may have anything from five to ten households. The largest Tangkhul village is Ukhrul (erstwhile Hunphun) with about a thousand households. Each household in the village belongs to a particular clan and, as already mentioned, occupies a particular area in the village called 'sangnao'. In the old days the 'sangnao' too had entrance and exit gates. In most villages, even today old 'sang' boundaries are respected but, there are no walls or gates separating one, 'sang' from another 'sang'.

"In every 'sang' there used to be a bachelors' house where a boy lived from the time he attained puberty to the time when he married and set up his own house. The Tangkhuls call their bachelors' house '*longshim*'. The practice was frowned upon by the early missionaries and hence it fell into disuse in converted the villages. With the disappearance of the '*longshim*' also went the only youth organised body in the village which taught the important and invaluable lessons of discipline, hardwork, and the spirit of service.

Each village has sufficient forest wealth and land. Land is owned individually by households and there is also common land belonging to the entire village. This common land is used by landless persons, if any. It is also used as grazing ground for cattle and for collection of firewood by all the villagers. The village is ruled by a chief whose office is hereditary. In actual practice, however, the village is not so much ruled as led by the chief and his councillors who represent the various clans of the village. The chief, as also the councillors, have many privileges but they have also to carry a weighty responsibility—act as advisers and judges and provide inspiring leadership in order that a village may stay united... "In common with other Naga tribes the Tangkhul Nagas too have the institution of a bachelors' or young men's dormitory, referred to by most writers as 'morung'. The word morung is probably of Assamese origin and was not used by the Naga tribes as each tribe has its own name for its dormitories. Today it is common currency among most tribes though the institution has vanished or has, at best, left only a vestige. Among the Tangkhuls the practice is revived in a limited way during 'Luira' as also during Christmas. But more of this later. The Aos call their morung '*arichu*', the Lothas call it '*champo*', the Angami word for morung is 'kichuki', and among the Semas it is known as '*dekha chang*'. The Tangkhul name for morung is 'Longshim' (*Long* meaning 'group' and *shim* meaning 'house').

"Most Naga tribes had separate or special houses to be used as 'morungs'. This was not the case with the Tangkhuls who, like the Sema Nagas, did not set any house apart for this purpose. The Angamis too did not always have exclusive houses to be used as *morungs*. The youth of a Tangkhul village used their chief's house as their *longshim* as did the Sema youth. The house of a Tangkhul chief (Awunga) was larger and more spacious than anybody's in a village. In a big village if the chief's house proved small, the youth from each clan would use the house of the clan head as their clan *Longshim*.

"A typical Tangkhul house, however small, is divided into three compartments: the outer, the middle, and the inner rooms, and it is the outer room which is used as the dormitory. Generally the outer room is given to relatives or strangers if any happen to sleep in the village while passing through the village. In the absence of any occupant, it houses the family animals including pigs, though most Naga homes have a separate enclosure for pigs at the side or the back of the house. Speaking of pigs, it is the practice to have always at least one pig in the enclosure so that the family can provide a feast at the shortest notice. Cows and buffaloes are no longer kept in the houses or even in the residential area in most Tangkhul villages but kept in the fields and enclosures away from the village. It is not, however, unusual to find cattle in the homes of the northernmost Tangkhuls as also among some Angami and other Naga villagers. A Tangkhul house may vary in size from a 25 feet by 18 feet dwelling of a widow to the massive 80 feet by 40 feet house of the Awunga. The walls are of wooden planks and the roof is either thatched or wooden for those who can afford it.

"The outer room of the *Awunga's* house has a plank carved out from a single tree and large enough to comfortably accommodate 20-30 boys. More than one such bed may be used. A similar arrangement may be made in the outer rooms of the houses of clan heads. The most popular clan head in the village is usually chosen to accommodate young men if the *longshim* of the *Awunga* gets crowded. The *longshim* used to be decorated with human and animal skulls and other trophies and insignia of war. Towards evening the inmates of the *longshim* congregate and the atmosphere is one of relaxation, leisure, and languid ease. The lengthening shadows enhance the subdued magic of the hour while the flames from the wood-fire in the centre of the room light up the faces of the young sitting around it. The greetings and chattering soon give way to humming in harmony and later into full-throated singing. Play, singing, and dancing are a regular feature of the *longshim.* Of all the activities, singing is most popular as it were, for with the Tangkhuls, as indeed with most Nagas, singing comes as naturally as breathing. But for a *yarnao* (*yar*—youth or grown-up, *nao*—

man, person) life is not all song and play. The *longshim* strikes a happy mean between education and fun. Time spent in the *longshim* is divided between pleasure and purpose, and the purpose is to prepare the young men for all the tasks and responsibilities of life.

"To give the reader a general idea of the importance and the usefulness of the morung system, I shall deal briefly first with the admission of a boy to the morung, then his initiation as a member of this body, and lastly his growing participation in its multifarious activities as well as the added responsibilities as he attains seniority as a member. It is said that in the bygone days a Tangkhul boy was ready to go to the *longshim* while he was yet quite young—at the age of 12 or as soon as he attained puberty. At that age he would consider it shameful to sleep in his parents' house. Once he joined the *longshim* he would leave it only when he married and set up a home of his own.

"Before the actual initiation there was a period of probation when the boy got to know what was expected of him as member of the club. Before he was accepted, the young aspirant had to prove his mettle and emerge unscathed out of the ordeals through which his seniors might be pleased to test his worth—mostly physical strength and moral courage. Much of this amounted to good-natured 'ragging', but in those days of superstition and fear of the myriads of spirits all around him, a young fellow with a youthful imagination would have to muster all his courage to qualify for the coveted membership of the *longshim*. A favourite task set for the new entrant was to send him all by himself to an eerie spot in the surrounding jungles to mark a tree or bring back a branch, etc. Once a member, the boy learned the easier jobs of the club, such as lighting the fire, sharpening the daos and other tools of the seniors, collecting fire-wood and especially the pine resin to be used as torches, fetching water, cooking, and other such drudgery. Later he graduated to performing any task that fell to his lot.

"Discipline, obedience, and efficiency are the hallmarks of a *longshim* youth. He is expected to be swift in discharging his duties. As the *longshim* is the social hub of the village, it becomes the centre of all activity during festivals, taboos, and religious ceremonies.

"It is the *longshim* members who attend to the detail and drudgery of village feasts, from collecting the fire-wood, slaughtering the animals, apportioning and distributing the meat, and providing entertainment after the feast. They sing and dance late into the night on such occasions and when the village has distinguished guests and visitors. They assiduously practise wrestling, spear-throwing and other items of sport to lend excitement and colour to all village fairs and to participate in inter-clan and in inter-village competitions. When a member decides to marry, all the wedding celebrations are arranged by his colleagues from the youth club. Handicrafts such as wood-carving, bamboowork, and dao-making also flourish among the youth. A spirit of keen competition and an ambition to excel pervade all *longshim* activity. The *longshim* is thus at once a school for the teaching of Tangkhul history in the form of folk-lore, song and dance, sports and games, discipline, hardwork, spirit of service in community living, and a resilience in all matters of life. Several early writers have borne testimony to this wonderful institution and have harped on the training in discipline that it imparts. To quote Mills: 'It is in the 'morung' that he fags for other boys and is taught his duties in life and generally hammered into shape. This means that 'morung' tends to take the place of his father as a disciplinarian. This is most important, for it is from a son's feelings towards his father as disciplinarian that one of the great stresses of the family complex arises. J.P. Mills, *The Rengma Nagas,* p. 50. The *longshim* had its own set of rules and regulations the violation of which was visited with punishments. Though the *longshim* was a self-governing body, the inmates understandably came within the pale of the village authority and were liable to be punished for breaking any customary law. A *longshim* may aptly be called a microcosm of the village for, like the village, it has its own leaders and laws. This provides excellent training for future clan or village leadership.

"... the *longshim* comes to life only after the members begin to arrive there after taking their evening meals in their own homes. Indeed during the day the boys belong to their families.

At daybreak a youth will go to his own home, take or cook his morning meal, and accompany the parents to the fields. No account of the *longshim* is complete without a reference to its activities in the affairs of the heart. It was customary for the youths from the *longshim* to pay noctural visits to the '*ngalalong*' (*ngala*—girl, *long*—group), *i.e.,* girls' dormitories. A member or members of the visiting group may be the admirers of a girl or girls. Where there were no '*ngalalong*', groups of boys would betake themselves to different houses. No individual visits were paid. A love-smitten youth would take his friends with him to the house of his sweetheart. There they would all sing, exchange stories, banter and small talk, laugh, joke, and indulge in making veiled declarations of love. This custom of oblique courtship persists even today. The lovers are adequately chaperoned and thus built-in safeguards are provided in Tangkhul society in which there are no bars for the mixing of the sexes. Surprising as it may sound, despite this freedom, Tangkhul society lays great emphasis on strict decorum and decency between men and women. Since there are no caste, creed, or class barriers between lovers, they can marry when they wish to. Consequently, pre-marital sex is not found among the Tangkhuls, and in the few cases, if any, it is difficult for a girl who flirts around to find a good husband.

"... There were as many *ngalalong* in a village as there were clans. This means that all girl cousins of one clan slept in the large outer room of the clan headman's house. There were no dormitories for girls at the village level, and in the clan dormitories there were no rigid or fixed regulations. A girl used it as soon as she had reached the age of puberty for as Mills says: 'It is as shameful for girls as it is for boys to sleep with their parents when they reach years of understanding. J.P. Mills, *The Rengma Nagas*, p. 52. Like the boys, the girls shared the family burdens during the day. After marriage a girl would leave the *ngalalong*. A touching send-off would be given to her by her cousins who would join the boys of the *longshim* to help in the marriage celebrations.

"The *longshim* system with a few modifications still exists in some non-Christian villages, but life and mirth have gone out of it due to the Christian influence of the neighbouring villages and other changes in Tangkhul society. To say that the *longshim* is extinct among the Tangkhuls would not be wholly correct, but it must be understood that changed circumstances have already altered and are everyday altering the Tangkhul life, and the *Longshim* cannot be an exception to this change. Yet even today, when visiting villages of the Tangkhuls, especially during the festival of Luira and Christmas, I cannot but help seeing vestige of the once all-important *longshim* system. Today in the Tangkhul villages, the Luira and Christmas festivities are the responsibility of temporary groupings of young men and women. These groups or Longs make all the arrangements for the Luira and Christmas and other village festivals and celebrations and attend to the drudgery that accompanies all big festivals involving the entire village. During such festivals the *Longshim* system is revived, but there being no separate building, a school building or a village hall is used for the purpose. Each member, however, sleeps in his or her own house, but all through the day a member is expected to work in and for the temporary Long. Contributions of rice are made by each member, and cash contributions go towards the purchase of pigs, cows, buffaloes, and fowls for the festival. This temporary revival, as it were, of the *longshim* system is common to all the Tangkhul villages where once *Longshim* existed, and though *Longshim* has lost its significance, to say that it has completely disappeared, would not be true.

"... It was the *Longshim* which fostered the Tangkhul arts, crafts, music, and dance. The disappearance of the '*Longshim*' tolled the death-knell of Tangkhul culture. For, in the worlds of Verrier Elvin, the dormitory-club was veritably the 'dear nurse of Arts'. To understand and fully appreciate the extent as well as the irreparable nature of the damage done, one has but to meet those Tangkhuls who are in the age-group 15-35. Their ignorance of the Tangkhul culture is colossal. They are the immediate products of an earlier generation which, though itself well versed in the indigenous culture of the hills, nevertheless had to give it up in the wake of conversion to a new religion. The missionaries sought to plant in these eastern hills a replica of the western concept of norms and standards of life, and these were conveniently introduced as part of Christianity. Such trends of pseudo-westernisation are to be found in many parts of India where Christian converts adopted the ways and habits of the European and other missionaries who converted them. There have of course been refreshing exceptions when converts in certain parts of India have been ardent advocates of their own culture and have found it perfectly natural to be a Christian without any way compromising with Indianness. It is a sad but true commentary that in Tangkhul hills this was not to be, and the Tangkhuls after initial hesitation and spirited opposition abandoned their customs with a speed which led an entire generation to be born into a world which was alien and totally foreign.

"The double tragedy of this generation was that not only were they denied the real culture of their forefathers but they were also never able to fully face up to the demands of the new norms. It is not difficult therefore to feel the urgency and enthusiasm with which they are trying today to recapture the old magic of their hills. Many of the young Tangkhuls have chosen to remain deeply committed to Christianity, but they have also realised that Tangkhul culture and Christianity are not incompatible. How far this cultural revivalism will be successful is yet to be seen, but it is a healthy trend and one which will utilise the energy of the Tangkhul youth towards constructive and creative ends. This will also partly relieve the political frustration suffered by this very same generation. A reaching out into the past and renewal of their cultural image can be a thrilling and rewarding experience for the present generation of the Tangkhul Nagas who finds in this continuity of traditions that lost rhythm of tribal life which was the secret of the vigour, discipline, and cheerfulness of the old Tangkhuls, and which is all but forgotten, till the Tangkhul hills again resound with the old songs and till the Tangkhul homes once again become schools for the teaching and dissemination of Tangkhul folklore and history."

Human Skulls and War Trophies in Morungs

About the present condition of Manipuri Morung or bachelors' sleeping house another scholar Jyotirmoy Roy noted, "An important characteristic feature of tribal life is its *Morung* system. Each village reserves two separate houses—one for the boys belonging to a certain age-group and the other for the unmarried girls of the village. Boys and girls reaching at puberty sleep in these houses or dormitories. These dormitories are maintained by the entire village and have different names in different tribes *e.g.* the *Ruongmei 'Khangchu'* is the dormitory of their boys and *'Luchu'* is of their girls, the Tangkhuls call it *'Longka'* and in Hmar it is 'Buonzawl'. These dormitories are the greatest centres of activities in the villages and the system as a whole plays a vital role in the entire tribal way of life.

"The *Morungs* are usually decorated with the trophies of war and games and representations of animals on wood. They are the headquarters of village defence, recreation clubs and the centres of education, art and ceremonial functions. Young men are trained here in various arts and crafts, dance and music, morality, discipline as well as in the arts of offence and defence. Discipline is strictly enforced. All the young men in the village sleep there sending out batches of armed sentries to watch and guard the village. They go round the village often singing songs, narrating the heroic deeds of the past or assuring complete security to their sweet-hearts and asking them to listen to their songs and spin peacefully. In case of impending danger villagers are alarmed and summoned by beating drums kept in the *Morung*. Festivals are also announced in the same way. In view of their importance Morungs receive due consideration from the elders of the village.

"Modern administrative system has succeeded in establishing peace in the hill-areas of Manipur. Government is there to maintain peace, assure security and administer justice. Inter-village and inter-tribal feuds have become things of the past. Moreover Christianity and modern education have brought a new age in the hills where the Morung finds no part to play. The system is fast withering away. With proper orientation it could still play a vital role in the hill-villages of Manipur." Roy adds.

Dimasa *Nodrang* Reverberates with Singing and Dancing

In the evening, people of the same sex and age-group generally gather in open places for singing, dancing and gossip.

Men were found gossiping for hours together sometimes upto 11 o'clock at night. In every village nodrangs or the bachelors' dormitory there are flute (*muri*) players who entertain people with their music every evening, who are accompanied by drummers with *kharam* (drum). The young boys cannot afford to have a drum of their own. They play drums only when the elders get tired and hand their drums over to them. Until then young boys indulge in traditional tribal tunes or Hindi film songs through a small flute called *supen* which they make from slim bamboo nodes. However, the girls never play flutes of any sort. Sometimes they play drums during midday leisure when the men are out but never publicly. Unmarried girls participate in dance. During the evening the gay girls practice dance along with the young boys in open spaces. Some unmarried girls were found playing melancholic tunes on the *topang-kharam* (a harp like instrument made of reed) an instrument played and made by women only. Usually the married women do not join this type of recreation and marry-making. Women having babies prefer to chat among themselves or with the elderly women. The evening congregations are devoid of any vocal music.

Among the Dimasa tribals there is no place for vocal music at public functions. Songs are sung in solo or in duet in *jhum* fields to ease the tiredness of physical labour. The Dimasa songs are composed by young boys during their leisure hours. In Barawaphu village the young boys were found composing songs for the next *busu* festival. Most of the cultural activities of the Dimasa are revolve around the *nodrang* or the bachelor's dormitory. It is a long house consisting of the sleeping arrangements for the young boys till their bachelorhood. It is usually situated at the centre of the village built by the village bachelors. At the age of 12 or 13 the tribal boys become eligible for *nodrang* membership. Nowadays, it is not a compulsion for the Dimasa youngsters to sleep in a dormitory, however they prefer to live there voluntarily. No formality or initiation ceremony is required for entering into a *nodrang* for the first time and there is no maximum age-limit for sleeping there. From adolescence, boys try to get familiar with the youth and the youthful activities of the village and work under their discipline and guidance during the social occasion. Thereby they get automatically admitted to the *nodrang*. A man can live there until his marriage. The *nodrang* is meant for only the bachelors which is also used as the club house of the village. There is no such dormitory for the young girls and the women are not allowed to enter a *nodrang*.

Thus, after taking their evening meal in their parental houses, boys assemble in the dormitory. Their sleeping mat, pillows, duilts and other personal belongings are kept there. In a dormitory youths enjoy their evenings in their own way. Some way have special fancy for singing dance and music. So they play their flute and drum, and the village girls sometimes join the party in the open courtyard of the *nodrang* for dancing. Often dancing is continued up to late night. The middle-aged married and even some old men also join the party. They usually do not participate in singing or dancing but beating of drums. Meanwhile, some of the youths prefer to gossip with others of their age-groups. A few of them are always industrious and spend their time in weaving baskets and mats. Some boys of marriageable age or those whose marriage has already been settled spend time in romantic discussion with their lovers.

As the young boys share major responsibility in farming in jhums individual village youth have their respective workload. But if the village is endangered by enemy they feel it is their joint responsibility to protect the village from the enemy attack. In normal times the *nodrang* members render free to the community like construction of roads and clearing of jungles. They are ready to carry out any order issued by the tribal chieftain. Any member of the village may ask for their joint service for house-building or clearing of jungle for agricultural purpose. Then it is the custom to make payment to them and to entertain them with feasts and rice-beer. The *nodrang* works as a highly systematized organization to celebrate the annual harvest festival: *busu*. The boys of the *nodrang* constitute a *busu* celebration committee every year. One secretary and one assistant secretary are selected from the senior members of the *nodrang* who further select another secretary and assistant secretary from the village girls who help them in organizing the *busu*.

The rest of the boys and girls of the village work under their leadership. The secretaries collect subscription for the purpose and organize the function. Though there is no formal age-grade system, in the composition of *nodrang* the villagers are divided into senior and junior groups according to the age where the junior members are always obedient to the seniors. Collection of firewood and lighting the fire in the dormitory during winter are the responsibilities of the junior members. They are also responsible for cleaning the dormitory and its premises regularly. Besides, a *nodrang* is also a seat for the village council.

Custom of Hnathlang

Tribals had certain obligations to do the community work for the village and the chieftain. This was in the shape of voluntary work called *hnathlang*. Everybody in the village would contribute voluntary labour to build the *zawlbuk*, clear and build all passages in and around the village, and clear and fence the source of water supply. A chieftain could call upon his villagers to contribute for his private work also. Some tribals would accompany and carry the load of a chieftain or a member of his family when he would be travelling. In case of a death in the family of a chieftain the tribals and members of Morung would dig the grave and erect the memorial stone.

The Lakher villagers and the *zawlbuk* members performed certain common duties. They would build the village fort in the centre of the village and keep watch by turns from the zawlbuk. They would keep the village free of jungle, erect fences and keep clear the water point and take all other action necessary for community use and welfare. This was similar to Lushai *hnathlang* and was called *tlaraihria* by the Lakhers. Anyone refusing or failing to do *tlaraihria* would be fined (*leu*) to pay rice, fowl, axe or dao or one rupee in cash.

If paid in cash or by rice, the chieftain and the elders would use it to have some beer. In Lakher villages, there were regular systems for obtaining contribution by village tribals for common entertainment general feast and other general purposes. By the custom of *sathi* a member of the tribe or *zawlbuk* was required to kill a pig for a common feast or for entertaining a visiting chieftain or for some other similar entertainment. By a custom called *vohle*, a piglet, immediately after its birth, would be collected for any purpose chosen by the tribals. *Sakhei* was custom of subscription of paddy for village entertainment to a distinguished visitor or for similar other purposes. The Lakhers followed the custom of providing hospitality, so very common in the hills. By custom of *tlongang* every Lakher was required to be hospitable.

However, when the mission work of evangelizing the tribals was first started among the Lushai villages it was carried on without training and without knowledge of the which customs of the people which led to the condemnation as 'heathen' and useless of some most excellent customs, which no one who had learnt them could have put to extinction and condemnation. No use was made of the *zawlbuk* or bachelor's house or of the custom of *tlwmngaihna* (the obligation on everyone to be unselfish and to help others). The *zawlbuk* was condemned quite wrongly by the Christian missionaries as an evil place where people drank and fornicated. The practice of *tlawmngaihna* was also neglected. Through lack of knowledge, therefore, excellent customs which would have strengthened the church while at the same time averting denationalization, were sneered at discouraged among the local tribals.

However, the Christianity brought about personal and collective cleanliness among the people. Under old Lushai customs no one was allowed to have a window in the house unless he had performed certain sacrifices and given large community feasts. Such customs have long been given up. After independence, the influence of Christianity has been more adapted to the indigeneous way of life and belief. The large scale abandonment of local clothes and dresses by the youths in favour of western style shorts, trousers, coats, etc., has, to some extent halted. Now there is a mixture of *puans*, traditional Mizo clothes, shirts, trousers and local Mizo hats. There is respect and liking for the old traditional Mizo clothings and dresses.

Tribal Feuds and Head Hunting

In the tribal life in the northeast, conflict and warfare could not be avoided as a measure for security and defense among the Nagas. If any neighbouring village raided another village without any provocation still lose lives of innocent person or suffer grievous injuries it was considered a sufficient ground for retaliation. However, proper explanation shall be called upon by the aggrieved party and due reparation as deemed proper shall be claimed failing which the defaulter faced the consequences. In the process inter-village tribe feud ensued culminating in warfare and killing each other. While the age-old practice of warfare was on, it was natural on the part of the combative groups to contest in their valour and skill of warfare by the number of person killed and the number of enemy head brought over. In those times valour of the warrior was highly honoured. Accordingly, the popular term "Head hunting' had been associated with the Naga warrior who participated in feuds. Killing a fellow human being with or without intention the first degree offence of murder to the Naga custom thereby appropriate punishment was given. As such, the general practice was to recover the head if killed to prove the skills and valour of a warrior.

However, the ancient practice of head-hunting no longer exists among the tribes of Manipur or anywhere else in the northeast. In those days when it existed, it was regarded as an act of heroism, more so when one could bring the head of women or children by dashing inside the enemy village or approaching very close to it. They believed that the spirit or vitality of man lies in his head and by its possession the fertility of its soil is increased yielding better harvests. The Nagas was also believed that the victim would serve as the slave of the hunter in the next world. But gone are the days when people frankly believed in the crime of head-hunting and indulged in it. About the Angami co practice of head-hunting and the use of Morung and its members in the warfare, Mr. J.H. Hutton wrote, "While war might be occasioned by a varied number of circumstances, a private feud, a land dispute, mere lust of blood, anything, in fact, from a rude remark to the taking of a head, the general cause usually ascribed to the outbreak of war by Angamis is increase in male population. War is regarded as the certain accompaniment of an increase in the number of the village bucks, and the conclusion of peace as the no less certain result of a marked diminution in the same. After the opening conflict a state of war must usually have meant no great drain in population, but merely the taking of occasional heads. It would ordinarily be ended by one side's happening to lose heavily either in raiding or by an epidemic of disease, or perhaps by a common desire on both sides to cultivate in safety... and the cessation of hostilities would be symbolised by the blunting of a dao, hammered upon a stone till the edge was destroyed. Among some of the Angamis the making of peace was also marked by the sacrifice of a cat. The two Phom villages of Hukpang and Ourangkong are often at war. When they make peace they kill a slave and hang up his head in the place where the fighting began. In many cases one side would agree to pay annual tribute to the other, the tribute being either merely a nominal one of a few beads or a substantial payment in mithan or salt. The contingency of conquest does not usually occur, though some of the Kacha Naga villages seem to have been entirely dominated by settlements of Khonoma Angamis who superimposed on them their own customs. This, no doubt, was partly due to the razing of Khonoma village and the dispersal of its population after the Angami rebellion. It was some time before the population was allowed to return at all, and many seem to have remained for good in Kacha Naga, and some Memi, villages.

"Head-hunting as an accompaniment of the blood feud and of war has been mentioned, but so much significance has been attached to the practice that it possibly deserves some special notice. Some recent writers on the tribes of North Borneo have sought for an explanation of the practice in a desire for the hair for the ornamentation of the shield and the sword-hilt, or in the custom of killing slaves to accompany a dead chief beyond the grave. Neither suggestion seems to hold good of the Angamis. The first would, at any rate if applied to the Angamis or other Naga tribes, appear as an inversion of cause and effect, while the second practice is not known in the Angami country. Head-hunting in one form or another is a wide-spread practice, and whatever the various incidents of head-hunting in various quarters of the globe, the ultimate reason of its existence in any particular spot must probably be sought in some deep-rooted and innate characteristic of human nature. Among the Naga tribes, at any rate, head-hunting, though associated with a vague idea of the benefits accruing from human sacrifice, must also be connected in no small degree with ordinary, everyday human vanity. What man, or at the least what Naga, who has killed his enemy does not want to boast about it? And unless he can show the body, where is the proof? Most savages are somewhat economical of truth; at any rate the Naga is when it comes to his exploits in war and the chase. If the slayer can produce the body of the slain his statement is likely to be accepted as true, and since retrieving the body would be a laborious, not to say often dangerous, proceeding, the head is the natural part of it to bring back as testimony, as it gives a definite assurance that the foe has been killed, not scotched. This at any rate is Angami explanation. Among the Lhotas any human flesh brought into the village on return from an expedition is 'vetted', so to speak, by a board of old men, who sit and hold a sort of inquest on the flesh produced to make sure that it really is what it is stated to be by the bringer. And until the trophy has been passed by this board no ceremony can be performed for the success. I am indebted to Mr. J.P. Mills for having drawn my attention to this point. Moreover, if it can be retrieved, the Angami does prefer the whole body, and if the whole body is not available he will take the arms, hands, legs, and feet of the corpse as well as its head. In any case cuts are made in the arms and legs of the victim in order to entitle the slayer to the armlets and leggings that form part of the warrior's *insignia*. And in this connection it must also not be forgotten that the Naga does not fight in the open country and under the eyes of his fellows, but in heavy jungle and in raiding parties of small numbers from one upwards, where none can observe his deeds of daring. Small and stealthy raids for heads are called "*Ruzutsu*" in contradistinction to "*Rudise*," a war expedition. The omens are taken in the same way for the former as for the latter already described. Nor does the Naga make so very radical a distinction between human heads and heads of game. Man is the biggest game and the most dangerous game, and his pursuit is therefore attended with precautions which may be unnecessary in the case of smaller game, but he is still game. There is, after all, not so much to separate a sportsman's desire for, say, a fine buffalo head and a Naga's desire for the head of a man. Most Britishers are head-hunters at heart, and to a Naga every sort of head is welcome. All the skulls of larger animals killed by him are religiously kept, from that of an otter to that of an elephant, while even the heads of small birds may often be seen nailed to his house. As the Naga kills primarily for food, he recognises no differences in sex or age, and although he undoubtedly takes a pride in killing, say, a sambhar with a fine head, yet the heads of does and fawns are hung up as trophies beside it. So it is with his human heads. He recognises no distinctions between human heads provided they have cut their teeth; if they have not cut their teeth they are not taken.

"Up to a certain point then, and with the exception that the flesh of most animals is eaten and man's is not, the distinction between the pursuit of man and of animals is one of degree rather than of kind. It is true that the successful hunting of man is followed by genna, but so in varying degrees is that of animals. A strict genna precedes the robbing of bees' nests—a somewhat more dangerous game than ordinary hunting; a genna follows a successful chase of a tiger or leopard. Again the killing of a man entitles the killer to certain distinctive articles of dress, but so does the killing of a leopard or tiger. Among the Angamis this only goes as far as the shield on which the skin may be worn, but among the Semas it entitles a man to wear a boar's tush collar, one of the recognised signs of head-taking, and among the Rengmas and some of the Lhotas to a distinctive cloth also usually associated with the killing of man. Of course, Naga tradition associates man and the tiger very closely together. It may be noticed in this connection that among the Konyak tribes it is common for a slave to be bought for the 'chief's son to kill in order that the boy may wear ceremonial dress without risking the dangers of war. The wretched slave is tied up and the boy kills him with a dao, pieces of his flesh being distributed throughout the young men of the Morung. This custom brings us nearer to another idea which underlies head-taking, and that is the idea of sacrifice, the notion that the killing of a human being is conducive to the prosperity of the community or of the crops. Here again we find among the

Lhotas a parallel between head-taking and fishing, as the yield of the harvest is connected, in some villages at any rate, Changsang, for instance, with the success or failure of village fish-'poisonings.' The idea, however, of the benefit conferred by human flesh, or the taking of human life, is a very strong one among Nagas, though it is perhaps disappearing under the present *regime* of peace. Major Butler mentions the sale of a Kachari boy by some Angamis to some men of a Lhota village: 'A man of the village having died immediately after the purchase, it was considered a bad omen, and that ill-luck had befallen them on account of this captive child. They, therefore, flayed the poor boy alive, cutting off his flesh bit by bit until he died . . . then divided the body, giving a piece of flesh to each man in the village to put into his 'dolu,' a large corn basket. By this they suppose all evil will be averted, their good fortune will return, and plentiful crops of grain will be ensured.' It is no doubt partially with the same notion that Naga coolies taken on trans-frontier expeditions so carefully save up little bits of 'meat' to put in the Morung when they return, and to divide among their kindred. Only quite recently some Lhotas of Chingaki were punished by the Deputy Commissioner for going across the frontier and buying some flesh of a person killed in a head-taking raid, and selling part of it to another village after their return. The Angamis too had a custom, to quote Major Butler, 'of cutting off the heads, hands, and feet of any one they can meet with, without provocation or pre-existing enmity, merely to stick them up in their fields and so ensure a good crop of grain.' Finally, the late Mr. A.W. Davis, writing in 1898 as Deputy Commissioner of the Naga Hills, says,

'There can be no doubt that all the tribes in this district consider that by killing a human being in certain cases they are doing the most effectual thing towards averting the displeasure of some particular evil spirit *(terhoma)*. Amongst the Angamis especially this idea is very prevalent, and there have been two cases of murders committed within the last five years near Kohima, the only object of which was to propitiate an evil spirit. I will describe these cases in detail.

(*a*) Kigwema Case—In the autumn of 1891, small-pox, which was very prevalent, attacked the two lower *khels* of

Kigwema village, and a large proportion of the inhabitants died. *Khel* here is the part of the village inhabited by a clan—*thino*, and the clan occupying it. The two upper *khels,* the people of which all had been vaccinated, remained free of the disease. As, however, Nagas had at that time but little faith in vaccination, the people of these two *khels* determined to make themselves as safe as possible. A village council was therefore called, and it was decided that four men should be sent out to bring in a head as offering to the '*terhoma*' in order that the plague of small-pox might be averted. Four men were accordingly sent. They went and lay in wait by the cultivation path of a neighbouring village, and killed a woman, a small boy, and the baby he was carrying as they were returning alone from their fields. The baby's head and an ear each from the other two were cut off, carried away, and buried in the vicinity of the murderers' village. This murder was, from the Naga point of view, eminently successful; the angry deity was appeased, and the two upper *khels* of Kigwema remained exempt from the disease, which decimated the two lower *khels.* A similar case under exactly similar circumstances is said to have occurred at the village of Jakhama near Kigwema during the previous epidemic of small-pox which occurred about twenty years ago.

(*b*) There is a very general superstition among the Angamis and Semas that to kill a human being and place a small portion of the flesh in the murderer's fields is a specific to ensure a good crop, and this is said to have been the reason that prompted certain men of Purobami to murder two men, a woman, and a child near the Sijju River towards the end of 1895. The two men were partially scalped, while the child was taken away alive and killed outside the village. Murders like these partake of the nature of sacrifices, as their object is to avert disaster and so to ensure good crops.

'Before we annexed their country, the Aos were great slave owners, and these slaves were occasionally made use of for a semi-sacrificial purpose, *e.g.,* two villages are at war and are desirous of making peace. It is found that one side has taken more heads than the other. To make things equal, and as a sacrifice to the spirits of the dead who have gone unavenged, an agreement would be arrived at that the village which had taken the fewest heads should receive one or more slaves from the other village. Longsa, when they attacked Kanching, lost many heads, and Kanching only one, but when making peace Longsa are said to have given Kanching a slave to kill in place of the man they had lost. These slaves were bound and left at a spot agreed upon beforehand. There they were found by the young men of the receiving village, who killed them and carried off their heads in triumph. Thus were the spirits of their dead restrained from troubling the living. A case of this kind, in which Kanching gave, and Ungma village received, slaves, occurred not very long before we took over the Ao country.

'I have been frequently told by Aos that human sacrifices are not infrequent among certain of the Trans-Dikhu tribes. The method is said to be as follows: When the village jhums are ready for firing, a slave is tied up in the middle of them. The jhums are then lighted, and the slave is burnt to death. A sacrifice like this ensures a good crop.' I have made many inquiries, but so far failed entirely to locate or find any trace of this practice. I am of opinion that the report was incorrect, and an Ao invention. The Aos are very particular liars where their enemies are concerned.

"As regards the disposition of heads, we find one frequent difference between the treatment of those of animals and those of human beings. The heads of domestic animals are, it is true, set up in the fields where they have been sacrificed by those tribes who sacrifice in the fields, but the heads of animals killed in hunting are invariably hung up in the house of the hunter, with the exception usually of the skulls of tigers and leopards. On the other hand, heads taken from human beings are, by the Lhotas, Rengmas, and Semas, always hung up in a tree, usually somewhere near the edge of the village. The skull is bored and hung up by a cane string. It has been suggested that the practice of hanging captured heads in a tree is a survival of tree-burial, but it is to be noticed that the Aos and the Konyak tribes, which regularly practise tree-burial in the ordinary way, do not put the heads they capture in trees, but hang them in their houses or their 'Morungs,' or in the house of their chief, while the heads of animals killed in the chase are often put up in the 'Morung' also. The Angamis bury the heads taken from their enemies face downwards in the earth.

"It has been remarked that the Naga knows no distinction between heads. That does not mean to say that he does not pride himself on the killing of a redoubtable enemy, as distinct from killing women and children, though his rather bloodthirsty omnivorousness in slaughter may be gathered from a report by Mr. Carnegy, Political Officer in the Naga Hills, of an incident in 1870: 'In the middle of July a party of forty men of Mozema went over to Kohima and were admitted by one of the khels (clans) friendly to them, living next to the Puchatsuma quarter, into which they passed and killed all they could find, viz., one man, five women, and twenty young children. The people of the other clans made no effort to interfere, but stood looking on... one of the lookers-on told me that he never saw such fine sport *(i.e.,* the killing of the children), for it was just like killing fowls!' Still it would seem that heads taken by deliberate treachery as opposed to surprise, *i.e.,* by inviting a man to partake in some friendly act and then killing him unawares, were reckoned as different in some way from heads taken in the ordinary raid, as they are said to be represented on the warrior's shield by inverted heads. Also as regards heads taken from women and children there is some reason to believe that under certain circumstances they were more highly valued than those taken from men, provided, in the case of children, that the teeth were cut. Hodson mentions this point, and Colonel Shakespear throws doubt on it, but there is a case worth recording which goes far to substantiate its truth.

I am indebted to Captain Porter for this incident, which was related to me by him shortly after it took place. Since writing the above another fact has come to my notice which seems to clinch the argument. The Semas have a regular formula of praise which they sing for a man whom they wish to honour, saying that he has taken the head of a *girl* of such and such a tribe or village. For instance, I heard the following sung in answer to a request for a Sema song :

O Sakhalu no Abor-limi i pu ghu ihoh, ihoh, ihoh-u.
O Kohazu asa likighil   ihoh, etc.
O Ilheli alho ve   ihoh, etc.

i.e., "Sakhalu took-and-brought-back (the head of) an Abor girl, Kohazu cut-off-and-put-in-his-ear (a bit of her) hair; Ilheli was pleased." This formula is applied to anyone else, substituting another tribe or village for Abor, the name of the hero's younger brother for *Kohazu,* and of his wife for Ilheli. The Sakhalu, it may be noticed, here mentioned, went on the Abor expedition as a scout and took six *male* heads, but the use of "*ilimi*" (a girl) is constant.

In 1911 Captain Porter, of the 17th Infantry, then quartered at Kohima, went on a shooting trip into the Lhota country. Accompanied by some men of Phiro he was benighted near the Rengma village of Infoma. The Gaonbura only admitted him and his Lhota companions to his house with great reluctance and flatly refused to feed the Lhotas. Afterwards, on inquiring the reason of this unlocked for lack of hospitality, Captain Porter discovered that there was an old enmity between his host and his 'shikari.' In the days of their youth there had been a very pretty girl in Phiro, all suitors to whose hand had been rejected. At last her mother said that she should marry whichever of her suitors would bring her the ears of an Angami girl. The ears were brought; the 'shikari' with Captain Porter was the eartaker and successful suitor; the wife of the headman of Infoma has no ears; *Hinc illae lacrimae.* The reason given to Captain Porter for the specification of an Angami *girl* was that the warriors worked at the cultivation furthest from the village, above them the young men, then the old men, then the old women, and then nearest to the village the young women and children, and to get a pair of ears from the latter meant penetrating the enemy's ranks at the risk of the aspirant's head, both going and coming back. Infoma is not really an Angami village, but it contains an admixture of Angami blood, while it is possible that the headman's wife may have come from one of the neighbouring Angami villages, as most tribes are bilingual along their marches and intermarry freely. Of course the heads of women and children were often taken under less romantic circumstances than these, a favourite method being to lie up at dawn by a neighbour's well, to take the head of the first woman or child coming to draw water, and to decamp with all speed, setting panjis to delay pursuit. And additional reasons for special value being attached to a woman's head are probably to be found in the greater amount of long hair to be obtained for the purpose of garnishing a warrior's insignia, and most of all in the inevitable reduction the killing of a woman would effect on the birth-rate of the hostile village. Surprise was essential to a head-taking raid, and if a party found a village prepared for them the valiant warriors would almost certainly turn back home again. It is agreed by all Angamis, as well as by other Nagas, that head-taking was essential to marriage in so far that a buck who had taken no head, and could not wear the warrior's dress at festivals, not only found it exceedingly difficult to get any girl with pretensions to good looks or to self-respect to marry him, but was held up to ridicule by all the girls of his clan.

"Among the Angamis the good old days of head-hunting have gone. Girls who wish to marry cannot now afford to be so particular. The distinctive marks of the successful warrior are assumed on the fictitious grounds of having thrust a spear into a corpse or even of having gone as a coolie upon an expedition on which killing took place. In the Konyak village of Auting, annexed about five years ago, the young men have already taken to wearing ceremonial dress with the *insignia* of the head-taker after spearing a wooden dummy, since the real thing is no longer obtainable. But though the flesh is withheld the spirit is willing. Surreptitious heads are still sometimes brought back from punitive expeditions, on which a crowd of interpreters and Naga coolies follow in the wake of the sepoys, uttering loud yells and transfixing with their spears the corpses of the slain. It is related that at the taking of Makware village a Naga clerk of the Deputy Commissioner's staff, educated in speech and civilised in dress, having failed to provide himself with a spear, was seen dancing in vociferous triumph over the corpse of an enemy and with horrid yells plunging his umbrella, again and again into the wounds.

"But it is not everyone who is so fortunate as to accompany, armed even with the humble umbrella, a trans-frontier expedition from which to bring back bits of scalp, or ears, or toes, while the desire to perform the ancient ceremonies comes to many, and among the Semas, Rengmas, and Lhotas, if not the Angamis, it is a favourite expedient to cut off the tail, or some of the hair of the tail, of a neighbour's mithan or cow, and to follow up this feat of chastened valour with the genna performed for the taking of a head. As an animal treated in this way loses at least half its value—it can no longer be slain for any ceremony—the almost invariable result is a case in court, and the culprit is not infrequently detected by his too hasty eagerness to perform the rites, though he sometimes waits until he thinks the affair has blown over so that he can celebrate in safety. Thefts, too, are sometimes regarded as fit occasions for the performance of the genna. The Ao regards stealing from the plains as a meritorious action, while the Sema is apt to take a similar view as regards the Ao, whose cattle serve the double purpose of giving him an excuse for a genna and the wherewithal to perform it. A lock of hair from the head of a living person is also made to serve as a substitute, at a pinch, for the head from which it is cut, and almost all Nagas except those in service are most unwilling to cut their hair, except in their own villages, as, of course, the utilisation of a lock of their hair as a substitute for a head would entail, as a result of the genna performed by the taker of the hair, death, or at least dire misfortune, to the man from whose head it was cut. Among the Changs a man who loses his way in the jungle cuts off a bit of his hair, and puts it in a stick as an offering to the spirit (believed to be that inhabiting the python) which has ensnared him, after which he never fails to find his way home. Semas similarly placed cut off a bit of the fringe of their cloth for the spirit of the forest.

"The taking of heads in this life, however, does not seem to have any connection in the Angami mind with life in another world, except in so far as the headless man cannot get to the abodes of Kepenopfu, whence the great unwillingness of all Nagas to allow the heads of their killed to be taken by the enemy, if it can possibly be helped. The Konyak tribes fight in pairs, so that if one man is wounded or killed the other can drag away his body and save the head. Losses also seem to be by all Nagas counted primarily in heads rather than in lives. The tale of a warrior's heads is recorded on his grave, but then so is that of the tigers he has killed, and it does not seem likely that he would wish to be accompanied and served by tigers in the life beyond, while the same principle, if applied to the tale of his *liaisons,* which is likewise recorded on his tomb, would cause a confusion among deceased Angamis seventyfold greater than that suggested in the famous riddle of the Sadducees, of the woman who had married seven brothers, at least if the deceased's own count were accepted. There is nothing in the Angami eschatology to suggest that he believes his victims in this world will accompany him into the next.

REFERENCES

1. Parry, NE, The Lakhers, Firma KLM Pvt. Ltd. and Tribal Research Institute Aizwal, Calcutta (reprint) 1976, originally Published 1932.
2. Endle, The Kacharis, Cosmo Publications, New Delhi 1987, Originally Published 1911.
3. Danda, Dipali G., Among the Dimasa of Assam; An Ethnographic Study, Sterling Publishers, New Delhi 1978.
4. Hutton, J.H., The Sema Nagas, Oxford University Press, Bombay 1968, (reprint), Originally Published 1921.
5. Roy, Jyotirmoy, The History of Manipur, East Light Book House, Calcutta 1973, first Published 1958.
6. Hodson, T.C., The Naga Tribes of Manipur, BR Publishing Corp., Delhi 1974 (reprint) Originally Published 1911.
7. Horam, M., Social and Cultural Life of Nagas; The Tangkhul Nagas, BR Publishing Corp., New Delhi 1977.
8. Hutton, J.H., The Angami Nagas, OUP, Bombay 1969, first Published 1921.
9. Mills, J.P., the Ao Nagas, OUP, Bombay 1973 (reprint) Originally Published 1921 by Macmillan & Co. London.

3

Betrothal

Customs regarding, courtship betrothal and marriage differ in the northeast region among the tribals and non-tribals according to the status of their level of civilization, social and economic status. Here are some of the customs adopted by both the tribals and non-tribal social groups in the states.

Child Marriage

Child marriage, to some extent, is still prevalent among the Brahmans and Kayasthas, more particularly in the Assam villages.

Brahmins ceremonise the three rites connected with a girls marriage at three stages: before the attainment of puberty, after puberty and when she attains motherhood as described by ET Dalton in his Descriptive Ethnology of Bengal. The do not allow widow-remarriage. In some Assamese villages, there is a custom in which a man called a *Dhoka* or *Chapaniya* goes to live with a widow as her husband. But he is very much looked down upon. On the other hand, a widower sometimes brings into his house a widow as his wife, who is known as a *Batalu*. On the night the widower comes to the widow s house, she places a bowl of fried cock-meat and a bowl of ricebeer on the threshold of her bedroom and seats herself outside with a tiny lamp and a stick. The suitor goes round and round the house seven times mewing like a cat. After each round he approaches the door only to be driven off by the woman. After the seventh round she asks if it is her children s father (her dead husband) and the man replies, yes. Then only can he enter the house, eat and drink, and after certain formalities become the master of the house. The Dhoka leaves his original home for good, discarding all rights to property. The Bodo tribals generally provide a good safeguard to their widows.

Courting of Girls Freely Allowed

Among the Lushai tribals, courtship or *nula rim* was freely permitted by the traditional custom in the society. The *tsangvals* would go round in the evening, courting their sweethearts in the village. During the initial period the young men and the girls, if they liked each other, would work together in a *jhum* and otherwise would go about together. Parents having grown up girls in the house would go out during the evening to some place where a beer party might be going on, leaving their daughters and suitors undisturbed in their houses. It was quite common for the young suitors and their chosen girls to sleep together in her parental house. There was an interesting custom in this matter. If they were found sleeping on the *kumai*, the sleeping place for girls and young children, no objection would be made. But if they were found on the sleeping place used by the parents called *kumpui*, on the other side of the hearth, the young men would be fined ten rupees, or else he would have to marry the girl. If a girl became pregnant thus before marriage, the young man would have to marry the girl, or pay a fine of forty rupees or a mithun called *sawn man*, to the parents and relatives of the girl. If the court continued without marriage and a second illegitimate child was born, generally the father was not required to pay any further fine. But in case of a third such child, he would again be fined with a *sawn man* of ten rupees. When the suitor has paid the *sawn man* he could claim the child and take him away when it was old enough to leave the mother.

While going to visit the woman paramour a youth would generally take with him a boy, known as *puarak*, who would act as a witness of their sleeping together. If the youth claimed such relationship, and it was denied by the girl the *puarak* would be called upon to give the testimony. In case there was no testimony by a *puarak*, the girl would be entitled to a compensation of forty rupees from the suitor for defaming her. In the Mizo tribal custom called *dawn puan phah*, a young woman would persuade her parents to allow spreading of a cloth for her and her boy friend to sleep on in her parent s house. After this permission, if the boy refused to marry the girl, he would be fined a *mithun* or forty rupees.

However, when a young man after courtship would want to marry a girl, he would approach her parents. If they were agreeable first the marriage price-consideration amount to be paid by the youth to the relations of the girl, would be negotiated. Thereafter, on consent of the girl, the young man and the girl would be treated as engaged. They could continue as betrothed for a few years when they could freely mix with each other and cohabit. The engagement could also be broken off during the period without any liability on either part. When the wedding day was fixed, both sides would prepare for marriage feast with an abundance of *zu*. On the wedding day the bridegroom would send his two members of his party known as *palai*, to pay the bride price in full or part, as already negotiated upon. Lot of *zu* would be offered by both the marriage parties. The bride would then be escorted by her friends to the bride groom s house. A fowl would be sacrificed by the *puithiam* in a ritual called *arzangtuak* and a prayer would be chanted to *khuarang*, spirit of the air for a long and happy married life of the couple. Over this ritual the marriage would be solemnized. The bride would then return to her parents house. Relations, friends and guests would have a grand feast of meat and plenty of *zu* in the bride groom s house.

In the bride s house all those who would get shares of the bride-price, would contribute pigs and fowls for a feast and half of the meat so collected would be sent of the bridegroom s house for the feast there. Next day the bridegroom s mother along with some elderly women and young girls would go to the bride s house to bring her back to her husband. For sometime after marriage, the bride would spend the night in the bridegroom s house and the day in her parent s place, till she gradually settled down in her new household. The Lushais were mostly monogamous; but if any one could afford, there was no bar to have more than one wife. The chieftains were generally polygamous. The Lushais married within the clan, but outside the consanguine kins. As the chieftains had matrimonial relationship only amongst their own clans, their choice was limited and marriage among first cousins was rather common.

As to the Lashais, marriage was a civil contract with a bride price which was paid by the bridegroom to the bride s parents.

Settlement of the bride-price was the first and essential step to marriage. But one could rarely pay up one s bride-price straightaway. Some amount would be paid on the eve of the wedding, but the bulk would remain to be paid in instalments over a long period 15 or 20 years or even more. The ritual debt would be carried on for payment by sons after the death of the father and it was usual that an adult son would be paying for her mother s bride-price before he could think of his own marriage. The principal marriage price or *manpui*, was payable to the bride s father or brothers and in their absence to the nearest male relative. The general rate of *manpui* among the Lushai was four *mithuns* or eighty rupees in cash. There were also various subsidiary bride-prices. *Sumhmahruai* was an amount of 20 rupees payable to the bride s father or brother. To them was payable another subsidiary price called *sumphang*, consisting of an amount of eight rupees. *Pusum* was payable to the nearest male relative on the bride s maternal side - generally, the bride s *pu*, the protector, who would be her maternal uncle. This amount varied between four rupees to ten rupees and in case of a chieftain s daughter it would be a *mithun*. Equivalent of *pusum* was *niman* amount payable to the paternal aunt of the bride. The bride s elder sisters would get *naupuakpuan* for having carried the bride during her childhood in their *puans* or clothes. If the bride happened to be the eldest sister or the only daughter, this price would be received by other female relatives. Price was also payable to a *palal* who would be a trustee or adoptive father of the bride to oversee her nurturing and well-being all through her married life. Voluntary amounts of ten rupees downwards would be considered for payment as *thianman* to other friends of the bride. Similar optional payment called as *lawichal* was paid to the leader of the escorts, when a girl was married to another village. The girl going over to the village of the bridegroom would spend the night before the marriage in a friend s or relative s house who would get a share of *manpui*. Otherwise, the person putting her up would get five rupees as charges for her stay, called *thlenin man*.

The custom prevails among the Lushai tribals of Mizoram.

Rules of Exogamy and Endogamy

Among the Mikir tribals the exogamous divisions are called as *kur* (a Khasi word: Assamese, *phoid*). Each of the three sections of the race has within it the same *kurs*, and the individuals belonging to these *kurs*, whether in Chintong, Ronghang, or Amri, follow the same rules of exogamy. The number and names of the *kurs*, or exogamous clans, are differently named by different authorities. The differences appear to be party explained by the fact that one author has taken for a principal group-name what another has entered as a sub-group under another larger section. Mr. Stack, found that the people recognized four *kurs*, called respectively *Ingti, Terang, Lekthe*, and *Timung*, under which the smaller groups (also called *kur*) are as follow:

I. Ingti	Taro, Katar, Hensek, and Ingleng.
II. Terang	Be, Kro, and lngjar.
III. Lekthe	Hanse, Tutso, Bongrun, and Kramsa.
IV. Timung	Tokbi, Sengnar, and Rongphar.

These *kurs* are exogamous: an individual belonging to *kur* Ingti must go outside that *kur* for his spouse; and similarly Terang, Lekthe, and Timung cannot marry wives drawn from within the *kur*. The sub-groups are, of course, as parts of the larger groups, also exogamous. All the *kurs* have now social equality, and have no discrimination as to eating together or intermarriage. *Ingti* is said to have been in former times the priestly clan; *Terang* also claims this status, but is thought to be of lower rank; but in both cases the office has fallen entirely into desuetude. Lekthe is said to have been the military clan, while Timung are the commoners.

The Mikirs, settled in the plains of Nowgong and practicing cultivation are called *Dumrali* by the Mikirs and *Tholua* by the Assamese. They also have the same *kurs* as the other three sections of hill Mikirs. In their patrilineal society, the children belong to their father s *kur*, and cannot marry within it. They may, however, marry their first cousins on the maternal side, and indeed this appears to have been formerly the most usual match. This absence of matriarchal system strongly marks off the Mikirs from the Khasis, with whom they have much in common.

The Mikir age for betrothal and marriage is from 14 to 25 for the man, 10 to 15 for the girl; 18 or 19 and 15 are the most usual ages. If a young man fancies a girl (from meeting her at dances and the like), he sends one or both parents to her parental house, and if the girl s parents agree, the boy s father leaves a betrothal ring or bracelet with the girl called as *ke-roi-dun*; sometimes a gourd of ricebeer is taken and accepted, and in that case, if she subsequently marries another man the village council fine her family from 25 to 35 rupees; otherwise only the betrothal ring or bracelet returned. The length of the engagement is uncertain, but the actual marriage does not take place till after her puberty. The custom is practiced among the Mikirs of Assam.

Fixing of Bride-Price

The Manipuri legend about the custom of bride-price goes thus: Chongthu was the younger brother of Noimangpa, the Chief of the underworld. As per Kuki custom, in the presence of the elder brother called *Upa* , the younger brother called *Naopa* cannot become a Chief. So, Noimangpa, being the elder, was the Chief. Chongthu also desired to become the Chief. Therefore, he went out in search of a suitable land where he could establish himself separately as a Chief. He found one. On his plan to become a Chieftain he wanted to go with his won close friends whom he could trust. Thus, he arranged for the marriage of each of his selected men. In doing so, he paid the price of each bride to their parents. In those times, no valuable property or cash was available. All the valuable items that one could think of was a *Paigen* , a belt made of leather and decorated with a kind of beads, called *Longchang* , in seven lines. This was considered to be a very rare and valuable property. This could only be afforded by the Chieftain alone. So, traditionally it became associated with the sole property, the right of which was vested only in the Chieftain, and was venerated very much being associated with a certain magical powers.

Being the younger brother of the Chief, Noimangpa, Chonghtu had access to it, and when he arranged for brides for his friends with whom he planned to go to his new found land, he paid the *Paigen* to the parents of the girls as bride-price. It so happened that though the commoners dared not refuse to accept the *Paigen* when offered to them as bride-price, they could neither dare to keep it with them owing to the superstitions attached to it nor could they dare refuse to give the bride in marriage. Thus, along with the bride, the parents returned the *Paigen* to Chongthu saying that this being a valuable property associated with the tribal Chieftain exclusively, they dared not to keep it, lest the wrath of the unseen supernatural power fall on them and bring misfortune. This process went on and on until Chongthu was able to arrange the marriage of 30 of his best and closes allies and friends with the payment of *Paigen* time and again as the bride-price.

Thereafter, the bride-price of every clan was paid in terms of seven *Mithuns* based on the seven lines of *Longchang* on the *Paigen* with the exception of Sitlhous and Singsons (Singsit) for reasons given thus: Jampi family is the head of all the Sitlhou clans. It so happened that the land of Jampi Chief s daughter was sought for by the Chief of Aithuh, a junior lineage of the Sitlhou clan, in marriage. As per their custom, the senior man of the clan, gets the topmost part of the back flesh of the animal killed called *Sating* . Now, the Chieftain of Aithuh, being junior, called *Naopa* , to the Chief of Jampi had so long been paying *Sating* of animal killed by the former. In the same way, sister s husband or sister s son or daughter s husband or daughter s son are known as *Tucha* . It was that the man was born out of the waist of a woman, and, as such, any man marrying the woman or one s sister or daughter was assigned to receive the waist portion of any animal killed by a man. This indicates that the man who receives it is married to the women of the family.

The Chieftain of Jampi felt that a man of his junior lineage, who gave him Sating , portion of flesh on top of the spinal cord, and with whom he formed an exogamous group, indicated their close relationship, dared ask for the hands of his daughter. By such marriage the normal social relationship would be disturbed. The Chieftain of Aithuh who was the junior collateral cousin of the Chieftain of Jampi would now be the *Tucha* as well. Weighed with the consideration that he could not refuse the request, lest the family relationship be strained and antagonistic over a trifling matter, he was in a dilemma. Thus, the relationship that was to emerge out of such marriage alliance was one of double relationship. The man who was a collateral parallel cousin was to become, at the same time, a son-in-law. Therefore, it was tantamount to breaking the law of exogamy for which a fine was imposed requiring him to pay double the number of all the leading bride-prices. Since then, the bride-price of the Sitlhous was raised from seven *mithuns* to ten *mithuns*. This meant that he was to pay more than what was normally in vogue as is shown: thus:

Normal Bride-price: One Dahpi (Big gong), One Khichong (necklace with rare beads representing precious stones), One pair of Khichong (Rare bead used as erring representing precious stones), and Seven Mithuns.

Bride-price with Fine: Two Dahpis, Two Khichongs, Two pairs of Khichongs, and Ten Mithuns.

Among the Kukis of Manipur, clans are divided and further subdivided, and as such, the rule of exogamy is applicable only to a smaller group of people among the collaterals within three generations beyond which marriage between two members of collateral cousins is permitted though such marriage is not considered permissible. Such was the situation of the above example which prompted the Sitlhous to charge higher rate of bride-price. There might have been many good reasons for taking the bride-price among the *Kukis*. A few among them are: Luong-Kaidoh-Man-Dragging away of a body (meant person): For the purpose one *Mithun* is always attached to the bride-price, and is considered to lead the whole lot of bride-price and is called *Manlamkai*. Secondly, as recompense to the economic loss, because of the girls being taken away from the family who, as is usual among the Kukis are the main working hands of the family economy. The loss of a girl in a family is heavy, because it is only the women who are associated with the welfare of the family economy, means of earning, growth and development of the family; and thirdly, being the bearer of children for the propagation of family lines of generation to which she goes.

Among them, the bride-price has an underlying social value in that it must by all means be not paid in full. Even if a wealthy groom can afford to pay the bride-price in full, he is not allowed to do so. A part of it is always kept as due, to be paid in future. By this, it has an implication to the effect that the man should always have obligation, love, and respect, etc., for his wife and her relatives thereby enlivened a sense of maintaining constant and good social relationship with his wife and in-laws.

It also has an implicit meaning on the importance of the wife and her relatives in the family circle of the man. It is believed that the components of bride-price, such as *Khichong* represents precious stones and ornaments, and *Dahpi* and *Dahbu* represent valuable assets which are not within the reach of man s capacity to acquire. Similarly, a man s wife is so valuable that her price is not within the limit of a man s capacity to pay in full. Thus, the unpaid portion or the due part of the bride-price is a constant reminder to the man and his relatives that his wife, and for that matter, her relatives, are as precious and valuable as the priceless precious stones and assets which are yet to be paid in full. As for the bride-price of the Singsons, it is 30 Mithuns flat without any other items, such as, *Khichong, Khichang, Dahpi,* and *Dahbu*, etc., unlike the other clans of the Thadou Kukis. The higher rate of bride-price among the Singsons has no origin. It is considered that the Singsons are the direct junior collaterals of the Sitlhous. Therefore, when their senior collateral (Sitlhous) raise the bride-price under these circumstances the Singsons also deemed it proper to follow suit.

Custom of Nong a Pahaw

Dwelling on the custom of betrothal and unmatched marriage among the Lakhers, Mr. NE Parry records, This is a curious custom entirely unknown, among the Lusheis. Either the parents of two children marry them at an early age when both are below the age of puberty, or else a young man aged eighteen or twenty is married to a girl child, or a girl who has reached puberty is married to a boy younger than herself, who has not reached the age of puberty. These marriages are more often between two children of about the same age than between a mature and an immature person, and in most villages are comparatively rare. There are said to be two ideas at the back of this custom, the first being the desire of Lakher parents for their sons to marry into a higher clan, to ensure which a parent reserves a girl of good clan for his son at a tender age; and the second that if a girl is married young she is less likely to be deflowered by some other youth than her husband before she gets married. When such a marriage is contemplated the parents who wish their son to marry send a woman to sound the girl s parents, and if the latter are agreeable, a male envoy or *leuchapa* is then sent to present the girl s father with one *pumtek* bead to be worn as an ear-ring by the girl. This is called *nachipaba.* The girl s father must give the *leuchapa* rice beer to drink. After this a *thuasang* is sent to the girl s father through the *leuchapa,* and if that night the girl s parents have good dreams the match is finally settled and the price fixed. The couple are then treated as betrothed, and if the man breaks off the engagement he must pay the *angkia.* After this the parties wait till the girl has tied her hair up, and then the *amakia* takes place, pigs are killed by both parties and the price is claimed. The girl is still probably immature, and so she spends her time partly in her father s house and partly in her husband s house, as she likes. When the girl reaches the age of puberty, her husband has to woo her and try to persuade her to let him sleep with her. This courtship after marriage is called *ngiapareu,* and nowadays, if the girl does not like her husband, and absolutely refuses to sleep with him, she is considered to have divorced him, and the whole of the price paid must be refunded to him.

If the husband forcibly sleeps with his girl wife before she has fully reached the age of puberty and she complains, he will have to pay a *hmiatla* or peace offering of a *racha,* a large earthenware pot, to her parents. Where the husband is younger than the wife, and the wife reaches the age of puberty first, the girl must wait until her husband is able to have intercourse with her. If prior to her husband being able to have intercourse with her the girl has intercourse with another man, she is treated as an adulteress, and is subject to all the pains and penalties incurred by adultery.

If when a husband reaches the age of puberty he refuses to have anything to do with his wife, he is considered to have divorced her, and her people will keep all the price they have received, and can claim any balance of the price for which they have killed pigs. If either party dies before the marriage can be consummated, the girl s people keep whatever amount of the price has been paid, but none of the unpaid balance can be claimed.

Formerly, if when a girl reached the age of puberty she refused to let her husband have intercourse with her, her father would tie her hands and feet and take her to her husband, saying, I have tied your wife up for you; now have intercourse with her.ƒ The husband then usually consummated the marriage while his wife was still tied up. It the husband refused to have connection with his wife while she was tied up, he was considered to have divorced her, and her parents kept all the price paid for her, and could claim any balance for which they had killed pigs.

Sometimes a girl induced her husband to release her before he had had connection with her, on the pretext that she would then let him have intercourse with her willingly, and, having been released, escaped before her husband could accomplish his purpose. When this happened the husband was held to have divorced his wife, and her people kept the whole of the price that had been paid, and could claim any balance for which they had killed pigs. It seems strange that the parents of a woman who had deceived her husband in this way should have been entitled to keep the price paid for her. The idea seems to have been that the parents had done all they possibly could by tying the girl up and handing her over to her husband, and that if the latter was so foolish or so tender-hearted as to let the woman go without consummating the marriage when he had the chance, he only had himself to blame, and could not claim back the price. If the woman ran away after consummation, her price had to be refunded. The custom of tying up a wife who refuses to yield to her husband s embraces has passed out of use, but if a girl refuses to allow her husband access to her she is soundly beaten by her parents and sent back to her husband well primed with good advice. Several instances have been recorded, however, within living memory. Chiachai, a sister of The ulai, chief of Saiko, was married as a child to Pilang, brother of the chief of Tisi. Having refused to let her husband have connection with her, she was tied up and sent back to him, but induced him to release her by promising to let him sleep with her freely as soon as she was released. In spite of her promise, Chiachai, without redeeming her pledge, ran back to her village. Thoulai kept all the price he had been paid, since he had done all that could be expected of him.

Nongpawh, daughter of Theulai, was married as a child to Dawlong. When she grew up she refused to let him have intercourse with her, so her parents tied her up and sent her back to him, and he consummated the marriage while she was tied up. After this they lived happily together, and had children, and the woman is still alive. A similar case is that of Chahnang and Teichai of Siaha. Chahnang consummated the marriage while Teichai was tied up.

Custom of Laisacharei or Courting

Mr. Parry continued, While courting all the world over follows much the same course, a Lakher s wooing savours rather more of direct action than that of a young man in the West.

The chief difference really is that the Lakhers frankly recognise facts which are camouflaged in England. The Lakher method of courting is similar to the Lushei, but as the Lakhers have no *zawlbuk,* and it is the custom for young men to sleep in the house of the girl they favour, their task is much easier, whether their intentions are serious or whether they are only contemplating a casual amour. The suitor spends his day with the girl; they help each other in their work and exchange tobacco and nicotine-water, and at night the suitor sleeps in the girl s house. When a girl is favourably inclined to a young man, she places her bed nearer to his than is usual, and he is not slow to take the hint. The chief of Chapi told me that a favourite occasion for a young man to bring his wooing to a head is when a party of men and girls are drinking and singing together. The lover puts his arms round the girl and fondles her, and if she makes no objection he proceeds to make further advances, and if these are not taken amiss, the couple leave the merry-makers and go to the girl s house. Lakhers, however, are comparatively secretive about their love affairs, and show far better feeling in these matters than the Lusheis. If a Lushei has succeeded with a girl, he proclaims his triumph on the housetops, entirely regardless of the feelings of his victim, like a cock on a dungheap. A Lakher, on the other hand, never says a word, and does all he can to keep the affair quiet.

Though the custom varies somewhat in the different villages, scandal is on the whole sternly discouraged. In the Saiko and Siaha Tlongsai groups, if any one accuses two young unmarried persons of having been too intimate, the scandalmonger is fined a *racha* or 10 rupees and a *vopia,* whether the charge is true or not. In Chapi and the other Sabeu villages a fine is inflicted only if the charge cannot be proved. In Savang and the other Zeuhnang villages, no fine is imposed for merely saying that two young persons have slept together. Again, in the Saiko and Siaha group, if a young man himself gives out that he has slept with a girl and she denies it, he is fined 10 rupees and a *vopia,* whether he can prove the truth of his statement or not. In the Zeuhnang villages, a young fellow who boasts of his success with a girl is fined a gong of eight spans and a *vopia* if it is found that his boast is true, but if it is found that there was no foundation for the boast no notice is taken. In Chapi and the other Sabeu villages, however, young men can boast with impunity, and no fine is inflicted even if the girl denies the soft impeachment and her self-styled lover cannot prove his statement.

The Sabeu custom in this, as in a number of other instances, differs from the custom followed by the other groups. On the whole, however, it must be admitted that Lakhers are far more discreet about these matters than Lusheis.

It is doubtless this dislike for publicity that accounts for the fact that the Lakhers have no equivalent to the Lushei *puarak,* a friend who always accompanies a young Lushei in amorous adventures, and who acts both as pimp and as witness to what occurred, if by evil chance a civil suit arises owing to the victorious lover s boasting of his prowess. However, apart from the fact that discretion in love is essential, there is no bar to the freest of intercourse between unmarried persons, and no fine is inflicted merely because a young man and a girl have slept together.*f*

Custom of Nonghia

Mr. Parry further recorded thus, As a rule A young man s bride is selected by his parents, and it is only in comparatively rare cases, generally where a love affair has ended in an undesired result, that a man chooses his own bride. Except in cases of *nongapahaw,* a form of child marriage[a] , a man usually marries between the ages of twenty and twenty-five, and a woman after the age of twenty. This reasonable marriage age is due largely to the fact that Lakhers always want to marry into a higher clan if possible, so that it is by no means easy to find a suitable bride, and partly to the high rate of marriage price, which renders it necessary for a man s relatives to save up for years before they can afford to buy him a wife. Even so, the Lakhers marry earlier than the Lusheis. There is a deep social gulf between the higher and the lower clans, and every Lakher wants to raise his status by marrying a wife from a clan higher than his own.

Very few restrictions are imposed on the choice of a wife. There is no bar to people of the same clan marrying. It is *ana* for a full brother and sister to marry, as the children would not thrive. The Lakhers, however, believe that the marriage of a brother to a sister will only have evil effects for the parties, and not for the rest of the village, while among the Lusheis incestuous marriages are believed to lead to a failure in the crops. Children of the same father but by different mothers may not marry, but children of the same mother by different fathers may marry. The children of a brother and sister may and do marry if the sister s child is a son and the brother s child a daughter, but a man should not marry his father s sister s daughter, though it is not actually *ana* for him to do so. I am told that the reason for this is purely utilitarian, a brother s son being his sister s daughter s *pupa,* and so entitled to her *puma* when she marries, so that if he himself married her he would lose her price. I think, however, that the prohibition is more probably really due to the peculiarly close relationship existing between a maternal uncle and his nephews and nieces, the tie between them being very nearly as close as that between a parent and his children[a] and I think that probably in former times a marriage between a maternal uncle and his niece would have been just as *ana* as a marriage between a nephew and the widow of his maternal uncle is to-day. It is believed that such a marriage will most probably be fruitless, and that if by any chance offspring are produced, they will be imbeciles or afflicted with congenital disease. I know only two instances of a man marrying his father s sister s daughter, one in Siaha and the other at Chholong, the names of the parties in the latter village being Pabu and Keuhlei. Both these marriages took place only because the young man had made the girl pregnant, their relationship had come to light, there had been a scandal, and the relations had thought the best way out of it was to make the miscreants marry.

The children of brothers do not marry, it is not absolutely *ana* for them to do so, but it is believed that the children will be few and unhealthy, and that the parties themselves will die prematurely. In the one instance of such a marriage that I know of, between Siatia and Nongkhai of Amoingbeu, no evil effects are yet apparent, and they have three children. There is no objection to the marriage of the children of two sisters.

It is not *ana* for a man to marry his father s widow, but it is considered disgraceful, Mawtheu of Siaha, a son of Kikhaw by a concubine, on his father s death married his father s widow, Dawpeu. This was regarded as a breach of custom, and Dawpeu died not long after. In a marriage of this kind the son does not have to pay the full marriage price, he has only to pay a due called *abanasong,* usually a gong of eight spans. Such marriages are very rare indeed. Marriages of this kind are frequent among the Sema Nagas, and regarded as quite correct and desirable.

Although I am assured that such marriages are contrary to custom, I think that the sentiment against them is probably of modern growth. I find in Phayre s Account of Arakan,*f* *J.A.S.B.,* 1841, No. 117, that among the Lungkhes and Tseindus a son can marry his father s inferior wife after his father s death. It is true that Mawtheu married his father s married wife, but I am inclined to think that formerly such marriages were much more common than they are now.

The marriage of a father to his deceased son s widow is allowed, and is not regarded as a breach of custom. Vachhong, chief of Savang, married Ngongkei, widow of his son Chhonlang. Vachhong badly wanted an heir, and, being an old man, would have had to pay a very heavy price for any one else, the widow was good looking and willing, and no additional price beyond an extra gong of eight spans as *abanasong* was required. The most favoured marriage is with a mother s brother s daughter, as it keeps the maternal avuncular relationship in the same line, but it is not obligatory.ƒ

The custom is prevalent among the Lakhers of Assam and Mizoram.

Child Marriages being Discontinued Gradually

About 25 strictly exogamous clans are found among the Ashings in Arunachal Pradesh. The main function of these clans is to regulate marriage alliances. Some of the important clans include Yalik, Medo, Nyodo, Panyi, Pangga, and Lonsung. Tribal endogamy and clan exogamy are the general rules of marriage among them. However, there may be some instances of tribal exogamy. Child marriages were prevalent at one time, but now adult marriages are preferred, the age of marriage for boys being 17 to 18 years whereas for the girls being between 15 to 17 years. Traditionally, there has been provision for bachelors dormitories, both for boys and girls. The boys dormitory was called *bango* and the girls dormitory is known as *rasheng*. Girls are not allowed to visit the *bango* however, the members of the *bango* have free access to the *rasheng*. The majority of the Ashings had marriage negotiated by parents but in recent years courtship has gained preference among the educated boys. Monogamy is the most acceptable form of marriage. Polygamy is permitted by the society and traditional custom but is rare. Earlier, there used to be a hefty bride price but now the amount has decreased considerably low. The marriage involved some kind of gift being presented to the bridegroom s side. The bride may stay with her parents after the wedding, generally for three years, before joining her husband. However, in case the bride groom is from the same village, he can regularly visit the bride. The residence after marriage is patrilocal and the family type is patriarchal. Divorce is permissible adultery, sterility and maladjustment being some of the main reasons for divorce. Both the partners have the right to seek a divorce, but a fine is payable in such cases. The amount of the fine is comparatively low if the wife has had no children or if she has not been brought to her husband s house. The amount of fine is generally fixed by the *kebang*. Widows, widowers and divorcees are permitted re-marriage. The children become the father s responsibility after a divorce, but minor children may stay with the mother till the age of five or six years. The Ashings have been nuclear and joint family structure. The older members of the family and the village elders are respected by the youngsters. Since marriages take place outside the village, within or outside the community, the inter-family linkages expand beyond the limit of the village. Only the sons inherit the parental property. At the time of separation, the *jhum* fields and the foodgrains are divided equally among all the sons, but the house goes to the eldest son because he is duty-bound to look after the parents. The daughters usually get ornaments as marriage gifts. In case there is no son, the daughter may get the property, provided her husband is ready to live in his father-in-law s house. The status of women in the Ashing society is low. They do not inherit any parental property. They are usually responsible for looking after the children, preparing food and drinks, bringing fuel looking after the children, preparing food and drinks, bringing fuel and fodder and doing other household chores. They have no place in political or religious affairs, but definitely play an important role in contributing to the family income by taking part in agricultural activities. They have no role to play in the mechanism of social control and in decision-making.

The custom is practiced among the Ashing sub-tribe of the Adi tribal group of Arunachal Pradesh.

Observing a Vast Number of Minute Rituals

Mr. J.H. Hutton wrote about the complex and varied customs and rituals practiced by different sub-groups among the Sema Negas of Nagaland, thus: The assumption of man s dress by a Sema boy is a matter of small account and is variously observed by the different clans. Thus the Yepothomi boy on the day that he first puts on the lengta merely abstains from wild vegetables, meat killed by wild animals, and any other sort of food which is spiritually dangerous. The Ayemi boy is stood upon the husking-table while the lengta is first put on by his parents; this is done to put him out of reach of lice, which might otherwise infest his lengta and trouble him. He observes no other rite or tabu. The Zumomi, also with the object of avoiding lice, refrain from the rice from which liquor has been brewed on the day on which they have first put on the lengta. They also refrain from vegetables. As, however, the lengta is usually first put on by them at night after the last meal, the actual abstention is rarely more than a nominal deprivation.

The Sema formalities in connection with marriage vary to a considerable extent among different clans and are characterised by a vast number of minute observances. The account below gives only the general details.

At the time of formal betrothal the prospective bridegroom goes to the house of the parents of the girl and eats and drinks there. He is accompanied by a person called *anisu*—in the Yepothomi clan an old man, in the Ayemi clan an old woman who drinks and eats before the prospective bridegroom does so and blesses the match. This is no doubt to assure, if possible, that any evil influences attending the proposed marriage shall fall on the *anisu,* who is old and therefore unimportant or less susceptible, rather than on the bridegroom, just as the reaping and sowing of crops are initiated by old persons who have in any case little to expect of life, are of little value to the community as fighting, working, or breeding units, or perhaps who are so tough as to be able the better to withstand evil influences, for it is clear that young infants are the most vulnerable. The *anisu* is asked whether he comes with the authority of the intending bridegroom s parents. He answers Yes, and asks for the girl. Assent is given, after which he kills a pig and cuts up the meat. After this a breach of the promise of marriage by either party without cause entails liability to a fine, usually of from Rs. 5/- upwards, according to the social position of the injured party.

The time that may elapse between the betrothal and the marriage may be almost anything from days to years, for in the Tizu valley the children of rich men are sometimes betrothed before they reach puberty, and though in such cases the actual marriage sometimes takes place before puberty, it is more common for a betrothal to take place and the marriage to follow when the parties are of a suitable age. Cohabitation does not take place in the case of such marriages until the parties are fit for it. They return to their parents houses for the time being, as a rule. Such early marriages usually take place for more or less political reasons.

Before the day fixed for the marriage the *anisu* takes a piece of salt and a dog and visits the house of the bride s parents. He (or she) puts the salt into the thatch of the roof from inside the house, where it remains untouched, and gives the dog to the bride s parents. This visit is followed by one by the bridegroom, who is accompanied by a friend or relative chosen for his cleverness, who argues the question of price with the bride s parents, doing his best to reduce it. When the price is finally fixed, the cattle, etc., are brought over the same evening from the bridegroom s house if the parties are in the same village. If the bride lives in a distant village, the approximate amount of the bride-price is conveyed by friends of the bridegroom some way behind, and if after all they have not brought enough they hand over what they have and indicate to the bride s parents other cattle in their village which they will add to the price. When the bride s parents have expressed themselves satisfied, a pig brought by the bridegroom s party and called *azazhunala* (? = way to mother-beholding) is killed and cut up. This completes the contract, and the essential transfer of the girl from the *potestas* of her father to her husband is complete. The fragments of the pig are given to the bride s relations (the bride may not taste it), and each one that receives a fragment pays a basket of paddy, which is sent with the bride to her new house. The bridegroom s party then name the date, not before the third day under any circumstances, on which they will come for the bride. Against that date the bride s relations get ready. Drink and food are prepared to entertain the bridegroom s party, all the paddy which is to be sent along with the bride is got ready, and whatever else she is to take with her.*f*

A Better Position of Women

About the position of women in the Sema tribe, Mr. Hutton records, thus: The position of women in the Sema tribe, though they are possibly more restricted in the matter of the possession of property and in sexual licence than the women of the Angami and Ao tribes, is probably higher socially, as it is morally, than in either of them, at any rate as far as the families of chiefs are concerned.

The Sema girl lives until marriage in the house of her parents unless she is sent to the house of her chief, or some other protector, where she lives as one of the family and pays for her keep by her services. In any case, though given plenty of freedom and going to the fields with her own *aluzhili,* which consists till her marriage of contemporaries of both sexes, she is carefully looked after and not allowed that freedom of sexual intercourse usual to unmarried girls in most Naga tribes. Lazemi is perhaps an exception to the general rule in this respect, and possibly one or two other villages in the Dayang Valley in which the Angami influence is pronounced. This is not to say that the unmarried Sema girl is invariably chaste, but she is a good deal more so than the girl of any neighbouring tribe. The care which is taken of her is partly due to the desire not to damage her value in the marriage market, as a girl who is known to have had an intrigue commands a much lower marriage price as a rule. Accordingly the fine for an adultery with a girl of position is much higher than that for a similar affair with the daughter of a man of none, since the marriage price of the latter is in any case much lower than that of, say, a chief s daughter.

A Sema girl s head is shaved until she is regarded as approaching a marriageable age, when the hair is allowed to grow. Marriage is of course always on exogamous principles, and it is regarded as very shameful to say anything at all improper before a woman of one s own clan and still more so of one s own kindred. Shameless men, however, who do this are not punished at any rate by any human agency. When she is betrothed she wears a plaited band of red cane and yellow orchid-stem round her forehead, which she leaves off shortly after her marriage. A girl s betrothal in the case of thc ordinary villagers does not usually last long, but in that of chiefs children marriages are sometimes arranged for a long time before they can take place. This arrangement is made as a rule by the parents, who are asked for their daughter by a go-between, acting usually at the instance of a young man who wants her, or at that of the parents of a young man who has not found a suitable wife, but normally the prospective bridegroom himself is the first to move in the matter. In any case the marriage is never made against the girl s will, though it may often happen that she does no more than passively acquiesce in the arrangements made by her parents or guardian. The arbitrary breaking off of a match by either party renders that party liable to a fine (usually about Rs. 5 or Rs. 10), which, in the case of the engagement being broken off by the girl or her people in order that she may marry someone else, is paid by the party last mentioned.

The prices paid for wives vary very considerably indeed according to their station in life, ranging in value from Rs. 20 or even less to as much as Rs. 400 or Rs. 500, but they are always paid largely in kind, and the girl in her turn brings with her beads and ornaments which become the property of her husband and which are to some extent proportionate to the price paid for her, though they do not by any means equal it in value. Besides the girl s birth, her capabilities are also taken into account, a girl who is thrifty, can weave, or is a hard and good worker in the fields commanding a higher price accordingly. Personal appearance has little bearing on the marriage price. The price of a widow who has gone back to her father s house is very much less than that of a girl not previously married, while a woman divorced for misconduct, or who for some other reason is generally undesirable, would command merely a nominal sum. On the other hand, the prices asked by important chiefs for their daughters are sometimes quite excessive. A daughter of Ghukiya is said to have fetched 50 head of cattle, a pair of ivory armlets worth Rs. 80, and Rs. 100 in cash, which might be in total value anything from Rs. 300 to Rs. 500 or more, and she blear-eyed, but the commoner who married her probably got beads worth Rs. 200 or so with her, as well as the distinction of an alliance with Ghukiya, which was as good as a life insurance policy[1] and was probably what he wanted. Because few would be rash enough to interfere too far with the man who had married the daughter of so powerful a chief.

The Sema woman is usually a good wife and a good mother, and though marriages are polygynous in the case of all who can afford it, the various wives get on well enough together, particularly if there are more than two. Separate houses are sometimes built for some of the wives, but not necessarily. The wife manages the house, entertains her husband s guests, works in his fields, and generally shares his entire confidence on matters of domestic economy. One of the wives is usually regarded as the head wife, but she does not necessarily take the lead in regulating her husband s household, and her position as the principal wife does not seem to be very definite. In the case of a chief s son or other *kekami,* she would normally be the one first married, though as it is not always easy to find a girl of suitable age and family, such marriages are often arranged a long way ahead, and thus it happens that sometimes the bridegroom takes one wife to himself before the important marriage comes off, but in such a case the wife married later would take formal precedence of the one married first.

As regards property, a man s widows are entitled to one-third of their husband s movable property, and if one or more of the widows remain unmarried in the late husband s house, she, or they, may get whatever free labour was due to the dead man for a period not exceeding three years. After that they may be given some free labour as a matter of courtesy, but they are not entitled to it. If a widow marries one of her husband s heirs, the latter enjoys the property without division for her lifetime, and in some cases widows are allowed to receive payments in cash on the score of dues to their late husband.

Although women can possess movable property in absolute ownership, they cannot, however, possess land unless they have bought it, and even then they do not seem able to bequeath it as they please, for the sons or other male heirs will claim the land in virtue of the disability of women to inherit or possess it.

An regards the guardianship of children, the children by her original husband of a wife divorced or of a widow who had married again could be claimed by the husband or his heirs when weaned, but the woman would have the right to keep unweaned children when she left her husband s house until they were weaned, which is usually at about three years old. If they were not claimed they might stay with their mother, but they might, unless specifically given up, be claimed at any time on payment of a sum to cover the cost of their keep in the interval. In the case of a girl who has been brought up by her mother independently of the father and his relations, or partly so, it is usual to divide the marriage price, the mother taking half and the father or his representatives taking half, and even if the paternal rights over a girl had been renounced, a payment of some sort would probably be made to him on the girl s marriage in recognition of the fact that he had begotten her.

Divorce is easy and fairly often occurs. In the case of a wife committing adultery, she may be simply put away, her husband keeping the ornaments he got with her and claiming a penalty of one head of cattle from her father or his heirs, together with repayment of the price which he paid for her if within three years of the marriage. Otherwise the husband may condone the offence, receiving a fine from her paramour, which varies according to the woman s position. This fine he could claim in any case, whether he kept his wife or not, but if the offended husband was a chief and the offender one of his own men, the latter would certainly be ejected from his village and, if in unadministered territory, would be in peril of his life if he did not anticipate trouble by fleeing fast and far.

A man who puts away his wife for incompatibility of temper or some minor fault may claim a repayment of the marriage price provided the divorce takes place before three years have expired from the date of the marriage. At any time, however, he must give back the woman s ornaments in case of a divorce of this sort.

A woman who objects to her husband can leave him at any time, but will not get her ornaments back if she does so against her husband s consent, unless he has seriously ill-treated her, in which case she could claim the return of her ornaments as well as a fine for the ill-treatment. In any case the marriage price would have to be repaid to him. Divorce is, however, probably less frequent among the Semas than among neighbouring tribes, of whom the Aos are particularly bad in this respect, almost making it the rule rather than the exception to be divorced at least once during their lives, and usually for infidelity. They are, as Hakluyt s voyager would put it, the most of them naughtie packes.

The position of women among the Semas is on the whole far from the degradation sometimes alleged of Nagas in general (*e.g.* Assam Census of 1891). The women have to work very hard in the fields, but their husbands do the same, and both as daughters, wives, and mothers they are treated with real affection and respect by their parents, their husbands, and their children. The writer remembers going into the house of Ivihe, the old Chief of Aochagalimi, who was very miserable, and noticing a long tally of knotted string. On asking what it meant he was told that each knot represented one day that had passed since the death of the old man s wife some months before.*ƒ* adds Mr. Hutton.

A Low Position of Women

About the Angami women, Mr. Hutton noted, The position of women among the Angamis would at first sight appear to be but a low one. By the Tengima proper and Chakroma she is debarred from inheriting land at all, while among the Eastern Angamis she can only inherit subject to the reversion of the property to the male line on the death of her sons, or to a substantial payment in lieu of such reversion. At the same time she is, of course, free to purchase and possess land and transmit purchased land to her posterity absolutely. Again, not only is relationship through the female side not recognised, but its very existence does not seem to be realised, and a man who can enumerate his male ancestors for fourteen generations cannot name his grandmothers for four. As for his collateral relatives on the female side, he knows nothing whatever about them. Mr. Davis, writing of Naga women in general, goes so far as to say that after marriage they become mere household drudges. Assam Census Report, 1891, p. 250.

With this latter proposition, however, we can in no wise agree, at any rate not in so far as Angami women are concerned, nor for that matter Sema women either. However low the legal status of the Angami woman may seem, her position in the household makes it true that in the Naga Hills, as elsewhere, women are a very strong folk. The husband expects absolute fidelity from his wife, but, at any rate in the case of the ordinary villager, he renders a fair measure of it himself in return, and while in all domestic matters the wife is an equal partner, consulted by and consulting with her man, a woman is, in Tengima villages, usually the holder of the village office of First Reaper *(Lidepfu)*. While hunting and warfare fall to her husband s lot, as weaving and cooking to hers, agriculture and, in some degree, trade are carried on by both together. When a guest is to be entertained the wife assumes the *role* of hostess; in family quarrels she is usually to the fore. In the question of the marriage she is allowed a freedom of choice that will easily bear comparison with the freedom of choice which she exercises in the most civilised of nations. Her parents, it is true, may resort occasionally to a good deal of persuasion in regard to matrimonial projects. They never resort to force, and cases of girls married against their inclinations are exceedingly rare. In the last resort she is always able to evade a distasteful alliance by conveniently dreaming dreams of ill-omen at the critical point. Polygamy is not practised, and Hurukhe of Kohima, formerly head interpreter to the Deputy Commissioner, is the only Tengima Angami known to have had two wives at the same time, though there is nothing to prevent their having a number in succession. The Memi do have two wives at the same time more frequently, but they too look on the practice with a good deal of disfavour. Among most Angamis the price of a bride is merely nominal, a few chickens, a couple of pigs, and a spear, but in some of the Chakroma villages, Chephama for instance, sums of from twenty to a hundred rupees are paid. Divorce is easy to obtain; incompatibility of temper is a quite sufficient reason; and unless she is herself divorced for adultery the woman always obtains a third of the joint property exclusive of land. As a widow, though entitled to nothing but her third (except in the Eastern Angami villages, where, if childless, she gets the whole of the property other than land), she is usually provided for by her husband s relations, that is, if the husband before death has not given directions for provision for her, which he usually does. She can also remarry where and when she pleases, provided only that she may not remarry from her deceased husband s house. She must go back to the house of her father or of his male representative. Mr. Davis remarks, It is wonderful how soon after marriage a Naga woman loses her good looks, if she ever had any. As soon as ever she has had a child she takes no further care about her personal appearance.*f* As far as the Angami woman goes this is absolutely true of most, and it possibly indicates the strength of her position.

The Angami woman before marriage is given a very great deal of liberty, though the extent to which she takes advantage of this has possibly been exaggerated. Mr. Davis, speaking not of Angamis in particular, but of Nagas generally, says: I should say that it was very rare for a girl not to have at least one lover. Assam Census Report, 1891. Customs, however, differ in this respect in a very great degree between different tribes. While the Ao girl is bound to admit men to the girls houses at night, chastity before marriage prevails among the Semas, where the marriage price of a girl is reduced at least 50 per cent, by the fact of her having had an intrigue. The Angamis would seem to fall somewhere between the Ao and the Semas, for while separate girls houses do not exist in Angami (Tengima) villages, though they are found in Memi villages, girls are not looked after with the same jealousy as that with which a Sema girl is watched until her marriage. In some Memi villages the girls share the same morung as the young men, the boys sleeping on an upper platform, the girls on a lower. Publicity is probably an efficient bar to flirtation. Accurate information as to the precise degree of chastity observed by Angami girls is very difficult to obtain. When asked about it, Angamis usually admit that it is common for a girl to have a lover, but they deny that it is the rule, and say that some do have one and some do not. It is also usually averred by them that public opinion is against it, and that a girl who is found out is subjected to a great deal of ridicule, while a girl believed to be fickle or known to have transferred her affections from one lover to another finds it very difficult to get anyone to marry her. Mr. Davis, still speaking of Nagas in general, has said that a girl s lover would as a rule belong to the girl s own *khel (i.e., thino)* and would be a man whom it would be impossible for her to marry in any case. In the copy of Assam Census Report for 1891 which belongs to the Subdivisional Office at Mokokchung, the late Mr. Noel Williamson, a careful observer, made the following marginal note against this statement: I think that this is rarely the case. Incest before marriage is as abhorrent to these people as that on marriage. My own opinion is that among the Angamis, as among other Naga tribes, the lover would as a rule be a man whom it *would* be possible for her to marry. It very frequently happens that a girl does marry her lover. Indeed, it is probably the rule rather than the exception. Possibly Mr. Davis was misled by the change in the exogamous unit from the original *thino* to its subdivision. Premarital intrigues and the subdivision of exogamous groups are in a way not unconnected, as it is certain that in a large exogamous group living as a community there would be many intrigues inside the group, if its members were Angami or indeed of almost any other Naga tribe. As far as the Sema, Chang, Lhota, and Ao countries go, Mr. Williamson was undoubtedly right. An Ao girl, although bound to admit any other man in the village, may not admit to her house a man of her own exogamous group. If she does so she is held jointly guilty with the man. The Lhotas have the same dislike of any *liaison* within the exogamous group. With the Angamis what appears to be really the case is that while a girl *might* take a lover from her own clan, she would at any rate be rigidly forbidden to take one from her own kindred, which is regarded as entailing great misfortune. As the kindred is now becoming the real exogamous unit of the Angamis, their practice in this respect is much the same as that of the Lhotas and Aos, only in the case of the Angamis the clan as a social unit has not yet disappeared, as it has done among the Lhotas, and in some villages still remains a more or less exogamous body. A theory of the origin of exogamy and marriage was advanced by Mr. S. E. Peal, who suggested that within the tribe all women were common property and that no single man could claim an exclusive right to any woman of the tribe, but that such a right was recognised in the case of women captured in war from other tribes. This theory, of course, would provide an explanation of the freedom of sex intercourse before marriage, but if we accept it, the prohibition of intercourse between unmarried members of the same kindred must be regarded as a comparatively recent growth, or as an extension to the kindred of a prohibition which formerly affected only the family. *Vide* Gait, Assam Census Report, 1891, p. 122, note. Among some of the Ndreng Lhotas it is common for a man going on a long journey to allow a near relative of his won kindred to cohabit with his wife during his absence. Such cohabitation, however, is usually only allowed by a definite arrangement, and only to a man of the husband s kindred. The Sema villages of Seromi and Tichipami have told me that they were allowed free intercourse with any of the women in the Sangtam village of Charr, as the men of that village wished to improve the stock by an admixture of more warlike blood, Charr being rather an inferior village with warlike neighbours. Seromi and Tichipami go there regularly to trade.

The licence allowed to unmarried girls raises another question. What of their children? Here again accurate information is exceedingly difficult to obtain. Illegitimate children are very rare, and Mr. Davis remarks that it is impossible to resist the conclusion that they are made away with immediately after birth, or that abortion is procured before the birth of the child. The practice of infanticide is denied by Angami men, but they admit that some method of procuring abortion may be known to and practised by the women, although they, the men, do not know about it. In Kohima illegitimate children were born in private and killed by their mothers; in the Eastern Angami country illegitimate children were forbidden by the village to be reared. Girls about to become mothers used to, and probably still do, though, of course, it is denied, procure abortion by twisting and squeezing the abdomen. Should a child be born it was invariably killed, though not in any particular manner, and the soles of the infants feet were pierced all over with thorns to prevent their returning to haunt their mothers dreams. It was believed that if they were allowed to grow up the village would be without success in war or hunting. Of course it is denied that this custom still prevails, and in support of such a denial the Kezabama Gaonburas point out a man born out of wedlock who is said to have been allowed to grow up as a result of the village s having been taken over by Government. It is, however, to say the least of it, curious that they should only point out one. The Kacha Nagas are related by Khonoma to kill children who are born with the placenta adhering to the neck by pouring boiling water into their mouths, and it is said that a woman of Lakema was sentenced to three years imprisonment for killing her child in this way when Mr. Porteous was Deputy Commissioner. The Aos undoubtedly procure the abortion of illegitimate children, and, as Mr. Davis suggests, it is only fair to assume that for every case of abortion or infanticide that comes to light many happen of which nothing is heard. The custom being one that is approved of by all Nagas, it is impossible to expect them to give information of the occurrence of such cases. A method used in the Ao village of Nankarn is to feel from the outside for the child s head a few days before birth and catching hold of that part of the mother s body together with the head of the child inside to give a sharp rap on it with a stone, which causes the child to be born dead. This method is said to be known to certain old women who practise it in privacy.

It is probable, however, that among the Angamis proper, at any rate, illegitimate children were not *necessarily* killed, as there is at present a definite custom with regard to their disposal. Male children go to the father when weaned, but no proper ceremony is performed for their birth. The women probably perform one on their own account in secret, but the men do not know what it is, as the father does not take part. He merely provides food and drink for the woman, who comes to his house to fetch it. This provision is tantamount to an acknowledgment of parentage, and a refusal to provide the food and drink according to custom gives great offence to the girl and her relations. The mother herself is not allowed to grow her hair and must remain shorn like the other unmarried girls. If she insists on growing her hair, no one is allowed to marry her except a man of the very poorest condition and of the lowest standing in the village.

Although Angamis do not admit that there is absolute freedom of intercourse between the unmarried, they readily admit that widows, unless quite aged, are in no way restrained in this matter, even by public opinion, which seems to be the only real check upon girls, while in some of the Eastern Angami villages there are regular prostitutes. This class appears to be sometimes recruited from unmarried girls as well as from the younger widows, and is most numerous in rich Eastern Angami villages like Kezabama. These women frequently acquire a good deal of land and take their fees in work. One of them died just after the Makware expedition, a number of days labour on her terraces being owed to her by different clients. Captain Butler, in his enthusiastic encomium on Angami women, is quite wrong in saying prostitution is a thing unknown here[a] A Naga woman would scorn to barter for her person ; but he was doubtless speaking of the Tengima villages, where it is not known except in so far as it has been introduced round Kohima. He also adds that the foul diseases that follow in its train are evils to which Naga flesh has not been born an heir. If this is so, they have unfortunately been inherited since Captain Butler wrote.

REFERENCES

1. Dalton, ET, Descriptive Ethnology of Bengal, office of superintendent of Govt. Printing Press, Calcutta, 1872 (reprint, Firma KLM, Calcutta 1960.
2. Singh, K.S. (Gen. ed) People of India: Arunachal Pradesh, Seagull Books, Calcutta 1995.
3. Stack, Edward and Lyall, Sir Charles, The Mikirs, United Publishers, Guwahati, first published 1908.
4. Endle, The Kacharis, Cosmo Publications, New Delhi, 1987, (Originally Published 1908).
5. Danda, Dipali, S., Among the Dimasa of Assam: An Ethnographic Study, Sterling Publishers, New Delhi 1978.
6. Hutton, J.H., The Sema Nagas, OUP, Bombay, 1968 (first Published 1921).
7. Roy, Jyotirmoy, History of Manipur, Eastlight book House, Calcutta (reprint) 1974), Originally Published 1911.
8. Chib, SS., The Beautiful India: Meghalaya, Life and Light Publishers, New Delhi, 1980.
9. Hutton, J.H., The Angami Nagas: With Short Notes on Neighbouring Tribes, OUP, Bombay, 1969 (first Published 1921).
10. Mills, JP, The Ao Nagas, OUP, Bombay, 1973, Originally Published 1926.
11. Gangte, Thangkhomang, The Kukis of Manipur: A Historical Analysis, Gyan Publishing House, New Delhi, 1993.

4

Marriage Ceremony

The marriage systems in the Northeast region vary vastly ranging from Vaidic type to the most primitive still practised in far-flung corners. Later additions to them were the Christian and Muslim marriage systems. Here we give an array of marriage systems practised in the region.

Approaching Girl's Father with a Measure of Salt

At the beginning of a negotiated marriage the boy's parents approach girls's father or in his absence her guardian with one *seer* of salt, known as *sandidangsingba*. Its acceptance indicates that he is inclined to establish the matrimonial relationship. Otherwise, he politely refuses to accept the salt.

If all goes well, then comes the ceremony of *laothailangba,* at this the bridegroom's father goes to the girls' house with ricebeer in four *laothai* (container made of small bottle gourd) and presents them to the girl's father. This formal visit is repeated three times on different occasions and discussions are carried through to complete the negotiation to settle the amount of bride-price, and arrange for wedding.

The Dimasa of Assam say the marriage should take place within a month after *laothailangba,* otherwise the married life of the would-be couple might not be a happy one. Usually, the marriage, is solemnised after the harvest, Tuesday, Wednesday, and Friday being considered as specially auspicious days.

On the preceding day to marriage an advance party from the bridegroom's side goes to the girl's house. They make necessary arrangements for their stay in the bridal village. At night the young boys of both the villages feint a mock fight. The next morning the bridegroom accompanied by his father and other relatives comes to the bride's village. There her would be father-in-law performs *mayofagarba* in presence of the village elders. This is done to secure a safe journey to the bride's village. The bridegroom is ceremonially dressed in finery and wrapper. The other members of the bridegroom's party are dressed in clean cloth. The bridegroom's father is specially dressed with head-gear and other wrappers.

Then they start for the bride's village. Before entering the bride's village a special ritual *lama-fungba* (*'lama'* means road and *'fungba'* means to close) is observed by bridegroom's father by breaking an egg, this will stop evil spirits from entering the village. The next is *midogarba,* in this ceremony a pig is sacrificed in honour of the gods; this is said to secure a prosperous life for the newly marred couple. The sacrifice is made on behalf of bridegroom's father. He carries the pig on his way to the bride's village and the flesh is consumed by the bridegroom's party on the wedding day. No food is supplied to the bridegroom's party by the bride's father, he treats them with drinks (mainly rice-beer) only.

The bridegroom's father then conducts *khaltiriba (khalti* means bride-price), in which he pays the bride-price to the bride's father and mother. Then the bridegroom begs *khilimba,* or blessings from all the elderly persons who had assembled there. The bride's parents and other patrilineal and matrilineal relatives sit according to their seniority and closeness. The bridegroom's father and relatives also sit facing the bride's relatives. The bride's father then narrates the virtues of the bride and that of her matriclan. The bridegroom then bows down to all elderly persons according to their seniority, everybody blesses them and wishes them a happy married life. After these rituals the guests are entertained with rice-beer. The bridegroom is taken to the first chamber of his father-in-law's house who he stays there. Leaving thus the bridegroom at his father-in-law's place all his companions return to their own village. The morning he meets the bride and is taken to the inner chamber of the house where cooking is done, considered to be a private place where none but the family members can have access, by which the Dimasa symbolises his acceptance as a member of the family.

After a few days of ceremony, the bride's party accompanying the newly married couple go to the bridegroom's village. On the way, bride' party also observe *mayofagarbe* and *lamafungba*. At the bridegroom's village they are welcomed by the bridegroom's parents and entertained with food and rice-beer. The bride's party leaves the next day leaving the couple there for about a week.

The ceremony that follows is called as *madaikhilimba*, conducted to worship clan gods which can be observed at any time within one year of marriage. Usually, it is performed by within one week of marriage when the couple stays at his place. At the ritual of *madaikhilimba*, a male goat or a fowl is slaughtered to propitiate the clan gods. By the ceremony the bride is formally accepted as a member of her husband's patriclan.

Then again, the couple returns to the bride's house they live there for one year, the period of this stay is called *minhabba*. Though it is obligatory for a newly married couple to stay at the girl's house for one year, nowadays there is a tendency among the Dimasa to reduce the period.

No Brahman priest is usually required to solemnise a Dhimasa marriage. No incantations were chanted either. However, in recent times, the Dimasa of Mikir Hills started to engage the village priest who performed certain rituals by setting a sacrificial dagger on the ground. He worshipped Shivrai and Kamadi as the presiding deity of marriage. The priest also chanted, "They are married today with kind permission of Shivrai and Kamadi. May God bless them. Today onwards they have got two fathers and two mothers". This was followed by the ceremony of *khilimba* or blessings. This employment of priest and worship of Shivrai and Kamadi at the time of marriage is still unknown in the villages of the North Cachar Hills situated in interior of the rural side. This seems a new introduction to the Dimasa customs due to the influence of Hinduism. The custom prevails amongst the Dimasas of Assam.

Rice beer Drinkings in Abundance

Dwelling on the custom of Mikir marriage ceremonies, Mr. Edward Stack noted. "When the marriage day is fixed, both families prepare beer and spirits; if the bridegroom is rich, he provides drink for the whole country-side (*hor-hak hor-tibuk*). The bridegroom's party, giving a gourd of beer to each village they pass through, arrive at the bride's house in the evening. There they sit a while, and then offer one gourd of beer and one glass bottle of spirits to the bride's father on the *hong*. A colloquy ensues : the bride's father asks the bridegroom's why they have come, and why these offerings. He answers, 'Your sister (*i.e.,* the wife of the speaker) is becoming old and cannot work, so we have brought our son to marry your daughter.' (The custom formerly was that a boy must marry is first cousin on the mother's side, and if he did not, the maternal uncle could beat the lad as much as he liked; but now they can do as they please). The replay follows: 'My daughter is unworthy, she does not know weaving and other household work'. 'Never mind, we will teach her ourselves'. The bride's father then asks his wife to enquire of the girl if she will take the lad; without her consent the beer and spirits cannot be accepted. If the wife reports consent, the beer and spirits are drunk by the two fathers. Sometimes they sit the whole night before the girl's consent is obtained. If any knowing old men are there, they sing in two parties : 'We cannot send our daughter to your house!' 'We cannot leave our boy to stay with you!' When the question of consent is settled, all eat together. Then the bride prepares the bed inside the house for the bridegroom, in the *kam;* in the *tibung* ...... if there is room : if not, in the *thengthor;* but if the lad is ashamed, he sends one of his garments to take his place in the bed.

"What follows depends upon the wealth and standing of the parties. If the wedding is *akejoi*—that is, if no payment is to be made for the bride—the girl goes with her husband next day to her new home. Her parents accompany her, and are entertained with food and drink, returning the following day. If the wedding is *akemen* (literally, ripe, *pakka*), the lad stays in his father-in-law's house. He rests one day, and then works for his father-in-law for a year, or two years, or even it may be for life, according to agreement. 'There is no money payment in any case. If the girl is an heiress or only daughter, the marriage is usually *akemen;* but in the great majority of cases it is *akejoi*. The neighbours of both villages assemble at the marriage, and when the bride goes to her husband's house, the neighbours of the village accompany her and are hospitably entertained."

"When Mr. Stack made his enquiries, there was little intercourse between the young men and girls. Seduction rarely occurred, but when it did, the parents of the girl had to give her to the lad in marriage and it was not punished. Old tribal men, however, could remember when the *terang* or 'bachelors' house' used to be the abode not only of the youths but also of the maids, and illegitimate births were common. The girls used even to work in the fields with the boys; there was not even a matron to look after then! Mr Stack further recorded.

"After marriage adultery is said to be rare. The case is judged by the *me,* or village council who inflict a fine. The guilty pair are tied up and exposed to the scorn of the neighbours until the fine is paid by the man. Adultery was never capitally punished. After the fine is paid, the husband has to take his wife back, unless there are no children, when he might refuse to do so. The fine is not given to the offended husband, but distributed among the elders who compose the *me.*"

As to the question whether more than one wife is allowed, Mr. Stack wrote, in 1883 the chapter on *"Castes and Tribes"* in the Report on the Assam Census of 1881 thus: "Polygamy is permitted if a man can afford it." His subsequent notes of 1885-86, however, record that monogamy is the rule, and no one is allowed to marry two wives. Writing in 1903, Mr. W.C.M. Dundas, Subdivisional Officer of North Cachar, says that an Arleng may marry only one wife. On the other hand, the Rev. P.E. Moore, who has a long experience of the Mikirs, writing in 1902, says, "Polygamy is not common. A man sometimes takes a second wife. In one instance which came to my notice recently the two wives were married on the same day. The man is usually fined Rs. 12.8 for this irregularity."

Simply Carrying Away Bride and Load of Dowry

About the marriage custom and its practice among the Sema Nagas of Nagaland, Mr. J.H. Hutton writes, "On the day appointed the bridegroom comes with a party of his relations to carry away the bride and her stuff. The latter, consisting of a considerable amount of paddy together with the bride's dowry of cloths and ornaments, is all arranged ready outside her parents' house. The bridegroom's party, having arrived, eat and drink with the bride's people, and after that start back to their own village. The *anisu* must be the first to pick up a load and give it to someone to carry. Then a procession starts to the bride-groom's house. First goes a warrior in full kit and carrying a spear in one hand and a dao in the other. He is called *akeshou.* After him goes the *anisu*, likewise, if a man, with spear and dao. After the *anisu* comes the bride, a narrow red and yellow circlet of plaited cane round her head, and a chicken in her hand, and a woman's staff which has a wooden top shod with a long iron butt-piece. In some cases the bride carries a dao instead, which she presents to her husband. After the bride comes her personal property, carried by a man specially chosen for the purposes and called *aboshou*. He also carries food for her to eat on the way, as she may not eat after her arrival. The *aboshou* is followed by the bride's paternal aunt (*ani*), preferably her father's elder sister, but a younger sister or, if no sister is a available, a female cousin on the father's side will do. She is called for the occasion *akawoku-pfu* in virtue of carrying the bride's *akawoku*—a 'work-basket' containing balls of thread, a spindle, etc., symbolical of her duty in life. This is carried even in the case of the Tizu valley Semas, who do not know how to spin or weave. After the *akawoku-pfu* come the bride's brothers and her mother and other relations, excepting her father, how is not allowed to accompany the bride, together with the bridegroom and his relations, in no particular order of precedence. All, of course, go in single file and march to the usual accompaniment of meaningless chants and loud cries. On arrival the property is put into the bridegroom's own house. The bride and her mother and relations sleep there, but may not eat in it. They eat (except the bride, who must fast) in the house of the bride groom's parents. The bridegroom may not sleep in his own house that night. The next morning the bride and the *aboshou* first eat together in the bridegroom's parents' house; then the *aboshou* and the whole of the bride's party, who eat after the *aboshou* and the bride, go home. Small presents are given to the *anisu,* the *akeshou,* the *aboshou,* and the *akawoku-pfu* by the bridegroom, and also to the *aluzhitoemi,* or captain of the working gang of which the bride was a member. The latter's present consists of a chicken and a handful of small beans, and is called *mini-lha-me* ('petticoat stripping-off price'). The *akeshou* and the *aboshou* usually get about Rs. 2 each, and the *akawoku-pfu* Rs. 5. The bride's mother is given a hoe by the bridegroom. This is not given if the bride has been married before. When the *anisu* is a woman she gets a basket of each sort of cereal brought by the bride, but these payments vary a good deal. For that day the newly-married pair observe *pini* and may not go to the fields, and the bride may not even go to cut wood or draw water. In the evening the *anisu* kills the chicken brought by the bride, and the bride gives liquor to the bridegroom's relations. The chicken is cooked and eaten by the newly-married couple, who sleep together in the bride groom's house that night, the ceremony being entirely concluded.

"By the custom called *agasho* a man, or his heir male, can claim a payment on the marriage of his sister's first child, male or female. The amount used to be a black cloth, but is now Rs. 5. Failing payment a field is liable to be confiscated and sold.

"No ceremony accompanies divorce, but if a woman is divorced for adultery she or her parents or their representatives have to pay a cow to the injured husband. Moreover, the marriage price has to be returned to him if such a divorce takes place within three years of the marriage. The paramour is beaten if he is caught, and if he has ventured to interfere with a chief's wife he is turned out of the village and his property confiscated. If the husband divorces his wife for any other fault within three years of marriage he may claim back the price paid for her, but not after that date, though he can claim it if she divorces herself by refusing to live with him. If, however, he systematically ill-treats her without cause he loses the claim." The custom is practised by the Sema Nagas of Nagaland.

Noting and Intrepreting Dreams of Young Couple

Dwelling on the Angami Tribals' Custom, Mr. J.H. Hutton, notes, "Price having been fixed by negotiation, the dreams of the young couple are noted; if those are favourable, both families prepare *zu.* An old woman goes from the bridegroom's house to that of the bride, taking with her two pots of *zu* and two hoes. She receives two pots of *zu* in exchange from the bride's house. On the day fixed for the marriage the bride is taken to the groom's house and they exchange leaf cups of *zu* which they have each made; the cups are hung on opposite walls of the house. The brice gives her cup with her left and the groom with his right hand. That night the pair remain chaste. The next morning the girl's ear-rings are removed and she bathes and fasts, taking only *zu.* She stays in her new home, her husband going elsewhere; he makes a new bamboo spoon and puts it is his house and goes back to the *Ikhuichi.* On the following day he returns to his house and makes a new hearth and brings a new pot and the pair eat together; then the bride goes to her home, but returns in the evening with friends carrying food and drink, and the elders of the *sagei* are called and drink, and then the younger members feast, and from then the young couple live together. After the marriage, in the month of *Sa-le-kluh* or *Chi-thu-ni-kluh,* June or December, *Salani* has to be performed. This is a two days' feast, during which the males of the *sagei* eat apart, using clean fire. The bride's parents send twenty or thirty loads of food and drink and all the males feast thoreon. The people of the goom's *sagei* make a collection, which the groom gives to his father-in-law."

On the Angami marriage customs, Mr. Hutton further notes, "The Angamis ..... are monogamous and exogamous. One case of bigamy, but only one, is known to have taken place among the Tengima Angamis, and although it is somewhat commoner among the Memi, it is looked on by them also which disfavour. The marriage by a man of two sisters concurrently is forbidden, and the second marriage is usually a non-ceremonial one. There are among all Angamis two forms of marriage, one celebrated with ceremony and formality, and one without, and although both form are equally binding and the informal marriage confers no social stigma or disability on the wife or on her issue, the ceremonial form is preferred by persons aspiring to the respect of themselves and their fellows. It entails, however, a certain amount of expense, though that is little enough, and a certain amount of formality, which is sometimes perhaps irksome.

"The informal marriage consists merely in a man's taking a girl to his house, where they remain *kenna* for one day. Where is takes place it is usually the outcome of an intrigue between the two, or is necessitated by the poverty of the parties.

"The ceremonial marriage is very much more formal. A man who intends to get married employs or gets his father to employ an old woman as a go-between with the girl's parents. She makes all the arrangements and there is no intercourse between the parties. First omens are taken by strangling a fowl and watching the position assumed by its legs as it dies. If the right leg crosses over above the left the omen is good. Then both the man and the girl must note their dreams on the same night. Dreams of weeping, of excretion, or of the sexual act are bad, but if the man's dreams have been good, the old woman goes and asks the girl what hers were like. If hers have also been good, the marriage price is discussed by the old woman with the girl's parents. The marriage price consists normally of a spear, two pigs, and fifteen or sixteen fowls. Whatever its significance here, the presentation of a spear is usually regarded among Nagas in general as in some sense the tribute of an inferior to a superior, or as signifying the recognition of some obligation under which the giver lies in regard to the recipient. It is commonly given by one village to another when the former cultivates land on sufference from the latter, and it often forms part of the penalty paid to an injured husband by his wife's paramour. The man will by a spear, pigs, chickens, and keep them in his house, while the girl starts making rice beer in readiness for the ceremony. At this point in the proceedings there is frequently some delay, but when everything is satisfactorily and finally arranged, young men of the girl's family and of her own age go on the day fixed to the bridegroom's house and carry off, as though by force, the spear and the pigs and chickens, which they kill and eat at the bride's house, and all the girl's kindred go and eat and drink there. One basket is filled with small pieces of flesh; one leg of pork is set aside; and four or five gourds are filled with liquor and set aside. At dusk two men take this meat and drink and take their places in a procession which goes to the bridegroom's house. This procession is thus composed : First the bride, next one boy and three girls from among her companions, then the two men carrying meat and drink, and finally a number of young men of the bride's kindred and clan, singing. Inside the bridegroom's house are the bridegroom and his parents, no one else. When the procession arrives the first seven persons mentioned as composing it go inside, but only the first five of these remain, and all talking must be in a whisper. A Kacha Naga bride has to step into the bridegroom's house with her right foot, placing it upon a piece of iron (a rupee is often used nowadays) laid on the threshold of the house. A Sema bride carries a dao in her hand which she give to her husband. She also has to step across the threshold with her right foot first. She always spends the night after arriving at her husband's house with her parents. First of all the bridegroom eats of the meat and drink brought by the men, which the bride eats a little piece of liver and rice, which she has brought with her, and drinks liquor brought by her in a little 'lao' and poured into a small leaf cup lifewise brought by her. Then the bridegroom's parents eat and drink, and then the rest; after they have all eaten the bridegroom goes to the 'morung' house and sits on the 'machan'. Next the bridegroom's kindred present the bride's escort with a big fowl and give one fowl each to the two who brought the meat and drink, after which all go away to their houses except the one boy and three girls, who spend the night in the bridegroom's house, the groom staying in the 'morung'. Next morning one of the bridegroom's kindred gives a fowl each to the boy and to the three girls. Then the bridegroom's mother gives the bride liquor in a leaf cup, which she drinks up. The bride must not leave the house before sunrise, after which she takes a pitcher and fetches water and cooks for the household.

'This day the household is *kenna,* but on the following day the bride and the bridegroom go to the field and work together on the part given to them by the latter's parents. They eat together in the fields. For the next three days they are confined to their own village and its lands, not being allowed to visit other villages, but after these three days the ceremony is complete. There is usually, however, no consummation of the marriage for at least two or three months, and it is said that this is delayed sometimes for as long as a year 'for shame,' during which time the bride-groom sleeps at the 'morung.' In the Khonoma group a delay of several months is normal.

"The marriage rites as performed by the Eastern Angamis are more elaborate, and an account of the Memi ceremony follows. It is taken from an unpublished note of Major Kennedy made during the *Assam Census of 1901*.

'The young man or his parents send an old man or woman to the girl's parents with a proposal of marriage. If the latter agree to the match, an answer is sent to that effect, and then both the girl and young man consult their dreams. Dreams of water, a tiger, *dhan*, etc., are considered lucky, while dreams concerning pigs, a dead person, etc., are unlucky. If the dreams of one party are bad, and those of the other party good, they consult their dreams again at the time of the next new moon. Should the dreams of both sides be auspicious, negotiations regarding the property to be contributed by each are entered upon. The girl is supposed to contribute at least half as much property as the man. Her dowry consists of *dhan* cattle, fields, and beads. Wen this is settled, a day is fixed for the wedding. On that day, an old woman of the husband's 'khel' is sent to bring the bride. *Khel* in this note means "clan", the Angami '*thino*'. The old woman takes two hoes as a present to the bride's mother. The old woman then brings the bride to her husband's house, the girl being unattended by any of her own people. The bride takes with her two laos of *dzu* and a *seer* or so of rice, together with her own clothes in her *khang* (basket). When the bride reaches the bridegroom's house, the old woman who accomanies her gives the bridegroom and bride a piece of plantain leaf, of which they make cups. The old woman then fills the cups with *dzu* from the bridegroom's house. The bride and bridegroom, without drinking the *dzu,* exchange the cups of *dzu*, which they then place in crevices of the wall, the man on the right side of the entrance door, and the woman on the left side thereof, inside the house. Any number of young girls belonging to the bridegroom's 'khel' are assembled, except seven, which is considered by the Memis, Angamis, and Kezhamas as an unlucky number. These girls consume the *dzu* brought by the bride. That night a young girl of the husband's 'khel' sleeps with the bride. The bride is not allowed to eat food cooked in her husband's house. That night the bridegroom sleeps in the young men's dormitory till about midnight, when he returns to his house, and calls the young girl who is sleeping with his bride, and conducts her back to her father's house. He then goes back to his house, and makes a noise at the door, on hearing which his father and mother and all occupants of the house, except the bride, leave the house. The bridegroom then enters and has connection with the bride, after which he returns to the young men's dormitory, his parents, etc., returning to the house. Next day the bride and bridegroom bathe at separate springs, the bride being accompanied by the girl who slept with her the night before, and her ablutions being performed in the morning. The bridegroom spends the whole of that night at the young men's dormitory and does not visit his wife. On the third day, the bride and bridegroom are not allowed to see each other, the bride remaining in the bridegroom's house and the latter at the house of a friend. That day the bridegroom selects three stones to form the fireplace, and makes two or four wooden spoons. These he sends to his house by a messenger, who gives the spoons into the hands of the bride, and leaves the stones in the house. That night again the bridegroom sleeps in the young men's dormitory and does not visit his bride. Next morning the bridegroom returns to his own house, when the bride makes a fireplace of the three stones sent the previous day by the bridegroom. She then cooks food for the bridegroom and herself in new utensils, and they eat the food together. That day the bride must remain in the house and do no work, but the bridegroom may work if he likes. That night they sleep together. On the following day in the early morning, the bride and bridegroom go to the fields together, and do a little nominal work, and then drink the *dzu* and eat the food which they have brought with them. They each bring back one small piece of firewood with them, which they burn that day. This concludes the actual marriage ceremonies. A few days after this, the bride goes to her father's house and brings from there two *'khalsis'* of *dzu* and 100 pieces of pigs' flesh. The bridegroom then first entertains his father-in-law with the *dzu* and flesh so brought, and then feasts his own friends. As among the Angamis, it is customary for the bride's friends to bring flesh and *dzu* to the house of the newly-married couple during the next succeeding Salegni (Angami Sekrengü) or Chitegni (Angami Terhengi) genna. I think Major Kennedy is possibly wrong in saying that the Saleni and

Sakrengi gennas correspond, but it is always difficult to be certain. In the morning the newly married couple go to the bride's father's house, and return from thence, the bridegroom carrying a piece of flesh, and the bride a *'khalsi'* of *dzu,* followed by the bride's friends with their offerings. It is customary for the bridegroom's friends to bring kodalis to the feast, which they present to the bride's friends, who have contributed the food and drink. When the first child is born, the wife takes it to her father's house, where all her relatives present her each with a fowl, a cock if the child is a boy, and a hen if the child is a girl. These fowls are taken back and are kept shut up till they are by degrees killed and eaten, it being considered most unlucky if one should escape. The above ceremonies are those observed in the case of persons previously unmarried. No part of the ceremony is more essential or binding than another, all being necessary to constitute a marriage between persons not previously married. If a man takes a second wife, without divorcing the first wife, the full ceremonies are observed, if the girl has been previously unmarried. Widows may marry, but they must obtain the permission of their late husband's heirs before doing so, else they lose their property brought as dowry. A widow can marry her husband's younger brother, but is not compelled to do so. She cannot marry her husband's elder brother. In the case of the remarriage of a widow, the ceremonies for the first day are the same, but the bride and bridegroom sleep together that night, and next day the new fireplace is constructed. The couple go to the fields on the following day for nominal work. It is not the custom for the presents of food and drink to be made by the bride's father and relatives after the marriage.

'Divorce is allowed and is common. Incompatibility of temperament is the chief reason. There is no ceremony. A woman, however, cannot leave her husband until more than five days after the marriage have elapsed. If she does so her husband can keep all her property. Otherwise the woman takes her property away with her, unless she is unfaithful or makes arrangements to marry another man, while under her husband's roof, in which cases she forfeits the property brought as dowry. Infidelity on the part of the man is not a ground for divorce, but if a man arranges to marry another woman, before divorcing his wife, the latter is entitled to a cow and a *dhuli* of *dhan* as compensation. When a man wishes to take a second wife without having divorced his first wife, he must first obtain the latter's permission. Divorced persons can marry, the ceremony being the same as that for the widowed persons'. The custom is practised among the Angami Nagas.

Maternal Uncle's Consent Binding

For the Sikkimese people the marriage ceremony is a gala event. Earlier this ceremony was spread over eighteen days but now has been limited to only three days. The bride's maternal uncle holds a very prestigeous position in the matrimony. At the time of bethrothal, unless his consent is obtained no marriage deal can be stuck. Obviously he is the first to receive gifts including money and liquor from the side of bridegroom. Only after he has accepted the gifts, the engagement stands binding, irrevocable and final. After betrothal, the would be bridegroom is required to work with his prospective in-laws. On the day of wedding, the would be couple and their parents gather together on a *watir* spring sprouting from beneath a massive monolith. At this spot the bride and bridegrom are blessed and it is prayed that the marriage may be as stable as the massive rock, and the new couple should have off-springs continuously like the flow of the spring. Bride price has to be paid by the bridegroom. The price usually consists of a milch cattle, a calf, bronze and brass utensils, ornaments, a poney or a horse. The bride is taken to her in-laws a year after the wedding ceremony. On all these occasions, the relatives of both the spouses are feasted on delicacies of meat and liquor. Till recently divorce had no sanction in this region. Chogyal Tashi Namgyal's wife lived separately but the king could not divorce her.

Dwelling on the Sikkimese marriage, Mr. C.Dc. Beavoir stocks notes; "The classificatory system of the Lap-cha tribe has, I believe, never been worked out, and as it is essential to give two forms of nomenclature to nearly every relation, a different term being applied to the same kinsman or kinswoman—according to their age—it has made the writing of the tables of generation very complicated.

"Tremendous sexual freedom exists among the Lap-chas, and they can be described as a race having polyandry, as well as being a tribe that is polygamous. Only the law of not marrying blood relations is strictly adhered to, and severe punishment is meted out to those who break this rule. In the cases of known incest, the man and woman are sent away from the village never to return. In this connection it is interesting to note that the mother's relations are considered to be of much nearer kin than the father's. The Lap-cha believe it to be only the father who transmits bone to his offspring, while from the mother they obtain their flesh and blood.

"Sir James Frazer tells us that though Tibetans and Lapchas forbid cousins-german to marry, Bhotias confine the prohibition to cousins on the father's side, and more particularly to the children of the father's brother. The reason given is that the bone inherited from the father in this case would be pierced resulting in course of time in various infirmities.

"Among the Lap-cha three brothers can marry three sisters, and all the wives are common. In such a case the children of the eldest girl belong to the eldest brother, while those of the youngest sister belong to the youngest brother. Should one or more of the women not bear children, the children are apportioned by arrangement, with certain restrictions, ... Two men who are not related may have one wife, but this is unusual.

"A man occasionally lends a wife to a visitor. In the antemarried state of the girl, virginity is not considered essential. Should she have a child and if he is a good worker, it is considered a valuable factor. An unmarried girl becomes a nun, she lives in seclusion for three years being taught to read and write by some woman. Her tuition is paid for by her parents and by those of the boy who would have married her. After learning she attends a Buddhist monastery for the whole day three times a month.

"Girls marry from the age of puberty.

"Occasionally a forcible abduction takes place. Should a man's wife run away, the husband is compensated by the wife's parents, who give him back half the sum he paid for her.

"A man when courting, gives the girl of his choice some handkerchiefs, and a few pieces of soap; a refusal of marriage is considered unlucky for him. As the bride-price the boy works in the girl's father's fields for one or two years, and unless he can pay the full amount they ask for their daughter then, and present them with a large brass pot, he must work for another year.

"In a case I investigated personally, the son had to pay Rs. 300 for his bride, and yet had to work for three years for his father-in-law. The eldest son of the Ate laama in Tumun. The man is allowed to cohabit with the girl; sometimes children are born before the man brings his wife home.

"Similar customs are observed among the tribes in Indo-China, which probably have an ethnological connection with the Lap-chas, the husband being treated more or less as a slave, and his services considered an economic factor.

"The custom among the Lap-chas is that should a man pay but a small amount for his wife, he will have to work for a longer period, though for several years after he helps his father-in-law in his fields in harvest time.

"In the *Rong*-tribe in order that a marriage may be arranged, two go-betweens are required, one acting for each family. They introduce the subject first of all by visiting the girl's parents and presenting them with a brass water-vessel. Should the parent accept this gift, the purpose of the visit is disclosed, and a day is fixed when they will come with the boy to introduce him. On the appointed day, the two go-betweens arrive with the boy, who brings with him a pig and a roll of white cloth from Assam. They also place several rupees before the parents, which is eventually deducted from the bride-price, and which varies according to the wealth of the boy. They bring a big copper pot to cook the food in, and a brass pot to boil '*chi*.' The drink is then made and a great feast is given to which all the villagers are invited. The young man brings a cock with him which he and the bride eat. *Nam* is a year in Lap-cha, the new year is *nam-bu,* which varies according to the date of the new moon, and according as the period is altered by the addition of an intercalary month. See Mainwaring, Grammar of the Rong (Lepcha) language (Calcutta 1876), p. 141. Marriage rules vary in every village, in some cattle is never exchanged, in others the bridegroom brings his future parents a bullock and the bride is given a cow. The custom alters with the wealth of the families.

In some cases the bridegroom may bring a cock, while the bride takes a hen to her new home. When families are too poor to pay for a bride, they effect an exchange, exchanging a daughter for a wife for their son. *Pa-zu* at *Song* told me the following:—*Tikung-tek* and *Nikung-ngal* were the first two who were married, they made a golden bride near Tibet for their wedding, which a spider helped them make, and that is why we Rong-folk give the first fruits of the harvest to them in remembrance. A year passes and then it is the turn of the boy's parents to give a feast. The go-betweens come with the boy to fetch the girl from her home. The parents do not follow her as it is considered unlucky were they to go with their daughter. This time it is the girl who brings a pig with her and a basket of '*chi*'. The boy's family kill two bullocks, one pig and seven fowls, and before eating offerings of food and drink are made to the *Rum*.

"The *lamas* and the village headman drink the health of the bride and bridegroom and are witnesses to the marriage, this being the only legal proceeding that is taken. At these feasts the girl sits between a '*nyom-mu*' and a '*nyom-byng*'. These are two sisters, generally of the mother—hand maidens they could be termed—the '*nyom-mu*' must, however, be married. They receive the remains of the bride-price which they give to the parents. That night, the visitors sing and dance till the day breaks, stamping their feet on the floor. (There is only sorrow when the bride leaves her home). The mother cries while the father gives her advice saying:—'Be nice to your husband's people, and work hard for them, remember we have sold you to them—'. For one week, the bride from supposed shyness does no work in her husband's home, but after seven days, she works in the house and the fields. Should she have some children already, they are taken over by the husband.

"The marriage tie is very slight, and can be theoretically dissolved at any time by the man or the woman, especially in the case of childlessness. The practice however I did not come across a single case in which divorce had taken place, even when the marriage was childless.

"It is considered lucky for a man who is born in the 'bullock' year to marry a girl who is born in the 'rat' year. It is said that they will become very rich. The man in that case being either her senior by eleven years or else one year her junior. A woman is never allowed to mention the name of her son's wife, who, never in return, can pronounce the name of her mother-in-law.. The mother calls her by the name of her first child, thus should the child be called *Guruck (Curly-locks),* the daughter-in-law is called *Guruck-bo,* (mother of *Curly-locks).* It is the same with the husband of a daughter, and with a nephew's wife or a niece's husband. It is never thought correct for the mother to stay with her daughter and son-in-law. The Lap-cha custom is for the husband to cohabit with the younger sisters of his wife during the lifetime of his wife, and even should they be married.

"These two customs, that Frazer has termed the Sororate and the Levirate, are observed in different tribes in many parts of the world, and it is curious to note that a Lap-cha man may marry the *younger* sister of his wife, though he can only cohabit with the wife of his *elder* brother. But though the custom of marrying in the order of seniority is usually observed in connection with Sororate and Levirate practices, it is not customary among the Rong-folk.

"The elder brother's wife is common to all the brothers, and should the second brother take a wife she is common to all the brothers younger than himself. The eldest brother is not allowed to cohabit with the wives of his younger brothers. It is only the wife of the youngest brother with whom no one can have access. Should the younger brother die, his wife returns home, marrying generally into another family; she may not like with any of her late husband's elder brothers. Hence the nomenclature for sisters is extensive : *nom-ren-bo* meaning the eldest sister (*ren*-eldest), *nom-hlen-bo* means the second eldest sister (*hlen*-between), whilst *nom-byek-bo* eans the third elder sister, and *nom-chum-bo* is the name given to the youngest (*chum*-younger).

"It is the youngest brother who has the monopoly of his wife, though it is hard to understand if this has any claim to ultimogeniture, inheritance of '*nasti*' and fields being divided amongst all the brothers who live together. Thus though a man may live with his brothers' wives, should the brothers be older than himself, he could not cohabit with his younger brother's wife, who is called a *nyom* meaning bride. The best view to take, it seems, is to adopt Frazer's opinions on the subject which he explains so clearly in the systems of the Sororate and Levirate. He thinks they are made clear by studying the terms used in a tribe for the Classificatory technical names of relationship. It will be seen that the same term is applied for the man's wife as is given to his wife's sister's *nom;* while the same term but with the masculine *'u' num* is used for himself the husband, and the brothers. Though the term for the brothers' wives and the sisters' husbands correspond, they are not the same as the two former, being *a-ngop* or *a-zong* in each case. But it can be understood that fraternal polyandry existed in the former days, and coincided with the force of sexual communism that took place then, though it has developed among the Lap-cha into the form of marriage they now have when they must have no connection with a blood relation" add Mr. Stocks. The custom is prevelent among the Lepchas tribals in Sikkim.

Visiting Girl in Sleeping Quarters before Proposing

Dwelling on the Ao Naga marriage customs in Nagaland, Mr. J.P. Mills notes, "Men usually marry between the ages of twenty and twenty-five, and girls between fifteen and twenty. Old men regard this as too young. They say that in their time men married when they were thirty and women when they were twenty, and had lusty children. Now mere boys marry because women no longer expect men first to show their valour, and the first children born are often puny and short-lived. The usual practice is for a man to visit a girl for some time in her sleeping quarters before he decides to marry her. Having sounded her parents informally and received the necessary encouragement he decides to ask formally for her hand in marriage. Among the Chongli he goes to an old man of his clan who is the father of many children and uses the well-understand formula : 'I am going to fish to-day. Come to my house in the evening.' He goes and catches some fish and comes back to his father's house in the evening, to find the old man and a number of friends waiting for him. He hands over the fish to the old man to carry, and walks behind him to the girl's parents' house, which both must enter right foot first. The fish is left and he and the old man are given a drink, but nothing is said about the marriage. In the morning he goes again to the girl's parents' house and is given a meal. If the girl's parents eat of the fish brought the day before it means that they agree to the marriage. I suppose that they give the girl some of this fish to eat (*cf. infra,* p. 273). Anyhow, this association of fish with marriage is common in parts of India and is also found in China (Kidd, *China,* p. 332), and it forms part of the bridegroom's gift among the Palaungs of Burma just as among the Aos (Milne, *op. cit.* p. 154). It is possibly due to the peculiar fecundity of fish, which are also commonly regarded in South India as repositories of the souls of the dead (*Man in India,* III 130 *sq.,* 1923). In Bengal the fish is the symbol of married life and widows may not eat it, while it is eaten by a woman whose husband is ill in order to prolong her married life and so bring about her husband's recovery (*id.* I. 73). Virgin widows, however, having lost their husbands before puberty, are allowed to eat fish in parts of Eastern Bengal (Mookerjee, *Travels in Bengal,* p. 272). The young man and the girl then go off and cut wood, which they bring to her parents' house. The marriage price is discussed and decided on within the next few days. It is not big as a rule, varying from five to sixty baskets of rice, with, in some villages, a leather shield and one or more 'daos'. The bridegroom builds a house in the cold weather and on the day of the marriage pays over the price agreed upon. This is returned if the girl leaves him within a year. In the evening his formal friends light a fire with a fire-thong for the first time in the new house, and the bridegroom sets ready by it some fermented rice and a pot, and leans a long hollow bamboo of water against the wall. Then, accompanied by men of his clan, he goes to the girl's parents' house. Outside he is met by a party of men who have married women of his clan, and he and his friends are given food and drink. An old man of the girl's clan then sacrifices a cock and takes the omens from its entrails. When this is over, the bride, in her best clothes and preceded by three old women of her clan, comes out of the house and goes to her new home, the first old woman carrying a bamboo spoon and an imitation tethering-rope made of bamboo slips. The bridegroom does not follow at once. The bride and three old women prepare and drink 'madhu' from the fermented rice, not without much broad jesting on the part of the old hags. While this is going on the bridegroom enters. With him are two or three formal friends, one of whom carries the bride's bed. There also come three girls, usually those who have shared the bride's sleeping quarters with her. They bring with them a cooking-pot, some salt and six *chabili*. After an old man of the bridegroom's clan has killed a cock and taken the omens outside the door all drink together, and the old women and formal friends of the bridegroom depart, but the three girls remain behind, and sleep in the house for three nights. The newly-married couple must not have connection for nine nights. For the first three mornings after the wedding they must remain in their house till the girls have brought them meat, fish and rice from the parents of both. The evening meals they eat in their respective parents' house, for nothing may be cooked in the new house for three days. On the fourth and fifth days they are no longer confined to the house in the morning, but they must still eat in their parents' houses, though 'snacks' may be cooked in the new house. On the sixth day the parents of both send pots and raw food, and the bride enters upon her life-long duty of cooking meals for her husband. In Mokongtsu and some other villages the newly-married couple eat in their parents' houses till the next *Moatsu* festival and only sleep together in the new house if they so desire. During this period each can consort with a former flame without incurring any censure.

"The Mongsen custom is rather different. Some time in the rains a young man lets it be known that he wishes to marry a certain girl, with whom he has probably been consorting for some time. The mothers of the two parties meet and talk, and if all goes well the man sends a friend as an intermediary (*langpathung*) to make a formal proposal to the girl's parents. At first they pretend to reject the proposal, saying that their daughter is ignorant and idle and not fit to be married. But the *langpathung* goes again, and this time they agree. The couple are then regarded as engaged. They sleep together in the girl's dormitory, and are expected to remain faithful to one another. The man works for about a month in the girl's parents' house, and she for a month in his house. The man then goes down with twenty or thirty friends and poisons a stream for fish. A large share of the catch is taken by the *langpathung* to the girl's parents. Of this they return a portion to him, and from the rest send presents to their relations, the man's relations, and the girls in their daughter's age-group. This is regarded as a public announcement of the engagement. In the cold weather the couple must help to cut the jungle, first on the girl's parents' fields and then on those of the man's parents. This done, the man sets to work to build a house. He pays all expenses, but the girl's parents give him one basket of fermented rice, a present of meat, and one bundle of thatch. Three days before the wedding the bridegroom sends the *langpathung* with two formal friends to ask finally what marriage price is required. This is little more than a formality, for the matter has already been thoroughly discussed. The price is called *chamen,* and consists of from ten to twenty baskets of rice and a good 'dao'. If the woman desert her husband within four months half this price is returned; if her husband leave her within four months she is entitled to all there is in the house; if the couple separate after four months the marriage-price is not returned and the contents of the house are divided. The day before the marriage the event is formally announced throughout the village by elderly relations on both sides. On the morning of the wedding-day all those who received fish from the girl's parents bring little return presents of cotton, rice, cooking-pots and so on. In return the girl's parents kill a pig and entertain them. On this day all the girls of the bride's age-group bring in two loads of firewood each. A little of this is given to the parents on either side, and the rest stacked at the new house. The girls then pound rice for the bride's parents. She in turn invites to her parents' house all the boys of the age-group corresponding to her own; they have been her companions in the fields from her childhood, and she now gives them 'madhu' in return for all the firewood they have cut for her in the past—for, as elsewhere in the world, a pretty girl never lacks devoted admirers who are ever ready to wait upon her. In the evening three old women of the bridegroom's clan enter the new house, light a fire with a fire-thong or iron and quartz, and send for the bride. She comes from her parents' house in procession, first five or six old women of her clan, then the bride, and then the girls of her age-group, carrying one wood basket, one rice basket, three baskets of husked rice, a leaf-parcel of meat, two new cooking-pots, one new winnowing-fan and one leaf parcel of salt. The bride wears her best clothes and ornaments and, if the daughter of rich parents, carries an

to the bridegroom's house. If on the journey she has to cross a river, road, or embankment (*áli*), etc. she is given at each such crossing nine areca nuts and nine pan-leaves as presents to overcome her assumed reluctance to proceed further. (Perhaps another relic of the 'marriage by capture' practice.) Before the bride enters the bridegroom's house, those who bring her are entitled to receive a jar of molasses as well as one of rice-liquor, and are hospitably entertained for the night. It is said that Kachári custom sanctions a certain interval of time, sometimes amounting to five days, between the bride's entering her husband's house and the consummation of the marriage. All expenses attending the marriage festival, which may extend to Rs. 200/- and upwards, are borne by the family of the bridegroom, the bride's people as a rule contributing nothing." add Mr. Endle. The custom is practised by the Kacharis in Assam.

Ritual of Sujen Luburuba

This is the *Ritual in connection with marriage by elopement.* In a marriage by elopement, the ritual known as *Sujen Luburuba* or *Meloni* is performed at the house of the bride's parents. A few cases have been observed where old men and women have conducted this ritual after many years of their marriage by elopement. Old men and women of both the sides, including the couple, gather at the residence of the bride's parents and offer *Sujen* to the ancesters' manes and *Kundimama.* The members of the bride's side say, 'we have offered our daughter today. She will not get her oblation from our side after her death'. The members of the bridegroom's party reply "we have accepted your daughter and she would be treated with oblation after her death at her husband's residence". The couple bow in front of the *Giras* and receive blessings from them.

It is considered that this ceremony enables a woman to change her affiliation from the natal *Jaku* to her husband's *Jaku,* which is merely a psychological fact. A woman cannot change her membership to a clan merely by performing this ritual. For all practical purposes, she retains the membership of the natal *Jaku.* this becomes obvious from the fact that she cannot be married to her natal *Jaku* after widowhood or being divorced. Moreover, the change would not have permitted junior member because of clan exogamy. If a woman dies before performing this ritual, a banana sheath is used as a representative of the deceased by her husband at the time of the ritual. This ritual signify that the dead woman would receive oblation after her death from the members of her husband's *Japa*.

Ritual of Chuchengna Laruba

This ritual is also a means of purifying a yough and a girl from their illicit relations. In both the cases, a she-pig and four are sacrificed by the *Boderi* at the house of the *Midiku*. A young she-pig and fowls are considered as pure. The *Boderi* prays to *Kundimama* and their associates to forgive the incumbent for the commission of the sin; he then sprinkles *Shuchi Ji* from his copper jar. Besides the expenses for this rituals by the transgressor, a cash fine of Rs. 25/- to Rs. 50/- is imposed on him by the priestly council. The custom is peculiar to the Dibongiya tribals.

An Easy Divorce

Divorce is easy in all primitive tribes. Among the Aos it is very common. It was very rare to meet an Ao man or woman who had married only once. The Sema Naga, however, is less inclined to change his spouse because of financial obligations which it would entail invariably. In case of a woman committing adultery, the husband could abandon her while he would keep with him the ornaments brought by her in marriage gifts and also claim fine, from the paramour. If this happened within three years of marriage, the husband could even demand return of the bride-price.) If the husband ill-treated the women, she could separate and demand the return of her personal jewellery. Among the Khemungan tribals, divorce is as easy as marriage. The girl desiring to separate gets up early one morning, clean the house, prepares the food and then just walks out.

However, sex-intrigues are not frowned upon among the Nagas, except those who have converted to Christianity. The Angamis and Chakhesangs have three lines of cowries embroidered on their kilt. A fourth line signifies powers not in war but love and could denote any of the following achievements : an intrigue with a married woman living with her husband; a simultaneous intrigue with two girls of the same name or with two daughters of one father, and or with a mother and her daughter at the same time.

An Ao tribal would not hesitate to make advances to a woman whose husband was away. Among the Lothas, if the man was going to be away from the village for a long time he could permit his brother or a near relative from the father's side to co-habit with his wife during his absence.

About the Ao custom of Ao Nagas, Mr. J.P. Mills notes, "Divorce is such a common sequel to an Ao marriage that any attempt to describe the life-cycle of the tribe must contain some account of it. It is exceptional to meet a middle-aged Ao man or woman who has kept the same partner throughout. One day I ventured to wish good luck to a boy who was just about to marry for the first time. He replied calmly that he did not suppose the marriage would last long. Nor did it. Within a year he had fallen in love with someone else's wife, got rid of his own, compensated the aggrieved husband and married his new flame. It is quite common for two men to fall in love with each other's wives and effect an exchange by a simultaneous divorce. The usual reason given when a couple do not get on is that the *tiya* are at variance (*tiya mecham* C and M). Certain acts make reconciliation difficult or impossible. If one of the couple during a quarrel deliberately breaks a hearthstone they will almost certainly separate, but reconciliation is possible. If, however, one of them swears that they will separate and breaks a *chabili* or other piece of iron, they can never live together again; Cf. *The Sema Nagas*, p. 166; Mills, *The Lhota Nagas*, p. 187; Herodotous, I. 165. The house-site must be abandoned and will probably never be used by anyone again—certainly not till a purificatory sacrifice has been performed on it. Commonly there is a woman in the case. If the wife at the time of divorce can prove that a certain woman is responsible for alienating her husband's affections her relatives can demand a fine from the intruder, who is then free to marry the man. Often a man ceases to care for his wife, but denies that she has any particular rival. She is then entitled on the day she leaves her husband to name any woman she suspects and to fix a sum, often as much as forty or fifty rupees, to be paid by the man if he marries that particular rival. The guess is generally a pretty shrewd one, and the man often decides that, the cat being out of the bag, there is no point in waiting, and pays down the money and takes the woman to his house the same day".

Return of Bride-price and Dowry

Divorce is an accepted social custom and tribals divorce as soon as it is found difficult to live together. Usually, divorce comes from husband's side but sometimes the wife also divorces the husband. If the marriage is based on bride-price then the divorce is related to the return of the bride-price if the failure or infidelity lies with the wife. If the wife divorces out of her own will and goes back to her parents, the parents are required to pay back all the presents and bride price, that is why with her paramour then the paramour is to pay back the bride-price as well as some fine imposed by the tribal elders and council. If husband divorces the wife for any reason, other than infidelity, barrenness or sickness of the wife, he is bound to pay some fine relating to the seriousness of the case. The return of bride-price or paying fine etc. are settled by negotiation by the parties concerned. Because of this bride-price system divorce among the Semas and Lotha Nagas is much less.

But in the tribes without bride-price, the process divorce is simple as much as lying separately is the divorce, and the parties can remarry or stay single as they like. Unlike marriage, divorce is unceremonial, it does not require going to any court or passing through any ritual. Among the Aos, divorce on the ground of fidelity is very common. (The Sema Nagas, JH Hutton, Pg. 187). Children remain with the father and so in any case of divorce the mother leaves behind all her children, except the suckling one if any, to be returned to the husband when he or she gives up suckling. For such suckling child, the husband is required to pay some money to be decided by mutual agreement. Among them, courting and marrying after pregnancy or childbirth is very common. But there are cases where the couple do not marry inspite of the child-birth. Earlier, and still now is some villages, the father of the child is required to bear the cost of up-bringing the child and even pay some fine in such cases. But nowadays social control being loose, it is difficult to impose and exact such fines from the erring spouses. In some cases the father accepts the paternity whether pays the up-bringing cost or not, but in some cases the father refuses the paternity too, and in that case the child becomes an absolute responsibility of the unwed mother and is known by her mother's name, and tribal society accepts it as a normal thing and does not look down on any such child.

The customs are prevalent among the Naga tribes of Assam. Among the Mizos, there were many ways of securing divorce or *inthem*. The most common forms of divorce were *mak* and *sumchhuah.* In *mak,* a Mizo could divorce his wife by simply saying that he was divorcing her. If the wife was with children (*thisenpal)*, the husband has to pay the balance of the bride price and if without children (*thisenpallo*), the husband did not have to pay the outstanding balance of price. The divorced woman could take with her all personal properties and her dowry or *thuam.* In *sumchhuah* form of divorce a woman would divorce her husband by refusing to remain with him and deserting him. A woman was free to divorce her husband in this way whenever she desires, but the entire price paid by her husband would have to be returned to him. In *sumchhuah* also the woman could take back all her personal property and her *thuam.* There had always been a dispute as to a particular divorce was a *mak* or *sumchhuah,* the woman claiming it to be a *mak* and the husband as *sumchhuah.* If after divorce, the husband wanted to call back his wife, she sometimes would come back on getting some money from him. This sum was called as *famghmanei.*

Sumlaition was a form of divorce by agreement. In this case the bride price, would be shared equally by both the spouses. Thus if a husband was still to pay the part of bride price, he would deduct what had already been paid and would pay the balance. If the had paid up the whole price he would get half of it back.

Peksachang was another form of divorce by agreement and in this cases there would not be any further transaction with regard to the bride price wholly paid or outstanding.

In the custom called as *pasal awn loh hlana chhuak,* in case of a divorce due to the husband remaining away from home for a long period old the wife was expected to remain in her husband's house and await his return. But this also could lead to divorce which would either be *mak* or *sumchhuah,* depending on the circumstances. In case of the husband abandoning wife and going away, *nupui tlansan,* the house, field and all other property would vest in the wife. Their children would also go to the wife and she would get the marriage price of the daughter if any. In case of his return the woman had the choice of taking him back or not, and in case of the latter, she could retain the house, the property and the children.

Lunacy could be one of the causes of divorce or *at na vanga inthen*. The normal spouse was expected to look after the lunatic person for three years. Divorce was allowed if there was no normalcy after this period. In case of impotence of a man (*zangzaw),* a woman could divorce the husband, if after some prescribed ceremonies by the puithian and after waiting for three months or negotiated period the husband did not become potent. If the wife's accusation was found to be false by witnesses appointed to see the sexual performances of the couple, she was fined forty rupees. In the reverse case called *chhuping* if a wife owing to physical peculiarities was unable to perform her merital duties to her husband, the husband, was entitled to a divorce her and to get back all prices he had paid.

Widowhood

When a woman's husband dies she performs a ceremony called as *thlaichhiah*. For three lunar months she would put aside a portion of rice out of her meal for the manes of her deceased husband *mirrhi chaw pek*. After this period she would usually return to her parent's or brother's house and perform another ceremony called as *thalhual* and then return to her husband's house to look after her children.

Custom of Hmei Thai pasal nei

Mizo custom allowed widow's remarriage as per their traditional custom call *hmei thai pasal nei.* A divorcee was free to remarry. Different terms were used in this respect. A *muthlawi* was a woman separated from her husband by any form of divorce. A *lengleh* was a woman who abandoned her husband after spending only one night in his house, widow is called as lusum.

The marriage price of a woman who had already been married once, would be reduced by a *tlai*. If however, the woman was attractive or industrious she might get the full price. A widow with children was expected to consult her children about her marriage if they were grown up before she would remarry. If they did not agree she could not get married from their house but would have to get married from her own parents' house. The widow's children who married again could go and live where they liked. They could continue to live with her or could go to live with their father's relatives or to their *pu,* maternal grand-father.

No bar on Widow Remarriage

"Dwelling the Lakhor practice of widow remarriage, Mr. NE Parry notes, "There is no bar whatever to a widow marrying again, she can do so immediately her husband died if she likes. A widow usually remains in her husband's house till the memorial stone has been erected, but the Lakhers have no equivalent to the Lushei *thla-hual* ceremony, before performing which a woman in considered to be still bound to her deceased husband, and a woman can marry while still living in herlate husband's house without any objection. A woman who has children usually remains in her late husband's house till she marries again, and her children generally go with her to her new husband, but if they prefer to go to their father's relations or to their *pupa* they are at liberty to do so. A dead man's brother have no rights over his widow unless they support her, and even then the widow will obey them only so long as she is living in their house. They cannot put any bar in the way of her remarrying. The price of a widow who remarries is as a rule less than that of a girl who has not been married before, but it is impossible to say what reducation, if any, will be made, as this will depend partly on the age, personal attractions and industry of the widow, and partly on the custom followed in different villages. A widow is called *nonghmei.* A woman who has been thrice married and all of whose husbands have died is called a *malusong*. A *malusong* is on the verge of being *ana*, and Lakhers are very shy of marrying *malusong*, as they believe that if a woman has outlived three husbands she is likely to outlive a fourth. An elderly spinster is known as *laitleu*.

"It is quite common among Lakhers for a man to marry his deceased brother's wife. The deceased's relatives do not like to send the woman away, also it is economical for the man's family, as it saves expenditure on marriage price. When a married man died, either his younger or his elder brother can, if he likes, ask to marry his deceased brother's wife. The widow can refuse, but more usually she accepts. If she accepts, her deceased husband's brother pays a small sum, called *abanasong*, which is usually between 10 and 30 rupees, to her relatives, and then marries her. In such a case a woman cannot claim a separate marriage price for this second marriage, but her new husband must pay any balance of the price that had not been paid by his deceased brother.

"If the deceased left sons, his sons inherit his property. If deceased left no sons, the brother who married his widow inherits his property, provided that he is the youngest brother; but if the deceased was the eldest of three brothers and his widow was married by the second brother, the youngest of the three inherits deceased's property, and not the brother who marries the widow; as eldest and youngest brother inherit in preference to those born in between them." The custom is practised by the Lakh tribals of Assam.

Adultery as a Great Disgrace

Adultery or *uire*, was considered a great disgrace for the Mizo women. In case of adultery by a woman while her husband was alive, all her bride price had to be refunded to the husband and he could keep her *thuam* or dowry and her other properties like clothes, and precious beads, etc. In case of adultery within three months of her husband's death, while she was expected to leave a portion of her meal for the spirit of the deceased husband, the misdemeanor was treated as if it was adultery during the husband's lifetime and she would also he turned out of her husband's house. If she committed adultery after the three-month period of her husband's death, she could not claim payment of the outstanding bride price. Her children could turn her out of the house, but she could keep the *thuam.* If the children allowed her to stay in their paternal house, they had to pay up the balance of her price. If a woman had no child, adultery after three months was not seriously viewed. In case, she did not perform *thlahual,* adultery would be viewed as if the husband was alive. In an adultery case only the woman was punishable, not her paramour. Wh is not required to pay any compensation. If a woman was accused of adultery and was not found guilty by the chieftain her husband would have to take her back at once or he would be considered to have divorced her *mak.*

Prior to the British administration adultery could be avenged by cutting off the ears or nose of the offending woman. During those days, the husband was free to kill his un-faithful wife and her paramour.

Impact of Christianity and Modernity

Among the Naga tribes it is the nuclear family system that prevails in contra-distinction to joint family system of the rest of India. When a son marries he goes away out of his paternal family and establishes his own house and hearth and that is why the son constructs a house of his own before marriage and after marriage the bride goes straight to her husband's new house, and not to her father-in-law's house. Formerly, when the economy was not so much exacting and the people were living in that house, it was possible to construct a house quickly and easily without spending any money through simply by collecting the materials like wood and canes from jungle. But now the modern educated young men do not like to live in the thatch house, on the other hand it may not be possible for a young man to construct a *pucca* or semi-*pucca* house of his choice so easily, and so very often the newly married son goes to his father's house to live line in with his bride. But this is generally for a few day because the educated young man has got a government job or at least a business or contract work and has got to his own quarter and so goes away there soon, or even he goes direct to his own quarter along with the bride.

The Nagas converted as the Christians are wedded by the pastor in church, and exchange of bridal rings between the bride and bridegroom takes place there and the marriage is considered being solemnised. In case of poor people exchange of ring may not take place also. In case of non-Christian the marriage is solemnised by the elderly people of the bridegroom's family, but there is no exchange of any thing except rice-beer and meat etc, however, details of this exchange varying from tribe to tribe.

Except the Sema, all Naga tribes practise monogamy. The Semas are allowed to take more than one wife and the wives stay in the same house peacefully and the first wife is incharge of the house. People of other tribes sometimes take more than one wife at a time, but it is not in good taste and in anyway they are needed to build separate house for each wife because no two wives will live under the same roof.

Under the primitive Mizo custom, marriages and divorces were easily gone through and these only entailed civil rights and duties and did not have any religious significance. With the advent of Christianity, marriage has attained a religious overtone. Monogamy has earlier been accepted totally. Although divorce continues liberally, it is rather frowned upon. Brideprice around which revolved the Mizo network of social relationships has almost become a matter of the forgotten past. This has released the society from a bondage of intricate relationships and obligation which has brought about long desired personal freedom.

Prior to the arrival of Christianity, if a mother died at childbirth, the living child would also be buried with the deceased mother. Since cow's milk was taboo in Mizo Society it was difficult to feed an infant and hence such a custom was practised. The Christian Missionaries started a home for the motherless babies to take care of them. With better medical facilities, such deaths of mothers a child birth have almost been eliminated, but the Mission's homes for motherless children continue, now to take care of the children from the unwed mothers. Practices regarding funeral ceremonies have changed totally. Earlier the corpses would be kept in the house for a number of days and burial would take place near the house itself. Now, burial takes place after the usual Christian funeral ceremony in the designated cemetry. Every village has now a graveyard where the bodies are buried. The unknown and gripping fear and superstition of the dead and of the evil spirits is totally gone. Death is accepted according to the usual modes of Christian faith and this has released the mourning familymen and relatives from old customs of intricate ritualistic behaviour and restrictions. However, following departure of the foreign missionaries after independence, the indigeous administration of the church is wholly with the Mizos now. They do not sneer at Mizo folk tradition customs relating to life cycle songs, dances and festivals etc. One of the functions of the Mizo District Council, which was set up after independence, was to uphold the old customs. The Council revived many of the old customs and festivals and upheld the customary rights and duties of the individuals and the society. The young Mizos also are taking pride in their roots and trying to revive and participate in many of the good old social customs and practices like *tlawmngaihna.*

REFERENCES

1. Parry, NE, The Lakhars, Firma KLM Pvt. Ltd., Calcutta (Repint) 1976, originally printed 1932.
2. Sukla, Brahma Kumar, People of NEFA : The Daflas of Subansiri Region, North-East Frontier Agency, Shillong 1959.
3. Endle, the Kacharis, Cosmo Publications, New Delhi 1987, originally Published 1911.
4. Stack Edward, & Lyall, Sir Charles, The Mikirs, United Publications, Guwahati first Published 1908.
5. Saikia, Paban Chandra, The Dibongiyas, BR Publications, New Delhi 1976.
6. Danda, Dipali G., Among the Dimasa of Assam: An Ethnographic Study, Sterling Publishers, New Delhi 1978.
7. Hutton, JH., The Sema Nagas, OUP, Bombay 1968 (first Published 1921)
8. Hutton, JH, The Angami Nagas; with Some notes on Neighbouring Tribes, OUP, Bombay 1969, first Published 1921.
9. Mills, JP, The Ao Nagas, OUP Bombay 1973, originally Published 1926.
10. Stocks, C. De. Beauvoir, Sikkim : Customs and Folklore, Cosmo Publications, New Delhi (Reprint) 1975.

5

Death Rituals : Cremation

In death rituals, the custom of cremation is practised mainly among the Hindu, Buddhist, Jain and Sikh communities in Assam, Sikkim and Arunachal Pradesh. Some of there customs are described hereunder :

Wearing of Mourning *attire dhara*

The Acharyas cremate their dead in Assam. A pollution period is observed for ten days. The day after the cremation a mourning attire called *dhara* is worn by the family or the deceased. During the mourning period, the mourners are not supposed to eat non-vegetarian food, and cannot use oil, species and salt. Besides, they cannot comb their hair, or use oil for massaging the body. Using an umbrella and putting on shoes or slippers is disallowed as well. As per their customs, the mourners must sleep on the floor, with straw spread on it. A purificatory shaving of the head, called *kaman,* is done on the tenth day, and *ghtat pinda* is offered to the deceased on the same day.

Sraddha is performed on the eleventh day, followed by *Brahman bhojan* and *ganti bhojan* (a feast for the kinsfolk and relatives). On the 15th day, since the death *matsadi* (a feast of rice and fish) is given to the kinspeople and relatives but this feast cannot be observed during the months of *Baisakh* (April-May), *Kartik* (October-November) and *Magh* (January-February), or on Sundays, Tuesdays, Saturdays, *Amabasya* (the new moon day), *Purnima* (the full moon day) and *Ekadashi.* No marked change has been observed in the Acharya rituals of the community, but the pomp associated with them has been cut down because of financial reasons. The custom is prevalent among the Acharyas of Assam, who constitute the high varna caste of Brahmans.

Cremation as a Religious Affair

The Bhils working as labourers in tea gardens of Assam cremate their dead. If a child below the age of three years dies, the body is buried. Their adult cremation assumes quite a religious character. A priest conducts it with incantation of *mantras.* The deceased's kinsfolk and relatives sing *bhajans* and offer fruits. The mourning period lasts for 13 days, followed by the *mundan* and *sraddha* rituals, as well as a feast for their community men. A piece of bone is immersed in the river Ganga at the holy confluence of Prayag. *Pinda dan* (offering of rice balls) is held at Gaya. With rising costs, the rituals are being cut short in the community. The bones of the dead are often immersed in a local river.

Abjuring Non-vegetarian Food

The pollution period after the death of a person in the community is fifteen days. The Basphor cremate their dead. During that the pollution period the members of the deceased's family eat only vegetarian food without fried in mustard oil. Shaving of head, beard and moustache, and paring of nails are also forbidden during the period. These restrictions are observed only by the blood relations from the father's side. Meanwhile, no religious or social functions are conducted by the family. On the sixteenth day, *sardha,* the purificatory rite, is observed. The rites and rituals in connection with this occasion are performed by saving their hair, beard and moustache shaved by a *napit* (barber). After end of the pollution period, a non-vegetarian feast is arranged. All the relatives and friends are invited to this feast, and with this, ritual pollution is deemed to be removed.

During the post-Independence period, customs rituals and ceremonies are becoming more expensive therefore being cut short. People now give less importance to the religious side of their functions. They simply conduct the function with the minimum expenditure. The custom is prevalent among the Basphore community.

Relatives Contributing Money for Cremation

On death the corpse is placed in an outside room and is covered by a white shroud. Flowers are spread over the cloth and visiting relatives also place money on it as their contribution for the funeral. The Buddhist monk chants prayers. The body is taken to the cremation ground where it is placed in a funeral pyre of wood. The eldest son set ablaze the pyre, after circling it seven times. The purification ceremony called *sraddha,* takes place six days after the cremation, when a feast is given to the Buddhist monks, relations and fellow members of the community.

When a wealthy person dies, a special ceremony is held by the family members of the deceased. The body is kept in a coffin which is placed in a chariot pulled by the mourners with the accompaniment of drum beats, fire works etc. and assembly of a large number of people.

They observe a special custom of offerings victuals for departed souls. In this ritual called *bhadya* a list of dead ancestors upto three or five pedigrees is prepared and small cremation pyres for them are also prepared in the cremation ground. The monks and the relatives invoke the spirits of the ancestors.

Buddhist Inheritance

After the death of patriarch, the family members solve the question of inheritance. About the inheritance custom of Buddhist in Arunachal Pradesh C. Von Furer – Hasimendorf notes, "The rules of inheritance vary from region to region and in minor details even from village to village. The distribution of a man's property begins usually before his death. Once his sons are grown up and married his land is divided. One share remains with the father, a somewhat larger share goes to the eldest son, and the remaining land is divided equally between the other sons. After the father's death the land which he had kept for himself is distributed among the sons, but all his movable property goes to the youngest son. These are the rules prevailing in the Dirang region.

"In the Seru-tso of the Tawang circle all sons get shares of the father's property, but the eldest son's share is larger than those of the other sons. Middle sons are expected to enter a monastery, but if any such son returns to secular life he can claim a share of the family property. The parental house goes normally to the eldest son, and the younger sons can either stay in it, even if married, or build separate houses on the family's land. In the absence of sons the daughters have a claim to their father's property, and no consultation with the male kinsmen is required at the time of division.

"In the Bomba *mang* of the Sher-tso most of the land goes to the eldest son, and even the movable property is largely given to him. If there is a middle son he is likely to become a monk, and the youngest son gets one plot of land and a share in the movable property. If there are no sons the eldest daughter gets the entire property and her sons will ultimately inherit from her.

"In Kitpi and the surrounding hamlets the sons inherit nearly equally though the eldest son may get one or two plots more than his brothers. As the eldest son is expected to remain in the family house during his father's life-time his marriage is normally arranged with his parents' consent, and the bride is expected to bring a dowry to the house of her parents-in-law. If the eldest son marries without his parents' knowledge they may still allow him to bring his wife to their house, but they will see whether she fits into the family and if they do not approve of her, she and her husband may be asked to leave the house, and the father may or may not give the eldest son a share of the land.

"An eldest son staying in the parental house and managing the family property may build a separate house for his aged parents, and in this case his father will retain one or two fields. These will ultimately go to the eldest son who will pay for the father's funeral.

"The youngest son has three options : (1) He can join the eldest son in a polyandrous marriage; (2) He can build a separate house with the help of his eldest brother; (3) He can marry a girl who has no brothers and enter as *makba* his father-in-law's house.

"An eldest son will never be allowed to become a *makba,* and the second son should become a monk and for this reason is not likely to become a *makba.* Any third, fourth or fifth son may become a *makba* and thereby relinquish any claim to the parental property.

"All such rules are adjusted to the actual situation in a family and this may necessities a deviation from the customary practice. Thus in the family of Tashi Lama the eldest brother died before he had any issue, the second brother became a monk but later left the monastery and went as *makba* to Lumla, the third and fourth brothers married one wife in a polyandrous union and took over the parental house. Tashi Lama, the youngest son, who is in government service and works in Tawang as Research Officer, has built a house of his own and purchased a nearby plot of communal land.

"It is not unusual for several brothers to remain unmarried. Such a situation is exemplified by the family of Tashi Kando of Kitpi. Tashi Kando was married and had three children when his wife died. He did not marry again. He has three brothers, one of whom is a monk in the Tawang monastery. Another had gone to Lhasa as a monk, but had returned after the Chinese had occupied Tibet and monastic life had come to an end there. He now lives at Kitpi in the family house and is engaged in trade. The youngest of the brothers, who is also a monk, has gone to India to study in one of the settlements of expatriate Tibetans. He was already thirty when he left for India. Thus only one brother out of four got married, and he did not remarry when he became a widower. He now shares the ancient family house with his eldest son and daughter-in-law and their small children." adds Furer Haimendorf.

Performing an Act of Feeding the Dead

Dwelling on the Kachari custom funeral rites, Endle notes : "Immediately after death occurs, the corpse is carefully washed by the nearest relatives, the arms and legs straightened out, the head anointed with oil, and the hair reverently combed. A fowl or a pigeon is killed, and from its flesh a curry is prepared with vegetables and condiments. A portion of this food is then placed close by the deceased's head, and the act of feeding him with a little of it is carried out up to a certain point, though no food is as a matter of fact actually placed within his lips. This act is repeated some ten or twelve times, and what remains of the curry, etc., is then thrown away, no one being allowed to consume it. The dead man's body is then clothed with the best garments he owned in his lifetime, and the whole covered with a perfectly new cloth; and in this condition it is taken outside the homestead for final disposal.

"There are two recognised way of disposing of the dead, i.e., (1) Burial and (2) Cremation. The latter is looked upon as the more correct and respectable, though from motives of economy the former is by far the more common. When burial is decided upon the corpse is carried to its last resting place, which is often but not always on the banks of a running stream, by the nearest surviving relatives, no women being permitted to attend. Should it be necessary for the burial party to cross a river or irrigation canal, a cord is usually stretched from bank to bank at the crossing place, either above or below the water, to serve a kind of bridge for the spirit (*jiwa*), should he be at any time disposed to revisit the scenes amid which his earthly life has been passed. Arrived at a suitable place (there are no recognised cemeteries for the interment), some pice are thrown on the spot to purchase the ground from the deity (*madai*) to whom it is supposed to belong. The body is laid on the ground and the grave duly dug, but before placing the corpse therein, the friends and relatives make a solemn procession around it, five times in the case of a man and seven in that of a woman. The body is then placed in the grave, a somewhat shallow one, and the nearest relatives proceed to fill it with earth. In carrying out this process a certain precaution is taken, i.e., a hollow reed or a stalk of jungle grass (*kher*) is placed perpendicularly in the grave extending from the nose of the deceased to a point somewhat above the natural level of the ground; and in filling the grave with earth, great care is taken not to injure or displace this reed, so that the deceased's spirit may be able to breathe should he so desire. After feeling the grave four posts are erected over it, one at each corner; and threads passed around them, in order to prevent the spirits of other men from interfering with the repose of the deceased. In the case of well-to-do people a certain number of rupees are usually buried with the corpse, and even the poorer classes make offerings of pice, etc. for this pious purpose; whilst brass and other utensils needed in everyday life are almost always left on the grave, it being supposed that the deceased may require the use of these things in the new state of existence on which he has recently entered. Finally, a rough shed of thatch is put up closed by the grave to shelter the deceased's spirit from the rain and sun.

"Very much the same procedure is in vogue in the case of cremation, which is looked upon as the more respectable method of disposing of the dead among the wealthier members of the community. Cremation usually takes place on or near the banks of running streams, and is prefaced by the formal buying of the land from the deity (*madai*) of the locality. Here too a certain difference is made in disposing of the corpse of a man and of a woman respectively; for in the case of a woman *seven* layers of wood are placed under the body and seven above it, whilst in dealing with a man's corpse *five* such layers under and five above the body are held to be sufficient. After placing the body on the funeral pile, the deceased's friends and relatives pass round it in procession, *five* times in the case of a man and *seven* in that of a woman. The funeral pile is then set on fire on all four sides at once, and the fire carefully fed until every vestige of the deceased's body is consumed. The ashes are not carried away, but four posts are usually placed in the ground enclosing the oblong space on which the cremation has been carried out; and on the tops of these a cloth is spread, which is held to shelter the spirit of the deceased from sun and rain.

"From what has been written above, it would certainly seem that the Kachari has some idea, however vague and unsatisfactory, of a life prolonged after the great change we commonly call 'death,' though his notion of the future life is merely that of the 'first (earthly) life renewed.' It has obviously little or nothing in common with the hope of life eternal in Christ, i.e. life *in* God, life *with* God, life *like* God, given us in the New Testament (see 1 Cor. xv.; Phil. iii. 20, 21; 1 John iii 2)." The custom is prevalent among the Kachari's of Assam.

Endle adds further the custom of cremation, thus, "The bodies of the dead are usually disposed of by burning, except in cases of epidemics, when through panic or like cause, they are thrown into the jungle, or left to perish where they fall. The cremation is generally followed by funeral feast, lasting for a period of from five to nine days, either at the deceased's house or at the river-side where the body was burnt. A shradh with feasting of the dead man's relatives takes place usually at the end of a month after the cremation. This shradh marks the closing of the period of mourning, which in the case of an adult extends over about thirty days, during which period no flesh or fish may be eaten, though rice, ghi and potatoes are allowed. In the case of those who die in childhood no shradh is observed, though the bereaved family usually go into mourning for some three days."

Rubbing of Oil and Turmeric Paste on the Dead

A man, in his last moments of life or when he is dead, is carried out of the house. Oil and *haldi* (turmeric) paste is rubbed over the body; it is then bathed and new clothes are put on it. Thus he is prepared for his last journey to the cremation ground. People returning from the cremation ground will take a bath, place their feet on stones and bask in the fire. Then only can they enter the house. If it is very late at night, they have to stay out of the house till morning. Otherwise, it is considered that the spirit of the dead may follow them inside the house. The custom is practised among the Hindus of Assam.

Dying a Wretched Death

Among the Dimasa tribals in Assam the old people are not at all cared and well looked after. During old age the Dimasa are deserted by their children as they get busy with their own respective families. Thus the old man have practically no companion to look after them except the little children if there are any, seldom visiting them. The old men and women arrange for their sustenance themselves, scarcely taking the help of others. Under unavoidable circumstances they are helped by the village youth under direction of the village headman. Sometimes the daughter or daughter-in-law helps the old persons through by cooking their food. Though the Dimasa may be a bit indifferent to the old people, they are never disrespectful to them. When they refer to their old parents they speak of them with affection and admiration, very high of valour and courageous acts of the old men of the community. In important social customs and ritual affairs their advice and opinion are earnestly sought.

The officials of the village council consult the experienced old persons to solve complicated cases. Not all the old men are, however, so fortunate. Only the really intelligent and experienced few can enjoy this privilege. This is more so because most of the aging people become senile, thus generally the middle-aged intelligent members of the community are consulted in solving problems of the beleaguered society.

Generally, the old men are peace-loving and stoic lot who try to avoid trouble. They do not take any active part in community affairs. However, they greatly enjoy social and ceremonial feasts and attend festivals very much. On such occasions they recall their past life and encourage youths by narrating colourful stories of their activities and achievements. The Dimasa youths are free with them and enjoy the colourful stories narrated by them. Though the old people had solitary life, at the time of death all their children and relatives assemble around them. After death sons, daughters and other kinsmen together with all the relatives conduct their funeral and observe mourning. The funeral and post-funeral rituals are observed with great reverence. For those who die without child or have no relatives, the villagers conduct their funerals in abbreviated form.

On death, a cock is sacrificed or an egg is broken near the head of the dead by a male member of the family. It is said that the soul of the cock will accompany the deceased to the next world. The Dimasa tribals cremate their dead. To carry the corpse to the cremation ground known as *mangphlang,* a bier or *bangfong* is made of bamboo and a piece of cloth. The number of bamboos used for making the bier is quite important to the Dimasa tribals. If more than one bamboo is used for making the bier two buffaloes have to be sacrificed at the feast of post-funeral ceremony and those who carry the cortege get four legs of these buffaloes. In case, one bamboo is used for making the bier only one pig is slaughtered as the sacrifice animal. The four legs of the animal, however, are given to those who carry the corpse to the cremation ground.

Before carrying the cortege to the cremation ground the corpse is ceremonially bathed in water and then placed on the bier. A *rino,* made of bamboo frame and a piece of cloth having a basket like appearance is carried by the mourners to lead the funeral procession. The Dimasa believe that after death the spirit of the dead takes shelter in the *rino.*

As per their old custom, both men and women can carry the coffin. While it is carried a woman continuously throws paddy and cotton thread on the way to the cremation ground. This ritual is called *maiokhrai,* i.e. making a bridge between the dead and the living. An advance party gathers at the cremation ground and collects firewood for making the pyre. They also prepare a temporary shelter for the spirit of the dead in the cremation ground called as *jara.* When the funeral procession arrives, there the *rino* is opened and the spirit is ceremonially transferred to the *jara.* The left over of cotton thread that is not required for *maiokhrai* is kept in the *jara* and preserved there till the post-funeral ceremony is over.

Before setting ablaze the pyre, rice-beer is offered to the spirit of the deceased at the *jara.* The body is then placed on the pyre arranged with twelve layers of logs with the head pointing to the west. The sons or in their absence, their representatives with torch in hand stand at either side of the dead (not towards the head or feet), touch each other's torch and then put fire to the pyre from both sides. Prior to that the relatives call the dead ancestors of the deceased and request them to accept and treat them sympathetically in the next world. The party waits till the body is burnt completely. Then, a piece of charred bone is preserved under the *jara.* The ashes and other remains are then washed away in the running water stream. After taking a purificatory bath the funeral party returns to the village.

There, two boys welcome the funeral party with sprinkling *dither,* i.e. holy water prepared by the village priest at the entrance of the village. Everyone touches the holy water in an act of purifing oneself. In the day following cremation, the sleeping mat and other articles that have been used by the deceased are carried away to the spot where cremation took place. If the deceased has a female, a complete loom or some part of it, her used hair oil, comb, and other articles are put there. All garments worn by the deceased are burnt along with the dead on the pyre. A plate or a pitcher made of bellmetal that has been used by the deceased is taken back home after touching it to the fire.

Among the Dimasas, there is no fixed period of mourning or any set restrictions to the mourners. Generally, the family members of the deceased eschew non-vegetarian or sour food for seven days following death. The mourning clan members observe pollution for one day only.

The post-funeral ceremony or *Maimutharba,* is held at a suitable time between the seventh day and a year of death depending on the economic condition of the family. In Dimasa language *maimu* means paddy and *tharba* means purification, thus the *teru* means purification of paddy. It is believed that the paddy gets polluted as soon as a death occurs in a family. The post-funeral ceremony can take place only on Tuesday, Wednesday and Thursday. Until the post-funeral ceremony is completed, *makhamgarba* or food offering is to be made to the spirit of the dead by one of the elderly members of the family. The cooked food is offered to the *jara* also believed to be the abode of the deceased's spirit. The relationship between the spirit and the living members of the family is completely severed following the final offering of food or *makhamgarkhaoba,* at the time of annual harvest festival or *busu.*

However, in case of unnatural death like accident, suicide, death at child-birth, etc., the post-funeral ceremony is performed just after the cremation. Only those persons who have taken part in cremation attend the post-funeral ceremony and feast. The restrictions and taboos associated with an unnatural death are more varied and strict than that of the natural death. In case of unnatural death, the deceased's clan members of the same village eschew eating fruit or vegetables that grow on creepers. They cannot tear any thread and the women members of the clan have to refrain from all kinds of weaving for one and a half months.

As for the unnatural deaths, killing by a tiger is considered to be the most unfortunate one. No cremation or funeral ceremony is permissible in such a case and the body is simply buried by the clan members at the outskirts of the village without any ceremony. None but the clan members are allowed to touch the corpse. If there is no clan member of the deceased in the village, the village headman would first touch the body.

All the clan members observe death pollution until the *dangphlaiba,* or the expiatory ritual is ceremonised.

In the case of death by diseases like leprosy, black fever, cholera, small pox and similar other diseases, the Dimasa bury their dead and no ceremony is performed. If a person suffers from *thampidiba* (mosquito laying eggs on a sore) he becomes polluted and the members of his family and clan are also considered to be polluted. A ritual offering to *Mongrang Daikho* is arranged for removal of the pollution. When there is no hope for recovery, an expiatory ritual is performed to enable the family to undertake the funeral ritual in the event of death. But if the expiatory rite is not conducted no funeral can take place.

In case of death of a woman at childbirth the body is cremated and an funeral ceremony is performed. Only the elderly persons and clan members can attend the funeral ceremony. Those who have little children are not permitted to attend any such ceremony. It is said that if they go there this may cause evil impact to their young children. In case of an unnatural death however, every belonging of the deceased is destroyed except the immovable property, cash, jewellery and weapons. It is said that if someone keeps his belongings, that may cause harm to the keeper. No religious rites are attached with Dimasa funeral ceremony except the offerings of food and libations of drinks to the spirit of the deceased. It is believed that the more the number of people entertained at the time of post-funeral ceremony and feast, the happier the spirit of the dead will be, and it would obtain a prosperous life on rebirth. The custom pertains to the Dimasa tribals of Assam.

Most Elaborate and Pompous Funeral

Well on the funeral customs, pertaining the Mikir tribals of Assam and neighbouring states, Edward Stack writes, "The funeral is the most elaborate, costly, and important of all the ceremonies performed by the Mikirs. Such ceremonies are considered obligatory in all cases except that of a child who has been born dead, or who has died before the after-birth has left the mother; such a child is buried without any ceremony. Victims of small-pox or cholera are buried shortly after death, but the funeral service is performed for them later on, the bones being sometimes dug up and duly cremated. When a person is killed by a tiger, if the body or clothes are found, they are buried at a distance from the village, because the tiger is supposed to visit the burial-place. Such persons cannot gain admittance to *jom-arong* unless there are elaborate funeral ceremonies performed for them. Being killed by a tiger is generally imputed to the victim's sin. His spirit is believed to dwell in the most dreary of the place where dead men's spirits go; there is no notion (such as is found among some races in India) that it animates the tiger who killed him. Except in these cases the dead are disposed of by cremation, the burnt bones being afterwards buried.

"The elaborateness of the funeral depends on the means of the family. The description which follows applies to a case where the household is well-to-do. In any case the body is kept in the house for one day after death; if a regular service is held, it may lie as long as from a week to twelve days.

"The body lies in the *kut.* The persons occupied with the funeral ceremonies live in the *hong-pharla;* the rest of the family cook and eat in the *kam,* but the officiants, male and female, must go across a stream or creek to cook and eat.. the old women of the family wash and lay out the corpse. Then beer is prepared, rice husked and got ready, and a convenient day fixed for the service. If the house has not a big enough *hong* (front platform), the neighbours join and build one on to it. From the date of the death, each household in the village gives a man to sleep in the house (in the *hong-pharla*). When it is settled that the beer and rice required can be provided in four or five days, the village lads are summoned about 8 o'clock in the evening. They bring their drum (*cheng*), and drum up to the *tikup* (front yard); they drum, dance by pairs, holding in their left hands shields (*chongkecheng-nan*), and in their right hands sticks. They go round twice in a circle; then they all dance round, holding each the other's hands (this is called *chomang-kan,* "Khasi dance). After an hour spent in this way they go back to the *gaonbura's* house to sleep. Early next morning they come without beat of drum, and dance the *chomang-kan* to the drum; they then dance the shield-dance as before (*chong-kechengnan*) to the drum, and go home. Next night they come as before, but a little later, and go through the same ceremonies. Next morning they proceed as before, and in the usual course they kill a fowl and roast it in pieces on spits in the *tikup,* and eat it there. The third and last night is that of the *kan-pi* ('great dance').

"Meantime, during the day, the *risomar* have to work at getting ready the *tele*—the stout bamboo to which the corpse is to be slung : the *banjar*—a bamboo ornamented with curied shavings (*bu*) hung in tufts to projecting arms; and the *seroso*—shorter bamboo sticks similarly ornamented and tipped with leaves. The men have to go the *theri* (village burning-place) and prepare there a *chang* or platform, with logs for burning the body arranged under it; this *chang* is built in a peculiar manner, known only to adepts. The *uchepi* (a skilled old woman) is summoned to prepare the *viaticum* for the dead, and the *duhuidi,* with an assistant, who beat the two drums which have now been hung up in the *kam-athengthot :* the *duhuidi* is one skilled in tolling on these drums. Then comes the girl called *obokpi* (not necessarily a maid), that is, the 'carrier' of the dead man; but in place of the dead she carries on her back a gourd for holding beer; she must belong to his mother's *kur.* Also the *nihu,* the maternal uncle or other male representative of the mother's *kur,* and the *ingjir-arlo,* sister's husband, or father's sister's husband, of the deceased; it is his office to kill the goat for the dead, if they can afford one.

"About midnight the villagers, with torches, drums, and the attendant *risomar,* assemble in the *tikup.* The neighbouring villages, if so minded, may come too (*arong ari* is the phrase for the rontingents as they arrive). Each contingent is welcomed with the drum, and joins in the drumming concert; the lads and girls are dressed in their best, and provided with betel. The chief of the village lads (*kleng-sarpo*) then calls the other *risomar* to *touch* (not taste) the beer, *hor kacheme.* Then follows the shield-dance, first by the *risomar* of the village, then by the outside contingents in order of arrival or merit. Then all together take hands and dance in a circle. The young women join in the line, taking hold of the lads' coats, while the lads take hold of them by the belt (*vankok*); the girls cover their heads and faces with a black scarf (*jiso-ke-ik*); the petticoat is a red-stripped Mikir *eri* cloth. Near the first cock-crow, seven young men go up on the *hong* or house-platform from the dancing, with the *duhuidi* and his assistant; one lad goes in and dances in the inside of *kam,* in the space by the partition-wall (*noksek*), while the six others stand at the door (*hongthu,* or *inghap angho* = 'door's mouth'), and dance there. The six whoop three times together as they dance. After a quarter of an hour they return to the circle of dancers in the *tikup.* At dawn they go up again, and dance till sunrise. The circle breaks up at daylight, and then follows the shield-dance. Then all the drums go round the circle where they dance ten to twenty times, playing a different tune each time. Then, while they all drum standing, a pig is brought forth, tied up for killing. The *risomar* in successive parties recount over the tied-up pig the history of the funeral service; this is called *phak aphu kacholang.* Then the pig is killed and cut up for the *risomar,* and for the men engaged in the funeral service. The latter have to cook and eat their shares of the meat, which is given in leaf-bundles (*ok-bor*) or on spits (*ok-kron*), beyond the river. The *risomar* also get their shares in the same way, and cook them in the dancing-ring. A small piece of flesh is cooked by the *uchepi* for the dead man, and this is put in the plate of the dead and carried by the *ingjir-arlo* up to the body in the *kut,* the *duhuidi* tolling the drum as he goes in; this ceremony is called *kasole.* Meantime the old experienced men, braving the horrid stench, have been performing certain rites about the body. The remainder of the cooked flesh, with rice, is distributed to the young girls. The *risomar* then, provided with rice, beer, salt, chillies, and greens from the dead man's house, disperse to houses in the village to eat, and the officiants go off beyond the river to prepare and eat their food. This part of the ceremony is called *riso kachiru,* 'the lads' entertainment.

"Then two or three of the *risomar* take a cock on the road to the burning-place, and kill, cook, and eat it there. A small pig is killed by the other lads where they dance, and the head and one leg are sent to the road-side *risomar.* The blood is caught in a bamboo-joint, and smeared on the *banjar,* which is set up in the road like a maypole; it is a thick bamboo about seven feet long, with sticks projecting on three sides, from which hang tassels of curled bamboo shavings (*banjar abu*). These shavings also are smeared with the blood, so as to look flowers like flowers. Six shorter pieces of bamboo, three feet long, also ornamented with tufts of shavings, are called *serosos,* and these too are smeared with blood : likewise the *tele* for carrying the corpse to the pyre. Six young men, each taking a *seroso,* dance round the *banjar.*

"The *uchepi* has now prepared all the food. The *obokpi* takes the beer-gourd on her back, and one egg in her hand, and the *uchepi* a beer-gourd, and they break the egg and the gourd against the *tele* as it lies upon the house-ladder (*dondon*). The *duhuidi* tolls the drum, and dancing as before takes place on the *hong* and in the *kam,* but not with the *serosos.* The *uchepi* and the *obokpi* then go on to the burning-place. The *tele* is now taken up by the old men into the house, and the corpse tied to it and brought down; all the dead man's clothes are hung over the bamboo. Then a pair of ducks and another of pigeons are killed by the *nihu,* and a goat by the *ingjir-arlo,* each previously going thrice round the dancing circle with the sun. The goat is called *hongvat-abi;* the heads are thrown to the *risomar,* the rest of the meat kept and cooked later on by those who remain. Preceded by the *duhuidi* and his assistant tolling the drums, they all march in procession, carrying the *banjar* and *serosos,* to the burning-place. The body is untied from the *tele* and placed on the pyre, which is lighted. While the pyre is burning, knowing women sing the *kacharhe*—a chant describing the dead man's life, whither he is going on leaving this earth, how he will see his dead relations, and the messages he has to carry to them. A few of the lads dance while the cremation is proceeding.

"The body is thoroughly burnt, and the bones that remain are tied up in a cloth and buried. The *tele* is either laid down whole or cut into three pieces, which are split again into six, and placed in the little house which is then erected over the grave. This is built with the *banjar* and the *serosos,* the former being in the middle and the latter used as props for the roof. The food prepared by the *uchepi* is now placed on a flat stone over the grave, and the ceremony is at an end.

"The company, returning, clean and wash the house, and cook and eat and drink on the *hong.* On coming back from the cremation, the *nihu* gets some money, clothes, salt, and a knife. He shares the salt with his own *kur,* if any are present. The *ingjir-arlo* next morning has to clean up the dancing ring (*rong-ru kangru,* or *tikup karkok*).

"The ceremonies of the funeral are performed by the neighbours and cunning men and women of the village, and the old people of the family. The wife, children, parents, brothers and sisters of the dead sit besides him and mourn, in spite of corruption, or even sleep beside the decomposing corpse. 'It is genuine grief, a national characteristic. Even after the funeral service, they remember and mourn; and the death of another renews their grief.' The mourners continue their lamentation, heedless of the dancing.

"If a great man, such as a *mauzadar* (*bikhoya*) or leading *gaombura* (*sarlar, sarthe*), dies, in addition to the ceremonial described above, there is another, called *Langtuk* ('the well') A well or pit is dug outside the village, four-square, with sides ten to fifteen feet : it need not be carried down to the water; stairs are made to the bottom. At the corners are planted various trees. A tall upright stone (*long-chong*) and a broad flat stone (*long-pak*), supported on short uprights, are brought and set up, as in the Khasi hills. The *risomar* come and dance there the whole day, with manifold apparatus. The *uchepi* sings and places food of different kinds on the flat stone for the dead man; his clothes and umbrella are put upon the tall stone, with flowers. A fowl is killed for the well at the bottom of the pit, and a goat, two ducks, and two pigeons are killed at the top, and their heads thrown to the *risomar.* Then the people of thirty to forty villages assemble. The *uchepi* sings extemporaneously before the memorial stone, and the people dance and eat there until dark. After dark the company go to the house and perform the usual service already described. The *langtuk* is very costly, for people have to be fed at two places, and double the quantity of food for an ordinary funeral has to be provided." adds Mr. Stack.

Differing of Funeral Customs

In sum, disposal of the dead, ancestor worship and funeral rites of the Hindus in Assam are intimately connected with the cult of fertility and the idea of rebirth. These elements were also the legacy of the pre-Aryans and non-Aryans in Assam as elsewhere in India. There is no record about the mode of disposal of the dead in ancient Assam. The practice of burial, particularly observed by the Khasi-Syntengs, Garo, Mikir (Karbi) and others, is attested by some ancients megaliths of Khasi-Jaintia Hills and North Cachar, where the human remains were excavated. The practice of stonecist burial of the skull, and urn burial of the remains parallel the local Aryan Hindu practice of keeping the bones in an earthen pot for ten days or atleast for some time after burning. The diverging practices of keeping the charred bones, as is done by some of the Kukis, throwing these into water as is done by some Kacharis, burial of bones as is followed by the Garos and the Mikirs (Karbi) or digging of graves in a rice field or near water all have parallels in similar Hindu practices; which are associated with the cult of fertility and ancestor worship. Whatever the other ideas associated with these funeral practices, the custom of offering food to the dead, like the erection of memorial stones by the tribals, suggest that besides the cult of fertility and ancestor worship, they entertained a belief in life after death. The Hindu *sraddha* ceremony, in fact, must have arisen from the same idea of feeding the spirit of deceased. Customs related to the rites and rituals differ according to the status of the mourner in the Hindu varna system, or the non-varna.

Here, certain non-Assamese Hindu groups, the Bangalis, the Biharis and the Punjabis for example, have been treated as communities, in spite of the fact that they include more than one, or all of the four *Varnas.* Among the Assamese Hindu communities also, there a mix of all the four *Varnas.* However, certain communities do not belong to any of the pure *Varnas.* For example, the *ahisya,* are believed to have originated from Kshatriya and Vaisya parenthood. All such mixed communities do not place themselves in *Varna* hierarchy, but consider themselves to be members of one *Varna* or the other. Then there are later entrant communities to the system, who, when they entered the Hindu fold, were assigned position in one *Varna* or the other. Whenever a royal tribal family or a group of tribal nobles became Hinduised, the Brahman priests fabricated elaborate genealogical charts proving status between these tribal families and mythical Kshatriya characters who had taken to jungles due to their repression. The Barman Kacharis, who were at one time rulers of Cachar, in spite of being scheduled as tribals, claim their entry into the *Varna* hierarchy through the lowest rung, as per the pan-Indian pattern.

As for the Hindu communities of Assam into four *Varna* system there are only two Brahman communities whereas the number of their *Sudra* counterparts are fifteen times as many. Such a pyramidal structure is similar to the pan-Indian situation. However, for example, qualitatively the social system is quite different. For example, untouchability is unknown among the high caste people of Assam and there is no indigenous caste of scavengers. The religious reform movement initiated by Sankardeva further helped to wither the rigidity of the *Varna* system by denying the Brahmanical supremacy in the Assamese society. As a result, of Shankardeva's movement and in the course of the Ahom rule, a number of occupational groups came into existence, which are unique to Assam and do not fit into the Brahmanical *Varna* system.

In brief, the *Varna* system of Assam can be described as liberal and incomplete. The communities of Assam, who stay outside the *Varna* system are the 'non-Hinduised' tribals the Christians, Buddhists and the Muslims. Sometimes there is found a semblance of *Varna* system in one or two of such communities also. For example, Bangali Muslims are divided into several endogamous groups, which are arranged in hierarchical order. The social customs situation, however, are not same in the tribal communities.

Beliefs Concerning the Life after Death

According to Mr. J.P. Mills, the Ao does not believe that death means his extinction of life but expects that his spirit will take up its abode in the village of the shades. Concerning the post-death life, his ideas are weak, vague and shadowy. In general the other life does not differ greatly from this; it is no better but if anything less desirable, because it is so indefinite and so uncertain. If the man has lived in comfortable circumstances on earth during his life time he will likewise be comfortable in the future. Rich men who had slaves in the old days will have them again in heaven. The men who did the cultivation work on earth would continue that occupation in heaven. However, some say that they will not have to work in the next existence. The coming of the British Government and the Christian missionaries has served to confuse their ideas.

In the times gone by they found a great pleasure in contemplating the cutting off of the heads in heaven during their head-hunting expeditions, but now, since the practice has been discontinued on earth, they are uncertain about the status of this pleasurable pursuit in the after-life. With a few exceptions, the spirits of all mankind go to this world of the departed shades. A man who has been killed by falling from a tree simply roams about and never arrives at *Mojing's* village. The spirit of a victim who has been killed by a tiger clings to the tiger's tail and follows that about never entering the abode of the blessed. The spirit of a woman who dies in childbirth will go to the lower realms of the other world and her lot will be far from happy. The spirit of a thief will be in disgrace, and so will sneak along some other path, avoiding the route frequented by the good people, but he would eventually reach the same destination.

In the world of spirits the dead men are supposed to live and toil as they did on earth for exactly the same number of years, whereupon the spirits end their real existence and pass into another realm being where they may live in the form of butterflies or locusts. Here they may have everlasting existence even though they may not find it highly enjoyable. While wandering about in this first stopping place in the realm of the departed, if a spirit stubs its toe against a rock. It will become a rock, and if it stumbles over a log, it will turn into a log; thus ending the existence as a spirit and wiping out all hope of an entrance into the second exaled state, of being.

Following the death a person's spirit goes to appear before *Mojing,* the ruler over the departed spirits. When the spirit of a male arrives at the judgement seat he must hurl a spear or gong at a tree. If he hits the object, this proves that he was a good man on earth, and is entitled to a good place; but if he misses the target, then, amid the jeers of the congregation of spirits, his spirit is sent to an undesirable place to atone for his evil life on earth. On the other hand, the spirit of a female hurls a weaver's batten instead of a spear. If a man has killed *mithan* for giving feasts of merit to his village, the spirits of the animals remain on earth hovering about the *mithan's* skull, which the owner keeps. Sometimes, the sacrifice of a fowl or a pig is made to this spirit lest it depart. When the man dies he takes these animal spirits along with him to the world of shadows and gives the largest one to the god *Mojing.* He is also supposed to take with him the skulls of the men he has killed in war and head hunting one of which he presents to *Mojing.*

Apparently the Aos do not fear death. They seem to accept it as a part of the programme which must be obeyed. At first there is some wailing by the women, but that also seems to be a part of the regular schedule that must occur. The mourning, however, is of short duration, because they soon forget all about their grief in the merry feasting that ensues. The widow soon desists from wailing and begins to sing the praises of her brave and noble husband, and enters into the task of preparing the symbols which are the insignia to the world what a noble man he was.

In primitive tribal beliefs, both diseases and death are the handiwork of maleficent agents and not to natural causes. Because of this the primitive mind turns to euphemisms, lest they offend the malevolent spirit concerned and it bring calamity upon them. It has been a practice among the Chinese tribes also instead of mentioning the word 'death' to call it 'the great sickness'. The shop that sell caskets and coffins do not mention them as 'coffins,' but advertise them as 'boards of old age'. The Aos also make use of euphemisms to some extent. For instance, if a man is killed by a tiger they prefer to say that he was 'eaten by the jungle', while cholera is called *motongtaker,* which signifies 'the thing which causes them not to arrive home'.

Something that Leaves the Body is Like Butterfly, bee or insect

About the general idea of death and the after death life of the Nagas of Manipur, Mr. T.C. Hodson records, "At death something leaves the body. That something is often regarded as a winged insect of some kind, now a butterfly, now a bee. In order to allow the insect to escape 'a hole is made in the roof directly above the bed of the deceased'. I cannot be quite sure whether what assumes the shape of the insect in question is to be identified with the soul or personal essence, or with the vital principle. A false impression may be created by the use of philosophical terms in reference to savage beliefs, which are vague, shifting shadows, not modern synthetic systems. Mr. Pettigrew remarks that 'after burial the form of the spirit as a 'kaha' (i.e., the honeybee) is lost and the spirit is supposed to enter the deceased's body again and in that condition remains under all circumstances'. Among other tribes in the vicinity it is believed, according to Dr. Brown, that transformation into an insect, especially a butterfly, is the last, not the first, stage in the progress of the cycle of life. So strongly is this idea held among the Angamis that 'they carefully refrain from injuring' some species of butterfly on this account.

"Something which on and by death is separated from the body and is treated in much the same way as when united with and immanent in the body, is believed to remain at or near the place of death or at the place where the wound which caused death was inflicted, for some time after death. This came to my notice in connection with a frontier raid where a young man of Manipur village had received his spear wound on ground belonging to another village. He actually died in his own village, but I was so fortunate as to witness the ceremony of calling his spirit home.

"A party of the young men of the village all in war paint went to the boundary of the village overlooking the village where the fatal affray had occurred. A dance was solemnly performed and then zu was poured on the ground, rice scattered about and they all shouted 'Nipone, come back, come back. Have no fear. We are your friends, here is food and drink. Come from that unlucky place'. On this occasion, perhaps because I was there, to keep the peace, there was no answer but I was told that some answer was usual.

"The 'ghost' of the deceased is regarded as an exact image of the deceased as he was at the moment of death, with scars, tattoo marks, mutilations, and all—and as able to enjoy and to need food and other sustenance—which are therefore given to it for a period. The psychology of the Karens has been described by Forbes (*British Burma,* p. 272, *et. seq.*). Everything, animate and inanimate, has a 'la' which is the case of human beings constantly wanders from the body, so that its persistent absence causes death. To the 'thah' or will, but not to the 'la' is attached moral responsibility. A third principle called 'tso' may be defined as Reason. How tempting to identify these terms with the psychical components of consciousness, feeling (la), will (thah), and thought (tso). In Lushai psychology, 'each person has three spirits. One of these is called khawrin, and this is the one that sometimes wanders; the other two are spoken of as thlarao, and one is supposed to be wise and one foolish, and the constant struggle between these two causes men's actions to be so unreliable.' (Shakespear, *Ethnography of India,* p. 226.) The Lushai term thla, which is translated by Lorrain and Savidge (*Lushai Grammar* p. 197), as a spirit or one's double, is no doubt identical with the Karen word 'la'. Here, at any rate, we have distinctly a belief in a sort of double, a soul to which responsibility is attached which uses the double as its vehicle, but it must be left to further investigation to decide the extent to which the beliefs of the Hill tribes of Manipur resemble those held by their neighbours and congeners, south and east of them.

"The Tangkhuls say that their dead go to a heaven by a path over the crest of Sirohifurar. This is the realm of the Deity Kok-thi-yong, Kok-thi-makha, Kok-thu, or Kokto as Mr. Pettigrew finds him to be called. The place is called Ka-zai-ram or the country (ram = lam = territory) of the zai. The Deity of Heaven is fain to keep them all out. By the gates there flits a woodpecker, the type of restless vigilance. The thin ghosts cannot themselves force a way in, and so it is uncumbent on the living to provide a buffalo for the burial feast in order that its mighty ghost may open the massy gates. To kill a pig were idle expense, because, as they know full well, 'to drive a pig to Dublin you must set his nose to Cork.' So, near the gates of Heaven, awaiting the arrival of the ghost of a rich man, there is a crowd of ghosts whose living kin are too poor or too selfish to slaughter a buffalo. The Deity judges them all, and on the occasion of the Kathi Kasham festival Dr. Brown notes that the 'spirits of the departed appear at a distance from the village in the faint moonlight wending their way slowly over the hills, and driving before them the victims they may have slain or the cattle stolen during their lives; the procession disappears over the distant hills amidst the wails of the villagers. Unless the village priests are well fed, it is said this appearance will not take place'. Mr. Pettigrew's account differs but slightly from that given above. He says that 'The king of Kazairam, what we might call the place of departed spirits, is named Kokto. He is supposed to live in a grand mansion, with sentries guarding all sides and nobody from the upper world dare enter. On the appearance of any spirit from above before the entrance to this mansion, they find him seated inside the door, and his first duty is to notice what kind of following the spirit has. They are of two kinds, one who has been a thief will be seen with the whole livestock which he has stolen trailing behind him and the other will be seen with a following of all the animals procured by honest hunting. As Tangkhul women do not hunt, it is difficult to find out how Kokto distinguishes the weaker sex. However, Kokto judges them all, and, after appropriating for himself all the best cloths brought along, he sentences the thieves to go by the road to the left where there are worms and everything dreadful, and the honest spirit turns off to the right, and follows a road which can only be described as clean. It seems, however, that these good and bad spirits meet again further on near the banks of a river. Here the spirits dispose of the gifts they have brought, some to those who have not yet departed from the village, and to those who have and who are on the other side of the river, the gifts are thrown across to them. After this performance, the difficulty comes in as to how the spirit gets back to the house of the deceased, but the only way out of it seems for the spirit to dodge Kokto and come up to the upper world another way'. So far as my memory serves me, there was some room for improvement in the attitude of Tangkhuls towards stray cattle.

"At Jessami I was told that the good go to a Heaven above but the bad are consigned to an abode beneath the earth. What exactly constituted goodness and badness, was not explained to me. At Mao there is a belief in a Deity named Pekujikhe with whom the ghost must strive in combat. Verily they take the kingdom of Heaven by violence. For this end two spears are placed in the grave and if the ghost succeeds in wounding the Deity or scores a hit, it is well with him, but if he fail, he is enslaved for ever. Then there is also a Deity named Kechira who sorts out the dead, some according to merit (though in what merit consists my informant knew not), others according to the manner of their death. In their Heaven are many mansions. In one such compartment are herded together those who died in battle, in another are those who in life have split their ears, being thus literally ear-marked by fate, while in another are the women who have died in childbirth. There is also said to be a nice place inside the earth to which the dead go, but I do not know whether it was a place of lasting abode or a temporary sojourn. At Maram the Heaven lies in the west and it too is divided into many compartments. The Quoirengs believe that the ghosts of the dead are despatched on and as a result of the annual festival of the dead to a Heaven in the north-east. Of the Kabuis we have from Dr. Brown the statement that 'After death the souls descend to an underground world where they are met by their ancestors, who introduce them into their new habitation; the life they lead in this underground world is an exact counterpart of what they have led in this—the rich remain rich, the poor, poor.' Heaven is in fact regarded down to the minutest details as an exact replica of this 'material' world. Among the Marrings the good dead up go above, while the bad go below to a place inside the earth. Those who have died in an extraordinary manner flit about between Heaven and earth.

"It is curious to note that as a matter of coincidence the tribes which claim to have sprung from the earth place their Heaven inside the earth. Maram is said to have had its origin from immigrants from the west and their Heaven is in the west. The Quoirengs say that they came from the north-east where they place their Heaven.

"Mr. Pettigrew wonders how Koktho, the Lord of the Tangkhul Heaven, distinguished the weaker sex. Is there a back door, for ladies only ? How would a poor old Naga woman fare in combat with the stout Guardian of the Mao Heaven, seeing that all she has to fight with are a digging stick and some cooking pots, part worn ? As I read Colonel Shakespear's account of the Lushai beliefs, much the same difficulty occurs there, since Pupaola always shoots at women whoever they may be (Shakespear JRAI, p. 379). There seems to be some hope for them, since in an earlier account. I find that Colonel Shakespear allows women to be taken by their husbands to Piel-ral—the comfortable after world.

"It is evident that the dead are sorted out by two methods which are not really inconsistent. In the first place there is a selection according to the life lived in this world, where the 'good' so-called go to one place and the 'bad' to another. Then the dead are sorted out according to the manner of the death they die. The common belief with respect to persons who meet with a violent or an extraordinary death is that were they to be buried in the ordinary place, their fate would overtake others. (As Marett says, 'there is plenty of proof that the savage is extremely unwilling to recognise the fact of natural death'. (*Threshold of Religion,* p. 26). The truth is that in these cases of 'extraordinary' death, as we call them, the mechanical cause is generally patent and intelligence to them. The cause of death is not so patent, not so intelligible, in cases of 'ordinary' death. Hence the dead in the first category are treated as dead, recognised as severed from the community, without delay.). Like follows like, and there is not a Naga who does not believe that there is a great deal of truth in the saying that the greatest of all misfortunes is always followed by one still greater. 'Death is a phenomenon which touches the communal life very deeply. Apart from all considerations of private grief, the mere occurrence of death puts the tribal nerves on the stretch. The explanation of this strange discrimination between the various kinds of death is to be found in the psychological attitude of these people towards all such social phenomena. In some of the cases of death the proximate or mechanical cause of death is clear... Behind these interpretations... which are specifically referable to animistic concepts, there is in all these cases and in all such 'extra natural' phenomena a vague sense of terror which gives rise to the thought that what has happened is due to somebody's default. Sin, sickness and death are not for them isolated, unconnected phenomena. Sin in their view consists primarily of breaches both by accident and by intent of the unwritten laws of society. What gives validity to these unwritten laws is the vague fear that something may happen if they are broken. Something, this terrible death of a tribesman, has happened. Why did it happen ? What more logical than the answer that it happened because a sin has been committed ? Thus they come to the belief that the occurrence of any of these 'extra natural' cases of death is good evidence of sin either in the sense of a breach of some precept of the communal law, the punishment for which follows, automatically, quasi-mechanically, without postulating the intermediary agency of spirits, or in some cases, of an offence against some power. If any such case occurs, some Naga tribes destroy the house and property of the deceased and drive the survivors into the jungle. This is in part due to blind terror, in part to the desire to banish from their midst all possible sources of danger, and in part to the hope of propitiating the power whose might has thus been manifested to them.'

"Among the Tangkhuls Dr. Brown found the belief that 'in the future state they live and die, men six times and women five times : after this they are turned into clouds.' At Jessami and at Mao I was assured that only the 'good' were reborn, and that thieves were turned into animals. Those who were killed by animals were never reborn. Of the Kabuis Dr. Brown states that 'after living their lives over again they return to the upper world and are born, live and die unconscious of their former state; the bad, however, are annihilated. Among the Marrings, the reward of a virtuous life is immediate, since 'after death the good are born again at once into this world.' I was often assured that it was evident that people were reborn since there were children in the village who were the exact image of some deceased relation. This belief may have some connection with the custom of naming children after deceased relations." adds Mr. Hodson. The custom of the belief, and rituals connected therewith pertain to the Naga tribes of Manipur.

Death Related Genna or Taboo

Death term *genna* is used in two ways : (*i*) it may mean practically a holiday, i.e., a man will say, 'My village is doing *genna* to-day,' by which he means that, owing either to the occurrence of a village festival or some such unusual occasion as an earthquake or burning of a village within sight of his own, his people are observing a holiday; (*ii*) *genna* means anything forbidden." Primarily the term means 'forbidden' or 'prohibited'. And *genna* applies to the large number of prohibitions which constitute so important an element in the social and religious life of the Aos as well as of the large number of the related hill tribes. Some are occasional, some come at regular times, some are of short duration, while some are permanent. Since all of the festivals, religious and funeral ceremonies have some prohibitions they may in reality be classed as *gennas*. At these times the normal activities of the individuals or groups are suspended or restricted in order that the gods, being thus propitiated, may shower prosperity upon them or withhold calamity. If any of these interdicts be violated by an individual, the proper body will punish him because his act is putting in jeopardy, not only his own welfare, but also that of entire community. However, in these matters it is the letter of the law that must be kept, while it matters less about the spirit. Since there is so little tribal unity there is no actual tribal *genna.* However, there are certain practices which approach it.

The Aos do not eat the cock, or black gibbon, neither do they eat the black crow. Until quite recently no person would drink cow's milk, but that custom is in process of breaking down. These taboos on food might be regarded as tribal *gennas* because they are so general. The Mongsen moiety will eat neither dog, or monkey of any kind, while the Chongli moiety is quite fond of dogs and certain species of monkey. Of course the *gennas* which affect individuals and the various communities are common in the entire tribe, but there is no taboo which affects the entire tribe at the same time unless by mere coincidence. The village is the largest unit affected by these taboos or *gennas.*

About the death-related gennas of Manipuri Nagas, Mr. T.C. Hodson records, "The village gennas which are observed in connection with cases of death, fall into two classes, the first being gennas of regular occurrence as the mangla tha, a genna which seems to contain the germ of some kind of ancestor worship, though celebrated only for those of the recent dead whose manner of death does not argue them to have sinned and to be excluded from the privilege of rebirth and the second being gennas which are necessitated by the deaths of individual members of the village. I may remark that with the notable exception of the Mao group where it is customary to hold a village genna on each occasion a villager dies, whatever the immediate cause of his death, it is not usual to have a village genna when the cause of death is what we should call regular and without mystery. A village genna for the death of an individual villager is held when the death is 'extra natural.' In both cases the idea is the same, to sever the living from the dead. At the annual festival they restore to the living those of their members who have been in jeopardy of the contagion of death. The dead from whom they then separate themselves are regarded as in a state of existence from which it is possible they may return to life. All seek to have done with the evil dead as soon as possible. They are denied rebirth. They are indeed dead. The wages of their sin is death. The society sets itself free at once, by an exertion of communal energy, from the taint of sin.

It reacts violently in opposition to the calamity, in order to restore the equilibrium of life. 'Here, then, is a twofold seed of religion—fear that prompts the immediate sepulture of the dead whose manner of death argues them to have sinned, while human affection retains its hold on the ghost of the good.' Yet there may be in this rite a desire to placate the ghost, almost to worship it, as well as to protect themselves against its wrathful malice. In an impressive passage, Hartland remarks that 'superstitious like those concerning ghosts in the West and *bhuts* in the East exhibit souls disembodied by other than a natural death as vindictive and often extremely dangerous beings who must be pacified and exorcised or even worshipped. The cult of executed criminals in... is therefore not an isolated example of the vagaries of human emotion. It is merely one of the many manifestations of the shock given to the collective mentality of any society by the death of a member. That shock is always deeper and more terrible where the severance from life is by violence... where it is imposed by arms or more mysterious terrors... then the shock and the terror reach their height, the whole sympathy of society goes out towards the victim and he is surrounded by a halo of more than common radiance." adds Mr. Hodson. The custom called gennas are practised by the Naga tribes of Manipur.

Lycanthropy

J.H. Hutton wrote, Magic power relating to "the Semas fancy that certain people have the power of changing themselves into tigers. According to them, half the soul of such a lycanthropist runs into the forest and takes shelter in a tiger, whereas the other half remains in the body of the man himself. When this tiger is chased by anybody, the half souled man instantaneously runs mad and the people suspect a lot of things. Some people change themselves into tigers in malice and in that form destroy the cattle of their enemies. If the tiger is killed by chance, the man also dies.

"It is very difficult to release half the soul from a tiger unless the lycanthropist can eat the remnant of the raw meat tasted by that particular tiger in which his soul resides. It is not known if the tiger dies at the death of man but it is unmistakably certain that the man dies at the death of the tiger. To make their belief well-founded they generally trace a similarity in the outward appearance of the tiger and the man by means of a few signs. Thus, if the lycanthropist has a wreath around his neck, the tiger also must have white and red signs across its neck looking like a wreath, etc. If the lycanthropist by chance meets the tiger in the forest, the latter generally runs circling about the former very eagerly.

"There is a rumour about a Naga of the Sarumi village that he ran away as a lycanthrope in the forest, and the people who ignorantly killed him were all drowned. When such a tiger is chased by the people the relatives of the man-tiger become conscious of it at once and they inform the chasers about it. My Naga servant 'Huvekey' has seen his eldest brother 'Luzatulukey' of the 'Khukia' village and 'shakutukey' of 'Hohibi' village turn themselves into tigers. He was himself one of the party when the villagers of 'Khukia' gave chase to the tiger possessed of the soul of the aforesaid 'Shakutukey'. He says that just when a very hot chase was given to the tiger the villagers of 'Hohibi' came running by the identified it to be Shakutukey whereupon they had to cease the chase and return home." adds Mr. Hutton.

Naga Belief and Witch-doctor

The Semas of Nagaland are monotheistic in belief and their name of God is 'Kunglin,' who has created this universe and dwells in the sky. He sees through the deeds of all. The Semas believe in 'Satan', ghosts and spectres. The Sema satan is known as 'Tagamy.' The favourite haunt of Tagamy monster is in the midst of gigantic boulders and rocks, in the rivers beds, dense forest and, according to some, in the very houses of men now and then. According to Sema belief the soul of a religious dead man goes up to the sky and becomes a *Deo* there, and the soul of an irreligious man walks down to an abysmal depth below and is born again as a human being or a fly there.

Auou is the principal witch-doctor of the Sema Nagas and in every village there is one of them. Being the hereditary priest of the Semas, and in respect second to the chieftain, the Auou is the authority on questions of the '*gena*' or religious rites of the Semas, and the sole person to fix the date for the celebration of such a *gena* and to order for its necessary publicity. He receives paddy from every villager and in time of *gena* he gets meat. Whenever a new village is going to be founded, the house of the Auou has first to be built, then that of the chieftain and then others. In every village there is a class of people called as 'Lapu' or *Apnou* whose business is to bury the dead of the village. The shovels used at the time of the burial come to the possession of these *Lapus,* whose secondary business is also to dig canals for the purpose of letting the water in and out whenever a new village is in the process of being built. In a *gena* called 'Afisata' the Lapu will suck honey first of all and will receive a cow's leg and a seer of salt. He also gets sufficient paddy for burying the dead.

Witchcraft

About causing death and sickness to a foe, and also curing illness, by the Mikir Shamans, Edward Stack and Sir Charles Lyall write, "Sickness, if long continued or severe, is frequently attributed to witchcraft (*maja*). A man suffering from long sickness is said to be *maja kelong*—'witchcraft has got hold of him.' To discover the author of the spell, or the god or demon who has brought the trouble and must be propitiated, the services of a diviner are necessary. *Uche,* feminine *uche-pi* (Hindi, *ojha*), is the general name for the cunning in such things. Of these there are two grades–the humbler, whose craft is acquired merely by instruction and practice, and the higher, who works under the inspiration or *afflatus* of divine powers. The former is the *sang-kelang abang,* 'the man who looks at rice,' in Assamese, *mangalsua;* the latter, invariably a woman, is the *lodet* or *lodet-pi.* In serious sickness or distress the latter is called in; on ordinary and less important occasions, the former.

'The *sang-kelang abang* picks out of the pot the unbroken grains of rice (*sang*), and places them by fives and tens, in pentacle or other fashion. He then counts by couples. If in the groups the odd numbers predominate, the omen is good. If there are no odd grains over, it is very bad. Then all are swept together again, and arranged in three or four heaps. Each heap is counted out, a god being named, and if after the counting, again by couples, three single grains remain, the god named is the one to be propitiated. If three grains do not remain, the process is tried over again. Cowries (*chobai*) are sometimes used instead of rice in the same way. Also, with cowries a handful is taken and spread out, and the number with the slits upwards counted; if they are the majority, the omen is good.

"Another mode of divination used by the *mangalsua* is to arrange in a circle, equidistant from a point marked on a board (*inghoi*), as many little heaps of clay as there are gods suspected in the case, each heap being called by the name of its god. An egg is then sharply thrown into the middle of the board at the marked point. When it breaks and the yolk is scattered, that clay heap which receives the largest splash of yolk, or towards which the largest and longest splash points, indicates the god responsible for the affliction.

"Another mode is to use the *nok-jir,* which is a long-handled iron *dao* with a cross-piece at the handle and two inclined projecting pieces higher up, before the blade...

"This is held upright in the hand. It shakes of itself when the charm is recited and the *nok-jir* invoked to become inspired : *Nang uche vang-phlot*! 'Let your spirit (*uche*) come!' The holder asks whether the sick person will recover, and goes over the names of the possibly responsible gods, and the *nokjir* shakes at the right answer and name. The charm (the Assamese word *montro* is used) recites the making of the *nokjir,* and ends—'if you tell lies, you will be broken up and made into needles' (—the lowest use to which iron can be put, to sew women's petticoats!)

"The *Lodet* is an ordinary woman (not belonging to any particular family or *kur*), who feels the divine *afflatus,* and, when it is upon her, yawns continually and calls out the names and the will of the gods. Another *lodetpi* is summoned in to question her, a ascertain if her possession is really divine; a *sang-kelang abang* may also be consulted. If the report is favourable, a purificatory offering of a fowl is made to Hemphu and Mukrang, the preservers of men, and the women is accepted as a *lodetpi.*

"She sits by the bewitched person (*maja-kelong*), and the neighbours come in after supper. The *lodetpi* bathes her hands and feet and face in water in which the *tulsi* plant (*Ocymum sanctum,* holy basil) has been steeped, and begins to shake and yawn. A gourd of rice-beer is brought, of which she drinks some, and beings to call out the names of gods, and they descend upon her. She is now inspired, and when questioned indicates, by indirect and riddling answers, the enemy who has bewitched the sufferer, or the gods who must be sacrificed to. When this is ascertained she goes away. The accusation of practising witchcraft is carried before the *me* or village assembly. The sacrifice to placate the gods proceeds next day, and is usually costly.

"To bewitch a person, it is necessary to have some of his hair, or a piece of his clothes; these are buried with one egg, some bones, and some charcoal. A good *lodetpi* can produce these things by the power of her inspiration. A white cloth is tied up into the shape of a bag. She conjures the things into it, and on opening the bag next morning they are found inside. When they are thus recovered, the spirit (*karjong*) of the sufferer returns with them, and he gets well.

"Charms (*pherem*) are much used for medicinal purposes, either alone or in combination with other remedies. For an ordinary stomach-ache (*pok-keso*), a little mud rubbed on the abdomen, with a muttered charm, is the specific. For rheumatism (*kechease*), a castor-oil leaf is struck on the place, and a charm muttered; if this fails, sacrifice must be offered to the god *Keche-ase*. The worker of these remedial measures is called *kangtok abang,* and the verb is *ingtok*. Charms are not, as a rule, carried on the person.

"The expression *vur kachethat,* 'to kill for oneself (a fowl) for disease,' means to prevent evil by sacrifice after a dream which had previously been followed by mischance.

"If a child does not thrive, it is imputed to the sin, or devil (*ahi-i*) of the maternal uncle (*ong*), or, if there is no maternal uncle, of one of the child's mother's *kur*. The family apply to the person held to be responsible, and he gives a brass ring to be hung round the child's neck, and a rice-ball (*an adum*).

"There is no entertaining of friends on recovery from sickness. The sick person is tended by his wife and relations.

"*Tekere, Thekere,* means a man who knows a spell or *montro,* especially one which protects him against tigers (*teke*)." They add. The custom is pertinent to the Mikir tribals.

About the Semas witchcraft, J.H. Hutton writes, "The *thumomi,* though a well-known and more or less indispensable person, has no official position in the village hierarchy. He (or she) is a private practitioner, self-appointed and independent. He acts as an intermediary between private persons and the spirits, and sometimes is, or claims to be, *clairvoyant.* He is a dreamer of dreams and skilled in the interpretation thereof, a curer of illness, and a discoverer of stolen property. Divining is a property often ascribed to books. A chief once came to me and asked me to look in my books and tell him the whereabouts of his brother, who had run away from the hospital into the jungle in delirium. I consulted the *sortes Homerianae* for him with the most appropriate results, opening the Odyssey at the passage where Telemachus asks for news of his father, and is told that he has visited the land of the dead and returned. Sometime he has, or is credited with, a knowledge of poisons not possessed by the ordinary man. Including that of the poison called *atsunigha,* the fruit of a plant, which when thrown at a person or secreted in his clothes enters into his body, causing him to die later on by the swelling of all his limbs. Yet he is not as a rule a man of any social standing or personal influence, and is almost invariably poor, so markedly so that it is generally held that a *thumomi* is unable to acquire riches, a belief which assists credulity in the *thumomi's* impostures, as it meets the most obvious criticism as to the *thumomi's* object in deceiving. No stigma attaches to the activities of a *thumomi* or to his practice of magic, and he is not necessarily regarded as being personally responsible for being a *thumomi,* which may befall him against his will." adds Mr. Hutton. The custom is pertinent to the Sema Nagas of Nagaland.

REFERENCES

1. Singh, KS (Gen. ed.) People of India : Arunachal Pradesh, Seagul Books, Calcutta, 1995.
2. Singh KS (Gen. ed.) People of India : Assam, Seagull Books, Calcutta, 2003.
3. Endle, The Kacharis, Cosmo Publications, New Delhi 1987, Originally Published 1911.
4. Stack Edward & Lyall, Sir Charles, The Mikirs, United Publishers, Guwahati, First Published 1908.

5. Danda, Dipali G., Among the Dimasas of Assam; Ethnographic Study, Sterling Publishers, New Delhi 1978.
6. Hutton, J.H. The Sema Nagas, Oxford University Press, Bombay 1968 First Published 1921.
7. Hodson, TC, The Naga Tribes of Manipur, BR Publishing Corp. Delhi (reprint) 1974, Originally Published 1911.
8. Hutton, J.H. The Angami Nagas : With some notes on Neighbouring Tribes, Oxford University Press, Bombay 1969, First Published 1921.
9. Mills, JP, The Ao Nagas, Oxford University Press, Bombay 1973, Originally Published 1926.
10. Furer–Haimendorf, C.V., Highlanders of Arunachal Pradesh, Vikas Publishing House, New Delhi 1982.

6

Death Rituals : Burial

The custom of burying of the dead seems to be common amongst all the non-Aryan people of the entire north-east and even in other regions, like Madhya Pradesh, Chhattisgarh and Jharkhand. Hindu influences have induced some of the tribes men to take a burning. Tribes like the Akas, the Adis, the Dafla's and most of the Nagas in Assam, Arunachal, Manipur, Mizoram, Nagaland, Tripura etc. bury the dead. The Ahoms before they embraced Hinduism used to bury their dead. The Mikirs and Deuris also burn their dead. But among the Bodos, all the three customs are prevalent : some of them cremate their dead, some bury them, a third section simply takes the dead to the burial ground and leaves them there. After burial, the Daflas take up arms and shoot arrows in all directions to drive the evil spirits away. The Dowaniyas will burn the dead if he is over 20 years of age and bury him if he is under 20 years; the Fakials will burn the deceased if he is above 15 years and bury him if he is under 15 years.

A person dying unnatural death is not given the usual funeral ceremony, the Adis will not offer food at the grave of pregnant woman or a man killed in an accident; the Deuris will not burn a man who has died of an epidemic like cholera, but first bury him and then exhume the skeleton and consign it to fire. The Khasis and the Rabhas follow both the custom of burying and burning. The Ao Nagas erect a high *machan* and place the corpse on it and expose it to be eaten by crows and vultures or to rot away; formerly they used to smolder a fire below corpse to render it dry and help it wither away.

Most of the tribes believe in the next world or life after death where the spirit of the dead goes. Some of them also believe in the rebirth of the spirit in another form. If a Lalung baby cries too much, they imagine that some dead member of the family must have been reborn. When a Mikir baby is named after its grandfather, it is imagined that the dead old man is reborn as his grandson.

The most wonderful speculation about rebirth is that of the Daflas and the Bodos. To the Daflas the colourful butterflies are the spirits of the dead. When an unmarried Bodo youth dies, a banana tree is planted near his grave so that his life after death becomes more fruitful than has been the case hitherto. When a Bodo woman dies, a pipal branch is planted near her grave in the hope that in her rebirth she will be blessed with a luxuriant growth of hair. Prior to burial or cremation, water is poured and red threads placed between the lips of the dead, that will make in rebirth, the lips thin and red, a sign of beauty.

When a Naga Christian dies in Nagaland, he is given a Christian burial, but usually an object that he particularly cherished is put into the coffin just as a deceased's prized possessions were displayed on his funeral platform. Before burial, family members bid farewell to the deceased with an emphasis on the statement that he should not grieve as he goes to the other world nor should he return to search for those he has left behind (Naga's believe that the dead returns to take with them members of their family). This faith is still in the traditional ways. In the post-Independence India, Naga Christians do not see their traditions that belong to a pre-Christian era as in any way clashing with Christian way of living.

Worrying about the Soul that is Liable to Stray

About the funeral customs of Sema Nagas of Nagaland, Mr. J.H. Hutton notes in detail. Thus, "the Sema views as to the soul and its survival after death have already been dealt with, but to understand the observances attending death it is necessary to bear them in mind. It has been seen that the episode of death is to some extent regarded as due to a voluntary desertion on the part of the departing soul, always a source of anxiety on account of its liability to stray. It would appear, however, that there is something contagious about dying, and that association with death is liable to cause it. Merely to spread an untrue report of a man's death may cause it in itself, and the penalty for doing this serious injury is a heavy fine, usually about four mithan. Possibly the fact of a man being reported dead gives malicious spirits some hold over him, just as to mention the name of an infant (or even of an adult if done often and persistently) is enough to cause death. Again the grave is begun as soon as a man is dead, but should he prove to be merely unconscious and recover, it is essential that some substitute should be buried, and his own stool (*alaku*) is wrapped in a cloth and put in the grave in his stead. This was done in the case of one Kiyakhu of Aochagalimi, an acquaintance of mine. Cf "The Golden Bough," Vol. viii (3rd ed.) pp. 98, 100).

The stool is chosen as, like the bed (*alipa*), it is so closely associated with its owner as to contain some part of his essence, as it were, in virtue of which it is absolutely genna at any time to cut or burn a person's stool or bed, while it is very bad form to sit on the bed of a Sema chief unless invited by him to do so. Until the actual burial the dead man's household may eat and drink as usual, but after the burial has once taken place no one of the household may eat again that day, and on the following morning *akini* seed (*Perilla ocimoides,* L.) is pounded up, made into a paste with hot water, and put into the mouth on a bit of thatching grass stalk. It is spat out, and after that all the dishes and vessels in the house are washed, to cleanse them, no doubt, from any death-pollution which might affect others using them. A meal is then taken as usual. (The ceremonies of death and burial are recorded as observed in the Zumomi village of Kiyeshes.)

"On the second day after the death a pig is killed, and the dead man's share of flesh, torn up into very fine fragments such as a ghost can manipulate, is put for him in a platter with rice, chillies, etc., covered up with leaves and set on a shelf for the ghost, who helps himself to minute particles. Pieces of meat not torn up are sometimes set there, and it is known that the ghost has partaken by his infinitesimal nibblings. For ten days not only the whole household but everyone in the village who belongs to deceased's clan observes *pini,* not going to the fields and abstaining from all vegetables. On the tenth day the house is cleaned out and the genna is at an end.

"The method of burial is as follows. A grave is dug breast deep in front of the house and usually a little to the left. A new-born child that dies, or one that is born dead, is buried inside the house in the *akishekhoh.* An American traveller relates that a Sema told him that he buried a young girl, his daughter, inside the house because she would be frightened to be left outside alone at night, but the actual age of the child is not given ("Ethnography of Nagas of Eastern Assam," Furness, *Journal of Anthropological Institute,* 1902, Vol. xxxii). This grave is lined with hewn planks of wood at the bottom and sides and with bamboo matting at the ends. The body is laid face upwards, the head at the end nearest the house, on the plank at the bottom at full length, with a spear at his side, a dao at his head, and a dao carrier, at least one string of conch shell beads (*ashogho*), cloths up to about seven or eight, and a spare 'lengta.' Asimi villages put a bead and some fragments of foodstuffs between all the fingers of their dead. In the ears are wads of fresh cotton put in by some near relation. This service is performed by any near relation, mother, wife, brother, etc. A peg-top (*aketsu*), a snare for birds (*akusu*), and a pipe and tobacco accompany the dead warrior. A boy is given a sharpened bamboo instead of a spear, while a woman, in place of spear and dao, is given the iron-shod stick that she used in her lifetime. In place of the the peg-top she takes a single bean of the pod of the great sword-bean (*alau*), together with a springy slip of bamboo taken from the wall of the house. This serves the same purpose to her as the peg-top does to the male, for she uses it to delude *Kolavo* when she comes to the narrow way where he lies in wait for passing souls seeking whom he may devour. Metsimo, the Angami equivalent, makes every passing soul eat a monster nit from his head unless he is already eating one, so that a black seed is put in the mouth of the dead to deceive him. He sits in the path with a truculent air. 'My head is full of lice' (*akhu*), says he. 'Oh,' says she, 'let me kill them for you.' Then she goes up to him and as he sits there searches his head and starts to click the bamboo slip from time to time as though it were the popping of squashed lice, monsters in size. Suddenly she flicks the bean to a distance. 'I will run and catch it,' she says, and so slips by and escapes. In the same way a man or boy gets by when pretending to go to fetch his errant peg-top. When the body has been laid in the grave a piece of resinous pinewood is taken and lit, and the body is fumigated to drive away worms and flies and insects by waving the torch round it to the words *'Ni'ya liki kumoike, Ina cheghi' ya ke, ina kuku 'ya ke',* which is, being interpreted. 'It befalls not our clan alone. Men of all villages that can be named come to this.' (Lit. 'Our clan (custom) alone is not. Villages ten custom is; villages call-call custom is.' The language is archaic. Ten is used as the equivalent of a very high number where the Sema ordinarily uses *ketonhye,* 'a thousand,' nowadays. Perhaps it dates from the time when counting did not go beyond ten. *Kuku* is the last clause is obscure, but is believed to be from the *ku* = to call. *Ina* = *ghana,* 'a village community.' *Aya* is the southern form of *aye* = 'clan,' 'custom'.) Cross-pieces of stick are then put across the grave over the body, being thrust into the earth on each side just above the planks that form the lining of the sides. Over these another plank is put to form the lid, as it were, of the grave, and on the top of that the earth is heaped in and piled up. In the process of this a chicken is killed and buried by stamping it into the earth that is being put into the grave. All the earth taken from the grave is put back so that when the grave is completed there is a mound over it. On this mound a piece of bamboo is set upright, the bottom sharpened and thrust into the earth, the top split, splayed out, and made into the form of a basket by the interweaving of horizontal strips. This is used as a stand for a gourd of liquor. For a man of importance a fence is made round the mound and a little roof of thatch put up.

"On the day of burial cattle and pigs are killed and the skulls put up on a sort of fence or rack erected for that purpose along with the skulls of those slaughtered by the dead man during his lifetime, the souls of which he either takes with him to the village of the dead or finds already awaiting him there. At right angles to this fence down another side of the grave is put a rail of bamboo on which cloths and ornaments belonging to the dead man are hung, as well as a miniature panji basket with 'panjis' and his shield, while a spear or two are stuck into the ground beside them. To the inside of the shield a fire-stick and thongs for making fire are tied. The disposal of a dead man's dog varies. The prevailing custom has been described, a dead man's favourite dog being killed and buried in his grave after his body has been put in and before the earth is thrown back. The Zumomi, however, cut up the dog together with the cattle and distribute its flesh to all guests at the funeral who are not of the same clan as the dead man. The Chophimi clan divides the flesh of a dog killed in this way among all the guests. A dead man is systematically keened by his female relatives, and his widows will often keen him for some time after his death and burial.

"Occasionally a wooden statue of the deceased nearly life-size is made and set up clothed in his ornaments over the grave, but this appears to be merely imitation of the Angamis and not a genuine Sema custom. It is rarely done. If the dead man is a warrior, a bamboo pole is erected from which dangles a string supporting a gourd for each head at the taking of which he has assisted, and an earthen pot for each head he has actually taken himself. (Mr. Mills tells me he has seen a tally of the dead man's liaisons put up on a Sema's grave in the form of little sticks carrying a tuft each of red hair. He was told that to touch a woman's breasts would qualify for one of these.) After a man has taken a head himself an enemy's cattle and even dogs killed by him are counted when reckoning the number of gourds to be put up. Besides these, little baskets are hung up representing the number of raids or warlike expeditions in which the dead man has carried panjis or otherwise taken part. In some Asimi villages the memory of a rich man is perpetuated by a shallow circle of flat stones set in the ground so as to slope away from the centre of the circle at an obtuse angle. Stone circles of this sort are called *atheghwo*. (Kacha Nagas build similar circles for the same purpose. There are circles also in the Sema village of Litsami; likewise at Yeshulutomi, where however the slabs are erect, instead of sloping, with a solitary standing stone at a slight distance.)

"When a woman *in extremis* is visited by her parents they take a bit of stick from the gable of her house. When they have said all they wish to say they place the stick by the dying woman's bed and cut it in two, thus releasing the life so that their daughter can die in comfort.

"In the case of a woman it is a matter of strict etiquette that as many should attend at her funeral as accompanied her on her wedding day from her father's to her husband's house.

"There is no positive orientation of the dead, but a negative orientation, as they must not, when buried, look towards the house in which they lived when alive.

"There remain a few miscellaneous items of semi-religious belief which it is difficult to assign to any particular category. The *thumomi* have already been mentioned in their connection with the healing of the sick, but their activities are not limited to this. The *thumomi* is essentially a seer,... an interpreter of omens, a dreamer, clairvoyant. Second sight he no doubt often has in some degree or other, and since it is an intermittent gift, he must simulate it when absent, for the sake of his reputation, and descend to deception just as a European medium does. In general the *thumomi* is in some degree possessed and is sometimes subject to fits somewhat resembling epilepsy. In particular, it is true, he diagnoses and recommends upon cases of sickness and also upon the probable success or failure of contemplated trading ventures, but he may be consulted on anything from the detection of theft to the foretelling of the future, though in the latter case he usually restricts himself to advising that good or bad will probably follow a certain course of action or the observing of certain gennas. Omens may be taken by anyone, though certain persons and *thumomi* in particular have the faculty of obtaining correct results. The commonest method is by the use of the fire-stick, the omen being taken from the disposition of the broken strands of the bamboo thong after it has been charred through to breaking point by the friction. Dreams, like omens, are not the exclusive province of the *thumomi,* and happen to anyone. Indeed most Semas believe in their own dreams, and take note of them as forecasting events to come, in particular those of hunting and war. A dream is not interpreted in the terms in which it occurs, but on a regular and known system. Thus to dream of bringing in a human head forecasts success in hunting, but the opposite in war. (And usually to dream of dead animals' flesh foretells human death. A curious parallel may be found in the superstition which causes Mr. Vachell in one of his novels to make a character dream of butcher's meat and therefore predict misfortune. This was pointed out to me by Mr. J.P. Mills. Mr. Vachell told Dr. Seligman that he had obtained the data for this from an Irish mother-in-law. *Cf.* Jenks, "The Bontoc Igorot", pp.

74, 78.) To dream of a man carrying a load means that someone will be injured, and so forth. Of course all dreams cannot be reduced to formulae, so that there is plenty of scope for the exercise of the imagination of the dreamer or of anyone he consults in the interpretation of them.

"Second sight also is far from being confined to *thumomi*. Very early in the morning before daybreak on April 13, 1918, some Sema scouts and carriers attached to the column operating against the Kuku Chief Chenjapao burnt a Kuki village after a brush with a Kuki patrol and succeeded in taking a head. They marched back to the camp singing paeans, arriving at about 8.15 a.m. The leaders of the party were Nikiye, Sakhalu's brother, and Sakhalu himself, and the carriers who went included a large proportion of men from that village, one of whom killed the Kuki, whose head Sakhalu cut off. The following night (April 13) many persons in Sakhalu's village (six marches distant) clearly heard the chanting of the paeans of the successful raiders. A number, however, were, even when their attention was directed to it, totally unable to hear the singing, but it was at once known and recognised throughout the village that their fellow villagers with the column had got a head. No natural explanation of this phenomenon is possible. Semas in administered villages do not take heads, or if they do, they do not advertise their wrong-doing by singing paeans that can be heard for miles at night, while verbal communication with the column was out of the question. Nor had any heads been taken or paeans sung by the independent villages across the other side of the Tizu valley. This instance cannot strictly perhaps be called second sight, but is clearly of that nature. Two or three cases also occured within the writer's knowledge in regard to labourers who had gone to France with the Naga Labour Corps. They may have been pure coincidence, but a similar explanation certainly suggests itself. It happened three times that relations of an absent labourer came to the writer to ask if it were true that So-and-so (in France) was dead, refusing to say any more than that they had heard that he was dead. On each occasion no casualty report had been received, nor could any news of the labourers' death have reached their relations by material channels, but the death reports were received in each case about two months later. (I am indebted to Mr. Mills for drawing my attention to these two incidents.)

"Wraiths of the living are also seen. On June 11, 1918, Hotoi and Luzukhu (two interpreters), with four servants, went out to meet some friends expected to arrive that day at Mokokchung from a distant village. They saw them coming towards them up the hill, called to them, and were answered. The approaching guests disappeared for a moment in a bend in the path. Hotoi and Luzukhu waited for some time and, being unable to conceive why they did not appear again, went to look. They found no one at all in the angle of the path, and it was not possible for them to have gone off in any other direction. The expected guests arrived the following day. A similar case occurred in Sheyepu about the same time. A man from another village came to the village to trade, spoke to several people, and was seen and recognised by many. It was, however, only a wraith, as the man himself came two days later and said the same things as his wraith had said to the same persons. He avowed that he had not been present at all on the previous occasion. One was a Chang, two were Semas. On the other hand a similar belief in the death of a Naga convict in the Andamans (March/April, 1922) proved unfounded.) The psychic experiences of Semas differ little on the whole from those of more cultured societies." adds Mr. Hutton. The custom is related to the Sema Nagas of Nagaland.

Challenging the Angel for taking Away Dead Man's Soul

About the burial customs of Angami Nagas of Nagaland, Mr. J.H. Hutton writes in his book the *Angami Nagas* (pp. 225-9). Thus : "By some Naga tribes the work of burying the dead seems to be regarded with a certain amount of repulsion, but the Angamis do not, like some others, relegate this function to a particular individual in each village. The office is usually performed by the deceased's male relatives. In the case of *seshoma,* however, only old men take part in the burial (*vide infra*).

"The first office performed after death is the washing of the corpse by a child of the same sex as the deceased, while the latter's most intimate friend, by no means necessarily a man of the same clan, brings flesh, rice, and rice beer to the dead man's house. After the washing the dead man is laid out upon the bed and covered from the eyebrows to the feet with his own cloth. His ceremonical dress is piled about him, and above his head a 'kang' (carrying basket) is placed containing seeds for wet rice, Job's tears, millet, and every other kind of grain and eatable, together with a lao of '*zu*' and the dead man's own cup. A share also of the flesh, rice, and '*zu*' brought by his best friend is put into this 'kang,' while the remainder is given to the living occupants of the house, who may on that day eat nothing provided from their own household. Next day the young men of the deceased's kindred bring cattle, including those of the dead man, or some of them, if he had any. The Zhevo or Pitsu, as the case may be, makes a would in each beast, after which it is killed by the young men, who, after setting aside the heads, livers, and certain other portions, divide the flesh as they believe the deceased would have done had he been alive; that is to say, large portions are given to those with whom he was specially intimate, and who during his lifetime received much from him, and *vice versa*. In Khonoma, men of the Thevoma or Semoma clans consider it obligatory to eat up any share they may receive within two days, provided they are of the same clan as the dead man, though if of a different clan they may keep it as long as they like. All this time the family of the dead man maintain a doleful howling. The young men of the kindred make the coffin, which is of wood and lidless. When it is ready the deceased's father-in-law, if he have one, if not a friend from another clan, or usually from another clan, enters the house of the dead man and stands on the left-hand side of the body. He then places a spear at the right of the corpse if a man's, a black cloth if it is a woman who had died. He also cuts off a lock of hair from the head of the corpse. Then the coffin is brought inside and a little thatching grass burnt inside it, after which the body is laid in the coffin. The grave is dug during the day, either in front of the house or alongside one of the village paths, and the corpse, covered with a cloth and lying in the coffin, is placed in the grave at dusk. With the body in the coffin are buried a fire-stick ('*segomi*') one or two spears, a dao, and a young chicken alive, and the bitter seed called '*gadzosi*' (it is used for killing leeches) is placed between the teeth. The object of the *gadzosi* is that the soul may be eating it when he meets with the spirit Metsimo, who guards the path to paradise. When Metsimo, sees the dead man eating *gadzosi* he let him pass by, but if the dead man has no *gadzosi* in his mouth, Metsimo makes him eat a monster nit from his (Metsimo's) head. Someone has reported of Angamis that they make wounds in the bodies of dead arriors so that they shall go to the next world as though killed in battle by an honourable death, but I have never met with the custom. If *gadzosi* or a leaf of the plant is not obtainable, any leaf will do, but it must be spoken of as '*gadzosi.*' In the case of woman, a few beads are buried with her, her cloths and a under-petticoat and a reaping hook, with the chicken and the *gadzosi* as in the case of males. Then the coffin is covered with flat stones, and on to the stones that cover the lower half of the corpse the contents of the 'kang' mentioned above are poured. Then the earth is heaped in and the grave levelled, to the accompaniment, in the case of males, of the firing of many guns, and to the howling and shrieking of the women, who beat upon the ground with their cloths, having tried to hold back the coffin as it was lowered into the grave. Mr. McCabe quotes in one of his diaries the cry raised at the disappearance of the coffin :

'Do not be afraid, do not mourn. You have only followed your parent's custom. Although you have died, let us remain happy. Although God has not been kind to you, and you have died, fear not!'

"On the next day the kindred of the deceased with someone from another clan come together at the deceased's house and eat of the meat previously set aside, except the livers. Ceremonial dress is worn and the men shout and leap by the grave, challenging the spirit that has carried off the dead man, asking him where he has hidden, and bidding him come that they may spear him and kill him. (See Butler, "Travels in Assam," p. 150, and compare Owen, "Notes on the Naga Tribes in Communication with Assam," p. 24. Owen's notes refer to Konyak tribes.) They then put up the skulls of the slaughtered cattle over the grave together with the shield, ornaments, clothes, weapons, eating and drinking utensils, and other such personal possessions of the dead man, a gourd of *zu,* and the empty flasks which contained the powder fired on the previous day. On a woman's grave a little basket is placed, containing her spinning and weaving utensils, and a diamond-shaped frame on which different coloured threads are stretched. They also build up over the grave a stone tomb. In the case of the Chakrima villages, a wooden effigy almost of life-size dressed in the ceremonial dress of the dead is set up over the tomb, which is by most Tengima merely hung with the clothes, skulls, etc. while in Viswema large white cloths stretched upon bamboo frames are erected high up off the ground to advertise the death of rich men cut off in the prime of youth. Food is then again taken at the house of the dead man, the livers of the cattle killed being cooked by members of a different clan. When cooked, a piece of liver with salt and chillies is given to each member of the deceased's family, who, without speaking, throw their pieces outside the house some yards away. After this everyone goes back to his own house.

"On the second day after the burying seventeen portions of cooked rice with a little salt are tied up in plantain leaves. These are buried outside the house on the fourth day. On the fifth deceased's platter and drinking cup are suspended by a string inside the house, the string being undone and thrown away after thirty days, when the cup and platter are given to one of deceased's intimate friends; about ten days later the deceased's family kill a cock and divide the flesh equally and eat it, the funeral ceremonies being then finished.

"This does not always entirely complete the ceremony. Sometime between the Tsungi and Terhengi gennas of the year in which the death occurs, or of one of the first two or three years following, one or two pigs are killed and the tomb built up with more solidity than at first. This additional ceremony is not essential, but if at any time the tomb breaks a pig must be killed and repairs executed; but this can only be done between the Tsungi and Terhengi gennas, and it is only between these gennas that a grave may be removed (graves are occasionally removed for the sake of convenience to a different site), or that a man's bones may be brought from another village for interment, as is done when a man dies away from home. (This rule is stated more precisely as follows :

Graves may only be repaired or moved : (1) between the end of the millet harvest and the beginning of the rice harvest; (2) between the end of the rice harvest and the sowing of the millet; i.e. between the reaping and sowing of the millet crop, except whilst the rice harvest is in progress.) The grave of a Kemovo is particularly sacred, and is only disturbed with extreme reluctance, at any rate in the case of the original founder of a village. There is no particular orientation of the dead, but if two persons are buried at the same time and place they are given the same orientation.

"In the case of persons killed in war, or whose bodies are for some similar reason not recoverable, a wooden image is made of the wood called '*hetho*' and, if obtainable, a piece of the deceased's hair affixed to the head. This is substituted for the real corpse and the ceremonies performed as usual.

"Persons killed by wild animals, or dying in childbirth, and suicides are not allowed to be buried within the precincts of the village, but the rites are the same subject to the proviso that the flesh of the cattle killed at the funeral and the beads worn by the dead may be taken only by the old man who buries the body, and may not be sold in the village, while the flesh is *kenna* to all young men. Such a death is called '*sesho*' and the victim of it '*seshoma.*' Death by a fall from or by the fall of a tree is regarded as akin to *sesho,* but though some extra ceremony is performed, the ordinary ceremonies are not affected as in the case of a gunuine *seshoma.* Suicide, it may be noted, is not common. The writer has only heard of three cases among the Angamis. (I have also known of one case among the Aos, a man who tried to spear himself, according to his own account, at the dictation of an evil spirit, but this man seemed to be more or less demented; and of one case of a Kacha Naga who hanged himself in the jungle, under the impression that he had killed a man, though in point of fact the man was only severely wounded and recovered. I have heard of other Nagas hanging themselves, and suicides by Lhotas are more frequent. I knew of one who speared himself after committing a murder, and of several cases of persons taking poison. The Lhotas know of the bitter root of a creeper which can be mixed with liquor. This is drunk in some quantity and intoxication ensues, followed by death while in that state. Lovers who for some reason cannot marry each other not infrequently make use of this way out of their troubles.) One of these was the result of debt. A man of the Semoma clan of Khonoma, being heavily in debt, bequeathed his terraced fields to his sister, dined unusually well, and went off saying that he was going to work on the railway. Next day he shot himself. He is said to have made himself more or less drunk before he actually did the deed. The second case was that of a man of Chephama who committed suicide by poisoning himself with the herb *'kwethi.'* The third was in Viswema, where a man hanged himself in June 1918. Mourning is observed by the deceased's near relatives not wearing ceremonial dress should a genna involving its use occur shortly after the death." adds Mr. Hutton. The custom is pertinent to the Angami Nagas of Nagaland.

Carriers of Coffin Living in Deceased's House

On death mourners gather at the dead man's house and bring along with them small load of firewood. If the deceased is male a *dao* is placed in his right hand and then the body covered with cloth. The blanket or bed sheet used by the deceased serves the purpose of shroud. Arrows are shot at regular intervals in all directions within the house to keep spirits of departed ancestors at bay who call on the spirit of the deceased. The family members prepare beer and rice bread in the night and all take food. The custom is called *uram dokke.* A wooden plate or metallic bowl is continuously beaten with a stick near the deceased's head by a mourner in the family till body is taken for burial. It is said that the noise made from beating of bowl would not allow the *olo* spirit from snatching the eyes of the dead. This beating is conducted by the family member assigned with the duties to carry the dead for burial. The corpse is buried along with his belongings such as utensils, and other articles used by him.

The persons who helped in digging the grave and carrying the coffin remain under a taboo and do not go out from the house of the deceased for five days. The family members also observes certain pollution related taboos such as abstaining from cultivation work for ten days. The family members would abstain from eating certain food items such as sweet potatoes, ginger, garlic, onions, gourd etc.

In case of accidental death outside the village the bodies are not brought at home instead buried at the site of the accident or in the forest away from the village. The Pailibo perform numerous rites and ceremonies associated with various economic, social, religious and domestic occasions. Among them, *Sobo Panan* is considered to be of immense importance. The family performing it spends considerable wealth, because it is believed that such ceremony brings emancipation of soul and helps in its movement straight to the land of departed ancestors. The ceremony of *Sobo-panan* or *mithun* sacrifice requires a number of *mithun,* pig, fowls, large quantity of maize, millet and rice in advance. In such ceremonial feast, the whole tribe in the village is invited to participate. The custom is related to the Pailibo sub-tribe of the Adis in Arunachal Pradesh.

Burying the Dead Close to House

About the funeral customs of Naga tribes of Manipur, Mr. TC Hadson writes, "All these tribes bury their dead... the custom of placing the heads of enemies may be a ceremonial survival of the practice common in other parts of this area of tree-burial. So far as my information goes, Jessami is the only village where the dead are regularly buried outside the village; although young children are there buried in front of the house. The Tangkhuls possess family vaults. Of the Kabuis Colonel McCulloch remarked that 'The village and its immediate precints form their graveyard and when for a time, from whatever cause, they have been obliged to desert their village, I have heard them more often express their wish to return to it as being the grave of their ancestors than as being their own birthplace.'

"But not all the dead are buried inside the village or in the usual burying place. In the first place the children of tender years who die before they are weaned are often not buried in the ordinary grave but close to the house. In the second place, those that die outside the village must as a general rule be buried outside the village, though there is either a ceremonial burial in the usual place or the burial of some part of the remains or belongings of the deceased. Mr. Pettigrew of the American Baptist Missionary Union, who has for many years enjoyed remarkable facilities for studying the customs of the Tangkhuls, states that 'in any case where the person dies away from home and where there is a difficulty in getting back—crossing a river, for instance—the person is buried near the place of death but the skull is brought to the village... On burying the skull they cover it with a black cloth, and in place of the trunk left behind a piece of wood, generally the wooden pillow of the deceased, is attached to the skull, and covered also with a piece of cloth, to represent the whole person.' (*J.A.S.B.* (N.S.), Vol. V, No. 2, 1909, p. 37). In the third place, under the influence of eschatological belief, the dead who die by violence, who are killed in war, whose death might, as we should say, argue a visitation of God, such as death by snake-bite, by drowning, by a fall from a tree, by a tiger in the jungle, or women who die in childbirth, are buried apart from the generality of the village. At Uilong a man killed in war is buried outside the village on the side of the village opposite to that on which live the enemies who inflict the fatal wound. Among the Quoirengs and Kabuis a woman who dies in childbirth is buried inside the house. The Quoirengs in such cases bury all the moveable articles and utensils in the house, while the Kabuis abandon the house and its contents completely. In the Kabui settlements in the valley of Manipur it is usual to carry the body out by the small door at the side of the house, or even through a special aperture cut for the purpose and then closed, and to bury it close to the house, within, so I understand, the limits of the shadow cast by the noontide sun.

"Among the Tangkhuls 'the dead are buried outside their houses to the depth of the length of the corpse, plus a margin for top dressing of stones, etc. Where there are no family graves near the house, other graves can be opened if there has been no burial during the past year. But before doing so a sort of ceremony has to be gone through with the bones of the departed. Some years ago one man of the village was set apart for this particular work, but now the custom is for each family to attend to same. On opening this family grave the bones are collected, cleaned with water, and then wrapped in a large cloth, new or old, and put on one side of the grave. When a great number of bones are collected and there is not sufficient room for a fresh corpse, they are taken out of the tomb; and when the fresh corpse has been buried and covered to the depth of a few feet, the bones are thrown in to help fill up the grave. The bottom of the grave is made circular to hold the corpse and the things buried with it. (Pettigrew, op. cit. p. 37) "Among the Kabuis 'the grave is thus prepared,' says Dr. Brown. (Op. *cit.* p. 106) 'A trench is first made and at right angles to this the ground is excavated and a recess made into which the coffin is inserted, the earth being afterwards filled in : this grave is used again and again before a new one is opened... A stone either flat or upright, resembling those so common in the Cossiah Hills, is placed over the grave... Amongst some of the Kowpoees the side of a hill is excavated for the reception of the coffin, and the vault filled and closed with earth and stones.'

"In ordinary cases of death, as we should classify them, the grave is dug by the Tangkhuls, at Maram by friends, among the Quoirengs by young male friends, as is also the practice among the Kabuis, (The grave is dug by those connected with the family by marriage with its females, McCulloch, *op. cit.* p. 52) while custom among the Marrings imposes this task upon the relatives of the family by marriage. In cases of extraordinary death among the Tangkhuls only the immediate relations dig the grave. Among the Quoirengs when a woman dies in childbirth, either women past the age of childbearing dig it or it is begun by old men past child-begetting age and is finished by the young men. The Kabuis assign this duty to the immediate male relations of the woman. The Chirus' custom is for the elders to dig the grave in all cases of mysterious death, and for childless old men to dig the graves of women dying in childbirth. Among the Marrings it is a general task in which every household participates.

"Burial takes place, as a rule, on the day following death except in the cases where children die or where death occurs before sunrise.

"In the graves are placed various articles for the use and comfort of the deceased in the world hereafter. Cloths, spears, daos, sometimes as at Maram the ornaments, the shield, the drinking cup and supplies of food and drink are buried with the men. The Tangkhuls bury two old and torn cloths with a man for his own use and a new untorn cloth as a present for the Deity of Heaven. Tobacco and a pipe are laid near at hand. In the grave of a woman are placed food and drink, her tail of false hair, her cooking pots, (*Cf.* Brown, *op. cit.* p. 106.) her digging stick and the brow-band which in life she used to carry loads from the fields. (This is not an apt comparison, the Khasi monuments being cenotaphs – P.R.G.) Among the Tangkhuls in the grave of a man whose parents have predeceased him it is customary to place food and drink as gifts for his relations. If a man dies of tiger bite, they put a bugle in his grave to scare away the tigers on the road to heaven. They also bury a thorn, or sharpened stake, rough and ready but useful weapons. Sometimes they provide a well-sharpened spear and kill a dog to keep him company on his long road. Over the body they play the bugle before burial. At Jessami they never kill an animal for a man who has met this death. At Maikel they put nothing in the grave, not even a cloth. At Maram they bury the body without a plank but put a white cloth on it and place a thorn and spear in the grave. No animals are killed.

"The Quoirengs wait for five days, and then in such cases kill a dog and a pig. In ordinary cases of death these animals are killed on the day of the burial. The Kabuis seem to leave them without weapons, although wrapping the corpse in the usual cloths.

"The detailed account given by Mr. Pettigrew of the burial ceremony practised by the Tangkhuls noteworthy :

"On the day of burial the rich kill a buffalo, others manage a cow, or a pig. They are killed before the grave is dug, and are left whole until the grave is finished. It is then cut up, the relations take half, and the grave-diggers the other half of the intestines. The head is taken always by the nearest male relative, the right hind leg is given to the eldest daughter, the left hind leg to the next daughter. If no daughters of their own, the nieces receive them. The forelegs are given to other distant female relatives. The heart, liver, kidneys, spleen, lungs, etc., are then handed to the 'Sherra,' the village priest. He first of all divides these portions up, six portions for a male and five for a female, and takes them to the next door neighbour's house and cooks same. He then brings them to the deceased's house and places them on top of the rice and vegetables which the relatives have brought in during the morning, and placed near the head of the corpse. His next duty is to offer up this food to the 'kameo' (evil spirit) by reciting this refrain : 'Thisan yamsanrava, shaiphung shap phungda thulu,' and calling upon the dead to eat this offering, takes the special portions on a plate of his own, and throws it away in the compound, where the dead's spirit and the 'kameo' are supposed to have appropriated it before touching the ground. The dogs, however, have a meal afterwards. Beer is also offered, and a small portion thrown away. After this ceremony of the priest, the rest of the meat and rice is divided amongst all and eaten before the burial. It is interesting to note here, that no matter what is killed in the village, or at whatever time, feast or otherwise, it is always offered to the 'kameo' before eating. The next act is for the 'sherra' to take the length and breadth of the bier, and if found too large for the grave, he alone is supposed to cut off any portion necessary. The bier is simply a plank of wood which lies outside ready. The body is then covered over with a clean white cloth before taking it out of the house. In the meantime one of the relations takes a pine torch from a house nearby, and descends into the grave, and twirling it round beseeches the ancestors of the dead to come and meet him on his way to 'Kazairam.' O awo ayi! ishava rarali, ungngaroklu' is the prayer made. Then after the 'sherra,' according to custom, has slightly raised the head of the bier the relations carry it out, and put it on the plank of wood, and on top of same whatever cloths are to be taken to 'Kazairam.' The top cloth is never torn, as it is meant for Kokto when they meet him. Then the hands of the corpse are washed with water. The bier is lifted by the palms of the hands and taken to the side of the grave. If lifted otherwise the relations will get ill. All the relations now gather round and make great lamentation, and tramp around the grave two or three times. After a final burst of the mourners' refrain by one of the old braves of the village, those who wish to stay and mourn stay on, and the rest leave. Then tightly fastening the body to the plank, it is placed, with all the gifts for the journey mentioned above, in the grave. The wife is allowed to enter and remain till the last moment. Then around and over the body, to prevent any earth from touching it, is built a stone wall. After filling up with earth the 'sherra' is again called to place a pole above the mound, while others place six prongs of wood around a small hole made in the mound, wherein is placed a pine torch. On lighting this they all leave the grave and enter the house. Here all fires have been put out, and all ashes cleared, and on their entering, fresh fire is brought from another house near by. Around this fire the family sit and wait for any sign in the fire-place, such as the print of a foot, to see if there are any more deaths to be expected. If there are none it is a favourable sign fortunately. As a final wind-up for the night, the relations' portion of meat is cooked and partly eaten, along with the rice and vegetables left over from the morning's feast. At the same time, small portions in six or five pieces, with a small quantity of beer, is offered to 'kameo' near the bed of the deceased by the nearest relation. Next morning and evening the pine torch on the grave is again lighted. This is continued for three days. The spirit, after it has had its interview with Kokto, and has handed over the gifts taken with it to the ancestors, is supposed to return the following day after burial. For this reason the family keeps all doors open from morning to night, and from that day until the final disposal of the spirit from the village at the great feast of 'Kathi Kasham,' the family prepare with their own meals a similar one for the spirit. It is then put into a plate used when alive by the deceased, and put on his or her own seat. This is done twice a day. After ten days or a month the parents if a child has died, the wife if a husband, or vice versa, search the village for a person as like as possible in features and size as the deceased to be their representative at the ceremonies of the great feast." (*op. cit.* p. 38)

"We have the authority of Dr. Brown for the statement that 'on the death of a warrior his nearest relation takes as spear and wounds the corpse by a blow with it on the head so that on his arrival in the next world he may be known and received with distinction." (*op. cit.* p. 121)

"But the obsequies are not really completed till the spirits of the deceased have been laid to rest finally and for ever by a second rite in which the community as a whole takes part. This rite is known to the Meitheis under the name Mangla tha or month belonging to the ghosts. It may be a form of ancestor worship, although celebrated only on behalf and in respect of the recent dead. It seems that they exclude from its purview those who have died by violence, as their deaths involve the whole village in a genna. At Mao it is usual to have a village genna whenever anyone dies and perhaps as a consequence of this there is there no such secondary funeral ceremony. This rite, which is held after the crops are gathered in, consists among the Tangkhuls of two parts, the 'Wonyai thing ceremony and the Kathi kasham ceremony which are thus described by Mr. Pettigrew :

"*The 'Wonyai thing' ceremony*—After the harvest in December has been gathered in, and all instruments in connection with same have been put on one side, in the evening the rich kill a cow, the rest pigs and dogs, and for those whose children have died, eggs are boiled. After cooking same the 'sherra' is called in as usual and offers up small portions to 'kameo.' Next morning the 'sherras' from each section of the village gather together in a compound and receive from the relations of the dead special portions of the meat killed the night before, and rice beer. On finding out the number of persons who died during the past year in each section, the plates and cups of each deceased are brought to them thoroughly cleaned and put in a row before them. In these plates, etc., are placed the meat and beer. On one side the 'sherras' tear off small portions, and arrange three small heaps of same. After all is divided out they take these portions as well as the beer and offer again to 'kameo' up and down the rows of plates. After this performance whatever is left they eat, and the plates, etc., are taken back to their respective houses. This being done all friends who come forward to help in erecting the 'wonyai thing' are counted, and to them a liberal supply of meat and beer is distributed. They then go off and bring in the wood and rope necessary to erect this structure. It is a lightly made structure, built outside the door of each deceased's house, and is shaped like a shield with a sort of small platform in front, on which the following day are placed various articles, such as Indian corn, roots, pumpkins, etc. The shield framework is covered with sheaves of rice corn, and so arranged that the birds cannot eat same. At the side of this structure is also placed a large clump of the orchid '*Cymbidium giganteum.*' All these articles are said to be for the departed spirit to show, as a sign, the fruits of the earth received during the past year. After four or five days friends from other houses and other villages who have not had any deaths during the past year present rice and beer to the mourners, and portions of same are first placed in the deceased's plate, etc., at evening. If this is not done by the friends it is feared it will be their share to receive death in their midst the following year." (*op. cit.* p. 41)

Stating about the *'Kathi Kasham' Feast,* Mr. Hodson writes, thus, "This takes place about the end of January of each year. The first thing for each family to do is to procure their buffaloes, cows, pigs, and dogs. After they have procured these from near and far, the headmen of the village give orders for the beer, weak and strong, to be prepared for fermentation, and they also, after a palaver, decide what day the feast shall commence. It is a ten-day feast, and I give below particulars of each day's work.

"*First day*—The rope for binding up the animals before killing is procured from the jungle, also the poles for hanging cloths up (see fifth day).

"*Second day*—These ropes are prepared so as to withstand any strain by the animals when being killed. This work of the first and second day is performed by the males, the women, in the meantime, gathering and stacking wood in each house.

"*Third day*—This is the day for killing buffaloes and cows. Their mode of killing is very cruel, and would not be tolerated for a moment in any civilised state. In the more northern villages the poor animals are tied down and subjected to much torture, the animal being cut to pieces piecemeal with knives and spears, and no attempt made to end its life before almost the last shred of flesh has been torn away and the limbs torn from their sockets. It is considered quite a sight, and crowds gather round, and even sit on the house-tops, and gaze on this horrible butcher's work. After the cutting-up process in the whole village is over, the division and distribution take place in the same way as performed on the death of the person and of course the 'sherra' is called in to offer to 'kameo.'

"*Fourth day*—Both males and females join together in getting in a plentiful supply of wood; and as there is much entertaining during this feast, and all night signing and dancing performed, there is need of plenty of fires, it being the coldest part of the year. The representative of the dead finds his first occupation on this day by collecting khamuina,' a kind of broad plantain leaf used for the unleavened bread made the next day.

"*Fifth day*—Unleavened bread is made into small cakes, and pigs and dogs killed, cut up into small pieces, cooked and offered to 'kameo' and then distributed with a small cake of bread wrapped in the 'khamuina' leaves amongst the mourners in each section of the village. On this day also cloths of all kinds and qualities are attached to long poles and erected outside each house of the dead. The more cloths displayed the greater one is thought of.

"*Sixth day*—This is occupied in preparing the rice beer which has been fermenting for some days in large casks, and any other work not finished on previous days is completed.

"*Seventh day*—This is the day when the real excitement commences. Friends and relations from villages around come in during the afternoon, and at sunset. Before their arrival the females only give an offering to 'kameo' in the shape of a sandwich of unleavened bread, sesamum seed concoction, and slices of pork, which after being offered to 'kameo' by the 'serra' is placed on the platform of the 'wonyali thing'. With this is also placed four pots of beer (weak and strong). After the arrival of villagers each family of the dead calls for its representative or 'thila kapo' as he is called. He in the meantime has been decked with bright head-gear, necklaces, armlets, and leglets. On his arrival at the house he performs a dance outside, and then on entering is introduced to the seat of the dead. From this point until the end of the feast he is looked upon as the dead person in life, and just as we would treat a friend or relation who was going on a long journey, with no prospect of seeing him again, so is this 'thila kapo' looked upon by the family and treated accordingly. He is presented with all the food cooked, and as the head of the house for the time being dispenses hospitality. On this evening in particular there are high jinks performed in each house. What with eating, drinking, and dancing, I am afraid they think more of their own enjoyment than of the dead. Before the day is over the cloths hung upon poles in each compound, after having been seen and admired, or otherwise, by the villagers, are taken down and brought into the house to be given to the representative later on.

"*Eighth day*—This day is mostly taken up with commercial pursuits, in the buying and selling of cloths, etc., brought in by the villagers. The representatives of the dead also give the villagers a specimen of their dancing powers in the large space called 'Laingapha kayang' situated in the midst of the village.

They are, of course, dressed up for the occasion. The 'sherras' during this performance cut up a portion of the skins of the pigs killed on the fifty day and offer to 'kameo.' The remaining skin of all the animals killed is eventually cooked and eaten with the other portions. After this exhibition by the 'thila kapo' they are taken and fed by the female relations, going from house to house, receiving the cloths brought in the previous night, so that by the time he has finished visiting there is a goodly pile, and he takes the first opportunity to sell all he does not require for himself, or for herself, if the representative happens to be a female.

"*Ninth day*—The great day of the feast. The first thing in the morning one of the family searches for plantain leaves to cover the pine torch handles etc. These torches are made extra large, and laid aside for use at sunset. A further dish of pig's meat and rice is next prepared and placed on large plates, with salt and fish, and brought on the compound. Next a great gathering of all friends and relations with each representative. They meet at the lowest point of the village where a death has occurred, each one carrying his or her load of meat, ginger, rice beer, and cloths already given to the representative. These are all placed on mats in a row. Empty plates and pots are placed in a row near, and are then filled up. Everybody is dressed up for the occasion, especially the representatives. When all is ready some old priest of the village gives a great shout, 'He hiaina tatang tarangsa,' and at this everybody suddenly takes hold of the plates and pots, etc., and holding them up above their heads, take all to the 'thila kapos' houses. They are supposed to have another meal here, but as it is a question of eating and drinking all day long, they, if they are not gluttonous, content themselves with a small portion. They now take the place of receiving guests, friends, and relations who wish to say farewell, as they are now on the point of leaving for good. First to receive a parting gift is the head of the deceased's house, who receives a cloth from the 'thila kapo.' Then come along the widows of the village, but instead of giving anything they receive a parting gift of meat and beer from him or her. After the widows come the female relations who entertained them the day before, and they also receive a present of meat and beer—a sort of mutual give and take before the final parting. It is sunset now, and a procession is formed. At the head of the same march the torch-bearers, with the leaves gathered early in the morning would round their heads and shoulders to keep off sparks from the flaming torches. Behind these march a crowd of elders dressed in their war garb, and lastly the 'thila kapo,' the representative of the dead, follow with relations crowding around them, and with much lamenting and grief the procession proceeds slowly on its way towards 'Zaiphar,' a spot at the north end of the village overshadowed by a large tree. To this spot the torch-bearers wend their way. The idea is that the spirits need to be led in the gathering twilight to show them the way to their final place of abode, 'Kazairam,' and the warriors are also needed as a guard to keep them from all harm on their way there. The spirit is supposed to enter into, or rather turned into these lighted torches as soon as they are thrown down at 'Zaiphar.' By the time these torches have reached this place, the 'thila kapo' have reached the limit of the village boundary, and on the supposition that the spirit has left to proceed on its way as a torch to 'Kazairam,' these representatives are at once denuded of all their finery. The head-gear is broken up on the spot, and as far as these individuals are concerned, their representative work is over. All the villagers return to their homes, the torch-bearers having already returned by another route. Before entering their houses, the 'wonyai thing' structure erected outside is pulled down, and the poles over the grave are pulled out and thrown away. At the front door, just inside the house, a pine torch is lighted and placed on a stone. This is done for the purpose of not allowing the spirits of the living to go off with the spirits of the dead just got rid of.

"The spirits after entering the torches are declared to wend their way during the evening towards the hills on the north, and finally disappear to find themselves crossing the river in 'Kazairam.' On that side of the river they are believed to commence and carry on an existence similar to that enjoyed, or, otherwise, when alive on earth. The wealthy enjoy their wealth again, and the poor eke out the precarious existence suffered on earth.

"*Tenth day*—This and the following few days are practically days of rest, and the only thing recognised is the supposition that the embodied spirits in 'Kazairam' cut all their hair off on the tenth day, and have a sort of 'wash and brush' up to remove all connection with mother earth. On this day, therefore, no one is supposed to bathe or touch water.

'I was informed by Manipuris that the Tangkhuls used to throw cloths away on these occasions which Manipuris collected and sold, thus exploiting the piety of the hillmen.

"In December, 1900, I witnessed a similar ceremony at the Quoireng village Lemta, and noted the events of the day as they passed before my eyes. The young bachelors, the youths from twelve to fifteen years of age, assumed their best attire and paraded outside the village. Most of them smeared their legs with white earth and made a criss-cross pattern on them. A few of them decorated themselves with a quaint picturesque head-dress which resembled the glory worn by Saints in medieval art. The lads all assembled outside the village carrying spears. As they entered at the lower gate, they commenced to sing. No sooner had the procession entered the village then the women began to wail and lament. Each woman lit two torches over the graves in front of the houses. As the procession passed them, they poured water from a bamboo chunga over one torch and threw the other away into the jungle. The empty bamboo chunga was also thrown on to the grave. The women then joined the procession and accompanied it to the other gate of the village. They stayed inside and the lads then finished their performance outside. They formed up into two lines moving one inside the other in opposite directions, singing all the while and then gathered to the centre and all shouted together to complete this part of the ceremony. They then indulged in sports, a long jump being the first event. All jumped one after another in rapid succession and then the village champions tried their skill. After that they 'put' the stone and set the younger lads to wrestle. By this time it was near sunset and they re-entered the village. Not a stroke of work was done during the day. The rice was pounded over-night. No woman or married man may leave the village from sunrise to the following sunrise. I noticed that the women when following the procession carried their best cloths on their arm, perhaps as a precaution. In prepartion for the ceremony they had erected a palisade of forked white carefully peeled sticks from ten to twelve feet high. On it hung imitation bears' beads with tusks of wood. There were semblances of men's heads fashioned from gourds, and swinging high above all from a long pole was a buffalo's head and horns." adds Mr. Hodson in his book *The Naga Tribes of Manipur*, (pp. 146–158)

Dying in Sitting Posture

Dwelling on the burial custom practised by the Lakher tribals of Assam Mr. N.E. Parry notes, "When a Lakher is ill he is taken off the bed and laid on the middle of the floor, and his friends and relations who are looking after him sit around him. The floor is preferred to the bed, as it is much lighter, and it is easier both for the sick man and for the people who are looking after him to see. When the sick man appears to be dying he is raised up into a sitting position and held there by his relations until he draws his last breath. It is considered better that a man should die in the arms of his relations than lying flat on the floor. As soon as death has taken place, if there is a gun in the house it is fired off, so that the dead man's spirit may take the spirit of a gun with it to *Atikhi,* and also that the villagers may know that the sick man has departed. After this the body is washed with warm water by some close relation, the hair is greased and properly tied, and the body is fully dressed as in life—if deceased was a man, with a loin cloth, a body cloth and a *puggree,* and if a woman, with all her best cloths. Two bamboos are placed sloping-wise against the wall at the back of the house, and a mat is placed across these bamboos, and the body is laid on the mat in a reclining position, with its feet on the floor. Against the wall above the dead man's head a small shelf is erected, on which rice and cooked eggs are placed for the spirit to eat. Special care is taken to see that flies do not settle on the body, as it is very disgraceful if they do so. A wake is held, which is attended by all the deceased's friends, who bring *sahma* beer, which on this occasion only is known as *bupa,* and *mithun,* pigs, or whatever animals may be available are killed as *riha* to accompany the spirit to *Athikhi.* The deceased's *pupa,* who is entitled to the deceased's *ru* or death due, must also kill a pig. Usually the body is kept in the house for two or three days, and on each day a little rice, meat and *sahma* are placed in deceased's mouth. Meanwhile the wake goes on, and a feast is held off the meat of the animals killed to go with the deceased to *Athikhi. Sahma* and rice are contributed by the deceased's friends, and dancing to the beating of drums and gongs goes on all the time. This feast is intended to make the deceased's spirit go off happily to *Athikhi.* During the wake, which is called *rikia,* the deceased's *pupa,* who is his maternal uncle, stands on the verandah; and, facing towards the dead body, calls out the name of the dead man and the names of his ancestors, in order to let the spirits in *Athikhi* know who is coming, and cries out, 'Go to Athikhi happily : do not worry about your relations.' Next the deceased's *pupa* makes cuts on the beams and doorways of the house with a *dao.* This is done to frighten the *Chhongchhongpipa,* who stands on the road to *Athikhi* and waylays all spirits, so as to make him allow the deceased's spirit to go to *Athikhi.* Having done this, the deceased's *pupa* dances round inside the house three times, and is followed by all the persons present in turn, one man dancing round at a time, followed by two women. The object of the dance is to please the deceased's ghost. At this dance beer is provided by the deceased's family and relations. Each trio dances round three times, and at the end of each round all stamp with their feet on the ground to show that the dance is ended. When the husband of a pregnant woman dances, he must not stamp with his feet at the end of the dance, or he will trample on the spirit of his unborn child. The old men chant a song without words, called the *athihla,* intoning, *A-ah E-eh A-eh E-eh.* Meanwhile the feast goes on; the women are served by women and the men by men, the young men who have been digging the grave being served last. On the day fixed for the burial the deceased's *pupa* comes and stands on the verandah of the deceased's house and sends an envoy (*leuchapa*) into the house to claim the *athiawrua,* which consists of a pig, and the *athiawruabawna,* which consists of 5 rupees. The deceased's relations then kill a pig and make it over with 5 rupees and a dao to his *pupa.* This is preliminary to claiming the death due, which is not demanded till later.

"Burials always take place in the evening, and before the corpse is taken out of the house the deceased's *pupa* again makes cuts on the beams and doorways as before. The grave is dug by the young men of the village, whether they belong to the deceased's clan or not, in front of the deceased's house or in the village street, except among the Sabeus of Chapi, Chakang and some Haka villages, who have cemeteries outside the village. The *pupa* first goes to the grave and climbs down into it; after him follow the young men carrying the body dressed in the cloths it was laid out in and wrapped in a blue cloth, and then come the deceased's relations. The body is laid on the edge of the grave, the deceased's wife or husband, as the case may be, taps the body gently with his hands and says, 'Do not worry about me; go off happily to *Athikhi,'* and places a little *sahma* in the deceased's mouth. The young men lift the corpse into the grave. If guns are available they are fired off, so that the dead man may take them with him to *Athikhi,* and the *pupa* lays down the corpse, pushes it feet first into the alcove hollowed out for it at one end of the grave, and closes the alcove with a stone. The *pupa* climbs out of the grave and goes off home. The young men fill in the grave and lay a flat stone along the top of it, on which to place a small portion of all the component parts of the morning meal, which is done every day until the memorial stone has been erected. A forked post is planted on the grave, on which are hung plantains, sugar-cane, limes and any other fruits that are available, and a gourd of nicotine-water is placed on the stone. Another straight post is erected on the grave, to which the heads of the animals killed for *riha* are attached. Some people, instead of placing the food for the spirit on the stone above the grave, place it in a pot which is kept for the purpose above the hearth.

"The dead man's relations now return home, and as they enter the verandah each steps on to a sieve containing a little rice, which has been placed ready for the purpose, and goes on into the house. This is to show that the soul of the dead has gone to *Athikhi,* and that his relations are again clean, rice being an emblem of purity. That evening the *pupa's* wife brings a fowl and some *sahmahei* (fermented rice), and sacrifices the fowl, to console the souls of the surviving members of the deceased's family, and anoints the big toe of each with the fowl's blood; she then gives each of them a little *sahmahei* to eat and returns home. This ceremony is called *Thlathleu,* and is an important sacrifice, as it is essential that the souls of the deceased's family should be at peace, as if any member of it sees any one in his dreams on the night of funeral, the person dreamed of will soon die also. The belief is that on the night of the funeral the spirit of the deceased comes to visit his family, and if they are dreaming of any one, the deceased's spirit meets the spirit of the person dreamed of and seizes it and carries it off with him to *Athikhi.*

"On the morning after the funeral one of the neighbours always asks the deceased's relatives whether they had any dreams during the night or not; if the answer is 'No', all is well, but if one of the family dreamt of any one that night, he must say so, as it is very unlucky for the person dreamt of. If the dream was that the dead man appeared again alive in the house, it means that another member of the family will die.

"A further precaution is often taken to prevent the deceased's relations or other villagers from dreaming on the night of the funeral. Each householder, before going to sleep, puts a little cooked rice into a pot, and each member of the household says, 'May my spirit not wander about to-night, let it remain within this pot'; having said this, each person puts his hand inside the pot, and touches the rice. By this means the spirits are kept imprisoned inside the pots, and as they cannot wander about and meet other people's spirits, the owners of the imprisoned spirits do not dream of any one that night, and so cause no one any harm. Another way of preventing the soul from escaping from its owner's house is to place a paddy pestle across the door, as the soul will fear to go under it, lest the pestle should fall on it.

"In Tisi, to prevent the deceased's spirit from re-entering his house on the night of the funeral, a hen is taken and some of its feathers are cut off while standing on the ladder leading into the house. The feathers fall on each side of the ladder, and act as a barrier which the spirit cannot cross. The cutting off of the feathers of a live hen is symbolical of the final separation of the spirit from its relations. The hen is not sacrificed, but is released after its feathers have been cut. I have found this ceremony only in Tisi; it is called *Awhhmichaikha,* and is to show the dead man's spirit that if it returns they will cut it in the same way as they cut the hen's feathers.

"When a death has taken place in a village, all the people are very afraid lest the spirit of the dead should enter their houses at night and do them harm. To prevent this each householder places his paddy pestle across the doorway. When the dead person's spirit comes along, it sees what it thinks is a huge snake, and retreats in terror. More intelligent spirits are said to recognise the pestle, but, fearing that it might fall and crush them if they attempt to enter, return whence they came.

"After the funeral all fires in the deceased's house must be quenched and fresh fire must be kindled. The old fire, having been used for cooking the meats for the funeral feast and for all kinds of purposes during the lifetime of the deceased, is held to be defiled. If new fire were not made, the *Khazangpiya* and *Zangda* sacrifices would be of no avail. *Khanzangpa* and *Zang* would know at once that the sacrifice had been cooked on an impure fire, and would get angry, and the sacrifice would do more harm than good. It is therefore *ana* to use fire on which funeral meats have been cooked for *Khazangpina* and *Zangda,* and new fire must be made immediately after a funeral. (Among the Tangkuls also all fires are put out after a funeral and fresh fires are kindled. *Cf.* Hodson, *op. cit.,* p. 151) The fowl sacrificed by the *pupa's* wife for *Thlatheu* is cooked on the new fire and eaten; no *phavaw* are set aside. All persons who have touched a corpse must cleanse themselves by washing their bodies with water and rice. Rice is the purest of all things, and removes the evil smell of the corpse and all other defilements. Unless this purificatory ceremony is performed a man must not touch his *anahmang,* the vessels dedicated to the service of *Khazangpa,* or they would be defiled, and *Khazangpa* would be annoyed and would wreck vengeance for the insult offered to him. It is *ana* to walk over a corpse. If any one does so, the spirit of the deceased removes the strength of the man crossing over his body and carries it off to *Athikhi.* People who disregard this prohibition become suddenly weak and feeble when on a journey, and are unable to proceed.

"The day after a funeral the deceased's family is said to be *sawpana.* This *pana* is strictly observed, as if it is disregarded the deceased's *saw* may cause misfortune or sickness to other members of the family. No member of the family may leave the village, no work may be done, and the women may neither spin nor weave. The day after this *sawpana* a bamboo fence is erected round the grave. If any of deceased's relations have been unable to attend the wake, they must come after the funeral and see the grave, and pour a little *sahma* on it, and must go and give the deceased's family *sahma* and condole with them. This is known as *Athiahmo.* If a deceased's *pupa* neither attends the wake nor visits his grave after the burial, the deceased's family will claim a *hmiatla* or atonement price of 2 or 3 rupees from him. When a Lakher attends the funeral of a friend or relation in another village, precautions are taken to ensure that he shall not carry home with him the spirit of the disease (*hri*) from which his relation died, and thereby infect himself and any of his fellow-villagers. Before leaving the lands of the village in which the funeral has taken place, a fire is kindled, and the visitors step over the fire. A disease-bearing spirit (*hri*) cannot pass over a fire, and so is unable to follow the visitors home. By this means the dangers involved in attending a funeral in another village can be averted.

"When a wealthy or an important man dies and a *mithun* or a cow is sacrificed for his *riha,* an additional ceremony, called *Rakhatla,* is performed while the body is in the house, and artificial flowers, called *tatangteuleupa,* are made out of small pieces of bamboo, which are placed crosswise one over the other and wound round and round with coloured threads. The Lusheis make similar flowers, which they call *lenglep* and use at the *Daibawl* sacrifice of a hen and a cock offered to a *ramhuai,* a spirit of the rivers or woods, when any one is ill, and hang them up over the place of sacrifice. *Lenglep* are not used by Lusheis at funerals. The *Rakhatla* is a peculiar dance, performed only on the occasion of funerals, and at no other time. A log is laid on the ground, and five people, men or women, sit opposite each other on each side of the log. Each person holds a bamboo in each hand, the other end of the bamboo being held by his *vis-a-vis.* The bamboos are struck against the log twice and then raised and struct against each other; the dancers have to skip in and out between the bamboos and avoid getting caught between the bamboo clappers, which requires a good deal of skill, the dance becoming faster and faster as it proceeds. The young men who dance wear their best cloths, and the first time they dance each carries a bag, a powder-flask and a gun; the girls each carry a new skirt, a new cloth, a man's loin-cloth, a new woman's coat and a bag. These articles are for the spirit of the deceased to take with him to *Athikhi.* The second time that each man and girl performs the dance, instead of the cloths he carries a tall bamboo from which all the leaves have been removed and replaced with *tatang-teuleupa.* This dance is performed each day that the body remains in the house. (A very similar dance to *Rakhatla* is performed by the Dyak women of Borneo, who dance between wooden paddy pestles clapped together by two other women, but the Dyaks do not seem to confine the dance to funerals. *Cf.* W.O. Krohn, *In Borneo Jungles,* pp. 210-211. Among the Haka Chins the dance is called *Rawkarrklak,* and is performed at *lam sher* (the death dance) when the ceremony is being held in honour of a woman. Only women take part in it. *Cf.* W.R. Head, *Haka Chin Customs*, p. 27) When the grave has been filled in, the bamboos with the *tatangteuleupa* are erected on it and the bamboos and log of wood used for the *Rakhatla* are thrown away outside the village. The Lushei *Cherokan* is danced in the same way by young men and girls, but purely for amusement, and without any religious significance. Instead of the log of wood in the middle and the bamboo clappers, the Lusheis use paddy pestles.

"Unnatural deaths are regarded as extremely unlucky, and are the occasion of special precautions designed to save other people from a similar fate. Any one who dies an unnatural death—being killed by a wild animal, drowned, killed by a fall from a tree or a precipice, killed in war or by a shooting accident—is known as a *sawvawpa.* A woman who dies in child-bed (*naweupasi*) is also said to be *sawvaw.* All *sawvaws* are *ana,* or unlucky, and when any one dies *sawvaw* there is a village *aoh* for from three to five days, starting on the day of the funeral, and neither men nor women may leave the village or do any work. (*Cf.* Hodson, *The Naga Tribes of Manipur,* p. 88) When a woman dies in child-bed (*naweupasi*), the women who go to draw water during the *aoh* must use men's carrying-bands for their water-tube baskets. The reason for this is that when a Lakher woman is giving birth to a child she holds on to the cane carrying-band of her water-tube basket, which is hung up on the beam above her, and the women fear that if they used their own head-bands during the *aoh* for a woman who died in child-bed they would suffer the same fate. The *aoh* for *naweupasi* applies to men as well as to women. The *aoh* for *sawvaw* is observed partly owing to sorrow for the deceased and sympathy for his relatives, and partly from fear that the same fate will befall others unless the *aoh* is observed.

"When the body of a man has died *sawvaw* is brought back to the village, it is wrapped up in bamboo matting and is left for one night outside the village fence, and the deceased's relations and friends light fires and watch the body all night. Next morning the body is brought into the village and laid in the verandah of deceased's house, but it does not sit in state. The body may not be taken inside the house, as it is believed to have a *saw,* or the property of causing sickness, and so if the body is taken inside the house the deceased's relations fear that they will suffer the same fate. A wake is held as usual, animals are killed to accompany the spirit to *Sawvawkhi,* and *sahma* is drunk, but there is no dancing. The body is buried outside the village to the west, so that the sun, as it sinks, may carry the evil away, and the funeral takes place before dawn by torch-light. The grave is dug differently from ordinary graves, and a *sawvawpa's pupa,* if he is living in another village, very often does not bother to come to bury him, as he will get no *ru.* (These customs approximate very closely to those of the Thado, *vide Notes on the Thado Kukis,* p. 56 n.) No memorial posts or stones are erected for a *sawvaw,* nor is any food for his spirit placed on the grave, but if an animal has been killed for *riha* its head is buried with the body. The spirits of people who have died unnatural deaths have a separate abode from ordinary spirits. They start along the ordinary road, but when they reach the *Chhongchhongpipa,* he stops them and turns them off by a branch road which leads to their special abode. If the parents of a *sawvawpa* are rich, when they die they can rescue his spirit and bring it to the abode of all normal spirits by paying a ransom to the *leurahripa* who caused his death. They cannot do this while alive, but only after death. In Chapi there are stricter prohibitions than in the other villages. The body is not taken even into the verandah, but is left at the foot of the ladder leading up to the house. Only members of the deceased's clan can touch the body or perform the funeral rites. Any one going to the wake must, if a man, empty the tobacco out of his pipe, and if a woman throw away the nicotine-water out of the bowl of her pipe before going home, lest the *sawvawpa's saw* should have got into the tobacco and should be carried home in it and cause illness. The body of a woman who has died in child-bed is never taken out of the house by the door, but through a hole cut in the back wall; this is done because, as the spirits of women who have died in child-bed do not follow the road taken by the spirits of those who have died natural deaths, but have to go by another path to the *Sawvawkhi,* it is considered that the body should not leave the house by the ordinary path, but should also take a different path to the grave. (*Sawvaw* and *thichhi may be compared with the Ao apotia* which covers botho these classes of deaths. *Cf.* Mills, *The Ao Nagas,* pp. 283 *et seq. Cf.* also J.H. Hutton, *The Sema Nagas,* p. 234. Semas take the body of a woman who died in childbirth out by the back door.) The Lushei *sarthi* is the same as *sawvaw,* but the Lusheis do not fear unnatural deaths to the same extent as Lakhers, and do not take so many precautions; but among them also no death due can be claimed for any one who has died *sarthi.*

"Among the Tlongsai, Zeuhnang and Hawthai a special hole is cut in the wall of the house leading on to the verandah, and the corpse of a woman who has died in child-birth is carried out through this hole instead of through the door, for the same reason. No *ru* can be claimed for any one dying *sawvaw,* and if a woman dies *sawvaw* the balance of her price cannot be claimed. Besides the *sawvawpa,* another class of unfortunates called *thichhi* are also condemned to go to the *Sawvawkhi.* Any one dying of dropsy, paralysis, owing to losing an arm or a leg, blind of both eyes, mad, or covered with sores due to leprosy, syphilis, or yaws is known as *thichhi.* The spirits of *thichhi* have a peculiar and unpleasant smell, which the ordinary spirits dislike, so the *Chhongchhongpipa* does not let them into *Athikhi.* No *ru* can be claimed from the heir of a person who has died *thichhi,* and if a woman dies *thichhi* the balance of her price cannot be claimed. As a matter of fact, no one would ever claim these dues on account of a *thichhi,* as it is *ana* to do so, and any one taking the dues would die or suffer great misfortunes. The corpse is buried in the same way as a *sawvaw,* but is never kept for more than one day.

If a man while on a journey dies in the house of any one belonging to a different clan, the man in whose house the death took place can claim a pig and a fowl from the deceased's relatives for a sacrifice to purify the house, which has been defiled by the death of a stranger and can also claim a fine, which varies in the different villages, but is usually an earthenware beer-pot (*racha*) or 10 rupees. The sacrifice is called *Angpataina.* (The Lusheis claim a due called *Insilman*=house-cleaning price, in similar circumstances. *Cf.* N.E. Parry, *Lushai Customs and Ceremonies,* p. 79. The Thado call it *inbo'man*=house-dirtying price.) The fowl is first killed, and thrown away towards the west outside the village fence, in the belief that the disease-bearing spirit (*hri*) which caused the death of the stranger will follow the chicken and disappear in the west. The pig is then killed and eaten. A little of the blood of the fowl and the pig is rubbed on the verandah and inside the house to purify it.

"A Lakher intensely dislikes a stranger dying in his house, and if a stranger falls ill in another's house, the owner of the house often causes the sick man to be carried outside when at the point of death to avoid the death taking place inside the house. Leichhia of Saiko went to Lungleh for work, on his way home he fell ill in Paitha, he grew rapidly worse, and when he seemed to be dying his friends carried him outside the house and laid him on the ground, where he died. They did this at the request of the host and also to save Leichhia's relations from having to pay a pig and a fowl as *Angpataina.*

"A young man of Bualpui while staying in the house of Hnangthlo of Saiko fell ill; before he died he was carried outside the house by his friends at the order of their chief Ngunlinga, who was with them. Ngunlinga and his villagers are Pois, but the Lakher and Poi customs in this respect are the same."

About The Graves, Mr. Parry Writes further,

"The Lakhers always bury their dead, and, so far as I can ascertain, there are no traces of either cremation or platform burial. Unlike the Lusheis, they never use coffins, the corpses being simply wrapped in a cloth. There are three kinds of graves. Chiefs and important persons generally have family vaults, which are called *thlapi* or *longang,* situated near the house. The Savang vault is in the chief's garden, between his house and hat of the dowager chieftainesses. The Saiko chief's vault is in front of the chief's house. *Longang* means literally 'stone house'.

"The Lakhers are not singular in liking to have their dead near them : in parts of Scotland I have noticed that a favourite burial-place is in the grounds not far from the house. This absence of dislike to the proximity of the dead seems to be common to many primitive races, certainly to those in the Assam hills. A vault is made by digging a pit about 6 feet deep, 8 feet long, and 6 feet wide. The floor, sides and roof are lined with stones; a small piece is left as a doorway and is closed with a large stone. When a vault has been made, a *mithun* must be killed for the *riha* of the first person buried in it, and after this all members of the family who die are laid to rest in the same vault. The Savang vault contains the remains of Keinang, Ngongthaw, Hmonglai, and Vachhong, the last four chiefs, and also of Keinang's wife, Nona and of Ngongthaw's wife, Nguhlia. The Saiko vault contains the bones of Theulai and his wife, and of Siatu's wife only, as Theulai's father was buried at Theiva. When a body is placed in a vault, valuable ornaments and guns are often deposited with it for the use of the spirit of the deceased in the next world, the articles selected being those that the dead man habitually used and liked. (The Haka Chins also do so. *Cf.* Carey and Tuck, *The Chin Hills,* p. 192) When Theulai of Saiko was buried, as he had been a great hunter and warrior in his youth, his spear, his sword and his *dao,* to which he was greatly attached, were buried with him. When a vault has to be opened to receive another inmate, this must be done by the sister or the sister's son of the person who is to be buried; if deceased had no sister, then his daughter or her son must open it. When she opens the vault this woman picks up the head and bones of the last person burried, wraps them in a cloth, and places them on one side of the vault; she then sweeps all the debris on the floor of the vault into one corner, and the corpse awaiting burial is placed inside by its *pupa* or his representative in the usual way.

"The woman who opens the vault is entitled to take all the articles buried with the last corpse; this is called *thupahama,* which means the price of touching the evil-smelling remains. When Vachhong, chief of Savang, died, many valuable ornaments and gongs that had been buried with his predecessor, Hmonglai, were taken by Ngongchia, mother of the Chapi chief, who was Vachhong's niece, and so opened the grave. These articles were thus all lost to the Bonghia family. When Theulai was buried, his sister Maicha opened the grave and took as *thupahama,* four metal belts which had been buried with Siatu's wife. The desecration of graves in order to steal the articles buried in them is quite unknown. It is very curious that articles of value buried in vaults should ultimately descend in the female line and so be lost to the family and clan that originally owned them, as this is the reverse of the ordinary Lakher custom of inheritance. It seems probable that this must have survived from a time when inheritance was matrilineal.

"On the day that a vault is opened the whole village is *pana* for a day, lest the paddy should rot in the same way as the corpses in the vault have rotted. This *pana* is known as *thlathupaheu.* Although Lewin states that a 'a chief or a woman of position is buried in a sitting posture, as among the Bunjoges,' (Lewin, *The Chittagong Hill Tracts and the Dwellers Therein,* p. 115.) I find that nowadays, at any rate, no Lakher is ever buried in any other way except lying straight out flat, and all those I have asked say that corpses never were buried in a sitting position. (Precisely the same information exists about the Thado. Brown, *Native State of Manipur,* p. 51, and *Annual Report of the Munnipore Political Agency,* 1868-69, p. 132, very definitely described the Thado as buried sitting, but the idea of such a practice is now scouted by men who might be expected to know. I think Brown's and Lewin's evidence too good to be rejected, and that the custom has changed since 1869, in which year Lewin also published the book referred to.) The corpse when it is lying in the house is in a reclining position, and it is possibly from this that Lewin got the idea that Lakhers were buried sitting. Their nearest relations, the Haka Chins, sit in state after death, like the Lakhers, and are also buried prostrate Carry & Tuck, *The Chin Hills*, p. 192). Another old authority, however, Sir Arthur Phayre, recording a report made to him by Lengkung, a Lungkhe chief, as regards Lungkhe and Tseindu customs, notes Lengkung as saying, 'We bury our dead; the corpse is placed in a sitting posture, with a pipe in its mouth, food by its side and *kung.'* (Phayre, "Account of Arakan," *J.A.S.B.,* 1841, No. 117, p. 709.) It would seem, therefore, that formerly either the Lakhers or one of the tribes allied to them must have buried their dead sitting, and that if the Lakhers did so, they have now entirely abandoned the practice. I am inclined to think, however, that this burial custom ascribed to the Shendus by Lewin and Phayre must have been followed by some other tribe, and not by the Lakhers, as no traces or traditions of burial in a sitting posture exist among them to-day.

"A commoner's grave is called *thlata,* and is generally dug in front of the deceased's house. A hole about 5 feet deep, 5 feet long, and 2.5 feet wide is first dug out; when this is complete, a narrow hole just large enough to hold the body is burrowed out at one end of the grave. When the burial takes place the body is lowered into the outer grave and then pushed feet first into the hole, which is closed with a large stone, the outer grave being filled in with earth. There is no particular mode of placing the corpse; the head may lie towards the north, south, east or west indiscriminately. The head is never disinterred and buried separately, and bamboo tubes are let down into the grave to let the soul escape. (As by, e.g., the Thado, where graves are made on the same plans but with the excavation, and therefore also the feet of the dead man, pointing northwards, except in the case of bad deaths, perhaps. I do not know on which side of the grave the Thados make their excavation in the latter case, but apart from orientation the plan is that shown by Mr. Parry for Lakher *Thlachhi.*)

"The grave of a person who has died an unnatural death is called *thlachhi,* and is always dug outside the village fence, on the west of the village, towards the setting sun. The grave is dug at first in the same way as a *thlatha,* but instead of the hole for the body being excavated at the end of the grave, it is excavated at one side; the body is placed in this alcove and kept in place by a log of wood or by bamboos. The grave is then filled up with earth. The head of the body may lie in any direction. The different construction of the graves of *sawvaw* and *thichhi* from those of persons dying a natural death is due to the fact that the spirits of these unfortunates go to a separate place.

"When a chief dies, the whole village goes into mourning and no music or merrymaking is allowed until heads, formerly human, now of animals only, have been taken for *machhipaina,* as has been explained elsewhere. Mourning for a commoner is less prolonged; the relatives generally go into mourning for two or three months, and during this period may not wash their bodies and may not put grease on their hair. (Haka Chins mourn in the same way. Cf. Head, *op. cit.* p. 26.) Until the memorial stone has been erected, food must be given to the spirit. A small portion of each daily meal is set aside and placed either near the hearth inside the house or else on the grave for the spirit to eat. Plantains, sugar-cane, nicotine-water and flour are also placed on the grave in case the spirit should have need of them in *Athikhi.* Lakhers worship their ancestors at *Laliachhia,* but these offerings are not at present, at any rate, of a propitiatory nature, but merely to meet the needs of the spirit. Whether or not they are a relic of ancestor-worship I am not prepared to say. As soon as the memorial stone has been erected, the offerings cease, as it is believed that after this the spirit goes off to *Athikhi* for good and does not return, and so will have no further use for food."

About the memorials, Mr. Parry writes, "The ceremonies held in connection with the erection of memorials are called *Athiteukhei,* which means 'sitting with the dead,' the idea being that on this occasion the dead man's spirit will visit its home for the last time before going off finally to the abode of the dead. There are several kinds of memorials. That ordinarily erected is a flat stone called *longphei,* and is always accompanied by a wooden memorial post called *thangri.* For chiefs and important persons pyramids called *phura pachang* and small stone walls called *longdong* are erected as well. If several memorials are prepared, they are all erected, or at any rate finished, on the day fixed for the *Athiteukhei* feast. For this all the deceased's relations and friends are invited. *Mithun* or pigs are killed, *sahma* is made, and a feast is prepared. Against the wall of the house which faces down the slope a tray is placed, covered with every sort of edible and drink; this is for the spirit of the deceased, who is supposed to come and sit with his friends and to partake of the good things provided. In the course of the day the memorials are finished, and then the women all have their feast inside the house and the men on the verandah. When the food is all consumed, the men join the women inside the house and they drink *sahma* together. In the evening after sunset all the edibles on the tray are collected in a small basket and hung on a forked stick planted on the grave near the *thangri;* this is to show the final separation of the dead man's spirit from the living. The next day the whole village holds an *aoh* called *Viachwpana;* no one may do any work, and the women may neither spin nor weave; it is believed that unless this *aoh* is observed, the dead man's spirit will carry off with it to *Athikhi* the spirits of rice and of all the other kinds of edibles and there will be a famine. The *aoh* need not be held on every occasion that a memorial post is erected, but only on the occasion of the erection of the first memorial post between the harvest and the burning of the new *jhums*. Memorials are erected by the deceased's heir. If the latter is very poor and cannot afford to pay for the sacrifice and feast required, a little of every kind of available edible is collected in a basket and hung up on a forked post over the grave.

"A *longphei* is a plain flat stone which is laid flat on the top of the grave, supported on all four sides by four stones of the same length planted on their sides. If at the funeral the *Rakhatla* dance was performed, it is repeated at the erection of the *longphei,* and if the ceremony is being held just before the *jhums* are burnt, it is customary to dance the *Pakhupila,* but not at any other season. On this same day the wooden memorial post called *thangri* is also erected over the grave. This post has to be prepared some days before the date fixed for its formal erection. A well-grown young *khaimei* tree (*Schima Wallich ii*) is cut down, the bark is all removed and it is roughly hewn into shape, so that the lower part of the post represents a body which is surmounted by a head. A man's *thangri* has no neck, the body runs straight up to the head; a woman's *thangri* has a sort of lozenge-shaped neck. The difference is clearly shown in the illustration. As soon as the post has been shaped, it is carried in procession to the dead man's house by the young men, who are accompanied by a crowd of boys, playing on drums and gongs. If the deceased was a man, his widow meets the procession and leads it into the house; if a woman, this is done by her brothers. The post is then carved with a chisel with conventional ornaments, which vary in the different villages." adds Mr. Parry. The custom is practised by the Lakher tribals in North-eastern region.

Memorial of the Dead in Manipur

Dwelling on the monuments raised for the dead in Manipur, Mr. TC Hodson notes, "The worship of stones in this area possesses an importance which will justify detailed treatment. Stone monuments consist of (1) monoliths, which are not as large as those in the Khasia Hills, (*Cf.* The Khasis, major Gurdon, p. 144-154) and which are found either singly or arranged symmetrically in rows, avenues, circles or ovals; (2) cairns or heaps of stones; (3) single smaller stones; and (4) the flat stones near Maram, supported on smaller stones.

"Monoliths abound in this area, but the symmetrical arrangements of monoliths are found, so far as I know, in only two portions, viz. at Maram and the village Uilong and in the Marring area. (At Konga Khul there are a few which reminded me of Marim. At a site further south, the name of which I have forgotten, I came on some monoliths in a regular avenue.) Outside the once large and prosperous village of Maram there is an avenue of stones, nearly all of which are still standing, and inside the village one can see the remains of, or parts of, a circle of stones. One particular monolith in the avenue is associated with hunting luck, and before a hunting party goes forth, they go down to the stone and endeavour to kick a pebble on top of it. If they succeed in this, their venture will be successful. At Uilong there is a very remarkable collection of stones, which is not mentioned in any of the earlier writers on Manipur, as McCulloch, Brown, Pemberton or Johnstone, though it is certain that more than once they were close to the village, which lies in a remote corner of the State. I visited this village in December, 1900, and to my regret had no instruments with me for determining the size and orientation of the stones. At my request Colonel H. St. P. Maxwell, C.S.I., deputed Babu Nithor Nath Banerji to measure the stones and prepare a plan which is now reproduced. By the side of the winding path up to the village I noticed small stones, perhaps a foot or eighteen inches high, with a larger one at regular intervals, then I came to a flight of stones steps, close to which was a circle of stones. On investigations being made, I found that there were two contiguous series, one having a circular shape and the other, the smaller, being nearly oval. The unmarried men dance and wrestle inside the large circle on the village genna for the annual festival of the dead. From the edge of the oval there starts a line of monoliths. There are now thirty-two stones standing, four in the small oval, fourteen in the circle, and fourteen in the long rows. (*Cf. Prog. Liverpool Geographical Society,* 1904, pp. 31 and 32 *Journal of Society of Arts,* Vol. LIII, No. 2733, p. 559.) These stones are said to have been erected three or four centuries ago, when the village is believed to have been much larger than it now is. The erection must have been very costly and would be impossible at the present time. From the traditions of the people themselves and from the actual practices as found elsewhere at the present time, we may obtain some idea of the expenditure of human energy and material resources required for the purpose.

"....On the fateful day the maiba pours zu on the stone, 'utters many mantras,' and lets loose a fowl, in order that there may be no difficulty in getting the stone into its appointed place. The villagers drag the stone up by sledges like those used by the Manipuris, attaching to them ropes made of the creeper. For a year the lungchingba lives apart from his family. Thereafter his descendants annually go to the stone, drink together, and clear the jungle growth away. They say that if a stone falls or cracks, it portends the ruin of the family of the lungchingba, a belief which will go far to explain the annoyance of the Nagas at Maram when some Public Works overseers broke up a stone in order to get road metal. At Mao I was informed that the father of a man who erected a stone would help his son, so that there it has the aspect of ancestor worship. In what way the help would be rendered by the deceased parent to his son, was not made clear to me.

"Among the Marrings we find stone circles, mostly dilapidated, inside the village.

"Cairns and heaps of stones are found among the Tangkhuls and Quoirengs, who build them in a beehive or conical shape. Some of these beehive cairns are to be seen in the Kaithenmanbi plain close to the cart-road.

"So far as I know, the flat stones, supported on three or four smaller vertical stones, are to be seen only near Maram, and I learnt that one of these flat stone monuments had been erected within comparatively recent times.

"Connected with some of the stones are various legends. At Hundung is a stone commemorating the subjugation of that turbulent Tangkhul village by Ching Thang Komba, and annually worship is paid to it. Near Ukrul is a stone from which they got fire when on their migration. At that stone they divided, some going to Sirohi, while the majority preferred to go to Ukrul. At Maikel is a stone on which I was told there were pictures of men and animals. I took measures to have this stone placed in a proper position, for it had fallen down, but its inscriptions, if it ever had any, had long disappeared. The curious weathering of the stone produced effects which the Nagas took for inscriptions. It is said that it stands on the very spot where their ancestor emerged from his sojourn in the earth. These stones are all regarded as laipham, places where a lai dwells. So, too, the heaps of stones in the Tangkhul villages and the rings of stones in the Marring villages are holy, so holy that no one dare swear falsely on them. Similar sanctity attaches to a meteor stone in a Kabui village. Good luck in war is associated with the Tangkhul cairns and with single stones such as those kept by the khullakpas at Mao and Maikel. That at Maikel is a mass of conglomerate and is always hidden inside the khullakpa's house, where, as a favour, I was allowed to see it. Heads taken on a raid were shown to these stones, and I specially observed that at Mao the khullakpa poured zu on a stone outside the village when performing a rite. There is a quaintly shaped stone in a Naga village west of the valley which receives pigs from various villages and is very holy. It is about 5 feet long.)

"Small stones are associated with sickness and it is legitimate to infer that they too are laiphams, i.e. not the actual spirit which causes the sickness, but the place in which he dwells.

"I may add that among some of the minor Kuki tribes an interesting form of sepulchral monument is erected in honour of a rich woman after her death. Small stones are erected in rows inside a fence of slightly larger stones and the heads of the creatures killed at her obsequies (a fowl, a goat, a pig, a cow) are placed on them.

"Dr. Brown mentions the erection by the Kabuis of upright or flat stones as marking the grave, and the only case I have known of the erection of a stone monument took place after the death of the man's father, so that the motive of honouring the dead and of exhibiting piety operates among them to the present day. (Among Lusheis, stones are only put up as memorials of the dead. I have known two occasions on which persons having no one to put up the stone for them have put them during their own lifetime. Stones are only put up to very important persons—chiefs or their children. Can the fear of not being honoured have led to the custom of putting up stones?)

"Mr. Pettigrew gives a lively account of the ritual employed by the Tangkhuls when erecting a memorial stone, which I reproduce verbatim.

"*The 'Onra' (memorial stone) ceremony*—Amongst the wealthy, the male member of the family makes a stipulation in his verbal will, that a monument should be erected in memory of him, and the wife and family suffer in consequence, as a great deal of money is spent over it. During the rainy season, before the rice begins to bear fruit, all the friends of the deceased gather together at a prominent spot outside the village which serves as a landmark and which the relations have before decided upon. The night before a cow is killed and cooked by the males only; half of the intestines is taken by the relations and the other half by the friends. It is then cooked and divided amongst them, and should there be a goodly number, say 100 or 150, their share is infinitesimal; still it has to go round. This division takes place in the morning, and after all is ready each person divides his small portion again into three pieces, and offers them to 'kameo.' The three pieces represent (1) the earth, (2) the heavens, (3) his self. With this meat weak rice beer is drunk, and after the feeding is over the strong rice beer is distributed. Then six friends are set apart to carry the wooden images shaped to represent buffalo and dogs heads, and in the case of a brave who has taken heads, an image of himself is made. These are all to be placed on top of the memorial. Following these six friends solemnly walks the 'sherra' with suitable portions of cooked meat, and offers up to 'kameo' on the proposed spot. His refrain or prayer on this occasion is as follows : 'Thinghum lungkarna katatit nana yengmira,' at first offering. At second : 'Ina mashai mashakranglaga, nathum shairilu.' At third : 'Iwui vang kho kharanosea ungphazak zaulu.' In the meantime the friends are gathering stones, and then, the 'kameo' offering being over, the earthwork is started and the stones built up all around to the height of 2 feet or more.

The artists of the village then paint the different images placed on the memorial, generally with charcoal and lime. The last article to be placed on this ceremony is a large stone slab, which is considered the most important stone of all, for on it the spirit is said to come and sit during big occasional peregrination around, to view his rice fields. Any removal of this stone by others means a heavy fine. The shape of this memorial is oblong, with one of the shorter sides more approaching an angle. They are about 20 feet long by 8 feet wide. Pine-trees and other trees likely to afford shade to the passer-by are planted on them at the same time. The stones on the sides are used a great deal by the villagers as resting places for themselves and for loads of wood etc., carried up from the jungle or rice field. The next day and for two days following the family take down a basket of meat and chillies and place it on a raised platform upon which the spirit is supposed to come and partake. They stay for half an hour or so, and go through the same performance at sunset." The custom is pertinent to the Naga tribes of Manipur.

REFERENCES

1. Parry, NE, The Lakhars, Firma KLM Pvt. Ltd. and Tribal Research Institute (Aizwal), Calcutta, (reprint) 1976, originally published 1932.
2. Rizvi, S.H.M. & Roy, Shibani, The Adi Tribes of Arunachal Pradesh, BR Publications, New Delhi 2006.
3. Stack, Edward & Lyall, Sir Charles, The Mikirs, United Publishers, Guwahati, first published 1908.
4. Hutton, J.H., The Sema Nagas, Oxford University Press, Bombay (reprint) 1968, first published 1921 by Macmillan & Co., London.
5. Roy, Jyotirmoy, History of Manipur, East Light Book House, Calcutta 1973 first published 1958.
6. Hodson, TC, The Naga Tribes of Manipur, BR Publishing Corp., Delhi reprint 1974, first published 1911.
7. Horam, M, Social and Cultural Life of Nagas : The Tangkhul Nagas, BR Publishing Corp., New Delhi 1977.
8. Hutton, J.H., The Angami Nagas, Oxford University Press, Bombay 1973 (reprint), first published 1926.

7

Social Customs

In the states like Nagaland and Manipur etc. the major social customs are *genna, kenna* and *penna,* in the approval and non-approval senses. About them Mr. T.C. Hodson wrote, as practised among the Naga Tribes of Manipur.

Social prohibition called *Genna*. Thus, "The term 'genna' means simply forbidden or prohibited. *A.C.R.* p. 249. (The word genna is used in two ways : (1) it may mean practically a holiday—i.e. a man will say, 'My village is doing genna today,' by which he means that, owing either to the occurrence of a village festival or some such unusual occurrence... his people are observing a holiday; (2) *genna* means anything forbidden.) It is therefore applied in its primary sense to the mass of prohibitions, permanent and temporary, periodic and occasional, which form so important a part of the tribal law of these societies. All the rites and festivals observed by socoial units in this area are characterised by a prohibition of the normal relations with other social units, so that the term has come to be applied to all occasions and festivals at and by which the social unit concerned consolidates and concentrates itself. It is not a new discovery. Colonel McCulloch remarked of the Kabuis that 'A whole village or individual members of it are often 'Neina' or under prohibition. Sometimes this state of things lasts a day, sometimes several. The 'Neina' may be against the entrance of strangers, or the exit of members or of both, or, allowing the entrance of strangers, disallow their going into houses, etc. Peculiar circumstances also induce prohibitions in food and drink, but to attempt describing them would be to pretend to more knowledge of minutiae than I possess.' So too Dr. Brown observed that 'There is one curious custom which has a religious significance and which is common not only to all the hill tribes
significance and which is common not only to all the hill tribes,

but also to the half Hindooised Loee population of the Munnipore valley : this is 'Namoongba' or a periodical closing of individual villages. This custom does not take place with any regularity, and its object is some kind of worship. One of the occasions is just before the jungle which has been cut down on their jhooms is fired : this lasts two days and the villagers are said to fast during that period : the village remains shut up during the two days, and no one is allowed either entry or exit, and it is also affirmed that anyone attempting to force an entrance during this period would be liable to be killed. On other occasions the proceedings are of a joyous nature and may take place after a successful hunt, a warlike expedition, a successful harvest, or other striking event: on these occasions feasting and drinking is the order of the day.

"I hope to set forth the facts which I have collected so as to show (1) the social units affected, thus giving to social structure its due prominance, (Gennas sometimes affect whole villages. Sometimes only chiefs or single households), (2) the occurrences which bring these customs into play, (3) the activities and relations which are so forbidden, and (4) as far as possible the nature of the sanctions which give validity to these customs. It may be that this method involves some repetition, but as I think, no more than is needed to display the ideas which inspire these customs. The real value of any social phenomenon cannot be estimated accurately by isolating methods but is largely determined by its relation to other social phenomena with which it forms part of an organic whole.

"There is so little tribal that it is difficult to assert positively that there are tribal gennas, customs affecting individuals as members of a tribe or homogeneous group of villages. Yet in the special prohibitions which deny pork to the Maram Nagas and forbid the Tangkhuls to keep or eat goats, there is something of the nature of a tribal genna. So far as I could learn, the penalty attaching to a breach of either of these regulations falls rather on the actual offender, though it might be fairly described as a social sanction because there is always the fear of some calamity happening in their midst as the result of disregard of any one of these ordinances.

"The village is an economic unit, so that all the ritual observed for the cultivation of the staple, rice, necessitates the expenditure of communal energy in the form of village gennas. Rain compelling ceremonies are naturally part of the cultivation ritual. Their economic life is rigidly and sharply divided into two periods, one for agriculture and the other for hunting, fishing and other such subsidiary industries, so that there is again an economic basis for the gennas which are intended to promote good hunting. In the next place the appearance of epidemic sickness occasions a genna, whose purpose is obviously prophylactic. The occurrence of mysterious 'extra natural' cases of death also necessitates a village genna for the purpose of separating the living as soon as possible from the dangerous dead. Except at Mao and its allied villages it is usual to hold an annual rite for the purpose of laying finally to rest the ghosts of those who have died within the year. At Mao any and every case of death is followed by a village genna. Events such as earthquakes, eclipses, probably also the appearance of a comet (though of this I have no personal knowledge (See Owen, *Notes on the Nagas,* p. 25) are of so serious a portent as to require the community to meet the danger which they threaten or betoken by an effort of all its energy. If a village be burnt, there is a genna against all ordinary work for a short period. In some cases village gennas are caused by what are otherwise regarded as domestic events, such as sickness, when a man can afford the luxury of a village genna, and in other cases they are caused by the deliberate intentional acts of individuals, as when a man erects a stone monument. There are village gennas connected with the first fruits and with the first death in the year of any domestic animal. These are very typical of the fear of 'la premiere fois'. (Van Gennep, *Rites de Passage,* p. 249 et. seq.) Some village gennas are therefore of periodic occurrence while others are held only after the occurrence of some abnormal event. The letter are as much part and parcel of the village customary law as are the former.

"At all these village gennas the ordinary routine of life is profoundly modified if not broken off altogether. There are special gennas imposed on these occasions which require abstinence from certain kinds of food. The duration of these gennas varies considerably, and some undoubtedly are of much less consequence than others. The ill effects of an interruption of a village genna are sometimes irremediable, while in other cases a repetition of the genna is adequate to prevent all harmful consequences. At all the village gennas the gates are shut when the genna begins so that the stranger that is within the gates may not go forth and the friend that is without must stay outside. At some stage in all the village gennas husband and wife cook and eat apart and the unmarried of both sexes are rigorously forbidden food cooked by the other. Thus the society concentrates itself. The male element is sharply separated from the female element of society, thus effecting a resolution of society into its components. Among all these tribes from the day of the first crop genna to the final harvest home all other forms of industry and activity are forbidden. All hunting, fishing, tree and grass-cutting, all weaving, pot making, salt working, games of all kinds, bugling, dancing, all trades are strictly forbidden—are 'genna' lest the grain in the ear be lost. Some of these prohibitions exert—indirectly—a beneficial effect. The game has a close-time which it sorely needs, for these sportsmen spare not the does. But after all necessity knows no law. I met a Mao villager once in the Sena Kaithel in Imphal at a time when by rights he ought to have been at home minding his fields. I taxed him with disregard of his genna rules but he told me that once he got past the Maram hills, fourteen miles from his village, he was free of all these restrictions upon his commercial energy. The hinterland of Mao morality was limited to the boundaries of its neighbour and the sanctions of the crop gennas ceased to operate for him when he got round the corner out of sight.

"Every stage of the rice cultivation is marked by a village genna the duration of which varies. (*Cf. U.B.G.* Vol. I, Part I, p. 425, where the Kachin and Chingpaw customs, which are very similar to those of the Nagas, are fully described.) At the end of March or the beginning of April the paddy is sown and the genna among the Tangkhuls lasts for five days. A month later they hold a genna for the prosperity of the rice before it is transplanted, and at this genna they celebrate the first rope-pulling festival, when the women and girls have a tug of war against the men and boys in order to take the omens for the future of the crops. This is followed by considerable license. (*Cf.* Frazer, *History of the Kingship,* p. 268.) In some cases the 'thauri chingba' or rope-pulling' takes place at the earlier genna when the rice is sown. In some villages, as at Sirohi, the khullakpa inaugurates the transplanting genna by sacrificing a fowl more to take the omens than to perform a sacrifice, although the connection between the slaughter of an animal for sacrifice and for omens is very close. When the transplantation is successfully completed, again a genna is held lasting for two days as does the previous one. Similarly both the beginning and completion of the harvest are marked by gennas lasting two days and there is also a repetition of the rope-pulling ceremony with its attendant license before the first fruits are cut by the hand of the khullakpa. (*Cf.* Frazer, *Golden Bough,* Vol. II, p. 460.) At Phadang, one of the cloth-weaving villages, I learnt that there was a village genna to institute the planting of the ginger, which is used in the preparation of zu. I have enumerated five crop gennas (as practised by the Tangkhuls), but I find that as a rule four only are observed, the one generally omitted being that marking the end of the transplantation.

"Rain compelling ceremonies are necessitated by the dependence of the rice crop (even in the best terraced fields) upon a seasonable and equable distribution of rain, and at the Tangkhul village genna for this purpose the khullakpa kills a pig and eleven rice cakes are made. Six men and five women with the khullakpa go outside the village where the sacrifices are duly offered up to the deity whom I believe to be Phiraoi the wife of Kamyou. At Chingai I found that in addition to this form of rain-compelling ceremony they practised the following rite. The khullakpa takes a water-worn pebble and wraps it in weeds from the river bed and killing a fowl, offers it to the deity.

"In the Mao group inclusive of Jessami we find four crop gennas usually observed which are called at Jessami, (1) Mongunge, (2) Killache kiche, (3) Aghrume, (4) Takkone. They last for five days each at Jessami, while at Liyai the first takes ten days, the transplantation genna one day, the genna marking the beginning of the harvest four days and the final genna of the harvest home occupies ten days. At Mao I gathered interesting information regarding the special food prohibitions associated with these crop gennas. At the gennas for sowing the rice, pigs are forbidden, salt is tabu at the transplantation genna and dogs are not to be eaten at the two last gennas. At Mao I learnt that they worshipped the Suo as a good deity and sacrificed a white cock to him. The gennas for this last for one day only.

"In most of the villages, I learnt that a sacrifice of zu was offered at the village gate by the khullakpa as a rain-compelling ceremony, but at Liyai the ceremony is more complicated. The khullakpa takes a brand from the fire puts it on the grave of mao who has died of burns extinguishes it with water and then prays for rain. The people of Mayang Khong though remote from Mao are said to be linguistically connected with them and when rain is needed dip their large wicker shields in the pond near the village and sprinkle the water on the fields. A hen and some eggs are sacrificed and I noted at the time that this rite was performed, not by the khullakpa but by an elder.

"If duration of time be any test of importance, in the Mao group we have a village genna of much importance for the purpose of securing an abundance of game in the hunting season which cannot commence till the crops are safely stored. This genna takes place at a date which in other village calendars is that of the Mangla Tha for which it may be a substitute or with which it may have been fused.

"At Maram we have six gennas for the crops and one for the game. The two additional crop gennas are held one when the rice begins to show through the ground, before transplantation, and the second in connection with the growth of the ginger root. Their form of rain ceremony is to descend to the river, the Barak, and there to fill vessels (bamboo chungas) with water, which they empty over their fields and pray for rain.

"The Quoirengs have only four crop gennas, but the exact occasions of these four seem to vary. In one village which had no terraced fields, the first genna was held when they were ready to start felling the jungle for the jhums, the second when the jungle was all ready to be fired, the third when the rice was to be sown, and the last when when the rice was about to be harvested. For a rain compelling rite they drown a pig in a pond or in the nearest river and ask for rain. At Lemta they told me that they took an eel from the river and cut it into small pieces, which they threw about on the top of the irrigation cuts. The sun and moon are worshipped here, but are malevolent deities. A pig is killed and omens are taken from its entrails. Apparently this rite is performed twice a year, and is associated with a village genna.

"Colonel McCulloch mentions a number of gennas among the Kabuis which he describes as festivals, and as connected with the crops, 'The Reengnai, in or about January, which lasts for three days. In one day during this festival the men and women fetch separately the water for their own use. The men having killed pigs, take a portion for themselves and give a portion to the women, and having cooked them separately they eat them separately, the men in the house of the head of the family, the women each in her own house. An effigy of a man made of a plantain is hung on a tree, and at it they throw pointed bamboos or sticks. Should the javelin strike it in the head, the thrower, it is said, will kill an enemy, but if it lodges in the belly the thrower is to be blessed with plenty of food. (The Quoirengs do this also, but with them this ceremony is performed just before the crops are cut, and must be performed outside the village gate.) On the termination of the Reengnai they go through the ceremony of taking the omens in regard to their place of cultivation, but this seems to have descended to them merely as a ceremonial relic of former times, for the circle of cultivation is never broken, let the omens be what they may... These festivals over (those for ear-piercing and the omen taking for the year), the cutting of the jungle for cultivation is commenced, which, when finished is crowned with the festival of 'Oodooee yung,' or drinking the juice of ginger... One night of the month of August and one of September they dedicate to feasting.' Dr. Brown adds the remark that 'the reason for the males and females bringing water separately during this festival (Reengnai) is to begin with this ceremony the making of new liquor and the separate eating and cooking of the sexes to be a mark of respect to their gods. After the festival of the 'Oodooee yung,' or 'Mahlong,' as it is also called, when the cutting down of the jungle on the jhooms is finished, a curious ceremony takes place. All the people bathe after the work is completed, and, in addition, their agricultural implements are also dipped in a running stream as they are supposed to be exhausted by their labours; thus refreshed, the tools are hung up in their houses until again required for use.' According to my information we have among the Kabuis at least five, if not six, crop gennas, the first of which occurs before the jungle is cut, and is named

'*Faidoutingan*,' and lasts for one day. A genna named *Taisoipa,* lasting for two days, at which no stranger may be present, is held before sowing. Strangers are also excluded from the *Phuphoi* genna, which happens when the crop is about a foot out of the ground. Private individuals of more than usual piety or plenty celebrate a private genna, named *Latang-mai,* and pluck an ear of paddy which they bring to their house. Before cutting the paddy there is a village genna named *Nakonna,* lasting for one day, at which a pig is killed and distributed. The last genna of all is named *Pumthummai,* which lasts for one day, and celebrates the end of the harvest. The cultivation omens are taken by two elders who wash their bodies very carefully and put on new clothes that day. They must not sleep with their wives the night before the ceremony. Overnight a bamboo (umu) is split lengthwise and laid ready. They sit opposite each other holding a portion of the bamboo in either hand. If the bamboos press together the cultivation will not be prosperous in the direction proposed. If the bamboos turn outwards, the fields will be good. But as Colonel McCulloch observed, the rotation of cultivation is fixed and known beforehand.

"Kabuis employ sacrifice as a means of bringing rain, and should this fail, it is necessary for the men to come out of their houses at the dead of night and then to bestride the roofs, and, stripping themselves of all their garments, to use the most obscene language to one another.

"The Chirus have six crop festivals, one of which, that before the crops are cut, is marked by a rope-pulling ceremony of the same nature as that observed among the Tangkhuls. In order to get rain, they catch a crab in a neighbouring river, put it in a pot with water, having fastened a thread to one of its claws, and then keep on lifting it out and letting it fall back into the pot.

"The Marrings, according to my notes, seem to have only one crop genna, that before the rice is sown; but I may be mistaken.

"I may here describe a rain puja which I saw in course of performance in a small Kom village. A fish was cut up on the embankment of the village weir and another fish hung up at the village gate, and all the men called upon the sky to give them rain. The maibas meanwhile smeared mud on small pieces of plank, which they dragged about the village.

"Village gennas are caused by the advent or near approach of epidemic sickness, and are prophylactic measures rather than part of a cure. At Jessami one of the regular village gennas has for its purpose the prevention of sickness throughout the year. A party of young men is sent out to catch a bird, and if they are so fortunate as to bring back to the village a fine big bird such as a toucan (or hornbill), it is an unerring omen that there will be no sickness in the coming year. This genna lasts for eight days. The Kabuis observe a genna in January in order to protect themselves specially from hurt by bamboos. It lasts for one day, and on it the young men are forbidden to drink outside their houses.

"In the Mao group either a cock is killed, as at Liyai and Maikel, or let go outside the village by the khullakpa who orders the genna. The Quoirengs sacrifice a goat or a cock at the village gate, and entreat the deity not to enter. The Kabuis kill either a fowl or a dog for this purpose, but on occasions when a python is killed, either a fowl or a pig or a goat may be sacrificed, but never a dog. The python is closely associated with sickness, and merely to see one is most unfortunate, while if they see it and kill it, some, if not all, the trouble may be avooided by a village genna which lasts for three days. All the able-bodied men are gathered at the village gate, and all together shoutout 'we are all here!' Then the genna begins as the dead python is dragged inside." adds Mr. Hodson. These social customs are prevalent among the Naga tribes of Manipur.

Social Custom called as *Kenna*

Mr. JH Hutton describes the Angami Naga customs called genna and kenna. Thus : "The Angami act of worship has been termed as '*gennas*' because there is no suitable English word which describes them, and the word genna, through by deviation from the Angami '*kenna*' signifying 'forbidden' merely, has become regularly used in the Naga Hills for the various incidents of a magico-religious rite. These may suitably be dealt with under the three heads which are in casual speech lumped together under the expression 'genna.'

"First of all we have *'Kenna'* (or *'kenyu'*), that is to say, 'prohibition.' Now this word *'kenna'* is used without any reference whatever to the sanction on which the 'prohibition' rests, and it is for this reason that the word *'tabu'* has been rather avoided, since there is nothing in the Angami word to suggest the reason of the prohibition. So loose is the use of word *'kenna'* that it may refer not only to the breach of the strict rule of a magico-religious observance or to the breach of a social law, theft for example, but to the most trivial matter of pure utility. An extreme instance of the latter came before the notice of the writer. One of his interpreters had shot a monkey and going on ahead had jestingly propped it up in a lifelike attitude against a fence. The writer coming along with a village headman inserted into the open mouth of the dead animal the stump of a Burma cheroot which he had been smoking. The Angami with him remarked at once *'hau tsu kennawe,'* it is forbidden to do that.' On being asked how such an act could be *kenna,* it was explained that it was highly improper to waste so precious a luxury as the stump of a cheroot. Leaving out of account, however, extreme cases of this sort of use, it is possible to distinguish classes of *kenna* according to the intention underlying the prohibition. A good example of such a distinction may be seen in the prohibitions associated with the use of wood. On the one hand the burning for firewood of the wood of trees used for building in *kenna.* Of course it is just possible that the reason underlying this may be a fear that the use of this wood as firewood might make the timber of houses more liable to conflagration, but the simpler and accepted explanation, that the object of this *kenna* is to preserve the building material from waste, is perhaps more likely to be the true one. On the other hand, and, whichever be the explanation of the *kenna* on timber trees, differing from it, is the *kenna* on the use as firewood of the tree *'hetho'* from which are made the wooden images substituted in burial ceremonies for the unrecovered corpses of those slain in battle. While it is *kenna* to burn the wood of the tree *'mela'* at weddings, because if burnt at weddings or touched by the bride or bridegroom it causes barrenness and necessitates a divorce. The story which explains the prohibition against burning *hetho* wood is told as follows :

'The wood called '*hetho*' is not to be burnt or brought to any dwelling for this reason : a man was once lost and no trace of him or of how he disappeared could be found. His relations wanted to perform the ceremonies for his death. It was much discussed as to how this should be done. At last it was decided to make a wooden image of the dead man, and an old woman' (she would be the dream-woman of the village) 'was consulted as to what wood should be used. She conversed with a spirit in a dream and the spirit advised her to make use of a thorny tree so that in future all should be afraid to touch it. Then the *hetho* was chosen' (it has thorny bark and crimson flowers. Its Assamese name is *Madar* (It is perhaps significant that this tree is preferred by the Garo for the pyre on which the dead are burned. See Playfair, *The Garos,* p. 109) as it was sufficiently large, soft, and thorny. Since then the *hetho* has not been burnt, as it is considered in some sense a man. When a man dies at a distance from his home, his companions cut off some hair and bring it home, and making a figure of *hetho* wood, affix the hair and perform the funeral ceremonies, substituting this figure for the corpse.'

"In the matter of dress we may compare the *kenna* which forbids a man who has not taken a head to wear the hornbill's feather, the insignia of the successful warrior, with the *kenna* which prohibits a man from not merely putting on but even laying across or against his body a petticoat which has once been worn by a woman. The fact that there is not the least objection to a man's putting against his body a new and unworn woman's petticoat shows that it is not the nature or meaning of the garment itself which, as in the case of the warrior's insignia, is the reason of the prohibition. A *kenna* similar perhaps to that against burning timber trees for firewood may be seen in the prohibition against cutting the stubble from the reaped field until the whole harvest of the village is gathered in. The idea here would seem to be that until the really valuable part of the harvest is gathered a man who has reaped his own grain should aid his neighbours. Delay would not hurt the straw, and it would not matter much if it did, whereas grain quickly spoils if unreaped and is of vital importance to the community. But perhaps the best instance of a purely utilitarian prohibition is the one by which a village in which there is some epidemic is put 'out of bounds' by the neighbouring communities purely to avoid risk of infection. (Compare also the *kenna* against taking paddy out of the 'duli' except in the morning and with the doors shut. The woman must do it if there is one in the household, and a stranger is absolutely prohibited from touching the paddy in the 'duli.' The object is purely utilitarian—to prevent the too rapid use of the rice supply, but the process of thought on which the tabu is based is less clear.)

"It should be added that by the word *kenna* used hereafter without specifying any particular act prohibited is meant a prohibition laid on persons or households from holding intercourse of any sort by word or by deed with others. This, in fact, is perhaps the commonest use of the word, and its corruption 'genna' has sometimes been used in this sense exclusively, though now usually having a much vagurer significance. *Kenna* in this sense is, however, subject to degrees. It may refer merely to speech, though it usually refers to all communication whatever. A bunch of green leaves is affixed to the front of a house when its inmates are *kenna* in this sense.

"While *kenna* is the prohibition laid on a unit of the community, *penna* is the prohibition laid on the whole community. It includes the idea contained in *kenna* and goes further. Besides entailing on the community a *kenna* towards strangers in a greater or less degree and for a longer or shorter period, *penna* entails entire abstention from work in the fields by the community as a whole, when such abstention is proclaimed by the Kemovo or Pitsu. The essence of it is that the individual should not leave the village to go to his fields or cultivate. It does not necessarily prevent the man's going out hunting or his wife's weaving or performance of household duties. The power ascribed to the observance of *penna* may be gathered from the effect which their observance with a definite object is believed to have upon the individual. For instance, two Sachema women went to catch snails in the Jotsoma terraces when the paddy was ripening, and some Jotsoma men, annoyed at the possibility of damage to their crop, threw mud at the women. They were not even struck by the mud, but when some of their fellow villagers threatened to do a genna consisting in this case of a day's *penna* (that is with *kenna* as regards strangers) 'for the loss of two heads,' the two women, fearing that they would die as a result of such a genna, hurried into Kohima to get orders against its observance. A precisely similar effect was ascribed to *penna* in the case already alluded to of the man of Nerhema who sacrificed a cat for illness, and instances might easily be multiplied. From time to time certain days (e.g., those on which there is no moon either new or old, those on which eclipses occur, etc.), at the instance of the Kemovo or Pitsu, are observed as days of *penna* as opposed to *'li-chu'* (= 'field-go'), much like the 'dies nefasti' of the ancient Roman Courts. In most Angami gennas a certain number of days are observed as *penna* and the rest as *nanu* merely without prohibitions other than that against going to work in the fields. *Penna* really is *kenna* applied to the community instead of to the individual. The word *kenna* would probably be hardly, if ever, applied by an Angami to a communal prohibition, at any rate when speaking of the community, though it might be used of the incidence of the communal prohibition upon an individual.

"Supplementary to *kenna* and *penna* in magico-religious observancs we find in some degree or other *Nanu,* the whole rite, the active side of the observance as well as the negative and passive sides exemplified in *kenna* and *penna. Nanu* is also used as the term for a whole genna in which *penna* is observed by the community or by the individual (accompanied by *kenna*) and followed by a period of similar abstention from work in which *penna* has not been actually proclaimed by the priest. The ceremony implied by *nanu* is at its minimum the offering of a little folded leaf containing a few grains of rice and a sip of liquor which is hung up in the house on all days of *penna,* the grains of rice having been held for a moment at the fire by way of a pretence at cooking it. Perhaps even the offering of a little liquor shaken from the cup or touched on to the forehead before drinking on all occasions might be held to be *nanu* at its minimum. At its maximum *nanu* consists of sacrifice of flesh, part of which is set aside for the spirits, wearing of ceremonial dress, dancing, singing, and the pounding of dhan, together with the total abstention from work in the fields involved by *penna,* and complete *kenna* to intercourse with strangers. But while offerings in a lesser or greater degree accompany all observances, they may amount to a mere drop of liqor set aside on the mourning of a genna day, or may be the head and entrails of a chicken or the snout and feet of a pig killed in case of illness. In the latter case parts of the animal killed are given to the Zhevo and sometimes also to the Kemovo, Tsakro, and Lidepfu. In the case of a genna conferring social status a number of cattle, more or less fixed according to the particular genna, are sacrificed and the whole clan, or at least the kindred, is feasted. The wearing of ceremonial dress accompanies some of the village gennas, but practice in this respect varies a good deal and is anything but a criterion of the importance of the genna. Different villages attach varying degrees of importance to different gennas, and it thus happens that a genna kept with great ceremony at one village is comparatively insignificant at another village which makes a great deal of a genna barely observed in the first. Dancing, singing, and dhan-pounding as a rule go hand in hand with ceremonial dress. Dhan-pounding at a small genna is done inside the *'theka ki,'* which is the house of some rich man who has a large pounding table and which is always used for this purpose at gennas; at a big genna it is done outside in the open, a large number of tables being collected for the purpose. Pounding is done in full dress and by both men and women, and in some cases, e.g. the Thekrangi genna at Khonoma, the girls and young men pound at the same trestle, standing on opposite sides of it and using the long straight pestle. In the Terhengi genna in Kohima the men doing gennas of social status pound separately, using a hook-shaped pestle.

"Dancing as practised by the Khonoma group is a very serious affair. It consists of a solemn procession of young men in full dress which moves at a slow pace describing circles, eights, and similar figures and splitting into two lines which work in and out of one another serpent-wise. The motions of the dancers are stiff and there is a certain amount of posturing with the arms and hands, the upper arms being kept close to the body and the fore-arms and open hand being moved up and down from the elbow, but not from side to side. Free movement is much restricted owing to the weight, cumbrous dimensions and instability of the head-dress worn. In the Kohima group, where the rather fragile wheel of hornbill feathers is not worn by the younger men, who wear less cumbrous erections of bamboo and paper, the movements of the dancers are freer, while in the Viswema group the dancers work up a gradually increasing pace, ending up by running very fast and leaping. In this ceremonial dancing the old men take little part, following for a time at the end of the line and directing operatings generally. They do not trouble to put on full dress, but carry weapons and any marks of particular distinction to which they are considered entitled.

"Both dhan-pounding and dancing are accompanied by singing, the nature of which has already been described. The songs sung include both particular songs traditionally associated with the occasion, and sometimes in archaic language not fully understood except by those skilled in them, as well as songs in common use which may be fancied by the singers is performed in ceremonial dress and rain is a serious disaster. These visits are paid about the month of March and at no other time of the year. The clan which issues the invitation is occupied for several days in preparing a vast quantity of liquor, and numbers of animals are killed for the feast. Males of all ages take part in the visit and the dancing.

"In addition to these and other recurrent gennas, any untoward or unusual occurrence may call for the observance of a genna by the village or clan, as, for instance, the fall of any earth on to a genna stone (*kipuchie*) or the dragging of a new door for the village gateway. The latter ceremony is performed at Sachema as follows :

"The door is dragged up beforehand to within half a mile or so of the village. This is done without ceremonial dress and is not attended by genna. On the day of the ceremony the Kemovo takes some new 'pita modhu' and a cock and goes early in the morning to the stump of the tree from which the door was cut. The cock is fed and let loose, while the 'modhu' is poured into a plantain-leaf cup. A little 'modhu' is also poured on to a plantain leaf and offered to the cock. If the cock takes the 'modhu' it is regarded as a good omen. The Kemovo then goes to the door itself, taking with him the Zhevo and Tsakro. The two former take grass (*kurhi*) and touch the door with it, addressing the door in the following terms :

"You must not stay here but go to the place appointed for you. Men shall be more in number, paddy and cultivation shall be more prosperous, cattle, dogs, etc. shall be more plentiful.'

"The Kemovo ties two thin strings to the door and drags at and breaks them. Then two boys, who have never had sexual intercourse, one Kepezoma and one Kepepfuma and both naked, the former on the right and the other on the left, tie on two string ropes, which must on no account subsequently break, and pull them. Then all the men may take hold of the ropes, and they proceed to drag up the door towards the gateway. On the way up the door is stopped and blessed by the Tsakro, the Zhevo and Kemovo having done so before as already described.

"No one is allowed to follow or get behind the door; and all spectators and women have to get inside the village walls before the door arrives at the gate. The clan to whom the door belongs drags the right rope and the other clan or clans drag the left rope. Every male in the village (including small boys) has to have his hand on the rope, though the dragging is really done by a dragging party.

"On arriving at the gate, the draggers being inside, the clan to whom the door belongs first drop their rope and go in procession to the *tehuba.* When they have all left, the others follow. Then the Kemovo, the Zhevo, and the Tsakro take a fowl and touch the door with its beak and repeat the blessing. The fowl is then killed with a piece of wood in the house of a man near the gate, where the 'modhu' for the genna has also been made, and it is eaten that night by the Kemovo only off plantain leaves.

"A dance called *sovi* follows.

"A large amount of a compound called *'hinu'* is prepared from maize, Job's tears, rice, beans, chillies, salt and *'kenya.'* This is the only food to be eaten that day after the dragging of the door until the evening meal.

"All the men wear dancing dress (without arms), except those who have had a death in the house, and they wear ordinary clothes, as at all gennas at which ceremonial dress is worn. Before the ceremony strangers are not allowed inside the houses where the preparations for the genna are going on.

"Should the clothes and miscellaneous stuff left on one side by persons working in the fields get burnt while they are doing so, a *mi-penna* (*mi* = 'fire') is kept by the whole village. One was observed in Kohima village on March 25, 1919. Should the stubble catch fire at harvest time, too, a *mi-penna* is observed, while if the wind should overturn the mat used for threshing and winnowing the grain a genna called *Thekrelhape* is observed.

"The gennas which attend the life of the individual Angami fall roughly into two divisions : the gennas which are more or less inseparable from his existence in the community, gennas, that is to say, which attend all ordinary individuals, at his birth, his marriage, and his death, and the gennas which are more or less optional and which determine his status in the society. It is perhaps simplest to deal first with the gennas that attend all individuals and afterwards with those that are not essential." adds Mr. Hutton. The customs are practised among the Angami and other neighbouring tribes of Nagaland.

Feast of Merit

The Lakhers tribals used to give feasts of Merit which would follow a certain order - the entire series of feasts together was known as *Khangchie.* The first feast was called *Phidong.* When a sow would be killed in the morning and the pork along with *Sahma* (rice beer) would be consumed with the invited relatives and friends. After about 3 months of *phidong,* the rich man would give the next feast called *vothawthi* when a boar would be killed in the evening and a large number of people would be invited to enjoy the meat and beer. The young boys and girls of the village would entertain the gathered people with songs and dances. The party would go on for the whole night and start afresh next day in the morning with heaps of meat, rice and gallons of beer. In the third feast called *vori* a sow would be sacrificed. Only the clans men would participate and the feast would be over in one night. The fourth feast was called *seichong* when a *mithun* calf would be killed after sunset. The villagers would participate in the feast for two nights and two days.

The fifth feast was called *beibei.* For a week before the feast the young boys and girls of the village *morung* would help the person giving the feast in collection of firewood for cooking the meat and otherwise prepare for the mood of the feast by presenting songs and dances. They would be rewarded by a pig which they would eat with lots of beer. The sacrifice for the feast would consist of two bull *mithuns* and three pigs. The feast given would last seven days when the entire village community would eat, drink and be merry.

The next feast was given when a tiger would be killed by any one of the village. The feast was called *chakei.* It would involve killing a boar on the first day and bull *mithun* and another pig on the second day. Only men would participate in the feast. The men would dance around the head of the killed tiger which would be placed on a platform in a road. After the dance, feast would start which would continue for a day. The last or the culminating feast was called *Khangchei.* To start with, a cow *mithun* would be killed and the feast would last three days. Thereafter the boys and girls would collect firewood and would get a pig and beer as their remuneration. In the feast five *mithun* would be slaughtered and the feast would last nine days. On the last night there would be a lot of merriment singing and dancing including free mixing of men and women without any inhibition in the darkness of night.

About the Angami feast of merit, Mr. J.H. Hutton writes, "The aspirant for fame must perform the Yuhongba ceremony before he can do the greater one of pulling a stone. He must give notice of his intention to do so in the month of *Bellu-khuh,* corresponding to October. He renews all his cooking pots and changes the hearth-stones, and for one month from the date of giving notice he remains chaste. During this time he is busy getting *zu* brewed; when all is ready he kills a pig and calls the villagers. His friends bring presents and contributions of *zu,* which are very welcome, for it is up to the giver of the feast to provide *zu* for all the village for the whole of the month of *U-klaw-kluh,* and if it runs short he would fall into dire disgrace. On the first of *Chi-thu-ni-kluh* he again renews his cooking pots and changes the hearth-stones, and having eaten from the new utensils he may sleep with his wife. The next or any succeeding *Bellu-kluh* he may give notice that he will perform the stone-pulling. New pots and new hearth-stones are procured and the stone-puller must keep chaste for the next ten months. In the month of *Chi-thu-ni-kluh* he gives a feast called *U-tuzur,* killing a big cow or two small ones and feeding the whole village and providing *zu* for the *sagei.* During the next month the village collects wood for *zu* making, and the puller has to provide them with *zu.* In the next month *zu* in quantities is made and stored. The stone has to be chosen during this month. Having selected the stone, he puts some *zu* and "Kollaw" leaves under it and goes home to dream; if he does not dream at all it is bad. When the stone has been approved of, the pulling is arranged. The puller wears a special dress with a head-dress, white cloth gaiters, and special cloths; the others all dress in their finest. Two old men dressed as the puller, except that they do not wear the special cloth *Zawshishu,* go to the stone, and one of them places some ginger and *zu* in a leaf by the stone and then lets a white chicken go that the stone may move as easily as the chicken runs away. The young men chase it and kill it. The *Mohvu* now walks round the stone with a spear in his hand and then gives the first pull. (The stone has been put on the sledge before the ceremony.) Then two chaste young men who have followed the *Mohvu* holding *Chhip-pe* wands and 'Kollaw' leaves and some cocks' feathers take up their position in front of the stone and throw the *Chhip-pe* wands in the direction in which it is intended to go. They mount on to the stone and shout to it to go quickly, after which they rejoin the *Mohvu* and give a pull at the ropes. They get on to the stone a second time, and then the hauling begins, and if possible the stone must be got to the site on that day, but certainly by the next. This done, all go and drink. The *Mohvu* and the old men of each *sagei* go into the puller's house with him and an old man who has pulled a stone sits outside. *Zu* is distributed in leaves; those inside the house except the *Mohvu* drinks theirs; the old sentry also does not drink his; the rest of the people assemble outside, and when they have drunk their portions all shout 'Ho!' The old sentry goes into the house and he and the *Mohvu* drink. Then all go home; the *Mohvu* and the old sentry must remain chaste that night. The next day but one more *zu* is made and five days later a pig is killed, and the day after a cow and buffalo, and two days later whatever meat has not been eaten by the puller and his household is divided among everyone with *zu*. The village is cleared of strangers. The unmarried girls and all males are called and come with their *zu* cups, get them filled, taken them home, and return and stand or sit in rows and are given drink in leaves; this goes on for four or five days, but the cups are not brouought on the later days. The puller receives small cash presents from his friends, to whom he gives a special drink. New *zu* is then prepared, and when it is ready everyone is again treated. Again *zu* is prepared, and when it is ready the villagers go and hoe the puller's field and erect the stone which all this time has been waiting on the sledge. This ends the show. The puller is not allowed to eat fowls, eggs, and certain vegetables. At every feast a Yuhongba gets two shares, a Lunchingba four, and one has pulled two stones ten shares." adds Mr. Hutton. The custom is related to the Angami Nagas of Nagaland.

U-klaw genna

"This month *U-klaw* is the genna of that name. The first day is *mi-kuru-kraw;* on this day offerings are made for those who have died by fire; on the second day, *Se-zur-kraw,* offerings are made for those who have been murdered; on the third day, *I-kraw-ji,* offerings are made for all other deceased during the preceding year. On each evening the offerings are thrown away. The three days are very strictly *penna.*" writes Mr. Hutton.

Rain making and stopping

The *Mohvu* of every village calls for rain or fine weather and a one day's genna is proclaimed, writes Mr. Hutton about the Angamis.

Custom of Head-Hunting

About the word custom of head-hunting among the wild Savages of Nagaland Mr. J.H. Hutton writes, "Disputes between villages in the still unadministered country, where there is no superior authority to settle them, must if an amicable agreement is not reached, be subject to the ultimate arbitrament of war. The real causes of war are probably not more than three in number in the Sema country—first, shortage of land necessitating forcible encroachment on that of neighbouring villages; secondly, the protection of trading interests, as an attempt on the part of one village to trade directly with another at some distance has often caused war with an intervening village through which the trade used to pass (much to the profit of that intervening village) and which retaliates for its loss by making war on the interlopers, cutting up their trading parties, destroying the intercommunication between the offending villages, and compelling their trade to return to its old channel. Trade routes east of the administered area are still jealously protected in this way, and each village on a route makes its little profit on all articles passing backwards and forwards—daos, salt, pigs, cloths, pots and the like. The third cause is found in the fits of restlessness that from time to time afflict most Naga villages, the desire of the young men as yet untried to prove their manhood and gain the right of wearing the warrior's gauntlets and boar's tush collar, all culminating in an overwhelming desire to get somebody's head, which not infrequently outweighs all riper considerations of policy and prudence. If this cause is at work the most trifling incident may become an occasion for a raid. Villages in this mood too will deliberately provoke hostilities by refusing some act of customary courtesy or right. And war has frequently been known to be occasioned by the refusal to give the customary feast to a person bound by formal ties of friendship, by a refusal to pay up the price agreed upon for a wife or to give a girl in marriage when it has been arranged, by the divorce of a chief's wife, the housing of a runaway and refusal to send him back, by selling the flesh of animals that have died of disease and so infecting another village, by the breach of a genna, such as taking some prohibited thing into the fields of another village at harvest time, or by a gratuitous insult, 'or any other reason why.' All such matters as these could be and often, probably usually, are settled amicably, but if the villages are in the mood for it they will and often do occasion war.

"War is of many sorts, and no fine distinction is made in the Sema mind between what is genuinely war and what we should call merely head-hunting. The following various tactics are distinguished by Semas :

"*Akuluh*—pitched battle. One village challenges another either by a message sent through a third village or shouted out on the occasion of a raid or called out from some safe spot within earshot of the opponents, but out of their reach. A time two or three days off is fixed for the two villages to meet at a given place with all the allies they can muster and fight. Heads are normally very difficult to get in this form of warfare, as the retreat of the weaker side is always covered by panjis and picked warriors. Seromi, however, in a pitched battle with the Aos of Longsa on the site where Sapotimi village now is, once managed to get seven heads. A challenge to a pitched battle sent through a third village would normally be accompanied by some symbolic message, generally a panji or part of one, but often accompanied by something else, generally a *chilli*, to signify the smarting in store for the recipients. The writer was once sent a *chilli* impaled on a bit of panji together with a challenge to personal combat, signifying not only war and the un-pleasantness in store for him if he accepted, but that if he failed to accept he was only fit for impalement like a sacrificed puppy. The Survey party in the Sema country in 1875 was several times met by the whole fighting strength of a village got up in full dress and prepared to give battle, though the only attacks actually made were apparently attempts at surprise attacks. In event of a battle taking place the women would probably support their menfolk at a safe distance with petticoats full of stones for use as missiles, which they would replenish from dumps previously collected along the most probable line of retreat.

"*Ashepe* is a raid on the fields of a hostile village, proved warriors being placed as sentries on the flanks and as a rear-guard to protect the raiding party from being cut off, while the raiders clean up those of the enemy village who have the misfortune to be surprised at their hoeing. Thus before their annexation Asukokhwomi took a woman's head from Sheyepu by an attack in this method, while Seromi took seven heads from Baimho in a similar raid.

"*Ahusu* (or *inahusu*) consists in laying an ambush for people of a hostile village as they emerge from their village in the morning when going to work on their fields. They are, if possible, cut off from their village and surrounded.

"*Tivetsate* is the laying of an ambush during the day to catch the people of a hostile village returning from their fields in the evening.

"*Apfulie* are raids on the village itself, and are divided up according to the circumstances under which they are made, thus :

"*Puchofile* is a raid at midday on a village the menfolk of which have gone to their fields to work. Thus in 1912 or thereabouts Tsukohomi raided Sheitz and got seven or eight heads in this way, and in 1914 Shietz raided Lumtami (Lumakami) and got the heads of one old man and two children. The latter raid was entirely gratuitous and unprovoked.

"*Tsuktofile* is a raid at cock-crow—just before dawn. An entry is made quietly into the hostile village and the raiders post themselves at the doors of the houses and cut down the inmates as they emerge at daybreak. So Churangchu, chief of the Angangba khel of Chisang, led a raid on Pakavi of Kumishe in 1914 which succeeded (owing to the treachery of one faction in Kumishe) in destroying twelve or thirteen households. Only two men escaped, and a woman and a child, who hid behind a door, till the raiders had gone through the house and then ran out into the jungle. So too in 1917 the Sangtam village of 'Chonomi' raided the newly-built Sema village of Zivihe, which consisted of elven houses. 'Chonomi' only got two heads, but frightened Zivihe into removing his village from their land.

"*Kighishi* consists in making an entry into a hostile village by night and merely spearing a man through the wall or roof of his house or entering the house and taking his head. In either case a departure is effected with all speed. Baimho and Yezami were for a long time at war, during which some men of Baimho killed Hovishe, chief of Yezami, by spearing him through the thatch of his house at night, and Viheshe, a man of Yezami, retaliated by killing Inache, a chief of Baimho, in the same manner.

"*Tinshi* is killing a cow of a hostile village, hiding in wait for the first pursuer, and taking his head and one's own departure as fast as possible. To provide an instance of *tinshi* and *kighishi* combined, Nikhui's villages made a joint raid on 'Lakomi,' a Tukomi Sangtam village, in 1914. They sent a warrior on ahead, who speared a man in his house in the early morning. The village braves hurriedly assembled for the pursuit and ran straightway into the ambush laid for them. A little later, however, Gwovishe's people thought they would try the same game on Kitsa, but their bait, who had missed his man in the hostile village, got wounded by the enemy, who suspected a trick and refused to follow him into the trap.

"*Tushwonei* (*tushwonu* = a stranger (*i.e.,* a man of another village) who is not an enemy and *yi* = to kill) means killing and taking the head of a person who is met casually on the path or even by arrangement. Nikashe, the present chief of Aichi-kuchumi, practised *tushwonei* when he incited a Yachumi chief to come with him to Mokochung in 1912 and get a red cloth, and then while fording the Tizu river fell upon him and smote him, and took his head.

"The names given by the Semas to these tactics suggest in several instances the perpetration of a grim jest. *Ashepe* is the same word as that meaning work in the fields, and only the faintest difference in accent is detectable. *Kighishi* means 'thatching,' and, in view of the tactics it denotes, the application is obvious. *Inahusu* (*ina,* an obsolete form of *inakhe* = early, and *hu* = going to the fields) means early rising to go to the fields. *Tivetsate* seems to mean 'letting go,' with the intent, of course, to catch on their way home, and *tinshi,* which means 'desire to die,' undoubtedly refers to the mentality of the silly ass who rashly pursues the killer of his cattle.

"With the exception of *akuluh,* all these tactics postulate surprise, and if the raiders find their prospective victims prepared, they come home rather ignominiously. This is called *aghuphipusho.*

"The tactics described above should give a fair idea of the Sema methods of warfare and head-hunting. Sudden raids, surprise, ambushes, and hurried evasion constitute most of it, and the pitched battle does not often occur. The throwing spear, the crossbow (for the simple bow has disappeared), the dao, and an occasional muzzle-loading gun are their weapons of offence, the shield and panjis those of defence, for a Sema on the warpath carries a basket of panjis, and sticks all the path with them, when retreating, to hinder pursuit. Booby traps are also popular, but are not developed to the extent that the Changs and Konyaks use them further north and east, as they consist mainly in panji-pits. A favourite variety is the *aghukhoh* or 'war-pit.' This is contrived by choosing a place where the path goes along the side of a hill and excavating a deep and long pit under the path perhaps as much as 6 feet long by 8 feet deep, without disturbing the surface, which is left intact for a considerable thickness.

"The bottom of the pit is filled with double rows of panjis, say 4 feet and 2 feet in length respectively, and the excavation is concealed. The *aghukhoh* may then just be left for the enemy to walk into, or the enemy may be lured to rush into it by a warrior on the far side, who apparently risks his head to wait about and shout insulting challenges. In this way, with good luck, sometimes even three of one's foes at a fall may be caused to go down together well perforated into the pit. The *apukukhoh* or 'leg-pit' is usually made by taking advantage of a depression in the ground, and this depression, or a shallow pit made for the purpose, is plant with short panjis in the ordinary way and filled up with bits of sticks, moss, grass, leaves, and earth, so that it lames people before they realise that the ground is panjied. The stone-chute (*zhuka,* 'flattener') is known to the Semas, but apparently not put into practice by them in warfare.

"Stones and sticks and sharpened bamboos are also used. When two neighbouring villages are at war large numbers of the former, and these including stones of all sizes, are collected near the hostile border by men, women, and children for days in advance of a projected battle or raid on the enemy. They are then used to throw or roll down at any who pursue the returning warriors of their own village. Similar collections of stones are made in houses built in large trees near the village overlooking any path which an enemy is likely to use. (Some tribes, the Phoms and Konyaks in particular, carefully train the suckers of the Bor tree (*Ficus Indica*) so as to grow into a natural scaffolding on which a large tree house may be built for this purpose. I once found the suckers being trained in this way in a small Ao village that had been administered for many years, and asked them why they did it. All they could tell me was that it was the custom, and it was only later that I found out the real reason, which the village itself had undoubtedly forgotten. Mr. Mills tells me that the Ao village of Longjang also trains these suckers with hollow bamboos 'because it is the custom.')

"The Semas have on many occasions shown themselves superior as warriors to their neighbours on the north and east, as indeed may be inferred from the way in which they have dispossessed them of their lands. Thus the 30 houses of Maghromi proved such a thorn in the flesh of the Ao village of Nankam (700 houses) that the latter determined on a serious effort to wipe out the village. Two hundred Aos surrounded Maghromi before daylight, and, having completed their preparations, sat down to wait till it was lighter. During the wait they laid down their weapons to eat and, Ao-like, started chattering. A Sema, up early and coming into the jungle near the village, heard them and slipped back to warn the village, which collected what men it could muster, who surprised and routed seven times their number of Aos, taking heads and capturing several guns, which they broke up as they did not know how to use them.

"Maghromi also supplied an instance of the Sema use of craft. Both the Aos of Nankam and the Lhotas of Lungtang claimed tribute from the chief, who was thus between two fires. By promise to both he managed to induce the Aos and Lhotas to fight about it, offering his tribute to the victor and egging on both disputants. As Lungtang was a small village and Nankam a large one, all the Lhota men had to turn out to fight the Aos in the pitched battle that took place by the stream selected by the Chief of Maghromi. While the Lhotas were engaged in the fight they suddenly spied a great column of smoke rising up from their village, where Maghromi had cut up all who were left behind and burnt the village. Having thus disposed for ever of one enemy (the site of Lungtang was occupied by Semas from Phusumi and is the present Litami), they were able successfully to resist the other.

"Many Sema raids, however, have and still do end in *aghuphipusho,* like a raid of Gwovishe's on Shipvomi; the raiding party found Shipvomi prepared, and when it got there came back again, like the fleet that went to Spain.

"In the administered village, however, war is gradually receding into the limbo of the forgotten past, except in so far as the desire to wear the warrior's pigs' tushes and cowrie gauntlets keeps the young men desirous of going as carriers on expeditions on which they hope for a chance of 'touching meat' and thus acquiring the right to put on the coveted ornaments. It is partly this desire, as well as loyalty, which at the time of writing (April 1917) has just taken 1,000 Semas to work in France. In their own villages they have to confine themselves to the more modest exploits of cutting off the tail of a neighbour's cow, a deed of chastened daring which is followed by the hanging up of the beast's tail and the performance of a genna as though for the taking of a head. Incidentally, the animal—it is usually a mithun—which is thus treated loses all its value for ceremonial purposes and becomes fit only for sale as meat, for the owner himself cannot even eat of it, much less kill it at a feast, so that they animal loses at least 50 per cent of its market value. A bit of another person's hair, if abstracted by stealth or force, may be likewise treated as the subject of a genna, with the dire effect of causing the death, or at least the illness, of the original grower of the hair. (In 1915 some men of Aochagalimi cut a bit of hair off a boy of Yeshulutomi. Though this was settled as between the principals in the dispute, Yeshulutomi village demanded a formal and public peace-making with Aochagalimi village.) The killing of an enemy's cattle, or even dogs, cannot, however, be counted as 'heads' by the killer unless he has actually taken part in the killing of an enemy. If a man does so take part, and probably if he succeeds at all in being 'in at the death,' he reckons as heads all the enemy mithun he may have killed previously, provided always that he has not eaten the flesh of such mithun. No cattle of which he has eaten the flesh can under any circumstances be counted.

"The principal gennas connected with head-taking are the *aghucho,* which inaugurates hostilities, and the *aghupfu,* which celebrates their success. The former centres on certain stones, themselves called *aghucho,* which are usually to be found lying about the village somewhere near the chief's house. These stones should strictly be water-worn black stones approximately spherical in shape and divided across the middle by a thin white stratum dividing each into two parts. (I have seen just such a stone venerated as a "healing stone" in Co. Donegal.) The size of the stone is immaterial. Of course, stones that really comply with this description are only occasionally met with, but anything that approaches the standard will serve, and very often any queer-shaped stone is taken to the village and preserved as an *aghucho.* Some *aghucho* were shown to the writer in Philimi which were just black stones worn into curious shapes by water, one or two faintly resembling the shape of a human neck and head. Like the charm stones kept in granaries to ensure the prosperity of the owner and as a guard against the depredations of mice, these *aghucho* breed and beget young, in witness where of there are numerous small stones always to be seen lying around the place where the *aghucho* are. These in time will grow up and become *aghucho* and breed in their turn. In most Sema villages *aghucho* are prized only as giving success in war, and, though in Philimi the chief would not let the writer take away an *aghucho* for fear it might hurt the crop, in most administered villages the *aghucho* have been neglected and lost, as now that there is no war they are of no further use.

"The genna preceding a raid consists in killing a pig and presenting six small scraps of the liver and of the flesh to the *aghucho* stones. The village is genna that day and no one may go to the fields. After this day is over anyone may start raiding. When an *aghucho* is found and brought to the village, this genna is observed whether it is intended to follow it by raiding or not.

"The *aghupfu* is celebrated by successful raiders, who come back singing a *yemale,* on the day of their return from the warpath. Till it is done they are unclean, genna, holy, and a village that is sowing etc., cannot entertain them. (Observed on operations against the Kukis in 1918, as also the custom referred to of counting enemy mithun as 'heads.') The whole village is circumambulated by the raiders, carrying the heads obtained. Then a chicken is killed by each man who has actually taken a head himself, and the most pre-eminent warrior in the village, whose duty it is to make holes in the crowns of enemy skulls—he is called (for this purpose) *akutsu-kegheheo,* 'the head-hanger'—is given the head of the chicken in virtue of his office. Tiny scraps of the fowl's flesh are set apart for the ghosts of the dead enemy. Eleven minute scraps in all, each placed on two crossed leaves, six pieces in the name of the victor and five in that of the victim, are laid out in a row before the head and in the place where the skull is to hang. (Mr. Mills tells me that eleven scraps of meat are used by the Lhotas in almost all ceremonies.) The rest of the fowl is eaten on the spot by the returned warriors; before returning to the village the scraps are again counted, and should one be found short the ghost of the dead has eaten it, and it is a sure omen of another successful expedition, the idea probably being that the dead man, gratified at his meal, will call his living friends to come and partake similarly. Some of the eastern Semas, following a Yachumi practice, skewer wads of meat to the mouth and eyes of the dead head, that the ghost may eat and be filled and call his friends to come and be killed, and that after all sorts of indignities both in word and deed have been showered on the trophy by the women and children of the village. It is essential, in laying out the scraps of meat for the ghost of the slain, that while six are brought in the name of the killer, only five are brought in the name of the killed, otherwise the former would not be victorious in the future. The raiders are genna on this day, and may not eat inside the village. They must observe chastity and may not even sleep in the inner room where their wives are, but in the *akishebokhoh.* If they are to eat at all they must be fed outside the village and before they enter it after returning from the raid. There is, however, no restriction on drinking. On the following day the warriors are still genna, and a pig is killed. The head is given to the *akutsu-kegheheo,* who now makes a hole through the head from the top of the forehead to the bottom of the skull at the back, after which the *lapu* strings it on a cane. A bamboo is cut and planted in the ground at the village Golgotha (*aghu-kutsu-kogho-bo,* 'the place of enemy heads') outside the fence. This bamboo must be cut off high enough from the ground to ensure its not surviving and taking root, as this would entail the success of the enemy. The head is strung up by the *lapu* to the top of the bamboo, after which it is genna to touch it. Those who do not bring back a head, but have shared in getting one, hang up an earthen pot to represent it. Gourds are also hung up for mithun, dogs, etc., and also for human heads.

"A Sema returning from the warpath with a head sings "*O, Yemusale, Yemale,*" probably in allusion to the piercing (*yema*) of the heads for their stringing up. *Ale* = *'sing.'* (But this is not certain, and some Semas do not profess to know the meaning. The Lhotas sing *'O Shamashari o smaiyali'* under similar circumstances, but do not know the meaning of the words.)

"For some reason or combination of reasons the heads of women are as highly prized as those of men, perhaps more so.

That this is so is demonstrated by the stock formula for songs in celebrations of a warrior's exploits. This formula runs as follows :

'Oh! So-and-so killed-and-brought-back-the-head-of a girl of Such-and-such (a village or tribe);

'Oh! So-and-so (the warrior's brother or, if none, his nearest male relative younger than himself) cut off the hair and put it in his ears;

'Oh! cut off and put in his ears the hair of the girl of Such-and-such;

'Oh! So-and-so (the warrior's wife) rejoiced' (or 'applauded').

"Thus a song celebrating the exploits of Sakhalu... being interpreted, tells how Sakhalu killed and brought back the head of an Abor girl, how Kohazu (his brother) cut off the hair and put it in his ears, and how Ilheli (Sakhalu's wife) rejoiced or applauded. Now Sakhalu was employed as a Scout ono the Abor Expedition of 1911-12 and took the heads of several male Abors, and, as far as is known, of no women, yet in celebrating his exploits he is described as taking the heads of women, and not of men. Similarly, the song in the same formula celebrating Inato's exploits fictitiously attributes to him the taking of the head of a girl of Nankam, although he had taken one or two genuine heads from men in his time. (I have gone into this, as the greater value put on women's heads has been asserted of other tribes and doubts have been raised as to the truth of such assertions. See Hodson, "Naga Tribes of Manipur," p. 114, notes 2 and 5.) The killing of idiots and similarly deficient persons, as hunchbacks and deaf mutes, is 'genna.'

"It is possible that the reason why women's heads are held in greater estimation is that they are harder to get, as a village in time of trouble sends the men to work where there is danger, while the women work only near the village, so that to get one of their heads entails venturing right up to the hostile village at great risk of being cut off on the return journey. It is also possible that the desire to cause a permanent reduction of the enemy population may have something to do with it. The killing of a man will not affect the birth-rate much, but the killing of a woman probably will. (Conversely, too, the acquisition of a female head plus a female ghost might increase the fertility of the successful village.) It is also possible that the desire for the woman's hair for ornaments may have contributed. Some men of Lumitsami made a successful raid on Nankam, but several of them were cut off on their way back owing to the delay caused by their squabbles as to the possession of a woman's head with long hair, which all of them wanted in order to adorn the tails they wore at festivities. (In 1919 I heard an accusation brought by the men of Iganumi, headed by their chief, who accused a woman of that village named Shikuli, and another, of bewitching and poisoning their fellow villagers with the aid of human hair taken in war from dead enemies by the ancestors of these women, who were alleged to put fragments of these heirlooms into food offered to their neighbours. They produced a *thumomi* named Kamli, who to prove the truth of her statement produced from Shikuli's hand a minute fragment of hair which she (Kamli) had hidden under her thumb nail and which she pretended to extract from under Shikuli's finger-nail after stroking along her finger as though drawing out the hair as by a magnet.

"The taking of a head or killing of an enemy entitles the warrior to wear cowrie gauntlets (*aouka ashuka*) and a collar of pigs' tushes, though strictly only one pair of these should be worn unless the wearer has taken more than one head. Nowadays it is enough to 'touch flesh' by spearing the body of an enemy shot by troops, since the administered Semas can no longer make war on their own account. A man who has speared or 'cut' a still living enemy whose head is taken by another man—for the first spear gets the whole head even if someone else cut it off—has an earthen pot hung up in place of a head with precisely the same ceremonial, while a man who has only 'touched meat' has a gourd hung up in the same way, the stringing being done by the *akutsu-kegheheo*. Should the string on which a head is hung break, it is regarded as an excellent omen, forecasting an early repetition of the success.

"The ceremony of peace-making between two villages that have been at war is an elaborate one. A place is fixed upon between the two villages at which the opposing hosts are to meet and make a formal peace. Each side prepares food and drink, and every man according to his ability gets ready flesh, a chicken, or eggs at least, while several large pigs are killed in plenty of rice-beer is brewed. All the flesh is cooked, and on the appointed day is taken to the spot with cooked rice and several gourds of liquor per head by the whole community of grown males. Women are not allowed to be present, and must not even go to the fields on that day by the path which the men are to use when they go to the peace-making.

"Meanwhile the *lapu* of each village has made ready a new fire-stick, and a single silver of pliant bamboo made from a plant most carefully sought and brought in from the forest by a selected unmarried youth and kept until needed in his house or, if the *lapu* has no wife, in the *lapu's* house. When the two parties have met at the appointed spot, a small party of the chief and leading men of both villages is formed at a distance from the main body of villagers, and in the presence of this select group the rival *lapus* proceed to make fire, using their new fire-sticks and the single thong. Each *lapu* when starting to make fire says to the other, '*Alhokesa kizhe a la wosala shipini,*' which, being interpreted, is 'All that there is of evil, shall it not be on thy head ?' (The use of the word 'head' here is not an absolutely literal rendering of the Sema, but probably conveys the sense of the expression as nearly as is possible in English. The word *wosala* is obscure and possibly archaic; *wo*-probably = o—the possessive of the second person—*sala* is possibly connected with *asa* = hair of the head.)

"After that, should either of the *lapu* fail to get fire with his single thong, then all the expiation to which either side or both have renderd themselves liable will be borne by the clan of those men, in the village of the *lapu* who has failed, who have lost their heads, or lives, to the other village, and some members of this clan will most certainly go blind, or lose their teeth, or get a cancer (particularly of the mouth or eye), or go lame or die of internal haemorrhage. The same happens to the rash man who eats the foods, smokes the pipe, or touches the dao of a man whose family has killed one of the former's clan before any formal peace has been made. It is also advisable always to sit on one's dao when eating or drinking in the house of a man with whose clan one's own clan used to be on head-taking terms, even if peace has since been made and many years have elapsed. Otherwise one's teeth decay and fall out and one's eyes become sore and watery. The idea which underlies the sitting on a dao is said to be that iron brakes all gennas, the evil effect of the forbidden act being neutralised by the iron of the dao.

"After the *lapus* have made (or failed to make) their fire, both villages collect fuel and make a fire, which they light from the fire made by their *lapu.* Should the *lapu* have failed to get fire, his fire-stick is chopped up and thrown away, and fire is made by some lusty young man, for since it is a serious matter if fire again fails, older men, like the now very unpopular *lapu,* are not trusted to try. Matches may not be used under these circumstances. (The Sangtams, who ordinarily possess flint and steel (or rather quartz and iron,) eschew these in the same way as Semas eschew matches when they perform their peace-making ceremonies. On this fire *aghu* is burnt, and each side expresses a wish that his village may be in future as sharp as thatching grass or sword-grass. The reason for burning *aghu,* which gives a very pungent odour when burnt, is probably to drive away evil influences, as it is burnt in time of illness to drive away evil spirits, and at most or all important gennas, presumably with the same purpose. Next the two villages exchange the food and drink they have brought and lay out their daos upon the ground, and the men of each side, putting a foot upon the dao of one of their late adversaries, start to eat and drink standing there, but presently sit down and eat as usual, still keeping a foot on the dao. While drinking, each side expresses a silent wish that all the evil which may have resulted from their hostility may be upon the heads of the other side. What or why exactly this evil is not clear, and the Sema himself has probably no precise notion of what he means, but it is possible that the anger of the dead killed in the war is roused at the making of peace by their fellow villagers and clansmen with the enemy, and that this anger is feared. It must be admitted, however, that there is nothing in Sema eschatology to suggest this. It is, however, clear that the performance of the peace-making genna is not regarded as ensuring the peacemakers absolute security against the toothlessness, cancers, lameness, and other judgements that follow reconciliation with an hereditary enemy. In any case it is highly advisable to express the wish in silence. When Sotoemi and the Sangtam (Tukomi) village of Yetsimi were making peace in the way described at the place where the village of Tokikehimi now is, a Sotoemi man of the Chophimi clan, which had lost eight heads to man of Yetsimi, expressed aloud and with emphasis the hope that the said man of Yetsimi should suffer the horrors detailed above. He said this in Sema, but one Yevetha, a runaway Sema who had acted as go-between, translated it into Sangtam, whereupon a man of Yetsimi clave the speaker's head in twain with a battle-axe (*ailaghi*), whereto a Sema of Sotoemi responded by cutting down Yevetha, and both sides incontinently fell a-fighting, and as they were all mixed up there was much slaughter, and Yetsimi got 50 heads off Sotoemi, and Sotoemi 75 off Yetsimi; but this is the Sema version.

"When eating and drinking are finished the gourds are given back to their owner and the villagers return home, usually abstracting many of each other's spears, as these are stuck into ground here and there in every direction, and the chiefs and elders cannot prevent looting, though they hunt out the stolen weapons afterwards and secure their return. Before reaching the village everyone has to wash himself, his clothes, and his weapons, though the old men sometimes restrict the washing of their clothes to one corner only for fear of catching cold. If any victuals or drink are left over from the ceremony, these must be partaken of by the old men before entering the village, after which nothing more may be eaten or drunk that day, while all must remain chaste that night.

"In the case of a man cutting off the tail of his neighbour's mithun, when regarded as head-taking in a minor degree as described above, he performs a peace ceremony of correspondingly reduced dimensions, which in its simplest form consists merely of the exchange, between the offender and the owner of the tail-cut mithun, of sips first of water, then of liquor from each other's plantain-leaf cups, and lastly of the burning of *aghu* on a fire outside the house, new fire not necessarily being made, though some insist on this. Failure to do this ceremony might entail unpleasant consequences. Recently one Khekuvi of Shevekhe cut off a bit of the ear of one of Sakhalu's mithun. This was found out, suitably atoned for, and the peace ceremony gone through in its simplified form by the offender and Sakhalu. Some months later (in April 1917) Hotoi, Sakhalu's son, was passing through Shevekhe village, and anon blood gushed forth from his nose and his mouth in a manner terrifying, at any rate, to Hotoi. This was put down at once to his not having been made a party to the peace ceremony, and a further ceremony was insisted on obetween Khekuvi and Hotoi.

"When fighting with nearly-related persons, as sometimes happens in a land dispute, sticks and stones are used, or the blunt backs of daos. And even if sharp weapons are used heads are not taken.

"A birth of any domestic animal prevents the owner going to war, but that of a human being in his house does not; on the contrary, it is rather lucky.

"Sexual intercourse while on the warpath is strictly genna." adds Mr. Hutton in his book *The Sema Nagas*. The custom pertains to the Sema Nagas of Nagaland.

Impact of Modernity

In the modern times, the Mizo tribes living in specific location in Mizoram have not maintained fixed relation in their mutual socio-economic life. Their mutual social relationship reflects social unity and harmonious ethnic relationship, exhibiting it as a close-knit Mizo society. Their social and religious customs are common with little local variations. However, the Buddhist Chakmas maintain distinct social customs due to difference in religious practices, still their agro-economic life shows a common outlook and a high sense of morality. The egalitarianism presents the Mizo society classless and casteless. The Mizos are also proud of their ideal of 'Tlawmaihna' or the (selfless service to needy persons.)

The introduction of Christianity in society in Mizoram and Nagaland had made an excellent impact on the socio-cultural life of the people. Their mode of life culture and customs were changed and their social structure was completely transformed. The Christianity spread education among the people, gave them lesson of love, sympathy, and a sense of value which were completely missing during their primitive life. Christianity taught the tribes the value of tolerance, peace, co-existence and universal brotherhood. It paved the way for modernity in the region. As a result, the life style, the way of thinking and doing, were radically transformed. Their menal horizon widened by its teaching, and the superstitions, faith in spirit and magico-religious practices vanished. In fact, the Christianity made them adaptable to modern civilisation and culture. Its impact on socio-economic activity is also significant. A sense of individualism and individualistic approach to life was inspired by the Christianity.

In the social life, arranging feast, animal sacrifice, offering drinks and inviting large number of guests are the common cultural traits of the regional life. These strengthen fellow-felling, stimulate interest in adventurous activities and promote spirit of selfless (*Tlawngmaihna*) service to the needy persons, irrespective of social, economic, political and other considerations. These are the most essential parts for their life in such a natural surrounding where people are leading an isolated life in the natural surroundings. The tribal society is an ideal one and the people help the poor, hungry, and needy persons in their respective communities. No begging is allowed in the Naga or Mizo society. The community life of the people is deeply embedded in agricultural activity which invites the whole community to share both pleasure, labour and pain. This ultimately, gives birth to a socio-cultural unity, harmony and cohesion.

REFERENCES

1. Chowdhury, J.N., Arunachal Through the Ages, Jaya Chowdhury, Shillong, 1982.
2. Burman, S.G. NEFA : Island and People, Indian Quarterly 19(4), 1963.
3. Chakravarty, R., People of Manipur, BR Publishing, Delhi 1986.
4. Shakespear, J., The Lushai Kuki clans, Macmillan & Co. London 1912.
5. Furer-Haimendorf, C.V. Highlanders of Arunachal Pradesh, Vikas Publishing House, New Delhi 1982.
6. Hutton, J.H., The Sema Nagas, OUP Bombay 1968 (reprint) first published 1921.
7. Parry, N.E. The Lakhers, Firma KLM Pvt. Ltd. (reprint) 1976, first published 1932.
8. Hodson, T.C. The Naga Tribes of Manipur, BR Publishing, Delhi (reprint) 1974, originally published 1911.
9. Hutton, JH, The Angami Nagas : with some notes on neighbouring tribes, OUP Bombay 1969, first published Macmillan & Co. London 1921.
10. Horan, M., Social and Cultural Life of Nagas : Tangkhul Nagas, BR Publishing, New Delhi 1977.
11. Thunga, LB, The Mizos : A Study in Racial Personality, United Publishers, Gauhati, 1978.

Bibliography

Abbot, A.K. 1881. Notes on the Naga Hills and the Narrative of a Military Expedition into Kacha Naga Country during February-April 1881. *Journal of the United Service Institute of India. no. 49-50. 1881-1882.*

Abbott, A.K. : *Indian States : North-east,* MacMillan, London, 1994.

Adhikari, O.S. 1988. *Four Immigrant Tribes of Tripura—Their Life and Culture.* Agartala:DirectorateofResearch,GovernmentofTripura.

Aier, L. IMTI. 1969. *Ao Naga Social and Customary Genealogy.* Mokokchung (Nagaland). Published by the author.

Aiyar, S.P. and Mehta, Usha : *Essays on Indian States,* Popular Prakashan, Bombay, 1965.

Ali, G.H., 1979. *The Manipuri Muslim* Banskandi : Assam.

Ali, S.M. 1954. *The History of Jaintia.* Dacca.

Allen, B.C. 1901. *Assam Report,* 1901. Shillong : Assam Secretariat Printing Press.

Allen, B.C. 1902. *Gazetteer of the Naga Hills and Manipur,* Shillong: Assam Secretariat. (Also published in 1905).

Allen, B.C. 1905 (1980. Reprint) *Gazetteer of the Khasi and Jaintia Hills, Garo Hills, Lushai Hills.* Gian Pub. New Delhi.

Allen, B.C. 1905. *Assam District Gazetteer,* Vol. VIII-Lakhimpur. Calcutta; The City Press.

Allen, B.C. 1905. Assam District Gazetteers. Vol. IX : Pt. II *Naga Hills and Manipur : Socio-economic History.* Calcutta, British Baptist Mission.

Allen, B.C. 1906-1907. *Assam District Gazetteer,* Vol. III, Goalpara.

Allen, B.C. 1912. *Assam.* Shillong : Assam Secretariat Printing Press.

Allen, B.C., 1905. *Assam District Gazetteers,* Vol. I, Lakhimpur. Shillong : Assam Secretariat Printing Press.

Allen, B.C., E.A. Gait, C.G.H. Allen and H.F. Howard. 1979 (Reprint). *Gazetteer of Bengal and North East India.* Delhi : Mittal Publications.

Anonymous, 1958. The Hill Tribes of Assam *Modern Review* Vol. 103, p. 245 : 1958.

Anonymous. 1856. "The Khasia Hills". *Calcutta Review.* 27 : 55-93.

Anonymous. 1924. *Handbook of Castes and Tribes employed in Tea Estates in North East India.* Calcutta 1924.

Anonymous. 1958. Naga Interlude. *Social Welfare* Vol. 5, no. 2. 1958.

Anonymous. 1965. Naga Hills *Encyclopaedia Americana,* Vol. 19.

pp : 679-80.

Antrobus, H.A. : *A History of Sikkim,* Edinbrough, 1975.

AO, M. Alemchiba, 1973. Significance of Cultural Research in Nagaland. *The Thinker,* Vol. I. no. 1. Kohima. Feb. 1973.

AO, Shilu. 1953. The Nagas, *Vanyajati,* Vol. I, no. 3, March 1953.

Aonok S. Wati. 1956. Morung Organisation Among the Nocte Nagas, *Vanyajati,* Vol. 4, No. 2. 1956.

Archer, W.G. 1948. The Attitude of Sema Nagas to Dancing by Women. *Man in India,* Vol. 28.

Avery, John : *The Hill Tribes of India,* American Antiquarium, New York, 1884.

Awasty, Indira. 1978. *Between Sikkim and Bhutan.* B.R. Publishing Corporation, New Delhi.

Ayerst, W. 1880. "The Garos". *Indian Antiquary.* 9 : 103.

Bacon, Elizabeth, E. 1965. Naga *Encyclopaedia Americana,* Vol. 19, p. 679 : 1965.

Bagchi, C.G. and S. Sinha. 1972. *Census of India 1961 : West Bengal, Upper Pedong : A village survey monograph.* Calcutta: Government of West Bengal.

Bagchi, R.N. 1979. Family system and inheritance of property among the tribes of Arunachal, *Resarun,* 5 (1) : 39-41.

Baily, F.M. 1945. *China-Tibet-Assam : A journey, 1911.* London : Jonathan.

Balfour, E. : *Cyclopaedia of India,* University of Madras, Madras, 1871.

Balfour, Henry. 1917. Some Types of Native Hoes, Naga Hills. *Man.* Vol. 17. no. 24.

Balfour, Henry. 1925. Thornlineal Traps and Their Distribution. *Man,* Vol. 22.

Balfour, Henry. 1926. Ceremonial Fire Making in Naga Hills. *Man,* Vol. 23. No. 65. June 1926. cultural link. *Custom is King,* London, 1936.

Bandopadhyay, B. 1961. Hira Potters of Assam. *Man in India.* 41: 25-44.

Bareh, H. : *Our Cultural Heritage,* Omas Pub., Tripura, 1999.

Bareh, H. 1967. 'The History and Culture of the Khasi People.' Shillong. Meghalaya Provisional Tables, *Census of India* 1981.

Bareh, H. 1970. Aspects of Social Change in Nagaland. *The Thiker,* Vol. 1, No. 1. Kohima.

Bareh, H. 1973. Nagaland's Pre-history *Highlander* Vol. 1. No. 1 Kohima. March 1973.

Bareh, Hamlet. 1974. *Meghalaya.* Shillong.

Barthakur, J.K. 1972. *Census of India 1971, Arunachal Pradesh Part IIA.* Shillong : Directorate of Census Operation.

Barthakur, J.K. 1972. *Census of India 1971, District Census Handbook : Lohit District Part X-A.* Shillong : Directorate of Census Operation, Arunachal Pradesh.

Barua, G. 1972. *Ahom Buranji.* Gauhati : Assam Govt. Press.

Barua, Hem 1954. *The Red River and the Blue Hill.* Gauhati : Lawyer's Book Stall.

Barua, Hem. 1956. *The red river and the Blue hill.* Guwahati : Lawyer's Book Stall.

Barua, S. 1986. Mating pattern among the Dirang Monpa of West Kameng District, Arunachal Pradesh, *Current Anthropology,* 27 : 188-190.

Barua, T.K.M. 1977. *The Singphos and their religion.* Shillong Directorate of Research, Arunachal Pradesh.

Baruah, B.K. 1951. *A Cultural History of Assam* (Early period), Vol. I., Nowgong : K.L. Barua.

Baruah, I., 1978. *Social Relations in an Ahom Village.* New Delhi: Sterling Publishers Pvt. Ltd.

Baruah, T.K.M. 1960. *The Idu Mishmi.* Shillong : North-East Frontier Agency.

Baruah, T.K.M. 1977. *The Singphos and their Religion.* Shillong: Research Department, Government of Arunachal Pradesh.

Basnet, L.B. 1974. *Sikkim : A Short Political History.* New Delhi: S. Chand and Co.

Basu, S. 1966. 'Bhots of Northern Sikkim', in *Man in India.* 46 (2), April-June.

Bhagabati, A., 1982. *Janajati.* Gauhati : Silver Jubilee Souvenir, M.E. School, Gauhati.

Bhattacharjee, J.B. : *North-east India History,* NEHU Publications, Delhi, 2000.

Bhattacharjee, J.B. 1977. *Cachar under British Rule in North East India.* Delhi : Radiant Publishers.

Bhattacharjee, J.B., 1991. *Social and Polity Formations in Pre-colonial North East India.* Delhi : Har-Anand Publications in association Vikas Publishing House.

Bhattacharjee, N. 1987. *Bharatiya Jati Varna Pratha.* Calcutta: Firma K.L.M.

Bhattacharjee, P.C. 1962. *Asomar Janajati* (in Assamese) Jorhat: Assam Sahitya Sabha.

Bhattacharya, J.N. 1896. *Hindu Castes and Sects.* Calcutta: Editions India (Reprinted in 1968).

Bhattacharya, P.K. 1973. Forests and the Naga Tribes. *Highlander.* Bull. of Cul. Res. and State Museum. Kohima. Government of Nagaland.

Bhattacharya, Pradip Nath. 1983. *The Jamatiyas of Tripura.* Agartala : Directorate of Research, Government of Tripura.

Bhattacharya, Suchinta. 1980. *The Kaipengs.* Agartala : Directorate of Tribal Research, Government of Tripura.

Bhattacherjee. T.K. 1965. *The myths of the Shimongs of the Upper Siang.* Shillong : Research Department, Government of Arunachal Pradesh.

Bhattacherjee. T.K. 1975. *The Tangams.* Shillong : Research Department, Government of Arunachal Pradesh.

Bhowmik, K.K., M.K. Chowdhuri, P. Das, & K.K. Chaudhuri. 1971. *Fertility of zemi women in Nagaland.* Calcutta : Institute of Social Studies.

Bigge, H. 1841. Despatch from Dimapur to Capt. Jenkins, Agent to the Governor General, N.E.F., with a brief general description of the Naga Hills and its People J.A.S.B. no. 110.

Billory, R.K. 1984. The Members of Arunachal Pradesh in *Tribes of North East India.* Edited by Sebastian Karotemprell, pp.

58-61. Shillong : Vendrame Missiological Institute.

Bor, N.L. and Hutton, J.H. : *The Use of Tones in Sema Naga,* J.R.A.S., Nagaland, 1927.

Bordoloi, B.N. and G.C. Sharma Thakur, 1988. *Tribes of Assam. Part II.* Gauhati : Tribal Research Institute.

Bordoloi, B.N., 1972. *District Hand Book, United Mikir and North Cachar Hills,* Gauhati : Tribal Research Institute.

Bordoloi, B.N., 1983. An Ethnographic note on the Hmar of North Cachar Hills District of Assam. *Bulletin of the Tribal Research Institute, Assam* 1 : 1 : 36-51.

Bordoloi, B.N., 1984. *The Dimasa Kachari of Assam.* Gauhati : Tribal Research Institute.

Bordoloi, M. 1964. *Land of the hornbill and myna.* Shillong :

Research Department, Government of Arunachal Pradesh.

Borgohain, H. 1982. Change and Development in the Socio-economic Life of the Adis of West Siang District, *Resarun,* 8 (2) : 36-40.

Bose, J.K. 1934. "Social Organisation of Aimol-Kukis." *Jr. Dept. Letters Univ.,* Calcutta.

Bose, S.C. 1968. *Land and People of the Himalayas.* Calcutta : Indian Publication.

Bower, U.G. 1953. *The hidden land.* London.

Bower, Ursula, G. 1939. The Kabui and Tangkhul Nagas *Journal of the Royal Central Asian Society* (Jan).

Bower, Ursula, G. 1950. *The Naga Path.* London : John Murray.

Brahma, M.M. 1986. 'Social Laws of the Boros.' *Bulletin of Tribal Research Institute* Vol. I. IV pp. 14-18. Gauhati.

Breton, P. ND. On the poison of the Nagas. *Trans. Med. and Phys. Soc.* IV. 235-41, Calcutta.

Briggs, G.W. 1920. *The Chamars.* Calcutta.

Brown, R. 1874. Report on the Exploration of the Angami Naga Country made in connection with the survey of the Naga Hills and Manipur Boundary. 1873 : 74.

Brown, R. 1874. Statistical Account of Manipur. Govt. Press, London.

Burman, S.G. 1963. NEFA : Its land and people, *Indian Quarterly,* 19 (4).

Butler, Capt. J. 1874. *Report on the Exploration Survey of the Naga Hills.* Shillong : Secretariat Press.

Butler, J. 1847. *A sketch of Assam.* London.

Cantlie, Audrey, 1984 *Assamese Religion, caste and set in an Indian village.* London : Curzon Press in collaboration with United Publishing, Gauhati.

Cantlie, Sir K. 1974 (Reprint). *Notes on Khasi Law,* Shillong.

Carey, P.S. and H.N. Tuck 1932. *The Chin Hills,* Calcutta, Firma KLM Pvt. Ltd. (Reprint).

Census of India 1891 Assam Vol. I Report, Shillong, India.

Census of India 1981, Series 19, Sikkim : District Handbook, p. 28.

Census of India. 1892. *Assam Report.* 1891 Vol. 1 Shillong.

Census of India. 1923. *Assam Report.* 1921, Vol. 3, Part I. Shillong.

Census of India. 1961. Assam Dist. Census Handbook. UK-J Hills. Gauhati.

Census of India. 1961. Registrar General Govt. of India, New Delhi.

Census of India. 1961. *Tripura* (General Report). Vol. XXVI. Part I (i).

Census of India. 1971. Meghalaya.

Census of India. 1981. Meghalaya.

Chaki-Sircar 1984. *Feminism in a Traditional Society.* New Delhi, Shakti Books.

Chakladar, H.C. and T.C. Raychoudhuri 1957. "The Kabui" *Man in India:* 37 : 192-198.

Chakravartti, R. 1986. *People of Manipur.* Delhi, B.R. Publishing Corporation.

Chakravarty, L.N. 1973. *Glimpses of the early history of Arunachal.* Shillong : Research Department, Arunachal Pradesh Administration.

Chandra, P.R. 1981. 'Sikkim : Its Old Laws and Customs', in *North Bengal University Review* (*Humanities and Social Science*).

Chari, R.B. 1975. *Census of India 1971, Scheduled Castes and Scheduled Tribes : Series I. Paper I of 1975.* Delhi : The Government of India Press.

Chari, R.V. 1971. *Census of India, Scheduled Castes and Scheduled Tribes.* Series 1. Delhi : Government of India, Delhi.

Chatterjee, S.N. 1984. *Tripura : a profile.* New Delhi : Inter-India Publications.

Chatterjee, Suniti. 1923. "Study of Kol." *Calcutta Review.* pp. 451-473.

Chatterji, N. 1975. *Status of Women in the Earlier Mizo Society,* Tribal Research Institute, Aizwal.

Chatterji, N. 1975. *Zawlbuk as a Social Institution in the Mizo Society,* Tribal Research Institute, Aizawl.

Chatterji, S.K. 1947. *The place of Assam in the History of Civilization of India.* Guwahati : Department of Publication, University of Guwahati.

Chatterji, S.K. 1950. *Kirata Jana-Kriti.* Calcutta : Asiatic Society.

Chatterji, S.K. 1974. *Kirata-Jana-Krti : the Indo-Mongoloids, their contribution to the History and Culture of India.* Calcutta : The Asiatic Society. Revised second edition.

Chattopadhyay, K. 1978. *Tribalism in India.* Vikas : New Delhi.

Chattopadhyay, S.K. (ed). 1985. *Tribal Institutions of Meghalaya.* Spectrum. Gauhati.

Chaudhuri, J.C. 1982. "The Halam : A study of a tribal community of Tripura." *Educational Miscellany.*

Chaudhury, J.N. 1978. *Kasi Canvas.* Shillong.

Chaudhury, P.C., 1959. *The History of Civilisation of the People of Assam to the Twelfth century A.D.* Gauhati : Department of Historical and Antiquirian Studies.

Chemjong, I.S. 1966. *History and Culture of the Kirat People.* 2 Vols. Kathmandu : Tumeng Hang.

Chib, S.S. : *Caste, Tribe and Cultural of India : Northeastern India,* Anil Pub., New Delhi, 1986.

Chib, Sukhdev Singh. 1988. *This beautiful India—Tripura.* New Delhi. Essess Publications.

Chie Nakane 1967. *Garo and Khasi : A Comparative Study in Matrilineal Systems.* Mouton & Co. Paris.

Chishti, S.M. A.W. : Christian Mission in Manipur (1926-29) *Soc. Research.* 2 (1) : 48-51.

Chopra, P.N. 1979. *Sikkim.* New Delhi : S. Chand and Co. Ltd.

Choube, S.K. (*ed.*). 1985. *The Himalayas : Profiles of Modernization and Adaptation.* New Delhi : Sterling.

Choudhuri, B. and Chanda, S. (ed). 1984. *Glimpses of Tripura.* Agartala: Tripura Darpan Publications.

Choudhury, B.N. 1868. *The Cultural and Linguistic Aspects of the Garos.* Guwahati.

Choudhury, P. 1966. *The History of Civilization of the People of Assam to the 12th century A.D.* Calcutta.

Choudhury, P.C. : *The History of the Civilisation of the People of North-east to the Twelfth Century A.D.,* Concept Pub., Madras, 1959.

Chowdhury, J.N. 1970. *The Hill Miris of Subansiri.* Shillong : Research Department, Government of Arunachal Pradesh.

Chowdhury, J.N. 1973. *Arunachal Panorama.* Shillong : Jaya Choudhury.

Chowdhury, J.N. 1982. *Arunachal through the Ages :* Shillong : Jaya Choudhury.

Chowdhury, K. 1976. *The Manipuri Mohammedan,* Silchar : Assam.

Chowdhury, Uma. 1953. Role of women among the Padam tribe, *March of India.* 6 (2) : 20-23.

Clark, M.M. 1907. *A Corner in India.* Philadelphia.

Coelho, V.N. 1967. *Sikkim and Bhutan.* New Delhi : Indian Council for Cultural Relations.

Constantine, R. 1981. *Manipur Maid of the Mountains.* New Delhi, Lancers Publishers.

Crawford, C.G. 1927. *Handbook of Kuki Customs.* Manipur.

Crooke, W. 1896. *Caste and Tribes of N.W.P. and Oudh.* Vol. IV. Calcutta.

Culshaw, W.J. 1949. *Tribal Heritage.* London : Lutterworth Press.

Dahotia, S.K. 2981. *Moran Matak Mayamora.* Tinsukia : Assam.

Dalton, E.T. 1872. *Descriptive Ethnology of Bengal,* Calcutta : Office of the Superintendent of Government Printing Press.

Dalton, E.T. 1872. *Descriptive Ethnology of Bengal.* Calcutta.

Dalton, E.T. 1960. *Descriptive ethnology of Bengal.* Calcutta : Firma K.L. Mukhopadhyay.

Damant, G.H. 1878-79. *Administrative Report of Naga Hills.* Shillong Government Press.

Danda, D., 1978. *Among the Dimasa of Assam : An Ethnographic Study.* New Delhi : Sterling Publishing Pvt. Ltd.

Das Gupta, K. 1968. *An introduction to Central Monpa.* Shillong: Research Department, Government of Arunachal Pradesh.

Das Gupta. P.K., 1984. *Tribe and Culture of Matrilineal Tribe of Meghalaya.* New Delhi : Inter India Publications.

Das, A.K. 1968. "Analysis of the social system of the Kharias". *Bulletin of Cultural Research Institute* VII (1 & 2), 85-88.

Das, B.M. (ed.) 1974. *Contemporary Anthropology in North East India.* Dibrugarh, Dibrugarh University, Publications.

Das, B.M. 1981. *Microevolution.* Concept Publishing House. New Delhi.

Das, B.M., 1956. A note on the Hira Potters of Assam. *Man in India* 36 : 3 : 199-202.

Das, B.M., 1985. *The peoples of Assam : Their Ethnic Composition.* Gauhati: Text Book Foundation Courses of Gauhati University.

Das, B.S. 1982. *Sikkim Saga.* Vikas, New Delhi.

Das, N.K. 1977. Urgent Anthropological Research in Nagaland. *Highlander,* No. 1 and 2. Vol. V.

Das, N.K. 1978. The Pattern of Social Change in Nagaland. *Highlander.* Nos. 1 & 2. March-September 1978.

Das, N.K. 1982c. "Tribe" As a Segmentary Social system : The Case of the Zounuo-Keyhonuo Naga. *Social Research.* Vol. IV

Das, N.K. 1983a. The Ritual Kinship and the Traditional Political System of the Ao Naga. Socioal Research. No. 1. Vol. 3.

Das, N.K. 1983b. The Emergence and Role of Naga Hills in Independent India in *The Emergence and role of middle class in North East India.* B. Dutta Roy (ed). New Delhi : Upal Publication.

Das, N.K. 1984. Angami Naga. *In Tribal Education in India.* B.K. Dasgupta and A.K. Danda (eds) Calcutta : Anthropological Survey of India.

Das, N.K. 1984. *The Social Organisation of the Angami Naga.* M/s. Anthropological Survey of India.

Das, N.K. 1985a. *The Politico-Jural Aspects of the Segmentary Social System of the Zuo-Keyhonuo Naga (The southern Angamis).* Unpublished Ph.D. Thesis, Gauhati University.

Das, N.K. 1988. Agnatic Descent, Matrifiliation and Endogamy: Implications of descent-Group in marriage among the Southern Angami Nagas. *Marriage in India.* Goswami, B.B., J. Sarkar, D. Danda (Eds) Calcutta : Anthropological Survey of India.

Das, N.K. 1988. *Special Study of the Anthropological Aspects of the Zeliangrong Area in North East India.* A report prepared for the Prime Minister's office, New Delhi. Office of the Director General, Anthropological Survey of India, New Delhi.

Das, N.K. 1989. *Ethnic Identity, Ethnicity and Social Stratification in North East India.* New Delhi : Inter India Publications.

Das, N.K. 1989. *Ethnic Identity, Ethnicity and Social Stratification in North East India.* New Delhi, Inter India Publications.

Das, N.K. and P.B.S. V. Padmanabham. 1983. *The Karbi of Assam.* Calcutta : Anthropological Survey of India. Report prepared under project Tribes in Contemporary India.

Das, T.C. 1945. *The Purums : An Old Kuki Tribe of Manipur.* Calcutta, University of Calcutta.

Dasgupta, Biman K., A. Basu, Bikash Roychoudhury & P. Gupta *Purum (Chote) Revisited.* Calcutta, Anthropological Survey of India.

Dasgupta, P.K. 1984. *Life and Culture of Matrilineal Tribe of Meghalaya.* Inter India Pub. New Delhi.

Dash, A.J. 1907. *Bengal District Gazetteers : Darjeeling District.* Calcutta : Bengal Government Press.

Datta, A.M. 1987. *A study on the Lushais of Jampui Hills in Tripura.* Agartala : Directorate of Research.

Davis, A.W. 1981. Naga Tribes, *Assam Census Report.* Shillong : Government Press.

Deb Barma, R. 1981. *The Tribes of Tripura.* Tripura : Directorate of Tribal Research, Government of Tripura.

Deb Barman, S. 1987. *The Chakmas and the Maghs,* Agartala : Kishore Press.

Deb-Roy, H.L. 1981. A *Tribe in Transition - the Jaintias of Meghalaya.* Cosmo Publication. New Delhi.

Deka, Anee 1978. *Reproductive Performance and Selection among the Jaintias of Village Saphai* (Unpublished).

Deuri, D. 1964. *Deori Sanskriti.* Jorhat : Janam Bhumi Press.

Deuri R.K. 1983. *Festivals of Kameng.* Shillong : Directorate of Research, Government of Arunachal Pradesh.

Deuri, R.K. 1982. *The Sulung.* Shillong : Research Department, Government of Arunachal Pradesh.

Deuri. R.K. 1983. Rituals, beliefs and practices of the Miju Mishmis of Lohit Valley, *Resarun,* 9 (2) : 1-4.

Dev Barman, T.J.M. 1958. "Origin of Tripura and its people". *Vanyajati,* 6 (3).

Dev. Bimal J. and D.K. Lahiri, 1984. *Cosmogony of Caste and Social mobility in Assam.* Delhi : Mittal Publication.

Dhar, B., 1985 Monpa Tribe : An inter-ethnic interaction. *Human Science* 34. 1 : 67-70.

Dhar, Bibhash. 1984. "The Monpas of Khalakthang area, alias the Tsangla. A brief ethnographic account", in *The Tribes of North East India.* Edited by Sebastian Karotemprell, pp, 290-306. Shillong : Vendrame Missiological Institute.

Dhasmana, M.M. 1985. *The Ramos of Arunachal Pradesh.* New Delhi : Concept Publishing Co.

Directorate of Research. 1980. *The Kaipengs.* Agartala : Government of Tripura. 1980 *Tripura Lushai Kukider Itikatha* (in Bengali), Agartala, Government of Tripura.

Ditcher. 1968. *Nagaland Capital,* April 25. 803.

Duara, D.K. : *Neolithic Celts from Subansiri District,* Arunachal News, A.P., 1979.

Dubey, S.M. 1975. Modernisations and elites in Arunachal Pradesh. *Census of India, 1971.* Delhi : Government of India Publications.

Dun, Capt. E.W. 1975 *Gazetteer of Manipur.* New Delhi, Vivek Publishing House, (first published in 1896).

Dunbar, G. 1916. *Abors and Gallongs.* Calcutta : Asiatic Society.

Dutta Choudhuri, S. Editor 1978. *Arunachal Pradesh, Tirap District Gazetteer.* Shillong : Government of Arunachal Pradesh.

Dutta Choudhuri, S. Editor 1981. *Arunachal Pradesh Subansiri District Gazetteer.* Shillong : Government of Arunachal Pradesh.

Dutta Chowdhury, S. 1978. *Gazetteer of India, Arunachal Pradesh. Lohit District. Shillong :* Government of Arunachal Pradesh.

Dutta, A. 1986. *Report on joint multi-disciplinary expedition of Subansiri.*

Dutta, D.K. 1983. Sajalong : The ancestor of the Mijis, *Resarun,* 9 (2) : 34-35.

Dutta, P., 1978. *The Noctes.* Shillong : Directorate of Research. Government of Arunachal Pradesh.

Dutta, P.N. *Impact of the West on Khasis and Jaintias.* Cosmo Publication. New Delhi.

Dutta, P.S. : *History of the North-east,* Omsons Publications, New Delhi, 1986.

Dutta, Parul. 1959. *The Tangsas.* Shillong : North-East Frontier Agency.

Dutta, Parul. 1969. *The Noctes.* Shillong : Directorate of Research, Government of Arunachal Pradesh.

Edgar, J.W. 1874. *Report on a Visit to Sikkim and the Tibetan Frontier in October, November and December 1873.* Calcutta: Bengal Secretariat Press.

Elwin, V. : *Sikkim in the 19th Century,* Popular Prakashan, Bombay, 1969.

Elwin, Verrier. 1965. *Democracy in NEFA.* Shillong : North-East Frontier Agency.

Elwin, Verrier. 1958. *Myths of the North-East Frontier of India.* Shillong : North-East Frontier Agency.

Elwin, Verrier. 1959. *A Philosophy for NEFA.* Shillong : Advisor's Secretariat, North-East Frontier Agency.

Elwin, Verrier. 1961. *Nagaland.* Shillong : Research Deptt. NEFA Administration.

Elwin, Verrier. 1969. *The Nagas in the Nineteenth Century :* Bombay : Oxford University Press.

Endle, S. 1911. *The Kacharis.* Macmillan and Co. Ltd. London.

Ering, O. 1971. Evil spirits in the Adi land, *NEFA Information,* 6 (2) : 24-28.

Ering, O. 1983. Adi belief and faith. *Arunachal News,* 12 (5) : 25-26.

Evans-Wentz, W.Y. 1957. *The Tibetan Book of the Dead.* London : Oxford University Press.

Fuchs, Stephen. 1966-67. Messianic Movements in Tribal India. *The Journal of the Asiatic Society of Bombay,* 20 (1-2) : 15-33.

Furer-Haimendorf, C. von. 1938. The Morung system of the Konyak Nagas, Assam, JRAI LXVIII, ii.

Furer-Haimendorf, C. von. 1938. Through the Unexplored Mountains of the Assam-Burma Border. *Geographical journal.* XCI, 3.

Furer-Haimendorf, C. von. 1939. Konyak Naga Head Hunters as agriculturists. *Illustrated London News.* 8 July.

Furer-Haimendorf, C. von. 1939. The Megalithic Culture of the Naga Tribes of Assam. *Research and Progress* Vol. 2. Berlin.

Furer-Haimendorf, C. von. 1939. *The Naked Nagas.* London : Methuen.

Furer-Haimendorf, C. von. 1946. *The Naked Nagas Head Hunters of Assam in peace and war.* Thacker Spink & Co. Ltd. Calcutta.

Furer-Haimendorf, C.V. 1947. *Ethnographic notes on the Eastern Himalayas, Diaries of travel in the Subansiri region, 1944 and 1945.* Shillong : North-East Frontier Agency.

Furer-Haimendorf, C.V. (Ed) 1981. *Asian Highland Societies.* New Delhi: Sterling Publications Pvt. Ltd.

Furer-Haimendorf, C.V. 1944. Culture types in Assam Himalayas, *Indian Geographical Journal,* 21 : 1-9.

Furer-Haimendorf, C.V. 1949. Anthropology and Administration in the tribal areas of the North-East Frontier, *Eastern Anthropologist,* 3 : 37-49.

Furer-Haimendorf, C.V. 1955. *Himalayan barbery.* London : John Murray.

Furer-Haimendorf, C.V. 1962. *The Apatanis and their neighbours.* London: Routledge and Kegan Paul.

Furer-Haimendorf, C.V. 1980. *A Himalayan tribe : From cattle to cash.* New Delhi : Vikas Publishing House Pvt. Ltd.

Furer-Haimendorf, C.V. 1982. *Highlanders of Arunachal Pradesh.* New Delhi. Vikas Publishing House Pvt. Ltd.

Furer-Haimendorn, C. and J.P. Mills. 1936. The sacred Founders Kin among the Eastern Angami Nagas. *Anthropos,* XXXI.

Furer-Haimendorn, C. von. 1946. *The Naked Nagas.* Calcutta Thacker Spink and Co. Ltd.

Furer-Haimendorn, C. von. 1974. *Return to the Naked Nagas.* New Delhi: Vikas Publications.

Gait E.A. 1965. *History of Assam.* Calcutta : Thacker Spink & Co.

Gait, E. 1967 (Reprint). *A History of Assam.* Thacker Spink Co. Calcutta.

Gait, E.A. 1892, *Assam, Census Report,* 1891. Shillong, Assam Sectt. Printing Press.

Gait, E.A. Davis. 1891. *Report on the Census of Assam* (237-251) Shillong: Assam Secretariat. Vol. I.

Gait, Edward. A. 1933. "Manipur" in *History of Assam.* Calcutta, Thacker Spink and Co.

Gait. E.A. 1906. *History of Assam.* Calcutta.

Gaite, A.E. : *History of Sikkim,* MacMillan, London, 1907.

Gan-Chaudhury, Jagadis : *Sikkim : The Land and its People,* DK Pub., Delhi, 1979.

Gan-Chaudhury, Jagadish, (Ed)., 1979. *Tripura : The land and its people.* Delhi : Leeladevi Publications.

Gan-Chaudhury, Jagadish. 1983. *The Riangs of Tripura.* Directorate of Research, Dept. of Welfare for Scheduled Tribes and Scheduled Castes. Government of Tripura.

Gangmumei, Kabui 1974. "Social and religious reform movement in Manipur in the 19th and 20th Centuries." *Bulletin of the Division of History :* Imphal Centre of Post Graduate Studies Jawaharlal Nehru University; pp. 53-75.

Ganguly, Milada. 1984. *A Pilgrimage to the Nagaland.* New Delhi; Oxford and IBH Publishing Co.

Ganguly, J.B. 1983. *Benigu Hills.* Agartala : Tripura Darpan Prakasan.

Ghose, B.B. 1979. *Nagaland District Gazetteer* Wokha District. Kohima. Government of Nagaland.

Ghose, B.B. 1980. *History of Nagaland.* New Delhi. S. Chand & Company Ltd.

Gimson, C. 1926. Some notes on the Maring Nagas of Manipur. *Man in India :* Vol. 6.

Gob, W.G., 1911. *The Lusei.* Reprinted in Census of India. 1961. Vol. 3 Assam Part V-A.

Godden, G.M. 1896. Naga and other Tribes of North East India, *J.R.A.I.* XXVI.

Godwin Austen, H.H. 1873. Report on the survey operations during the field season 1872-73 in the Nagas Hills and Manipur, Calcutta Survey of India.

Godwin Austen, N.H. 1875. On the Rude stone monuments of certain Naga Tribes *JRAI* IV.

Gogoi, L., 1971. *Tai Sanskriti Rup Rekha* (in Assamese) Calcutta : Firma K.L.M.

Gogoi, P., 1966. *The Tai People of Assam. 'Lik Fan Tai.'* Vol. I. Guwahati: Department of Historical and Antiquarian Studies.

Gorer, G. 1967. *Himalayan Village, An account of the Lepchas of Sikkim.* Second edition. London : Thomas Nelson and Sons.

Goswami, B.B. 1962. "Mizo laws of inheritance". *Bulletin of the Tribal Culture and Folklore Research.* Guwahati University.

Gougin, T. 1984. *History of Zomi,* Zomi Press, Manipur.

Government of India 1971. *Census of India : Manipur,* New Delhi, Government of India Press.

Government of Manipur n.d. *Manipuri Customs* (Codified by the Codification Committee). Imphal, Government Press, Manipur Administration.

Grange, E.R. 1840. Extracts from the Journal of an expedition into the Naga Hills *J.A.S.B.* 1840, Vol. IX, pp. 953-8.

Grange, G.R. 1839. Narrative of an expedition into the Naga Territory of Assam *J.A.S.B.* VIII. I. 70.

Grierson, A (ed.) 1903. *The Linguistic Survey of India.* Calcutta.

Grierson, G. 1903. *Linguistic Survey of India,* Superintendent, Govt. Printing. Calcutta : Government Press.

Grierson, G.A. 1923. *Report on the Linguistic Survey of India.* Calcutta.

Grierson, G.A. 1968. *Linguistic Survey of India,* 5 (1) : 321. New Delhi : Gyan Publication (reprint).

Grierson, G.A., 1903. *Linguistic Survey of India,* Vol. III Parts II and III and VI. Superintendent. Govt. Printing. Calcutta : Government Press.

Grierson, G.A., 1904. *Linguistic Survey of India,* Vol. II Part II. Calcutta: Government Printing Press.

Grierson, G.A., 1987. *Languages of North Eastern India—A Survey,* Vol. II. Delhi : Gian Publishing House.

Grover, B.S.K. 1974. *Sikkim and India, Storm and Consolidation.* New Delhi : Jain Brothers.

Guha, B.S. 1973. *Racial Ethnology of India,* The Field Science of India.

Gupta, Kali Prasanna. *Rajmala* (First part, Trilochan Khanda chapter).

Gupta, S.P. 1955. "Riang shradh". *Vanyajati.* Vol. 3 (1), 6-9.

Gurdon P.R.T. 1907. *The Khasis* London : David Natt.

Gurdon, P.R.T. 1895. On the Khamtis. *Journal of the Royal Asiatic Society.* 27 : 157-163.

Gurdon, P.R.T. 1904. 'Note on the Khasis, Syntengs, and Allied Tribes, Inhabiting the Khasi and Jaintia Hills District in Assam', *Journal of the Asiatic Society of Bengal,* Vol. LXXIII part III no. 4.

Gurdon, P.R.T. 1980 (Reprint). *The Khasis.* Cosmo Publication. New Delhi.

Gyaltshen, K.T. 1977. 'Note on Buddhist Communities of Sikkim', in *Orient,* 6 : 1-2.

Gyanchand : *India's Teeming Million,* MacMillan, London, 1939.

Hajger, N., 1974. *Dimasa* (in Assamese). Jorhat : Assam Sahitya Sabha.

Haldipur, K. 1985. *Around the Hills and Dales of Arunachal Pradesh.* Shillong : North Eastern Hill University.

Hambers Capt. O.A. 1889. *Handbook of the Lushai Country.* Calcutta : Government Printing Press.

Hamilton, A. 1912. *In Abor jungles.* London : Eveleigh Nash.

Hamlet, Barch. 1967. *The history and culture of the Khasi people.* Calcutta.

Hefley, James and Marti, 1976. *God's Tribesman, The Rochunga Pudaite Story,* Viclor Books.

Hesselmeyer, C.H. 1968. The hill tribes of North-East Frontier of Assam, *Journal of Asiatic Society of Bengal,* 37 : 192-208.

Highlander, Vol. II, no. 369, Aizawl.

Hodson, T.C. : *The Primitive Culture of India,* Royal Asiatic Society, New Delhi, 1922.

Hodson, T.C. 1908. Funerary Customs and Eschatological Belief among Hill Tribes of Assam. *Transactions of the Third International Congress of Religions.* Oxford.

Hodson, T.C. 1908. *The Meteis.* Delhi. (Reprinted in 1975).

Hodson, T.C. 1910. Some Naga customs and Superstitions. *Folklore,* XXI.

Hodson, T.C. 1921. "The Garo and Khasi marriage systems contrasted". *Man in India.* 1 (2) : 106-127.

Hodson, TC. 1905. Genna among the Tribes of Assam *J.R.A.I.* XXXVI 92-103.

Hooker, J.D. 1854. *Himalayan Journals : Notes of a Naturalist in Bengal, the Sikkim and Nepal Himalayas, the Khasia Mountains etc.* 2 vols. London : John Murray. 1954. *'Himalayan Journal',* chapter V of above reprinted in Mitra, A., *Census of India 1951 : West Bengal : District Census Handbook : Darjeeling.* Calcutta : West Bengal Government Press.

Hussain, M. : *Sikkim,* Reema Pub., New Delhi, 1988.

Hussain, M., 1987. The Muslim of the contemporary Assam : A Sociological Introduction. *Journal of the North East India Council for Social Science Research.* 11 : 2 : 21-28.

Hutton, J.H. 1920. Leopard-men in the Naga Hills. *Journal of the Royal Anthropological Institute of Great Britain and Ireland.* January to June. 1920.

Hutton, J.H. 1921. *The Angami Nagas.* London : MacMillan and Co. Ltd.

Hutton, J.H. 1921. *The Sema Nagas,* London : Oxford University Press.

Hutton, J.H. 1922. A Type of Snare from the Phom Country, Divide and Decorated Heads As Trophies : A Konyak Naga snare *Man,* XXII. vii. viii. xii.

Hutton, J.H. 1922. Carved Monoliths at Dimapur and an Angami Naga Ceremony Meaning and method of the Erection of the Monoliths by the Naga Tribes : *J.R.A.I.* III.

Hutton, J.H. 1922. Leopard Men in the Naga Hills *Smithsonian Institute's* report, 1921.

Hutton, J.H. 1923. Carved Monoliths at Jamuguri. *J.R.A.I.* LIII.

Hutton, J.H. 1925. Some Astronomical beliefs in Assam *Folkore* Vol. XXXVI, No. II, June 1925.

Hutton, J.H. 1927. The Nagas of Assam and the Children of Sun *Man,* July.

Hutton, J.H. 1929. *Diaries of two tours in the Unadministered area East of Bengal.* Vol. XI, No. 1, 1929. Calcutta : Baptist Mission Press.

Hutton, J.H. 1931. Wild men in Assam. *Journal and Proceedings,* Asiatic Society of Bengal (New Series) Vol. XXVII, No. 2.

Hutton, J.H. 1939. The Rengma Nagas. Review. *Man.* XXXIX. 25 (Feb.)

Hutton, J.H. 1951. *Caste in India.* Bombay : Oxford University Press.

Hutton, J.H. 1965. The Mixed Culture of the Naga Tribes. *J.R.A.I.* XCV.

Hutton, J.H. 1969. *The Angami Nagas.* Bombay : Oxford University Press.

James Long. 1850. "Analysis of the Rajmala". *Journal of Asiatic Society of Bengal.* Calcutta.

Jaswal, I.J.S. and Susma Jaswal. 1981. Age at Menarche among the Apatanis of Arunachal Pradesh, *Bulletin of the Department of Anthropology,* Dibrugarh University, 10 : 55-60.

Jenkins, Major : *A Sketch of our Relations with the Angami Nagas,* Oxford, New York, 1994.

Jha, S.D. 1986. *Arunachal Pradesh,* New Delhi : Omsons Publications.

Johri, B. : *Art and Culture of North-east India.* Publications Division, New Delhi, 1998.

K. Cantlie, 1974 (Reprint). *Notes on Khasi Law.* Shillong.

Kabui, Gangmumei. 1985. *Anal : a transborder tribe of Manipur.* Delhi, Mittal Publications.

Kakati, B.K. 1962. *Kalita Jatir Itibritta* (in Assamese). Gauhati : Lawyer's Book Stall.

Kamkhemthang, H. 1986. An Introduction to Tribal Culture and Language in Manipur, Imphal.

Kamkhenthang, H. 1988. *The Paite,* (A trans-border tribe of India) Delhi, Mittal Publications.

Kandell, A.S. and Salisbury, C.Y. 1977. *Mountaintop Kingdom : Sikkim.* New Delhi : Vikas.

Kapadia, K.M. 1950. The Matrilineal Social System of the Nagas of Assam, Bombay.

Kar, R.K. and B. Mahanta. 1975. Menarche and menopause among the Singpho women of Arunachal Pradesh. *Indian Journal of Physical Anthropology and Human Genetics,* 1 : 51-57.

Karan, P.P. and Jenkins, W.M. 1963. *Himalayan Kingdom : Bhutan, Sikkim, Nepal.* New Jersey : D. Van Nostrand.

Karotemprel, S., 1984. *The Tribes of North East India,* Calcutta: Firma K.L.M.

Kennedy, R.S. 1914. *Ethnological reports on the Akas, Khowas and Mijis and the Memba of Tawang.* Shillong.

Kent, D. 1971. *Census of Nagaland,* Director of Census Operation, Kohima; Nagaland.

Khan, Abdul Majeed. 1969. *The Transition in Bengal.* Cambridge.

Khasi, 1978. *The Illustrated Encyclopedia of Mankind.* Marshall Cavendish Ltd. London.

Khongphai, A.S. (ed). 1974 (Reprint). *Principles of Khasi Law,* Shillong.

Kotturen, G. 1983. *The Himalayan Gateway : History and Culture of Sikkim.* New Delhi : Sterling.

Kumar, K. 1978. *The Boris.* Shillong : Research Department, Government of Arunachal Pradesh.

Kumar, K. 1979. *The Pailibos.* Shillong : Research Department, Government of Arunachal Pradesh.

Laitanga, C. (ed.) 1981. *Know your own land* (Mizoram series-I-III), Calcutta, Firma KLM Private Ltd. (on behalf of Tribal Research Institute, Aizawl, Mizoram).

Lal, J.S. 1981. *The Himalaya : Aspects of Change.* Delhi : Oxford University Press.

Lal, P. and B.K. Dasgupta. 1979. *Lower Siang People.* Calcutta : Anthropological Survey of India.

Lall, K. 1966. 'The Thami', in *The Rising Nepal.* Kathmandu.

Lalthangliana, B. 1975. *History of Mizo in Burma.* Mandalay History Department, Arts and Science University.

Lehman, F.K. 1979. Review of Lalthangliana's book *History of Mizo in Burma* in *Thu Leh Hia* Sept. 1979, Aizawl.

Lehman, T.K. (n.d.) *Kuki : The structure of Chin Society)- a tribal people of Burma adopted to a non-Western Civilization:* Urbana, University of Illinois (Studies in Anthropology).

Lepper, C.H. 1882. Notes on the Singpho and Khampti country. North-East Frontier, *Proceedings of the Asiatic Society of Bengal.*

Lewin, T.H. 1896. *The Hill Tracts of Chittagong and the Dwellers therein.* Calcutta.

Lewin, T.H. *Wild races of South-Eastern India.*

Little C.B. and J. West 1884. *Gazetteer of Manipur,* Calcutta.

LLoyd, G.T. 1923. *Assam Report-1921.* Shillong Census of India. Government Press.

Luthra, P.N. 1964. *Mishmis of Lohit Frontier Division,* Folklore, 5 (2) : 62-66.

Lyall, C. 1908. *The Mikirs.* London : David Nuff (Reprinted) United Publishers, Panbazar, Gauhati (Assam).

Lyall, Sir Charles. 1908. *The Mikirs.* London : David Nutt.

Lyngdoh, F.B. and B.K. Roy Burman. 1961. Mikirs of Assam, *Census of India, 1961,* Vol. 1, monograph series. New Delhi: Office of the Registrar General of India, Ministry of Home Affairs.

M'Cosh, J. 1836. Accounts of the mountain tribes on the extreme North-East Frontier of Bengal, *Journal of the Asiatic Society of Bengal,* 5.

Macaulay, C. 1885/1977. *Report of a Mission to Sikkim and the Tibetan Frontier, 1884.* Calcutta : Bengal Secretariat Press. Reprinted Kathmandu : Ratna Pustak Bhandar.

Macgregor, C.R. 1884. Notes on Akas and Akaland. *Proceedings of the Asiatic Society of Bengal.*

Mackenzie, A. 1869. *Memorandum on the North East Tribes,* Calcutta : Bengal Secretariat Press.

Mackenzie, A. 1884. *History of the Relations of the Government with the hill tribes of the North-East Frontier of Bengal.* Calcutta (reprint 1979). *North-East Frontier of India.* Delhi : Mittal Publications.

Maitland, P. 1880. Detailed Report on the Naga Hills Expedition of 1879-80. Simla.

Majumdar, B.C. 1936. *Elements of Social Anthropology.* Calcutta: University of Calcutta.

Majumdar, D.N. 1968. 'An Account of Magico-religious Rites and Beliefs of Rongdani Rabha.' *Bulletin of the Anthropological Suvery of India* 17.

Majumdar, D.N. 1968. 'A Study of the Clan Organisation of the Rabha.' *Bulletin of the Anthropogical Survey of India* 17.

Majumdar, D.N. 1972. Acculturation among the Hajong. *Man in India.* 54 : 46-83.

Majumdar, S.N. 1924. The Ao Nagas. *Man in India.* IV 1 and 2.

Male, P.F. 1971. *Sikkim.* Calcutta : Oxford and I.B.H.

Mallo, D.M. 1989. Inter-tribe marriage. *Arunachal Newsletter,* March 27: 4.

Mathew, T. : *North-east,* Spectrum Publications, Gauhati, 1980.

Maxwell, H. 1878. *Administrative Report of the Naga Hills.* London.

M. Call, A.G. 1949. *Lushai Chrysalis.,* Luzac and Company Ltd., London.

MC. Rae, John. 1801. Account of the Kookies or Lunctas *Asiatic Researches.* VII. VI.

McCormack, Anna P. 1969. 'The Khasis'. *Ethnic Groups of Mainland South East Asia.* F.M. Lebar et al ed., New Haven.

McCulloch, Major W. 1859. "Account of the Valley of Manipore and the Hill Tribes with a comparative vocabulary of the Manipore and other languages." In *Selection from the Records of Government of India (Foreign Deptt.) XXVII,* Calcutta.

Mills, J.P. & J.H. Hutton. 1930. Ancient Monoliths of North Cachar, *J.A.S.B.* XXV.

Mills, J.P. 1922. *The Lhota Nagas,* London : Macmillan.

Mills, J.P. 1923. The lesson of the Red Man, *Man in India* III, IV.

Mills, J.P. 1926. The Head Hunters of Assam. *Illustrated London News,* February.

Mills, J.P. 1928. Hill Tribes of Assam. *Assam Review,* I, nos. 1 to 8, and no. 10. Silchar.

Mills, J.P. 1935. Sanctuary of Savages, *Geographical Magazine,* July.

Mills, J.P. 1935. The Effect of Ritual upon Industries and Arts in Naga Hills, *Man* 35.

Mills, J.P. 1937. *The Rengma Nagas.* London : Macmillan & Co. Ltd.

Mills, J.P. 1947. Note on head hunting among the Mishmis of the Lohit Valley Assam, *Man in India,* 27 : 74-75.

Mills. J.P. 1952. Mishmis of Lohit Valley of Assam, *Journal of the Royal Anthropological Institute,* 82.

Minattur, J. 1955. "Khasi religion". *Man in India.* 35 (3) : 233-236.

Miri, Sujata 1979. 'Rituals and War Jaintia', Journal of the NEICSSR. Vol. III, no. I.

Misra, R.C. 1977. *Sikkim Joins The Motherland.* Ajay Bandhu Fort, Bharatpur.

Mitchell, H.J. 1928. Report on the Naga Hills (Upper Chindwin) Expedition for the Abolition of Human Sacrifice, Rangoon.

Mitra A., 1961. *Census of India* Vol. I, Part II-C (4). Language Tables. New Delhi : Govt. of India Press.

Mitra, A. 1951. *Census of India, 1951, West Bengal. The Tribes and Castes of West Bengal.* Calcutta.

Mitra, A. 1954. *Census of India 1951 : West Bengal : District Census Handbook : Darjeeling.* Calcutta : West Bengal Government Press.

Mitra, A.K. 1956. "The Riang of Tripura". *Bulletin of the Department of Anthropology*. 5 (2).

Morris, C.J. 1938. *Living with the Lepchas : A Book about the Sikkim Himalayans.* London : William Heinemann.

Morris, C.J. 1985. *The Gurkhas : an Ethnology*. Delhi : B.R. Publications.

Mukherjee, B. 1956. "The cult of dead and funerary customs of the Riang". *Bulletin of the Department of Anthropology*. 4 (2).

Mukherjee, B. 1959. "Trends of changes in Riang culture since independence". *Bulletin of the Department of Anthropology*. 8 (2).

Mukherjee, B. 1960. "Cross-cousin marriage among the Riang". *Anthropologist.*

Mullan, C.S. 1932. *Assam Report 1931.* Calcutta, Census of India, Pub. Branch.

Munshi, S. and Lama, U. 1978. 'The Tamangs of Darjeeling. A Study of a Group Identity', in *Journal of the Indian Anthropological Society.* 13 (2).

Nair, P.T. 1985. *Tribes of Arunachal Pradesh.* Guwahati : Spectrum Publications.

Nakani, C. 1966. 'Plural society in Sikkim : A Study of the interrelations of Lepchas, Bhutias and Nepalis', in Furer Haimendorf, C. (*ed.*). *Caste and Kin in Nepal, India and Ceylon: Anthropological Studies in Hindu-Buddhist Contact Zones.* Bombay : Asia Publishing House.

Nanda, N. 1982. *Tawang-The land of Mon.* Delhi : Vikas Publishing House Pvt. Ltd.

Nath, R.M. 1948. *The Background of Assamese Culture.* Shillong.

Needham, Rodney. 1959. "Analytical note on the Kom of Manipur." *Ethnos : 24.*

Needham, Rodney. 1962 "Chawte Social Structure." *American Anthropol.* April. 60 : 236.

Nepali, G.S. 1965. *The Newars.* Bombay : United Asia Publication.

Odi, Dai 1989. Property rights of women in Arunachal Pradesh, *Arunachal Newsletter,* March 27 : 3.

Oliver, G. 1956. Anthropology of the Naga head-hunters of Assam. *Bull. Soc. anthrop.* 6.6. 373-417.

Pakem, B. 1972. 'The Socio-political System of the Jaintia Tribe of Assam.' *An Analysis of Continuity and Change in Tribal Situation in India.* K.S. Singh (ed.) Simla.

Pakem, B. 1984. *The Tribes of Northeast India,* B. Karotemprel (ed.), Firma KLM Private Limited, Calcutta.

Pakrasi, K. 1953. Note on the Kurs and sub-Kurs of the Arlengs (Mikirs), *Man in India,* 33 (4) : 307-314.

Pakyntein, E.H., 1964. *Census of India.* 1961. *District Census Handbook, Cachar, Assam,* New Delhi, Govt. Publication.

Pakyntein, E.H., 1965. *Census of India.* 1961. Vol. III, Assam, pt. V-A, Scheduled Tribes and Scheduled Castes (Reprints from old Census Reports and Special Tables). Faridabad : Govt. Press.

Pandey, B.B. 1974. *The Hill Miris.* Shillong : Government of Arunachal Pradesh.

Parry, N.E. 1982. *A Monograph on Lushai Customs and Ceremonies.* Assam Govt. Press, Shillong.

Pathak, L.P., 1984. The enliced immigrants : Imported Tribal Tea labour in Assam. *Journal of Social Sciences and Humanities.* II : 4 : October-December.

Paul, Gemini. 1958. The Sherdukpens, *Vanyajati,* 6 : 61-69.

Peal, S.E. 1872. Notes on a visit to the Tribes inhabiting the Hills south of Sibsagar, Assam *J.A.S.B.* XLI.

Peal, S.E. 1893. On the Morung as possibly a Relic of Pre-marriage Communism. *J.R.A.I.* XXX, iii.

Peal, S.E. 1896. On some traces of the Kol-Mon. Anam in the Eastern Naga Hills, *J.A.S.B.* i.

Pearl, S.E. 1896. Eastern Nagas of the Tirap and Mamtsik, *Journal of the Asiatic Society of Bengal,* 65.

Pegu, N.C. 1956. *The Miris or Mishings of the Brahmaputra Valley.* Guwahati : The Tribune Press.

Pegu, N.C., 1986. *The Miris or the Mishings of the Brahmaputra Valley.* Dhermaji : D. Pegu.

Pembarton, R.B. 1966 (Reprint). *Report on the Eastern Frontier of British India.* Gauhati.

Pemberton, R.B. : *Memoirs and Journals of Survey in Sikkim,* Rohi Pub., Kolkata, 1827.

Pettigrew, W. 1909. "Social departure feast as practised by the Tangkhul Nagas, Manipur, Assam." *J. Royal Asiatic Soc. Bengal,* 5 : 37-46.

Playfair, A. 1909. *The Garos.*

Porter, A.E. (1933) 1987. *Census of India 1931 : West Bengal and Sikkim.* New Delhi : Usha Publications.

Prain, David. 1887. The Angami Nagas *Revue Coloniale Internationale,* V. vi. 472-292.

Pruett, Gordon E. 1974. Christianity, History and Culture in Nagaland. *Contribution to Indian Sociology.* No. 8. 1974.

Pudaite, R. 1963. *Education of the Hmar People,* Manipur.

Querry, B. : *Studies in the History of North-east India,* MacMillan, London, 2000.

Rai, M.B. 1981. *Census of India, 1981, District Handbook, West Kameng District, Arunachal Pradesh,* Series 25. Shillong : Directorate of Census Operation, Arunachal Pradesh.

Rajput, A.B. *The Tribes of Chittagong Hill Trats.*

Ram, R. 1969. *The Himalayan Borderland.* Delhi : Vivek Publications. 1978. *The Himalayas as a Frontier.* New Delhi: Vikas.

Ram, R. 1970. *The Himalayan Borderland.* New Delhi : Vikas Publishers.

Rammuny, M. 1988. *The World of Nagas,* New Delhi : Northern Book Centre.

Ramsharma, S.N. 1985. Miju Mishmi marriage system and festivals, *Arunachal Review,* 1 (4) : 20-21.

Rawlins, J. : *On the Manners, Religion and Laws of the Cucis, or Mountaineers of Tipra,* Asiatic Researches, Nagaland, 1792.

Ray, P.C. 1957. "The effect of culture contact on the personality structure of two Indian tribes : The Riang of Tripura and the Baiga of Madhya Pradesh". *Bulletin of the Department of Anthropologyy.* 6 (2) : 1-84.

Reid, R. 1942. *History of the Frontier Area Bordering on Assam, 1833-1941.* Shillong : Government Press.

Risley, H.H. 1891. *The Tribes and Castes of Bengal.* Vol. 1 & 2. Calcutta : Firma Mukhopadhyay. (Reprinted in 1981).

Risley, H.H. 1891/1981 reprinted. *Tribes and Castes of Bengal : Ethnographic Glossary,* Vol. 2. Calcutta : Firma K.L. Mukhopadhyay.

Risley, H.H. 1894/1985. *Gazetteer of Sikkim.* New Delhi : B.R. Publishing.

Risley, H.H. 1903. *Census of India, 1901, Vol. 1, India part 1. Report of Ethnographic Appendices.* Calcutta : Supdt. Government Printing.

Risley, Sir Herbert, 1969. *The people of India,* Delhi, Oriental Book. Reprint Corporation (First published in 1915).

Rizvi, S.H.M. and S.K. Mukherjee 1984. *Tribes in Contemporary India a study of Paite tribe of Manipur south,* Project Report, Calcutta. Anthropological Survey of India (unpublished).

Rizvi, S.H.M. and Shibani Roy 1984. *Muslims bio-cultural Perspective* New Delhi, B.R. Publishing Corporation.

Rizvi, S.H.M., 1988. "Study of Consanguinity among the Hmar of Manipur." In *Current Anthropological and Archaeological Perspectives* (ed.) K.L. Bhowmik, New Delhi, Inter Publications. pp : 251-258.

Robinson, W. 1841. *Descriptive Account of Assam.* Calcutta. Ostell & Lepage, London : Thos. Ostell & Co.

Rodborne, Rev. T. 1979. *U Khasi.* Shillong.

Roland, Y.L. 1988. *Comparative History of the Nagas* (from ancient period). Delhi : D.K. Distributors.

Ronaldshay, L. 1923. *Lands of the Thunderbolt, Sikkim, Chumbi and Bhutan.* London : Constable.

Rose, H.A. 1936. "Garo marriage", *Folklore*. 47: 375-393.

Rownew, H.B. 1882. *The wild tribes of India*. Delhi : B.R. Publishing Corporation. (Reprinted in 1974).

Roy Burman, B.K. (ed.) *Census of India 1961, Demographic and Socio-economic profiles of the hill area of North East India*. New Delhi, Govt. of India.

Roy Chowdhury, D. 1957. "Palmar main lines and configuration types of the Riangs of Tripura". *Bulletin of the Anthropological Survey of India*. 6 (1) : 67.

Roy Chowdhury, N.R. *Tripura through the ages*. Calcutta, 1977.

Roy, Amitesh : *Sikkim, Dynamics of Change*, Pearl Publishers, Calcutta, 1982.

Roy, Jyotirmoy. 1958. *History of Manipur*, Calcutta, Firma K.L. Mukhopadhyay.

Roy, S.C. 1912. *The Mundas and their country*. Calcutta : City Bode Society.

Roy, S.C. 1915. *The Oraons of Chotanagpur*. Ranchi : Author (Bar Library).

Roy, S.C. 1950, The *Munda and their Country*. Ranchi : Asia Publishing House.

Roy, S.C. and Ramesh Chandra Roy. 1937. *The Kharias*. Vol. 1 & 2. Ranchi.

Roy, S.C., 1937. *The Kharias*. Asia Publishing House, Ranchi.

Roy, S.N. 1927. "The Savaras of Orissa". *Man in India*. 7 : 277-336.

Roy, Sachin. 1956. Abor weapons of war and chase, *Journal of the Asiatic Society*, 22 (2) : 139-159.

Roy, Sachin. 1958. Dress, ornaments and decoration of the Adis, *Vanyajati*, 6 (1) : 4-21.

Roy, Sachin. 1958. Lohit-Wasi Mishmi (In Hindi), *Uttar-Purav Simanchal Vanyajati*, 6 (3) : 107-113.

Roy, Sachin. 1960. *Aspects of Padam-Minyong Culture*. Shillong: North-East Frontier Agency.

Roy, U Hipshon (ed). 1969, *Khasi Heritage*, Shillong.

Rukbo, T. 1985. Donyi-Poloism : A religion, *Arunachal Review*, 1 (4) : 1-4.

Russel, R.V. and Hiralal. 1975. *Tribes and Castes of the Central Provinces of India*. Rajdhani Book Centre. Delhi.

Russell R.V., and Hiralal, 1916. *The Tribes and Castes of the Central Province of India*. Vol. IV, London : Macmillan & Co. Ltd.

Rustomji, N.K. 1971. *Enchanted Frontiers : Sikkim, Bhutan and India's North Eastern Borderlands*. Delhi : Oxford University Press.

Rymbai, R.T. 1980. 'Some Aspects of the Religion of the Khasi Pnars', *Religion and Society of Northeast India,* S. Miri (ed.), New Delhi.

Sachchidananda. 1979. *The changing Munda.* New Delhi : Concept Publishing Co.

Saha, N. 1984. Ethnographic Study of the Zeliangrong Tribe of North East India in *Tribes of North East India,* Karotemprel S. (Ed). Shillong : Vendrame Missiological Institute.

Saha, N. 1986. Role of the Christian Missionaries in all round Development of a Nagaland village. Unpublished Ph.D. Thesis. Gauhati University.

Saha, S.B. 1986. *Socio-economic Survey of the Noatia Tribes.* Agartala : Tribal Welfare Department.

Saigal, Omesh. 1978. *Tripura—its history and culture.* Delhi. Concept Publishing Company.

Saikia, A.K., 1976. *Census of India 1971.* A Portrait of Population, Assam, Series 3. Howrah : Govt. of India Press.

Saikia, A.K., 1971. *Census of India.* Vol. III Assam Pt. VI., Delhi: Govt. Press.

Saikia, P.C., 1976. *The Dibongya.* Delhi : B.R. Publishing Co.

Sangma, M., 1984. History and culture of the Garos. *In Garo Hills Land and the People.* ed. by L.G. Gassah. Gauhati : Omsons Publication.

Sangma, Milton, S., 1994. *Essays on North-East India.* Presented in memory of Professor V. Venkata Rao. New Delhi : Indus Publishing Company.

Sankrityayan, Kamila. 1973. *Manipur, Tripura.* (Hindi). New Delhi

Sardeshpande, S.C. 1987. *The Patkoi Nagas.* Delhi. D.K. Distributors.

Sarkar, Jayanta. 1986. The Na of Arunachal Pradesh, A written communication to the Regional Officer, NERO, Shillong.

Sarkar, Jayanta. 1987. *Society, Culture and Ecological Adaptation among three tribes of Arunachal Pradesh.* Calcutta:Anthroplogical Survey of India.

Sarkar, N. 1980. *Buddhism among the Monpas and Sherdukpens.* Shillong: Research Department, Government of Arunachal Pradesh.

Sarkar, N. 1981. *Tawang Monastery.* Shillong : Research Department, Government of Arunachal Pradesh.

Sarma, K.K., 1985. A note on the Aiton - a Buddhist population of Assam. *Journal of North East India Council for Social Science Research.* 9 : 2: 36-38.

Sen, Namita C.S. 1981. *The Origin and Early History of Khasi-Synteng People,* Calcutta.

Sen, S.P. (ed.) 1979. *Sources of the History of India,* Vol. II. Indian Historical Studies.

Sen, Soumen. 1985. *Social and State Formation in Khasi-Jaintia Hills.* B.R. Pub. New Delhi.

Shadwell, J.B. e.d., 1986. *Notes on Khasis.*

Shakespear, J. (Lt. Col.). 1912. *The Lushai-Kuki clans.* London : Macmillan.

Shakespear, J. 1912. *The Lushai Kuki clans,* MacMillan and Co. Ltd. London; Reprint 1975, Tribal Research Institute, Aizawl, Mizoram.

Shakespeare, J.E. 1927. The Ao Nagas review. *Folklore.* Vol. XXXVIII; 92-98.

Shakespeare, L.W. 1914. *History of Upper Assam and the N.E. Frontier,* London : Macmillan.

Shakespeare, Maj. 1903. *Census of India, 1901, Vol. 1.* pp. 222-29. India (Ethnographic Appendices). Calcutta.

Sharma Thakur, G.C. 1972. *The plains Tribes of Lakhimpur, Dibrugarh. Sibsagar and Nowgong.* Gauhati : Tribal Research Institute, Assam.

Sharma, J.L. 1982. *Hamro Samaj : Ek Adhyayan.* Kathmandu : Sajha Prakashan.

Sharma, R.R.P. 1961. *The Sherdukpens.* Shillong : Research Department, Government of Arunachal Pradesh.

Sharma, Rajesh. 1983. *The Images of Sikkim : The Land, People and Culture.* Gangtok : Rigeum Publications.

Sharma, T.C. and D.N. Mazumdar. (Eds) 1980. *Eastern Himalayas: A Study on Anthropology and Tribalism.* New Delhi : Cosmo Publications.

Shasmal, K.C. 1972. *The Bauris of West Bengal.* Calcutta : Indian Publications.

Shaw, William. 1928. "Notes on the Thadous Kukis." *Jr. of Asiatic Soc. Bengal.* 1-175.

Sherring, M.A. 1914. *Hindu Tribes and Castes as represented in Banaras.* Vol. 1. Delhi.

Shimray, R.R. 1985. *Origin and Culture of Nagas.* New Delhi : Aruna Printing Press.

Shukla, B.K. 1965. *The Daflas of Subansiri Region.* Shillong : North-East Frontier Agency.

Siiger, Halfden. 1967. *The Lepchas, Culture and Religion of Himalayan People.* Parts I and II. Copenhagen : The National Museum of Denmark.

Simon, I.M. 1976. The Status of Women in some North East Indian Tribal Communities, *Arunachal News,* 4 (5) : 34-39.

Singh, R.G. *The Kukis of Tripura.* Agartala : Directorate of Research, Department of Welfare for Scheduled Tribes and Scheduled Castes.

Singh, B.P. 1987. *The Problem of Change : A Study of North East India.* Delhi : Oxford University Press.

Singh, Chandrika. 1989. *Emergence of Arunachal Pradesh as a State.* Delhi: Mittal Publications.

Singh, K. Suresh. (ed.) 1972. *Tribal Situation in India.* Simla, Indian Institute of Advanced Study.

Singh, K.B. 1963 "Manipuri Vaishnavism." *Soc. bull.* Bombay : 12 : 2.

Singh, K.M. 1974. *Bishnupriya Manipuri* (in Assamese). Guwahati: Assam Sahitya Sabha.

Singh, K.S. (ed). 1972. *Tribal Situation in India.* IIAS, Simla.

Singh, K.S., B.N. Mukherjee et.al. 1986. "Genetic markers among Meities and Brahmins of Manipur, India." *Hum. Hered.* 36 (3): 177-87.

Singh, Kynpham, 1980. 'Khasi Religion and Khasi Society', *Religion and Society of North East India,* S. Miri (ed)., New Delhi.

Singh, N. Tombi 1975. *Manipur : The Mainstream.* New Delhi, Rajesh Printing Press.

Singh, N. Tombi. 1972 *Manipur : A Study,* Delhi, Rajesh Printing Press.

Singh, N. Tombi. 1975. *Manipur-TheMainstream,* Imphal : Chitrabiram Tombichandd Khorjeirup.

Singh, O.K. and T.C. Sharma 1969. "Discovery of Stone Age Relics from Manipur." *Jr. Assam Sc. Soc.* XIII : 36-48.

Singh, Prakash, 1970. *Nagaland,* New Delhi : National Book Trust of India.

Singh, Ranjit R.K. 1985. *The Monsang Tribe of Manipur : A Study of Changing Social Orientation of a small tribal group.* Dibrugarh, Dibrugarh University (Unpublished Ph.D. Thesis).

Singh, S. 1977. *The Beautiful India—Sikkim and Life.* New Delhi.

Sinha, A.P. 1974. 'Status-role of the Matrilineal Pnar husband.' *Tribe Caste and Peasantry.* K.S. Mathur and B.C. Agarwal (eds.), Ethnographic and Folk Culture Society, Lucknow.

Sinha, K.P.N.D. *The Bishnupriya Manipuris.* Silchar : Aja Babaisena Prakasani.

Sinha, Raghuvir. 1962. *The Akas.* Shillong : Research Department, Advisor's Secretariat.

Smith, W. Carlson. 1925. *The Ao Naga Tribe of Assam,* London : Macmillan.

Songate, Hranglien 1956. *Hmar History : Hmar Chanchin.* Imphal, Mao Press.

Soppitt, C.A., 1885. *A Historical and Descriptive Account of the Kachari Tribes in N.C. Hills with specimen of tables and folklore.* Shillong. Assam Secretariat Press.

Soppitt, C.A. 1884. *Short Account of the Kuki and Lushai Tribes on the N.E. Frontier.* Shillong : Assam Government.

Soppitt, C.A. 1885. *A Short Account of the Kachcha Naga (Empeo) Tribe in the North Cachar Hills.* Shillong : Assam Secretariat Press.

Soppitt, C.A. 1887. *A short account of the Kuki-Lushai tribes on the N.E. Frontier District* : Cachar, Sylhet, Naga Hills, etc. and North Cachar Hills. Shillong.

Srivastava, L.R.N. 1962. *The Gallongs.* Shillong Research Department, Advisor's Secretariat.

Srivastava, L.R.N. 1973. *Among the Wanchos.* Shillong : Research Department, Government of Arunachal Pradesh.

Stack, E. 1883. Koch. *Report on the Census of India, 1881.* Calcutta.

Stack, E. 1883. *Miri, Daphlas and Abors, A report on the Census of India 1881, Assam.* Calcutta.

Sten, H.W. 1977. *Meghalaya Year Book.* Shillong.

Stewart, R. 1885. Notes on Northern Cachar. *J.A.S.B.* Vol. XXIV, pp. 607-17.

Stocks, C de B. *Sikkim : Customs and Folklore.* New Delhi : Cosmo.

Stonor, C.R. 1952. The Sulung Tribe of the Assam Himalaya, *Anthropos,* 47.

Stonor, C.R. 1957. Notes on religion and rituals among the Dafla tribe of the Assam Himalayas, *Anthropos,* 52 : 1-23.

Stracly, P.D. : *History of Indian States,* Popular Prakashan, Bombay, 1958.

Subba, Tanka B. 1989. *The Nepalis in Darjeeling and Sikkim Himalayas: Dynamics of a Hill Society.* Delhi : Mittals.

Swney, J.M.C. 1912. *Assam Census Report* 1901; Shillong : Assam Secretariat Printing Press.

Tayeng, A. 1976. "The Millang", *Resarun,* pp. 238-239. Shillong : Directorate of Research, Government of Arunachal Pradesh.

Temple, R. 1977 (reprint). *Journals kept in Hyderabad, Kashmir, Sikkim and Nepal, A Historical and Political Record.* Vols. I and II.

Terhuja, K. 1972. The Christian Church among the Angami Nagas. In *Tribal Situation in India.* K.S. Singh (ed.) Shimla : IIAS.

Thanga, L.B. 1978. *The Mizos : A Study in Racial Personality.* United Publishers, Gauhati.

Thanga, L.B. : *Sikkim:A Study in Racial Personality,* Suresh Pub., Gauhati, 1978.

Thanhlira, R. 1969. The Mizos. *In Tribes of Assam.* Ed. S. Barkataki. National Book Trust, New Delhi.

Thaosen, S.R., 1962. *Dimasa Kachari* (in Assamese). In *Asamar Janajati* ed. by P.C. Bhattacharjee : Jorhat : Assam Sahitya Sabha.

Thoma, R, 1963. *Moyon Monsang Customs,* Liwachangning. Kumlathabi.

Thusu, N.K. 1980. *Gond Kingdom of Chanda.* Calcutta : Anthropological Survey of India.

Tucci, G. 1962. *Nepal, The Discovery of the Malla.* London : George Allen and Unwin Ltd.

Valley (1974-75), *Subansiri District, Arunachal Pradesh.* Itanagar: Regional Geology Division.

Vansittart, E. 1890 (Revised 1980). *The Gorkhas.* New Delhi : Ariana Publishing House.

Waddel, L.A. 1900. *The Tribes of Brahmaputra Valley.* J.A.S.B. Vol. LXIX, part III.

Waddel, L.A., 1901. The Tribes of Brahmaputra Valley : A Contribution of their physical types and affinities *Journal of Asiatic Society of Bengal* 69 : 31-127.

Waddell, L.A. 1895. Notes on the poisoned arrows of the Akas, *J.A.I.*, 24.

Waddell, L.A. 1973 (reprint). *Lamaism in Sikkim.* New Delhi : Cosmo.

Ward, Kingdon. 1928. In the Naga Hills'. *The Times,* 16th April.

Watson, J.F. and J.W. Kaye. 1868. *The People of India.* Vol. 2. Delhi : B.R. Publishing Corporation. (Reprinted in 1974).

Watt, G. 1887. "The Nagas of Manipur." In *The Nagas in the Nineteenth Century :* (ed) Verrier Elwin, Bombay Oxford University Press, pp. 447-463.

Weiner, M. : *Sons of the Soil,* MacMillan, London, 1978.

White, J.C. 1909. *Sikkim and Bhutan, Twenty-one Years on the North-East Frontier 1886-1 908.* London : Edward Arnold. 1920/1977. *Himalayan Bhutan, Sikkim and Tibet.* Reprinted Delhi: ESS Publications.

Wiener, M., 1978. *Sons of the Soil.* Delhi : Oxford University Press.

Wood, W.H.S. 1929-30. British Relations with the Angami Nagas. *Assam Review* (July 29-July 30).

Woodthorpe, R.G. 1881. Note on the wild Tribes inhabiting the so-called Naga Hills on our N.E. Frontier of India : Pt. *I.J.R.A.I.* XI. i. ii. iii.

— 1887. "Aboriginal Tribes of Manipur." *Journal of Anthropol. Instt.* 16 : 346-70.

— 1911. *The Naga Tribes of Manipur,* London, MacMillan & Co. Ltd.

— 1912. *The Lushai Kuki Clans,* London, MacMillan & Co., Ltd.

— 1915. *The People of India.* Calcutta & Simla : Thacker, Spink & Co. London : W. Thacker & Co.

— 1975. "Slavery in Manipur." *Folklore :* XVIII : 7-9.

1971. *District Census Handbooks : North, South and West Tripura.*

1971. *Tripura—a portrait of population.*

1980 *Socio-economic Survey of the Cobblar Communities of Agartala Municipality and Adjacent Areas.* Agartala, Government of Tripura 1980. *Tripura LushalKukider Itikatha* (in Bengali), Agartala, Government of Tripura.

Index

J

K

L

M

■■■